In Memory of Eric Sears

Donated by the Carlsbad City Library Staff

BACKCOUNTRY ADVENTURES

SOUTHERN CALIFORNIA

Warning: While every effort has been made to make the 4WD trail descriptions in this book as accurate as possible, some discrepancies may exist between the text and the actual trail. Hazards may have changed since the research and publication of this edition. Swagman Publishing, Inc., and the authors accept no responsibility for the safety of users of this guide. Individuals are liable for all costs incurred if rescue is necessary.

Printed in Korea.

Publisher's Cataloging-in-Publication
(Provided by Quality Books, Inc.)

Massey, Peter, 1951-
Backcountry adventures. Southern California: the ultimate guide to the backcountry for anyone with a sport utility vehicle / Peter Massey and Jeanne Wilson. —1st ed.
p.cm.
Includes bibliographical references and index.
ISBN 1-930193-04-1

1. Automobile travel—California, Southern—Guidebooks. 2. Four-wheel drive vehicles. 3. Trails—California, Southern—Guidebooks. 4. Ghost towns—California, Southern—Guidebooks. 5. Plants—California, Southern—Identification. 6. Animals—California, Southern—Identification. 7. California, Southern —Guidebooks. I. Wilson, Jeanne (Jeanne Welburn), 1960- II. Title.

GV1024.M37 2002 917.94'904'54
QBI02-200180

BACKCOUNTRY ADVENTURES

SOUTHERN CALIFORNIA

THE ULTIMATE GUIDE TO THE
BACKCOUNTRY FOR ANYONE
WITH A SPORT UTILITY VEHICLE

PETER MASSEY AND JEANNE WILSON

Acknowledgments

Many people and organizations have made significant contributions to the research and production of this book. We owe them all special thanks for their assistance.

The production of the book has been a team effort, and we would especially like to thank the following people who have played the major roles in its production.

Project Editor:	**Timothy Duggan**
Senior Field Researchers:	**Donald McGann, Maggie Pinder**
Assistant Field Researchers:	**Sarah Swanson, Timothy Duggan**
Researchers:	**Chris Munden, Amy Volker**
Copy Editing and Proofreading:	**Robin Loveman, Sallie Greenwood**
Graphic Design and Maps:	**Deborah Rust**
Finance:	**Douglas Adams**
Office Administration:	**Peg Anderson**

We received a great deal of assistance from many other people and organizations. We would like to thank Alfredo L. Casillas, public information officer at the United States Border Patrol, Yuma, for guidelines on encounters with undocumented aliens; Thomas B. Egan (Lead Wildlife Biologist), Sally Cunkelman, and the rest of the staff at the Bureau of Land Management's Barstow Field Office; Carol Leigh for consulting on the flora and fauna sections and reviewing final photographs; Sue Hirschfeld for consulting on the geology section; staff at the California Desert Information Center in Barstow; and staff at Jawbone Station for information on the OHV area.

Staff at many offices of the National Forest Service also provided us with valuable assistance. Special thanks also to Meredith Wilson for his support of this project.

The book includes more than five hundred photos, and we are most thankful to the following organizations and people who have helped to research photographs or allowed us to publish the wonderful photographs they have taken: Lori Swingle and Coi Gehrig, Denver Public Library; Linda Fisk and Ken Hedges, San Diego Museum of Man; Dace Taube, University of Southern California; Carrie Burroughs and Karren Elsbernd, California Academy of Sciences (CalPhotos); Barbara Pitschel, Strybing Arboretum & Botanical Gardens; Tanya Hollis, Abby Bridge, and Crissa Van Vleck, California Historical Society; Professor Ron Olowin, Department of Physics and Astronomy at Saint Mary's College and curator of the Alfred Brousseau Collection; staff at Denver Botanical Gardens; staff at Tucson Botanical Gardens; Alison Sheehey, James Cokendolpher, Earle Robinson, Doug Von Gausig, Don Baccus, Lauren Livo, Steve Wilcox, and Paul Berquist.

For maintaining our vehicles, we would like to thank Dave's European, Denver, Colorado.

We would like to draw our readers' attention to the website (www.bushducks.com) of our senior researchers, the Bushducks—Donald McGann and Maggie Pinder. It provides information on current 4WD trail conditions and offers their valuable assistance to anyone who is planning a backcountry itinerary.

Publisher's Note: Every effort has been taken to ensure that the information in this book is accurate at press time. Please visit our website to advise us of any changes or corrections you find. We also welcome recommendations for new 4WD trails or other suggestions to improve the information in this book.

Swagman Publishing, Inc.
P.O. Box 519, Castle Rock, CO 80104
Phone: (303) 660-3307
Toll-free: (800) 660-5107
Fax: (303) 688-4388
www.4WDbooks.com

Contents

The Desert Region

Appendix: Trail Lists

Introduction

For most people, Southern California evokes images of Hollywood glamour, densely populated cities, and freeways jammed with cars inching toward their destinations. However, the same region that is home to some of America's largest metropolitan areas also boasts vast expanses of backcountry wilderness. From desolate desert stretches to rugged coastal roads and the towering Sierra Nevada, Southern California is an area of unique and varied natural beauty. The extreme diversity in climate and elevation—14,494-foot-tall Mount Whitney is less than a hundred miles from Badwater Basin, which is 282 feet below sea level—means that at least part of the region's backcountry is accessible year-round.

Mountains, deserts, and ocean formed a formidable natural boundary around California for centuries. Because of this relative isolation, many species of plants and animals that exist nowhere else in the world can be found in Southern California. Majestic giant sequoias and unruly Joshua trees dot the edges of many trails in this book. A lucky traveler might also spot a recently reintroduced California condor, a desert tortoise, or an elusive mountain lion. In spring and summer, much of California's backcountry is covered in dazzling swathes of wildflowers.

In addition to the region's natural beauty, countless relics of human history can be found in Southern California. Evidence of millennia of Native American habitation can be seen in acorn grinding bowls chiseled into rocks. Along the coast, huge mounds of seashells are the remains from meals of countless generations. In select areas, elaborate rock paintings and mysterious ground formations communicate cultures now lost forever. Life for many of California's Indian tribes changed irrevocably when Spanish explorers and priests began to colonize the region in the late 1700s. The Spanish, too, left their mark on the landscape. Many towns and landmarks retain Spanish names and pronunciations. Most of California's oldest buildings were constructed along the chain of Franciscan missions that spreads along the Pacific Coast. Other old structures are reminders of the huge ranches that covered California during its period of Mexican rule.

The discovery of gold near Sutter's Fort in January 1848 changed California forever. In a few years sites of untouched arcadia were transformed into bustling mining camps. The mineral resources that sparked the largest mass migration in American history—the gold rush—are illustrative of California's geological diversity. Gold, silver, lead, mercury, borax, and oil deposits have all been major factors in the region's development.

Some communities that sprang up around a mining claim remain population centers today, but many faded when all the mineral wealth was extracted from the vicinity. Often, a backcountry driver may stumble upon the remains of a mining operation or abandoned settlement without warning. These dilapidated buildings and hidden adits conjure images of a youthful state far removed from modern California.

We have selected 153 of our favorite unpaved roads and 4WD trails to take you off the highways and into the wild backcountry where much of Southern California's most interesting history has taken place. Our trails often retrace the routes taken by gold rush era migrants as they completed their long journeys into the state. Other trails follow old wagon roads, abandoned train lines, and disused mining roads. All the trails in this book are within the capabilities of stock sport utility vehicles, allowing you to escape into remote wilderness in the same car that you take to work and the grocery store. The trails range in difficulty from unpaved scenic drives with easily negotiated obstacles to exciting routes that provide a challenge for experienced off-highway drivers.

Many SUV owners are unaware of the opportunities their vehicles offer. With this book, readers can discover the immense rewards of backcountry touring. We are certain that you will get the same enjoyment we have as you travel through the most remote, scenic, and historic locations in Southern California.

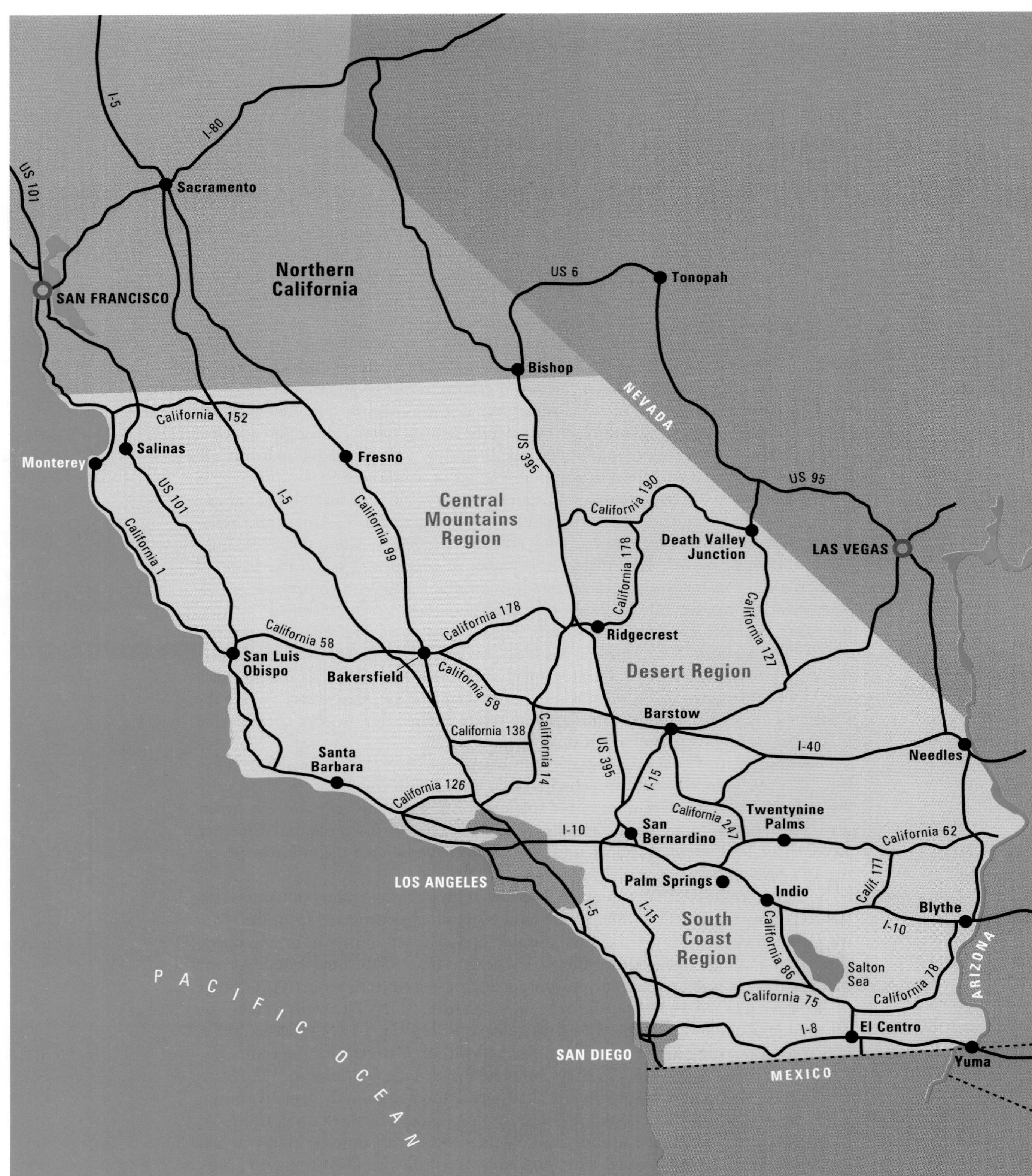

Northern California
Central Mountains Region
Desert Region
South Coast Region
NEVADA
ARIZONA
MEXICO
PACIFIC OCEAN
SAN FRANCISCO
Sacramento
Tonopah
Bishop
Monterey
Salinas
Fresno
Death Valley Junction
LAS VEGAS
Ridgecrest
San Luis Obispo
Bakersfield
Barstow
Needles
Santa Barbara
Twentynine Palms
San Bernardino
LOS ANGELES
Palm Springs
Indio
Blythe
Salton Sea
El Centro
SAN DIEGO
Yuma
I-5
I-80
US 101
US 6
US 395
US 95
California 152
California 1
California 99
California 190
California 178
California 127
California 58
California 138
California 14
California 126
I-40
I-15
California 247
I-10
California 62
Calif. 177
California 86
California 78
California 75
I-8

Before You Go

Why a 4WD Does It Better

The design and engineering of 4WD vehicles provide them with many advantages over normal cars when you head off the paved road:

- improved distribution of power to all four wheels;
- a transmission transfer case, which provides low-range gear selection for greater pulling power and for crawling over difficult terrain;
- high ground clearance;
- less overhang of the vehicle's body past the wheels, which provides better front- and rear-clearance when crossing gullies and ridges;
- large-lug, wide-tread tires;
- rugged construction (including underbody skid plates on many models).

If you plan to do off-highway touring, all of these considerations are important, whether you are evaluating the capabilities of your current 4WD or are looking to buy one; each is considered in detail in this chapter.

In order to explore the most difficult trails described in this book, you will need a 4WD vehicle that is well rated in each of the above features. If you own a 2WD sport utility vehicle, a lighter car-type SUV, or a pickup truck, your ability to explore the more difficult trails will depend on conditions and your level of experience.

A word of caution: Whatever type of 4WD vehicle you drive, understand that it is not invincible or indestructible. Nor can it go everywhere. A 4WD has a much higher center of gravity and weighs more than a car and so has its own consequent limitations.

Experience is the only way to learn what your vehicle can and cannot do. Therefore, if you are inexperienced, we strongly recommend that you start with trails that have lower difficulty ratings. As you develop an understanding of your vehicle and of your own taste for adventure, you can safely tackle the more challenging trails.

Using This Book

Route Planning

Regional maps at the beginning of each section provide a convenient overview of trails in that portion of the state. Each 4WD trail is highlighted in color, as are major highways and towns, helping you to plan various routes by connecting a series of 4WD trails and paved roads.

As you plan your overall route, you will probably want to utilize as many 4WD trails as possible. However, check the difficulty rating and time required for each trail before finalizing your plans. You don't want to be stuck 50 miles from the highway—at sunset and without camping gear, since your trip was supposed to be over hours ago—when you discover that your vehicle can't handle a certain difficult passage.

You can calculate the distances between Southern California towns by turning to the Southern California Distance Chart at the end of this chapter.

Difficulty Ratings

We use a point system to rate the difficulty of each trail. Any such system is subjective, and your experience of the trails will vary depending on your skill and road conditions at the time. Indeed, any amount of rain may make the trails much more difficult, if not impassable.

A few of Southern California's national forests rate their trails with the green, blue, and black ratings based on the system employed for downhill ski runs. However, even easy green-rated trails can provide an interesting drive for stock vehicles and should not be underestimated.

We have rated the 4WD trails on a scale of 1 to 10—1 being passable for a normal passenger vehicle in good conditions and 10 requiring a heavily modified vehicle and an experienced driver who expects to encounter vehicle damage. Because this book is designed for owners of unmodified 4WD vehicles—who we assume do not want to damage their vehicles—most of the trails are rated 5 or lower. A few trails are included that rate as high as 7, while those rated 8 to 10 are beyond the scope of this book.

This is not to say that the moderate trails are easy. We strongly recommend that inexperienced drivers not tackle trails rated at 4 or higher until they have undertaken a number of the lower-rated ones, so that they can gauge their skill level and prepare for the difficulty of the higher-rated trails.

In assessing the trails, we have always assumed good road conditions (dry road surface, good visibility, and so on). The factors influencing our ratings are as follows:

- obstacles such as rocks, mud, ruts, sand, slickrock, and stream crossings;
- the stability of the road surface;
- the width of the road and the vehicle clearance between trees or rocks;
- the steepness of the road;
- the margin for driver error (for example, a very high, open shelf road would be rated more difficult even if it was not very steep and had a stable surface).

The following is a guide to the ratings.

Rating 1: The trail is graded dirt but suitable for a normal passenger vehicle. It usually has gentle grades, is fairly wide, and has very shallow water crossings (if any).

Rating 2: High-clearance vehicles are preferred, but not necessary. These trails are dirt roads, but they may have rocks, grades, water crossings, or ruts that make clearance a concern in a normal passenger vehicle. The trails are fairly wide, so that passing is possible at almost any point along the trail. Mud is not a concern under normal weather conditions.

Rating 3: High-clearance 4WDs are preferred, but any high-clearance vehicle is acceptable. Expect a rough road surface; mud and sand are possible but will be easily passable. You may encounter rocks up to 6 inches in diameter, a loose road surface, and shelf roads, though these will be wide enough for passing or will have adequate pull-offs.

Rating 4: High-clearance 4WDs are recommended, though most stock SUVs are acceptable. Expect a rough road surface with rocks larger than 6 inches, but there will be a reasonable driving line available. Patches of mud are possible but can be readily negotiated; sand may be deep and require lower tire pressures. There may be stream crossings up to 12 inches deep, substantial sections of single-lane shelf road, moderate grades, and sections of moderately loose road surface.

Rating 5: High-clearance 4WDs are required. These trails have either a rough, rutted surface, rocks up to 9 inches, mud and deep sand that may be impassable for inexperienced drivers, or stream crossings up to 18 inches deep. Certain sections may be steep enough to cause traction problems, and you may encounter very narrow shelf roads with steep drop-offs and tight clearance between rocks or trees.

Rating 6: These trails are for experienced four-wheel drivers only. They are potentially dangerous, with large rocks, ruts, or terraces that may need to be negotiated. They may also have stream crossings at least 18 inches deep, involve rapid currents, unstable stream bottoms, or difficult access; steep slopes, loose surfaces, and narrow clearances; or very narrow sections of shelf road with steep drop-offs and potentially challenging road surfaces.

Rating 7: Skilled, experienced four-wheel drivers only. These trails include very challenging sections with extremely steep grades, loose surfaces, large rocks, deep ruts, and/or tight clearances. Mud or sand may necessitate winching.

Rating 8 to 10: Stock vehicles are likely to be damaged and the trail may be impassable. Trails with these difficulty ratings are for highly skilled, experienced four-wheel drivers only.

Scenic Ratings

If rating the degree of difficulty is subjective, rating scenic beauty is guaranteed to lead to arguments. Southern California contains a spectacular variety of scenery—from its coastal cliffs and oak forests to its desert wilderness. Despite the subjectivity of attempting a comparative rating of diverse scenery, we have tried to provide a guide to the relative scenic quality of the various trails. The ratings are based on a scale of 1 to 10, with 10 being the most attractive.

Remoteness Ratings

Many trails in Southern California are in remote mountain or desert country; sometimes the trails are seldom traveled, and the likelihood is low that another vehicle will appear within a reasonable time to assist you if you get stuck or break down. We have included a ranking for remoteness of +0 through +2. Extreme summer temperatures can make a breakdown in the more remote areas a life-threatening experience. Prepare carefully before tackling the higher-rated, more remote trails (see "Special Preparations for Remote Travel," page 12). For trails with a high remoteness rating, consider traveling with a second vehicle.

Estimated Driving Times

In calculating driving times, we have not allowed for stops. Your actual driving time may be considerably longer depending on the number and duration of the stops you make. Add more time if you prefer to drive more slowly than good conditions allow.

Current Road Information

All the 4WD trails described in this book may become impassable in poor weather conditions. Storms can alter roads, remove tracks, and create impassable washes. Most of the trails described, even easy 2WD trails, can quickly become impassable even to 4WD vehicles after only a small amount of rain. For each trail, we have provided a phone number for obtaining current information about conditions.

Abbreviations

The route directions for the 4WD trails use a series of abbreviations as follows:

SO **CONTINUE STRAIGHT ON**
TL **TURN LEFT**
TR **TURN RIGHT**
BL **BEAR LEFT**
BR **BEAR RIGHT**
UT **U-TURN**

Using Route Directions

For every trail, we describe and pinpoint (by odometer reading) nearly every significant feature along the route—such as intersections, streams, washes, gates, cattle guards, and so on—and provide directions from these landmarks. Odometer readings will vary from vehicle to vehicle, so you should allow for slight variations. Be aware that trails can quickly change in the desert. A new trail may be cut around a washout, a faint trail can be graded by the county, or a well-used trail may fall into disuse. All these factors will affect the accuracy of the directions.

If you diverge from the route, zero your trip meter upon your return and continue along the route, making the necessary adjustment to the point-to-point odometer readings. In the directions, we regularly reset the odometer readings—at significant landmarks or popular lookouts and spur trails—so that you won't have to recalculate for too long.

Most of the trails can be started from either end, and the route directions include both directions of travel; reverse directions are printed in blue below the main directions. When traveling in reverse, read from the bottom of the table and work up.

Route directions include cross-references whenever two 4WD trails included in this book connect; this allows for an easy change of route or destination.

Each trail includes periodic latitude and longitude readings to facilitate using a global positioning system (GPS) receiver. These readings may also assist you in finding your location on maps. The GPS coordinates were taken using the NAD 1927 datum and are in the format dd°mm.mm'. To save time when loading coordinates into your GPS receiver, you may wish to include only one decimal place, since in Southern California, the first decimal place equals about 165 yards and the second only about 16 yards.

Map References

We recommend that you supplement the information in this book with more-detailed maps. For each trail, we list the sheet maps and road atlases that provide the best detail for the area. Typically, the following references are given:

- Bureau of Land Management (BLM) Maps,
- U.S. Forest Service (USFS) Maps,
- *California Road & Recreation Atlas,* 2nd ed. (Medford, OR: Benchmark Maps, 2000)—Scale 1:300,000,
- *Southern & Central California Atlas & Gazetteer,* 5th ed. (Yarmouth, ME: DeLorme Mapping, 2000)—Scale 1:150,000,
- Maptech-Terrain Navigator USGS Topo Maps—Scale 1:100,000 and 1:24,000,
- *Trails Illustrated* Topo Maps; National Geographic Maps—Various scales, but all contain good detail.

We recommend the *Trails Illustrated* series of maps as the best for navigating these trails. They are reliable, easy to read, and printed on nearly indestructible plastic paper. However, this series covers only a few of the 4WD trails described in this book.

The DeLorme atlas is useful and has the advantage of providing you with maps of the state at a reasonable price. While its 4WD trail information doesn't go beyond what we provide, it is useful if you wish to explore the hundreds of side roads.

U.S. Forest Service maps lack the topographic detail of the other sheet maps and, in our experience, are occasionally out of date. They have the advantage of covering a broad area and are useful in identifying land use and travel restrictions. These maps are most useful for the longer trails.

In our opinion, the best single option by far is the Terrain Navigator series of maps published on CD-ROM by Maptech. These CD-ROMs contain an amazing level of detail because they include the entire set of 2,815 U.S. Geological Survey topographical maps of California at the 1:24,000 scale and all 116 maps at the 1:100,000 scale. These maps offer many advantages over normal maps:

- GPS coordinates for any location can be found, which can then be loaded into your GPS receiver. Conversely, if you have your GPS coordinates, your location on the map can be pinpointed instantly.
- Towns, rivers, passes, mountains, and many other sites are indexed by name so that they can be located quickly.
- 4WD trails can be marked and profiled for elevation changes and distances from point to point.
- Customized maps can be printed out.

Maptech uses 14 CD-ROMs to cover the entire state of California, which can be purchased individually or as part of a two-state package at a heavily discounted price. The CD-ROMs can be used with a laptop computer and a GPS receiver in your vehicle to monitor your location on the map and navigate directly from the display.

All these maps should be available through good map stores. The Maptech CD-ROMs are available directly from the company (800-627-7236, or on the internet at www.maptech.com).

Backcountry Driving Rules and Permits

Four-wheel driving involves special driving techniques and road rules. This section is an introduction for 4WD beginners.

4WD Road Rules

To help ensure that these trails remain open for all four-wheel drivers to enjoy, it is important to minimize your impact on the environment and not be a safety risk to yourself or anyone else. Remember that 4WD clubs in California fight a constant battle with federal, state, and local governments and various lobby groups to retain the access that currently exists.

Although many vehicle manufacturer advertisements depict high-speed rally-style driving as proof of the automobile's off-highway abilities, these commercials are misleading—such driving techniques would only result in vehicle, occupant, and environmental damage. For all concerned, this style of driving is best left to professionals in controlled driving events. The fundamental rule when traversing the 4WD trails described in this book is to use common sense. In addition, special road rules for 4WD trails apply:

■ Vehicles traveling uphill have the right of way.

■ If you are moving more slowly than the vehicle behind you, pull over to let the other vehicle by.

■ Park out of the way in a safe place. Blocking a track may restrict access for emergency vehicles as well as for other recreationalists. Set the parking brake—don't rely on leaving the transmission in park. Manual transmissions should be left in the lowest gear.

Tread Lightly!

Remember the rules of the Tread Lightly! program:

■ Be informed. Obtain maps, regulations, and other information from the forest service or from other public land agencies. Learn the rules and follow them.

■ Resist the urge to pioneer a new road or trail or to cut across a switchback. Stay on constructed tracks and avoid running over young trees, shrubs, and grasses, damaging or killing them. Don't drive across alpine tundra; this fragile environment takes years to recover.

■ Stay off soft, wet roads and 4WD trails readily torn up by vehicles. Repairing the damage is expensive, and quite often authorities find it easier to close a road rather than repair it.

■ Travel around meadows, steep hillsides, stream banks, and lakeshores that are easily scarred by churning wheels.

■ Stay away from wild animals that are rearing young or suffering from a food shortage. Do not camp close to the water sources of domestic or wild animals.

■ Obey gate closures and regulatory signs.

■ Preserve America's heritage by not disturbing old mining camps, ghost towns, or other historical features. Leave historic sites, Native American rock art, ruins, and artifacts in place and untouched.

■ Carry out all your trash and even that of others.

■ Stay out of designated wilderness areas. They are closed to all vehicles. It is your responsibility to know where the boundaries are.

■ Get permission to cross private land. Leave livestock alone. Respect landowners' rights.

Report violations of these rules to help keep these 4WD trails open and to ensure that others will have the opportunity to visit these backcountry sites. Many groups are actively seeking to close public lands to vehicles, thereby denying access to those who are unable, or perhaps merely unwilling, to hike long distances. This magnificent countryside is owned by, and should be available to, all Americans.

Remember that you are sharing the road with other users. It is courteous to slow down when you encounter travelers on foot, mountain bike, or horseback, and also sensible for safety reasons and to prevent a dust hazard. Pulling over and turning off your vehicle—whether it is a 4WD, ATV, or motorbike—is a simple gesture appreciated by those with horses. Offering water to people on foot or mountain bikes is a small act of generosity that may be much valued by those engaged in physically demanding activities in remote locations.

Special Preparations for Remote Travel

Because of the remoteness of some areas in Southern California and the very high summer temperatures, you should take some special precautions to ensure that you don't end up in a life-threatening situation:

■ When planning a trip into the desert, always inform someone as to where you are going, your route, and when you expect to return. Stick to your plan.

■ Carry and drink at least one gallon of water per person per day of your trip. (Plastic gallon jugs are handy and portable.)

■ Be sure your vehicle is in good condition with a sound battery, good hoses, spare tire, spare fan belts, necessary tools, and reserve gasoline and oil. Other spare parts and extra radiator water are also valuable. If traveling in pairs, share the common spares and carry a greater variety.

■ Keep an eye on the sky. Flash floods can occur in a wash any time you see thunderheads—even when it's not raining a drop where you are.

■ If you are caught in a dust storm while driving, get off the road and turn off your lights. Turn on the emergency flashers and back into the wind to reduce windshield pitting by sand particles.

■ Test trails on foot before driving through washes and sandy areas. One minute of walking may save hours of hard work getting your vehicle unstuck.

■ If your vehicle breaks down, stay near it. Your emergency supplies are there. Your car has many other items useful in an emergency. Raise your hood and trunk lid to signal "help needed." Remember, a vehicle can be seen for miles, but a person on foot is very difficult to spot from a distance.

■ When you're not moving, use available shade or erect shade from tarps, blankets, or seat covers—anything to reduce the direct rays of the sun.

■ Do not sit or lie directly on the ground. It may be 30 degrees hotter than the air.

■ Leave a disabled vehicle only if you are positive of the route and the distance to help. Leave a note for rescuers that gives the time you left and the direction you took.

■ If you must walk, rest for at least 10 minutes out of each hour. If you are not normally physically active, rest up to 30 minutes out of each hour. Find shade, sit down, and prop up your feet. Adjust your shoes and socks, but do not remove your shoes—you may not be able to get them back on swollen feet.

■ If you have water, drink it. Do not ration it.

■ If water is limited, keep your mouth closed. Do not talk, eat, smoke, drink alcohol, or take salt.

■ Keep your clothing on, despite the heat. It helps to keep your body temperature down and reduces your body's dehydration rate. Cover your head. If don't have a hat, improvise a head covering.

■ If you are stalled or lost, set signal fires. Set smoky fires in the daytime and bright ones at night. Three fires in a triangle signal "help needed."

■ A roadway is a sign of civilization. If you find a road, stay on it.

■ If hiking in the desert, equip each person, especially children, with a police-type whistle. It makes a distinctive noise with little effort. Three blasts signal "help needed."

■ To avoid poisonous creatures, put your hands or feet only where your eyes can see. One insect to be aware of in Southern California is the Africanized honeybee. Though indistinguishable from its European counterpart, these bees are far more aggressive and can be a threat. They have been known to give chase for up to a mile and even wait for people who have escaped into water to come up for air. The best thing to do if attacked is to cover your face and head with clothing and run to the nearest enclosed shelter. Keep an eye on your pet if you notice a number of bees in the area; many have been killed by these Africanized honeybees.

■ Avoid unnecessary contact with wildlife. Some mice in California carry the deadly hantavirus, a pulmonary syndrome fatal in 60 to 70 percent of human cases. Fortunately the disease is very rare—by November 2001, only 33 cases had been reported in California and 288 nationwide—but caution is still advised. Other rodents may transmit bubonic plague, the same epidemic that killed one-third of Europe's population in the 1300s. Be especially wary near sick animals and keep pets, especially cats, away from wildlife and their fleas. Another creature to watch for is the western black-legged tick, the carrier of Lyme disease. Wearing clothing that covers legs and arms, tucking pants into boots, and using insect repellent are good ways to avoid fleas and ticks.

Special Note on Travel Near the Mexican Border

California's southern border forms part of the international boundary with Mexico. This location can present a unique set of situations that the traveler may encounter. Every month, thousands of undocumented aliens attempt to gain unauthorized entry into the United States from Mexico. It is estimated that approximately 70 percent of all border jumpers are apprehended and returned to Mexico immediately.

What does this mean for you? Any remote area traveler who spends any time in the deserts of Southern California is likely to encounter undocumented aliens. First and foremost, it should be stressed that the majority of meetings pose absolutely no threat to the traveler. You are most likely to meet people just like you who want little more than food and water before they move on, leaving you alone. However, many people find these meetings worrisome and upsetting, and some even feel threatened.

It is suggested that travelers adopt the following guidelines compiled from advice given by the U.S. Border Patrol.

■ If possible, avoid all contact with suspected undocumented aliens. Do not go out of your way to offer unsolicited assistance.

■ If it is impossible to avoid contact—for example if you are approached and asked for help—then stop. Remain in your vehicle. Most of the time you will be asked for food and water. Give them what you can safely spare without running your own supplies dangerously low and move on as soon as possible. The border patrol does not see this as aiding and abetting; this is humanitarian aid and you may be saving someone's life. Many people die each year trying to cross the desert.

■ Do not give anyone a lift in your vehicle unless you see it is a life-threatening situation.

■ As soon as is practical, notify the border patrol or sheriff's department of the location, number, and physical condition of the group so that they can be apprehended as soon as possible. Be as specific as you can; GPS coordinates are extremely useful. Again, by doing this you may be saving someone's life.

■ Do not attempt to engage people in conversation and avoid giving exact distances to the nearest town. Many undocumented aliens arrive in the United States by paying a "coyote" to bring them safely across the border. They are often deliberately misled and woefully unprepared for the desert conditions they encounter and the distances they will have to travel to safety. Giving exact distances, especially if it is many miles away, is putting yourself and your vehicle at risk. Carjackings are *extremely rare* but should not be discounted.

■ Be extremely wary of groups traveling in vehicles, because these are likely to be professional smugglers of both humans and drugs. However less than 5 percent of encounters are with the actual smugglers themselves; most are with individuals or groups after the coyotes have dropped them off.

■ If traveling exceptionally remote routes in areas of high activity, consider traveling as part of a large group. Individual vehicles and small groups stand a higher chance of being approached.

■ Always lock your vehicle when you leave it, even for a short period of time, and carry as few valuables as possible.

■ Finally, do not let this be a deterrent to exploring the wonderful trails in Southern California. Be alert and aware but not paranoid. Many thousands of recreationists safely travel these trails every year.

Obtaining Permits

Backcountry permits, which usually cost a fee, are required for certain activities on public lands in California, whether the area is a national forest, a national park, a state park, a national monument, an Indian reservation, or BLM land.

Restrictions may require a permit for overnight stays, which can include backpacking and 4WD or bicycle camping. Permits may also be required for day use.

When possible, we include information about permit requirements, but these regulations change constantly. If in doubt, check with the most likely governing agency.

One of the most common permits required for trails in this book is the Forest Adventure Pass, which can be purchased from any national forest office. It is required for all recreational activities within a specific national forest and must be displayed on your vehicle's windshield anytime you are parked within the bounds of the forest.

Assessing Your Vehicle's Off-Road Ability

Many issues come into play when evaluating your 4WD vehicle, though most of the 4WDs on the market are suitable for even the roughest trails described in this book. Engine power will be adequate in even the least powerful modern vehicle. However, some vehicles are less suited to off-highway driving than others, and some of the newest, carlike sport utility vehicles (SUVs) simply are not designed for off-highway touring. The following information should enable you to identify the good, the bad, and the ugly.

Differing 4WD Systems

All 4WD systems have one thing in common: The engine provides power to all four wheels rather than to only two, as is typical in most standard cars. However, there are a number of differences in the way power is applied to the wheels.

The other feature that distinguishes nearly all 4WDs from normal passenger vehicles is that the gearboxes have high and low ratios that effectively double the number of gears. The high range is comparable to the range on a passenger car. The low range provides lower speed and more power, which is useful when towing heavy loads, driving up steep hills, or crawling over rocks. When driving downhill, the 4WD's low range increases engine braking.

Various makes and models of SUVs offer different drive systems, but these differences center on two issues: the way power is applied to the other wheels if one or more wheels slip and the ability to select between 2WD and 4WD.

Normal driving requires that all four wheels be able to turn at different speeds; this allows the vehicle to turn without scrubbing its tires. In a 2WD vehicle, the front wheels (or rear wheels in a front-wheel-drive vehicle) are not powered by the engine and thus are free to turn individually at any speed. The rear wheels, powered by the engine, are only able to turn at different speeds because of the differential, which applies power to the faster-turning wheel.

This standard method of applying traction has certain weaknesses. First, when power is applied to only one set of wheels, the other set cannot help the vehicle gain traction. Second, when one powered wheel loses traction, it spins, but the other powered wheels don't turn. This happens because the differential applies all the engine power to the faster-turning wheel and no power to the other wheels, which still have traction. All 4WD systems are designed to overcome these two weaknesses. However, different 4WDs address these objectives in different ways.

Full-Time 4WD

In order for a vehicle to remain in 4WD all the time without scrubbing the tires, all the wheels must be able to rotate at different speeds. A full-time 4WD system allows this to happen by using three differentials. One is located between the rear wheels, as in a normal passenger car, to allow the rear wheels to rotate at different speeds. The second is located between the front wheels. The third differential is located between the front and rear wheels to allow different rotational speeds between the front and rear sets of wheels. In nearly all vehicles with full-time 4WD, the center differential operates only in high range. In low range, it is completely locked. This is not a disadvantage because when using low range the additional traction is normally desired, and the deterioration of steering response will be less noticeable because the vehicle will be traveling at a slower speed.

Part-Time 4WD

A part-time 4WD system does not have the center differential located between the front and rear wheels. Consequently, the front and rear drive shafts are both driven at the same speed and with the same power at all times when in 4WD.

This system provides improved traction because when one or both of the front or rear wheels slip, the engine continues to provide power to the other set. However, because such a system doesn't allow a difference in speed between the front and rear sets of wheels, the tires scrub when turning, placing additional strain on the whole drive system. Therefore, such a system can be used only in slippery conditions; otherwise, the ability to steer the vehicle will deteriorate and the tires will quickly wear out.

Some vehicles offer both full-time and part-time 4WD in high range.

Manual Systems to Switch Between 2WD and 4WD

There are three manual systems for switching between 2WD and 4WD. The most basic requires stopping and getting out of the vehicle to lock the front hubs manually before selecting 4WD. The second requires you to stop, but you change to 4WD by merely throwing a lever inside the vehicle (the hubs lock automatically). The third allows shifting between 2WD and 4WD high range while the vehicle is moving. Any 4WD that does not offer the option of driving in 2WD must have a full-time 4WD system.

Automated Switching Between 2WD and 4WD

Advances in technology are leading to greater automation in the selection of two- or four-wheel drive. When operating in high range, these high-tech systems have sensors to monitor the rotation of each wheel. When any slippage is detected, the vehicle switches the proportion of power from the wheel that is slipping to the wheels that retain traction. The proportion of power supplied to each wheel is therefore infinitely variable as opposed to the original systems where the vehicle was either in two-wheel drive or four-wheel drive.

In recent years, this process has been spurred on by many of the manufacturers of luxury vehicles entering the SUV market—Acura, Mercedes, BMW, Cadillac, Lincoln, and Lexus have joined Range Rover in this segment.

These higher-priced vehicles have led the way in introducing sophisticated computer-controlled 4WD systems. While each of the manufacturers has its own approach to this issue, all the systems automatically vary the allocation of power between the wheels within milliseconds of the sensors detecting wheel slippage.

Limiting Wheel Slippage

4WDs employ various systems to limit wheel slippage and transfer power to the wheels that still have traction. These systems may completely lock the differentials, or they may allow limited slippage before transferring power back to the wheels that retain traction.

Lockers completely eliminate the operation of one or more differentials. A locker on the center differential switches between full-time and part-time 4WD. Lockers on the front or rear differentials ensure that power remains equally applied to each set of wheels regardless of whether both have traction. Lockers may be controlled manually, by a switch or a lever in the vehicle, or they may be automatic.

Manual lockers are the most controllable and effective devices for ensuring that power is provided to the wheels with traction. However, because they allow absolutely no slippage, they must be used only on slippery surfaces.

An alternative method for getting power to the wheels that have traction is to allow limited wheel slippage. Systems that work this way may be called limited-slip differentials, posi-traction systems, or in the center differential, viscous couplings. The advantage of these systems is that the limited difference they allow in rotational speed between wheels enables such systems to be used when driving on a dry surface. All full-time 4WD systems allow limited slippage in the center differential.

For off-highway use, a manually locking differential is the best of the above systems, but it is the most expensive. Limited-slip differentials are the cheapest but also the least satisfactory, as they require one wheel to be slipping at 2 to 3 mph before power is transferred to the other wheel. For the center differential, the best system combines a locking differential and, to enable full-time use, a viscous coupling.

Tires

The tires that came with your 4WD vehicle may be satisfactory, but many 4WDs are fitted with passenger-car tires. These are unlikely to be the best choice because they are less rugged and more likely to puncture on rocky trails. They are particularly prone to sidewall damage as well. Passenger vehicle tires also have a less aggressive tread pattern than specialized 4WD tires thus providing less traction in mud.

For information on purchasing tires better suited to off-highway conditions, see "Special 4WD Equipment" below.

Clearance

Road clearances vary considerably among 4WD vehicles—from less than 7 inches to more than 10 inches. Special vehicles may have far greater clearance. For instance, the Hummer has a 16-inch ground clearance. High ground clearance is particularly advantageous on the rockier or more rutted 4WD trails in this book.

When evaluating the ground clearance of your vehicle, you need to take into account the clearance of the bodywork between the wheels on each side of the vehicle. This is particularly relevant for crawling over larger rocks. Vehicles with sidesteps have significantly lower clearance than those without.

Another factor affecting clearance is the approach and departure angles of your vehicle—that is, the maximum angle the ground can slope without the front of the vehicle hitting the ridge on approach or the rear of the vehicle hitting on departure. Mounting a winch or tow hitch to your vehicle is likely to reduce your approach or departure angle.

If you do a lot of driving on rocky trails, you will inevitably hit the bottom of the vehicle sooner or later. When this happens, you will be far less likely to damage vulnerable areas such as the oil pan and gas tank if your vehicle is fitted with skid plates. Most manufacturers offer skid plates as an option. They are worth every penny.

Maneuverability

When you tackle tight switchbacks, you will quickly appreciate that maneuverability is an important criterion. Where a full-size vehicle may be forced to go back and forth a number of times to get around a sharp turn, a small 4WD might go straight around. This is not only easier, it's safer.

If you have a full-size vehicle, all is not lost. We have seen many of the trails in this book traveled in a Suburban. That is not to say that some of these trails wouldn't have been easier to negotiate in a smaller vehicle! We have noted in the route descriptions if a trail is not suitable for larger vehicles.

In Summary

Using the criteria above, you can evaluate how well your 4WD will handle off-road touring, and if you haven't yet purchased your vehicle, you can use these criteria to help select one. Choosing the best 4WD system is, at least partly, subjective. It is also a matter of your budget. However, for the type of off-highway driving covered in this book, we make the following recommendations:

■ Select a 4WD system that offers low range and, at a minimum, has some form of limited slip differential on the rear axle.

■ Use light truck, all-terrain tires as the standard tires on your vehicle. For sand and slickrock, these will be the ideal choice. If conditions are likely to be muddy or traction will be improved by a tread pattern that will give more bite, consider an additional set of mud tires.

■ For maximum clearance, select a vehicle with 16-inch wheels, or at least choose the tallest tires that your vehicle can accommodate. Note that if you install tires with a diameter greater than standard, the odometer will undercalculate the distance you have traveled. Your engine braking and gear ratios will also be affected.

■ If you are going to try the rockier 4WD trails, don't install a sidestep or low-hanging front bar. If you have the option, have underbody skid plates mounted.

■ Remember that many of the obstacles you encounter on backcountry trails are more difficult to navigate in a full-size vehicle than in a compact 4WD.

Four-Wheel Driving Techniques

Safe four-wheel driving requires that you observe certain golden rules:

■ Size up the situation in advance.

■ Be careful and take your time.

■ Maintain smooth, steady power and momentum.

■ Engage 4WD and low-range gears before you get into a tight situation.

■ Steer toward high spots, trying to put the wheel over large rocks.

■ Straddle ruts.

■ Use gears and not just the brakes to hold the vehicle when driving downhill. On very steep slopes, chock the wheels if you park your vehicle.

■ Watch for logging and mining trucks and smaller recreational vehicles, such as all-terrain vehicles (ATVs).

■ Wear your seat belt and secure all luggage, especially heavy items such as toolboxes or coolers. Heavy items should be secured by ratchet tie-down straps rather than elastic-type straps, which are not strong enough to hold heavy items if the vehicle rolls.

California's 4WD trails have a number of common obstacles, and the following provides an introduction to the techniques required to surmount them.

Rocks

Tire selection is important in negotiating rocks. Select a multiple-ply, tough sidewall, light truck tire with a large-lug tread.

As you approach a rocky stretch, get into 4WD low range to give maximum slow-speed control. Speed is rarely necessary, since traction on a rocky surface is usually good. Plan ahead and select the line you wish to take. If a rock appears to be larger than the clearance of your vehicle, don't try to straddle it. Check to see that it is not higher than the frame of your vehicle once you get a wheel over it. Put a wheel up on the rock and slowly climb it, then gently drop over the other side, using the brake to ensure a smooth landing. Bouncing the car over rocks increases the likelihood of damage, because the body's clearance is reduced as the suspension compresses. Running boards also significantly reduce your clearance.

It is often helpful to use a spotter outside the vehicle to assist you with the best wheel placement.

Steep Uphill Grades

Consider walking the trail to ensure that the steep hill before you is passable, especially if it is clear that backtracking is going to be a problem.

Select 4WD low range to ensure that you have adequate power to pull up the hill. If the wheels begin to lose traction, turn the steering wheel gently from side to side to give the wheels a chance to regain traction.

If you lose momentum, but the car is not in danger of sliding, use the foot brake, switch off the ignition, leave the vehicle in gear (if manual transmission) or park (if automatic), engage the parking brake, and get out to examine the situation. See if you can remove any obstacles, and figure out the line you need to take. Reversing a couple of yards and starting again may enable you to get better traction and momentum.

If, halfway up, you decide a stretch of road is impassably steep, back down the trail. Trying to turn the vehicle around on a steep hill is extremely dangerous; you will very likely cause it to roll over.

Steep Downhill Grades

Again, consider walking the trail to ensure that a steep downhill slope is passable, especially if it is clear that backtracking uphill is going to be a problem.

Select 4WD low range and use first gear to maximize braking assistance from the engine. If the surface is loose and you are losing traction, change up to second or third gear. Do not use the brakes if you can avoid it, but don't let the vehicle's speed get out of control. Feather (lightly pump) the brakes if you slip under braking. For vehicles fitted with ABS, apply even pressure if you start to slip; the ABS helps keep vehicles on line.

Travel very slowly over rock ledges or ruts. Attempt to tackle these diagonally, letting one wheel down at a time.

If the back of the vehicle begins to slide around, gently apply the throttle and correct the steering. If the rear of the vehicle starts to slide sideways, do not apply the brakes.

Sand

As with most off-highway situations, your tires are the key to your ability to cross sand. It is difficult to tell how well a particular tire will handle in sand just by looking at it, so be guided by the manufacturer and your dealer.

The key to driving in soft sand is floatation, which is achieved by a combination of low tire pressure and momentum. Before crossing a stretch of sand, reduce your tire pressure to between 15 and 20 pounds. If necessary, you can safely go as low as 12 pounds. As you cross, maintain momentum so that your vehicle rides on the top of the soft sand without digging in or stalling. This may require plenty of engine power. Avoid using the brakes if possible; removing your foot from the accelerator alone is normally enough to slow or stop. Using the brakes digs the vehicle deep in the sand.

Air the tires back up as soon as you are out of the sand to avoid damage to the tires and the rims. Airing back up requires a high-quality air compressor. Even then, it is a slow process.

In the desert backcountry of Southern California, sandy conditions are commonplace. You will therefore find a good compressor most useful.

Slickrock

When you encounter slickrock, first assess the correct direction of the trail. It is easy to lose sight of the trail on slickrock, because there are seldom any developed edges. Often the way is marked with small cairns, which are simply rocks stacked high enough to make a landmark.

All-terrain tires with tighter tread are more suited to slickrock than the more open, luggier type tires. As with rocks, a multiple-ply sidewall is important. In dry conditions, slickrock offers pavement-type grip. In rain or snow, you will soon learn how it got its name. Even the best tires may not get an adequate grip. Walk steep sections first; if you are slipping on foot, chances are your vehicle will slip, too.

Slickrock is characterized by ledges and long sections of "pavement." Follow the guidelines for travel over rocks. Refrain from speeding over flat-looking sections, because you may hit an unexpected crevice or water pocket, and vehicles bend easier than slickrock! Turns and ledges can be tight, and vehicles with smaller overhangs and better maneuverability are at a distinct advantage—hence the popularity of the compacts in the slickrock mecca of Moab, Utah.

On the steepest sections, engage low range and pick a straight line up or down the slope. Do not attempt to traverse a steep slope.

Mud

Muddy trails are easily damaged, so they should be avoided if possible. But if you must traverse a section of mud, your success will depend heavily on whether you have open-lugged mud tires or chains. Thick mud fills the tighter tread on normal tires, leaving the tire with no more grip than if it were bald. If the muddy stretch is only a few yards long, the momentum of your vehicle may enable you to get through regardless.

If the muddy track is very steep, uphill or downhill, or off camber, do not attempt it. Your vehicle is very likely to skid in such conditions, and you may roll or slip off the edge of the road. Also, check to see that the mud has a reasonably firm base. Tackling deep mud is definitely not recommended unless you have a vehicle-mounted winch—and even then, be cautious, because the winch may not get you out. Finally, check to see that no ruts are too deep for the ground clearance of your vehicle.

When you decide you can get through and have selected the best route, use the following techniques to cross through the mud:

- Avoid making detours off existing tracks to minimize environmental damage.
- Select 4WD low range and a suitable gear; momentum is the key to success, so use a high enough gear to build up sufficient speed.
- Avoid accelerating heavily, so as to minimize wheel spinning and to provide maximum traction.
- Follow existing wheel ruts, unless they are too deep for the clearance of your vehicle.
- To correct slides, turn the steering wheel in the direction that the rear wheels are skidding, but don't be too aggressive or you'll overcorrect and lose control again.
- If the vehicle comes to a stop, don't continue to accelerate, as you will only spin your wheels and dig yourself into a rut. Try backing out and having another go.
- Be prepared to turn back before reaching the point of no return.

Stream Crossings

By crossing a stream that is too deep, drivers risk far more than water flowing in and ruining the interior of their vehicles. Water sucked into the engine's air intake will seriously damage the engine. Likewise, water that seeps into the air vent on the transmission or differential will mix with the lubricant and may lead to serious problems.

Even worse, if the water is deep or fast flowing, it could easily carry your vehicle downstream, endangering the lives of everyone in the vehicle.

Some 4WD manuals tell you what fording depth the vehicle can negotiate safely. If your vehicle's owner's manual doesn't include this information, your local dealer may be able to assist. If you don't know, then avoid crossing through water that is more than a foot or so deep.

The first rule for crossing a stream is to know what you are getting into. You need to ascertain how deep the water is, whether there are any large rocks or holes, if the bottom is solid enough to avoid bogging down the vehicle, and whether the entry and exit points are negotiable. This may take some time and involve getting wet, but you take a great risk by crossing a stream without first properly assessing the situation.

The secret to water crossings is to keep moving, but not too fast. If you go too fast, you may drown the electrics, causing the vehicle to stall midstream. In shallow water (where the surface of the water is below the bumper), your primary concern is to safely negotiate the bottom of the stream, avoiding any rock damage, and maintaining momentum if there is a danger of getting stuck or of slipping on the exit.

In deeper water (between 18 and 30 inches), the objective is to create a small bow wave in front of the moving vehicle. This requires a speed that is approximately walking pace. The bow wave reduces the depth of the water around the engine compartment. If the water's surface reaches your tailpipe, select a gear that will maintain moderate engine revs to avoid water backing up into the exhaust; and do not change gears midstream.

Crossing water deeper than 25 to 30 inches requires more extensive preparation of the vehicle and should be attempted only by experienced drivers.

Snow

The trails in this book that receive heavy snowfall are closed in winter. Therefore, the snow conditions that you are most likely to encounter are an occasional snowdrift that has not yet melted or fresh snow from an unexpected storm. Getting through such conditions depends on the depth of the snow, its consistency, the stability of the underlying surface, and your vehicle.

If the snow is no deeper than about 9 inches and there is solid ground beneath it, crossing the snow should not be a problem. In deeper snow that seems solid enough to support your vehicle, be extremely cautious: If you break through a drift, you are likely to be stuck, and if conditions are bad, you may have a long wait.

The tires you use for off-highway driving, with a wide tread pattern, are probably suitable for these snow conditions. Nonetheless, it is wise to carry chains (preferably for all four wheels), and if you have a vehicle-mounted winch, even better.

Vehicle Recovery Methods

If you do enough four-wheel driving, you are sure to get stuck sooner or later. The following techniques will help you get back on the go. The most suitable method will depend on the equipment available and the situation you are in—whether you are stuck in sand, mud, or snow, or are high-centered or unable to negotiate a hill.

Towing

Use a nylon yank strap of the type discussed in the "Special 4WD Equipment" section. This type of strap will stretch 15 to 25 percent, and the elasticity will assist in extracting the vehicle.

Attach the strap only to a frame-mounted tow point. Ensure that the driver of the stuck vehicle is ready, take up all but about 6 feet of slack, then move the towing vehicle away at a moderate speed (in most circumstances this means using 4WD low range in second gear) so that the elasticity of the strap is employed in the way it is meant to be. Don't take off like a bat out of hell or you risk breaking the strap or damaging a vehicle.

Never join two yank straps together with a shackle. If one strap breaks, the shackle will become a lethal missile aimed at one of the vehicles (and anyone inside). For the same reason, never attach a yank strap to the tow ball on either vehicle.

Jacking

Jacking the vehicle allows you to pack under the wheel (with rocks, dirt, or logs) or use your shovel to remove an obstacle. However, the standard vehicle jack is unlikely to be of as much assistance as a high-lift jack. We highly recommend purchasing a good high-lift jack as a basic accessory if you decide that you are going to do a lot of serious, off-highway four-wheel driving. Remember, a high-lift jack is of limited use if your vehicle does not have an appropriate jacking point. Some brush bars have two built-in forward jacking points.

Tire Chains

Tire chains can be of assistance in both mud and snow. Cable-type chains provide much less grip than link-type chains. There are also dedicated mud chains with larger, heavier links than on normal snow chains. It is best to have chains fitted to all four wheels.

Once you are bogged down is not the best time to try to fit the chains; if at all possible, try to predict their need and have them on the tires before trouble arises. An easy way to affix chains is to place two small cubes of wood under the center of the stretched-out chain. When you drive your tires up on the blocks of wood, it is easier to stretch the chains over the tires because the pressure is off.

Winching

Most recreational four-wheel drivers do not have a winch. But if you get serious about four-wheel driving, this is probably the first major accessory you should consider buying.

Under normal circumstances, a winch would be warranted only for the more difficult 4WD trails in this book. Having a winch is certainly comforting when you see a difficult section of road ahead and have to decide whether to risk it or turn back. Also, major obstacles can appear when you least expect them, even on trails that are otherwise easy.

Owning a winch is not a panacea to all your recovery problems. Winching depends on the availability of a good anchor point, and electric winches may not work if they are submerged in a stream. Despite these constraints, no accessory is more useful than a high-quality, powerful winch when you get into a difficult situation.

If you acquire a winch, learn to use it properly; take the time to study your owner's manual. Incorrect operation can be extremely dangerous and may cause damage to the winch or to your anchor points, which are usually trees.

Navigation by the Global Positioning System (GPS)

Although this book is designed so that each trail can be navigated simply by following the detailed directions provided, nothing makes navigation easier than a GPS receiver.

The global positioning system (GPS) consists of a network of 24 satellites, nearly 13,000 miles in space, in six different orbital paths. The satellites are constantly moving at about 8,500 mph, making two complete orbits around the earth every 24 hours.

Each satellite is constantly transmitting data, including its identification number, its operational health, and the date and time. It also transmits its location and the location of every other satellite in the network.

By comparing the time the signal was transmitted to the time it was received, a GPS receiver calculates how far away each satellite is. With a sufficient number of signals, the receiver can then triangulate its location. With three or more satellites, the receiver can determine latitude and longitude coordinates. With four or more, it can calculate elevation. By constantly making these calculations, it can determine speed and direction. To facilitate these calculations, the time data broadcast by GPS is accurate to within 40 billionths of a second.

The U.S. military uses the system to provide positions accurate to within half an inch. When the system was first established, civilian receivers were deliberately fed slightly erroneous information in order to effectively deny military applications to hostile countries or terrorists—a practice called selective availability (SA). However on May 1, 2000, in response to the growing importance of the system for civilian applications, the U.S. government stopped intentionally downgrading GPS data. The military gave its support to this change once new technology made it possible to selectively degrade the system within any defined geographical area on demand. This new feature of the system has made it safe to have higher-quality signals available for civilian use. Now, instead of the civilian-use signal having a margin of error of 20 to 70 yards, it is only about one-tenth of that.

A GPS receiver offers the four-wheeler numerous benefits:

- You can track to any point for which you know the longitude and latitude coordinates with no chance of heading in the wrong direction or getting lost. Most receivers provide an extremely easy-to-understand graphic display to keep you on track.
- It works in all weather conditions.
- It automatically records your route for easy backtracking.
- You can record and name any location, so that you can relocate it with ease. This may include your campsite, a fishing spot, or even a gold mine you discover!
- It displays your position, allowing you to pinpoint your location on a map.
- By interfacing the GPS receiver directly to a portable computer, you can monitor and record your location as you travel (using the appropriate map software) or print the route you took.

However, remember that GPS units can fail, batteries can go flat, and tree cover and tight canyons can block the signals. Never rely entirely on GPS for navigation. Always carry a compass for backup.

Special 4WD Equipment

Tires

When 4WD touring, you will likely encounter a variety of terrain: rocks, mud, talus, slickrock, sand, gravel, dirt, and bitumen. The immense variety of tires on the market includes many specifically targeted at one or another of these types of terrain, as well as tires designed to adequately handle a range of terrain.

Every four-wheel driver seems to have his or her own preference when it comes to tire selection, but most people undertaking the 4WD trails in this book will need tires that can handle all of the above types of terrain adequately.

The first requirement is to select rugged, light-truck tires rather than passenger-vehicle tires. Check the size data on the sidewall: it should have "LT" rather than "P" before the number.

Among light-truck tires, you must choose between tires designated "all-terrain" and more-aggressive, wider-tread mud tires. Either type will be adequate, especially on rocks, gravel, talus, or dirt. Although mud tires have an advantage in muddy conditions and soft snow, all-terrain tires perform better on slickrock, in sand, and particularly on ice and paved roads.

When selecting tires, remember that they affect not just traction but also cornering ability, braking distances, fuel consumption, and noise levels. It pays to get good advice before making your decision.

Global Positioning System Receivers

GPS receivers have come down in price considerably in the past few years and are rapidly becoming indispensable navigational tools. Many higher-priced cars now offer integrated GPS receivers, and within the next few years, receivers will become available on most models.

Battery-powered, hand-held units that meet the needs of off-highway driving currently range from less than $100 to a little over $400 and continue to come down in price. Some high-end units feature maps that are incorporated in the display, either from a built-in database or from interchangeable memory cards. Currently, only a few of these maps include 4WD trails.

If you are considering purchasing a GPS unit, keep the following in mind:

- Price. The very cheapest units are likely outdated and very limited in their display features. Expect to pay $125 to $400.
- The display. Compare the graphic display of one unit with another. Some are much easier to decipher or offer more alternative displays.
- The controls. GPS receivers have many functions, and they need to have good, simple controls.
- Vehicle mounting. To be useful, the unit needs to be placed where it can be read easily by both the driver and the navigator. Check that the unit can be conveniently located in your vehicle. Different units have different shapes and different mounting systems. If you are considering attaching a GPS unit to the dashboard of your vehicle, be sure not to obstruct the safe deployment of air bags. A GPS unit could cause serious bodily harm to an occupant of the vehicle at the speed at which air bags deploy.
- Map data. More and more units have map data built in. Some have the ability to download maps from a computer. Such maps are normally sold on a CD-ROM. GPS units have a finite storage capacity; having the ability to download maps covering a narrower geographical region means that the amount of data relating to that specific region can be greater.
- The number of routes and the number of sites (or "waypoints") per route that can be stored in memory. For off-highway use, it is important to be able to store plenty of waypoints so that you do not have to load coordinates into the machine as frequently. Having plenty of memory also ensures that you can automatically store your present location without fear that the memory is full.
- Waypoint storage. The better units store up to 500 way-

points and 20 reversible routes of up to 30 waypoints each. Also consider the number of characters a GPS receiver allows you to use to name waypoints. When you try to recall a waypoint, you may have difficulty recognizing names restricted to only a few characters.

■ Automatic route storing. Most units automatically store your route as you go along and enable you to display it in reverse to make backtracking easy.

After you have selected a unit, a number of optional extras are also worth considering:

■ A cigarette lighter electrical adapter. Despite GPS units becoming more power efficient, protracted in-vehicle use still makes this accessory a necessity.

■ A vehicle-mounted antenna, which will improve reception under difficult conditions. (The GPS unit can only "see" through the windows of your vehicle; it cannot monitor satellites through a metal roof.) Having a vehicle-mounted antenna also means that you do not have to consider reception when locating the receiver in your vehicle.

■ An in-car mounting system. If you are going to do a lot of touring using the GPS, consider attaching a bracket on the dash rather than relying on a Velcro mount.

■ A computer-link cable and digital maps. Data from your GPS receiver can be downloaded to your PC; maps and waypoints can be downloaded from your PC; or if you have a laptop computer, you can monitor your route as you go along, using one of a number of inexpensive map software products on the market.

Yank Straps

Yank straps are industrial-strength versions of the flimsy tow straps carried by the local discount store. They are 20 to 30 feet long and 2 to 3 inches wide, made of heavy nylon, rated to at least 20,000 pounds, and have looped ends.

Do not use tow straps with metal hooks in the ends (the hooks can become missiles in the event the strap breaks free). Likewise, never join two yank straps together using a shackle.

CB Radios

If you are stuck, injured, or just want to know the conditions up ahead, a citizen's band (CB) radio can be invaluable.

CB radios are relatively inexpensive and do not require an FCC license. Their range is limited, especially in very hilly country, because their transmission patterns basically follow lines of sight. Range can be improved using single sideband (SSB) transmission, an option on more expensive units. Range is even better on vehicle-mounted units that have been professionally fitted to ensure that the antenna and cabling are matched appropriately.

Winches

There are three main options when it comes to winches: manual winches, removable electric winches, and vehicle-mounted electric winches.

If you have a full-size 4WD vehicle—which can weigh in excess of 7,000 pounds when loaded—a manual winch is of limited use without a lot of effort and considerable time. However, a manual winch is a very handy and inexpensive accessory if you have a small 4WD. Typically, manual winches are rated to pull about 5,500 pounds.

Electric winches can be mounted to your vehicle's trailer hitch to enable them to be removed, relocated to the front of your vehicle (if you have a hitch installed), or moved to another vehicle. Although this is a very useful feature, a winch is heavy, so relocating one can be a two-person job. Consider that 5,000-pound-rated winches weigh only about 55 pounds, while 12,000-pound-rated models weigh around 140 pounds. Therefore, the larger models are best permanently front-mounted. Unfortunately, this position limits their ability to winch the vehicle backward.

When choosing between electric winches, be aware that they are rated for their maximum capacity on the first wind of the cable around the drum. As layers of cable wind onto the drum, they increase its diameter and thus decrease the maximum load the winch can handle. This decrease is significant: A winch rated to pull 8,000 pounds on a bare drum may only handle 6,500 pounds on the second layer, 5,750 pounds on the third layer, and 5,000 pounds on the fourth. Electric winches also draw a high level of current and may necessitate upgrading the battery in your 4WD or adding a second battery.

There is a wide range of mounting options—from a simple, body-mounted frame that holds the winch to heavy-duty winch bars that replace the original bumper and incorporate brush bars and mounts for auxiliary lights.

If you buy a winch, either electric or manual, you will also need quite a range of additional equipment so that you can operate it correctly:

- at least one choker chain with hooks on each end,
- winch extension straps or cables,
- shackles,
- a receiver shackle,
- a snatch block,
- a tree protector,
- gloves.

Grill/Brush Bars and Winch Bars

Brush bars protect the front of the vehicle from scratches and minor bumps; they also provide a solid mount for auxiliary lights and often high-lift jacking points. Additionally, they are an ideal place to fit a tall whip-antenna with a brightly colored flag atop, something that reduces safety concerns on trails with restricted visibility. The level of protection brush bars provide depends on how solid they are and whether they are securely mounted onto the frame of the vehicle. Lighter models attach in front of the standard bumper, but the more substantial units replace the bumper. Prices range from about $150 to $450.

Winch bars replace the bumper and usually integrate a solid brush bar with a heavy-duty winch mount. Some have the brush bar as an optional extra to the winch bar component. Manufacturers such as Warn, ARB, and TJM offer a wide range of integrated winch bars. These are significantly more expensive, starting at about $650.

Remember that installing heavy equipment on the front of the vehicle may necessitate increasing the front suspension rating to cope with the additional weight.

Portable Air Compressors

Some portable air compressors on the market are flimsy models that plug into the cigarette lighter and are sold at the local discount store. These are of very limited use for four-wheel driving. They are very slow to inflate the large tires of a 4WD vehicle; for instance, reinflating from 15 to 35 pounds typically takes more than 10 minutes for each tire. They are also not rated for extended use, which means that they will overheat and cut off before completing the job. If you're lucky, they will start up again when they have cooled down, but this means that you are unlikely to reinflate your tires in less than an hour. By comparison good quality models will take one to five minutes to fill each tire and have a duty cycle of at least 30 minutes.

The easiest way to identify a useful air compressor is by the price—good ones cost from around $200 to as much as $400. Viair and Quickair both manufacture an extensive range of portable and hard-mount compressors. These pumps draw between 10 and 45 amps. Those drawing more than 10 amps should not be plugged into the cigarette lighter socket.

Auxiliary Driving Lights

There is a vast array of auxiliary lights on the market today, and selecting the best lights for your purpose can be a confusing process.

Auxiliary lights greatly improve visibility in adverse weather conditions. Driving lights provide a strong, moderately wide beam to supplement headlamp high beams, giving improved lighting in the distance and to the sides of the main beam. Fog lamps throw a wide-dispersion, flat beam; and spots provide a high-power, narrow beam to improve lighting range directly in front of the vehicle. Rear-mounted auxiliary lights provide greatly improved visibility for backing up.

For off-highway use, you will need quality lights with strong mounting brackets. Some high-powered off-highway lights are not approved by the Department of Transportation for use on public roads.

Roof Racks

Roof racks can be excellent for storing gear, as well as providing easy access for certain weatherproof items. However, they raise the center of gravity on the vehicle, which can substantially alter the rollover angle. A roof rack is best used for lightweight objects that are well strapped down. Heavy recovery gear and other bulky items should be packed low in the vehicle's interior to lower the center of gravity and stabilize the vehicle.

A roof rack should allow for safe and secure packing of items and be sturdy enough to withstand knocks.

Packing Checklist

Before embarking on any 4WD adventure, whether a lazy Sunday drive on an easy trail or a challenging climb over rugged terrain, be prepared. The following checklist will help you gather the items you need.

Essential

- ❒ Rain gear
- ❒ Small shovel or multipurpose ax, pick, shovel, and sledgehammer
- ❒ Heavy-duty yank strap
- ❒ Spare tire that matches the other tires on the vehicle
- ❒ Working jack and base plate for soft ground
- ❒ Maps
- ❒ Emergency medical kit, including sun protection and insect repellent
- ❒ Bottled water
- ❒ Blankets or space blankets
- ❒ Parka, gloves, and boots
- ❒ Spare vehicle key
- ❒ Jumper leads
- ❒ Heavy-duty flashlight
- ❒ Multipurpose tool, such as a Leatherman
- ❒ Emergency food—high-energy bars or similar

Worth Considering

- ❒ Global Positioning System (GPS) receiver
- ❒ Cell phone
- ❒ A set of light-truck, off-highway tires and matching spare
- ❒ High-lift jack
- ❒ Additional tool kit
- ❒ CB radio
- ❒ Portable air compressor
- ❒ Tire gauge
- ❒ Tire-sealing kit
- ❒ Tire chains
- ❒ Handsaw and ax
- ❒ Binoculars
- ❒ Firearms
- ❒ Whistle
- ❒ Flares
- ❒ Vehicle fire extinguisher
- ❒ Gasoline, engine oil, and other vehicle fluids
- ❒ Portable hand winch
- ❒ Electric cooler

If Your Credit Cards Aren't Maxed Out

- ❒ Electric, vehicle-mounted winch and associated recovery straps, shackles, and snatch blocks
- ❒ Auxiliary lights
- ❒ Locking differential(s)

Southern California Distance Chart

	AMBOY	BAKER	BAKERSFIELD	BARSTOW	BIG BEAR CITY	BIG SUR	BISHOP	BLYTHE	BORREGO SPRINGS	CAJON JUNCTION	CALEXICO	CARMEL	DEATH VALLEY JUNCTION	EL CENTRO	FRESNO	FURNACE CREEK	LAS VEGAS, NV	LONE PINE	LOS ANGELES	MARICOPA	MOJAVE	MONTEREY	NEEDLES	OCOTILLO	PALMDALE	PALM SPRINGS	PALO VERDE	PASO ROBLES	PISMO BEACH	PORTERVILLE	RANDSBURG	RIVERSIDE	SALTON CITY	SAN BERNARDINO	SAN DIEGO	SAN FRANCISCO	SAN LUIS OBISPO	SANTA BARBARA	SANTA MARIA	TWENTYNINE PALMS	VENTURA	VISALIA
BAKER	75																																									
BAKERSFIELD	209	193																																								
BARSTOW	80	63	131																																							
BIG BEAR CITY	108	117	184	55																																						
BIG SUR	419	403	210	339	410																																					
BISHOP	290	275	255	210	265	356																																				
BLYTHE	105	169	333	240	178	530	417																																			
BORREGO SPRINGS	168	246	262	184	157	459	361	144																																		
CAJON JUNCTION	130	114	144	52	59	357	229	188	132																																	
CALEXICO	182	310	346	248	186	543	426	107	89	196																																
CARMEL	456	440	247	376	447	25	336	567	497	394	581																															
DV JUNCTION	159	83	277	147	200	486	193	292	329	197	393	524																														
EL CENTRO	177	342	338	280	182	535	457	102	80	228	12	572	425																													
FRESNO	317	301	108	237	292	182	224	439	368	252	453	157	385	444																												
FURNACE CREEK	191	115	243	179	232	453	161	313	361	229	425	491	32	421	352																											
LAS VEGAS, NV	133	92	285	155	209	495	267	209	337	206	315	532	94	311	393	126																										
LONE PINE	233	217	168	153	208	378	57	360	303	172	368	415	135	363	276	103	233																									
LOS ANGELES	194	179	112	117	104	309	267	224	152	65	236	346	262	228	218	294	271	209																								
MARICOPA	242	227	48	162	213	202	258	333	263	160	347	249	310	338	154	277	319	201	113																							
MOJAVE	149	133	60	69	124	270	172	272	216	84	280	307	217	321	168	190	225	115	95	93																						
MONTEREY	453	437	244	373	444	29	332	564	494	391	578	4	521	569	155	487	529	412	344	246	304																					
NEEDLES	81	124	273	144	197	483	355	99	215	194	205	520	184	201	381	216	112	297	258	306	213	517																				
OCOTILLO	205	315	311	253	227	508	430	129	66	201	36	545	398	27	417	430	407	373	200	311	294	542	228																			
PALMDALE	162	147	95	85	95	298	207	236	179	48	244	335	230	288	203	225	239	149	62	101	35	332	227	261																		
PALM SPRINGS	107	187	218	125	72	415	302	118	88	73	126	452	270	122	323	302	279	245	109	218	157	449	189	149	120																	
PALO VERDE	124	188	346	253	191	543	430	20	135	201	87	580	301	82	451	333	229	373	237	346	285	557	119	109	248	136																
PASO ROBLES	317	302	109	237	309	101	334	429	358	256	443	117	385	434	115	352	394	277	208	101	169	115	382	407	197	314	441															
PISMO BEACH	369	353	136	292	279	121	351	399	327	240	411	160	437	403	151	369	446	294	177	92	186	158	433	376	209	285	412	43														
PORTERVILLE	261	245	51	181	235	258	239	382	312	196	396	233	289	387	73	257	337	182	162	97	112	230	325	361	146	268	395	127	159													
RANDSBURG	141	125	99	61	116	309	149	267	211	79	276	346	208	271	207	139	217	92	144	132	46	343	205	281	81	153	280	208	232	151												
RIVERSIDE	159	143	168	81	55	365	259	170	106	29	211	402	227	202	274	258	235	201	58	168	113	399	223	176	77	56	183	264	232	217	109											
SALTON CITY	160	245	276	183	121	473	361	117	28	131	58	510	329	49	382	361	337	303	167	276	215	507	188	81	179	67	104	372	342	325	211	114										
SAN BERNARDINO	148	132	169	70	45	366	248	170	114	18	178	403	216	210	275	247	224	190	60	169	102	400	212	183	66	56	183	265	235	218	98	11	113									
SAN DIEGO	255	239	233	177	151	430	355	214	87	125	120	467	323	112	339	355	331	297	122	233	216	464	319	85	183	142	194	329	297	282	205	100	120	109								
SAN FRANCISCO	491	475	282	411	482	146	296	602	532	429	616	121	559	607	186	457	567	353	382	284	342	118	555	581	371	488	615	204	245	268	381	437	546	440	502							
SAN LUIS OBISPO	330	314	121	250	292	107	346	412	340	252	424	145	397	415	136	364	406	289	189	105	181	143	394	389	209	297	424	28	13	147	220	246	355	250	310	233						
SANTA BARBARA	289	273	148	211	198	200	333	319	247	159	331	238	336	322	254	351	365	276	96	103	161	236	353	296	129	204	331	121	81	198	207	153	262	157	217	326	94					
SANTA MARIA	351	335	127	273	261	138	338	381	309	221	393	176	419	385	167	356	427	281	159	79	173	174	415	358	191	267	394	59	19	177	212	215	324	219	279	264	32	63				
TWENTYNINE PALMS	49	125	252	99	59	449	309	117	119	108	140	487	208	136	358	240	182	252	143	253	192	484	131	163	155	50	130	348	318	302	160	90	91	92	175	522	331	238	300			
VENTURA	260	245	120	182	170	228	305	290	218	131	302	266	328	294	226	323	337	247	68	85	133	264	324	267	100	176	303	149	109	169	178	124	233	128	188	389	122	29	91	210		
VISALIA	288	273	79	208	263	227	226	410	339	223	424	202	356	415	42	323	364	247	189	125	139	199	352	388	174	295	422	113	146	30	178	245	353	248	310	237	133	225	164	329	197	
YUMA, AZ	191	345	394	283	221	559	461	87	137	231	61	628	428	59	500	460	296	403	283	394	315	625	187	84	279	167	67	490	458	443	311	213	106	215	168	663	471	378	441	159	350	471

Distances are calculated using major highways

Along the Trail

Towns, Ghost Towns, and Interesting Places

Amboy

Amboy, south of I-40, was established as a siding for the Atlantic & Pacific Railroad in 1883. Little happened here until Route 66 was built through this section of the Mojave Desert in the 1930s.

Around that time, Buster Burris and his partner Roy opened a motor vehicle service station. The town flourished and soon supported a school, café, motel, and major repair shop to cater to the increasing passing trade of the 1940s. Amboy's population grew to almost 100 at its peak in the late 1940s. However, the town's days were numbered after the construction of Interstate 40. The new and faster highway took the passing motor trade north, bypassing Amboy. The town faded. Property was hard to sell, and some people ended up walking away from their properties. Burris stuck with the settlement and ended up owning most of the nearly deserted town.

A reawakening of interest in classic travel routes across the nation has brought attention to many small abandoned towns located along the long, quiet stretches of Route 66, now also referred to as National Trails Highway. In the late 1990s, Burris finally sold out to a duo from the East Coast. White and his partner Wilson are slowly returning a 1940s atmosphere to this once important desert crossroads. Movie location hunters are also starting to appreciate the remote feeling of its gas station and motel, set in the depths of the sweltering Mojave Desert.

Amboy is a few miles from the picturesque Amboy Crater, which was created by volcanic activity at least 500 years ago. The same lava flow that formed the crater also removed one side of it, leaving a horseshoe formation.

GPS COORDINATES: N34°33.52' W115°44.67'
TRAIL: Desert #9: Amboy Crater Road
MAP: Page 476

Ashford Mill

Ashford Mill, just off California 178 in Death Valley, is named after three brothers—Henry, Harold, and Louis Ashford. In 1907, the brothers discovered a gold ore deposit in the Black Mountains and founded the Golden Treasure Mine. The Ashfords soon sold their mining claim to a Hungarian nobleman for $60,000. He then sold it to Benjamin McCausland for $105,000.

In 1914, McCausland and his son built a stamp mill to support their mine as well as the nearby Carbonite Mine. Twice the ordered amount of cement was brought to the construction site. Reluctant to refuse the extra material, the McCauslands decided to build extra thick foundations and walls. The mill, however, was not profitable. After only a few tons of ore had been milled, the site was abandoned. Because the mill walls were so sturdy, much of the original structure remains to this day.

GPS COORDINATES: N35°55.12' W116°40.95' (approximately)
NEAREST TRAIL: Desert #32: Death Valley West Side Road

Atolia

Atolia was one of the last towns to be settled in the Rand mining area of the Mojave Desert. One of three tiny communities off US 395, it lies southeast of the famous Rand (Yellow Aster) Mine and the town of Randsburg, where Southern California's mining boom began.

In 1905, while men who had made their fortunes at Randsburg witnessed a decrease in production, prospectors discovered rich tungsten deposits at nearby Red Mountain. The discovery triggered the second mining boom in the area, and in 1907 Atolia was established. The mill in Barstow was converted to process the tungsten ore found near Atolia. By 1915, the town's population reached 2,000 because of the demand for tungsten during World War I.

Atolia flourished and failed a number of times. At its peak, the town contained Donker's Sunshine Dairy, which produced nonfat milk, a rarity in those days. Although townspeople questioned the milk's value, they didn't complain because the beverage was a scarce commodity in the desert.

GPS COORDINATES: N35°18.99' W117°36.46'
NEAREST TRAIL: Central Mountains #27: Government Peak Trail

Bakersfield

The settlement of Bakersfield was named in 1868 after a corral (Baker's field) owned by an early settler, Colonel Thomas Baker. Baker was a civil and hydraulic engineer who attempted to build a canal from Kern Lake to San Francisco in the early 1860s. Baker's lands were flooded by the Kern River in 1866, and he was widely admired for his reclamation efforts after the flood.

The town started as a small agricultural community, but by 1871 it already boasted a population of 800. The first railroad line reached east Bakersfield in 1874. The town saw a jump in population after gold was discovered in the Kern River Valley in 1885. More significant were the discoveries of oil in the region in the late 1800s. Bakersfield has also established itself as a major market and distribution center for the region's agricultural produce. Oil and agriculture remain the backbone of the town's economy.

A fire destroyed much of the original downtown in 1889, but the city was rebuilt within two years. Bakersfield has since

Bakersfield, circa 1896

been forced to battle several disasters, such as a flood in 1893 and another major fire in 1919. The worst disaster was an earthquake that seriously damaged parts of the town in 1952. Yet the region continued to grow and develop throughout the latter half of the twentieth century. Bakersfield remains the major city in Kern County; the 2000 census registered a population of 247,057, almost four times the 1970 count. Today's population is quite diverse; it is more than one-third minority, including 28 percent Hispanic. Tourist attractions include the County Museum and the reconstructed Pioneer Village.

GPS COORDINATES: N35°22.80' W119°01.06'

NEAREST TRAIL: Central Mountains #12: Rancheria Road

Ballarat

Ballarat, once described as the "wraith of the desert," sits in the Panamint Valley at the western edge of Death Valley National Park. Australian immigrant George Riggins proposed the name, after the rich Ballarat goldfields in Victoria, Australia. The Australian goldfields were well known, and townspeople hoped that the Ballarat name would attract investors to the Panamint Valley.

From 1897 to 1917, Ballarat served as a supply center for the mines in the Argus, Panamint, and Slate Ranges, although it was mainly supported by the Ratcliff and World Beater Mines in Pleasant Canyon. In 1896, Henry C. Ratcliff identified the Never Give Up claim, later known as the Ratcliff (Radcliff or Radcliffe) Mine. Workers then set up a small mining camp at Post Office Springs, one of only a few sources of potable water in the area. Meanwhile, the Montgomery brothers were starting up their own profitable mine, the World Beater. Together, the two mines required a collective labor force of approximately 200. Post Office Springs could no longer accommodate this many men; thus, in July 1897, workers established Ballarat below the canyon at the base of Panamint Valley. The boom lasted several years.

Ballarat's population grew to nearly 500 people. Soon the town supported several saloons, a Wells Fargo station, the Calloway Hotel, a post office, and a school. It had a jail and a morgue, but no churches. By 1900, seven mills were operating in the area. However, in 1905, the Ratcliff Mine suspended operations, and the Montgomery brothers found further mining success at Skidoo. Much of the workforce in Ballarat relocated. The town continued to serve as a supply center for the region, but by 1917, it was all but abandoned. Today, it consists of a small general store.

Ballarat has played host to many famous (and infamous) people. In 1930, Michael J. "Jim" Sherlock bet local gamblers that he could break the speed record between Ballarat and Los Angeles. What gamblers didn't know was that Sherlock's wagon could be broken down and bundled into a relatively manageable size. Instead of going around a mountain, Sherlock packed his wagon on a team of burros and headed straight over it. He ended up beating the old record by a full day. Sherlock died in 1935 and is buried in the Ballarat Cemetery.

Charles "Seldom Seen Slim" Ferge settled in Ballarat around 1915. A philosopher and poet, Slim claimed he hadn't taken a bath in 20 years because water was too scarce to waste. He quickly became the subject of many Death Valley tales. Soon after his death in 1968, the U.S. Department of the Interior designated one of the peaks in the Panamint Range as Slim's Peak.

Ballarat was also the home of Frank "Shorty" Harris, a prospector who discovered the massive $650 per ton Bullfrog Gold Mine near Beatty, Nevada. Rumors were that while inebriated he sold the claim for $500 and a mule. His tombstone in Death Valley reads "Here lies Shorty Harris, a single blanket jackass prospector."

Charles Manson, one of America's most notorious criminals, and his "family" hid from authorities in the Panamint Range. The Manson Family relocated several times, eventually setting up camp at the Barker Ranch. While there, the group traveled throughout Death Valley, frequenting Ballarat regularly. In October 1969, Manson and eight of his followers were captured at Barker Ranch. He and four others were sentenced to death, but because of changes in California law, they are now serving life sentences.

GPS COORDINATES: N36°02.89' W117°13.40'

TRAIL: Desert #33: Mengel Pass Trail; Desert #35: Pleasant Canyon Loop Trail

MAPS: Pages 568, 576

Banner

Banner was the sister city of Julian, the nucleus of San Diego County's only significant mining operations. Around 1870, Louis Redman was searching for wild grapes in the shadow of Volcan Mountain in the San Diego Mountains when he discovered a deposit of gold. To mark his find, Redman planted a small American flag, hence the name Banner. Banner grew with each successive gold strike and reached a peak of almost 1,000 residents, complete with a hotel, three general stores, and four saloons. Nearby Banner Grade Road was considered the most dangerous road in Southern California in the 1870s, and it is still inadvisable to travel it at more than 25mph. Unlike its companion town, Banner did not

Banner

outlast its gold mining days, and today little remains at the original site, now a campground 6 miles east of Julian on California 78.

GPS COORDINATES: N33°04.11' W116°32.77' (approximately)

NEAREST TRAIL: South Coast #23: Grapevine Canyon Trail

Barstow

The area around Barstow has long been a resting point for weary travelers making their way across the Mojave Desert. Evidence of Native Americans found in the vicinity has been dated back more than 3,000 years. The area became important for silver mining in the 1860s when ore was discovered in nearby mountains. It was in this decade that the town was first settled.

In 1882, the Southern Pacific Railroad extended its line from Mojave to Daggett, which was already connected to the mining center in Calico. For some time, these towns eclipsed Barstow in terms of population and importance. But when silver, and later borax, deposits were depleted, the rival settlements faded. Before the completion of the Southern Pacific line, Barstow was known as Fishpond, after a waterhole. The name was changed to Waterman after Robert W. Waterman, president of the Southern Pacific and later governor of California (1887–91). It was renamed for the last time four years later for the president of the Atchison, Topeka & Santa Fe Railroad, William Barstow Strong, whose surname was already used for Strong City.

Santa Fe Hotel in Barstow

As a vital railroad junction, Barstow grew in importance in the early years of the twentieth century. Route 66 (now called the National Trails Highway) also passed through the expanding city, and Barstow became a jumping off place for migrants entering California. This route into the state was made famous by novelist John Steinbeck in his book *The Grapes of Wrath*. Barstow's Main Street preserves some of the historic traveling facilities from an earlier era.

Unlike many settlements on Route 66, Barstow did not decline with the advent of the interstate highway system. Interstate 40, Interstate 15, and California 58 all pass through the town. Barstow remains an important supply junction and stopping point for travelers. It is situated almost exactly midway between Los Angeles and Las Vegas in San Bernardino County. Barstow was incorporated in 1947 and in the 2000 census it boasted a population of 23,050. It lies in an extremely dry region of California and receives an average yearly rainfall of less than six inches. Daytime summer temperatures regularly exceed 100 degrees Fahrenheit, although nights and winters can get quite cold.

GPS COORDINATES: N34°53.18' W117°01.32'

NEAREST TRAIL: South Coast #16: Daggett Wash Trail

Belleville

The mining community of Belleville was established during the 1860s rush to southwestern San Bernardino County. Gold was first discovered in the area by Indiana native William F. "Uncle Billy" Holcomb, after whom Holcomb Valley is named. Holcomb found deposits in the San Bernardino Mountains in May 1860 and within a few weeks hopeful miners were streaming into the region. One of the first prospectors to arrive was Jed Van Dusen, who spent $1,500 to build a road into town. His wife gave birth to the first baby born in the settlement, Belle Van Dusen, after whom the town was named.

At its peak, Belleville's population was about 1,500 and miners were extracting an estimated 50 ounces of gold a week from the nearby hills. Most of the gold was found in easily worked placer deposits. In September 1861, the town lost the county seat election by just two votes to San Bernardino.

Belleville quickly gained a reputation for being quite violent. The surrounding region was a stronghold of Confederate sympathizers during the Civil War and a gathering place for volunteers eager to fight for the secessionist cause. One man was killed in a shootout between Union sympathizers and Rebels in 1861, and further violence was prevented only when four companies of infantry and a regiment of cavalry were dispatched from San Francisco.

There were also a fair number of less politically motivated shootings, and a tall juniper tree in town bears testimony to the fate of captured perpetrators. Every time someone was hanged from one of the limbs, the branch was sawed off. The tree is missing quite a few of its lower branches! Other ruins in Belleville include an entrance to the Mitzger Mine, Two Gun Bill's Saloon, some mining equipment, and the grave of a miner named Ross, whose friends hand-carved a picket fence around his final resting place. Like other mining camps,

Belleville faded when local gold deposits played out. By 1880, only a handful of residents remained. Before long, the rich settlement that almost became the San Bernardino county seat was a ghost town.

GPS COORDINATES: N34°18.07' W116°53.07'
TRAIL: South Coast #13: Big Pine Flat Trail
MAP: Page 333

Berdoo Camp

The name Berdoo comes from a common shortening of San Bernardino. Unlike most ghost towns in California, Berdoo Camp was never a mining community. It was established in 1933 as division headquarters for the Colorado River Aqueduct Project, being built to carry water from Parker Dam to Los Angeles. Workers were housed at Berdoo Camp while constructing the East Coachella Tunnel, an 18.3-mile section of the project.

By 1935, Berdoo Camp had more than 35 buildings, the dominant structure being a modern 35-bed hospital, complete with air-conditioning and an X-ray machine. By the time it closed in October 1936, the hospital had treated only 12,000 patients, a low number considering the dangerous work.

Each morning, workers descended 2,042 feet into the Little San Bernardino Mountains to work on the tunnel. The section of the East Coachella Tunnel completed by the men stationed at Berdoo Camp was about 5.5 miles long, the longest of the whole Colorado River Aqueduct Project. After their shifts, workers retired to company dormitories, for which they paid a quarter a day. They were also served hearty meals in the dormitories, at an additional cost of $1.15 per day.

Work on the East Coachella Tunnel was completed by 1937. Buildings and equipment were sold, and the town was abandoned. The Colorado River Aqueduct was finished in 1939. Today little remains of Berdoo Camp, just some roads, a few concrete foundations, and some crumbling walls. The site is north of Indio in Riverside County.

GPS COORDINATES: N33°50.06' W116°08.74'
TRAIL: South Coast #39: Berdoo Canyon Trail
MAP: Page 407

Big Bear Lake, Big Bear City

Two settlements are situated on the banks of man-made Big Bear Lake—Big Bear City and Big Bear Lake. The reservoir inundated a large area of Bear Valley, which was named by John Frémont in 1848 after he noticed a large number of bears in the area.

The valley was first flooded in 1885. Frank Elwood Brown organized construction of the original dam in order to create a reliable water source for nearby citrus farmers. Brown's dam was a unique single-arch rock dam, made entirely from local granite. Granite from surrounding hillsides was cut by hand into huge blocks, each weighing two to three tons. The dam was 20 feet wide at the bottom and only 3 feet wide at the top. At the time, the 52-foot-tall dam created the largest man-made lake in the world. The walls were relatively thin, but extremely strong. Despite the reservoir's size, plans began almost immediately to build a newer, bigger dam. In 1910, construction started on Eastwood Dam, 150 feet upstream from the rock dam. The new dam was only 20 feet higher than the old one, but it increased the amount of water in Big Bear Lake by three times.

Bear Valley Dam

The shores of Big Bear Lake soon became a popular vacation spot for people from all over Southern California. Lodges and camps sprang up along the lakeshore to accommodate the visitors, many of whom were among the wealthiest in the state. Big Bear City was originally called Van Dusen. Founded in 1927, it took its name from Jed Van Dusen, an early settler in the area. The name changed to Big Bear City in 1928. The settlement has never incorporated.

The town of Big Bear Lake was founded in 1891 as a logging camp. Trees around Bear Valley provided lumber for construction projects in San Bernardino and Los Angeles. Large-scale logging continued in the surrounding San Bernardino Mountains until the second decade of the twentieth century. Until 1905 the camp was called Pinelake. From 1912 until 1938 it took the name Pine Knot. From 1938 onward the settlement was officially called Big Bear Lake. However, throughout its early years, people were already referring to the settlement as Big Bear Village, Big Bear Lake Village, or simply the Village. In its early years, the village was crowded during summer but virtually abandoned during winter. The seasonal imbalance started to change in the 1930s, when townspeople began to promote skiing and other winter activities around Big Bear Lake. One prominent citizen, Judge Clifford L. Lynn, raised money to build a 3,000-foot-long chairlift. The project was completed in 1949, a few months after Lynn's death. The chairlift marked the beginning of Big Bear Lake as a major ski area in Southern California. The city of Big Bear Lake was incorporated in 1980.

Today, the settlements around Big Bear claim to be "four season resorts." Summer and winter activities now attract many thousands of visitors every year.

GPS COORDINATES: Big Bear Lake: N34°14.39' W116°54.63'
Big Bear City: N34°15.66' W116°50.68'
NEAREST TRAIL: South Coast #13: Big Pine Flat Trail
MAP: Page 333

Big Sur

Big Sur is a coastal region of central California approximately 25 miles south of Carmel. It gets its name from the Spanish *el pais grande del sur,* which means "the big country to the south." For many years, the region was removed from all settlement by the rugged coastline and the natural barrier of the Santa Lucia Range. The same factors that prevented people from inhabiting the region in previous years make it a wonderful place to live or visit today: the high cliffs abutting the fierce ocean, the scenic mountains, and the steep canyons of Los Padres National Forest.

Juan Bautista Alvarado (later a Mexican governor of California) received a land grant for the region in 1834, but the area remained unsettled until European-Americans began to enter Big Sur in the 1850s. Over the next two decades, a number of ranchers took advantage of the isolated region to raise cattle. George Davis is thought to be the first American to homestead in the region. He built a cabin along the banks of the Big Sur River in what is now Pfeiffer Big Sur State Park.

Michael Pfeiffer was also an early settler in Big Sur. He arrived with his 16-year-old wife, Barbara, in fall 1869. The couple raised cattle, sheep, and pigs and planted crops in Sycamore Canyon. They eventually raised eight children; their second son, John, opened the first lodge in the region. In 1934, John Pfeiffer sold 706 acres of his land to the state at a reduced price to form the nucleus of the Pfeiffer Big Sur State Park. Other area residents have also entrusted land to the government, helping to preserve parts of the scenic coast.

The first reliable road into Big Sur was completed in the 1870s under the guidance of Charlie Bixby, but it was not until 1937 that the first highway cut along the coastline. California 1 increased access into Big Sur, but its construction angered some residents, who thought it threatened some of the region's natural beauty.

Big Sur was still underpopulated in the middle of the twentieth century, when it became popular among artists and writers fleeing an increasingly commercialized Carmel-by-the-Sea. Poet Robinson Jeffers wrote extensively about the scenic beauty of Big Sur. Beat author Jack Kerouac published his critically acclaimed novel *Big Sur* in 1962. The insightful personal work chronicles Kerouac's three-week stay in the region in the summer of 1960. Playwright Henry Miller published a number of works while living there, including *Big Sur and the Oranges of Hieronymus Bosch.*

For a time, Big Sur was host to an annual folk festival organized by legendary performer Joan Baez. Today, the musical tradition continues with the Big Sur Jazz Festival, held every May. Recently, the region has become home to an increasing number of quality restaurants and guesthouses, though it still retains much of its unique rural atmosphere.

GPS COORDINATES: N36°16.18' W121°48.39'
NEAREST TRAIL: Central Mountains #51: Coast Road

Blythe

Blythe is a pleasant little town situated on the Colorado River, near the border between California and Arizona. It was founded in 1908 by the Palo Verde Land and Water Company and was incorporated on July 21, 1916. The settlement was named after Thomas H. Blythe, who first came to the area in 1877. Blythe was a San Francisco entrepreneur interested in diverting water from the Colorado River to the arid desert to the west. He began construction of a canal for this purpose, the first project of its kind on the river. However, he died of a heart attack before his plans could be realized. Water rights froze after Blythe's death, and it was some years before work was restarted.

By 1950, the Palo Verde Land and Water Company had been successful in irrigating the surrounding area, which now produces lettuce, melons, alfalfa, and barley and provides grazing land for livestock. The 2000 census counted 21,500 residents of Blythe, but this number more than triples in the winter when visitors arrive seeking refuge from harsher climates. The river east of Blythe is part of the Colorado River Recreation Area, a 650-mile section of the waterway that offers fishing, boating, and other water-sport opportunities. Hiking, rockhounding, and backcountry driving are all popular in the Blythe region. The town promotes itself as "the City of the Outdoors." Blythe has also recently constructed the Palo Verde Historical Museum to celebrate the region's history.

About 15 miles north of Blythe on US 95, visitors can view some remarkable examples of Native American art—the Blythe Intaglios. The large designs are thought to be at least 1,100 years old.

GPS COORDINATES: N33°36.49' W114°36.26'
NEAREST TRAIL: Desert #2: Blythe Intaglios Trail

Borrego Springs

Borrego Springs is a unique desert community surrounded on all sides by the Anza-Borrego Desert State Park, whose headquarters are 1.5 miles northwest of downtown. The region has been continually inhabited by humans for at least 6,000 years. When one of the first European visitors, Juan Bautista de Anza passed through the area in 1774, two subtribes of the Yuma (the Kumeyaay and the Northern Diegueno) and the Cahuilla Indians all lived in the vicinity. Anza, for whom the state park is named, was scouting an overland route from Sonora, Mexico, to San Diego and Monterey. His route, which came close to the present-day town of Borrego Springs, was soon closed by the Yuma uprising of 1781.

The Butterfield Overland Stage passed through this region of desert. The stagecoaches delivered mail until 1861 and the advent of the Civil War. Ranchers began grazing cattle in the Borrego Valley in the 1870s. The place was called Borrego Springs as early as 1883 because it was an important watering point for local bighorn sheep. (*Borrego* is the Spanish word for "yearling lamb.") The small community lay in an isolated part of San Diego County. It was scarcely populated well into the 1900s, although hopeful prospectors often trekked the arid region seeking gold. The most famous rainbow-chaser of the Anza-Borrego Desert was Pegleg Smith. Pegleg's stories about a lost fortune of black gold in the local mountains continue to attract hopeful treasure-seekers to Borrego Springs. Every year in April, "pegleggers" hold a Pegleg Smith Liars' Contest to regale one another with fictional stories about the legendary character.

The army and the navy used the Borrego Springs area as a

training ground during World War II and constructed many of the first paved roads and electrical lines in Borrego Springs. After the war, helped by the arrival of air conditioning, the region's population grew. Borrego Springs got its first post office in 1947. The Anza-Borrego Desert State Park was established around this time to preserve the vast open spaces and limit population growth.

Interestingly, Borrego Springs has never been incorporated, so it still has no mayor or any form of municipal government.

GPS COORDINATES: N33°15.38' W116°22.43'

NEAREST TRAIL: South Coast #25: South Coyote Canyon Trail

Brawley

The city of Brawley is located north of El Centro in Imperial County. The Imperial Land Company first laid out the settlement in 1902. Los Angeles resident J. H. Braly had previously owned the property upon which the town was situated and the settlement became known as Braly. Fearing the project would fail, Braly refused to give his name to the town, so a substitute, Brawley, was suggested by the general manager of the Imperial Land Company, A. H. Heber, who had a friend in Chicago by that name. It seemed unlikely that anything would grow in the desert environment, but extensive planning by the land company enabled the region to become one of the most productive in the state.

Brawley was incorporated in 1908. Today, the town has a population of about 22,000. Residences are generally less expensive than elsewhere in Southern California. Brawley lies in the Colorado Desert, 10 miles south of Salton Sea, 25 miles north of Mexico, and 125 miles east of San Diego. It enjoys a warm year-round climate. Winter temperatures are especially enticing, averaging in the low 70s. Water from the Colorado River, 30 miles to the east, has enabled Brawley to escape water shortages common in Southern California. The city is currently offering tax credits to businesses in an effort to persuade them to relocate to, or start up in, this pleasing little town. One highlight of Brawley's annual calendar is the Cattle Call Rodeo, held every November since 1956. The Cattle Call Arena is supposedly one of the finest of its type in the world.

GPS COORDINATES: N32°58.73' W115°32.44'

NEAREST TRAIL: South Coast #26: Truckhaven Trail

Calexico

Until the early 1900s, inland Southern California was largely uninhabitable. The Imperial Land Company sought to change the desert landscape by channeling water from the Colorado River to irrigate land in what is now Imperial County. Calexico was established in 1900 by George Chaffey as a tent city of the Imperial Land Company on the California-Mexico border. Prior to its use in the irrigation project, Calexico was the site of Salvation Camp. The camp acted as a refugee center for forty-niners seeking a southern route into California during the gold rush.

Calexico took its name from a combination of California and Mexico. Its sister city in Baja California, Mexico, is called Mexicali. The city was incorporated in 1908 and soon gained a reputation as a rowdy border town. During Prohibition, in the 1920s, workers flocked to adjacent Mexicali in search of the intoxicating activities made illegal by the Volstead Act of 1919.

Cotton gin in Calexico, circa 1914

Today, Calexico's economy is still based upon its position on the Mexican border, but its atmosphere is much less tawdry. Trucking companies ship many tons of produce into the United States through Calexico and many binational companies have their headquarters in town. Because of its location, the region retains a strong multicultural identity. Mexicali, literally right across the street, is a booming metropolis and the capital of Baja California.

GPS COORDINATES: N32°40.20' W115°29.84'

NEAREST TRAIL: South Coast #34: Painted Gorge–Carrizo Mountain Trail

Calico

Humans first inhabited the Calico area more than 10,000 years ago. Evidence of early inhabitants was discovered in 1942 by some amateur archaeologists. The artifacts included many stone tools, such as knives, scrapers, and saw-like utensils. Famed paleontologist Dr. Louis Leakey, who discovered the oldest human remains ever found at Olduvai Gorge in East Africa, visited the site on several occasions. The age of the artifacts is debated. Some experts claim they could be 200,000 years old, which would make them by far the earliest evidence of humans in the Western Hemisphere.

Mining has occurred in the Calico Mountains, named for their multicolored rock formations, since the 1860s. It began in earnest in 1881 with the discovery of the Silver King Mine. Soon the roads from San Bernardino were full of hopeful young men seeking a fortune in the hills. The town of Calico sprang up on a narrow ledge below the Silver King. Just one year after the discovery of rich silver ore, the settlement bustled with more than 2,000 residents and many saloons and stores. Many of the newcomers were former tin miners from Cornwall, England.

Although Calico was never as violent as some western mining towns, it had its fair share of colorful characters. One hotel owner named Bill Harpold ran a dilapidated establishment on the outskirts of town. Much of the building was constructed from old liquor barrels. Breakfast was chili and whisky. When the ceiling collapsed on some visitors, Harpold apologized, saying, "Sorry about the leaky roof." Another famous Calico resident was Dorsey, the mail-carrying dog, who faithfully delivered letters for many years.

Calico was one of the towns that used the famous 20-mule teams (see page 101) to transport goods and ore. Until 1898, the closest railroad station was several miles away in Daggett. The railroad was eventually constructed not to carry silver, but borax. The silver industry was just beginning its decline when the first samples of calcium borate were discovered in the hills east of Calico. Soon the area became as prosperous from borax mining as it ever had from silver.

Eventually, however, the borax trade went bust and the town was slowly deserted. By 1929 it was a ghost town. In the early 1950s, the land was bought by former miner Walter Knott, the founder of Knott's Berry Farm southeast of Los Angeles. Today, Calico is a reconstructed commercial ghost town that is more famous than it ever was during its mining peak. One-third of the buildings are original, but the rest are careful replicas. Recent prices for admission were $6 for adults, $3 for children 6–15, and free for children 5 and under. Visitors can take a walking tour, visit an underground silver mine, and ride a narrow gauge railroad.

Graveyard in the desert at Calico

GPS COORDINATES: N34°56.93' W116°51.89'
NEAREST TRAIL: South Coast #16: Daggett Wash Trail

California City

In the late 1950s, progressive college professor Nat Mendelsohn purchased 80,000 acres of land in Boron Valley and started to plan a model desert city. The California City Development Company was formed to sell lots and homes. The Gold Ribbon Days Celebration in October 1958 marked the opening of the first 20 homes in the planned community. Before long, the settlement had a hotel, motel, supermarket, gas station, and four stores.

From this humble beginning, California City grew rapidly. The 80-acre Central Park was laid out, complete with an 18-acre lake. Soon the town had a 3-par golf course, a ski area, and a sports arena. Incorporated on November 16, 1965, the city has grown to a population around 9,000. It is the closest town to both Edwards Air Force Base and NASA's Dryden Research Center. In acreage, California City is the third largest incorporated city in the state, encompassing 204 square miles. Attractions include the California City Skydiving Club, one of the largest in North America, and Tierra Del Sol, an 18-hole championship golf course. Planning for every new city expansion is extensive, so California City has become a favored town for both families and businesses. A mid-1990s state retail survey picked the town as one of the best retail markets in all of California.

GPS COORDINATES: N35°07.56' W117°58.39'
NEAREST TRAIL: Central Mountains #26: Koehn Lake Trail

Camp Coxcomb

Control of North Africa was vitally important during World War II because the region was a gateway to the British-controlled oil fields on the Arabian Peninsula. Upon entering the war, the United States decided to send troops to aid its allies in Africa. The Southwestern deserts provided an ideal training ground in which to train for this arena. Camp Coxcomb was one of 11 subcamps of the Desert Training Center (DTC) set up in California, Nevada, and Arizona. From 1942 to 1944, the DTC prepared more than 1 million troops for battle.

Operation of the camps was overseen by General George S. Patton, later famous for commanding the Third Army, which swept through northern France in the final stages of the European war. Patton was unfamiliar with the desert and was assisted by Roy Chapman Andrews, an explorer of the American Museum of Natual History who had made many expeditions into the Gobi Desert. The environment faced by trainees was truly daunting; the land was dry and inhospitable and accommodations were primitive. Troops quickly learned the importance of a good supply line.

Evidence of military operations can still be seen in the vicinity of Camp Coxcomb. Piles of stones are the remnants of makeshift bunkers. The area has been swept for unexploded ammunition several times, but caution should still be used. Digging is prohibited and certainly ill advised. Report any dud bombs to the authorities.

Troops trained at the DTC, later renamed the California-Arizona Maneuver Area (CAMA) were instrumental in securing North Africa for the Allies. From Africa, Allied armies were able to invade Italy, opening a southern front in Europe and forcing Mussolini from power. With the Nazis occupied in Italy and on the Russian front, the Allies were able to liberate France and later defeat Germany itself. Attentions then turned to America's original instigator, Japan, which finally capitulated in August 1945. Troops from CAMA were employed in all these theaters. A monument at Camp Coxcomb thanks "all the soldiers that served here, and especially... those who gave their lives in battle, ending the holocaust & defeating the armed forces of Nazi Germany, Fascist Italy and Imperial Japan."

GPS COORDINATES: N33°54.49' W115°14.82' (historical marker)
NEAREST TRAIL: Desert #1: Palen Pass Trail

Camp Young

Camp Young was the headquarters of the Desert Training Center (DTC), 18,000 square miles of land in California, Nevada, and Arizona where American troops trained for combat in World War II. It was named after Lieutenant General S. B. M. Young, the First Army chief of staff. In addition to Camp Young, eleven subcamps were created: Camp Coxcomb (see above), Camp Iron Mountain, Camp Granite, Camp Ibis, Camp Hyder, Camp Horn, Camp Laguna, Camp

Pilot Knob, Camp Clipper, Camp Rice, and Camp Bouse. They were established in the spring of 1942 by General George S. Patton.

Conditions were primitive at the camps. There was no time to set up proper facilities because the camps' sole purpose was field training for troops. Tent life was the norm. Patton also lived at the camp, though he had been offered accommodations not too far west, at Indio. His wife, Beatrice, stayed at a nearby ranch during the general's time in the desert. She donated a piano to the troops for entertainment purposes. It is currently on display in the nearby General George S. Patton Memorial Museum. From 1942 until the camps were deemed unnecessary on March 16, 1944, more than 1 million U.S. troops were trained on the DTC, the largest military training ground ever to exist. Thirteen infantry divisions, seven armored divisions, and numerous smaller units grew accustomed to the desert environment in the American Southwest before they were sent to fight in North Africa. The museum was opened in 1988 to educate the public about the important contributions made by these troops.

GPS COORDINATES: N33°40.50' W115°43.37' (museum)
TRAIL: South Coast #44: Red Canyon Trail
MAP: Page 422

Carmel

The town of Carmel-by-the-Sea, now generally referred to as Carmel, lies on the south side of the Monterey Peninsula while Monterey is on the north side. The peninsula was first visited by Europeans in 1602, when Sebastián Vizcaíno (see page 70) landed there on his voyage of discovery. Vizcaíno was very impressed with Monterey Bay and held a ceremony on the peninsula to celebrate claiming it for Spain. The ceremony was conducted under an oak tree close to the shore. Vizcaíno also named the Carmel River as Río del Carmelo. Carmelo is the name for Mount Carmel near Jerusalem; it is based on the Hebrew *Kerem-El*, which means "Vineyard of God."

For the next 150 years, the area was not visited by the Spanish, and Costanoan Indians lived there much as they had for centuries. Colonization around Monterey Bay began in 1770 when the renowned Franciscan missionary Junípero Serra (see page 71) held another ceremony under Vizcaíno's oak tree and dedicated the presidio of Monterey and the Mission San Carlos Borroméo de Carmelo. The first building for the new mission was constructed on the site where the San Carlos Church stands today. The mission became Serra's favorite, and he spent much of his remaining life there, although he traveled a great deal throughout Southern California. The surviving church was finished in 1797, 13 years after Serra's death. The mission was abandoned in 1836 and its buildings fell into ruin until restoration was begun in the 1880s. Today, the Carmel Mission is a National Historic Landmark. In 1960, the Vatican raised the church to the rank of a minor basilica.

The town of Carmel-by-the-Sea, which stretches north of the mission to the beautiful golf courses of Pebble Beach, began as a writers' and artists' colony in the early years of the twentieth century. Creative artists such as poets Robinson Jeffers and George Sterling settled here, enticed by the area's quiet beauty and isolation. Although the community still retains some of its early atmosphere, it has become a popular tourist destination. Visitors continue to be drawn by the nearby golf courses, sunny beaches, picturesque streets, and historic mission. Just south of the city lies Point Lobos State Reserve, which encompasses 1,250 acres of coastal inlets for wildlife and includes a stand of Monterey cypress and several sea lion rookeries.

Actor Clint Eastwood served as mayor of Carmel from 1986 to 1988 after winning a staggering 72 percent of the vote. In his two years in office, he pushed through the construction of several beach walkways and a library annex. Despite his popularity, "Dirty Harry" assured his constituents that his concern was for Carmel and that he had no wider political aspirations. Eastwood's continued absence from politics since leaving office seems to have confirmed his claim.

GPS COORDINATES: N36°33.12' W121°55.42'
NEAREST TRAIL: Central Mountains #51: Coast Road

Cerro Gordo

Cerro Gordo was the most important mining discovery of the 1860s. It contributed to the economic growth of Los Angeles much as the Comstock find did for San Francisco. Pablo Floras, a Mexican prospector, is attributed with having worked the first claim in this region of the Inyo Mountains east of Lone Pine in 1865. The lack of water and firewood in this remote, high elevation location were definite deterrents in the mine's development. The promising silver veins gave rise to the name Cerro Gordo, meaning "fat hill" in Spanish, yet little development occurred.

In 1866, Victor Beaudry, a merchant from nearby Fort Independence, noticed promising ore reaching the mill near his store. His interest was piqued. Within a year, he opened a store in Cerro Gordo and attracted financial interest from as far away as San Francisco. An engineer from San Francisco named Mortimer Belshaw bought in, too, and lost no time in constructing a toll road down from the mountain. Called the Old Yellow Grade Road, the toll road traveled via the least steep descent. The toll caused massive financial stress to poorer independent prospectors, as they had little option but to pay the high fee in order to get their ore off the mountain.

Belshaw and Beaudry joined forces, creating a near monopoly on the mountain. Next came the need to improve transportation to the markets in Los Angeles. Remi Nadeau's mule teams managed to freight massive quantities of silver and lead down the treacherously steep Yellow Grade, around the water-filled Owens Lake, and on to Los Angeles. Santa Barbara, Visalia, Ventura, and Bakersfield all fought hard to gain the freighting business but Los Angeles won, reaping millions for the developing pueblo. The ore-laden freight wagons would return from Los Angeles fully loaded with freshly grown produce from the San Fernando Valley for the ever-expanding Cerro Gordo camp. With alarming regularity, wagon trains leaving Cerro Gordo with 85-pound slabs of silver were held up.

With rising production in 1870, and a camp of nearly 2,000 people living and working in Cerro Gordo, thousands of ingots were stockpiled, awaiting transportation by Nadeau's mule teams to Los Angeles. After two years of increased min-

Cerro Gordo, circa 1872

ing production, mine operators realized they needed to shorten the difficult transportation route. They decided to ferry the ingots across Owens Lake. A lengthy wharf was constructed and the steamboats *Bessie Brady* and *Molly Stevens* were built to ferry the goods to the southwestern shores of the lake. Shipment of the ingots increased, despite the earthquake of 1872 that rocked the region, tilting the Owens Lake bed to the west. The new, altered water level forced settlers to build an extension to the wharf.

Greater demands for charcoal and timber at the booming mines created a lumber industry on the western side of Owens Lake. Cottonwood Canyon provided the transportation route for timber harvested from high up in the Sierra Nevada. Additional investors came to Cerro Gordo, developing more wharves and steamboat ferries, and helping millions of dollars' worth of silver to reach Los Angeles.

Cerro Gordo's frenzied mining activity may have peaked about the mid-1870s, as did its growing business rivalries. Expanding markets brought bitter competition within the region until a sequence of fires, landslides, and lawsuits, and a shifting of interest to the nearby mining town of Bodie brought about a general slowdown. By 1882 the steamboats had disappeared from Owens Lake, and the mines were being abandoned.

Ironically, the Carson & Colorado Railroad, which had been racing ahead to construct a line to Keeler to secure the transportation business for the Cerro Gordo mines, did not complete its line until 1883; by that time Cerro Gordo was winding down operations. Plans to complete a railroad through to Mojave were abandoned, and Keeler was officially the end of the line.

Little happened at Cerro Gordo until 1906, when the Great Western Ore and Reduction Company began mining for high-grade zinc. Aerial tramways still evident today were built to transport the ore to a terminus beside the lower section of the Yellow Grade Road. The immense weight of the ore traveling downhill was more than enough of a counterweight to haul supplies uphill to the mines in the emptied buckets. Cerro Gordo was back on the map and Keeler was a busy railroad depot. A standard gauge rail connection was constructed from Mojave to Owens Lake, where it connected with the old narrow gauge at Owenyo in 1910.

By 1913, Owens Lake was dry following the completion of the Los Angeles Aqueduct, which caught the Owens Valley waters, preventing them from flowing to the natural lake. Cerro Gordo improved its operations to extract silver and zinc from old workings, made profitable because of increasing metal prices. Limestone mining produced millions for Cerro Gordo in the 1920s. But by the late 1930s, large-scale mining was coming to a close in Cerro Gordo, and investors once again moved out. Much of the mining equipment and town has been recycled or has weathered away, leaving little evidence of the once bustling mining town that played a major part in the growth of early Los Angeles.

Today, the town is privately owned by Jodie Stewart, who has refurbished much of the site. She has already restored a 12-bed bunkhouse and a full house, which are both available to rent. The income generated from these rentals is reinvested to preserve Cerro Gordo for future generations.

GPS COORDINATES: N36°29.19' W117°51.94'

TRAILS: Desert #47: Cerro Gordo Road; Desert #48: Swansea–Cerro Gordo Road

MAPS: Pages 612, 616

Chloride City

Prospector August J. Franklin discovered the rich silver-lead ore deposits on Chloride Cliff in 1871. Franklin was wandering through Death Valley looking for minerals when he encountered a rattlesnake. To kill the snake, he picked up a rock and discovered a shiny metal beneath it. He established the Chloride Cliff Mine to extract the wealth from the hill. Unfortunately, the cost of transporting ore out of Death Valley made the operation prohibitively expensive; San Bernardino was 180 miles away, and the metals had to be hauled by mule train.

Franklin died in 1904 and passed the mine on to his son, George. Operations had ceased several years before, but new discoveries nearby, such as the profitable Bullfrog Mine, brought about renewed interest in Chloride Cliff. Three new companies, the Bullfrog Cliff Mining Company, the Mucho Mining Company, and the Death Valley Mining and Milling Company, arose to exploit the area around Chloride City. The settlement itself quickly grew and soon included a bunkhouse for miners, an assayer's office, a blacksmith, and a house for the mine superintendent. As was the case elsewhere in Death Valley, water was scarce in Chloride; it had to be transported from Keane Spring in the Funeral Mountains.

Mining was halted in 1906, when the great San Francisco earthquake tied up investors' money. It resumed in 1909, but ended again after a few decades. Most structures in Chloride City were not permanent, so little has survived the years.

GPS COORDINATES: N36°42.29' W116°52.92'

TRAIL: Desert #41: Chloride City Trail

MAP: Page 592

Claraville

In 1860, a prospector from Missouri named Robert Palmer found a rich vein of gold on Piute Mountain. To extract the metal from the mountain, Palmer founded the Hamp Williams Mine, named after his part-Cherokee partner. Other mines were soon being worked on Piute Mountain. The town of Kelso, which took its name from a nearby creek, sprang up to accommodate miners. The town was later renamed Claraville in honor of a miner's daughter, Clara Munckton.

The most profitable enterprise in the area was the Bright Star Mine, which was operated by three brothers who took everything they could from the mine and spent their earnings on the debaucheries available at every western mining camp. Their bad management sank the operations into debt.

Claraville's peak was short, but the town was the biggest one in the area during its boom. It had several saloons, hotels, and stores. It even played host to a local opera company. When the mines were played out, the town faded, and by 1880 it was deserted. No buildings remain from its early days; the last structure, a dilapidated courthouse, was moved to Bakersfield's Pioneer Village. Visitors can still view foundations and mining remains, though Piute Mountain is becoming wilderness once again.

GPS COORDINATES: N35°26.65' W118°19.50'
TRAIL: Central Mountains #16: Piute Mountain Road
MAP: Page 185

Coolgardie

Gold was discovered in easily obtainable deposits in the Mojave Desert around 1900, and a small settlement of several hundred miners soon sprang up. Coolgardie was named after the rich Western Australian mining town that became large and famous both for its wealth and its rough nature. California's Coolgardie never reached the same status, although it was one of the few placer mining districts in the desert. When the gold ran out after just a few short years, there was nothing in the desolate place to entice its residents to stay. Gradually the wooden structures crumbled, and today little remains except some rusted cans and piles of lumber where buildings used to stand. Coolgardie is 19 miles north of Barstow, and it is necessary to drive along a narrow dirt road to reach it. Visitors should exercise extreme caution because many mining shafts have not been filled in and a fall would leave a victim stranded in the middle of the desert.

GPS COORDINATES: N35°06.03' W117°03.12' (approximately)
NEAREST TRAIL: Desert #21: Black Canyon Road

Cudahay Camp

Cudahay Camp was the settlement founded by the Cudahay Packing Company as the headquarters for the Old Dutch Cleanser Mine. Miners from the camp extracted pumice seimotite. Activated seimotite was sold in the early 1900s for a variety of household tasks, primarily surface cleaning. The pumice was located under a layer of volcanic ash. A series of tunnels was cut into the white, chalky rock layer through openings in the cliff face. The large tunnels sloped nearly 45 degrees down to a transverse tunnel deep within the volcanic layer. A tramway carried the diggings through the main tunnel and down the steep cliff face into Last Chance Canyon. Mining trucks would transport the diggings all the way down Last Chance Canyon. Some sections of the old road that have endured decades of natural erosion are still visible in the canyon.

Advertisements for Old Dutch Cleanser featured a bonneted Dutch woman in a blue dress and white apron chasing dirt away with a wooden stick. The signs were very common until around 1950. They are now collectors' items, selling on the internet for greatly inflated prices.

Cudahay Camp was located in an old petrified wood forest. Early miners took most of the prize specimens, but small broken pieces can still be seen. Some larger segments are occasionally revealed by erosion, but it is illegal to remove any of the petrified wood because the area is under the jurisdiction of Red Rock Canyon State Park.

GPS COORDINATES: N35°24.66' W117°55.55'
TRAILS: Central Mountains #21: Opal Canyon Road; Central Mountains #23: Last Chance Canyon Trail
MAPS: Pages 202, 208

Daggett

Daggett, originally known as Calico Junction, was founded in the 1860s. In 1882, the Southern Pacific Railroad renamed it Daggett after John Daggett, the lieutenant governor of California at the time. The name was changed to avoid confusion with Calico, located just to the north. John Daggett built one of the first houses in the settlement, and it was he who laid out the original street design. The Atchison, Topeka & Santa Fe retained the name when it assumed control of the railroad junction several years later.

As the Calico and Death Valley mines developed, so did Daggett. A 10-stamp mill was in operation north of town near Elephant Hill by the early 1880s. Transportation to and from Calico and Death Valley was a major barrier until the famous 20-mule teams (see page 101) were put into action hauling supplies to the mines and returning with ore. *Old Dinah*, the steam-driven workhorse, was less successful at hauling ore and its failure brought about the return of the mule team. Calico went on to be the driving power behind Daggett. When trains were introduced, transportation costs fell from $2 per ton to less than 20 cents per ton. Fortunately, just as the silver mines played out, borax deposits were found to keep the trains in operation. Daggett had a rougher reputation than Calico; it was described by some as "the worst place between Mojave and New York."

By the early 1900s, Daggett supported a lumberyard, restaurants, three saloons, and several stores. The Stone Hotel was constructed in the early 1870s and was a favorite resting place for John Muir, the famous writer, conservationist, and first president of the Sierra Club, whose son-in-law was a native of the town. The hotel still stands, as do several other remnants from Daggett's heyday. Today, the town has a small historical museum to inform visitors about the area's past. Historic Route 66 passes through Daggett, so the small settlement (population, 200) still sees some tourist traffic.

GPS COORDINATES: N34°51.29' W116°53.61'
TRAIL: South Coast #16: Daggett Wash Trail
MAP: Page 344

Dale

There are actually three town sites with the name of Dale, all situated within several miles of each other in San Bernardino County. The town was moved through the Dale mining dis-

Dale

trict to be closer to whatever was the most productive mine at the time. Gold deposits were first discovered in the area in the early 1880s, the most productive of which was worked by the Virginia Dale Mine. The mine was quite profitable until about 1900, by which time it was largely depleted. Nevertheless, prospectors scoured the surrounding Pinto Mountains, and mining would continue in the area on a small scale well into the twentieth century.

The demise of the Virginia Dale Mine coincided with the development of the Supply Mine, several miles southeast of the original Dale settlement. Town residents, mostly miners, moved closer to the new mine and called the site New Dale. From that point on, the first Dale became known as Old Dale. Another settlement, Dale the Third, was also developed on a nearby bajada. All three towns obtained their water from a deep well in the dry bed of Dale Lake. By 1920, the major gold deposits had all been worked, and only minor operations continued in the region. Some housing remains survive at each of the three Dale sites, with the most remaining at Dale the Third. There are also adits and remnants of mines scattered around the area.

GPS COORDINATES: N34°07.33' W115°47.64' (Old Dale)
TRAILS: South Coast #41: Old Dale Road; South Coast #42: Brooklyn Mine Road
MAPS: Pages 412, 417

Darwin

In 1874, Rafael Cuervo discovered the first recorded mine in the vicinity of Darwin, the Promontoria. That same year, prospectors organized the New Coso Mining District and created the town of Darwin at the base of Ophir Mountain. The settlement was named after Dr. E. Darwin French, an early explorer of the area.

Once considered the gateway to Death Valley, Darwin featured more than 70 businesses, including two butcher shops, three restaurants, a doctor's office, and a lawyer's office. It had two smelters and twenty mines and supported two baseball teams. It quickly became the primary commercial center for the developing district; more than 3,000 residents occupied the town by 1877. But Darwin's success was short-lived. Promising gold strikes to the north at Bodie coupled with the nation's economic downturn signaled the beginning of the end of this lively community. Several other factors also contributed to Darwin's collapse: Mine production began to decline as rapidly as it had boomed; a violent labor dispute broke out; and the *Coso Mining News* shut down and moved its printing press to Bodie. But the town's true demise came in 1879 when a fire broke out in the commercial area, burning more than a dozen businesses to the ground.

Despite Darwin's ill-fated history, a shifting market rejuvenated the town in the early 1900s. Copper was extracted from mine tailings beginning in 1906, significant silver production marked the town in the 1910s, and by the 1920s, Darwin was producing a number of metals, including the majority of California's lead. In all, the area produced more than $3 million worth of metal.

The most productive mine in the area was the Defiance Mine, named after the many legal battles that took place over its ownership. A lurid county lawyer eventually acquired the property as payment for legal fees.

Today, geologists periodically probe the Defiance Mine for more ore. But Darwin is no longer considered the gateway to Death Valley. Construction of California 190 bypassed the town in 1937, thereby eliminating tourist traffic. These days, there is little to attract settlers to Darwin except the enticement of an isolated desert existence. In 1967, Superior Court Judge McCurry offered lots in the town for just $5 apiece! The current residents pride themselves on their close-knit community. Life in Darwin is a challenge, but the town continues to attract a stream of retirees and others seeking the isolation it provides.

GPS COORDINATES: N36°16.10' W117°35.47'
TRAIL: Desert #44: Darwin Falls Trail
MAP: Page 600

Doble

Not much is left of Doble except the remains of a cemetery and a mine headframe overlooking the dry Baldwin Lake. Once, a small community of miners flourished at the site. The settlement grew around the workings of Gold Mountain Mine, which was purchased by Elias Jackson "Lucky" Baldwin in 1876. Lucky had previously made a small fortune in mining near Virginia City and had spent a rumored $6 million to buy the rich mine. The community had previously been known as Bairdstown, but changed to Gold Mountain after Lucky bought the mine. Lucky put his son-in-law in charge of operations, and the town took its final name from this manager, Budd Doble.

Lucky also owned and operated a cyanide works and stamp mill in the area; remains of a 40-stamp mill can still be seen on the mountainside. Little else remains of Doble, which drifted into ghost town status when the nearby mine played out.

In addition to the dry lake, Lucky gave his name to the city of Baldwin Park, which is situated on what was once one of his many ranches.

GPS COORDINATES: N34°17.90' W116°49.25' (approximately)
TRAIL: South Coast #13: Big Pine Flat Trail
MAP: Page 333

El Centro

W. F. Holt and C. A. Barker bought the land on which El Centro was plotted in 1906 for about $40 an acre. They originally called the settlement Cabarker, after Barker, but soon changed it to El Centro to indicate that their new town was in the center of Imperial County. Holt's real estate company invested $100,000 in El Centro and the settlement grew rapidly. By 1910, El Centro had 1,610 residents. By 1920, the figure was 5,646.

Expansion was largely due to the irrigation of Imperial Valley, which enabled a variety of crops and livestock to thrive in the area. El Centro attracted more residents after it was chosen as Imperial County's seat and the site of the Imperial Irrigation District's administrative offices. A number of fruit and vegetable packers and produce shipping companies chose to locate in El Centro. Government offices and wholesale traders continue to be the largest employers in the area.

El Centro is still the county seat and most populous city in Imperial County. Because of its low elevation (-50 feet) it is sometimes known as the "largest city below sea level in the Western Hemisphere."

GPS COORDINATES: N32°47.50' W115°33.62'

NEAREST TRAIL: South Coast #34: Painted Gorge–Carrizo Mountain Trail

Escondido

Escondido is Spanish for "hidden." A creek near the present-day town was named Agua Escondido (Spanish for "hidden water") by the expedition of Spanish explorer Juan Bautista de Anza in 1776. The area was part of the Rancho Rincon del Diablo (Spanish for "The Devil's Corner Ranch"), a land grant given to the former Mexican governor of California, Juan Bautista Alvarado, by his successor, Manuel Micheltorena, in 1843.

The land grant was acquired in 1885 by the Escondido Land and Title Company, a syndicate of Los Angeles and San Diego businessmen. The company laid out a town site named after the nearby creek and divided the surrounding valley into small farms. Soon the region was flourishing with vineyards and citrus plantations. The city was incorporated on October 8, 1888.

Escondido, with hotel in distance, circa 1880

Located just 30 miles north of San Diego, Escondido expanded as the metropolis grew. The 2000 census registered a population of 133,559, of which 52 percent of those polled identified themselves as white and 39 percent as Latino. The cultural diversity gives the city a vibrant atmosphere. Family-owned businesses are still common in this pleasant Southern California town, but one of the biggest attractions is the California Center for the Arts, which attracts almost 300,000 visitors a year. The San Diego Wild Animal Park is also located close to Escondido.

GPS COORDINATES: N33°07.46' W117°04.53'

NEAREST TRAIL: South Coast #22: Santa Ysabel Creek Trail

Fresno

Fresno, the seat of the county of the same name, is the largest city in the San Joaquin Valley. Although the name comes from the Spanish word for "ash tree," Spanish and Mexican settlers ignored the area because it was too dry. The Central Pacific Railroad established a town at the present-day site in 1872 as a stopping point on its new line. Irrigation begun in the 1860s allowed for agricultural development of the arid region, which soon became renowned for its grapes.

The raisin industry in Fresno County started accidentally in 1875 when leading wine producer Francis Eisen let his grapes dry on the vines. The county is now the leading agricultural region in the nation, producing $3 billion a year in more than 200 commercial crops, including 60 percent of the world's raisins.

The city of Fresno grew steadily, aided by its central location amid fertile surroundings. Gold and oil discoveries in the late 1800s and a thriving lumber industry supplemented the burgeoning agricultural production. Fresno was incorporated on April 19, 1885. Several disasters—fires in 1882 and 1883 and a flood in 1884—stunted growth, but by 1900 Fresno was already the major market and shipping center in the San Joaquin Valley. California's first junior college, Fresno Junior College, was established in 1910 and later incorporated into the state school system.

One prominent citizen of the young city was Martin Theo Kearney. Kearney, president of the California Raisin Growers Association from 1898 to 1904, built a beautiful tree-lined avenue from Fresno to his vast estate. Kearney Avenue remains one of the most appealing urban drives in the state. Kearney Mansion, the agriculturalist's home, is open as a museum in the recreation area of Kearney Park.

Other attractions in Fresno include the Victorian Meux home, the Fresno Metropolitan Museum, and the unique Forestiere Underground Gardens. The underground gardens were built by the eccentric Sicilian Baldasare Forestiere between 1909 and 1949. They include 65 rooms, gardens, and grottoes.

Fresno remains one of the fastest growing cities in California. Since 1980, the population has almost doubled. Many of the more than 400,000 residents have relocated from crowded Los Angeles and San Francisco, attracted by Fresno's relatively low cost of living. Although there are few good backcountry trails in the immediate vicinity of the city,

The early days of Fresno

it serves more as a gateway to Yosemite, Sequoia, and Kings Canyon National Parks.
GPS COORDINATES: N36°45.03' W119°46.30'
NEAREST TRAIL: Central Mountains #2: Delilah Fire Lookout Trail

Garlock

Garlock came into being when an enterprising settler made the unlikely decision to dig a well on the edge of the barren El Paso Mountains. Surprisingly, water was found only 30 feet below the surface. For decades, the settlement then known as Cow Wells was a reliable watering stop for travelers through Death Valley. The town's ample water resources prompted Eugene Garlock to install a 5-stamp gold mill, the Garlock Pioneer Mill, in 1895, the same year prospectors struck gold at Randsburg. Garlock's mill processed the first ore from Randsburg's Yellow Aster Mine and other burgeoning mines in the area.

By 1899, six stamp mills and several hundred people resided in town. The legendary 20-mule teams hauled ore from the Yellow Aster Mine across the Fremont Valley. Garlock thrived. Two hotels offered accommodations to travelers. The town supported assayers, two saloons, a couple general stores, a Wells Fargo office, a school, and mine promoters. The two-story Doty Hotel gave the best view of the region, but that apparently was not terribly impressive. As one guest commented, "one could look farther and see less than at any point in the surrounding country."

Garlock's prosperity was short lived. In 1898, a railroad spur was completed to connect Johannesburg in the Rand Mining District to the Atchison, Topeka & Santa Fe line at Kramer. In the same year a water pipe was extended from Goler Wash to Randsburg. These two projects eliminated the region's need for Garlock's mills and water. By 1903, its little school had only three pupils; the post office closed in 1904. Garlock, once a town full of activity, was now deteriorating. Many of Garlock's residents and structures relocated to Randsburg.

Garlock did have two small revivals. In 1911, workers laying track for the Southern Pacific's line from Mojave to Keeler camped in the abandoned buildings. The crews moved on when the section of track was completed. Then in the early 1920s a salt company started to work deposits in nearby Kane Lake. The post office reopened in 1923, but by 1926 the salt project had failed and the office was forced to close again. Today, a rock and adobe structure known as Jennie's Bar remains, as does an automated Mexican arrastra.

Approximately 5 miles northwest of Garlock is evidence of a prehistoric Indian village, discovered in the 1880s. Some experts believe the same tribe who built the sites in Arizona and New Mexico inhabited the village. (Stone carvings resemble those found on the famous Posten Butte near Florence, Arizona.) Other experts believe the site was a religious center used intermittently.
GPS COORDINATES: N35°24.14' W117°47.42'
NEAREST TRAIL: Central Mountains #24: Burro Schmidt Tunnel Trail

Goffs

Goffs was originally built in the 1880s as a railroad depot on the Atlantic & Pacific line. It was named after a town in the East, as were all the stations on that stretch of line. One inventive railroad employee, probably a locating engineer named Lewis Kingman, decided to designate the towns alphabetically, starting with Amboy and continuing through Bristol, Cadiz, Danby, Edson, Fenner, Goffs, Homer, Ibex (later Ibis), and Klinefelter. Goffs became an important junction when the Nevada Southern Railroad was constructed, linking the Atlantic & Pacific line to the Eldorado, Goodsprings, and Ivanpah mining district, first as far as Manvel but later all the way to Ivanpah. The line was not abandoned until the 1920s. Another line connected Goffs to the mining district around Searchlight, Nevada, whose production peaked in the first decades of the twentieth century. Tons of gold, iron, and copper ore passed through Goffs at this time.

Goffs re-emerged as a waypoint for travelers after Route 66 was dedicated in 1926. The historic road, now known as the National Trails Highway, passed through Goffs and brought business to the small town. The military used the area for desert training in World War II and obliterated many of the buildings. An interestingly designed schoolhouse has been restored. It is filled with information on the surrounding desert region and its history.
GPS COORDINATES: N34°55.18' W115°03.89'
TRAIL: Desert #14: East Lanfair Valley Trail
MAP: Page 504

Goldstone

About 33 miles northeast of Barstow stand a few remnants of the town of Goldstone. The Goldstone area had attracted prospectors as early as 1850, but it was not until 1881 that the first gold frenzy occurred here. The town boomed for a while as interested miners flooded the region. The initial rush was short lived, but Goldstone's mining days were not finished. In December 1915, another discovery of gold brought prospectors back to the area and soon the town was dotted with claims. By 1920, these too had played out, and Goldstone was once again deserted.

Renewed interest in Goldstone surfaced in 1958, when the U.S. Army Ordinance Corps, Jet Propulsion Laboratory Division chose this radio reception-free environment as a deep-space communications center. The area is now leased by NASA, which has installed some large antennas and other equipment to monitor interplanetary spacecraft and satellites, and perhaps to listen for other noises from the deep reaches of space.

GPS COORDINATES: N35°17.95' W116°54.98'
NEAREST TRAIL: Desert #20: Starbright Trail
MAP: Page 526

Goler

In 1867, a German prospector named John Goler (Galler or Goller) discovered gold while traveling out of Death Valley. Weak, hungry, and fearful of an attack by Indians, he charted his find and headed south to the San Fernando Valley. With the help of Los Angeles financier Grant Price Cuddeback, Goler completed several expeditions back to the area. Although he struck gold in Red Rock Canyon and mined there for many years, he never found his original strike. It wasn't until 1893 that prospectors began to believe Goler's story when one of their finds seemed to match his claim. The area was named Goler Gulch, and the nearby mines in the El Paso Mountains became known as the Goler Mining District. John Goler himself never profited from the mines.

A few hundred miners briefly settled into the rough camp of Goler. The settlement mushroomed for a few years until the Rand discovery of 1895. That strike proved to be much richer, and prospectors hurriedly departed to Randsburg. Few permanent structures were ever constructed at Goler, so little remains today.

GPS COORDINATES: N35°24.67' W117°45.50' (approximately)
NEAREST TRAIL: Central Mountains #24: Burro Schmidt Tunnel Trail

Harrisburg

Harrisburg was named after the itinerant desert prospector Shorty Harris (see page 84). Harris and his partner, Pete Aguereberry, discovered a gold outcropping in the Panamint Range on July 1, 1905. The pair were traveling together on their way to Ballarat for a Forth of July celebration.

Word of the duo's find spread across Death Valley, mostly because of Harris's loose tongue. At first, the settlement near the claim was called Harrisberry in honor of both discoverers, but this was changed to Harrisburg, probably by Shorty. At its peak, the mining camp of Harrisburg was home to about 300 prospectors, but most fortune seekers were soon drawn to other discoveries, including those at nearby Skidoo. Harrisburg supported a general store and a saloon during its brief boom.

Most of the surviving structures at Harrisburg were the property of Aguereberry, who returned to the area years after the original rush. Aguereberry was a former sheepherder of Basque origin who turned to prospecting in search of fortune and excitement. During his career, Aguereberry faced recurrent problems common for small-time Death Valley miners. He and Shorty disagreed on ownership of the claims; some of Aguereberry's best ore was stolen from him while he attended church; and the prospector suffered from silicosis, a disease of the lungs often caught by miners from breathing in dust. Nevertheless, Aguereberry worked a small-scale mining operation at Harrisburg until his death in 1945 at the age of 72. Some maps identify the site as Aguereberry Camp.

GPS COORDINATES: N36°21.74' W117°06.36' (approximately)
NEAREST TRAIL: Desert #43: Skidoo Road

Havilah

Havilah was the first county seat of Kern County, which was formed in 1866 from parts of Los Angeles and Tulare Counties. The town was founded in 1864 by Kentucky native Asbury Harpending, a devout Christian who named the town after the biblical golden land of Havilah, discussed in Genesis 2:11. Before establishing the town, Harpending had served time in a San Francisco jail for outfitting a Confederate privateer during the Civil War. He made a fortune—$800,000—from Havilah, but not through gold mining. Harpending sold lots for $20 a front foot.

During its brief heyday, the town was a busy mining center. It had a population of more than 2,000 and was home to 147 businesses. In 1874, Havilah lost the county seat to Bakersfield in a closely contested election. Bakersfield, which retains the honor today, won by just 34 votes. Even before its loss, Havilah was in decline. The mines were depleted and many residents moved away. The post office closed in 1918. Still, not everyone left; the settlement has been continually inhabited for more than 130 years. Most of the current residents are ranchers or retirees.

Few structures remain from Havilah's peak, and one might never imagine it was once a county seat. The only important old landmark is the pioneer cemetery, although reproductions of the courthouse and schoolhouse have been constructed.

GPS COORDINATES: N36°31.00' W118°31.04'
NEAREST TRAIL: Central Mountains #16: Piute Mountain Road

Hedges (Tumco)

In pre-colonial times, Indians carved petroglyphs on the rocks near the twin cones of the Cargo Muchacho Mountains. They also did some crude mining; ancient tools are still found sometimes near the Tumco town site.

In the modern era, gold was first discovered in the desolate Cargo Muchacho Mountains of what is now Imperial County in the 1860s. For several years, Mexican prospectors quietly worked the mountains, extracting small amounts of gold and drawing little attention. In 1884, a trackwalker inspecting a line for the Southern Pacific Railroad was neglecting his job when he found a deposit of gold-laced mica schist in a canyon some distance from the company tracks. A mine was soon set up, operated by the now former railroad employee, C. L. Hedges. The camp that arose around the mine was initially called Gold Rock Camp, but by the 1890s it was known as Hedges, the name it would keep for most of its active existence.

At its peak, Hedges was home to more than 3,000 people. Most of the residents worked for the Golden Cross Milling and Mining Company, and violent disputes were somewhat

Hedges

uncommon. Hedges did have a less salubrious area of town on its outskirts. One particularly renowned establishment was the Stingaree Saloon, whose owner, Billy Horan, was also constable for Hedges.

In 1906, the Golden Cross Company was suffering financial strain and was forced to sell the Hedges mining operation to The United Mining Company. The new owners changed the settlement's name to an acronym of the company, Tumco. The new company closed operations just three years later and the town was quickly deserted. Mining was attempted sporadically, but generally unprofitably, until 1941. Since then, the settlement has drifted into its ghost town status. Today, a few stone ruins remain. Stone was the most abundant building material in this barren region. The most poignant sight in Tumco is probably the old cemetery. The graveyard looks quite well populated for a small town, but none of the final resting places for the town's inhabitants have kept any marker. The unmarked graves seem to highlight the desolation of the once bustling town.

GPS COORDINATES: N32°52.82' W114°49.59'
NEAREST TRAIL: South Coast #49: Indian Pass Road

Ibex

Ibex Spring was an important oasis for early desert travelers. Centuries-old Indian artifacts have been excavated around the spring. Mining in the region began in the 1880s. Gold, silver, and lead were all found in the hills around the spring. The Ibex Mine was founded in 1882 to extract silver-lead ore, and a small settlement called Ibex arose for mine workers. The operations were short lived, however, as transportation costs in the remote region proved insurmountable. Attempts to reopen the mine in the early 1900s were also foiled by the isolated location.

Another mine near Ibex Spring was located in 1901 by Judge L. Bethune. Sadly, the judge died alone in 1905, and the mine went amiss, acquiring a "lost" status until the following year. The new investors from Rhyolite, Nevada, incorporated under the name of the Lost Bethune Mining Company and sank more than a million dollars into developing their mines. Bunkhouses were constructed for the employees, and the ores were paying relatively well. However, as activity slowed in nearby Rhyolite, investors were scared away from the mines and haulage costs rose dramatically. By 1910, the Ibex Spring mines were quiet once again. The late 1910s saw a period of revival for the region. The old Ibex Mine was active for several years, with trucks hauling ore on a daily basis. These were promising times, yet by the early 1920s most of the mines lay idle. Lone prospectors would come and go as late as the 1970s, putting their efforts in for a time, then moving on.

Most of the remains at Ibex are from the talc-mining boom that began in the 1930s. The Moorehouse Mine was the most important of the area's operations. It yielded almost 62,000 tons before it played out in 1959. The ruins at Ibex were obtained by the Mojave River Museum in Barstow and are still maintained by the museum.

GPS COORDINATES: N35°45.92' W116°24.49'
TRAIL: Desert #30: Ibex Spring Road
MAP: Page 559

Ivanpah

The name Ivanpah comes from the Ute-Chemehuevi word *aavimpa*, meaning "white clay water." The appellation also referred to a supply center on the Nevada Southern Railroad, but this was a separate entity. In 1869, the Paiute Company of California and Nevada discovered silver ore in San Bernardino County's Clark Mountain, close to the Nevada border. By the following year, Ivanpah was the only center of civilization in the Mojave Desert. In its short existence, almost $4 million worth of ore was taken from the hills around the town.

The harsh environment was not suited to support a large population, and Ivanpah never had more than about 500 residents, its peak coming in 1872. By 1875, the population had dropped to 100. It never grew much above that, even after the 10-stamp Bidwell Mill was built in 1876. Competition from other strikes drew miners away from Ivanpah, and by 1882 the town was mostly deserted. A store remained opened for another 16 years, finally closing in 1898. The town's post office closed a year later. Today the remains of two mills, a smelter and ten or so stone and adobe houses mark the site, situated in a shallow canyon in the shadow of Clark Mountain.

GPS COORDINATES: N35°32.47' W115°31.63' (approximately)
TRAIL: Desert #24: Colosseum Gorge Trail
MAP: Page 543

Johannesburg

Named after the famous mining district in Transvaal, South Africa, Johannesburg, popularly known as Joburg, was the transportation hub of the Rand mining region. It was established in 1897, and in 1898 crews expanded the railroad from the Santa Fe line in Kramer north to Johannesburg. Randsburg and other surrounding mining communities began using the railway to receive goods and transport gold from the Yellow Aster Mine. By 1906, the Rinaldi & Clark shipping company was established in Johannesburg. Its stagecoaches transported passengers, goods, and mail from Johannesburg's depot to distant areas, such as Panamint City. But the company's business suffered with the onset of World War I and the production of the first Ford and Moreland trucks.

When Randsburg expanded its processing capacity from 30 to 100 stamps with the addition of a second mill, the railway's value decreased greatly. In 1903, the Santa Fe Railroad purchased the tracks, eventually tearing them up for use elsewhere.

Unlike the adjacent towns of Red Mountain and Atolia, Johannesburg was a planned community that consisted of churches, inns, and only a few saloons. It even boasted a nine-hole golf course, which encircled the town.

Today, Johannesburg shows little evidence of its past. Some renovated buildings are still occupied, but the only remnants from the town's peak are the abandoned cemetery and a mine headframe. Buried in the cemetery is William Henry "Burro" Schmidt, who is famous for tunneling 1,872 feet through nearby Copper Mountain by hand.

GPS COORDINATES: N35°22.29' W117°38.16'
TRAIL: Desert #22: Grass Valley Trail
MAP: Page 536

Julian

The famous California gold rush of the mid-nineteenth century largely bypassed Southern California and left San Diego County quiet and underpopulated. Nevertheless, hopeful prospectors scoured the San Diego Mountains. Evidence of gold was finally discovered in 1869 on the lands of Mike Julian. More miners began to search the surrounding hills for a big bonanza.

The first strike came the following year on February 22, the anniversary of George Washington's birthday, and the resulting mine was named after the first president. Other rich strikes followed close behind. Word of the finds spread up California's coast and prospectors began to pour in from the north. They settled in Julian City, which was at first just a tent camp. Julian was laid out by Mike Julian's cousin Drury Bailey. The town grew slowly because court battles disputing the mines' ownership and new rushes to Tombstone, Arizona, and other areas grabbed miners' attention. Still, Julian was large enough to make a strong bid for county seat in the early 1870s and mining continued in the region into the twentieth century. Gold production from the area totaled an estimated $5 million.

By the time the gold ran out, Julian was already a major agricultural center, known especially for its choice apples. The town held its first Apple Day in 1909, starting an annual tradition that continues to this day. Julian never succumbed to ghost town status, and it continues to prosper. Visitors can still admire several intact buildings from the 1870s and 1880s, including the Witch Creek School, completed in 1880, and a brewery from 1876. The town retains a gold camp atmosphere and celebrates its history in the Julian Pioneer Museum on Fourth and Washington Streets.

GPS COORDINATES: N33°04.68' W116°36.03'
NEAREST TRAIL: South Coast #23: Grapevine Canyon Trail

Keeler

The village of Keeler, situated on what were once the shores of Owens Lake, began its life as a shipping point for the Cerro Gordo mines. Silver was discovered near Cerro Gordo in 1865, and by the mid-1870s the town was a hotbed of mining activity. Keeler was one of the sites from which the valuable ore was shipped across Owens Lake to be transported by mule teams to Los Angeles. The Carson & Colorado Railroad rushed to build a line through Keeler all the way to Mojave, but by the time the line reached Keeler in 1883, mining operations were coming to a halt. A plaque opposite the old railroad station celebrates this miscalculation; it reads, "Keeler—End of the Line." Before the coming of the railroad, the town had been called Cerro Gordo Landing, and then briefly Hawley. It was renamed after Julius M. Keeler, owner of a mill in town. Keeler's mill used wood shipped from the Sierra Nevada side of Owens Lake, brought down the mountains by a flume through Cottonwood Canyon.

Cerro Gordo saw a revival in 1906 when the Great Western Ore and Reduction Company began to exploit zinc deposits in the area. The railway line to Keeler again saw some use. Aerial tramways carried the zinc ore from Cerro Gordo to Keeler, whence it could be hauled to Los Angeles or Mojave. The last train came to Keeler in 1960, but the town has never been completely deserted. Many dilapidated buildings remain today, including the train station, the Sierra Talc Company plant, and a few old stores.

GPS COORDINATES: N36°29.35' W117°52.18'
TRAIL: Desert #47: Cerro Gordo Road
MAP: Page 612

Leadfield

The ghost town of Leadfield sits in Death Valley close to Titus Canyon. Gold was discovered in the area as early as 1904, and the following year Clay Tollman of Rhyolite was extracting profit-making ore from the region. Still, no settlement was built here until 1926, when a cunning entrepreneur named Charles C. Julian began to promote Titus Canyon as a district rich in gold. Julian constructed a road to town at a cost of $60,000 and sold 300,000 shares in a mining company he had not yet incorporated. As many as 93 blocks were planned for the town and 300 people rushed to the area. Shops and houses were constructed to accommodate the influx of hopeful miners. But although there were small de-

Leadfield, circa 1962

posits of gold in the area, there was nothing like the rich bonanza that Julian promoted. After just six months the gold ran out; the post office closed, and angry residents left town. Julian was forced to flee and went to Shanghai, China, where he committed suicide a year later at age 40. Today several metal buildings and some mine remains survive at the site, which was placed on the National Register of Historic Places in 1975.

GPS COORDINATES: N36°50.90' W117°03.50'
TRAIL: Desert #40: Titus Canyon Trail
MAP: Page 589

Lee

A mining company town named Lee started just over the Nevada state line in late 1906 as surrounding mines were experiencing a mild boom. In a real estate battle, a rival company called Lee Hidden Treasure Mining Company started its own town—Lee, California. The California site took off faster and merchants from Rhyolite, Nevada, set up shop in an effort to catch early business from the miners. The Kimball brothers established a stage service to Rhyolite. Town site advertisements for Lee, California, and Lee, Nevada, continually tried to outdo each other, and permanent timber structures soon began to appear in both settlements. The only noticeable difference between the towns was that gambling was legal in Lee, Nevada. But with no law enforcement in either settlement, this was of little consequence.

Lee, California, overtook its namesake rival when water was found close to the surface. The promise of running water enabled the settlement to steam ahead in real estate sales. Saloons, meat markets, a lumberyard, an icehouse, and other structures were hastily erected. Four months after the initial battle began between the two developing towns, another rival stepped in and established the town site of Lee Addition. This town was laid out farther from the wash and claimed to offer a more permanent location. Within months Lee, Nevada, faded. The adjacent town sites in California combined and continued to boom. A two-story hotel was constructed, and by 1907 the mining camp had attracted its own red light district.

Lee, California, just managed to pull through the financial panic of 1907, but as local mining activity slowed down the settlement dwindled. By early 1912, most of the townspeople had moved away, never to reappear. All that remains of Lee today are the low rock foundation walls that outline the three main streets crisscrossed by half a dozen side streets. The town site is named Lees Camp on recent maps. The low stone wall laid out in a large rectangular shape was located in Lee Addition. It is thought to have been a corral and feed lot. Many mineshafts surround the ghost town; the largest is the remains of the Hayseed Mine.

GPS COORDINATES: N36°34.88' W116°40.06'
TRAIL: Desert #39: Funeral Range Trail
MAP: Page 587

Lone Pine

The Inyo County town of Lone Pine was settled in the 1860s as a supply point for local miners. The first cabin was con-

Lone Pine ruins after the earthquake of 1872

structed in the area in 1862, and a post office was established in 1870. When mining slowed at Cerro Gordo and Darwin, Lone Pine evolved to cater to farmers and ranchers. An adobe wall behind the La Florista flower shop is a remnant of an 1860s building. Lone Pine got its name because of a pine tree that stood alone at the entrance to Lone Pine Canyon. The lonely tree was destroyed many years ago by a flood.

The beautiful Alabama Hills are near town and were discovered by Hollywood in the 1920s. Many Westerns and war movies have been set against this backdrop. TV shows, feature films, and commercials continue to be filmed in the area. It is not uncommon to see camera crews in Lone Pine capturing the ambience of a typical western town. An annual film festival pays homage to the movie industry's history in the area.

Still, Lone Pine's biggest attraction is the surrounding backcountry. Within two hours of the settlement one can visit the highest point in the continental United States, Mount Whitney (14,496 feet above sea level), or the lowest point, Badwater Basin (246 feet below sea level). A 100-mile bike race held every March requires participants to complete a two-day ride from Stovepipe Wells in Death Valley to the Mount Whitney trailhead. The overnight stop is in Lone Pine. The hundreds of dirt roads through Owens Valley make the area perfect for backcountry driving. Mountain bikers also enjoy the region, which is also well known for its trout fishing, some of the best in the eastern Sierra. Fishing season begins the first Saturday in March, earlier than in most areas.

Lone Pine has no municipal government, but the town's Chamber of Commerce organizes many community events and promotes the surrounding area. The chamber occupies a historic building in town—the old Lone Pine Hotel, completed in 1918. The hotel used to house movie stars when many Westerns were being filmed in the area. At the time of the last census, Lone Pine had a population of 2,257.

GPS COORDINATES: N36°36.30' W118°03.71'
TRAIL: Central Mountains #1: Movie Flat Trail
MAP: Page 150

Lookout

Established in 1875 in the Argus Range, Lookout (also known as Lookout City) is considered one of the most prolific desert mining locations of the 1870s. It sits atop a mountain overlooking the Minnietta and Modoc Mines, the latter of which was owned by George Hearst, father of William Randolph Hearst (see page 83). The Minnietta Mine is on the south side of Lookout Mountain; the Modoc Mine is in a deep gorge on the east side of the mountain, approximately a mile down. A pack trail connected the town and mines, and the silver-lead ore was hauled by mule to the Modoc furnaces. Ten charcoal kilns in Wild Rose Canyon, 25 miles away, supplied fuel to the furnaces via a continuous stream of burros. The unique structures are still standing and are a popular tourist attraction to this day.

According to the U.S. Bureau of Mines, the Modoc Mine alone produced $1.9 million between 1875 and 1890. During its heyday, Lookout City included a few general stores, three saloons, and offices. Today, evidence remains of more than 40 foundations along with remnants of the Modoc furnaces.

GPS COORDINATES: N36°14.75' W117°26.03' (approximately)

NEAREST TRAIL: Desert #44: Darwin Falls Trail

Los Angeles

Los Angeles County was the ancestral homeland of the Gabrielino Indians (see page 92). The tribe settled several dozen villages within the county's present-day borders, including one named Yang-na, situated in modern downtown Los Angeles. In 1542, Juan Rodriguez Cabrillo (see page 70) became the first European to enter the future city's bay. Another Spaniard, Gaspar de Portolá, camped in the area on an expedition into California in 1769. In the next few years, the Spanish created several Franciscan missions in Southern California, including San Gabriel Arcángel near present-day Los Angeles in 1771. Forts and towns soon followed.

In 1781, 44 settlers, many of them black or Indian, under the leadership of Felipe de Neve, established the fourth civic municipality in California. They called the new settlement Pueblo de Nuestra Señora la Reina de Los Angeles de Porciúncula (Town of Our Lady the Queen of the Angels of Porciúncula). This was soon shortened to Los Angeles. Though still small, the town became the most populous settlement in Mexican California, and at times was its unofficial capital.

The United States captured Los Angeles early in the Mexican War, but incompetent rule led to a rebellion by Hispanic Angelinos. The town's Spanish-speaking population successfully defended itself for some time before being forced to capitulate in January 1847.

Los Angeles was made the seat of Los Angeles County when California became a state in 1850. At first the county was much bigger, incorporating all of what is now Orange County, and parts of Kern, Ventura, San Bernardino, and San Diego Counties. Still, the area did not enjoy the population boom that hit Northern California during the gold rush. In 1880, the town's population was just 11,000, but the following decade saw the first period of Los Angeles's remarkable growth. The completion of two railroads connecting Los Angeles with the larger San Francisco and the East, combined with inexpensive land in a fertile and hospitable climate, resulted in a 500 percent increase in population in just 10 years. By the second decade of the twentieth century, Los Angeles began to surpass its northern rival in terms of population. Later periods of growth were strongly affected by a new technological innovation—the automobile. Los Angeles grew outward; highway arteries linked surrounding communities into a contiguous metropolis. Today, the sprawling development is in no way confined to the city's municipal boundaries.

Nevertheless, the large urbanized region is far from homogenous. The high-powered movie business and fruitful orange growing industry made millions of dollars for some Angelenos, while others, predominantly minorities, floundered. The suburban bliss of Beverly Hills flourished in stark contrast to dilapidated neighborhoods like Compton and Inglewood. Twice in recent history, in 1965 and again in 1992, the city erupted into riots as dissatisfied African-Americans took to the streets. Los Angeles has also been home to many immigrants, including millions of Mexicans and Central Americans. Los Angeles continues to draw migrants from the south, as well as from the eastern United States. The 2000 census gave Los Angeles County's population as 9,519,338, and the Los Angeles metropolitan area (including Orange County and parts of Riverside County) a count of 16,373,645, second only to the New York City area.

View of Los Angeles, circa 1873

Los Angeles continues to be an entertainment mecca, producing an endless stream of blockbuster movies and television shows from its famous Hollywood studios and spawning such musical acts as the Doors, NWA, and Snoop Dogg. Nearby Anaheim is the site of world famous Disneyland. Los Angeles is also home to several universities, including the University of California at Los Angeles (UCLA) and the University of Southern California (USC). The area enjoys a pleasant climate and generally high standard of living (although not for some), diminished somewhat by recurrent smog conditions

and difficulty sustaining its water and electricity supply. The city is also located within a reasonable drive from some of California's most scenic backcountry regions.
NEAREST TRAIL: South Coast #7: Rincon-Shortcut OHV Route

Ludlow

About 50 miles east of Barstow sits the old railroad town of Ludlow. The settlement began in 1882 as a watering stop for the Atlantic & Pacific Railroad. It was named after William B. Ludlow, master car-repairer for that railroad. Two other railroads branched out from the small town—the Tonopah & Tidewater and the Ludlow & Southern.

Ludlow grew after gold was discovered nearby in the late 1880s. The town became a popular drinking spot for miners from the Bagdad Chase Mine; their company town of Rochester had no saloons.

An interesting anecdote from Ludlow's history involves a shipment of frogs' legs waylaid in the town. The frogs' legs were headed to Goldfield, Nevada, but they missed a connection. Sold cheaply in Ludlow, they became a favored dish. Future shipments also mysteriously failed to make their connections until a railroad investigator discovered what was going on and put a stop to it.

Ludlow declined when the railroads proved financially unviable. Neither of the two branch lines survived the Great Depression, and the Atchison, Topeka & Santa Fe, the new owners of the Atlantic & Pacific, no longer retained a station in the town. Ludlow did see renewed business with the dedication of Route 66 through its boundaries, but Interstate 40 bypassed the settlement and it once again dwindled. About 20 residents still live in Ludlow, and the town has a gas station and a cafe for travelers who drive the historic route. Remains of buildings abandoned throughout the settlement's history continue to attract visitors.

GPS COORDINATES: N34°43.24' W116°09.67'
NEAREST TRAIL: South Coast #17: Rodman Mountains Trail

Millerton

Gold was discovered in the Sierra Nevada foothills of present-day Fresno County in the early 1850s. One of the major mining camps in the area was Millerton, founded in 1851 as Rootville. Millerton became Fresno County's first seat of government when the county was organized in 1856 out of parts of Mariposa, Merced, and Tulare Counties. The town was named after a nearby fort, Fort Millerton, established by Lieutenant Tredwell Moore. Moore named his fort in honor of Major Albert S. Miller, a veteran of the Mexican War (1846–48).

Millerton was the victim of several floods. In 1861, the San Joaquin River overflowed, destroying half the town. Six years later another flood washed away almost every structure. A few residents returned to rebuild the settlement, but a fire in 1870 compounded the damage. Government officials moved the Fresno County seat to the town of Fresno in 1874; by then Millerton was already becoming a ghost town.

The town site is now submerged under the waters of Millerton Lake, which was created by the Friant Dam. Before the site was flooded, the Native Sons and Daughters of the Golden West disassembled the Millerton Courthouse. The impressive two-story structure has been reassembled near the banks of the lake and is all that remains of the historic mining camp.

NEAREST TRAIL: Central Mountains #2: Delilah Fire Lookout Trail

Millwood

Fresno County's Millwood was the first major logging camp in the area. Its first building was a sawmill constructed by the Sanger Lumber Company to saw wood cut from nearby forests. The town grew as lumberjacks moved to the area and businesses (and brothels) sprang up to accommodate them. Wood was in great demand in the 1880s for use in building and as fuel. The lumber company was responsible for felling hundreds of enormous old redwoods, leaving just one giant standing. The huge tree is called the Boole Tree, and it can still be seen today. Giant sequoias were seen as a miracle tree by nineteenth century lumber companies. The trees grew 20 feet or more in diameter and about 200 feet high. However, they did create some considerable problems. Their huge trunk size made them difficult to fell using a two-man saw, and almost impossible with an axe. When they did come down, they often shattered under their own weight, so beds of smaller trees had to be assembled to break the fall. Transporting a sequoia was no easy task, either. Huge flumes were constructed to get the trees down hills. From Millwood, the sequoias would be sent by flume to Sequoia Lake, then sent downriver to a finishing mill in the San Joaquin Valley.

Because of its cool climate and picturesque location, Millwood soon became a popular summer getaway spot for people from the hotter Central Valley. Hotels were built and houses were upgraded for wealthy vacationers. In the summer, a stagecoach ran daily from Sanger up the steep hill to Millwood.

By World War I, most of the best trees in the area had been felled, and the sawmill was no longer economically viable. Soon Millwood was deserted, and little remains today. The surrounding forest is recovering, but slowly. A giant sequoia takes much longer than a human lifetime to go from a seed to a full-grown tree.

GPS COORDINATES: N36°44.68' W119°00.18' (approximately)
NEAREST TRAIL: Central Mountains #2: Delilah Fire Lookout Trail

Mission La Purísima Concepción

The eleventh settlement in the Spanish mission system that dotted coastal Southern California was La Purísima Concepción, founded on December 8, 1787, just nine years after Junípero Serra and Gaspar de Portolá first landed in San Diego. In a short period of time, Franciscan priests had converted thousands of Native Americans, introduced agriculture to the region for the first time, and established Alta California as a distant outpost in the vast Spanish Empire. The site of La Purísima was chosen by the second president of the Californian missions, Fermín Francisco de Lasuén, as a convenient waypoint between Mission San Luis Obispo and Mission San-

Mission La Purísima Concepción

ta Barbara. A church was completed by 1802 and other facilities followed. Unfortunately, the buildings were constructed directly atop a fault line. Major earthquakes struck Southern California in 1812 damaging many missions, but Mission La Purísima was almost completely leveled.

Fearing a repeat disaster, the priests and Indians decided to rebuild the mission 4 miles northeast of its original location. Father Mariano Payeras supervised the reconstruction. The mission flourished at its new site, but Indian neophytes were clearly disenchanted with their new life. Traditional ceremonies were banned by priests who viewed them as pagan; European disease had killed untold numbers of local Chumash Indians; and the converts, although treated kindly, were looked upon as inferior beings by their Spanish "benefactors."

When an uprising occurred at Mission Santa Inés in 1823, the Indians of La Purísima Concepción decided to seize their mission. The craftsmanship taught to them by the Franciscan priests proved invaluable during the ensuing siege. The Chumash built a wooden fort with holes for two cannons and held out against a military guard for over a month. It was not until a force of 100 Spanish soldiers arrived from Monterey that the Indians could be persuaded to surrender. The fighting resulted in the deaths of six Spanish and seventeen Chumash; four of the uprising's ringleaders were later executed.

Daily life at La Purísima went back to normal after the siege, but this was not to last. In 1834, mission lands were secularized. The Indians abandoned the settlement, and its buildings were left to ruin. Over the years the structures were home to wandering bandits and were later used as a horse stable and to house sheep. By 1934, when Santa Barbara County acquired the lands, little remained. The government embarked on a massive reconstruction project. Workers of the Civilian Conservation Corps made 110,000 adobe bricks, 32,000 roof tiles, and 10,000 floor tiles using the same methods as the earlier Indian builders. The original mission plans were carefully followed; surviving walls were incorporated into the general design and are now almost indiscernible from the reconstructions. Today, the rebuilt mission is a state historical monument operated by the Division of Beaches and Parks.

GPS COORDINATES: N34°40.29' W120°25.27'

NEAREST TRAIL: Central Mountains #34: Camino Cielo Road

Mission San Antonio de Padua

San Antonio de Padua was the third of the Spanish missions founded in California. Two summers previous, in 1769, the redoubtable Franciscan Father Junípero Serra had established a Christian settlement in San Diego, followed the next year by his future home mission at Carmel. For the third summer in a row, Serra set out to find a good location for the conversion of Native Americans. Accompanied by two fellow priests, Serra walked until he came across a beautiful oak-mantled valley in the Santa Lucia Range. On July 14, 1771, the three priests made camp and secured a large bronze bell to a nearby oak. For some time the elderly Serra energetically swung the heavy clapper and a wholly new sound resounded around the riparian forest. His younger companions begged their superannuated superior not to overexert himself, but he ignored their pleas. The unusual clanging did reach the ears of at least one local Indian that day, and the curious young man brought the priests gifts of pine nuts and seeds.

Nevertheless, the new mission named after Saint Anthony of Padua began inauspiciously. The first year's harvest failed and the river dried the following summer. The priests moved the mission 3 miles away and began again, making sure to irrigate the land well. The settlement attracted increasing numbers of Indians, who were impressed by the Spanish method of constructing adobe buildings and by the increasingly abundant food supply. Mission San Antonio became especially renowned for its fine flour, ground in a newly constructed stone mill, and for its large and tasty pears. The mission was also famous for its specially bred golden horses. Despite one attack on the settlement by non-neophyte Indians, San Antonio continued to prosper until the Mexican government secularized mission lands in 1834. Afterwards it went into a period of rapid decline, and by 1882 it was completely abandoned. The elements and thieves left the adobe buildings in a state of ruin. Reconstruction began in 1948 using a portion of a fund established by William Randolph Hearst. Many of the original structures were rebuilt using the same techniques employed by the Spanish and the native converts.

GPS COORDINATES: N36°00.90' W121°14.91' (approximately)

NEAREST TRAIL: Central Mountains #49: South Coast Ridge Road

Mission San Antonio de Padua, shortly before its restoration

Mission San Gabriel Arcángel

In the summer of 1771, two years after the establishment of the first California mission, another 10 Franciscan priests landed on the Monterey Peninsula. At the time, a considerable distance separated the only two missions in San Diego and Carmel. Mission founder Junípero Serra wanted to fill that gap with some new settlements. That summer he established two new missions, San Antonio de Padua and San Gabriel Arcángel. Mission San Gabriel became one of the most successful of all the Franciscan settlements in California, housing 8,000 converts at its peak. The local Gabrielino Indians took their name from San Gabriel. Baptisms began as early as the second day, but the mission did not really start growing until it moved to its present location in 1776.

he Bell Tower at Mission San Gabriel

The new location, 9 miles east of present-day downtown Los Angeles, proved to be a good one. Fields of grain soon stretched out on all sides and thousands of cattle and horses grazed the surrounding land. Hundreds of cattle were slaughtered every week just to feed the large Indian population of the settlement.

San Gabriel was hit by earthquakes on several occasions. Cattle belonging to the mission were branded with a large letter "T" that stood for *temblores* (Spanish for "earthquakes").

A major annual event for residents of San Gabriel was the springtime journey for salt. Hundreds of Indians accompanied priests to the desert country to the east. The journey to the salt fields was quite arduous because no roads existed to mark the route, and it took a month of travel to complete the roundtrip. On the return journey, the travelers hauled enough cartloads of salt to last a whole year.

The settlement became wealthy and prosperous, and it seemed the biggest problem for the native residents was interference from secular colonists in the nearby pueblo of Los Angeles. By 1834, pressure from civilians in Los Angeles brought secular control to San Gabriel. Most of the mission land is now sprawling metropolis, but several of the main buildings still remain, including the unique bell tower wall, constructed after the earthquakes of 1812.

GPS COORDINATES: N34°05.83' W118°06.44' (approximately)

NEAREST TRAIL: South Coast #13: Big Pine Flat Trail

Mission San Luis Rey de Francia

The "King of the Missions," San Luis Rey was established on June 13, 1798. It was the eighteenth Franciscan settlement in California, and the last one founded by Fermín Francisco de Lasuén, the second president of the missions. Named in honor of Louis IX, a thirteenth-century French king, San Luis Rey was soon recognized as the richest of all the missions.

The leader of San Luis Rey was Father Antonio Peyri, who proved himself to be a great organizer and noble friend to his Indian converts. He implemented quarantine procedures to limit deaths from diseases among the local Luiseño. The Indians were taught farming techniques, which were put to good use in the pleasant Southern California climate. Before long, vast fields of wheat swayed in the breeze, huge vegetable gardens supplied ample food, thousands of cattle roamed the mission lands, and acres of grape vines produced the finest wine in California.

A huge cross-shaped church with elaborate structures around it gave the impression of an enormous white palace. San Luis Rey produced so much that it was able to trade tallow (reduced fat from cattle) and wheat with foreign traders. The death rate at the mission was perhaps the lowest of any in California, and the Indians sincerely admired their Franciscan protectors. San Luis Rey became the most populous settlement of any Franciscan mission. When Mexico secularized the missions, Father Peyri secretly left San Luis Rey to return to Spain. The Indians realized he had fled, and 500 Luiseño rushed to the San Diego harbor to persuade him to stay. They arrived just as he was leaving, and although they could not get him to stay, two Indians did accompany the priest to Europe. They later enrolled in seminary school in Rome.

President Abraham Lincoln returned mission lands to the Franciscans in 1861, but San Luis Rey was largely ignored until 1892. In that year, two Franciscans from Mexico decided to establish a novitiate in Southern California. They thought the old mission site would be a perfect location. The buildings were restored, and by 1950 much of their original grandeur

Mission San Luis Rey de Francia

had been recovered. Today, Mission San Luis Rey de Francia remains a center for Franciscan learning.
GPS COORDINATES: N33°13.92' W117°19.15'
NEAREST TRAIL: South Coast #21: Palomar Divide Road

Mission San Miguel Arcángel

The sixteenth Franciscan mission in California was founded on July 25, 1797, by Father Fermín Francisco de Lasuén. Mission San Miguel Arcángel (Spanish for the "Mission of St. Michael the Archangel") was the farthest inland of the Roman Catholic settlements. It was situated to the north of the present-day city of Paso Robles. The soil in the area was not as fertile as in other parts of California, so the mission never grew to the extent that its founders had envisioned. Nevertheless, the settlement attracted more than 1,000 Indians.

The converts embarked on a large construction project, which was slowed by a fire in 1806. The large church that stands today was not completed until 1818. The church was decorated with many beautiful paintings, drawn by Indians under the direction of Monterey artisan Estévan Munras. The paintings have never been retouched.

Attempts by the priests at San Miguel to attract Indians from the Central Valley were unsuccessful and had to be abandoned when California came under Mexican rule. The new regime secularized the missions, and the last Franciscan left the settlement in 1840. Governor Pío Pico sold the land to William Reid, a naturalized Mexican citizen with a Hispanic wife. The Reids were murdered by Mexican soldiers, who stole the family's gold.

During the 1860s and 1870s, the mission buildings were occupied by a variety of stores, including a popular saloon. In 1878, the Catholic Church regained control of the lands; Franciscans returned to San Miguel in 1928. The mission has been restored and is now a museum.
GPS COORDINATES: N35°44.67' W120°41.81'
NEAREST TRAIL: Central Mountains #47: Parkfield Grade Trail

Mission Santa Inés

One of the last of the Franciscan missions established in Southern California was Mission Santa Inés (also spelled Ynez). It was founded on September 17, 1804, and named in honor of Saint Agnes, an early Roman Christian martyr. Located in a beautiful oak-mantled valley in what is now Los Padres National Forest, the mission grew quickly. The earthquakes of 1812 slowed construction, but Chumash builders managed to construct several sturdy stone structures despite this setback. Still, the mission failed to fulfill its initial expectations. In its 32 years of existence, the population never exceeded 800. The agricultural output was adequate, but only meager surpluses were produced. One thing the Indians of Santa Inés were known for was their exquisitely designed saddles.

In the early 1800s, Spanish military forces in California were isolated from Spain, which had lost its navy in battles against England. Soldiers became increasingly dependent on the missions, and they took control of Santa Inés. Their rule angered both mission residents and inland Tulare Indians. The soldiers left California after it came into Mexican control in 1821 and jurisdiction returned to the priests. In February 1824, Indians attacked and set fire to many of the mission buildings.

In 1836, Santa Inés was taken from the Franciscans. Unlike other missions, Santa Inés continued to house priests and the church was never abandoned. In the early 1900s, emigrants from Denmark settled the area around the mission. The town they developed was named Solvang, which is still in existence as a popular tourist stop. Today, Mission Santa Inés is home to an excellent historical museum.
GPS COORDINATES: N34°35.66' W120°08.13'
NEAREST TRAIL: Central Mountains #34: Camino Cielo Road

Mojave

Mojave was founded in 1876 by the Southern Pacific Railroad. The town took its name—that of a native Indian tribe—because it was situated on the edge of the Mojave Desert. The first passenger train arrived on August 8, 1876, and Mojave celebrates that day as its birthday. From its inception, Mojave provided welcome hospitality to desert travelers. Between 1884 and 1889, it was the rail terminus for 20-mule teams that hauled borax from mines in Death Valley. At first, the town was located on just one line, the track that ran from Los Angeles to San Francisco. In 1883, a line was completed linking Mojave with Needles on the Arizona border. In 1910, a branch to the north was constructed to transport supplies for the Los Angeles Aqueduct project. Mojave remains an important railway junction today.

In 1894, gold was discovered on Soledad Mountain, not far from town. A succession of mines sprang up in the Mojave area. By the time the mines were no longer profitable, a cement industry had taken root in town. Cement was necessary for the Los Angeles Aqueduct, and tons of it were produced in Mojave. Cement production continues to this day. The Creal plant to the west of town is one of the most modern cement plants in the world.

Mojave is especially proud of its airport, which began in 1940 as a training ground for navy and marine pilots. Today the East Kern Airport District is home to the National Test Pilots School and the Civilian Flight Test Center.

Mojave is located at the intersection of California 58 and California 14, as well as the junction of America's two biggest

Harvey House and Wells Fargo Express office, circa 1896 or 1897

railroads, the Burlington Northern Santa Fe, and the Union Pacific. The town is only 90 miles from Los Angeles and so remains an important supply center and an ideal location for distribution-oriented businesses. Its location on the edge of the Mojave Desert also makes Mojave a great departure point from which to explore Southern California's backcountry.

GPS COORDINATES: N36°02.88' W118°10.26'

NEAREST TRAIL: Central Mountains #17: Jawbone Canyon Road

Monrovia

Europeans first visited the San Gabriel Valley in 1769, when Gaspar de Portolá trekked through it on his first expedition into California. Two years later, Spanish missionaries established Mission San Gabriel in the valley. Mission lands were vast and prosperous, and the settlement attracted many Gabrielino Indians. When Mexico gained control of California from Spain, the missions were secularized. In 1841, Governor Juan Bautista Alvarado gave out two land grants in the area, Azura de Duarte and Santa Anita. The modern California town of Monrovia is composed of parts of these two ranches.

Monrovia's horse and buggy days

The town was named after William N. Monroe, who bought part of the Santa Anita Ranch in 1884 for $30,000. Monroe, a former schoolteacher and Civil War officer, first came to California in 1875. Between 1879 and 1882, he served on the Los Angeles City Council. Monroe had made a good deal of money working for the Southern Pacific Railroad and was able to invest quite a bit in his ranch. In 1885, he finished construction of his family home. The next year, Monroe and four other local landholders decided to establish a town on their combined holdings. They laid out a 60-acre town site, naming the streets after various flowers, trees, and ladies. The first lots went on sale on May 17, 1886.

Monrovia became known as the "Gem City of the Foothills" because of its beautiful location. Incorporated in 1887, it was the fourth-oldest general law city in the Los Angeles Basin. One of the first orders of the city government was a prohibition on the sale of alcohol. Rather than becoming a rowdy western town, Monrovia grew as a quiet community of farmers and fruit growers. In 1903, the Pacific Electric Railway Company opened transportation to Los Angeles, and Monrovia residents have been able to commute to the bulging metropolis ever since. The fabled American highway Route 66 ran through town, and it has now been superseded by Interstate 210. As Los Angeles has grown, urban sprawl has reached this once rural community. Still, Monrovia borders the natural wilderness of Angeles National Forest to the north. The town is unique among Los Angeles suburbs in that it retains the stability, tradition, and heritage characteristic of a small residential community.

GPS COORDINATES: N34°08.86' W117°59.89'

NEAREST TRAIL: South Coast #7: Rincon-Shortcut OHV Route

Monterey

Monterey was discovered by Spanish explorer Sebastíon Vizcaíno in 1602, although it is likely that Juan Rodriguez Cabrillo sighted the Monterey Peninsula 60 years earlier. Vizcaíno named the bay in honor of Gaspar de Zúñigo y Acevedo, Count of Monterey, who was then viceroy of New Spain in Mexico. The explorer's descriptions of the bay's beauty and calm were so enthusiastic that subsequent explorers did not recognize the place.

The presidio of Monterey was founded 168 years later, in 1770, during an expedition by Franciscan missionary Junípero Serra and the first governor of the Spanish province of Alta California, Gaspar de Portolá. The presidio was the political capital of California during the era of Spanish and Mexican rule, as well as its social and military capital. The town that grew up around the presidio was never very large or pretentious. English explorer George Vancouver was struck by the simplicity of the governor's wooden house when he visited in 1792, and by 1800 the town had fewer than 500 residents.

In 1821, Spain relinquished control of California to Mexico in a peaceful transfer of power. The period of Mexican rule, while quiet socially, was politically turbulent, and governors were rarely secure in their jobs.

Monterey was captured by U.S. forces under Commodore John Drake Sloat on July 7, 1846, and held for the duration of the Mexican War. Sloat was honored in 1910 with a monument to him erected on the presidio grounds. The presidio, with the rest of California, was ceded to the United States by Mexico in 1848, and California quickly became a state following the discovery of gold and ensuing rush to the region. Although California's constitutional convention was held in Monterey, the town was bypassed as the state's capital, an honor that went to Sacramento. In 1873, the town also lost its role as seat of Monterey County to Salinas, where the county archives retain many Spanish language documents from the pre-statehood era.

A controversial event took place in 1859, when 30,000 acres around Monterey and a large portion of the town itself were sold to David Jacks and his partner for just $1,002.50. Jacks went on to develop the only native California cheese, Monterey Jack. At this time Monterey was impoverished, having seen little of the gold-rush boom that ensured San Francisco's growth.

Monterey's major industry was whaling. By the 1870s, overhunting and decreased demand meant that conventional fishing eclipsed whaling. Monterey became the center of a huge sardine canning industry. Novelist John Steinbeck dramatized life in and around the canning factories in his book *Cannery Row*, published in 1945. By the 1940s, however, overfishing had again depleted resources to a point where the industry was no longer viable.

Monterey's decline was halted by development of the adjacent Del Monte forest into a series of world-class golf courses and a renovation of the downtown area focusing on the city's historic and cultural heritage. Visitors today flock to the "Golf Capital of the World." Its superb aquarium, historic Fisherman's Wharf and Cannery Row, and numerous parks, galleries, and shops give Monterey a unique and pleasant atmosphere.

GPS COORDINATES: N36°36.36' W121°53.79'

NEAREST TRAIL: Central Mountains #51: Coast Road

Needles

Needles was established in 1869 as a port on the Colorado River. The Mojave people have lived in the valley by the Colorado River for generations. Trails, petroglyphs, pictographs, and mortise working areas are all evidence of their life in this area. The Yuma, another Indian tribe, also trace their origins to the region. The Spanish priest Francisco Garcés passed through the site of Needles under the guidance of the Mojave in 1776. The fur trapper Jedediah Smith also used this native trail in 1826 and was the first American to cross the Colorado River at what would later be named Needles.

In the late 1800s, steamboats plied the river, carrying passengers and freight. The settlement developed as a supply center for mining prospectors and early settlers. By 1883, the Atlantic & Pacific Railroad had established a station on the Arizona side of the river. Later that same year the company transferred operations to the California side, stating that it better suited its needs for a future division depot. The railroad's arrival took the place of the steamboat transport system to a large degree.

The name Needles was derived from the peaks near town. Early railroad survey crews mentioned these prominent features, to the east and south of the locality, as a reference point. The name seemed appropriate when the post office was established in 1869.

Needles flourished as the railroad depot grew in importance. Highways brought automobiles, and like many desert locations, this spawned a multitude of motels and restaurants. The ornate two-story Garces Building near the railroad resembled a Southern mansion, inviting all who passed. Today the mansion awaits restoration. It was part of a series of Harvey Houses located along the Santa Fe Railroad system, from Chicago to Los Angeles. These welcoming houses provided meals to rail passengers and railroad crews on their long journey to the West Coast. The houses were later the subject of a Judy Garland movie, *The Harvey Girls* (1946).

Front Street, Needles

Early bridges were often washed away in floods. The building of dams on the Colorado River and dredging of the river in the 1950s brought a more reliable water level to the river, encouraging agriculture, and future development of the town. Less flooding meant increased vegetation, a more stable embankment, and clearer water. The river has gone on to be one of the city's biggest draws, with two marina parks and many water-sport opportunities. Other local attractions include the Mitchell Caverns, the Havasu National Wildlife Refuge, and the AVI Casino on the Mojave Indian Reservation.

GPS COORDINATES: N34°50.53' W114°36.67'

TRAIL: Desert #12: Eagle Pass Trail

MAP: Page 486

Newberry Springs

Humans have lived in the area around Newberry Springs for thousands of years. Tools and bone fragments found at the nearby Calico Early Man Site date back about 19,000 years. Some experts have speculated that they are much older, a notion that would change current concepts about when humans first arrived in North America. Evidence of Paleo-Indian life, such as pictographs and petroglyphs, is most commonly found near streams and springs in the vicinity of Newberry Springs.

The famous Indian trade route, the Mojave Road (see page 61), passes through this area. American traders and early settlers also used this route, often stopping at water sources near Newberry Springs. The gold rush brought increased traffic as forty-niners came to California in hordes, braving long arid stretches and possible Indian attacks. Freight lines and railroads would later choose a similar route into California.

The town of Newberry Springs was established in 1883 as a stop on the Southern Pacific Railroad, now known as the Santa Fe line. At first, the station was known as Newberry. In 1919, the name was changed to Water because the town supplied most of the water for the Southern Pacific. In 1922, the name reverted to Newberry. The word "Springs" was added to the name in 1967 to avoid confusion with Newberry Park.

Newberry Springs is situated on historic Route 66. The Great Depression brought an influx of migrants hoping to take advantage of farming opportunities in the area. In later years, Route 66 provided a steady stream of tourists and truckers, and Newberry Springs supported a variety of businesses that catered to travelers. At one time, the town had five gas stations and four hotels along the highway.

Interstate 40 bypassed the small community and most of its stores went out of business. Today, Newberry Springs is a growing agricultural and retirement community. Melons, alfalfa, and farmed catfish are all produced in large quantities in the area. Water remains a major attraction. Hundreds of man-made lakes draw visitors from all over Southern California and beyond.

GPS COORDINATES: N34°49.61' W116°41.19'

TRAIL: South Coast #17: Rodman Mountains Trail

MAP: Page 348

New Idria

The New Idria Mine in the Diablo Mountains was formed to work a quicksilver deposit discovered in San Benito County in 1853. The surrounding community officially adopted the name when a post office was established on March 22, 1869. New Idria was named after Idria, a famous quicksilver mining center in Slovenia, which was then part of the Austrian Empire. The postal service shortened the name to Idria in 1894, but residents continued to use the longer appellation.

The great California gold rush heightened the need for quicksilver because it was useful in smelting gold and silver ore. Forty-niners had good reason to be thankful for the mercury discoveries in California; without them, smelters would have relied on foreign quicksilver deposits. At its peak, New Idria was the second largest producer of mercury in California. It was a relatively nonviolent company town with a population of around 500. Most of its residents were from Mexico or the Basque region of Spain.

Today, more than 20 buildings remain in this well-preserved ghost town. The dominant structure is the mill and smelter, built out of tin with a huge concrete base. There is a two-story wooden hotel, a dance hall, a post office, a school, and a mine rescue station. A few residents still make their homes in the area. New Idria is about 66 miles southwest of Hollister.

GPS COORDINATES: N36°24.96' W120°40.34'

NEAREST TRAIL: Central Mountains #47: Parkfield Grade Trail

Ojai

Ojai is located about 80 miles northwest of Los Angeles and 45 miles east of Santa Barbara in Ventura County. Founded in 1874 by R. G. Surdam, the settlement was originally called Nordhoff, in honor of author Charles Nordhoff. In 1916, the town was renamed after the beautiful Ojai Valley in which it sits. Ojai is derived from a Chumash Indian word *a'hwai*, which means "nest" or "moon."

Ojai was incorporated as a city on August 5, 1921. The 1920s proved to be a good decade for the town. The United States economy was booming, and many Californians were wallowing in prosperity. Ojai has miles of coastline on Lake Casitas and stunning natural beauty all around, with views to the Pacific, the surrounding mountains, or both. Visitors flocked to the El Roblar Hotel and the beautiful Foothills Hotel. The Ojai Valley Country Club became famous as one of the finest in the nation. The onset of the Great Depression stunted Ojai's growth, as people were no longer willing to spend money on leisure activities, but when the economy recovered after World War II, so did the town.

Today about 8,000 people live in Ojai; many have chosen to retire there. Orange groves and avocado farms spread out from town, giving the air a sweet smell. The climate is great; temperatures stay cool but are rarely cold. Many businesses are

The Ojai Library, Casa de Piedra, circa 1952

located outdoors, including the renowned Bart's Books. The Arcade shopping center has both indoor and outdoor establishments. Despite being the smallest and slowest-growing city in Ventura County, or perhaps because it is, Ojai remains an extremely pleasant place to live or visit. It retains a village atmosphere, relying much less on the automobile than elsewhere in Southern California.

GPS COORDINATES: N34°26.88' W119°14.55'

NEAREST TRAIL: Central Mountains #32: Nordhoff Ridge Trail

Olancha

The site of Olancha was inhabited by Panamint Indians prior to the discovery of some rich silver deposits in the Coso Range. Minnard Farley had come to the area hoping to find a lost mine first stumbled upon during the gold rush era. Instead he found some new veins of silver ore, and in 1863 he constructed a sawmill, an 8-stamp processing mill, and a blacksmith shop. Local Panamint Indians were not impressed with the intrusion into their ancestral homeland, and in 1867 they burned Farley's mill. Operations at Olancha continued. The town began to get increased business as a stage stop for supplies en route from Los Angeles to Cerro Gordo. Silver bullion from Cerro Gordo was ferried across Owens Lake (before it dried up) to Cartago, a few miles north of Olancha.

Mining operations in the Inyo Mountains did not last, but Olancha survived as a farming community. The Southern Pacific extended a line into town in 1910; the line was used until 1982. The town was also used as a supply depot while work progressed on the Los Angeles Aqueduct, a huge project that robbed Owens Lake of its water to supply the growing Southern California metropolis. The Olancha post office, established in 1870, has never had to close, but ruined buildings blend with it and current residences. One less savory visitor was Charles Manson, who spent some time nearby in the 1960s. Remains of Farley's mill can still be seen. One popular site was the abandoned Calloway Restaurant, but an 18-inch snowfall in 1998 caused the fragile structure to crumble. Today, Olancha provides access from US 395 to the back roads of Death Valley National Park.

GPS COORDINATES: N36°16.95' W118°00.32'

TRAIL: Desert #45: Cactus Flat Road

MAP: Page 603

Oro Grande

Oro Grande was established near the Mojave River in 1878 as a gold mining camp for newcomers who rushed to the area after deposits of the precious metal were discovered in the Old Silver and Granite Mountains. *Oro grande* means "big gold" in Spanish, but when the post office was established here on January 3, 1881, the settlement was named Halleck, after the chemist in the town's only stamp mill. Oro Grande reached its peak in the 1880s, and although it dwindled thereafter, it never became a ghost town. Its name was officially changed in 1925, but by then it had been known as Oro Grande for some time, taking the name of a nearby mine. The town saw some resurgence when its main street was designated as part of Route 66. Today, Oro Grande is marked mainly by a large cement plant. Its stores are generally abandoned, with the notable exception of Stubbs Auction, which contains a delightful collection of antique road signs and other treasures. It has seen increased traffic in recent years with renewed interest in the National Trails Highway (old Route 66).

GPS COORDINATES: N34°35.95' W117°19.99'

NEAREST TRAIL: South Coast #9: Upper Lytle Creek Ridge Trail

Palmdale

In 1886, German and Swiss Lutherans founded the first settlement in the vicinity of present-day Palmdale in the Antelope Valley. The valley was on a popular Indian trade route for centuries prior to this. The town was originally named Palmenthal because the German families mistook local Joshua trees for palm trees. The name was changed to Palmdale when a post office was established in 1890.

The late 1890s were a period of drought in the Antelope Valley. Most residents were unable to make a living from farming, and Palmdale was largely abandoned. A new settlement arose several miles away near the location of a Southern Pacific Railroad station, previously known as Harold and Alpine Station.

The arid climate of the Antelope Valley had discouraged human settlement for many years and it continued to make life difficult for Palmdale's residents until 1913, when the Los Angeles Aqueduct (see page 101) was completed. The aqueduct, which carried water from Owens River Valley, made irrigation of Antelope Valley possible. Agriculture quickly became the primary livelihood in the region, and Palmdale's population grew in response.

The aerospace industry became Palmdale's dominant industry after World War II with the establishment of Edwards Air Force Base and U.S. Air Force Plant 42. Lockheed, McDonnell Douglas, Rockwell, and Northrop all maintain facilities in Palmdale. The Federal Aviation Administration's Air Traffic Control Center, which handles air traffic for the western United States, is also located in town.

The first paved road to Los Angeles, the Sierra Highway, was completed in 1921, and Palmdale's growth since then has been tied to that of California's biggest metropolis. Located just 60 freeway miles from central Los Angeles, Palmdale is now home to many workers who commute to the city each day. The town is one of the fastest growing in California; residents are attracted by its beautiful high desert location, low crime rate, and pleasant temperatures. Palmdale is also a great place from which to access Southern California's backcountry—several trails in this book begin nearby.

GPS COORDINATES: N34°34.79' W118°06.94'

NEAREST TRAIL: South Coast #2: Grass Mountain Trail

Palm Springs

Agua Caliente Indians, a subtribe of the Luiseño-Cahuilla, lived in the region of present-day Palm Springs for centuries before Euro-American entry into California. American influence permeated the area as early as 1852, when Mormons settled in San Bernardino. Palm Springs was established as Palmetto Springs, named after the palm trees that dotted the area. It was also known as Big Palm Springs, Seven Palms, and later Agua Caliente (Spanish for "hot water") after the hot springs. The post office, established in 1890, chose the name Palm Springs because an Agua Caliente already existed in Sonoma County.

The Southern Pacific Railroad built a station here in 1875, but the town still grew quite slowly. Palm Springs was incorporated in 1938. By 1940, it had little more than 5,000 year-round residents, although this jumped to 8,000 seasonally.

Hollywood celebrities took a fancy to Palm Springs after the hot springs became open to the public in 1957. Previously, the springs were the sole property of the Agua Caliente Indians. A hospital completed in 1952 and an airport opened in 1958 made the town even more attractive to outsiders. Kirk Douglas, Frank Sinatra, Liberace, and Elvis Presley all spent time in Palm Springs. Long-term resident Bob Hope was even named honorary mayor. Hope founded one of the many golf tournaments in the Palm Springs area.

Many U.S. presidents have vacationed in Palm Springs. Presidents Eisenhower, Ford, and Reagan all held properties nearby. Ford retired here after his election defeat in 1976. He and his wife, Betty, continue to be active in the area. The former president is a regular participant in regional golf tournaments. Mrs. Ford brought attention to Palm Springs when she founded the Betty Ford Clinic in Rancho Mirage. The clinic is world-renowned for the treatment of drug and alcohol addiction.

Palm Springs was revolutionized in the 1960s by Jack Weis and his son, Dick. Together, Jack and Dick introduced the idea of second-home condos. Today, there are more than 12,000 condominiums in the Palm Springs Valley. Many residents also own a home elsewhere.

Palm Springs is still a favored locale for celebrities. At least 28 of the Forbes 400 list of the most-wealthy people in America have homes in the valley. Many hotels and golf courses in town cater to snow birds who enjoy the elegant winter resort.

GPS COORDINATES: N33°49.82' W116°32.76'

NEAREST TRAIL: South Coast #20: North Coyote Canyon Trail

Panamint City

Panamint City (also known as Panamint) was founded in 1873 after the discovery of silver chloride ore by Richard Jacobs and two partners. A town quickly sprang up as optimists rushed to the area. After just one year, the settlement had a population of about 2,000. The main street bustled with a variety of businesses—a brewery, more than twenty saloons, six general stores, a meat market, a bank, and a newspaper office for the *Panamint News*. The main investors in the mining district were two Nevada politicians, John P. Jones and William M. Stewart, known as the "Silver Senators." Jones and Stewart had financed and made fortunes from the Comstock Lode, a rich silver mine in Nevada.

Panamint City was in remote Surprise Canyon in Death Valley. Its isolation caused considerable problems in the transportation of ore. Remi Nadeau made a sizable profit in hauling the metal by mule to Los Angeles. To prevent theft along the lonely 200-mile journey, the silver was smelted into ingots weighing more than 400 pounds each.

Protection from theft was very necessary in Panamint City. Before mining operations collapsed in 1876 after just three years, there were about 50 killings in the small town. One Wells Fargo employee described the settlement as a "suburb of hell." The owners of two of the town's saloons, Ned Reddy and Dave Neagle, had already escaped prosecution for killings elsewhere in the West. Jim Bruce, another violent gunman, was said to have a private cemetery for his shooting victims, although this was probably an exaggeration.

Panamint City's boom was remarkably short lived. By 1877, the last mines were closed and the town was dead. A flood in 1901 destroyed many of the decaying buildings, and all that remains today are a few ruins and a crumbling smelter chimney.

GPS COORDINATES: N36°07.11' W117°05.72'
NEAREST TRAIL: Desert #35: Pleasant Canyon Loop Trail

Parkfield

Parkfield calls itself "the earthquake capital of the world." It rests in a valley dotted by oaks on the San Andreas Fault and has traditionally been struck with a serious earthquake about every 20 years. The last major tremors were felt in 1966, so seismologists have flocked to the area, predicting a quake at any time. Local businesses have incorporated this uncertainty into their advertisements; a sign on the Parkfield Café reads, "Eat Here When It Happens," and a sign on the Parkfield Inn states, "Sleep Here When It Happens."

Sign for Parkfield

Yokuts Indians lived in the area of Parkfield for centuries before white settlers arrived. They called the valley Cholame, which translates to either "the beautiful one" or "evil people," depending on which source you believe. American ranchers first came to the region in 1854. Initially, the settlement was called Russelsville, but the postal service asked that another name be chosen when the name was submitted in 1883. Residents decided on Parkfield because they thought the surrounding area was as beautiful as a park. In the late 1800s, coal was discovered near Parkfield. The town's population peaked at 900, but mines soon played out.

Only a few ranchers remain in this picturesque central California town. Recently they have been joined by a slew of scientists eager to study seismic activity. The United States Geological Survey keeps an eye on the area, which now has the largest array of earthquake monitoring equipment in the world.

GPS COORDINATES: N35°54.08' W120°25.90'
TRAIL: Central Mountains #47: Parkfield Grade Trail
MAP: Page 276

Paso Robles

Paso Robles began as an outpost for Mission San Miguel. The Spanish Mission Trail, or El Camino Real (see page 59), passed by the outpost. The mineral hot springs at this site were well known to Indians before the Franciscans found them and constructed a crude wooden pool at the edge of the main spring in 1797. The priests later built a log house over the pool. In 1844, the lands around the hot springs were granted to Pedro Narváez as part of the Rancho El Paso de los Robles. In Spanish, *El paso de los robles* means "the passage of the oaks." The name was given to the site in 1776 by Pedro Font, cartographer and chaplain for the second expedition of Juan Bautista de Anza.

In 1857, the old Mexican land grant was purchased by James H. and Daniel D. Blackburn. The two brothers built some of the first substantial structures in the area. Their brother-in-law, Drury James, was the first to develop the tract of land where present-day Paso Robles now stands. The town itself was founded in 1886 and became an agricultural center. An elegant resort spa was established at the hot springs in 1889; it remained in business until 1941.

Today, Paso Robles is one of the largest towns in San Luis Obispo County and the closest settlement to Camp Roberts, headquarters of the California Army National Guard. The city lies in the midst of cattle, wheat, apple, and almond country. Local attractions include the Mission San Miguel, Hearst Castle at San Simeon, and many vineyards.

GPS COORDINATES: N35°37.69' W120°41.36'
NEAREST TRAIL: Central Mountains #47: Parkfield Grade Trail

Picacho

Picacho was located on the Colorado River, 25 miles upstream from Yuma in what is now Imperial County. The town, originally a Mexican settlement named El Rio ("The River" in Spanish), housed placer miners from the surrounding area. José Maria Mendivil of Sonora, Mexico, first discovered gold in the area in 1852. He quickly sold his interests in the mine and planned out the nearby town. The major strike in the area was at Picacho Mine. *Picacho* means "peak" in Spanish (making the nearby Picacho Peak somewhat redundantly named). The mine took its name from the distinctive landmark to its west. The strong influence of the mine on the town's development led it to adopt the same name.

At first, the settlement retained a very Spanish flavor with regular bullfights and fiestas, but as mining operations grew, more Anglo Americans moved into town. Yuma storeowner

David Neahr built a processing mill on the banks of the Colorado and invested heavily in the burgeoning mine. The mine grew even more when it became the possession of Stephen W. Dorsay's California King Gold Mines Company. The company built another, larger mill and constructed a 5-mile-long railroad to connect it to the mine. Railroads and steamboats transported an estimated $15 million of ore to Yuma.

By 1900, Picacho had a population of 2,500. However, the town's days were numbered; the decreased value of gold, combined with a mine explosion and floods, hurt production severely. In 1909, the completion of the Laguna Dam isolated Picacho from Yuma, and the Imperial Dam, finished in 1938, flooded what remained of the town. Today, much of the site lies below water, but small sections of the railroad grade can still be seen. The area is now part of Picacho State Recreation Area.

GPS COORDINATES: N32°58.01' W114°38.11'
TRAIL: South Coast #49: Indian Pass Road
MAP: Page 442

Porterville

Porterville began in 1859 with a stage stop operated by R. Porter Putman. Putman's store and hotel were called Porter's Station; when he began laying out a town in 1864 he called it Portersville. By the time it was incorporated as a city in 1902, the settlement was known as Porterville.

To encourage people to come to Porterville, the first settlers were given a free lot for every lot they purchased. The town soon became an important trading center for local farmers after the surrounding area was irrigated. The Southern Pacific Railroad extended a branch line to Porterville in 1888.

Agriculture has always been the backbone of the town, with orange, other fruits, vegetable, and cotton growing and dairy farming all thriving in the warm climate. The early 1900s saw an extra boost to Porterville's slowly rising population when magnetite ore was found nearby. By 1920, the population exceeded 5,000. Many more migrants came to the Central Valley during the 1930s for agricultural work. Porterville continues to attract newcomers, perhaps drawn by the city's motto, "The Good Life." The 2000 census counted 40,625 residents.

Porterville, circa 1912

Porterville is situated along the western foothills of the Sierra Nevada and provides an excellent outlet to explore the surrounding backcountry. The headquarters of Sequoia National Forest is located in town.

GPS COORDINATES: N36°04.25' W119°00.94'
NEAREST TRAIL: Central Mountains #8: Solo Peak Road

Pozo

The village of Pozo (population 52) is 18 miles southeast of Santa Margarita on Pozo Road. It was named by G. W. Lingo after the Spanish word for well and began as an agricultural community in the mid-1800s. The settlement was located in a depression that stayed moist and was good for farming. Most of its early residents spoke Spanish.

In the 1860s, Pozo was the site of both a Wells Fargo office and a Pony Express delivery stop. The town's most famous building is the Pozo Saloon, built in 1858 as a stage stop overlooking the Pozo Valley. The saloon was forced to close during Prohibition, but it reopened in 1967 and remains a popular bar with locals and tourists. It provides good drinks and wonderful oak pit–barbecued food. The house drink is a Pozo Martini, which is a pint of beer with olives in it. Pozo Saloon hosts an annual Scottish Highland Games, where competitors can try their hand at activities like the caber toss (throwing a long heavy log underhand for distance). The bar is also a popular concert venue, with such guests as Willie Nelson, John Mayall, Country Joe McDonald, and George Thorogood.

Pozo's peak came around 1878 when gold was discovered in the area. The town post office opened that year and remained in service until 1942. At that time, the town had (in addition to the saloon) a two-story hotel, dance hall, school, blacksmith shop, general store, and barbershop. Remains of the old school can still be seen.

GPS COORDINATES: N35°18.22' W120°22.62'
TRAIL: Central Mountains #44: Pozo Road
MAP: Page 268

Providence

About 25 miles north of Interstate 40 and old Route 66 are a few foundations and crumbled white softstone walls, all that remains of the settlement of Providence. This was the company town of the Bonanza King Mine, one of the richest silver mines in California's history. In the 1870s, silver ore was discovered nearby in the Providence Mountains. The mine was heavily developed in the early 1880s and extracted $1 million of ore in its first 18 months of operation. By 1883, the town boasted three saloons, two hotels, a post office, and two general stores, though a miner risked losing his job if he conducted business anywhere but the company shop. The town's existence was extremely short-lived; in 1885 the 10-stamp mill burned down and the company decided there was insufficient ore to warrant the construction of another one. Miners left town and the buildings fell into ruin. Enough remains of the settlement today to make a visit there quite worthwhile.

GPS COORDINATES: N34°58.82' W115°30.20' (approximately)
NEAREST TRAIL: Desert #13: Mojave Road

Ramona

The small, pretty town of Ramona is situated in the area Native Americans referred to as Mutarati, meaning "The Big Valley." The valley has undergone several name changes, including Valley de Pamo Santa Maria, which means "Warm Valley of Saint Mary," which in turn was shortened to Santa Maria Valley.

The settlement began when a Basque sheep rancher, Bernard Etchenverry, gave a parcel of land to Amos Verlaque. Verlaque opened a general store, and soon other businesses started in the area. In 1883, the town took the name of Nuevo (*nuevo* means "new" in Spanish). It was renamed Ramona in either 1884 or 1886 by a man named Milton Santee, after the Indian girl in the book *Ramona*, written by Helen Hunt Jackson. Jackson named her character after her friend Ramona Wolf, the wife of the storekeeper at Temecula.

Ramona briefly lost its name to a new division of Los Angeles County, but regained it in 1895 when the division closed. The present town of Ramona has retained the name ever since. It is now a semi-rural outer suburb of San Diego, combining the amenities of a metropolitan area with a small town charm. It is situated 40 miles from downtown San Diego, and 40 miles from the beaches of the Pacific Ocean. The town is growing rapidly, with population up 40 percent from 1990 to about 40,000, making Ramona the fastest growing community in San Diego County.

Ramona's inland climate is more seasonal than most of the county. Summer temperatures average between 53 and 90 degrees Fahrenheit, slightly warmer than on the coast; and winter temperatures average between 35 and 67 degrees Fahrenheit, slightly cooler than on the coast.

To this day, the nearby town of Hemet hosts the Ramona Bowl, the state's oldest continuing outdoor pageant. Started in 1920 and based around Jackson's best-selling novel, it is hosted in the natural open-air amphitheater known as the Ramona Bowl. The bowl has been improved over the years, with a museum being added in 1952.

GPS COORDINATES: N33°00.57' W116°57.41'

NEAREST TRAIL: South Coast #22: Santa Ysabel Creek Trail

Randsburg

For years, prospectors had been exploring the Mojave Desert northeast of Los Angeles. Although their search produced little gold, it did generate enough profit for them to survive. One prospector, a German named John Goler, discovered significant amounts of gold in the El Paso Mountains in the 1850s. Eager to escape the desert, he charted his find but did not develop a mine. In 1893, prospectors found what they believed to be Goler's strike in a place they named Goler Gulch, north of what was to become the town site of Randsburg.

Frederick Mooers and John Singleton came to the vicinity of Goler Gulch in 1893 and discovered placer gold on the side of an unnamed mountain to the south of the gulch in the Rand Mountains. They returned in 1895 with Charles Burcham in hopes of locating the source. At the top of the mountain, they fractured a piece of a rock outcropping and found extraordinary amounts of metal. "We've struck it rich," exclaimed Mooers. The mountain, once bypassed by prospectors because it showed few signs of mineralization, was entirely ore. The men named their claim Rand (later called Yellow Aster), after South Africa's rich Rand Gold Mining District. Yet Mooers, Singleton, and Burcham couldn't afford the registration fee for the claim without extracting some of the gold or gold dust. Too broke to develop the mine, the men resolved to sell their claim. Mooers's wife, however, prohibited the sale and began mining the mountain with the men. By 1904, some 10 miles of tunnels ran through the mine, and by 1911, the mine's production reached more than $6 million worth of gold.

Gold Hill, Randsburg

Within hours of the Rand discovery, prospectors arrived to stake their own claims. What began as a small mining camp with a few tents north of the mine quickly evolved into the town of Randsburg. Its population reached 3,500 by the start of the twentieth century. The town had hotels, saloons, a general store, an Orpheus theater, and even a brass band. Each evening residents convened at local bars and dance halls. More than one fire besieged the town, but Randsburg's many celebrations never subsided.

The colossal ore deposits found at the Yellow Aster warranted construction of a railway. By 1898 the Randsburg Railroad was up and running. That same year Barstow built a 50-stamp mill and began receiving ore from the mine via the rail. By 1901, the Yellow Aster Mine was operating its own mills, which had a total capacity of 130 stamps. To refine the ore, men piped water from Garlock.

Today, several businesses remain in Randsburg, including the original general store, which contains an authentic vintage soda fountain, and the White House Saloon, a full service bar. The Yellow Aster Mine, now an open pit, heap leach mine, is operating under Rand Mining Company, a subsidiary of Glamis Gold Ltd. In 2000, the mine produced a record 100,000 ounces at $176 per ounce of gold. At year's end, its proven and indicated resources were 232,700 ounces and 429,300 ounces, respectively.

GPS COORDINATES: N35°22.14' W117°39.47'

TRAIL: Central Mountains #27: Government Peak Trail

MAP: Page 224

Red Mountain

In 1919, the Kelly silver deposit was discovered and the town of Red Mountain was born. It was originally named Osdick, after Pete Osdick, the first miner to stake claims here. While Osdick attempted to create a reputable community, another settlement, referred to as Inn City and Sin City, was making its own history a few yards away. As the names imply, Inn City was a place of brothels and wild times. Liquor flowed freely, and Prohibition had little effect. The town attracted plenty of outsiders. With the two factions so close together, a controversy arose over what to call the local post office. In 1922, the postal service chose the appellation Red Mountain after a neighboring peak.

The Kelly Mine, which included an onsite mill, was one of the greatest silver producers in California, generating more than $15 million worth of metal. Most of the town's buildings were ultimately abandoned; the few saloons that remain are now antique stores.

GPS COORDINATES: N35°21.47' W117°36.99'

NEAREST TRAIL: Central Mountains #27: Government Peak Trail

Sageland

Sageland was a small settlement in what is now Kern County. It gained its first post office in 1860, when it was established as a supply point for miners working in the nearby ranges. It took its name from the aromatic sagebrush. Sageland supplied much of the labor force for local mines, such as the St. John, Burning Moscow, and Hortense. The town grew to a population of more than 200 after the El Dorado Mining District was organized in 1866. The settlement attracted many storekeepers from Havilah, one of whom was George Bodfish. His name lives on to this day in the settlement of Bodfish.

In 1863, Sageland was the scene of an ambush of one of the haulage drays from Los Angeles. A group of Indians set upon five teamsters, killing two. The remaining three men scattered and managed to escape. One took refuge at Weldon, which was named after settler William Weldon. Sageland suffered from the closure of the Bright Star Mine and was deserted by the early 1870s.

A store and a bar in Sageland were washed away by flood in the 1960s. Today, several more recent houses mark the site. There are also some old ore workings and a typical ghost town cemetery complete with a Victorian picket fence.

GPS COORDINATES: N35°28.79' W118°12.70'

TRAIL: Central Mountains #16: Piute Mountain Road

MAP: Page 185

San Bernardino

San Bernardino is the seat of the county of the same name. San Bernardino County is the largest county (in terms of area) in the United States. Indeed, nine of the fifty states are smaller. Any *two* of the following states could fit into the county: Vermont, Rhode Island, New Jersey, New Hampshire, Massachusetts, Maryland, Hawaii, Delaware, and Connecticut. The city of San Bernardino is by far the most populous in the county, with a 2000 census count of 185,401, up 13 percent from 1990.

San Bernardino

San Bernardino was established on May 20, 1810 as an *asistencia* for Mission San Gabriel. (An *asistencia* is an outlying branch of a mission with a church but no permanent priest.) It was named by a Spanish priest, Father Dumetz, for San Bernardino of Sienna, a famous Franciscan preacher whose feast day is May 20. After the missions were broken up, the name was applied to a land grant given by the Mexican governor of California in 1842. The San Bernardino Rancho was purchased in the early 1850s by a group of Mormons. The Mormons built a fort to protect themselves from Indian attacks and gradually developed a community. By 1854, when the city of San Bernardino was incorporated, its population was around 1,200, nearly all members of the Church of Latter-day Saints. Many Mormons left in 1857 at the request of Brigham Young, who wanted them to help settle the Salt Lake City, Utah, area. This stunted San Bernardino's growth at a time when much of California was seeing explosions in population.

Gold was discovered in the Holcomb Valley in 1860 by William F. Holcomb, sparking a sudden gold rush into San Bernardino County. For a while, San Bernardino was somewhat dwarfed by the mining town of Belleville. A close race for the county seat in 1861 gave San Bernardino a victory by just two votes. Rumors abounded that a ballot box from Belleville mysteriously disappeared in the hands of San Bernardino supporters.

San Bernardino started to take off as a railway junction in the final years of the 1800s. The Atchison, Topeka & Santa Fe, the Union Pacific, and the Southern Pacific all laid lines into the town. By 1910, the city had a population of about 13,000. In the 1900s, the automobile replaced the train as the preferred mode of transportation, and San Bernardino benefited from this change. Historic Route 66 passes through town. In the 1930s the route saw thousands of migrants making their way into the Golden State; San Bernardino was a destination for many. Today, the main highway through town is Interstate 15. Because of its accessibility and proximity to the Mojave Desert, San Bernardino is an excellent departure point for a variety of backcountry adventures.

GPS COORDINATES: N34°06.34' W117°17.29'

NEAREST TRAIL: South Coast #11: Sugarpine Mountain Trail

San Diego

In 1542, Juan Rodriguez Cabrillo became the first European to set foot on California soil when he landed on Point Loma near the mouth of San Diego Bay. The Cabrillo National Monument commemorates the spot today. Sebastían Vizcaíno named the site in 1602. The name originates not from Saint James (Santiago) as is often thought, but from Saint Didacus, a fifteenth-century Spanish priest whose name also adorned Vizcaíno's flagship. San Diego was the site of the first Spanish mission and the first non-native town in California. The intrepid Franciscan priest Junípero Serra founded the mission on July 16, 1769. Its beginnings were inauspicious; Serra established the settlement by raising a single wooden cross on the projected site of the first chapel. He enticed local Indians to join the community by handing out gifts. The Indians responded by raiding the new mission. Eventually, they did flock to the settlement and by 1797 they numbered more than 1,400, peaking at 1,800 in 1824. A second church, dedicated in 1813, still stands in the old town area of the city. The nearby presidio fared somewhat less well; in 1800 there were only 167 non-Indian residents of San Diego.

The mission was secularized in 1834 by the Mexican government, and it lost much of its land and resources. San Diego was made the unofficial capital of the province for a period during Mexican rule, but even after the town fell into the hands of the United States following the Mexican War, growth was slow and sporadic. The arrival of the transcontinental Santa Fe Railroad in 1885 made the city more accessible, but it was not until the twentieth century that it started to experience a real population explosion.

San Diego benefited greatly from the establishment of several major army and navy bases in the area. Electronic companies, aerospace businesses, oceanographic research facilities, and other scientific enterprises followed. Its location near the Mexican border made it a natural destination for immigrants from the south. Especially since World War II, San Diego has grown astronomically both economically and in population. In the 1940 census, just under 150,000 residents were counted; by 2000 that figure was 2,813,833, making it one of the 20 biggest metropolitan areas in the nation. The city has spread northward to include La Jolla, inland to El Cajon, and southward through suburban Chula Vista almost to Mexico's Tijuana. Along the coast lie some beautiful beaches warmed by its sunny climate. The Spanish mission church, maritime museum, and world-famous zoo are some of San Diego's premier attractions.

San Diego, circa 1850

NEAREST TRAIL: South Coast #38: Otay Mountain Truck Trail

San Juan Capistrano

San Juan Capistrano has managed to retain a village quality despite its close proximity to America's second largest city. It is the site of the oldest surviving church in California, a little chapel dating from 1776 that is often known as "Father Serra's Church."

Mission San Juan Capistrano has the interesting distinction of being established twice. The original founding took place on October 30, 1775, with Father Fermín Francisco de Lasuén leading ceremonies. Rumors of an impending Indian attack caused the new camp to be abandoned, the priests left, burying bronze bells they had brought with them. Father Junípero Serra was in the party that returned the following year, and the mission was founded for a second time on November 1, 1776. It was named after Saint Giovanni de Capestrano, a fourteenth-century Italian theologian and warrior priest whom Serra greatly admired. This time the settlement proved more long lasting, and several buildings from the mission's early years still survive. In 1806, a huge stone church was dedicated. This was the prize of San Juan Capistrano until its destruction by earthquake in 1812. A reproduction of the great building was completed in 1984.

Mission San Juan Capistrano

Like other Franciscan sites, Mexican independence from Spain ended mission life. At first, many Indians stayed in the community, but gradually the land was given to Mexican rancheros, including Governor Pio Pico's cousin, Juan Forster. Still, the surrounding community remained small. President Abraham Lincoln returned mission lands to the Catholic Church in 1864.

In 1881, railroads connected San Juan Capistrano to Los Angeles, and it instantly became a favored destination for those interested in California's pre-statehood history. The town's population was still small when the San Diego Freeway was finished in 1958. Rapid development in the following decade persuaded city officials to enact some of the first growth management legislation in the state. Much of the town is now designated as historic area or open space, and the 2000 census counted just 33,826 residents. San Juan Capistrano is famous for the large flock of swallows that arrive every year on St. Joseph's Day, March 19, and stays until October 23. The Fiesta de las Golondrines celebrates their arrival. A renovated and restored mission area and a Native American museum are some of San Juan Capistrano's most visited attractions. Despite pressure from surrounding urban sprawl, the city has lived up to its motto, "Preserving the Past to Enhance the Future," and it still makes for a pleasant visit today.

GPS COORDINATES: N33°30.10' W117°39.64'

NEAREST TRAIL: South Coast #18: Main Divide Road

San Luis Obispo

The town of San Luis Obispo, seat of San Luis Obispo County, grew around the fifth California mission, established by Junípero Serra on September 1, 1772. Serra chose a scenic valley previously visited by Gaspar de Portolá for the location of the mission. The valley was inhabited by an astonishing number of bears, and the Spanish were able to win the goodwill of local Indians by killing the feared beasts and sharing their meat. The site was named Mission San Luis Obispo de Tolosa ("the mission of Saint Louis, bishop of Toulouse"). San Luis Obispo began to attract some Indian converts immediately, although others thrice burned the mission buildings. The wood and grass structures were eventually replaced with clay. The settlement was especially well known for the clothing it manufactured, including coatlike serapes.

Like other Californian missions, Mission San Luis Obispo deteriorated during Mexican rule, although the town itself became a ranching center. It was isolated from the effects of the 1849 gold rush, and its seclusion continued until the construction of the Southern Pacific Railroad through town in 1894.

Mission San Luis Obispo de Tolusa

Today, San Luis Obispo is situated at the convergence of US 101 and scenic California 1, but it remains a sufficient distance from the metropolises of San Francisco and Los Angeles to retain a rustic quality. San Luis Obispo County is still relatively underpopulated. It did attract U.S. military interest in World War II, and more than 100,000 personnel were stationed nearby at Camp Roberts, Camp San Luis Obispo, and the naval training center at Marco Bay. The city recently renovated its downtown area, the heart of which is Mission Plaza. The mission church is still in use for congregational services, and the old priest's residence is now a historical museum. Parts of the mission lands are rumored to be haunted by ghosts of Native Americans massacred by Spanish soldiers for refusing to convert to Catholicism; several businesses opened near the site of the killings have met with strange misfortune. Tourists can also visit nearby Hearst Castle at San Simeon, opened to the public since 1958.

GPS COORDINATES: N35°17.21' W120°39.70'

NEAREST TRAIL: Central Mountains #44: Pozo Road

Santa Barbara

Sebastían Vizcaíno named the passageway between the mainland and the Channel Islands the Canal de Santa Barbara on December 4, 1602, the feast day of Saint Barbara, a Roman virgin beheaded by her father for accepting Christianity. As early as 1777, Serra had requested funds to build a new mission on the site of what is now the modern city. However, the first Spanish settlement, the Presidio de Santa Barbara, founded in 1782, was military rather than religious in nature. The presidio consisted of a small square enclosure surrounded by a ditch and an earthen wall. Inside was a small church, housing for both soldiers and civilians, and some warehouses and workshops. The military value of the fortification was mostly symbolic; only a few cannons and several hundred soldiers defended it, but an attack on the presidio was an attack on Spain itself.

The presidio was followed in 1786 by the establishment of the tenth Franciscan mission in California, and the first to be set up after Junípero Serra's death in 1784. The architecture of Mission Santa Barbara was superb and has led many to call it the "Queen of the Missions." It bears a heavy Roman influence, inspired by a book on classical buildings obtained in reprint by one of the mission's priests. The surviving structures were built after the earthquakes of 1812, which ravaged many of the coastal missions. More recent earthquakes have necessitated repairs several times since then. A complete reconstruction was carried out after a 1925 earthquake.

Santa Barbara County was one of the state's original 27 counties, and the county seat has always rested in the city of the same name. Santa Barbara prides itself on its history. Many prestatehood adobe buildings have been reconstructed and a fiesta celebrates Old Spanish Days every summer. American traders began to arrive in Santa Barbara during the period of Mexican rule that was ended when volunteer forces led by John Frémont captured the city peacefully on Christmas Day 1846.

Landmarks include the beautiful mission, a remarkable courthouse finished in 1929, the Botanic Gardens, and the Museum of Natural History. The downtown area has been carefully zoned to retain a pleasant charm and the waterfront still boasts an active harbor.

GPS COORDINATES: N34°25.30' W119°41.86'

TRAIL: Central Mountains #33: Big Caliente Spring Trail

MAP: Page 242

Schwab

The town site of Schwab is located in the northern, or upper, branch of Echo Canyon in Death Valley National Park. This ambitious settlement was established in 1906 in response to the growth of mines in the vicinity. The most productive mine in the area was the Inyo Gold Mine, discovered in 1905 by Chet Leavitt and Maroni Hicks. Production at the mine began in 1906, with ore assaying anywhere between $300 and $650 per ton. Leavitt and Hicks retained ownership of most of the mine and constructed a boardinghouse to accommodate their workers.

The new settlement was named after Charles Schwab, the steel and mining magnate from Pennsylvania who was developing mining interests in this region. Large newspaper advertisements described a town with an assured future. Freight lines, water sources, boardinghouses, and more would soon be in place in this booming mining region.

In just three months, Schwab had a population nearing 200; a post office was opened in March 1907. However, Schwab was in direct competition with Lee, located just west of the California border. Merchants found it hard to compete, as most supplies came in via Lee. Lee, being closer to Rhyolite, was a busier town that catered to the various mines on the state line. Schwab's town government came under the control of three strong-minded women led by Chicago stockbroker Gertrude Fesler. The women embarked on a crusade to raise the moral standards of the small settlement. The city government closed several saloons and gambling houses and kicked out the town's female "entertainers." A good portion of Schwab's male population also left.

In the financial panic of 1907, many of the mines around Schwab were forced to close. Most merchants simply dismantled their tent stores and moved to bigger settlements. After less than a year, the town of Schwab was dead, joining a long list of short-lived mining camps in California.

The Inyo Gold Mine was worked intermittently until 1941; most of the ruins in the area are remnants of that operation. In 1938, a ball mill was constructed onsite. The mill, near the parking area at the mining complex, once consisted of a 50-ton ore bin, a jaw crusher, a reciprocating feeder, a ball mill, and associated fixtures. Water for the mill and camp was carted from Furnace Creek at great expense. The building that lies flat on the ground close to the mill is the old cookhouse. The ore bin high above the mill site marks the main complex of the Inyo Mine. Of Schwab itself, little remains.

GPS COORDINATES: N36°30.33' W116°43.37'

TRAILS: Desert #39: Funeral Range Trail; Desert #38: Echo Canyon Trail

MAPS: Pages 584, 587

Silver Lake

About 8 miles north of Baker are the sparse remains of Silver Lake. The settlement was founded in March 1906 as a station on the Tonopah & Tidewater Railroad line. By 1907, Silver Lake hosted a post office, boardinghouses, a telegraph office, and (of course) several saloons. At its peak it was home to about 100 people. Situated on the banks of dry Silver Lake, wells in the town supplied all the drinking water for Baker in the early years of the twentieth century.

The settlement served as a center for many regional mines, including the Riggs silver mines and the Avawatz Mountains mines. Workers were attracted to the many saloons and the regular dances held in a large tent by "Ma" Palmer.

Silver Lake started to decline rapidly in the 1920s, following the completion of the Arrowhead Trail Highway (present-day I-15) connecting Los Angeles to Salt Lake City, Utah, a major thoroughfare that bypassed Silver Lake. When the Tonopah & Tidewater line ceased service in 1940, the settlement quickly became a ghost town. All that remains today are a few adobe walls and a small cemetery.

GPS COORDINATES: N35°22.26' W116°06.83' (approximately)

NEAREST TRAIL: Desert #13: Mojave Road

Skidoo

During 1905, two prospectors lost in rare Death Valley fog stumbled upon gold-bearing ledges near the town of Harrisburg. John "One-eye" Thompson and John Ramsey attempted to keep their discovery secret, though news of the new gold traveled quickly and eventually reached the Nevada mining town of Rhyolite. Bob Montgomery, co-owner of the World Beater Mine, reportedly paid $60,000 for the men's claims and what became known as Skidoo. To power a 15-stamp mill, Montgomery piped pure mountain water from Bird Spring, some 23 miles away on the top of Telescope Peak. The aqueduct resulted in the popularity of the slang phrase "twenty-three, Skidoo." Altogether, Montgomery spent more than twice his original investment.

Skidoo's 400-plus inhabitants benefited from a telephone line and a stagecoach connecting them to Rhyolite, as well as the usual saloons, inns, and trading posts. Although it was known for its quiet, almost dreary nature, the town did have at least one moment of notoriety. On a Sunday in April 1908, Joe "Hootch" Simpson, co-owner of Skidoo's Gold Seal Saloon, shot and killed Jim Arnold, the manager of a local store. Within days, Simpson was seized from jail and lynched. Several days later, his body was exhumed and hanged again for the sake of newspaper photographers from Los Angeles.

When mining operations at Skidoo ceased, residents found it hard to leave; the settlement was one of the last gold camps in Death Valley. Today, Skidoo is listed on the National Register of Historic Places. Only a few buildings remain.

GPS COORDINATES: N36°26.20' W117°08.61'

TRAIL: Desert #43: Skidoo Road

MAP: Page 597

Soledad

Soledad began as the thirteenth Franciscan mission in California. It was named Nuestra Señora de la Soledad (Spanish for

"Our Lady of Solitude") by Gaspar de Portolá in 1769. Portolá decided on the name after attempting a conversation with a local Indian who kept repeating a phrase that sounded like *soledad* to the Spaniard. The mission was founded two decades later, on October 9, 1791.

The weather around Mission Soledad proved harsh on the adobe buildings; frequent rains melted their walls. By the time secularization orders were received in 1834, many were already in ruin. The population at the mission never exceeded 700. Many converts died or fled during an epidemic in 1802. When the site was sold in 1846 it raised just $800. The structures slowly crumbled away, though in recent years several buildings have been reproduced and now house a museum.

Mission Nuestra Señora de la Soledad

The town of Soledad, in Monterey County, began in 1874 as a base for local farmers. Its first businesses were a feedlot, post office, general store, and two hotels. The arrival of the Southern Pacific Railroad in 1872 inspired growth in the town. Soledad was officially incorporated as a city on March 9, 1921. At this time, the area was seeing an influx of temporary agricultural workers. John Steinbeck portrayed the itinerant lifestyle in his classic novelette *Of Mice and Men*, published in 1937. The work used Soledad as its backdrop. The same seasonal work later attracted many migrants from Mexico and the Philippines.

Despite its isolation, Soledad continues to attract new residents. The Salinas Valley State Prison and the California Department of Corrections's Soledad Training Facility provide employment for many in the area. In the 2000 census, the city had a population of more than 15,000.

GPS COORDINATES: N36°25.56' W121°19.46'

NEAREST TRAIL: Central Mountains #52: Tassajara Road

Stedman

Eight miles south of Ludlow lie what little remains of the mining settlement of Stedman. In 1898, the Atchison, Topeka & Santa Fe Railroad instructed its local roadmaster, John Suter, to search for a source of water in the area for its trains. While Suter was looking for water he stumbled upon several rich deposits of gold.

The Pacific Mine was soon built to extract the metal. This name still marks the site on some of today's maps. At first the surrounding settlement was called Rochester, but the name was soon changed to Stedman, the origin of which is unknown. The Ludlow & Southern Railroad was constructed to haul ore and transport workers from Stedman to Ludlow on the Santa Fe line. One mine just south of Stedman, the Bagdad Chase Mine, is credited with producing more than half the total recorded gold from San Bernardino County. However, like many mining communities, when the gold was depleted the residents moved on. Until the 1960s, several wooden houses survived at the town site, but unfortunately these have since been destroyed by vandals.

GPS COORDINATES: N34°37.82' W116°10.07' (approximately)

NEAREST TRAIL: Desert #9: Amboy Crater Road

Swansea

Swansea is situated on the old shoreline of Owens Lake, which dried up early last century when the Los Angeles Aqueduct diverted the tributaries that fed it. The town is named after a city in Wales from which many Welshmen immigrated to California to exploit mining opportunities. Swansea was built in 1870 to smelt ore mined from the hills around Cerro Gordo. The small settlement lay at the bottom of the steep Yellow Hill; mules and wagons hauled ore from the mining area. The brick smelter, which survives today in a ruined state, was owned by the Owens Lake Company. The company was the chief rival of Mortimer Belshaw, who owned many of the mining operations in Cerro Gordo. At its height, the smelter's output was 150 83-pound bars of silver every 24 hours. A great quantity of fuel was necessary for this enterprise. The Inyo Range was not densely forested, so timber was cut from the Sierra Nevada on the west side of the lake. Kilns in the camp of Cartago turned the wood into charcoal.

After the ore was converted to silver, it was transported by the ferries *Bessie Brady* and *Mollie Stevens* across Owens Lake to Cartago. Mule teams operated by Remi Nadeau then picked up the metal and transported it to Los Angeles. When the silver and lead deposits had all been extracted from the Cerro Gordo area, Swansea lost its reason for being. Today Swansea is a ghost town. Visitors can still view the remains of a furnace and mill and two small stone buildings, one of which was originally a stage stop. The ruins are in a beautiful location, near dry Owens Lake opposite the Sierra Nevada and towering Mount Whitney.

GPS COORDINATES: N36°31.46' W117°54.23'

TRAIL: Desert #48: Swansea–Cerro Gordo Road

MAP: Page 616

Twentynine Palms

San Bernardino County's Twentynine Palms is situated near a desert oasis known to Paleo-Indians for centuries before its discovery by American Colonel Henry Washington in 1855. Washington named the oasis after the number of Washingtonia palms he found in the area.

Prospectors began to stream into the area in the 1870s. They often rested at the oasis while they sought gold in local hills. Large-scale settlement started after World War I. Local physician Dr. James B. Luckie promoted Twentynine Palms as an ideal environment for rehabilitation for veterans suffering

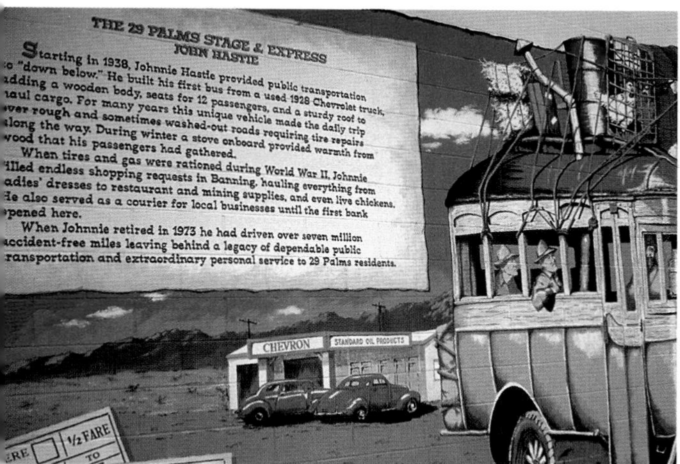

Mural in Twentynine Palms

the effects of mustard gas poisoning. The federal government provided 160-acre parcels free of charge to former soldiers. William Campbell was one of the veterans who came to Twentynine Palms. He arrived in 1924 and built a stone home that still stands today—Roughly Manor, now a bed and breakfast. Together with his wife, Elizabeth, Campbell discovered thousands of important archaeological sites in the area.

Twentynine Palms is home to a United States Marine Corps base, established in 1952 for glider training. The base is the fastest growing in the nation, and now houses about 20,000 military personnel. The city is also the site of the Joshua Tree National Park headquarters and a community college.

Twentynine Palms was incorporated on November 23, 1987, and now has a population in excess of 26,000, more than double the number in 1987. It is located on California 62, 57 miles east of Palm Springs. Although Twentynine Palms's history is relatively short, the city is proud of it. Large historical murals can be seen painted on buildings around the town.

GPS COORDINATES: N34°08.14' W116°03.22'
NEAREST TRAIL: South Coast #41: Old Dale Road

Vallecito

Vallecito was originally named Murphy's Diggings after two brothers, Daniel and John Murphy, who discovered gold here in 1848. For several months, the Murphy brothers panned for the precious metal along Coyote Creek, but they soon left to seek fortunes elsewhere. The place became known as Murphy's Old Diggings to distinguish it from the brothers' new prospects at Murphy, a few miles to the north. Mexicans who occupied the site Daniel and John left renamed it Vallecito, which means "little valley" in Spanish. However, when the post office was established in August 1854, the name was misspelled as Vallecita, an error that was not rectified until 1940.

Vallecito gained some regional attention in 1852 when a rich vein was discovered that was worth far more than the placer pickings of the streambed. Soon the town had a miner's hotel, fandango hall, school, bank, and (of course) many saloons. Several buildings remain from this brief flurry of excitement, including a ruined Wells Fargo office. The town was also a stopping point for the Jackass Mail, whose stage station was used as a supply station for the California Volunteers during the Civil War. By 1877, Vallecito was largely abandoned, but some residents remain in the sleepy community today.

In front of Union Church on Main Street, visitors can admire the town monument, complete with a bronze bell that hung in a large oak tree from 1854 until the tree was felled by winds in 1930. The bell, known as "ship's bell," was cast in Troy, New York, in 1853 and was left on a ship in the San Francisco harbor when its owner hurried to the goldfields. It was hung in a tree because Vallecito's church had no steeple. The trunk of the oak can still be seen near the monument.

GPS COORDINATES: N32°58.51' W116°20.99' (approximately)
NEAREST TRAIL: South Coast #32: Vallecito Wash Trail

Ventura

The present-day town of Ventura rests on the site of an old Chumash Indian settlement. The Chumash were known as accomplished boat builders. They inhabited a stretch of the Pacific Coast in what is now Ventura County and had settlements on several of the Channel Islands. Spanish explorer Juan Rodriguez Cabrillo landed nearby in 1542, as did Gaspar de Portolá in 1769. The site was suggested quite early as a possible location for a Franciscan settlement, but limited Spanish resources delayed construction until 1782. On March 31 of that year, Junípero Serra established his ninth and final mission, naming it Mission San Buenaventura in honor of a thir-

Vallecito stage station intact

...and in ruins, circa 1924

Ventura, circa 1875

teenth century Franciscan saint. San Buenaventura grew quickly and was especially praised for its agricultural output. After his visit in 1793, English sea captain George Vancouver claimed that he had never seen anywhere with crops so beautiful and varied.

The decline of Mission San Buenaventura was not as precipitous as that of other Franciscan missions, but nevertheless by 1845 the lands had been completely broken up. The town of Ventura grew up slowly in the 1860s and 1870s, then more rapidly after the arrival of the railroad in 1887. In 1891, the name was shortened from San Buenaventura at the behest of the post office, though some residents used the longer name for some time afterwards. The town profited from the discovery of oil in the 1920s and expanded considerably in the twentieth century. It is the county seat of Ventura County, created in 1872 from part of Santa Barbara County.

GPS COORDINATES: N34°16.78' W119°17.41'

NEAREST TRAIL: Central Mountains #32: Nordhoff Ridge Trail

Visalia

In November 1852, a group of settlers from Iowa and Texas built a fortified settlement on the north bank of Mill Creek. Nathaniel Vise, one of the town surveyors, suggested the name Fort Visalia, after his hometown, Visalia, Kentucky, which had been named after members of Vise's family.

Main Street, Visalia

An election in 1853 moved the county seat of the newly formed Tulare County (the area was originally part of Mariposa County) from Woodsville to Fort Visalia. County officials changed the name of the settlement to Buena Vista, but the appellation reverted to Visalia in March 1854.

Visalia was a center for Confederate sympathizers during the Civil War (1861–65). Violence erupted after a garrison of the pro-Union California Cavalry was stationed in town in 1862. Additional companies arrived to quash the situation. The pro-South newspaper was closed, and several prominent citizens were arrested, including state Senator Thomas Baker, who later founded Bakersfield.

Visalia was incorporated as a city in 1874 and had 3,000 residents by 1900. The town continued to grow slowly through the first half of the twentieth century. By 1960, the population was about 16,000 and the county seat was a center for local fruit and dairy products. Tulare County consistently ranks as one of the three most productive agricultural counties in the nation (at last count it was second).

The 1960s saw the beginning of rapid growth for Visalia. The population more than doubled in that decade and has continued to rise. At least 96,000 people now live within the city limits. Visalia enjoys warm summers and mild winters and its agricultural-based economy continues to flourish. The town is also close to several excellent backcountry trails in the Sierra Nevada.

GPS COORDINATES: N36°19.74' W119°17.52'

NEAREST TRAIL: Central Mountains #4: Whitaker Research Forest Trail

Wrightwood

Wrightwood is situated in beautiful Swarthout Valley. Serrano Indians resided in the area for thousands of years before Spanish priests brought them into the mission system. When the missions were broken up during Mexican rule of California, many Serrano returned to the valley. The area was then part of the Lugo land grant. Mormons purchased part of the grant in 1851. Two Mormons, Nathan and Truman Swarthout, homesteaded the valley that now bears their name. They abandoned their ranch in 1857 to return to the larger Mormon colony in Salt Lake City.

Sumner Wright, after whom Wrightwood is named, first came to the Swarthout Valley in the 1880s. He and his family eventually acquired two-thirds of the land in the valley. Other settlers came to the area and collectively pushed the few remaining Indians from the land. The settlers also hunted local wildlife; it is said that the last grizzly bear in California was killed in Swarthout Valley. Wright established the Circle Mountain Ranch, which included 1,000 acres of land in the eastern end of the valley. He planted thousands of apple trees on the ranch; parts of his orchard still exist today. Cattle and horses were also raised on the ranch. Other, smaller cattle ranches dotted the valley, and logging and mining were attempted on a small scale.

In 1924, Wright subdivided the Circle Mountain Ranch into a series of smaller lots and a small residential community arose. The settlement grew slowly. Tourism gradually replaced ranching as the area's major industry. Today, Wrightwood remains a center for recreation—several ski resorts attract thousands of people to the area every winter. The town also attracts summer visitors—the Angeles Crest Highway, a National Forest Scenic Byway, begins a few miles east of Wrightwood and winds through Angeles National Forest.

GPS COORDINATES: N34°21.48' W117°37.42'

TRAIL: South Coast #9: Upper Lytle Creek Ridge Trail

MAP: Page 318

Historic Trails

El Camino Real

California's mission trail, better known as El Camino Real (The King's Highway), was composed of a series of roads that connected the 21 Franciscan missions scattered along the Pacific Coast. Rather than being a single formed road, the mission trail grew as the mission system expanded. Parts of it were probably dirt paths used by Native Americans. It began at the church of San Diego de Alcalá, in what is now the Mission Hills area of modern San Diego. This was the first of California's missions, established by Junípero Serra (see page 71) in 1769. The mission has been restored and is open to visitors, as is the nearby Junípero Serra Museum.

From its southernmost point, the trail wound through coastal California to missions in or around the present-day towns of Oceanside (Mission San Luis Rey de Francis), Los Angeles (Mission San Gabriel Arcángel), Ventura (Mission San Buenaventura), Santa Barbara (Mission Santa Barbara Virgen y Mártir), Soledad (Mission Nuestra Señora de la Soledad), Monterey/Carmel (Mission San Carlos Borromeo), and San Francisco (Mission San Francisco de Asís, better known as Mission Delores). The northernmost mission was in Sonoma Valley. Spanish priests and soldiers would travel along the connecting paths to deliver food and supplies to the dispersed missions. In 1783, the year before his death, Junípero Serra walked a staggering 500 miles in a tour of the nine completed settlements.

When large-scale migration into California began in the mid-nineteenth century, the only passable roads were those of the mission trail, which was unfortunate for the gold-seekers because the paths ran north-south instead of east to the goldfields. The original mission trail has long since disappeared, but California 1 and US 101 follow the general route. Several of the missions along the way have been recently restored and make for a pleasant visit. One of them, Mission San Juan Bautista, located north of Carmel, preserves a trace of the original El Camino Real.

For more information on California's missions, see page 96 or the individual sections in "Towns, Ghost Towns, and Interesting Places."

Gila Trail

The Gila Trail bears the dusty footprints of some of the most colorful characters in U.S. and Mexican history. Francisco Vásquez de Coronado, Juan de Oñate, Estavanico, General Stephen Kearny, James Pattie, and Ewing Young all ventured on or crossed the famous trail. Its route followed the Gila River until it reached the Colorado near Yuma, Arizona. From here the trail wound westward to San Diego. The Gila Trail was the first overland route into California, having been opened in 1775 by Juan Bautista de Anza under the guidance of Fray Francisco Garcés. Before this, Hohokam and Pima Indians had traversed parts of the trail. The fact that California was now connected to the bulk of New Spain might have eased the province's isolation, but the trail was closed in 1781 by an uprising of Yuma Indians.

During the Mexican War, General Stephen Kearny and guide Kit Carson led an army regiment west along this route. For a brief time the trail was known as Cooke's Wagon Trail in honor of Lieutenant Colonel Philip Cooke. After the war, in 1848, President James K. Polk decided that California needed to be more closely linked to the Union. A new Gila Trail was born—one that differed somewhat from that followed by Spanish explorers along the Gila River. In 1851, Fort Yuma was constructed to protect the crossing of the Colorado River. Some of the forty-niners, especially those from the southern states, used this route to reach the goldfields of California.

The ravages and upheaval of the Civil War touched the Gila Trail. Whoever controlled the trail controlled the flow of communications and wagons to Southern California. Most importantly, whichever side could control and capture the California mines could keep its currency from deflating in the eyes of world powers. When Texas, in which the far east reaches of the trail lay, became the seventh state to secede, the bat-

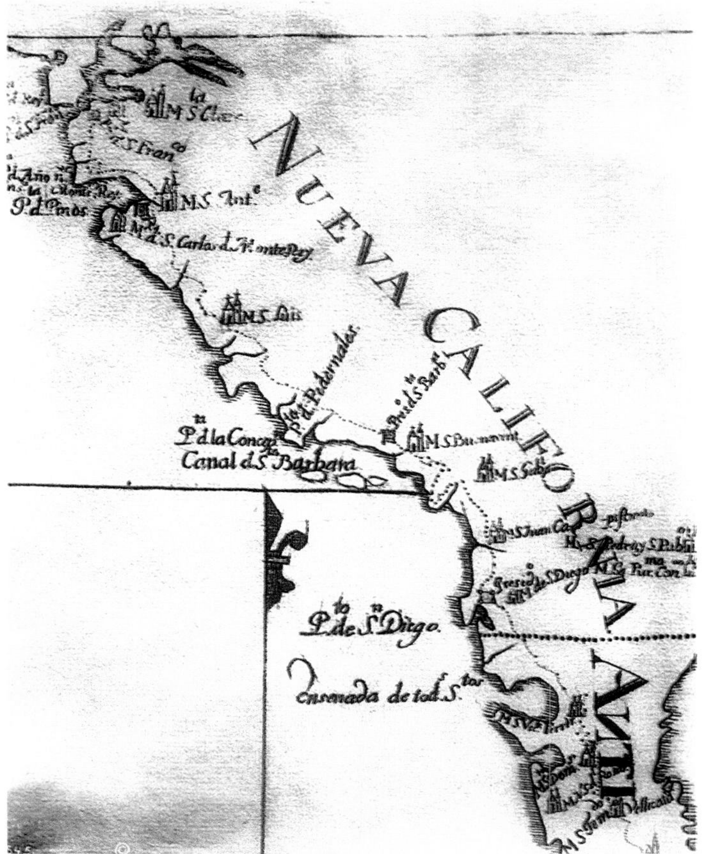

Old map of El Camino Real

tleground was set. Three hundred Union soldiers under the command of Major Isaac Lynde marched from their federal outpost to besiege Lieutenant Colonel John Robert Baylor's 258 Texans at Mesilla, New Mexico. The Texans prevailed. The territories of Arizona and New Mexico, already sympathetic to the Southern cause, joined the Confederacy. News of Arizona's rebellion against the Union had spread to nearby California. General James H. Carleton raised 2,000 Union soldiers and blazed his way through Arizona and into Tucson, thereby recapturing the territory, and the trail, for the Union.

In the years after the Civil War, the trail became the principal route for the Butterfield Overland Mail Company, whose stages were brimming with passengers and mail. Eventually, the company would merge with William G. Fargo's firm—Wells, Fargo & Company. The completion of the transcontinental railroad in 1869 and the line between San Diego and Tucson did not immediately cripple the stagecoach industry. Coaches were needed to service small towns not linked to the railroad. Still, it was only a matter of time before this well-used trail became a railroad line. The respective owners of the Southern Pacific Railroad, the San Antonio Railroad, and the Texas and Pacific Railroad (owned by Jay Gould) decided to avoid a bitter railroad war and to cooperate in creating a line from Los Angeles to New Orleans, with spurs to Dallas and Marshal, Texas. In 1878, the Southern Pacific began laying tracks in Yuma that followed the Gila Trail. Stagecoaches, freight wagons, and mule trains disappeared from the frontier West. Parts of the route were eventually paved. The federal Highway Act of 1956 incorporated the Gila Trail into the superhighway system that includes it as Interstate 8 from San Diego to Casa Grande, Arizona, and Interstate 10 to El Paso, Texas.

Old Spanish Trail

The Spanish Trail was the first major thoroughfare in the American Southwest. It extended 1,120 miles, across six states, in a northward-looping route from Santa Fe, New Mexico, to Los Angeles. It entered California south of what is now Death Valley National Park and wound southwest to Barstow, south to San Bernardino, and then west to Los Angeles. Despite its name, the Spanish Trail was never traversed in its entirety during the period of Spanish rule. It was named by American explorers who mistakenly assumed that it had been opened by Spaniards.

Spanish explorers did travel along sections of the trail attempting to find overland routes into California. The Domínguez-Escalante Expedition followed part of its course in 1776, as did Francisco Garcés. Garcés had earlier opened the first route into California, the Gila Trail. However, this was closed in 1781 by an uprising of Yuma Indians. American mountain man Jedediah Smith was the first to travel through the mountain interior into California. He did so twice, in 1826 and 1827. By 1831 the newly blazed trail was the major overland route to the Pacific.

The Spanish Trail was not a wagon road, but was instead used by mule trains and horses. The whole trail took about two and a half months each way. The route was used by trappers roaming the hills in search of beaver, by merchants from Santa Fe, and by California ranchers. Trains of up to 2,000 animals traveled along the road. However, the looping line it took from Los Angeles to Santa Fe was far from the most direct. When the Southwest came into American hands in 1848, more direct routes were blazed and the Spanish Trail fell out of use. Today, Interstate 15 generally follows the path of the trail between Los Angeles and Barstow.

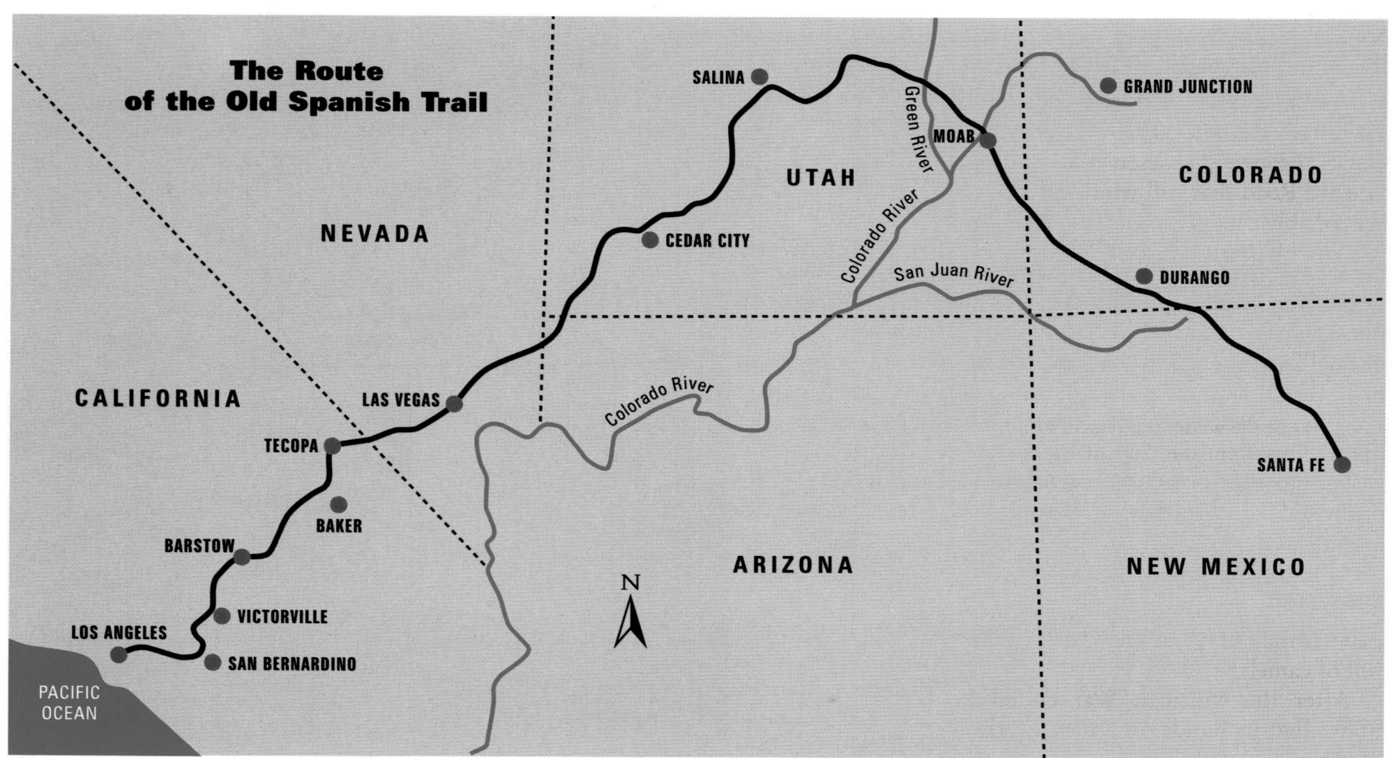

Mojave Road

The Mojave Desert was for many years as formidable a natural barrier to the Pacific Coast as the Sierra Nevada. Between the Colorado River and the coast, water was scarce. The trick to completing a safe passage through the arid barrenness was to follow a line connecting sequential watering spots. Paleo-Indians found an adequate route through the desert thousands of years ago and used it to trade with coastal tribes. The first European to travel the Indian path was probably Fray Francisco Garcés, who was guided over the desert by members of the Mojave tribe in 1776. Garcés described some of the Indians he met along the way as extremely hardy travelers, men who could survive without water for up to four days.

American traders began to take an interest in the desert route in the 1820s. Legendary explorers such as Jedediah Smith, Kit Carson, and John Frémont used the road to trade with Spanish settlements on the coast. At times the itinerant trappers came under attack by Indians. Fort Mohave was built to control the Indians along the Colorado River.

After gold was discovered in 1848, thousands of migrants began entering California. Most chose a more northerly route to the gold fields, but many wagon caravans were forced to cross the desert after snow closed Sierra Nevada passes. In the years following the Civil War, the Mojave Road, as it was already known, became an important thoroughfare connecting California with Arizona. Most of its users were tradesmen rather than migrants. Although Fort Mohave was successful in suppressing the Mojave Indians, inland tribes still plagued desert travelers. In response to attacks by the Ute-Chemehuevi, the U.S. military established a series of redoubts along Mojave Road. The remains of one outpost from the 1860s, Fort Piute, can still be seen today along Desert #13: Mojave Road.

The completion of the southern transcontinental railroad in 1883 spelled an end for Mojave Road as a major transport route. Unlike with other old wagon trails, the new railway did not follow the road, but traveled to the south. Later roads and tracks through the desert also chose different routes, so the Mojave Road that still winds through the California desert is remarkably similar to that traveled by early pioneers. Even today the trail passes through some of the most remote areas in the entire state. The landscape is largely unchanged from prehistoric times. Mojave Road is truly a living piece of history.

Beale Wagon Road

> A year in the wilderness ended! During this time I have conducted my party from the Gulf of Mexico to the shores of the Pacific Ocean, and back again to the eastern terminus of the road through a country for a great part entirely unknown, and inhabited by hostile Indians, without the loss of a man.
>
> —*Journal of E. F. Beale, February 21, 1858*

Where the buffaloes roam, where the camels and the antelope play? It may have happened thanks to three men and a boat full of camels.

After the Mexican War ended in 1848, the United States had its hands on a new southwest territory that was ready to be surveyed and utilized. Congress also saw that the new land could provide better access to the burgeoning California. A federally funded interstate road was soon commissioned.

A trek through Indian country was interesting enough; the addition of camels made things bizarre. Jefferson Davis, who was the secretary of war but would later become president of the Confederate States of America during the Civil War, proposed that camels should be the animals for the expedition. Major Henry C. Wayne was ordered to investigate and import some camels from the Middle East in order to discern whether the animals could be used for military purposes. After some research, what first seemed like a ludicrous idea was deemed a pearl of wisdom. Dromedaries were docile, needed little water, and could carry excessive loads—these useful features fit the southwest climate to a tee. Amiel Whipple had surveyed the Arizona area and excitedly told Congress that a road could be built. On May 1, 1856, Wayne and 33 camels landed in Powder Horn, Texas. Now all Davis needed was someone to put up with the animals and construct the highway.

Lieutenant Edward Fitzgerald Beale (see page 73), the western hero and companion of Kit Carson, was selected. On June 25, 1857, Beale and party left San Antonio, Texas, arriving at the Colorado River on October 18. The expedition crossed the river and continued west to Fort Tejon and then Los Angeles. In January 1858, Beale and his party headed back east to further improve the road. They reached the Colorado River on January 23, just in time to see the *General Jesup* (see page 64) on its journey back down the river. Beale's expedition came to a successful finish at Albuquerque on February 21, 1858.

The expedition went without a hitch. No men were lost, nor did anyone get sick along the way. Beale bragged that their medicine chest just encumbered the mission. The weather was even agreeable—Beale never once pitched his tent. He then commenced work on the wagon road and at a cost of $210,000 created a route to the Colorado River.

Yet the importance of this route is disputed. Some historians argue that the road superseded the Oregon/California Trail, while others downplay the trail's importance, stating that it never outdid the Oregon/California Trail because of the disruption of the Civil War and the trail's dangerous course through Indian country. In fact, the first immigrant party to attempt the trail had to turn back after Indians killed nine members of the party. What remains certain is that the Beale Wagon Road was well traveled then, and is well traveled today. Route 66, Interstate 40, and the Santa Fe Railroad all help mirror Beale's trek. Later, between 1858 and 1859, Beale created a wagon road that followed his camel expedition, but lengthened it so that the road stretched from Los Angeles to Fort Smith, Arkansas.

What became of the camels? Mule skinners hated the beasts; Beale fell in love with them. On September 21, 1857, he wrote in his diary, "I look forward to the day when every mail route across the continent will be conducted and worked altogether with this economical and noble brute." Even with such praise, camels would never come to be the pack animal of choice. The Civil War took attention away from the Southwest's experiments with the camels. Troops were needed and no one gave the animals a second thought. They were released into the desert, where they were seen for many years. Eventually, some were rounded up, others were shot, and some just disappeared. One descendent of the original camel herd, Topsy, lived until 1934, when she had to be put to sleep by the Los Angeles Zoo. Fittingly, her ashes rest in the monument to Hadjii Ali (often called "Hi Jolly"), who cared for the camels during Beale's expedition. Like a distant mirage, camels faded from the Southwestern deserts.

Bradshaw Trail

In 1862, Pauline Weaver, the famous prospector and explorer, discovered gold at La Paz, close to present-day Ehrenburg, Arizona. Yuma was the first town to hear of the gold strike and many prospectors headed north as soon as they could get their supplies together. Tales of nuggets the size of fists and instant fortunes being made reached towns on the West Coast within a couple of months. A gold rush was on.

The discovery, close to the Colorado River, was made on January 12, which was the feast day of Our Lady of Peace for Roman Catholic Mexicans. The name La Paz, Spanish for "The Peace," stuck with the newly founded gold-mining town.

Los Angeles immediately started losing a lot of its labor force to the new gold field by the river. Merchants also rushed to the area. The biggest obstacle they faced was actually getting to the mines in Arizona from the coast. You could go the long way via ship, sailing south around Baja California to the mouth of the Colorado River. From there you could board a paddlewheeler and steam upriver to La Paz. The only overland trails at the time were terribly uncomfortable and followed long and circuitous routes. The main overland routes traveled west from San Diego to Fort Yuma and north alongside the Colorado River to La Paz, or along the Mojave Trail to the Colorado River at Fort Mohave then south, running parallel with the river, to La Paz. These options were proving all too slow for the fever-struck miners and impatient merchants.

Los Angeles explorer William Bradshaw saw the obvious need for an improved route and set about finding one. Bradshaw had served under John C. Frémont and was familiar with opening up new territories. He quickly realized that to cross the California deserts in a successful manner, travelers needed water. This became the basis for his shortened route. With guidance from the people who knew these deserts, the Cahuilla Indians (see Cahuilla, page 93), Bradshaw followed an old Indian trail that crossed the desert to the Colorado River in a direct eastbound route, touching on waterholes as it went.

Bradshaw returned to Los Angeles and set about pushing through a wagon road from the Pueblo de Los Angeles. The route followed the existing trail through the San Georgio Portal and southeast toward the rim of the Salton Sea depression. From here Bradshaw's trail turned east, climbing the stony bajada up the wide and sandy wash of Salt Creek, running close to the Chuckwalla Mountains, and arriving at the Colorado River at Palo Verde Valley. Here the trail swung north for the last short section alongside the Grand River, as the Colorado River was then known, to La Paz.

The finances necessary for establishing a proper road through such desolation were enormous, hence most of the wagon "road" received only basic improvements and was rough going through deep sand, dust, and desert rocks. Yet nobody complained, as the new wagon trail cut several days off the time involved in reaching La Paz. By late 1862, the Colorado Stage and Express Line was running stages on the remote trail. The journey from Los Angeles to La Paz took five days and cost $40. The U.S. mail used the trail en route to Prescott, Arizona, and Santa Fe, New Mexico.

La Paz really boomed in the 1860s, and the Bradshaw Trail won over most of the traffic to it. Thousands of people used the trail, passing by several strikes that would not be discovered for decades to come. Bradshaw's Ferry was put into action on the south side of La Paz, in the region of today's I-10, to transport travelers over the Colorado River. The primitive ferry could just manage to carry small wagons and a few animals at a time.

At its peak, La Paz had more than 5,000 men working the mines. As the ore played out, workers moved on, and the town became a ghost town that never recovered. The completion by the late 1870s of the Southern Pacific Railroad that ran west to Yuma provided too much competition for Bradshaw's desert trail. Trains now took passengers to Yuma, and no one needed to reach La Paz anymore; the Bradshaw Trail gradually faded from the desert landscape. Usage by passengers and freight diminished greatly, though the trail continued to be traveled by prospectors in the Chuckwalla and Orocopia Mountains.

William Bradshaw did not live to see his trail fall into disuse; he committed suicide in La Paz just two years after his trail was opened.

Transhumance Sheep Trails

Although never as widespread as cattle, sheep were an important agricultural commodity in California's early history. Large flocks of the animals were kept in Southern California, especially around San Bernardino and San Gabriel. Spanish settlers brought much of the original stock to the New World. In Spain, sheep farmers generally graze their flocks in lowlands during the winter and lead them to the mountains in late spring. This practice was continued in California, often with Basque shepherds as the guides.

The transhumance sheep trails generally began in San Bernardino, San Gabriel, or Bakersfield, where the sheep were lambed, sheared, and dipped in the spring. After dipping, the flocks where driven in groups of 1,000 to 4,000 to the high valleys of the Sierra Nevada. The bands averaged 8 to 10 miles per day and took 30 to 40 days to reach their mountain destinations. Each group had to be moved at least five times daily, to prevent any one band from overgrazing a section of the trail.

From Southern California the trails passed through Antelope Valley, entered the mountains through Tehachapi or Walker Passes, then followed the general route of the Los Angeles–Owens River Valley Aqueduct and US 395. The trails narrowed for a per-head toll near Owens Lake, then began to separate again after Bishop, sometimes heading eastward into Nevada. For most of the summer, shepherds tended their flocks on the eastern slopes of the Sierra Nevada before leading them through Tioga Pass and homeward through the Central Valley.

Sheep numbers in California have declined drastically since the late nineteenth century, but the route from Bakersfield to the Mono Lake area has been marked by the Bureau of Land Management and is still in use today. The journey home in the fall is now by truck.

Route 66

> If you ever plan to motor west
> Travel my way, take the highway that's the best,
> Get your kicks on Route 66!
>
> It winds from Chicago to L. A.
> More than two thousand miles all the way.
> Get your kicks on Route 66!
>
> —"Route 66" *by Bobby Troup*

Route 66 was the idea of Tulsa, Oklahoma, highway commissioner Cyrus Stevens Avery, who wanted a road that would link his state to the metropolises of Chicago and Los Angeles. Avery was asked by the U.S. Bureau of Public Works to develop a system of interstate highways. On November 11, 1926, Route 66 was created, weaving together hundreds of existing roads. Improvements to the route, touted as "The Mother Road" and the "Main Street of America," began immediately. By 1936 the entire route from Chicago to Santa Monica was paved. Its completed length was 2,278 miles, 320 of which wound through California.

Beginning on the shore of Lake Michigan and stretching across eight states before concluding on the shore of the Pacific Ocean, Route 66 helped link California to the rest of the nation. Towns along the route prospered, providing gasoline, lodging, and cheap food to weary long-distance travelers. The very first McDonald's restaurant was opened on Route 66 in San Bernardino in 1940.

John Steinbeck made the fabled road a backdrop for his Pulitzer Prize–winning novel, *The Grapes of Wrath* (1939), chronicling the journeys of a family moving to California from Dust Bowl-era Oklahoma. Thousands of "Okies" used the route to escape the devastating drought that hit the Great Plains during the 1930s. From 1960 to 1964, Route 66 was the setting for a popular television series of the same name. *Route 66*, starring Martin Milner and George Maharis, followed two companions as they traveled through America's heartland in their red Corvette. Bobby Troup's song "Route 66" was recorded by several musical acts, including the Rolling Stones.

Gradually, Route 66 was superseded by new interstate highways, most notably Interstate 40. Towns began to dwindle as stores lost business. In 1984, Route 66 was officially decommissioned. Today the route, known as National Trails Highway, is seeing a resurgence of use as tourists, many of them Europeans or RV drivers who are retired, cruise its remains seeking a lost America. Ghost towns and glimpses of kitsch Americana make a trip along the remaining stretches of the road an interesting experience. The California Historic Route 66 Association was formed to protect and provide information in the Golden State.

Several of the trails in this book begin on Route 66, including South Coast #17: Rodman Mountains Trail, which commences in Newberry Springs, near the Bagdad Cafe. Bagdad Cafe is an old truck stop celebrated in a 1988 movie of the same name.

Pacific Crest Trail

The Pacific Crest National Scenic Trail is relatively young but historically important. In 1968, Congress adopted the National Trails System Act, which made the route one of two national scenic trails (the other being the Appalachian Trail that runs from Georgia to Maine). Nevertheless, the California portion of the Pacific Crest Trail, which extends from Canada to Mexico, was not fully completed until just before the dedication ceremony on June 25, 1993.

The idea for a hiking route that traversed the entire West Coast of the United States was suggested at least as early as 1926. By that time there were already several small trails spread across the mountains of California and Oregon. In the 1930s, Clinton C. Clarke, who formed and headed the Pacific Crest Trail System Conference, proved the feasibility of a connected border-to-border route. Teams of young volunteers explored the proposed course under the guidance of a YMCA secretary, Warren L. Rogers. Clarke and Rogers continually promoted the idea of a Pacific Crest Trail. In the 1960s the suggestion began to gain public support. Congress finally designated the Pacific Crest Trail in 1968, but it was left to a citizen advisory council to work out the complete route.

The biggest problem facing the committee was private lands that interrupted the proposed route. It often took years to negotiate a right of way through someone's land; at times permission was never granted, and the trail had to bypass a homestead. The trail's dedication in 1993 was meant to emulate the 1869 celebrations at Promontory Point, Utah, where tracks of the transcontinental railroad were joined.

The trail begins in Southern California on a low hill near the border town of Campo. It passes through Anza-Borrego Desert State Park, Cleveland National Forest, parts of the Mojave Desert, and into the Sierra Nevada. In all, the path runs through 24 national forests and 7 national parks. The southern section is one of the most difficult. Summer temperatures often exceed 100 degrees Fahrenheit, and water sources are scarce. Still, hundreds of hikers walk this section every year, some on their way to completing the 2,600-mile through-hike. Those who hike here are greeted with beautiful desert and mountain scenery where they can spot lizards, snakes, coyotes, cougars, and a variety of birds and plant life.

The Steamboat Trade

For those lucky enough, wealth could be discovered in California during the gold rush of 1849. For those enterprising enough, wealth could be gleaned from those in search of that elusive California gold. In 1849 or 1850, Indians destroyed the only ferry crossing the Colorado River and massacred about a dozen whites, including the disreputable owner John Glanton. With hordes of eager prospectors wanting to cross the river and no ferry, entrepreneurs saw an opportunity on the banks of the Colorado River. Lured by this prospect, George Alonzo Johnson sailed in from San Francisco and beat out his competition by re-establishing the ferry at the junction of the Gila and Colorado Rivers. The Yuma Indians, who were responsible for the massacre, still threatened the area. Eventually, troops led by Major Samuel P. Heintzelman arrived to protect the ferry. Heintzelman, not one to pass up a good deal, soon discovered the profitable prospect of ferrying and built Fort Yuma (in 1851) to completely encompass Johnson's ferry, thereby cutting Johnson out from any hopes of business. Disgruntled, and understandably annoyed, Johnson and his partners sold their land to Heintzelman for $3,000 and a mule each. In the end, though, Johnson would have the last laugh.

As the years passed, Fort Yuma verged on disaster. Starvation constantly threatened the garrison because of a lack of a substantial supply route. As he dropped off supplies for the fort near the mouth of the Colorado, the great western humorist Lieutenant G. H. Derby wondered if steamships could steer up the river. The famous trapper Antoine Leroux, who had navigated the river by raft, said it could be done. Excitement was buzzing around this opportunity; even Mormon leader Brigham Young wondered if steamships could make the journey because of the great possibilities that a sea-route could have for the new Mormon colonies. In November 1852, the first steamboat puttered its way up the Colorado River.

The *Uncle Sam*, powered by a 20 horse-power locomotive engine, sagged under 35 tons of freight. It carefully made its way to Fort Yuma thanks to its captain, James Turnbell. Much to Heintzelman's chagrin, George Johnson financially backed Turnbell and the *Uncle Sam*. Steamboating the Colorado could be done—here was Johnson's gold mine. He launched the *General Jesup* to help the frumpish *Uncle Sam* service Fort Yuma.

In 1856, Johnson asked the California legislature and the Secretary of War Jefferson Davis for funding to see just how far he could make it up the river in a steamboat. The funding was passed, but the honor went to Lieutenant Joseph Christmas Ives. Johnson was infuriated. Not to be denied, he secretly journeyed ahead of Ives in the *General Jesup*. Ives eventually caught wind of Johnson's lead and, seeing fame slipping through his fingertips, he plowed on in his own steamship, *Explorer*. The race was on. The *Explorer* ran into difficulties, repeatedly striking the many sandbars along the river. Meanwhile, *General Jesup* and Johnson had run into a submerged rock, but still held a comfortable lead. Johnson reached the head of Pyramid Canyon (north of present-day Bullhead City, Arizona). He traveled 300 miles and finally turned around triumphant: He proved that the Colorado was indeed navigable by steamboat. Ives reached the same conclusion after he ventured up to Black Canyon, but he was dismayed to find that his own venture was overshadowed by Johnson and the *General Jesup*. With the Colorado deemed navigable, Fort Mohave was established farther up the river, which Johnson too would service.

In 1862, trappers Johnny Moss, Pauline Weaver, and Joseph Walker discovered silver in Eldorado Canyon, and Johnson's monopoly over the riverway paid off tenfold. Tons of equipment, ore, miners, and soldiers used Johnson's steamships, and the Colorado River became a lifeline for Southern California and Arizona. Johnson and his associates began to enjoy their new wealth and turned their attention away from their ships. In turn, the industry suffered. More steamships were needed, and a solid month was needed before a ship could steam its way up the river. Miners grumbled and protested about the monopoly. One of the most vocal was Samuel Adams, who successfully created a rival company called the Union Line. Additional competition surfaced when Alphonzo Tilden put his own steamer in the river to better serve his Eldorado mines.

Competition was fierce enough to pull Johnson away from his political endeavors and return him to his steamships. In the end, Johnson proved to be the most ruthless. As he was firmly established as the freighter for both Fort Yuma and Fort Mohave, Johnson cut his shipping charges by half to root out his rivals. The only thing that could save them was to open trade with Utah. But sandbars and low water prevented this route from opening. Competition went belly-up; Johnson secured his monopoly and bought more steamers to better serve the river. He was once again the king of the Colorado, until the arrival of the Southern Pacific Railroad.

The boom of the steamships quickly waned. In 1877 the Southern Pacific Railroad joined with Yuma. This cut deeply into Johnson's newly incorporated company, the Colorado Steam Navigation Company. Johnson's sea-faring steamers, which freighted from San Fransisco to Yuma, were suddenly antiquated, slow, and expensive for travelers. Profits plummeted by 50 percent. In the wake of the great Iron Horse, Johnson and his partners knew they couldn't prevail. They sold their shares to the Western Development Company, which continued a light freighting service up the Colorado River. But the increasing number of railroad lines continued to cut away business. The river was now being dredged in order to remove silt and sandbars, but dredging and the use of ill-prepared canals doomed the waterways. In 1905, the Colorado flooded, broke loose from a canal, engulfed part of the Southern Pacific Railroad line, and turned the Salton Sink into the Salton Sea. It would take millions of dollars and three years of effort to return the river to its proper bed. The devastating erosion from this flood can still be seen today. The construction of the Laguna Dam in 1909, just 9 miles above Yuma, signaled the end of steamships in the waterway.

Railroads

Central Pacific Railroad Company and the First Transcontinental Railroad

Prior to May 10, 1869, individuals who wished to travel from one coast of the United States to the other had only three options. Travelers could journey six months via boat around the length of South America; they could walk, a grueling experience that took at least six months; or they could take a very

onness locomotive #6, Central Pacific Railroad, circa 1865

bumpy and expensive twenty-four-day stagecoach ride. However, after the fateful day when two trains met in Promontory, Utah, travelers could buy a first-class ticket on the transcontinental railroad for $100 and make the journey in four comfortable days.

In 1862, Congress approved a venture to create the first coast-to-coast railroad in the United States. Two railroad companies were authorized for its construction: the Union Pacific Railroad in the east and the Central Pacific in the west. After delays due to disagreements over financing, Congress passed the Railroad Act of 1864, which allowed larger land grant offerings and 30-year loans to the companies. Pleased with the deal, the railroads began major construction in late 1865.

The Central Pacific had been conceived and incorporated in 1861 by Theodore D. Judah, who served as its chief engineer until his death in 1863. Its major investors were Charles Crocker, Mark Hopkins, Collis Huntington, and Leland Stanford—known collectively as the "Big Four." The four were already prominent Sacramento businessmen when they heard Judah's idea for a western railroad route. Even before it received federal funding, the company began to survey a route through the Sierra Nevada and purchase adjacent lands.

The Civil War was winding down and the California gold rush was still on when construction commenced. The railway companies were faced with a labor shortage, so they hired large numbers of immigrants to begin the work. Union Pacific hired more than a thousand Irishmen, while Central Pacific shipped in 15,000 Chinese laborers to work for just $30 a month. Once the Civil War ended, German and Italian immigrants, war veterans, and ex-slaves also became railroad employees.

Construction in the east began in Omaha, Nebraska, with Union Pacific workers laying an average of a mile of rail per day over the flat Nebraska plains. The Central Pacific began in Sacramento. Its employees experienced a much different and taxing job of laying rail over the treacherous Sierra Nevada. Each company had the same goal in mind: to lay more rails in less time than its competitor. The population of the traversed land was sparse, and little shantytowns were built along the way to accommodate the workers. Following in their wake were gamblers, saloon owners, and merchants. Towns were settled, but when the tracks out-distanced the town, the workers got up and left, leaving economic ruin behind.

As the two railways grew closer, competition became even fiercer. Congress allowed the companies to send their respective graders up to 300 miles ahead of the end of their tracks. At one point, the Union Pacific and Central Pacific graders actually passed each other and proceeded to create parallel grades for 200 miles. Most of the parallel grades can still be observed today. Realizing the wastefulness, Congress ended this competition and set the official meeting place at Promontory Summit, Utah. In addition to the railroad, a second transcontinental telegraph was simultaneously constructed. This enabled workers to keep in constant communication with their headquarters during construction.

Near the end of the building, Union Pacific workers boasted to their competitors that they had put down an extraordinary 8 miles of rail in one day. Never to be outdone, the Central Pacific waited until the distance between the two was too short for Union Pacific to defeat them again and laid 10 miles and 56 feet in one incredible day. What makes this almost inconceivable is the fact that each 28-foot section of rail weighed approximately 522 pounds.

Although the railroad was actually completed on May 8, 1869, the commemorative ceremony was not held until two days later. Seven years after the railway's initial planning, Leland Stanford drove in a solid gold stake to mark the completion of the first transcontinental railroad. Two trains, Central Pacific's *Jupiter* and Union Pacific's *119*, triumphantly came together, facing each other, joining two oceans and a world of individuals across what had previously been a daunting space. From that moment on, the Great West would no longer be such a mystery to the rest of the nation. Engraved on the famous gold spike were the words, "May God continue the unity of our country as this Railroad unites the two great oceans of the world." The transcontinental railroad would not only unite two oceans but would change the lives of Americans forever. Much of the route through California is still used by railroad companies today and is generally mirrored by Interstate 80.

C. P. Huntington, **the original Central Pacific engine No. 3, circa 1864**

In later years, the Central Pacific extended the railroad's course to San Francisco. The Big Four acquired rival Southern Pacific in 1868 and the tracks of these two corporations made up much of the early infrastructure in California's railroad system. In 1899 the companies were joined as one as the Southern Pacific Company, which was purchased the following year by the Union Pacific. This merger was later reversed and government regulations preserved the Central Pacific as a corporate entity until 1959.

Southern Pacific Railroad Company

As early as 1852, Southern congressmen had proposed a southern railroad route to California. In 1853, Congress decided to sponsor the survey of four routes. The Gadsden Purchase of 1853–54 (which extended the U.S. border farther to the south) had made the southern route feasible. Agreement could not be reached on the best route until the Civil War quashed any prospect of a southern route. In 1862, Congress passed the long-awaited Pacific Railroad Bill, which gave contracts for the line's construction to the Union Pacific and Central Pacific, the latter of which was controlled by the Big Four merchants from California: Leland Stanford, a Sacramento wholesale grocer; Charles Crocker, a dry goods merchant; and Collis P. Huntington and Mark Hopkins, partners in a hardware store. These men had all met by 1857, having already made fortunes from supplying the prospectors who flooded into California after the discovery of gold in 1848.

The Central Pacific's strategy for making a profit was not from running the line, but instead from selling it after completion. The trouble was that no one wanted to buy such an expensive project. In order to make a profit, the leaders of the Central Pacific decided they needed to maintain a monopoly on railroads into California. Even before the first transcontinental railway was completed in 1869, the Big Four acted to ensure that their monopoly was protected. In 1868, they acquired the Southern Pacific Railroad Company, which had been formed three years earlier to build a line from San Francisco to San Diego and east to the Colorado River.

The Big Four then obtained the charter to build a southern transcontinental railroad. They chose to depart from Los Angeles instead of San Diego. The route taken is similar to that of Interstate 10 as far as Coachella, where the railroad moves southeast toward Yuma, Arizona. Congress gave the Southern Pacific permission to build across the Fort Yuma Reservation, and steel tracks soon followed along the old Gila Trail (see page 59). Railroading history was made along the Southern Pacific. The steel track had the longest curve (5 miles) and the longest portion of straight track (47 miles) in the country.

Southern Pacific Railroad crossing the Salton Sea on the California-Arizona route

The second transcontinental route was completed on January 12, 1883, near the Pecos River in Texas. The Big Four had maintained their monopoly on railroading into California. Increasingly, they controlled the major routes inside California as well. Southern Pacific trains ran from Portland, Oregon, to San Diego, with two routes from Los Angeles to San Francisco (close to those followed by US 101 and US 99). Eventually, its carriages sped all the way to New Orleans. Its partnership with the Central Pacific remained close until the latter was purchased in 1899 and officially absorbed into the Southern Pacific in 1959. The Southern Pacific itself continued in operation until 1996, when it merged with the Union Pacific.

Atlantic & Pacific Railroad

Although it began slowly, the Atlantic & Pacific Railroad would eventually make significant contributions for trade and the settling of California. The company eventually completed the third transcontinental railroad, laying tracks as far as the Southern Pacific line in Mojave. The company was organized in 1866 to build a railroad from Springfield, Missouri, to Albuquerque, New Mexico, and then to the Pacific by way of the thirty-fifth parallel route first surveyed by Amiel W. Whipple in 1854. By 1873, after only 327 miles of track had been laid in Missouri and eastern Oklahoma, financial difficulties forced the railroad into bankruptcy.

Early in 1880, the Atchison, Topeka & Santa Fe Railroad Company was laying tracks toward Albuquerque on its way to connecting with the Southern Pacific Railroad at Deming, New Mexico. However, it was keen to establish a more direct route to California. In January 1880, the Atchison, Topeka & Santa Fe joined with the St. Louis

The first locomotive built in California ran on the San Francisco & San Jose Railroad, a predecessor of the Southern Pacific line

and San Francisco Railway Company to rescue the Atlantic & Pacific by financing the stalled expansion of its tracks westward from Albuquerque. The small town of Gallup, New Mexico (which was settled in 1880 as a Westward Overland Stagecoach stop), became the construction headquarters of the railway. In fact, the town was named after David L. Gallup, the railroad paymaster.

Laying tracks through desert is not an easy feat, and it certainly wasn't for the Atlantic & Pacific. Water sources were needed, so storage reservoirs had to be constructed along the route. The line did have one thing going for it—an abundance of trees that could be used for railroad ties. Although construction was arduous, the surveys proved to be so good that today the track continues along most of the original route's 575 miles. (Recently there was only a slight change in course to allow for double-tracking.)

While the Atlantic & Pacific was hard at work, the Southern Pacific Railroad beat it to the quick by completing its own line to Needles (named after a group of needlelike peaks in nearby Arizona). Although the Southern Pacific had built its line over the proposed route of the Atlantic & Pacific, begrudgingly, a compromise between the two was reached. The Atlantic & Pacific could lease that portion of the Southern Pacific line in order to enter California. Thus, the thirty-fifth parallel transcontinental line was completed in August 1883, and yet the Southern Pacific was able to retain its monopoly over railroad access into California.

In June 1897, after having been forced into bankruptcy for a second time, the Atlantic & Pacific was sold at foreclosure to the recently reorganized Atchison, Topeka & Santa Fe Railway Company.

San Diego & Arizona Eastern Railroad

This regional railroad company was incorporated in 1906 as the San Diego & Arizona Railway Company and operated its first train on March 11, 1911. Tracks ran from San Diego to Tijuana, through northern Mexico to Campo, then through Southern California as far as El Centro. The trains carried mainly passengers and produce. Although the entire length was just 140 miles, the railroad took 13 years and $19 million (a staggering sum in 1919) to complete, making it one of the most expensive railroads ever built. Over its course, the track rises and falls more than 3,700 feet.

The area of track in the Carrizo Gorge near Dos Cabezas was particularly impressive. In just 11 miles, the railroad crosses 14 trestle bridges and goes through 21 tunnels, an engineering feat that earned it the nickname "the impossible railroad." It was the organizational genius of its owner, millionaire John D. Spreckles, that made the construction possible. Spreckles was frustrated by the absence of an eastern line from San Diego, leaving the city reliant on its northern neighbor, Los Angeles. With the completion of the line to El Centro, San Diego passengers could connect to the Southern Pacific transcontinental railroad without having to travel through Los Angeles. This made the city more accessible and helped contribute to the town's population growth.

The San Diego & Arizona Eastern Railroad Company continued to operate until 1984, although the last passenger train ran in 1951. During its existence, it was the victim of several floods, fires, and landslides. Several bridges and tunnels had to be reconstructed. Storm damage in 1976 and again in 1982 helped persuade the company to discontinue use of the line.

San Diego & Arizona Eastern locomotive

Nevada Southern Railroad

The Nevada Southern Railway Company was incorporated on December 15, 1892, and began laying tracks the following month. The line from Goffs to Manvel was completed by 1893, and freight trains began to haul goods to and from the Eldorado, Goodsprings, and Ivanpah Mining Districts. The station at Goffs connected to the Santa Fe line operated by the Atlantic & Pacific Railroad. The town of Manvel, named after the railroad's owner, soon flourished as a supply terminal with two general stores, a blacksmith, a butcher shop, several saloons, and a small school. Ivanpah replaced Manvel as the main supply center for the region when the Nevada Southern was extended in 1902. By this time the company had changed its name to the California Eastern Railway, a designation it would keep until 1911, when it was consolidated into the Atchison, Topeka & Santa Fe. The line was abandoned in the 1920s, but part of the region it served can still be accessed using Desert #15: New York Mountains Trail.

San Pedro, Los Angeles & Salt Lake Railroad

The San Pedro, Los Angeles & Salt Lake Railroad ran a total of 1,260 miles (350 of which were in California) northeast from San Pedro to Salt Lake City, Utah. The direct trip from Salt Lake City to San Pedro took more than 24 hours. The local train took 9 hours more and stopped in 112 towns, including Los Angeles, Riverside, San Bernardino, Barstow, and Las Vegas, Nevada. Construction began in 1901 and was not completed until four years later. Eighteen tunnels were built, totaling more than 9,000 feet in length. More than 300 people worked on the project. Steep grades were necessary in some areas, especially at Cajon Summit near San Bernardino, but the terrain traversed varied greatly, from mountain curves to desert flats. Temperatures along the line could also be extreme, ranging from below zero in winter to 120 degrees Fahrenheit in summer.

The railroad was an important supply route for a number of towns and mines. Its trains hauled copper, zinc, silver, gold, and other products. Passengers also enjoyed the route; the company boasted that all cars were fitted with electric lights! By 1911 the railroad had been bought by the Union Pacific, which changed the name to the Los Angeles & Salt Lake Railroad Company in 1916. Desert #17: Nipton Desert Road retraces part of its route near the California-Nevada border.

Tonopah & Tidewater Railroad

When it incorporated in 1904, the Borax Consolidated Company, owners of the Tonopah & Tidewater Railroad, intended the line to stretch from Los Angeles (hence the name "Tidewater") to Tonopah, Nevada. The first tracks were laid in November 1905, but only the 169-mile middle section of the intended route, from Ludlow to Gold Center, Nevada, was ever completed. Its unfinished state led some to call it "the railroad with no beginning and no end." Much of the problem with the construction came from the area near the Amargosa River, along a stretch of railroad retraced by Desert #26: Sperry Wash Route. The heat along this wash was stifling and the ground was sandy and inconsistent. Many workers fled from the work site, and those who stayed faced 140-degree heat. This section of the route delayed construction and pushed it well over budget, costing over $40,000 per mile.

Tonopah & Tidewater locomotive

Even when it was completed, the line struggled to make a profit. From 1928 to 1937, the company reported a loss every single year. Flash floods and sandstorms often forced major repairs. By 1933, the line from Ludlow to Crucero was idle, and seven years later the entire route was abandoned. In 1942, the tracks were torn up and shipped to Egypt for use in World War II.

Stagecoach Lines and Mail Routes

San Antonio and San Diego Mail Line

In the 1800s, the vast Great Plains and the daunting Rocky Mountains posed such natural obstacles to travel that they literally split the country in two. By the 1850s, California was clamoring for a decent line of communication with the eastern United States. So great were these land barriers that there was talk of California splitting from the Union and becoming its own country. Trade and communication between California and the eastern United States was a long and costly process that involved a ship sailing to Panama, paying a caravan to reach the Atlantic, then making its way to a suitable port.

In 1853, Congress decided to solve the problem. Surveys were taken for a suitable land route for a transcontinental railroad. After careful consideration, four possible routes were chosen, but Congress couldn't decide which one to take. The Southern states wanted a route that started in Memphis or New Orleans; the Northern states demanded that the route meet with St. Louis or Chicago; and Texas thought a route running from Galveston would be very cost effective. The U.S. Treasury certainly couldn't afford multiple routes. As the debate continued, California was becoming increasingly unhappy. Numerous petitions were signed, all revolving around the government's negligence. Finally, on June 22, 1856, Congress awarded a four-year contract to James Birch.

Birch quickly decided on a route that started in San Antonio, went through El Paso, and ended in San Diego. Why? This route was well traveled and well marked. Plus, he wouldn't have to deal with snow. The only problem was the lack of way stations. Military forts could be used, but beyond El Paso the population grew very sparse. Seven new sod-house stations had to be built to accommodate the stagecoach line. Isaiah Woods, Birch's new employee in charge of purchasing, bought new stagecoaches. Instead of horses, he bought mules because he thought they would do better in the dry climate. For this reason, the San Antonio and San Diego was soon nicknamed "Jackass Mail." This line carried mail and passengers overland in 38 days or less. Two hundred dollars bought a passenger a one-way fare on the Jackass Mail. Conditions were rough. The new way stations that passengers had to sleep in were nothing more than hovels, and the food that Birch supplied was sometimes inedible. Though he succeeded in what he set out to do, Birch wouldn't get to enjoy his success. On August 20, 1857, he concluded business in San Francisco and boarded the *Central America*, which was bound for New York. He would never arrive. The ship was lost at sea.

After his death, the San Antonio and San Diego fell into fi-

A Concord stagecoach advertised by Abbot Downing Company (its inventors) as having "pinstriping and retractable window covers," circa 1885

nancial ruin and eventually was acquired by the firm of Giddings & Doyle. The mail dwindled and the business was not as financially prosperous as the firm hoped. Congress opened the floor for another bidding on a transcontinental stagecoach route. John Butterfield accepted the contract and started the famous Butterfield Overland Mail. However, the honor of being the first to create a transcontinental stagecoach line will always belong to James Birch and his Jackass Mail.

Butterfield Overland Mail

> Remember, boys, nothing on God's earth must stop the United States mail.
>
> —*John Butterfield*

When, on March 3, 1857, John Butterfield and his business associates received a contract from the U.S. Congress to build a transcontinental stagecoach line, the Butterfield Overland Mail was created. One of Butterfield's associates was William G. Fargo, who would later play a key role in stagecoach history. Butterfield Overland Mail was not the first transcontinental stagecoach line; that title belonged to the San Antonio and San Diego Mail Line. Instead, Butterfield was taking the reins away from the ailing San Antonio and San Diego.

Time was of the essence. Butterfield had only one year to get his stagecoaches rolling. A route was chosen that followed along the old Gila Trail (see page 59) but also crossed Texas and reached St. Louis and Memphis—a considerable extension from the previous San Antonio and San Diego route. From the Gila Trail the Butterfield Overland Mail would stop in San Diego, and then continue north to San Francisco. Butterfield hired Indian-friendly frontiersmen to work for the company. Trying to avoid using way stations, he paid farmers along the route to board passengers at night. In the sparsely settled Southwest, where hardly any farmers could be found, sod houses were used as way stations. Drivers were stationed along the route. Each one had to memorize his 60-mile route because they would drive the stagecoach during day and night. A conductor, who had to make a 120-mile run, would ride along with the driver.

On September 15, 1858, the first Butterfield stage left San Francisco to make its way overland. The stagecoach arrived in St. Louis 23 days, 23 hours, and 30 minutes later. Regular mail had finally been provided across the continental United States. Two hundred dollars bought a ticket from St. Louis to San Francisco. Because hardly anyone was leaving California, $100 bought a ticket from San Francisco to St. Louis. Food was not provided, so it had to be either carried along or purchased at way stations or farmhouses. Passengers also had to help if trouble arose, ranging from getting stuck to the prospect of an Indian attack. The coach's speed depended on the smoothness of the road and ranged from three-and-a-half to nine miles an hour. For those who were hardy, the trip was exciting. For those of lesser stock, the trip was a grueling nightmare. One traveler remarked that he knew what hell was like because he'd just spent 24 hours there. Waterman L. Ormsby, a reporter for the *New York Herald*, took the challenge and reported that during the ride he had subsisted on beans, salt pork, and black coffee. He slept very little, constantly breathed in trail dust, and lived in fear of an Indian attack. Indian attacks rarely occurred though.

A typical Concord stagecoach used on the Overland Trail (United States Express Company)

In 1860, John Butterfield left the Butterfield Overland Mail after a successful career and was replaced by William B. Dinsmore. In the 1860s, William G. Fargo's firm (Wells, Fargo & Company) took an interest in the mail route. Fargo's stagecoaches were running both mail and gold across the continent and gradually dominated the express business. Butterfield Overland Mail was then absorbed into Wells, Fargo & Company.

Wells, Fargo & Company

In March 1852, this great freighting and banking firm was established in New York City by two experienced expressmen, Henry Wells and William G. Fargo. Wells, Fargo & Company established a main office in San Francisco and began transporting mail and freight to the booming mining camps of California and back to the eastern seaboard. The company bought up many smaller express companies, and by the 1860s, it had a monopoly on California's express business. For a brief time, Wells Fargo also operated a passenger line between San Francisco and Sacramento.

San Mateo & Pescadero Stage Company coach in front of a Wells Fargo & Co. Stage Office, Western Union Telegraph Office, and post office

In 1866, Wells, Fargo & Company combined with several interstate stage companies and for the next few years it ran a transcontinental express company. While work was being completed on the first transcontinental railroad, Wells Fargo connected the lines with stagecoaches. The dedication of the finished railroad in 1869 rendered the express line superfluous.

Because the most important freight shipped from California was gold, Wells, Fargo & Company branched into banking quite early in its career. At first, the chief enterprise was the trafficking of gold dust, which could be bought in mining camps at a cheaper price than it could be sold to the U.S. mint. Soon the company extended its operations into general banking. A banking crisis in California in 1855 led to the collapse of many rivals, and the company emerged as the leading financial institution in the West. The bank was separated from the express business in 1905 and remains prominent today. The headquarters, which include a small historical museum, are located on California Street in San Francisco.

People

Explorers, Mountain Men, and Surveyors

Juan Rodriguez Cabrillo

Born in Portugal around 1495, Juan Rodriguez Cabrillo became an able sailor for the Spanish Empire. He served with Cortés in the conquest of Mexico but is best known for making the European discovery of California.

Seeking an elusive northwest passage from the Pacific to the Atlantic, Cabrillo set sail from Navidad on the west coast of Mexico in June 1542. He landed at San Diego Bay on September 28, the first white man to set foot in present-day California. The expedition continued northward to the islands of Santa Cruz, Santa Rosa, and San Miguel. On San Miguel Island, Cabrillo fell and broke his arm. Nevertheless, he continued the voyage until January 3, 1543, when he died, most likely from an infection in his injured arm.

Juan Rodriguez Cabrillo

Cabrillo left his captain, Bartolomé Ferrelo, with instructions to continue the expedition. Ferrelo sailed as far as the modern Oregon-California border before turning back, short of supplies. The mission concluded in Navidad on April 14, 1543.

Cabrillo named many of the islands and bays that he encountered along his voyage, but another explorer, Sebastían Vizcaíno, renamed them 60 years later. Today, Point Cabrillo in Mendocino County and Cabrillo Point in Monterey County honor him, and a national monument marks the probable site of his first landing on California soil.

Sebastían Vizcaíno

One of the first European visitors to California, Sebastían Vizcaíno named many of its coastal bays, including San Diego and Monterey. He was born in Spain around 1548. After serving the empire in the invasion of Portugal (1580), he sailed to Mexico and the Philippines as a merchant. He later returned to Mexico and began to explore the coast of California.

In 1602, he set out from Acapulco to explore the shoreline for a suitable harbor for Spanish galleons and to seek the fabled Strait of Anian, or Northwest Passage. His expedition sailed as far north as the forty-third parallel (present-day Oregon) but missed San Francisco Bay. Along the way Vizcaíno named the islands and bays of the coast, changing the names that Juan Rodriguez Cabrillo had given them 60 years earlier. He named Monterey Bay after the Count of Monterey, Spanish viceroy in New Spain, giving the inlet such lavish praise that later explorers failed to recognize it. However, bad weather and scurvy made the journey severely laborious and the ships returned to Mexico in 1603 in a state of distress.

Vizcaíno's route was barely retraced in the next 150 years. His attempts to persuade Spanish authorities to establish a port at Monterey Bay were unsuccessful. Vizcaíno continued in the service of the crown, mapping the coast of Japan and fighting Dutch pirates in the Pacific, until his death in 1629, possibly in Mexico City.

Eusebio Francisco Kino

Eusebio Kino was a prominent figure in the Southwest because of his exploration, trail-blazing, devout religious genius, and missionary work. Kino was born in the Austrian-Italian Alps near Trent on August 10, 1645. He was well educated and he particularly excelled in mathematics. In adolescence he became very sick with a mysterious illness. Just when he appeared to be at death's door, he recovered. The recovery was so miraculous that Kino was imbued with faith and entered the Jesuit Order. He volunteered for missionary service in the Orient, but instead was sent to the New World. On May 9, 1681, Kino landed at Vera Cruz on the Gulf of Mexico.

In 1683, Kino accompanied an exploration party and set out to create a mission in lower (Baja) California. Indian hostility toward the encroaching Spaniards doomed the mission, but Kino was not deterred. In the next 24 years, he made many trips along the Gila and Colorado Rivers, proving conclusively that California was not an island, a fact that would open the area to new missions and settlement. Many of Kino's frontier missions became starting points for new explorations of the West. He was the first to travel along parts of El Camino del Diablo, and his maps of the area were not bettered for 100 years.

Artist's rendering of Eusebio Kino

The number of Indians Kino converted is outstanding—about 30,000. He baptized 4,000 Indians. He introduced many tribes to cattle and agriculture for the first time. Kino later explained that he could have further spread the Gospel, but he lacked priest coworkers and orders from the Church limited his progress. Still active at the age of 65, he rode out to Magdalena, Sonora, to dedicate a new chapel. During the Mass of Dedication on March 15, 1711, Padre Kino became ill and that night he passed away.

Friar Junípero Serra

Junípero Serra is often called the founder of California. He was born November 24, 1713, on the Spanish Mediterranean island of Majorca. Christened Miguel José Serra, he changed his name to Junípero when he joined the Franciscan order of monks at age 17.

In 1749, he volunteered as a missionary in Mexico, landing in the New World on December 7 that same year. Within a few years of his arrival, Jesuit monks were expelled from the Spanish Empire, and their missions were given to the Franciscans. In 1768, Serra was made president of the missions in Baja California.

Father Junípero Serra

From the Baja peninsula, Serra traveled north to Alta California (the Spanish name for present-day California). Spanish authorities at the time feared Russian and British encroachment along the Pacific Coast and sought to further establish their control of the empire's northern dominions. On July 16, 1769, Serra founded the mission of San Diego de Alcalá. He waited there while his party, under the command of Gaspar de Portolá, continued north, discovering the natural harbor of San Francisco Bay.

When Portolá returned to San Diego in January 1770, spirits and supplies were running low. He urged a return to Mexico, but at Serra's insistence agreed to stay for nine days of prayer. While the group waited, a supply ship appeared and the Spanish presence in California was saved. Serra sailed to Monterey and established a second mission in Carmel. He lived in Carmel for most of his remaining years, though he traveled much, despite suffering from a severely ulcered leg. He either founded or co-founded nine of the twenty-one missions in California, including Mission Delores in San Francisco and Mission San Juan Capistrano. A church at the latter site is the state's oldest surviving building.

Serra baptized thousands of Indians during his time in California. Although his Franciscan successors are widely blamed for the epidemics that ravaged native populations, Serra himself treated the converts well, once trekking all the way to Mexico City to plead on their behalf. Descendants of the cattle he brought to the missions would stock California's herds for years to come. Today, his bust is one of two chosen to represent the state in the National Statuary Hall in Washington, D.C., and he is often suggested as a candidate for sainthood. A significant step toward that was taken in 1988 when Serra was beatified by the Vatican. Junípero Serra died near Monterey on August 28, 1784. He is buried at the Mission San Carlos Borroméo in Carmel.

Gaspar de Portolá

In 1723, Gaspar de Portolá was born into a noble family in Catalonia, Spain. He served in the imperial military in Italy and Portugal before moving to the New World in 1767 as governor of California. At the time, the term "California" was applied to the peninsula we call Baja California. Modern California, Alta California to the Spanish, was still unsettled by Europeans. As governor of the province, Portolá was determined to change this. The Spanish authorities feared interference by British or Russian traders unless they established their dominance in the area.

In 1769, accompanied by the great Franciscan priest Junípero Serra, Portolá traveled north overland, sending two ships to meet his party with supplies. Portolá's group arrived at San Diego Bay in June 1769. Serra established the first Spanish mission on present-day Californian soil near the landing site. Portolá's party continued its trek up the coast, searching for Monterey Bay. They missed it, but instead discovered the natural harbor of San Francisco Bay. They were the first Europeans to do so. The weary party returned to San Diego in January 1770. Portolá was ready to return to Mexico City, but Serra persuaded him to remain in the area long enough for supplies to arrive. The governor agreed, and in June 1770 he established the presidio of San Carlos at Monterey, which became the first military and religious capital of Alta California.

Portolá left California later that year and arrived in Mexico City as a hero. In 1777, he became governor of Puebla, Mexico, and subsequently returned to Europe. An account of his travels, *Diario Histórica*, was published shortly before his death in Spain in 1786. He is remembered today as California's first governor.

Juan Bautista de Anza

Juan Bautista de Anza was born in 1735, a third-generation Spanish frontier soldier. When he was 17 he joined the army. Military life suited him, and by 1759 he had become a captain and commander of the Tubac (modern Arizona) Presidio. Over the course of the next decade, he led several successful military campaigns against the troublesome Apache Indians.

As more and more world powers set their hooks into the New World, the Spanish began to worry about their claims. They felt the Pacific Coast needed to be protected from infringing British and Russian explorers. Mission sites, like that at Monterey Bay, were isolated from Spanish dominions by a lengthy sea journey. A land connection was necessary to better establish Iberian dominance in the area. Anza heard his country's call. In 1774, he financed his own exploratory trip and, after an arduous trek, proved that an overland route from Sonora to Alta California was possible. This mission, consisting of 34 men and guided by Francisco Garcés, was the first sizeable land expedition by Europeans into present-day California. It opened a 2,200-mile route across the desert, crossing the Colorado River. The viceroy in Mexico City was so impressed that he commissioned Anza to return to California with a colonizing force.

In October 1775, the explorer left Tubac with 240 men, more than 1,000 cattle, and the blessing of Viceroy Bucareli. On September 17, 1776, while colonial revolution was breaking out in the East, Anza formally dedicated the Presidio of San Francisco de Asís on the site of today's modern city. Anza had successfully opened up Alta California (present-day California) for settlement and missionaries. However, a revolt of Yuma Indians in 1781 closed his route and the Spanish never reopened it. Alta California was destined to remain isolated from Mexico proper.

Nevertheless, officials were so impressed with Anza that he was made the governor of New Mexico in 1778. He left Santa Fe in 1787 to become the commander and captain of the Tucson Presidio, a position he held until his death on December 19, 1788. Juan Bautista de Anza was buried beneath the floor of the church of Nuestra Senõra de la Asunción in Arizipe, Sonora, Mexico, where he lies to this day. Anza deserves to be remembered alongside Lewis and Clark and Kit Carson as a trailblazer in the opening of the American West for European settlement.

Francisco Garcés

On April 12, 1738, Francisco Garcés was born in Aragon, Spain. As a young man, Garcés was very pious. He entered holy orders when he was about 16. He was ordained as a Franciscan priest when he was 25 and volunteered to work with the Indians of Sonora, Mexico. On June 30, 1768, the young priest arrived in Mexico, eager to spread the word of God.

Garcés instantly took to his work. His friendly demeanor and unselfish attitude won him friendships with many Indians, and the priest was even welcomed by Indian chiefs. Preaching from the Bible, he set up missions and administered to those suffering from the measles epidemic. However, it was as an explorer and adventurer that Garcés entered California history. In 1771, while searching for mission sites, he traversed the Colorado River at Yuma Crossing and trekked across the Colorado Desert to the San Jacinto Mountains. This extremely dry trail, nicknamed El Camino del Diablo, Spanish for "the Devil's Road," became the main overland route to the Pacific in the Spanish era. In 1774, Captain Juan Bautista de Anza followed this path on his quest to open a route of communication between Sonora and the mission settlement at Monterey. Garcés accompanied Anza's party as far as the Colorado, then set off on his own in an unsuccessful attempt to find an alternate route to Monterey.

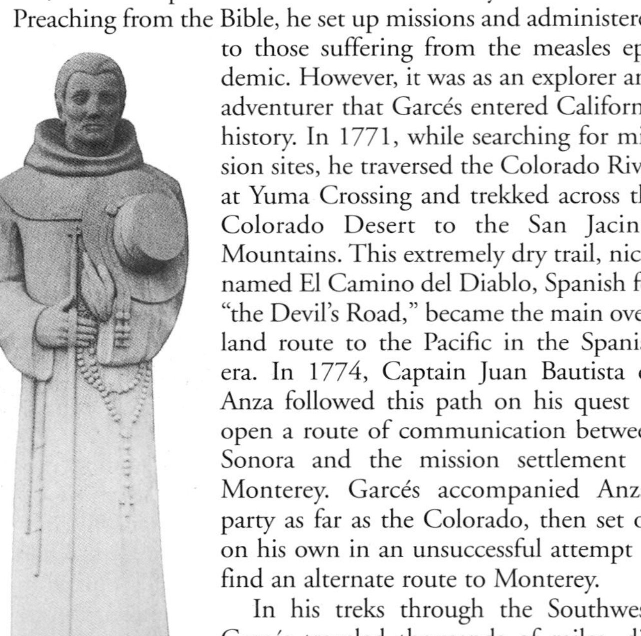

Fray Francisco Garcés

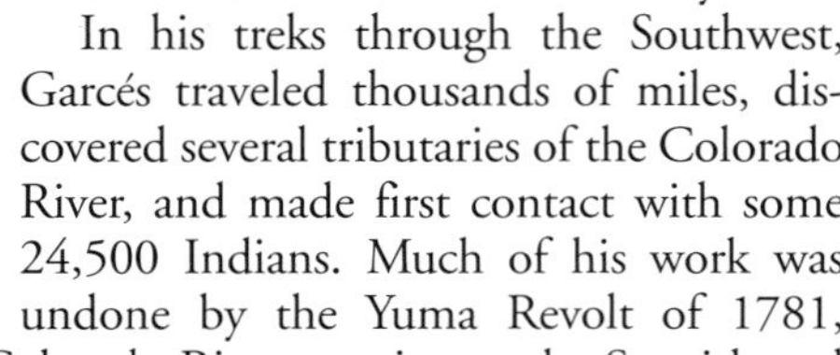

In his treks through the Southwest, Garcés traveled thousands of miles, discovered several tributaries of the Colorado River, and made first contact with some 24,500 Indians. Much of his work was undone by the Yuma Revolt of 1781, which closed the Colorado River crossing to the Spanish and resulted in the death of this intrepid priest. However, having previously gained their respect, he was buried by the Yuma, and piles of flowers were placed over his gravesite.

Sylvester Pattie and James Ohio Pattie

Sylvester Pattie and James Ohio Pattie are a father and son team whose exciting and daring adventures represent a period of time when the West was truly wild. On July 20, 1825, 42-year-old Sylvester Pattie and his 20-year-old son, James, left Council Bluffs, Iowa, with 114 men to hunt and trade in the area of New Mexico. The stories that were to come are documented in *Personal Narrative of James Ohio Pattie of Kentucky*, written by Timothy Flint as explained to him by James Pattie.

The Pattie party traveled along the Salt and Gila Rivers, trapping as much beaver as they could along the way. Several times they were attacked by Indians, often suffering heavy losses. Undaunted and aching for adventure, James Pattie and his father headed through Arizona and eventually wound up in San Diego. The Mexican authorities were not happy to see them and immediately tossed them into prison. Sylvester Pattie died May 24, 1828, within the confines of the Mexican jail. According to his narrative, James Pattie was spared jail time because of his knowledge of smallpox—he was entrusted to wander the vicinity and try to help those suffering from the rampant disease. In this way he was able to see much of the still unexplored province.

Although James never found the fortune he sought, the publication of his travelogue in 1831 brought him fame and helped raise interest in California and the Southwest among American readers. The last solid record of him comes from an 1833 Kentucky tax roll. It is likely that he died in the cholera epidemic of that year, although possibly he fled the disease and returned to the western frontier. Whatever his fate, his remarkable journey lives on.

Ewing Young

Ewing Young was born in 1792 in Tennessee. A third generation frontiersman, he received training as a carpenter. Soon, however, the lure of the American wilderness took him west. As a mountain man, Young was persistent and single-minded in acquiring wealth from trapping. By the time he was 30, he had traveled to Santa Fe and was catching beaver along the Pecos River.

Young was already a successful trapper when he reached Los Angeles with a group of 36 men in 1832. After a failed trip hunting coastal sea otters, the party traveled north to trap the Kings River and the San Joaquin River. They made it all the way into Oregon before returning south, where Young chose to settle. Two years later, he decided to migrate to Oregon with livestock and 50 horses. The Mexican governor of California, José Figueroa, sent word to Oregon officials that the horses were stolen. The accusations were likely false, but Young's new life was made more difficult by the wild claims. It was a hard time for northern settlers, and there was an acute shortage of cattle. To rectify the situation, Young was sent back to California with orders to buy 650 head. His journey overland with the herd predated the great cattle drives of the 1880s by more than 40 years and established Young as a prominent rancher and an important figure in early Oregon history. His many Californian expeditions also demonstrated the accessibility of the state to future emigrants. He died in 1841.

Joseph Reddeford Walker

Joseph Reddeford Walker was born December 13, 1798, in eastern Tennessee's Roan County. Soft-spoken, disciplined, and

oseph Reddeford Walker

never a braggart, Walker stood 6 feet tall. For four years he served as a sheriff in Jackson County, Missouri, before leaving the area to head west. Here, on the frontiers of North America, he established his reputation as one of the greatest figures of American expansion.

In 1832, Walker met Captain Benjamin Bonneville, who was planning a trapping expedition in the Rocky Mountains. Walker joined Bonneville's party as they moved west toward Green River. After wintering on the Salmon River, Walker and a group of 40 men left the main party and headed to California. The motives for the trip are unknown, but the exploration was a resounding success. The group found the Humboldt River, in what is now Nevada, crossed the Sierra Nevada, and made its way to the Pacific Coast. On the way, they passed through the Yosemite Valley and its huge sequoia trees. It was along Walker's route that many of the forty-niners reached California during the gold rush.

Once rested in the Mexican mission of San Juan Bautista (near present-day Monterey), the group moved down the San Joaquin Valley and through the mountains at Walker Pass, before heading north to reconnect with Bonneville's party. California 178 roughly retraces his steps today.

Walker returned to California many times, often as a guide to migrants from the East, and notably as a member of John Frémont's explorative expeditions. He mined gold in the state for several years. A prospecting trip to southern Arizona in the 1860s yielded much wealth and sparked a gold rush to the area around present-day Prescott. In 1867, Walker retired to his nephew's ranch in Contra Costa County, California. The old pathfinder died in 1876 at the age of 78. By then, his trailblazing had helped open California to many Americans.

Jedediah Smith

Jedediah Smith was born January 6, 1799, in New York State. A natural explorer, Smith answered an ad in the *St. Louis Gazette and Public Advertiser* in 1822 calling for young men who wanted to explore the West. He soon became part of William Ashley's great fur trapping and exploration venture.

On one of Smith's first expeditions he was attacked by a grizzly bear that ripped off one ear and part of his scalp. Undeterred, he commanded his companions to sew back his dangling parts and returned to the trail after just 10 days' rest. For the rest of his life he wore his hair long to conceal his wounds.

Jedediah Smith

In 1824, while searching for the fabled Buenaventura River, Smith and his party became the first Americans to cross overland into California. Upon his arrival in the Mexican mission of San Gabriel, he was taken to the authorities in San Diego. The Mexican governor was fearful of American intrusion into the area and ordered the party to leave California immediately. Instead of leaving, Smith entered the San Joaquin Valley via Tejon Pass and headed north. At the Stanislaus River, he left most of his party and crossed the Sierra Nevada on his way back to Utah, becoming the first American to do so. Upon returning to the group in California, Smith again ran into trouble with authorities while attempting to trade for supplies in San Jose. After a stint in a Monterey jail, he was released with strict orders to leave California immediately. This time Smith obeyed, and his party trekked north, following the Sacramento River into Oregon.

In Oregon, Smith's party was decimated by an Indian attack, one of many that the great mountain man faced in his short career. Having lost most of their supplies, the remainder of the group almost did not survive; at one point they resorted to eating horses.

In 1831, Smith's party was attacked by Comanche Indians near the Cimarron River. Smith was slain in the ensuing fight. He died before publishing an autobiography. A highly religious and strong willed man, Jedediah Smith is remembered as one of the most important figures in the opening of the American West.

Edward Fitzgerald Beale

Regarded as "Mr. California," Edward Beale played many successful roles throughout his life. Born in 1822, he had a variety of professions, ranging from naval officer and prominent explorer to bureaucrat and politician. Those who knew him described him as a thin, wiry man whose outspoken thoughts were often very frank. Status, wealth, and a thirst for adventure seemed to drive E. F. Beale in his many exploits.

Edward F. Beale

Beale first gained prominence in the Mexican War of 1846–48. He and Kit Carson slipped through enemy lines at San Pasqual (see Mexican War, page 97) and fetched relief for the embattled American troops. Over the course of that war, he made many transcontinental journeys with dispatches to Washington. On one of those trips, he carried the first sample of California gold to President Polk, helping to inspire the gold rush of 1849.

Beale left military service in 1851 after a promotion to lieutenant. The following year he entered politics as California's first superintendent of Indian affairs. He used the post to promote humanitarian solutions in disputes between whites and Indians, but also connived to purchase some Indian lands for himself at a greatly reduced price. In 1856, he resigned the position to become brigadier general of the California state militia. He proposed the formation of a camel corps to better supply forts across the dry deserts of the Southwest. In 1857, he accepted a job as superintendent for a transcontinental wagon road, which led to the creation of the Beale Wagon Road and the introduction of camels in the American Southwest. When the State Department sold the animals, Beale relocated them to his ranch near Bakersfield. He spent the Civil War in the West as surveyor general of California and Nevada.

Beale stayed in politics through his later years. He was active in the Pennsylvania movement for African-American suffrage. During the 1870s, he climbed the Republican political ladder and soon became one of President Ulysses S. Grant's personal friends, serving a year as ambassador to Austria-Hungary. He died April 21, 1893, at the age of 71.

Famous Soldiers

Stephen Watts Kearny

Stephen Watts Kearny was born in Newark, New Jersey, in 1794. After attending Columbia University he entered the military as a lieutenant in the War of 1812. He rose quickly in rank, and when hostilities began between Mexico and the United States in 1846 he was a general in command of the western forces. President James Polk instructed Kearny to capture Santa Fe and California. The conquest of New Mexico succeeded without bloodshed. Kearny divided his forces in Santa Fe and proceeded to California with a force of 100 men.

Kearny's dragoons were weary indeed when they encountered a force of Mexicans near the Indian village of San Pasqual. The Americans lost 20 men in the fiercest battle of the California conflict. However, this was to be the last victory for the Californio Mexicans. When Kearny reached San Diego, he combined forces with Commodore Robert Stockton and the mainly volunteer militia of Captain John Frémont. On December 29, 1846, Kearny set out for Los Angeles with more than 600 men. He won a series of light skirmishes near the San Gabriel River, forcing General Andrés Pico to surrender to Frémont on January 13, 1847, thus ending hostilities in California.

Stephen Watts Kearny

Commodore Stockton left the new territory, placing Frémont in charge as governor. Kearny set up his own civil government and Frémont refused to yield power. Eventually, Kearny had his subordinate court-martialed, forcing him to retire from the military. Kearny went to Mexico, serving as military governor for Mexico City before returning to his home in St. Louis, where he died of yellow fever in 1848.

John Charles Frémont

A native of Savannah, Georgia, John Frémont was born in 1813 to French and American parents. He grew up primarily in Charleston, South Carolina, where he attended the College of Charleston's scientific department before being expelled in 1831. After teaching math to midshipmen in the navy for a few years, Frémont joined the U.S. Corps of Topographical Engineers as a second lieutenant.

It was during this time that Frémont met Missouri senator Thomas Hart Benton, a man who would have great influence in the young explorer's life. Frémont also met and fell deeply in love with the senator's 16-year-old daughter, Jessie Benton. Despite the couple's 11-year age difference, they happily eloped and were married in October 1841. After each of his many explorations, Frémont returned home to his wife and energetically dictated his tales to her. Her elaborate stories became national best sellers and even caught the attention of members of Congress, who were impressed by Frémont's scientific and topographical abilities.

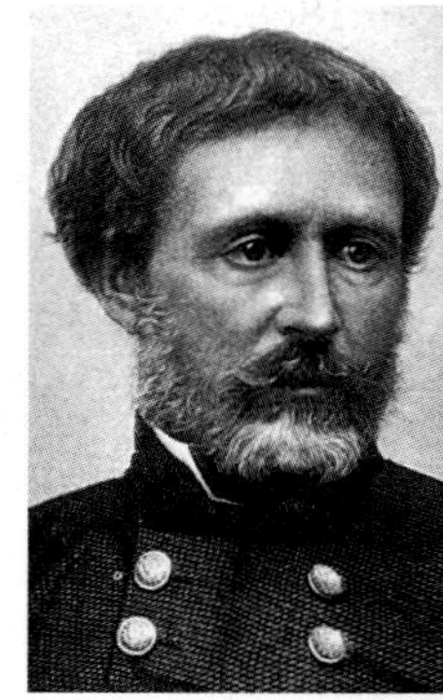
John Charles Frémont

Arriving in California during an 1843–44 mapping expedition, Frémont eventually became embroiled in the political tensions erupting between Mexico and the United States. Although ordered by Mexican authorities to leave, he stayed in the area with a unit of the U.S. Army. When settlers began a revolt on June 10, 1846, Frémont sent his troops in support of the rebels. The rebellion became known as the Bear Flag Revolt after the banner raised by the civilian forces. Under Frémont's command, the settlers captured Sonoma. The outbreak of the Mexican War called Frémont south to assist in fighting around Los Angeles.

Uniting with the main body of United States forces, Frémont was appointed military governor of California by Commodore Robert Stockton. However, a dispute with the newly arrived General Stephen Kearny led to Frémont's court-martial. Although acquitted of any wrongdoing, he left the military and returned to California to take part in the gold rush. He was appointed as a senator for the new state and ran for president in 1856 as the first candidate on the Republican Party ticket. Despite making a fortune in gold, Frémont's fortune dwindled in his later years and he died in 1890 a virtual pauper.

Robert Field Stockton

Born in New Jersey in 1795, Robert Stockton (known to some as "Gassy Bob") began his naval career in 1811 and served in the War of 1812. He arrived in California on July 15, 1846, as commodore of the USS *Congress*. In August of that year, Stockton's forces entered Los Angeles and left Captain Gillespie with a force of 50 to occupy the city. Gillespie's policies soon alienated the populace, who revolted, surrounding his garrison on a hilltop. Reinforcements sent in to aid the beleaguered troops landed at San Pedro and suffered a humiliating defeat at the hands of Californio locals armed with a single cannon. As a result, all Southern California lay in the hands of Mexicans.

Commodore Stockton, now military governor of the province, was preparing to retake Los Angeles when he received a message from General Stephen Kearny. Kearny had entered California with a small force and was now surrounded near San Pasqual. Stockton sent 200 soldiers to his aid. Kearny reached San Diego and joined with Stockton's troops. The combined force moved to Los Angeles, where they met 400 volunteers commanded by Captain John Frémont. Stockton's men engaged the Mexicans near the San Gabriel River. He outmaneuvered the enemy commander and re-entered Los Angeles. The remainder of the Mexican forces surrendered to Frémont on January 13, 1847.

Stockton sailed to Mexico, naming Frémont as his successor, a move opposed by General Kearny. After the war, Stockton resigned from the navy and settled again in New Jersey. He served as a senator for that state from 1851 to 1853. He died in 1866.

George S. Patton

George S. Patton Jr. was born in San Gabriel, California, in 1885 and went on to become one of the greatest generals in American history. Patton knew from an early age that he wanted not just to enter the armed forces, but also to become a combat leader. By age 7 he could read military topographic maps; his only educational weaknesses were spelling and grammar. After graduating from high school, Patton attended Virginia Military Institute before being accepted to the U.S. Military Academy at West Point. He left the prestigious military academy in 1909, ranked 46th out of 103, and joined the cavalry as a lieutenant. The following year he married Bee Ayer, whom he met while studying at West Point.

In 1912, Patton represented the United States in the Stockholm Olympics, placing fifth in the modern pentathlon. When World War I began in Europe, Patton requested permission to serve with the French cavalry, but he was turned down. Instead, he accompanied General Pershing in his raids against Pancho Villa in Mexico. For his actions during the engagements, which included killing one of Villa's bodyguards, Patton was promoted to captain. When the United States declared war on Germany, Patton served in France with the new U.S. Tank Corps. During the conflict he was wounded by machine gun fire; but he received several promotions and rose to the rank of colonel.

George S. Patton

Between the wars, Patton spent time in Hawaii and Texas. He was a determined proponent of increasing America's armored strength in preparation for a conflict he felt sure was inevitable. By the time World War II began, he had attained the coveted rank of brigadier general. Patton was put in charge of training U.S. troops for Operation Torch (the Allied offensive in North Africa). He set up a series of camps in California and other Southwestern states that were collectively known as the Desert Training Center. In 1942, Patton's forces recaptured Algeria and Morocco from the Vichy French. Patton then attacked German forces to the east while his British counterpart, General Bernard L. Montgomery, attacked to the west.

Following the victory in North Africa, Patton commanded the new U.S. Seventh Army in the successful invasion of Sicily. He became perhaps the most feared Allied general in German eyes. General Dwight Eisenhower, head of operations in Europe, used this fact to his advantage. Although Patton was not put in charge of another offensive until the invasion of France, Hitler repeatedly sent Nazi forces to areas near where the fearsome general was stationed.

When Allied forces landed in Normandy, German leaders were convinced the invasion was a decoy because Patton was not committed to the battle. With the beachheads secured, Patton and the Third Army were unleashed on northern France. Patton used German *Blitzkrieg* tactics to advance 600 miles in just two weeks. His strategies were crucial in rebuffing the Nazi counteroffensive in early 1945. By this time, his offensive prowess was legendary.

Patton's army liberated the concentration camp at Buchenwald. The general forced local German citizens to tour the camp, a policy later adopted by other Allied commanders. With Hitler defeated in Europe, Patton asked for a transfer to the Pacific theater. The War Department refused his request. Patton remained in Europe, where his controversial remarks recommending the rearming of Germany for a combined attack on the Soviet Union lost him command of the Third Army.

Throughout his military career, Patton predicted that he would die on foreign soil. The general always led his forces from the front and took many risks that seemed to ensure the fulfillment of his auguries. In December 1945, his predictions came true when he died from injuries sustained in a Luxembourg automobile accident. He was buried in Luxembourg, where he is still praised as the small country's liberator.

Lawmen, Gunfighters, and Outlaws

Joaquin Murrieta

Church records indicate the birth of a Joaquin Murrieta (also spelled Murieta) in 1830 near Alamos in Sonora, Mexico. After marrying a fellow Mexican named Rose Felix, Murrieta followed the northern exodus of 1848 in search of gold. His wife, half-brother, and three brothers-in-law, including the outlaw Claudio Felix, accompanied him on his migration to California. The group settled in the tent city of present-day Sonora, California.

Legend has it that Joaquin was forced from his claim by a group of Americans who lynched his brother and raped his wife. Though this story is likely a fabrication, it is probable that Murrieta was mistreated by Anglos and developed a disliking for them. By 1850, Cladio Felix was leading a murderous outlaw gang that committed a series of thefts and killings around San Jose. Murrieta's involvement in these crimes is unknown, but according to legend he was in a gunfight on April 5, 1852, which led to the serious wounding and arrest of his wife's brother.

Joaquin Murrieta

Three weeks after Claudio's imprisonment, Murrieta led a group of outlaws in the murder of a young farmer named Allen Ruddle. Ruddle's family was wealthy and offered a large reward for Joaquin's capture. Respected lawman Harry Love gathered a posse to hunt for the outlaw, but it would be some time before he was successful. In the meantime, Murrieta's reputation grew. He was blamed for a multitude of robberies and murders across the Mother Lode. By January 1853, his gang was the bloodiest and most feared of the gold rush. They would ride into mining camps—often Anglo, but also Chinese and Hispanic—and steal all the gold in the town, killing those who resisted.

In May 1853, the state legislature formed the California Rangers, headed by Harry Love, to capture the "five Joaquins," as the gang was known. Love arrested another of Murrieta's brothers-in-law, Jesus Felix, who led the Rangers to the outlaws' hideout. On July 25, 1853, Love's men awakened the gang and shot Murrieta dead. His head and the hand of a companion, Bernadino "Three-fingered Jack" Garcia, were removed and paraded around the state as evidence of their deaths.

In 1854, John Rollin Ridge published *The Life and Adventures of Joaquin Murieta, the Celebrated California Bandit*, a highly fictionalized account of Murrieta's violent career. His myth grew until he was idealized as a modern Hispanic Robin Hood, avenging injustice in the Old West. In 1967, Chilean poet Pablo Neruda wrote a play about the outlaw. As accounts of Murrieta's life grew increasingly fictionalized, historians began to question whether he had ever really existed. Recent works have helped restore a historical view of the bandit, but his legend persists.

Harry Love

Harry Love was born in Vermont in 1810. In his youth, Love served as a scout in the Seminole wars in Florida and the Blackhawk War of 1832. He also worked as a mariner before serving as an express rider in the Mexican War of 1846–48. Love arrived in California in December 1850 and began mining. None of his mining projects succeeded, but Love was recognized as a capable lawman, becoming deputy sheriff of Santa Barbara and then Los Angeles. He was living in Mariposa County when Joaquin Murrieta's gang murdered Allen Ruddle in April 1952. On May 17, 1853, the state legislature authorized the formation of the California State Rangers to catch the Mexican bandits. Love was asked to command the 20-man group.

The Rangers, a mix of professional men and hardened adventurers, tracked Murrieta across Mariposa County. The gang members refused to lie low—they continued to commit daring robberies, even as the law closed in on them. Love successfully captured several of the bandits, but his real break came when Murrieta's brother-in-law Jesus Felix was brought into custody. On July 25, 1853, the Rangers were able to confront Murrieta. The outlaw was killed in the ensuing firefight. Love ordered his men to decapitate Murrieta's body. The detached head and the hand of another gang member, Bernadino "Three-fingered Jack" Garcia, were displayed at towns across the Mother Lode.

For his efforts, Harry Love and his Rangers received a reward of $6,000. With the money, Love bought a sawmill in the Santa Cruz Mountains. In 1858, he married the sawmill's previous owner, a wealthy widow named Mary Bennett. Before long, Love's excessive drinking placed undue strain on the marriage. On July 29, 1868, Love confronted Christian Eiverson, a German immigrant, and accused the poor man of stealing his 300-pound wife's affections. Seeing the lawman's shotgun, Eiverson drew his pistol and shot him in the right arm. Love died after surgery to amputate his wounded limb. He was buried in the Santa Clara Mission Cemetery.

Tiburcio Vasquez

One of the most feared and notorious outlaws in California history, Tiburcio Vasquez was born in Monterey on August 11, 1835. He apparently came from a respectable family and was bilingual at an early age. Nevertheless, Vasquez found himself an outlaw at just 19 years old after he was involved in the killing of a police constable. In 1857, he was convicted of horse theft and sentenced to five years at San Quentin, where he was treated roughly because of his ethnicity. He participated in the mass escape of June 1859 but was recaptured and resentenced the following year.

Tiburcio Vasquez

Upon his release in 1863, Vasquez moved on to more serious crime, killing an Indian butcher in a robbery attempt. By 1871 he was head of a bandit gang that included Procopio Bustamente, the nephew of Joaquin Murrieta. The group proceeded to rob a couple of stages. Vasquez and Procopio used their proceeds for a debauched stay in rural Mexico. They soon tired of the "quiet" life, however, and Vasquez returned to California once more. Over the next several years his gang conducted a series of daring and well-publicized heists. Although numerous murders were committed during the course of the robberies, Vasquez was reportedly reluctant to take life. His civilized character is further revealed in an incident that took place in a bank raid. Vasquez ordered a lady's watch returned, stating, "We didn't come here to rob women." Indeed, the outlaw was quite a ladies' man, and was almost as famous for his many spurned female partners as for his bold thefts. On at least one occasion, a member of his band turned informer after finding Vasquez in a compromising position with his wife.

The band's exploits increasingly angered state law enforcement. At times, Vasquez would rob entire towns, shop by shop. By 1874 there was a reward of $8,000 on his head and a multitude of posses scouring Central California on his trail. The vigilante atmosphere took its toll on California's Mexican community, whose members were frequently hassled just for looking "suspicious." But instead of retiring from his life of crime, Vasquez continued to conduct audacious raids even as he was being pursued. His luck ended on May 14, 1874, when a posse surrounded the house in which he was staying, in the area now known as Hollywood. The outlaw tried to shoot his way out, but was felled by a reporter's buckshot. The wounds were not serious, but he was tried and convicted of three murders and hanged in Santa Clara County on March 19, 1875.

Richard A. "Rattlesnake Dick" Barter

Rattlesnake Dick was born Richard Barter in Quebec, Canada. His father was a British army officer. Dick migrated to California in 1850 with his elder brother and settled in the mining camp of Rattlesnake Bar, from which he gained his nickname. A contemporary report describes him as a young man who was "nearly six feet in height, and weighed about 160 pounds, slight of build, but...very muscular." Other sources testify to his handsome appearance. Rattlesnake Dick's criminal career began in 1853 when he was arrested for stealing some clothes from a store. The following year he was convicted of grand larceny and sentenced to a year at San Quentin.

It was during his imprisonment that Dick met Tom Bell. Dick joined Bell's outlaw gang and participated in a string of horse thefts, robberies, and killings in California's mining country. Following Bell's death in 1856, Rattlesnake Dick took control of the gang. Under Dick's guidance, the group conducted several daring thefts, including the February 1857 burglary of a Wells Fargo safe in Fiddletown and robberies of three stagecoaches for a heist of more than $30,000. Huge rewards were issued for the arrest of the bandits, but the gang continued to evade law enforcement.

Several times Rattlesnake Dick was captured and brought to justice, but he repeatedly managed to escape custody. In 1858, he was caught trying to break out of Auburn prison while there awaiting trial. Reluctant to return to San Quentin, Dick repeatedly filed for a continuance, delaying his court date. Before the trial could take place, Dick had successfully escaped! Once free, the outlaw sought to avenge his capture. He camped all night outside the house of lawman John Boggs. The constable was absent and did not return until the following morning, at which time he found a threatening note from Rattlesnake Dick pinned to his front door. Time was short for the young bandit, however. On July 11, 1859, a posse caught up with Dick and a companion on a stage road near Auburn. The outlaws shot their way out of the ambush, killing one posse member, but not before Dick had taken two bullets. Rather than be imprisoned once more, he finished the job with a self-inflicted shot to the head.

Tomas Procopio Bustamente

Procopio was born near Jose de Guadalupe, Mexico, around 1840. His mother was the older sister of famed outlaw Joaquin Murrieta. Following the death of Procopio's father at the hands of Indians in 1852, his mother took him to join Murrieta in California. Although Joaquin was killed the following year, the outlaw atmosphere had rubbed off on young Procopio, and he began his life of crime at an early age.

His first brush with the law came in 1862 when he was detained in the investigation of the murder of prominent Southern California rancher John Rains. Although Procopio was more than likely at least an accomplice to the crime, he was released because of a lack of evidence against him. He was soon implicated in another killing, this time of rancher Aaron Golding and his family in the Livermore Valley. Again, lawmen lacked sufficient evidence to imprison the young bandit. That was not the case the following summer, when Procopio and a companion stole a herd of cattle in Alameda County. The outlaw was arrested as he sold the livestock to a local butcher. He was sentenced to nine years at San Quentin.

After his release in 1871, Procopio wasted no time in resuming his criminal ways. In August of that year he stole two steer from a Bay Area rancher, but fled south before he could be captured. Somewhere on the southern coast of California, Procopio joined famous highwayman Tiburcio Vasquez. Together, the pair committed a series of robberies before fleeing to Mexico to spend their new wealth. Upon his return to California in April 1872, Procopio was again arrested. Convicted of cattle theft, he served another five years in San Quentin.

Prison had far from a rehabilitating effect on Procopio. Within five months of his parole, he was once more leading a gang of bandits in raids around Fresno. The gang moved south and was captured near Tejon Pass. Procopio escaped unharmed but his companions were all lynched. Procopio quickly assembled another band of outlaws and robbed a store in Hanford, stealing $300 and some jewelry. A posse caught up with the new gang a few days later. Procopio was surprised while sleeping, but managed to grab two revolvers and shoot his way out of trouble, killing one deputy in the process. Other posses followed the outlaw, but failed to corner him again.

Details about Procopio's later life are somewhat cloudy. He was still thieving and murdering as late as 1882. He possibly died in Sonora, Mexico, in that year, although many accounts have him dying as much as ten years later.

Dick Fellows

Dick Fellows was born George B. Lyttle in Kentucky in 1846. His father was a state legislator there. While still below the age of majority, Dick joined the Confederate Army. He was captured and spent the final months of the Civil War in a Union prison. After his release he tried to study for a law degree, but heavy drinking thwarted any career plans. In part to try to kick his alcoholism, Dick moved to California in 1867. But the change of scene only exacerbated his problem, and he was soon in the company of criminals. At age 23, now going by the name Dick Fellows, he was already an outlaw wanted for several stage robberies.

At this time Dick seems to have made an attempt to quit thievery in exchange for pig farming. When a fire destroyed the ranch's winter food supply, the robber returned to his criminal ways. He soon gained a reputation as the "lone highwayman" because he committed his raids alone, although he often acted as though he had companions waiting in the bushes. After one holdup of a Wells Fargo coach in which he netted $435, Dick was recognized in a nearby road station and shot in the foot. While resting at a friend's house in Los Angeles, he realized he was about to be captured, so he persuaded his friend to turn him in for the now-hefty reward. He was sentenced to eight years in San Quentin for robbery and assault. In April 1874, he was released after serving four years of his sentence. He settled in Caliente, east of Bakersfield, and while there robbed the Los Angeles stage to the tune of $1,800. Unfortunately for the outlaw, he broke his ankle in his escape and was quickly captured. Before he was returned to state prison, Dick tunneled out of his county cell and evaded his pursuers for a week. But a reward of $550 ensured his recapture, and he was sent back to San Quentin for another eight-year term in January 1876.

Dick was a model prisoner, and his good behavior got him

paroled in May 1881. He resumed stage robbery, holding up a series of coaches around San Luis Obispo. Wells Fargo issued a large reward for him, and posses began to chase him. He was captured, he escaped, he was recaptured, and he escaped again before he was hurried to Folsom Prison for a life sentence. He served 25 years of that sentence, again as an ideal prisoner. In 1908, the Wells Fargo president recommended him for clemency and he was released on March 8 of that year. By then an old man, Dick returned home to Kentucky, where he presumably spent his final days.

Chris Evans

Chris Evans was born near Ottawa, Canada, in 1847 to parents of Welsh and Irish descent. He left home at age 16 and joined the Union Army during the Civil War. After the war ended, Evans stayed in the army and fought Indians under the command of Lieutenent Colonel George A. Custer. In 1869, he deserted and made his way to California where he met and married Molly Byrd.

Evans worked as a miner, farmhand, teamster, lumberjack, and railroad employee before settling down on his own farm near Visalia in the San Joaquin Valley. As a farmhand he hired a former Southern Pacific Railroad brakeman named John Sontag. Sontag had been fired by the railroad company after being badly injured on the job in 1887. Evans and Sontag became close friends. When Evans bought a livery stable in Modesto in 1890, Sontag helped him with the down payment. A fire destroyed the stable in 1891, bankrupting both men. The pair returned dejectedly to Visalia.

Around this time a series of train robberies struck the San Joaquin Valley. In January 1890, $20,000 was stolen from an express car at Goshen, near Visalia. The was a robbery in February 1891 at Pixley, and in September of the same year two more hold-ups were attempted near Ceres. In all cases the culprits were two masked men.

In 1892, Evans and Sontag were in Minnesota visiting Sontag's bother, George Contant (Contant kept his father's name when his mother remarried), when a train was held-up at Kasota Junction by three bandits. Evans, Sontag, and Contant were back in California on August 3, 1892, when $50,000 was stolen from a Southern Pacific train near Fresno. The robbers' tracks led back to Visalia.

George Contant was picked up for questioning, and officers proceeded to the Evans farm to interrogate Evans and Sontag. Railroad detective Will Smith and Deputy Sheriff George Witty were confronted by the pair wielding shotguns. Both lawmen were wounded in the gunfight that ensued, and another deputy was killed later that day. A huge manhunt began for the fugitives. A $10,000 reward offered for their capture lured many bounty hunters.

On September 11, 1892, a posse tracked the duo to Jim Young's cabin in the mountains southeast of Visalia. As the posse approached the door, Evans and Sontag jumped out onto the porch and began shooting, killing two lawmen. The fugitives escaped into the mountains, where they spent the winter in camps.

The following spring, U.S. Marshall George Gard assembled a well-qualified posse to search for the outlaws. The posse moved stealthily through the mountains, eating dried food to avoid making campfires and visiting places where Evans and Sontag had previously been seen. On June 11, 1893, the posse surprised the pair at Stone Corral, close to Visalia. The resulting gunfight lasted eight hours, and left Sontag mortally wounded. Evans was captured the following day with bullet wounds that led to the loss of an arm and an eye.

Evans repeatedly denied any connection with the train robberies, but he could not explain why it was necessary to shoot several inquisitive lawmen. His wife Molly claimed he had just "gone crazy." It was true that the Evans remained a poor farming family and no loot was ever recovered. Nevertheless, Chris Evans was sentenced to life imprisonment and held at the Fresno County jail. Evans quickly escaped but was recaptured and sent to Folsom Prison. While there he shared a cell with fellow outlaw Dick Fellows.

Evans was released from jail in May 1911 on the condition that he leave California forever. He spent his remaining days with his family in Portland, Oregon, where he died on February 9, 1917.

Wyatt Earp

A controversial icon of the West, Wyatt Berry Stapp Earp, was born on March 19, 1848, in Illinois. His father, Nicholas Porter Earp, had served in the Mexican War under Wyatt Berry Stapp and young Wyatt was named in honor of his father's revered commander. Wyatt spent most of his early life in Illinois and Iowa. When the Civil War broke out in 1861, he dreamed of enlisting. Wyatt often ran off in hopes of joining, but his father would catch up to him and bring him back home. He was one of five rough-and-tumble brothers who were dubbed the Fighting Earps.

Wyatt Earp

Wyatt worked on his father's farm but soon learned to hate the backbreaking labor. Upon Virgil's return from the Civil War, Wyatt took off with him and took such jobs as loading freight wagons and working on the Union Pacific Railroad. The Earps, including Wyatt and Virgil, settled down on their father's farm in Lamar, Missouri. Wyatt married Urilla Sutherland there in 1870 and got his first taste of dispensing law and order when he was elected the local constable. Urilla died suddenly of typhoid just a year later. Grief-stricken and fleeing accusations of fraud, Wyatt left Lamar. In 1871, he wandered into controversy in present-day Oklahoma. Wyatt Earp's actions are unclear, but he was arrested for horse stealing. He jumped bail and fled into Kansas, where he may have worked briefly as a buffalo hunter.

Wyatt continued to drift from one frontier town to the next. In 1875, he became a policeman in Wichita where he gained a reputation as an excellent lawman. He rarely smiled, had nerves of steel, and never killed unless he had to. Once Wyatt imprisoned a drunken man, on whom he discovered a roll of bills adding up to $500. To the drunk's surprise, when he woke up Wyatt returned the money. The local newspaper, the *Beacon*, heralded Wyatt's honesty, noting that the drunk was lucky to be tossed into the Wichita prison because in any other jurisdiction the money would have disappeared. Yet Wyatt was by no means a saint, and he often let his fists do the talking. Wyatt was eventually kicked off the force for assaulting the former marshal, Bill Smith.

In 1876, Wyatt joined the police force in the wild and morally destitute Dodge City—the Babylon of the West. He frequently chased criminals and tracked them over the countryside. One such case involved robber Dave Rudabaugh, who escaped into Indian Territory (present-day Oklahoma) with Wyatt nipping at his heels. His trail led Wyatt to Fort Griffin, Texas. Once there, Wyatt met a slender, gambling dentist by the name of Doc Holliday, who had information that helped Wyatt find his man. The friendship between Doc and Wyatt would prove to be invaluable. In April 1877, Wyatt followed the gold rush to the Black Hills, but was back in Dodge before the end of summer. In 1878, he spent a couple of months in Texas gambling, before returning to serve briefly as assistant city marshal to Charles Bassett.

Wyatt left Dodge City for good on September 9, 1879 to travel to Las Vegas, New Mexico, where he joined up with Doc Holliday and Morgan and Virgil Earp. The four, along with their families, including Wyatt's second wife, Celia "Mattie" Baylock, soon moved to Tombstone, Arizona. Wyatt worked as a shotgun guard for Wells Fargo until July 1880, when he became the deputy sheriff of Tombstone. After the town marshal was shot in October 1880, Virgil Earp took over that job.

From the first days when the Earps entered Tombstone, a feud began to develop between them and the Clantons and McLaurys, two families of cattle rustlers. It exploded with the famous shoot-out at O.K. Corral on October 26, 1881, in which three of the Earps' enemies were killed. In the months that followed, Virgil and Morgan Earp were both shot; Morgan's wounds proved fatal. Before Wyatt left Tombstone, he tracked down his brothers' assailants and killed them.

Wyatt's experiences in Tombstone had established him as the most famous lawman of the West. In 1882, he came to California, where he would spend most of his remaining life. That year, Wyatt married his third wife, Josie, in San Francisco and was elected marshal of Colton. Earp left California briefly to visit Doc Holliday, who was dying of consumption in a Colorado sanatorium. He returned to San Francisco in 1886 and ran a saloon there until 1890.

Throughout most of the 1890s, Wyatt raised thoroughbreds in San Diego and officiated several boxing fights. In 1896, he refereed the heavily publicized Bob Fitzsimmons–Tom Sharkey world championship bout, on the condition that he could wear his six-shooter. In a controversial decision, he awarded the win to the out-boxed Sharkey—a move that outraged Fitzsimmons's supporters. Earp called the fight in the eighth round after Sharkey was hit with a crippling blow below the belt. Perhaps it was the presence of his six-shooter, but Wyatt avoided anything more than being charbroiled in the newspaper and heralded as a cheat. He was arrested for carrying a concealed weapon into the ring and his reputation suffered.

In 1897, the Earps trekked to Alaska to exploit the northern gold rush. Wyatt operated a saloon in Nome before returning to the contiguous states for the Nevada mining boom in 1901. In 1906, Wyatt and Josie finally settled down in Los Angeles. Wyatt made investments in oil and mining ventures but was often forced to work as a bounty hunter or hired tough; his reputation was usually enough to ensure a criminal's compliance. The Los Angeles Police Department often hired Earp for special jobs. In one instance he shrewdly halted a run of withdrawals from an overstretched bank by entering the bank carrying bags of iron slugs labeled as gold. Wyatt also served as an honorary deputy sheriff of San Bernardino County, where he would often spend his winters. On only one occasion did he have to make an arrest.

Toward the end of his life, Wyatt tried to attract the attention of the burgeoning Hollywood film industry, but met with little success. However, his stories did interest many young actors. A young extra named Marion Morrison was particularly impressed by the old lawman. Morrison, who later changed his name to John Wayne, credited Earp as the inspiration behind some of his most famous characters. During his time on the movie lots, Earp became friends with the two biggest cowboy stars of the era—Tom Mix and William S. Hart. Nevertheless, during the 1920s Wyatt had to battle a barrage of slanderous accounts of his earlier life. To counter these he endeavored to get his own version of his adventures published. In 1928, Stuart N. Lake took an interest in the project, but the fanciful account of Wyatt's life did not appear until after his death at age 80, on January 18, 1929. Lake's biography was the first of many, and over the decades Hollywood's interest has repeatedly turned to the Wyatt Earp story, most recently in *Tombstone* (1993) and *Wyatt Earp* (1994), starring Kurt Russell and Kevin Costner, respectively. To this day, Earp remains one of the most famous figures of the frontier West.

Charles Manson and his Family

The story of Charles Mills Manson and his followers is well known to many people. Traveling in his black bus, Manson collected a number of social misfits, indoctrinating them into his satanic beliefs and setting himself up as their leader. Many of his followers were young women, a number of whom subsequently bore his children, often with Manson as their only midwife. The group existed on the fringes of society, scavenging from supermarket trashcans; the women often traded sexual favors for rent and goods. They were heavy drug users and practiced many black magic rituals led by Manson.

Charles Manson

Before moving to the Barker Ranch, the "family" lived in Canoga Park in the San Fernando Valley, an old movie set called Spahn Ranch in Chatsworth, and many other abandoned premises. Manson's personal belief was that a racial war was imminent. He embraced this idea with fervor and used it to incite his followers to commit several brutal murders.

To escape attention, Manson moved his group to the high

desert. Some time was spent hiding out at the southern end of the Owens Valley in the Olancha area. Eventually, they ended up at the Barker Ranch. Manson had apparently spent time in the Death Valley region before, painting his name on rocks and old structures in the region, including high in the range at Panamint City.

Manson attempted to affiliate his group with a biker club called The Straight Satans, hoping that this would scare the public away from his ranch. One of its members stayed at the ranch, receiving special attention from the women in exchange for his mechanical services. The rest of the club disliked and distrusted Manson. When the bikers paid a group visit to the ranch to retrieve their friend, they threatened to kill the entire family if the man didn't leave with them. Manson apparently offered his own life to spare the others, but the biker group left without causing any harm.

Manson and four of his followers were convicted of multiple homicide in 1971. They were given death sentences that were later commuted to life in prison. To date, all attempts at parole have failed. One result of the case is that public horror and fascination with Manson continue in almost equal measures. Manson has acquired a cult status among many people, with public interest continuing to grow to this day.

Leaders, Ranchers, Settlers, and other Colorful Characters

Pío de Jesus Pico

Pío Pico, the last Mexican governor of California, was born at the Mission San Gabriel in 1801. Pico's ancestry included Spanish, Italian, African, and Native American roots. His family was one of the most prominent in California's early history. Pico moved to San Diego in 1819 and set up a small shop there. He later moved to Los Angeles and ran a tavern, serving liquor in unique ox-horn cups.

Pío de Jesus Pico

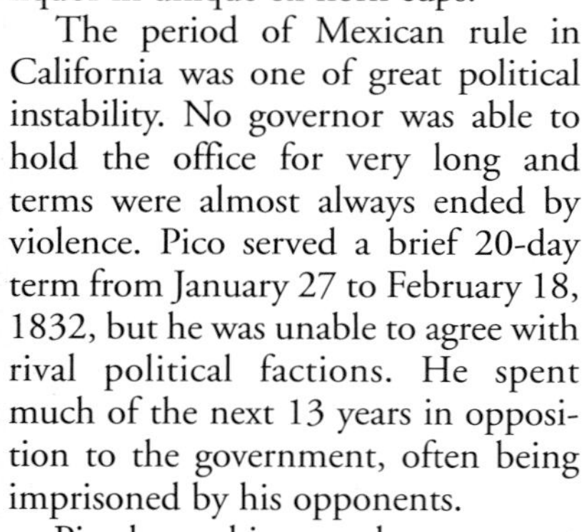

The period of Mexican rule in California was one of great political instability. No governor was able to hold the office for very long and terms were almost always ended by violence. Pico served a brief 20-day term from January 27 to February 18, 1832, but he was unable to agree with rival political factions. He spent much of the next 13 years in opposition to the government, often being imprisoned by his opponents.

Pico began his second term as governor of California in March 1845 after his predecessor Manuel Micheltorena was expelled after a bloodless battle at Cahuenga Pass. Today Campo de Cahuenga, opposite Universal Studios, marks the spot. Pico feared the influx of Americans that accelerated during his term; he thought another European power, perhaps France or Britain, would be more suited to rule California. The governor briefly relocated California's capital from Monterey to Los Angeles. From there, he completed the ongoing secularization of the Franciscan missions and gave thousands of acres of land away in land grants, many to his own family. Pico fled California when U.S. troops overran Los Angeles in 1846, but he later returned to reclaim his ranch lands. Although he built a fortune, floods destroyed his family home and gambling lost him much more. Pico died a pauper in Los Angeles on September 11, 1894.

John Bidwell

John Bidwell was born in 1819 in Chatauqua County, New York, and raised in Pennsylvania and Ohio. After a brief stint teaching, he moved west to Missouri where he established a ranch. He lost his land to a claim jumper in 1840. Bidwell spent the following winter preparing for an expedition to California. A group of 69 people led by John Bartleson embarked on a journey west in the spring of 1841. Half the party followed a trapping group into Oregon, but 32 people completed the trail into California.

John Bidwell

The Bartleson-Bidwell expedition was the first wagon party to traverse overland from the Missouri River to the Sierra Nevada, but their journey was not without hardships. None of the group was an experienced trailsman, and there were few established routes through the vast western wilderness. The trek took the migrants across stretches of desert and over icy mountains. At one point, they were forced to abandon their wagons and resorted to eating horses. It was not until November 1841 that the tired pioneers completed their journey.

Once in California, Bidwell found work at Sutter's Fort, the site of the big 1848 gold discovery. In 1844, he became a Mexican citizen and gained a large land grant. He joined in the Bear Flag Revolt of 1846, fighting with John C. Frémont in his volunteer force.

The rush of 1848 led Bidwell to prospect for gold, and by 1849 he was able to purchase a 22,000-acre ranch in Northern California. Bidwell established himself as one of the state's finest agriculturists. He used his wealth to embark on a political career, serving California in the House of Representatives. An unsuccessful bid for president for the Prohibition Party in 1892 ended his sojourn in politics. In 1900, the year of his death, Bidwell published *Echoes of the Past*, recounting his journey to California and earlier life there. That pioneering trek had paved the way for the mass overland migrations of subsequent years, something for which Bidwell is remembered to this day.

James Wilson Marshall

Born October 8, 1810, James Wilson Marshall was raised in Lambertville, New Jersey, where his childhood home still stands. In his early life he had a falling out with his Baptist father and was jilted by the woman he loved, events that led the young man to head west. He wandered until he reached western Missouri, where he built a cabin, started to farm, and fell in love again. When his intended wife married another man, Marshall picked up and moved to California.

Once in California, he sought employment at the fort built by John A. Sutter in the Sacramento Valley. Sutter hired Marshall as a woodworker for the growing community. It was a job in which the new arrival could utilize skills he had learned back East. Marshall soon established his own ranch nearby, where he kept livestock.

When American settlers began to revolt against Mexican rule, Marshall volunteered to serve with Captain John C. Frémont (see page 74). He served as chief military carpenter before his discharge early in 1847. Upon returning to his farm, he found it plundered. Again he looked to Sutter's Fort for work. Sutter sent Marshall to build a sawmill on the banks of the Cullomah River, about 45 miles from the settlement.

On January 24, 1848, James Marshall was tweaking the flow in the mill's tailrace when he saw pieces of a shiny metal glistening in the sunlight. Seizing a small nugget, he placed it on the ground and began pounding it with a rock. Instead of shattering like fool's gold (pyrite or mica), the nugget thinned under the beating. Convinced he had found gold, Marshall rushed to tell his colleagues. The next day he traveled back to the fort to consult with Sutter. The pair conducted a series of tests until they felt indubitably that the metal was gold.

Sutter quelled Marshall's excitement at the discovery, urging him to keep it a secret until work on the mill was completed. However, by the time the mill began sawing logs in mid-spring, rumors were spreading across the area. When Samuel Brannan announced the discovery, first orally on the streets of San Francisco and then in his own newspaper, prospectors began rushing to the valley.

Soon the area around the mill became a bustling town called Coloma. Marshall kept sawing logs and only dabbled in gold mining. When he tried unsuccessfully to extract a percentage from other miners, he was virtually driven from town. He returned in 1850 to find the mill crippled by lawsuits. The litigation would eat at Marshall's wealth, eventually forcing him to sell the last of his real estate.

ames Wilson Marshall

The rest of Marshall's life was spent in the shadow of his first gold discovery. He tried his hand at wine producing; his grapes even won prizes at the state fair. In 1862, however, his cabin burned down, destroying his valuable papers and perhaps a historically priceless diary. He became a little too keen on his own drink and was forced to quit the wine business. In the mid-1870s, the state legislature granted him a humble pension, but this was halted when it was discovered that the money was spent mostly on booze. Nevertheless, the allowance did enable Marshall to establish a small blacksmith shop in Kelsey, El Dorado County. The man who started the world's greatest gold rush was squeaking out a living in this little store when he died peacefully on August 10, 1885. A charitable group, The Native Sons of the Golden West, built a statue of Marshall on a hill overlooking his original discovery. The Marshall Gold Discovery State Historic Park in Coloma now honors him as well.

John A. Sutter

John Augustus Sutter was born in February 1803 in Kandern, Germany, and raised in Switzerland. He married a fellow Swiss, Annette Dubeld, in 1826. She bore him five children. In order to support his family Sutter joined the Swiss Army, where he achieved the rank of lieutenant. However, Sutter was not as successful in his later civilian life. For several years he ran a dry-goods business his mother-in-law set up for him, but it was soon crippled by debts. He liquidated the business and departed for America, leaving his family in Europe.

Landing in New York in 1834, Sutter quickly headed west, for a while living as a trader in Missouri. He arrived in California in 1839, having traveled via the Oregon Trail to the Pacific Northwest, and by boat to Hawaii and Alaska before finally sailing to Monterey. While in Monterey he persuaded the Mexican governor to give him a large land grant, upon which he planned to establish a settlement called Nueva Helvetia (New Switzerland). In return he applied for and received Mexican citizenship.

John A. Sutter

The new settlement soon grew, bolstered by Indian and Hawaiian workers and new arrivals from the American East. Hundreds of adobe-brick buildings were built, fields were planted with wine grapes and other crops, and vast meadows were irrigated for livestock. Sutter was appointed *alcade*, or chief law enforcement officer, for his entire 50,000-acre land grant. His wealth and stature grew enormously. In 1840, he began construction of a huge, high-walled adobe fort, built to protect his interests from Indians and Mexican authorities. By the time Sutter's Fort was completed in 1844, New Helvetia was a bustling community.

Around this time Sutter became entangled in a small-scale civil war between allies of the penultimate Mexican governor, General Manuel Micheltorena, and his successor, Pío Pico. Sutter had gathered a force to fight for Micheltorena. When Pico took control of the government, Sutter was imprisoned, tried, and later freed.

Upon his return to the fort, Sutter met and hired a young carpenter from New Jersey named James Wilson Marshall. Soon, however, he was embroiled in another conflict when United States forces under John C. Frémont took control of the fort during the Mexican War. In the course of the war many of the fort's workers, including Marshall, left to fight with Frémont.

When Marshall returned in 1847, Sutter sent him to construct a water-powered mill on a partnership basis. Marshall selected a spot in the Cullomah Valley, about 45 miles from the fort and took a group of workers to build the sawmill. On January 24, 1848, the mill was nearing completion when Marshall discovered several gold nuggets in the tailrace. He hurried back to the fort with samples for Sutter. Sutter consulted an encyclopedia and conducted several tests on the metal before he was convinced that it was indeed gold.

Sutter was unsurprisingly excited at the discovery, but he feared that his workers would flee in search of gold if word got out. He urged Marshall to finish work on the mill, telling the laborers that they could prospect in their free time. The men agreed and the mill began sawing logs in March. Nevertheless, rumors about the discovery were beginning to spread and migrants flooded the area. All John Sutter's fears were realized when his workers deserted their jobs to mine gold, leaving crops in the ground, stealing livestock, and leading him to financial ruin.

Around this time, Sutter brought his estranged family over from Europe after a 16-year separation. The family was forced to sell Sutter's Fort and move to a farm on the Feather River. Slowly, Sutter sold off his real estate interests. Much of present-day Sacramento is built on plots of land auctioned by him during the gold rush. He served in California's constitutional convention in 1849 and lost a close race for governor of the new state. He was appointed general in the state militia in 1850. Still, Sutter was hounded by creditors. A fire on the family farm in 1865 persuaded him to relocate to Lancaster County, Pennsylvania. He was buried there upon his death on June 18, 1880.

Samuel Brannan

Samuel Brannan was born in Maine in 1819, and later moved with his sister and her husband to Ohio. While there, he married and converted to the Mormon faith. His marriage was unsuccessful, however, and he soon relocated to Connecticut, where he met his second wife. In 1844, the Mormon Church paid him to go to New York and set up a printing press. There he produced the paper *The Prophet* with the younger brother of Mormon founder Joseph Smith.

Samuel Brannan

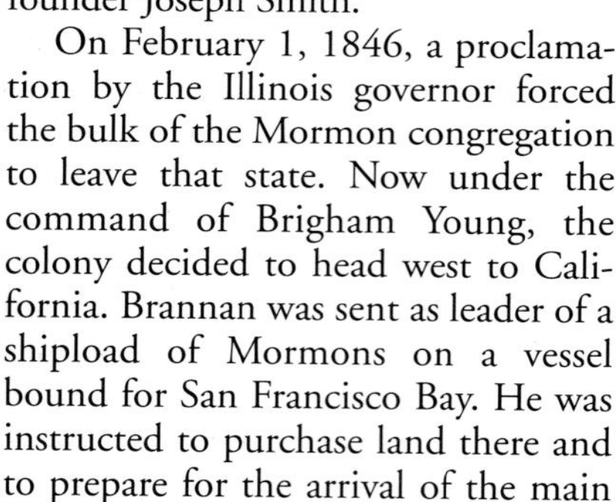

On February 1, 1846, a proclamation by the Illinois governor forced the bulk of the Mormon congregation to leave that state. Now under the command of Brigham Young, the colony decided to head west to California. Brannan was sent as leader of a shipload of Mormons on a vessel bound for San Francisco Bay. He was instructed to purchase land there and to prepare for the arrival of the main body of the church. The émigrés arrived in California only to discover that the province had been seized by U.S. forces. Undeterred by the presence of his oppressors, Brannan established the state's first flourmill and first newspaper, *The California Star*. He knew, though, that Brigham Young would prefer the isolated banks of the Great Salt Lake as the site of the new Mormon settlement. Brannan trekked east and tried unsuccessfully to persuade the religious leader to come to California.

On his journey back, Brannan stopped at Sutter's Fort. Several Mormons were working there, and Brannan visited quite often. He was present in January 1848 when James Marshall arrived to announce his discovery of gold. Although it is unlikely that Brannan was informed at this time, he was nevertheless soon aware of the metal's presence in the region. An astute businessman, Brannan proceeded to corner the market in mining equipment and opened several general stores. When he was fully prepared, he sent 2,000 copies of a newspaper confirming gold's discovery to the East and stood on a San Francisco street corner with a glass bottle of the shiny metal shouting, "Gold! Gold from the American River!" Within a few days the small town was almost deserted as its inhabitants rushed to the mines.

Hordes of migrants began arriving in California. Brannan soon made a fortune selling them necessary supplies and providing transportation to the goldfields. Now excommunicated from the Mormon Church, he became a prominent citizen of San Francisco. He organized the Society of California Pioneers, a vigilante group, to help combat the city's growing crime rate. Despite his newfound wealth, Brannan's marriage was increasingly strained. Partly because of his earlier polygamy, but also because of his heavy drinking and adultery, the relationship ended in divorce. The settlement left Brannan with heavy debts from which he never recovered. California's first millionaire died lonely and destitute on May 5, 1889, in San Diego County.

Leland Stanford

Leland Stanford was born in 1824 in Watervliet, New York, and studied law before moving to Wisconsin with his wife, Jane. The couple relocated again in 1852, migrating to Sacramento to work with Leland's brothers in their retail store. Stanford quickly became a prominent citizen of the new state and in 1861 launched a successful bid for governor. In this role he helped keep California in the Union as the Civil War erupted in the East.

Stanford was known as one of the "Big Four," a group of businessmen who built the Central Pacific and Southern Pacific Railroads. As president of the Central Pacific, he drove the final gold spike that connected the line to the Union Pacific on May 10, 1869, thus completing the first transcontinental railroad. It was his political clout that helped smooth the way for the track's construction. He remained president of the Central Pacific until his death and held the same title in the Southern Pacific Railroad Company from 1885 to 1890.

Leland Stanford

In 1885, Stanford was elected Republican senator for California. Stanford was not a great senator. During his first term he gave much of his attention to the endowment of a new college, the Leland Stanford Junior University. Named after his only son, who died at age 15 of typhoid fever in Florence, Italy, in 1884, Stanford University opened in 1891 and today is arguably the West Coast's finest educational institution.

Stanford was also an agriculturist. He grew vast vineyards on the future site of the university and kept many horses. To settle a bet with a friend on whether all four legs ever left the ground during a horse's movement, he commissioned Eadward Muybridge to take a series of photographs of a galloping stallion. Muybridge's study, when viewed through an invention called a zoopraxiscope, proved that all four legs do leave the ground and formed the basis of the motion picture.

Leland Stanford died in 1893, still a senator of California. His wife was left to preserve Stanford University from the economic depression of the period, ensuring that Stanford's name would be remembered today.

William Mulholland

William Mulholland was born in Ireland in 1856. He left his native country for the sea at age 15. He arrived in California in 1877 and found work maintaining ditches for the Los Angeles City Water Company. While he was keeping ditches clear of debris during the day, Mulholland dedicated his free time to studying mathematics, hydraulics, geology, and engineering. With his self-taught learning, he quickly rose through the ranks of the city's water department. By 1886, he was chief engineer of the department.

Mulholland is best known for the great aqueduct that transported water 233 miles from the Owens River Valley to Los Angeles. Begun in 1907, the aqueduct was the greatest engineering feat attempted by an American to date. The project required 5,000 employees working for five years, digging an astounding 142 tunnels. Mulholland was the first engineer in America to make use of hydraulic sluicing in the construction of a dam. The aqueduct cost $25 million, but was completed on time and under budget.

The first water from the Owens River Valley flowed into a San Fernando Valley reservoir on November 5, 1913. The city held a spectacular ceremony to mark the occasion. Mulholland uttered a brief declaration, "There it is. Take it." Those five words would become among the most famous in Los Angeles history.

The increased water supply enabled the burgeoning metropolis to increase its population to an extent that would have been unthinkable relying solely on local water sources. Still, Mulholland foresaw that other sources of the precious commodity would be necessary. In 1923, at age 68, the engineer initiated a six-year survey of the desert region between Los Angeles and the Colorado River. The survey selected the route of the Colorado River Aqueduct, a project that Mulholland did not live to see finished.

Mulholland is indubitably a hero in the growth of Los Angeles, now the second most populated metropolitan area in the United States. His legacy in other parts of Southern California is considerably less great. The Los Angeles–Owens River Valley Aqueduct robbed rural residents of their water supply, making once-blooming agricultural areas dry and unworkable. Still, the furor sparked by the aqueduct was nothing compared to that which followed the St. Francis Dam collapse of 1928. The dam, one of several built to store water from the Owens River, collapsed on March 12, 1928, sending 12 billion gallons of water surging down San Francisquito Canyon. The disaster killed more than 400 people and led to Mulholland's resignation from the water department seven months later.

Mulholland was a good-humored and intelligent supervisor, a family man who married and raised five children, an excellent engineer, and a generous fighter for the improvement of public welfare. However, his later years were overshadowed by memories of the dam collapse. After his death in 1935, the city of Los Angeles named its most scenic highway, Mulholland Drive, after this legendary and controversial individual.

William Randolph Hearst

Born in San Francisco on April 29, 1863, William Randolph Hearst was the only son of George and Phoebe Hearst. George Hearst came to California during the gold rush and made a fortune in mining. He was a senator representing California in the 1880s. In 1887, George gave control of the *San Francisco Examiner* to his son. William Randolph Hearst soon became known for his sensationalist editorial style. Hearst and his paper prospered and soon he owned a chain of dailies and weeklies around the nation. Hearst used his newspapers to press his own political agenda, which included extreme nationalism. He helped secure a second presidential term for Theodore Roosevelt and gave excessive coverage to the sinking of the battleship *Maine*, an event that helped spark the Spanish-American War (1897–98). Hearst was also accused by many of racism. His papers often published diatribes against minorities, including Japanese and Filipinos. He seems to have felt particular animosity toward Mexicans, portraying them as marijuana-smoking job stealers. His isolationism during World War II was criticized by many but praised by others as patriotic.

William R. Hearst

Hearst always kept a home in California, but for a while his principal residence was in New York City. He served as a congressman for New York from 1903 to 1907 and ran unsuccessful campaigns for mayor and governor of that state. In addition to his political interests, Hearst expanded his business empire to include magazines, motion picture studios, radio stations, and real estate. His eccentric and lavish lifestyle was the basis of Orson Welles's classic film *Citizen Kane*, released in 1941.

Hearst's greatest love interest was movie star Marion Davies. The two spent many years together at Hearst's mansion at San Simeon. The vast estate included a zoo, an airport, a private theater, and several beautiful guesthouses. William Randolph Hearst died on August 14, 1951, in Beverly Hills.

The Hearst family came into the national spotlight again in 1975 when a fringe terrorist group calling themselves the Symbionese Liberation Army kidnapped the heiress to the family fortune, Patricia Hearst. The story took a strange twist when Patricia sided with her captors in staging a bank robbery. The group was later cornered and caught after a bloody shootout. Patricia was released from custody and still resides in California today.

Hiram Warren Johnson

Hiram W. Johnson was born in Sacramento in 1866. He attended the University of California at Berkeley before leaving to marry his girlfriend. He continued his studies in the law offices of his father, a state legislator and supporter of the powerful railroad companies. Hiram defied his father when he joined the anti-railroad movement growing in the state.

Hiram Warren Johnson

In 1902, Johnson moved to San Francisco, where he helped prosecute the defendants in the city's graft trials. When the leading attorney was assassinated, Johnson took control of the case and secured the conviction of political boss Abe Ruef. The trial brought the young lawyer much public attention. He ran for governor in 1910 on the Progressive Party ticket and won. Johnson used the office to decrease the power of the Southern Pacific Railroad, to enact some of the nation's first conservation statutes, and to introduce the initiative and referendum to California—tools that still shape the state's politics. Teddy Roosevelt selected him as the vice presidential candidate for his Bull Moose Party in 1912. The pair lost the election to Woodrow Wilson, but carried California and four other states, becoming the only third party ticket to place second in a twentieth-century presidential campaign.

Johnson rejoined the Republican Party as a senator in 1916. He declined Warren Harding's offer of the vice presidency in 1920 and lost the Republican presidential nomination to Calvin Coolidge in 1924. He served in the Senate for another 20 years, his politics moving slowly to the right. He opposed Wilson's League of Nations, isolating America from a troubled Europe; he supported anti-Japanese legislation limiting the rights of Asian immigrants and citizens; and he attacked Franklin Roosevelt's New Deal aimed at easing the national depression. By the time Hiram Johnson died in 1945, the once powerful California Progressive movement had perished too.

Frank "Shorty" Harris

Frank Harris was born in Rhode Island in 1857 and was orphaned at the age of seven. He moved west in the 1870s, living in mining camps such as Tombstone, Arizona, and Leadville, Colorado, before coming to Death Valley. Although he never became rich, mostly because he shunned the hard labor of mining, he gained a reputation as an exemplary prospector by discovering several profitable claims.

As his nickname suggests, Harris was a small man. He measured just five feet four inches tall and was generally forced to wear clothes several sizes too big. He had large protruding ears, a bushy mustache, and sparkling blue eyes. Shorty roamed the harsh environs of Death Valley for decades, "a single-blanket-jackass prospector," as his self-penned epitaph proclaims. It was his discovery in 1904 that sparked a mini gold rush into the Bullfrog Mountains. Harris was traveling through the mountains with fellow prospector Ernest Cross when the pair found a large quantity of quartz on a hill. Breaking the rocks open with a pick, the prospectors discovered the quartz was rich with gold. One of the first nuggets they freed was the size of a hen's egg! The vein was imbedded in a green rock that reminded Shorty of a bullfrog, and so the mountain range in which it was found became the Bullfrog Mountains.

Word soon spread of the strike, fueled largely by Shorty's infamous loose tongue, and before long thousands of hopeful rainbow-chasers flocked to the area. The town of Rhyolite, just over the Nevada border, sprang up to accommodate the newcomers. Shorty did not capitalize on his rich find; in a drunken stupor he sold his claim for just $1,000, his partner Cross later made $125,000 on his stake. Shorty continued to roam the desert mountains and consistently found good claims. The ghost town Harrisburg (named after Shorty) grew around another of his finds. But the hardy wanderer loved the prospecting life more than the wealth it could provide. Each time he found riches he spent his money on booze or lost it gambling. People who encountered him remembered an extremely talkative, generous man, always willing to buy a drink (if his luck was up) and tell a story. A statue in Rhyolite depicts a short miner (Harris) with a penguin walking behind him. Apparently, Shorty often talked about the penguins that followed him when he'd had one drink too many. One of the last of the desert old-timers, Harris died in Lone Pine in 1934. As he had requested, he was buried in Death Valley, south of Furnace Creek, beside his friend Jim Dayton, who had passed away more than 30 years earlier.

Walter "Death Valley Scotty" Scott

One of the most colorful characters in California history, Death Valley Scotty was born Walter Perry Scott in 1872. He left his childhood home in Kentucky at an early age and worked for a while on his brother's ranch in Nevada. In 1890, he joined Buffalo Bill Cody's Wild West Show and spent the next 12 years as a cowboy in the road show. After leaving the Wild West Show he tried unsuccessfully to prospect for gold in Death Valley. Undaunted by his failures, Scotty began to boast of a rich mine deep in the desert. He managed to persuade several wealthy businessmen to invest in his imaginary mine and used their money to fund lavish spending sprees.

Death Valley Scotty

Scotty's best investor was Albert Mussey Johnson, a millionaire Chicago insurance magnate. Johnson poured thousands of dollars into the fictitious project, even after he realized that it was a scam. In 1904, Johnson visited Death Valley to see the gold mine he was generously funding. Scotty led his benefactor on a circuitous journey through the desert, hoping that the city dweller would tire of the grueling travel. Instead, Johnson became truly enamored with Death Valley and the good-natured, though thoroughly dishonest Scotty.

In 1922, Johnson initiated construction of a huge mansion in Grapevine Canyon. Death Valley Scotty boasted that the building was being funded by profits from his mine. When reporters investigated the story, Johnson pretended he was Scotty's banker and confirmed that the house belonged to him. The ranch became known as Scotty's Castle.

When Johnson died, he willed the ranch to a charity called the Gospel Foundation. The foundation allowed Death Valley Scotty to live in the mansion until his death in 1954. He was buried on a hill overlooking the famous structure. Today, Scotty's Castle is owned by the National Park Service, which gives daily tours of the building.

Walt Disney

Walter Elias Disney was born in Chicago in 1901. As a youth he was interested in drawing and sketching, but he dropped out of high school to join the Red Cross in World War I and received no further education. Disney apparently covered the ambulance he drove during the conflict with colorful cartoons. After the war, he lived in Kansas City and worked as an advertising cartoonist.

Walt Disney

In 1923, Walt Disney moved to Hollywood to join his brother, Roy. The brothers set up their first animation studio in their uncle's garage. Disney married one of the studio's first employees, Lillian Bounds, in 1925. The couple had two daughters, Diane and Sharon.

On November 18, 1928, Disney premiered the world's first fully synchronized sound cartoon, "Steamboat Willie." The star of the short feature was an animated rodent called Mickey Mouse, later to become an icon of Walt Disney Studios and a much-loved character for millions of children around the world.

Disney released the first full-length animated musical feature, *Snow White and the Seven Dwarfs,* in December 1937. This was followed by *Pinocchio*, *Fantasia*, *Dumbo*, and *Bambi*, all of which are considered classics today. By 1940, when construction began on the company's Burbank studios, Disney's staff exceeded 1,000. Disney and his employees would go on to win a staggering 48 Academy Awards.

Disney Studios soon branched out into live-action features, releasing *The Three Caballeros* in 1945 and the critically acclaimed *Mary Poppins* in 1964. In 1955, the company launched Disneyland, a $17 million amusement area in Anaheim. In its first six months, the park attracted more than a million visitors. The amusement park has since been replicated at Disney World in Florida and at newly constructed Disney parks near Paris, France, and Tokyo, Japan. Disney was also very successful in television, producing one of the first color programs and the enormously popular program "The Mickey Mouse Club." Walt Disney passed away December 15, 1966, but his company continues to expand; it is now one of the biggest entertainment corporations in the world and still dominates the market for animated features.

Before his death, Disney founded the California Institute of the Arts, an educational institution for a variety of performing arts. Disney left a large portion of his fortune to the school.

John Steinbeck

John Steinbeck, arguably California's most revered novelist, was born in Salinas in 1902. He studied at Stanford University and worked as a farmhand and fruit picker before publishing his first novel, *Cup of Gold*, in 1929. This work romanticized the life of a seventeenth-century Welsh buccaneer, Sir Henry Morgan.

Steinbeck's most remembered writings were set against a contemporary California backdrop and generally dealt with people who depended on the soil for their livelihood. The critically acclaimed novelette *Of Mice and Men*, which focuses on two itinerant farm workers yearning for some land of their own, was released in 1937. This was followed two years later by the Pulitzer Prize–winning book *The Grapes of Wrath*. Probably his most famous novel, *The Grapes of Wrath* chronicles the migration to California of the Joads, a farming family escaping the Oklahoma dust bowl. The work, now an American classic, highlighted the exploitation of migrant workers on California ranches.

Steinbeck's later writing was somewhat inconsistent. Among his best work was *Cannery Row*, published in 1945, which depicts idlers associated with the Monterey sardine-packing industry. *The Pearl* (1948) is an excellent novelette, an allegorical story about a young Mexican fisherman who discovers an enormous pearl. *East of Eden* (1952) and *The Winter of Our Discontent* (1961) are also considered classic works. In 1962, Steinbeck became the first Californian to receive the Nobel Prize for literature. He died in 1968.

César Estrada Chávez

Born in Yuma, Arizona, in 1927, César Chávez became one of the nation's great union organizers. His grandparents had migrated from Mexico in the 1880s, and in Chávez's youth his father owned a small farm in Arizona. The Great Depression forced the family from their land, and they became transitory seasonal farm workers. At age 19 Chávez joined his first labor organization, the National Agricultural Workers' Union. In 1944, he left the Southwest to serve in the navy but returned to California after the war.

Chávez married Helen Fabela in 1948 and spent the next several years as a sharecropper in the strawberry fields around San Jose, where he became involved with the Community Service Organization (CSO). As chairman of that organization he conducted voter registration drives in Chicano towns and worked to secure citizenship for Mexican immigrants. He resigned from the CSO in 1962 and formed the National Farm Workers' Association, which later evolved into the United Farm Workers' Organizing Committee (UFWOC). This union was the first to represent the harshly treated seasonal workers. Chávez organized strikes, boycotts, marches, and hunger strikes to promote the cause of farm laborers. He drew on the lives of Mahatma Gandhi and Henry David Thoreau for inspiration for his nonviolent protests.

Robert Kennedy praised Chávez and picked him as a delegate to the Democratic National Convention in 1968. Chávez decided not to attend after RFK was assassinated in June of that year. Still, he continued to work for the rights of agricultural workers. In 1970 he led a successful national boycott for the grape pickers of California, and in 1975 he pressured the state legislature into the first collective bargaining agreement for farm workers. Although the UFWOC faced increasing competition from the Teamsters Union for representation among laborers, Chávez remained a spokesman for migrant farmers. When he died after a hunger strike in 1993, 35,000 mourners attended his funeral. He is recognized as a great Hispanic leader. California recently designated March 31 as César Chávez Day.

Ronald Reagan

The fortieth president of the United States was born in Illinois in 1911. He worked as a sports announcer in Iowa before moving to Hollywood in 1937 to work in the burgeoning film industry. Reagan became a popular movie star, performing in more than 50 films. He left the industry to serve in the army in World War II, but he returned to be president of the Screen Actors Guild. This position thrust him into politics, where he established himself as a fierce anticommunist.

Ronald Reagan, 1968

Reagan was elected governor of California in 1966, having held no previous public office. He enforced an ideologically conservative agenda, strongly repressing the student activism erupting at Berkeley and across the California university system. Having established himself as a spokesman for the right wing of the Republican Party, Reagan left the governor's mansion in 1975 and tried to gain the GOP nomination for president the following year. He lost the nomination to the incumbent president, Gerald Ford, but this loss did not deter Reagan. He ran again for the office in 1980, this time securing the Republican nomination and the presidency.

Reagan's two-term incumbency became known as the Reagan Revolution because he shifted American politics to the right. The period was one of great economic boom, though this was largely fueled by federal deficit spending, vastly increasing the national debt. Although he began his presidency calling the Soviet Union the "Evil Empire," Reagan held earnest talks with the last Soviet leader, Mikhael Gorbachev. This opening of relations, combined with the highly competitive military spending of the Reagan administration, helped end the long-standing Cold War.

Reagan was, and remains, one of the most popular modern presidents. He won re-election in 1984 by a landslide and was succeeded in 1989 by his vice president, George H. Bush. Soon after he left office, Reagan was diagnosed with Alzheimer's disease, something from which he now acutely suffers, forcing him to end his public appearances. He now lives in Bel Air with his wife, Nancy.

Indian Tribes of Southern California

Humans likely first arrived in the area of present-day California 10,000 to 15,000 years ago, though anthropologists differ on the date. Once there, they were generally cut off from interaction with native peoples in neighboring regions by mountain and desert boundaries. Isolated, the varied tribes developed unique lifestyles fitted to their individual environments. The diverse climate and geography of California meant that many different cultures developed, from the seafaring Chumash to the mountain-dwelling Serrano. Evidence of precolonial Indian life can still be seen just northwest of Santa Barbara at the Chumash Painted Cave, and at other sites scattered around the state. Classification of the different California tribes has always been extremely complicated; most communities were organized by village, and allegiance to a larger tribal entity varied greatly. Colonization of the area further confused the issue as different Native American bands were lumped together into a mission or vanished under the threat of imported diseases. Names for tribal units are also vague and in coastal areas often just denote the mission to which the designated Indians belonged (i.e. the Gabrielino, Luiseño, and the Yuman subtribe the Diegueno).

For most native Californians, life was fairly idyllic. Resources were plentiful in the form of abundant edible plant life, most notably the acorn (a primary food source for nearly all California tribes). Oftentimes the acorn gathering festival in fall was an important ritual for the village community. Some tribes developed elaborate storage baskets, and most carved grinding bowls into stones. Evidence of these mortars can still be found today. Small and large mammals, birds, and fish were also readily available for consumption. Hunters used a variety of tools—bows and arrows, antler-tipped spears, and hemp snares were the most common.

Generally, native Californians did not practice agriculture until the arrival of the Spanish missionaries, but some forms of land management were common. Wild plants were often pruned to encourage growth, and forests and grasslands were burned to clear debris and open areas for hunting. These controlled burns also reduced the risk of dangerous wildfires, an occurrence now much feared throughout the western United States. The plant that was most commonly farmed among aboriginal residents of the state was tobacco, which was used to induce sleep and as a painkiller.

Life for Native Americans in California changed drastically with the arrival of Europeans and Americans. The population was decimated and traditional culture destroyed. In 1500, the aboriginal population of the state numbered an estimated 300,000; by 1900 it was one-tenth of that. Illness, starvation, and outright murder had killed untold thousands.

The eradication of the native peoples took place in two

waves. The first began in 1769, when Junípero Serra established the first of 21 Franciscan missions at San Diego de Alcala. The elaborate mission system, which extended along the coastal regions north to San Francisco Bay, sought to convert the inhabitants of the region to Catholicism and eventually to incorporate the Indians into the society of the Spanish Empire. The second aim failed; the first succeeded in varying degrees. Still, the missions changed the lives of the coastal Indians irrevocably. Spanish priests and the soldiers sent to protect them created epidemics of disease for which the long-isolated Californians had little natural defense. Smallpox and measles killed thousands and syphilis, often spread by forced sexual contact, resulted in the death or sterilization of many more.

The missions also altered the coastal environment by turning vast tracts of land into farms. The farms served to feed the missionaries and native populations, and their surplus provided for local soldiers and for trade with foreign visitors. Indeed, the constant supply of food helped draw many of the local Indians into the missions. However, huge herds of cattle and sheep now occupied land on which they had hunted game. Fields of corn and wheat took the place of native plants upon which Indians had depended for survival. Inhabitants of the regions around the missions were often left with little choice but to enter the religious communities. Once there, residents were forever indentured to the missions. Escapees were pursued with force. And, although forbidden to do so, bands of soldiers often brought back additional prisoners as well as fugitives, at times killing those who refused to come.

The second wave of intrusion began in earnest with the discovery of gold in 1848. The next few years saw an amazing influx of migrants, mostly from the Eastern states. The forty-niners settled in the gold-rich regions of Central and Northern California. Indians in these areas had been largely untouched by the Spanish missions but now faced white encroachment at its worse. Again, disease ravaged the population—one smallpox epidemic around Nevada City destroyed one-fifth of the region's native population. Despite California's admittance into the Union as a free state in 1850, Indians were often used as forced labor in the mines. In other instances, the native peoples of Central California were seen as an unwanted nuisance. Violence against Indians was largely condoned, and the indigenous tribes were often stripped of their traditional homelands without compensation.

Because of the speed with which the alterations in their life took place, or perhaps because the tribal groups were not unified, California's Indians presented little organized opposition to the white settlers. The revolt at San Diego in 1775 did not herald rebellion in other missions, and the Modoc War in the north of the state that raged from 1872 to 1873 was a small, isolated resistance. Instead, centuries-old cultures vanished silently from the California landscape. In a relatively short span of time, some of the most diverse and distinct aboriginal populations in the world disappeared, and others lost much of their unique identity. Unlike in other Western states, few reservations were established for the displaced Indians. Tribes were forced to struggle to preserve their traditional character. In 1969, a group of Native Americans calling themselves the Indians of All Tribes seized the abandoned federal prison on Alcatraz Island in San Francisco Bay, giving the plight of native peoples national attention once again. The remaining population of California Indians has survived much and endures to this day. In the 1980 census, California passed Oklahoma as the state with the highest population of Native Americans.

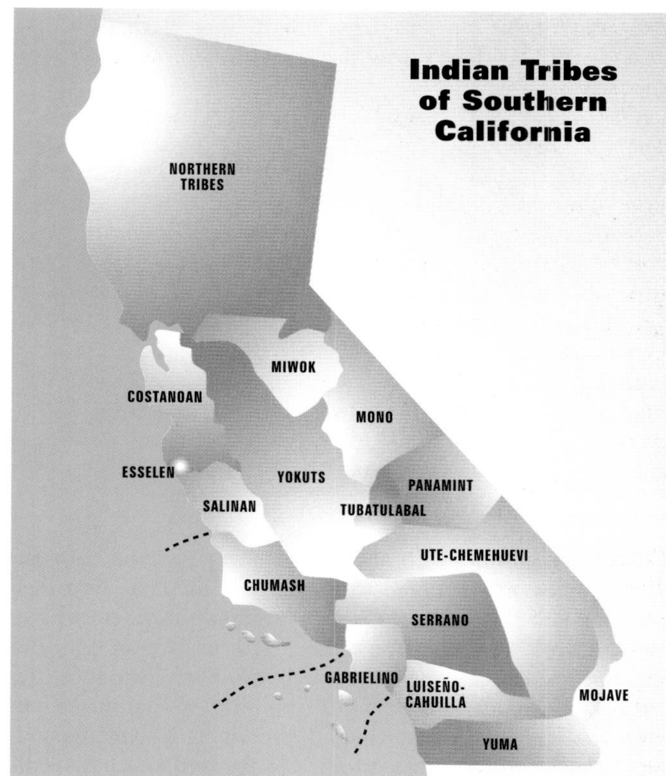

Miwok

The Miwok lived in Central California, predominantly in the western foothills of the Sierra Nevada. They also had relatives to the northwest, even as far as the Pacific Coast north of San Francisco Bay. The name Miwok merely means "people" in their Penutian dialect. The tribe was spread over more than 100 villages and numbered approximately 9,000 souls before European intrusion. There was no overall tribal leader and the society was apparently decentralized.

Like many other tribes in California, the Miwok valued the acorn as a valuable food source. They supplemented this item by collecting local plants and hunting small game and fish. The usual Miwok house consisted of a pole frame over which was spread grass or brush. Each village had an earth-covered assembly chamber where religious rituals and performances were held. The Miwok celebrated their beliefs with a variety of ceremonial dances, performed to the accompaniment of a large foot drum. Each dance had a different cast of characters, with performers dressing in feather costumes, animal skins, or paint. One common character was the *Wo'ochi*, a type of clown who would appear at interludes to shout *woo*.

Until the gold rush brought hordes of outsiders into their homeland, the Miwok had little interference from Europeans.

Miwok woman cooking acorn mash

Their relationship with the Spanish was peaceful, but the colonists never attempted to incorporate the tribe into their mission system. After the discovery of gold, however, the Miwok suffered great hardships. Their lack of immunity to European diseases left them extremely prone to introduced illnesses, and much of their population died as a result. Miners exploited the land upon which the surviving Miwok depended. Some prospectors, accustomed to the warlike tribes of the Great Plains, shot innocent Indians on sight. Eventually the Miwok became so enraged that they resisted the newcomers with force. Their uprising was known as the Mariposa War.

Miwok now inhabit three small reservations in California—Jackson Rancheria, Sheep Ranch Rancheria, and Tuolomne Rancheria.

Costanoan

The Costanoan occupied a large area of the central California coast, from San Francisco Bay south to Point Sur. Their name is derived from the Spanish *costaños*, meaning "coast people." Most of the tribe's villages were situated near the ocean shore or along inland rivers. Some settlements had thatched assembly houses that could seat up to 200 people and large ritual dance enclosures surrounded by a circular brush fence. Tribesmen generally wore no clothes; women wore a short deerskin skirt. Facial tattooing in the form of a row of dots was customary for females.

The Pacific was an important source of food for the Costanoan. Early explorers saw tribe members navigating the waters of San Francisco Bay in small tule rafts. The ocean waters provided oysters, clams, mussels, crabs, and other shellfish. Mounds of discarded shells up to 30 feet high can still be seen along the central California coast. This is debris piled up over centuries of feasts.

The Costanoan also supplemented their diet by hunting small game and gathering a variety of plants. As was the case for many California Indians, the staple food was the acorn. The Costanoan calendar was based on counting the number of months, or "moons," since the autumn acorn harvest, and anticipating the number of months until the next one. The harvest was the central event in Costanoan life. Several villages would camp together in the oak groves while the nuts were collected. The whole population worked from sunrise to sunset gathering the acorns. Young boys would climb trees to shake acorns down and the smallest children would join in collecting them. At night, the gathered tribe members would celebrate with dancing and feasting. Men from the villages took advantage of the congregation to trade and gamble. The harvest festival was also important for adolescent courtship, and many marriages were arranged during its brief duration.

The pre-colonial Costanoan population was probably about 7,000. The population was greatly reduced during the period of Spanish missions. Five Franciscan settlements were established on Costanoan land. Eventually the whole tribe was subjected to Christian conversion. Soldiers would hunt down runaways from the missions and often forced other Indians to join against their will. European disease killed thousands of Coastanoan. By the time Mexican rulers secularized the missions, many Costanoan had died and their way of life was lost forever.

Mono

The Mono Indians of California were part of a larger group of Paiute Indians known as the Northern Paiute. Northern Paiute Indians ranged over northwest Nevada, eastern Oregon, southern Idaho and parts of eastern California. The Northern Paiute of Central California were known as Mono; the origin of this name is unknown.

The Mono probably numbered about 6,000 souls before the gold rush. Most lived in the Great Basin area around Mono Lake and the Owens Valley. Others lived in the high Sierra Nevada of Central California. The Mono were probably relatively new to California compared to other tribes, having moved into the area from Nevada.

Mono Indians in Owens Valley and around Mono Lake lived an itinerant lifestyle. They moved constantly in search of seasonal foods—pine nuts, grass seeds, and fish. Their possessions were light and portable—carrying baskets, bows and arrows, and rabbit blankets. The Mono supplemented their diet by hunting creatures ranging in size from insects to bighorn sheep.

Little was recorded of aboriginal Mono culture, although evidence suggests it was influenced by the neighboring Yokuts

Mono basket maker

A Mono windbreak shelter erected for field collecting

tribe. Pottery and basketry similar to that of the Yokuts has been excavated in Mono territory.

One notable Paiute Indian, Wovoka (or Jack Wilson) from Nevada, is responsible for creating the Ghost Dance in 1888. This mystical religion uses chanting and dancing in a spiritual cleansing of self. It prophesies an end to the white man and his reign over the land, and an eventual return of the Indians and the buffalo. The religion caught on with many other tribes throughout the West and has even excited the curiosity of mystics outside of Indian cultures. Attempts to ban the Ghost Dance resulted in the last significant Indian violence of the century, culminating in the massacre of Wounded Knee (1890).

The Mono in the Sierra Nevada suffered persecution during the gold rush, but the Mono population has never been endangered. Sizeable numbers of present-day Californians still identify themselves as Mono. The tribe has given its name to a county and a lake in California.

Yokuts

The Yokuts occupied the San Joaquin Valley and the western Sierra Nevada foothills. They were not a centralized tribal unit but rather were organized into at least 50 "tribelets," themselves divided into several villages. The tribelets were united by a common language, culture, and religion, although disagreement among groups led to intratribal warfare at times. Total aboriginal population was probably in excess of 15,000.

The Yokuts' diet was fairly omnivorous. They ate a variety of small game, including skunks, which many tribes shunned. They fished the streams and rivers and collected many wild plant foods, most importantly the acorn. They were also adept at catching birds. A Yokuts prayer, invoked before killing an eagle, has been recorded: "Do not think I will hurt you/ You will have a new body/ Now turn your head northward and lie flat." Yokuts agriculture was very limited, although they undoubtedly exercised passive control over their environment. One crop planted was tobacco, which was smoked as a painkiller, as a soporific, or in rituals. The Yokuts interacted with neighboring tribes, influencing the Salinan and Tubatulabal and trading melons, pigment, tobacco, herbs, and salt with the Chumash.

The Yokuts are generally recognized as superb artisans. Their basketry is exemplary, they drew elaborate pictographs on rocks, and they fashioned tule rafts on which they explored river valleys. One Yokuts band, the Choinimni, built huge floating barges, 50 feet in width, upon which whole families could live for long expeditions. Other bands constructed large thatch buildings, 35 feet long and 12 feet high, the largest of their kind in North America. In summer, villagers might construct tule shade mats; sometimes mats would cover the entire settlement.

The Yokuts were quite religious. Families would mourn their dead in weeklong ceremonies. Another surviving prayer was invoked during cremation: "You are going to another land/ You will like that land/ You will not stay here." After the ceremony, it was forbidden to speak the name of the deceased. Young men were initiated into adulthood in a *toloache*-drinking ritual, during which they drank the powerful hallucinogen jimson weed.

Yokuts culture was largely unaffected by Spanish missions, but it was devastated by the gold rush. Much of the Yokuts territory was part of the Mother Lode, the area richest in the precious metal. Prospectors stole Yokuts land, plundered the natural resources, and at times even enslaved Yokuts for mine labor. In 1850, together with the Miwok, the Yokuts fought in one of the few California Indian wars, the Mariposa War. The combined bands attacked mining camps and trading posts in Central California before the uprising was quashed by a volunteer battalion.

Yokuts women with baskets, perhaps collecting mushrooms

Today, the surviving Yokuts live on two reservations—the Santa Rosa Rancheria and the Tule River Indian Reservation. Tribe members still come together annually for traditional ceremonies.

Esselen

Little is known today about the Esselen. They were a small tribal group whose homeland was located on Central California's coast, just south of present-day Big Sur. Nearly all of their territory was rocky and mountainous, so it is unlikely that the group occupied more than a few villages. The land would have supported some small game and fishing opportunities, as well as acorns and a variety of other edible plants.

Most of what we know about the Esselen comes from their language. It was a Hokan dialect, as were the languages spoken by the Salinan and the Chumash. Nevertheless, the Esselen language was sufficiently different from these related tongues to imply a separate and perhaps earlier migration into California. Linguists also speculate that the Esselen once occupied a significantly larger area of land, although the cause of territorial shrinkage is unknown.

The Esselen were incorporated into the Carmel mission. Their small population shrank further and intermingled with neighboring tribes to such an extent that they are often described as the first California tribe to become extinct.

Salinan

To the north of the Chumash lived the Indian tribe we know as the Salinan, a name that refers to the river that drained the bulk of their territory; their actual name has long been forgotten. When Spanish explorers first contacted them in 1769, the Salinan numbered approximately 2,000, scattered in 20 or more villages near the Pacific Coast in present-day San Luis Obispo County and southern Monterey County. They spoke a Hokan dialect similar to that of the Chumash and Esselen. Despite this, they held closer ties to the inland Yokuts than to either of the coastal tribes. The Costanoan, who lived to the north of the Salinan, were considered enemies. Much of Salinan culture was influenced by the Yokuts. Salinan basketry shows much Yokuts influence, as do their reed smoking pipes and grooved arrow straighteners, and several of their recorded rituals.

The Salinan built boats with which they negotiated coastal inlets, streams, and rivers. Unlike the Chumash, they generally refrained from seafaring. Instead they hunted a variety of land mammals; almost all species were eaten, with the exception of the skunk. They also caught birds and fish. In addition to meat, the Salinan gathered acorns, clover, berries, grasses, pine nuts, chia, wild oats, and other plant life.

The Salinan were brought into the Spanish mission system in the late 1700s. Two missions were established for the tribe—San Antonio and San Miguel. The effect of the missions was to submerge traditional customs into Christian beliefs. By the time the missions ceased to exist, Salinan culture had been effectively extinguished. A century later, in 1925, only 40 tribal members remained.

Chumash

The Chumash were the first of California's tribes encountered by Europeans. Portuguese conquistador Juan Rodriguez Cabrillo (see page 70) landed in Chumash territory in 1542. At that time, the tribal group, a network of 75 to 100 villages united by common language and culture, numbered between 20,000 and 30,000 members. They inhabited a 7,000-square-mile region of Southern California, along the shore between present-day San Luis Obispo and Ventura, on several of the Channel Islands, and inland along the streams and valleys of what is now Santa Barbara County. The Chumash are thought to have entered California quite early, perhaps 10,000 years ago. The last 1,000 years of pre-colonial Chumash civilization was a golden age for the culture, and evidence of their expressive artwork can be seen scattered around their ancestral homeland, most famously at Painted Cave northwest of Santa Barbara.

The Chumash survived by exploiting the abundant resources of this region. They were the best seafarers of the California Indians and stood alone among those tribes in their use of boats made out of conjoined plants, instead of carved tree trunks or hide-covered frames. From these boats, the Chumash caught ocean fish using both nets and spears. They made harpoons by putting an antler tip or bone on a wooden spear and tying a string to it. With these weapons they hunted sea otters, seals, and sea lions.

The Chumash were technically advanced when compared to their neighbors. Spanish missionaries viewed them as the most "civilized" of the various mission tribes. The British Museum in London has preserved a Chumash bow, harpoon, and spear-thrower obtained by George Vancouver on an early expedition in the Pacific. All three weapons reveal a craftsmanship superior to that of other Southern California tribes. Chumash basketry and stone working were also quite advanced.

Chumash village of Wihatset

Five Spanish missions were established on Chumash territory—San Buenaventura, Santa Barbara, Santa Inés, La Purísma Conception, and San Luis Obispo. Though the tribe was apparently quite receptive to Spanish influence, mission life seems to have somewhat demoralized the Chumash. Missionaries complained that abortion became alarmingly common among the tribe. Clearly the Indians were reluctant to bring new members into a world so removed from their traditional life. Secularization of the missions only led to disorder for the Chumash, and by the time California became a U.S. state in 1850, their survivors were scattered and few. Nevertheless, there remain today a relatively large number of people who claim at least partial Chumash ancestry.

Tubatulabal

The Tubatulabal tribe lived in a small, landlocked domain in Central California along the Kern River, near present-day Bakersfield. Though their culture largely disappeared after European-American entry into California, the linguistic evidence implies that the tribe inhabited the same area for many millennia. The transcribed words that survive to this day are unlike those of their neighbors, such as the Yokuts, the Mono, the Chemehuevi, and the Panamint. Though their native terrain goes some way toward explaining this phenomenon, ethnologists also conclude that the Tubatulabal's ancestors came to California in an earlier, separate migration.

The area in which they settled, around the Kern River and its forks, was pleasant and fertile. Most Tubatulabal villages were situated along the water in clean-cut valleys high in the mountains. Today, the Kern River waters have been drawn off into irrigation canals and ditches, and the Tulare Lake, into which it flowed, has mainly disappeared. In the Tubatulabal's time, however, the waters were abundant with fish, which was a major component of the Indians' diet. This was supplemented with a variety of small game and plants. In all, the region probably supported about 1,000 people before European contact.

Little is recorded of Tubatulabal society. Interaction and intermarriage with the larger Yokuts tribe were common, and the smaller tribe's culture took on many attributes of the larger. Basketry and pottery followed Yokuts design, and the Tubatulabal also buried their dead. One remarkable activity in Tubatulabal society was the keeping of pets. Young eagles were caught and tamed, but later released unharmed. Condors, crows, hawks, geese, and even young coyotes were all kept as lifelong companions, in some cases even inherited when their keeper died. The religious practices of the tribe are scarcely recorded, although a female coming of age ceremony has been described. Mourning ceremonies were also important, and could last for up to two years after the death of a person of importance. Unfortunately, fewer than 100 Tubatulabal remained by the end of the nineteenth century. Today, the tribe has been lost as a distinct entity.

Panamint

The Panamint Indians lived along the present-day California-Nevada border, in Death Valley, and in the Panamint Mountains to which they gave their name. This area was indubitably the most inhospitable of any native homelands in California. In many cases the land was inhabitable only at isolated oases. For this reason, the native Panamint population was small, perhaps as few as 500 souls.

The Panamint survived in the harsh environment by utilizing every resource available. They were part of the group of Ute Indians (like their relatives, the Ute-Chemehuevi) who became known to white settlers by the derisive term "digger Indians." They got this name because of the long pointed sticks they used to dig for roots and vegetation. Their diet consisted of roots, seeds, and nuts. Acorns, the principal food source for many California Indians, were unavailable in the Panamint land, and were partly replaced by pine nuts. Meat, too, was scarce in the tribe's homeland, but the Panamint ate rabbits, rats, lizards, squirrels, insects, and grubs when available. Desert vegetation requires more preparation than other plants. The Panamint learned how to boil, wash, or squeeze the yuccas, prickly pear joints, and crucifers that they ate, in order to remove the bitter and dehydrating salts.

Panamint Indians used plants for more than just food. They wove baskets tight enough to hold water when treated. They constructed hemp carrying nets and rarely went anywhere without their bows and arrows. The bow was generally made of juniper, with a hemp string. The arrows were willow or cane with a sharpened greasewood tip. Panamint clothing was either simple or absent, but they did value the large eagle-quill headbands for which Native Americans are stereotypically famous. Because the tribe was so isolated, they were little affected by colonial civilization. Nevertheless, their small population dwindled, and little remains of their culture today.

Chemehuevi mother with a child

Ute-Chemehuevi

The Chemehuevi are members of the Paiute family of Indians. The Paiute Indians, one of the Shoshonean subdivisions, included many bands scattered over a vast area from present-day Arizona to Oregon. The Chemehuevi name comes from a Yuman word for Paiute. The Chemehuevi referred to themselves as *Nuwu*, meaning "the people."

The territory of the Chemehuevi was one of the largest of any occupied by California's Indians, but it was also mostly inhospitable desert. Much of their population, perhaps 1,000 people, was concentrated near the Colorado River. The Chemehuevi were separated from other California tribes by vast deserts and mountains, so their culture was more similar to Indians in the Southwest.

The Chemehuevi were semi-nomadic hunter-gatherers, so the dwellings they constructed were often temporary. Their architecture was similar to that of the Apache wickiup—huts of brush spread over pole frames. A village consisted of up to ten of these houses. Each band elected its own leader; the tribe had no overall chief.

Religion and ceremonies were important to the Chemehuevi. Funerals could last up to four days, with mourning rituals continuing for up to a year. Both sexes adorned themselves with tattoos and piercings. Indeed, Paiutes believed that the dead could not pass into the next world without an ear piercing.

Abandoned Chemehuevi dwelling

In 1907, the United States government set aside a reservation for the Chemehuevi on the California side of the Colorado River, northwest of Parker, Arizona. In 1938, the reservation's area was effectively reduced when it was flooded after the construction of the Parker Dam. Many Chemehuevi moved to the Colorado River Indian Reservation, which straddles the river downstream near Parker. The relatively undeveloped Chemehuevi Indian Reservation offers a striking contrast to the expanding settlement of Lake Havasu City, Arizona, across the river, and home of the imported "London Bridge."

Serrano

Serrano is a broad term applied to the collection of similar subtribes and bands who inhabited the area of Southern California around the San Gabriel Mountains. The various bands spoke different dialects of the Shoshonean language groups. Most of these dialects became extinct some time ago. The name Serrano is derived from Spanish and means "mountaineers," or more specifically "those of the Sierra."

The Serrano were incorporated into the Franciscan mission system quite early. Once missionized, they were forced to converse in Spanish and adopt imported Iberian farming techniques. For this reason, much evidence of their aboriginal culture has been lost. Like other California Indians, the Serrano also suffered from European disease epidemics.

Some aspects of Serrano culture are known to modern ethnologists, largely from the accounts of Spanish priests. Francisco Garcés (see page 72) first encountered the tribe in 1776. He described small villages of 25 to 80 people. Often the entire settlement would live in a single square communal house. Each family had its own room, complete with a separate door and a fireplace. The rooms opened out into a central courtyard, but not to the outside of the house. The courtyard had two entrances, with guards posted at each.

For sustenance, the Serrano grew a variety of plants; beans, grapes, and acorns were among the most important. They fashioned snares from wild hemp plants, with which they captured small game. Garcés relates that the tribe members also ate tobacco, apparently to relieve fatigue. Serrano pottery was reportedly quite impressive, although no examples have survived.

The entire Serrano population at the time of European contact was small, perhaps as low as 1,500. The tribe had no chief, and subtribes often fought each other. Villages were headed by a *kika*, who was assisted by a *pala*, the positions being inherited along different family lines. Interestingly, Serrano villages were all labeled as either "wild cat" or "coyote" settlements, and each had a corresponding totem design. Members of the two designations would taunt each other. To their opposites, "wild cats" were stereotypically dull and lazy, whereas "coyotes" were stereotypically swift but unreliable.

Following the break-up of the missions, the Serrano received several large land grants from the Mexican authorities. Although they subsequently lost much of this land, some of it is retained to this day. In the 1900 census, the Serrano population was just 100, but it has rebounded somewhat in the last century.

Gabrielino mortar for pounding acorns

Gabrielino

The Gabrielino were named after the mission of San Gabriel, situated outside present-day Los Angeles. Traditionally, they inhabited the fertile area of Southern California around present-day Los Angeles County and into Orange County. Gabrielino also lived on the coastal islands of Santa Catalina and San Clemente. They developed quite an advanced culture, one that influenced surrounding tribes. In particular, many of the religious beliefs and practices of Southern California Indians are thought to have originated with the Gabrielino. The ritualistic drinking of hallucinogenic *toloache* (jimson weed) started in the islands of Santa Catalina and San Clemente and spread throughout the region. Associated Gabrielino deities were worshiped by other tribes; some even sang their ritual songs in the Gabrielino language, a tongue they would not have understood. *Toloache* was mixed with salt water, and in addition to its spiritual qualities, it was valued as a strength-giver and as a hunting aid.

Gabrielino houses were pole-framed and covered in grass mats. Like other native Californians, the Gabrielino also built sweathouses, which they heated by fire and smoke. Their homeland was very fertile, and the tribe collected a variety of plants, including the ubiquitous acorn. The Gabrielino were unique among California's Indians in that they ground acorns in portable stone mortars, instead of ones in carved rock. They also manufactured different types of bowls and goblets from steatite. Gabrielino domain reached the ocean, and the Indians utilized the Pacific's vast resources. They dug for clams, netted fish in the ocean's waves, and pulled mussels from rocks at low tide.

Compared to other tribes in California, the Gabrielino were quite violent and often attacked other tribes. The tribe possessed two unique weapons. The most common was the war club—really just a heavy, carved stick. The other, more often used for hunting, was called a *makana*. This was a curved throwing stick, similar to the boomerangs used by aboriginal Australians. In 1785, a young Gabrielino woman named Toypurina led six Indian groups in an attack on Mission San Gabriel. The raid was the largest in the history of the Spanish missions and resulted in the deaths of all the priests and resident soldiers. The Spanish troops stationed several miles away never heard the attack. Nevertheless, the uprising did not last and Gabrielino culture was soon submerged into the mission system. Today, most of the remaining evidence of this once flourishing society comes from reports written by early Spanish priests.

Luiseño

Midway between Los Angeles and San Diego is the ancestral homeland of the Luiseño. The Luiseño, named after Mission San Luis Rey de Francia (Spanish for "the mission of Saint Louis, king of France"), are part of the Shoshonean, Takic-speaking group, whose ancestors probably came to California about 7,000 or 8,000 years ago. The Luiseño were among the earliest California tribes contacted by Europeans, and they became integrated into the mission system when Mission San Luis Rey was established in 1798.

This mission was quite successful and pleasant compared to others in New Spain, largely because of the foresight and compassion of its head priest, Father Antonio Peyri. During his time in California, Peyri noticed that Spanish missions generally had two-thirds more burials than baptisms. He sought to reverse this trend and implemented a series of measures to do so. He demanded that his Indian neophytes take daily baths. Although it was an alien concept to the Indians, the public baths (one for men, one for women) soon became a favorite spot among mission residents. Peyri also had special agents watch for any sickness among the population. When an Indian became ill, he was hurried to a special sick-wing and cordoned off from the rest of the mission. The Luiseño at San Luis Rey lived in small individual huts around the grounds. When someone died in a hut, the entire structure was burned and a new one built. These measures led to the mission being the most populous and perhaps most successful of all the California missions.

uiseño woman with pots

Even before Christian penetration into their homeland, religion was an integral part of Luiseño culture. Shamanism was widely practiced, the main ritual being a rain dance. The tribe believed that the world was created by two deities, Brother Sky and Sister Earth. Changichngish, an imported deity from the island Gabrielinos, was important to the Luiseño. Tied into *toloache*-drinking rituals (see section on Gabrielino), Changichngish was an all-powerful being, not unlike the Christian God. He was believed to have molded the first humans out of riverbank clay—one male, one female. Changichngish's teachings were also a moral compass for the Luiseño; they believed that he punished the wicked and rewarded the good. Despite this religion's similarities to Christianity, mission priests decried it as paganistic Satanism. Nevertheless, the Luiseño arranged secret meetings and managed to preserve a cultural continuity that outlasted the missions.

Today, the Luiseño number around 3,000 and are one of the largest Indian communities in Southern California, with numbers that rival pre-European populations. Most Luiseño live on reservations, where they preserve many ancient traditions, rituals, and their language as well. Luiseño reservations include La Jolla, Pala, Pauma, Pechanga, and Rincon.

Cahuilla

The ancestral homeland of the Cahuilla, east of present-day Los Angeles, included parts of the Mojave Desert and the Salton Sink. Cahuilla is probably a Spanish name, although its origins are unknown. Like the Luiseño, the Cahuilla are part of a Shoshonean, Takic-speaking group. Unlike the Luiseño, the Cahuilla largely escaped European influence during the mission period, although Spanish soldiers did sometimes enter Cahuilla land looking for runaway Indians or seeking to capture new recruits for the mission at San Luis Rey.

Although they were never part of the mission system, the Cahuilla suffered from European presence. Eighty percent of their population died of imported diseases, and the tribe endured hardships under Mexican rule of California. The land grants of the new regime robbed the Indians of much of their land, and Mexican landowners used the native population as virtual slave labor, treating them much worse than the Spanish priests ever did.

Their plight did not change much under United States rule, and by the 1870s the tribe had lost almost all of its native land. However, in 1875, President Ulysses S. Grant created several reservations for the group. The reservations varied in size, from the relatively large Agua Caliente Indian Reservation to the small, village-size San Pasquat.

With a legal land base, the Cahuilla have flourished. Today the Cahuilla number about 2,500, a figure that rivals their pre-European population. On reservations, the Cahuilla have fought to preserve their culture and language. Cahuilla vocabulary indicates the importance of family ties to the tribe. The language has at least 65 terms to distinguish family relationship (like "father," "aunt," or "great-grandmother" in English). The Cahuilla also have a telling saying: "I am related everywhere."

The Cahuilla have always been active in the struggle for Native American rights. In 1964, Cahuilla tribal leader Rupert Costo formed the American Indian Historical Society. The society pushed for, and achieved, changes in California school history textbooks to more accurately communicate the plight of the state's Native Americans to young Californians. It also established several museums and cultural centers, including the Malki Museum on the Morongo Indian Reservation, the first of its type in California.

Kumeyaay

The Indians who lived in present-day Imperial and San Diego Counties called themselves the Kumeyaay. In 1769, Spanish missionaries led by Junípero Serra established the first mission within modern California's borders. Serra named the mission San Diego, and the Kumeyaay who were converted

A Kumeyaay woman grinding clay to make pottery, circa 1928

there were known as the Diegueno. The tribal names are generally considered synonymous. Like the Colorado River Yuma, who spoke a similar language, the Diegueno were a proud people.

The mission at San Diego was not very successful. Indians in the area largely resisted Spanish influence, and in their first year at the mission, Franciscan priests were unable to baptize a single person. The mission was attacked several times during its 65-year existence. A revolt in 1775 led to the deaths of three Spaniards, including one priest. Another uprising in 1826 resulted in the deaths of 26 Kumeyaay.

The population at the mission never exceeded 3,000. The San Diego mission did not control as large an area as other Franciscan settlements in California. This was partially because of the determination of the Diegueno, but also because the area was unsuitable to the large-scale agriculture practiced at the other missions.

Before Spanish influence, the Kumeyaay spoke a Yuman dialect, but differed culturally in many ways from the Yuma. They followed the *toloache*-drinking rituals that originated with the Gabrielino. Many Kumeyaay songs were sung in the Gabrielino language. New Kumeyaay parents (both mother and father) had a taboo against working or eating meat for a month after the birth of a child.

The southeastern bands of Kumeyaay who escaped Spanish influence preserved tribal customs better than bands nearer the coast. Even missionized Kumeyaay were more independent than tribes on other Franciscan missions. Their population was not depleted as much as that of other California tribes. In the years after California became part of the United States, the Kumeyaay were given control of several small reservations. Today, the Kumeyaay Nation holds thirteen rancherias, small reservations, in San Diego County and another four in Baja California.

Yuma (Quechan)

The Yuma, or Quechan as they prefer to be called, trace their ancestral home to a sacred mountain near Needles, California, called Avikwamé. Sometime before Spanish explorers made contact with the tribe in 1540, they moved to the area around the confluence of the Colorado and Gila Rivers and controlled the Yuma crossing, an important passage across the Colorado River.

Conditions in the region were harsh; temperatures often exceeded 100 degrees Fahrenheit. The Quechan lived along the banks of the river, moving to higher lands to avoid spring floods. Their dwellings varied from open, rectangular structures to Apache-like wickiups. They supplemented their diet of fish and wild plants by farming corn, beans, squash, and grasses in the silt left over from floods.

In the late 1700s, Spanish missionaries established two settlements near Yuma crossing. Soldiers from the missions mistreated the Indians, stealing food, supplies, and land. On July 17, 1781, Chief Palma and his brother Ygnacio Palma led their people in a revolt. Local settlements were burned to the ground and about 95 priests, settlers, and soldiers were killed. The Yuma rebellion shut down the Spanish route into Alta California that had been created by Juan Bautista de Anza. Spanish soldiers tried to regain the lost land, but the Quechan fought them off and were never subdued.

By the 1840s, Americans began to pass through Quechan territory. At first, the Quechan were able to exploit the situation, charging travelers for passage across the Colorado River. However, non-Indian ferry companies soon challenged Quechan control of the crossing. When Indians attacked a rival ferryman, a California lawyer named John C. Morehead raised a volunteer militia and destroyed Quechan crops and boats. Skirmishes between Indians and travelers became frequent. Those who traversed the Yuma crossing did so with trepidation. Fort Yuma was built in 1850 to quell the situation, but a poor supply line and frequent attacks led to its abandonment. Not until the following year did a stronger garrison return to secure the crossing.

Quechan Yellow Sky on left

In 1884, the Quechan were put on a reservation along the Colorado River. Later, the Cocopah Reservation was established for them in 1917. Since then, the Quechan have had to continually battle for land. By the 1950s, the federal government had taken or sold 8,500 acres of Quechan territory. Twenty-five thousand acres of land were returned to the reservation in 1978, but the 1,000 remaining Indians still fight for water rights.

Mojave (Mohave)

The Mojave Desert, named after this Southwestern tribe, is one of the harshest environments in the United States. Temperatures regularly exceed 100°F during the day, then drop sharply at night. The Mojave adapted to the tough conditions

Lithograph of three Mojave Indians in body paint

by settling along the banks of the lower Colorado River, an area they occupy to this day. Mojave Indians call themselves the *aha macave (*meaning "people along the water"). Near the river they were able to farm corn, pumpkins, squash, melons, and (after Spanish influence permeated the area) wheat. The runoff from melting snows in the Rocky Mountains into the Colorado River flooded their lands annually, and they adjusted their crop cycles accordingly, producing double harvests of many crops. The Mojave supplemented their diet with local game, nuts, and protein-rich fish.

Traditionally, the Mojave lived in two types of dwellings constructed from brush and earth. For the winter months they built low rectangular houses; in the summer they made open flat-roofed structures. They dressed in sandals and rabbit skin robes. Both males and females took pride in body art, adorning their bodies with tattoos and body paint. The Mojave were very interested in dreams. Interpretations of dreams exerted influence over much of their daily life.

A traditional Mojave boy's cradle board (left) has feathers; girl's (right) has red cloth and beads

One of the Mojave's first contacts with Europeans came when Spanish explorer Juan de Oñate met with them on January 25, 1605. The Mojave Indians regaled the conquistador with strange stories, which Oñate's companion Escobar jotted down in his journal. They told about a rich island on Lake Copalla where the people wore gold bracelets, and another island whose fat, big-footed queen ruled over a tribe of bald-headed men. The stories became more and more fantastic; the most bizarre was about a tribe that purposely slept underwater. By the time Oñate left, his head was full of outlandish visions of the New World, and the Indians had eaten half of his party's horses.

However, much of the Mojave's contact with white men was less friendly. They became known as the "wild Indians" because of their frequent raids on Spanish settlers. With the Mexican Cession of 1848, and the California gold rush of the following year, more Americans were traveling through Mojave territory. When Captain Lorenzo Sitgreaves surveyed the land in 1851, the Indians attacked, killing one member of his party and wounding another. Mojave were also responsible for many ambushes and slaughters along the Beale Wagon Road. In 1858, members of the tribe massacred a group of immigrants, killing nine and wounding sixteen. In response, Fort Mohave was created and the Indian raids were steadily reduced.

The Mojave never signed an official treaty with the government, and they continue to live on and have rights to their homeland on the Colorado River. A congressional act in 1934 officially recognized the Fort Mojave Indian Reservation and the Colorado River Indian Reservation, though the sites were laid out as early as 1865. Today, most of the 2,900 Mojave live on the two reservations, along the California-Arizona border, or on the Fort McDowell Reservation in Maricopa County, Arizona.

Events

Painted Cave and Chumash Rock Art

The Chumash Indians prospered for thousands of years along the south-central coast of California. Although Chumash populations dwindled and much of their cultural identity was lost during the period of Spanish missions, the tribe left an indelible mark on the California landscape in the form of several cave paintings. In order to protect these historical treasures, state authorities generally refrain from releasing their locations. One notable exception is Painted Cave, in the hills above Santa Barbara.

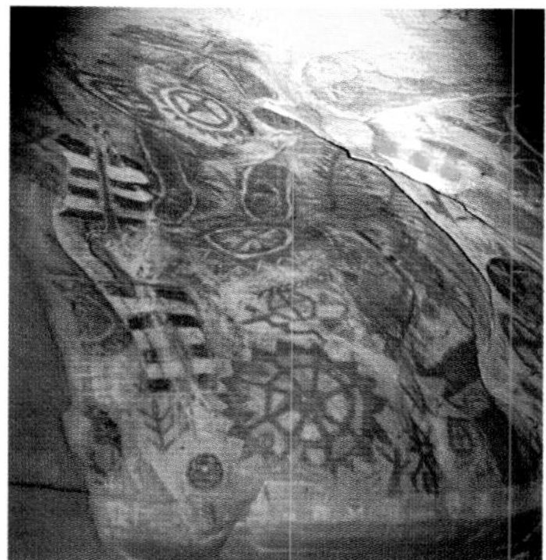
Rock art at Painted Cave

Painted Cave was likely a religious site, with drawings representing spiritual themes. The painting also appears to mark the winter solstice; a triangular beam of light shines onto the panel on the first day of winter each year. One theory, supported by dating of the paint substances, claims that the central black disc outlined in white commemorated a solar eclipse that took place on November 24, 1677. Other symbols include wheels, halos, crosses, horned animals, humans, and fantastical beasts.

Most Chumash paintings were drawn on sandstone cave walls using natural materials. Red paint was made from hematite, an iron oxide; black paint was made from charcoal or manganese oxide. The pigments were mixed with animal fat or plant juices and the resulting substance was applied to the rock using fingers or brushes made from feathers or animal tails. At other times, the pigment was dried and applied directly as a type of chalk.

The Painted Cave can be viewed, free of charge, every day in the Chumash Painted Cave State Historic Park. The cave is protected by a gate, but the paintings are clearly visible from outside. Some visitors claim that at sunrise and sunset, the echoes of bone flutes and soft chanting resound around the painted walls. Painted Cave can be found along Central Mountains #33: Big Caliente Spring Trail.

Era of the Spanish and Mexican Missions and Presidios

By 1769, Spain had claimed California as part of New Spain for more than 200 years. Despite this, no Spaniards had visited the land they knew as Alta California since Vizcaíno's voyage in 1602. But when Russian trappers began to visit North America's Pacific shores in search of furs, Spanish officials decided the area needed to be placed under firmer imperial control. For this and other reasons, Father Junípero Serra and his civilian counterpart, Governor Gaspar de Portolá, were sent from Mexico to establish a series of Franciscan missions and related presidios.

Two land parties and two sea parties left La Paz, on the Gulf of California, after arranging to meet in San Diego Bay. In July 1769, after months of hard traveling, the four parties met on the shore of California. Of the 219 men who had departed, only about a hundred had survived, and many of those were exhausted and sick. Father Serra was undeterred. On July 16, 1769, he erected a tall wooden cross on a hill overlooking the bay. In doing so, he established San Diego de Alcalá, the first of 21 missions in California. By the time Serra built his first brushwood church, Portolá was already marching north in search of Monterey Bay.

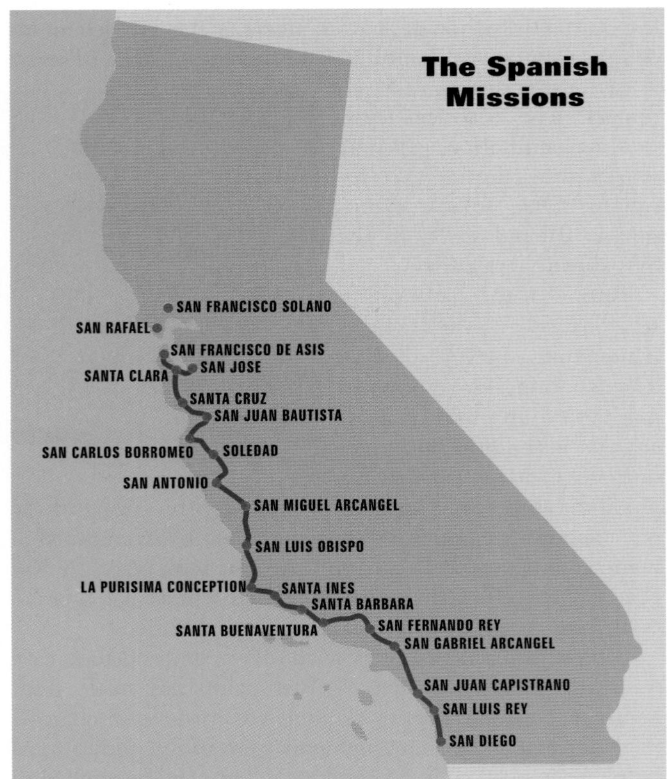

Chain of missions during the period of Spanish rule (1769–1821)

When Portolá returned to San Diego six months later after failing to find the elusive bay, the mission was in dire straits. Serra's attempts to befriend the local Indians had failed. He had tried handing out food and beads, but this only encouraged the Indians to raid the vulnerable settlement. Food and supplies were running dangerously low, and 19 graves had already been filled. Not a single Indian had been persuaded to convert to Christianity. Portolá's men were also suffering after their long, unsuccessful journey. The governor wanted to return to Mexico; Serra persuaded him to wait for a supply ship. On the very last night before they were due to depart, the *San Antonio's* sail appeared on the horizon; the Franciscan presence in Alta California was saved.

Leaving Father Jayme in charge of the Mission San Diego, which was moved 6 miles upstream to more fertile soil, Serra sailed north in another attempt to find Monterey Bay. Portolá reached the bay first, by land, and this time he recognized it. He began construction of a presidio, or fort, where soldiers could be stationed to protect a nearby mission and secure the Spanish claim to the land. Three more military presidios were eventually built in California. Father Serra decided to build the second California mission a few miles from the bay, in the Carmel Valley. San Carlos Borromeo was officially established on June 3, 1770. It was here that Serra would spend the majority of his time as the leader of the California missions, until his death in 1784.

Serra went on to establish another seven missions and traveled thousands of miles along El Camino Real. (Spanish for "the King's Highway," El Camino Real was the name given to the trail that connected the various missions.) By the time of his death, many of the settlements had begun to flourish. The Spanish were becoming accustomed to California's climate and growth cycles. Indians started to enter the missions, encouraged by the ready supply of food. Sturdy adobe buildings replaced crude brushwood structures. Three civilian pueblos had also been established, at San Luis Obispo (1772), San Juan Capistrano (1776), and Los Angeles (1781). Four more were added after Serra's death.

Life at the missions was often hard. Supply ships came infrequently, and the settlements were forced to be self-sufficient. Workdays were long and hard, especially for Native Americans unused to agricultural labor. Discipline was strictly enforced by whipping and daily life was rigorously regimented. Any neophyte (as the Indian converts were called) who attempted to escape was tracked down and returned to the mission. Sanitation was also a problem and many Indians, with no immunity to European ailments, died of imported diseases. Treatment of neophytes by nearby soldiers was harsh, to the dismay of most priests. Rape of Indian women was not uncommon.

Recent historians have strongly criticized the Franciscan mission system in California for squashing native culture and oppressing Indian converts. Although it is true that the neophytes were viewed with condescension by their Spanish guardians, it should be remembered that most of the priests were genuinely concerned about their subjects' welfare. Treatment of the California Indians is abhorrent when viewed through modern eyes, but the flagellation, poor sanitation, and cultural elitism were standard practice in the eighteenth century. Also, most Indians entered the mission system voluntarily and some settlements, notably San Gabriel Arcángel near Los Angeles, developed quite large populations. Nevertheless, the missions indisputably had a devastating effect on the culture of coastal Indian tribes, much as the gold rush would destroy the inland tribes decades later. Traditional practices were forgotten, populations were decimated, and at least one cultural group, the Esselen, was lost forever.

The breakup of the mission system, which came after Mexican independence from Spain in 1821, only exacerbated the Indians' problems. The government ceded large tracts of mission land to civilian settlers, who stole much more. Some Indians worked on the new Mexican ranches, often as virtual slaves; others returned to the wilderness whence they had come.

For years, the buildings of the missions lay in a state of decay. Some, such as the Mission Santa Barbara, were continuously inhabited by Franciscan priests, but most were abandoned. Many are now just ruins, but a few have been restored and can be viewed today. The Mission Delores in San Francisco remains a tourist attraction; in Southern California, San Diego County's Mission San Luis Rey is particularly picturesque and the mission at San Juan Capistrano is famous for its annual festival celebrating the return of the swallows.

Mexican Land Grants

On February 21, 1821, revolutionaries took control of Mexico City and declared independence from Spain. Without its knowledge, California had become part of a new Mexican nation. Mexican rule was uneasy; political rivalry was rife in a province accustomed to paternalistic authority, and the governorship of the province changed regularly. Still, it was during the period of Mexican control that the region saw its most far-reaching land reform—the land grant, or rancho.

Land grants began in the Spanish era as early as 1784, but the imperial government retained title to the lands given. After 1821, the ranchos were given outright. Any Catholic citizen of Mexico could petition to receive a holding of up to 11 square leagues (48,400 acres). At first, land grants were uncommon, but after the Franciscan missions were secularized in 1834, they increased rapidly. Mission Indians sometimes retained small holdings, but much of the mission land became privately owned. At times, the Indians resisted this theft with force, but no organized resistance proved sustainable.

Life on the ranchos was simple. Manufactured goods were as scarce as natural produce was abundant. More than half of each land parcel was devoted to cattle. Cow hides were produced in great quantities and were a valuable trading commodity, as was tallow, the rendered fat of a cow. From a herd of just 200 brought to California by Gaspar de Portolá in 1769 and supplemented by Juan Bautista de Anza a few years later, the province's stock had mushroomed. Ranchos on the old mission lands also exploited surviving crop agriculture and each grant was generally self-supporting.

By 1846, there were around 700 ranchos, mostly along the southern coast. The last Mexican governor, Pío Pico, made dozens of grants. At the time of American conquest his family held 532,000 acres of Southern California. Non-Mexicans, like John Sutter (see page 81), often became citizens and accepted Catholicism in order to receive land. The rancho borders were often vague, however, and many of the larger grants were broken up when California became a state in 1850. But even to this day many land titles are based on Mexican grants made when California was a different place altogether.

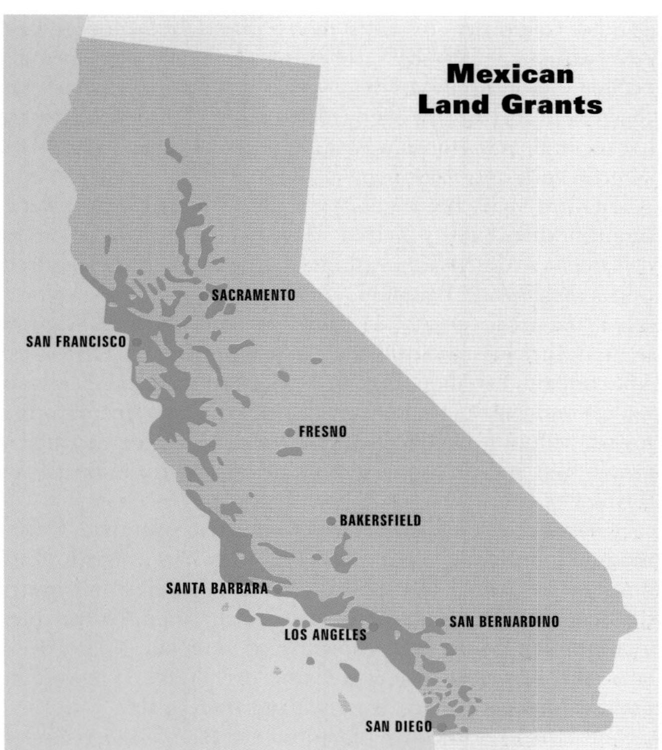

Land grants under Mexican rule extended throughout Alta California

Mexican War (1846–48) and the Bear Flag Revolt

The American annexation of Texas in 1845 set the stage for war between Mexico and the United States. Continued border disputes fueled anger between the two nations. Mexico severed relations in March 1845. President James Polk would not be refused. He sent John Slidell on a secret mission to Mexico City. His orders were to settle U.S. claims and to purchase California and the New Mexico territory for $30 million. Slidell's mission wasn't a complete secret. Mexican officials knew he was coming and would not talk to him about an issue they considered irrelevant to the more immediate boundary question. Polk ordered Zachary Taylor to occupy the disputed territory between the Nueces and Rio Grande Rivers in Texas. Mexican troops crossed the Rio Grande and fired on American soldiers, killing 16. Polk proclaimed that Mexico "invaded our territory and shed American blood on American soil." On May 11, 1846, Congress overwhelmingly supported a declaration of war.

As Taylor began his march into the heart of Mexico, Colonel Stephen Kearny (later brevetted brigadier general) was to march through Mexican territory and take New Mexico and California. Kearny's march through the Southwest went without a hitch. Mexican citizens generally welcomed his occupation and only a few resented it. Hearing reports that the American flag was flying throughout California, Kearny left the bulk of his force in Santa Fe and proceeded toward Los Angeles with only 100 men.

Fighting had been going on in California for several months when Kearny arrived. Even before the United States declared war on Mexico, volunteer Americans had organized into a "California Battalion" under the guidance of explorer John Charles Frémont (see page 74), son-in-law of Thomas Benton, the chairman of the Senate Committee on Territories. The unpaid battalion captured Mexican General Mariano Vallejo and began to raise their distinctive flag over California towns, declaring a California Republic. The banner depicted a grizzly bear and the uprising became known as the Bear Flag Revolt.

Even as the Bear Flaggers were conquering Sonoma, Commodore John Drake Sloat was sailing with 250 troops to California. On July 7, 1846, he landed in Monterey and raised the Stars and Stripes above the provincial capital. By the time Commodore Robert F. Stockon arrived to replace Sloat a week later, the American flag was flying over Yerba Buena (San Francisco), Sutter's Fort, Sonoma, and Bodega Bay.

Commodore Stockton organized the Bear Flaggers under the United States banner and entered Los Angeles, conquering the town and leaving a force of 50 to guard it. However, the local Californios (Hispanic Californians) were soon angered by the occupying force and on September 23 they surrounded the American garrison and forced the troops to flee. Reinforcements arrived two weeks later, but these too were rebuffed by the Angelenos. The engagement became known as "The Battle of the Old Woman's Gun," after the unique tactics with which it was won. During the earlier occupation of Los Angeles, a superannuated lady had buried an antique cannon in her yard. Unearthed for the uprising, the Mexicans tied the weapon to a mud wagon. They rushed it along their defenses, disorienting the U.S. forces and convincing them that their adversaries were well armed.

Meanwhile, General Kearny was having problems of his own. South of Los Angeles, near present-day Escondido, Kearny's forces were surrounded by Mexican troops. The Americans were already short of supplies and their gunpowder was damp. In the hand-to-hand combat that ensued, Kearny lost a quarter of his small force. The besieged Americans ate mule meat for four days before Commodore Stockton sent relief from San Diego. Together, Stockton, Kearny, and Frémont planned to retake Los Angeles with a combined force of 1,000 men. On January 13, 1847, Mexican commander Andrés Pico surrendered to Frémont. His brother, Pío Pico, the last Mexican governor, had already fled. The war in California was won.

The main conflict, however, was still raging. General Taylor was confronted several times in his march through Mexico. His troops emerged victorious, but their march south was slow. President Polk decided to send General Winfield Scott with an army by sea to capture the seaport of Veracruz. After a three-week seige, the city fell. Scott now had a clear path to Mexico City, which he took on September 14, 1847.

On February 2, 1848, just a few days after the discovery of gold near Sutter's Fort, Mexico signed the Treaty of Guadalupe Hidalgo, thereby relinquishing control over the huge parcel of land that now comprises New Mexico, Utah, Nevada, Arizona, western Colorado, Texas, and California. For this vast territory the United States paid just $15 million. Although the United States gained a large stretch of land, the acquisition nearly vaulted the nation into civil war. Discussions raged over which states should be slave states. The country slipped further into feelings of separation between North and South, but the Compromise of 1850 settled the immediate argument. This agreement also allowed California to enter the union as a free state.

Gold Rush

The greatest mass migration the United States had ever seen, and the defining moment in California's history, began rather inauspiciously one morning in 1848. On Monday, January 24, James Wilson Marshall (see page 80) was inspecting the flow in the newly constructed tailrace of an isolated sawmill deep in the Sierra Nevada. Nestled on the floor of the race were several flakes of yellow rock. Marshall hurried to Sutter's Fort, the home of his employer, John Sutter (see page 81). Together they determined that the yellow flakes were gold.

Despite Sutter's best efforts to keep the strike secret until preparations could be made, news began to spread through the surrounding area. Sutter's workers abandoned their posts to pan for the precious metal. In May, entrepreneur Sam Brannan walked through the streets of San Francisco carrying a jar of gold dust and shouting, "Gold! Gold! Gold from the American River!" (Brannan had already purchased any available mining supplies and set up a store near the gold strikes.) Within two weeks the small port was deserted as residents fled to the goldfields. Nearby soldiers left their posts to seek riches. Boats carried newfound gold to Hawaii, Mexico, Asia, and South America. Ranchers streamed down from the Oregon Territory. By the end of 1848, 10,000 people were mining in California.

Prospector posing with his gear

Letters began to arrive in the East telling of California's natural wealth. At first, news was treated with great suspicion. But when President James Knox Polk included word of the gold mines in his address to Congress on December 5, 1848, gold fever became international. Young men across the world dreamed of easy wealth and began to plan routes to California. Forty-niners (as the migrants became known) from the eastern United States had three main options. From the eastern seaboard, most chose one of two sea routes: either a boat all the way around South America and Cape Horn or one vessel to the Isthmus of Panama, a treacherous wagon trip across the isthmus, then an uncertain sail north to California. The former journey could take up to a year, depending on winds. Travelers across Panama began arriving as early as February 1849. Less expensive but no less difficult was the overland route through the Midwestern plains. This involved careful timing in order to reach California before the winter snows blocked mountain passage.

Before the gold rush, California's non-native population was small, around 25,000. By 1850 it was 115,000. In the first census of the state in 1860, the population had skyrocketed to more than 300,000. The newcomers included thousands of non-Americans. Chinese came to the land they called "Golden Mountain" in great numbers, although they often faced much discrimination. Mexicans and other Latin Americans flocked to the goldfields, where their superior mining knowledge was often much resented. Frenchmen and Englishmen also arrived by the boatload. Once in California, new arrivals found conditions far removed from what they had envisioned. Roads were poorly developed and generally ran up the coast instead of to the goldfields. Almost everything had to be imported by ship and prices were astronomical, even for basic supplies. And the gold, though plentiful, required more hard work and good luck to find than many had been led to believe.

There is the occasional tale of a fortuitous strike by a solitary miner. One prospector tied his mule to a stake overnight and when he took the stake out in the morning he found a rich deposit of gold in the hole. Another discouraged fellow kicked a rock in anger, rolling it aside to expose a large nugget. But for the majority of forty-niners, especially those who arrived after the initial rush, riches were scarce. The inexperienced young men who did stumble upon a good placer often squandered their wealth on gambling, liquor, and women. Sometimes the best money could be made in supplying the miners. Food, alcohol, and entertainment fetched a good price in gold rush California. Young women flocked to the mining camps and often made a small fortune plying the world's oldest trade.

Soon the streams and rivers were all panned out. The "easy pickings" were gone. Mining increasingly became a corporate industry. Newcomers found they could extract more gold by pooling their resources, and some of these conglomerates became large companies. Corporate mining further ravaged the already strained environment. Entire mountains were torn up, whole rivers were diverted, and huge hydraulic machines tunneled into the earth, leaving gaping holes in their wake. (For more information on mining techniques, see page 105) Waters became poisoned, forests were felled to provide fuel and shelter, and hastily constructed shantytowns spread across California's mountainsides.

The Indian population of the region suffered equally. The tribes in the mining districts had generally seen little contact with white men, being removed from the area of Spanish missionary influence. Early experiences with the new settlers who invaded their homeland en masse were unfavorable. The Indians saw their land stolen, the natural resources upon which they depended destroyed, and their way of life irrevocably altered. Some unfortunate tribe members were used as virtual slaves in mining enterprises. Still others were used as target practice by bored prospectors. Entire bands of people who had lived in their homeland for centuries became extinct over the course of a single decade. In the span of a single generation the native population of California dropped from an estimated 125,000 to just 32,000. Nevertheless, the disunity of the California Indian tribes prevented any organized resistance of the type undertaken by Arizona's Navajo.

Lawlessness flourished in the mining camps. In the predominantly male society, traditional moral compasses were mute. Rowdy young men often became embroiled in brawls, which sometimes blossomed into knife or gun fights. Theft was scarce when the gold was plentiful, but rampant when the mines dried up. Several bandits became legendary; Joaquin Murrieta, Black Bart, and Tiburcio Vasquez were all famous outlaws of the day. In the absence of an established judicial system, crime was often combated by vigilantism. Lynchings were at times as common as murders. Still, the majority of miners were law abiding, and most towns had a church in addition to several saloons.

Though many unlucky prospectors returned to their homes poor and disillusioned, most chose to stay in California. When the mining camps declined, miners flocked to the cities. Although the metropolitan population of Southern California remained small, villages like San Francisco and Sacramento became cities overnight. Ranches were established across California and immigrants continued to flood into the new state. The person who sparked the gold rush, James Wilson Marshall, died a pauper. John Sutter saw his fort ruined and his dreams destroyed, with little gain for himself. But their discovery had changed California, and the United States, forever.

First Death Valley Wagon Train

The story of the first wagon train to enter Death Valley is mixed with heroism and tragedy. Most of the train belonged to a group of forty-niners who had left a large party led by Captain Jefferson Hunt. Hunt was an experienced trailsman paid to guide groups to the California goldfields. He strongly cautioned his party not to attempt a supposed shortcut recommended by O. K. Smith, the leader of a passing pack train. Nevertheless, a third of Hunt's party decided to deviate from the known route west of Salt Lake City.

Included in the fated wagon train were a group of about 40 men known as the Jayhawkers. The Jayhawkers discovered that the uncharted route added several months to their journey and led them through forbidding desert expanses. They reached Death Valley late in December 1849, and spent a hot Christmas Day trudging down Furnace Creek Wash. Forced to burn their wagons and eat their oxen, the Jayhawkers escaped Death Valley by a northerly route via Towne's Pass. Jayhawker Canyon is named after the unfortunate group. Several members perished during the journey, but several survivors later returned to Death Valley as some of the region's first prospectors.

Accompanying the Jayhawkers were Reverend Brier, his wife, and their three sons—the youngest just four years old. The trip was especially hard for the family, who were particularly ill suited to desert travel. Juliet Brier later described her travels: "I was sick and weary and the hope of a good camping place was the only thing that kept me up." Despite having to abandon their possessions, eat all their beasts of burden, and carry their exhausted children, the Brier family made it through Death Valley intact. On February 5, 1850, the Briers and Jayhawkers found civilization at the San Francisquito Ranch.

Several groups had split from Hunt's original party. One group included two families—the Bennetts and Arcanes—and 11 bachelors. Hopelessly lost in the arid wilderness, this party was also forced to slaughter their oxen to survive. On Christmas Day 1849, the group reached Travertine Springs at the base of the Panamint Range. They decided to camp there while two bachelors, William Lewis Manly and John Rogers, set out to look for a settlement. They succeeded in obtaining supplies and pack animals from Mission San Fernando. When they made it back the group's campsite, they found the Bennetts and Arcanes alone; the bachelors had left to attempt their own escape from Death Valley. One man perished in the journey.

Manly and Rogers guided the families through Galena Canyon, Warm Spring Canyon, and Butte Valley before exiting Death Valley via Redlands Canyon. Fresh water was extremely limited along the route and the terrain was deadly. Leather boots on the oxen's feet soon wore out. The adults' shoes were destroyed, too, and all group members trudged on with blistered feet. It took three weeks and 250 miles of travel before the families reached civilization. Despite their ordeal, the group was happy to escape with their lives. As she departed the area she thought would be her grave, one woman cried "goodbye, Death Valley." This was the first recorded usage of the region's present-day name.

Manly and Rogers had saved the group from the well-known fate of the Donner Party. Their heroism in this tragic journey is remembered by several regional place names, including Rogers Peak, Manly Peak, Manly Fall, and Manly Pass. Manly later published his recollections of the ordeal in *Death Valley in '49*. Several trails in this book follow sections of the Bennett-Arcane escape route.

California Statehood

U.S. forces captured California from Mexico in 1846 and for some time after that the province was ruled as a conquered territory, subject to military law. However, with the end of the Mexican War in 1848 and the huge migration into California that followed the discovery of gold, it became clear that a more permanent governance was necessary. Although there had been talk of establishing a California Republic, the majority of residents felt allegiance to the United States. Because of its large population growth, California was able to skip the territorial stage of its entry into the Union.

A constitutional convention opened in Monterey in September 1849 to draft a state constitution that could be submitted to Washington. The convention had to decide whether to allow slavery, a practice still active throughout the South. Delegates chose to enter the Union as a free state. They also had to draw boundaries for the new state. Some argued that California should include the desert area east of the Sierra Nevada, perhaps even as far as Salt Lake City, which had been settled recently by Mormon pioneers. Eventually delegates decided a smaller California would be more palatable to federal lawmakers, and its present boundary lines were drawn just east of the mountains. On September 9, 1850, California became the nation's thirty-second state.

The decision about where to locate the new state's capital was not an easy one. Several cities presented proposals, including San Francisco and Monterey, the latter being the province's seat of government during Mexican rule. The first legislature was held in San Jose, but in 1851 the government archives were moved to a new town site named Vallejo. By 1853, Benicia had become California's third state capital, only to be superseded by Sacramento the following year. It is in that city that the state government still sits.

From its inception, California has endured a rivalry between residents in the north and south. In Mexican times, the more populous south sought to move the provincial capital from Monterey to Los Angeles. The huge population growth of the mid-nineteenth century switched the balance, as most new migrants moved north of the Tehachapi Mountains. In 1859, a plan by southern Senator Andrés Pico to split California in two won the approval of the state senate, but died in a federal Congress preoccupied by the nation's slip toward civil war. The 1880s saw another southern proposal for partition when unfavorable water laws and domination by northern companies angered separatists. By this time, however, Southern California was booming and beginning to catch the north in terms of population. Fearful of an expanding Los Angeles, it was the northerners' turn to request separation in a squashed 1915 bill. In 1964, the U.S. Supreme Court further jolted northerners with a ruling that effectively handed control of the state legislature to the now more populous south. The last bid for partition came as recently as 1978, when northern lawmakers proposed an "Alta California" state north of the Tehachapi. Although most Californians today still hold strong regional affiliations, few actively support a separation of the state.

Development of a Reliable Communications Network

In 1861, San Francisco was connected to the East by the first transcontinental telegraph line. The line then spread throughout the West, linking major cities like Los Angeles and San

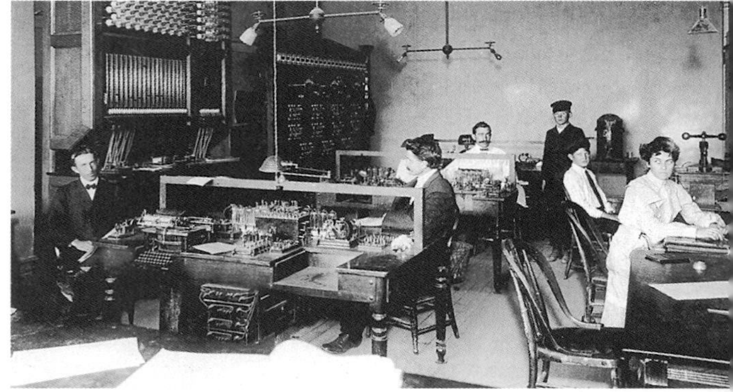

Western Union telegraph office, circa 1900

Diego. The telegraph was intended mainly for military use, but civilians could also receive messages. With this in mind, businesses flourished. Goods could be ordered faster, and the line increased the networking range of businesses. The telegraph became so popular that commercial telegraph companies were established to better serve the people. In 1877, for instance, there was about 1,000 miles of military telegraph lines. By 1882, only 532 miles remained; the rest had been taken over by commercial enterprises. Eventually, military telegraph lines would cease to exist after they had been bought up or replaced by commercial lines.

20-Mule Teams

Around 1880, a lone prospector named Aaron Winters was scouring Death Valley when he found a rock on the desert floor. Camping that night with his wife, Winters heated the rock over his fire and was delighted when it began to turn green. The prospector had discovered a rich deposit of borax, a mineral used in the manufacture of glass and ceramics. The discovery sparked a period of intense borax mining in Death Valley.

A 20-mule team

Mining companies soon found that it was quite difficult to transport the mineral out of Death Valley. The only viable method was to use mule-drawn wagons. From 1883 to about 1907, 20-mule teams (actually two horses and 18 mules) carried some 2.5 million pounds of borax a year from the mines to a railroad depot in Mojave. Each 16-foot wagon traveled 165 miles across harsh desert with a load of up to 30 tons.

Eventually trucks replaced the mule teams, but their mystique survived. Ronald Reagan hosted a television series dramatizing their treks. Members of the Boron Chamber of Commerce opened the Twenty Mule Museum, where visitors today can see exhibits about the mule teams and the mines they helped support.

Los Angeles–Owens River Valley Aqueduct

From its inception, Los Angeles was plagued by a shortage of water. Periods of drought were common; one report from 1841 claims that no rain fell on the town for 18 months. Still, for many years, Angelenos could meet their water needs by using water from the Los Angeles River. The population explosion at the end of the nineteenth century meant that the city was starting to outgrow its water supply. William Mulholland, superintendent of the city's water department, decided to look for an alternative source. Mulholland soon noticed the Owens River Valley, a picturesque agricultural region to the north of Los Angeles on the east side of the Sierra Nevada. Farmers in the area had a large surplus of water, and the Bureau of Reclamation was already considering damming the Owens River for future irrigation use.

Mulholland began to secretly purchase land in the quiet valley. He persuaded business associates such as Fred Eaton to do the same. The purchases prevented a dam from being built without angering local farmers. Many willingly sold their land to the Los Angeles prospectors, unaware of their intentions. Eventually the Los Angeles Department of Water and Power controlled 302,000 acres of land in Inyo and Mono Counties. Before long it became apparent what the city intended to do with the land and water rights.

Construction of the Los Angeles Aqueduct began in 1907 and was completed in 1913. At the time it was considered quite an engineering feat; 233 miles long, including 52 miles of tunnels, it carried 320,000 acre-feet of water annually to Los Angeles. A second aqueduct, finished in 1970, increased the supply.

In 1928, disaster struck the San Francisquito Canyon. The Saint Francis Dam, part of the system that provided Los Angeles with its water, began to reveal a fault in its wall. Mulholland and his inspectors rushed to inspect the dam but decided the structure was secure and returned to Los Angeles. That night, the dam gave way and water flooded 7,900 acres of land. Many downstream communities were destroyed and at least 385 people lost their lives in the torrent of water. Although Los Angeles gave $1 million for relief, local residents were infuriated, blaming poor engineering for the dam's failure. Some Angelenos countered, implying the disaster was the result of terrorism by Owens Valley activists. Only years later was a natural landslide revealed to have been the cause of the dam's collapse.

Before the aqueduct to Los Angeles, the Owens River Valley was a fertile and prosperous farming region, but this changed when the land was robbed of its water. Owens Lake dried, and local residents suffered economically. Beautiful Mono Lake has also lost much of its water because streams feeding it have been diverted to feed the coastal metropolis. The aqueduct was bombed several times during the 1920s. In addition to an increased water supply, Los Angeles had gained the ill will of some of California's rural inhabitants.

Geology

The Geological Timeline

The southern half of California is possibly the most geographically diverse region in the United States, from its miles of scalloped shoreline, to its multiple mountain ranges, through its fertile Central Valley, and into the forbidding deserts of the south and east. The forces shaping the region have been dramatic and deadly, such as the earthquake that heavily damaged much of the San Fernando Valley city of Northridge in 1994.

California lies on two tectonic plates—the continental North American plate and the oceanic Pacific plate. About 200 million years ago, the Pacific plate, with its covering of sedimentary layers, was overridden by the North American plate. Where these two great plates collide, the oceanic plate slides under the continental plate. At depth, so much heat is generated that the underside of the continental plate melts. Over the millennia, this pool of molten rock (magma) cooled deep beneath the surface and became granite. Over time, the rocks were uplifted and exposed by erosion, creating the dramatic range of the Sierra Nevada. With the magma came the minerals, most famously gold, that would shape California's more recent history.

The movements of the plates also caused the North American plate to scrape rocks off the ocean floor as it overrode the Pacific plate. The results, in part, are the crumpled Coast Ranges that extend north from Santa Barbara County to Oregon. About 25 million years ago, the direction of the plates changed. Instead of colliding with one another, they began to slide by one another creating the San Andreas Fault. The Pacific plate now grinds northward past the North American plate.

Sometime between 2 and 3 million years ago, during multiple cycles of ice ages, huge glaciers carved into the Sierra Nevada, further sculpting the landscape. When the glaciers retreated once and for all, the land began to assume the forms we see today. Worldwide, the forming and melting of glacial ice cause sea levels to rise and fall. Coastlines reflect these climatic changes, and the Channel Islands, for example, became isolated from mainland California.

Humans first entered California some time after the last ice age, perhaps 15,000 years ago, and began to alter the natural surroundings. The gold rush of the mid-nineteenth century brought a huge influx of people into the region. Today one in ten Americans resides in California, and an estimated 2,000 migrants move there daily. The newcomers have chopped down 80 percent of the state's riparian woodlands, developed 99 percent of the native grasslands, changed water flow for irrigation, and settled 94 percent of the coastal wetlands. Nevertheless, California is a land of immense and varied natural beauty, a sampling of which you will be able to experience by following the trails in this book.

The Regions

Southern California can be divided into five geological regions: the Pacific Coast, the Coast Ranges, the Central Valley, the Sierra Nevada, and the desert.

Pacific Coast

The beach pervades popular images of California, from the Beach Boys to *Baywatch*. Most of the state's ever-growing population resides along the coast, with 15 million people in the four southernmost coastal counties alone. The coast region of Southern California is far from a uniform series of surf resorts. California has 1,100 miles of coastline, and one road, California 1, meanders along most of it. Some have remarked that the scenery seems to change at every milepost. Much of it is composed of dramatic rocky cliffs; some areas are prized for rock climbing and bouldering. Other parts contain beautiful sandy beaches, now often overdeveloped, but sometimes protected as state beaches or parks. The pounding sea has cut the cliffs and bluffs from the rock of the Coast Ranges. Most of the sand on the beaches is deposited river sediment. Beaches are in a constant state of flux; violent winter storms can strip the sand overnight only to have it replenished by gentle summer swells. Attempts to stabilize a beach are generally costly and unsuccessful.

The shore is home to an eclectic collection of wildlife. Seals and sea lions bask on the ocean rocks, hundreds of species of birds thrive on the cliffs and beaches, and rare plants like the Torrey pine grow near the water's edge. Also rich in life are the Channel Islands, which can be seen from along the coast. Cut off from the mainland for thousands of years, the islands' plants and animals have evolved uniquely. Several species exist only on these small islands, and others have developed distinct features. The northernmost islands, including the largest, Santa Cruz Island, are now part of the Channel Islands National Park. A trip to the park is a worthwhile experience for any visitor to, or resident of, Southern California.

The Mediterranean climate of Southern California is unique in North America. South of Point Conception, the shoreline angles eastward. The relatively shallow Californian Bight formed by this angle causes warm water to circulate, affecting onshore temperatures. In general, the winters are wet but mild and the summers are dry and warm.

Coast Ranges

Rising from the majestic Pacific Ocean are three ranges of coastal mountains: the longest chain, extending from Santa Barbara north to the vicinity of the Oregon border, are the Coast Ranges. The Transverse Ranges, south of the Coast Ranges, extend inland, marking the southern limit of the Sierra Nevada. These include the Santa Ynez, Santa Monica, San Gabriel, and San Bernardino Mountains. The Peninsular Ranges, such as the San Jacinto and Santa Ana Mountains, encompass San Diego and stretch west to the Colorado Desert.

Unlike the Sierra Nevada, the Coast Ranges were not formed as a result of tectonic plates creating an upwelling of magma. Rather, these ranges are a result of the continental North American plate scraping off sediments and the upper part of the oceanic Pacific plate. The mountains, mostly crushed and crumpled marine sediments, do not have the vast stock of granitic rocks that comprise the Sierra Nevada.

The coastal forests are magnificent. Huge redwoods grow in the northern part of the state and the dry hills of the Big Sur rise dramatically above the ocean in the area south of Monterey. The valleys, mostly running parallel to the San Andreas Fault, are pretty and well cut. As in the rest of the state, there is an abundance of wildlife, much it native to California alone.

Central Valley

The Sacramento Valley in the north and the San Joaquin Valley to the south comprise the Central Valley of California. The valley lies between the Coast Ranges to the west and the Sierra Nevada to the east. The rivers of this valley are a vast watershed that empties into the San Francisco Bay.

This well-watered valley supports much of California's astounding agriculture. Perhaps more crops of fruits, vegetables, and nuts are grown here that any other valley in the world. The Sacramento Valley and the foothills of the Sierra Nevada are the site of the Mother Lode, the rich gold mining area of the late 1800s. In the south, the San Joaquin River was once a rich fishery, particularly for trout, that Indians and settlers relied upon before pollution, irrigation, and dams diminished fish populations.

Sierra Nevada

The remarkably scenic Sierra Nevada (Spanish for "white" or "snowy mountains") is a 400-mile-long mountain range that extends from Tehachapi Pass in the south to Lassen Peak and the beginning of the Cascade Range in the north. The range, encompassing eight national forests, three national parks, fourteen wilderness areas, and numerous state parks and recreation areas, has eleven peaks with elevations above 14,000 feet, including the highest mountain in the coterminus United States, Mount Whitney (14,494 feet).

The mountains of granitic and metamorphic rock were formed by molten rock (magma) that intruded into overlying rock some 185 to 65 million years ago when the oceanic Pacific plate was overridden by the continental North American plate. Over millions of years, these rocks have been uplifted and eroded, exposing the granite at the surface. The mountains have been shaped by rivers and glaciers and weathered into the domes and spires we see today.

The range is habitat for the largest living things on earth —the sequoia trees. Although the related redwoods grow taller, no other species has as great an overall weight and volume. These magnificent trees, remnants from the age of dinosaurs, are protected in Sequoia National Park, Giant Sequoia National Monument, and Kings Canyon National Park. The largest of the large is a tree named General Sherman, which is about 275 feet tall, with a base diameter of 36 feet, a weight of about 2.7 million pounds, and an estimated age of 2,300 years.

Because of its elevation, the Sierra Nevada has several different life zones. At its eastern base, the mountains border the deserts of the Great Basin. Conditions become almost arctic at the higher reaches. Vegetation and animal life vary at different elevations, depending on temperature, precipitation, and soil composition. At the lower levels live coyotes and jackrabbits; mountain lions and black bears inhabit the middle elevations; and marmots and bighorn sheep survive in the area above and around tree line. Unfortunately, much of the forests have been felled for lumber, and many species are becoming increasingly endangered. Still, the Sierra Nevada is a truly wild and rugged area of California. Traversing the mountains can be difficult, even in an automobile.

Deserts

To the east of the Sierra Nevada lies the vast Great Basin, which stretches to western Colorado and encompasses the Mojave and Colorado Deserts to the south. Part of the Great Basin, the Basin and Range province of mountains separated by valleys includes Death Valley. The Garlock Fault at Death Valley's southern border marks the boundary between the Basin and Range and the Mojave and Colorado Deserts, which extend into Arizona, Nevada, and Mexico and lie in the rain shadows of the Peninsular and Transverse Ranges. These extremely dry regions are sparsely populated, but they encompass beautiful scenery and exotic plants and animals uniquely adapted to survival in this harsh environment.

Much of the land is owned by federal and state agencies. The National Forest Service and the Bureau of Land Management administer vast stretches of land; national parks include Death Valley and Joshua Tree; and recently an area of the Mojave Desert has been designated the Mojave National Preserve. The Anza-Borrego Desert State Park, in the southern part of the state, is an easy drive from San Diego.

The deserts were formidable and daunting barriers to emigrants who dared travel a southern route instead of taking the California Trail, which lay farther to the north. Many died. Those who survived had a grudging respect for its stern and unrelenting character.

Although barren, the deserts are far from lifeless. Many plant and animal species have adapted to its little water, high temperatures, wind, sand, and rocky terrain. In addition to the tormented shapes of Joshua trees, many cacti thrive, some of which produce amazingly colorful flowers in spring. Some lizards "swim" under sand to avoid predators. Desert tortoises, protected by their shells, can easily ignore hungry coyotes and kit foxes. Roadrunners prey on rattlesnakes and lizards. For the careful and astute backcountry traveler, California's deserts hold countless wonders to discover and explore.

Famous Geological Features of Southern California

Death Valley

Located on the northern edge of the great Mojave Desert, Death Valley is characterized by one of the harshest climates in the world. It was a thoroughfare for some early travelers into California, but one that they may have preferred to avoid. Water is scarce, and the few oases are widely spaced. The region receives less than 2 inches of rain per year, and daytime summer temperatures regularly exceed 120 degrees Fahrenheit. Truly the area has earned its name; more than 500 people have perished in the heat. Local place names express the forbidding nature of the land: Hells Gate, Coffin Peak, Funeral Peak, Badwater Basin, and Dante's View. Local Indian tribes called the area To-me-sha, which means "ground on fire."

Situated between the Amargosa Range and Black Mountains to the east and the Panamint Range to the west, Death Valley is a youngster in geological terms. Like the coastal ranges and the Sierra Nevada, it was created by a complex se-

Moving rocks, a Death Valley phenomenon

ries of tectonic movements. It sits on the continental North American plate and has faults that occur as the plate stretches and moves. The result is what geologists call a pull-apart basin. The bordering mountains rise as the valley sinks or subsides.

Volcanic activity is frequently associated with such tectonic movements, and there are numerous lava flows and craters throughout the region. The Ubehebe Crater, along Desert #51: Racetrack Road in the north-central part of the park, is just one example.

Also found along that trail are Death Valley's famous moving rocks (pictured above). Within the park, Telescope Peak (11,049 feet) is not far from Badwater Basin (-282 feet), the lowest point in the Western Hemisphere. Mount Whitney, the highest point in the coterminus United States, is less than 100 miles away. These extremes typify the astounding difference in relief and the wide variety of landforms within the park. From Zabriskie Point, you can see badlands, evidence of volcanic activity, salt flats, and alluvial fans.

Mount Whitney

Mount Whitney is one of almost a dozen peaks in the Sierra Nevada that rise above 14,000 feet. Geologist Clarence King named it after Josiah Dwight Whitney (1819–1896), the well-respected chief of the California State Geological Survey. The first people known to scale the towering peak were three local fishermen, Charley Begole, Johnny Lucas, and Al Johnson. They reached the summit in August 1873. Today, thousands of hikers make the ascent every year. There is a paved road to the trailhead, 13 miles west of Lone Pine, at 8,361 feet. From there, a maintained hiking trail winds 11 miles to the summit at 14,494 feet (4,418 meters). The hike is best undertaken over a period of three days, although some very fit (and perhaps crazy) mountaineers make the journey in a single day. Between May 22 and October 15, both day and overnight hikers are required to obtain a U.S. Forest Service wilderness permit. Permits can be reserved up to six months in advance. It is best to book early, as quotas for weekends and holidays are met quickly. Between October 16 and May 21, only overnight hikers need a permit. Recent rates were $3 per group for an overnight pass plus $1 per person, or $2 per person for a day pass. Contact the Inyo National Forest for more information at (760) 873-2483.

Joshua Tree National Park

The Joshua Tree National Park spans 734,000 acres of wilderness and is a transition zone between the Mojave and Colorado Deserts. It provides a perfect opportunity for visitors to see the different characteristics of these deserts. The area in the east of the park, generally situated below 3,000 feet, is dominated by the abundant creosote bush. The west of the park, however, is higher, moister, and slightly cooler. This is the habitat of the largest of all yucca plants, the Joshua tree, after which the park is named. To Mormon pioneers trekking across the Mojave Desert, the branches looked like the outstretched arms of Joshua welcoming them to the promised land. These huge yuccas can reach heights of 30 feet or more, and they can live for many hundreds of years. Their spiny leaves once fed the giant sloth (now extinct) and the plant is still a vital food source for many species of birds.

Scattered across the park are several oases, where a third ecosystem provides contrast to the arid surroundings. Five fan palm clusters in the park indicate places where water occurs naturally, either above or near the earth's surface. These areas abound in wildlife.

Animals that can be seen within the park include golden eagles, roadrunners, jackrabbits, burrowing owls, bobcats, rattlesnakes, kangaroo rats, and tarantulas. Most species avoid excessive daytime temperatures, preferring the relatively cool nights.

Steep mountains rise along the park's edges. A drive along the 40-mile tour from the visitor center in Twentynine Palms is a rewarding one indeed. To preserve the wilderness of this area, Franklin D. Roosevelt declared it a national monument on August 10, 1936. President Clinton redesignated it a national park on October 31, 1994.

San Andreas Fault

Faults, fractures in the earth's crust, occur in California because the state is situated on the boundary of the oceanic Pacific plate and the continental North American plate. Earthquakes occur when the plates shift and grind against each other along the faults. The San Andreas Fault is the most significant one in California. It extends nearly 700 miles from Cape Mendocino in the north, through San Francisco, west of San Jose, south through Parkfield and Tejon Pass, east of the San Jacinto Mountains, and into Mexico.

The San Andreas Fault revealed itself dramatically during the legendary San Francisco earthquake on April 18, 1906. The powerful quake and the ensuing fire claimed the lives of at least 700 people and moved land on either side of the fault as much as 21 feet. Another powerful earthquake, perhaps just as strong, occurred in 1857 near Fort Tejon.

Approximately 20 million people now live in the vicinity of the San Andreas Fault. Hundreds of small earthquakes occur along the fault each year, though most are very low in magnitude. The fault is clearly visible from the air, marked by a linear arrangement of lakes and valleys. One of the best places to see it from the ground is on the Carrizo Plain, west of Bakersfield.

Salton Sea

The Salton Sea is a relatively recent addition to the California landscape. It was formed between 1905 and 1907 by floodwaters from the Colorado River. The river flooded because silt blocked an irrigation canal that was part of a project to provide water for farming in Imperial Valley.

This flooding of the Salton Sink was the first to occur as a result of human intervention, but sediments confirm that the area was submerged by water dozens of times before. The biggest historical lake in the region was Lake Cahuilla. It was formed around A.D. 700 by floodwaters and was replenished several times until about 1700. When the first Europeans entered the area in the 1770s, the Salton Sink was a dry lakebed.

After its formation, the Salton Sea probably would have dried up if not for irrigation runoff. Fights continue to ensure that saline levels remain low enough to support the lake's wildlife. Congressman Sonny Bono was an important campaigner for the preservation of the Salton Sea, a cause adopted by his widow and successor, Mary Bono.

The lake is the largest in California, extending over 35 miles and covering 376 square miles. It remains a much-visited tourist destination. The Salton Sea Recreation Area on the northern shore is favored for water sports, while the Sonny Bono Salton Sea National Wildlife Refuge along the southern shore preserves the biological life of the lake.

Mining

California achieved statehood in the wake of the biggest mass migration in American history—the gold rush. The cause of this huge western exodus was the discovery of gold near Sutter's Fort in January 1848. For years, gold-hungry Spaniards had sailed California's coastline and settled its shore, unaware of the fortunes that lay buried in its hills and scattered along its riverbeds. It was up to a young New Jersey native named James Wilson Marshall to unearth the first nugget of the region's natural wealth. Mining has since played an elephantine role in California's history. In addition to gold, the state has silver, copper, zinc, borax, and petroleum operations, to name but a few. Still, it is from the shiny yellow metal that the Golden State takes its name.

Gold and silver deposits are frequently found together. They are formed when molten minerals are forced from deep within the earth into the bedrock. Because of California's position on active faults, such movements have been common, forcing up many rich veins of metal. Other minerals such as pyrite (fool's gold) and galena (which has a silvery appearance) coexist with gold and silver. Commonly, the host rock is quartz.

Over time, erosion breaks down the rock deposits and the gold is freed. Water then disperses the free gold along streambeds. In its free form, gold exists in a variety of shapes: nuggets, scale, shot, grains, and dust. These free deposits are known as "placers" when the gold is found in streambeds or along stream banks. A deposit of gold that is still contained in a rock formation is called a "lode." It was the abundant placer deposits that attracted the hordes of forty-niners to the Sierra Nevada with dreams of quick wealth.

Placer Mining

Because placers are relatively easy to find, they are normally the first gold deposits discovered in any area. Miners typically follow placers upstream to a mother lode.

Placer mining is the simplest form of mining operation, because it merely involves separating the free gold from dirt, mud, or gravel with which it is mixed. The process takes a number of forms:

- panning
- sluicing to process a larger volume, using the same principle as panning
- dredging to process even larger volumes of rock (Dredge mining utilizes a power-driven chain of small buckets mounted on a barge. Processing tons of rock and soil quickly, dredges overcame the problem of large quantities of low-grade gravel. Dredges could move up to three-quarters of a million yards of earth per annum.)
- hydraulic mining, used where the ancient riverbeds had long since disappeared, leaving the gold some distance from any existing stream on dry land (hydraulic mining uses hoses

Gold dredge

Sluicing for gold in California

to bring water from up to 3 miles distant and wash away the extraneous material to recover the gold.)

Placer mining was known as "poor man's mining," because panning a creek could be done with very little capital. Nevertheless, despite the popular image of the California miner as a solitary figure with a gold pan and a burro, most mining ventures involved several prospectors with at least some machinery. Placer mining was generally only practiced for the extraction of gold and was not effective for the recovery of other minerals.

Hard-Rock Mining

When the easily found placer mines were all panned out in California, prospectors had to pool their resources to extract harder-to-reach mineral deposits. This involved a process called hard-rock mining.

Hard-rock mining involves digging ore out of the ground and recovering it from the quartz (or other minerals) surrounding it. In its simplest form, hard-rock mining required tunneling horizontally under a vein (either directly or from an initial vertical shaft), then digging out the ore into mine cars

Rock crusher

placed beneath it. In the 1800s, mining cars were pulled by mules along tracks laid in the mines. If the mine incorporated a vertical shaft, then a hoist would lift the ore to the surface. Digging the shafts was made much easier during the 1870s, when machine drills and dynamite made hand-drilling techniques obsolete.

Once extracted from a mine, gold had to be separated from the host rock. To do this economically in the latter half of the nineteenth century, mining companies made use of stamp mills. Large structures that processed the ore in stages, stamp mills required water and a downhill slope. Mine workers brought the ore into the mill and fed it into a stamper, which weighed up to a ton. The stamper crushed the host rock; the resulting slurry of crushed ore and water was fed over a series of mercury-coated amalgamation plates, which captured the precious metal.

Because hard-rock mining required substantial capital, only large mining corporations normally undertook this kind of operation. The men who worked the mines were employees of the larger corporations. They often received small reward for the immense wealth they extracted. More unscrupulous mine owners even used Indians as slave labor in their operations.

Southern California's Lost Mines

Pegleg's Black Gold

Of all the legends of lost gold in Southern California, none is more famous than the tale of Pegleg Smith. So much time has passed since this now-famous discovery that the facts of the find have become distorted. Over the years, several characters claimed to be the real Pegleg Smith, but most sources credit the story's origin to a Thomas Long Smith, a successful trapper and early American visitor to California.

Smith was born in 1801 in Garrard County, Kentucky. At age 23 he joined a caravan bound for Santa Fe and began working for various trapping companies. On one expedition his company was attacked by Indians. Smith was attempting to carry an injured friend to safety when he was struck in the leg by an arrow. None of his companions was willing to amputate the badly injured limb, so Smith did it himself, cutting off the leg just below the knee with a butcher knife. After recovering in an Indian village of a different tribe, he fashioned a wooden stump from an ash tree. From this time on, Thomas became known as "Pegleg" Smith.

When he was adequately healed, Pegleg resumed trapping. In 1829, he and a companion were entrusted with the task of transporting beaver pelts to sell at Spanish settlements along the Pacific Coast. The trappers were hardy mountain men, but they were unused to the rigors of desert travel and became hopelessly lost near the Salton Sink (this was before the sink filled with water to become the Salton Sea). Leaving his friend at their camp, Pegleg limped up the central peak of three nearby buttes, hoping to get perspective and perhaps locate some water. While on the hill, he noticed a multitude of peculiar black stones. He picked up a few of the heavy rocks and placed them absentmindedly in one of his pockets. After examining the stones, Pegleg decided they were probably copper and decided to hold on to them, reasoning that they could be made into crude bullets if necessary. However, when he showed them to a miner in Los Angeles, he was surprised to hear that they were almost pure gold, coated black with a thin film of manganese.

This was 20 years before the great gold rush revealed just how wealthy a good gold strike could make someone, and Pegleg did not realize the potential of his find. Instead, he waited years before trying again to find the hill of black gold. Unfortunately, by this time his memory had dimmed, and his only companion on the day of the original discovery had died. Several times Pegleg looked in vain for the black butte, but to no avail; he died a pauper in San Francisco in 1866.

Since then, hundreds of hopeful treasure hunters have scoured the desert around Salton Sea hoping to stumble upon three small buttes, one of which contains a fortune in undiscovered gold. Several have likely been successful. A dying Indian woman staggered into the Southern Pacific Railroad's construction camp in Salton in 1876 clutching a sack full of black gold. Around the same time, a farm laborer who lived on the northern edge of the Anza-Borrego Desert made several trips into the mountains, each time returning with a sizable amount of the same black pebbles. He was killed in a bar brawl before he could stake a claim to the find, but a posthumous search of his bunk revealed $4,000 worth of the rocks. Treasure buff John D. Mitchell, former editor of *Desert Magazine*, also claimed to have found the site while looking for a meteorite in the Chuckwalla Mountains. In 1965, a subscriber to the same publication wrote to the magazine alleging that he had rediscovered the gold-bearing butte. He sent several black cobbles as proof and asserted that $300,000 worth had already been pulled from the hill. Unfortunately, the writer was anonymous and his story was unverifiable. So perhaps the legendary treasure still sits on a hidden peak, waiting for a lucky prospector. Or perhaps, as some sources have suggested, the butte never really existed, and Pegleg was just a lying drunkard who told his fabrications to anyone who would buy him a drink.

Lost Arch Diggings

Perhaps the second most famous tale of lost gold in Southern California is the story of the Lost Arch Diggings. Again, the facts of the find may have been lost to legend, but an enduring story nevertheless remains. The tale begins during the height of the gold rush with a group of Mexican prospectors traveling through the Turtle Mountains to the placer fields of La Paz. The Mexicans stopped to camp a night in a wash in the area north of the present-day town of Rice, in San Bernardino County, and west of US 95. When they awoke in the morning, members of the group noticed that the bottom of the wash was glittering with gold. The travelers quickly forgot their intended destination and hastened to set up a mining operation in the mountains. For living quarters, they constructed a two-room adobe building with a large connecting arch.

The prospectors had with them all the equipment necessary for a successful placer operation and over the course of several months, they extracted an impressive $30,000 worth of gold from the little streambed. However, as spring progressed into summer, the water in the bed became increasingly sparse. By midsummer, the searing desert sun had evaporated the water required for sluicing. Dismayed, the miners hid their equipment and continued their journey eastward to the Colorado River, intending to return to the diggings the following spring.

As is common in the tales of lost mines, the discoverers parted ways, some heading to Los Angeles or the Mother Lode, some returning to their homes in Mexico. In the following years, several members of the original party made individual efforts to relocate the placer, but always unsuccessfully. Subsequent searches have been further confused by rumors of another rich strike in the Turtle Mountains, this one in the vicinity of a natural arch!

The adobe arch of the Mexican placer was still standing in the early 1900s, when a German naturalist named Peter Kohler camped under it, unaware of its significance. Today, the arch has probably crumbled, but a fortune in gold could still lie in the area around its rubble.

Lost Ship of Pearls

In the second half of the nineteenth century, thousands of migrants crossed the Colorado Desert of Southern California. This was a harsh journey, and many travelers perished along the way. Some of the survivors arrived with a story of a strange sighting—a Spanish galleon resting upright in the sands of the great desert.

The presence of an ocean vessel in an arid, landlocked region thousands of miles from Europe is somewhat incredible, but not impossible. Just 100 years ago, the large body of water we call the Salton Sea was nonexistent. It was formed by runoff from the Colorado River. Similar floods have indubitably produced other inland seas, and it was into one of these that a Spanish pearl ship may have sailed hundreds of years ago.

The most likely candidate as the lost ship is a vessel once commanded by Alvarez de Cordone. Cordone was a successful captain stationed in Mexico City when he received orders from Phillip III of Spain to find pearls with which to stock the royal treasury. The seaman had three ships constructed, and shipped 50 experienced pearl divers from Africa to help with the mission. In July 1612, the three vessels left Acapulco to seek pearls. One of the ships was commanded by a young officer named Juan de Iturbe.

The expedition went extremely well, and the Spanish collected huge quantities of pearls from diving and through trade with local Indians. During one trade dispute, Cordone was shot with an arrow. The ship's doctor urged the commander to return to Acapulco. Cordone did so, taking with him one of the three boats. The other two ships were ordered to continue northward up the Gulf of California. The expedition lost another vessel when it sailed onto a reef. Hurriedly, the sailors transferred its treasure onto the surviving ship, the one captained by Juan de Iturbe. The boat headed west into a large inland sea where the Colorado River reaches the gulf.

Iturbe's men explored the sea for several weeks, but they found few oysters and decided to sail back to Acapulco. Unfortunately, when they returned to the sea's entry point, they found the outlet closed. Iturbe searched frantically for a way out of the now rapidly evaporating waters. Eventually, the ship became grounded, and the crew had to trudge to the ocean, where a passing galleon picked them up. In the hull of the boat they left millions of dollars worth of pearls, what one source estimated would be the wealth of several modern nations.

An old Indian legend corroborates this story. The legend takes place in the time of a great flood. One day, after a lengthy ritual dance, tribe members spotted a great bird with outstretched white wings moving slowly along the surface of the water. When the wings were lowered, the Indians saw many ants scurrying across the bird's body. When the bird moved no more, the ants unloaded onto dark objects and made their way to the shore. Here they became more visible, and the Indians realized that they were not ants but rather strange light-skinned people. Soon, the visitors left, the waters receded, and the bird (boat) lost its wings (sails) and was buried by sand. Sporadically, wind would uncover the bird, but the tribe took it as a harbinger of evil and avoided it.

Hundreds of other sightings further support the presence of an old treasure ship in the California desert. One old-timer even claimed to have slept in its hull, unaware of the massive wealth that lay in the sands beneath him. The winds of the desert are constantly changing the arid landscape, which is probably the reason that no expedition has ever successfully located the lost vessel. Perhaps one day a backcountry explorer will stumble across the decaying ship and claim its fortune in pearls.

Underground River

For more than a century now, Californians have heard tales of a mysterious cave with a large body of water edged by gold-bearing black sands. Early prospectors dismissed these stories as Indian myths but several witnesses have borne evidence that such a place exists, nestled somewhere in the Mojave Desert of southeastern California.

Of the various claims, two stand out as most believable. The first is a story of two Paiute Indian brothers wandering through Death Valley at the northern end of the Funeral Mountains. The brothers stopped to rest in a cave and noticed cool air coming from an opening in the cave's rear. They struggled through the opening into a small passageway that led to a large, dome-shaped cavern. At the bottom of the cavern was a dark lake that slowly receded from the terraced sides. Collected along the terraces were large quantities of black sand. The Indians quickly realized that the sand contained many shining shards of pure gold. The brothers collected handfuls of gold and headed back to camp. The next day they carried several sacks into the cave and filled them with the golden-flecked sand. Content with their treasure the young men decided to explore the cave. One brother spotted a rocky island in the center of the underground lake and chose to swim to it. While he was crossing, the water suddenly rushed out of the lake, taking the poor Indian with it. His brother waited for several days, and although the water level rose and fell several times, his partner never returned. The surviving Indian carried his gold from the cave but never returned, respecting the tribal tradition that avoided places of death.

In another part of the great Mojave Desert, an American prospector made a similar discovery. In the late 1920s, Earl Dorr was given a map by two strange Mojave Indians. The Indians often rode into town with enough gold to buy ammunition and food. One night, while sharing a camp with Dorr, they sketched a map with the location of the hidden wealth. Dorr journeyed into the area described on the map, around Crystal Mountain. For days he combed the mountainside searching for a hidden cave, which his benefactors had described as being rich with gold. Eventually he discovered a crack in the rock. Over the next several days he explored the cave, descending far into its depths. Soon he found himself in a large cavern with a huge flowing river in the center. Along the riverbank was the same black and gold sand that the Paiute brothers had found.

Dorr extracted some of the gold from the underground cave but was unable to find investors to remove the sand in bulk. Through his own efforts, he inadvertently closed the only entrance to the cavern. At one point he persuaded a mining company to drill another tunnel, but while digging the company hit a rich vein of zinc and chose to extract that instead. Later mining engineers have looked at the original passageway, but judged it too dangerous to reopen. Some local Indians claim to know a second entrance to the cave but hold it as a tribal secret.

So it is quite likely that a veritable Eldorado of treasure lies in a cavern deep below the California desert. The caves are quite dangerous, however, and two spelunkers died in 1959 in the very cave system in which Earl Dorr made his discovery.

Golden Eagle Mine

Death Valley is also the site of the legendary Alkali Jones's lost Golden Eagle Mine. Alkali Jones was an old-time prospector and desert wanderer who set off from Skidoo, California, bound for Searchlight, Nevada, in the summer of 1902. Jones took only what his single burro could carry, which included just a gallon of water. After two days in the desert, the prospector was caught in a sandstorm. He staggered across the swirling sands until he found shelter behind a low hill, where he and his burro waited out the storm.

After the winds subsided, Jones decided to climb the little butte in hopes of regaining his bearings. On the way back down the slope, he saw a large vein of white quartz. Out of habit, Jones took a pickax and chiseled into the quartz. He was surprised to find it riddled with streaks of bright gold. The vein was very rich indeed; it was 3 feet wide and over 100 feet in length. As Jones stood enthralled by his discovery, a lone bird flew overhead. Seeing the bird as a good omen, he named his find the Golden Eagle Mine. Jones collected about 10 pounds of the valuable ore into a bag and, now desperate for water, resumed his journey. Before he left the site, he scribbled a note on a piece of paper and left it in a coffee can on top of the hill.

Jones was a hardy desert traveler, and after a few more days he made it safely to the mining town of Searchlight. While there he had his find assayed at a staggering $41,000 per ton. He sold his remaining gold for $180 (some sources quote an unlikely $180,000) and purchased supplies with which to extract his newfound wealth. Unfortunately, Alkali Jones died without reaching his lucky strike, and its whereabouts was lost with his death. His body and pack were found many years later.

Countless others have scoured the desert looking for the now-fabled Golden Eagle Mine. One geologist even found Jones's coffee can with a faded letter enclosed, but he could see no evidence of the rich vein that the late prospector had described. Others have concluded that the strong desert winds must have covered the low hill. Perhaps one day the same winds will again reveal the little butte and its wealth in gold, and a fortunate backcountry adventurer will be lucky enough to find the hill. If so, the finder will be confronted by another formidable force: The supposed area now lies within the confines of the Death Valley National Park, and the mine would come under the control of the federal government!

Animals

Mammals

Badger

Badgers measure about 2 feet long with short legs, clawed feet, and shaggy gray-brown coats. A white stripe reaches from midway on their pointy snouts back to their shoulders. They have bushy, short, yellowish tails. Found in open grasslands, sagebrush, and brushy areas, badgers use their powerful legs and front claws to dig out ground squirrels and other rodents. They are most active at night and make burrowed homes in the ground.

Badger

Beaver

Beavers are North America's largest rodents. They have thick brown fur, chunky bodies, short legs, rounded heads, small rounded ears, yellowish orange front incisors, webbed hind feet, and flat, hairless, paddle-shaped tails. Their weight ranges from 30 to 60 pounds. Beavers live in lakes, streams, ponds, and rivers, and eat bark and twigs. Because they do not hibernate, they collect large caches of twigs and branches to eat in their lodges during winter. Beavers have thick layers of fat and waterproof fur, so icy waters do not bother them. Skin flaps close over their ears and nostrils when they are submerged. Their webbed feet aid in swimming. Their eyes have clear membrane covers that enable them to see in water and protect them from floating debris. A beaver can remain submerged for up to 15 minutes without coming up for air.

Beaver

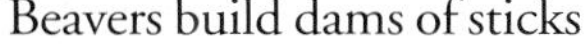

Beavers build dams of sticks and mud across streams and slow rivers. They gnaw down trees, strip them, cut them into small sections, and weave them into dams, holding the logs in place with mud. They build lodges in the dams with one or more entrances below water and the living chamber well above waterline. Beavers mate for life, which can be as long as 20 years. In the spring, furry beaver kits are born in the lodges with their eyes open.

The beaver population almost died out during the nineteenth century because of unregulated trapping for their fashionable fur (used primarily for hats). However, the beaver population has recovered and is thriving.

Bighorn Sheep

Bighorn sheep are grayish brown with yellowish white rump patches and short brown tails. Some have whitish fur around their muzzles, eyes, bellies, and calves. They have muscular bodies and thick necks. Ewes weigh around 150 pounds, and rams range from 150 to 250 pounds. Both the male and female have horns that grow continually and never molt. The ram's horns are massive and coil up and back around his ears in a C shape up to 40 inches long. The ewe's horns are thin and only slightly curved—no more than a half curl. Bighorn sheep are active by day, dwelling on cliffs, mountain slopes, and rolling foothills. They feed on a wide variety of grasses and shrubs. Rams challenge each other in butting contests in which they simultaneously charge each other. Their combined speed can be more than 40 miles per hour just before impact, and their foreheads meet with a crack that can be heard a mile away. These contests can last for as long as 20 hours. Horn size determines status among rams, but these ramming contests establish hierarchy among rams with horns of similar size.

Bighorn sheep (ram)

Many bighorns died in the twentieth century from hunting, habitat fragmentation, and diseases contracted from domestic livestock. Reintroduction programs and habitat protection have assisted in increasing their populations, but they are still endangered. Today, bighorn sheep can be seen in the high Sierra, the Owens Valley, and the desert mountains of southeastern California.

Black Bear

Black bears can actually be black, brown, or cinnamon. Their bodies are powerful and densely furred, with slight shoulder humps, small rounded ears, small close-set eyes, and five dark, strongly curved claws on each paw. Females range in weight from 120 to 200 pounds, and males range from 200 to 400 pounds. Nocturnal and solitary, black bears prefer forested habitats throughout the year, although they can sometimes be seen on open slopes searching for fresh greens. They usually make their dens in tree cavities, under logs, in brush piles, or under buildings; the dens are lined with leaves or grass. Black

Black bear

bears are omnivorous. They feast on grasses, sedges, berries, fruits, tree bark, insects, honey, eggs, fish, rodents, and even garbage. In the fall they go into a feeding frenzy to gain as much weight as possible to get them through their winter hibernation, often adding a 4-inch layer of fat to keep them warm and nourished. During hibernation, black bears crawl into their dens, and their bodies go dormant for the winter; they do not eat, drink, urinate, or defecate during their long sleep. Their kidneys continue to make urine, but it is reabsorbed into their bloodstream. They awaken by an internal clock in the spring and wander out in search of food. The black bear has a lumbering walk but can actually travel up to 30 miles per hour in a bounding trot. Black bears are powerful swimmers, able fishers, and agile tree climbers. They breed in the summer; the females undergo a phenomenon in which the fertilized egg passes into the uterus but changes very little until late fall, when it implants and then begins to grow quickly. Females commonly give birth to a litter of one to five cubs in January or February.

Despite its appearance on the state flag, the grizzly bear is extinct in California, and the black bear is the only bear that is encountered here today.

Black-tailed Jackrabbit

Jackrabbits, also known as hares, are very similar in appearance to cottontail rabbits, but are larger and have longer ears, bigger feet, and longer hind legs. It is suggested that the name jackrabbit originated because their large ears resemble those of jackasses. Black-tailed jackrabbits have fur that is mottled gray and brown, grizzled with black. The tail has a black stripe above, which extends onto the rump, and a white border.

Black-tailed jackrabbit

Their very long ears are brown with black tips. Does (females) are larger than bucks (males), which is unusual in mammals. Their weight varies from four to eight pounds. In summer, jackrabbits eat mostly green plants, such as clover and flowers. In winter, they rely more on shrubs and dried vegetation. Their ears are so sensitive that they can detect the muted sound of a coyote as its fur brushes against the grass. When threatened, they first freeze, laying their ears back to be less conspicuous; their coats assist with camouflage. If this fails, they can move from a hiding place like lightning, running at speeds up to 35 miles per hour and changing direction instantly. If they are running at moderate speeds, every fourth or fifth leap is higher so they can get a broader view of their surroundings. Unlike cottontails, young hares are born fully furred, with their eyes open. The female puts each young hare into an individual form, or depression, in the ground, thus decreasing a predator's chance of taking her entire litter. She keeps her distance by day and comes several times to nurse at night so that she attracts less attention. The related white-tailed jackrabbit is found mainly in Northern California.

Bobcat

Bobcats are reddish brown (grayer in winter) with dark spots on their bodies and legs. Their ears are slightly tufted; their bodies are usually buff and spotted. Bobcats get their name from their short, stubby, bobbed tails that have three horizontal, dark stripes. Females range in weight from 15 to 25 pounds, and males range from 20 to 35 pounds. The most common wildcat in North America, bobcats live in virtually every habitat below 10,000 feet—from dry, rocky mountainsides to forests to brushy, arid lands. Bobcats have also been known to adapt to swamps and farmlands. Although more gregarious than mountain lions, bobcats are still secretive and are seldom seen or heard. When threatened, they make a cough-bark sound, and during mating season they yowl. Bobcats are efficient predators with keen eyes and ears to help them locate prey in poor light. When hunting, they stalk and move at blinding speed for short distances, then pounce and make the kill. Their primary diet consists of rabbits and hares, ground squirrels, mice, birds, insects, lizards, and frogs. Generally solitary animals, bobcats come together mainly for mating. Litters of two or three kizttens are born in April and May in maternity dens, which are usually in hollow logs or under rock ledges or fallen trees and lined with dry leaves. The bobcat population is currently stable, although trapping by humans once nearly eradicated the species.

Bobcat

Burro

Native to Africa, burros, or donkeys, are small asses with large ears and short, erect manes. Spanish explorers originally brought burros to the Southwest in the 1500s. Present populations are descendants of this stock, which have thrived in the wild because of their adaptability to arid environments. Although burros are primarily forb and grass eaters, they are opportunistic and will beg for food from motorists—eating almost anything offered. They can tolerate high water losses and will rehydrate quickly when drinking water becomes available.

Burro

Burros compete with native fauna for food and water and have been known to drive bighorn sheep from waterholes, thus contributing to the decline of these animals in some areas. Burros have a lifespan up to 25 years. A lack of predators has helped to preserve their population. They give birth to a single young at a time. Breeding does not appear to be seasonal.

Chipmunk

The several varieties of chipmunks in Southern California share similar characteristics and are not easily discerned from one another. Ranging in color from chestnut to yellowish gray to light gray, chipmunks are small rodents with dark and light stripes on their faces. Dark stripes line their backs from the neck to the base of the tail, with white stripes running parallel on the back portion only. The palest chipmunks tend to be found in arid environments. They measure about 3 to 6 inches long, with 3- to 4-inch tails, and weigh a mere one to four ounces. Chipmunks are most active during the day. Their diet consists of a variety of vegetation, including seeds, leaves, fruits, flower components, and other plants. They have large, fur-lined internal cheek pouches used for carrying food. Chipmunks stow away much of their food; instead of relying on stored body fat to sustain them during hibernation, they awaken periodically throughout winter and early spring to eat from their caches. They dig burrows underneath rocks, logs, and roots, and line them with grass; these burrows become the nests where they have their young. Babies are born blind and naked after a gestation period of about 30 days.

Chipmunk

Cottontail

One of the most abundant animals in nature, cottontails are very similar in appearance and behavior to jackrabbits. However, they tend to be smaller and have shorter ears, smaller feet, and shorter hind legs. They do not turn white in winter. The buff-brown desert cottontail is found in grasslands as well as in creosote brush and desert areas. It will climb sloping trees and is known to use logs and stumps as lookout posts after dark. Nuttall's cottontail, also known as mountain cottontail, is grayish, with a white belly and black-tipped ears. It inhabits rocky, wooded or brushy areas, often with sagebrush, throughout the higher elevations of California. It uses dense vegetation for shelter or, when not available, it uses burrows and rocky crevices. Because of their vulnerability at birth, cottontails are born in maternal nests, which the pregnant female finds and prepares about a week before giving birth. She locates a suitable spot, where brush or high grass provides protection, and makes a saucerlike depression in the ground, lining it with her own downy fur, soft grasses, and leaves. In a good habitat, adults may have three or four litters per year. Unlike hares, cottontails are born hairless, with their eyes closed.

Cottontail

California is also home to the similar, but smaller, brush rabbit and the smallest rabbit in North America, the pygmy rabbit.

Coyote

Coyotes have grayish brown bodies with rusty or tan fur on their legs, feet, and ears. Doglike in appearance, with pointed muzzles and bushy tails, coyotes range in weight from 30 to 50 pounds. Their tracks look much like those of a domestic dog but in an almost straight line. Paws are slightly smaller and strides are slightly longer than a dog of similar size. Coyotes rarely seek shelter and remain in dens only when they have pups. They are carnivores and scavengers, and their opportunistic diet includes rabbits, mice, squirrels, birds, frogs, snakes, grasshoppers, fruits, berries, sheep, and other domestic livestock. In winter they often eat carrion from larger animals, especially deer, which is an important food source. They are vocal animals whose call is commonly heard at dusk or dawn. It typically consists of a series of barks and yelps, followed by a prolonged howl and short yaps. Coyotes howl as a means of communicating with one another; one call usually prompts other coyotes to join in, resulting in a chorus audible for significant distances. They are stealthy runners and can cruise at 25 to 35 miles per hour, making leaps as high as 14 feet. They hunt singly or in pairs, acting as a relay team to chase and tire their prey. Coyotes are monogamous and often mate for life. Their maternal dens are usually found or dug by the female under large boulders, in caves, on hillsides, or along river embankments. The openings, or mouths, of these dens usually measure several feet wide and are often marked by a mound of earth and tracks. A coyote might use the same den from year to year, unless it is disturbed. Coyotes breed in February, March, and April and give birth to a litter of four or more pups by May.

Coyote

The population of coyotes is flourishing, despite the popular demand for their fur in the 1970s and 1980s. Their main enemies are humans.

Foxes

Gray foxes are recognizable by their salt-and-pepper gray coat, rust-colored legs and feet, white throat and belly, black-tipped tail, and dark streak down the spine. The gray fox weighs 7 to 13 pounds and is about 22 to 30 inches long with a 10- to 15-inch tail. This animal prefers heavier cover and is more nocturnal than the red fox, so it is rarely seen. It lives in wooded and brushy slopes in valleys. It is the only fox that commonly climbs trees and has been known to rest, hide, or escape into them. Gray foxes sometimes raise their young in large, hollow trees, some of which have entrance holes as high as 20 feet. More often, dens are located among rocks, in cliffsides, or in hollow trees or logs. Because the gray fox's pelt is undesirably bristly, it has never been heavily hunted or trapped for its fur. Like other foxes, its worst enemies are humans. The gray fox is the most abundant fox in Southern California.

Kit foxes, about the size of a house cat, are one of North America's smallest canids. These nocturnal animals have yellow eyes, buff yellow fur with grayish areas above, and white chins, throats, and bellies. Most have a black tip on their tail, and all have especially large ears. Well adapted to desert conditions, kit foxes avoid extremes of temperature and drought by hunting at night, using their extra-large eyes and ears to navigate through the darkness. Hot days are spent in a cool, humid, underground burrow. Kit foxes rarely drink water; instead they obtain dietary water from the food they consume. Their heavily furred paws give good traction on loose, dry, desert soils and insulate the pads from the hot ground. Their diet consists of nocturnally active rodents including kangaroo rats, as well as jackrabbits, lizards, scorpions, and insects. They can be found throughout the southeastern deserts and the San Joaquin Valley.

Common gray fox

Red foxes are rusty red in color, with white underparts, chins, and throats. Their tails are very bushy, long, and red with white tips. Their lower legs and feet are black. The red fox weighs 8 to 12 pounds and measures about 2 feet long with a 15-inch tail. They were introduced into southern regions of the state from Northern California and are now relatively common in the southern coastal regions. Red foxes are primarily nocturnal, elusive animals, making them difficult to spot. Their favorite foods are voles and mice, followed by almost anything that is available—including rabbits, birds, reptiles, fruits, berries, eggs, insects, and carrion from larger animals. An adult red fox can eat up to a hundred mice per week. Red foxes have keen hearing and can listen for burrowing or gnawing animals underground and then dig into the soil or snow to capture them. They continue to catch food even when they are full, burying the excess in the dirt or snow for later.

Kit foxes

Javelina

The javelina, or collared peccary, is descended from large pigs that inhabited North America about 25 million years ago. At a height of about 2 feet, the javelina is smaller than domestic and wild pigs, with straight tusks, an erectable mane, and a whitish collar. Average weight varies between 30 and 65 pounds. The javelina has a large head and shoulders, relatively small legs and hindquarters, a piglike snout, and heavy, bristly, grizzled gray hair. Only the tips of their tusks protrude beyond their lips but in full, the tusks measure about 1 to 2 inches. Javelinas are becoming common in the southeast corner of California. They form herds, ranging from 6 to 30 animals, which may break up into temporary subherds for feeding purposes. These social animals will often stand side by side, head to tail, each grooming the other by rubbing its head along the rump, legs, and scent gland on their back. Prickly pear is a favorite food, and it also provides a water source. Javelinas usually give birth to twins during the summer; they are born with yellowish or reddish hair. Humans should use caution, as families with young may charge when approached or disturbed.

Javelina

Kangaroo Rat

Kangaroo rats are so named for their upright hopping gait, their huge hind legs and feet, and a long furry tail on which they balance. Generally, they have buffy-reddish or blackish color above with white underparts, and a 6- to 8-inch tail. Their large eyes enable them to see in minimal light. Kangaroo rats can survive in arid country without ever consuming water as a result of several amazing conservation features nature has given their bodies. Their nasal passages are elongated to cool outgoing breath and recapture moisture; their kidneys concentrate salts and urea from 10 to 20 times before eliminating them; and their feces are concentrated to contain 50 percent less water than similar rodents. These nocturnal creatures spend their days in underground burrows with the opening plugged up, so as to maintain a stable temperature. Kangaroo rats eat seeds and when out foraging, can store up to a teaspoon in their cheeks for later caching. As defense against predators (rattlesnakes, owls, badgers, skunks, foxes, coyotes), kangaroo rats kick sand into the face of their attacker. When pursued, the kangaroo rat speeds off in a zigzag pattern, changing course quickly, using its tail as a rudder—sometimes leaping as far as 10 feet. Adults live a solitary existence except during mating, when males vie with one another for females. The reproductive season is concurrent with rainfall and new vegetative growth. Heermann kangaroo rats inhabit most of Southern California, whereas the desert kangaroo rats are mostly confined to the desert regions.

Kangaroo rat

Mountain Lion

Also known as cougars or pumas, mountain lions have brown fur that is shaded gray, yellow, or red, with buff areas on their bellies, necks, and faces. They are feline in appearance, with long heavy legs, padded feet, retractable claws, long black-tipped tails, small round heads, short muzzles, small rounded ears, and supple, strong bodies. Females range in weight from 80 to 150 pounds, and males range from 120 to 180 pounds. Mountain lions are good climbers and jumpers, able to leap more than 20 feet. Elusive and rarely seen, they are territorial loners that live in the wilderness throughout the mountains, foothills, and canyons. Carnivorous eaters, they thrive on large mammals such as deer and elk as well as on porcupine, mice, rabbits, and grouse. They locate prey, slink forward close to the ground, then spring onto their victims' backs, holding and biting the neck. They may bury the leftovers of a large kill and return one or more times to eat. Mountain lions typically live together only for a few weeks while breeding. Each mountain lion has its home range and rarely ventures outside it. Mountain lions breed every other year, and although there is no fixed breeding season, it often occurs in winter or early spring. Their maternity dens are lined with vegetation and may be located in caves, in thickets, under rock ledges, or in similarly concealed places. Two to four spotted kittens are born in maternity dens from May to July.

Mountain lion

Mule Deer

Gray in winter, the mule deer's coat changes to reddish brown in summer. Some have a whitish throat and rump patch. Their tails are either black-tipped or black on top. Mule deer have large mulelike ears that move almost constantly. They are medium-sized deer with stocky bodies and long, slim, sturdy legs. Does range in weight from 100 to 180 pounds, and bucks range from 150 to 400 pounds. Only the buck has antlers; he sheds them in the winter and begins to grow another set in the spring. Summers are spent in alpine meadows and sometimes logged areas. The onset of winter drives them to lower slopes, where food supplies are more abundant. Summer forage includes grasses, sagebrush, serviceberry, and chokecherry. In winter they eat twigs, shrubs, and acorns. Mule deer are mostly active in the mornings, evenings, and on moonlit nights. A social group generally consists of the doe and her fawn or twins; bucks often remain solitary. During the November breeding season, bucks become increasingly active and intolerant of one another, sometimes engaging in vigorous fights during which each tries, with antlers enmeshed, to force down the other's head. Injuries are rare, and usually the loser withdraws. Mule deer breed in mid-November; fawns usually arrive in June, July, and August, with spotted coats for camouflage. A doe giving birth for the first time normally produces a single fawn, whereas an older doe tends to have twins. Together with the similar, but smaller, black-tailed deer, the mule deer is the primary big game animal in California.

Mule deer

Opossum

A species that is common throughout Southern California, opossums are the only pouched mammals in the United States. They have grayish black furred bodies with a ratlike, hairless tail and thin black, hairless ears. Their snouts are long and pointed. Most opossums range from 25 to 40 inches long, including the tail and weigh between 4 and 14 pounds. Opossums make their nests in hollow trees, logs, brush piles, and under houses. They are known to hang upside-down in trees with their tails wrapped around a branch. Their diet includes fruit, vegetables, nuts, insects, bird eggs, and carrion. They pretend to be dead when frightened or when approached by a predator. Nocturnal and solitary, opossums do not hibernate, but they are considerably less active in winter and may remain in the den for several weeks to wait out cold weather. Opossums have one to two litters per year and are unique in the manner they give birth; 1 to 14 embryos (which are collectively small enough to fit on a teaspoon) crawl out of the womb and somehow find their way into the mother's pouch. There, they nurse for approximately two months; only about half of the infants survive to the juvenile stage. After detaching themselves, the young venture out of the mother's pouch and may be seen riding on her back.

Opossum

Porcupine

Porcupines have gray-brown, chunky bodies, high arching backs, and short legs. Yellowish hair covers long quills all over their backs, rumps, and tails. These rodents measure up to 2 feet in length, have an 8-inch tail, and range in weight from 10 to 28 pounds. After the beaver, they are the largest rodents in California. Found throughout the state, even in very scrubby desert areas, where they eat cactus and other available foods, porcupines are active year-round. They are slow-moving animals with poor eyesight, but are equipped with thousands of barbed quills for

Porcupine

protection against predators. Contrary to popular belief, porcupines do not throw their quills; quills are released from the porcupine's body and penetrate the attacker's skin. Quills are hard to pull out, they readily work themselves in farther, which can produce painful and even fatal results. Porcupines are primarily nocturnal, but they can occasionally be seen resting in treetops during the day. They make their dens in logs or caves and use them for sleeping and birthing. Kits are born in May and June, after a gestation period of seven months. They are born headfirst, with quills aimed backward.

Pronghorn

Pronghorns are pale or reddish tan in color on the upper body and outer legs, with two white bands across the throat, a white rump patch, white chest, white lower sides, and white inner legs. Bucks have vertical black markings from eyes to snout and on the cheeks. Does range in weight from 75 to 110 pounds, and bucks range from 110 to 130 pounds. Both sexes have sets of horns; the doe's horns are seldom longer than 3 or 4 inches, but a buck's horns can grow as long as 20 inches, curving back and slightly inward. Horn sheaths are shed each year. Pronghorns are common and highly visible, preferring open rolling plains or grasslands. Active night and day, they alternate bits of sleep with watchful feeding. Pronghorns feed on grasses and forbs in summer and sagebrush and other shrubs in winter. They are the fastest animal in the Western Hemisphere and have been clocked at 70 miles per hour, although 35 miles per hour is more usual. Pronghorns run with their mouths open, not from exhaustion but to gasp extra oxygen. When it senses danger, a pronghorn snorts and erects the white hairs on its rump (twice as long as the body hairs), which creates a flash of white as it flees, warning other pronghorns of danger. If a surprise attack forces a pronghorn to fight rather than flee, it uses its sharp hooves, which can effectively drive off a coyote. Adult bucks establish territories in March and hold them through the September breeding season. Throughout the spring and summer, non-territorial bucks gather into bachelor herds, while does and fawns drift on and off the territories. By late September, territorial bucks attempt to hold groups of does and fawns in their territories for breeding and keep other bucks away. These territories are abandoned after the breeding season, horns are shed, and all ages and both sexes congregate on the winter range. The young are usually born in April, May, and June.

Pronghorn

Pronghorn populations were reduced significantly in the mid-1920s due to the fencing of range land, which hampered migration and foraging (pronghorns cannot leap fences like deer—they crawl under them instead). Most barbed wire fences in pronghorn territory now have an unbarbed bottom wire to accommodate their movement. Despite the fact that some 40,000 are taken annually as popular game animals, with management and transplantation of herds by game departments, the pronghorn population is steadily increasing.

Raccoon

Raccoons have salt-and-pepper coloring with black masks across their eyes and black-and-white ringed tails. They are about 2 feet long with a 10-inch tail, and they appear slightly hunchbacked. They range in weight from 10 to 25 pounds. Raccoons are found near water, living in dens in hollow trees, logs, rock crevices, or ground burrows. They feed mostly along streams, lakes, and ponds, and their favorite foods include fruits, nuts, grains, insects, eggs, and fish. They appear to wash their food before eating it; they either dip it in water or rub it in their paws. The reason for this activity is unknown. It is conjectured that they moisten their food because they are so used to getting it from water. Other scientists claim they are feeling for the edible parts. Raccoons do not hibernate in winter, although they may sleep for several days during cold weather. Raccoons give birth in April and May to litters of two to seven young. Raccoons have adapted well to life near humans and naturalists estimate that there are 15 to 20 times as many raccoons now as there were in the 1930s.

Raccoon

Ringtail

Also called ringtail cat, the ringtail is appropriately named for the black and white rings encircling its bushy, 15-inch tail. Their catlike bodies are yellowish brown or gray, with whitish buff below. Their heads resemble those of foxes, with big eyes and pointy ears. They inhabit rocky areas, canyons, and large trees with hollows, from deserts to lower mountain forests. Solitary and nocturnal, ringtails spend their days in a den—usually a crevice in rocks, padded with grass, moss, or leaves. They emerge at night to hunt insects, scorpions, lizards, snakes, birds, eggs, and small animals. Despite their short legs, ringtails are excellent tree climbers and they have the traction to scale rock walls. They are particularly nimble on rock ledges and can turn around with a surefooted hop if the ledge runs out. When threatened, ringtails will scream at their

Ringtail

predator and they might secrete a foul-smelling liquid. Females typically give birth to three or four young in May or June in their dens. They are born white, fuzzy, and stubby-tailed. Ringtails were once called miner's cats because of their propensity for catching and eating mice in and around mines.

River Otter

Dark brown in color, with silvery fur on their underparts, river otters have long, cylindrical bodies; small, rounded ears; large noses; small, beady eyes; long whiskers; and thick, furry tails. River otters are about 3 feet long, with 10- to 18-inch tails; they range in weight from 10 to 25 pounds. River otters live in large rivers, streams, and beaver ponds and feed primarily on fish, frogs, and aquatic invertebrates. River otters can stay under water for two to three minutes because their pulse slows and skin flaps close over their ears and nostrils. They have powerful feet and webbed toes to propel them through the water. Stiff whiskers help them hunt by feel under water. Cold waters do not bother them because their dense fur and oily underfur do not allow water to reach their skin. River otters tend to use beaver and muskrat burrows as their own. They are very playful animals that spend much time frolicking and chasing each other. Pups are born—furry, blind, and helpless—in litters of one to four in March, April, and May.

River otter

Squirrels

Several different types of squirrels inhabit Southern California. The different varieties are often quite similar and difficult to distinguish. Among the most common are antelope squirrels. The two types of antelope squirrels found in California are the white-tailed antelope squirrel, found mostly in the desert regions of the state, and Nelson's antelope squirrel, found in Kern County and the San Joaquin Valley. Both of these ground squirrels are pale buff in summer and turn gray in winter, with a single white stripe along the sides of their bodies. Neither have stripes on their faces. These squirrels hold their tails vertically when running, as the American antelope or pronghorn does when it flees. Nelson's antelope squirrels are slightly larger than white-tailed antelope squirrels and the two species do not occur together. Both live in the burrows they dig. White-tailed antelope squirrels are most active in midmorning and late afternoon, becoming dormant during hot or dry periods. Nelson's antelope squirrels are also averse to warmth and can go into a fatal frenzy in temperatures over 90 degrees. Both of these omnivorous creatures eat seeds, nuts, and fruits, although they may also feed on insects. Water is generally metabolized from food. Their calls are easily recognized loud trills that sound like a mix between a bird and a large grasshopper.

Rock squirrel

Golden mantled ground squirrels resemble chipmunks, except chipmunks are smaller and have facial stripes. Golden mantled ground squirrels' backs are brownish gray, with head and shoulders coppery red, forming the "golden mantle." Bellies are white or buff. They have one white stripe bordered by black stripes on each side. Also called copperheads, these little squirrels live in moist forests, on mountains, and sometimes in sagebrush country or rocky meadows. They hibernate through winter, putting on a layer of fat in the fall. They have well-developed cheek pouches, where they carry food to their dens to be stored and eaten in spring when they awaken. Occasionally, some individuals awaken to feed. Their diet consists of pinyon nuts, fruits, seeds, and fungi. They live in shallow burrows up to 100 feet long.

Antelope squirrel

Rock squirrels are the largest of the ground squirrels. They are 17 to 21 inches, with a 6- to 10-inch tail. Coloring is mottled gray-brown in front and darker behind, with buff bellies. Tails are long and bushy with sprinklings of brown and buff edges. True to their name, rock squirrels dwell in rocky locales in the mountains of the Mojave Desert. They dine on berries, nuts, plants, or carrion and often collect food to transport and store back in their dens. Rock squirrels are often seen sitting on or running among rocks, but they are also good tree climbers. Vocalizations include an alarm call, which is brief and followed by a lower-pitched trill. They have a sharp, sometimes quavering whistle. Females normally bear two litters during the year, one in late spring or early summer and the other in late summer or early fall.

Golden mantled ground squirrel

California ground squirrels are endemic to the state. They live throughout California, with the exception of the desert regions, preferring open oak forests as their habitat. They are brown in color, speckled with paler buff spots and bars, with a silver patch around the neck and sides.

Other types of squirrels include the small Mojave ground squirrel, found in the namesake desert; the round-tailed ground squirrel; and the common western gray squirrel.

Striped Skunk

A member of the weasel family, the striped skunk has a black coat, usually with two broad white stripes on the back that meet at the head and tail. Striped skunks have a narrow vertical stripe on their foreheads, a white cap, and bushy tail, which can range from black to varying amounts of white. Striped skunks are typically 2 feet in length, with 9-inch tails.

The western spotted skunk has a smaller body, approximately 16 inches in length, with a 9-inch tail. Their bodies are

Striped skunk

black with small horizontal white stripes on the neck and shoulders and irregular stripes and spots on their sides.

The contrast of a skunk's coloration with that of its environment demonstrates nature's protection; instead of blending, the boldness is a way of advertising to potential enemies that the skunk is not to be contended with. If appearance fails to be a deterrent, the skunk will face an intruder, arch and elevate its tail, chatter its teeth, and stomp the ground with its front feet in a show of aggression. Finally, the skunk will emit an oily, foul-smelling sulphurous spray from its anal glands, which is repulsive enough to drive away predators. When a direct hit is scored to the eyes, the irritating substance causes a temporary loss of vision. A skunk's primary predator is the great horned owl. Both the striped skunk and the spotted skunk are omnivores with a widely varied diet, ranging from insects, small mammals, and eggs to seasonal fruits. They are primarily nocturnal and live in underground burrows that they have either dug themselves or taken over from other animals. Young are usually born in the spring to fiercely protective mothers. Skunks are currently the main carriers of rabies in the United States.

Tule Elk

Tule elk are the smallest subspecies of elk in North America. Males grow much larger than females, but neither sex regularly exceeds 5 feet in height. Because of their size, uncharacteristically small for elk, they have also been known as dwarf elk.

Tule elk

Tule elk have buffy brown backs; males often have a grayish brown mane of long throat hairs. They feed on grasses, herbs, twigs, and bark.

Before human interference, tens of thousands of Tule elk roamed the grasslands of California. The depletion of their natural habitat and excessive hunting during the gold rush seriously depleted their population. Perhaps as few as two tule elk survived. The remaining population, certainly no more than a handful, was carefully protected and their numbers slowly grew. Twenty separate herds have now been introduced into the wet grasslands of the Central and Owens Valleys.

Woodrat

Also known as the pack rat, woodrats are brownish gray above, with tawny-colored sides. Their feet, bellies, undersides of tail, and throats are white. They measure about 12 inches in length and have a 4- to 6-inch tail. The nickname pack rat was given because of the animal's tendency to accumulate all sorts of objects, such as cow pies, newspaper, aluminum cans, coins, and jewelry. Pack rats have a particular fondness for shiny objects. They line their dens with a collection of treasures, which serve as insulation to maintain consistent internal temperatures. Their houses are bulky, approximately 5 feet wide by 2 feet tall with a nest inside—constructed of various materials, mostly stacks of cacti, twigs, and cow droppings. Often the houses are built at the base of a cactus, the needles of which are used by the woodrat to cover its entrance. Only one adult inhabits each house. Badgers are the only animals that tear woodrat nests apart but other predators include snakes, coyotes, owls, ringtails, and weasels. Woodrat diets consist of prickly pear, juniper, yucca, cholla, and other leafy plants. They obtain water from the foods they consume. Woodrats are believed to communicate by drumming their hind feet. Females give birth to two to four litters per year, usually yielding two or three young per litter. In Southern California, the dusky-footed woodrat inhabits the western woodlands, whereas the lighter-colored, grayer desert woodrat is found primarily in the desert regions.

Woodrat

Desert woodrat nest

Marine Mammals

Dolphins

Eleven of the world's thirty-two species of dolphin have been spotted in California's coastal waters. The different members of the dolphin family are fairly heterogeneous, but are often distinguishable by the shape of their noses, which ranges from blunt to pointed. The common dolphin, often seen in southern waters, is about 8 feet long and has a distinct beak. This species and the similar bottle-nosed dolphin regularly ride in the waves of coastal ships. Other regional dolphins include the Pacific white-sided dolphin, the northern right-whale dolphin, and Risso's dolphin, recognizable by its bluntly sloped nose. The killer whale, not uncommon in California waters, is also a member of the dolphin family.

Dolphin

Dolphins eat a variety of fish and squid. They often feed in large herds, sometimes comprising several different subspecies. They are highly intelligent creatures and are also quite playful. They can be spotted leaping out of the water along California's shoreline.

Sea Lions

Sea lions are generally larger than seals, and are distinguished by their external ear flaps. They breed along parts of the California coast, and are well protected on the Channel Islands. The California sea lion is a playful inhabitant of the coastal waters. Males are about 7 feet in length and dark brown in color. Females are about a foot smaller and lighter in color. Their numbers have increased in recent years and they are sometimes a nuisance to salmon fishers, at times becoming entangled in the nets. Females give birth to a single pup in June. The dominant males form harems, leaving younger, weaker males with no mate. They mainly breed on the Channel Islands.

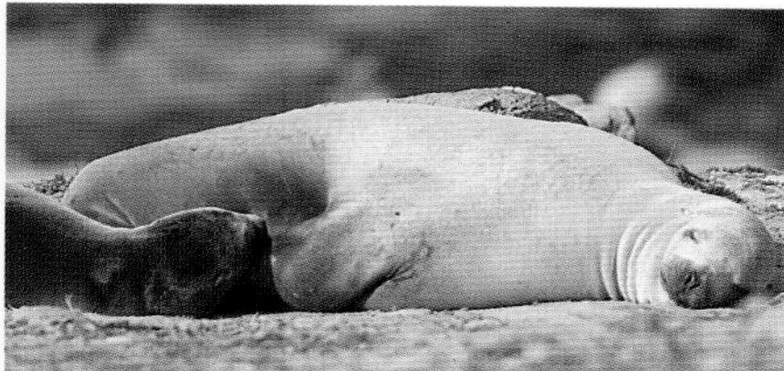

California sea lion

The northern sea lion is larger in length and heavier than the California sea lion. They are buff-colored and shy. Northern sea lions are less commonly sighted than California sea lions because they generally stay in deep ocean water. Recently, however, they established a breeding colony on San Miguel in the Channel Islands.

Seals

Seals are more adapted to life in water than sea lions. Their bodies are more compact and their limbs are smaller. This makes them better swimmers, but more awkward and slower on land. The two common types of seals in California waters are the large northern elephant seal and the harbor seal. Male northern elephant seals reach lengths in excess of 15 feet; females are about two-thirds that size. They are brown or gray with a lighter-colored underbelly. Males have a distinct pendulous snout, which earned the species its name. They are excellent hunters, feeding on fish, squid, and octopus. They can remain submerged for up to 80 minutes. In breeding season, males fight over the best beaches and build up harems. The seals depart for the open ocean after winter breeding season.

Northern elephant seal

The smaller harbor seals mainly inhabit shallow coastal waters along the entire California shore. They breed on the Channel Islands. They are playful and curious, though somewhat shy. They range in color from pale to gray to dark brown and have a cute, doglike face. They grow to about 5 feet in length. Breeding season is late summer and females give birth to one pup in April or May.

Sea Otter

Sea otters were responsible for much of the early exploration of California prior to the gold rush. They were widely and irresponsibly hunted and pushed close to extinction. Their population has rebounded somewhat, and their numbers now exceed 2,000 in California. Sea otters are larger than river otters, with larger and blunter heads. Their fur is long, brown, and insulated from the cold. Their front paws are webbed and their back paws are almost flipperlike. They eat, sleep and give birth at sea, hunting sea urchins, crabs, mussels, and fish. Sea otters are one of the few animals to use tools; they are known to break open mollusks with rocks. They are most common in Monterey Bay, but can be spotted south of there. An extensive sea otter refuge has been established in the area of Big Sur.

Sea otter

Whales

Several species of whales can be seen along the California coast, including the largest mammal ever to have existed, the 90-foot-plus blue whale. Other commonly spotted species include gray whales, fin whales, and humpback whales. Nineteenth-century whaling decimated the worldwide whale population, but it is recovering somewhat today. Whales feed on plankton and sometimes small fish. They breed infrequently, often only biennially. Each individual whale has distinct markings on its tails and marine biologists can identify whales by these markings.

Whale

Reptiles and Amphibians

Alligator Lizard

The alligator lizard may have been named for its likeness to a miniature alligator, but its habitats and size bear no resemblance. The southern alligator lizard has a long, slender body—up to 7 inches—with relatively small legs. Alligator lizards regenerate their tails if lost to a predator. The new tail will be shorter and usually a different color from the rest of its

Alligator lizard

body. An individual that has never lost its tail may have a tail nearly twice the length of its body, making the largest alligator lizards about 21 inches from end to end. The body and tail color varies from brown to yellow-ochre. Adult lizards are marked with dark crossbands; juveniles are not. The scales on the back are large, which gives the skin texture a rough appearance. Males in particular have large, triangular-shaped heads, giving them a formidable appearance. Confrontational when caught, alligator lizards will thrash around, often delivering a painful bite. They are active during the day, when they feed mainly on insects and small animals. Like a snake, these lizards shed their skin in one piece.

Bullfrog

Bullfrogs grow to about 6 inches, which is large for a frog. They are yellowish green above, with dark mottling; bellies are pale yellow. Their legs are long and dark-banded, ending in webbed feet. They make a distinctive *jug-o-rum* call, often repeated throughout the night.

The bullfrog was introduced into California from the eastern United States in order to supplement the diet of early settlers. Apparently, settlers did not like the idea of eating frogs, so the appetizer never caught on. The frogs were let loose, and they eventually made their way into the waterways. Now bullfrogs are devouring practically everything in sight, including other frogs, insects, and even birds. They are common throughout California except in the deserts or in mountains above 4,000 feet. Bullfrogs have few predators and compete with native frogs and toads for food and space. There are some legislative proposals to exterminate bullfrogs.

Bullfrog

Chuckwalla

A harmless member of the iguana family, the stout-bodied chuckwalla is the second largest lizard in the United States, second in size only to the Gila monster. Chuckwalla males grow to a length of 18 inches; females are slightly smaller. Adult males have reddish or gray backs and blackish heads, necks, and legs. Young chuckwallas have four or five broad bands across the body and three or four on the tail. Although these bands are usually lost when the males reach adulthood, females tend to retain them. Small scales cover the body, with larger scales protecting ear openings. Chuckwalla bodies have loose folds of sandpapery skin around the neck. Their tails are thick, long, and blunt. This lizard is able to change colors somewhat in response to changes in light, temperature, and other variables. The diurnal lizard emerges in the morning and before seeking food, basks in the sun until its optimum body temperature of 100 degrees is reached. It is not unusual to see several chuckwallas sunning themselves at the same time. Strictly herbivorous, chuckwallas eat fruit, creosote bush, leaves, buds, and flowers. When a chuckwalla senses danger, it scurries between rocks and lodges itself tightly in crevices by taking a breath and inflating itself—making forced extraction nearly impossible. If a predator in pursuit grabs a chuckwalla by its tail, the tail separates from the body and proceeds to wriggle, thus distracting the predator and giving the lizard a chance to escape. Another tail will grow back, smaller than the previous one. This phenomenon can occur several times. Females lay an average of eight eggs in rock crevices every year or perhaps every other year.

Chuckwalla

Collared Lizard

These robust lizards have bodies that measure 3 to 5 inches, with large heads, narrow necks, and long tails. Including tails, collared lizards reach lengths of about 12 inches. The males have blue-green bodies with yellow spots. The females are typically gray or brown with creamy spots. Found in rocky canyons, rocky ledges, and boulder-strewn areas, collared lizards also seek out boulders to serve as areas for basking, warmth, and lookouts. They spring from boulders to seize lizards and insect prey. Collared lizards run from danger on their hind legs with tails in the air.

Collared lizard

Desert Tortoise

Desert tortoises have high-domed shells and stocky legs that are covered with large conical scales. Adult males grow to about 15 inches and weigh about 20 pounds; females are slightly smaller. These completely terrestrial creatures are masters at conserving water and energy in the harshest of conditions. They derive most of their water from food and can store up to a cup in their bladders for use during dry seasons. After heavy rains, tortoises will drink so much water that one tortoise was documented as having weighed 43 percent more after drinking! To minimize water loss they incur from breathing, desert tortoises hibernate in humid burrows, occupied by one or many individuals, as far as 30 feet underground—ideally beneath a wash. Their hard, domed shells serve as insulation against moisture loss and temperature fluctuation in addition to providing armorlike protection from predators. Tortoises breed after 15 years of age. Their eggs—which are

Desert tortoise

the size and shape of Ping Pong balls—hatch into fully formed, self-sufficient young turtles. However, youngsters remain vulnerable to predators because their protective shells do not develop until after the first five years. It takes 15 to 20 years for one to reach maturity. Desert tortoises prefer rocky foothills; they live in burrows they have dug in firm soil or between and under large rocks. Native Americans considered their meat a delicacy but never seriously endangered their population. Desert tortoises have become threatened in recent years because native plants have been replaced by less nutritionally satisfying foreign species.

Two of the tortoises' relatives, the western pond turtle and the spiny softshell turtle, can be found in California lakes and ponds.

Garter Snake

There are several types of garter snakes found in California. Among them are the common garter snake and the western aquatic garter snake, both found in the southern portion of the state outside the desert regions. The western aquatic, as its name suggests, prefers ponds and rivers.

The moderately slender bodies of adult garter snakes range from 24 to 45 inches in length. They have light stripes down the sides of their bodies, sometimes with a distinctive light stripe down the back of some individuals. The color between the stripes is brownish, marked with dark spots. Underneath they are brownish, bluish, or gray, with reddish blotches. These snakes feed on fish, tadpoles, frogs, earthworms, snails, lizards, small mammals, and occasionally insects, birds, and carrion. Unlike other snakes, garter snakes give birth to live young. When captured, they emit a foul-smelling fluid from vent glands.

Garter snake

Gecko

Geckos are small lizards with a distinct appearance and coloration. Western banded geckos are found in much of Southern California, especially in chaparral, deserts, and canyons. They are light tan, with yellow or red-brown spots or bands, and a white underbelly and pinkish legs. They have a thick tail and long, slender toes. Their eyes protrude and their eyelids are moveable. Geckos are generally nocturnal, which allows them to survive in hot environs. They live under rocks or in crevices and hunt insects and spiders. They can be spotted on blacktop roads at night, illuminated by headlights. Some of the geckos seen during the day are not western banded but rather introduced Mediterranean geckos. Mediterranean geckos are similar in appearance to western banded geckos. The European variety is more active during the day than its North American counterpart.

Gecko

Gopher Snake

Also called a bullsnake, this common snake is long, reaching 5 to 6 feet in length. The head is oval and slightly flattened, with a somewhat pointed snout and an enlarged scale on the front of the nose. Varying in color by region, gopher snakes have smaller blotches on the sides, with a prominent dark stripe across the top of the head that reaches from eye to eye. In southeastern California, they are predominantly reddish, whereas in the western part of the state, they are generally dark brown. Their habitats range from grassland, gravelly soil, coniferous forests, deciduous forests, riparian areas, and agricultural areas, to sagebrush and rabbitbrush. Gopher snakes can appear threatening by mimicking the coiling and hissing of a rattlesnake. However, these formidable-looking snakes are harmless. They are considered desirable to have around because they consume large numbers of rodents. Diet includes assorted rodents, small rabbits, birds and their eggs, and occasionally lizards. Females lay 5 to 20 eggs under rocks or in burrows.

Gopher snake

Horned Lizard

A member of the iguana family, the horned lizard is common throughout Southern California, the main varieties being the coast horned lizard and the desert horned lizard. It has sharp-pointed horns along the back of its head and is often referred to as a horned toad. About 3 or 4 inches in length, the horned lizard has a squat, somewhat flat body. Horned lizards can be brown or bluish gray, with the color matching the local soil. Their sides and quite short tails are edged with whitish spines. They inhabit rocky and sandy open areas, remaining active throughout the warm days but when it is

Short horned lizard

Regal horned lizard

too hot, restricting activity to mornings. Although most lizards rely on speed and break-away tails to avoid predators, the horned lizard is slow and sluggish. Instead, its defenses are camouflage and the ability to inflate itself like a blowfish. These lizards are far from sumptuous meals to predators—their spike-like scales make them difficult to swallow. Horned lizards feed on insects—primarily ants—but also are known to eat small snakes. Females give live birth of up to 30 offspring.

King snake

The common king snake is a non-venomous member of the Colubridae family, which includes gopher snakes, garter snakes, and whip snakes. Mature adults are 3 to 4 feet long and come in a variety of colors and patterns, usually chocolate brown to black. Common king snakes vary in pattern and color. Although most have a pattern of alternating black and white bands, these colors may vary to brown, white, cream, or pale yellow, depending on the region. Some individuals have black bellies, while others are nearly all black. The king snake was named because it eats other snakes—particularly rattlesnakes, copperheads, and coral snakes—and is immune to their venom. They also eat lizards, birds and their eggs, small mammals, turtles, and frogs. They will even climb trees in pursuit of prey. King snakes use their keen sense of smell to locate food at night, then quickly bite and surround the victim with suffocating coils. They swallow their prey whole, while it is still alive. Generally regarded as a gentle snake, a king snake will hiss, strike, and vibrate its tail when threatened. If attacked, king snakes roll into a ball with their heads in the center and smear attackers with musk and feces. Females lay up to 20 eggs in the spring or summer; once the eggs are laid, she shows no further interest.

King snake

Native Frogs

Many of California's native frogs are suffering from competition with introduced bullfrogs, but the state still supports a variety of frog species. One unique type of frog is the Pacific tree frog, a small amphibian about 1½ inches in length, with the ability to cling to trees. Its skin is rough, and its toes are not webbed but are instead long and pointed. Its color is generally green, but it can change to shades of brown and red in a few minutes. Pacific tree frogs and gray California tree frogs are common throughout the state, except in the deserts. They emit a recognizable, high-pitched, *kre-eek* sound.

Pacific tree frog

California red-legged frogs are quite large, about 4 inches in length, and can jump up to 3 feet in one leap. They are brown in color, with red bellies, sides, or legs. They like low-elevation wooded areas, preferring humid forests and slow moving streams or ponds. During breeding season, the frogs deposit up to 4,000 eggs at one time.

California tree frog

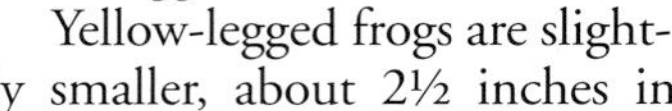

Yellow-legged frogs are slightly smaller, about 2½ inches in length, with yellow legs and sides. The mountain yellow-legged frog is dark brown with black spots. It lives in mountain regions, rarely more than a jump or two from water. It lacks the ability to vocalize, unlike the foothill yellow-legged frog, which makes a deep guttural noise.

Night Snake

The night snake is common in Southern California and is comfortable in a variety of habitats—oak woodlands, deserts, sagebrush, chaparral, and mountains as high as 7,000 feet. As its name implies, the night snake is a nocturnal hunter; it kills frogs and lizards with poisonous saliva secreted from glands in its grooved back teeth. Night snakes are patterned with dark gray and brown spots that are arranged over a lighter gray or brown background. They grow to a length of about 20 inches. Female night snakes lay up to six eggs in summer.

Night snake

Rattlesnake

There are six species of rattlesnake found throughout California, all of which are dangerous to humans. They are typically gray (although individual colors will vary, depending on how long it has been since the last molt), with darker blotches along the back. The tail is ringed with black and white bands. They have a triangular head, narrow neck, and grow to lengths of more than 4 feet, including the rattle. In hot summer weather they usually prowl at dusk and at night. Pores in their heads pick up scents and heat to help detect prey. The snake kills its prey by injecting it with venom through hollow fangs that snap downward and forward as the snake strikes. To human beings, a rattler's bite is painful and can cause infection and illness. There have been few fatalities documented among adults who have been bitten. They are relatively docile snakes—most frequently they lie still and allow danger to pass, only coiling and rattling if they sense they've been seen and feel threatened. Even then, they often do not rattle. If left alone, they crawl away and seek a hiding

Rattlesnake

place. Exercise caution in tall grass, rocky areas, and around prairie dog towns, especially in the mornings, evenings, and after summer thunderstorms. Females give birth to as many as 15 live young in late summer.

Sidewinder

Sidewinders are members of the rattlesnake family. They look much like other rattlesnakes, but have a triangular horn over each eye. Their coloration gives a dusty appearance and blends with their environment; they range in color from sand to pale gray. They have rough scales with brown or gray blotches along their back and sides. They usually reach a length ranging from 17 to 33 inches. The name sidewinder is derived from the unique way this snake moves: rippling sideways and keeping minimal contact between its body and the hot sand. Sidewinders leave parallel, J-shaped tracks in the sand. These nocturnal snakes are found in the deserts, sand dunes, and rocky hillsides of Southern California. Adults feed primarily on kangaroo rats and pocket mice, while youngsters prefer lizards. Rodents are bitten, released, and tracked down, while lizards are held until the venom takes effect. Sidewinders mate in April and May or sometimes in the fall. Females give birth to 5 to 18 young in late summer or fall.

Sidewinder

Skink

Sold in pet stores as a combination of a snake and a lizard, skinks are shiny-skinned, small-legged reptiles with a long tail and a fondness for water. They generally feed on insects. Two species of skink are common in California: Gilbert's skink, which inhabits the riparian woodlands of the central and southern mountain regions, and the western skink, common in coastal regions. Gilbert's skinks are pale brown in color; the head is pink in breeding seasons. The tail is pinkish or sometimes blue. Their average length is about 10 inches. Western skinks are slightly smaller, about 8 inches in length. They have brown, tan, black, or red-brown stripes running the length of their bodies.

Skink

Spiny Lizard

Spiny lizards occur practically statewide, from low deserts to pinyon-juniper woodlands; they prefer a habitat with rocks, shrubs, and trees. Although good climbers, they are often found on the ground where they forage for insects, leaves, berries, and occasionally smaller lizards. They sometimes use the nests of woodrats for shelter.

Spiny lizard

The Sonoran spiny lizard is the largest spiny lizard found in North American deserts—reaching up to 10 inches in length. The stocky lizard has sharp-tipped spiny scales, grayish to yellowish in color, with black triangular patches on the sides of the neck. Males have blue patches on the throat and on each side of the belly.

Toads

California is home to several species of toads, which are distinguishable from frogs by their shorter legs and warty skin, as well as their tendency to survive outside of the water. The western spadefoot is a medium-small toad that grows to 3 inches. Its color is dusky brown, green, or gray. The eyes protrude and have vertical elliptical pupils. Spadefoot toads are named for their built-in digging tools—a black sickle-shaped spade on each hind leg, which they use to "swim" through mud.

Spadefoot toad

The Sonoran desert toad, which is also known as the Colorado River toad, is olive green to dark brown, with white warts near the corners of its mouth. It grows to about 6 inches. These amphibians are rather well protected against predators. The toad's skin produces toxins that react with mucous. If a dog mouths a toad, it will suffer severe discomfort and the possibility of paralysis or death. If a toad sits in a dog's water dish and the pet subsequently drinks the water, illness or death can result. Sonoran desert toads spend most of the year underground, having dug themselves in or usurped abandoned rodent burrows. Summer rains trigger emergence and signal the beginning of breeding season. After mating, toads feed on insects, spiders, smaller toads, and small vertebrates that are abundant after summer rains. After storing an adequate supply of fat, toads again burrow into the ground where they remain through winter.

Sonoran desert toad

The western toad is grayish green or brown with a bold yellow stripe along its back. It tends to walk instead of hopping and lacks the ability to vocalize except for small peeps. It is common in the low mountains, where it is active during the day. In warmer regions it is predominantly nocturnal. Western toads feed on insects, shooting out a long sharp tongue to capture them.

Other Californian toads include the red-spotted toad and the southwestern arroyo toad. The arroyo toad has lost much of its natural habitat and is now a protected species.

Whiptails

Western whiptails are slender lizards found throughout most of California, except in the high mountain areas. They are yellow to grayish brown, sometimes with dark markings. Under-

Whiptail lizard

bellies are white or yellow. Adult males have a black throat and chest. Predators include birds, snakes, and small mammals. For protection, whiptails dig burrows that provide a safe retreat. Their agility and speed help them escape danger; they travel up to 15 miles per hour. In addition, they have break-away tails, which help them elude capture. Whiptails are constantly in motion—almost hyperactive. They are known to run upright on their hind legs, swiveling their head rapidly from side to side, sniffing the air with their forked tongue as they forage ceaselessly for termites, spiders, and other insects. Some all-female species of whiptail lizard do not reproduce sexually but by parthenogenesis, which means that all of their offspring are female. Their eggs require no fertilization, and the offspring are exact and complete genetic duplicates of the mother.

Invertebrates

Ant Lion

Ant lion larvae are sometimes referred to as doodlebugs because they have a clumsy, backward motion that leaves doodling tracks in the sand. When larvae hatch, they immediately begin digging individual ant traps with their sickle-shaped jaws. After they reach the bottom of their pitlike trap (approximately 2 by 2 inches), they open their jaws and wait for ants to slip on the edge of the pit and tumble inside—right into the ant lion larvae's mouth. Victims are then injected with venom and eaten. Eventually, the larvae spin cocoons and metamorphose to emerge in late summer as winged dragonflylike creatures with one single mission—to mate. Adults die almost immediately after mating, but not before females lay their eggs directly onto the soil surface, where her larvae will hatch and repeat the life cycle.

Ant lion larva

Ant lion adult

Butterfly

There are many species of butterflies in California, some of which, like the California tortoiseshell and the beautiful California sister, are rarely found elsewhere. Dependent on plants for their survival, butterflies lay eggs on host plants, which then become food for the caterpillars after they hatch. Mature caterpillars spin cocoons on the host plants. After weeks or months a butterfly emerges to mate, sip flower nectar, lay eggs, and die. With wingspans of 4 to 6 inches, the giant swallowtail is the largest butterfly in the United States. Their forewings have a diagonal band of yellow spots, and their tails are edged with black and filled with yellow. The caterpillars, which are sometimes called orangedogs, feed mostly on citrus and prickly ash. Hairstreak butterflies are small, and have cobalt blue wings with black margins dotted red and white. Hairstreaks fool predators into attacking a false head on their hind wings, which they rub up and down. Birds will bite the false head, allowing the butterfly to escape with minimal damage. Monarch butterflies have striking reddish brown wings with black veins and black borders with two rows of white dots. The wingspan may reach 4 inches. When monarch larvae feed on milkweed plants, they accumulate a poisonous substance in their bodies that makes them distasteful to birds and other predators. Birds learn to recognize the butterflies' bright pattern and avoid them. Tiger swallowtails are yellow with black stripes and have black wing margins. Some females are all black with a bluish iridescence. They are called swallowtails because they have long "tails" on their hind wings, which look a bit like the long, pointed tails of swallows (a type of bird). When it is very young, the caterpillar is camouflaged to look like bird droppings. Later, it develops distinctive eyespots that make it look like a snake, which scares off some predators.

Monarch

Acmon blue

California sister

Edith's checkerspot

Blue copper

Pipe vine swallowtail

Mourning cloak

Damselflies and Dragonflies

Damselflies and dragonflies belong to the Odonata order. These insects have biting mouthparts, short antennae, and very large eyes. Their legs are attached to the body just behind the head. This makes walking almost impossible but greatly facilitates gripping. Damselflies have broad heads with widely

Damselfly

Dragonfly

spaced eyes; dragonflies have rounded heads with eyes that are closer together. Damselflies have two similar pairs of wings that they hold close to their bodies and fold together when at rest. Dragonflies' hind wings, which they hold outstretched when at rest, are broader than their forewings. In both insects, the powerful wings move independently. Damselflies sit and wait for prey; dragonflies actively pursue their prey in air. Both creatures lay their eggs on aquatic plants in the water.

Darkling Beetle

Also called stinkbugs, these desert beetles are blackish, about an inch long, and walk with their rear ends raised in the air. This posture serves two purposes: It gets the beetles up and away from the hot ground, and it allows them to drink the drops of nighttime dew that collect on their backs by channeling the liquid into their mouths. Darkling beetles repel predators by spraying a foul-smelling liquid from their abdomens while standing on their heads and aiming directly at the target. The odor can remain in the air for 15 minutes. Not all enemies, however, are deterred by this kerosene-scented repellent. Black widow spiders tie the beetle down and stay out of range until the supply of spray has been depleted. Before consuming the insect, grasshopper mice press the beetle's abdomen into the soil to disarm the sprayer.

ırkling beetle

Giant Desert Centipede

Centipedes belong to a class arthropods called Chilopods. Centipede literally means "100 legs," although they do not actually have that many. At lengths of 6 to 9 inches, the giant desert centipede is North America's largest centipede. It is mostly brown with a bluish head and tail segments. It has a segmented body with a pair of legs attached to each segment. Each leg of the first pair is slightly shorter than the body width, but each leg of the twentieth pair is twice as long as the body width. The last pair of legs faces backward, giving the impression that the centipede has a head on either end. Like many Chilopods, centipedes can inflict a painful, but not fatal, venomous bite with the pincers at the end of their first pair of legs. They are not considered dangerous to humans, although handling one is likely to be an unpleasant experience. Giant desert centipedes are most active at night, when they prey upon vertebrates such as small lizards and mice. During hot days they retreat to burrows in the arid desert.

Giant desert centipede

Harvester Ant

Ants are related to wasps and bees. They are social creatures, found in colonies with populations ranging from a few dozen to millions of members. All colonies have a queen—the large, fertile female—in addition to numerous, sterile, wingless females. The queen is the only one to reproduce. The cycle of a colony begins when the queen lays eggs that are both male and female. The eggs hatch into winged ants, which leave the nest and mate. The males die and the females go on to become new queens, which build nests, lay eggs, and begin the cycle again. Individual ants can live as long as 5 years; queens live up to 15 years. Only old workers leave the nest. When they are killed, a defensive scent is emitted that draws others from the colony to attack the killer of the worker. They will inject a venom that produces a painful sting. Most creatures will not eat harvester ants because of their venom. An exception is the horned lizard, which has an antitoxin in its blood specific to harvester ants. Harvester ants get their name because a colony can collect as many as 7,000 seeds in one day. Some plants, such as jimson weed, rely on harvester ants to gather and scatter their seeds before rodents eat them from the vine. Harvester ants do not eat jimson weed seeds because of their thick coating. The California harvester ant is reddish, with a large head. Other ants in the state include the red mound ant, a rusty red ant with a painful stinger, and the Argentine ant, which was introduced from South America in coffee shipments and has thrived.

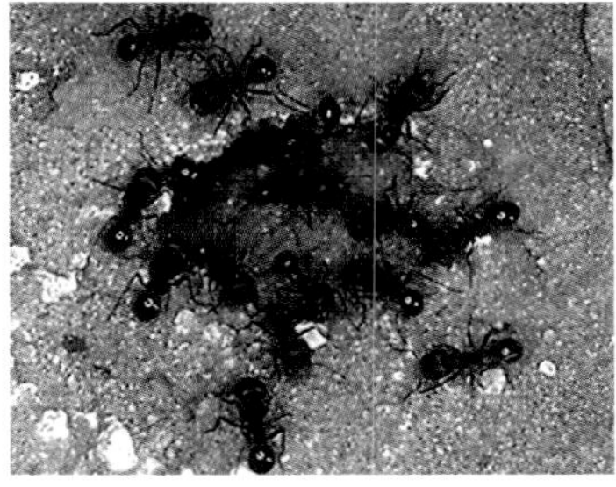

Harvester ants

Scorpions

Scorpions, venomous relatives of spiders, mites, and ticks, belong to the class Arachnida. They look a bit like miniature lobsters, with elongated bodies, four pairs of legs, pincers, and a segmented tail (actually the abdomen), which is tipped with a stinger. A scorpion stings by thrusting its "tail" forward over its head and impaling the prey held in its pincers. Scorpions are covered with several layers of wax in order to conserve body water. Most scorpions are nocturnal predatory insects with diets that include crickets, spiders, centipedes, other scorpions, snakes, and mice. They locate prey by sensing vibrations. The primary purpose of a scorpion's venom is to capture prey—self-defense is secondary. A scorpion would much prefer to be left alone or to retreat than sting. Caution should be exercised when camping or participating in other outdoor activities; be sure that scorpions have not crawled into footwear, clothes, or sleeping bags. First aid for a scorpion sting should include cleaning the site with soap and water, applying a cool compress, elevating the affected limb to approximately heart level, and ingesting aspirin or acetaminophen as needed for minor discomfort. Children or anyone experiencing severe symptoms from a sting should be taken to a health care facility immediately.

Giant desert hairy scorpion

Sphinx Moth

Sphinx moths are also known as hummingbird moths for their ability to hover in front of flowers and sip the sweet nectar. The humming noise that is made by the rapid beating of wings, along with an extremely long proboscis (feeding tube) tongue, increase the similarity to hummingbirds. Sphinx moths are stout-bodied with long, narrow forewings and shorter hind wings; wingspans range from 2 to 8 inches. Sphinx moths emerge at dusk from their hiding places and begin feeding on the nectar of flowers. Many species pollinate flowers such as orchids, petunias, and evening primroses while sucking their nectar with a proboscis, which exceeds 10 inches in some species. Caterpillars of this group are known as hornworms because of a sinister-looking barb on the rear; they are the culprits that eat all the leaves in tomato and petunia gardens. Sphinx moth larvae change into adult moths underground and then dig their way to the surface to mate. Females lay up to 1,000 eggs on the underside of food plants; the eggs hatch within a few days. Sphinx moth males and females die after they have completed the reproductive process. Two species of sphinx moths in California are the white-lined sphinx moth and Cerisy's sphinx moth (also known as the eyed sphinx moth). Other moths common in the state are California tent caterpillar moths, whose caterpillars build silken tents in willows and oaks; polyphemus moths; and the brightly colored ceanothus silk moth. Moths are distinguishable from butterflies in several ways. Butterflies fly only during the day, whereas moths come out both day and night; moths' antennae lack the clubbed tip of butterfly antennae; and moths rest with their wings angled or outstretched while butterflies rest with their wings held vertically, like a sail.

Sphinx moth

Tarantula

Desert tarantulas are large hairy spiders found throughout the deserts of California. Despite their multiple eyes, tarantulas are nearly blind, relying on smell and touch to help them "see." They have gray-brown bodies up to 3 inches long with 4-inch legs. Males have thinner, longer legs; the first pair has hooks that are used to hold the female's venomous fangs during mating. Males and females do not become sexually mature until about eight or nine years. Following copulation, the male scrambles away because females occasionally kill their mates. Tarantulas are most active during their mating season, which lasts from June to October. The tarantula, which does not spin a web but instead catches its prey by pursuit, feeds on mice, lizards, and snakes. A bite from the quarter-inch fangs injects venom along with a digestive fluid to liquefy the victim's soft tissues. Then the tarantula sucks the body dry, leaving an empty shell. Tarantulas are timid creatures but will bite if provoked. To humans, their bites can be extremely painful but are not usually dangerous. Tarantulas live underground in burrows, where they are protected from extreme weather conditions. They can plug the entrance and go dormant, even going without food for up to two years and without water for seven months. Females may live to about 20 years, but males live only half as long—they die after their one season of sexual activity. Other arachnids in California include the western black widow, the common house spider, the common orb weaver, and the crab spider, none of which are deadly to humans.

Tarantula

Tarantula Hawk Wasp

These wasps are easily identified by their dark bodies, which have a black metallic appearance, and their bright orange wings. Females can be as long as 4 inches. Tarantula hawks are nectar feeders and can often be found in gatherings of a dozen or more feeding on plants. Their name is derived from their fascinating means of reproduction. After mating, a female is ready to lay her eggs. She seeks out a tarantula, immobilizes it with a paralyzing zap from her half-inch stinger, and then maneuvers the comatose victim to an underground chamber. Instead of killing the tarantula, the venom she injects causes only paralysis. Then she lays one large white egg on the spider, which hatches within five days. The larva feeds on the spider, saving the vital organs for last so that the spider remains alive for about a month, or until the larva is ready to pupate. The larva then spins a cocoon, in which it spends the winter. When mature, it has transformed into an adult wasp, completing the cycle. California is also home to ichneumon wasps, live oak gall wasps, golden paper wasps, and the easily recognizable yellow jackets.

Tarantula hawk wasp on top of her victim

Birds

American Coot

The American coot can be found throughout California. In summer it rests on freshwater lakes and ponds; in winter it also comes to coastal bays and inlets. Similar to a duck, the American coot is distinguished by its smaller size (15 inches), dark coloring and white chickenlike bill. Coots are expert swimmers, propelling themselves over the water with wide lobed toes. They feed by diving underwater or foraging near the shore. Coots are gregarious birds and are often seen gathered in rafts (flocks). They vocalize with a variety of harsh clucks, cackles, and

American coot

grunts. Their nests, shallow platforms of dead plant matter, are usually secured to reeds on the water. Females lay 8 to 10 pinkish eggs with brown spots.

American Kestrel

The American kestrel is a commonly seen bird of prey that was formerly known as the sparrow hawk. Kestrels can be spotted hovering in search of prey in the open country of the deserts, prairies, and farmland. The American kestrel is identified by two distinctive facial stripes. The male has a rusty back with blue-gray wings and crown. The female has a rusty back and rusty wings. The female's tail is rusty with black banding and the male's is solid rust with a black tip. At about 8 to 12 inches long, the American kestrel is the smallest, most common falcon in Southern California. It is similar to a robin in size but fiercely preys on insects, small rodents, reptiles, and amphibians. It has a loud voice and when excited, lets out a shrill *killy, killy, killy.* Kestrels make their nests in the cavities of saguaros or trees, or in abandoned nest cavities of flickers.

American kestrel

Blackbirds

Red-winged blackbirds are about 8 or 9 inches long. Males are black with crimson shoulder patches above a white slash, while females are mottled brown, with heavily streaked underparts and a faint red shoulder patch. The red coloration serves as a flag in courtship and also in aggression. In an experiment, males whose red shoulders were painted black soon lost their territories to rivals they had previously defeated. These birds inhabit marshes, wetlands, and open fields. Their nests—woven of dried grass and soft materials—are found among grasses or cattails. Another species, the tricolored blackbird, is unique to California. Similar in appearance to the red-winged blackbird, tricolored blackbird males have a white slash below the crimson shoulder patch. Brewer's blackbirds and yellow-headed blackbirds are also found in the state. The yellow-headed blackbird is distinguished by its colored head and a white patch near the bend of its wings. Male Brewer's blackbirds are almost entirely black with hints of purple; females are grayish brown.

ed-winged blackbird

Cactus Wren

The cactus wren is the largest wren in North America. At about 8 inches, this large speckled and striped wren has a brown head, white eye line, light-colored underparts spotted with black, and a long tail. The cactus wren has a long beak, which it uses to search out termites and other insects from bark or cacti. Found in the deserts, the cactus wren builds domed ovular straw nests in a cholla or yucca. Females lay four to seven pinkish, speckled eggs from March to June.

Cactus wren

California Condor

The California condor is a large, majestic bird. It can be 4 feet in length and its wingspan is the largest in North America, often approaching 9 feet. Adult condors are black with a naked orange head. Immature birds have a gray head. From below, observers will notice white wing linings. California condors eat a variety of small animals, mostly rodents. They should not be fed as this increases their reliance on humans and decreases their chances of independent survival.

In prehistoric times, the range of the California condor extended from British Columbia to Florida, but by the twentieth century it was confined to the mountains north of Los Angeles. By the 1980s a combination of factors had reduced its numbers to just five. Lead poisoning from eating pellets imbedded in game was a major killer. The surviving birds were placed in captivity, where attempts are being made to breed the species. Condors have been reintroduced into the wild in limited areas, but for now the main battle is merely to prevent extinction. In spring 2000, the total population of California condors was 176, only 53 of which were flying free. Several trails in this book, such as Central Mountains #45: Pine Mountain Road, provide opportunities for viewing these rare and beautiful raptors.

California condor

California Gull

Found along the coast and in western inland valleys, the fully grown California gull reaches 18 to 23 inches in length. California gulls tend to nest on islands. They need very little cover because the open water keeps them safe from terrestrial predators. Nests are often on open beaches or shorelines on the ground in a shallow hole lined with plants, grass, feathers, and small sticks. Similar in appearance to other gulls, California gulls are mostly white, with gray wings and backs and black tails. Their legs and beak are yellow.

California gull

The California gull is, paradoxically, the state bird of Utah. They are credited with saving Mormon pioneers in that state by eating insects during the locust plague of 1848. The California gull is one of several types of gull found along California's shoreline.

California Quail

The California quail was officially adopted as California's state bird on June 12, 1931. They are found in the foothills, often near a river or lake. Males have a brown crown and buff forehead with a bluish brown, scaled belly. Females' markings are less bold. During the mating season, birds pair to mate and build nests on the ground beneath a low shrub. Females lay from 12 to 16 cream-colored eggs. Because of their vulnerability in ground nests, on average more than half the youngsters die within their first year. The adult cry is distinctive. It sounds like *chi-ca-go*, with an emphasis on the middle note. Whole families will take to trees for breeding. After breeding they become quite gregarious, often grouping in city parks and gardens.

California quail

Other quails in California are the mountain quail and the desert-dwelling Gambel's quail.

Cliff Swallow

These small birds grow to 6 inches. They have a square tail; blue-gray head and wings; cream-colored rump, forehead, and breast; and rusty cheeks, nape, and throat. Cliff swallows build gourd-shaped, all-mud nests on rocky cliffs, as well as under many low-elevation bridges. They consume enormous quantities of bugs, entirely during flight. Their migration schedule is so regular that it was used as a calendar reference for missionaries at Mission San Juan Capistrano.

Cliff swallow

Common Raven

The common raven is entirely black and looks a bit like the American crow, but is much larger. Common ravens are 20 to 27 inches long with thick black bills that are heavier than most birds of similar size. They have a wedge-shaped tail and shaggy throat feathers. When in flight, they often soar like hawks. Common ravens have an opportunistic diet, ranging from berries and other birds' eggs and nestlings to other small vertebrates. They inhabit cliffs and canyons, where they build large nests of sticks or bones, lined with fur or plant materials on steep cliffs or in tall trees. Females usually lay four to seven eggs, which are green with brown spots.

Common raven

Curve-billed Thrasher

Curve-billed thrashers are brownish gray with long, down-curved bills and bright orange eyes. Their size ranges from 9 to 12 inches in length. Common year-round in California's deserts, these birds prefer extensive thickets of thorny shrubs and large dense cacti. Curve-billed thrashers are ground feeders, who use their long curved bills to ferret out bugs. They vie with cactus wrens for food and nesting sites; thrashers have been known to tear up cactus wren nests. Curve-billed thrashers build cuplike nests in the protection of shiny chollas or yuccas, where they lay two to four bluish green eggs. Males and females are similar in appearance. Le Conte's thrasher is the palest of the several species in Southern California. The California thrasher is darker and prefers riparian woodland. Thrashers have similar calls to mockingbirds, to whom they are related.

Curve-billed trasher

Gambel's Quail

The most common quail in the arid regions of California is the desert-adapted Gambel's quail. These plump game birds are 10 to 12 inches and have a distinctive comma-shaped, forward-leaning black head plume, or topknot. Their coloring is grayish-brownish gold. Males have a black face and throat with rusty sides, diagonal white stripes, and a buff white belly. Females are somewhat drabber. Gambel's quails can withstand severe dehydration, losing up to half their body weight. When possible, they consume green, succulent plants that provide water, but when the plants they eat are dry—especially in winter—they will seek water, and large convoys can be found at waterholes. During mating season, birds pair to mate and build nests on the ground beneath a cactus or low shrub. Females lay from 12 to 15 eggs. Because of their vulnerability in ground nests, it is common for more than half the youngsters to die within their first year.

Gambel's quail

Golden Eagle

Golden eagles are truly magnificent birds, ranging in length from 30 to 40 inches with a wingspan of 6 to 8 feet. Males and females are similar in appearance, with brown bodies that have a golden tint, especially on the neck and head. Their feet are yellow and their hooked bills are dark. While soaring above, golden eagles swoop down onto prey, which includes ground squirrels, marmots, and grouse. They are also capable of killing young goats, sheep, and deer. Normally they build nests of sticks, branches, and roots atop a cliff that overlooks an open area with a reasonable population of small mammals. Despite suffering population loss, golden eagles are still regularly seen in much of Southern California.

Golden eagle

Great Blue Heron

The great blue heron stands nearly 5 feet tall with blue-gray feathers, a long curving neck, and a straight yellowish bill. Great blue herons are occasionally mistaken for cranes because of their similarity in size and proportion, but in flight, cranes hold their necks outstretched while herons fold their necks back onto the shoulders. These birds are adept at catching aquatic fauna with a spearlike bill. Great blue herons nest in trees, in flimsy to elaborate stick-and-twig platforms that are added to over the course of many years. These nests can be up to 4 feet in diameter to accommodate the heron pair as they incubate three to seven blue-green eggs.

Great blue heron

Greater Roadrunner

Perhaps the desert's best-known bird, the greater roadrunner is a super-speedy, long-legged, crested bird with an oversized bill. Adult birds measure about 20 to 24 inches in overall length. These members of the cuckoo family are grayish brown, with streaks of black and white, tinged with shiny green. A blue and red patch is behind each eye. Roadrunners have long tails, which they sometimes flick vertically. They are shy and reclusive. Although they can fly, roadrunners prefer to run for cover instead of taking flight, sprinting as fast as 15 miles per hour when startled. They feed on a wide variety of desert life including insects, scorpions, lizards, snakes (including rattlesnakes), and rodents. Females lay three to five ivory-colored eggs in a flat stick nest lined with grass, usually in a thick shrub or cactus close to the ground. When food is scarce, older hatchlings selfishly devour it, leaving younger hatchlings to starve. The siblings and parents then consume the dead hatchlings' bodies.

Greater roadrunner

Hummingbirds

The name hummingbird originated from the noise the birds' wings make while in flight. Hummingbirds, only a few inches long, are the smallest of all birds. There are a number of species in California, including black-chinned, Anna's, Allen's, Costa's, and rufous. The most common are Anna's hummingbirds, recognizable by the red hood of the males. Hummingbirds feed mainly on nectar; they also regularly consume small insects. They obtain nectar by inserting their bills and tongues into a flower, accumulating pollen on their bills and heads; this pollen is then transferred from flower to flower. Hummingbirds are strong fliers and have exceptional flight characteristics for birds: They can hover and fly backward. The extremely rapid beating of their wings can reach 80 beats per second. Some hummingbirds save energy on cool nights by lowering their usually high body temperature until they become sluggish and unresponsive—a condition termed torpor. In contrast, during daylight hours, hummingbirds are often very active and can be highly aggressive, sometimes attacking much larger potential predators, such as hawks and owls.

Costa's hummingbird

Rufous hummingbird

Anna's hummingbird

Jays

The western scrub jay is commonly found in Southern California. This 11- to 12- inch crestless jay has sky blue upper parts, a long tail, and grayish buff underparts. It is found in the open country and dry habitat of California. The western scrub jay is aggressively intolerant toward the Steller's jay and drives it away.

The Steller's jay is the only western jay to have a crest. Because of its large size (10 to 12 inches), blue coloration, and crest, the Steller's jay is quite distinctive. Male and female Steller's jays look similar: The head and upper breast are brownish or grayish black to jet black. The underparts below the breast are greenish blue, turning brighter blue under the tail. Wings are bright purplish blue to sky blue with narrow black barring; the rump and tail are bright blue with black barring that becomes more prominent toward the end. Under the wings and tail, the body is gray. The Steller's jay prefers conifer forests in the mountains of California. Like other jays, the Steller's jay consumes a wide variety of foods, including small vertebrates, seeds, berries, nuts, and especially acorns and pine seeds when available. They commonly take the eggs and nestlings of small birds, and they have even been observed attacking and eating adult birds. Normally a shy and wary bird, the Steller's jay can become accustomed to humans at campgrounds and picnic areas. They build bulky nests of sticks and twigs, which are lined with mud, grass, and conifer needles. The nests are found in conifer trees. Females typically lay four eggs.

Western scrub jay

Pinyon jays, another small blue bird, prefer pinyon forests, but will traverse a variety of habitats in search of food. They store pine nuts for winter and spring. Pinyon jays are friendlier than other jays, and tend to gather in flocks. Adults are almost completely dull blue with a black beak. Their tails are somewhat shorter than those of other jays.

Mountain Bluebird

These beautiful, sky-blue birds are found in Southern California at elevations above 5,000 feet. They normally take over nests abandoned by woodpeckers because their beaks are not strong enough to hollow out their own nest cavities. Their sur-

Mountain bluebird

vival is becoming more difficult, as the logging industry cuts down many standing dead trees that the birds would normally use as homes. They readily adapt to whatever homes they can find, including chipmunk burrows, abandoned car bumpers, and fence posts in open areas. When not nesting, mountain bluebirds are often spotted in sizable flocks. They hunt by flying slowly, low to the ground, and swooping down to catch insects and spiders.

Western bluebirds, distinguished by chestnut colorings on their bodies, are found at most elevations.

Mountain Chickadee

The mountain chickadee is a small, energetic bird that sings its name: *chick-a-dee-dee-dee.* Identified by its black cap and bib, black eye line, white cheek, and gray underparts and tail, it grows to about 5 inches. Mountain chickadees must consume nearly their body weight in seeds and insects each day because of their amazingly fast heart rate of 500 beats per minute. During cold weather, it puffs out its feathers so that it resembles a fluffy ball with a beak. Nests are usually in natural cavities or abandoned woodpecker nests.

Mountain chickadee

Mourning Dove

Mourning doves are one of the most common wild doves native to North America. They are members of the same family as pigeons and bear a resemblance to them, except that mourning doves are grayish brown, with thinner, pointed tails. Their outer tail feathers have white tips with a black marking midway, so that the tail is edged with a black and white stripe. Both male and female mourning doves look alike but females have more of an overall brown coloring. Mourning doves are named for their sad-sounding, long calls most often heard in the mornings. This melancholy song has been compared to a person mourning the loss of a loved one. Mourning doves produce up to six broods per year—the most of any native bird. Typically, two eggs are laid in a nest made in an evergreen tree, although a wide variety of nest sites are used, including clumps of grass.

Mourning dove

Northern Flicker

The northern flicker, a type of woodpecker, can be identified in flight by a flash of salmon red under its wings and tail. Viewed at rest, the northern flicker has a brown crown, a brownish body, and a red streak behind its bill. Northern flickers are the most terrestrial of North American woodpeckers—they are found anywhere from tree line to sea level. They are occasionally spotted bathing in dusty depressions, as dust particles absorb oils and bacteria from their feathers. Northern flickers feed mostly on insects—particularly ants. They also eat berries. Northern flickers use their powerful beaks to create nesting holes in dead or dying deciduous trees and line the cavity with wood chips.

Northern flicker

Northern Mockingbird

Northern mockingbirds are long, streamlined gray birds reaching up to 9 inches in length, with white undersides and flashy white wing patches and outer tail feathers. Males and females look alike. Of all North American birds, the mockingbird is most famous for vocal imitations—its repertoire has been known to include more than 40 different sounds. These talented birds can also mimic sounds such as those of a barking dog, squeaky hinges, notes from a piano, and even a cackling hen. During mating season the male will mark his territory with song. Mockingbirds sing incessantly, both night and day, hopping from one song post to another. They are known to be aggressive when defending their nests and territories. However, if you see them jumping up and down in the air, they may be catching a few insects. Mockingbirds live year-round throughout Southern California.

Northern mockingbird

Nuthatches

Nuthatches are small birds, only about 4 to 6 inches in length. They are the only tree-climbing birds that descend headfirst. While foraging on a tree trunk, a nuthatch might pause in mid-descent, arch its head, and call out noisily. Nuthatches clasp the trunk with their feet, which are equipped with a back claw to help them traverse the undersides of branches. They nest in natural cavities in trees or in abandoned woodpecker nests. They line their nests with bark, grass, fur, and feathers. Females lay five to eight eggs and incubate them for up to two weeks. The white-breasted nuthatch has bluish gray coloring on its back and a white breast; males have a black crown. This nuthatch, the only one with an entirely white face, lives throughout the forests of Southern California. Red-breasted nuthatches are primarily confined to higher elevations. Pygmy nuthatches reside mainly in yellow pine forests.

White-breasted nuthatch

Orioles

Orioles are members of the blackbird family. The brightly colored hooded oriole is commonly found in California. The male's head and underparts are bright yellowish orange; it has a black back, tail, and throat. Females are olive-gray with greenish yellow underparts. Two other orioles, Bullock's oriole and Scott's oriole, also migrate to California in the spring and summer from Mexico and Central America. Bullock's oriole males are bright orange and black—distinguishable from other black and orange orioles by their black eye line. Scott's oriole males have solid black heads and backs with lemony yellow underparts. Females and their young are more subtly colored with an olive-green to grayish back and yellowish breast. Orioles create beautifully woven hanging nests of plant fibers, suspended pouchlike from the very tips of tree branches. They eat insects, fleshy fruits, berries, nectar from hummingbird feeders, and nectar from flowers.

Hooded oriole

Owls

California is host to several owl species, from the large and imposing great horned owl to the diminutive burrowing owl. Owls are truly unique birds. They are characterized by large heads; round, penetrating eyes; acute hearing and eyesight; generally nocturnal hunting habits; and slow, silent flights. They accomplish their quiet movement using specially adapted serrated feathers that allow air to pass through them slowly. Owls also have a wide range of vision; in some species the neck can rotate nearly 180 degrees. They are equipped with excellent night vision. Many owls make a distinctive *hooting* sound, and often respond to imitations of their call. Around the nests of owls, one can find regurgitated pellets, revealing the bones of the predators' last meal.

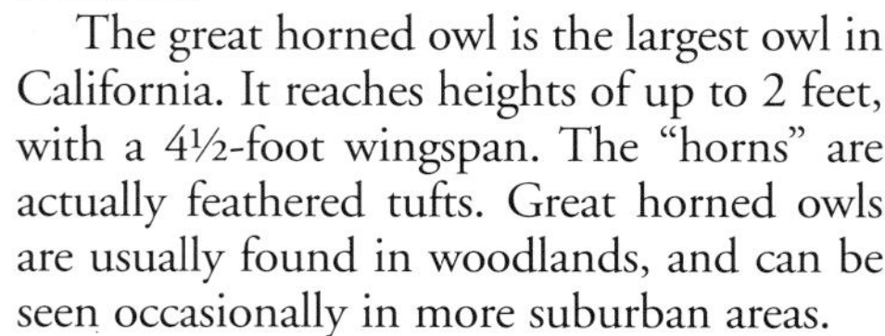
Great horned owl

The great horned owl is the largest owl in California. It reaches heights of up to 2 feet, with a 4½-foot wingspan. The "horns" are actually feathered tufts. Great horned owls are usually found in woodlands, and can be seen occasionally in more suburban areas.

Also common is the barn owl, which has a recognizable heart-shaped facial disc and white- or cream-colored plumage. Barn owls are very beneficial to humans because they primarily eat rodents. However, as humans have urbanized increasingly large areas of Southern California, barn owls have lost much of their habitat. They can still be spotted in rural areas, where they earn their name nesting in barns.

Barn owl

Western screech owls are small, cute owls that inhabit a variety of terrain in Southern California, from desert to woodland. They nest in natural cavities or abandoned woodpecker holes. They are quite numerous in the state, but, like other owls, they are nocturnal and thus infrequently seen.

Burrowing owl

The aptly named burrowing owl, which lives in peculiar ground nests that they guard by day, inhabits the open country of Southern California. It can often be seen standing on its long legs on fence posts or at golf courses.

Some California owls have become endangered in recent years. An increasingly uncommon owl is the northern spotted owl, whose plight has attracted the attention of environmentalists, much to the chagrin of logging companies and developers. The tiny elf owl has also pretty much disappeared from its desert habitat, and the clearing of riparian woodland has robbed the long-eared owl of its primary breeding ground.

Screech owl

Owls often played a part in Native American spirituality. They were viewed alternatively as a bringer of fortune, an omen of evil, or a harbinger of death. Although their image is common in modern popular culture as a symbol of wisdom, nighttime, or nature, owls are rarely seen in the wild. Still, the backcountry adventurer should be watchful for a chance sighting of these beautiful raptors.

Pelicans

California is one of the few states in which one can view pelicans. Two species of this distinctive water bird winter in Southern California. American white pelicans, the largest birds in the state with a length of about 5 feet, visit the inland lakes of the region, including the Salton Sea; smaller, but more colorful, brown pelicans can be seen in coastal areas. American white pelicans are mostly white with a long, flat orange bill. Brown pelicans are brown with a yellow head and black underbody. Unlike brown pelicans, which dive from great heights to capture fish, American white pelicans cooperate to surround fish in shallow water where they can be easily scooped up. The population of brown pelicans fell dramatically because of agricultural runoff containing DDT, but recent years have seen some reversal of the decline.

White pelican

Brown pelican

Phainopepla

The phainopepla is a slender elegant bird with lustrous feathers, a crest, and a long tail. Males are glossy black with two white wing patches that show in flight; females and ju-

Phainopepla

veniles are gray. Adults grow to about 8 inches. Male phainopeplas build a nest to attract females, who, if impressed, then lay and incubate the eggs. The pair disbands after its young are raised. In summer, phainopeplas seek relief from the hot deserts by migrating to cooler regions of southern Nevada and Utah, and to the Pacific Coast. They usually breed in the deserts, producing one brood, and a second upon migrations to cooler habitats. These birds eat mistletoe berries, which provide both nutrition and water. When seasonal berries are not available, phainopeplas pluck insects from the air.

Red-tailed Hawk

The red-tailed hawk is a big, powerful bird that reaches lengths of about 24 inches. The red-tailed hawk goes through several color phases, which can make identification difficult. Generally, the bird has dark upper parts, light underparts, and a red tail. Females are larger than males. Red-tailed hawks like open country, fields, and mixed woodlands. These predatory birds perch in trees, overlooking open fields with a sit-and-wait hunting technique. They swoop down on their prey, ripping it apart with their hooked beaks and sharp talons. They are also known to dive after prey while soaring. Diet ranges from small rodents to medium-size birds, amphibians, and reptiles. Red-tailed hawks normally make their nests in trees; bulkily constructed with sticks, the nests are usually added to each year. Both parents incubate the eggs, but only the female raises the young. Cooper's hawks are also fairly common in Southern California. They are grayer in color, smaller than red-tailed hawks, with a rounded tail. They prefer woodland areas.

Young red-tailed hawk

Sandhill Crane

This native of northern Canada migrates south to winter in Southern California's Central Valley. Sandhill cranes are very tall birds, up to 4 feet in length, with long legs and neck. Coloring is mostly gray, though the cheeks and throat are white and the forehead is red. Young birds are a paler gray-brown color. Sandhill cranes emit a distinctive *gorooooo-ah-ah-ah* call, often when in flight. The birds glide in flight and flap with a rapid upstroke of the wings. They breed to the north but return annually in large flocks.

Sandhill cranes

Sparrows

The black-throated sparrow, previously called desert sparrow, thrives year-round in desert scrub environments. These distinctive birds reach a length of about 5 inches, have a dark conical bill, black throat and mask, gray crown, back, and wings, white belly, and a long black tail with a small amount of white on outer tail feathers and outer corner. Both sexes are similar in appearance.

Black-throated sparrows were named for their black throats, which resemble a V-shaped bib on their chest. They drink less water than any other seed-eating birds; they obtain most of their water from food. After rains, they eat new vegetation and seeds. During dry seasons, they switch to juicy insects. To conserve water during very hot days, black-throated sparrows will retreat to cool underground rodent burrows. They can drink saltier water than other birds.

White-crowned sparrow

A common sparrow found throughout Southern California during the winter months is the white-crowned sparrow—large flocks of them arrive during fall. White-crowned sparrows range from 6 to 7 inches in length. This bold, colorful, and vocal bird has a white crown ringed with black stripes, a white eyebrow, black eye line, gray face, gray back streaked with brown, and gray underparts. White-crowned sparrows scratch the ground to expose insects and seeds, although they also eat berries.

Another very common sparrow found in California is the slightly smaller chipping sparrow, which is distinguished by its rufous cap and black eye line. Chipping sparrows prefer woodland areas in the mountains. The largest sparrow in the state is the fox sparrow, which migrates to California from elsewhere in North America. Lark sparrows are resident throughout the year and are known for their lovely songs and beautiful plumage. They nest on the ground, concealed by dense vegetation. The English sparrow is also common in the state, having been introduced from Europe in the 1800s.

Towhees

The California (or brown) towhee, spotted towhee, Abert's towhee, and green-tailed towhee are all found in Southern California. These birds range from approximately 7 to 8 inches in length and are members of the sparrow family. Towhees scratch the ground vigorously for insects and seeds. They nest low in a bush, on the ground under cover, or in a brushy pile in a cup nest made of leaves, grass, and bark shreds. California

Spotted towhee

Abert's towhee

towhees are friendly and populous. They are small gray birds often seen in suburban gardens. They prefer heavily brushed coastal areas, and their range does not extend far beyond the state borders. Spotted towhees are slightly less common, but more brightly colored, with red sides and white underparts. Abert's towhees are found throughout the desert regions of Southern California, while green-tailed towhees prefer mountain areas.

Turkey Vulture

This scavenger bird is predominantly black, with a featherless red head. Its legs and feet are orange and its hooked beak is yellow. Turkey vultures are large birds with bodies as long as 32 inches and wingspans as wide as 6 feet. They soar over open areas, seldom flapping their wings, in search of carrion they sense by utilizing their keen sight and smell. They gather for communal roosts on fence posts or in dead trees at night. Instead of building nests, turkey vultures lay their eggs in logs or under protective ledges. They are mostly seen in spring or fall.

Turkey vulture

Western Kingbird

Western kingbirds are 8 or 9 inches long, gray above, and white, gray, or yellow below, with whitish edges on the outermost tail feathers and a blackish mask through the eye. They have a red spot (usually concealed) on the crown, which is flared in courtship displays or during confrontation with rivals. Western kingbirds are somewhat social; two or more pairs have been found nesting in the same tree. They will attack hawks, crows, ravens, and other birds that fly near their nest; they will even ride on the larger bird's back and peck at its head. The western kingbird is usually found in the summer months in open country around ranches and towns. A large flycatcher, it perches upright on tall weeds, exposed branches, or wires before sweeping forward to catch insects in midair. Western kingbirds occasionally eat berries. An entertaining tumble-display takes place during courtship when males fly to about 60 feet, then stall and tumble, free-falling toward the ground. Kingbirds build nests in cottonwood, oak, sycamore, and willow trees, and on utility poles, water towers, and barns. Made of weed stems, twigs, and string, the nests are lined with sheep's wool, cotton, hair, and feathers. Four eggs are laid between April and July; incubation is usually 12 to 14 days. Fledglings can usually fly about two weeks after hatching.

Western kingbird

Western Tanager

The colorful male western tanager is exotic and tropical-looking with a red head, yellow body, black back, black wings, and black tail. The female is yellow-green above with yellow below. Her coloring is more subdued. Both males and females have horizontal bars on their wings; the top one is thin yellow and the bottom one is white. They eat insects and fruit and grow to about 7 inches in length. Found in coniferous mountain forests, the western tanager is a migratory bird that prefers conifer forests in the summer and warm spots in the winter. Western tanagers build frail cup nests out of twigs, grass, or other plant materials, on horizontal branches or in the fork of high trees. The hepatic tanager is another of the species found (infrequently) in Southern California. The male has an orange-brick color. The female is olive-green with yellow under parts.

Western tanager

White-throated Swift

The white-throated swift is a 6- or 7-inch bird with a long forked tail and a black upper part with white below that tapers down the belly. These remarkable little birds spend most of their lifetime in flight; they feed, drink, bathe, and even mate while flying! One of the fastest birds in the world—and certainly one of the fastest in California—white-throated swifts like open habitat, where they feed almost entirely on flying insects. They build nests within cracks or crevices of cliffs.

Woodpeckers

California is home to several species of woodpeckers. Woodpeckers bang their strong bills on trees and utility poles, generally as a way of establishing territory and probing for insects in the barks of trees. They have thick, chisellike bills and long tongues for this purpose. The males' plumage is similar to the females', but the male often has a patch of red on his head. Acorn woodpeckers live in oak forests and eat acorns, which they sometimes bury in tree trunks for later consumption. For other woodpeckers, diets consist mostly of insects, seeds, and berries. Woodpeckers make holes in trees in which to nest. The nests are used for just one season before being appropriated by other birds, often owls. Females lay three to five eggs; the young can fly in about a month. Nuttall's woodpecker is perhaps the most common, it usually nests in riparian woodlands, unlike the visually similar ladder-backed woodpecker, which prefers desert areas, as does the uncommon Gila woodpecker. The downy woodpecker has a fairly large population in California and is often seen in residential areas and parklands.

Acorn woodpecker

Gila woodpecker

Yellow-Billed Magpie

Yellow-billed magpies are found only in California, from the Sacramento Valley to Santa Barbara County. Magpies' black-

Yellow-billed magpie

and-white coloration and long tails make them easy to identify. This California variety is distinguished, as its name suggests, by its yellow bill. Magpies are big, flashy, boisterous, and loud birds, with a reputation for raiding the nests of other birds, picking sores of cattle, and attacking the eyes of injured animals. Their sturdy nests, made of mud and reeds, are used from year to year; they also mate with the same partners from year to year. They can often be seen in parks and picnic areas feeding on food scraps.

Plants

Wildflowers

Bindweed

Bindweed is a twining plant found throughout North America. Common bindweed and field bindweed were introduced from Europe. Related to morning glory, bindweed's white or cream-colored flowers resemble those of that vine. In Southern California, it is often found in gardens, fields, roadsides, and waste areas. Many people consider it a weed and its deep root system makes it difficult to eradicate. Length: 1 to 3 feet.

Field bindweed

Bladderpod

Bladderpod is a tall, dense, rounded shrub that grows from Southern California down through the Baja Peninsula. It flourishes in coastal sagebrush regions, along the western edge of the deserts, and in the southern Sierra Nevada foothills. Also known as burro fat, bladderpods sprout bright yellow flowers almost year-round. The flowers are about 1 inch long with 4 petals and long stamens. The inedible fruit grows in inflated green pods that give the plant its common name. Bladderpods emit a strong, distinctive skunky smell. Height: 2 to 6 feet.

Bladderpod

California Poppy

The California poppy is the state flower of California. It is a common sight throughout Southern California, with the exception of the Colorado Desert. It can be a perennial (surviving for several years) or an annual (completing its life cycle in one year). Flowers start to bloom in February or March and continue to form until September. They are usually deep orange in color, but are often pale yellow by the end of summer. The flowers are bowl-shaped and about 2 inches in height. They often close at night or during bad weather. The preferred habitat for the California poppy is open grassy areas. Height: 18 inches.

California poppy

Chuparosa

Chuparosa means "rose sucker" or "hummingbird" in Spanish, and this wildflower is indeed a favorite for hummingbirds. The diminutive birds help to pollinate the plant as they feed from it. Chuparosa is a common sight at the low elevations of the Colorado Desert in southeastern California. It blooms between February and June. Flowers are about 1 inch long and look like narrow red tubes. The shrub itself is densely branched, wide, and tall. Leaves are scarce and, when flowerless, the plant has a dull gray-green appearance. Height: to 5 feet.

Chuparosa

Common Mullein

Also known as flannel mullein, blanketweed, woolly mullein, and velvet plant, common mullein is a naturalized weed from Europe. It is an erect, stout, woolly biennial with matted layers of short, starlike hairs that cover the entire plant. Leaves form a woolly rosette on the ground in the first year, from which the stem arises in the second year. Its large woolly stem is very leafy. Greenish yellow flowers, which bloom from June to September, are crowded on a long, thick spike at the top of the plant, 1 to 3 feet long and ¾ to 1¼ inches thick. Egg-shaped seedpods contain numerous tiny, dark brown seeds. Common mullein grows in dry disturbed soil in waste places or fields and along roadsides, railroad embankments, and old dwellings. This widespread plant has no value as forage. Colonists and Native Americans lined their footwear with the leaves of this plant for warmth. Height: 2 to 6 feet.

Common mullein

Common Sunflower

Common sunflowers are tall, robust, branched annuals with coarse, rough stems. Hairy leaves are heart-shaped and pointed at the tip; the edges are usually toothed. Sunflowers have large 2- to 5-inch flower heads that bloom from March to October or November. Flower heads follow the sun as it moves across the sky during the day. The sunflower was introduced in California and is native to the Great Plains area. This showy and somewhat ornamental plant is abundant in moist soils throughout most of the state along roadsides and in waste places, aban-

Common sunflower

doned fields, lowlands, and barren spots. It can be a pest near cultivated crops. Birds, rodents, and humans eat sunflower seeds. Native Americans have been known to make purple and black dye from the seeds, and yellow dye from the flowers. Height: 3 to 7 feet.

Desert Globemallow

This year-round blooming plant is also known as apricot mallow and desert mallow. Desert globemallows are bushy, somewhat woody perennials, covered by minute star-shaped hairs that may be very irritating to the eyes. Desert globemallows have bright orange or apricot flowers, with five petals each. These cup-shaped flowers grow along upper stems to 2 inches wide. Petals can be white, pink, peach, purple, or blue. The plant has erect branches and three-lobed, scalloped-edged leaves that resemble the maple. Desert globemallow is the most drought-resistant member of the mallow family. It is found along roadsides, in sandy washes, and on rocky hillsides, sometimes among pinyon and juniper. Height: 1 to 4 feet.

Desert globemallow

Desert Lupine

In Latin, *lupine* means "wolfish," as members of this family were once believed to destroy the soil. The opposite is in fact true; many members of the pea family actually improve soil fertility through nitrogen fixation. Desert lupine, often called Coulter's lupine, is a favorite among bees. Like other peas, the plants have distinctive flowers with one petal on top and two on the bottom. They have ½-inch-long blue to lilac flowers that bloom on slender, erect stems from January through May. The upper petal has a yellow spot, which changes to reddish after pollination. The two bottom petals are short and wide; they are hairy on the bottom edge and curve upward to a slender tip. When ripe, the seedpods explode, scattering their seeds to the wind. This annual herb has dark green compound leaves with five to nine leaflets arranged like the spokes of a wheel. Lupines can be toxic and should never be eaten. Height: to 16 inches.

Desert lupine

Desert Marigold

Also called wild marigold, paperdaisy, and desert Baileya, desert marigolds are attractive spring annuals of the sunflower family. The name marigold is derived from "Mary's Gold," in honor of the Virgin Mary. Desert marigolds grow in large clumps, with daisylike, brilliant yellow flowers—from five to many per head. The leaves and stems are a dull grayish green; they are woolly and densely matted to protect the plant from ultraviolet rays and to help it retain water. Desert marigold is found on roadsides, slopes, sandy and gravely areas, and overgrazed land. Feeding on this plant has poisoned sheep and goats. Height: to 2 feet.

Desert marigold

Desert Trumpet

A perennial herb, desert trumpet is a member of the buckwheat family. Desert trumpet stems are inflated or flared just below the point of branching, vaguely reminiscent of several wind instruments. According to Dr. James L. Reveal of the University of Maryland, the stem is swollen because it has high concentrations of carbon dioxide. If you look very carefully, you may see a small hole near the top of the inflated area. This is the entrance to a miniature food storage room and incubator for minute wasps. The female wasp packs the cavity with insect larvae and then lays her eggs upon them, thus ensuring a food supply for her young. Desert trumpets have tiny yellow flowers on very slender, almost leafless, gray-green stems. In Southern California, they generally bloom between March and July. Native Americans used the dried stems as pipes; another name for Desert trumpet is Indianpipe weed. Height: to 3 feet.

Desert trumpet

Fairy Duster

A member of the pea family, fairy duster is a low, thornless, densely branched shrub. It remains inconspicuous for much of the year, but when the spring bloom arrives, it sends out the ball-shaped clusters of pink flowers that give the plant its name. These light pink to orange puffs contain many flowers, which are darker toward the center, from which long stamens radiate. It is a food source to a variety of desert animals, birds, and insects. Fairy dusters are a particular favorite of hummingbirds. Height: 8 inches to 4 feet.

Fairy duster

Fiddleneck

Fiddleneck is a common annual found in open, disturbed areas of Southern California, such as roadsides and fields. Part of the forget-me-not family, fiddleneck was named because its curved flower spike resembles the head of a violin. The orange-yellow flowers grow in a cluster at the end of bristly, coiled branches that sprout from a long, erect stem. As the flowers bloom, the coil opens. Blooming generally occurs in April and May. Height: 1 to 3 feet.

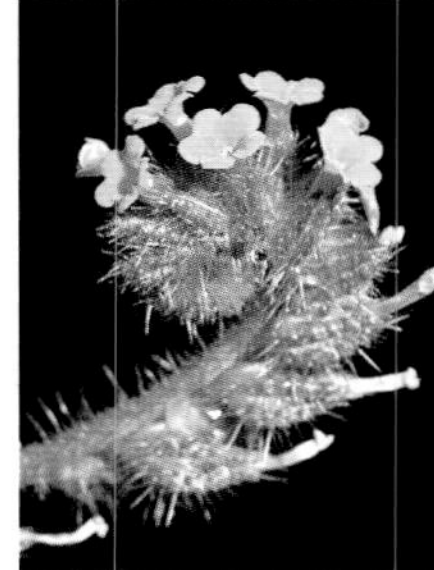

Fiddleneck

Filaree

Early Spanish settlers introduced filaree, a member of the geranium family, into the United States from Eurasia. Also called heron bill because of the way a ripening seedpod re-

Filaree

sembles a heron's beak, this plant is one of the earliest to bloom in the desert. Flowers are pinkish violet, about ¼ to ½ inch wide, with five petals that drop off the plant very quickly. The unusual needlelike fruits split into five one-seeded fruits at maturity. One seed is enclosed in each of these single, spindle-shaped, very hard fruits. The plant has red creeping stems that sprawl along the ground up to 20 inches, fernlike leaves, and small sword-shaped fruits. Mature seedpods turn into a spiral as they dry. But when moisture is available, the pod untwists, pushing the seedpod into the soil. Height: to 15 inches —spreads horizontally.

Filaree flower

Goldenrod

Also known as yellowweed, goldenrod is a genus in the sunflower family. It typically has a slender unbranched stem with short-stalked or stalkless leaves and small yellowish flower heads in complex clusters. It is one of the later-blooming plants, usually flowering from July to September. Medicinal applications of this plant include use as an astringent and diuretic for kidney stones. In powder form it has been used for cicatrization of ulcers. Height: 1 to 5 feet.

Goldenrod

Goldfield

Goldfields are small annual flowers that thrive throughout California, ranging from northern Baja California to Oregon. When there is adequate moisture, they can cover entire slopes or fields with a golden yellow hue. Goldfields bloom from March to May. Flowers are a little over 1 inch wide, with about 13 pale-tipped petals spreading from the central disc. Height: 6 inches.

Goldfields

Indian Paintbrush

Indian paintbrush flowers are small modified leaves called bracts, which have colorful tips of fiery orange, pink, maroon, red, or yellow, giving the appearance of a dipped paintbrush at the end of the stems. The roots of these plants are semiparasitic and steal food from other plants. Found most often in habitats with dry, open soil, sometimes with sagebrush, this plant blooms from May to September. Height: 1 to 3 feet.

Indian paintbrush

Jimson Weed

Also called *toloache* or sacred datura, all parts of this plant are poisonous and can prove fatal. Jimson weed has white, foul-smelling, trumpet-shaped flowers that open after dusk and close the next morning. The fruit is round and thorny, with many small spines. Leaves are up to 6 inches long, greenish gray, and covered by tiny hairs. Jimson weed is often seen along roadsides and desert sandy flats. The ingestion of this plant, which is a powerful though dangerous hallucinogen, was popular among California Indian tribes. Height: to 24 inches.

Jimson weed

Milkweed

Showy milkweeds have small but complex flowers in rounded clusters that vary from white or yellowish to red or purplish. Their leaves are paired and their fruit pods are filled with seeds. The sap has toxic properties that are destroyed by boiling; Native Americans used to cook and eat the shoots, leaves, buds, flowers, and seedpods. Monarch butterfly larvae consume the toxic foliage, which makes them less vulnerable to predators. The seedpod's down, which is five or six times more buoyant than cork, was used to stuff pillows and, during World War II, life jackets and flight suits. Milkweed is commonly found in clumps beside streams, ditches, and roads. Height: 18 to 72 inches.

Milkweed

Mission Bells

Mission bells were named by early Spanish priests who thought the dark purple-brown and yellow drooping flowers resembled church bells. Their preferred habitats are open woodlands and grassy areas. Mission bells' stems are very long and erect. The leaves separate in a circle around single points along the stalk, generally occurring more toward the top of the stem. Flowers bloom between February and July. Height: 1 to 4 feet.

Mission bells

Monkeyflower

Monkeyflowers are extremely variable plants, ranging from tiny and spindly to large and bushy. They are characterized by their trumpet-shaped flowers. In Southern California, monkeyflowers come in a variety of colors including yellow, scarlet, and orange. The common monkeyflower blooms from March to September and prefers a wet environment. This plant is also called wild lettuce because Native Americans and early settlers ate the bitter

Monkeyflower

leaves. Tiny Fremont's monkeyflower, which blooms from April to June, thrives in fire-swept chaparral but decreases in abundance as other vegetation reclaims the burned land. Height: 1 inch to 3 feet.

Owl's Clover

The Spanish name for owl's clover is *escobita*, which means "little broom," referring to the broomlike flower cluster. The clusters range in color from cream to a deep magenta, increasing in hue toward the top. The leaves are 1 to 2 inches long and are divided into a few narrow segments. Owl's clover is very common after a wet spring, when it blankets whole fields. After blooming, which occurs between March and May, the plant forms a small fruit. Height: 4 to 16 inches.

Owl's clover

Prickly Phlox

The woody stems of this plant are covered in small, prickly leaves. Pink flowers form in clusters near the top; less common colors include white, cream, and lilac. The flowers, which bloom from March to June, are about 1 inch wide and flare into five rounded petals. Prickly phlox prefers dry slopes and stream banks below 5,000 feet. They range from San Luis Obispo County to the Santa Ana and San Bernardino Mountains. Height: to 2 feet.

Prickly phlox

Prickly Poppy

This very branchy, pale green plant is covered with yellow prickles. Long, lobed, spiny leaves resembling thistles grow to 8 inches. Flowers are white and papery, with a single eye of yellow stamens and six broad, delicate, wrinkled petals. Seedpods are prickly and grow to 2 inches in length. All parts of this plant contain alkaloids that are poisonous. Prickly poppy grows wild throughout Southern California deserts because no animals will eat it. Height: to 4 feet.

Prickly poppy

Purple Nightshade

This woody member of the nightshade, or potato, family is a sticky glandular perennial. Nightshade is a native subshrub with deep purple, starlike flowers that have a crinkly appearance and a small cluster of yellow stamens in the center. Leaves are hairy and dark green. All parts of the plant are toxic. Purple nightshade grows in several habitats, including chaparral and oak woodlands. Height: 3 to 5 feet.

Purple nightshade

Salsify

Also called goat dandelion, this member of the sunflower family looks much like a tall, large dandelion after it goes to seed. Its yellow flowers bloom in the morning and close by noon. (There is also a purplish variety.) The plants are found in meadows, fields, waste areas, and roadsides. Salsify was brought by European settlers to use as a garden vegetable; roots were soaked to remove the bitterness, then peeled and eaten raw or stewed. Their flavor is similar to that of oysters. In our research, we have found many recipes for salsify dishes on the internet. Height: 1 to 4 feet.

Salsify

Shooting Star

Also known as birdbill, shooting star is a member of the primrose family. In appearance, shooting star resembles a colorful rocket. It has a yellow circle in the center with backward-curving magenta petals that point down to form the nose. There is a rosette of leaves around the base of the stalk. Elk, deer, and cattle graze on the young shoots, which grow in rich soil and partial shade along streams and in wet meadows. Height: 6 to 16 inches.

Shooting star

Thistle

There are several species of thistle in Southern California, all members of the sunflower family. The most unique is probably yellow star thistle, an extremely invasive, non-native plant found in most of California outside the deserts. It is characterized by long yellow thorns below the flower. These spines are painful to touch. Another common thistle is the creeping thistle, a pink-flowered, tall plant that blooms all summer. The Latin name for thistle, *Cirsium,* means "a swollen vein," for which the plants were thought to be a remedy. Height: 2 to 4 feet.

Red thistle

White Virgin's Bower

Also known as clematis, traveler's joy, or pepper vine, white virgin's bower is a woody vine that clambers over other vegetation in the canyons and gullies of Southern California. Its stems and leaves have a peppery taste. Native Americans chewed them as a remedy for colds and sore throats. However, a similar species is poisonous, so self-medication is not recommended. The roots of the plant have also been put to practical use; they were placed in a tired horse's nostrils to revive them. In summer, the vines produce hundreds of cream-colored flowers, less than an inch wide. Length: up to 10 feet.

White virgin's bower

Trees and Shrubs

Bigleaf Maple

As their name implies, bigleaf maples have the largest leaves of all maple trees, often 8 inches long. Bigleaf maples thrive in the woodlands of Southern California, especially on stream banks. They grow to heights between 30 and 80 feet. The broad, rounded crown of drooping branches and large leaves provides good shade and beautiful autumn colors. Their wood is the only western maple used commercially. Native Americans used it to fashion canoe paddles.

Bigleaf maple

Box Elder

The box elder is a member of the maple family (it is also known as ashleaf maple). Although they are more common in the eastern United States, box elders flourish in the coastal mountains of Southern California. They prefer streamside woodlands and valleys. Box elder is a medium-sized tree, usually reaching heights between 30 and 60 feet. The trunk is relatively short, and the slender, light green branches account for most of its height. The leaves, unlike those of other maples, are compound (divided into more than one leaflet).

Box elder

Brittlebush

Spanish missionaries in California's first churches called this common, rounded leafy bush *incienso* for its use as incense. Found on dry slopes and in desert washes, the deciduous shrub is a member of the sunflower family. These 2- to 5-foot plants have long, ovate silver-gray leaves and clusters of yellow flower heads that bloom from March to June. As its name suggests, brittlebush has breakable woody branches. The branches contain a fragrant resin.

Brittlebush flowers

Brittlebush

California Sycamore

These large, pretty trees thrive in the valleys of Southern California at elevations below 6,500 feet. They have large, stout trunks. The trunk often forks early and branches separate into picturesque shapes. The bark is mottled and distinctive and the leaves are light green and star-shaped. The fruit forms small bristly, red-brown balls grouped in stalks of three to seven. Its range is almost exclusively confined to California.

California sycamore

California Fan Palm

The California fan palm (also known as the desert palm) is the largest native species of palm in the continental United States. It is commonly planted as an ornamental tree along the streets of Southern California's cities, but it is also found in nature. Joshua Tree National Park has several groves of this palm. California fan palms grow quite tall, up to 60 feet. The trunk does not branch, but dead leaves often hang along its length. Native Americans enjoyed both its seeds and berries.

California fan palms

Catclaw Acacia

Catclaw acacia is a low shrub that is a member of the pea family. It has curved thorns that lend this species its name. The stems are lined with sharp curved "claws," which dig into whatever brushes against them. This shrub, or small tree, produces yellow blooms in spring that are densely formed on a cylindrical spike, about 2½ inches long. Catclaw acacia also has twisted pods that grow to 6 inches. Catclaw patches are important to wildlife habitats. They are found on slopes, canyons, desert grasslands, and along washes and streams at elevations below 5,000 feet.

Catclaw acacia

Chamise

Chamise is the most common shrub of the California chaparral. It is also known as greasewood, a designation it received because of its oily, stringy wood. Chamise grows as an erect shrub or small tree, to heights of about 10 feet. The leaves are needlelike and evergreen. It is most prominent in May and June, when it blooms in dense clusters of tiny white flowers.

Chamise

Coulter Pine

The species Coulter pine, found only in Central, Southern, and Baja California, was identified in 1831 by the Irish botanist Thomas Coulter. It is often known by the appellation bigcone pine because of the extraordi-

Coulter pine

nary weight of the cones, which often have a mass of 4 to 5 pounds. The needles are evergreen and come in bunches of three. The shape of the tree is often similar to a Christmas tree. The wood is often used as a rough lumber and as firewood. Native Americans collected the large, elliptical seeds as a food source; they are also a favorite for squirrels.

Coulter pine cone

Creosote Bush

The yellow foliage of the creosote bush is followed by white fuzzy seedpods. The leaves are naturally varnished to slow evaporation and to conserve water. Stems are gray and ringed with black. This abundant evergreen shrub is covered with an aromatic resin that smells like creosote. When older stems in the middle of the plant die off, new growth comes up around the edge. This process allows a plant, which is essentially a clone, to grow for centuries. It is believed that the creosote produces a toxic substance that prevents other plants from growing too close, thereby dictating local water rights. Only when the soil below a creosote bush has been cleansed by rain will other plants grow for a brief time beneath it. The sweet, refreshing smell of the desert after a rain results partly from wet creosote bush foliage. The plants are found primarily in the desert and on mesas below 4,500 feet.

Creosote bush

Desert Ironwood

Desert ironwood makes a colorful addition to the wildlife of the Mojave Desert. Early settlers in California called it ironwood because its wood is very dense, so dense that it will not float in water. Desert ironwood is a small tree, about 25 feet tall, with a broad rounded crown of blue-green leaves. It survives in desert washes. In May or June, it blooms in a beautiful display of small purple flowers.

Desert ironwood leaves

Desert ironwood

Desert Mountain Mahogany (Curl-leaf Mountain Mahogany)

Desert, or curl-leaf, mountain mahogany is a small pretty tree, usually about 20 feet tall. The twisted branches spread outward into a rounded crown. Its leaves are aromatic, a little over 1 inch long, and (as the name suggests) curled. The plant blooms in spring; flowers are small and yellowish. The flowers are succeeded by fruits with a red or white feathery plume at the tip. Desert mountain mahogany prefers dry rocky slopes in elevations between 4,000 and 9,000 feet.

Desert mountain mahogany

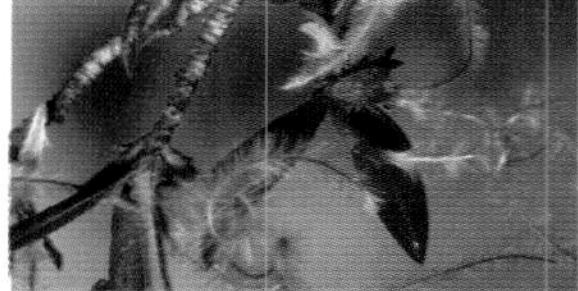
Desert mountain mahogany leaves

Desert Willow

Despite its drooping appearance, the desert willow is not a member of the willow family; rather it belongs to the bignonia family. Desert willow is an upright shrub or small tree that grows to a height of 25 feet. The trunk has a dark brown scaly bark; twigs are hairy and sticky. Narrow light green leaves with pointed ends grow from 3 to 6 inches. Desert willow flowers, which are pinkish purple, large, and fragrant, normally bloom from April to August. Long brown, cigarlike pods, from 4 to 8 inches long, contain numerous flat tan seeds. Desert willows grow along washes, creeks, stream banks, and drainages. This deciduous plant is tolerant to drought.

Desert willow

Douglas Fir

Douglas fir, also known as red pine, is a conical evergreen with flattened, needle-like leaves that are yellow-green or blue-green. Trees are pyramid-shaped when young, but the crown becomes irregular with age. The bark is dark red-brown and smooth on young trees; it becomes thick, furrowed, and corky on older trees. At the end of the twigs there is usually one, though sometimes more than one, cone-shaped, sharp-pointed, reddish brown, oblong cone with three-pronged tongues sticking out between the cone scales. The cones are 3 to 4 inches long. Douglas firs are long-lived conifers that grow in vast forests, often in pure stands, in well-drained soil at elevations from sea level to 9,000 feet. They are also found in canyons below 6,000 feet. Among the world's most important timber trees, Douglas firs are often used for reforestation. In California, height ranges from 60 to 180 feet.

Douglas fir

Douglas fir cones

Ferns

California is host to myriad species of fern. Ferns thrive in shady forests and valleys, where they often make up much of the underbrush. Ferns are seedless plants; they reproduce by releasing spores from tiny sacks on the underside of leaves. In spring, small young ferns sprout as fiddleheads. They are

Bracken fern

called fiddleheads because their coiled heads resemble the end of a violin. Fiddleheads of some species are considered delicacies, but only experts can distinguish the edible varieties from poisonous look-alikes. The most common fern is called bracken. It is a deep green plant with long, triangular leaflets. Most other ferns bear a general resemblance to bracken.

Fremont Cottonwood

Cottonwoods are deciduous members of the poplar family. The Fremont cottonwood is named for Major John Charles Frémont, an early explorer of the West. Frémont found these trees useful throughout his expeditions because their presence indicates nearby water and the trees provide shady resting spots. They are short-lived, fast-growing trees that produce an abundance of seeds. Male and female flowers bloom on separate trees in clusters of tiny petal-less flowers (catkins) in spring before leaves appear. The cotton-haired seeds, produced in small capsules, are carried to new locations by the wind. In suburban areas, this tree is sometimes prohibited because of the mess caused by the amount of "cotton" it yields. Fremont cottonwood foliage is dark, shiny green above and paler below, and turns dull yellow in the fall. Sometimes confused with aspen, the Fremont cottonwood is distinguished by larger, coarser, more deeply toothed triangular leaves; the trees are also larger than aspens and have coarser bark, except when young.

Fremont cottonwood

The bark is whitish and smooth on young trees and thick, rough, and light gray or brownish on mature trees. Found along streams and in moist places below 6,000 feet, Fremont cottonwoods are important to riparian areas and coniferous forests. Mule deer and cattle often browse the twigs and foliage. Frémont referred to it as "sweet cottonwood" because horses can eat its inner bark. This handsome hardwood usually reaches a height between 40 and 90 feet. Its cousin, black cottonwood, reaches similar heights.

Giant Sequoia

The giant sequoia trees of California are among the largest, and oldest, living things on earth. Almost all of these magnificent giants, remnants from the age of dinosaurs, are protected in Sequoia, Kings Canyon, and Yosemite National Parks. The trees have a tall, bare, reddish brown trunk; the diameter at the base sometimes exceeds 20 feet. The leaves are evergreen and scalelike, and the cones are pinelike. Sequoias grow to astonishing heights: usually between 150 and 250 feet tall. The largest of the species is a tree in Kings Canyon National Park named General Sherman, which is 275 feet tall, with a base diameter of 36 feet, a weight of about 2.7 million pounds, and an estimated age of 2,300 years. Rings on other trees imply ages of over 3,200 years old. Sequoia wood is no longer used as lumber, but many of these ancient trees were irresponsibly felled in earlier times.

Sequoias

The trees were named after a Cherokee Indian, Sequoya, the only inventor of a tribal alphabet in North America. Sequoya was the grandson of George Washington's personal guide, Christopher Gist.

Hollyleaf Cherry

Hollyleaf cherry is a small, shrublike evergreen found near the Pacific Coast from Central California to the northern region of the Baja Peninsula. Early Spanish missionaries planted hollyleaf cherry as an ornamental hedge, a practice that continues today. Its preferred habitat is along streams, and in chaparral and foothill woodlands. The shiny, evergreen leaves are spread out into a dense crown. The berries are red and edible, although they are generally eaten only by birds and other wildlife.

Hollyleaf cherry

Hollyleaf cherry fruit

Jeffrey Pine

Also known as western yellow pine or bull pine, Jeffrey pine was named after the man who discovered the species, John Jeffrey, a nineteenth-century Scottish botanist. Jeffrey pine is found almost solely in the state of California, most commonly on the slopes of the Sierra Nevada at elevations between 6,000 and 9,000 feet. It grows to heights of 130 feet. The long, evergreen needles come in bundles of three. The cones are egg-shaped or conical. They are 5 to 10 inches long and end in a sharp, bent-back prickle. The bark is purplish or reddish brown and furrowed into scaly plates. When crushed, both the bark and the twigs give off a pleasant odor that is commonly likened to vanilla or lemon.

Jeffrey pine

Jeffrey pine cones

Juniper

California juniper

Members of the cypress family, both western juniper and California juniper are found throughout plateaus, plains, foothills, and the pinyon-juniper belt. Similar in appearance, they grow from 10 to 40 feet tall with rounded crowns. These trees often have several branches that are as large as the main stem extending from ground level. The yellowish green foliage is scale-shaped and is pressed tightly against the twigs. Bark ranges from grayish brown to gray, growing whiter as the tree ages. It is fibrous and tends to shred in long strips. California junipers have coppery cones, about ½ inch in diameter, covered with a bluish waxy substance. The way the branches rise from the base of the trunk gives the tree a globular appearance. All juniper berries serve as an important food source for some birds and small wildlife.

alifornia juniper berries

Manzanita

Manzanita

Manzanita is a California peculiarity. There are about 40 species of this native shrub, mainly found in the north of the state, but also in the southern Sierra Nevada. A few of the species, including the common manzanita, grow to the size of small trees (often 20 feet or more). Botanists disagree on whether the common manzanita should be classified as a tree or a shrub. The contention is that manzanitas branch near the ground and thus lack the single trunk that characterizes a tree. *Manzanita* is a Spanish word that means "little apple." The fruit is enjoyed by a variety of wildlife and was also eaten by Native Americans, who often fermented a manzanita cider. Manzanita provides a dense foliage refuge for birds and small mammals. Its reddish brown branches twist into aesthetically pleasing shapes; they are termed "mountain driftwood" and trimmed into collectors' items.

lanzanita fruit

Mesquite

A member of the pea family, mesquite is a spiny deciduous shrub or small tree that grows up to 30 feet tall. Two species of mesquite in Southern California are western honey mesquite and screwbean mesquite. Both have bean pods, which are used by humans, wildlife, and livestock as a food source. Many birds, insects, and mammals eat the beans (some estimates are that 80 percent of a coyote's diet is made up of mesquite beans in the late summer and fall). Native Americans relied on sweet mesquite pods as a dietary staple from which they dried, cooked, and ate the beans, made teas, syrup, and a ground meal called *pinole.* Mesquite produces small, fragrant, greenish yellow flowers that are crowded on stalked spikes. The bark separates into dark strips and the wood is hard, reddish brown, with thin yellow sapwood. Native Americans found a wide variety of applications for the bark, such as making baskets, fabrics, and medicine. Mesquite burns slowly and is smokeless, making it one of the best sources of firewood in the desert. It is a common tree along watercourses, washes, and alluvial bottoms where groundwater is available. In some areas, the roots may penetrate to depths of 60 feet.

Velvet mesquite

Western honey mesquite

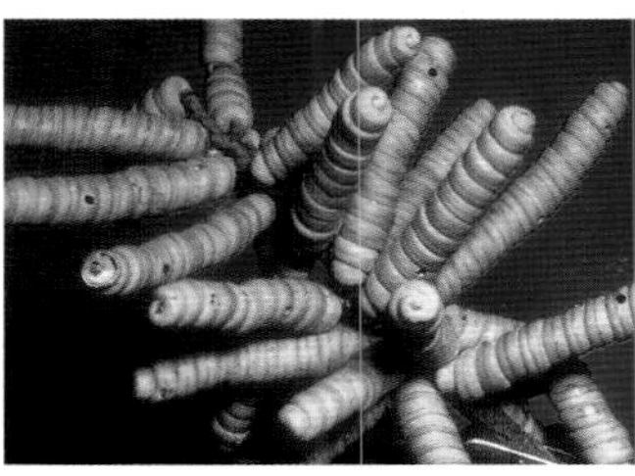
Screwbean mesquite

Oaks

California is home to 20 species of oak, more than half of which can be found nowhere else in the wild. Oak trees are a prominent vegetation feature throughout the state. The oak acorn was a staple of aboriginal Californians' diet; it was ground and rinsed to remove tannin, then prepared as a bread or in soup. Most Central California Indian tribes celebrated some sort of acorn harvest ritual. Oak is an important hardwood, prized as a timber source.

California black oak

The largest of California's oaks is probably valley oak (or California white oak), which grows in wooded inland foothills. It reaches heights over 100 feet. By contrast, California scrub oak rarely exceeds 10 feet. The most common oak of Southern California's coast and foothills is the coast live oak, whose well-spaced groves make for beautiful

Canyon live oak

scenery and whose acorns were among those preferred by Indians. A particularly recognizable species of oak is the blue oak, whose bluish foliage can be picked out from a distance. Perhaps the most beautiful of the varied oak species found in California is the canyon live oak, whose crown spreads out into broad picturesque shapes. Other common varieties include the interior live oak and the California black oak. The different oaks occur in pure stands and in mixed forests. Certain varieties have suffered heavily from disease in recent years and efforts are now underway to replenish them.

California scrub oak

Palo Verde

In Spanish, *palo verde* means "green pole" or "green stick." Palo verde is not a normal tree—it is actually a legume from the pea family. It has green bark and stems in which photosynthesis (the process plants use to make the "food" they need to grow) is carried out. The green bark enables the tree to continue photosynthesis even during its leafless stage. Palo verde can survive in its desert habitat because it has tiny leaves that help reduce water loss through transpiration. The leaves drop off during dry periods, further reducing the need for water. After substantial rains, new leaves grow. Masses of yellow flowers bloom in spring. In midsummer, seedpods are full of hard, brown seeds. Palo verde branches, pods, and seeds are browsed by wildlife; pocket mice and kangaroo rats bury the seeds to eat them later. The wood is soft and makes for poor firewood. These trees grow to 30 feet.

Palo verde

Pinyon (Piñon) Pine

The pinyon is a bushy evergreen with a short trunk and compact, rounded crown. The gray to red-brown bark is rough and scaly. Needles range from ¾ to 3 inches long, usually two to a bundle, with blue-green foliage on the younger trees and dark yellow-green foliage on more mature ones. Cones are 1 to 2 inches long and have edible seeds, known as Indian nuts or pine nuts, that can be eaten raw or roasted. Pinyon pines rarely grow taller than 30 feet and they are the most drought-resistant of all the pines in California. They are usually found in woodlands (often with juniper), mesas, and plateaus at elevations lower than 7,000 feet.

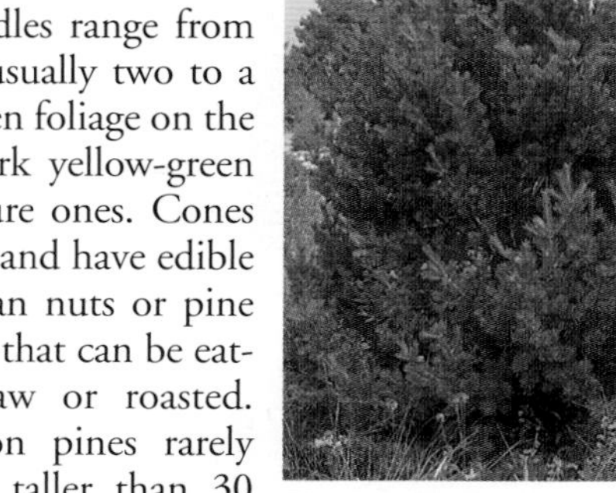
Pinyon pine

Pinyon pine cone

Ponderosa Pine

Also called western yellow pine, the ponderosa pine has long needles (5 to 11 inches), which grow in clusters of three from a single point. The bark of young trees is yellowish brown to cinnamon; older trees develop orange flaky bark. The spiky red-brown cones are about 3 to 6 inches long. Seed cones provide an important food source for wildlife. Ponderosa pines can grow 60 to 125 feet tall and are usually found at elevations of 6,000 to 8,500 feet.

Ponderosa pine

Ponderosa pine cone

Shrubby Cinquefoil

Also known as yellow rose, these shrubs have yellow flowers that measure about 1 inch across, with five petals each. Cinquefoils keep their leaves in winter; some animals eat them when food is scarce, although they don't enjoy the taste. Cinquefoils are found during the summer in open woods and meadows. Height ranges from 1 to 3 feet.

Shrubby cinquefoil

Smoke Tree

Also known as smokethorn, the smoke tree was named because of the smoky gray appearance of the plant in its leafless state. Leaves appear for a few weeks in spring and early summer and shed soon afterwards. The gray twigs produce most of the smoke tree's energy, performing photosynthesis during the long leafless months. Smoke tree is well suited to the desert environment in southeastern California; the light coloring of the twigs has evolved as a protection from the heat. Flowers are small, purple, and fragrant; blooming occurs between April and July. Because of its beauty while flowering, smoke tree is sometimes grown as an ornamental.

Smoke tree

Smoke tree close-up

Southern California Walnut

The Southern California walnut's range is confined to the coastal foothills in the southern portion of the state. It was not identified until 1850, when it was found just north of Los Angeles. Planned planting has increased its small range. It grows to a height of about 40 feet. The Northern California walnut is slightly taller.

Southern California walnut

Southern California walnut's bark is dark brown and the leaves are shiny green. Its nuts are edible.

Sugar Pine

Sugar pine has been called the "king of the pines." It regularly reaches heights over 100 feet and has been recorded as tall as 241 feet. The trunk diameter is also impressive, often 8 feet. The cones are extremely long, often 18 inches. Sugar pine is quite beautiful; the large trunk often extends quite high without branches, then spreads out in long, almost horizontal branches. It is found in the Sierra Nevada and most of the southern mountain ranges. The lumber is much admired and was used extensively by forty-niners in mining operations. Native Americans gathered the large, sweet seeds and also ate the sweet resin that comes from the cut or burned heartwood that gives the species its name.

Sugar pine cones

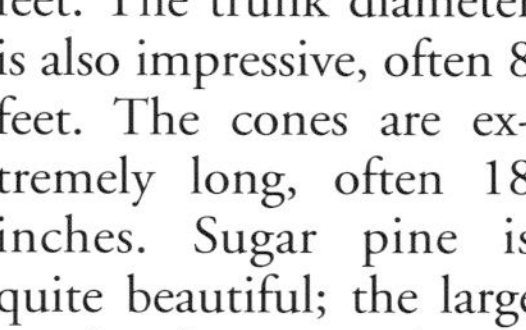

ugar pine

Torrey Pine

Only several thousand of these rare native conifers still exist. Most of their natural grove is contained within Torrey Pine State Park, north of San Diego. There is also a pure stand of Torrey pines on Santa Rosa Island and cultivated examples are grown elsewhere. The trees can reach heights of 50 feet, although they may be much smaller in exposed areas. Their gray-green needles are long, up to 10 inches, and are bunched in groups of five. The cones are also quite large, 5 inches in length.

Torrey pine

Two-petal Ash

Two-petal ash is a small tree common in the foothills of Southern California. It grows to heights of about 15 feet. Two-petal ash is a native of the state and is rarely found elsewhere. It is recognizable by its snowy white flowers and is often planted as an ornamental shrub. The petals of this ash are divided into two at the end of a narrow lobe. Leaves are dark green, about 5 inches long, with 1½-inch leaflets.

Two-petal ash flowers

wo-petal ash

Western Poison Oak

Western poison oak is a shrub or climbing vine that can cause great discomfort if touched. The leaves are recognizable by the three shiny ovate leaflets that often have a reddish green or crimson color. The flowers are very small and greenish white. Berries come in clusters of tiny whitish balls. Western poison oak is common in Southern California's oak woodlands.

Western poison oak leaf

Western White Pine

Western white pine ranges from Central California to Canada. It is one of the tallest pines in North America, recorded at a height of 239 feet in southern Oregon. In Southern California it is found in the snowy upper montane and subalpine areas between 6,000 and 9,000 feet. Needles come in bunches of five; like other white pines with this trait, the western white pine has been hit by white pine blister rust, caused by an introduced fungus. Its cones are long, curved, and cylindrical and hang down, ending in a small point. Western white pine is an important timber tree; it is of a uniformly high grade and rarely knots or twists.

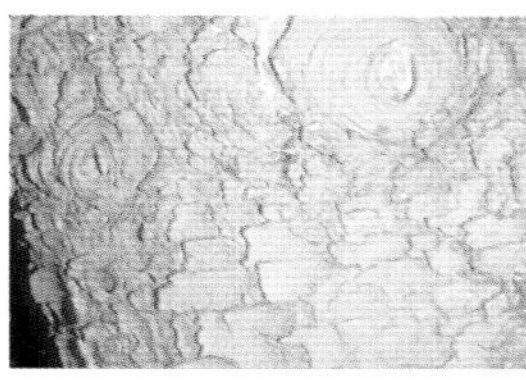

Western white pine

Winter Fat

Winter fat is also called white sage, sweet sage, or winter sage, although it is not related to sage at all. The plant has many erect, woolly branches that arise from a woody base. It has flowering clusters that when gone to seed fluff out to look like cottonballs. The plant has a fuzzy, white, and hairy appearance because of the dense woolly leaves that cover the entire plant. Leaves are dry in the fall but remain on the plant throughout winter. Winter fat serves as an important winter food source for wildlife and livestock.

Winter fat

Cacti and Succulents

Barrel Cactus

True to their name, barrel cacti are cylindrical or barrel-shaped and are among the largest cacti of the North American deserts. But they grow very slowly—a 4-year-old barrel cactus might only be 3 inches high. Once established, they can live to be 100 years old. Members of this genus have prominent ribs and are armed with heavy spines. Most have 1½- to 2½-inch yellow-green or red flowers growing in a crown near the top of the plant. They normally grow to heights of

Barrel cactus

2 to 3 feet, but they have been known to reach heights up to 10 feet. Fruits become fleshy and often juicy when mature, but they are not usually considered edible. Barrel cacti typically grow along desert washes, on gravelly slopes, and beneath desert canyon walls. Most species bloom from April through June, depending on local conditions. Native Americans boiled young flowers in water to eat like cabbage and mashed the flowers for a drink. They also used the cactus as a cooking pot by cutting off the top, scooping out the pulp, and combining hot stones with food inside. The pulp has been used to make cactus candy, a popular treat.

Beavertail Cactus

The beavertail cactus is so called because its flat, pad-like stems resemble beaver tails. The stems lack large spines seen in other desert plants. Instead, they have little tufts of barbed bristles that can be quite difficult to remove from human skin. The flowers are pink and showy, about 3 inches tall, with many petals. They bloom in May or June. Beavertail cacti thrive in the desert regions on the eastern side of Southern California's mountain regions.

Beavertail cactus

Century Plant

Members of the agave family, century plants take many years to flower, although not a century. The plant actually lives about 25 years before it sends up a flowering stalk, which happens only once in its lifetime. The blossoming spike grows so large and so quickly that it entirely saps the plant's resources. New century plants are formed from the root system. Normally found on rocky desert slopes, this unique plant has a tall thin stalk from 10 to 14 feet high that grows from a thick basal rosette of gray-green leaves. The leaves are 10 to 18 inches long with sharp spines. The century plant provided Native Americans with a source of soap, food, fiber, medicine, and weapons.

Century plant

Cholla

Pronounced "CHOY-ya," the cholla is a common cactus of the Southern California deserts. Both the prickly pear and cholla are shrubby cacti belonging to the genus *Opuntia*, which has a greater number of species with more variation than any other cactus group. The most common cholla in California is teddybear cholla (also known as jumping cholla because the spiny joints detach easily, seeming to jump off and penetrate passersby). For the most part, cholla grows in well-drained sandy and gravelly soils in desert plant communities at lower elevations. Take care as you walk in the desert—the spikes can penetrate your shoe soles and are extremely painful to remove.

Staghorn cholla

Teddybear cholla

Engelmann's Hedgehog

Engelmann's hedgehog is another spiky cactus found in the Mojave and Colorado Deserts of Southern California. Its spines are very sharp and reach lengths over 2 inches. The plant itself is usually a clump of cylindrical stems clustered in a mound that is wider than it is tall. Average width is 3 feet; average height is 2 feet. Engelmann's hedgehog blooms in April or May, when it produces reddish flowers. It is found on dry gravelly slopes and desert flats and in dry washes.

Hedgehog cactus

Joshua Tree

The Joshua tree, the largest of the yuccas, is a member of the lily family. These picturesque, spike-leafed evergreens grow in dry soils on plains, slopes, and mesas, often in groves. They range from 15 to 40 feet in height with a diameter of 1 to 3 feet. Flowers are bell-shaped, 1 to 1½ inches long, with six creamy, yellow-green petal-like sepals. The flowers are crowded into 12- to 18-inch, many-branched clusters with an unpleasant odor; they blossom mostly in the spring. Not all trees flower annually. Joshua tree fruit is elliptical, green-brown, 2 to 4 inches long, and somewhat fleshy. It dries and falls soon after maturity in late spring, revealing many flat seeds. Joshua trees (and most other yuccas) rely on the female pronuba moth (also called the yucca moth) for pollination. No other animal visiting the blooms transfers the pollen from one flower to another. In fact, the female yucca moth has evolved special organs to collect and distribute the pollen onto the surface of the flower. She then lays her eggs in the flowers' ovaries, and when the larvae hatch, they feed on the yucca seeds. Without the moth's pollination, the Joshua tree could not reproduce, nor could the moth, whose larvae would have no seeds to eat. Although an old Joshua tree can sprout new plants from its roots, only the seeds produced in pollinated flowers can scatter far enough to establish a new stand.

Joshua tree

Joshua trees can live 100 to 300 years. In Southern California, Joshua Tree National Park provides protection for this unique species. Early Mormon visitors to California named them. The outstretched branches of Joshua trees reminded the Mormon pioneers of a biblical Joshua reaching out to heaven.

Ocotillo

Not a cactus but a shrub, ocotillo is sometimes called coachwhip for its bare, 8- to 15-inch-long stems. Ocotillos are leafless most of the year, except immediately after rain, when the slender thorny branches sprout tiny green leaves. Ocotillos photosynthesize while the soil is moist because the leaves quickly wither and drop as the ground dries out. This drought-responsive process may be repeated several times during warm months. Narrow oval leaves grow to 2 inches, appearing in bunches above the spines. Ocotillos bloom annually to produce dense spikes of bright red, tubular blossoms in the late spring. Hummingbirds and other nectar feeders are attracted to the flowers. Native Americans ate the flowers like sweet candy and rubbed the flower stems on their cheeks for rouge. The ocotillo is one of the few flowering plants confined to a desert habitat.

Ocotillo

Our Lord's Candle

Our Lord's candle is a Californian yucca. It is most common on the desert edges but is found in brushy hill environs from Monterey County south. The plant is easily recognizable by its tall stalks topped with a large clump of white to purplish flowers. It blooms from April to June and its stature often dominates nearby plants. The plant dies after flowering. Like all yuccas, Our Lord's candle relies on the yucca moth for its survival. The moth collects pollen from the yucca flower, rolls it into a ball and deposits it, with its eggs, into another flower. The moth larvae feed on some of the yucca's seeds, but pollination has already been assured.

Our Lord's candle

Parry's Nolina

Also known by an Indian name, sacahuista, Parry's nolina is a large, showy plant found in the dry brushy areas of Southern California. Native Americans wove the long narrow leaves into baskets or mats and ate young stems. At maturity, stems can reach lengths up to 10 feet. A dense cluster of yellowish white flowers forms above the stalk. The 2- to 3-foot leaves form a rosette around the bottom of the stem. They grow as tall as 15 feet, but are often considerably smaller.

Parry's nolina

Short Coastal Prickly Pear

Prickly pear is a member of the genus *Opuntia*, plants in the cactus family that typically have round pads with prickly spines. The pads, covered with a thick layer of wax to prevent water evaporation, are actually modified branches or stems that serve several functions including water storage, photosynthesis, and flower production. The short coastal prickly pear is the most common of these plants in Southern California. It thrives in coastal chaparral south of Santa Barbara County. Flowers are pale yellow; the blooms appear from May to June and last only a few days. The flowers turn into a warty edible pear-shaped and spine-covered fruit with sweet flesh. The plants can be 4 feet tall.

Short coastal prickly pear

Saguaro

Some saguaros reach a height of 50 feet, making them the largest cacti in the United States. A saguaro has a tall, thick columnlike stem, 18 to 24 inches in diameter, with several large "arms" curving upward. Smooth waxy skin is covered with spines. Saguaros begin life near a "nurse" tree or shrub (perhaps a palo verde or mesquite), which provides a moist, shaded habitat. Ironically, the nurse plant will die when the growing saguaro outrivals and kills it off. The saguaro is the state flower of California's neighbor, Arizona, and is more associated with that state, but it also grows sporadically on the California side of the Colorado River.

Saguaro cactus

Saguaro cactus flower

Soaptree Yucca

An agave, the soaptree yucca has a tall, dense cluster of creamy whitish or greenish globe-shaped flowers atop stout, leafy stems. Numerous leaves grow from the base, up to 2 or 3 feet in length. Yuccas are members of the agave family and are pollinated by yucca moths. The moths, which cannot reproduce without yuccas, lay eggs during pollination and their larvae feed upon the seeds. Yuccas grow in sandy, rocky places, on dry mesas, and on slopes. The soaptree yucca derives its name from the material in its roots and trunk that people have used as soap. Native Americans ate the fruits, seeds, and flower buds—raw, roasted, or dried. They wove the fibrous leaves to make mats, sandals, baskets, and cloth. Cattle eat the tender young stalks, and chopped trunks and leaves are still utilized as emergency cattle feed in times of drought.

Soaptree yucca

The Central Mountains Region

Trails in the Central Mountains Region

- **CM1** Movie Flat Trail *(DR: 1; 11.7 miles; page 148)*
- **CM2** Delilah Fire Lookout Trail *(DR: 2; 7.5 miles; page 151)*
- **CM3** Davis Flat Trail *(DR: 2; 16.1 miles; page 152)*
- **CM4** Whitaker Research Forest Trail *(DR: 1; 5.4 miles; page 155)*
- **CM5** Cherry Flat Trail *(DR: 3; 9.9 miles; page 157)*
- **CM6** Buck Rock Fire Lookout Trail *(DR: 2; 11.8 miles; page 159)*
- **CM7** Buck Road *(DR: 5; 3.6 miles; page 162)*
- **CM8** Solo Peak Road *(DR: 2; 14.3 miles; page 164)*
- **CM9** Windy Gap Trail *(DR: 1; 13.5 miles; page 166)*
- **CM10** Packsaddle Meadow Trail *(DR: 2; 7.5 miles; page 168)*
- **CM11** Capinero Saddle Trail *(DR: 1; 8.2 miles; page 170)*
- **CM12** Rancheria Road *(DR: 1; 35.3 miles; page 172)*
- **CM13** Rhymes Road *(DR: 2; 22.1 miles; page 176)*
- **CM14** Portuguese Pass Trail *(DR: 1; 6.9 miles; page 179)*
- **CM15** Bull Run Basin Trail *(DR: 3; 2.3 miles; page 181)*
- **CM16** Piute Mountain Road *(DR: 2; 30.5 miles; page 182)*
- **CM17** Jawbone Canyon Road *(DR: 2; 30.3 miles; page 187)*
- **CM18** Dove Spring Canyon Trail *(DR: 3; 18.1 miles; page 191)*
- **CM19** Bird Spring Pass Trail *(DR: 3; 20.8 miles; page 194)*
- **CM20** Chimney Peak Byway *(DR: 1; 14 miles; page 198)*
- **CM21** Opal Canyon Road *(DR: 5; 6.3 miles; page 201)*
- **CM22** Nightmare Gulch Overlook Trail *(DR: 4; 5 miles; page 204)*
- **CM23** Last Chance Canyon Trail *(DR: 5; 10.6 miles; page 206)*
- **CM24** Burro Schmidt Tunnel Trail *(DR: 2; 14.9 miles; page 210)*
- **CM25** Sheep Spring Trail *(DR: 3; 12 miles; page 215)*
- **CM26** Koehn Lake Trail *(DR: 3; 24.9 miles; page 218)*
- **CM27** Government Peak Trail *(DR: 5; 7.9 miles; page 222)*
- **CM28** Frazier Mountain Trail *(DR: 4; 15.3 miles; page 225)*
- **CM29** San Emigdio Mountain Trail *(DR: 4; 14.9 miles; page 229)*
- **CM30** Cuyama Peak Trail *(DR: 3; 16.3 miles; page 232)*
- **CM31** Potrero Seco Trail *(DR: 3; 13.7 miles; page 234)*
- **CM32** Nordhoff Ridge Trail *(DR: 4; 28.8 miles; page 237)*
- **CM33** Big Caliente Spring Trail *(DR: 1; 28.9 miles; page 240)*
- **CM34** Camino Cielo Road *(DR: 2; 25.2 miles; page 244)*
- **CM35** Miranda Pine Road *(DR: 2; 25 miles; page 248)*
- **CM36** Buckhorn Ridge Trail *(DR: 3; 3.6 miles; page 251)*
- **CM37** Sierra Madre Road *(DR: 2; 29.7 miles; page 252)*
- **CM38** Bates Canyon Trail *(DR: 2; 11.9 miles; page 255)*
- **CM39** Big Rocks Trail *(DR: 2; 4.4 miles; page 257)*
- **CM40** Twin Rocks Trail *(DR: 7; 5.6 miles; page 259)*
- **CM41** Branch Creek Trail *(DR: 5; 7.3 miles; page 261)*
- **CM42** Paradise Road *(DR: 3; 3.4 miles; page 263)*
- **CM43** Sand Highway *(DR: 3; 5.3 miles; page 264)*
- **CM44** Pozo Road *(DR: 1; 18.2 miles; page 266)*
- **CM45** Pine Mountain Road *(DR: 4; 8.8 miles; page 269)*
- **CM46** Hi Mountain Road *(DR: 1; 12.1 miles; page 272)*
- **CM47** Parkfield Grade Trail *(DR: 1; 18.4 miles; page 275)*
- **CM48** Willow Creek Road *(DR: 1; 7.4 miles; page 277)*
- **CM49** South Coast Ridge Road *(DR: 2; 26.5 miles; page 279)*
- **CM50** Cone Peak Trail *(DR: 1; 6.4 miles; page 281)*
- **CM51** Coast Road *(DR: 1; 10.1 miles; page 282)*
- **CM52** Tassajara Road *(DR: 2; 13.6 miles; page 285)*

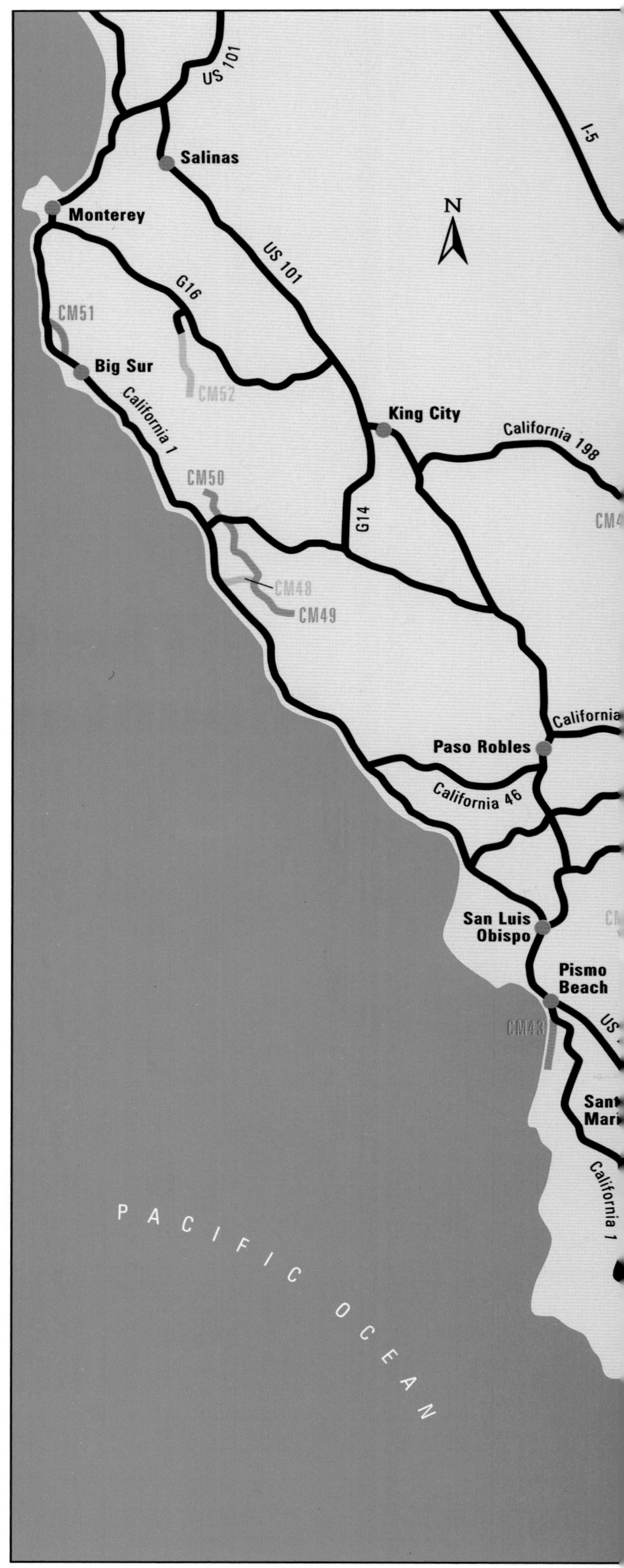

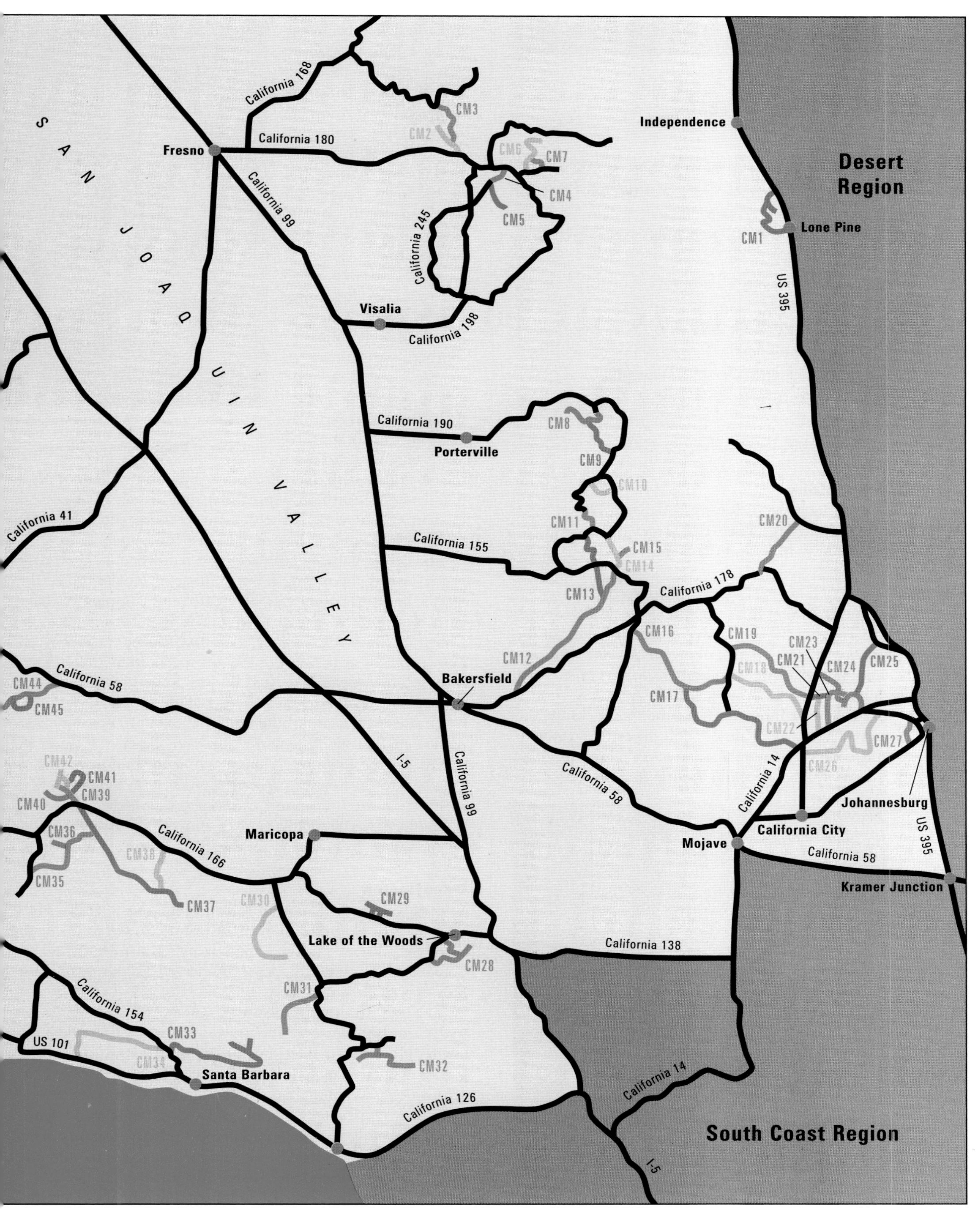

California 168
California 180
Fresno
SAN JOAQUIN VALLEY
California 99
CM3
CM2
CM6
CM7
CM4
CM5
California 245
Independence
Desert Region
Lone Pine
CM1
US 395
Visalia
California 198
California 190
Porterville
CM8
CM9
CM10
CM11
California 155
CM15
CM14
CM13
California 41
CM20
California 178
CM16
CM19
CM23
CM21
CM24
CM25
CM12
CM18
Bakersfield
CM17
CM22
CM27
CM26
California 58
CM44
CM45
I-5
California 99
CM42
CM41
CM39
CM40
Johannesburg
California City
CM36
California 166
Maricopa
Mojave
California 58
CM38
CM35
CM37
CM30
CM29
Kramer Junction
Lake of the Woods
California 138
CM28
CM31
California 154
CM33
US 101
CM34
CM32
Santa Barbara
California 14
California 126
South Coast Region

CENTRAL MOUNTAINS #1

Movie Flat Trail

Starting Point:	**US 395 at the intersection with Moffat Ranch Road, 6 miles north of Lone Pine**
Finishing Point:	**US 395 at Lone Pine**
Total Mileage:	**11.7 miles, plus 1.5-mile spur to Old Abe Mine**
Unpaved Mileage:	**8.5 miles, 1.5-mile spur**
Driving Time:	**1 hour**
Elevation Range:	**3,800–5,000 feet**
Usually Open:	**Year-round**
Best Time to Travel:	**Fall to spring in dry weather**
Difficulty Rating:	**1**
Scenic Rating:	**9**
Remoteness Rating:	**+0**

Special Attractions

- Scenic drive through the picturesque Alabama Hills.
- Road passes the locations where many movies were filmed.
- Views of Mount Whitney and the Sierra Nevada.

History

The low granite Alabama Hills were formed around 100 million years ago, roughly the same time as the formation of the neighboring High Sierra. Their striking shapes and outcroppings are the result of weathering and erosion from summer heat and winter snows.

In the early 1860s, conflict between the native Paiute and settlers came to a head. The Paiute found the settlers' cattle to be a convenient food source during the harsh winter months. The settlers retaliated by attacking and killing several of the Indians, who reciprocated by killing several settlers. The Owens Valley Indian wars ended in the winter of 1862 in the Alabama Hills, when settlers destroyed the Paiute's food reserves. In the spring of 1863, the Paiute were relocated south to Fort Tejon in the Tehachapi Mountains.

Passing through the boulder outcrops on Movie Flat Trail evokes the feel of many Western movie settings

Headframe, engine, and dangerous, deep open mine shaft—not a movie set, but a reminder of busier times on the trail

The Alabama Hills were named after mines in the region that, in turn, were named by southern sympathizers after the Confederate battleship *Alabama,* which was a scourge to northern shipping during the Civil War. The Yankee battleship *Kearsarge* sank the *Alabama* in 1864 off the coast of Normandy. Local northern sympathizers made their feelings clear by naming a new mining settlement Kearsarge after their battleship. Kearsarge can be found east of Independence.

Today the Alabama Hills are most renowned for their continued use as the setting for a number of movies. Since the 1920s, hundreds of movies, TV series, and commercials have been filmed in the Alabama Hills, including *The Lone Ranger, Gunga Din, Tremors, Joshua Tree,* and a number of other Westerns. A plaque at the start of the dirt road commemorates the feature films. It was dedicated by Roy Rogers, who made his first starring feature here in 1938.

Located at the end of the trail, the town of Lone Pine was named after a solitary pine tree that grew beside the creek. In the 1870s, the town was a supply point for mining towns to the east such as Kearsarge, Cerro Gordo, and Darwin.

In 1969, the Bureau of Land Management created the Alabama Hills Recreation Area in an effort to preserve the natural and cultural significance of the hills for future generations.

Description

This extremely popular road runs through the Alabama Hills Recreation Area, along a low range of hills on the west side of the Owens Valley. The road's popularity stems from the rocky, boulder-strewn hillsides that have served as the setting for movies and TV series.

The trail is an easy graded road, suitable for a passenger car in dry weather. However, the large jumbled boulders of the Alabama Hills are anything but ordinary. The trail follows the graded Moffat Ranch Road before climbing to Movie Flat, where many Westerns have been filmed. A number of side trails invite further exploration and a closer look at the landscape. Most of these are more suitable for high-clearance vehicles. Typically, these side trails either loop back to join the main trail or dead-end after a short distance.

One 3-rated spur goes 1.5 miles past the remains of a mine,

where there is a substantial loading hopper, headframe, adits, and shafts. It eventually ends at the Old Abe Mine, high above Owens Valley. Care should be taken in this region—the shafts are deep and unmarked. In addition, the final section of trail to the Old Abe Mine is narrow and very off-camber. In some places it will tilt vehicles toward the drop.

The main Movie Flat Trail joins Whitney Portal Road, which is the major paved road that offers hiking access to Mount Whitney, the highest point in the contiguous United States (14,494 feet). Hiking permits are required for day and overnight hikes; advance permit reservations are essential.

Current Road Information

BLM Bishop Field Office
785 North Main Street, Suite E
Bishop, CA 93514
(760) 872-4881

Map References

BLM Mt. Whitney
USFS Inyo National Forest
USGS 1:24,000 Manzanar, Union Wash, Lone Pine
1:100,000 Mt. Whitney
Maptech CD-ROM: Kings Canyon/Death Valley
Southern & Central California Atlas & Gazetteer, p. 27
California Road & Recreation Atlas, p. 87

Route Directions

Mileage		Direction	Description
▼ 0.0			From US 395, 6 miles north of Lone Pine, zero trip meter and turn southwest on paved Moffat Ranch Road at the sign. Cross over cattle guard; then track on left and track on right.
	2.8 ▲		Trail ends at T-intersection with US 395. Turn right for Lone Pine; turn left for Independence.
			GPS: N36°41.02' W118°06.35'
▼ 0.2		TL	Cross over Los Angeles Aqueduct; then immediately turn left, remaining on Moffat Ranch Road, and cross cattle guard. Road is now graded dirt.
	2.6 ▲	TR	T-intersection. Cross cattle guard and turn right onto paved road. Immediately cross over Los Angeles Aqueduct.
			GPS: N36°41.05' W118°06.58'
▼ 0.4		SO	Track on right and track on left; then cross over Hogback Creek. Two tracks on left. Remain on main graded road.
	2.4 ▲	SO	Two tracks on right. Cross over Hogback Creek; then track on right and track on left.
▼ 1.1		SO	Track on left.
	1.7 ▲	SO	Track on right.
▼ 2.2		SO	Track on right crosses through Hogback Creek.
	0.6 ▲	SO	Track on left crosses through Hogback Creek.
			GPS: N36°40.01' W118°08.22'
▼ 2.8		BL	Bear left onto graded dirt road marked Moffat Ranch Road and zero trip meter. Main graded road continues on right.
	0.0 ▲		Continue to the north.
			GPS: N36°39.49' W118°08.34'
▼ 0.0			Continue to the south.
	0.9 ▲	SO	Main graded dirt road enters on left. Remain on Moffat Ranch Road and zero trip meter.
▼ 0.4		SO	Track on left; then track on right.

Green vegetation at a creek crossing stands out against the otherwise arid landscape along Movie Flat Trail

Mileage		Direction	Description
	0.5 ▲	SO	Track on left; then track on right.
			GPS: N36°39.14' W118°08.23'
▼ 0.5		SO	Track on right.
	0.4 ▲	SO	Track on left.
▼ 0.7		SO	Track on right; then track on left.
	0.2 ▲	SO	Track on right; then track on left.
▼ 0.9		BR	Small track on left up hill. Zero trip meter at second track on left, which runs along shallow valley and is the start of 3-rated spur to Old Abe Mine. Continue along main trail.
	0.0 ▲		Continue to the northwest and pass second track on right, which climbs up hill.
			GPS: N36°38.94' W118°07.82'

Spur to Old Abe Mine

Mileage	Direction	Description
▼ 0.0		Start of spur.
▼ 0.1	BL	Track on right.
▼ 0.2	SO	Track on left across wash goes to mine visible on hillside to the left.
▼ 0.6	SO	Track on right goes to old stone walls and remains of stone cabins alongside creek.
		GPS: N36°38.94' W118°07.21'
▼ 1.3	SO	Remains of old stone cabin and mining shafts on left. From here, trail is extremely narrow.
		GPS: N36°38.77' W118°06.76'
▼ 1.5	UT	Trail ends at Old Abe Mine. Room for only one vehicle to turn at end.
		GPS: N36°38.67' W118°06.63'

Continuation of Main Trail

Mileage		Direction	Description
▼ 0.0			Continue to the southwest past small track on right.
	5.4 ▲	BL	Small track on left; then track right, which runs along shallow valley and is start of 3-rated spur to Old Abe Mine. Zero trip meter and continue along main trail.
			GPS: N36°38.94' W118°07.82'
▼ 0.2		SO	Track on left.
	5.2 ▲	SO	Track on right.
▼ 0.4		TL	Join wide graded dirt road, which continues on right.
	5.0 ▲	TR	Join graded dirt road, leaving main dirt road on left.
			GPS: N36°38.66' W118°08.12'
▼ 0.5		SO	Cross through wash.
	4.9 ▲	SO	Cross through wash.

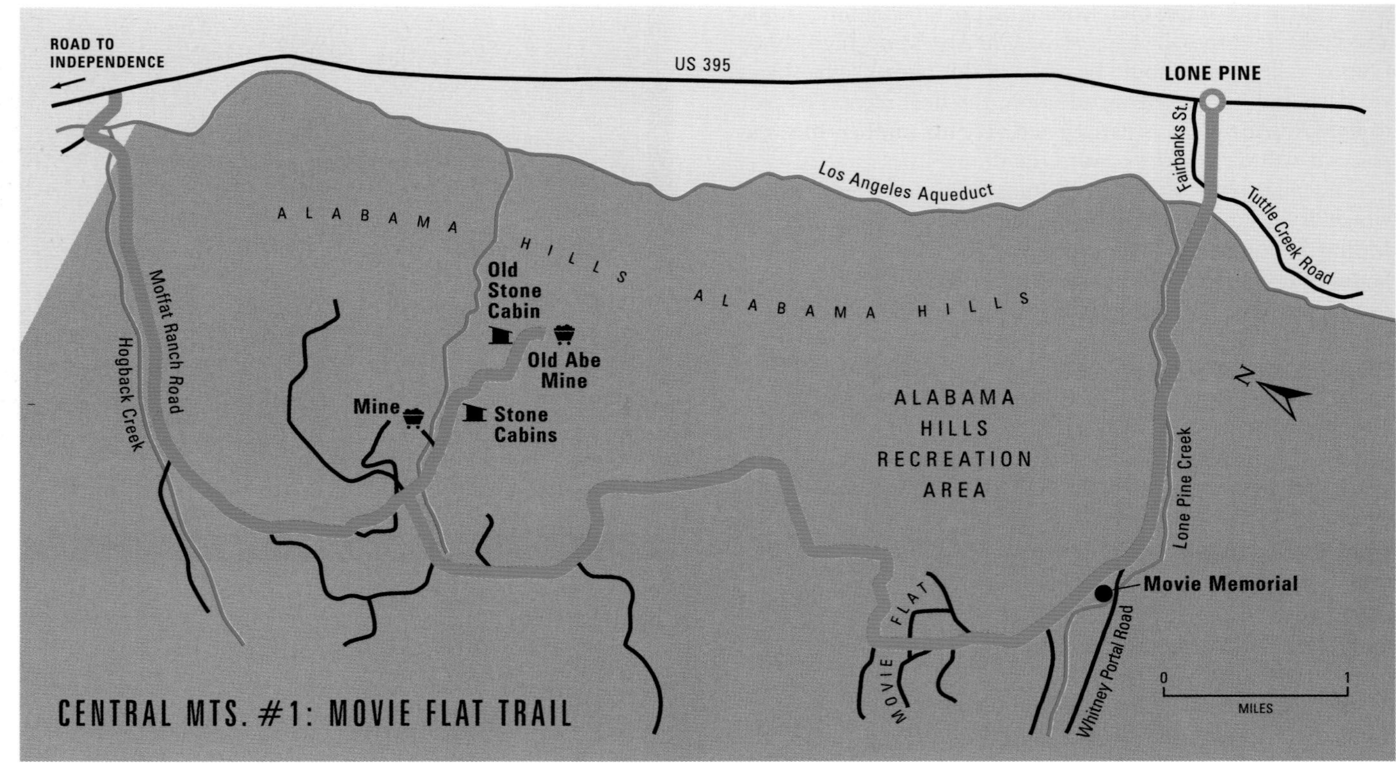

▼ 0.7		SO	Track on left.
	4.7 ▲	SO	Track on right.
▼ 1.1		SO	Track on right.
	4.3 ▲	SO	Track on left.
▼ 1.9		SO	Track on right.
	3.5 ▲	SO	Track on left.
▼ 2.5		SO	Cross through wash.
	2.9 ▲	SO	Cross through wash.
▼ 2.6		SO	Track on left.
	2.8 ▲	SO	Track on right.
▼ 3.0		SO	Track on left.
	2.4 ▲	SO	Track on right.
▼ 3.2		SO	Two tracks on left and track on right.
	2.2 ▲	SO	Two tracks on right and track on left.
▼ 3.6		SO	Track on right and track on left.
	1.8 ▲	SO	Track on right and track on left.
▼ 3.9		BL	Track on left; then bear left, remaining on major graded dirt road. Graded dirt road also goes straight ahead.
	1.5 ▲	BR	Bear right past graded dirt road on left; then track on right.
			GPS: N36°36.66′ W118°07.48′
▼ 4.0		SO	Track on left.
	1.4 ▲	SO	Track on right.
▼ 4.1		SO	Track on left.
	1.3 ▲	SO	Track on right.
▼ 4.2		SO	Track on right.
	1.2 ▲	SO	Track on left.
▼ 4.3		SO	Track on right.
	1.1 ▲	SO	Track on left.
▼ 4.4		SO	Two tracks on right and two tracks on left.
	1.0 ▲	SO	Two tracks on right and two tracks on left.
▼ 4.5		SO	Track on left.
	0.9 ▲	SO	Track on right.
▼ 4.6		SO	Track on right and track on left.
	0.8 ▲	SO	Track on right and track on left.
▼ 4.8		SO	Two tracks on right. Road is now paved. Remain on major road. Many tracks on left and right.
	0.6 ▲	SO	Two tracks on left. Road is now graded dirt.
			GPS: N36°35.95′ W118°07.01′
▼ 4.9		SO	Two tracks on left.
	0.5 ▲	SO	Two tracks on right.
▼ 5.2		SO	Road is now graded dirt.
	0.2 ▲	SO	Road is now paved. Remain on major road. Many tracks on left and right.
▼ 5.4		TL	T-intersection with paved Whitney Portal Road. Turn left toward Lone Pine. There is a movie memorial at the intersection. Zero trip meter.
	0.0 ▲		Continue to the north.
			GPS: N36°35.75′ W118°06.48′
▼ 0.0			Continue to the east.
	2.6 ▲	TR	Turn right onto graded dirt Movie Road at signpost. There is a movie memorial at the intersection. Zero trip meter.
▼ 2.0		SO	Leaving Alabama Hills Recreation Area; then cross over Los Angeles Aqueduct.
	0.6 ▲	SO	Cross over Los Angeles Aqueduct; then enter Alabama Hills Recreation Area.
▼ 2.1		SO	Tuttle Creek Road on right and Fairbanks Street on left. Entering edge of Lone Pine. Remain on major paved road.
	0.5 ▲	SO	Leaving Lone Pine. Tuttle Creek Road on left and Fairbanks Street on right. Remain on major paved road.
▼ 2.6			Trail ends in Lone Pine at stoplight on US 395.
	0.0 ▲		From Lone Pine on US 395, zero trip meter and turn southwest on paved Whitney Portal Road at stoplight. Remain on paved road, ignoring turns on left and right.
			GPS: N36°36.30′ W118°03.71′

CENTRAL MOUNTAINS #2

Delilah Fire Lookout Trail

Starting Point:	**Kings Canyon Road (California 180), 4.8 miles west of Sequoia Lake settlement**
Finishing Point:	**Delilah Fire Lookout**
Total Mileage:	**7.5 miles (one-way)**
Unpaved Mileage:	**6 miles**
Driving Time:	**45 minutes (one-way)**
Elevation Range:	**4,300–5,200 feet**
Usually Open:	**Year-round**
Best Time to Travel:	**Year-round**
Difficulty Rating:	**2**
Scenic Rating:	**8**
Remoteness Rating:	**+0**

Special Attractions

- Delilah Fire Lookout.
- Panoramic views from a narrow ridge trail.

Description

This short trail leads up a well-formed road to the Delilah Fire Lookout. From the lookout there are panoramic views over the Kings River Valley to Patterson Bluffs and over the forest toward Fresno. In dry weather, this trail is generally suitable for a high-clearance 2WD vehicle.

One of the highlights is the section of trail that runs through oaks and manzanitas along the narrow Pine Ridge, offering spectacular views to the east and west. The early stages of the trail pass through private property. Remain on the main trail and take it slow to keep dust to a minimum. The trail follows a small, formed road past some cabins.

Delilah Fire Lookout is still used and has excellent 360-degree views

The trail ends at the Delilah Lookout Tower at 5,176 feet. The steel and timber tower is not gated at the bottom and it is normally possible to climb up most of the way. The views are well worth the effort.

Current Road Information

Sequoia National Forest
Hume Lake Ranger District
35860 E. Kings Canyon Road
Dunlap, CA 93621
(559) 338-2251

Map References

BLM Fresno
USFS Sequoia National Forest
USGS 1:24,000 Miramonte, Verplank Ridge
1:100,000 Fresno

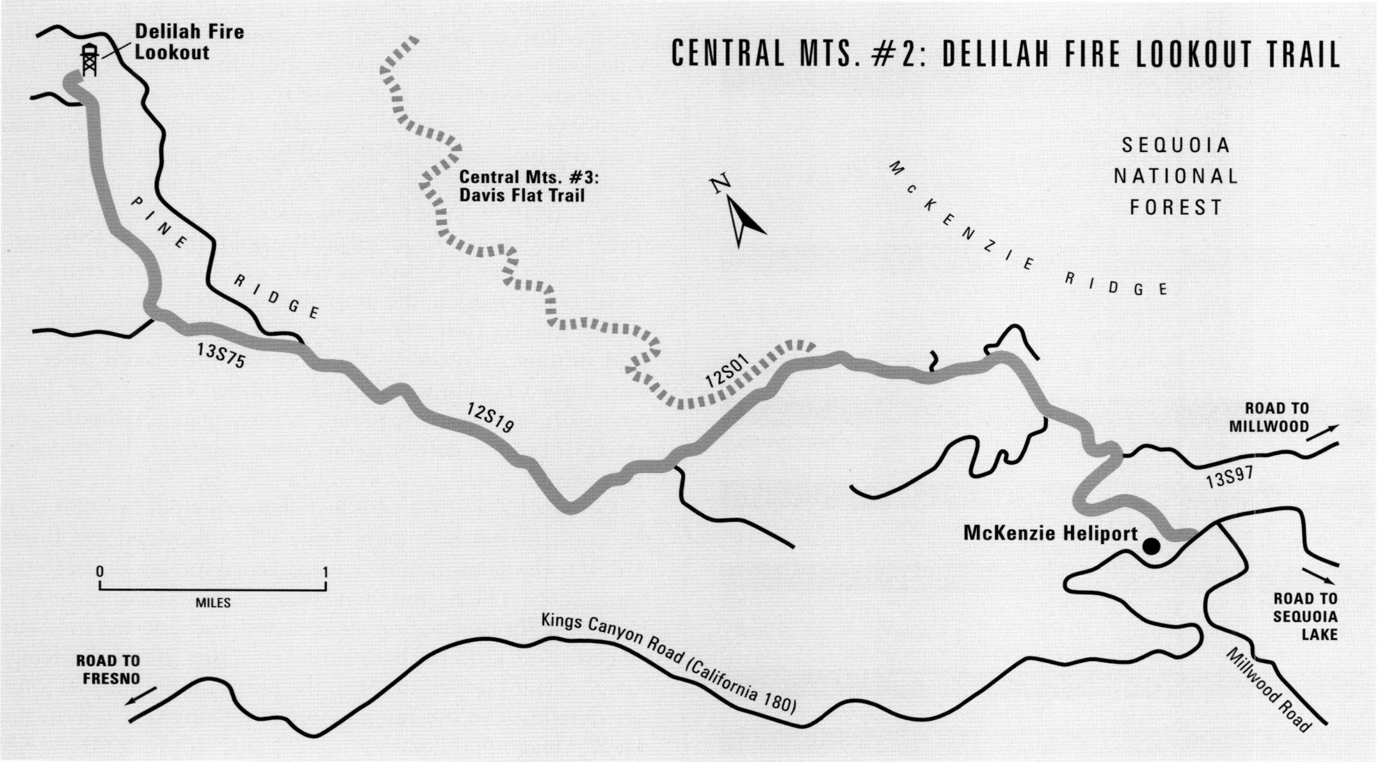

Delilah Fire Lookout Trail runs along the narrow Pine Ridge with views to the west and east

Maptech CD-ROM: Central Coast/Fresno
Southern & Central California Atlas & Gazetteer, p. 25
California Road & Recreation Atlas, p. 78

Route Directions

▼ 0.0		From Kings Canyon Road (California 180), 4.8 miles west of Sequoia Lake, zero trip meter and turn west on small paved road, following sign to Delilah Lookout. Remain on main paved road.
		GPS: N36°44.86' W119°03.04'
▼ 0.2	SO	McKenzie Helipad on left.
▼ 1.0	BL	Paved road on right is 13S97 to Millwood.
		GPS: N36°45.27' W119°03.28'
▼ 1.2	SO	Cattle guard.
▼ 1.5	BR	Bear right onto graded dirt road, following sign for Delilah Lookout and Kings River.
		GPS: N36°45.55' W119°03.50'
▼ 1.8	BL	Track on right through gate.
▼ 2.1	SO	Track on right is private.
▼ 2.6	SO	Two tracks on right.
▼ 2.7	BL	Track on right is Central Mountains #3: Davis Flat Trail (12S01). Also small track on right. Zero trip meter.
		GPS: N36°46.09' W119°04.39'
▼ 0.0		Continue to the northwest.
▼ 0.8	BR	Track on right; then cattle guard. Entering private property; then track on left. Remain on main graded road through private property for next mile.
		GPS: N36°45.94' W119°05.25'
▼ 1.9	SO	Cattle guard; then closure gate. Exiting private property.
		GPS: N36°46.42' W119°06.05'
▼ 2.8	BL	Bear left onto 13S75. Trail starts to climb toward lookout.
		GPS: N36°46.93' W119°06.58'
▼ 3.5	SO	Track on left.
▼ 4.6	BR	Continue to Delilah Fire Lookout. Road is now marked 13S75A. Small track on left.
		GPS: N36°48.12' W119°07.00'
▼ 4.8		Trail ends at the Delilah Fire Lookout.
		GPS: N36°48.27' W119°06.99'

Davis Flat Trail

Starting Point:	**Trimmer Springs Road, 1.6 miles east of Kirch Flat USFS Campground**
Finishing Point:	**Central Mountains #2: Delilah Fire Lookout Trail, 2.7 miles north of California 180**
Total Mileage:	**16.1 miles**
Unpaved Mileage:	**16.1 miles**
Driving Time:	**1.5 hours**
Elevation Range:	**1,000–4,400 feet**
Usually Open:	**April to December**
Best Time to Travel:	**April to December**
Difficulty Rating:	**2**
Scenic Rating:	**9**
Remoteness Rating:	**+1**

Special Attractions

- Boating and fishing at Pine Flat Reservoir.
- Excellent choice of campsites along the Kings River.
- Whitewater rafting and kayaking on the Kings River.
- Long, winding trail through Sequoia National Forest.

History

Mill Flat Camp was a junction point on a remarkable flume that transported lumber from McKenzie Ridge down to Sanger. This feat of engineering belonged to the Sanger Lumber Company, which constructed a sawmill at what is now the site of Millwood (located east of the southern end of this trail). Millwood was the first major logging camp in the region, and it expanded to include accommodation houses and a variety of businesses, including a red light district a mile down the road from the main camp. Millwood became a popular summer getaway spot for people from the hotter Central Valley. The accommodation houses were upgraded to cater to the tastes of these vacationers. A stagecoach would leave from Sanger shortly after dawn and travel east to Dunlap for a change of horses before making the long, steep climb to Millwood.

The lumber industry was growing hand in hand with the gold mining industry in Northern California and investors were eager to claim the abundant timber. Loggers cut down pines, firs, and giant sequoias. Narrow gauge railroads and beasts of burden delivered the fallen giants to the blades of the sawmill.

Sequoia Lake was established above the mill in 1889 with the construction of a dam. Lake water provided the flume with the momentum to float rough-sawn lumber down to the Kings River. The 62-mile-long flume followed alongside Mill Flat Creek for much of the descent and was reported to be the longest of its kind in the world. The flume joined the Kings River at Mill Flat. From there, the lumber continued its journey downriver to the Sanger Company's finishing mill in the flat San Joaquin Valley.

The lumber company expanded, developing additional sawmills, settlements, and reservoirs. Converse Basin, near Long Meadow, was one region that supplied the mills with more timber. In the early 1900s, the Hume Bennett Lumber Company created Hume Lake (located to the east of this trail) in only four months, using reinforced concrete for the dam. This lake was large enough to act as a storage pond for the massive logs, something that was not practical at the Millwood site.

The flume was extended and more railroads were built to bring in timber from farther afield. However, dwindling returns and increased expenses meant that by 1910, the big timber-cutting days were on the wane. Fires, World War I, and labor problems hastened the industry's decline. Some sections of the flume were burned down; other sections were dismantled. When the sawmill was no longer viable, it closed. With its closure, Millwood dwindled and eventually disappeared.

Crabtree, another site found along this trail, got its name from John F. Crabtree. He settled here in 1911, working a total of 157 acres around the junction of Davis and Mill Flat Creeks.

The Kings River has a simple Spanish explanation behind its name. The river was called Río de los Santos Reyes (Spanish for Holy Kings River). It was named after the three kings from Christian religion who brought gifts to the newborn Jesus.

Description

This long trail begins near Pine Flat Reservoir, a beautiful convoluted reservoir with many arms. The man-made lake is set in a deep valley along the boundary between the Sierra and Sequoia National Forests. The reservoir has a marina, which is popular for water skiing, boating, and fishing. There are semi-developed campgrounds along the lakeshore that are open for part of the year. The river is also popular with whitewater rafters and kayakers who ride the rough stretch of water from Garnet Dike to Kirch Flat. The rapids are rated as class III to IV, and the best conditions are normally found in late May and early June.

The trail starts near the eastern end of the reservoir, leading east on the south bank of the Kings River along a well-used but unmarked dirt road. Initially it travels above the river, but by the time it reaches Camp 4 1/2 it is traveling alongside it. The river is wide and is a designated Wild and Scenic River. It is managed for wild trout, and there are many places to cast a line.

Davis Flat Trail accesses many fishing points along Kings River

Davis Flat Trail commences on the south side of the steel bridge that spans Kings River

There are also many places for a quiet camp along the riverbank. Surprisingly, this trail is seldom used. It passes other camping spots, both national forest campgrounds and informal sites, before it moves away from the Kings River and follows the tight valley along Mill Creek.

Looking to the north as the trail climbs reveals striking views over the Kings River valley, Sierra National Forest, and gray Patterson Bluffs. The vegetation is a mixture of oaks, pines, and California walnuts.

The trail crosses Davis Flat and Sampson Flat, passing a few scattered pieces of private property before finishing at the intersection with Central Mountains #2: Delilah Fire Lookout Trail. From there, it is a short distance to California 180.

The trail is suitable for high-clearance 2WDs in dry weather. In places it is eroded and rocky with some fairly deep ruts, but the grade is moderate throughout.

Current Road Information

Sequoia National Forest
Hume Lake Ranger District
35860 E. Kings Canyon Road
Dunlap, CA 93621
(559) 338-2251

Map References

BLM Fresno
USFS Sequoia National Forest
USGS 1:24,000 Luckett Mt., Verplank Ridge
1:100,000 Fresno
Maptech CD-ROM: Central Coast/Fresno
Southern & Central California Atlas & Gazetteer, p. 25
California Road & Recreation Atlas, p. 78

Route Directions

▼ 0.0	From Pine Flat Reservoir, continue east along paved Trimmer Springs Road. Zero trip meter 1.6 miles east of Kirch Flat USFS Campground and turn southeast on unmarked graded dirt road that heads along south bank of the Kings River. Turn

is at the steel bridge that crosses river.

2.6 ▲ Trail finishes on paved Trimmer Springs Road. Turn left for Pine Flat Reservoir; turn right over steel bridge for Balch Camp.

GPS: N36°52.25′ W119°07.81′

▼ 0.8 SO Cattle guard. Passing through Camp 4 1/2 Workstation corral and cabin; then Camp 4 1/2 USFS Campground on left and right alongside river.

1.8 ▲ SO Camp 4 1/2 USFS Campground on left and right alongside river; then Camp 4 1/2 Workstation corral and cabin.

GPS: N36°51.73′ W119°07.26′

▼ 1.9 SO Camp 4 USFS Campground on left and right alongside river.

0.7 ▲ SO Camp 4 USFS Campground on left and right alongside river.

GPS: N36°51.43′ W119°06.37′

▼ 2.1 SO Green Cabin Flat Group Area on left.

0.5 ▲ SO Green Cabin Flat Group Area on right.

GPS: N36°51.55′ W119°06.16′

▼ 2.6 SO Cattle guard; then Mill Flat USFS Campground on left at confluence of Kings River and Davis Creek. Trail leaves Kings River and follows Mill Flat Creek. Zero trip meter.

0.0 ▲ Continue to the northwest.

GPS: N36°51.39′ W119°05.78′

▼ 0.0 Continue to the south.

12.2 ▲ SO Mill Flat USFS Campground on right at the confluence of Kings River and Davis Creek. Cross cattle guard and zero trip meter. Trail now leaves Mill Flat Creek and follows alongside Kings River.

▼ 0.6 SO Cross over creek.

11.6 ▲ SO Cross over creek.

▼ 1.8 SO Small track on right and cabin on left.

10.4 ▲ SO Small track on left and cabin on right.

GPS: N36°50.52′ W119°05.30′

▼ 1.9 SO Cross over Davis Creek on concrete ford at Crabtree; then private property on right.

10.3 ▲ SO Private property on left; then cross over Davis Creek on concrete ford at Crabtree.

▼ 2.2 SO Track on left turns into hiking trail almost immediately.

10.0 ▲ SO Track on right turns into hiking trail almost immediately.

▼ 4.1 SO Private property on right.

8.1 ▲ SO Private property on left.

GPS: N36°49.30′ W119°05.23′

▼ 4.5 SO Cross over Davis Creek.

7.7 ▲ SO Cross over Davis Creek.

▼ 4.7 SO Corral on left; then gate.

7.5 ▲ SO Gate; then corral on right.

▼ 5.7 SO Track on left.

6.5 ▲ SO Track on right.

GPS: N36°48.68′ W119°05.27′

▼ 6.0 SO Cross over creek.

6.2 ▲ SO Cross over creek.

▼ 6.4 SO Cross over creek.

5.8 ▲ SO Cross over creek.

▼ 7.5 SO Track on right.

4.7 ▲ SO Track on left.

GPS: N36°48.58′ W119°05.87′

▼ 7.8 SO Cross over creek.

4.4 ▲ SO Cross over creek.

▼ 8.6 SO Track on left.

3.6 ▲ SO Track on right.

GPS: N36°48.05′ W119°05.29′

▼ 9.0 SO Track on right.

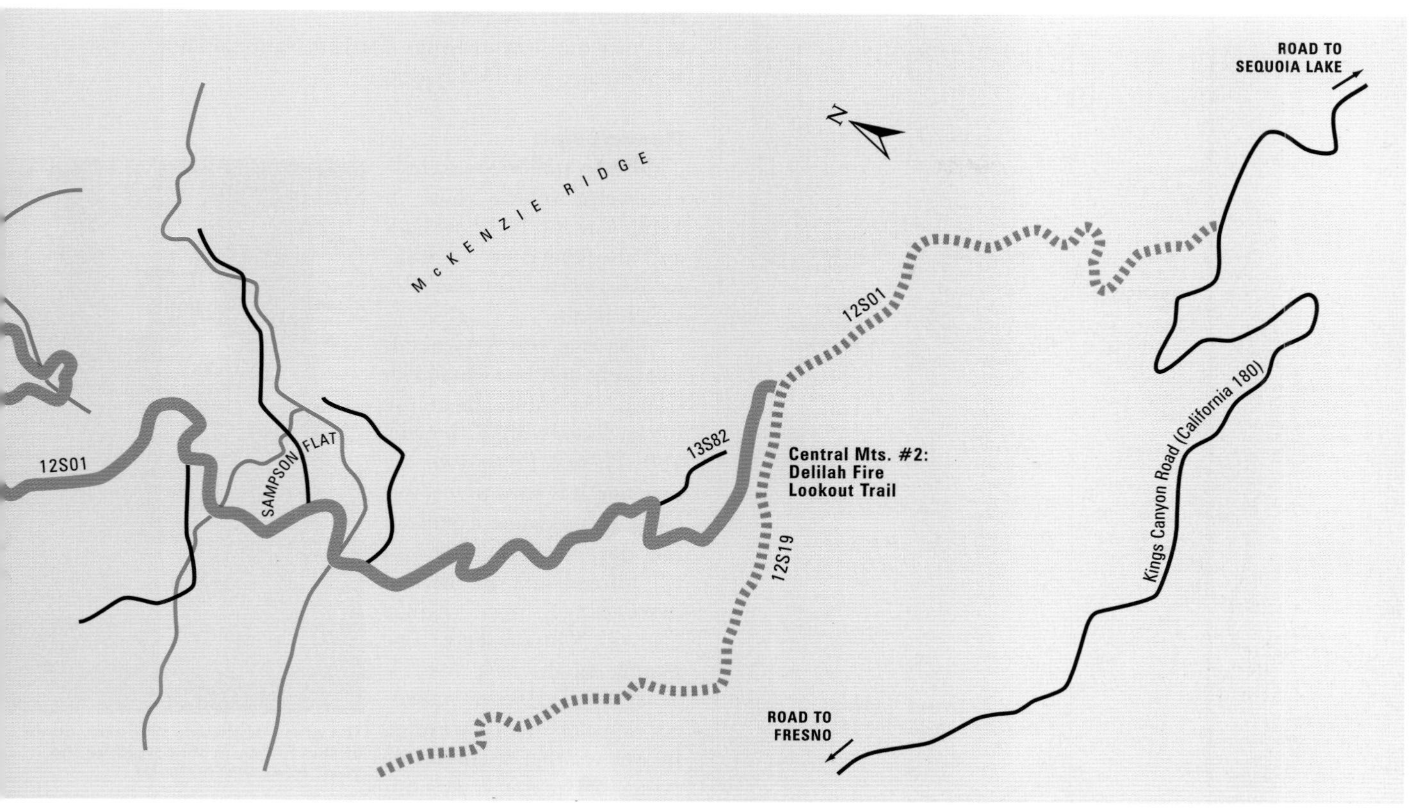

3.2 ▲	SO	Track on left.
		GPS: N36°47.93′ W119°05.52′
▼ 9.4	SO	Cross over creek.
2.8 ▲	SO	Cross over creek.
▼ 9.6	SO	Cross over creek.
2.6 ▲	SO	Cross over creek.
▼ 9.9	SO	Track on left.
2.3 ▲	SO	Track on right.
▼ 10.2	SO	Cross over creek.
2.0 ▲	SO	Cross over creek.
▼ 10.3	SO	Track on right.
1.9 ▲	SO	Track on left.
▼ 10.4	SO	Track on left.
1.8 ▲	SO	Track on right.
▼ 11.7	SO	Track on right.
0.5 ▲	SO	Track on left.
		GPS: N36°46.58′ W119°05.33′
▼ 12.2	SO	Closure gate; then track on left is 13S82. Zero trip meter.
0.0 ▲		Continue to the northwest.
		GPS: N36°46.36′ W119°05.03′
▼ 0.0		Continue to the southwest.
1.3 ▲	SO	Track on right is 13S82; then closure gate. Zero trip meter.
▼ 0.2	SO	Private property on right.
1.1 ▲	SO	Private property on left.
▼ 0.4	SO	Track on right.
0.9 ▲	SO	Track on left.
▼ 1.3		Track on left; then trail ends at intersection with Central Mountains #2: Delilah Fire Lookout Trail. Turn right to continue along the trail; turn left to exit to Kings Canyon Road (California 180).
0.0 ▲		From Central Mountains #2: Delilah Fire Lookout Trail, 2.7 miles north of California 180, zero trip meter and turn northwest onto smaller graded road, marked 12S01—suitable for 4WDs, ATVs, and motorbikes. Zero trip meter. Track on right at intersection.
		GPS: N36°46.09′ W119°04.39′

CENTRAL MOUNTAINS #4

Whitaker Research Forest Trail

Starting Point:	**Generals Highway, 3.6 miles east of California 180**
Finishing Point:	**Central Mountains #5: Cherry Flat Trail, 0.1 miles from Eshom USFS Campground**
Total Mileage:	**5.4 miles**
Unpaved Mileage:	**3.6 miles**
Driving Time:	**30 minutes**
Elevation Range:	**4,900–6,900 feet**
Usually Open:	**Mid-April to November 15**
Best Time to Travel:	**Dry weather**
Difficulty Rating:	**1**
Scenic Rating:	**9**
Remoteness Rating:	**+0**

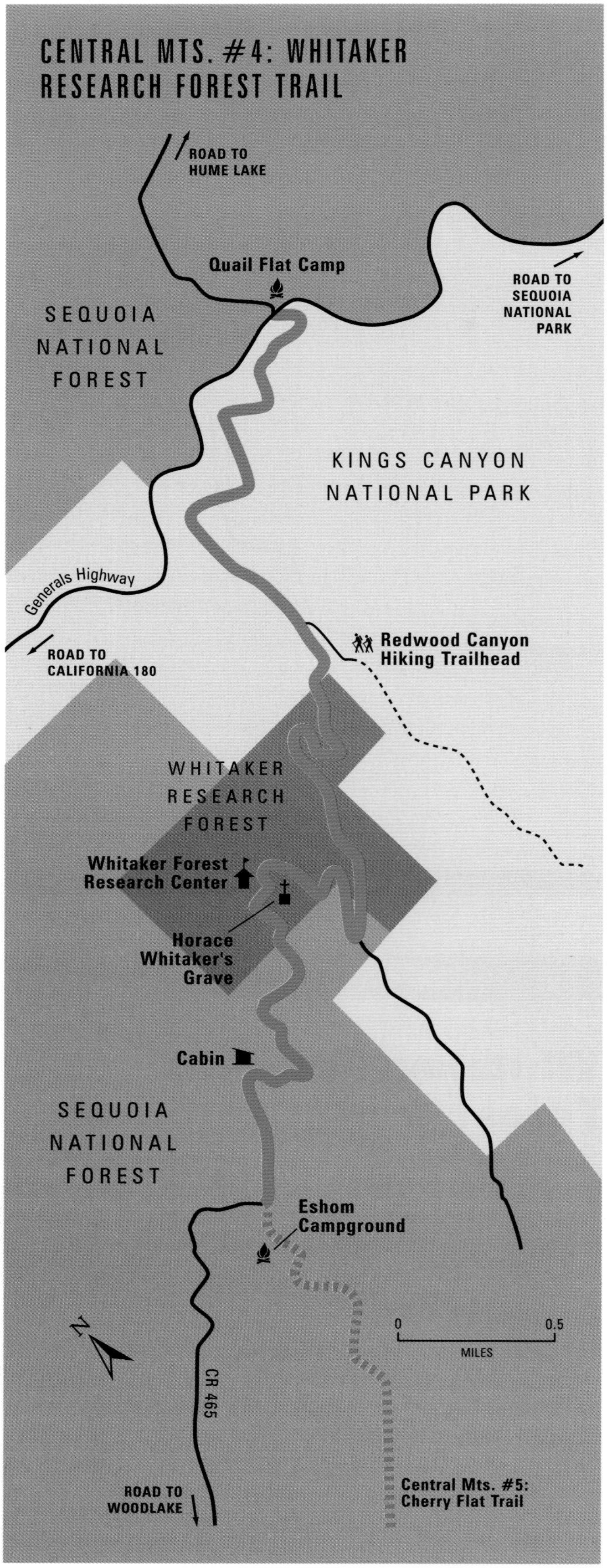

CENTRAL MTS. #4: WHITAKER RESEARCH FOREST TRAIL

ROAD TO HUME LAKE
Quail Flat Camp
ROAD TO SEQUOIA NATIONAL PARK
SEQUOIA NATIONAL FOREST
KINGS CANYON NATIONAL PARK
Generals Highway
ROAD TO CALIFORNIA 180
Redwood Canyon Hiking Trailhead
WHITAKER RESEARCH FOREST
Whitaker Forest Research Center
Horace Whitaker's Grave
Cabin
SEQUOIA NATIONAL FOREST
Eshom Campground
0 0.5 MILES
N
CR 465
ROAD TO WOODLAKE
Central Mts. #5: Cherry Flat Trail

Special Attractions

- Quiet trail within Kings Canyon National Park.
- Whitaker Research Forest.

Description

This short trail follows a lesser-traveled vehicle route in Kings Canyon National Park and the University of California-owned Whitaker Research Forest.

The grave of Horace Whitaker, donor of this forest, is shadowed by the giant trees that he loved

The trail leaves Generals Highway opposite Quail Flat Camp, 3.6 miles from the intersection with California 180. There is no sign for the turn and it is hard to see; initially, it looks like a pull-in, but once over the rise you will immediately see the trail descending into Kings Canyon National Park. The mainly single-track road is generally suitable for passenger vehicles in dry weather. In wet weather it should be avoided. The trail travels under the shady canopy of the forest, passing many large trees and granite outcroppings. The start of the Redwood Canyon Hiking Trail is passed on the edge of the national park before the main trail enters Whitaker Research Forest. The area is owned by the University of California and is dedicated to the study of forestry. The land was donated by Horace Whitaker, who is buried opposite the center's gates beside the trail.

Several felled trees and a number of enormous old-growth stumps can be seen in the forest. Some of these stumps bear slots that were cut by loggers to use for the planks they balanced on as they worked. It was not uncommon for loggers of that time to spend days felling a single tree.

Hand-hewn sequoia felled from old-growth forest—lumberjacks balanced on planks inserted in the slots

From the research facility, the road becomes roughly paved for the final couple of miles before it ends at the intersection with Central Mountains #5: Cherry Flat Trail, 0.1 miles from Eshom USFS Campground. Continue along the paved road for 7.5 miles to exit to Sierra Glen.

Current Road Information
Sequoia National Forest
Hume Lake Ranger District
35860 E. Kings Canyon Road
Dunlap, CA 93621
(559) 338-2251

Map References
BLM Mt. Whitney
USFS Sequoia National Forest
USGS 1:24,000 General Grant Grove
1:100,000 Mt. Whitney
Maptech CD-ROM: Kings Canyon/Death Valley
Southern & Central California Atlas & Gazetteer, p. 25
California Road & Recreation Atlas, p. 85

Route Directions

▼ 0.0		From Generals Highway, 3.6 miles east of California 180, zero trip meter and turn southeast on unmarked dirt road. Turn is immediately before a closure gate and opposite the turn to Hume Lake and Horseshoe Bend Trail at Quail Flat Camp. Turn looks like it is just a pull-in, but the trail continues over the rise and immediately enters Kings Canyon National Park.
1.7 ▲		Trail ends at the intersection with Generals Highway. Turn left for Kings Canyon Visitor Center and Fresno; turn right for Sequoia National Park.
		GPS: N36°43.28' W118°54.51'
▼ 1.7	SO	Track on left goes to Redwood Canyon Hiking Trailhead. Zero trip meter.
0.0 ▲		Continue to the north.
		GPS: N36°42.54' W118°55.27'
▼ 0.0		Continue to the south.
3.7 ▲	SO	Track on right goes to Redwood Canyon Hiking Trailhead. Zero trip meter.
▼ 0.4	SO	Leaving Kings Canyon National Park. Entering Whitaker Research Forest.
3.3 ▲	SO	Leaving Whitaker Research Forest. Entering Kings Canyon National Park.
		GPS: N36°42.44' W118°55.32'
▼ 1.5	BR	Track on left through closure gate.
2.2 ▲	BL	Track on right through closure gate.
		GPS: N36°41.91' W118°55.96'
▼ 1.7	SO	Examples of cut trees showing slots made for planks below trail on right. Cross over creek.
2.0 ▲	SO	Cross over creek. Examples of cut trees showing slots made for planks below trail on left.
▼ 2.1	SO	Whitaker Forest Research Center on right. Horace Whitaker's grave is on the left, adjacent to a large sequoia and surrounded by a wooden fence.
1.6 ▲	SO	Whitaker Forest Research Center on left. Horace Whitaker's grave is on the right, adjacent to a large sequoia and surrounded by a wooden fence.
		GPS: N36°42.16' W118°56.02'
▼ 2.7	SO	Gate. Exiting Whitaker Research Forest.
1.0 ▲	SO	Gate. Entering Whitaker Research Forest.
▼ 3.2	SO	Cabin on right behind fence.
0.5 ▲	SO	Cabin on left behind fence.
▼ 3.7		Trail ends at intersection with Central Mountains #5: Cherry Flat Trail, 7.5 miles northeast of Sierra Glen. Turn left to travel the Cherry Flat Trail; continue straight to exit to California 245 to Woodlake.
0.0 ▲		Trail commences on paved CR 465 at intersection with Central Mountains #5: Cherry Flat Trail, 7.5 miles northeast of Sierra Glen. The intersection is marked with a sign. Zero trip meter and continue north, following sign for Whitaker Forest.
		GPS: N36°41.49' W118°56.80'

CENTRAL MOUNTAINS #5

Cherry Flat Trail

Starting Point:	**CR 465, 2 miles southwest of Whitaker Research Forest**
Finishing Point:	**Cherry Flat**
Total Mileage:	**9.9 miles**
Unpaved Mileage:	**9.9 miles**
Driving Time:	**1.25 hours**
Elevation Range:	**4,200–5,100 feet**
Usually Open:	**May to December**
Best Time to Travel:	**Dry weather**
Difficulty Rating:	**3**
Scenic Rating:	**8**
Remoteness Rating:	**+1**

Special Attractions

- Views into Kings Canyon National Park and Kaweah River Valley.
- Small reed-fringed lake in Pierce Valley.

Description

This trail runs south from CR 465 near the Whitaker Research Forest and travels a lightly traveled trail to end near the national park boundary at Cherry Flat.

Spur trail off Cherry Flat Trail leads to a tranquil lake in Pierce Valley

Cherry Flat Trail opens out of the forest toward the endpoint overlooking Kaweah River

The first section of the trail is a well-used, graded dirt road, but after passing the last of the private property the trail is less maintained and becomes a formed, rutted trail. The ruts are deep, making wet-weather travel inadvisable. A few short sections through the manzanita and mountain mahogany vegetation can be a little brushy, but they are not long and with a bit of care the worst may be avoided.

The scenery is fairly typical of trails in this part of the Sierra Nevada—the views toward the granite domes of Kings Canyon National Park are worthwhile, as is the final view into the Kaweah River Valley.

The trail finishes on a spur overlooking the Kaweah River Valley. There is a small campsite here; otherwise camping along the trail is very limited because of the abundant vegetation. Other trails lead slightly farther toward Cherry Flat and the large granite domes, but these are narrow and brushy.

One short, interesting spur from the main trail leads 0.4 miles to a small, unnamed lake in Pierce Valley. The reed-fringed lake has a couple of pleasant campsites nearby, but the tracks that continue past the lake quickly lead to dead ends. The coordinates of the lake are N36°39.03' W118°56.36'.

Current Road Information

Sequoia National Forest
Hume Lake Ranger District
35860 E. Kings Canyon Road
Dunlap, CA 93621
(559) 338-2251

Map References

BLM Mt. Whitney
USFS Sequoia National Forest
USGS 1:24,000 General Grant Grove
1:100,000 Mt. Whitney
Maptech CD-ROM: Kings Canyon/Death Valley
Southern & Central California Atlas & Gazetteer, p. 25
California Road & Recreation Atlas, p. 85

Route Directions

Mileage	Direction	Description
▼ 0.0		Trail starts on California 465, 7.5 miles northeast of Sierra Glen. Zero trip meter and turn south on small paved road sign-posted to Eshom Campground. Road immediately turns to graded dirt.
4.2 ▲		Trail ends at intersection with CR 465. Turn right for Whitaker Research Forest and Kings Canyon National Park; turn left for Sierra Glen.
		GPS: N36°41.49' W118°56.78'

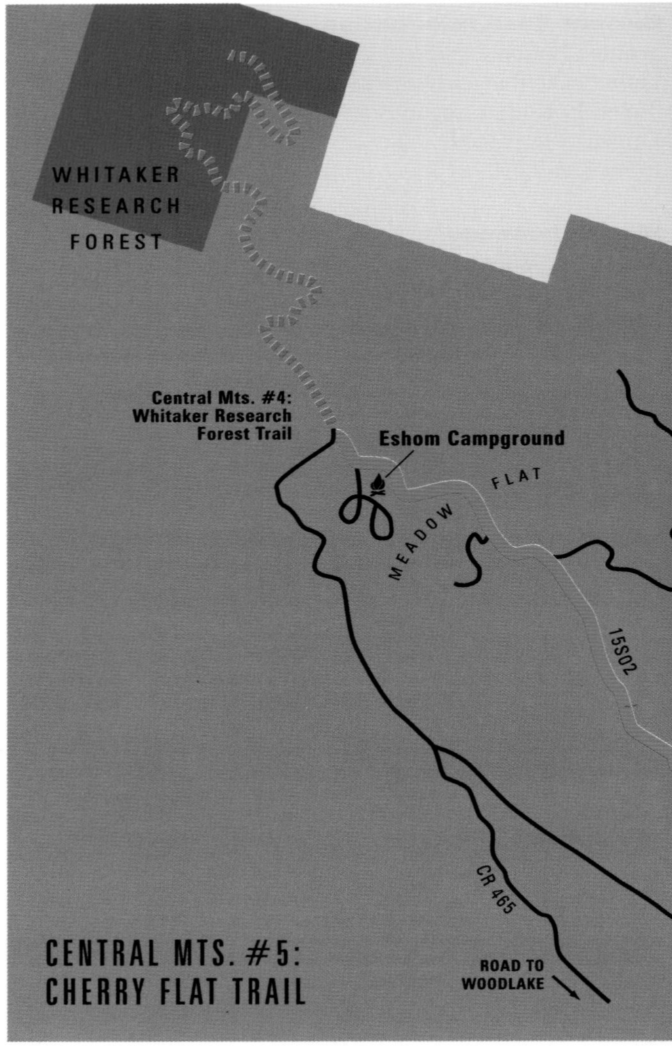

Mileage	Direction	Description
▼ 0.1	BL	Track on right into Eshom USFS Campground. Bear left through closure gate.
4.1 ▲	SO	Closure gate; then track on left into Eshom USFS Campground.
		GPS: N36°41.41' W118°56.82'
▼ 0.6	SO	Track on right.
3.6 ▲	SO	Track on left.
▼ 0.8	BR	Bear right onto smaller graded road.
3.4 ▲	SO	Join larger graded dirt road.
		GPS: N36°40.89' W118°56.92'
▼ 0.9	BR	Track on left.
3.3 ▲	BL	Track on right.
		GPS: N36°40.85' W118°56.99'
▼ 1.2	SO	Cross over creek.
3.0 ▲	SO	Cross over creek.
▼ 3.4	SO	Track on left is 15S05.
0.8 ▲	BL	Track on right is 15S05.
▼ 3.5	BR	Bear right past track on left; then closure gate.
0.7 ▲	BL	Closure gate; then bear left past track on right.
		GPS: N36°39.23' W118°57.07'
▼ 4.2	TL	T-intersection. Turn left and join 15S01. Track on right returns to CR 465. Zero trip meter.
0.0 ▲		Continue to the northwest.
		GPS: N36°38.68' W118°56.79'

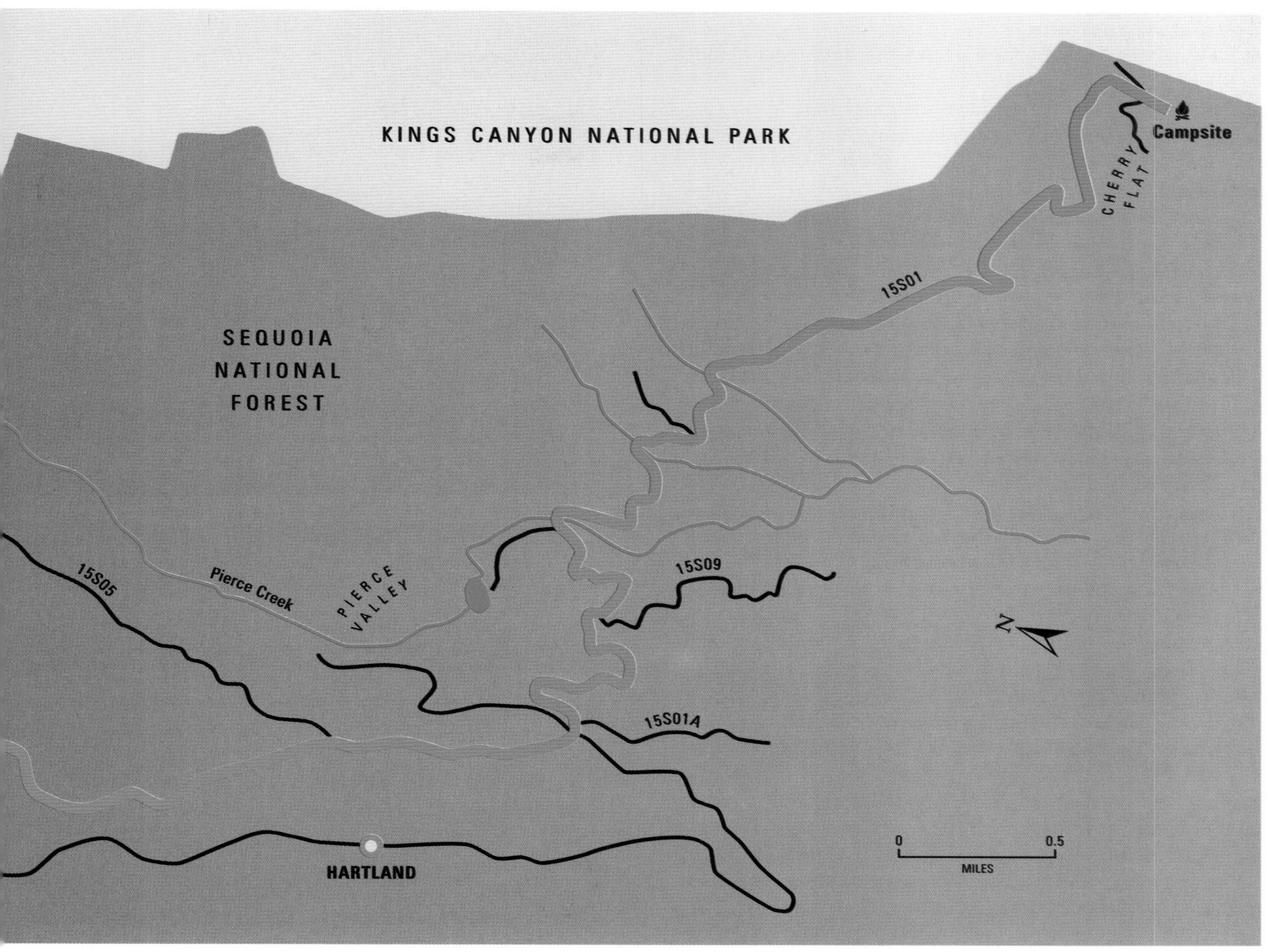

▼ 0.0	BL	Continue to the east. Immediately track on left; then bear left onto 15S01. Ahead is private road 15S01A.
		GPS: N36°38.65′ W118°56.75′
▼ 1.1	SO	Track on right is 15S09.
		GPS: N36°38.70′ W118°56.33′
▼ 1.5	BR	Track on left goes 0.4 miles to a small lake in Pierce Valley. Bear right through closure gate.
		GPS: N36°38.86′ W118°56.10′
▼ 1.6	SO	Cross over Pierce Creek.
▼ 2.3	SO	Cross over creek.
▼ 2.4	BR	Private road on left.
		GPS: N36°38.65′ W118°55.63′
▼ 2.6	SO	Cross over creek.
▼ 2.9	SO	Cross over wash.
▼ 5.5	SO	Track on left is a dead end.
		GPS: N36°37.85′ W118°53.91′
▼ 5.6	BL	Track on right.
		GPS: N36°37.78′ W118°53.93′
▼ 5.7		Trail ends at a campsite with views to the south over the Kaweah River Valley. Pierce Creek is to the west.
		GPS: N36°37.72′ W118°53.93′

CENTRAL MOUNTAINS #6

Buck Rock Fire Lookout Trail

Starting Point:	**Paved road14S11, 2.5 miles north of Generals Highway**
Finishing Point:	**Monarch Wilderness boundary**
Total Mileage:	**11.8 miles**
Unpaved Mileage:	**11.7 miles**
Driving Time:	**1 hour**
Elevation Range:	**6,700–8,200 feet**
Usually Open:	**Mid-April to November 15**
Best Time to Travel:	**Dry weather**
Difficulty Rating:	**2**
Scenic Rating:	**9**
Remoteness Rating:	**+0**

Special Attractions

- Unusual fire lookout location on the large granite Buck Rock.
- Fantastic views on either side of the ridge trail.
- Wilderness access at several points along the trail.

History

The wonderfully located fire lookout on Buck Rock was constructed in 1923. It is referred to as a 4A construction-style tower, being approximately 14 feet by 14 feet in its layout. It is one of only three remaining 4A towers in California.

Burton Pass and Burton Meadow are named after an early rancher who worked in the region. Another local name appears farther down the trail at Evans Creek and Evans Grove. John Evans is remembered for having lived near this grove of sequoias and protecting the trees from the ravages of fire.

Groves of sequoias often take their names from nearby features. Horseshoe Bend Grove is named after a nearby bend in the Kings River. Windy Gulch Grove takes its name from the Windy Cliffs on the Kings River. The names of both Horseshoe Bend and Windy Gulch were first recorded on USGS topographic maps after a survey team worked its way through the rugged terrain in 1903.

Close to the point where Windy Gulch drains into the Kings River is a cave that lay hidden to pioneer settlers until after the turn of the twentieth century. Around 1907, Peter H. Boyden discovered a strikingly beautiful cave and started development. He intended to turn the cave into a tourist attraction. In 1912, the *Inyo Register* reported that Boyden was installing ladders to access the various chambers and electricity to illuminate the features within. Boyden Cavern is a series of interconnecting rooms with many natural features including an underground stream, stalactites and stalagmites, shield formations, crystalline helictites, and a bat cave.

Boyden Cavern is located within the 8,000-foot-deep Kings River Canyon, the deepest canyon in the United States.

Buck Rock Fire Lookout perched like an eagle's nest

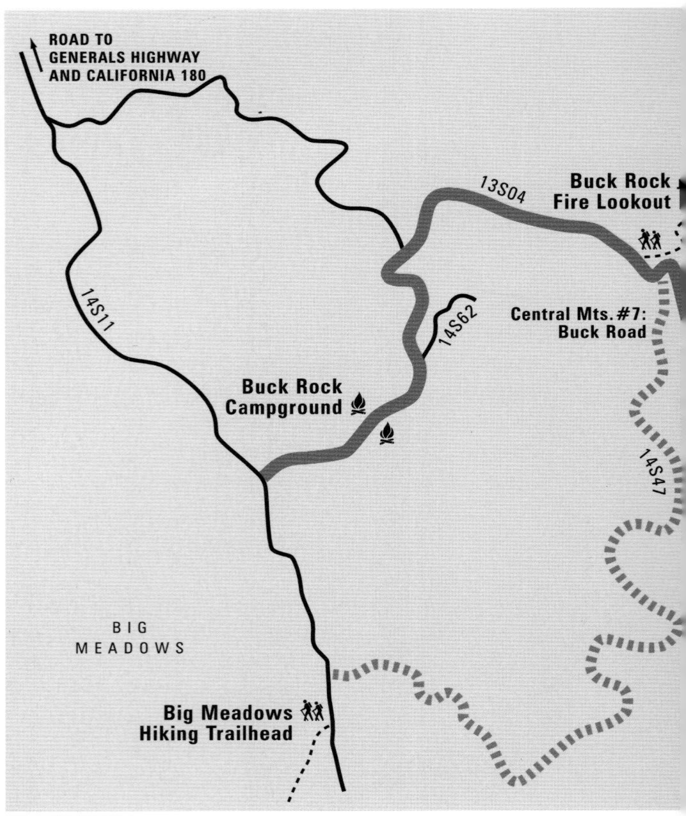

It is now open to the public between May and October and offers walking tours.

Description

The highlight of this trail is undoubtedly the Buck Rock Fire Lookout, perched as it is atop a large granite outcrop. It is accessible by a precarious ladder leading up the face of the rock.

The trail leaves from the small paved road that accesses the Big Meadows Hiking Trailhead. This extremely popular trail accesses the Jennie Lakes Wilderness. Initially the trail to the Buck Rock lookout is roughly graded as it passes Buck Rock USFS Campground. This is a relatively undeveloped camping area, with no numbered sites and only a few tables and fire rings. There are plenty of pleasant places to pitch a tent on either side of the road.

The trail past the campground is slightly rougher and better suited for high-clearance 2WD vehicles as it approaches the lookout.

As you drive north along the narrow ridge, there are fantastic views to the east and west. The lookout can be seen ahead, perched precariously on the large Buck Rock. Reaching the lookout requires a short, somewhat strenuous hike from the parking area at the bottom. The views from the lookout are well worth the effort.

Past the lookout, the trail is slightly rougher. The more difficult Central Mountains #7: Buck Road leads off into the boulder-strewn landscape to the east. The main trail continues as a formed trail down from the lookout to briefly cross the small paved road that travels over Burton Pass. It then follows the dirt road past the Kennedy Meadow Hiking Trailhead,

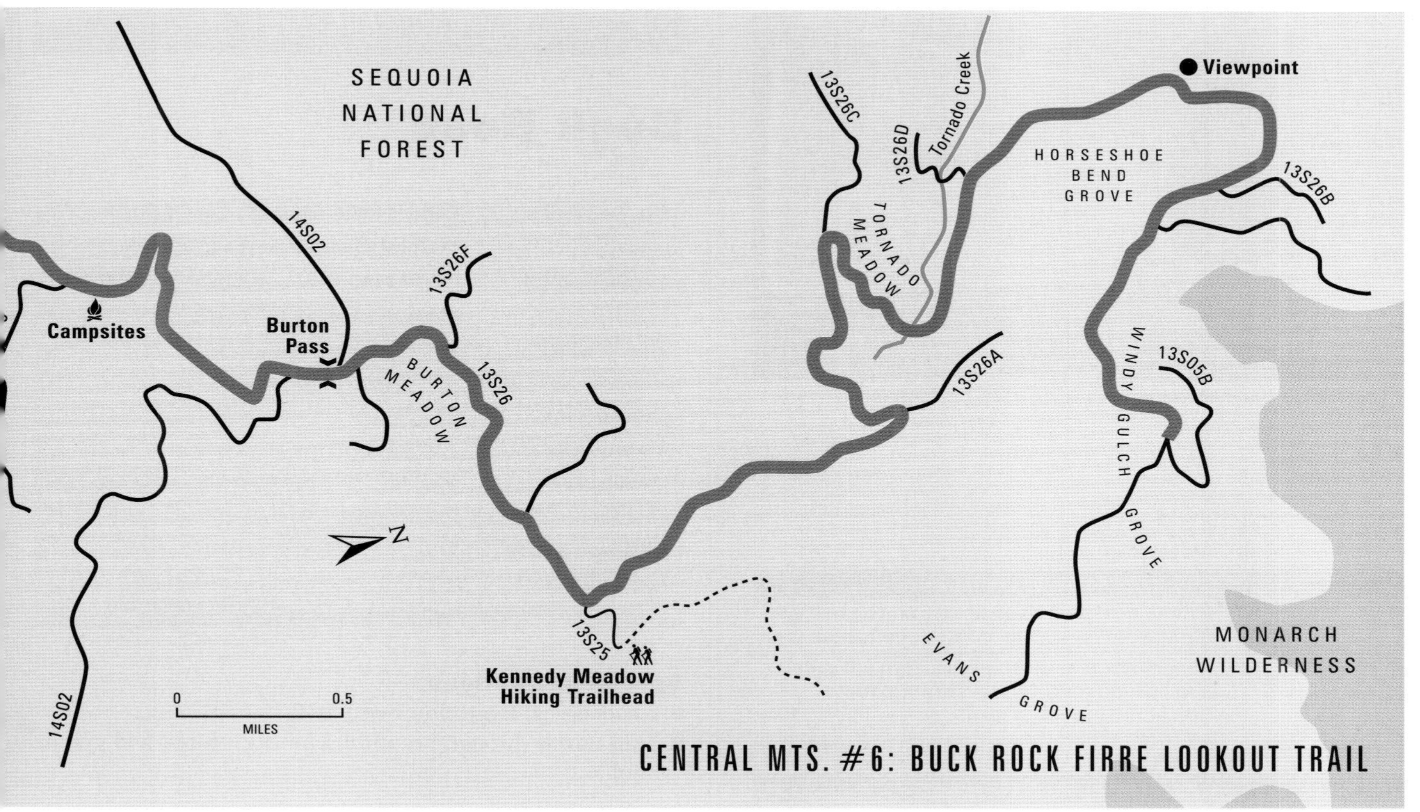

CENTRAL MTS. #6: BUCK ROCK FIRRE LOOKOUT TRAIL

which gives access to the Monarch Wilderness. The road continues as a small dirt trail past Tornado Meadows and meanders around the hillside before becoming brushy. The trail ends at the boundary of the Monarch Wilderness.

Current Road Information

Sequoia National Forest
Hume Lake Ranger District
35860 E. Kings Canyon Road
Dunlap, CA 93621
(559) 338-2251

Map References

BLM Mt. Whitney
USFS Sequoia National Forest
USGS 1:24,000 Muir Grove, Wren Peak
1:100,000 Mt. Whitney
Maptech CD-ROM: Kings Canyon/Death Valley
Southern & Central California Atlas & Gazetteer, p. 25
California Road & Recreation Atlas, p. 86
Trails Illustrated, Sequoia and Kings Canyon (205)

Route Directions

▼ Mileage	▲ Mileage	Action	Directions
▼ 0.0			Trail starts on small paved road 14S11, 2.5 miles north of Generals Highway. 14S11 is the road that leads to Big Meadows Hiking Trailhead. Zero trip meter and turn northeast onto graded dirt road, following sign to Buck Rock Lookout. There is a corral and picnic area at intersection.
	2.2 ▲		Trail ends at T-intersection with small paved road 14S11. Turn left for Big Meadows Hiking Trailhead; turn right to exit to Generals Highway.
			GPS: N36°43.02′ W118°50.89′
▼ 0.1		SO	Turnout area on left.
	2.1 ▲	SO	Turnout area on right.
▼ 0.3		SO	Entering Buck Rock USFS Campground. Pull-in areas for camping on right and left.
	1.9 ▲	SO	Leaving Buck Rock USFS Campground.
			GPS: N36°43.34′ W118°50.99′
▼ 0.5		SO	Cross over creek; then track on left. Leaving Buck Rock USFS Campground.
	1.7 ▲	SO	Track on right; then cross over creek. Entering Buck Rock USFS Campground. Pull-in areas for camping on right and left.
▼ 0.7		SO	Track on right is 14S62.
	1.5 ▲	SO	Track on left is 14S62.
			GPS: N36°43.47′ W118°51.21′
▼ 1.1		SO	Track on left.
	1.1 ▲	SO	Track on right.
▼ 1.2		BR	Well-used track on left. Follow sign to lookout.
	1.0 ▲	SO	Well-used track on right.
			GPS: N36°43.50′ W118°51.56′
▼ 2.1		BR	Track on left is 13S04B, which goes to Buck Rock Lookout—hiking access only. Parking for the tower on right. Remain on 13S04.
	0.1 ▲	SO	Track on right is 13S04B, which goes to Buck Rock Lookout—hiking access only. Parking for the tower on left. Remain on 13S04.
			GPS: N36°44.11′ W118°51.45′
▼ 2.2		BL	Track on right is Central Mountains #7: Buck Road (14S47). Zero trip meter.
	0.0 ▲		Continue to the southwest.
			GPS: N36°44.14′ W118°51.41′

Bear necessities! Good advice at Buck Rock USFS Campground

▼ 0.0			Continue to the northwest.
	2.3 ▲	SO	Track on left is Central Mountains #7: Buck Road (14S47). Zero trip meter.
▼ 1.0		SO	Track on right is 13S10.
	1.3	SO	Track on left is 13S10.
			GPS: N36°44.53' W118°51.23'
▼ 1.1		SO	Turnout on right with campsites and a great view.
	1.2	SO	Turnout on left with campsites and a great view.
▼ 2.3		TL	T-intersection at Burton Pass. Turn left onto small paved road 14S02. Zero trip meter.
	0.0		Turn southwest onto small formed trail 13S04, following sign to Buck Rock Lookout. Zero trip meter.
			GPS: N36°45.08' W118°50.84'
▼ 0.0			Continue to the north.
▼ 0.1		TR	Turn right onto dirt road 13S26, following sign to Kennedy Meadow.
			GPS: N36°45.19' W118°50.82'
▼ 0.2		SO	Closure gate.
▼ 0.3		BL	Bear left, following sign to Tornado Meadow.
			GPS: N36°45.26' W118°50.83'
▼ 0.6		SO	Track on left is 13S26F.
▼ 1.2		SO	Track on left.
▼ 1.6		SO	Track on right is 13S25, which goes 0.25 miles to Kennedy Meadow Hiking Trailhead.
			GPS: N36°45.76' W118°49.96'
▼ 2.8		BL	Track on right is 13S26A.
			GPS: N36°46.65' W118°50.45'
▼ 3.7		BR	Track on left is 13S26C.
			GPS: N36°46.54' W118°51.09'
▼ 4.2		SO	Cross over Tornado Creek. Tornado Meadow on left.
▼ 4.7		BR	Track on left is 13S26D. Zero trip meter.
			GPS: N36°46.92' W118°51.20'
▼ 0.0			Continue to the north.
▼ 0.8		SO	Exceptional viewpoint with views over Kings River Canyon and the mountains and forest to the north.
			GPS: N36°47.56' W118°51.46'
▼ 1.4		SO	Track on left is 13S26B.
			GPS: N36°47.59' W118°51.07'
▼ 1.7		SO	Track on left.
			GPS: N36°47.37' W118°50.95'
▼ 2.0		SO	Trail crosses old landslide area.
▼ 2.6		SO	Track on left is 13S05B. Trail continues past this point as far as the Monarch Wilderness boundary, but it can be brushy.
			GPS: N36°47.33' W118°50.22'

CENTRAL MOUNTAINS #7

Buck Road

Starting Point:	**Central Mountains #6: Buck Rock Fire Lookout Trail, below lookout tower**
Finishing Point:	**Paved road 14S11, 0.2 miles west of Big Meadows Hiking Trailhead**
Total Mileage:	**3.6 miles**
Unpaved Mileage:	**3.6 miles**
Driving Time:	**45 minutes**
Elevation Range:	**7,600–8,200 feet**
Usually Open:	**Mid-April to November 15**
Best Time to Travel:	**Dry weather**
Difficulty Rating:	**5**
Scenic Rating:	**9**
Remoteness Rating:	**+0**

Special Attractions

- Challenging, loose, and twisty trail.
- Trail travels through beautiful semi-open forest and granite boulders.

Description

This trail is one of only a few designated 4WD trails through the recently dedicated Giant Sequoia National Monument. It is suitable for high-clearance 4WDs because of the loose surface, steep ascents and descents, and large rocks that need to be negotiated. In addition, there are off-camber sections that run around the hill where care must be taken; it is easy to slip sideways on the loose surface. The small formed trail is predominantly sandy.

The very twisty trail is exceptionally scenic and travels through semi-open forest past large granite boulders. There

Outcrops of granite and views deep into the Sierra Nevada are a feature of this trail

he loose gravel on the steep rock
nclines will cause traction difficulty for
ome vehicles

are also panoramic views and a couple of pleasant camping places.

The 5-rated part of the trail is the western end, where it leaves Central Mountains #6: Buck Rock Fire Lookout Trail. Here the dips, descents, and loose surface will challenge some vehicles. Decent tires are recommended. The second half of the trail is easier. It follows along smoother trails that were once used for logging to emerge on the small paved road near the Big Meadows Hiking Trailhead, a popular access point for the Jennie Lakes Wilderness. Big Meadows got its name from hunters who found abundant game in the area over the years.

Current Road Information

Sequoia National Forest
Hume Lake Ranger District
35860 E. Kings Canyon Road
Dunlap, CA 93621
(559) 338-2251

Map References

BLM Mt. Whitney
USFS Sequoia National Forest
USGS 1:24,000 Muir Grove
1:100,000 Mt. Whitney
Maptech CD-ROM: Kings Canyon/Death Valley
Southern & Central California Atlas & Gazetteer, p. 25
California Road & Recreation Atlas, p. 86
Trails Illustrated, Sequoia and Kings Canyon (205)—route not shown

Route Directions

▼ 0.0 From Central Mountains #6: Buck Rock Fire Lookout Trail, directly below the lookout tower, zero trip meter and turn east on 14S47, marked as a designated vehicle route for 4WDs, ATVs, and motorbikes.
1.7 ▲ Trail ends on Central Mountains #6: Buck Rock Fire Lookout Trail, directly below the lookout tower. Turn left to visit Buck Rock Lookout and exit via Generals Highway.

GPS: N36°44.14′ W118°51.41′

▼ 0.5 BR Trail forks and rejoins. At times, the right-hand fork can be easier but this may change.
1.2 ▲ BL Trail forks and rejoins. At times, the left-hand fork can be easier but this may change.

▼ 1.1 TL Trail continues ahead. Turn left to avoid off-camber side slope.
0.6 ▲ TR Tracks rejoin.

GPS: N36°44.06′ W118°50.59′

▼ 1.2 SO Tracks rejoins.
0.5 ▲ SO Track on left. Continue straight ahead to avoid off-camber side slope.

GPS: N36°44.03′ W118°50.57′

▼ 1.6 SO Pull-off area on right. Remain on main trail marked by orange markers.
0.1 ▲ SO Pull-off area on left.

GPS: N36°44.06′ W118°50.24′

▼ 1.7 TR Track continues ahead. Zero trip meter.
0.0 ▲ Continue to the southwest.

GPS: N36°44.07′ W118°50.19′

▼ 0.0 Continue to the south.
1.9 ▲ TL Well-used track on right. Zero trip meter.

▼ 1.0 TR Well-used track on left.
0.9 ▲ TL Well-used track ahead.

GPS: N36°43.61′ W118°49.72′

▼ 1.6 SO Closure gate.
0.3 ▲ SO Closure gate.

▼ 1.7 TL T-intersection. Track on right is 14S01B. There are a couple of campsites with picnic tables opposite the intersection.
0.2 ▲ TR Turn right onto unmarked trail. Track straight ahead is marked as 14S01B. There are a couple of campsites with picnic tables on left.

GPS: N36°43.24′ W118°50.20′

▼ 1.9 Trail ends at T-intersection with paved road 14S11. Turn right to exit to Generals Highway.
0.0 ▲ Trail starts on small paved 14S11, 3.6 miles north of intersection with Generals Highway.

Zero trip meter and turn northwest on small unmarked dirt trail at an informal camp area, 0.1 miles west of Big Meadows Workstation and 0.2 miles west of the Big Meadows Hiking Trailhead, which leads into Jennie Lakes Wilderness.

GPS: N36°43.14' W118°50.19'

CENTRAL MOUNTAINS #8

Solo Peak Road

Starting Point:	**California 190 at Camp Nelson**
Finishing Point:	**Solo Peak**
Total Mileage:	**14.3 miles**
Unpaved Mileage:	**12.7 miles**
Driving Time:	**2 hours**
Elevation Range:	**4,500–6,700 feet**
Usually Open:	**May to December**
Best Time to Travel:	**May to December**
Difficulty Rating:	**2**
Scenic Rating:	**8**
Remoteness Rating:	**+1**

Special Attractions

- Many large sequoias along the trail.
- Lightly traveled trail.

History

Camp Nelson was named after pioneer John Milton Nelson, who first settled in the area in the early 1880s. He built a small sawmill and established an apple orchard. In the summer, ranchers moving their stock to higher meadows, hunters, and other travelers would visit Nelson on their way up the mountain. With so many visitors, Nelson built a two-story guesthouse and vacation cabins. The first post office was established in 1910 and operated until 1967. Rough mule train roads brought in the much-needed workforce for the sawmills in the summertime. A trafficable road was built by 1922, which opened up the area for further development. Many people built mountain retreats to escape the summer heat down in the valley. The area has many summer homes to this day.

Slate Mountain towers above Solo Peak Road near Camp Nelson

Coy Creek and Coy Flat are named after Milton Coy, who settled this land in 1891. Rogers Camp is named after Henry Rogers, the original settler on land that is still privately owned.

Sequoias stand out along Solo Peak Road

Description

This trail through the Sequoia National Forest leaves the small settlement of Camp Nelson and travels along the north side of Solo Peak. It passes the forest service campground at Coy Flat, where there are very shady sites available under large pine trees. The trail turns to graded dirt at this point and follows a shelf road through dense forest. The road is mainly single vehicle width, but there are ample passing places.

Past the private property at Rogers Camp are some huge red-barked sequoias. The massive trees continue to be scattered throughout the forest until the end of the trail.

Past the turnoff for Central Mountains #9: Windy Gap Trail, the road continues to a dead end at Solo Peak. It follows along a shelf road for 7 miles before turning into small trails that become brushy, although they do continue farther than what is shown on maps.

Current Road Information

Sequoia National Forest
Tule River Ranger District
32588 Highway 190
Springville, CA 93265
(559) 539-2607

Map References

BLM Three Rivers
USFS Sequoia National Forest
USGS 1:24,000 Camp Nelson, Sentinel Peak, Solo Peak, Camp Wishon
1:100,000 Three Rivers
Maptech CD-ROM: Kings Canyon/Death Valley
Southern & Central California Atlas & Gazetteer, p. 38
California Road & Recreation Atlas, p. 86

Route Directions

▼ 0.0	From Camp Nelson on California 190, zero trip meter and turn east on paved Nelson Drive, following sign for Camp Nelson and Coy Flat. Immediately, paved road on left and paved road on right. Continue straight, following sign to Coy Flat. Remain on paved Coy Flat Drive, ignoring turns on right and left.

1.6 ▲		Trail ends at T-intersection with California 190 in Camp Nelson. Turn left for Porterville.
		GPS: N36°08.19′ W118°37.10′
▼ 0.5	SO	Cross over Middle Fork Tule River on bridge.
1.1 ▲	SO	Cross over Middle Fork Tule River on bridge.
		GPS: N36°08.14′ W118°36.66′
▼ 1.2	SO	Bear Creek Trail (31E31) on left for hiking only; then cross over Bear Creek.
0.4 ▲	SO	Cross over Bear Creek; then Bear Creek Trail (31E31) on right for hiking only.
		GPS: N36°07.81′ W118°37.07′
▼ 1.6	SO	Coy Flat USFS Campground on right. Zero trip meter. Road turns to graded dirt.
0.0 ▲		Continue to the southwest.
		GPS: N36°07.67′ W118°37.09′
▼ 0.0		Continue to the east, following sign for Solo Peak Road through closure gate. Road is now marked 21S94.
4.4 ▲	SO	Pass through closure gate. Coy Flat USFS Campground on left. Zero trip meter. Road is now paved.
▼ 1.2	SO	Cross over Coy Creek.
3.2 ▲	SO	Cross over Coy Creek.
▼ 2.4	SO	Track on right; then cattle guard.
2.0 ▲	SO	Cattle guard; then track on left.
		GPS: N36°06.76′ W118°37.67′
▼ 2.6	SO	Cross over creek.
1.8 ▲	SO	Cross over creek.
▼ 3.8	SO	Track on left is private property; then start of large sequoias.
0.6 ▲	SO	Track on right is private property.
		GPS: N36°06.54′ W118°38.26′
▼ 4.0	SO	Track on left.
0.4 ▲	SO	Track on right.
▼ 4.4	TR	Turn right onto 21S12. Ahead is Central Mountains #9: Windy Gap Trail (20S94), which enters the Tule River Indian Reservation. Zero trip meter.
0.0 ▲		Continue to the northeast.
		GPS: N36°06.24′ W118°38.65′
▼ 0.0		Continue to the north.
▼ 0.3	SO	Closure gate.
▼ 1.2	SO	Small trail on right is 21S58.
		GPS: N36°06.53′ W118°39.18′
▼ 1.4	SO	Track on right.
▼ 1.9	SO	Track on left.
		GPS: N36°06.73′ W118°39.63′
▼ 2.7	SO	Closure gate.
		GPS: N36°07.17′ W118°39.75′
▼ 6.0	BL	Well-used track on right. Remain on 21S12. Marker post at intersection.
		GPS: N36°07.97′ W118°40.96′
▼ 6.6	BL	Major track on right is 21S12. Bear left onto 21S25 and zero trip meter.
		GPS: N36°07.61′ W118°41.46′
▼ 0.0		Continue to the south.
▼ 0.5	SO	Track on left dead-ends in 1 mile at a previously cleared area where there are some large redwoods. Trail is used past this point, but it is narrow and brushy.
		GPS: N36°07.32′ W118°41.26′
▼ 1.1	BL	Track on right through fence line. This is the site of Redwood Camp.
		GPS: N36°06.86′ W118°41.28′
▼ 1.7		Trail ends in small clearing. Track does continue past this point, but is narrow, brushy, and little used.
		GPS: N36.06.77′ W118°40.76′

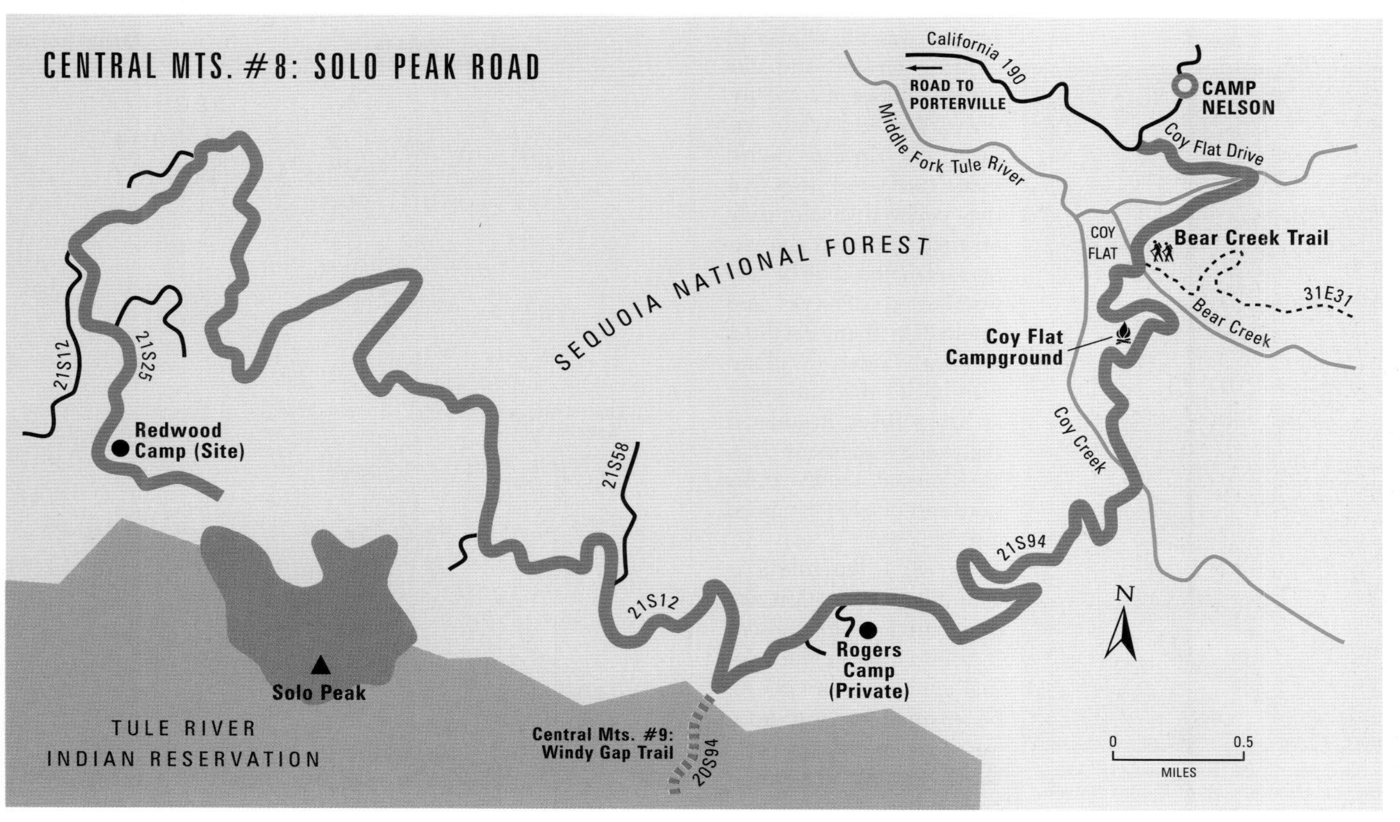

Windy Gap Trail

Starting Point:	**Central Mountains #8: Solo Peak Road, 6 miles south of Camp Nelson**
Finishing Point:	**Western Divide Highway**
Total Mileage:	**13.5 miles**
Unpaved Mileage:	**Approximately 7 miles**
Driving Time:	**1 hour**
Elevation Range:	**6,000–7,500 feet**
Usually Open:	**May to December**
Best Time to Travel:	**May to December**
Difficulty Rating:	**1**
Scenic Rating:	**8**
Remoteness Rating:	**+1**

Special Attractions

- Access to Summit Hiking Trail at Windy Gap.
- Views of Slate Mountain.
- Quiet, lightly traveled trail connecting two areas of Sequoia National Forest.

History

The Tule River Indian Reservation was established in 1857 at a location close to Porterville. Initially known as the Monache Reservation, it accommodated Native Americans relocated after the Tule River War of 1856. The war was the climax of growing tension and discontent between local Indian tribes and white settlers. The Indians killed many cattle and hogs that they believed were grazing on their land and the settlers retaliated. The bloody war lasted six weeks and resulted in many fatalities on both sides. William Campbell, the sub-agent at Kings River, negotiated the peace settlement. Battle Mountain, a few miles northeast of Milo, is named after this war.

The tea-color stain from water trickling down the granite rock of Mount Nelson along Windy Gap Trail

In 1873, the Tule River Indian Reservation was designated at its present location, because the original spot was thought to be unsuitable. Unscrupulous local merchants sold whisky on the reservation and some intoxicated Indians were subsequently responsible for the death of Mrs. J. Bonnsall and both of her young children. Those responsible were hanged and the local people demanded the relocation of the reservation.

The move to the new location involved hundreds of Indians from the Tejon, Kaweah, Kings Tule, and Monache tribes. A school opened at the new location and farming knowledge was passed on to members of the tribes.

Description

Many of the trails within the Sierra Nevada are fairly short and link major areas with hiking and motorbike trails. This trail, an alternative to the paved Western Divide Highway, links the trails around Camp Nelson to the southern trails around California Hot Springs. It travels mainly through Sequoia National Forest and briefly into the Tule River Indian Reservation.

The trail leaves Central Mountains #8: Solo Peak Road, 6 miles south of Camp Nelson, and immediately enters the reservation. Travel is permitted on designated roads only. Please observe the regulations posted on entry. As the trail leaves the reservation and heads back into the national forest, the road surface is alternately graded dirt and single-lane paved. A passenger vehicle can generally travel this trail in dry weather. However, the trail is remote for the Sierra Nevada, and vehicles should be well prepared.

The shelf road winds its way along the west side of Slate Mountain, at times giving good views of the bare-topped mountain towering above. It then climbs up to Windy Gap to

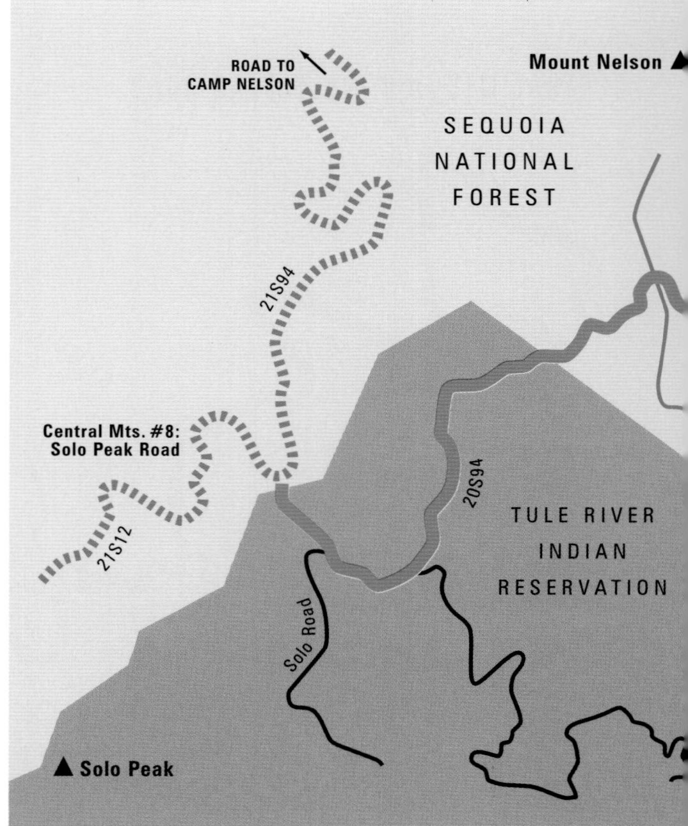

intersect with the Summit Hiking Trail, a popular trail that runs along the ridge tops of this part of the Sierra Nevada. From Windy Gap, it is an easy descent to join the Western Divide Highway.

Current Road Information

Sequoia National Forest
Tule River Ranger District
32588 Highway 190
Springville, CA 93265
(559) 539-2607

Map References

BLM Three Rivers
USFS Sequoia National Forest
USGS 1:24,000 Solo Peak, Sentinel Peak
1:100,000 Three Rivers
Maptech CD-ROM: Kings Canyon/Death Valley
Southern & Central California Atlas & Gazetteer, p. 38
California Road & Recreation Atlas, p. 86

Route Directions

▼ 0.0 From Central Mountains #8: Solo Peak Road, 6 miles south of Camp Nelson, zero trip meter and turn southwest on 20S94. Trail immediately enters the Tule River Indian Reservation. Regulations are posted at the gate.

9.8 ▲ Trail finishes at intersection with Central Mountains #8: Solo Peak Road. Turn left to continue to the end of this trail; continue straight to exit to Camp Nelson.

GPS: N36°06.24' W118°38.65'

▼ 0.4 SO Well-used track on right is Solo Road. Remain on 20S94.

9.4 ▲ SO Well-used track on left is Solo Road. Remain on 20S94.

GPS: N36°05.87' W118°38.84'

The trail approaches the open western slope of Slate Mountain

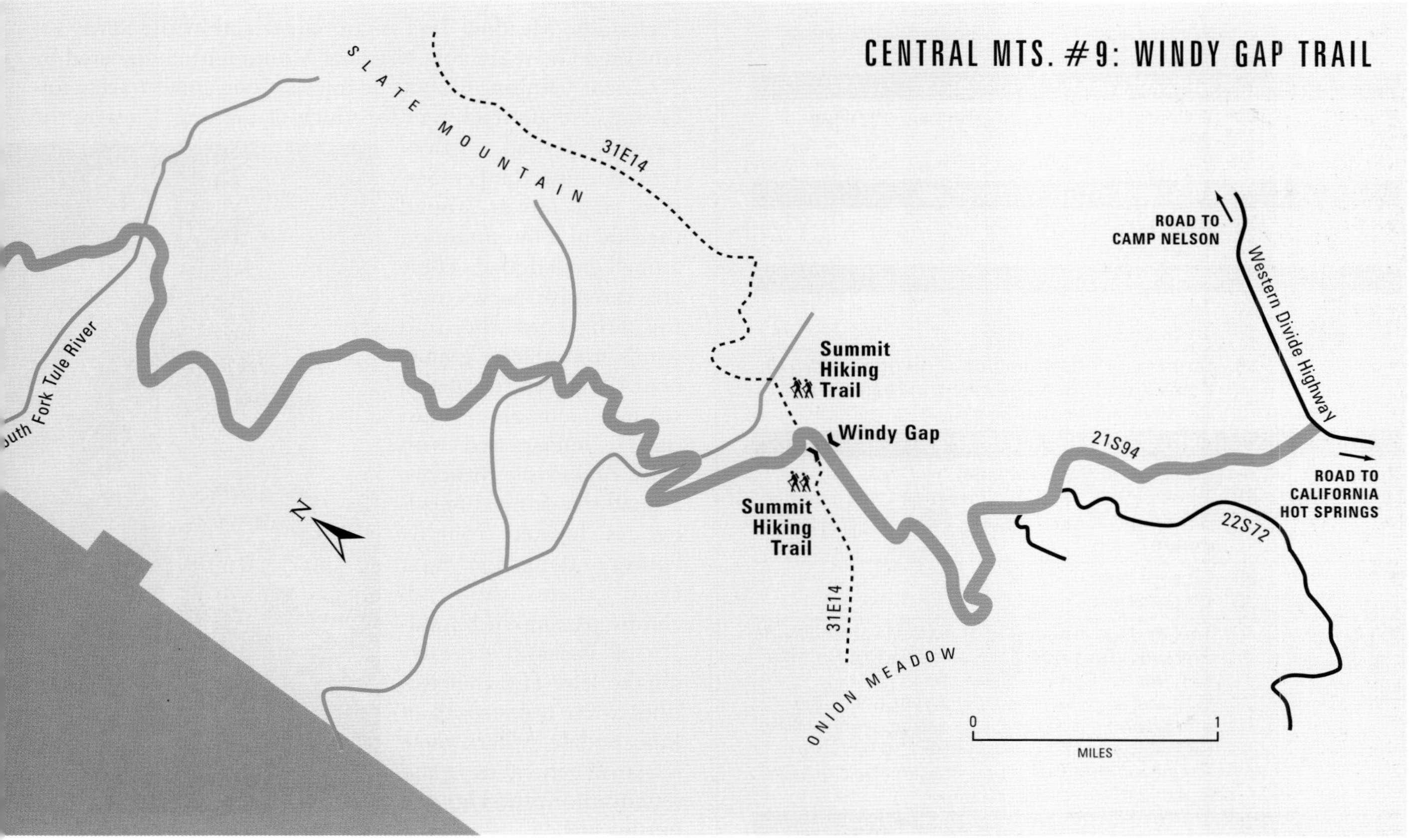

CENTRAL MTS. #9: WINDY GAP TRAIL

SLATE MOUNTAIN
31E14
ROAD TO CAMP NELSON
Western Divide Highway
South Fork Tule River
Summit Hiking Trail
Windy Gap
21S94
ROAD TO CALIFORNIA HOT SPRINGS
22S72
N
Summit Hiking Trail
31E14
ONION MEADOW
0 1
MILES

▼ 0.7		TL	Turn left, remaining on 20S94 through closure gate. Track ahead goes to Cholollo Camp.
	9.1 ▲	TR	Closure gate; then immediately turn right. Track on left goes to Chololo Camp.
			GPS: N36°05.68' W118°38.73'
▼ 2.7		SO	Cross over creek.
	7.1 ▲	SO	Cross over creek.
			GPS: N36°05.62' W118°36.99'
▼ 4.4		SO	Cross over South Fork Tule River.
	5.4 ▲	SO	Cross over South Fork Tule River.
▼ 7.7		SO	Cross over creek.
	2.1 ▲	SO	Cross over creek.
			GPS: N36°03.54' W118°35.62'
▼ 8.5		SO	Cross over creek.
	1.3 ▲	SO	Cross over creek.
▼ 8.7		SO	Well-used track on right. Windy Creek on right of trail.
	1.1 ▲	BR	Well-used track on left. Windy Creek on left of trail.
			GPS: N36°03.01' W118°35.69'
▼ 8.8		SO	Cross over Windy Creek.
	1.0 ▲	SO	Cross over Windy Creek.
▼ 9.8		SO	Summit Hiking Trail (31E14) on left goes to Quaking Aspen. Trail now follows along road for a short distance. Zero trip meter at sign.
	0.0 ▲		Continue to the southwest.
			GPS: N36°02.71' W118°35.18'
▼ 0.0			Continue to the southeast.
	2.4 ▲	SO	Summit Hiking Trail (31E14) on right goes to Quaking Aspen. Zero trip meter at sign.
▼ 0.1		SO	Cattle guard; then Summit Hiking Trail (31E14) on right goes to Onion Meadow. This is Windy Gap.
	2.3 ▲	SO	Summit Hiking Trail (31E14) on left goes to Onion Meadow; then cattle guard. This is Windy Gap. Trail now follows along road for a short distance.
			GPS: N36°02.63' W118°35.19'
▼ 1.3		BL	Well-used track on right. Remain on major road.
	1.1 ▲	BR	Well-used track on left. Remain on major road.
			GPS: N36°01.76' W118°35.28'
▼ 1.6		SO	Track on left is 21S94A.
	0.8 ▲	SO	Track on right is 21S94A.
			GPS: N36°01.90' W118°35.23'
▼ 2.2		SO	Track on right.
	0.2 ▲	SO	Track on left.
▼ 2.4		SO	Small track on left and track on right is 22S72. Remain on 21S94 and zero trip meter.
	0.0 ▲		Continue to the southwest.
			GPS: N36°01.85' W118°34.69'
▼ 0.0			Continue to the northeast.
	1.3 ▲	BR	Track on left is 22S72 and small track on right. Bear right, remaining on 21S94 and zero trip meter.
▼ 1.2		SO	Closure gate.
	0.1 ▲	SO	Closure gate.
▼ 1.3			Trail ends at T-intersection with Western Divide Highway. Turn right for California Hot Springs; turn left for Camp Nelson.
	0.0 ▲		Trail starts on Western Divide Highway, 5.5 miles south of the turnoff to Peppermint USFS Campground. Zero trip meter and turn northwest on graded dirt road, marked as Crawford Road (21S94) to Windy Gap.
			GPS: N36°01.27' W118°33.80'

CENTRAL MOUNTAINS #10

Packsaddle Meadow Trail

Starting Point:	**M50, 9 miles north of Hot Springs Ranger Station**
Finishing Point:	**Paved road 23S16, 4.6 miles south of Johnsondale**
Total Mileage:	**7.5 miles**
Unpaved Mileage:	**7.5 miles**
Driving Time:	**1 hour**
Elevation Range:	**5,800–7,200 feet**
Usually Open:	**May to December**
Best Time to Travel:	**May to December**
Difficulty Rating:	**2**
Scenic Rating:	**9**
Remoteness Rating:	**+0**

Special Attractions

- Trail skirts the edge of a giant sequoia grove.
- Small, seldom-used trail within Giant Sequoia National Monument.
- Access to many trails suitable for hiking, horse, mountain bike, and motorbike use.

Description

Packsaddle Meadow Trail is contained within the newly established Giant Sequoia National Monument, designated by President Clinton in 2000. It travels along small tracks, following a single-track trail for much of the way. It leaves the paved M50 road, north of Hot Springs Ranger Station, and travels around the side of a mountain on a small graded road. There are extensive views over the ranges as the trail winds around large granite boulders, passing through a sequoia and pine forest that is interspersed with oaks. Packsaddle Meadow, a small tree-fringed meadow, is located roughly halfway along the trail. From there the trail climbs, passing the boundary of Packsaddle Grove on the left. The trail finishes a few miles south of Johnsondale, where there is a small general store and restaurant (limited hours), but no fuel.

Lichen cover the trunk of this sequoia

Current Road Information

Sequoia National Forest
Hot Springs Ranger District
43474 Parker Drive
Route 4, Box 548
California Hot Springs, CA 93207
(661) 548-6503

Map References

BLM Isabella Lake
USFS Sequoia National Forest
USGS 1:24,000 California Hot Springs, Johnsondale
1:100,000 Isabella Lake
Maptech CD-ROM: Barstow/San Bernardino County
Southern & Central California Atlas & Gazetteer, p. 50
California Road & Recreation Atlas, p. 86

Route Directions

▼ 0.0		From M50, 9 miles north of Hot Springs Ranger Station, zero trip meter and turn east on graded dirt road marked 308018 and 23S64. Immediately track on right.
4.7 ▲		Track on left; then trail finishes on paved road M50. Turn left to exit to California Hot Springs.
		GPS: N35°56.35' W118°38.42'
▼ 0.1	SO	Closure gate.
4.6 ▲	SO	Closure gate.
▼ 2.1	SO	Track on left is 23S64E.
2.6 ▲	SO	Track on right is 23S64E.
		GPS: N35°56.43' W118°37.25'
▼ 2.5	SO	Trail on left is 31E50 for hikers, horses, mountain bikes, and motorbikes.
2.2 ▲	SO	Trail on right is 31E50 for hikers, horses, mountain bikes, and motorbikes.
		GPS: N35°56.23' W118°37.01'
▼ 2.6	SO	Trail on right is 31E50.
2.1 ▲	SO	Trail on left is 31E50.
▼ 4.2	SO	Closure gate.
0.5 ▲	SO	Closure gate.

Packsaddle Meadow is a quiet and pretty spot along the trail

		GPS: N35°55.29' W118°36.32'
▼ 4.5	SO	Track on right and small track on left.
0.2 ▲	SO	Small track on right and track on left.
		GPS: N35°55.25' W118°35.96'
▼ 4.7	BR	Fork in trail at Packsaddle Meadow. Track on left is 23S64. Zero trip meter.
0.0 ▲		Continue to the south.
		GPS: N35°55.40' W118°35.87'
▼ 0.0		Continue to the northeast.
1.5 ▲	SO	Track on right at Packsaddle Meadow is 23S64. Zero trip meter.
▼ 0.1	SO	Closure gate.
1.4 ▲	SO	Closure gate.
▼ 0.6	SO	Trail on right is Pup Meadow Trail (31E53) to Frog Meadow.
0.9 ▲	SO	Trail on left is Pup Meadow Trail (31E53) to Frog Meadow.
		GPS: N35°55.34' W118°35.33'
▼ 0.8	SO	Track on left.
0.7 ▲	SO	Track on right.

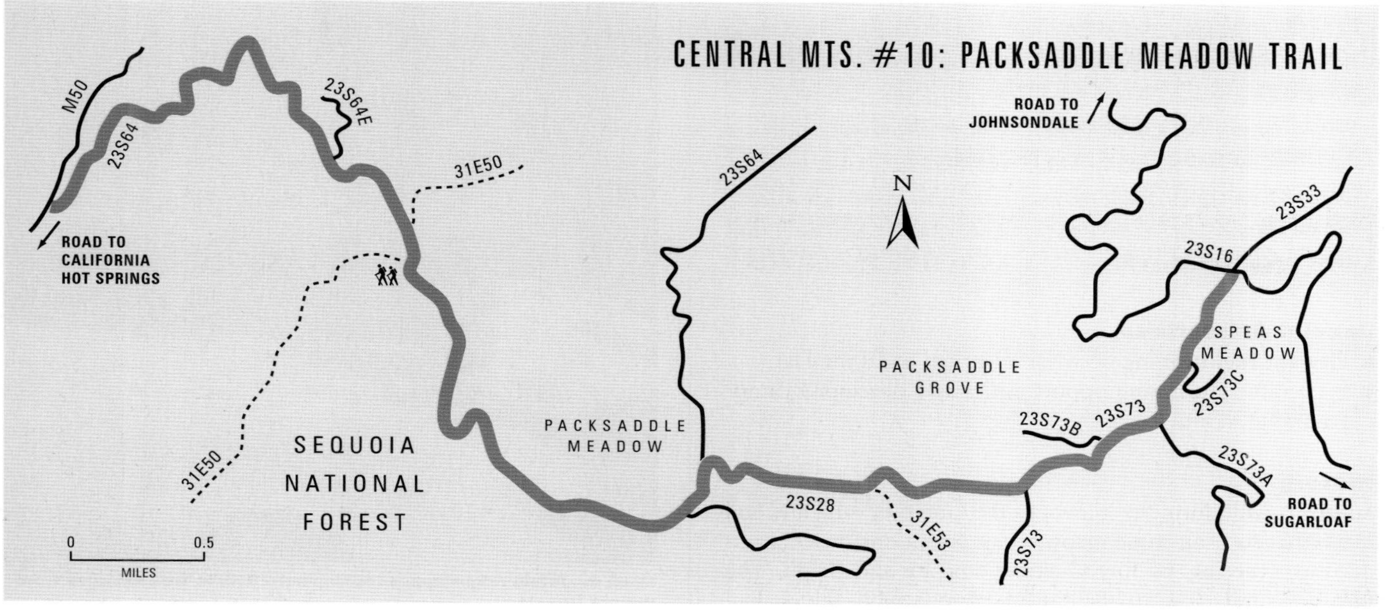

▼ 1.5		TL	Turn left and join 23S73. Track on right is also 23S73. Zero trip meter.
	0.0 ▲		Continue to the west.
			GPS: N35°55.29' W118°34.58'
▼ 0.0			Continue to the north.
	1.3 ▲	TR	Turn right, joining 23S28. Ahead is the continuation of 23S73. Zero trip meter.
▼ 0.4		SO	Track on left is 23S73B.
	0.9 ▲	SO	Track on right is 23S73B.
			GPS: N35°55.44' W118°34.25'
▼ 0.6		BL	Track on right is 23S73A. Remain on 23S73.
	0.7 ▲	BR	Track on left is 23S73A. Remain on 23S73.
			GPS: N35°55.50' W118°34.03'
▼ 0.9		SO	Track on right is 23S73C to Speas Meadow.
	0.4 ▲	SO	Track on left is 23S73C to Speas Meadow.
			GPS: N35°55.68' W118°33.89'
▼ 1.3			Closure gate; then trail ends on small paved road 23S16. Turn left for Johnsondale; turn right for Sugarloaf. Small paved road 23S33 is opposite.
	0.0 ▲		Trail commences on small paved road 23S16, 4.6 miles south of Johnsondale, at the intersection with SM 99. Zero trip meter and turn southwest on graded dirt road, following sign for Speas Ridge Trail. Route is marked 23S73. Small paved road 23S33 is opposite.
			GPS: N35°56.00' W118°33.70'

CENTRAL MOUNTAINS #11

Capinero Saddle Trail

Starting Point:	**CR 50, 0.8 miles north of Sugarloaf Sawmill, 6.7 miles north of Portuguese Pass**
Finishing Point:	**Intersection of M50 and M56, at the Hot Springs Ranger Station**
Total Mileage:	**8.2 miles**
Unpaved Mileage:	**6.1 miles**
Driving Time:	**45 minutes**
Elevation Range:	**3,600–5,300 feet**
Usually Open:	**April 15 to November 15**
Best Time to Travel:	**April 15 to November 15**
Difficulty Rating:	**1**
Scenic Rating:	**7**
Remoteness Rating:	**+0**

Special Attractions

- Pleasant trail running between Sugarloaf and Pine Flat.
- Backcountry camping opportunities and developed campground at White River.

History

Sugarloaf Mill, formerly known as the Guernsey Mill and still marked as such on some maps, began operations in 1923 under the ownership of Roy Guernsey and his son Ralph. The mill was built close to the site of Parson's Mill, which had ceased operations in 1905. The Guernseys improved many of the primitive roadways in the region in order to get their heavy milling machinery into place. However, truckers of the era still had their work cut out for them, sometimes taking a full day to travel a quarter of a mile through the worst areas. Getting stuck was a common occurrence. Pines, cedars, and firs were cut from the surrounding forests as well as from additional lands on Sugarloaf Mountain, which was the property of George Dooley, who had taken over some of Parson's former properties. The Guernseys sold their wood to traders in the region, who in turn brought the timber out of the forests to markets in Porterville and Bakersfield. The mill ran on gasoline until electricity was connected in 1947.

White River flows among pines, aspens and oaks

The Guernseys sold out to the Alexander family, who improved the mill to allow for proper finishing of the lumber on-site. The Alexanders had visited the area as early as 1908, and they constructed their first cabin in Spears Meadow around 1920. By the late 1930s, the Alexanders purchased some land and a cabin from the Guernseys and started constructing what would become the Sugarloaf Ski Lodge. Although low snowfalls hampered business during some winters, the Sugarloaf Ski Lodge soon became a popular resort. The lodge also attracted hunters who went after the region's abundant game. In later years, snowplows kept the roads open to allow guests to reach the lodge, which still used

Open mountain ridges appear as Capinero Saddle Trail emerges from mature forests

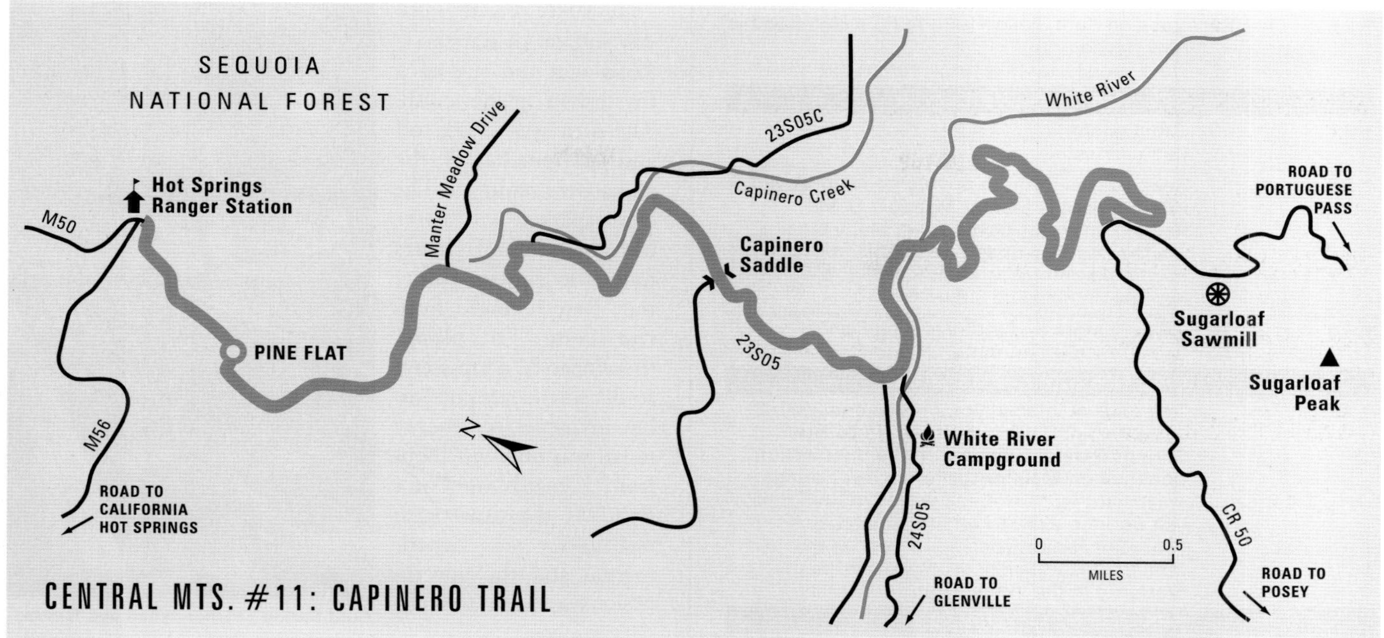

lanterns for lighting and wood-fired ranges for cooking until 1947. The Alexanders retired in the mid-1960s and sold the resort, which has changed hands several times since then and, when last visited, was closed.

Description

This short trail is one of a number of easy graded roads that crisscross Sequoia National Forest. Initially it travels through lush forest before entering more open, rolling hills, vegetated with small oaks and manzanitas. It continues to travel through a mixture of sugar pines, black pines, oaks, and giant sequoias, offering good views and quiet backcountry driving. A number of smaller trails, unmarked on most maps, lead off from the main route. There are also a number of good backcountry campsites, as well as a forest service campground alongside the White River. The forest service closes this trail in the winter and when there is any danger or trail damage, such as after heavy rains.

Current Road Information

Sequoia National Forest
Hot Springs Ranger District
43474 Parker Drive
Route 4, Box 548
California Hot Springs, CA 93207
(661) 548-6503

Map References

BLM Isabella Lake
USFS Sequoia National Forest
USGS 1:24,000 Tobias Peak, Posey, California Hot Springs
1:100,000 Isabella Lake
Maptech CD-ROM: Barstow/San Bernardino County
Southern & Central California Atlas & Gazetteer, p. 50
California Road & Recreation Atlas, p. 93

Route Directions

Mileage		Direction
▼ 0.0		From CR 50, 0.8 miles north of Sugarloaf Sawmill, zero trip meter and turn northwest on graded dirt road 23S05, sign-posted to California Hot Springs.
3.5 ▲		Trail ends on CR 50, 0.8 miles north of Sugarloaf Sawmill. Turn right for Posey.
		GPS: N35°50.46′ W118°36.95′
▼ 0.2	SO	Closure gate.
3.3 ▲	SO	Closure gate.
▼ 0.3	SO	Track on right.
3.2 ▲	SO	Track on left.
▼ 1.8	SO	Turnout on left.
1.7 ▲	SO	Turnout on right.
▼ 2.9	BL	Cross over White River on bridge; then track on right leads to a dead end.
0.6 ▲	BR	Track on left leads to a dead end; bear right and cross over White River on bridge.
		GPS: N35°50.95′ W118°37.39′
▼ 3.5	SO	Graded road 24S05 on left crosses White River on bridge and goes to White River Campground and Glenville. Follow sign to Pine Flat. Zero trip meter.
0.0 ▲		Continue to the east on 23S05.
		GPS: N35°50.80′ W118°37.87′
▼ 0.0		Continue to the west on 23S05.
4.7 ▲	SO	Graded road 24S05 on right crosses White River on bridge and goes to White River Campground and Glenville. Follow sign to Sugarloaf. Zero trip meter.
▼ 0.1	SO	Track on left.
4.6 ▲	SO	Track on right.
▼ 1.0	SO	Track on left.
3.7 ▲	SO	Track on right.
▼ 2.1	SO	Track on right alongside Capinero Creek is 23S05C into camping area; then cattle guard.
2.6 ▲	SO	Cattle guard; then track on left alongside Capinero Creek is 23S05C into camping area.
		GPS: N35°52.00′ W118°38.14′

▼ 2.6		SO	Track on right. Follow sign to Pine Flat. Road is now paved.
	2.1 ▲	SO	Track on left. Road is now graded dirt.
			GPS: N35°52.09' W118°38.36'
▼ 2.7		SO	Cattle guard.
	2.0 ▲	SO	Cattle guard.
▼ 2.8		SO	Road passes through private housing. Paved road on right is Manter Meadow Drive. Remain on major paved road. Many small roads to houses on left and right.
	1.9 ▲	SO	Paved road on left is Manter Meadow Drive. Remain on Pine Flat Drive.
▼ 4.0		SO	Grocery store and motel at Pine Flat.
	0.7 ▲	SO	Grocery store and motel at Pine Flat.
			GPS: N35°52.65' W118°39.05'
▼ 4.7			Trail ends at intersection of M56 and M50, 2 miles east of California Hot Springs. Hot Springs Ranger Station is at the intersection. Continue on M56 for California Hot Springs.
	0.0 ▲		Trail starts on M56, 2 miles east of California Hot Springs. Zero trip meter at intersection with M50 and proceed southeast on paved M56 toward Pine Flat. Hot Springs Ranger Station is at the intersection.
			GPS: N35°53.17' W118°38.83'

CENTRAL MOUNTAINS #12

Rancheria Road

Starting Point:	**California 178, 3 miles northeast of intersection with California 184**
Finishing Point:	**California 155 at Alta Sierra, 7.2 miles west of Wofford Heights**
Total Mileage:	**35.3 miles**
Unpaved Mileage:	**29 miles**
Driving Time:	**3 hours**
Elevation Range:	**600–6,800 feet**
Usually Open:	**April to November**
Best Time to Travel:	**Dry weather**
Difficulty Rating:	**1**
Scenic Rating:	**9**
Remoteness Rating:	**+0**

Special Attractions

- Historic Oak Flat Fire Lookout.
- Alternative entry/exit for Sequoia National Forest.
- Long trail through a variety of vegetation and scenery.
- Access to a wide variety of backcountry campsites as well as 4WD, hiking, and equestrian trails.

History

At the start of the trail, a historical marker indicates that Francisco Garcés crossed the Kern River near this point on May 1, 1776. He was on an expedition to find a shorter route from Sonora, Mexico, to Monterey. Garcés named the river the San Felipe.

In 1986, private property just off of Rancheria Road was the site of a mysterious plane crash. The area was closed off and all remains of the plane were removed. The crash sparked a 120-acre blaze that firefighters fought to contain before they were removed from the scene. The plane, thought to be a top-secret stealth plane designed to be invisible to enemy radar, was on a test flight from Edwards Air Force Base. At the time, such technology was experimental and the government was keen to keep details secret.

Cold Spring catches fallen oak leaves

Oak Flat Fire Lookout was constructed in 1934 as part of a chain of lookouts built to assist the forest service with communications and the detection of forest fires. This lookout tower ceased operations in 1984 because aircraft and truck patrols rendered it obsolete.

The idea for a ski area in the mountains of Kern County was first put forward in 1939. Possible locations were scouted by Kern County officials (initially by air) with the help of Wilfred Wiebe, president of the Bakersfield Ski Club. The team decided on Shirley Peak, and the location was developed for downhill skiing. In due course, the area opened, initially using an old towrope to pull skiers up the mountain. The first skier down the runs was Wilfred Wiebe.

Approaching Oak Flat Fire Lookout as morning haze fills the valley below

Description

Rancheria Road is a highly scenic alternative route connecting Bakersfield to Alta Sierra. The graded dirt road is suitable for passenger vehicles in dry weather. There is no snow removal along the route, so it closes naturally with snowfall anytime from late November on. In addition, the forest service may gate it shut because of snow or rain.

Initially, the road passes through citrus groves and private land as it climbs up the valley alongside Rattlesnake Creek. These tight valleys and grassy hills are very pretty and an easy drive.

After 14 miles, the road enters Sequoia National Forest (the boundary is unmarked). A short spur trail leads to the historic Oak Flat Fire Lookout. The spur is gated shut after 0.4 miles, but the tower can be reached on foot, via a short walk from the gate. The 14-by-14-foot cabin is available for overnight rental for a small fee, which includes vehicle access to the tower. Contact the Greenhorn Ranger District in Lake Isabella (760-379-5646) for details.

Oak Flat Fire Lookout

The graded trail climbs gradually as it passes a number of oak trees and open boulder-strewn landscape. At the higher elevations near the end of the trail, the vegetation changes to pines and firs. There are many good campsites to be found along the trail in the open fire-safe areas as well as the developed campground at Evans Flat.

The northern end of the trail levels off as it travels near the top of the ridge in the Greenhorn Mountains. Isabella Lake can be glimpsed through the trees from this end of the trail.

Shirley Meadows Ski Area operates during the winter months, with 70 percent of its runs catering to beginning and intermediate skiers. The quality of the season depends on snowfall—this quiet ski area has no snowmaking equipment.

A popular trail for hikers, mountain bikers, and equestrians is the Unal Trail, which heads off from the north end of Rancheria Road and climbs gently to travel over Unal Peak before dropping down past the site of a typical Native American home site. The entire trail is a loop of 3 miles and is dedicated to the Tubatulabal, early Native American occupants of the area.

Current Road Information

Sequoia National Forest
Greenhorn Ranger District
4875 Ponderosa Drive
PO Box 3810
Lake Isabella, CA 93240
(760) 379-5646

Map References

BLM Isabella Lake, Tehachapi
USFS Sequoia National Forest
USGS 1:24,000 Rio Bravo Ranch, Pine Mt., Democrat Hot Springs, Miracle Hot Springs, Alta Sierra
1:100,000 Isabella Lake, Tehachapi
Maptech CD-ROM: Barstow/San Bernardino County
Southern & Central California Atlas & Gazetteer, pp. 63, 49, 50
California Road & Recreation Atlas, p. 93

Route Directions

Mileage		Direction
▼ 0.0		From California 178, 3 miles northeast of intersection with California 184, zero trip meter and turn north on paved two-lane road marked Rancheria Road.
14.3 ▲		Trail ends at T-intersection with California 178. Turn right for Bakersfield; turn left for Lake Isabella.
		GPS: N35°25.01' W118°49.83'
▼ 4.0	SO	Road turns to graded dirt.
10.3 ▲	SO	Road is now paved.
		GPS: N35°28.33' W118°49.66'
▼ 6.2	SO	Cattle guard.
8.1 ▲	SO	Cattle guard.
▼ 6.5	SO	Graded road on left.
7.8 ▲	SO	Graded road on right.
		GPS: N35°29.50' W118°47.72'
▼ 6.9	SO	Road on right.
7.4 ▲	SO	Road on left.
▼ 7.1	SO	Road on right.
7.2 ▲	SO	Road on left.
▼ 7.9	SO	Graded road on left.
6.4 ▲	SO	Graded road on right.
▼ 8.1	SO	Cross over Rattlesnake Creek.
6.2 ▲	SO	Cross over Rattlesnake Creek.
		GPS: N35°30.31' W118°46.44'
▼ 8.6	SO	Track on left.
5.7 ▲	SO	Track on right.
▼ 8.7	SO	Cross over creek; then cattle guard.
5.6 ▲	SO	Cattle guard; then cross over creek.
▼ 10.3	SO	Cattle guard.
4.0 ▲	SO	Cattle guard.
▼ 13.6	SO	Cattle guard. Entering Sequoia National Forest.
0.7 ▲	SO	Cattle guard. Leaving Sequoia National Forest.
		GPS: N35°32.21' W118°42.59'
▼ 14.1	SO	Track on left.
0.2 ▲	SO	Track on right.
▼ 14.3	SO	Track on right is 27S20 to Oak Flat Fire Lookout. Closure gate at start of trail. Zero trip meter.
0.0 ▲		Continue to the west.
		GPS: N35°32.38' W118°42.02'
▼ 0.0		Continue to the north.
6.5 ▲	SO	Track on left is 27S20 to Oak Flat Fire Lookout. Closure gate at start of trail. Zero trip meter.
▼ 0.3	SO	Track on right.
6.2 ▲	SO	Track on left.
▼ 0.4	SO	Cattle guard.
6.1 ▲	SO	Cattle guard.
▼ 1.1	SO	Badger Gap Trail (31E76) on right for hikers, mountain bikes, horses, and motorbikes only.
5.4 ▲	SO	Badger Gap Trail (31E76) on left for hikers, mountain bikes, horses, and motorbikes only.
		GPS: N35°32.91' W118°41.39'

Mileage		Action	Description
▼ 2.3		SO	Fence line.
	4.2 ▲	SO	Fence line.
▼ 2.4		SO	Cattle guard.
	4.1 ▲	SO	Cattle guard.
▼ 3.7		SO	Cattle guard.
	2.8 ▲	SO	Cattle guard.
▼ 4.6		SO	Cross over creek.
	1.9 ▲	SO	Cross over creek.
▼ 4.8		SO	Cross over creek.
	1.7 ▲	SO	Cross over creek.
▼ 5.0		SO	Track on right is private.
	1.5 ▲	SO	Track on left is private.
▼ 5.6		SO	Cattle guard.
	0.9 ▲	SO	Cattle guard.
▼ 6.5		SO	Delonegha 4WD Trail (31E22) on right for 4WDs, ATVs, motorbikes, mountain bikes, horses, and hikers—rated black. Zero trip meter.
	0.0 ▲		Continue to the southeast.
			GPS: N35°35.70' W118°39.35'
▼ 0.0			Continue to the northeast. Road is now marked 25S15.
	1.9 ▲	SO	Delonegha 4WD Trail (31E22) on left for 4WDs, ATVs, motorbikes, mountain bikes, horses, and hikers—rated black. Zero trip meter.
▼ 0.2		SO	Track on left.
	1.7 ▲	SO	Track on right.
▼ 0.6		SO	Cold Spring on left; then track on right.
	1.3 ▲	SO	Track on left; then Cold Spring on right.
			GPS: N35°35.86' W118°38.89'
▼ 1.6		SO	Cattle guard.
	0.3 ▲	SO	Cattle guard.
▼ 1.9		SO	Graded road on left is Poso Flat Road. Remain on 25S15. Zero trip meter.
	0.0 ▲		Continue to the southwest, following sign to State Highway 178.
			GPS: N35°36.38' W118°38.23'
▼ 0.0			Continue to the northeast, following sign to State Highway 155.
	5.3 ▲	BL	Graded road on right is Poso Flat Road. Remain on 25S15. Zero trip meter.
▼ 0.6		SO	Re-entering Sequoia National Forest at sign.
	4.7 ▲	SO	Leaving Sequoia National Forest at sign.
			GPS: N35°36.70' W118°37.83'
▼ 0.9		SO	Track on left.
	4.4 ▲	SO	Track on right.
▼ 1.1		SO	Track on right; then small track on left.
	4.2 ▲	SO	Small track on right; then track on left.
▼ 1.4		SO	Track on left is Basket Pass Road. Continue on Rancheria Road, following sign to Highway 155.
	3.9 ▲	SO	Track on right is Basket Pass Road. Continue on Rancheria Road, following sign to Bakersfield.
			GPS: N35°36.91' W118°37.26'
▼ 1.6		SO	Cattle guard.
	3.7 ▲	SO	Cattle guard.
▼ 1.7		BL	Track on right and Davis Camp on right.
	3.6 ▲	BR	Track on left and Davis Camp on left.
			GPS: N35°36.93' W118°37.00'
▼ 1.8		SO	Track on left is 26S13. Davis Camp Fire Safe Area on left; then track on right is 26S30 to Greenhorn Creek.
	3.5 ▲	SO	Track on left is 26S30 to Greenhorn Creek; then Davis Camp Fire Safe Area on right. Track on right is 26S13.
			GPS: N35°37.00' W118°36.93'

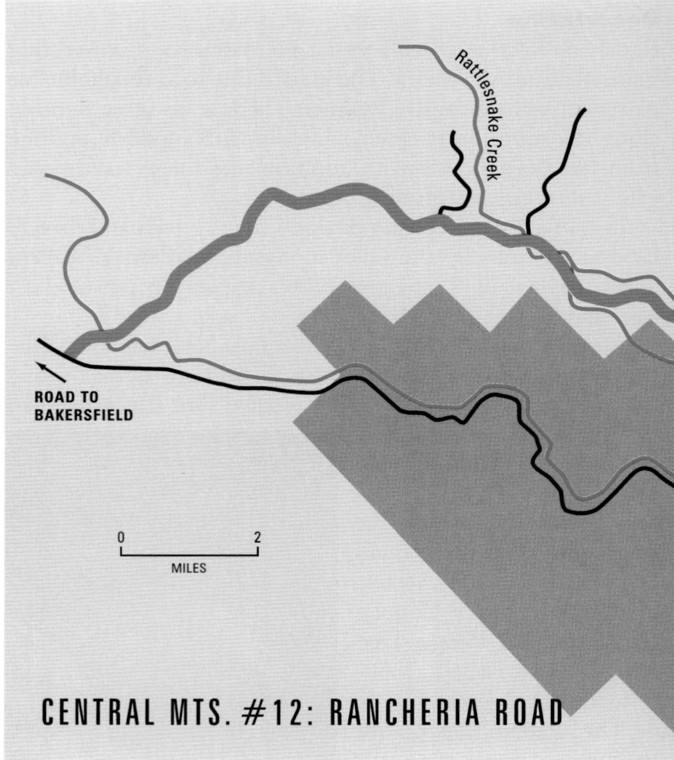

Mileage		Action	Description
▼ 2.5		SO	Track on left is 26S13; then second track on left.
	2.8 ▲	SO	Track on right; then second track on right is 26S13.
			GPS: N35°37.48' W118°36.61'
▼ 3.1		SO	Track on right is Bradshaw Creek Road (26S04); then small track on left.
	2.2 ▲	SO	Small track on right; then track on left is Bradshaw Creek Road (26S04).
			GPS: N35°37.41' W118°36.23'
▼ 3.5		SO	Closure gate.
	1.8 ▲	SO	Closure gate.
▼ 3.7		SO	Track on right; then track on left is 26S05 marked to Basket Pass. Continue on 25S15.
	1.6 ▲	SO	Track on right is 26S05 marked to Basket Pass; then track on left. Continue on 25S15.
			GPS: N35°37.92' W118°36.02'
▼ 4.3		SO	Track on left is 26S18.
	1.0 ▲	SO	Track on right is 26S18.
▼ 4.9		SO	Track on right is 26S27. Evans Flat USFS Campground on right; then track on left.
	0.4 ▲	SO	Track on right; then Evans Flat USFS Campground on left. Track on left is 26S27.
			GPS: N35°38.64' W118°35.48'
▼ 5.3		SO	Track on right is Sawmill Road to California 178. Zero trip meter.
	0.0 ▲		Continue to the south, remaining on Rancheria Road.
			GPS: N35°39.07' W118°35.29'
▼ 0.0			Continue to the north, remaining on Rancheria Road.
	2.9 ▲	SO	Track on left is Sawmill Road to California 178. Zero trip meter.
▼ 1.0		SO	Track on left is 26S20 and track on right.
	1.9 ▲	SO	Track on right is 26S20 and track on left.
			GPS: N35°39.87' W118°35°21'

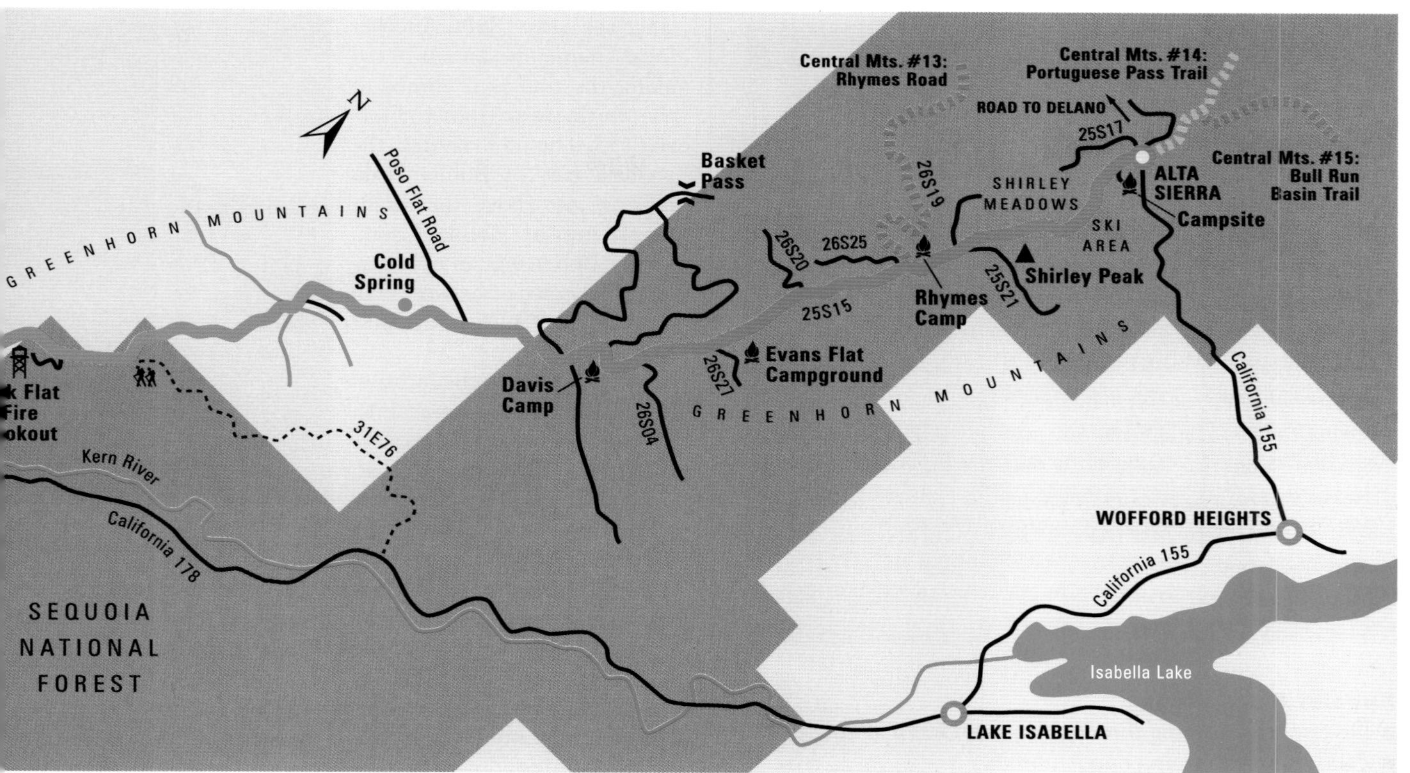

▼ 2.9 SO Small track on left is 26S25. Second track on left is Central Mountains #13: Rhymes Road (26S19). Zero trip meter.

0.0 ▲ Continue to the south, following sign to Bakersfield.

GPS: N35°41.10′ W118°34.40′

▼ 0.0 Continue to the northeast, following sign for State Highway 155. Rhymes Camp on left and track on right is Just Outstanding Trail.

4.4 ▲ SO Rhymes Camp on right and track on left is Just Outstanding Trail. Track on right is Central Mountains #13: Rhymes Road (26S19). Second smaller track on right is 26S25. Zero trip meter.

▼ 0.2 SO Track on left is 25S15D.

4.2 ▲ SO Track on right is 25S15D.

▼ 0.8 SO Track on left is 26S07 and track on right is 25S21.

3.6 ▲ SO Track on right is 26S07 and track on left is 25S21.

GPS: N35°41.65′ W118°34.13′

▼ 1.1 SO Just Outstanding Trail crosses road. Track on left is 25S15B.

3.3 ▲ SO Just Outstanding Trail crosses road. Track on right is 25S15B.

▼ 1.7 SO Just Outstanding Trail (32E46) crosses road—no 4WDs or ATVs permitted.

2.7 ▲ SO Just Outstanding Trail (32E46) crosses road—no 4WDs or ATVs permitted.

▼ 2.0 SO Seasonal closure gate; then track on right.

2.4 ▲ SO Track on left; then seasonal closure gate.

▼ 2.1 SO Road becomes paved. Pass through Shirley Meadows Ski Area. Remain on paved road for next 2.3 miles.

2.3 ▲ SO Exit ski area. Road turns to graded dirt.

▼ 2.2 SO Seasonal closure gate. Exit ski area.

2.2 ▲ SO Seasonal closure gate. Pass through Shirley Meadows Ski Area.

GPS: N35°42.73′ W118°33.52′

▼ 2.3 SO Track on left; then track on right.

2.1 ▲ SO Track on left; then track on right.

▼ 2.4 SO Track on left is used by snowmobiles and cross-country skiers in winter.

2.0 ▲ SO Track on right is used by snowmobiles and cross-country skiers in winter.

▼ 2.6 SO Track on right is 25S31.

1.8 ▲ SO Track on left is 25S31.

▼ 2.9 SO Track on right is 25S21.

1.5 ▲ SO Track on left is 25S21.

▼ 3.1 SO Turnout on right with views over Isabella Lake.

1.3 ▲ SO Turnout on left with views over Isabella Lake.

▼ 4.3 SO Track on left is 25S17 and track on right into campground. Unal Trail (31E58) for hikers, horses, and mountain bikes on left. Information boards mark the start.

0.1 ▲ SO Track on left into campground and track on right is 25S17. Unal Trail (31E58) for hikers, horses, and mountain bikes on right. Information boards mark the start. Follow sign for Shirley Meadows Ski Area.

▼ 4.4 Trail ends at T-intersection with California 155 at Greenhorn Summit, Alta Sierra. Turn right for Wofford Heights; turn left for Delano. Trail opposite is the start of Central Mountains #14: Portuguese Pass Trail.

0.0 ▲ Trail commences on California 155 at Greenhorn Summit, Alta Sierra, 7.2 miles west of Wofford Heights. Trail is opposite the start of Central Mountains #14: Portuguese Pass Trail at Kern County mile marker 53. Zero trip meter and turn south on paved road, following sign for Shirley Meadows Ski Area. Remain on paved road for next 2.3 miles.

GPS: N35°44.32′ W118°33.31′

CENTRAL MOUNTAINS #13

Rhymes Road

Starting Point:	**Central Mountains #12: Rancheria Road, 2 miles south of Shirley Meadows**
Finishing Point:	**Intersection of Poso Park Drive and Old Stage Drive, 0.5 miles south of Poso Park**
Total Mileage:	**22.1 miles**
Unpaved Mileage:	**22.1 miles**
Driving Time:	**2.5 hours**
Elevation Range:	**4,000–6,100 feet**
Usually Open:	**May to December**
Best Time to Travel:	**May to December**
Difficulty Rating:	**2**
Scenic Rating:	**9**
Remoteness Rating:	**+0**

Special Attractions

- Diverse trail running through Sequoia National Forest.
- Backcountry camping opportunities.

History

Rhymes Road commemorates James J. Rhymes, one of three people elected to office in the first Kern County election, which took place in 1866. That year, Democrats soundly defeated Republicans. Rhymes had been ranching in the area since the early 1860s. Another local name is encountered along the trail as it climbs to the north, away from California 155. The trail traverses the western face of Bohna Peak, passing just above the catchment area of Bohna Creek. Henry Bohna was an early settler who ranched between Rag and Gordon Gulches, just west of Glenville.

Shirley Peak is just visible among the pines on the southern end of the tra

Peel Creek was the location of a sawmill by the same name. Previously, it was known as Greene Mill and prior to that, Redfield Mill. The mill operated from the late 1880s, and the lumber produced there was used for the construction of early properties in this mountain region. Ox teams used to haul timber and machinery were a common sight on the steep-sided hills. The difficult terrain, combined with the distance from markets in Bakersfield, Visalia, and Porterville, was a major factor contributing to the closure of the mill.

After sitting idle for some years, the Peel Mill was brought back to life in the early 1910s by the popular Jack Ranch Resort. Jack Ranch attracted campers who came on horseback to camp along Poso Creek. When automobiles started making the trek, the number of visitors increased. To accommodate these extra visitors, the owner came up with an ingenious way of increasing its water supply. The ranch utilized the steaming

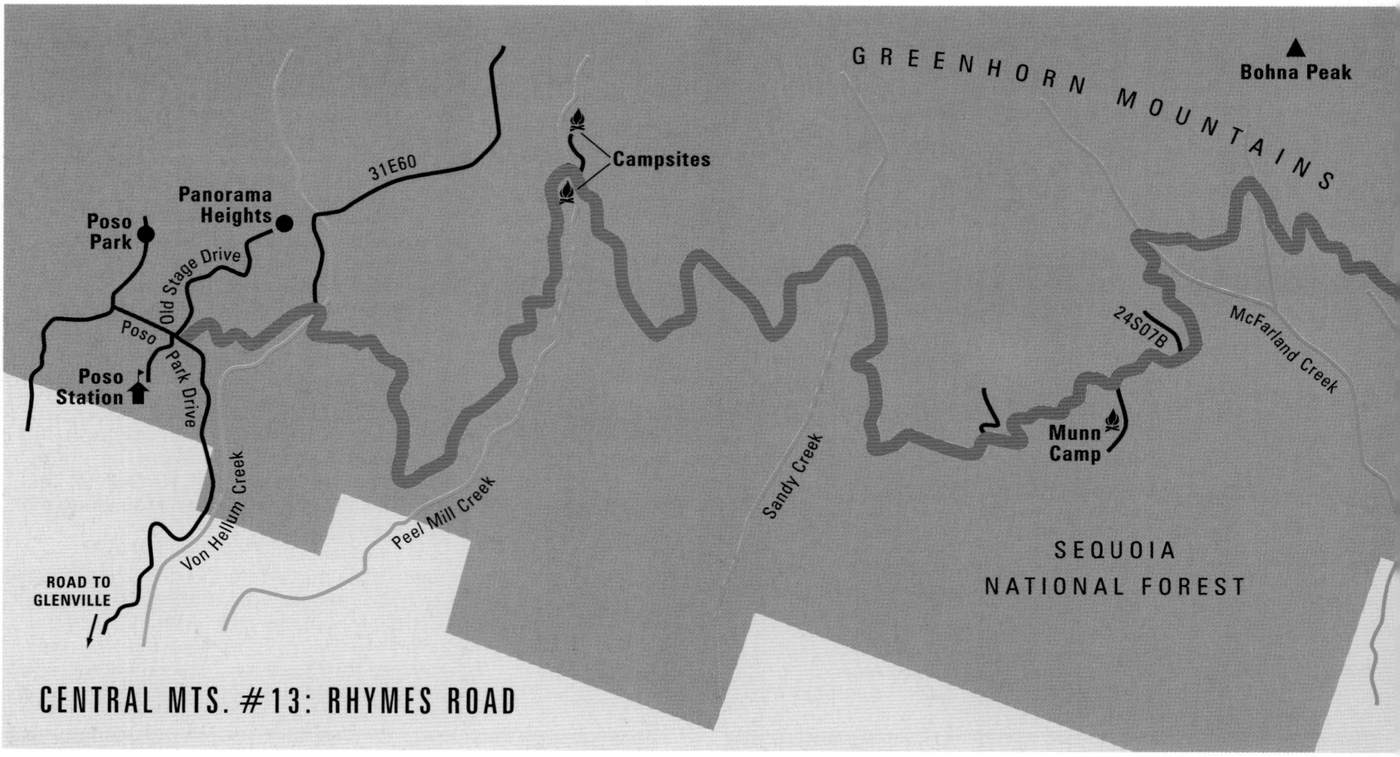

CENTRAL MTS. #13: RHYMES ROAD

tubes and smokestack from the old abandoned mill to run water from Poso Creek to the kitchen. Mrs. Berry, who ran the kitchen in its early days, now had running water. The addition of heating coils to the furnace of the wood-fired range also provided hot water. Her excellent cooking gained a reputation among travelers. Soon, a number of fishermen, hunters, and campers were stopping for one of her home-cooked meals.

The ranch utilized the remaining lumber from the Peel Mill to construct platforms upon which campers could erect their canvas tents. During the summer, these campsites would attract 200 to 300 people at a fee of $1 to $1.50 per week, depending on the size of the platform base used. Many visitors became enamored of the region and returned in later years to purchase small plots for summer cabins. Many subdivisions, such as Panorama Heights and Poso Park, developed over the following decades.

Description

Rhymes Road is a small, single-track trail that runs down from Shirley Peak to follow alongside Alder Creek. At the start of the lightly traveled trail are sections of shelf road with good views back to Shirley Peak.

The very pleasant Alder Creek Campground is at the confluence of Alder Creek and Cedar Creek, with some shady sites down by the water. From here, the trail is well used as it climbs steadily to intersect with California 155.

North of the highway, the trail continues around the western side of the Greenhorn Mountains. There is a well-used, primitive camping area at Munn Camp. The trail finishes at Poso Park, opposite Poso Station, a forest service property that is available for recreation rental. The cabin, constructed in 1933 as a base for national forest fire personnel, has one bedroom and sleeps five, with additional room outside for tents or a recreational vehicle. There is an overnight fee and reservations are required.

Rhymes Road winds in and out of the forest, descending to Alder Creek

Current Road Information

Sequoia National Forest
Greenhorn Ranger District
4875 Ponderosa Drive
PO Box 3810
Lake Isabella, CA 93240
(760) 379-5646

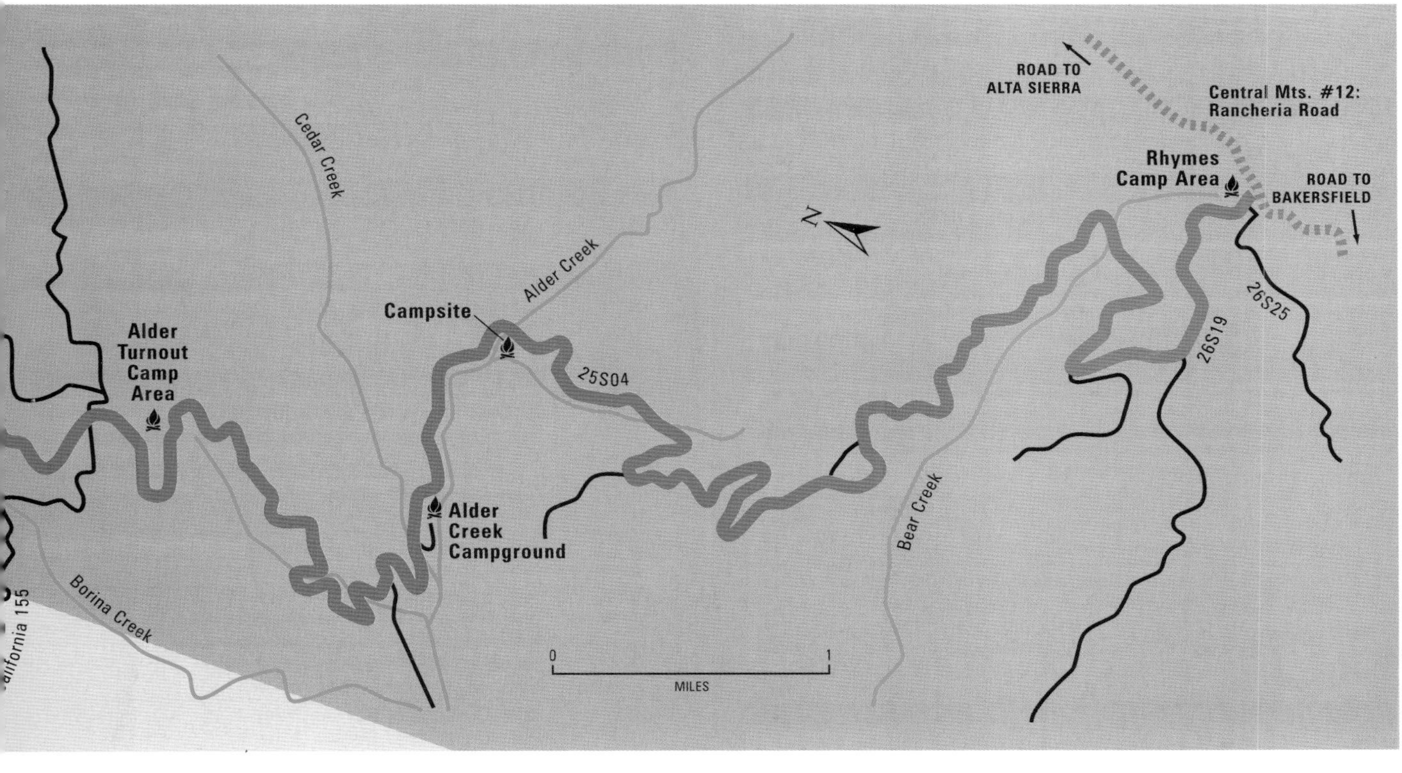

Map References

BLM Isabella Lake
USFS Sequoia National Forest
USGS 1:24,000 Alta Sierra, Tobias Peak, Posey
1:100,000 Isabella Lake
Maptech CD-ROM: Barstow/San Bernardino County
Southern & Central California Atlas & Gazetteer, p. 50
California Road & Recreation Atlas, p. 93

Route Directions

Mileage		Direction
▼ 0.0		From Central Mountains #12: Rancheria Road, 2 miles south of Shirley Meadows, zero trip meter and turn west on graded dirt Rhymes Road, following sign to California 155. Rhymes Camp area is at the intersection. Immediately, track on left is 26S25. Rhymes Road is marked 26S19.
7.6 ▲		Trail ends at intersection with Central Mountains #12: Rancheria Road. Turn right to travel the trail to Bakersfield; turn left for Alta Sierra.
		GPS: N35°41.10′ W118°34.40′
▼ 0.1	SO	Closure gate.
7.5 ▲	SO	Closure gate.
▼ 0.8	SO	Track on left. Continue straight ahead on 25S04.
6.8 ▲	SO	Track on right.
		GPS: N35°41.14′ W118°35.06′
▼ 1.1	SO	Track on left on right-hand switchback.
6.5 ▲	SO	Track on right on left-hand switchback.
▼ 1.9	SO	Cross over Bear Creek.
5.7 ▲	SO	Cross over Bear Creek.
▼ 2.0	SO	Boy Scouts of America Camp entrance on right.
5.6 ▲	SO	Boy Scouts of America Camp entrance on left.
▼ 2.4	SO	Track on right.
5.2 ▲	SO	Track on left.
		GPS: N35°41.63′ W118°35.09′
▼ 3.0	SO	Faint track on right.
4.6 ▲	SO	Faint track on left.
▼ 3.5	SO	Track on right.
4.1 ▲	SO	Track on left.
		GPS: N35°41.96′ W118°35.86′
▼ 3.8	SO	Track on right and track on left.
3.8 ▲	SO	Track on right and track on left.
		GPS: N35°42.03′ W118°36.04′
▼ 4.3	BR	Track on left. Remain on main trail.
3.3 ▲	BL	Track on right. Remain on main trail.
▼ 5.2	SO	Track on left to viewpoint.
2.4 ▲	SO	Track on right to viewpoint.
▼ 5.6	SO	Cross over creek.
2.0 ▲	SO	Cross over creek.
▼ 6.6	SO	Track on right; then cross over Alder Creek.
1.0 ▲	SO	Cross over Alder Creek; then track on left.
		GPS: N35°43.16′ W118°35.88′
▼ 6.8	SO	Campsite on left.
0.8 ▲	SO	Campsite on right.
▼ 6.9	SO	Cross over creek.
0.7 ▲	SO	Cross over creek.
▼ 7.1	SO	Entering Alder Creek Fire Safe Area.
0.5 ▲	SO	Leaving fire safe area at sign.
		GPS: N35°43.27′ W118°36.27′
▼ 7.4	SO	Cattle guard.
0.2 ▲	SO	Cattle guard.
		GPS: N35°43.19′ W118°36.51′
▼ 7.6	SO	Track on left into Alder Creek Campground; then main trail exits campground across bridge over Cedar Creek. Zero trip meter.
0.0 ▲		Continue to the northeast.
		GPS: N35°43.17′ W118°36.81′
▼ 0.0		Continue to the southwest.
3.0 ▲	SO	Entering Alder Creek Campground across bridge over Cedar Creek; then track on right into campground. Zero trip meter at bridge.
▼ 0.1	SO	Exiting fire safe area; then cattle guard.
2.9 ▲	SO	Cattle guard; then entering Alder Creek Fire Safe Area around campground.
▼ 0.3	SO	Track on right and track on left.
2.7 ▲	SO	Track on right and track on left.
▼ 1.1	SO	Cross over creek.
1.9 ▲	SO	Cross over creek.
▼ 2.7	SO	Two tracks on right.
0.3 ▲	SO	Two tracks on left.
▼ 2.9	SO	Alder Turnout Camp on right.
0.1 ▲	SO	Alder Turnout Camp on left.
		GPS: N35°44.20′ W118°36.72′
▼ 3.0	SO	Closure gate; then intersection with paved California 155. Zero trip meter and continue across paved road onto graded dirt Safety Creek Fire Road, following sign to Panorama Heights. Immediately pass through closure gate.
0.0 ▲		Continue to the south.
		GPS: N35°44.25′ W118°36.71′
▼ 0.0		Continue to the northwest. Road is marked 24S07.
3.8 ▲	SO	Closure gate; then intersection with paved California 155. Zero trip meter and continue across paved road onto graded dirt road signposted to Alder Creek Campground. Immediately pass through closure gate.
▼ 0.9	SO	Track on right.
2.9 ▲	SO	Track on left.
▼ 1.9	SO	Cross over creek.
1.9 ▲	SO	Cross over creek.
▼ 2.0	SO	Track on right.
1.8 ▲	SO	Track on left.
		GPS: N35°45.30′ W118°36.49′
▼ 2.3	SO	Cross over creek.
1.5 ▲	SO	Cross over creek.
▼ 2.9	SO	Cross over McFarland Creek.
0.9 ▲	SO	Cross over McFarland Creek.
		GPS: N35°45.76′ W118°36.67′
▼ 3.4	SO	Track on right is 24S07B.
0.4 ▲	SO	Track on left is 24S07B.
		GPS: N35°45.49′ W118°37.05′
▼ 3.8	BR	Track on left goes 0.1 miles to Munn Camp—primitive camp and corral. Zero trip meter.
0.0 ▲		Continue to the southeast.
		GPS: N35°45.66′ W118°37.23′
▼ 0.0		Continue to the northeast.
7.7 ▲	BL	Track on right goes 0.1 miles to Munn Camp—primitive camp and corral. Zero trip meter.
▼ 0.1	SO	Cross over creek.
7.6 ▲	SO	Cross over creek.
▼ 0.5	SO	Cross over creek twice.
7.2 ▲	SO	Cross over creek twice.
▼ 0.7	SO	Track on right.
7.0 ▲	SO	Track on left.
▼ 1.1	SO	Cross over creek.
6.6 ▲	SO	Cross over creek.
▼ 2.3	SO	Cross over Sandy Creek.
5.4 ▲	SO	Cross over Sandy Creek.

▼ 3.6	SO	Track on left through clearing.
4.1 ▲	SO	Track on right through clearing.
		GPS: N35°47.09' W118°37.68'
▼ 4.3	SO	Leaving Greenhorn Ranger District at sign.
3.4 ▲	SO	Entering Greenhorn Ranger District at sign.
		GPS: N35°47.47' W118°37.23'
▼ 4.4	SO	Track on right to campsite; then cross over Peel Mill Creek; then campsite on left.
3.3 ▲	SO	Campsite on right; then cross over Peel Mill Creek; then track on left to campsite.
		GPS: N35°47.50' W118°37.22'
▼ 6.2	SO	Track on left to viewpoint.
1.5 ▲	SO	Track on right to viewpoint.
▼ 6.9	SO	Cross over Von Hellum Creek; then trail on right is 31E60 to Portuguese Pass.
0.8 ▲	SO	Trail on left is 31E60 to Portuguese Pass; then cross over Von Hellum Creek.
		GPS: N35°48.09' W118°38.02'
▼ 7.1	SO	Cross over creek.
0.6 ▲	SO	Cross over creek.
▼ 7.2	SO	Cattle guard; entering private property.
0.5 ▲	SO	Cattle guard; leaving private property.
▼ 7.6	SO	Cattle guard.
0.1 ▲	SO	Cattle guard.
▼ 7.7		Trail ends at intersection of Poso Park Drive and Old Stage Drive, 0.5 miles south of Poso Park. Continue straight ahead to exit to Poso Park.
0.0 ▲		Trail starts at the intersection of Poso Park Drive and Old Stage Drive, 0.5 miles south of Poso Park, 11.5 miles northeast of Glenville. Zero trip meter and turn east on unmarked graded dirt road. Turn for Poso Station is opposite, and the CDF fire station and Panorama Heights are to the southeast. The turn is unmarked.
		GPS: N35°48.47' W118°38.35'

CENTRAL MOUNTAINS #14

Portuguese Pass Trail

Starting Point:	**California 155 at Alta Sierra**
Finishing Point:	**CR 50 at Portuguese Pass**
Total Mileage:	**6.9 miles**
Unpaved Mileage:	**6.8 miles**
Driving Time:	**45 minutes**
Elevation Range:	**5,900–7,400 feet**
Usually Open:	**April to November 15**
Best Time to Travel:	**April to November 15**
Difficulty Rating:	**1**
Scenic Rating:	**8**
Remoteness Rating:	**+0**

Special Attractions

- Views of the Kern River Valley.
- Easy trail through the Greenhorn Mountains.
- Snowmobile, cross-country skiing, and snowshoe route in winter.

New growth of oak and manzanita is evident in fire ravaged areas above Bull Run Creek

History

Cattle were driven on government trails past the old Parson Mill (located near the site of present-day Sugarloaf Mill) to summer pastures at Tobias Meadow to the north and Portuguese Meadow to the south. Early hunting and fishing pack trains carried visitors from the Jack Ranch on the western side of the Greenhorn Mountains through this region. Horses and mules were picked for their quiet demeanor and confidence on the narrow trails. Going rates were around $2 a day for a pack animal. Hiring a guide who would tend the animals cost about $5 a day. It was apparently quite an art to keep the animals moving in the correct direction and to keep them grouped at night. These pack trains continued until approximately 1950, when the construction of better roads enabled visitors to visit the region in their own vehicles.

Portuguese Pass Trail passes through mature forests along the ridge of the Greenhorn Mountains

The Greenhorn Mountains were thought to hold gold and were named after two miners who prospected there—one called Green, the other called Horn.

Description

This short, easy trail travels through Sequoia National Forest between the community of Alta Sierra and the paved road on top of Portuguese Pass. The trail meanders through the forest, passing through stands of sequoias, sugar pines, and black pines. It travels alongside Penney Plantation, where a fire decimated the vegetation about 10 years ago. There are views over the Kern River Valley to the mountains beyond. Black bears, coyotes, and deer are often seen in this region.

Like all of the trails in the national forest, this trail is closed by the forest service if there is any danger of trail damage from

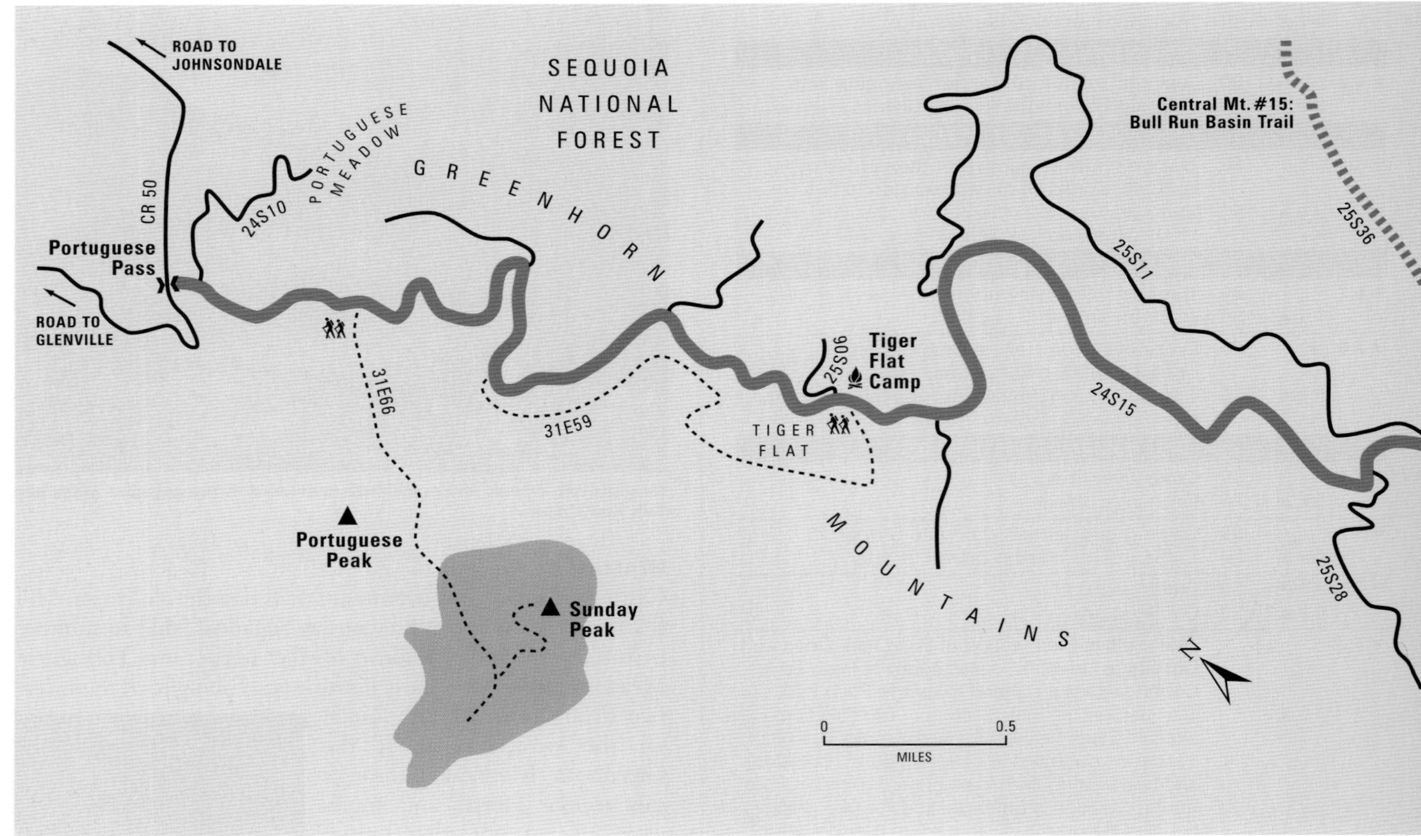

rain or snow. In winter, the trail is marked as a snowmobile route and is also used by snowshoers and cross-country skiers.

Current Road Information

Sequoia National Forest
Greenhorn Ranger District
4875 Ponderosa Drive
PO Box 3810
Lake Isabella, CA 93240
(760) 379-5646

Map References

BLM Isabella Lake
USFS Sequoia National Forest
USGS 1:24,000 Alta Sierra, Tobias Peak
1:100,000 Isabella Lake
Maptech CD-ROM: Barstow/San Bernardino County
Southern & Central California Atlas & Gazetteer, p. 50
California Road & Recreation Atlas, p. 93

Route Directions

▼ 0.0			From California 155 at Greenhorn Summit, Alta Sierra, 7.2 miles west of Wofford Heights, zero trip meter and turn north on small paved road. Trail is opposite Central Mountains #12: Rancheria Road. There is a sign after the intersection for Portuguese Pass. Route is marked as 24S15.
	1.1 ▲		Trail ends at California 155 on Greenhorn Summit, Alta Sierra, opposite Central Mountains #12: Rancheria Road. Turn right for Glenville; turn left for Wofford Heights and Lake Isabella.
			GPS: N35°44.32' W118°33.31'
▼ 0.1		SO	Closure gate. Road is now graded dirt.
	1.0 ▲	SO	Closure gate. Road is now paved.
▼ 1.1		BL	Two tracks on right are 25S16 to Black Mountain Saddle and Central Mountains #15: Bull Run Basin Trail (25S36). Follow sign to Tiger Flat. Zero trip meter.
	0.0 ▲		Continue to the west.
			GPS: N35°45.19' W118°33.24'
▼ 0.0			Continue to the northeast.
	5.8 ▲	SO	Two tracks on left are 25S16 to Black Mountain Saddle and Central Mountains #15: Bull Run Basin Trail (25S36). Remain on main graded road. Zero trip meter.
▼ 0.2		SO	Track on right is 25S11 and track on left.
	5.6 ▲	SO	Track on left is 25S11 and track on right.
			GPS: N35°45.36' W118°33.26'
▼ 0.5		SO	Track on left is 25S28.
	5.3 ▲	SO	Track on right is 25S28.
▼ 2.1		SO	Track on right is 25S11.
	3.7 ▲	SO	Track on left is 25S11.
			GPS: N35°46.55' W118°33.65'
▼ 2.6		SO	Track on left is marked Rockpile.
	3.2 ▲	SO	Track on right is marked Rockpile.
▼ 2.8		SO	Portuguese Trail (31E59) on left for hikers, horses, mountain bikes, and motorbikes.
	3.0 ▲	SO	Portuguese Trail (31E59) rejoins on right.
			GPS: N35°46.58' W118°34.04'
▼ 2.9		SO	Track on right is 25S06, which leaves through Tiger Flat Camp.
	2.9 ▲	SO	Track on left is 25S06, which leaves

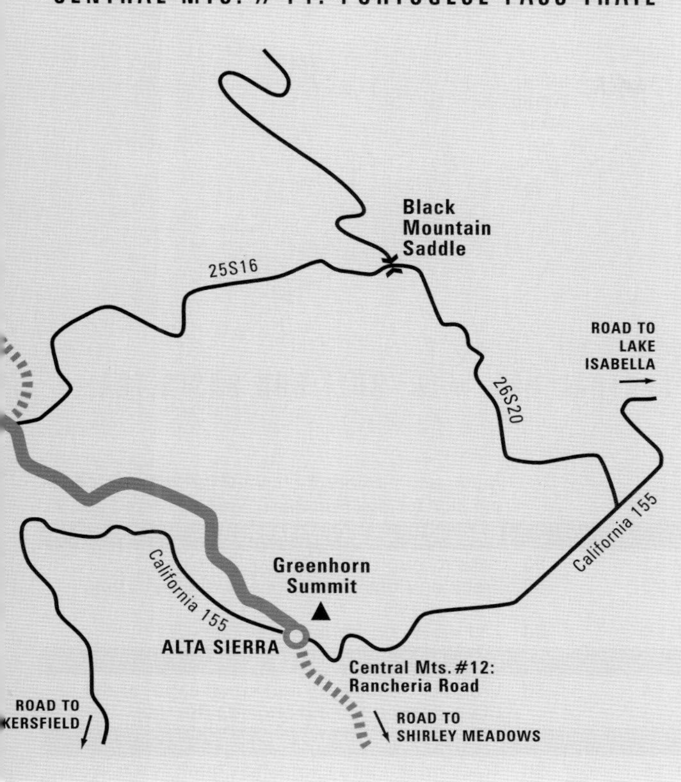

			through Tiger Flat Camp.
▼ 3.1		SO	Track on right.
	2.7 ▲	SO	Track on left.
▼ 3.5		SO	Track on right.
	2.3 ▲	SO	Track on left.
▼ 4.2		SO	Portuguese Trail (31E59) rejoins on left.
	1.6 ▲	SO	Portuguese Trail (31E59) on right for hikers, horses, mountain bikes, and motorbikes.
			GPS: N35°47.37' W118°34.57'
▼ 4.5		SO	Two tracks on right on left-hand bend.
	1.3 ▲	SO	Two tracks on left on right-hand bend.
			GPS: N35°47.45' W118°34.24'
▼ 5.2		SO	Track on left is Sunday Peak Trail (31E66) for hikers, horses, mountain bikes, and motorbikes. Also track on left is 24S28 and track on right.
	0.6 ▲	SO	Track on right is 24S28 and track on left. Second track on right is Sunday Peak Trail (31E66) for hikers, horses, mountain bikes, and motorbikes.
			GPS: N35°47.69' W118°34.56'
▼ 5.7		SO	Closure gate; then track on right is 24S10 and track on left.
	0.1 ▲	SO	Track on left is 24S10 and track on right; then closure gate.
			GPS: N35°48.04' W118°34.82'
▼ 5.8			Trail ends at T-intersection with small paved CR 50 at Portuguese Pass. Turn right for Johnsondale; turn left for Glenville.
	0.0 ▲		Trail commences on CR 50 at Portuguese Pass, 8 miles east of Sugarloaf Village. Zero trip meter and proceed southeast on graded dirt road at sign for Portuguese Pass, following sign for Greenhorn Summit and California 155.
			GPS: N35°48.12' W118°34.81'

CENTRAL MOUNTAINS #15

Bull Run Basin Trail

Starting Point:	**Central Mountains #14: Portuguese Pass Trail, 1.1 miles from the southern end**
Finishing Point:	**Silver Strand Mine**
Total Mileage:	**2.3 miles (one-way)**
Unpaved Mileage:	**2.3 miles**
Driving Time:	**20 minutes (one-way)**
Elevation Range:	**5,000–6,000 feet**
Usually Open:	**May to December**
Best Time to Travel:	**May to December**
Difficulty Rating:	**3**
Scenic Rating:	**8**
Remoteness Rating:	**+0**

Special Attractions

- Remains of the Black Sambo Mine.
- Access to the Bull Run Motorbike Trail.

History

The Black Sambo Mine was originally staked as an antimony prospect but in 1954 it was thought to contain tungsten. However, neither mineral was successfully mined from it. Two single-compartment shafts 20 to 30 feet deep were dug along the fault line; they have since caved in. Two open cuts were also made along a gully on the eastern side of Cow Creek. These open cuts, named Susie Q, were set about 300 feet apart and had faces 10 to 15 feet in height with the longest cut being about 75 feet. A pump station operated just below the lowest Susie Q cutting. It pumped water to a holding tank that was located above the upper cutting.

The Silver Strand Mine was also a tungsten mine seemingly with little recorded success.

The headframe of the Black Sambo Mine near Cow Creek amoung slender sequoias

Description

This short trail travels a much smaller track than many of the trails within this region of the Sierra Nevada. The surface is formed, undulating, and rough in spots as it descends along the narrow valley of Cow Creek. The trail passes beside large granite boulders as well as the creek as it travels through part of an area burned in a

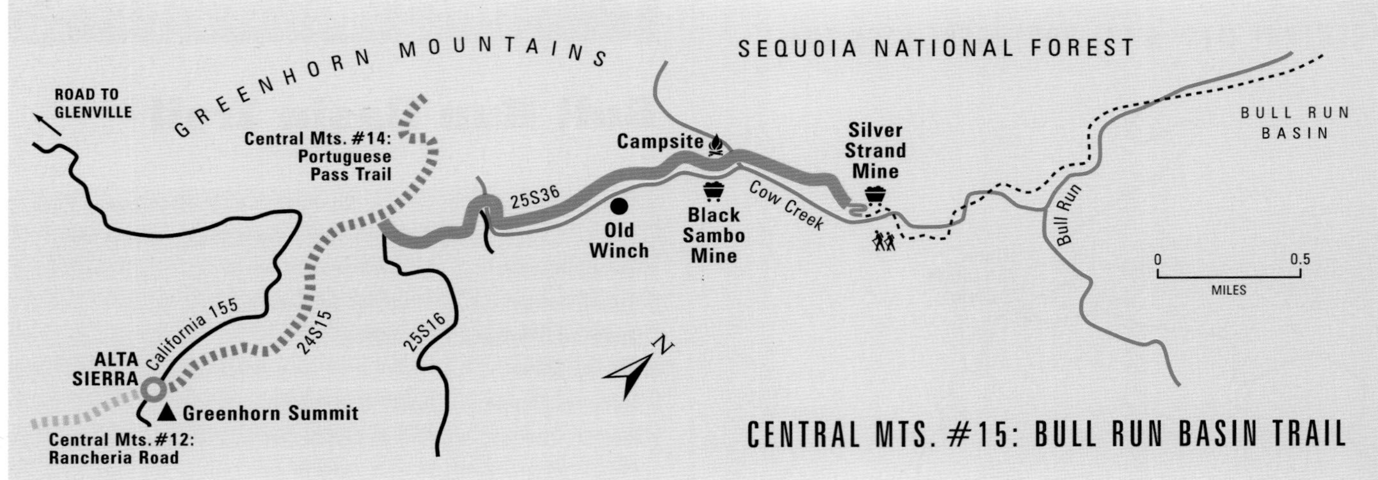

fire a few years ago. The creek contains trout but is not stocked for fishermen.

The large wooden headframe of the Black Sambo Mine can be found alongside the trail in the narrow valley. A short distance from the trail on the left are more mining remains, including an old crusher perched on the hillside.

Bear paw prints indicate that the Greenhorn Mountains are still habitat for these shy creatures

As the valley opens out slightly for the final vehicle section, the trail becomes narrower and more brushy. It ends for vehicles alongside the creek at the Silver Strand Mine. The adits at the mine have steel gates on them. Motorbikes, hikers, and horses can follow the trail to connect through to Bull Run Basin and farther to finish at road 24S35.

Current Road Information

Sequoia National Forest
Greenhorn Ranger District
4875 Ponderosa Drive
PO Box 3810
Lake Isabella, CA 93240
(760) 379-5646

Map References

BLM Isabella Lake
USFS Sequoia National Forest
USGS 1:24,000 Tobias Peak
1:100,000 Isabella Lake
Maptech CD-ROM: Barstow/San Bernardino County
Southern & Central California Atlas & Gazetteer, p. 50
California Road & Recreation Atlas, p. 93

Route Directions

▼ 0.0		From Central Mountains #14: Portuguese Pass Trail, 1.1 miles from the southern end, zero trip meter and turn north on small formed trail following sign for Bull Run Basin. Trail is marked 25S36.
		GPS: N35°45.21′ W118°33.23′
▼ 0.2	SO	Pass through fence line.
▼ 0.5	SO	Track on right; then cross over creek; then track on left.
▼ 1.0	SO	Old winch on right of trail.
		GPS: N35°45.77′ W118°32.75′
▼ 1.4	SO	Wooden headframe and small cabin of the Black Sambo Mine alongside the trail.
		GPS: N35°46.06′ W118°32.51′
▼ 1.5	SO	Track on left and campsite on left; then cross through creek. Track on left goes short distance to many mine remains on hillside.
▼ 1.6	SO	Adit below trail on right.
▼ 1.8	BR	Track on left stops just over the rise.
		GPS: N35°46.26′ W118°32.28′
▼ 2.3		Trail ends for vehicles beside Cow Creek at the Silver Strand Mine. From here the trail continues for hikers, horses, and motorbikes only.
		GPS: N35°46.30′ W118°32.07′

CENTRAL MOUNTAINS #16

Piute Mountain Road

Starting Point:	**Kelso Valley Road at Sageland, 17 miles south of California 178**
Finishing Point:	**California 483, 2.5 miles south of Bodfish**
Total Mileage:	**30.5 miles**
Unpaved Mileage:	**30.5 miles**
Driving Time:	**3.5 hours**
Elevation Range:	**4,000–8,200 feet**
Usually Open:	**March to December**
Best Time to Travel:	**Dry weather**
Difficulty Rating:	**2**
Scenic Rating:	**9**
Remoteness Rating:	**+0**

Special Attractions

- Trail traverses a wide variety of vegetation and scenery.
- Long shelf road offers views of Isabella Lake and the Sierra Nevada.
- Access to wilderness areas and the Pacific Crest National Scenic Trail.

History

The first section of the route, from Kelso Creek to the Piute Mountains, partly follows a trail that early prospectors traveled while exploring the mountains. A prospector named Bob Palmer made his way west from Missouri, hoping to cash in on the mineral boom in California. In 1860, he staked his first claim near Erskine Creek, on the northwest side of the Piute Mountains. The claim didn't pay off so he moved on, feeling there were too many miners in that general area. Palmer made his way to Kelso Creek, which is named after John W. Kelso, an early settler who carted much-needed goods to and from Los Angeles during the years of the Kern River gold rush.

Palmer found that the specks in his pan grew in size as he worked his way up Kelso Creek toward Piute Mountain. He joined with a part-Cherokee friend of his, Hamp Williams, and together they established what became known as the Hamp Williams Mine. This mine flourished and was joined by others such as the Bright Star Mine, which was located in the canyon of the same name to the north of the trail. By 1862, mining and logging activities in the region encouraged the development of a settlement originally known as Kelso. By 1864, it was known as Claraville, renamed after Clara Munckton, a miner's daughter. The town grew to a population of nearly 500 by the mid-1860s.

Climbing out of Kelso Valley near the Harris Grade

By 1868, Claraville was quite the place to be. Besides having the obligatory saloons, stores, and hotels, it had its own courthouse and even an opera company that gave performances in town as well as in Sageland. However, the Bright Star Mine was running into financial problems around that time because its owners were ignoring their investment and were instead squandering their fortunes living the high life. It was declared bankrupt a year later and Claraville suffered from the lack of trade. By the early 1870s, the town died out and its residents moved on to more profitable ventures. Landers Creek and Landers Meadow, to the east of Claraville, are named after early settlers who grazed their cattle on the high pastures in the favorable summer months.

The starting point for the trail is marked as Sageland on some maps. This was the site of a small settlement that supplied miners working in the mountain ranges. Sageland supplied much of the labor force for nearby mines, including the St. John, Burning Moscow, and Hortense Mines. Like Claraville, Sageland suffered from the closure of the Bright Star Mine and was deserted by the early 1870s.

Blind corners are encountered as the shelf road cuts around massive granite outcroppings

Liebel Peak, located close to the trail, was named in the 1930s in remembrance of prospector-turned-settler Michael Otto Liebel, who entered the region in the 1870s. Liebel married an Indian girl and settled on land near the base of this mountain to raise a large family of 11 children.

The name Walker is also prominent in the region. The Joe Walker Mine and Walker Basin are both named after renowned explorer Joseph Reddeford Walker (see page 72). His earliest trip through the region took place in 1833. During this expedition, he located what is now Walker Pass (northeast of the trail in the Scodie Mountains). In 1844, John C. Frémont suggested that the pass be named after Walker in recognition of the discovery of such an important route.

Description

This long trail traverses Piute Mountain, running from Kelso Valley to Rancheria Creek Valley. The trail leaves paved Kelso Valley Road and follows a roughly graded dirt road that climbs steadily into Sequoia National Forest. This section of trail is also known as the Harris Grade. Initially the trail climbs through a pinyon and juniper forest before entering a pine forest on top of the plateau. The trail gradually narrows to a single-lane dirt road as it enters the forest and passes the small settlement of Claraville—now private property and cabins. There are many side trails for 4WDs to explore, as well as an alternative exit back to Kelso Valley via Central Mountains #17: Jawbone Canyon Road.

The long Pacific Crest National Scenic Trail crosses the road a couple of times. There are also many pleasant backcountry campsites, although you do need to be aware of bears.

Eventually the trail descends a long shelf road, dropping nearly 4,000 feet in the last few miles down a steady grade to the highway near Isabella Lake. The views are excellent; the lake can be seen far below and the southern tip of the Sierra Nevada can be seen to the north.

The grade is moderate all the way, and although some sections are only wide enough for a single vehicle, there are ample passing places. Parts of the original trail (a harder, alternative 4WD route) are still open to travel up the ridge from Kelso Valley Road. This route runs close to the graded road and occasionally crosses it. The trail is best suited to high-clearance vehicles because of the eroded surface and some ruts that would make it difficult for passenger vehicles.

Current Road Information

Sequoia National Forest
Greenhorn Ranger District
4875 Ponderosa Drive
PO Box 3810
Lake Isabella, CA 93240
(760) 379-5646

Map References

BLM Tehachapi
USFS Sequoia National Forest
USGS 1:24,000 Pinyon Mt., Claraville, Piute Peak, Lake Isabella South, Miracle Hot Springs
1:100,000 Tehachapi
Maptech CD-ROM: Barstow/San Bernardino County
Southern & Central California Atlas & Gazetteer, pp. 65, 64, 51
California Road & Recreation Atlas, pp. 93, 94

Route Directions

▼ 0.0		From California 178, 5 miles southwest of Onyx, zero trip meter and turn southeast on paved Kelso Valley Road. Remain on paved road for 17 miles; then zero trip meter and turn southwest on graded dirt road sign-posted for Piute Mountain. This is Sageland town site
4.9 ▲		Trail ends at T-intersection with paved Kelso Valley Road. Turn left for Weldon and California 178; turn right for Mojave.
		GPS: N35°28.80′ W118°12.71′
▼ 1.0	SO	Track on right.
3.9 ▲	SO	Track on left.
▼ 1.1	SO	Track on right.
3.8 ▲	SO	Track on left.
▼ 2.1	SO	Two tracks on right.
2.8 ▲	SO	Two tracks on left.
		GPS: N35°28.31′ W118°13.60′
▼ 2.8	SO	Track on left.
2.1 ▲	SO	Track on right.
▼ 2.9	SO	Track on right.

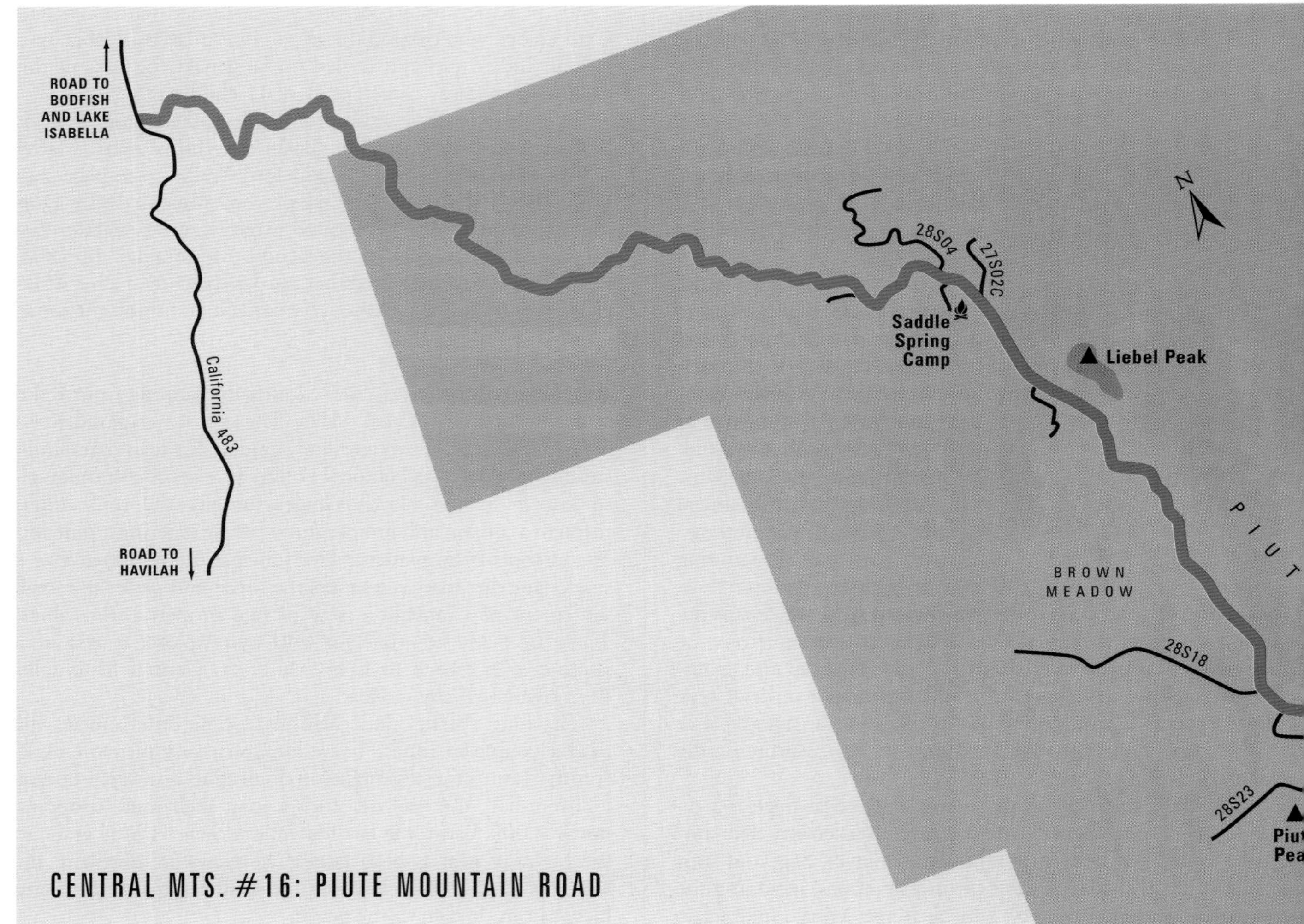

2.0 ▲	SO	Track on left.
▼ 3.4	SO	Track on left.
1.5 ▲	SO	Track on right.
▼ 3.6	SO	Track on right.
1.3 ▲	SO	Track on left.
▼ 4.1	SO	Track on left.
0.8 ▲	SO	Track on right.
		GPS: N35°27.78′ W118°15.14′
▼ 4.9	SO	Entering Sequoia National Forest at sign. Zero trip meter.
0.0 ▲		Continue to the south.
		GPS: N35°27.89′ W118°15.83′
▼ 0.0		Continue to the west. Road is now marked 27S02. Immediately track on right.
2.2 ▲	SO	Track on left; then leaving Sequoia National Forest. Zero trip meter.
▼ 0.4	SO	Track on right.
1.8 ▲	SO	Track on left.
▼ 0.7	SO	Cross over wash.
1.5 ▲	SO	Cross over wash.
▼ 1.2	SO	Track on right.
1.0 ▲	SO	Track on left.
▼ 1.5	SO	Pacific Crest National Scenic Trail crosses road. Left goes to Kelso Valley Road, Willow Spring, and Sequoia National Forest.
0.7 ▲	SO	Pacific Crest National Scenic Trail crosses road. Right goes to Kelso Valley Road, Willow Spring, and Sequoia National Forest.
		GPS: N35°27.39′ W118°16.64′
▼ 2.1	SO	Track on left.
0.1 ▲	SO	Track on right.
▼ 2.2	SO	Graded road on left is Sorrell Peak Road (27S04). Zero trip meter.
0.0 ▲		Continue to the northeast, remaining on 27S02 and following the sign for Kelso Valley Road.
		GPS: N35°26.95′ W118°17.18′
▼ 0.0		Continue to the southwest, remaining on 27S02 and following the sign for Jawbone Canyon Road.
2.2 ▲	SO	Graded road on right is Sorrell Peak Road (27S04). Zero trip meter.
▼ 0.9	BL	Graded road on right is 29S05 to Landers Station Camp.
1.3 ▲	SO	Graded road on left is 29S05 to Landers Station Camp.
		GPS: N35°26.93′ W118°18.16′
▼ 1.2	SO	Entering private property.
1.0 ▲	SO	Entering national forest.
▼ 1.4	SO	Corral on left.
0.8 ▲	SO	Corral on right.
▼ 1.5	SO	Re-entering national forest.
0.7 ▲	SO	Entering private property.

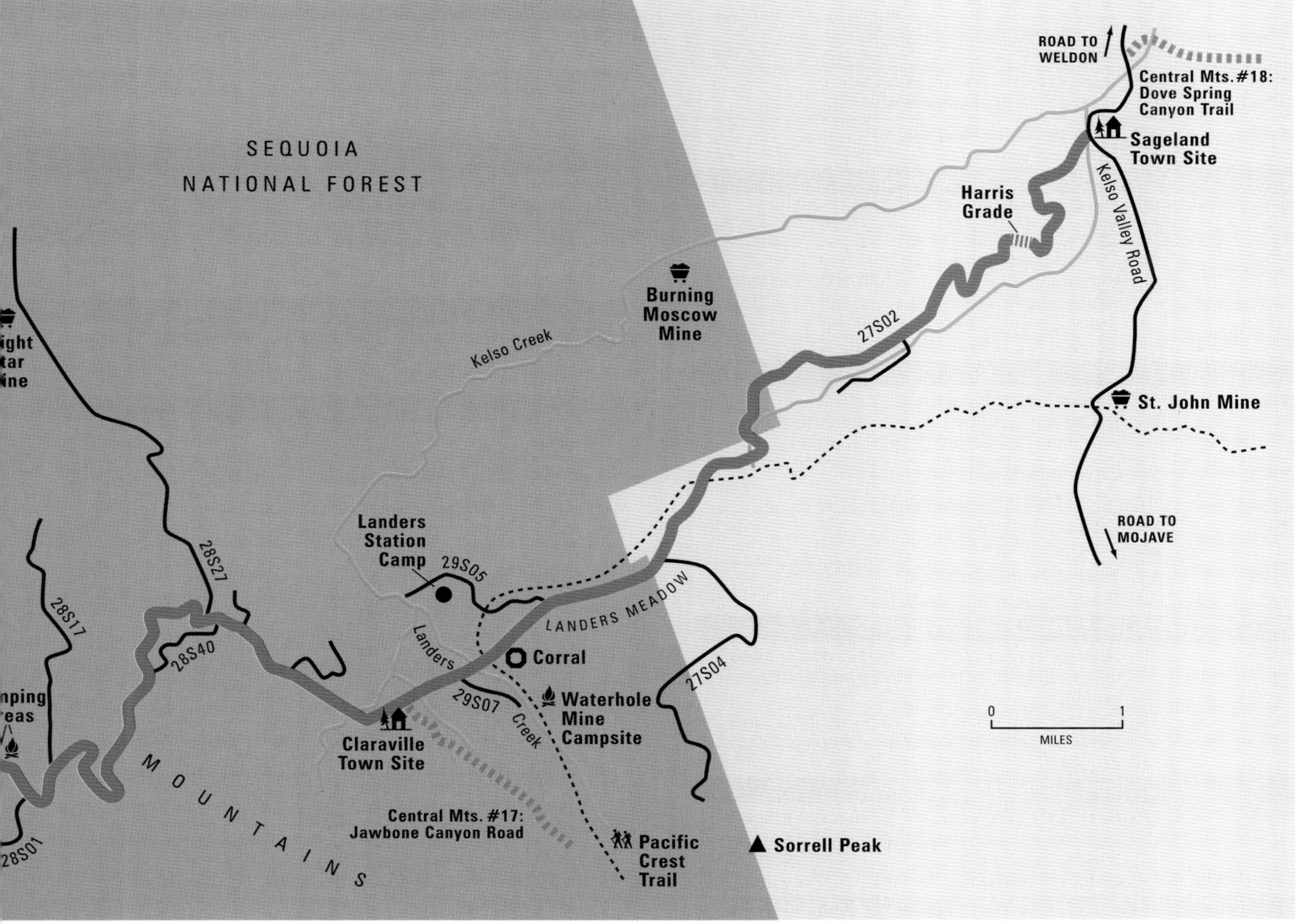

▼ 1.6	SO	Pacific Crest National Scenic Trail crosses road. Left goes 0.75 miles to Waterhole Trail Camp.
0.6 ▲	SO	Pacific Crest National Scenic Trail crosses road. Right goes 0.75 miles to Waterhole Trail Camp.
		GPS: N35°26.69' W118°18.83'
▼ 1.7	SO	Track on right; then cross over Landers Creek.
0.5 ▲	SO	Cross over Landers Creek; then track on left.
▼ 1.8	SO	Track on left is 29S07, which goes 0.6 miles to Waterhole Mine Campsite.
0.4 ▲	SO	Track on right is 29S07, which goes 0.6 miles to Waterhole Mine Campsite.
		GPS: N35°26.69' W118°19.03'
▼ 1.9	SO	Entering private property.
0.3 ▲	SO	Entering national forest.
▼ 2.1	SO	Cross over wash.
0.1 ▲	SO	Cross over wash.
▼ 2.2	SO	Graded road on left is Central Mountains #17: Jawbone Canyon Road to Kelso Valley. Zero trip meter. This is the site of Claraville.
0.0 ▲		Continue to the east.
		GPS: N35°26.65' W118°19.50'
▼ 0.0		Continue to the west. Remain on main road through private property.
1.8 ▲	SO	Graded road on right is Central Mountains #17: Jawbone Canyon Road to Kelso Valley. Zero trip meter. This is the site of Claraville.
▼ 0.5	SO	Cross over wash.
1.3 ▲	SO	Cross over wash.
▼ 0.7	SO	Re-entering national forest.
1.1 ▲	SO	Entering private property. Remain on main road.
▼ 1.1	SO	Track on right and track on left.
0.7 ▲	SO	Track on right and track on left.
▼ 1.3	SO	Track on left is 28S40.
0.5 ▲	SO	Track on right is 28S40.
		GPS: N35°27.22' W118°20.51'
▼ 1.6	SO	Track on right.
0.2 ▲	SO	Track on left.
▼ 1.8	BL	5-way intersection. Take the second left, remaining on 27S02 and following the sign to Walker Basin. Major track on right is 28S27 to Steve Spring. Zero trip meter.
0.0 ▲		Continue to the southeast.
		GPS: N35°27.59' W118°20.69'
▼ 0.0		Continue to the west.
3.6 ▲	BR	5-way intersection. Take the second right, remaining on 27S02. Zero trip meter.
▼ 0.3	SO	Cross over wash.
3.3 ▲	SO	Cross over wash.
▼ 0.7	SO	Cross over creek.
2.9 ▲	SO	Cross over creek.
▼ 1.2	SO	Track on left is 28S40.
2.4 ▲	SO	Track on right is 28S40.
		GPS: N35°27.45' W118°21.45'
▼ 3.3	SO	Graded road on right is 28S17, which goes 2 miles to Piute Vista and then stops. Also track on left.
0.3 ▲	SO	Graded road on left is 28S17, which goes 2 miles to Piute Vista and then stops. Also track on right.
		GPS: 35°26.98' W118°22.43'
▼ 3.6	BR	Bear right, remaining on 27S02 and following sign to Lake Isabella. Graded road on left is 28S01. Zero trip meter.
0.0 ▲		Continue to the southeast.
		GPS: N35°26.88' W118°22.64'
▼ 0.0		Continue to the north.
5.8 ▲	SO	Remain on 27S02, following sign to Kelso Valley Road. Graded road on right is 28S01. Zero trip meter.
▼ 0.2	SO	Track on right.
5.6 ▲	SO	Track on left.
▼ 0.3	SO	Camping areas on right and left as trail travels around Piute Peak.
5.5 ▲	SO	Camping areas on right and left as trail travels around Piute Peak.
		GPS: N35°27.14' W118°22.79'
▼ 0.6	SO	Closure gate; then turnout on left.
5.2 ▲	SO	Turnout on right; then closure gate.
▼ 1.2	SO	Track on left is 28S23; also track on right.
4.6 ▲	SO	Track on right is 28S23; also track on left.
		GPS: N35°27.73' W118°23.23'
▼ 1.4	BR	Track on right; then track forks. Track on left is 28S18 to Brown Meadow.
4.4 ▲	SO	Track on right is 28S18 to Brown Meadow; then track on left.
		GPS: N35°27.88' W118°23.34'
▼ 1.7	SO	Track on right.
4.1 ▲	SO	Track on left.
▼ 3.4	SO	Track on right is 27S02F and track on left is 27S02D.
2.4 ▲	SO	Track on left is 27S02F and track on right is 27S02D.
		GPS: N35°29.56' W118°23.66'
▼ 4.7	SO	Track on right is 28S19; then track on left.
1.1 ▲	SO	Track on right; then track on left is 28S19.
		GPS: N35°30.39' W118°24.26'
▼ 4.8	SO	Track on right is 27S02G.
1.0 ▲	SO	Track on left is 27S02G.
		GPS: N35°30.49' W118°24.33'
▼ 5.2	SO	Track on left is 27S02B.
0.6 ▲	SO	Track on right is 27S02B.
		GPS: N35°30.82' W118°24.43'
▼ 5.5	SO	Track on right is 27S02C; then track on left.
0.3 ▲	SO	Track on right; then track on left is 27S02C.
		GPS: N35°31.06' W118°24.51'
▼ 5.8	SO	Saddle Spring Camp on left at the start of 27S02A. Zero trip meter.
0.0 ▲		Continue to the east.
		GPS: N35°31.25' W118°24.67'
▼ 0.0		Continue to the west.
6.9 ▲	SO	Saddle Spring Camp on right at the start of 27S02A. Zero trip meter.
▼ 0.1	SO	Track on right is 28S04.
6.8 ▲	SO	Track on left is 28S04.
▼ 0.8	SO	Track on left.
6.1 ▲	SO	Track on right.
▼ 0.9	SO	Track on left.
6.0 ▲	SO	Track on right.
▼ 1.2	SO	Entering private property through closure gate. Remain on main road.
5.7 ▲	SO	Re-entering national forest through closure gate.
▼ 1.5	SO	Re-entering national forest.
5.4 ▲	SO	Entering private property. Remain on main road.
▼ 4.1	SO	Start to descend shelf road.
2.8 ▲	SO	End of climb.
▼ 6.9	SO	Leaving Sequoia National Forest at sign. Zero trip meter.
0.0 ▲		Continue to the south.
		GPS: N35°33.45' W118°28.82'

▼	▲		
▼ 0.0			Continue to the north.
	3.1 ▲	SO	Entering Sequoia National Forest at sign. Zero trip meter.
▼ 1.2		SO	Track on right.
	1.9 ▲	SO	Track on left.
▼ 2.1		SO	Track on right; then second track on right.
	1.0 ▲	SO	Track on left; then second track on left.
▼ 2.5		SO	Three tracks on right.
	0.6 ▲	SO	Three tracks on left.
			GPS: N35°34.20′ W118°30.04′
▼ 3.0		SO	Closure gate.
	0.1 ▲	SO	Closure gate.
▼ 3.1			Trail ends at T-intersection with California 483, 2.5 miles south of Bodfish. Turn left for Havilah; turn right for Lake Isabella.
	0.0 ▲		Trail starts on California 483, 2.5 miles south of Bodfish. Zero trip meter and turn south on graded dirt road. There is a sign after the intersection for Kelso Canyon.
			GPS: N35°34.16′ W118°30.36′

CENTRAL MOUNTAINS #17

Jawbone Canyon Road

Starting Point:	**California 14 at Jawbone Station, 19.1 miles northeast of the intersection with California 58**
Finishing Point:	**Central Mountains #16: Piute Mountain Road, 10 miles west of Kelso Valley Road**
Total Mileage:	**30.3 miles**
Unpaved Mileage:	**29.4 miles**
Driving Time:	**2 hours**
Elevation Range:	**2,100–6,900 feet**
Usually Open:	**April to November**
Best Time to Travel:	**April to November**
Difficulty Rating:	**2**
Scenic Rating:	**9**
Remoteness Rating:	**+0**

Special Attractions

- Jawbone Canyon OHV Area-an open area with a number of trails for 4WDs, ATVs, and motorbikes.
- Trail travels through a variety of scenery from desert to pine forest.
- The historic Geringer Grade.

History

In the 1860s, a German emigrant named Frederick Butterbredt settled in the region, took a Native American wife, and worked as a ranchero. Butterbredt Spring, Well, Peak, and Canyon are all named after his large family. In the late 1990s, the Jawbone-Butterbredt Area of Critical Environmental Concern was established on some of the weathered landscape once frequented by the family.

Trail crosses into Kelso Valley with the Piute Mountains in the distance

Jawbone Canyon Trail drops down through Kelso Valley at the foot of the Piute Mountains. John W. Kelso was a merchant who operated a store in the small mining town of Keyesville. Jawbone Canyon Trail follows a section of the trail used by Kelso to transport his merchandise into these mountains. His route took him through Jawbone Canyon, on to Kelso Valley, and then up and over St. John Ridge, which is visible from the trail at the northern end of Kelso Valley. From there he traveled down Kelso Creek to the South Fork Valley, and farther west to Keyesville. His ox team was a familiar sight to the miners and settlers of the Kern River region. Even in the worst weather conditions, he and others managed to bring supplies from Los Angeles to the gold rush camps in the area.

St. John Ridge is named after a gold mine of the same name, which was established in 1860 by a Mr. St. John and Jonnie Bonner. The partners sold out for an estimated $30,000. However, the mine flourished, supporting two mills and producing nearly $700,000 worth of gold by 1875.

The Geringer Grade on the southeast side of the Piute Mountains was a route established to connect the mining settlement of Claraville with Kelso Valley. The steep grade was named after Ott and Jack Gehringer, mining engineers who ran the Gwynne Mine, located 3 miles south of Claraville just west of the trail. They mined gold- and tungsten-bearing quartz that could be found in veins throughout the granitic bedrock. They staked six claims with a total recorded output of $770,000 in gold. Operations ceased in 1942.

In the late 1940s, the White Rock Mine was one of the active mines in the Jawbone Canyon region. Rhyolite, or pottery clay, was extracted with the use of earthmoving machinery and trucks. Antimony was also mined at Antimony Flat, just south of the prominent Cross Mountain, at the head of Jawbone Canyon.

The eastern end of the trail passes over a huge black pipeline known as the Jawbone Siphon, which is part of the Los Angeles Aqueduct. Also visible at the eastern end of the trail are the thousands of windmills that form the Tehachapi Pass Wind Farm. Scattered along the ridge tops around Tehachapi Pass, in one of the world's windiest areas, more than 5,000 wind turbines supply electricity for more than 500,000

The trail riding the ridge within the Sequoia National Forest

people in Southern California. Winds over Tehachapi Pass average 14 to 20 miles per hour, and the various kinds of wind turbines operate individually, depending on conditions and the needs of each turbine.

Description

Jawbone Canyon Road is a roughly graded dirt road that connects the desert areas of Jawbone Canyon with the pine-covered Piute Mountain region in the Sequoia National Forest. Initially the road is paved as it travels through the Jawbone Canyon OHV Area, where there are formed trails and open areas for 4WDs, ATVs, and motorbikes. At the start of the trail, the staffed Jawbone Station offers an excellent selection of maps, books, and free information.

One noteworthy feature along the early stages of the trail is Blue Point—a prominent ridge of rock that gains its distinctive blue color from copper in the rock. Blue Point was considered sacred to the Native Americans who lived in Jawbone Canyon. The scenery within the canyon is spectacular in its own right, with rugged hills surrounding the open canyon. The windmills of the Tehachapi Pass Wind Farm are visible on the ridge to the southwest.

Once outside the open Jawbone Canyon OHV Area, the route climbs alongside Hoffman Canyon, offering spectacular views back over Jawbone Canyon, Blue Point, and the Fremont Valley beyond. It continues to wind through boulder-strewn hills before descending to cross the wide, flat Kelso Valley. To the west of the valley, the Piute Mountains rise up behind it. The route passes through some private property within Kelso Valley, which is not clearly marked; be sure you are on public land before following any side trails or setting up camp.

Upon entering Sequoia National Forest, the road starts to climb up the Geringer Grade, a series of narrow steep switchbacks that swiftly takes the road up 2,500 feet to the upper reaches of the Piute Mountains. Once on top, the trail travels through pine forests before finishing at the T-intersection with Central Mountains #16: Piute Mountain Road.

Typically, the trail surface is fairly even and graded with areas in Jawbone Canyon that can be sandy in spots. At the

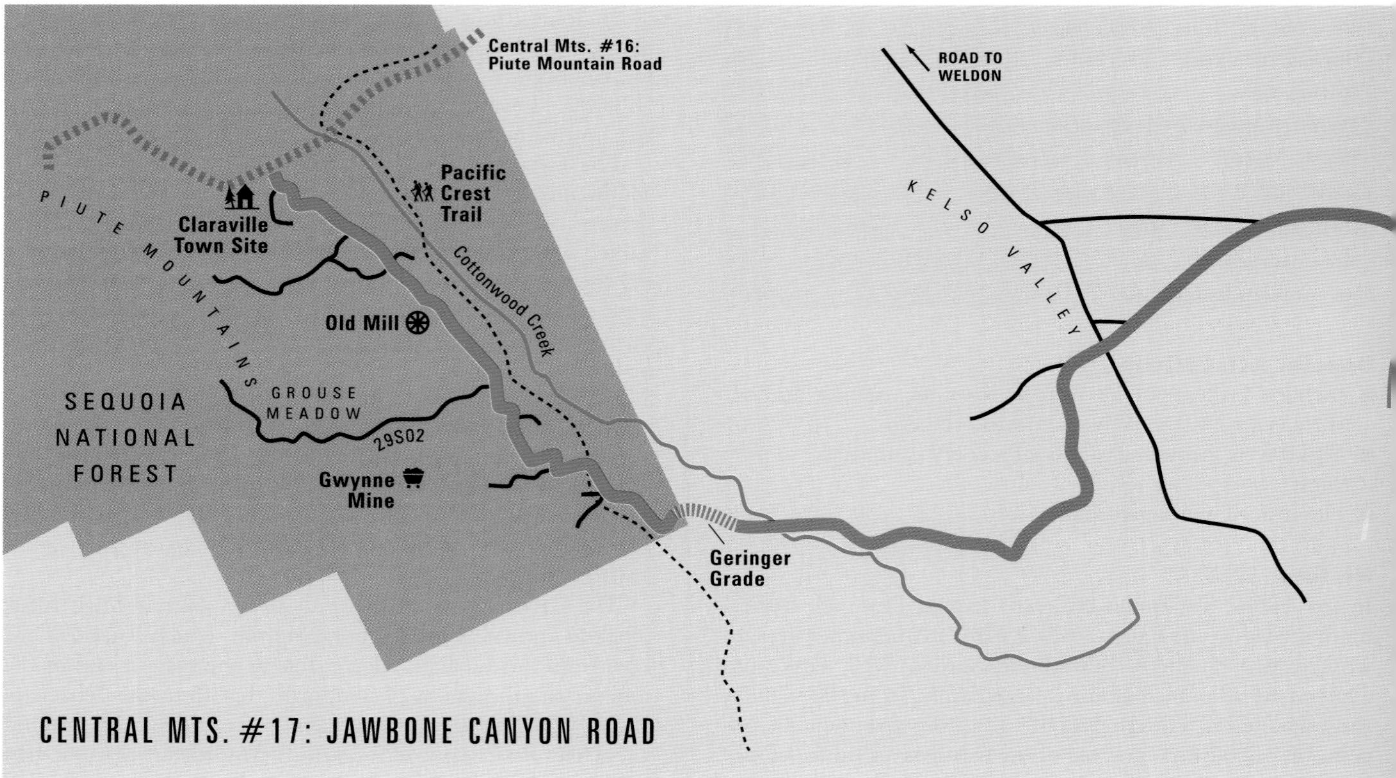

Central Mts. #16: Piute Mountain Road
ROAD TO WELDON
Pacific Crest Trail
PIUTE MOUNTAINS
Claraville Town Site
KELSO VALLEY
Cottonwood Creek
Old Mill
SEQUOIA NATIONAL FOREST
GROUSE MEADOW
29S02
Gwynne Mine
Geringer Grade

CENTRAL MTS. #17: JAWBONE CANYON ROAD

higher elevations, the trail is narrower and receives less maintenance. However it is still easily passable in dry weather by high-clearance vehicles. There are no closure gates along the trail; it closes naturally during the winter months depending on snowfall. It is often open for longer than the stated times. Check with the Sequoia National Forest for details.

Current Road Information

Sequoia National Forest
Greenhorn Ranger District
4875 Ponderosa Drive
PO Box 3810
Lake Isabella, CA 93240
(760) 379-5646

BLM Ridgecrest Field Office
300 S. Richmond Road
Ridgecrest, CA 93555
(760) 384-5400

Map References

BLM Tehachapi
USFS Sequoia National Forest
USGS 1:24,000 Cinco, Cross Mt., Pinyon Mt., Emerald Mt., Claraville
1:100,000 Tehachapi
Maptech CD-ROM: Barstow/San Bernardino County
Southern & Central California Atlas & Gazetteer, pp. 65, 64
California Road & Recreation Atlas, p. 94
Other: East Kern County OHV Riding Areas and Trails—Jawbone Canyon

Route Directions

▼ 0.0			From California 14, 19.1 miles northeast of intersection with California 58, zero trip meter and turn northwest at the sign for Jawbone Station. The paved road immediately passes beside Jawbone Station on right—BLM and OHV information and maps are available. Trail initially passes through Jawbone Canyon OHV Area. Remain on paved road. Many small tracks on left and right through open area.
	4.5 ▲		Trail passes Jawbone Station on left before finishing at T-intersection with California 14. Turn left for Randsburg; turn right for Mojave.
			GPS: N35°18.01′ W118°00.00′
▼ 0.6		SO	Graded road on right goes to Dove Spring.
	3.9 ▲	SO	Graded road on left goes to Dove Spring.
			GPS: N35°18.34′ W118°00.51′
▼ 1.1		SO	Graded road on right follows pipeline.
	3.4 ▲	SO	Graded road on left follows pipeline.
▼ 1.2		SO	Graded road on right.
	3.3 ▲	SO	Graded road on left.
▼ 1.9		SO	Graded road on right is SC175 for 4WDs, ATVs, and motorbikes.
	2.6 ▲	SO	Graded road on left is SC175 for 4WDs, ATVs, and motorbikes.
			GPS: N35°18.76′ W118°01.71′
▼ 2.7		SO	Cross over pipeline.
	1.8 ▲	SO	Cross over pipeline.
▼ 3.1		SO	Track on left.
	1.4 ▲	SO	Track on right.
▼ 3.8		SO	Cattle guard.
	0.7 ▲	SO	Cattle guard.
▼ 3.9		SO	Road turns to graded dirt.
	0.6 ▲	SO	Road is now paved.
▼ 4.5		SO	Track on right is SC176 for 4WDs, ATVs, and

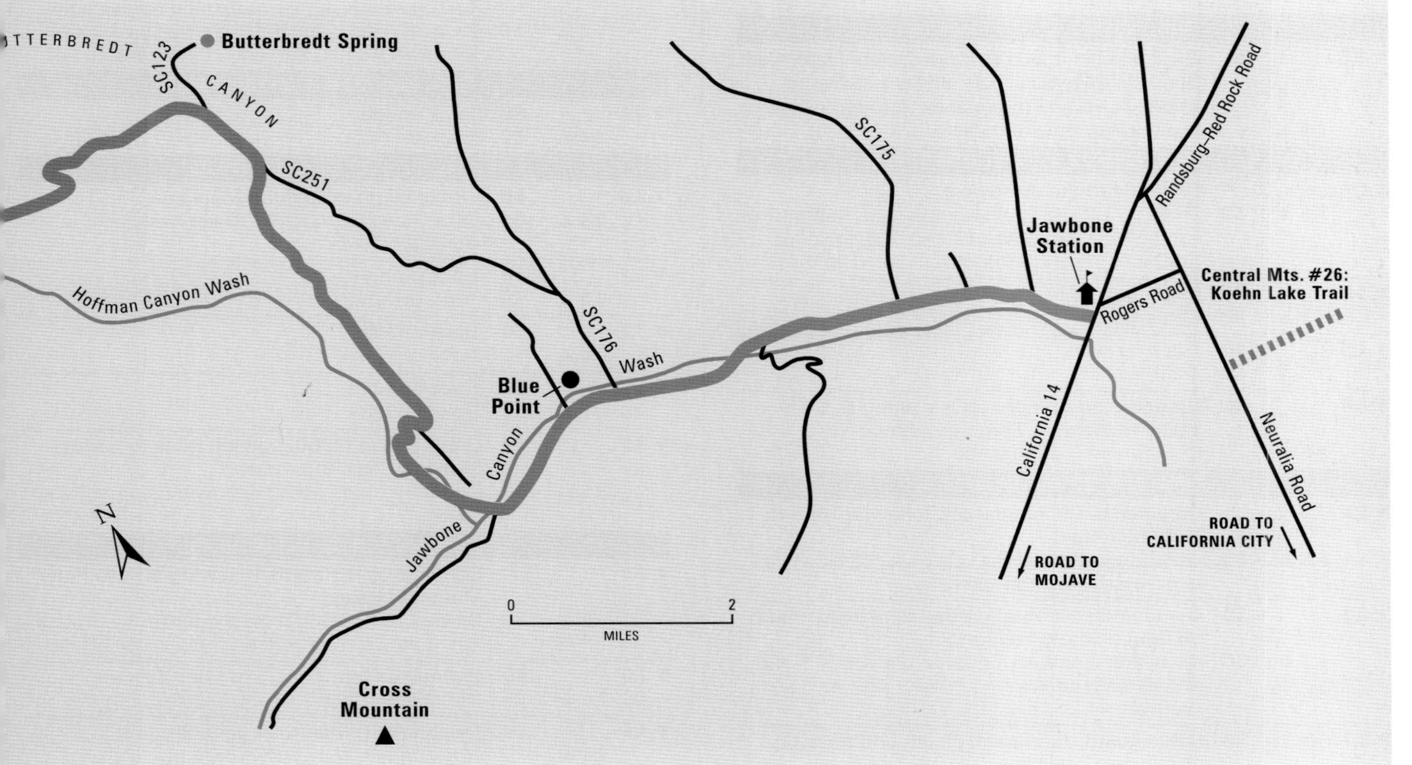

motorbikes. Zero trip meter. Blue Point is directly ahead.

0.0 ▲ Continue to the southeast.

GPS: N35°19.02' W118°04.49'

▼ 0.0 Continue to the northwest.

6.8 ▲ SO Track on left is SC176 for 4WDs, ATVs, and motorbikes. Zero trip meter.

▼ 0.4 SO Blue Point on right; then track on right.

6.4 ▲ SO Track on left; then Blue Point on left.

GPS: N35°19.06' W118°04.97'

▼ 1.4 BR Graded road on left leads through a closed area.

5.4 ▲ BL Graded road on right leads through a closed area.

GPS: N35°18.53' W118°05.89'

▼ 1.6 SO Cross through Jawbone Canyon Wash.

5.2 ▲ SO Cross through Jawbone Canyon Wash.

▼ 2.0 SO Cross through Hoffman Canyon Wash.

4.8 ▲ SO Cross through Hoffman Canyon Wash.

▼ 2.1 SO Exiting Jawbone Canyon OHV Area at sign.

4.7 ▲ SO Entering Jawbone Canyon OHV Area at sign. Many tracks on left and right through open area.

GPS: N35°18.91' W118°06.47'

▼ 2.3 SO Cross through wash.

4.5 ▲ SO Cross through wash.

▼ 3.1 SO Track on right.

3.7 ▲ SO Track on left.

▼ 3.3 SO Track on right.

3.5 ▲ SO Track on left.

▼ 3.5 SO Track on right.

3.3 ▲ SO Track on left.

▼ 6.0 SO Cross through wash; then track on right.

0.8 ▲ SO Track on left; then cross through wash.

GPS: N35°21.77' W118°06.72'

▼ 6.2 SO Two tracks on right are both SC251 for 4WDs, ATVs, and motorbikes.

0.6 ▲ SO Two tracks on left are both SC251 for 4WDs, ATVs, and motorbikes.

GPS: N35°21.92' W118°06.69'

▼ 6.8 BL Track on right is SC123, which enters Butterbredt Spring Wildlife Sanctuary, and is suitable for 4WDs, ATVs, and motorbikes. Zero trip meter.

0.0 ▲ Continue to the southeast.

GPS: N35°22.35' W118°06.95'

▼ 0.0 Continue to the northwest.

6.0 ▲ SO Track on left is SC123, which enters Butterbredt Spring Wildlife Sanctuary, and is suitable for 4WDs, ATVs, and motorbikes. Zero trip meter.

▼ 0.1 SO Cattle guard.

5.9 ▲ SO Cattle guard.

▼ 4.6 SO Track on right.

1.4 ▲ SO Track on left.

▼ 6.0 BL Graded road on right travels along Kelso Valley to Weldon. Zero trip meter.

0.0 ▲ Continue to the northeast.

GPS: N35°22.76' W118°12.64'

▼ 0.0 Continue to the southwest, following sign to Piute Mountain.

6.5 ▲ SO Graded road on left travels along Kelso Valley to Weldon. Zero trip meter.

▼ 0.3 SO 4-way intersection of graded dirt roads. Road on right leads to Weldon.

6.2 ▲ SO 4-way intersection of graded dirt roads. Road on left leads to Weldon. Follow sign to Highway 14.

▼ 0.7 SO Cattle guard; then track on left and track on right along fence line.

5.8 ▲ SO Track on left and track on right along fence line; then cattle guard.

▼ 1.7 SO Track on left and track on right along fence line; then cattle guard.

4.8 ▲ SO Cattle guard; then track on left and track on right along fence line.

▼ 2.1 SO Track on left.

4.4 ▲ SO Track on right.

▼ 2.2 SO Track on right.

4.3 ▲ SO Track on left.

▼ 3.0 SO Track on left; then track on right.

3.5 ▲ SO Track on left; then track on right.

▼ 3.7 SO Track on right.

2.8 ▲ SO Track on left.

▼ 3.8 SO Track on right.

2.7 ▲ SO Track on left.

▼ 4.9 SO Cross through Cottonwood Creek. Trail now starts to switchback up the Geringer Grade.

1.6 ▲ SO End of descent. Cross through Cottonwood Creek.

GPS: N35°22.41' W118°16.48'

▼ 6.5 SO Entering Sequoia National Forest at sign. Zero trip meter.

0.0 ▲ Continue to the east.

GPS: N35°22.80' W118°17.24'

▼ 0.0 Continue to the west.

3.5 ▲ SO Leaving Sequoia National Forest at sign. Zero trip meter.

▼ 0.9 SO Track on right to campsite.

2.6 ▲ SO Track on left to campsite.

▼ 1.3 TR Track on left and track straight ahead. Remain on main graded road.

2.2 ▲ TL Track on right and track straight ahead. Remain on main graded road.

GPS: N35°23.18' W118°17.87'

▼ 1.7 SO Track on right; then Pacific Crest National Scenic Trail crosses road, for hikers and horses only.

1.8 ▲ SO Pacific Crest National Scenic Trail crosses road, for hikers and horses only; then track on left.

GPS: N35°23.43' W118°17.89'

▼ 2.1 SO Track on left.

1.4 ▲ SO Track on right.

GPS: N35°23.54' W118°18.16'

▼ 2.6 SO End of climb onto Piute Mountain.

0.9 ▲ SO Begin descent to Kelso Valley along the Geringer Grade.

▼ 3.1 SO Track on right.

0.4 ▲ SO Track on left.

▼ 3.2 SO Track on left.

0.3 ▲ SO Track on right.

▼ 3.3 SO Track on right.

0.2 ▲ SO Track on left.

▼ 3.5 SO Graded road (29S02) on left goes to Grouse Meadow. Zero trip meter.

0.0 ▲ Continue to the south, following sign to Kelso Valley.

GPS: N35°24.33' W118°18.43'

▼ 0.0 Continue to the north, following sign to Piute Mountain Road.

3.0 ▲ SO Graded road (29S02) on right goes to Grouse Meadow. Zero trip meter.

▼ 1.0 SO Old mill on left.

2.0 ▲ SO Old mill on right.

▼ 1.6 SO Track on left; then track on right.

1.4 ▲ SO Track on left; then track on right.

▼ 1.9	SO	Track on right.
1.1 ▲	SO	Track on left.
▼ 2.1	SO	Track on left.
0.9 ▲	SO	Track on right.
▼ 2.9	SO	Track on left.
0.1 ▲	SO	Track on right.
▼ 3.0		Trail ends at T-intersection with Central Mountains #16: Piute Mountain Road. Turn right to return to Kelso Valley Road and Weldon; turn left for Bodfish.
0.0 ▲		Trail commences on Central Mountains #16: Piute Mountain Road, 10 miles west of Kelso Valley Road. Zero trip meter and turn east onto Jawbone Canyon Road, following sign for Kelso Valley.
		GPS: N35°26.64′ W118°19.52′

CENTRAL MOUNTAINS #18

Dove Spring Canyon Trail

Starting Point:	Kelso Valley Road, 17 miles south of Weldon
Finishing Point:	California 14, 7.6 miles north of Jawbone Station
Total Mileage:	18.1 miles
Unpaved Mileage:	17.4 miles
Driving Time:	1.5 hours
Elevation Range:	2,700–5,300 feet
Usually Open:	Year-round
Best Time to Travel:	Year-round
Difficulty Rating:	3
Scenic Rating:	8
Remoteness Rating:	+0

Special Attractions

- Dove Springs OHV Area.
- Picturesque sandy trail situated within a high desert area.
- Red Rock Canyon State Park.

History

The red-striped, tilted layers of Red Rock Canyon are the result of an uplift that occurred approximately 10 million years ago. The sediments packed within these layers are the remnants of earlier geological activities that had occurred in the surrounding regions. Time has compacted the layers and the elements have weathered them into the striking fluted shapes we see today.

Located along an old Indian trade route, the red canyon has been used as a meeting point by the native Kawaiisu people for thousands of years. In 1850, the spot was used as a resting and watering point for Illinois Jayhawkers who were escaping the harsh conditions of Death Valley.

Heading south from Death Valley in 1867, a German prospector named Goler stumbled upon gold nuggets while drinking at a spring. Unfamiliar with the land and fearful of an attack by Indians, he quickly mapped his find and headed for Los Angeles. He arranged Grant Price Cuddeback as his financial backer and made two unsuccessful expeditions back to the area in search of his original find. However, on their third attempt, Cuddeback and Goler struck gold in Red Rock Canyon. They mined in the canyon for several years, but Goler eventually moved on, still disappointed at not finding his original strike of 1867. In time, a collection of rich mines in the nearby El Paso Mountains became known as the Goler Mining District, seemingly at the location of the prospector's original find. However, Goler himself was long gone by then and never profited from the mines.

Some of the specatular formations in Red Rock Canyon State Park

Red Rock Canyon was also a watering point for cattle and sheep drovers on their way to greener pastures and markets. El Tejon Ranch was one of a number of ranches whose teamsters took advantage of this rest stop. As the Kern River goldfields grew, Red Rock Canyon became a stage stop for travelers coming from Los Angeles. A trade route developed from Owens Valley and Cerro Gordo through to Bakersfield and Ventura. The station was run by a gold miner named Rudolf Hagen, who named it after his son. The station, of which no trace remains, offered relief from the sweltering summer heat and icy winter winds. Hay and water were available for pack trains and a teamster could take a welcome rest after he tended to his stock. Stories were shared of events along the harsh trail, what conditions lay ahead, and where the latest washout or gunfight had occurred. A post office opened at Ricardo in 1898. A railroad was put through the canyon and at one time, a truck stop as well.

The railroad was constructed to bring cement, piping, and equipment to Dove Spring, where a small city was built as the center of construction for the Los Angeles Aqueduct. The project, which began in 1907, was completed in 1913.

Hollywood took advantage of the badlands scenery for movie backdrops. Red Rock Canyon has been the setting for many Westerns. Episodes of *Bonanza* and a number of TV commercials have also been filmed there.

A sandy section of trail descending to Dove Spring Canyon

Description

Dove Spring Canyon Trail connects Kelso Valley Road with California 14 and the old settlements in Kern County. For those with a high-clearance 4WD, the trail makes an easy and picturesque shortcut between the two areas.

The trail leaves Kelso Valley Road up one of the clearly marked OHV trails that traverses BLM land. It follows a formed sandy trail through stands of Joshua trees, and runs mainly in a wash until it reaches a saddle at the high point of the trail at a little over 5,300 feet. A side trail to the north at that point leads to the remains of the Sunset Mine.

The main trail gradually descends along Dove Spring Canyon, passing by Dove Spring, before entering the open OHV area at Gold Peak Well. Within the open area there are many unmarked trails to the right and left. Only numbered routes are mentioned as side trails in the route directions unless there is the potential for confusion. Remain on the major through-route, which is periodically marked with posts that read SC103.

The trail finishes in the extremely picturesque Red Rock Canyon State Park (which was established in 1968 as the first state park in Kern County), at the entrance to Ricardo Campground and the old site of the Ricardo Stage Station. The campground is situated at the base of the eroded White House Cliffs and makes a wonderful place to camp for the night. Alternatively, undeveloped backcountry campsites can be found at other points along the trail.

Current Road Information

BLM Ridgecrest Field Office
300 S. Richmond Road
Ridgecrest, CA 93555
(760) 384-5400

Map References

BLM Tehachapi, Cuddeback Lake
USGS 1:24,000 Pinyon Mt., Dove Spring, Saltdale NW
1:100,000 Tehachapi, Cuddeback Lake
Maptech CD-ROM: Barstow/San Bernardino County
Southern & Central California Atlas & Gazetteer, p. 65
California Road & Recreation Atlas, p. 94
Other: East Kern County OHV Riding Areas and Trails—Jawbone Canyon

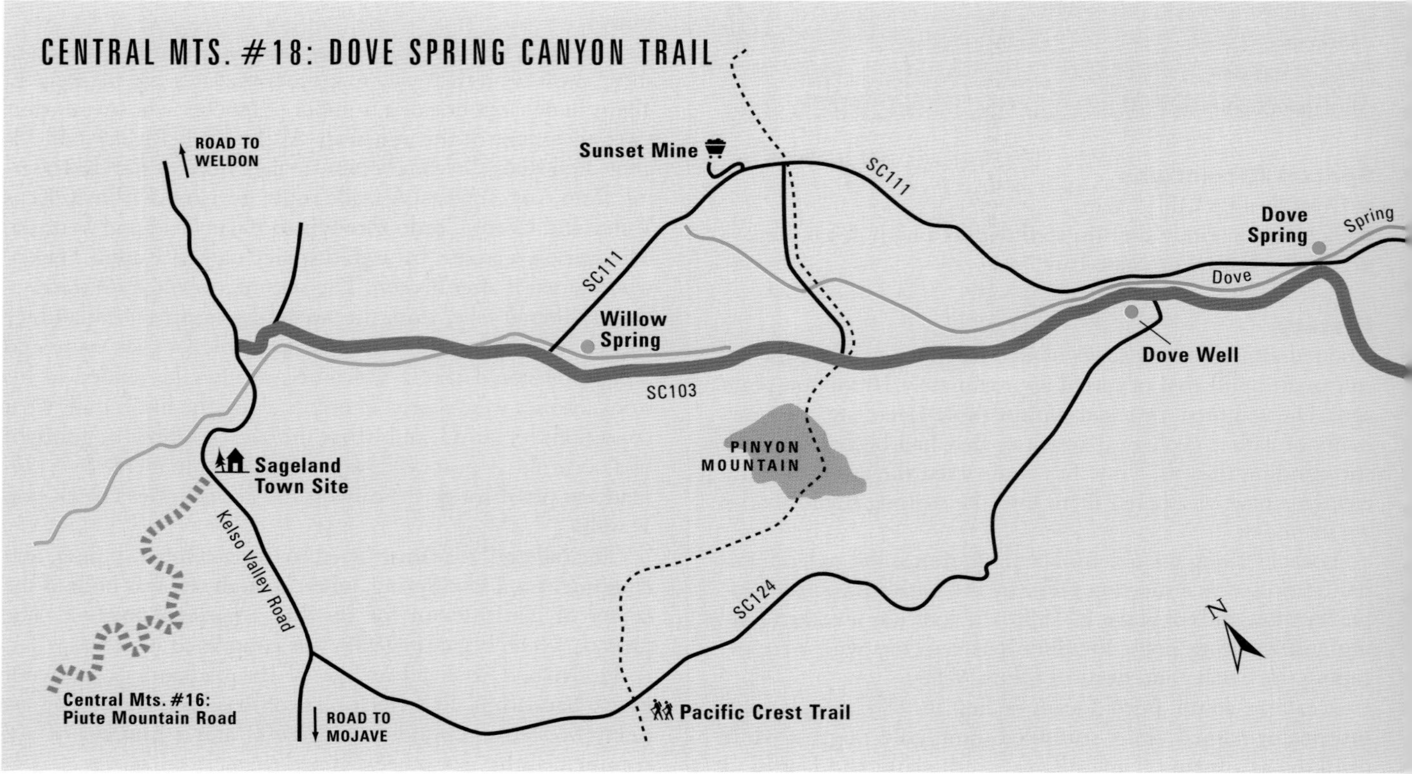

CENTRAL MTS. #18: DOVE SPRING CANYON TRAIL

ROAD TO WELDON
Sunset Mine
SC111
SC111
Dove Spring
Spring
Dove
Willow Spring
Dove Well
SC103
Sageland Town Site
PINYON MOUNTAIN
Kelso Valley Road
SC124
N
Central Mts. #16: Piute Mountain Road
ROAD TO MOJAVE
Pacific Crest Trail

Route Directions

▼ 0.0		From Kelso Valley Road, 17 miles south of Weldon on California 178, zero trip meter and turn southeast on formed dirt trail marked SC103 for 4WDs, ATVs, and motorbikes.
3.8 ▲		Trail ends on Kelso Valley Road. Turn right for Weldon; turn left to continue to Central Mountains #17: Jawbone Canyon Road or Central Mountains #16: Piute Mountain Road.
		GPS: N35°29.30′ W118°12.21′
▼ 0.4	SO	Track on left.
3.4 ▲	SO	Track on right.
▼ 0.5	SO	Track on left is SC36 for 4WDs, ATVs, and motorbikes.
3.3 ▲	SO	Track on right is SC36 for 4WDs, ATVs, and motorbikes.
		GPS: N35°29.22′ W118°11.88′
▼ 0.6	SO	Track on left is SC102 for ATVs and motorbikes only.
3.2 ▲	SO	Track on right is SC102 for ATVs and motorbikes only.
▼ 1.6	SO	Cross through wash.
2.2 ▲	SO	Cross through wash.
▼ 1.9	BR	Bear right and enter wash, remaining on SC103; then track on left is SC111 for motorbikes only.
1.9 ▲	BL	Track on right is SC111 for motorbikes only; then bear left and exit wash, remaining on SC103.
		GPS: N35°28.62′ W118°10.59′
▼ 2.2	SO	Willow Spring on left.
1.6 ▲	SO	Willow Spring on right.
		GPS: N35°28.39′ W118°10.40′
▼ 2.8	SO	Exit wash.
1.0 ▲	SO	Enter wash.
▼ 3.8	SO	Saddle. Track on left goes to the Sunset Mine. Pinyon Mountain is on the right. Pacific Crest National Scenic Trail crosses the road at this point. Zero trip meter.
0.0 ▲		Continue to the northwest.
		GPS: N35°27.85′ W118°08.95′
▼ 0.0		Continue to the southeast.
1.7 ▲	SO	Saddle. Track on right goes to the Sunset Mine. Pinyon Mountain is on the left. Pacific Crest National Scenic Trail crosses the road at this point. Zero trip meter.
▼ 1.2	SO	Track on left.
0.5 ▲	SO	Track on right.
▼ 1.7	SO	Track on left, which runs parallel with main route, is SC111 for 4WDs, ATVs, and motorbikes. Track on right is SC102 for ATVs and motorbikes only. Trail now enters Dove Spring Canyon Wash. Dove Well on right. Zero trip meter.
0.0 ▲		Continue to the west, remaining on SC103.
		GPS: N35°27.52′ W118°07.23′
▼ 0.0		Continue to the east, remaining on SC103.
3.3 ▲	SO	Track on right, which runs parallel with main route, is SC111 for 4WDs, ATVs, and motorbikes. Track on left is SC102 for ATVs and motorbikes only. Trail leaves Dove Spring Canyon Wash. Dove Well on left. Zero trip meter.
▼ 0.2	SO	Track on right is SC124 for 4WDs, ATVs, and motorbikes.
3.1 ▲	SO	Track on left is second entrance to SC124.
▼ 0.3	SO	Track on right is second entrance to SC124.
3.0 ▲	SO	Track on left is SC124 for 4WDs, ATVs, and motorbikes.
▼ 1.2	SO	Track on left is SC111 for 4WDs, ATVs, and motorbikes.
2.1 ▲	BL	Track on right is SC111 for 4WDs, ATVs, and motorbikes.
		GPS: N35°27.17′ W118°06.05′

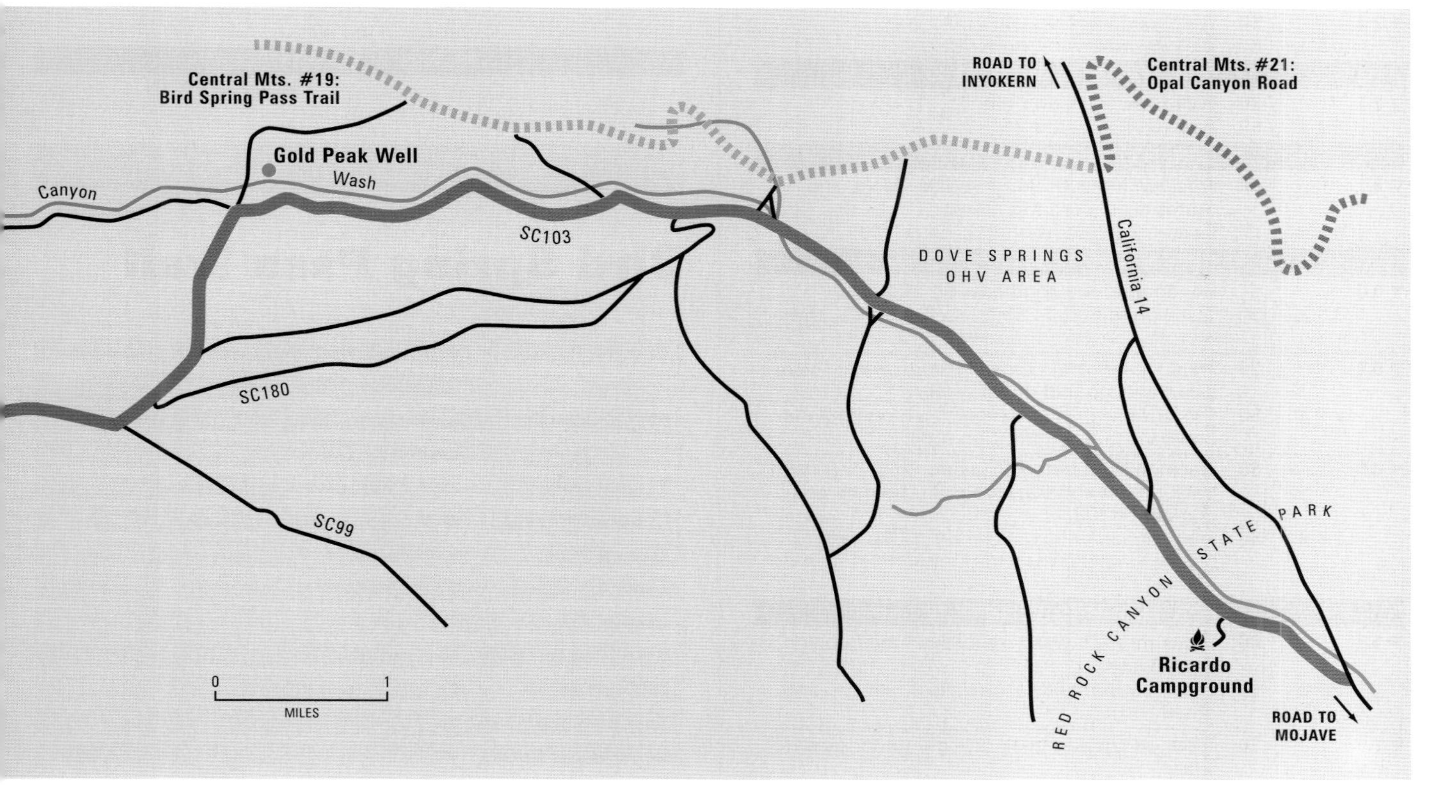

▼ 1.3 BR Track ahead is SC328 for 4WDs, ATVs, and motorbikes. Remain on SC103. Dove Spring on left.

2.0 ▲ BL Track ahead is SC328 for 4WDs, ATVs, and motorbikes. Remain on SC103. Dove Spring on right.

GPS: N35°27.17' W118°05.97'

▼ 1.4 SO Cattle guard.

1.9 ▲ SO Cattle guard.

▼ 1.5 SO Track on left.

1.8 ▲ SO Track on right.

GPS: N35°27.04' W118°05.94'

▼ 3.3 BL Track ahead is SC99 for 4WDs, ATVs, and motorbikes. Remain on SC103 and zero trip meter.

0.0 ▲ Continue to the northwest.

GPS: N35°25.87' W118°04.92'

▼ 0.0 Continue to the northeast.

1.7 ▲ BR Track on left is SC99 for 4WDs, ATVs, and motorbikes. Remain on SC103 and zero trip meter.

▼ 0.2 SO Track on right opposite rocky outcrop is SC180.

1.5 ▲ SO Track on left opposite rocky outcrop is SC180.

▼ 0.8 TL 4-way intersection. Remain on SC103. Track on right and track straight ahead.

0.9 ▲ TR 4-way intersection. Remain on SC103. Track on left and track straight ahead.

GPS: N35°26.00' W118°04.03'

▼ 1.7 BR Marked track on left; then enter Dove Springs OHV Area at sign. Track on left goes to Gold Peak Well. Zero trip meter at sign.

0.0 ▲ Continue to the southwest on SC103.

GPS: N35°26.61' W118°03.58'

▼ 0.0 Continue to the southeast. Many tracks on right and left in open area. Remain on main trail, which travels along the valley floor.

3.1 ▲ BL Leave Dove Springs OHV Area at sign. Track on right goes to Gold Peak Well; then second marked track on right. Zero trip meter at sign.

▼ 2.3 SO Well-used track on left.

0.8 ▲ BL Well-used track on right.

GPS: N35°25.83' W118°01.49'

▼ 2.7 SO Well-used track on right.

0.4 ▲ SO Well-used track on left.

GPS: N35°25.65' W118°01.21'

▼ 3.1 BR Track on left is SC94 for 4WDs, ATVs, and motorbikes. Zero trip meter.

0.0 ▲ Continue to the northwest on SC103.

GPS: N35°25.45' W118°00.82'

▼ 0.0 Continue to the southeast on SC103.

3.8 ▲ SO Track on right is SC94 for 4WDs, ATVs, and motorbikes. Zero trip meter.

▼ 0.2 SO Track on left; then cross through wash—vehicles travel up and down wash.

3.6 ▲ SO Cross through wash—vehicles travel up and down wash; then track on right.

▼ 0.9 SO Track on right before pipeline; then well-used track on left and track on right. Remain on marked SC103.

2.9 ▲ SO Track on left and well-used track on right before pipeline; then track on left. Remain on marked SC103.

GPS: N35°24.69' W118°00.38'

▼ 1.7 SO Cross through wash—vehicles travel up and down wash.

2.1 ▲ SO Cross through wash—vehicles travel up and down wash.

▼ 1.8 SO Track on left and track on right under power lines.

2.0 ▲ SO Track on left and track on right under power lines.

▼ 2.0 SO Track on right.

1.8 ▲ SO Track on left.

▼ 2.2 SO Cattle guard; entering Red Rock Canyon State Park. End of OHV area.

1.6 ▲ SO Leaving state park and entering Dove Springs OHV Area over cattle guard. Many tracks on right and left in open area. Remain on main trail, which travels along the valley floor.

GPS: N35°23.74' W117°59.75'

▼ 2.4 SO Cross through wash.

1.4 ▲ SO Cross through wash.

▼ 2.9 SO Old section of US 6 on left is being re-vegetated. Enter wash.

0.9 ▲ SO Old section of US 6 on right is being re-vegetated. Exit wash.

▼ 3.8 TR Turn right out of wash; then turn left onto paved road. Vehicles can continue in the wash, which exits at the end of the trail. Zero trip meter. Paved road on right goes immediately into Ricardo Campground.

0.0 ▲ Continue to the northeast.

GPS: N35°22.45' W117°59.28'

▼ 0.0 Continue to the west.

0.7 ▲ TR Turn right opposite parks work area and sign for Ricardo Campground; then turn left up wash. Vehicles travel to the right down wash. Zero trip meter. Paved road continues into Ricardo Campground.

▼ 0.7 Track on left is alternate exit from wash and track on right. Trail ends at T-intersection with California 14. Turn right for Mojave; turn left for Inyokern.

0.0 ▲ Trail commences on California 14, 7.6 miles north of Jawbone Station. Zero trip meter and turn northwest onto paved Abbott Drive at sign for Red Rock Canyon State Park, Ricardo Campground. Track on left. Track on right is alternate beginning that avoids paved road by traveling up the wash.

GPS: N35°21.89' W117°58.88'

CENTRAL MOUNTAINS #19

Bird Spring Pass Trail

Starting Point:	**California 14, 3.5 miles north of the turn to Ricardo Campground**
Finishing Point:	**Kelso Valley Road, 10.7 miles south of California 178**
Total Mileage:	**20.8 miles, plus 2.9-mile spur**
Unpaved Mileage:	**20.8 miles, plus 2.9-mile spur**
Driving Time:	**2 hours**
Elevation Range:	**2,600–5,500 feet**
Usually Open:	**Year-round**
Best Time to Travel:	**Year-round**
Difficulty Rating:	**3**
Scenic Rating:	**9**
Remoteness Rating:	**+0**

Special Attractions

- Historic route through Bird Spring Pass.
- Dove Springs OHV Area.
- Joshua tree forest and spectacular high desert scenery.

History

Located at the eastern end of the trail, Indian Wells Valley was known to Native Americans for many years. However, a waterhole farther up the valley was a welcome surprise to the Manly-Rogers Death Valley escape party of 1850 (see page 99) because it was the first water they had found since crossing the Argus Range north of Trona.

By the 1860s a stage station was located at Indian Wells. Operated by James Bridger, it catered to the mule teams coming from the mines in the Cerro Gordo and Coso regions.

Stagecoach holdups, bandits, and outlaw activity seemingly came hand in hand with any region being settled in the West. Indian Wells was an important stopping point for many travelers in the region, and it managed to attract its share of shady characters. One of these marauding outlaws was Tiburcio Vasquez. After he attacked a number of travelers, a warrant was issued for his arrest. Vasquez and his mob took to a hiding place that would later come to be known as Robber's Roost (located close to Freeman Junction near Indian Wells). In the 1870s, they would lie in wait behind the roost's rocky crags before ambushing stagecoaches, travelers, and pack trains. By the time a military party was sent to end their activities, the Vasquez gang had relocated to the thriving community of Los Angeles. In 1875, Vasquez was finally cornered at what would later become known as Hollywood. From there he was transported to San Jose to face trial for murder. He was convicted and hanged in March of the same year.

Crossing the creosote-covered flats en route to Bird Spring Pass

The Los Angeles Aqueduct and Second Los Angeles Aqueduct, which supply water from the Owens Valley to Los Angeles, pass just below the crags of Robber's Roost.

Joseph Reddeford Walker, a renowned pathfinder of the American West, is credited with finding a passage through the Scodie Mountains in 1833. The pass chosen by Walker is situated north of Bird Spring Pass along the ridge tops of the Scodie Mountains. The Pacific Crest National Scenic Trail crosses this trail at Bird Spring Pass, and takes hikers to Walker Pass—now on the busy route of California 178.

On his fifth trip to California in March 1854, John Charles Frémont was blocked by snow at Walker Pass. He found an alternate, southern route through the Scodie Mountains that crossed over Bird Spring Pass.

A remote stretch of trail approaching Bird Spring Pass

In 1874, a former forty-niner from Boston, Freeman S. Raymond, established a stage station at the important junction that gained his name. Located at the eastern end of the route over Walker Pass, the station adopted Raymond's first name in 1889 when it received a post office. Raymond passed away in 1909 and the post office was moved south to Ricardo, located in Red Rock Canyon. California 14 now runs along the original north-south stage route.

Description

Bird Spring Pass Trail travels between the Dove Springs OHV Area and the Kelso Valley. Along the way, it traverses some spectacular high desert country.

The well-formed sandy trail leaves California 14 at the main entry point into Dove Springs OHV Area. This popular area has a wide variety of trails and is designed to handle 4WDs, ATVs, and motorbikes. Throughout the OHV area there are many unmarked trails; these are not mentioned in the route directions unless there is a chance for confusion with the main route.

The trail leads north of Central Mountains #18: Dove Spring Canyon Trail and follows the smaller, sandy SC94 toward Bird Spring Pass. The trail is well formed and gets its difficulty rating from the frequent sections of loose sand that must be negotiated. Although it is in a popular area, the trail has a remote feel and once away from the OHV area is seldom traveled. A good portion of the trail passes through thick Joshua tree forests before swinging west to travel along the southern boundary of the Kiavah Wilderness toward Bird Spring Pass.

The Pacific Crest National Scenic Trail crosses on the pass, and a spur trail to the south climbs higher up to the communications towers on Wyleys Knob. From the towers there are excellent views in all directions: east over the Indian Wells Valley, west over the Kelso Valley to the Piute Mountains, and south over the high desert hills.

Motorbikes have the option of traveling one of the smaller

Trail SC44, for dirt bikes only, crosses Bird Spring Pass Trail and follows the sandy wash between Joshua trees and granite outcroppings

marked trails from this spur that allows them to cross over to the Dove Springs OHV Area.

West of the pass, the trail is less sandy as it switchbacks down a narrow shelf road to Kelso Valley Road. Passing places are limited on the shelf road, so you may need to back up if you encounter oncoming traffic. The trail passes around the boundary of the Jawbone-Butterbredt Area of Critical Environmental Concern, which was established to protect the region's desert wildlife and Indian artifacts. The area is also used for livestock, with sheep and cattle allowed to graze under a permit system.

Current Road Information

BLM Ridgecrest Field Office
300 S. Richmond Road
Ridgecrest, CA 93555
(760) 384-5400

Map References

BLM Cuddeback Lake, Tehachapi, Isabella Lake
USGS 1:24,000 Saltdale NW, Dove Spring, Horse Canyon, Cane Canyon
1:100,000 Cuddeback Lake, Tehachapi, Isabella Lake
Maptech CD-ROM: Barstow/San Bernardino County
Southern & Central California Atlas & Gazetteer, pp. 65, 51
California Road & Recreation Atlas, p. 94
Other: East Kern County OHV Riding Areas and Trails—Jawbone Canyon

Route Directions

▼ 0.0			From California 14, 3.5 miles north of the turn to Ricardo Campground in Red Rock Canyon State Park, zero trip meter and turn northwest on SC94 at sign for Dove Springs OHV Area. Central Mountains #21: Opal Canyon Road is opposite.Road turns to graded dirt over cattle guard. Many tracks on left and right through OHV area.
	1.9 ▲		Trail ends on California 14. Central Mountains #21; Opal Canyon Road is opposite. Turn left for Inyokern; turn right for Mojave.
			GPS: N35°24.85′ W117°58.81′
▼ 0.7		SO	Track on left and track on right under power lines. Remain on SC94.
	1.2 ▲	SO	Track on left and track on right under power lines. Remain on SC94.
▼ 1.1		SO	Well-used track on left and track on right. Continue on Bird Spring Road.
	0.8 ▲	SO	Track on left and well-used track on right. Continue on Bird Spring Road.
			GPS: N35°25.33′ W117°59.86′
▼ 1.9		TR	Cross through wash; then turn sharp right, following marker for SC94. Track straight ahead and small tracks at intersection. Zero trip meter.
	0.0 ▲		Continue to the northeast.
			GPS: N35°25.43′ W118°00.64′
▼ 0.0			Continue to the north.
	7.0 ▲	TL	Turn sharp left; then cross through wash, remaining on SC94. Track on right and small tracks at intersection. Zero trip meter.
▼ 0.3		BL	Roughly graded road on right. Follow sign for SC94.
	6.7 ▲	SO	Roughly graded road on left.
			GPS: N35°25.70′ W118°00.72′
▼ 0.8		SO	Track on right; then tank on left. Cross cattle

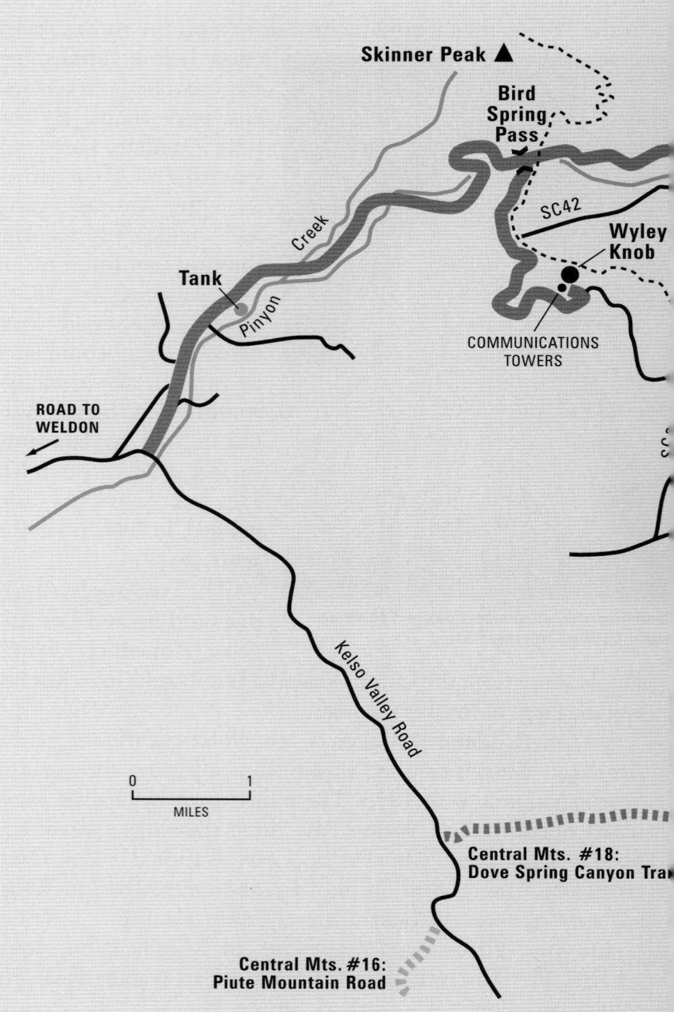

Mileage	Direction	Description
		guard, remaining on SC94. Track on right after cattle guard is SC5.
6.2 ▲	BR	Track on left is SC5; then cattle guard. Tank on right; then track on left. Remain on SC94.
		GPS: N35°26.05' W118°00.86'
▼ 2.7	SO	Track on left and track on right are both SC161 for ATVs and motorbikes only.
4.3 ▲	SO	Track on left and track on right are both SC161 for ATVs and motorbikes only.
		GPS: N35°27.08' W118°02.60'
▼ 2.9	SO	Track on left and track on right.
4.1 ▲	SO	Track on left and track on right.
▼ 3.1	SO	Track on left and track on right.
3.9 ▲	SO	Track on left and track on right.
▼ 5.1	SO	Track on left and track on right.
1.9 ▲	SO	Track on left and track on right.
▼ 6.1	BR	Track on left.
0.9 ▲	BL	Track on right.
		GPS: N35°28.94' W118°05.69'
▼ 7.0	SO	4-way intersection. Tracks on left and straight ahead are SC47 for 4WDs, ATVs, and motorbikes. Track on right is SC44 for motorbikes only. Zero trip meter.
0.0 ▲		Continue to the south on SC94.
		GPS: N35°29.63' W118°05.72'
▼ 0.0		Continue to the north on SC47.
1.4 ▲	SO	4-way intersection. Track on right is SC47 for 4WDs, ATVs, and motorbikes. Track on left is SC44 for motorbikes only. Track ahead is SC94 for 4WDs, ATVs, and motorbikes. Zero trip meter.
▼ 1.0	SO	Track on left. Stone and concrete foundations at intersection. Then track on right.
0.4 ▲	SO	Track on left; then track on right. Stone and concrete foundations at intersection.
		GPS: N35°30.10' W118°04.90'
▼ 1.1	SO	Track on left.
0.3 ▲	SO	Track on right.
▼ 1.4	TL	4-way intersection. SC47 continues ahead. Track on right is SC161 for 4WDs, ATVs, and motorbikes. Track on left is SC120 for 4WDs, ATVs, and motorbikes. Zero trip meter.
0.0 ▲		Continue to the west on SC47 and leave the boundary of the Kiavah Wilderness.
		GPS: N35°30.15' W118°04.50'
▼ 0.0		Continue to the northwest on SC120 along the southern boundary of the Kiavah Wilderness.
5.2 ▲	TR	4-way intersection. Tracks on left and right are SC47 for 4WDs, ATVs, and motorbikes. Track ahead is SC161 for 4WDs, ATVs, and motorbikes. Zero trip meter.

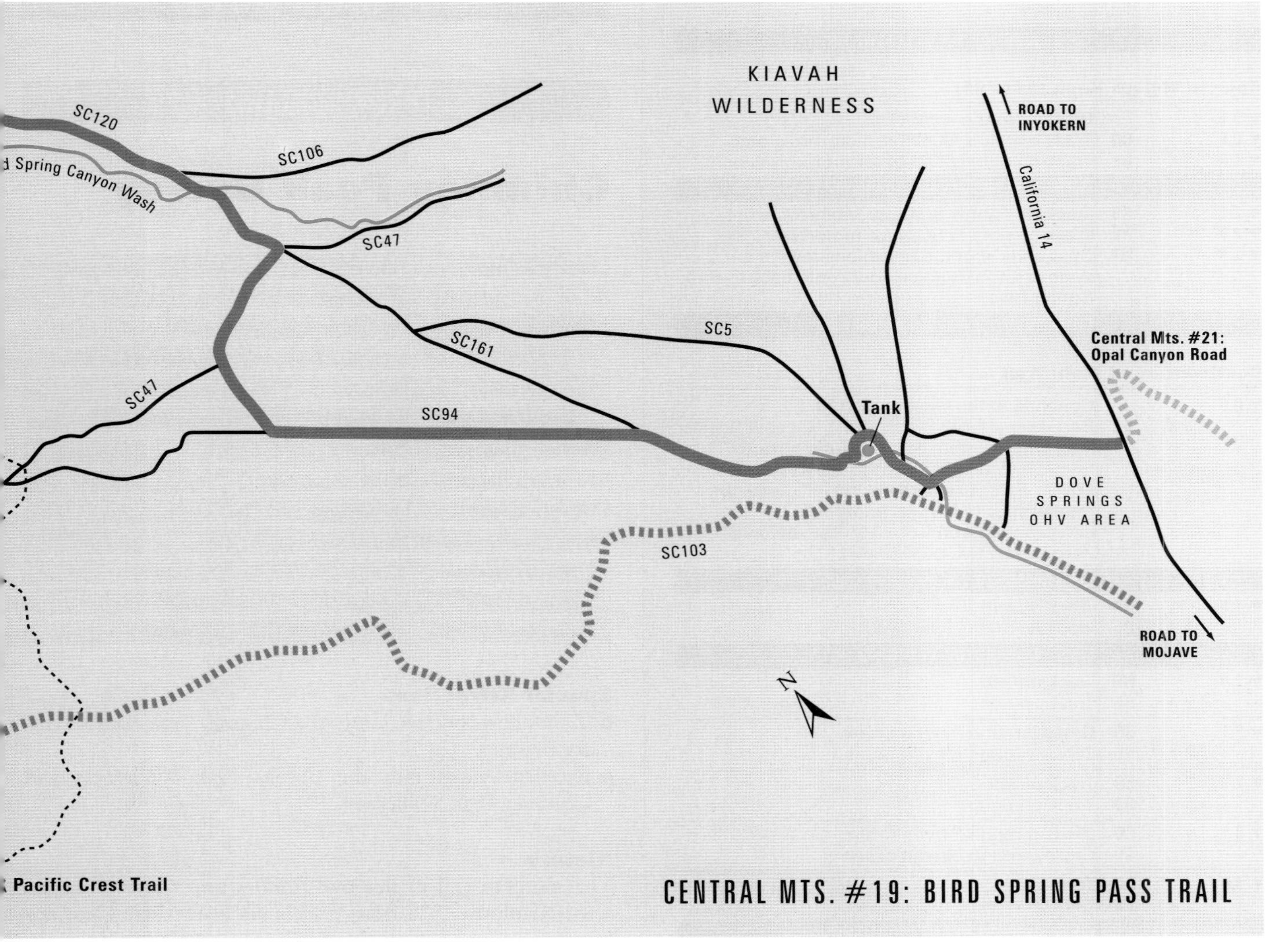

CENTRAL MTS. #19: BIRD SPRING PASS TRAIL

▼ 0.1		SO	Track on left.
	5.1 ▲	SO	Track on right.
▼ 0.6		SO	Track on left and track on right.
	4.6 ▲	SO	Track on left and track on right.
▼ 0.8		SO	Track on left.
	4.4 ▲	SO	Track on right.
▼ 0.9		SO	Track on left; then cross through Bird Spring Canyon wash.
	4.3 ▲	SO	Cross through Bird Spring Canyon wash; then track on right.
			GPS: N35°30.90' W118°04.77'
▼ 1.4		SO	Track on right is SC106 for 4WDs, ATVs, and motorbikes.
	3.8 ▲	BR	Track on left is SC106 for 4WDs, ATVs, and motorbikes.
			GPS: N35°31.21' W118°05.00'
▼ 1.6		SO	Track on left.
	3.6 ▲	SO	Track on right.
▼ 3.4		SO	Track on left.
	1.8 ▲	SO	Track on right.
▼ 5.2		BR	Bird Spring Pass. Pacific Crest National Scenic Trail crosses road. To the left it goes to Sequoia National Forest; to the right it goes to Walker Pass. Skinner Peak on right. Track on left is spur to Wyleys Knob (SC0228) for 4WDs and motorbikes only. Remain on SC120. Zero trip meter.
	0.0 ▲		Continue to the east on SC 120.
			GPS: N35°33.18' W118°07.98'

Spur to Wyleys Knob (SC0228)

▼ 0.0		Proceed to the southwest.
▼ 0.8	SO	Track on left is SC42 for motorbikes only.
▼ 1.8	BL	Track on right is SC124 for motorbikes only.
		GPS: N35°32.35' W118°09.03'
▼ 2.0	SO	Track on right is SC48 for motorbikes only.
▼ 2.7	BL	Track on right is SC34 for motorbikes only.
▼ 2.9	UT	Spur ends at communications towers on Wyleys Knob. Retrace your route back to Bird Spring Pass.
		GPS: N35°32.15' W118°08.38'

Continuation of Main Trail

▼ 0.0			Continue to the west on SC120.
	5.3 ▲	SO	Bird Spring Pass. Pacific Crest National Scenic Trail crosses road. To the right it goes to Sequoia National Forest; to the left it goes to Walker Pass. Skinner Peak on left. Track on right is spur to Wyleys Knob (SC0228) for 4WDs and motorbikes only. Remain on SC120. Zero trip meter.
			GPS: N35°33.18' W118°07.98'
▼ 1.0		BR	Track on left.
	4.3 ▲	BL	Track on right.
			GPS: N35°33.30' W118°08.36'
▼ 1.4		BR	Track on left.
	3.9 ▲	BL	Track on right.
▼ 2.1		SO	Cross through Pinyon Creek.
	3.2 ▲	SO	Cross through Pinyon Creek.
▼ 2.9		SO	Track on left.
	2.4 ▲	SO	Track on right.
▼ 3.1		SO	Cross through Pinyon Creek.
	2.2 ▲	SO	Cross through Pinyon Creek.
▼ 3.8		SO	Tank on left.
	1.5 ▲	SO	Tank on right.
			GPS: N35°33.58' W118°10.90'
▼ 4.1		SO	Track on left.
	1.2 ▲	SO	Track on right.
▼ 4.3		SO	Track on left.
	1.0 ▲	BL	Track on right.
			GPS: N35°33.46' W118°11.50'
▼ 4.5		SO	Two tracks on right.
	0.8 ▲	SO	Two tracks on left.
▼ 4.7		SO	Track on right.
	0.6 ▲	SO	Track on left.
▼ 4.8		SO	Track on left.
	0.5 ▲	SO	Track on right.
▼ 5.0		SO	Track on left is SC36 for 4WDs, ATVs, and motorbikes.
	0.3 ▲	SO	Track on right is SC36 for 4WDs, ATVs, and motorbikes.
			GPS: N35°33.12' W118°12.04'
▼ 5.3			Trail ends at T-intersection with paved Kelso Valley Road. Turn right for Weldon and California 178; turn left for Central Mountains #16: Piute Mountain Road.
	0.0 ▲		Trail commences on Kelso Valley Road, 10.7 miles south of California 178. Zero trip meter and turn east on well-used formed trail at sign for Bird Spring Pass. The Jawbone-Butterbredt Area of Critical Environmental Concern is on south side of road.
			GPS: N35°32.97' W118°12.39'

CENTRAL MOUNTAINS #20

Chimney Peak Byway

Starting Point:	**Kennedy Meadows Road, 11 miles west of US 395**
Finishing Point:	**California 178, 2 miles east of the South Fork Fire Station, 7.8 miles east of Onyx**
Total Mileage:	**14 miles**
Unpaved Mileage:	**14 miles**
Driving Time:	**1 hour**
Elevation Range:	**3,300–6,600 feet**
Usually Open:	**Year-round**
Best Time to Travel:	**Year-round**
Difficulty Rating:	**1**
Scenic Rating:	**8**
Remoteness Rating:	**+0**

Special Attractions

- Trail follows one section of the Chimney Peak Back Country Byway.
- Excellent views into the Owens Peak Wilderness and Chimney Peak Wilderness.

History

The southern end of this trail finishes near Canebrake, just across California 178 from Canebrake Flat, where Chimney Creek flows into Canebrake Creek. This was a popular gathering place for the local Tubatulabal Indians. The spot had remained unknown to settlers until Captain Joseph Reddeford Walker traveled through the region in 1834. He was responsible for finding a reliable route across the Sierra Nevada through what is now called Walker Pass. Today, California 178 traces Walker's route through the mountains.

The name Canebrake Creek is attributed to Lieutenant Robert S. Williamson, who passed by here in 1853 while surveying a potential railroad route through the Sierra Nevada. Williamson witnessed the Indians gathering the cane-like bulrush in the creek bed and learned that they referred to the creek in their native tongue as Chay-o-poo-yapah, which he understood to mean a creek of bulrushes. The route through Canebrake Creek Valley and Walker Pass was to become an important commercial route for early ox teams heading east to supply the developing mines on the eastern side of the Sierra Nevada. By the 1860s miners and ranchers were finding the South Fork Valley (located west of Walker Pass along present-day California 178) to be a suitable place to settle. In the 1870s, stagecoaches were kicking up dust as they crossed the dry Canebrake Flat at the start of the climb to Walker Pass.

In 1910, Billy and Ava James developed a stage station nearby and grew vegetables, which they sold to miners in Randsburg and other communities east of the Sierra Nevada.

A Tubatulabal Indian named Quigam, who as a child had witnessed Captain Walker passing through the region in 1834, remained in the area as an adult. He lived in the tribe's Canebrake tribal rancheria with his wife and family. One of their children was swept away in a flashflood in Canebrake Creek shortly after the turn of the twentieth century. Quigam died when their shanty home accidentally burned down a number of years later. Reminders of the Tubatulabal people and their long residence here linger on in the form of grinding circles worn into the rocks near the creek. The area was also a traditional gathering place for harvesting pinyon nuts and was later used for mining, cattle grazing, and barite mining.

The green around Canebrake Creek makes it hard to imagine the fires that recently ravaged the upper reaches of this trail

Description

This trail forms part of the designated Chimney Peak Back Country Byway. The graded dirt road travels through a wide variety of scenery between Chimney Peak Wilderness and Owens Peak Wilderness. Although the road is often washboardy, it is generally suitable for a passenger vehicle in dry weather.

Chimney Peak Byway winds through a green valley below Lamont Peak

The trail passes by the popular Chimney Creek BLM Campground. It enters Lamont Meadow and travels briefly alongside Chimney Creek, before climbing to Lamont Saddle where the Pacific Crest National Scenic Trail crosses again. The trail then descends a series of switchbacks to finish on California 178.

The route described is not the complete byway. A major loop, which travels past Chimney Peak itself, is not included but is well worth visiting. The trail is normally open year-round, but sections may become impassable in the winter and early spring.

Current Road Information

BLM Ridgecrest Field Office
300 S. Richmond Road
Ridgecrest, CA 93555
(760) 384-5400

Map References

BLM Isabella Lake
USFS Sequoia National Forest
USGS 1:24,000 Lamont Peak
1:100,000 Isabella Lake
Maptech CD-ROM: Barstow/San Bernardino County
Southern & Central California Atlas & Gazetteer, p. 51
California Road & Recreation Atlas, p. 94

Route Directions

▼ 0.0		From Kennedy Meadows Road, 11 miles west of intersection with US 395, zero trip meter and turn south onto graded gravel Chimney Peak Back Country Byway. Intersection is sign-posted and is immediately north of the Chimney Peak Work Center and Fire Station.
3.6 ▲		Trail ends on Kennedy Meadows Road. Turn right to exit to US 395; turn left to travel to Kennedy Meadows.
		GPS: N35°52.16' W118°00.74'
▼ 0.2	SO	Track on left.
3.4 ▲	SO	Track on right.
▼ 1.6	SO	Two tracks on right into weather site.
2.0 ▲	SO	Two tracks on left into weather site.
		GPS: N35°51.04' W118°01.55'

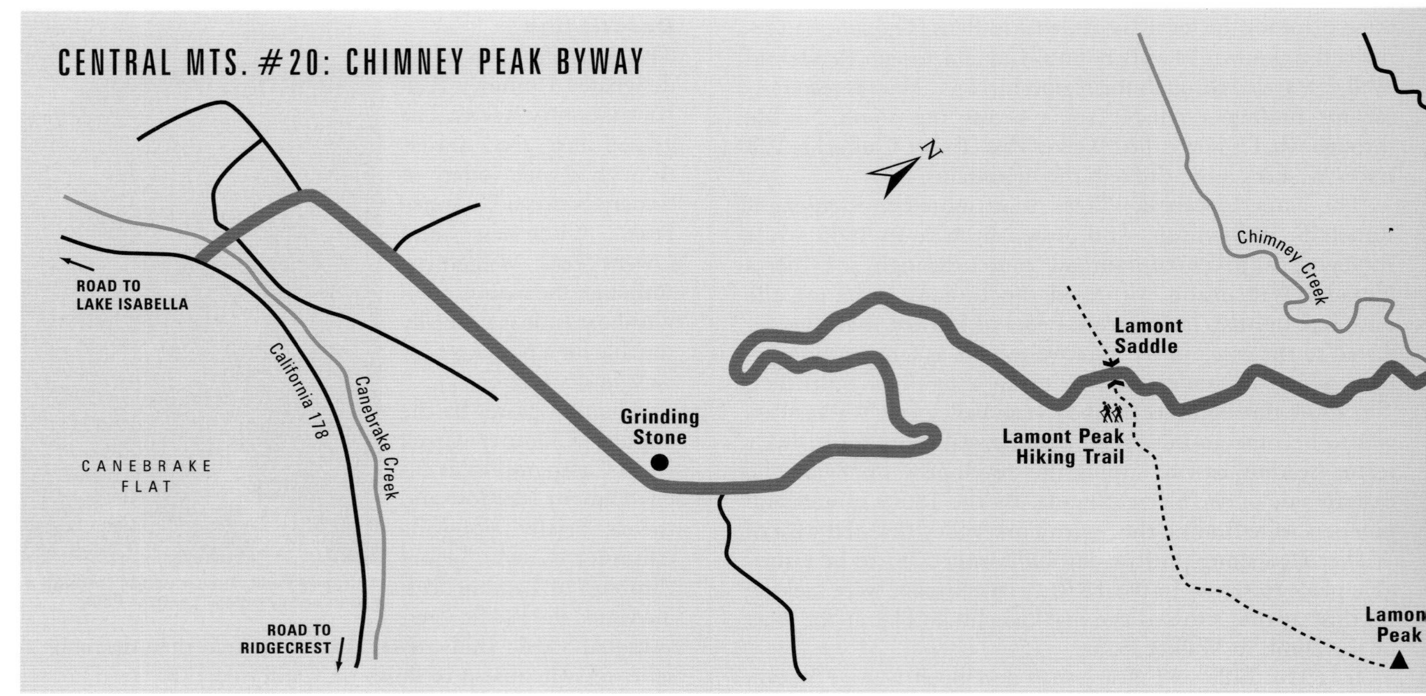

▼ 3.6		SO	Chimney Creek Campground on left of trail. Zero trip meter.
	0.0 ▲		Continue to the west.
			GPS: N35°50.34′ W118°02.53′
▼ 0.0			Continue to the east.
	1.8 ▲	SO	Chimney Creek Campground on right of trail. Zero trip meter.
▼ 0.3		SO	Pacific Crest National Scenic Trail crosses road.
	1.5 ▲	SO	Pacific Crest National Scenic Trail crosses road.
			GPS: N35°50.15′ W118°02.59′
▼ 1.8		SO	Graded road on right is the end of Chimney Peak Byway loop to Rock House Basin Trail. This is Lamont Meadow. Lamont Peak on left. Zero trip meter.
	0.0 ▲		Continue to the north, following sign to Kennedy Meadows.

Chimney Peak Byway landscape

			GPS: N35°48.89′ W118°03.18′
▼ 0.0			Continue to the south, following sign to Highway 178.
	2.4 ▲	SO	Graded road on left is the start of Chimney Peak Byway loop to Rock House Basin Trail. Lamont Peak on right. Zero trip meter.
▼ 0.1		SO	Track on left.
	2.3 ▲	SO	Track on right.
▼ 0.8		SO	Cross over Chimney Creek.
	1.6 ▲	SO	Cross over Chimney Creek. This is Lamont Meadow.
▼ 2.4		SO	Lamont Saddle. Lamont Peak Hiking Trail leads off on left and right. Zero trip meter at sign.
	0.0 ▲		Continue to the north.
			GPS: N35°47.27′ W118°04.27′
▼ 0.0			Continue to the south.
	6.2 ▲	SO	Lamont Saddle. Lamont Peak Hiking Trail leads off on left and right. Zero trip meter at sign.
▼ 2.9		SO	Track on left.
	3.3 ▲	SO	Track on right.
			GPS N35°46.66′ W118°04.41′
▼ 3.2		SO	Turnout on right.
	3.0 ▲	SO	Turnout on left.
▼ 3.7		SO	Cattle guard; then track on left.
	2.5 ▲	SO	Track on right; then cattle guard.
▼ 4.0		SO	Turnout on right is the site of an Indian grinding stone.
	2.2 ▲	SO	Turnout on left is the site of an Indian grinding stone.
			GPS: N35°45.79′ W118°04.86′
▼ 5.7		SO	Track on right.
	0.5 ▲	SO	Track on left.
▼ 6.0		SO	BLM information board on left and track on left. Road is now paved.
	0.2 ▲	SO	Road turns to graded dirt. BLM information board on right and track on right.
▼ 6.1		SO	Track on left and track on right; then cross through wash.

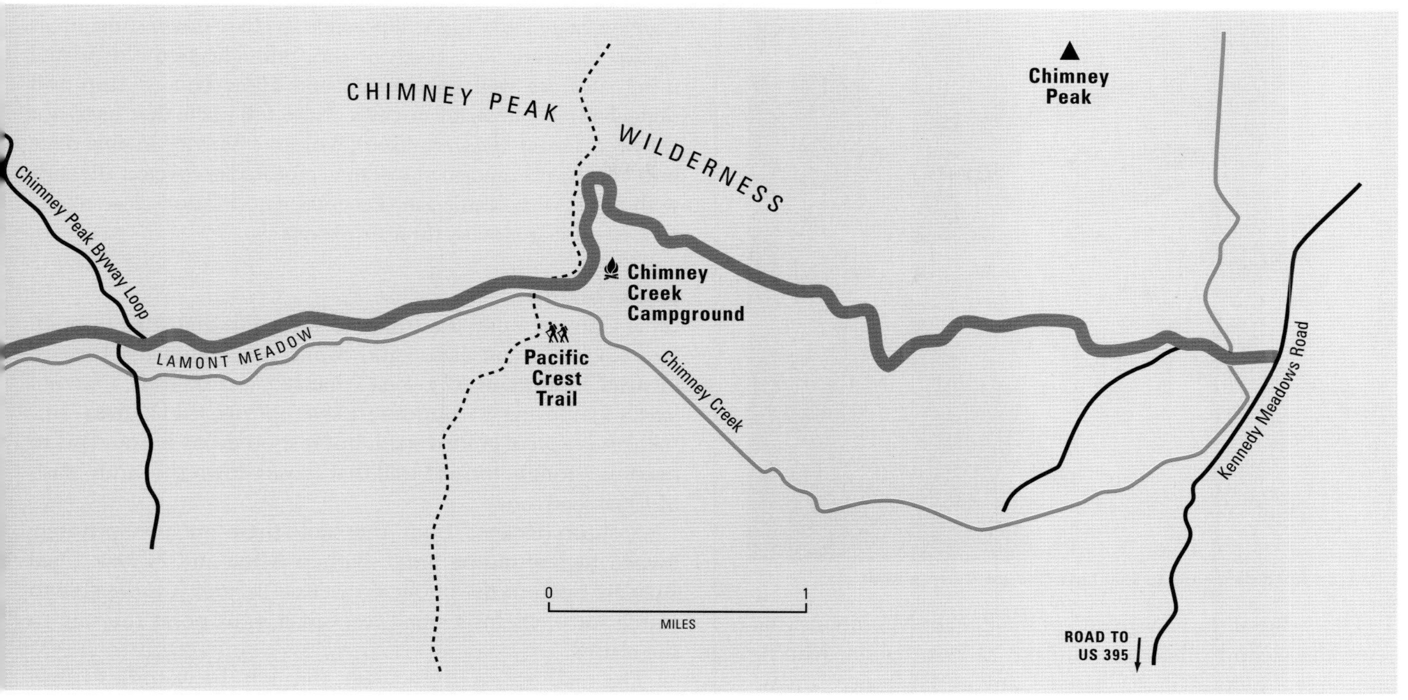

	0.1 ▲	SO	Cross through wash; then track on left and track on right.
▼ 6.2			Trail ends at T-intersection with California 178. Turn left for Ridgecrest; turn right for Lake Isabella.
	0.0 ▲		Trail commences on California 178, 2 miles east of the South Fork Fire Station and 7.8 miles east of Onyx. Zero trip meter and turn north on paved road. Intersection is well marked for Chimney Peak Recreation Area.
			GPS: N35°44.93' W118°06.70'

CENTRAL MOUNTAINS #21

Opal Canyon Road

Starting Point:	**California 14, 7.4 miles north of intersection with Randsburg–Red Rock Road**
Finishing Point:	**Central Mountains #23: Last Chance Canyon Trail at Cudahy Camp, 4.4 miles north of Randsburg–Red Rock Road**
Total Mileage:	**6.3 miles**
Unpaved Mileage:	**6.3 miles**
Driving Time:	**1 hour**
Elevation Range:	**2,700–3,300 feet**
Usually Open:	**Year-round**
Best Time to Travel:	**Year-round**
Difficulty Rating:	**5**
Scenic Rating:	**9**
Remoteness Rating:	**+0**

Special Attractions

- Rough, scenic trail within Red Rock Canyon State Park.
- Can be combined with Central Mountains #23: Last Chance Canyon Trail and other trails in the area for a full day's outing.
- Rockhounding for opals at two sites (fees required).

History

John Goler, one of the forty-niners who struggled out of Death Valley, also lived to tell of the gold he had seen in the El Paso Mountains during his epic trip. After regaining his strength, Goler took a job as a blacksmith in the San Fernando Valley, but he could never forget the memory of gold in the El Paso Mountains. Goler traveled back toward Death Valley time and time again for nearly 20 years, sticking as close as he could remember to his original route. However, he never found the gold he talked of so much. Fellow prospectors finally believed his story when a find in 1893 seemed to match Goler's description. The miners decided to call the location Goler Gulch.

The dry and rugged El Paso Mountains

Opal Canyon Road descends to join Last Chance Canyon Trail

This strike at the eastern end of the El Paso Mountains triggered the second mild rush into the El Paso region. Mining camps sprang up in Last Chance Canyon, Jawbone Canyon, Summit Diggings, and Red Rock Canyon. With little water to work their ores, miners turned to the mushrooming town of Garlock on the south side of the range. The town had an ample water supply and as many as a half dozen mills were operating at its peak in the late 1800s. Up to a thousand men were combing the hills in search of a big strike. As usual, most of the prospectors had little luck and moved on to the next promising sign of fortune.

As the trail's name suggests, opals are plentiful in this region. Though much of the area is off-limits to rock collecting, because of its location within the boundaries of Red Rock Canyon State Park, it is still possible to chase down some opals at two locations just north of the trail. The two old private mine sites are well sign-posted and allow you to chip and sledgehammer away to uncover those fire opals that have not yet been found (fees required). Volcanic activity in this once lush region resulted in flows that repeatedly covered the area with layers of volcanic ash. Petrified wood found close to the trail is associated with these ash layers.

Description

Opal Canyon Road is a small, formed trail that runs through Red Rock Canyon State Park, connecting California 14 with Central Mountains #23: Last Chance Canyon Trail. The trail leaves California 14 opposite Dove Springs OHV Area. Initially, it is a wide graded road, but it soon drops in standard to become a rough, formed trail that travels down the sandy wash of Opal Canyon.

A short distance from the trail, there are two privately owned rockhounding areas. Barnett Mine and Nowak Opal Area are open to the public on weekends, and it is possible to search for opals for a small fee. Small signs point the way to the claims.

The road travels in the wash, through the western El Paso Mountains, before swinging sharply and steeply out of the wash to climb a ridge. This section of the trail is where it earns its difficulty rating of 5. Low-traction, steep climbs, and off-camber side slopes will test the tire tread and wheel articulation of your vehicle. Although the trail is narrow, most vehicles will be able to negotiate this section with care.

There are panoramic views from the ridge top over the Nightmare Gulch Area, the El Paso Mountains, and east to the pink- and rose-colored rocks of Last Chance Canyon.

The trail passes the northern end of Central Mountains #22: Nightmare Gulch Overlook Trail, and drops down to

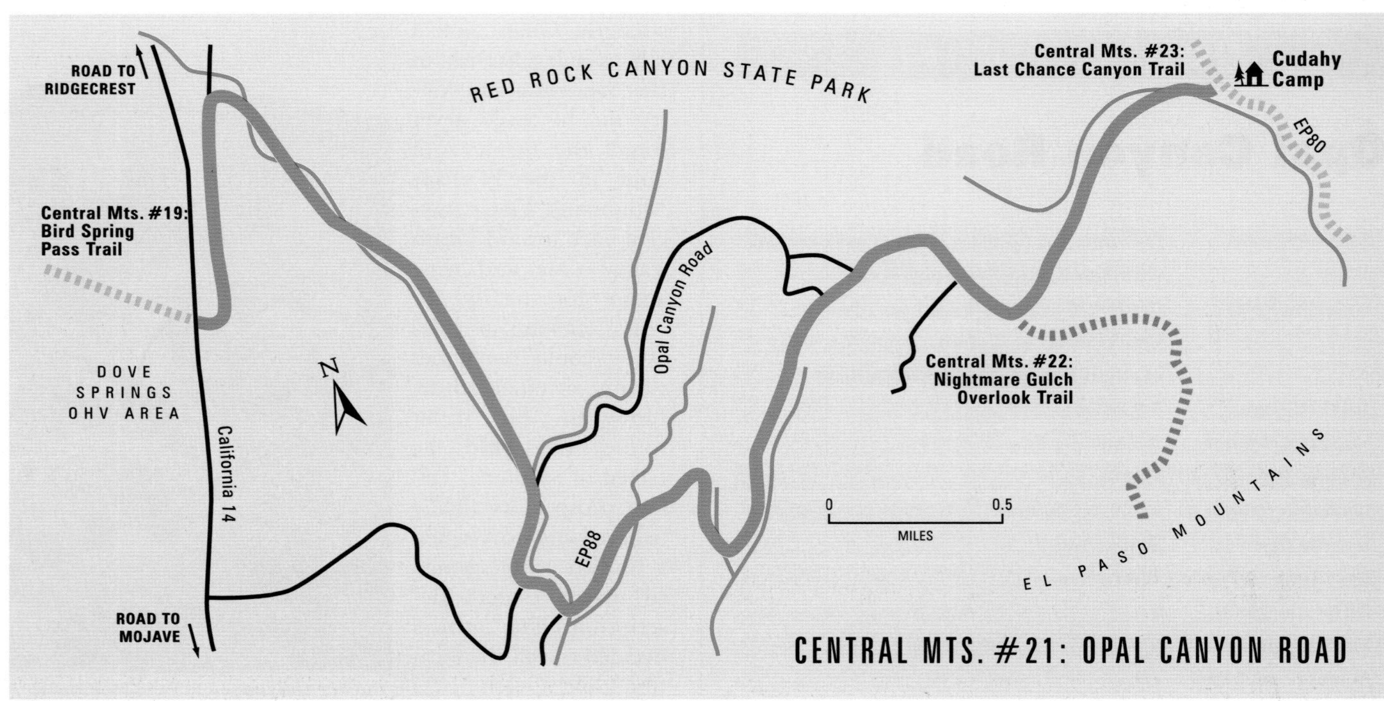

travel along a small wash to Cudahy Camp, located along Last Chance Canyon Trail. The final steep pinch to join this trail can have deep holes and the sandy soil offers little traction. However most high-clearance 4WD vehicles with good tires will manage the ascent.

Current Road Information

BLM Ridgecrest Field Office
300 S. Richmond Road
Ridgecrest, CA 93555
(760) 384-5400

Map References

BLM Cuddeback Lake
USGS 1:24,000 Saltdale NW
1:100,000 Cuddeback Lake
Maptech CD-ROM: Barstow/San Bernardino County
Southern & Central California Atlas & Gazetteer, p. 65
California Road & Recreation Atlas, p. 94
Other: East Kern County OHV Riding Area and Trails—Jawbone Canyon

Route Directions

Mileage		Directions
▼ 0.0		At mile marker 44 on California 14, 7.4 miles north of intersection with Randsburg–Red Rock Road, zero trip meter and turn east onto graded dirt road over cattle guard. The entrance to Dove Springs OHV Area and Central Mountains #19: Bird Spring Pass Trail is opposite. Road immediately swings north, following alongside the highway.
2.7 ▲		Trail ends on California 14, opposite the entrance to Dove Springs OHV Area and Central Mountains #19: Bird Spring Pass Trail. Turn left for Randsburg and Mojave; turn right for Ridgecrest.
		GPS: N35°24.83' W117°58.77'
▼ 0.5	SO	Enter Red Rock Canyon State Park at sign.
2.2 ▲	SO	Exit Red Rock Canyon State Park at sign.
▼ 0.7	BR	Track on left.
2.0 ▲	BL	Track on right.
		GPS: N35°25.37' W117°58.55'
▼ 0.9	SO	Cross through wash.
1.8 ▲	SO	Cross through wash.
▼ 1.0	SO	Cross through wash.
1.7 ▲	SO	Cross through wash.
▼ 1.3	SO	Enter wash.
1.4 ▲	SO	Exit wash.
▼ 2.1	SO	Well-used track on left up side wash is Opal Canyon Road, which goes to Barnett Opal Mine (privately owned, fee required).
0.6 ▲	BL	Well-used track on right up side wash is Opal Canyon Road, which goes to Barnett Opal Mine (privately owned, fee required).
		GPS: N35°24.20' W117°57.93'
▼ 2.5	BL	Track on right. Bear left and join unmarked EP88, remaining in wash.
0.2 ▲	BR	Track on left. Bear right, remaining in wash.
		GPS: N35°23.92' W117°58.08'
▼ 2.7	TL	Turn left and climb steeply out of wash. Track continues ahead in wash. Zero trip meter.
0.0 ▲		Continue to the north.
		GPS: N35°23.84' W117°57.97'
▼ 0.0		Continue to the southeast.
2.5 ▲	TR	Descend and turn right up wash. Track on left down wash. Zero trip meter.
▼ 0.2	SO	Enter wash.
2.3 ▲	SO	Exit wash.
▼ 0.4	SO	Exit wash up ridge to the right.
2.1 ▲	SO	Enter wash.
		GPS: N35°24.01' W117°57.68'
▼ 0.7	BR	Small track on left.
1.8 ▲	BL	Small track on right.
▼ 0.8	SO	Cross through wash.
1.7 ▲	SO	Cross through wash.
▼ 1.1	SO	Enter wash.
1.4 ▲	SO	Exit wash.
▼ 1.2	SO	Exit wash to the left.
1.3 ▲	SO	Enter wash.
▼ 1.3	SO	Enter wash.
1.2 ▲	SO	Exit wash to the right.
▼ 1.6	SO	Exit wash.
0.9 ▲	SO	Enter wash.
▼ 1.8	SO	Two tracks on left join main Opal Canyon Road.
0.7 ▲	SO	Two tracks on right join main Opal Canyon Road.
▼ 1.9	SO	Opal Canyon Road on left. Track on right on saddle goes 0.1 miles to viewpoint.
0.6 ▲	SO	Track on left on saddle goes 0.1 miles to viewpoint. Opal Canyon Road on right.
		GPS: N35°24.46' W117°56.83'
▼ 2.3	SO	Track on left goes to mine; then track on right.
0.2 ▲	SO	Track on left; then track on right goes to mine.
		GPS: N35°24.36' W117°56.51'
▼ 2.5	TL	Small track on right; then turn left on well-used trail descending to the northeast. Track ahead is Central Mountains #22: Nightmare Gulch Overlook Trail. Zero trip meter.
0.0 ▲		Continue to the northwest.
		GPS: N35°24.23' W117°56.39'
▼ 0.0		Continue to the northeast.
1.1 ▲	TR	T-intersection. Central Mountains #22: Nightmare Gulch Overlook Trail on left; then small track on left. Zero trip meter.
▼ 0.2	SO	Enter line of wash.
0.9 ▲	SO	Exit wash.
▼ 0.6	SO	Track on right.
0.5 ▲	SO	Track on left.
▼ 1.0	SO	Exit line of wash; then track on left by old water tank joins Central Mountains #23: Last Chance Canyon Trail. Track on right.
0.1 ▲	SO	Track on left. Track on right by old water tank joins Central Mountains #23: Last Chance Canyon Trail; then enter line of wash.
▼ 1.1		Cross through Last Chance Canyon Wash; then trail ends at T-intersection with Central Mountains #23: Last Chance Canyon Trail at Cudahy Camp. Turn right to exit via Last Chance Canyon Trail to Randsburg–Red Rock Road; turn left to continue along Last Chance Canyon Trail to either Central Mountains #24: Burro Schmidt Tunnel Trail or Central Mountains #25: Sheep Spring Trail.
0.0 ▲		Trail commences on Central Mountains #23: Last Chance Canyon Trail at Cudahy Camp, 4.4 miles north of Randsburg–Red Rock Road. Zero trip meter and turn southwest on unmarked trail that immediately dips down to cross through Last Chance Canyon Wash.
		GPS: N35°24.66' W117°55.55'

Nightmare Gulch Overlook Trail

Starting Point:	**Central Mountains #21: Opal Canyon Road, 1.1 miles from Cudahy Camp**
Finishing Point:	**Randsburg–Red Rock Road, 4.5 miles northeast of California 14**
Total Mileage:	**5 miles, plus 1.1-mile spur**
Unpaved Mileage:	**7.2 miles**
Driving Time:	**1 hour**
Elevation Range:	**1,900–3,400 feet**
Usually Open:	**Year-round**
Best Time to Travel:	**Year-round**
Difficulty Rating:	**4**
Scenic Rating:	**8**
Remoteness Rating:	**+0**

Special Attractions

- Access to the difficult canyon trail along Nightmare Gulch.
- Panoramic ridge top views.
- Scenic, small trail within Red Rock Canyon State Park.

History

Nightmare Gulch Overlook Trail offers a unique insight into the region's ancient landscape. The area, once full of lush vegetation, displays signs of high erosion. Early Native Americans may have camped by lakeshores in the vicinity prior to evolving climatic changes. Local volcanic activity resulted in heavy layers of ash that settled throughout the surrounding region. Nearby pumice mines such as the Holly Ash Cleanser Mine and Dutch Cleanser Mine, active from early last century, were dug deep into these fine white, chalk-like layers to produce the finest abrasive cleansing agents. Petrified wood, a result of such volcanic activity, can still be seen in the region. Early miners in the El Paso Mountains discovered petrified forests, and carted pieces off for collectors. Today, there are only sparse reminders of these once lush forests, and the remnants are just for looking and admiring. No rock collection of any sort is permitted within Red Rock Canyon State Park.

The slightly off-camber trail runs high above Nightmare Gulch

Description

Nightmare Gulch is a small, highly scenic canyon in Red Rock Canyon State Park. The area attracts many raptors, which can often be seen riding the thermals above the canyons and mountains. A difficult 4WD trail leads down into Nightmare Gulch. However, to protect raptor nesting sites, the gulch is closed to vehicle travel for the first 15 days of each month. Please respect this closure to ensure that the trail remains open to vehicles on its current basis.

Tumbleweed gathers at the old talc mine above Nightmare Gulch

The trail travels around the ridge tops between Nightmare Gulch and Last Chance Canyon, offering panoramic views of both. Some of the climbs are steep and eroded, and there are several sections that are off-camber, tilting a vehicle toward the drop. The trail descends from the first ridge to pass alongside the extensive workings of an old mine. Many trails leave in all directions here, and the route makes a sharp turn to climb a rough, uneven trail to the top of the ridge. Once on the ridge there are 360-degree views: To the east is Last Chance Canyon and the Rand Mountains, to the west is Nightmare Gulch and the Piute Mountains, to the north are the Scodie Mountains, and to the south is the Fremont Valley.

The trail descends the ridge again to rejoin the track it left a short distance south of the mine. Those not wanting to take the ridge top route can remain on the main trail through the mining area.

A spur leads off from this point and climbs to another panoramic viewpoint that looks south over the canyons to Koehn Lake. The difficult trail into Nightmare Gulch leaves through the mining area a short distance to the north.

From here, the trail follows a roughly graded road down to the canyon to exit to Randsburg–Red Rock Road.

Current Road Information

BLM Ridgecrest Field Office
300 S. Richmond Road
Ridgecrest, CA 93555
(760) 384-5400

Map References
BLM Cuddeback Lake
USGS 1:24,000 Saltdale NW, Cantil
1:100,000 Cuddeback Lake
Maptech CD-ROM: Barstow/San Bernardino County
Southern & Central California Atlas & Gazetteer, p. 65
California Road & Recreation Atlas, p. 94
Other: East Kern County OHV Riding Area and Trails—Jawbone Canyon

Route Directions

▼ 0.0			From Central Mountains #21: Opal Canyon Road, 1.1 miles from the eastern end at Cudahy Camp (the intersection with Central Mountains #23: Last Chance Canyon Trail), zero trip meter and turn southeast onto unmarked, well-used formed trail; then track on right.
	1.6 ▲		Track on left; then trail ends at intersection with Central Mountains #21: Opal Canyon Road. Turn right to exit to Central Mountains #23: Last Chance Canyon Trail; continue straight to exit to California 14.
			GPS: N35°24.23′ W117°56.39′
▼ 0.1		SO	Track on left.
	1.5 ▲	SO	Track on right.
▼ 0.5		BR	Track on left.
	1.1 ▲	BL	Track on right.
▼ 0.7		BR	Track on left.
	0.9 ▲	BL	Track on right.
			GPS: N35°23.89′ W117°55.94′
▼ 0.8		BL	Track on right.
	0.8 ▲	SO	Track on left.
▼ 0.9		SO	Enter wash; track on left.
	0.7 ▲	SO	Track on right; exit wash.
▼ 1.1		SO	Exit wash up ridge to the left.
	0.5 ▲	SO	Drop down to enter wash.
▼ 1.6		TL	Track on right toward mine. Large adit is visible directly ahead; then turn sharp left up unmarked, rough uneven trail and zero trip meter. Track straight ahead rejoins main trail in a short distance. Track ahead also passes the start of limited-access Nightmare Gulch Trail.
	0.0 ▲		Continue to the northwest past track on left toward mine.
			GPS: N35°23.30′ W117°56.23′
▼ 0.0			Continue to the north.
	0.9 ▲	TR	Turn sharp right onto well-used trail and zero trip meter. Large adit is visible ahead. Track straight ahead rejoins main trail (in opposite direction) in a short distance.
▼ 0.2		SO	Two tracks on left and two tracks on right.
	0.7 ▲	SO	Two tracks on left and two tracks on right.
▼ 0.4		TR	T-intersection. Turn right along ridge.
	0.5 ▲	TL	Turn left and descend from ridge. Track continues straight ahead.
			GPS: N35°23.25′ W117°56.02′
▼ 0.5		SO	Track on left.
	0.4 ▲	SO	Track on right.
▼ 0.9		TL	5-way intersection. Track straight ahead is spur to viewpoint. Turn first left and zero trip meter. First track on right rejoins main trail (in opposite direction) in a short distance. Second track on right is private.
	0.0 ▲		Continue to the northeast.
			GPS: N35°22.92′ W117°56.36′

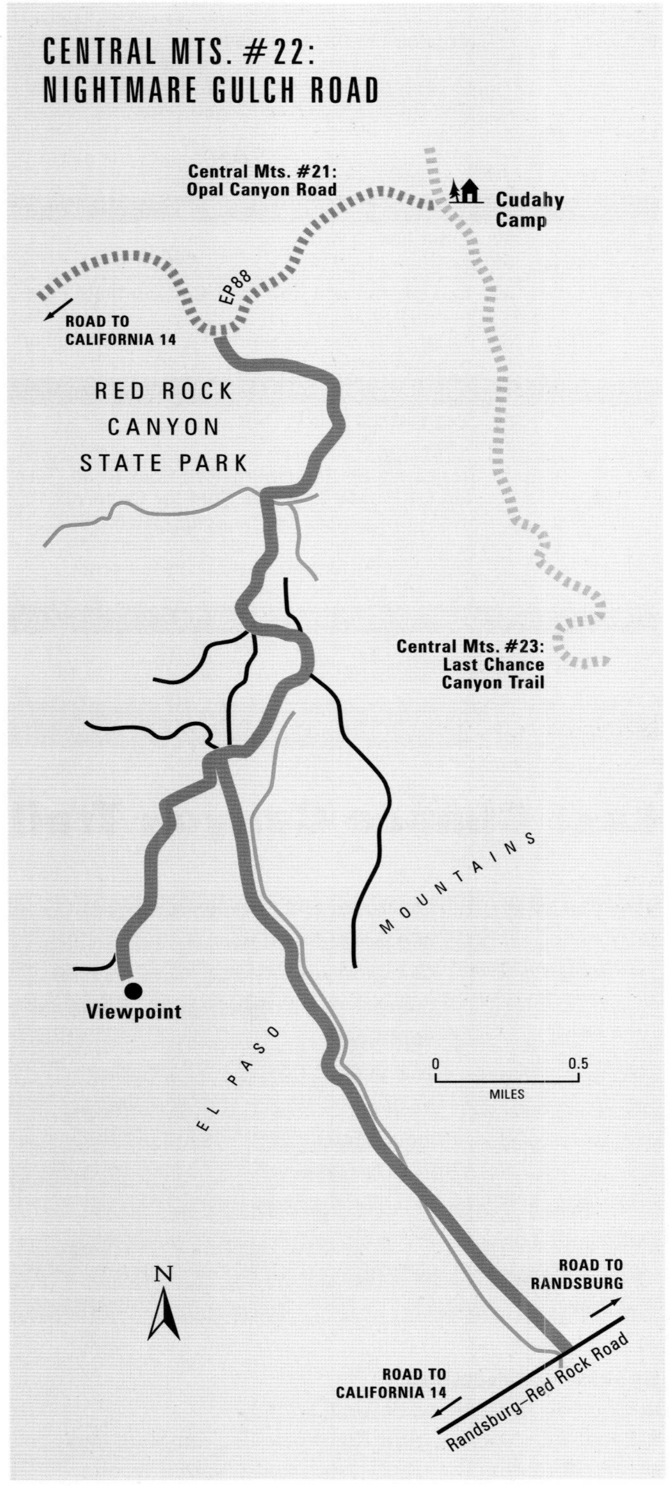

Spur to Viewpoint

▼ 0.0		Proceed to the southwest.
▼ 0.3	BL	Two tracks on right go to private property.
▼ 0.4	BL	Track on right.
▼ 1.0	BL	Track on right.
▼ 1.1	UT	Spur ends at viewpoint. Retrace your steps back to the 5-way intersection.
		GPS: N35°22.23′ W117°56.71′

Continuation of Main Trail

▼ 0.0			Continue to the southeast.
	2.5 ▲	TR	5-way intersection. First track on left is spur to viewpoint. Second track on left is private. Turn first right and start to climb up ridge. Zero trip meter. Track ahead rejoins main trail in a short distance. Track ahead also passes the start of limited-access Nightmare Gulch Trail.
			GPS: N35°22.92' W117°56.36'
▼ 0.1		SO	Enter line of wash.
	2.4 ▲	SO	Exit line of wash.
▼ 1.6		SO	Exit canyon and Red Rock Canyon State Park at small sign.
	0.9 ▲	SO	Enter canyon and Red Rock Canyon State Park at small sign.
			GPS: N35°21.65' W117°55.74'
▼ 1.7		SO	Exit wash.
	0.8 ▲	SO	Enter wash.
▼ 2.5			Trail ends on Randsburg–Red Rock Road. Turn left for Randsburg; turn right for California 14.
	0.0 ▲		Trail commences on Randsburg-Red Rock Road, 4.5 miles northeast of California 14. Zero trip meter and turn northwest onto unmarked formed trail.
			GPS: N35°21.04' W117°55.13'

CENTRAL MOUNTAINS #23

Last Chance Canyon Trail

Starting Point:	Randsburg–Red Rock Road, 6 miles northeast of California 14
Finishing Point:	Central Mountains #24: Burro Schmidt Tunnel Trail, 4.8 miles from the eastern end
Total Mileage:	10.6 miles
Unpaved Mileage:	10.6 miles
Driving Time:	2 hours
Elevation Range:	2,000–3,600 feet
Usually Open:	Year-round
Best Time to Travel:	September to May
Difficulty Rating:	5
Scenic Rating:	10
Remoteness Rating:	+0

Special Attractions

- Open-air museum at Bickel Camp.
- Beautiful scenery within Red Rock Canyon State Park.
- Rockhounding for agate, jasper, and opalized wood.

History

North of Cudahy Camp is the Old Dutch Cleanser Mine. The pumice found here is a result of ongoing volcanic activity in the region. Many layers of fine volcanic ash settled on an area that was once lushly vegetated. Early miners removed petrified wood, and only small segments are still visible today. These pieces are not for collecting anymore, just admiring. A series of tunnels were cut into the white, chalky rock layer through openings in the cliff face. The large tunnels sloped nearly 45 degrees down to a transverse tunnel deep within the volcanic layer. A tramway carried the diggings through the main tunnel and down the cliff face into Last Chance Canyon. Mining trucks then transported the diggings all the way down Last Chance Canyon. Some sections of the old road that have endured decades of erosion are still visible in the canyon.

Red rocks and an undulating trail make for an interesting ride

In the early 1900s, storekeepers across the country proudly hung metal "Old Dutch Cleanser" signs above their doors. The same signs are now prized antiques. Dutch Cleanser as a brand name is still popular as a fine polishing and cleansing agent. It has a multitude of uses, including the meticulous preparation of fish for *gyotaku,* the oriental art of fish printing.

The name Last Chance is generally associated with explorers and prospectors who found water at the brink of death by dehydration. In some prospectors' cases, it also referred to finding worthwhile ore deposits during their last search of a region. In this instance, Last Chance Canyon also may have reflected how hard it was for prospectors to find anything worth mining. Near the northern end of the canyon lies what was called Grubstake Hill. Prospectors who had spent all their time and money searching the El Paso Mountains and had run dry in all respects would turn to Grubstake Hill. The locality was known to contain gold, but the ore was so hard to extract that prospectors turned to it only as a last resort. It was their last chance to buy the new supplies it would take to move on to more promising areas.

Description

Last Chance Canyon is a beautiful, remote canyon within Red Rock Canyon State Park that combines breathtaking scenery, historical interest, and an exciting drive.

The trail leaves Randsburg–Red Rock Road opposite the dry Koehn Lake and the site of Saltdale. The trail is a clearly defined, formed road as it climbs up the bajada, providing views back over Koehn Lake and the Fremont Valley, before it drops down to enter the wash in Last Chance Canyon. It follows in or alongside the wash for the next few miles. For the most part, the trail is well formed and remains out of the wash itself. Some sections offer the choice of traveling in the sandy wash or along the formed trail. The sand in the wash is deep and loose; some will slow down a vehicle. The sand is interspersed with rocky sections that will require careful wheel placement to avoid underbody damage. However, the most challenging rocky section can be avoided by remaining on the formed trail.

All that remains of Cudahy Camp are concrete and stone foundations scattered around an open area. Central Mountains #21: Opal Canyon Road leaves the old mining camp to the west, heading toward California 14. A short distance farther, the adits of the Dutch Cleanser Mine can be seen high on the cliffs to the northwest. This mine can be reached via a network of small trails on the west side of the cliffs.

North of Cudahy Camp, the trail leaves the wash, where work is under way to re-vegetate the area. Be sure to remain on the correct trail to avoid damage to the wash area. This is one of the most scenic parts of the canyon, with pink- and rose-colored canyon walls and sculpted rock formations. Rock hounds can search the side washes in the area, where it is possible to find samples of agate, jasper, and petrified wood. However, collecting is prohibited in Red Rock Canyon State Park, and any specimens should be admired and left in place.

leathered sign guides the way to chmidt Tunnel

The trail leaves the wash area and heads up a short, steep low-traction climb. This stretch is the part that earns the trail its 5-rating for difficulty. The remainder of the trail is rated up to a 4 for difficulty. Farther north, the standard becomes easier and smoother as you approach Bickel Camp.

Walt Bickel donated the open-air museum at Bickel Camp to the BLM upon his death in 1995. Walt used to prospect in the region, and he lived in the cabin, which was built in 1937. The cabin and mining memorabilia are open for people to enjoy. There is a caretaker on site.

North of Bickel Camp, the trail becomes smooth and well-used as it loops around to finish near the eastern end of Central Mountains #24: Burro Schmidt Tunnel Trail. You have the choice there of exiting a short distance to the south to the paved Randsburg–Red Rock Road, or meeting up with Central Mountains #25: Sheep Spring Trail and heading north to exit near Ridgecrest.

Walt Bickel's Camp, now an open-air museum

Current Road Information

BLM Ridgecrest Field Office
300 S. Richmond Road
Ridgecrest, CA 93555
(760) 384-5400

Map References

BLM Cuddeback Lake
USGS 1:24,000 Cantil, Saltdale NW, Garlock
1:100,000 Cuddeback Lake
Maptech CD-ROM: Barstow/San Bernardino County
Southern & Central California Atlas & Gazetteer, pp. 65, 66
California Road & Recreation Atlas, p. 94
Other: East Kern County OHV Riding Areas and Trails—Jawbone Canyon

Route Directions

▼ 0.0		From paved Randsburg–Red Rock Road, 6 miles northeast of California 14 and 0.3 miles southwest of small signed Saltdale Road, zero trip meter and turn northwest onto well-used, formed Last Chance Canyon Road (EP80). Road is marked by a Red Rock Canyon State Park OHV sign.
4.4 ▲		Trail ends at T-intersection with paved Randsburg–Red Rock Road, opposite the dry Koehn Lake. Turn left for Randsburg; turn right for California 14 and Mojave.
		GPS: N35°21.70' W117°53.86'
▼ 0.8	SO	Track on right up ridge.
3.6 ▲	SO	Track on left up ridge.
▼ 0.9	SO	Cross through wash.
3.5 ▲	SO	Cross through wash.
▼ 1.0	SO	Enter Last Chance Canyon wash.
3.4 ▲	SO	Exit Last Chance Canyon wash.
▼ 2.0	SO	Start of rocky sections in canyon wash.
2.4 ▲	SO	End of rocky sections.
▼ 2.4	SO	Track on right.
2.0 ▲	SO	Track on left.
		GPS: N35°23.28' W117°55.08'
▼ 2.5	SO	Short, rocky 4-rated section.
1.9 ▲	SO	Short, rocky 4-rated section.

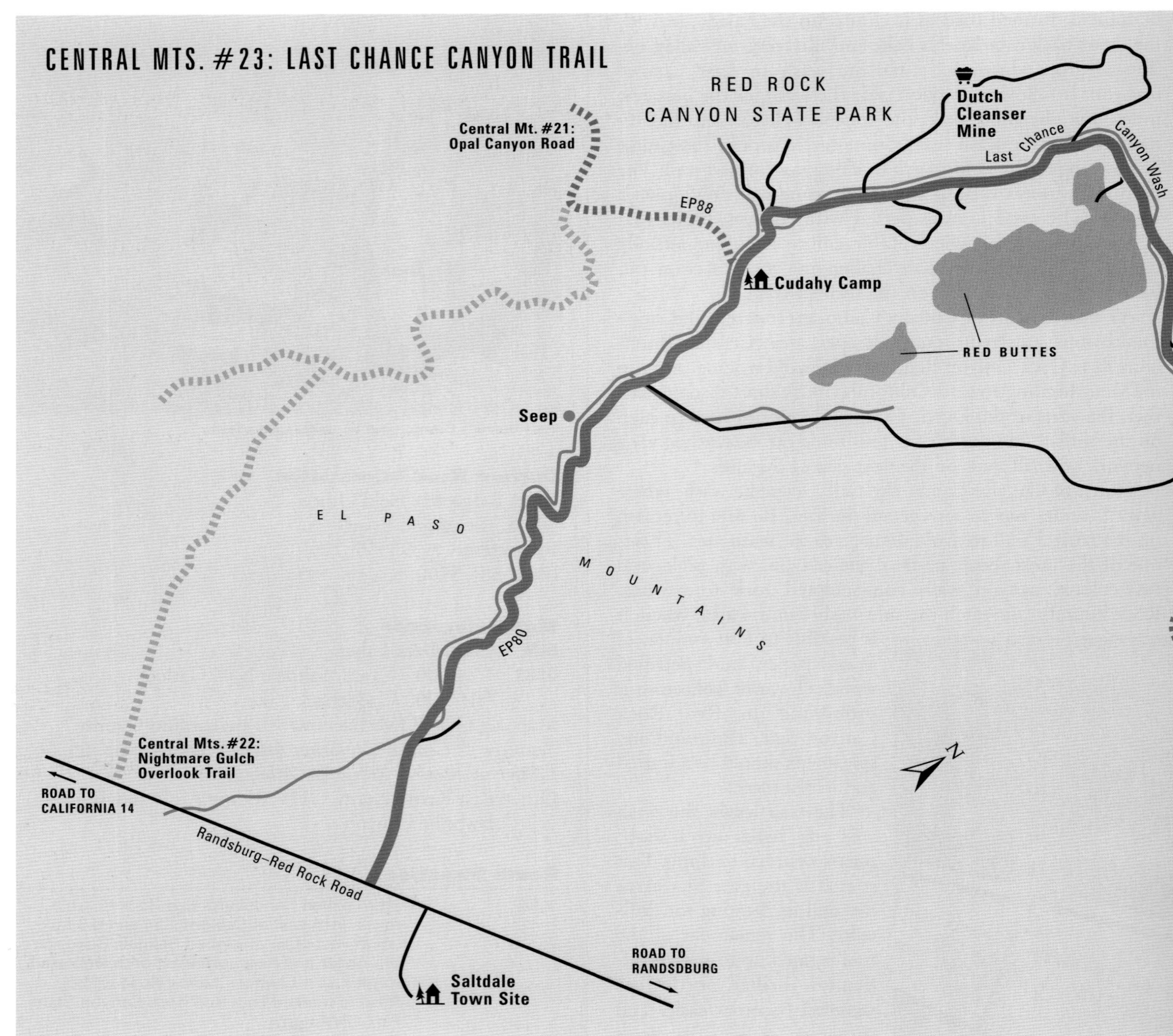

▼ 3.2 SO Seep on right.
1.2 ▲ SO Seep on left.

GPS: N35°23.70′ W117°55.29′

▼ 3.6 SO Well-used track on right travels up side wash, south of Red Buttes.
0.8 ▲ SO Well-used track on left travels up side wash, south of Red Buttes.

GPS: N35°23.98′ W117°55.35′

▼ 4.3 SO Open area is Cudahy Camp. Track is generally less rocky.
0.1 ▲ SO Open area is Cudahy Camp. Track ahead is somewhat more rocky.

GPS: N35°24.60′ W117°55.51′

▼ 4.4 SO Track on right and concrete slab foundations from Cudahy Camp. Then track on left is Central Mountains #21: Opal Canyon Road (EP88). Intersection is unmarked but well used. Zero trip meter.
0.0 ▲ Continue to the southeast.

GPS: N35°24.66′ W117°55.55′

▼ 0.0 Continue to the northwest.
3.2 ▲ SO Track on right is Central Mountains #21: Opal Canyon Road (EP88). Intersection is unmarked but well used. Track on left and concrete slab foundations from Cudahy Camp. Zero trip meter.

▼ 0.2 BL Bear left out of wash up steep, loose pinch. Track on left to mine at top of rise.
3.0 ▲ BR Track on right to mine on top of rise. Descend steep pinch and bear right along Last Chance Canyon wash.

▼ 0.4 SO Cross through side wash; then well-used track on left past tanks. There are three tracks ahead at this point. Take the right-hand track, bearing north, and re-enter wash.
2.8 ▲ SO Exit wash, bearing south, past tracks on right. Well-used track on right past tanks. Continue

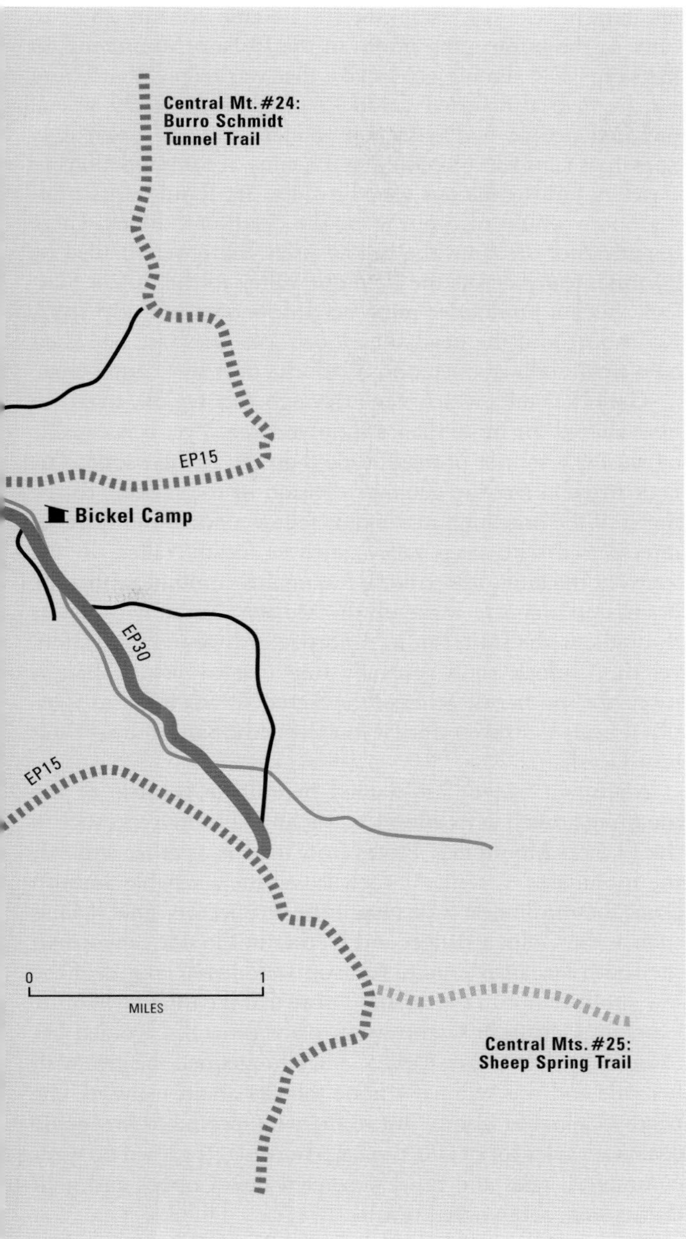

			straight ahead and cross through side wash to climb a small rise on the far side.
			GPS: N35°24.88′ W117°55.66′
▼ 0.9		SO	Track on right goes to mining camp and track on left.
	2.3 ▲	SO	Track on left goes to mining camp and track on right.
▼ 1.0		SO	Track on left.
	2.2 ▲	SO	Track on right.
▼ 1.1		SO	Track on right to private mining camp.
	2.1 ▲	BR	Track on left to private mining camp.
			GPS: N35°25.38′ W117°55.42′
▼ 1.4		SO	Track on right to mine adits.
	1.8 ▲	SO	Track on left to mine adits.
▼ 1.5		SO	Track on right and track on left.
	1.7 ▲	SO	Track on right and track on left.
▼ 1.7		SO	Track on right.
	1.5 ▲	BR	Track on left.
▼ 1.9		SO	Track on left; then trail forks and rejoins in a short distance.
	1.3 ▲	SO	Trail rejoins; track on right.
			GPS: N35°26.03′ W117°55.09′
▼ 2.0		SO	Trail rejoins; then track on left.
	1.2 ▲	SO	Track on right; then trail forks and rejoins in a short distance.
▼ 2.1		SO	Track on left.
	1.1 ▲	SO	Track on right.
			GPS: N35°26.22′ W117°55.07′
▼ 2.6		SO	Track on right.
	0.6 ▲	SO	Track on left.
▼ 2.7		SO	Small track on left.
	0.5 ▲	SO	Small track on right.
▼ 3.2		SO	Two well-used tracks on left. Zero trip meter and continue straight ahead, following wooden sign for Schmidt Tunnel.
	0.0 ▲		Continue to the west.
			GPS: N35°26.22′ W117°54.17′
▼ 0.0			Continue to the east.
	0.8 ▲	SO	Two well-used tracks on right. Zero trip meter and continue straight ahead. There is a small wooden sign for Schmidt Tunnel at the intersection.
▼ 0.4		SO	Small track on right; then well-used track on left. Follow sign for Schmidt Tunnel, leaving the wash.
	0.4 ▲	SO	Well-used track on right; then small track on left. There is a sign for Schmidt Tunnel at the intersection. Enter line of wash.
			GPS: N35°25.99′ W117°53.86′
▼ 0.6		SO	Leaving Red Rock Canyon State Park at sign.
	0.2 ▲	SO	Entering Red Rock Canyon State Park at sign.
			GPS: N35°25.95′ W117°53.68′
▼ 0.7		SO	Enter line of wash.
	0.1 ▲	SO	Exit line of wash.
▼ 0.8		SO	Track on left; then 4-way intersection. Continue straight ahead on well-used trail in wash, following BLM sign for EP30. Track on right and left is Central Mountains #24: Burro Schmidt Tunnel Trail (EP15). Zero trip meter.
	0.0 ▲		Continue to the southwest past track on right.
			GPS: N35°25.99′ W117°53.39′
▼ 0.0			Continue to the northeast on EP30.
	2.2 ▲	SO	4-way intersection. Continue straight ahead on well-used trail marked by a BLM sign designating the trail suitable for 4WDs, ATVs, and motorbikes. Track on left and right is Central Mountains #24: Burro Schmidt Tunnel Trail (EP15). Zero trip meter.
▼ 0.1		SO	Track on left beside mine adits in hillside.
	2.1 ▲	SO	Track on right beside mine adits in hillside.
▼ 0.3		SO	Bickel Camp on left—many old, interesting mining remains. Please do not take anything. Track on right.
	1.9 ▲	SO	Bickel Camp on right—many old, interesting mining remains. Please do not take anything. Track on left.
			GPS: N35°26.14′ W117°53.17′
▼ 0.6		SO	Track on left.
	1.6 ▲	SO	Track on right.
▼ 0.9		SO	Track on left.
	1.3 ▲	SO	Track on right.
			GPS: N35°26.13′ W117°52.57′
▼ 1.4		SO	Track on left.

0.8 ▲	SO	Track on right.
▼ 1.7	SO	Exit line of wash.
0.5 ▲	SO	Enter line of Last Chance Canyon wash.
▼ 2.1	SO	Track on left and track on right.
0.1 ▲	SO	Track on left and track on right.
		GPS: N35°26.14' W117°51.28'
▼ 2.2		Trail ends at intersection with Central Mountains #24: Burro Schmidt Tunnel Trail (EP15). Turn right to continue to Burro Schmidt Tunnel; turn left to exit to Randsburg–Red Rock Road.
0.0 ▲		Trail commences on Central Mountains #24: Burro Schmidt Tunnel Trail, 4.8 miles from intersection with Randsburg–Red Rock Road. Zero trip meter at 4-way intersection and proceed east on small formed trail marked EP30. Burro Schmidt Tunnel Trail continues to the southwest, following EP15. Also small track on left and pull-in on right.
		GPS: N35°26.13' W117°51.20'

CENTRAL MOUNTAINS #24

Burro Schmidt Tunnel Trail

Starting Point:	**California 14, 13.5 miles north of intersection with Randsburg–Red Rock Road**
Finishing Point:	**Randsburg–Red Rock Road at mile marker 11, 1.1 miles west of intersection with Garlock Road**
Total Mileage:	**14.9 miles, plus 0.9-mile spur**
Unpaved Mileage:	**14.9 miles, plus 0.9-mile spur**
Driving Time:	**1.5 hours**
Elevation Range:	**2,100–4,000 feet**
Usually Open:	**Year-round**
Best Time to Travel:	**Year-round**
Difficulty Rating:	**2**
Scenic Rating:	**9**
Remoteness Rating:	**+0**

Special Attractions

- Remains of the Holly Ash Cleanser Mine and Bonanza Gulch post office.
- Trail intersects with other 4WD, ATV, and motorbike trails in the El Paso Mountains.
- Burro Schmidt Tunnel and cabin.

History

Garlock, located near the eastern end of the trail, was formerly known as Cow Wells and it was just that. Early settlers and teamsters used it as a watering hole and staging station for haulage teams headed north to the Panamint Mines on the edge of Death Valley. After the 1893 gold strike at Goler Gulch, Cow Wells flourished because of the availability of water. Eugene Garlock established a 5-stamp mill in 1895 to cater to the burgeoning mines in the El Paso Mountains. In the same year, the big gold strike that was to put Randsburg on the map also fueled Garlock's progress. By 1899 several hundred people had taken up residency in the town now known as Garlock. Hotels offered quality accommodations to travelers and the saloons were bustling. Yet Randsburg's mining boom would turn out to be the death of Garlock. Large quantities of ore from the Yellow Aster Mine were hauled by 20-mule teams across the Fremont Valley to the mill at Garlock. Such a productive mine needed its own mill. By 1897, Randsburg and the newly developed Johannesburg had their own small mills in operation. Garlock's days were numbered.

Garlock Fault, which runs through this region, may not have shifted for more than a thousand years, yet it is capable of causing a tremor of magnitude 8 on the Richter scale. The fault marks a striking geologic division in the region. To the north of the line, high mountains follow a north-south trend, interspersed with deep valleys such as Death Valley. To the south of the fault, less striking mountains combine with wide basins and plains to make up the Mojave Desert. Most faults throughout the state run in a north-northwesterly direction, yet the Garlock Fault generally runs east to west. Where it meets the southern reaches of the Sierra Nevada (close to Cantil), it bears southwest until it intercepts the San Andreas Fault near Gorman.

Mesquite Canyon, so-named by miners because of the mesquite growth at its entrance, was an old Indian entrance to the El Paso Mountains. Prospectors used it to enter and exit the mountains as well. As such it became a reliable ambush point for gunslingers who sought the prospectors' gold. Mines such as the Golden Badger and Decker in the side canyons on the south face of Mesquite Canyon were just a couple of the low-profit claims in the region. Located at the top of Mesquite Canyon, Gerbracht Camp was a place generally avoided because in her later years, Della Gerbracht guarded the area with her rifle and was reputedly none too shy about using it! The nearby Colorado Camp, just to the west, produced low-grade coal that took a lot of effort to keep burning. It gained no great commercial sales and quickly petered out. Copper and gold claims were also worked nearby.

William Henry Schmidt, born in Rhode Island in 1871, moved to California in his early twenties, just before the gold strike in the Rand Mining District. Like several other rookie prospectors enticed by the 1893 Goler gold find, Schmidt established mining claims in the Last Chance Canyon area. As the years passed, Schmidt toiled in the remote location as small finds made him ever hopeful of an eventual "big one." He worked in the Kern River region during the warmer months, saving every penny he could earn as a hired hand. Every winter he took his meager wages and returned to work his own claims.

It occurred to Schmidt that he might need a better transportation route out of the El Paso Mountains if he ever did find a mother lode. He thought to himself, "Why not dig a tunnel through the mountain to the southwest and look for precious metals along the way?" Though seemingly a good idea at the time, no worthwhile seams were revealed in the entire 1,872 feet of the monumental tunnel he finally built. It seems tunnel fever overtook his gold fever. Schmidt, who was of slight build, had moved from back East partially for health reasons. (Several members of his family had died of tuberculosis, and he was advised to move to a better climate.) Yet he managed to dig the tunnel almost entirely by hand. His main tools were a pick, a four-pound hammer, and a hand drill. These were later complemented by occasional use of dynamite, a wheelbarrow, and later still a set of rails and an ore cart.

Over the years, Schmidt was forced to sell off his other claims in order to survive. He led the life of a hermit in his lone cabin and was known as Burro Schmidt to others because his main companions were his burros. Schmidt started his tunnel in 1906 and saw daylight on the south side of Copper Mountain in 1938. Although many people asked him his reasons, he would never say exactly why he kept digging. Schmidt sold his tunnel claim and moved to his other claims in the region. He died in 1954 and was laid to rest in the Joburg Cemetery.

Toward the northeastern end of the trail lies the Holly Ash Cleanser Mine. Discovered in the early 1930s, this large ledge of volcanic ash and white pumice became a direct competitor of the Dutch Cleanser Mine, located just to the south. Their products were used in a variety of items; the finest quality ore went into polishing substances and the coarser forms were used in plaster and agricultural products.

Description

The trail leaves California 14 and bears southwest across the wide Indian Wells Valley. It gradually rises along a steady grade toward the El Paso Mountains. At the base of the mountains are the remains of the old Holly Ash Cleanser Mine. A tank and several mining relics surround huge white caverns hollowed into the cliff.

The trail enters the El Paso Mountains, passing the sturdy wooden building of the Bonanza Gulch post office before descending into Bonanza Canyon. The trail crosses Central Mountains #23: Last Chance Canyon Trail, immediately southwest of Bickel Camp. If you do not intend to travel the full length of Last Chance Canyon Trail, it is worth the short detour to see the cabin and open-air museum at Bickel Camp.

Burro Schmidt's cabin, built in 1902

The main trail continues in the wash to the start of the spur to Burro Schmidt's cabin and tunnel. Pass by the private property and follow signs to the tunnel itself. There are two cabins side by side, the second of which is Burro Schmidt's old one-room house. The cabin still has a stove and the walls and ceiling are lined with old magazine and newspaper pages dating back to the 1920s. Outside there is a spread of old artifacts to admire. Stop here and register; donations are appreciated. An on-site caretaker lives in the first cabin.

Burro Schmidt's hand-dug tunnel took 32 years to complete

The tunnel itself is a short distance past the cabin. Past the tunnel, a network of steep narrow trails crisscrosses the ridge to many fine vantage points.

The main trail passes the eastern end of Last Chance Canyon Trail and the southern end of Central Mountains #25: Sheep Spring Trail, before swinging south into Mesquite Canyon. It passes by the remains of a few old mines before crossing the bajada to end on the Randsburg–Red Rock Road near the settlement of Garlock.

Current Road Information

BLM Ridgecrest Field Office
300 S. Richmond Road
Ridgecrest, CA 93555
(760) 384-5400

Map References

BLM Cuddeback Lake
USGS 1:24,000 Saltdale NW, Garlock
1:100,000 Cuddeback Lake
Maptech CD-ROM: Barstow/San Bernardino County
Southern & Central California Atlas & Gazetteer, pp. 65, 66
California Road & Recreation Atlas, p. 94
Other: East Kern County OHV Riding Areas and Trails—Jawbone Canyon

Route Directions

▼ 0.0	From California 14, 13.5 miles north of intersection with Randsburg–Red Rock Road, zero trip meter and turn southeast onto graded dirt road. There is a small wooden sign for Schmidt Tunnel at the intersection and the trail

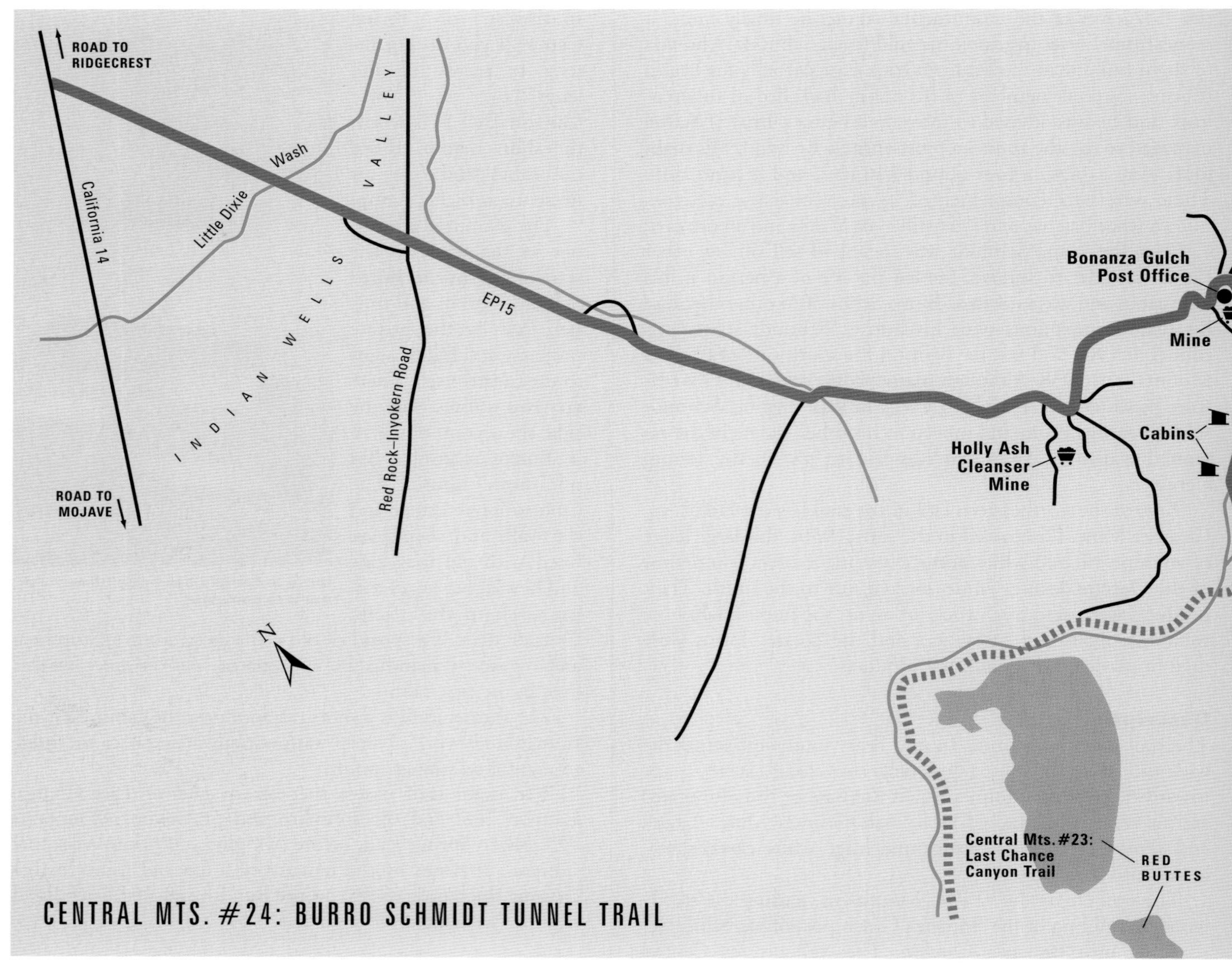

CENTRAL MTS. #24: BURRO SCHMIDT TUNNEL TRAIL

		is marked EP15 by a BLM marker. Trail is suitable for 4WDs, ATVs, and motorbikes. Cross cattle guard.
3.3 ▲		Cross cattle guard; then trail ends on California 14. Turn right for Ridgecrest; turn left for Mojave.
		GPS: N35°30.04' W117°56.87'
▼ 1.0	SO	Cross through Little Dixie Wash.
2.3 ▲	SO	Cross through Little Dixie Wash.
▼ 1.3	SO	Track on right.
2.0 ▲	SO	Track on left.
▼ 1.6	SO	Cross over graded dirt Red Rock–Inyokern Road. There is a sign at the intersection for Bonanza Trail and Burro Schmidt Tunnel.
1.7 ▲	SO	Cross over graded dirt Red Rock–Inyokern Road. There is a sign at the intersection for Bonanza Trail and Burro Schmidt Tunnel.
		GPS: N35°28.84' W117°55.84'
▼ 1.9	SO	Track on right.
1.4 ▲	BR	Track on left.
▼ 2.5	SO	Track on left.
0.8 ▲	SO	Track on right rejoins.
▼ 2.7	SO	Track on left rejoins.
0.6 ▲	SO	Track on right.
▼ 2.8	SO	Track on right.
0.5 ▲	SO	Track on left.
▼ 3.3	BL	Well-used track on right. Zero trip meter.
0.0 ▲		Continue to the northwest.
		GPS: N35°27.49' W117°54.63'
▼ 0.0		Continue to the east and cross through wash. Track on right up wash.
1.2 ▲	BR	Cross through wash. Track on left up wash. Then well-used track on left. Zero trip meter.
▼ 0.2	SO	Track on right.
1.0 ▲	SO	Track on left.
▼ 0.6	SO	Track on right.
0.6 ▲	SO	Track on left.
▼ 0.8	SO	Two tracks on right at tank.
0.4 ▲	SO	Two tracks on left at tank.
▼ 1.0	SO	Track on right to large stone tank and many mining remains of the Holly Ash Cleanser Mine; then second track on right.
0.2 ▲	SO	Track on left; then second track on left to large stone tank and many mining remains of the Holly Ash Cleanser Mine.
		GPS: N35°27.06' W117°53.76'
▼ 1.2	TL	5-way intersection. Turn first left on saddle,

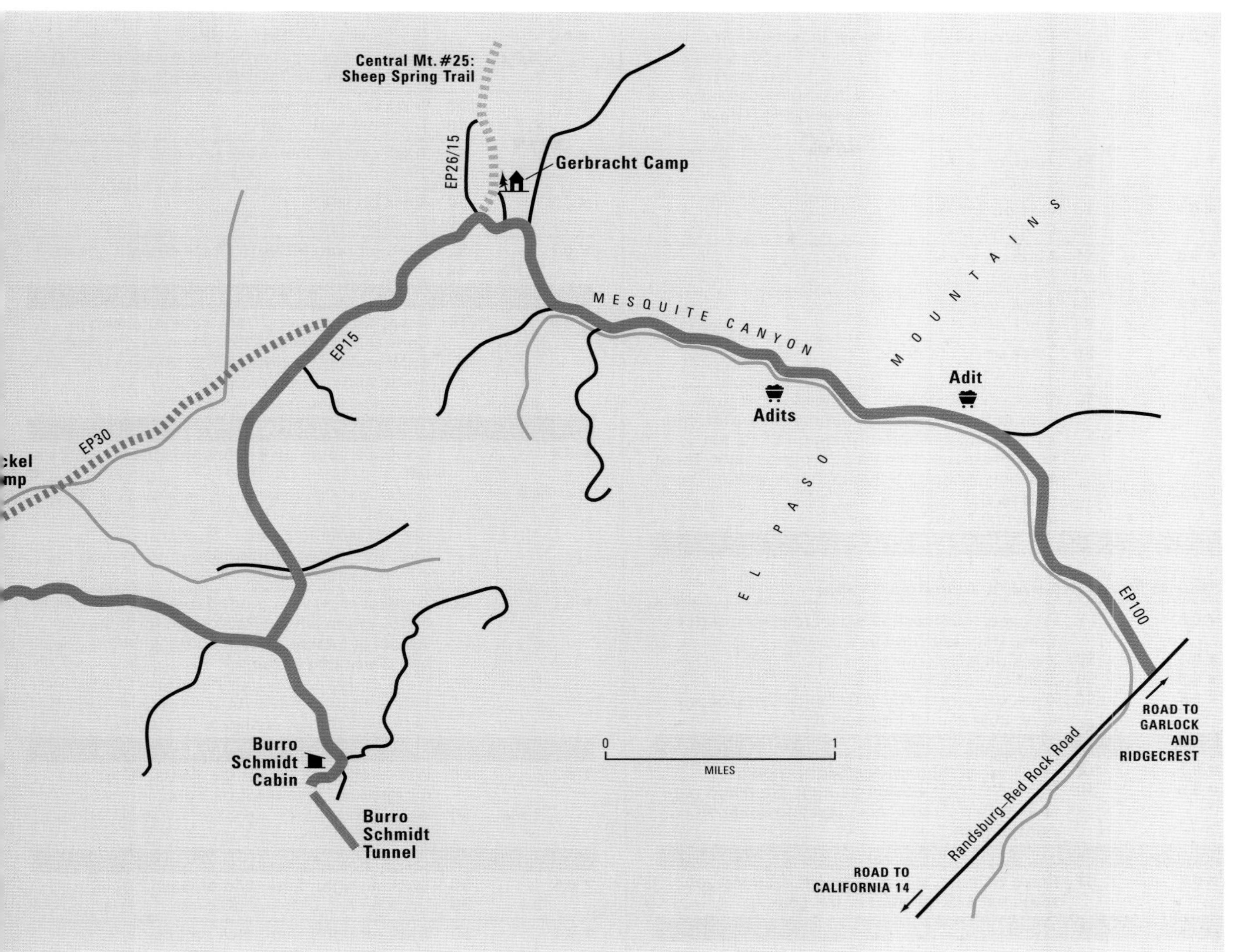

		remaining on marked EP15. Also second track on left, track on right, and track straight ahead. Zero trip meter.
0.0 ▲		Continue to the north.
		GPS: N35°26.93' W117°53.67'
▼ 0.0		Continue to the northeast.
2.5 ▲	TR	5-way intersection. Turn first right on saddle, remaining on marked EP15. Two tracks on left and track straight ahead. Zero trip meter.
▼ 0.7	SO	Track on right.
1.8 ▲	SO	Track on left.
▼ 1.0	TL	4-way intersection. Turn left; then rusty corrugated iron cabin on right is Bonanza Gulch post office; then enter Bonanza Canyon.
1.5 ▲	TR	Trail has exited Bonanza Canyon. Rusty corrugated iron cabin on left is Bonanza Gulch post office; then 4-way intersection.
		GPS: N35°27.02' W117°52.86'
▼ 1.1	TR	Track on left. Remain on EP15.
1.4 ▲	TL	Track on right. Remain on EP15.
▼ 1.2	SO	Track on left. Enter line of wash.
1.3 ▲	SO	Track on right. Exit line of wash.
▼ 1.3	SO	Mine on right; then track on right; then track on left to cabin.
1.2 ▲	SO	Track on right to cabin; then track on left; then mine on left.
		GPS: N35°26.84' W117°52.81'
▼ 1.7	SO	Stone and timber cabin on right.
0.8 ▲	SO	Stone and timber cabin on left.
		GPS: N35°26.57' W117°53.05'
▼ 1.8	SO	Track on right up side wash.
0.7 ▲	SO	Track on left up side wash.
▼ 2.0	SO	Corrugated iron cabin on right.
0.5 ▲	SO	Corrugated iron cabin on left.
		GPS: N35°26.40' W117°53.21'
▼ 2.4	SO	Track on left and track on right. Remain on EP15.
0.1 ▲	SO	Track on right and track on left. Remain on EP15.
▼ 2.5	SO	Exit Bonanza Canyon and cross through wide Last Chance Canyon wash. Central Mountains #23: Last Chance Canyon Trail crosses here. To the left it is marked EP30. Zero trip meter and continue straight ahead, remaining on marked EP15.
0.0 ▲		Continue to the northwest up Bonanza Canyon wash.
		GPS: N35°25.99' W117°53.37'

▼ 0.0			Continue to the southeast up side wash.
	1.4 ▲	SO	Central Mountains #23: Last Chance Canyon Trail crosses here. To the right it is marked EP30. Zero trip meter and continue straight ahead, remaining on marked EP15. Cross through wide Last Chance Canyon wash.
▼ 0.1		BL	Track on right.
	1.3 ▲	SO	Track on left.
▼ 0.4		SO	Adit on left.
	1.0 ▲	SO	Adit on right.
▼ 0.8		SO	Mine on left.
	0.6 ▲	SO	Mine on right.
▼ 1.2		SO	Track on right.
	0.2 ▲	SO	Track on left.
▼ 1.3		SO	Track on left to mine.
	0.1 ▲	SO	Track on right to mine.
▼ 1.4		TL	Track continuing straight ahead up wash is spur to Burro Schmidt's Tunnel and cabin. Turn left and exit wash, remaining on EP15, to continue along main trail. Zero trip meter. There is a sign for Burro Schmidt Tunnel at the intersection.
	0.0 ▲		Continue to the northwest.
			GPS: N35°25.20' W117°52.28'

Spur to Burro Schmidt's Tunnel and Cabin

▼ 0.0		Proceed southeast up wash, following sign to Burro Schmidt Tunnel.
▼ 0.1	SO	Track on left.
▼ 0.5	SO	Track on right.
▼ 0.6	SO	Track on right to Burro Schmidt Camp is private. BLM sign at intersection.
		GPS: N35°24.70' W117°52.35'
▼ 0.7	TR	Track on left and track straight ahead.
▼ 0.8	SO	Burro Schmidt's cabin on right. Stop and register in Burro's old cabin (second cabin on right of trail).
		GPS: N35°24.63' W117°52.43'
▼ 0.9	UT	Burro Schmidt's Tunnel on left. Retrace your steps back to the start of the spur.
		GPS: N35°24.64' W117°52.51'

Continuation of Main Trail

▼ 0.0			Continue to the northeast.
	1.7 ▲	TR	T-intersection with track in wash. Track on left up wash is spur to Burro Schmidt's Tunnel and cabin. Turn right down wash, remaining on EP30, to continue along main trail. Zero trip meter. There is a sign for Burro Schmidt Tunnel at the intersection.
			GPS: N35°25.20' W117°52.28'
▼ 0.1		SO	Track on right.
	1.6 ▲	SO	Track on left.
▼ 0.3		SO	Cross through wash. Track on left and track on right in wash.
	1.4 ▲	SO	Cross through wash. Track on left and track on right in wash.
			GPS: N35°25.34' W117°52.02'
▼ 1.0		SO	Track on right.
	0.7 ▲	SO	Track on left.
▼ 1.5		SO	Track on right.
	0.2 ▲	SO	Track on left.
▼ 1.7		SO	Track on left is Central Mountains #23: Last Chance Canyon Trail. Zero trip meter.
	0.0 ▲		Continue to the southwest on EP15.
			GPS: N35°26.13' W117°51.20'
▼ 0.0			Continue to the east on EP15.
	0.8 ▲	BL	Track on right is Central Mountains #23: Last Chance Canyon Trail. Zero trip meter.
▼ 0.1		SO	Track on left to mine.
	0.7 ▲	SO	Track on right to mine.
▼ 0.2		SO	Track on left; then track on right.
	0.6 ▲	SO	Track on left; then track on right.
▼ 0.5		SO	Track on left.
	0.3 ▲	SO	Track on right.
▼ 0.7		BL	Bear left onto EP26/15. Track straight ahead.
	0.1 ▲	BR	Track on left.
			GPS: N35°26.19' W117°50.51'
▼ 0.8		TR	4-way intersection. Track straight ahead is Central Mountains #25: Sheep Spring Trail; track on left is marked EP26/15. Zero trip meter and turn right onto EP26.
	0.0 ▲		Continue southwest on EP26/15.
			GPS: N35°26.20' W117°50.42'
▼ 0.0			Continue south on EP26. Immediately track on left.
	4.0 ▲	TL	Track on right; then 4-way intersection. Track straight ahead is EP26/15. Track on right is Central Mountains #25: Sheep Spring Trail. Zero trip meter and turn left onto formed trail, also marked EP26/15.
▼ 0.1		TL	T-intersection with graded road. To the right is EP15; to the left is EP100. Sign for Schmidt Tunnel at intersection; then track on left goes into Gerbracht Camp.
	3.9 ▲	TR	Track on right goes into Gerbracht Camp; then turn right onto EP26/15. Track ahead is EP15. Sign for Schmidt Tunnel at intersection.
			GPS: N35°26.15' W117°50.42'
▼ 0.2		SO	Well-used track on left for 4WDs, ATVs, and motorbikes. Also track on right.
	3.8 ▲	SO	Well-used track on right for 4WDs, ATVs, and motorbikes. Also track on left.
			GPS: N35°26.05' W117°50.26'
▼ 0.6		SO	Track on right. Enter line of wash.
	3.4 ▲	SO	Track on left. Exit line of wash.
▼ 0.8		SO	Track on right; then track on left.
	3.2 ▲	SO	Track on right; then track on left.
▼ 1.1		SO	Track on left.
	2.9 ▲	SO	Track on right.
▼ 1.3		SO	Track on right; then track on left.
	2.7 ▲	SO	Track on right; then track on left.
▼ 1.7		SO	Adits on right.
	2.3 ▲	SO	Adits on left.
▼ 1.8		SO	Track on right is old road.
	2.2 ▲	SO	Old road rejoins on left.
▼ 1.9		SO	Old road rejoins on right.
	2.1 ▲	BR	Track on left is old road.
▼ 2.1		SO	Track on right.
	1.9 ▲	SO	Track on left.
▼ 2.5		SO	Adit on left.
	1.5 ▲	SO	Adit on right.
			GPS: N35°24.54' W117°49.08'
▼ 2.6		SO	Track on left.
	1.4 ▲	SO	Track on right.
			GPS: N35°24.44' W117°48.96'
▼ 3.2		SO	Track on right.
	0.8 ▲	SO	Track on left.
▼ 3.5		SO	Track on right. Exiting Mesquite Canyon.
	0.5 ▲	SO	Track on left. Entering Mesquite Canyon.
▼ 3.8		SO	Two tracks on left.

0.2 ▲	SO	Two tracks on right.
▼ 4.0		Trail ends at T-intersection with RandsburgRed Rock Road. Turn right for California 14 and Mojave; turn left for Ridgecrest.
0.0 ▲		Trail commences on Randsburg–Red Rock Road at mile marker 11, 1.1 miles west of intersection with Garlock Road. Zero trip meter and turn north on well-used formed trail, marked EP100.
		GPS: N35°23.32′ W117°48.96′

CENTRAL MOUNTAINS #25

Sheep Spring Trail

Starting Point:	**Browns Road, 4 miles northeast of intersection with US 395**
Finishing Point:	**Central Mountains #24: Burro Schmidt Tunnel Trail, 4 miles north of the Randsburg–Red Rock Road**
Total Mileage:	**12 miles**
Unpaved Mileage:	**10.9 miles**
Driving Time:	**2 hours**
Elevation Range:	**2,700–4,000 feet**
Usually Open:	**Year-round**
Best Time to Travel:	**Year-round**
Difficulty Rating:	**3**
Scenic Rating:	**9**
Remoteness Rating:	**+0**

Special Attractions

- Petroglyphs near Sheep Spring.
- Remote trail through the El Paso Mountains.
- Sites of Gerbracht Camp and Colorado Camp.
- Collecting petrified wood.
- Hiking through the rugged Black Hills.

History

The old railroad grade at the northern end of the trail was once the route of the Nevada & California Railroad. Construction began in 1908 on the line that was needed to deliver construction materials for the ambitious Los Angeles Aqueduct project. The railroad was built from Mojave, passing through Inyokern, on its way to Lone Pine. The line also connected with the Carson & Colorado Railroad, which came in from Nevada and passed through Owenyo Station near Lone Pine. Union Pacific took over the railroad at a later stage.

Construction of the aqueduct continued until 1913. In 1914, increasing production at the Searles Lake chemical plant required an improved system of transportation. The mule teams that were in operation at the time could no longer meet the needs of the expanding industry. The American Trona Corporation financed and built its own railroad from Searles Lake to Searles Station. From the station it joined the Union Pacific Railroad (located east of this trail).

Many petroglyphs adorn the boulders near Sheep Spring

Gold was discovered close to the trail in 1893, in what became known as Goler Canyon. It gained its name from forty-niner John Goler, one of many prospectors on their way to the California goldfields in the winter of 1849 who just managed to escape death while on a shortcut through Death Valley. Goler survived to tell the tale of sighting gold nuggets in the general area, but fearful of an attack by the Indians, he had moved on in a lost and confused state of mind. Goler spent the following two decades looking for the elusive gold, but to no avail. News of the 1893 discovery prompted a rush of prospectors into the El Paso Mountains. Three of those prospectors would go on to find what would become the Yellow Aster Mine, giving birth to the nearby settlement of Randsburg.

Evidence of Native Americans in the region dates back thousands of years. Pottery shards and grinding stones appear to the west of this trail in the Black Mountain region. Petroglyphs can be found along the trail, often etched into the black rock near watering points. Many of the rock art designs are difficult to interpret. However, other images are more readily deciphered, often depicting wild animals that were encountered and hunted. As you travel through these colorful canyons and mountains, it becomes obvious that you are not the first to sample the breathtaking land.

Sandstone rock formations along the trail

This stone chimney and diggings are all that remain of the Colorado Camp

Description

Sheep Spring Trail winds alongside the eastern edge of the El Paso Wilderness, passing through some exceptionally beautiful and rugged scenery. The trail leaves Browns Road southwest of Ridgecrest. To reach the trailhead from Ridgecrest, proceed south on South China Lake Boulevard to the intersection with US 395. Continue southwest, across US 395, onto the unmarked paved Browns Road, CR 655 (on some maps this is called Randsburg-Inyokern Road) and drive 4 miles to the start of the trail.

The first mile of the road is paved because it serves as access for a sandpit. Afterwards, it turns into a well-used, winding formed trail. Navigation is generally easy because the El Paso Mountains Wilderness limits vehicle trails leaving to the west. However, there are many opportunities for hikers to head west into the wilderness.

One very interesting feature of the trail is the large group of petroglyphs that can be found up and down the shallow wash near Sheep Spring. The images are etched into darker volcanic boulders along the sides of the wash. You will find quite a few interesting figures and shapes, including many images of bighorn sheep, after which the spring is named.

Rock hounds will enjoy hunting for agate, petrified wood, and jasper in dry washes and around the base of sandstone domes along the trail.

The trail is best traveled in dry weather. Rain or snow can turn stretches of road into sticky mud. The surface is rough and undulating, but it has no major obstacles along the way. In dry weather, stock SUVs should encounter no difficulties.

South of Sheep Spring the trail follows along ridge tops and wash lines, at times providing panoramic views into the El Paso Mountains. The rock formations are both colorful and interesting, with many weathered holes in the sandstone domes that border the trail. At the site of Colorado Camp, a stone chimney and some scattered stone foundations are all that remain of this once active mining camp. Even less remains at the site of Gerbracht Camp, located at the trail's southern end.

The trail ends at the intersection with Central Mountains #24: Burro Schmidt Tunnel Trail. From here you can exit via the easy Mesquite Canyon or to the west by following the more difficult Central Mountains #23: Last Chance Canyon Trail.

This trail is considered to be part of Mesquite Canyon Road on some maps.

Current Road Information

BLM Ridgecrest Field Office
300 S. Richmond Road
Ridgecrest, CA 93555
(760) 384-5400

Map References

BLM Ridgecrest, Cuddeback Lake
USGS 1:24,000 Inyokern SE, Garlock
1:100,000 Ridgecrest, Cuddeback Lake
Maptech CD-ROM: Barstow/San Bernardino County
Southern & Central California Atlas & Gazetteer, pp. 52, 66
California Road & Recreation Atlas, p. 94
Other: East Kern County OHV Riding Areas and Trails—Jawbone Canyon

Route Directions

▼ 0.0		Trail commences on Browns Road, 4 miles northeast of intersection with US 395. Zero trip meter and turn southwest on unmarked paved road and immediately cross over old railroad grade. Trail is marked as EP26 a short distance from the start.
6.6 ▲		Trail finishes on paved Browns Road. Turn right for Ridgecrest; turn left for Inyokern.
		GPS: N35°34.03' W117°46.68'
▼ 0.5	SO	Track on left.
6.1 ▲	SO	Track on right.
▼ 1.1	SO	Road turns to graded dirt.
5.5 ▲	SO	Road is now paved.
▼ 1.6	SO	Track on right.
5.0 ▲	SO	Track on left.
▼ 1.8	SO	Track on right is EP18 for 4WDs, ATVs, and motorbikes.

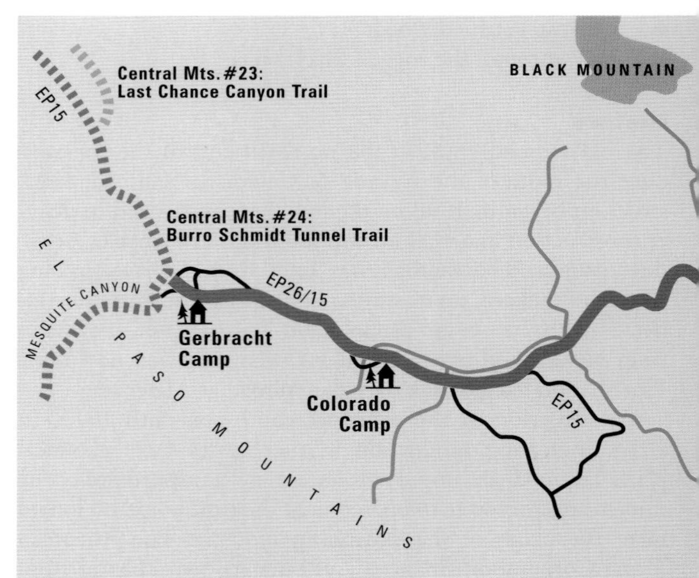

4.8 ▲	SO	Track on left is EP18 for 4WDs, ATVs, and motorbikes.
		GPS: N35°32.68' W117°48.01'
▼ 2.0	SO	Track on left into sandpit and small track on right. Trail is now small, formed trail.
4.6 ▲	SO	Track on right into sandpit and small track on left. Trail is now graded dirt.
		GPS: N35°32.62' W117°48.05'
▼ 2.2	BR	Trail forks; track on left.
4.4 ▲	SO	Track rejoins on right.
▼ 2.3	SO	Track rejoins on left.
4.3 ▲	BL	Trail forks; track on right.
▼ 2.4	SO	El Paso Mountains Wilderness on right.
4.2 ▲	SO	End of El Paso Mountains Wilderness on left.
▼ 2.7	SO	Track on left. Remain on marked EP26.
3.9 ▲	BL	Track on right. Remain on marked EP26.
▼ 3.0	SO	Enter line of wash.
3.6 ▲	SO	Exit line of wash.
		GPS: N35°31.83' W117°48.19'
▼ 3.2	SO	Track on left.
3.4 ▲	SO	Track on right.
▼ 4.1	SO	Exit line of wash; then track on left.
2.5 ▲	SO	Track on right; then enter line of wash.
▼ 4.9	SO	Track on left. Remain on marked EP26. On the right at this point is a sign for a closed vehicle trail. Park here and hike 0.2 miles in a southwest direction along old vehicle trail down into the wash. Petroglyphs are on the dark volcanic rocks along west bank of the wash. The easiest ones to find are facing down into the wash. Coordinates of petroglyphs are GPS: N35°30.11' W117°48.22'
1.7 ▲	SO	Track on right. Remain on marked EP26. On the left at this point is a sign for a closed vehicle trail. Park here and follow the above directions to find the petroglyphs.
		GPS: N35°30.23' W117°48.10'
▼ 5.0	SO	Track on left. Remain on marked EP26.
1.6 ▲	SO	Track on right. Remain on marked EP26.
▼ 5.1	SO	Track on left. Bear right into wash toward Sheep Spring, remaining on EP26.
1.5 ▲	TL	Track continues straight ahead. Remain on EP26.
▼ 5.2	SO	Campsite on right. More petroglyphs can be found on boulders above the wash, both to the north and south of the campsite. Enter line of wash.
1.4 ▲	SO	Campsite on left. More petroglyphs can be found on boulders above the wash, both to the north and south of the campsite. Exit line of wash.
		GPS: N35°29.99' W117°48.18'
▼ 5.3	SO	Cross through wash. More petroglyphs can be found on boulders on hill to the right.
1.3 ▲	SO	Cross through wash. Petroglyphs can be found on boulders on hill to the left.
▼ 5.4	SO	Cross through wash; then Sheep Spring on left and track on left opposite El Paso Mountains Wilderness sign.
1.2 ▲	SO	Sheep Spring on right and track on right opposite El Paso Mountains Wilderness sign; then cross through wash.
		GPS: N35°29.84' W117°48.23'
▼ 5.8	SO	Exit line of wash.
0.8 ▲	SO	Enter line of wash.
▼ 5.9	SO	Track on left. Remain on marked EP26.
0.7 ▲	SO	Track on right. Remain on marked EP26.
		GPS: N35°29.45' W117°48.35'
▼ 6.6	BR	Well-used track on left is EP11 (signed by BLM marker post) for 4WDs, ATVs, and motorbikes. Remain on marked EP26 and zero trip meter.
0.0 ▲		Continue to the northwest.
		GPS: N35°28.94' W117°48.25'
▼ 0.0		Continue to the south.
3.5 ▲	BL	Well-used track on right is EP11 (signed by BLM marker post) for 4WDs, ATVs, and motorbikes. Remain on marked EP26 and zero trip meter.
▼ 0.1	SO	Cross through wash.
3.4 ▲	SO	Cross through wash.
▼ 0.6	SO	Cross through wash.
2.9 ▲	SO	Cross through wash.
▼ 0.7	SO	Track on left. Remain on marked EP26.
2.8 ▲	BL	Track on right. Remain on marked EP26.
		GPS: N35°28.66' W117°48.75'

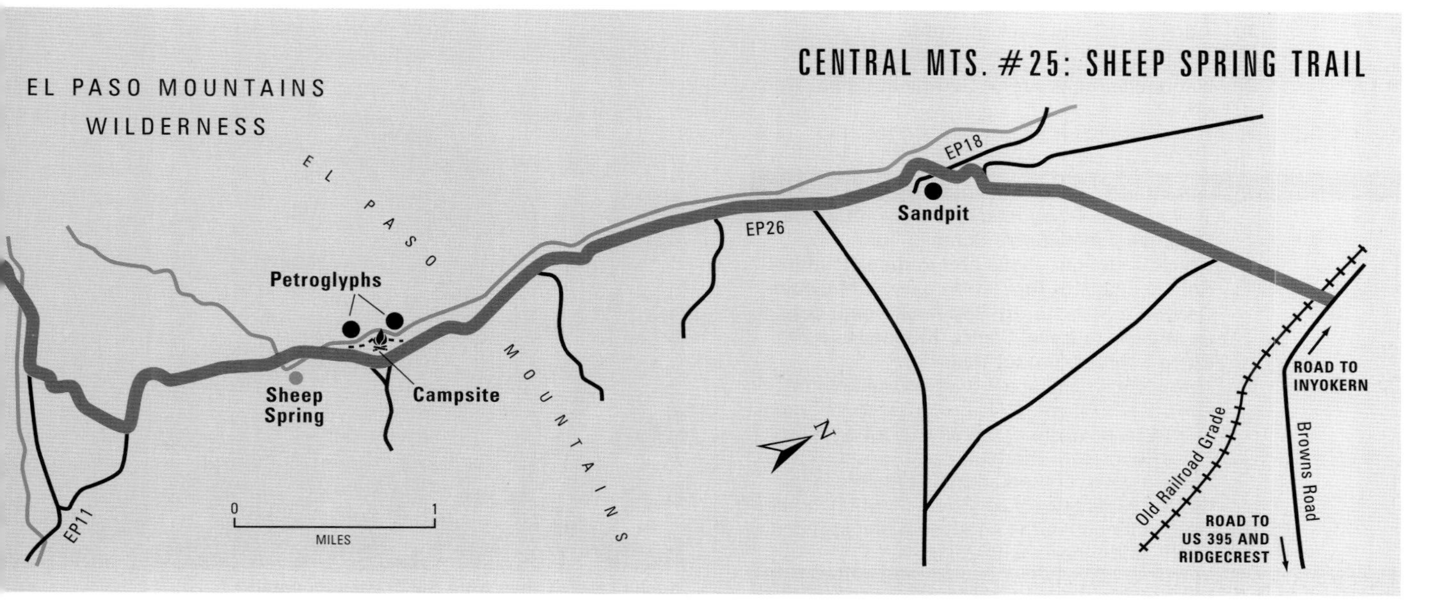

▼ 1.1		SO	Cross through wash.
	2.4 ▲	SO	Cross through wash.
▼ 1.7		SO	Cross through wash.
	1.8 ▲	SO	Cross through wash.
▼ 3.0		SO	Cross through wash.
	0.5 ▲	SO	Cross through wash.
			GPS: N35°27.70' W117°49.32'
▼ 3.1		SO	Track on left.
	0.4 ▲	SO	Track on right.
▼ 3.5		TR	T-intersection with EP15. Zero trip meter and turn right onto EP15. Intersection is marked with trail numbers.
	0.0 ▲		Continue to the west.
			GPS: N35°27.47' W117°49.27'
▼ 0.0			Continue to the south.
	1.9 ▲	TL	Turn left onto EP26 and zero trip meter. EP15 continues ahead. Intersection is marked with trail numbers.
▼ 0.4		SO	Track on left; then cross through wash; then second track on left.
	1.5 ▲	SO	Track on right; then cross through wash; then second track on right.
▼ 0.7		BL	Bear left, leaving main EP26/15 to pass beside remains of Colorado Camp.
	1.2 ▲	SO	Rejoin main EP26/15.
▼ 0.75		SO	Remains of Colorado Camp on left at sign—stone chimney and various diggings. Track on left.
	1.15 ▲	SO	Remains of Colorado Camp on right at sign—stone chimney and various diggings. Track on right.
			GPS: N35°26.88' W117°49.63'
▼ 0.8		SO	Rejoin main EP15.
	1.1 ▲	BR	Bear right, leaving main EP15 to pass beside remains of Colorado Camp.
▼ 0.9		SO	Track on right and track on left.
	1.0 ▲	SO	Track on right and track on left.
▼ 1.2		SO	Track on right.
	0.7 ▲	SO	Track on left.
▼ 1.4		BL	Small track on left; then bear left, leaving EP15/26 to the right.
	0.5 ▲	SO	Track on left is EP15/26. Continue straight ahead, joining EP15/26; then small track on right.
			GPS: N35°26.53' W117°50.15'
▼ 1.7		SO	Track on left and track on right.
	0.2 ▲	SO	Track on right and track on left.
▼ 1.8		BR	Flat open area is site of Gerbracht Camp. Track on left.
	0.1 ▲	BL	Flat open area is site of Gerbracht Camp. Track on right.
			GPS: N35°26.22' W117°50.32'
▼ 1.9			Trail ends at 4-way intersection with Central Mountains #24: Burro Schmidt Tunnel Trail, which is straight ahead and to the left. To the right is EP26/15. Turn left to exit via Mesquite Canyon to Randsburg–Red Rock Road; continue straight to travel Central Mountains #24: Burro Schmidt Tunnel Trail.
	0.0 ▲		Trail commences at a 4-way intersection on Central Mountains #24: Burro Schmidt Tunnel Trail, 4 miles north of paved Randsburg–Red Rock Road. Zero trip meter and turn northeast on well-used, unmarked trail at intersection. Central Mountains #24: Burro Schmidt Tunnel Trail continues to the southwest along marked EP15. To the north is EP26/15.
			GPS: N35°26.20' W117°50.42'

CENTRAL MOUNTAINS #26

Koehn Lake Trail

Starting Point:	**Neuralia Road at Rancho Seco**
Finishing Point:	**Randsburg–Red Rock Road, 1.5 miles east of intersection with Garlock Road**
Total Mileage:	**24.9 miles**
Unpaved Mileage:	**21.1 miles**
Driving Time:	**2 hours**
Elevation Range:	**1,900–3,900 feet**
Usually Open:	**Year-round**
Best Time to Travel:	**Year-round**
Difficulty Rating:	**3**
Scenic Rating:	**8**
Remoteness Rating:	**+0**

Special Attractions

- Wildlife viewing for desert tortoise.
- Access to a network of 4WD, ATV, and motorbike trails.

History

A German emigrant named Charley Koehn was en route to the goldfields of the Panamint region in search of work when opportunity came knocking. Koehn set up a way station near Red Rocks to supply passing freight teams traveling south from the Panamint Range. He was also fortunate enough to be in operation before the Goler gold rush of 1893 hit the nearby El Paso Mountains. Realizing another market was close at hand, Koehn would load up his newly

Koehn Lake as seen from the El Paso Mountains

purchased wagon and head for the hills to sell his wares. As the local mines flourished, so did Koehn's market. His way station also delivered news of the latest mineral strikes throughout the surrounding region. The Rand Mine was getting under way by the late 1890s, and he could relate its progress to miners while out selling wagonloads of food and merchandise around the El Paso and Randsburg mining regions.

The desert region surrounding Koehn Lake Trail is home to the desert tortoise. Not always visible, this animal retreats to its cool underground burrow during hotter parts of the summer and hibernates there during long, cold winters. The desert tortoise is currently protected to help increase the number of maturing animals. They are most vulnerable when young. As they age, their shells thicken, and by age 10, they have a good chance of survival. Desert tortoises can live as long as humans. To the early Native Americans the desert tortoise was a delicacy when roasted over a bed of hot ashes. Tortoise population numbers are thought to have been even lower then than now.

Description

Koehn Lake Trail takes a winding path through the Rand Mountains, traveling mainly through the Rand Mountain Fremont Valley Management Area. This area is prime habitat for the desert tortoise, and patient travelers will have a good chance of seeing one of these elusive animals, particularly when traveling between March and September.

To reach the trailhead, turn east on the paved Rogers Road from California 14, opposite Jawbone Station and the entrance to the OHV area, 1 mile south of the intersection with Randsburg–Red Rock Road. After 0.7 miles, turn south on Neuralia Road. Proceed 0.9 miles to Rancho Seco and then turn east on Munsey Road. The trail leaves along the paved Munsey Road before swinging north along the shores of the dry Koehn Lake. The Desert Tortoise Natural Area is on the east side of the trail at this point; no vehicles are allowed within the area, but hikers may walk inside and attempt to spot one of the creatures. Many tracks to the west lead down to the edge of Koehn Lake. Only hikers are allowed on the surface of the lake.

The trail enters the Rand Mountain Fremont Valley Management Area—another prime desert tortoise habitat. Vehicle travel within the area is restricted to roads and trails that are designated with numbered brown posts. Camping is restricted to areas marked with white signs and camping symbols. There are five such spots within the management area, although none of them are located along this trail. Camping is not permitted outside of these areas. Firearm use is limited to shotguns for seasonal hunting of upland game birds.

The route follows a mixture of sandy and rocky trails, traveling in wash bottoms and along ridge tops. The area has a very remote feel and is normally very quiet. There are panoramic views along the trail: into the Rand Mountains, north to the El Paso Mountains, and west to Koehn Lake. The trail ends by dropping down to finish on Randsburg–Red Rock Road.

The flat expanse of dry Koehn Lake sits on the western side of the Rand Mountains

Current Road Information

BLM Ridgecrest Field Office
300 S. Richmond Road
Ridgecrest, CA 93555
(760) 384-5400

Map References

BLM Cuddeback Lake
USGS 1:24,000 Cantil, Saltdale SE, Garlock, Johannesburg
1:100,000 Cuddeback Lake
Maptech CD-ROM: Barstow/San Bernardino County
Southern & Central California Atlas & Gazetteer, pp. 65, 66
California Road & Recreation Atlas, p. 94
Other: East Kern County OHV Riding Areas and Trails—Jawbone Canyon

Route Directions

▼ 0.0			Trail commences on Neuralia Road in Rancho Seco. Turn east onto paved Munsey Road and zero trip meter.
	5.6 ▲		Trail ends at the intersection with Neuralia Road in Rancho Seco. Turn right to exit to California 14.
			GPS: N35°17.20' W117°59.09'
▼ 3.8		SO	Road turns to graded dirt.
	1.8 ▲	SO	Road is now paved. Remain on paved road until end of trail.
▼ 5.2		SO	Track on left.
	0.4 ▲	SO	Track on right.
▼ 5.3		SO	Track on right.
	0.3 ▲	SO	Track on left.
▼ 5.5		SO	Track on right.
	0.1 ▲	SO	Track on left.
▼ 5.6		BL	Track on right goes to the edge of Desert Tortoise Natural Area. Zero trip meter.
	0.0 ▲		Continue to the west.
			GPS: N35°17.23' W117°52.93'
▼ 0.0			Continue northeast around the shores of Koehn Lake. Desert Tortoise Natural Area is now on the right and Rand Mountain Fremont

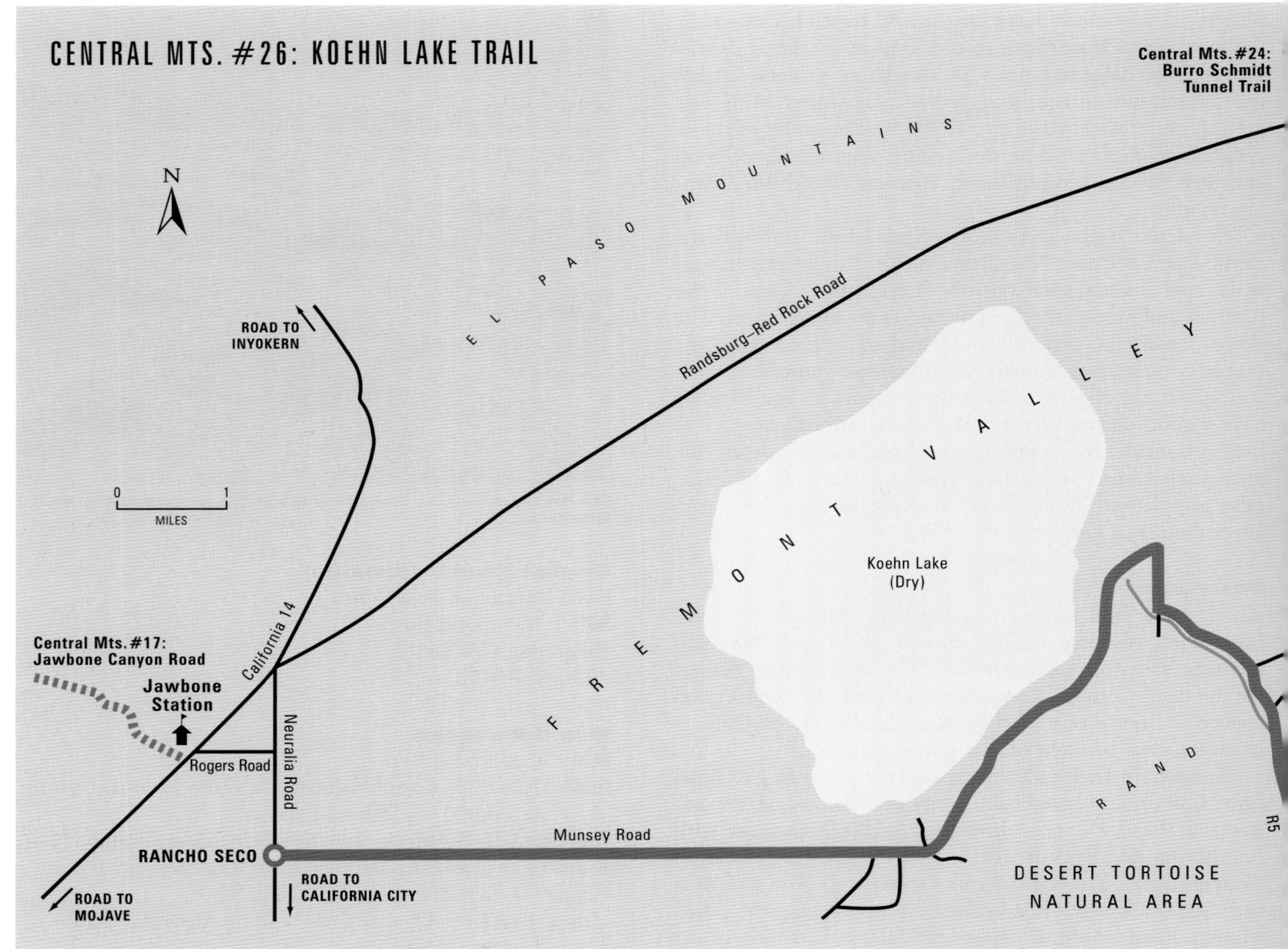

			Valley Management Area is on the left. Track on left.
	3.9 ▲	SO	Track on right; then track on left goes to the edge of Desert Tortoise Natural Area. Bear right and zero trip meter.
0.3		SO	Track on right and track on left.
	3.6 ▲	SO	Track on left and track on right.
1.9		SO	Track on left.
	2.0 ▲	SO	Track on right.
2.2		SO	Track on left. Many tracks on left to edge of lakeshore for next 1.7 miles. Vehicle travel on lakebed is prohibited.
	1.7 ▲	SO	Track on right.
3.9		TR	Turn sharp right around fence line that marks the boundary of Desert Tortoise Natural Area onto small formed trail marked R5, suitable for 4WDs, ATVs, and motorbikes. Entering Rand Mountain Fremont Valley Management Area. There is an information board at the intersection. Vehicle travel in this area is limited to trails marked with brown numbered posts. Zero trip meter.
	0.0 ▲		Continue southwest, following shoreline of Koehn Lake. Many tracks on right to edge of lakeshore for next 1.7 miles. Vehicle travel on lakebed is prohibited.

GPS: N35°19.88' W117°50.57'

▼ 0.0			Continue to the south.
	3.5 ▲	TL	Turn sharp left around fence line that marks the boundary of Desert Tortoise Natural Area onto large graded road. There is an information board at the intersection. Desert Tortoise Natural Area is now on the left. Zero trip meter.
▼ 0.6		BL	Bear away from the edge of Desert Tortoise Natural Area. Enter line of wash.
	2.9 ▲	BR	Fence on left marks the boundary of Desert Tortoise Natural Area. Exit line of wash.
▼ 1.6		SO	Track on left is R50 for 4WDs, ATVs, and motorbikes.
	1.9 ▲	SO	Track on right is R50 for 4WDs, ATVs, and motorbikes.

GPS: N35°18.80' W117°49.74'

▼ 2.0		SO	Track on left is R50 for 4WDs, ATVs, and motorbikes.
	1.5 ▲	BL	Track on right is R50 for 4WDs, ATVs, and motorbikes.

GPS: N35°18.46' W117°49.51'

▼ 3.3		BR	Track on left is R6 for 4WDs, ATVs, and motorbikes.
	0.2 ▲	SO	Track on right is R6 for 4WDs, ATVs, and motorbikes.

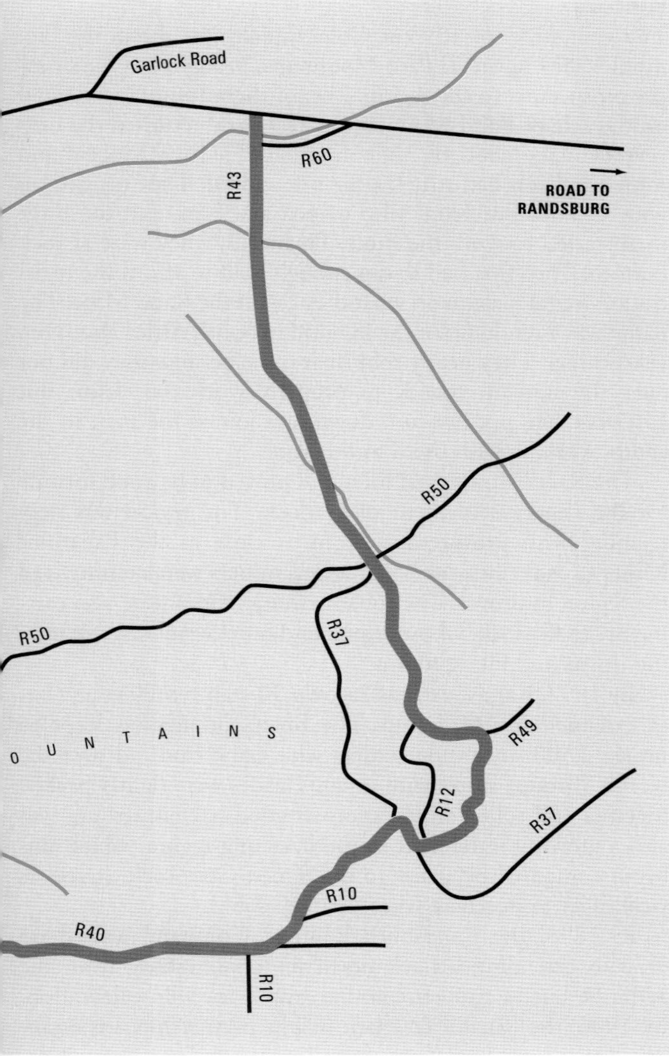

GPS: N35°17.35' W117°49.26'

▼ 3.5 **TL** Turn left up side wash onto R40 for 4WDs, ATVs, and motorbikes. Zero trip meter.
0.0 ▲ Continue to the northwest.

GPS: N35°17.21' W117°49.20'

▼ 0.0 Continue to the east.
4.2 ▲ **TR** T-intersection with R5. Turn right down main wash and zero trip meter.

▼ 1.7 **SO** Track on left and track on right are both R15 for 4WDs, ATVs, and motorbikes.
2.5 ▲ **SO** Track on left and track on right are both R15 for 4WDs, ATVs, and motorbikes.

GPS: N35°17.18' W117°47.36'

▼ 2.0 **SO** Exit line of wash.
2.2 ▲ **SO** Enter line of wash.

▼ 2.5 **SO** Pass through fence line, leaving Rand Mountain Fremont Valley Management Area. Track on right is R10 for 4WDs, ATVs, and motorbikes. Continue straight ahead on R 40/10.
1.7 ▲ **SO** Track on left is R10 for 4WDs, ATVs, and motorbikes. Continue straight ahead through fence line on R40, re-entering Rand Mountain Fremont Valley Management Area.

GPS: N35°17.20' W117°46.54'

▼ 2.7 **TL** Turn left along fence line, remaining on R40/10. Track straight ahead.
1.5 ▲ **TR** T-intersection. Turn right along fence line, remaining on R40/10.

GPS: N35°17.20' W117°46.32'

▼ 2.8 **TL** Turn left onto R40 and pass through fence line, re-entering Rand Mountain Fremont Valley Management Area. R10 continues straight ahead. Track on right.
1.4 ▲ **TR** Pass through fence line, leaving Rand Mountain Fremont Valley Management Area. T-intersection. Track on left is R10. Turn right onto R40/10. Small track straight ahead.

GPS: N35°17.27' W117°46.24'

▼ 3.2 **SO** Track on right and track on left are both R25 for 4WDs, ATVs, and motorbikes.
1.0 ▲ **SO** Track on right and track on left are both R25 for 4WDs, ATVs, and motorbikes.

GPS: N35°17.55' W117°46.00'

▼ 4.2 **TR** T-intersection with R37. Track on left goes 0.4 miles to viewpoint. Zero trip meter.
0.0 ▲ Continue to the southwest.

GPS: N35°18.08' W117°45.23'

▼ 0.0 Continue to the south.
3.9 ▲ **TL** R37 continues 0.4 miles to viewpoint. Zero trip meter and turn left onto R40.

▼ 0.3 **TL** Turn left onto R48. R37 continues straight ahead.
3.6 ▲ **TR** T-intersection with R37.

▼ 0.5 **SO** Track on left and track on right are both R12. It is marked as suitable for 4WDs, ATVs, and motorbikes but to the left it becomes too narrow for vehicles after 1 mile.
3.4 ▲ **SO** Track on left and track on right are both R12. It is marked as suitable for 4WDs, ATVs, and motorbikes but to the right it becomes too narrow for vehicles after 1 mile.

GPS: N35°17.86' W117°45.07'

▼ 0.7 **BL** Trail forks; both are marked R48.
3.2 ▲ **SO** Track on left is R48.

▼ 0.8 **BL** Bear left onto wider formed trail R43 for 4WDs, ATVs, and motorbikes, and proceed down line of wash in canyon.
3.1 ▲ **BR** Exit line of wash and bear right onto smaller formed trail R48 for 4WDs, ATVs, and motorbikes.

GPS: N35°17.95' W117°44.80'

▼ 1.9 **BL** Track on right is R49.
2.0 ▲ **BR** Track on left is R49.

GPS: N35°18.73' W117°44.49'

▼ 2.2 **SO** Game water tank on right.
1.7 ▲ **SO** Game water tank on left.

▼ 2.4 **SO** Track on left is R12. Although marked for 4WDs, ATVs, and motorbikes, it becomes too narrow for vehicles.
1.5 ▲ **SO** Track on right is R12. Although marked for 4WDs, ATVs, and motorbikes, it becomes too narrow for vehicles.

GPS: N35°18.81' W117°45.05'

▼ 3.0 **SO** Track on right is R45 for 4WDs, ATVs, and motorbikes.
0.9 ▲ **SO** Track on left is R45 for 4WDs, ATVs, and motorbikes.

GPS: N35°19.29' W117°45.12'

▼ 3.1 **SO** Track on right is R46 for 4WDs, ATVs, and motorbikes.
0.8 ▲ **SO** Track on left is R46 for 4WDs, ATVs, and motorbikes.

GPS: N35°19.41' W117°45.21'

▼ 3.7	SO	Track on left is R37 for 4WDs, ATVs, and motorbikes. Exit canyon, but continue in line of wash.
0.2 ▲	SO	Track on right is R37 for 4WDs, ATVs, and motorbikes. Enter canyon.
		GPS: N35°19.90' W117°45.27'
▼ 3.9	SO	Track on left and track on right are both R50 for 4WDs, ATVs, and motorbikes. Zero trip meter.
0.0 ▲		Continue east, entering line of wash.
		GPS: N35°20.04' W117°45.38'
▼ 0.0		Continue west, exiting line of wash.
3.8 ▲	SO	Track on left and track on right are both R50 for 4WDs, ATVs, and motorbikes. Zero trip meter.
▼ 0.7	SO	Cross through wash.
3.1 ▲	SO	Cross through wash.
▼ 2.8	SO	Cross through wash.
1.0 ▲	SO	Cross through wash.
▼ 3.6	SO	Cross through wash. Track on right up wash is R60 for 4WDs, ATVs, and motorbikes.
0.2 ▲	SO	Cross through wash. Track on left up wash is R60 for 4WDs, ATVs, and motorbikes.
		GPS: N35°23.19' W117°46.30'
▼ 3.8		Trail ends at intersection with paved Randsburg–Red Rock Road, 1.5 miles east of intersection with Garlock Road. Turn right for Randsburg; turn left for California 14.
0.0 ▲		Trail commences on paved Randsburg–Red Rock Road, 1.5 miles east of intersection with Garlock Road. Zero trip meter and turn south onto graded dirt road marked R43. R43 also goes north of Randsburg–Red Rock Road. Enter Rand Mountain Fremont Valley Management Area. There is an information board at the intersection.
		GPS: N35°23.39' W117°46.30'

CENTRAL MOUNTAINS #27

Government Peak Trail

Starting Point:	Randsburg–Red Rock Road, 1.5 miles west of Randsburg
Finishing Point:	Randsburg–Mojave Road, 4.7 miles west of US 395
Total Mileage:	7.9 miles
Unpaved Mileage:	7.9 miles
Driving Time:	1.5 hours
Elevation Range:	3,100-4,700 feet
Usually Open:	Year-round
Best Time to Travel:	Year-round
Difficulty Rating:	5
Scenic Rating:	10
Remoteness Rating:	+0

Special Attractions

- Far-reaching views from Government Peak.
- A network of trails around the mining region.
- Famous Yellow Aster Mine.

History

The gold strike of 1893 at Goler Gulch, just across the Fremont Valley in the El Paso Mountains, brought a surge of eager prospectors to the region. Two of them found placer gold on the side of Rand Mountain in 1894 and returned the next year to make good on their findings. Fredrick Mooers and John Singleton had struck a big one indeed. They teamed up with Charles Burcham, who owned a wagon, and the three men started to work the mine. Financially, they were at rock bottom. They first had to dig enough gold to afford the registration fee for a claim on what they called the Rand Mine. The name was a reminder of the big find in South Africa about ten years earlier. They nearly sold their mine because they did not have the start-up money to properly work the claim. But Mooers's wife put her foot down and joined the men in the camp, working with them in the mine.

The Rand Mine's need for a mill proved to be good fortune for the nearby settlement of Garlock. The region was now teeming with prospectors. From as close as the Panamint Mines to as far away as Los Angeles, miners were coming into the region in droves. The Johannesburg Mines were also carting ore to Garlock, whose saloon and hotel were busy quenching thirsts and filling rooms.

By 1897, Randsburg had its own 30-stamp mill, which later extended to 100-stamp. The town's population leapt to nearly 2,500, including settlers who came from all over the world. Wooden stores with ornate facades were tightly packed together and sold a wide variety of goods. Johannesburg was also a growing settlement in the booming region, which was being compared by many to the famed Comstock. Investors were eager to purchase wherever they could.

In 1898, the Randsburg Railroad Company wasted no time in extending a track north to Johannesburg from the Santa Fe line at Kramer, another reason for wild celebration. By 1906, the Rinaldi & Clark freight partnership was established locally and teams were hauling goods from the rail depot at Johannesburg all the way to the Panamint Mines. Their stagecoaches carried passengers, feed, supplies, and much-welcomed mail deliveries. The World War I years brought competition to the freight teams in the form of the Ford and Moreland trucks. Transportation modes in remote regions were about to change.

In 1905, tungsten was discovered at Red Mountain, and the town of Atolia was born. Another boom followed for the Randsburg Mining District. The Rand Mine, later known as the Yellow Aster Mine, which is the name shown on maps today, had produced over $6 million in gold by 1911. By 1919, it was silver that was making history at the Kelly Silver Mine near Red Mountain. This mine went on to produce more than $15 million worth of silver, making it one of the largest producers in California. The 1930s marked the decline of the mining district. In 1933, the rail line was torn up between Kramer and Johannesburg in order to be used elsewhere. The old embankment is still visible.

The 1940s rekindled life in the Randsburg region with the War Department's demand for tungsten, molybdenum, and potash. Once again, the mines reportedly ran 24 hours a day and Randsburg teemed with life.

Fire has plagued Randsburg since its earliest days, and the wooden houses and stores were reduced to ash on several occasions. Though the population continued to grow to 3,500 by the start of the twentieth century, most of the buildings are now gone.

Today, as you climb the shelf trail to the top of Government Peak (4,755 feet), you can overlook the modern mining activity of the Yellow Aster Mine, in full swing once again. The Rand Mining Company (now called Glamis Gold Limited) brought in heavy machinery in 1984. Using a cyanide leaching process, the company extracted more than 94,000 ounces of gold by 1997. Like many mining districts, the claim names in this region keep you wondering—Red Bird Mine, Tam O' Shanter Mine, Ben Hur Mine, Orphan Girl Mine, Sophie Moren Mine, and Winnie Mine are only a few of the colorful names.

Description

This short, high-interest trail takes the intrepid traveler high into the Rand Mountains along the face of Government Peak. The trail passes several mines before dropping down on the south side of the mountain to finish on graded dirt Randsburg-Mojave Road.

The trail leaves Randsburg–Red Rock Road 1.5 miles west of the ghost town of Randsburg. It travels through the Rand Mountain Fremont Valley Management Area; vehicle travel is restricted to roads and trails that are designated by brown, numbered posts. Camping is restricted to areas marked with white signs and camping emblems. There are five such sites within the management area, two of which are near the start of this trail. Firearm use is limited to shotguns for seasonal hunting of upland game birds.

The brown marker posts aid in navigation, but there are still a number of intersecting side trails that make it easy to miss a turn. The trail heads toward the base of Government Peak and ascends a wash for a short way before wrapping around the large, recently reworked Yellow Aster Mine. The narrow road is well formed with a limited number of passing places. As it starts the steep climb around the face of Government Peak, the trail passes several old mining remains—mainly wooden ore hoppers and tailings piles. Sections of the trail are rough and uneven, which, combined with the loose traction and narrow shelf road, gives the trail its difficulty rating of 5.

Expansive views over Fremont Valley as you descend from Government Peak

Randsburg post office

From Government Peak, there are panoramic views over the open-pit Yellow Aster Mine, Fremont Valley, and El Paso Mountains. The trail continues along the ridge tops before descending a rough track down to Randsburg-Mojave Road. The final off-camber descent will tilt vehicles toward a drop-off, with side slopes up to 20 degrees.

Note that because of recent mining activity, the route does not completely follow trails marked on topographic maps of the region.

Current Road Information

BLM Ridgecrest Field Office
300 S. Richmond Road
Ridgecrest, CA 93555
(760) 384-5400

Map References

BLM Cuddeback Lake
USGS 1:24,000 El Paso Peaks, Johannesburg
1:100,000 Cuddeback Lake
Maptech CD-ROM: Barstow/San Bernardino County
Southern & Central California Atlas & Gazetteer, p. 66
California Road & Recreation Atlas, p. 94
Other: East Kern County OHV Riding Areas and Trails—Jawbone Canyon

Route Directions

▼ 0.0	From Randsburg-Red Rock Road, 1.5 miles west of Randsburg and 6.9 miles east of intersection with Garlock Road, zero trip meter and turn southwest on formed dirt trail marked R44. Trail is suitable for 4WDs, ATVs, and motorbikes. There is an information board at the intersection and R110 also crosses paved road at this point. Enter Rand Mountain Fremont Valley Management Area.

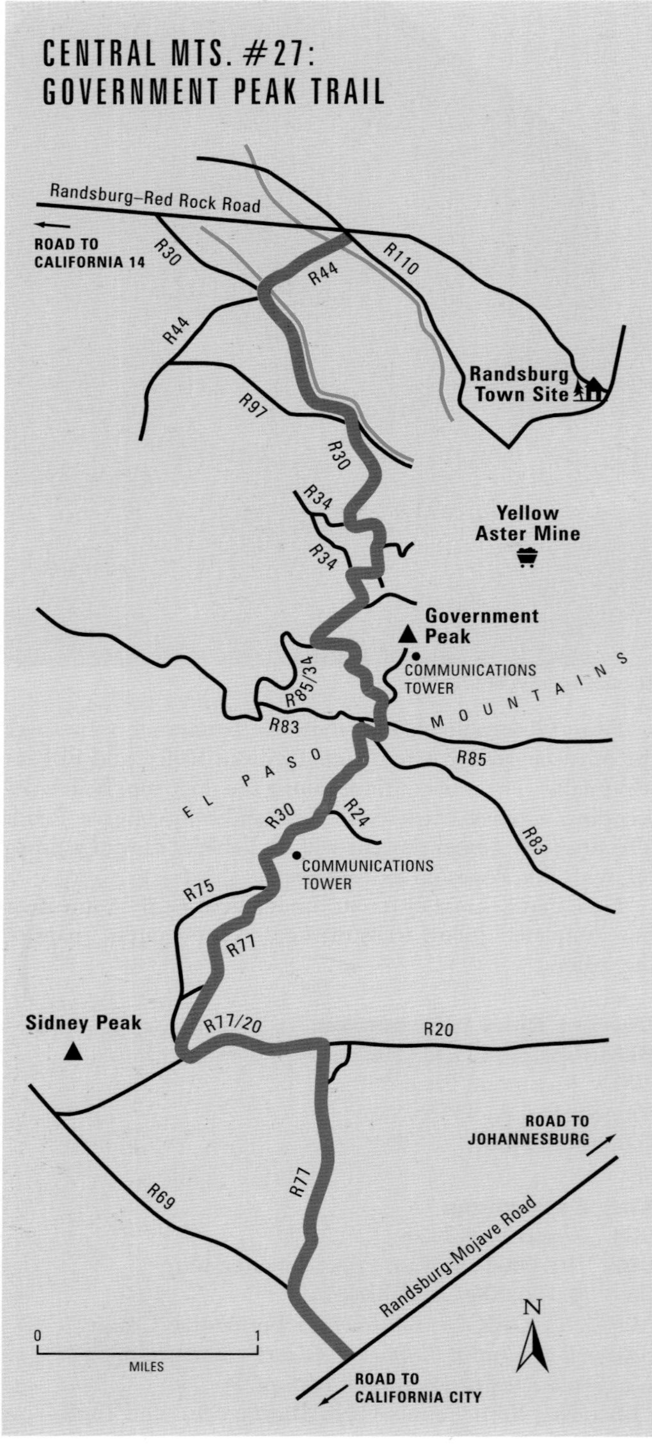

3.4 ▲		Trail ends at paved Randsburg-Red Rock Road. Turn right for Randsburg; turn left to exit to California 14.
		GPS: N35°22.82′ W117°40.61′
▼ 0.1	**SO**	Cross through wash.
3.3 ▲	SO	Cross through wash.
▼ 0.2	**SO**	Cross through wash.
3.2 ▲	SO	Cross through wash.
▼ 0.5	**TL**	Cross through wash; then turn left up wash onto R30 for 4WDs, ATVs, and motorbikes. R44 continues straight ahead. Track on right is also R30.
2.9 ▲	TR	Turn right out of wash onto R44 for 4WDs, ATVs, and motorbikes. R30 continues straight ahead. Track on left is also R44.
		GPS: N35°22.60′ W117°41.02′
▼ 1.1	**TR**	T-intersection. Turn right and exit wash, remaining on R30. Mining works on left.
2.3 ▲	TL	Turn left down wash, remaining on R30. Mining works at intersection.
		GPS: N35°22.13′ W117°40.56′
▼ 1.2	**BL**	Track on right is R97. Remain on R30.
2.2 ▲	BR	Track on left is R97. Remain on R30 and drop down to the wash.
▼ 1.7	**BL**	Track on right is R34 for 4WDs, ATVs, and motorbikes. Remain on R30.
1.7 ▲	BR	Track on left is R34 for 4WDs, ATVs, and motorbikes. Remain on R30.
		GPS: N35°21.66′ W117°40.65′
▼ 2.1	**BR**	Graded track on left. Trail leaves mining area.
1.3 ▲	BL	Graded track on right. Trail follows edge of mining area.
		GPS: N35°21.53′ W117°40.47′
▼ 2.2	**BR**	Bear right in front of wooden ore hopper, remaining on R30.
1.2 ▲	BL	Bear left in front of wooden ore hopper.
		GPS: N35°21.43′ W117°40.51′
▼ 2.3	**TL**	Track on right is R34.
1.1 ▲	TR	Track straight ahead is R34.
		GPS: N35°21.42′ W117°40.62′
▼ 2.5	**BR**	Track on left goes to ore hopper.
0.9 ▲	BL	Track straight ahead goes to ore hopper.
		GPS: N35°21.28′ W117°40.55′
▼ 2.8	**SO**	Viewpoint on right on tight left-hand switchback.
0.6 ▲	SO	Viewpoint on left on tight right-hand switchback.
▼ 2.9	**SO**	Track on right is R85/34 for 4WDs, ATVs, and motorbikes.
0.5 ▲	BR	Track on left is R85/34 for 4WDs, ATVs, and motorbikes.
		GPS: N35°21.10′ W117°40.81′
▼ 3.1	**SO**	Track on left to mine.
0.3 ▲	SO	Track on right to mine.
▼ 3.3	**SO**	Saddle. Track on left to communications tower and overlook above Yellow Aster Mine. Turnout on right. Remain on R85/30.
0.1 ▲	BL	Saddle. Track on right to communications tower and overlook above Yellow Aster Mine. Turnout on left. Remain on R85/30.
		GPS: N35°20.87′ W117°40.50′
▼ 3.4	**TR**	4-way intersection. Track on left. Track straight ahead is R85. Remain on R30 and zero trip meter.
0.0 ▲		Continue to the northwest.
		GPS: N35°20.80′ W117°40.47′
▼ 0.0		Continue to the southwest.
0.8 ▲	TL	4-way intersection. Track straight ahead. Track on right is R85. Remain on R30 and zero trip meter.
▼ 0.1	**SO**	Track on right and track on left are both R83 for 4WDs, ATVs, and motorbikes.
0.7 ▲	SO	Track on right and track on left are both R83 for 4WDs, ATVs, and motorbikes.
▼ 0.5	**SO**	Track on left is R24 for 4WDs, ATVs, and motorbikes.
0.3 ▲	SO	Track on right is R24 for 4WDs, ATVs, and motorbikes.

Mileage		Direction	Route
			GPS: N35°20.50' W117°40.75'
▼ 0.7		BR	Track on left to communications tower.
	0.1 ▲	BL	Track on right to communications tower.
▼ 0.8		BL	Communications tower on left; then bear left onto R77 for 4WDs, ATVs, and motorbikes. Track on right is R30/77. Zero trip meter.
	0.0 ▲		Continue to the northeast. End of climb.
			GPS: N35°20.31' W117°40.99'
▼ 0.0			Continue to the southeast. Trail starts to descend.
	3.7 ▲	BR	Track on left is R30/77 for 4WDs, ATVs, and motorbikes; then communications tower on right. Bear right onto R30 and zero trip meter.
▼ 0.3		SO	Track on right is R75 for 4WDs, ATVs, and motorbikes.
	3.4 ▲	0	Track on left is R75 for 4WDs, ATVs, and motorbikes.
			GPS: N35°20.12' W117°41.04'
▼ 0.9		BL	Track on right is R20 for 4WDs, ATVs, and motorbikes. Bear left onto R77/20.
	2.8 ▲	SO	Track on left is R20 for 4WDs, ATVs, and motorbikes. Bear right onto R77/20.
			GPS: N35°19.72' W117°41.40'
▼ 1.2		SO	Track on right is R75 for 4WDs, ATVs, and motorbikes.
	2.5 ▲	BR	Track on left is R75 for 4WDs, ATVs, and motorbikes.
▼ 1.3		BL	Track on right goes to private property.
	2.4 ▲	BR	Track on left goes to private property.
▼ 1.8		SO	Track on left to mine.
	1.9 ▲	SO	Track on right to mine.
▼ 2.0		TR	Turn right, remaining on R77. R20 continues straight ahead.
	1.7 ▲	TL	Turn left at T-intersection onto R77. R20 is on the right.
			GPS: N35°19.55' W117°40.77'
▼ 2.1		SO	Track on left.
	1.6 ▲	BL	Track on right.
▼ 2.2		SO	Track on left goes 0.1 miles to mine.
	1.5 ▲	SO	Track on right goes 0.1 miles to mine.
▼ 2.7		SO	Trail starts to descend to Randsburg-Mojave Road.
	1.0 ▲	SO	End of climb.
▼ 2.8		SO	Cross through wash.
	0.9 ▲	SO	Cross through wash.
▼ 3.2		SO	Tailings heap on right. End of descent.
	0.5 ▲	SO	Tailings heap on left. Start to climb.
▼ 3.3		TL	Turn left onto graded dirt road, which is also R77. R69 is on the right.
	0.4 ▲	TR	Turn right onto small formed trail R77. Straight ahead is R69.
			GPS: N35°18.46' W117°40.97'
▼ 3.7			Trail ends at intersection with graded dirt Randsburg-Mojave Road. Turn right for California City and California 14; turn left for Johannesburg and US 395.
	0.0 ▲		Trail commences on graded dirt Randsburg-Mojave Road, 4.7 miles west of US 395. Note that Randsburg-Mojave Road leaves US 395 as Osdick Road, which then becomes Randsburg-Mojave Road. Zero trip meter and turn northwest on graded dirt road. Road is marked R77 and immediately enters Rand Mountain Fremont Valley Management Area. There is a notice board at the intersection.
			GPS: N35°18.21' W117°40.69'

CENTRAL MOUNTAINS #28

Frazier Mountain Trail

Starting Point:	**Lockwood Valley Road, 5.5 miles southwest of Lake of the Woods**
Finishing Point:	**Lockwood Valley Road, 1 mile southwest of Lake of the Woods**
Total Mileage:	**15.3 miles, plus 4.1-mile spur**
Unpaved Mileage:	**15.3 miles, plus 4.1-mile spur**
Driving Time:	**3 hours**
Elevation Range:	**5,000–8,000 feet**
Usually Open:	**April to November**
Best Time to Travel:	**Dry weather**
Difficulty Rating:	**4**
Scenic Rating:	**8**
Remoteness Rating:	**+0**

Special Attractions

- Rocky 4WD route through Los Padres National Forest.
- Frazier Mountain Fire Lookout.
- Access to other trails for 4WDs, ATVs, and motorbikes.

History

William T. Frazier is the man after whom this mountain and associated trails are named. Frazier was a miner in these hills in the 1850s; the remains of one of his mines are located a short distance away from the trail. Names such as Arrastra Flat, at the bottom of the canyon below Frazier Mountain, and Gold Dust Mine farther to the south are reminders of the predominant pioneer activity in this region.

In anticipation of a mining boom, a town by the name of Lexington was laid out in 1887. The settlement was located on Piru Creek, south of Frazier Mountain. However, the town never developed, and little remains of it.

Borax deposits were found at the southern end of the trail in Lockwood Valley and have been mined by the Frazier Borate Company. A settlement in the valley was named Stauffer after John Stauffer, cofounder of the borax business. Stauffer and

Mine shaft and boiler remains on mountainside off Frazier Mountain Trail

his partner, Thomas Thorkildsen, established a company camp and store, which lasted until they were surpassed by the larger borax mines of Death Valley in the 1880s. A post office was established at Stauffer in 1905. It temporarily closed between 1933 and 1937, and shut its doors for good in 1942.

Frazier Mountain overlooks Tejon Pass and Peace Valley to the east. One of the major early routes to and from Los Angeles crossed the San Emigdio Mountains through these valleys.

The decommissioned Frazier Mountain Lookout Tower sits high above historic Tejon Pass

Tejon Pass was formerly called Fort Tejon Pass, in association with the historic Fort Tejon to the north in Kern County. The fort was established in the summer of 1854. By 1855, Phineas Banning's wagon trains were carting supplies from Los Angeles via Fort Tejon to Fort Miller in Fresno. With the Kern River gold rush also luring many away from the city, traffic out of Los Angeles was becoming heavy.

For a few years, a herd of camels was maintained at Fort Tejon. Under the suggestion of Edward F. Beale (see page 73), the camels were shipped from Africa and stationed at Fort Tejon. Beale had convinced Secretary of War Jefferson Davis that a camel corps would be well suited for duty in the California desert. The camels remained at Fort Tejon until 1861.

Fort Tejon was located along the Butterfield stagecoach route. The first stagecoach stopped there in the middle of the night on October 8, 1858. The stage was en route from St. Louis, heading for San Francisco via Los Angeles. From the fort, the journey became quite dangerous. It followed the shelf road through Grapevine Canyon past Comanche Point, and then went on to cross the San Joaquin Valley. The fort finally closed in September 1864. The property was later to become an important part of Edward Beale's ranch.

After his discharge in 1864, a soldier by the name of Henry Gorman settled in the area. Having served at Fort Tejon, Gorman knew the region well. In 1877, he operated the first post office south of the pass, Gorman's Station. This post office opened and closed five times by the 1910s.

A settlement to the north of Tejon Pass, Lebec, gained its first post office in 1895. In its early days, many bears roamed the region around Lebec. A carved inscription on an old oak tree related the tale of Peter Lebeck, a traveler who was killed by a bear in October 1837. It is thought that Lebeck, possibly spelled Lebec, may have been part of a Hudson's Bay party led by Michael La Framboise.

Description

The route past Frazier Peak combines a number of different trails to form a loop. The standard varies slightly, ranging from 2 to 4 over the course of the trail.

The trail commences on Lockwood Valley Road and initially follows a graded dirt road that runs alongside Seymour Creek. It then turns off onto one of the designated 4WD routes that crisscross the region, the blue-rated West Frazier Mine Route. This trail gradually climbs around some of the lower slopes of Frazier Mountain, becoming more uneven and eroded as it climbs through scrub oak, pine, and juniper. The grade is moderate and should not cause any trouble. The surface alternates between loose gravel and embedded rocks.

The route then turns onto West Frazier Tie Route, again blue-rated, which climbs a steeper grade onto Frazier Mountain. In places the grade reaches 25 percent, but it is usually more level. Although a bit loose and rocky in places, the trail will be within the crawling capabilities of most 4WDs.

On top of the mountain, the trail standard is easier as it travels around the eastern edge of Frazier Mountain through open pine forest. There are views south to Hungry Valley State Vehicular Recreation Area and Angeles National Forest. An old wooden fire lookout still stands on Frazier Mountain, now dwarfed by communications towers surrounding it. Like other lookouts in the region, it is no longer in use; the fire watch is carried out more efficiently from airplanes.

The trail follows a less direct route down from the mountain along a smaller road than others in the area. A spur trail heads off from this point, running out for 4 miles to end at a small loop. A popular blue-rated motorbike route connects through to Hungry Valley State Vehicular Recreation Area. All other vehicles must travel the roughly graded road back down to rejoin Lockwood Valley Road. The route exits past the Chuchupate National Forest Ranger Station near Lake of the Woods.

The trails in this region are closed during winter depending on snowfall, and they may close during or after heavy rains the rest of the year.

Views through Lockwood Valley, an old borax mining area

Current Road Information
Los Padres National Forest
Mt. Pinos Ranger District
34580 Lockwood Valley Road
Frazier Park, CA 93225
(661) 245-3731

Map References
BLM Cuyama, Lancaster
USFS Los Padres National Forest: Mt. Pinos, Ojai and Santa Barbara Ranger Districts
USGS 1:24,000 Cuddy Valley, Lockwood Valley, Frazier Mt.
1:100,000 Cuyama, Lancaster
Maptech CD-ROM: Barstow/San Bernardino County; San Luis Obispo/Los Padres National Forest
Southern & Central California Atlas & Gazetteer, p. 77
California Road & Recreation Atlas, p. 102

Route Directions

▼ 0.0 From Lockwood Valley Road, 5.5 miles southwest of Lake of the Woods, zero trip meter and turn south on graded dirt road 8N12 at sign for Lockwood Creek Campground.
1.4 ▲ Trail ends at T-intersection with Lockwood Valley Road. Turn left for California 33; turn right for Lake of the Woods.

GPS: N34°45.58' W119°02.94'

▼ 0.3 SO Cross through Seymour Creek wash.
1.1 ▲ SO Cross through Seymour Creek wash.

▼ 0.4 SO Cattle guard.
1.0 ▲ SO Cattle guard.

▼ 0.8 SO Track on right.
0.6 ▲ SO Track on left.

▼ 0.9 SO Cross through creek.
0.5 ▲ SO Cross through creek.

▼ 1.0 SO Closure gate.
0.4 ▲ SO Closure gate.

GPS: N34°44.89' W119°02.68'

▼ 1.3 SO Cross through wash.
0.1 ▲ SO Cross through wash.

▼ 1.4 TL Track on right is Lockwood Mine Road. Turn left onto West Frazier Mine Road #118—rated green for motorbikes and ATVs, rated blue for 4WDs. Zero trip meter.
0.0 ▲ Continue to the west.

GPS: N34°44.74' W119°02.32'

▼ 0.0 Continue to the north through closure gate.
3.4 ▲ TR Closure gate; then track straight ahead is Lockwood Mine Route. Turn right, joining graded road, and zero trip meter.

▼ 0.1 SO Cross through wash.
3.3 ▲ SO Cross through wash.

▼ 0.2 SO Cross through wash.
3.2 ▲ SO Cross through wash.

▼ 0.4 SO Track on left.
3.0 ▲ SO Track on right.

GPS: N34°45.04' W119°02.13'

▼ 0.6 SO Cross through two washes.
2.8 ▲ SO Cross through two washes.

▼ 0.8 SO Cross through wash.
2.6 ▲ SO Cross through wash.

▼ 1.0 BR Turnout on left.
2.4 ▲ BL Turnout on right.

▼ 1.6 BL Track on right. Follow trail route marker.
1.8 ▲ SO Track on left.

GPS: N34°45.61' W119°01.17'

▼ 1.8 SO Cross through wash and start to climb.
1.6 ▲ SO End of descent. Cross through wash.

▼ 2.1 SO Cross over creek.
1.3 ▲ SO Cross over creek.

▼ 2.2 SO Trail does a sharp switchback to the left. Remains of mine ahead—little remains except adit in hillside.
1.2 ▲ SO Trail does a sharp switchback to the right. Remains of mine ahead—little remains except adit in hillside.

GPS: N34°45.71' W119°00.80'

▼ 2.4 BL Two tracks on right go 0.1 miles to mine adits.
1.0 ▲ SO Two tracks on left go 0.1 miles to mine adits.

GPS: N34°45.79' W119°00.81'

▼ 3.2 SO Track on right.
0.2 ▲ SO Track on left.

GPS: N34°46.02' W119°00.23'

▼ 3.3 SO Gate.
0.1 ▲ SO Gate.

▼ 3.4 BR Track on left is continuation of West Frazier Mine Trail for 4WDs, ATVs, and motorbikes—rated green. Bear right onto West Frazier Tie Trail for 4WDs, ATVs, and motorbikes—rated blue. Zero trip meter.
0.0 ▲ Continue to the southwest. End of descent.

GPS: N34°46.17' W119°00.13'

▼ 0.0 Continue to the northeast and start to climb steeply.
3.1 ▲ BL Track on right and left is West Frazier Mine Trail for 4WDs, ATVs, and motorbikes—rated green. Zero trip meter.

▼ 0.7 SO End of climb.
2.4 ▲ SO Trail starts to descend.

▼ 1.1 TL T-intersection. Track on right. Turn left onto 8N41.
2.0 ▲ TR Turn right onto West Frazier Tie Trail for 4WDs, ATVs, and motorbikes—rated blue. Trail continues ahead.

GPS: N34°45.78' W118°59.48'

▼ 2.3 BR Track on left is continuation of 8N41. Bear right, following trail sign.
0.8 ▲ SO Track on right is 8N41. Continue straight, joining 8N41.

GPS: N34°46.21' W118°58.40'

▼ 3.0 SO Track on left and communications tower on left.
0.1 ▲ BL Track on right and communications tower on right.

▼ 3.1 BR Frazier Mountain Fire Lookout and two communications towers on left. Bear right onto trail sign-posted to East Frazier Road. Zero trip meter. Track on left is 8N04.
0.0 ▲ Continue to the east.

GPS: N34°46.53' W118°58.13'

▼ 0.0 Continue to the northwest.
1.0 ▲ BL Track on right is 8N04. Zero trip meter and bear left toward communications towers. Two towers and Frazier Mountain Fire Lookout on right.

▼ 0.4 BR Track on left.
0.6 ▲ BL Track on right.

▼ 1.0 TL T-intersection with roughly graded dirt East Frazier Road. Turn left to continue along main

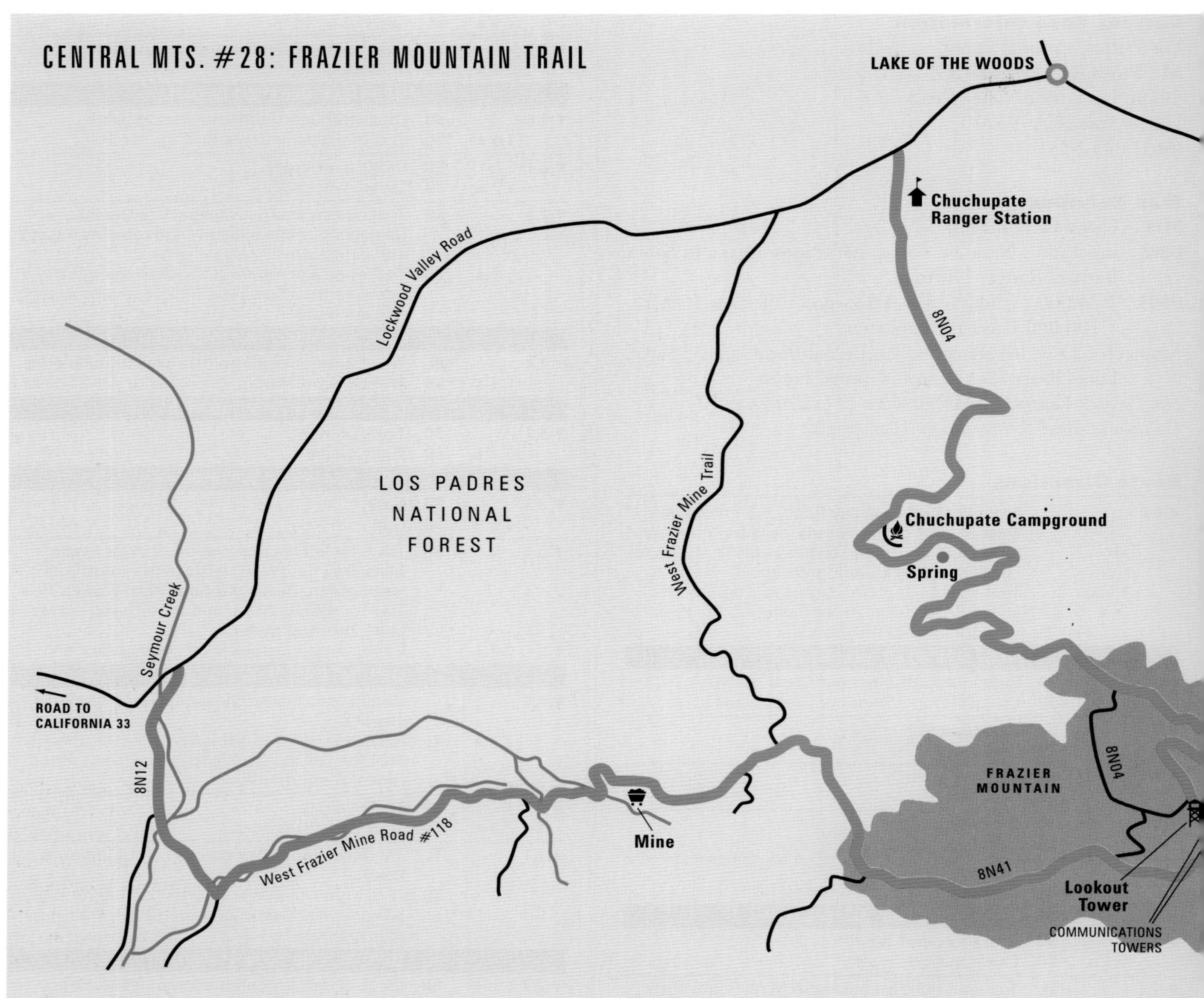

		trail; turn right to travel the Frazier Mine Spur. Zero trip meter.
0.0 ▲		Continue to the southwest.

GPS: N34°46.78' W118°57.92'

Frazier Mine Spur

▼ 0.0		Continue to the east.
▼ 0.5	SO	Track on right is Arrastra Trail #121. It is a vehicle route for 0.4 miles before becoming a black-rated trail for motorbikes only. Frazier Mine is below the motorbike trail.

GPS: N34°46.85' W118°57.51'

▼ 4.0	SO	Track on left is East Frazier Trail #120 for motorbikes only—rated blue. This trail accesses Hungry Valley State Vehicular Recreation Area.

GPS: N34°46.92' W118°55.76'

▼ 4.1	UT	Trail ends at a small loop. Retrace your steps back to the main trail.

GPS: N34°46.85' W118°55.81'

Continuation of Main Trail

▼ 0.0		Continue to the west.
4.0 ▲	TR	Turn right onto smaller, formed trail marked with a trail sign to continue on main trail. Zero trip meter. Continue straight ahead to travel Frazier Mine Spur.

GPS: N34°46.78' W118°57.92'

▼ 0.9	SO	Track on left is 8N04 to Frazier Mountain Fire Lookout. Continue straight, joining 8N04.
3.1 ▲	SO	Track on right is 8N04 to Frazier Mountain Fire Lookout. Continue straight on 8N24, following sign to East Frazier Trail.

GPS: N34°46.88' W118°58.70'

▼ 3.4	SO	Tank and spring on left.
0.6 ▲	SO	Tank and spring on right.

GPS: N34°47.16' W118°59.78'

▼ 3.6	SO	Closure gate.
0.4 ▲	SO	Closure gate.
▼ 4.0	SO	Track on right goes into Chuchupate USFS Campground. Zero trip meter.

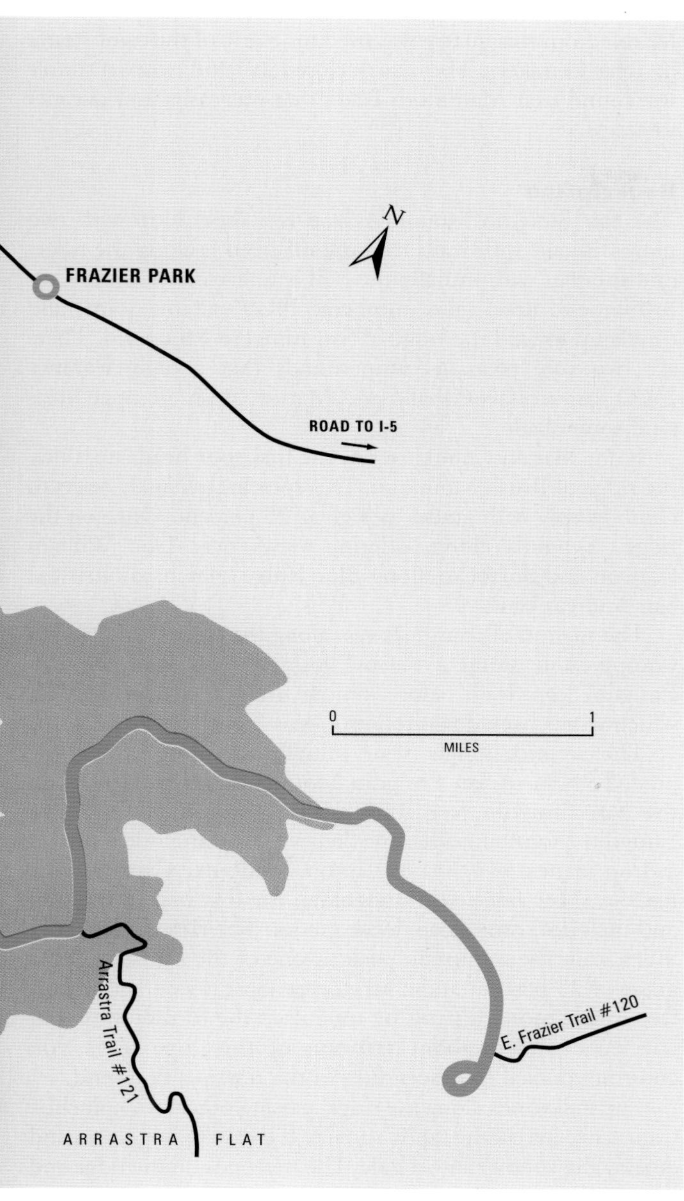

	0.0 ▲		Continue west on 8N04. Road is now graded dirt.
			GPS: N34°47.17′ W119°00.06′
▼ 0.0			Continue to the northeast on 8N04. Road is now paved. Remain on paved road, ignoring turns on left and right.
	2.4 ▲	BR	Track on left goes into Chuchupate USFS Campground. Zero trip meter.
▼ 2.2		SO	Closure gate; then Chuchupate Ranger Station on left.
	0.2 ▲	SO	Chuchupate Ranger Station on right; then closure gate.
▼ 2.4			Trail ends at intersection with Lockwood Valley Road. Turn left for California 33 and Ojai; turn right for Lake of the Woods.
	0.0 ▲		Trail commences along Lockwood Valley Road, 1 mile west of Lake of the Woods. Zero trip meter and turn southeast on paved road at sign for Chuchupate Ranger Station and Frazier Mountain Lookout.
			GPS: N34°48.57′ W119°00.69′

San Emigdio Mountain Trail

Starting Point:	**Cerro Noroeste Road, 4 miles west of Pine Mountain Club**
Finishing Point:	**Cerro Noroeste Road, 2.2 miles west of Pine Mountain Club**
Total Mileage:	**14.9 miles (round-trip) including both spurs**
Unpaved Mileage:	**14.9 miles**
Driving Time:	**2 hours (round-trip) including both spurs**
Elevation Range:	**5,700–7,400 feet**
Usually Open:	**Year-round**
Best Time to Travel:	**Dry weather**
Difficulty Rating:	**4, 5 for spur to San Emigdio Peak**
Scenic Rating:	**8**
Remoteness Rating:	**+0**

Special Attractions

- Loop trail offering two more-challenging spurs.
- National forest campgrounds and backcountry campsites.
- Wide-ranging views from the narrow ridge trail.

History

Considering that this trail runs mainly within the San Andreas Rift Zone, it is no surprise that there are frequent earth movements in the region. The name San Emigdio Mountain was chosen with this in mind. St. Emidius was a German martyr believed to offer protection from earthquakes. The name San Emigdio, also known as San Emidio, first appeared on a land grant in 1842. In July of that year, California governor Juan B. Alvarado granted a total of 17,709 acres of land to José Anto-

Descending San Emigdio Mountain with El Camino Veijo 3,000 feet below

A steep climb west from Marian Campground provides views of San Emigdio Mountain

nio Dominguez. In 1866, half of this parcel was patented to John C. Frémont, and the other half went to the heirs at law of José Antonio Dominguez, who had died of smallpox about one year after gaining the original land grant. It is commonly thought that this particular San Emigdio land grant was, in effect, the start of rancho days in what was to become Kern County. This property is visible way below the trail as it passes over San Emigdio Mountain. Look down through Doc Williams Canyon on the northern side of the range.

Beginning with San Diego in 1769, Spanish missionaries and soldiers established a string of missions and presidios in what was then known as Alta California. Jesuit missionaries had been expelled from Baja California by the king of Spain and were instructed to explore and settle the coast to the north. As missions developed up and down coastal California, they began to have a noticeable effect on native lifestyles. Some Indians chose to move away toward the San Joaquin Valley. Many traveled along El Camino Viejo. Spanish deserters moving between the San Francisco Bay area and Los Angeles also traveled this road in the late 1700s because it enabled them to travel from north to south without detection by the coastal missions. El Camino Viejo (literally "the old road" in Spanish) climbs up the spectacular eastern side of San Emigdio Mountain and enters the San Andreas Rift Zone. It roughly follows the course of San Emigdio Creek through what is known as Devils Kitchen, which is below the eastern spur off this trail. From there, El Camino Viejo followed close to today's Mil Potrero Highway, passing by Frazier Park en route to Los Angeles.

Traffic along the inland route varied over the years. Beaver trappers and missionaries were among the more frequent travelers along the road. However, their presence in the area began to push the native Yokuts farther inland. The Yokuts quickly adapted to the European intrusion. They found that the settlers' horses, as well as being good eating, were an excellent form of transportation that made it easier to avoid conflict with troops or rancheros. The Yokuts, with the assistance of other native people who had moved inland to avoid the missionaries, stole the settlers' horses. The settlers retaliated, often taking the Yokuts for slave labor.

Pine Mountain Club, a residential development begun in the mid-1970s, was once a marble quarry that produced a very pure white marble with a fine gray vein running through it. Marble from this quarry was used for many of the tombstones in Taft's Cemetery. The quarry closed in 1962, when a source was found near Mammoth Lakes that was easier and cheaper to access.

Description

The San Emigdio Mountain Trail is a short loop with two more difficult spur trails running off from it along the ridge, one at either end. Initially the trail is uneven as it leaves Cerro Noroeste Road (also numbered FR 95 at this point) and travels up toward the ridge of San Emigdio Mountain. There are two very pleasant campgrounds that a high-clearance 2WD can access—Caballo and Marian. Both are open areas with some shade.

From Marian Campground, the first spur heads up along the ridge to Brush Mountain. This spur immediately starts to climb steeply with grades as high as 25 percent. Once on the ridge, it winds along, offering views over Doc William Canyon and northeast along Blue Ridge, which parallels the San Andreas Fault.

The main trail continues east along the ridge from Marian Campground along a narrow formed section of the San Emigdio Jeep Trail, before joining the graded road, 9N34, which winds back down to join Cerro Noroeste Road.

The second, longer spur initially continues along the graded 9N34 to San Emigdio Mountain, where it picks up the San Emigdio Jeep Trail again. Viewpoints from San Emigdio Mountain offer excellent views to the north, down a drop of nearly 3,000 feet into Cloudburst Canyon. The narrow, sheer ridge continues along the first part of the trail and includes some steep, loose grades. The first descent, 0.3 miles from the mountain peak, is one of the steepest with a grade of 25 percent and a very deep, loose, low-traction surface, made more difficult by moguls at the top. Be sure that you feel confident about returning up this slope before you commit yourself to descending it; the trail is a dead end.

The trail winds along the ridge, passing other steep pinches. Care is needed on the sandy surface. It is easy to bog down and quickly dig yourself into a hole. The trail ends on the ridge and turns into an area for nonmotorized recreation only.

Current Road Information

Los Padres National Forest
Mt. Pinos Ranger District
34580 Lockwood Valley Road
Frazier Park, CA 93225
(661) 245-3731

Map References

BLM Cuyama
USFS Los Padres National Forest: Mt. Pinos, Ojai and Santa Barbara Ranger Districts
USGS 1:24,000 Sawmill Mountain, Eagle Rest Peak
1:100,000 Cuyama
Maptech CD-ROM: San Luis Obispo/Los Padres National Forest
Southern & Central California Atlas & Gazetteer, p. 76, 77
California Road & Recreation Atlas, p. 101

Route Directions

▼ 0.0			From Cerro Noroeste Road (FR 95), 20 miles southeast of the intersection with California 33/166 and 4 miles west of Pine Mountain Club, zero trip meter and turn west onto graded dirt road 9N27, following sign for Marian Campground. Immediately pass through closure gate. Cerro Noroeste Road is 9 miles south of Maricopa along California 33/166.
	1.8 ▲		Pass through closure gate; then trail finishes on Cerro Noroeste Road (FR 95). Turn left for Pine Mountain Club; turn right for California 33/166 and Maricopa.
			GPS: N34°51.80' W119°13.63'
▼ 0.5		SO	Caballo Campground on right and left.
	1.3 ▲	SO	Caballo Campground on right and left.
			GPS: N34°52.12' W119°13.53'
▼ 1.8		TR	Turn right at sign into Marian Campground. Track ahead is the start of Brush Mountain Spur along San Emigdio Jeep Trail #107. Zero trip meter.
	0.0 ▲		Continue to the southwest.
			GPS: N34°52.83' W119°12.99'

Brush Mountain Spur

▼ 0.0			Continue north at sign for Marian Campground.
▼ 0.1		TL	T-intersection. Turn left onto San Emigdio Jeep Trail #107—rated green for ATVs and motorbikes, rated blue for 4WDs. Track on right goes into Marian Campground.
			GPS: N34°52.88' W119°12.96'
▼ 1.0		SO	Track on left.
▼ 1.4		UT	Track on left is the end of small loop. Trail runs around a small loop and returns to this point. Retrace your route back toward the campground.
			GPS: N34°53.51' W119°13.68'

Continuation of Main Trail

▼ 0.0			Continue to the east.
▼ 1.2		TL	Turn left at sign for Marian Campground. Track on right is the start of Brush Mountain Spur along San Emigdio Jeep Trail #107. Zero trip meter.
			GPS: N34°52.83' W119°12.99'
▼ 0.1		BR	Keeping the campground on your left, bear right past sign for the San Emigdio Jeep Road, suitable for 4WDs, ATVs, and motorbikes—rated green.
	1.1 ▲	BL	Keeping the campground on your right, leave track on right through campground.
			GPS: N34°52.81' W119°12.93'
▼ 1.2		TR	Turn right onto better graded trail 9N34 (unmarked), and zero trip meter. Road ahead is San Emigdio Mountain Spur.
	0.0 ▲		Continue to the northwest.
			GPS: N34°52.33' W119°12.12'

San Emigdio Mountain Spur

▼ 0.0			Proceed southeast on graded road from intersection with San Emigdio Jeep Trail #107.
▼ 1.6		SO	Track on right goes to quarry.
▼ 1.8		SO	Turnout on left is San Emigdio Peak. Continue onto San Emigdio Trail—rated green for motorbikes, rated blue for ATVs and 4WDs. Zero trip meter.
			GPS: N34°52.32' W119°10.48'
▼ 0.0			Continue to the east.
▼ 0.3		BL	Trail forks.
			GPS: N34°52.18' W119°10.27'
▼ 1.6		SO	Suggested turnaround point. The last 0.4 miles of the trail are tight, twisty, and brushy, and do not go to a particular viewpoint.
			GPS: N34°51.93' W119°09.31'
▼ 2.0		UT	Trail ends at closure sign.
			GPS: N34°51.90' W119°09.06'

Continuation of Main Trail

▼ 0.0			Continue to the west.
	1.5 ▲	TL	Turn left onto San Emigdio Jeep Trail #107 at sign. Trail is suitable for 4WDs, ATVs, and motorbikes—rated green. Track on right is San Emigdio Mountain Spur. Zero trip meter.
			GPS: N34°52.33' W119°12.12'
▼ 1.4		SO	Closure gate.

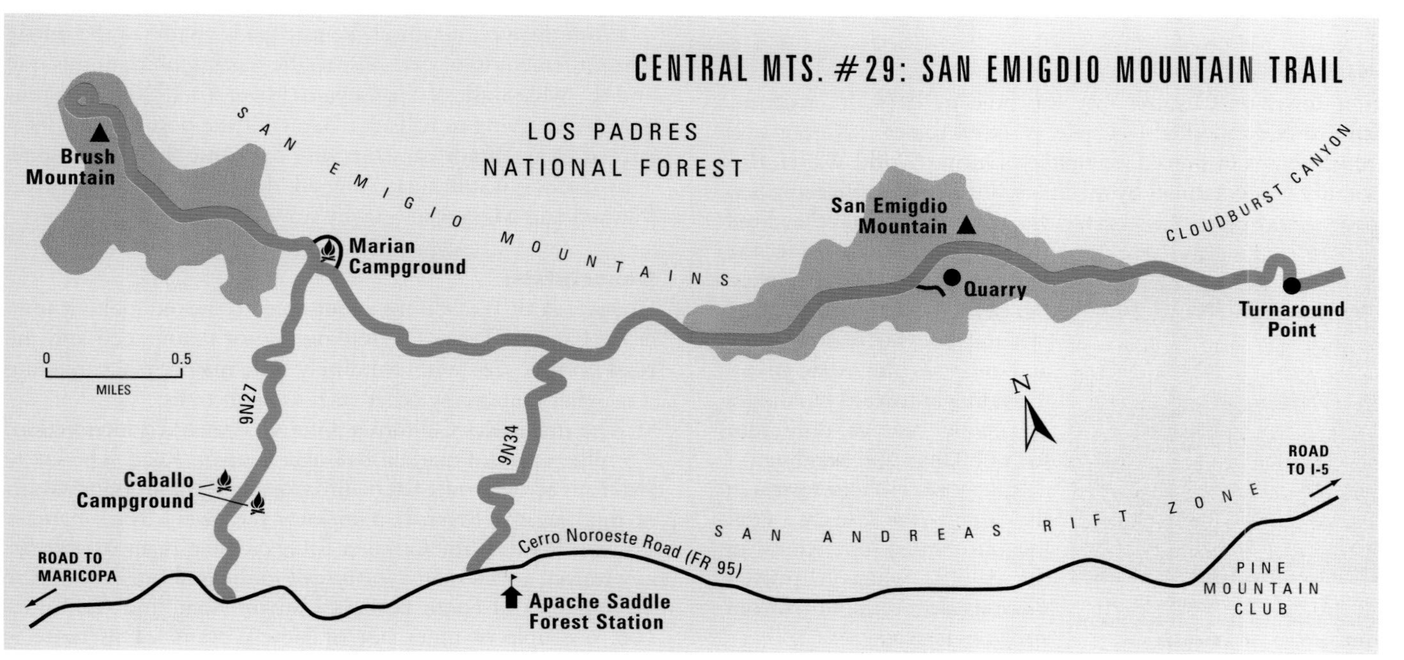

0.1 ▲	SO	Closure gate.
▼ 1.5	SO	Trail ends at T-intersection with Cerro Noroeste Road. Turn left for Pine Mountain Club; turn right for Maricopa and California 33/166.
0.0 ▲		Trail commences on Cerro Noroeste Road (FR 95), 0.2 miles west of Apache Saddle Forest Station and 2.2 miles west of Pine Mountain Club. Zero trip meter and turn north on unsigned, graded dirt road 9N34.

GPS: N34°51.69′ W119°12.71′

CENTRAL MOUNTAINS #30

Cuyama Peak Trail

Starting Point:	**California 33, 0.5 miles south of the intersection with Ballinger Canyon Road**
Finishing Point:	**Cuyama Peak Fire Lookout**
Total Mileage:	**16.3 miles (one-way)**
Unpaved Mileage:	**12.1 miles**
Driving Time:	**1.5 hours (one-way)**
Elevation Range:	**2,700–5,800 feet**
Usually Open:	**Year-round, may be closed briefly after snowfall**
Best Time to Travel:	**Dry weather**
Difficulty Rating:	**3**
Scenic Rating:	**8**
Remoteness Rating:	**+0**

Special Attractions

- Cuyama Peak Fire Lookout and shingle cabin.
- Rough, unmaintained shelf road climbing to Cuyama Peak.
- Popular trail for hunters (in season) and bird-watchers.

History

The tower on Cuyama Peak was built in 1934. Its structure, known as a modified L-4 style, is set on top of a 20-foot steel tower that is H-braced for rigidity. During World War II, this facility was occupied by members of the Aircraft Warning Service. The small cabin they lived in still stands alongside the lookout tower. Unfortunately, the cabin has attracted its share of vandals, who remove more and more as the years go by. This shingle-covered building is apparently one of only four such buildings still standing.

Cuyama Peak Fire Lookout—its fire-spotting days are over, but it remains rewarding for bird-watchers

Like most lookout towers in the region, the Cuyama Peak lookout ceased operations in the 1960s, when it proved more efficient to spot fires from airplanes instead.

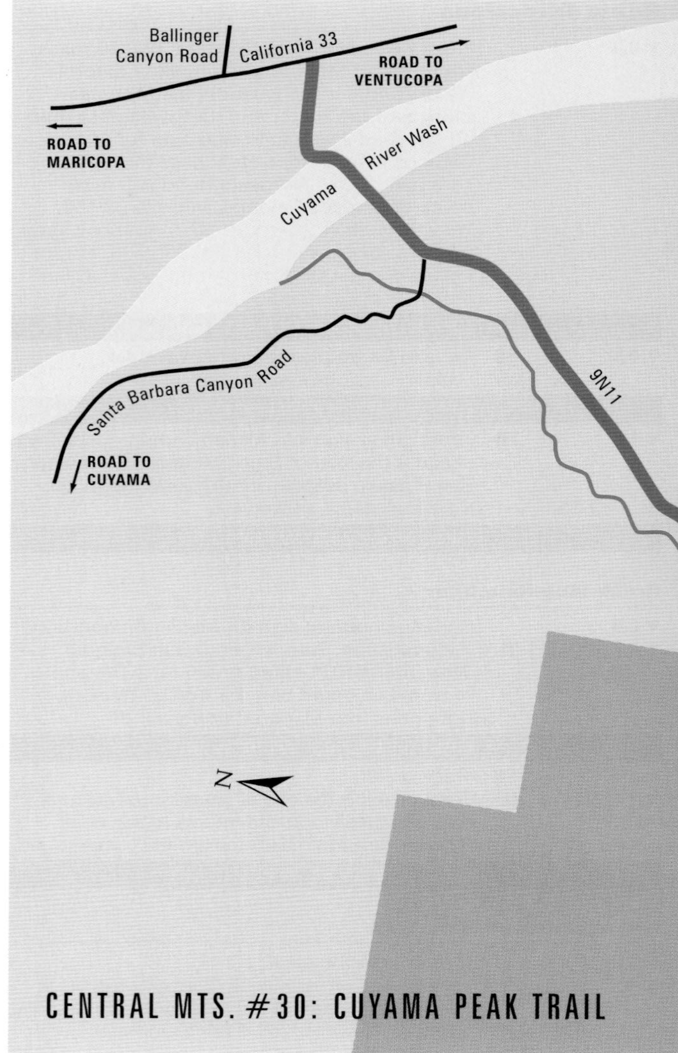

From the lookout tower, Ventucopa is visable to the north. The settlement is located close to the starting point of this trail and the wide wash of the Cuyama River. In 1926, when residents were trying to register a name for the post office, a local named Dean Parady came up with the name that was laughed at by many, but still stuck. After all, the settlement lay between Ventura and Maricopa. So why not call it Ventucopa?

Description

Cuyama Peak Trail climbs a long spur to the old lookout tower on Cuyama Peak. The lookout is not maintained and the road up to it sees correspondingly little maintenance, making it rougher than many other such lookout trails.

The trail leaves California 33 at an unmarked intersection, 0.5 miles south of marked Ballinger Canyon Road. The sandy trail runs across a river flat before crossing the wide, sandy wash of the Cuyama River. It then joins the paved Santa Barbara Canyon Road. If the Cuyama River crossing is impassable for any reason, an alternative entry/exit to the trail can be found at the junction of Santa Barbara Canyon Road and California 166, a couple of miles east of New Cuyama. This route is

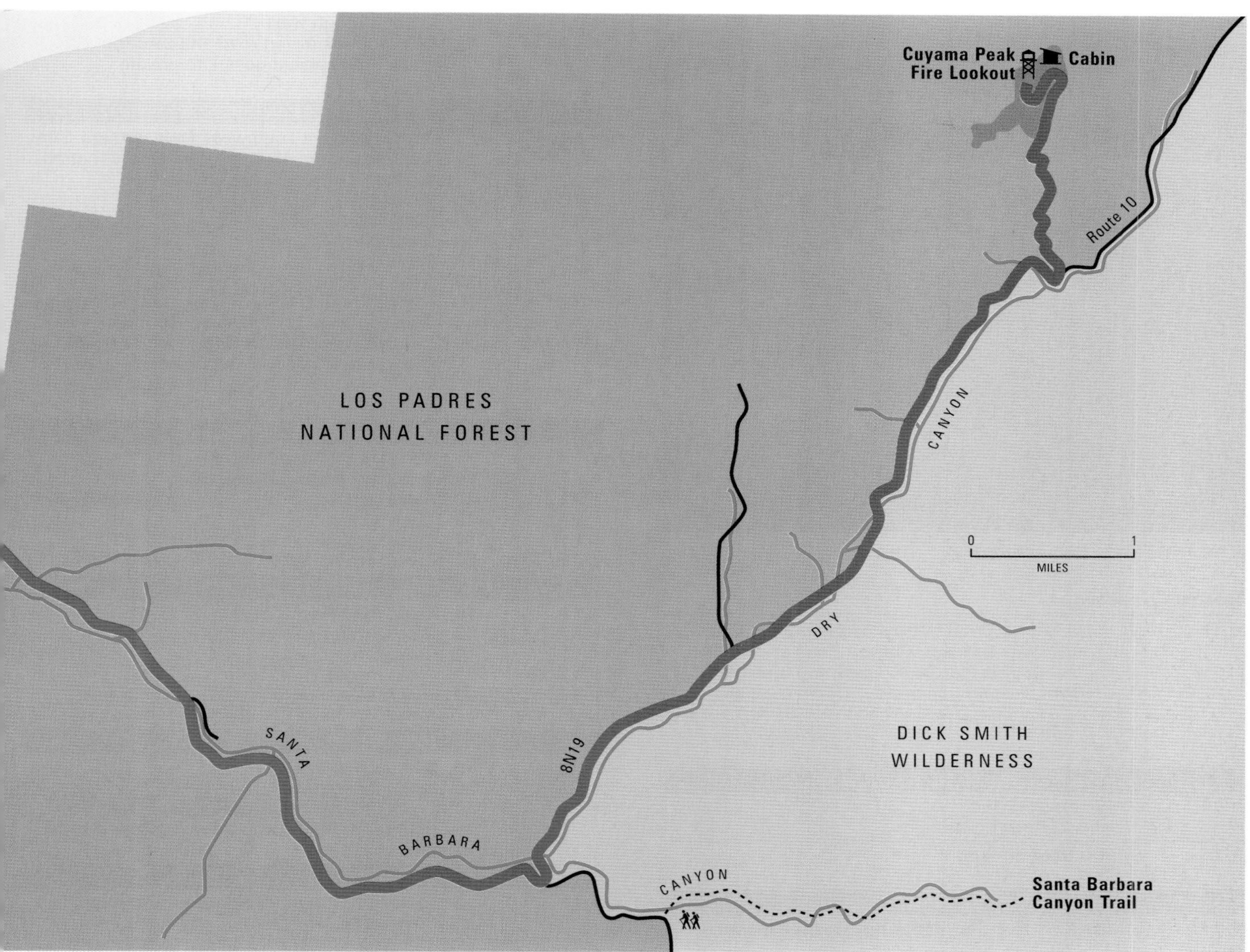

longer but avoids the sandy river crossing.

Initially, the trail passes through ranchland before entering Los Padres National Forest. It follows Santa Barbara Canyon before turning off into the narrower, rougher Dry Canyon. The Santa Barbara Canyon Trail, for hikers and horses, can be accessed from a major intersection near the start of Dry Canyon. There are some reasonable campsites along this spur, which goes 1.8 miles before stopping at a closure gate. Hikers can continue past the closure gate to McPherson Peak.

The main trail crosses the creek a number of times as it winds along Dry Canyon. Campers are better off selecting a site in the lower portion of the canyon; as it climbs and becomes tighter, there is less space available. The creek crossings can be rough and sandy. Water can race down this canyon, rearranging the creek crossings as it does so.

The trail climbs away from the creek for the final 3 miles to the old Cuyama Peak Fire Lookout and shingle cabin. The grades are moderate, but the shelf road can be loose in places. There are panoramic views from the lookout over the Dick Smith Wilderness, Chumash Wilderness, Cuyama Valley, and Los Padres National Forest.

The trail is popular with deer hunters (in season) and birdwatchers, who keep a special eye out for the pinyon jay.

Current Road Information

Los Padres National Forest
Mt. Pinos Ranger District
34580 Lockwood Valley Road
Frazier Park, CA 93225
(661) 245-3731

Map References

BLM Cuyama
USFS Los Padres National Forest: Mt. Pinos, Ojai and Santa Barbara Ranger Districts
USGS 1:24,000 Ballinger Canyon, Cuyama, Fox Mt., Cuyama Peak
1:100,000 Cuyama
Maptech CD-ROM: San Luis Obispo/Los Padres National Forest
Southern & Central California Atlas & Gazetteer, p. 76
California Road & Recreation Atlas, p. 101

View from the Cuyama Peak Fire Lookout

Route Directions

▼ 0.0 From California 33, 0.5 miles south of intersection with Ballinger Canyon Road and 4 miles south of California 166, zero trip meter and turn west on unmarked, formed dirt trail.

1.4 ▲ Trail ends at T-intersection with California 33. Turn left for Maricopa; turn right for Ventucopa.

GPS: N34°52.78' W119°29.79'

▼ 0.3 SO Track on left.

1.1 ▲ SO Track on right.

▼ 0.6 BL Track on right.

0.8 ▲ BR Track on left.

GPS: N34°52.76' W119°30.37'

▼ 0.7 SO Start to cross wide sandy wash of Cuyama River.

0.7 ▲ SO Exit Cuyama River Wash.

GPS: N34°52.68' W119°30.34'

▼ 1.0 SO Exit Cuyama River Wash.

0.4 ▲ SO National forest route marker—road not maintained for low-clearance vehicles. Start to cross wide sandy wash of Cuyama River.

▼ 1.4 SO Track on right opposite private property; then bear left on small paved road, following sign to Santa Barbara Canyon Road, and cross cattle guard. Road is now marked 9N11. Road crosses private property. Remain on main road. Road on right is also Santa Barbara Canyon Road to Cuyama. Zero trip meter.

0.0 ▲ Continue to the north.

GPS: N34°52.12' W119°30.81'

▼ 0.0 Continue to the south.

▼ 0.8 SO Two cattle guards.

▼ 2.6 SO Cattle guard. Entering Los Padres National Forest. Track on left to well.

GPS: N34°50.38' W119°32.50'

▼ 2.7 SO Second track on left to well.

▼ 3.0 SO Cross through wash.

▼ 3.1 SO Cattle guard.

▼ 3.3 SO Cattle guard. Entering private property. Remain on paved road.

GPS: N34°49.83' W119°32.88'

▼ 3.7 SO Cross through wash.

▼ 4.2 BR Bear right on paved road and zero trip meter. Road ahead goes into private property.

GPS: N34°49.13' W119°33.37'

▼ 0.0 Continue to the southwest. Pass through gate; then cross through creek. Road turns to graded dirt.

▼ 0.3 SO Cattle guard.

▼ 0.7 SO Cattle guard.

▼ 0.8 SO Cross through wash.

▼ 2.0 SO Cattle guard.

▼ 2.4 SO Track on right.

▼ 3.1 TL Turn left onto 8N19, following sign to Cuyama Peak Lookout. Track ahead passes some campsites and accesses the Santa Barbara Canyon Trail for hikers and horses before reaching a locked gate in 1.8 miles. Zero trip meter.

GPS: N34°47.13' W119°34.25'

▼ 0.0 Continue to the northeast.

▼ 0.2 SO Cross through wide wash.

▼ 0.3 SO Gate.

▼ 1.7 SO Track on left.

▼ 2.1 SO Cross through wash and track on left.

▼ 2.2 SO Cross through wash.

GPS: N34°46.27' W119°32.44'

▼ 2.3 SO Cross over wash.

▼ 2.7 SO Cross through wash.

▼ 3.1 SO Cross through wash.

▼ 3.9 SO Cross through wash.

▼ 4.9 SO Trail leaves creek and starts to climb shelf road.

GPS: N34°45.36' W119°30.02'

▼ 5.1 SO Saddle.

▼ 5.2 SO Cross through wash.

▼ 5.5 SO Cross through wash. Lesser-used track on right at left-hand switchback is Route #10 for motorbikes.

GPS: N34°44.96' W119°29.80'

▼ 7.6 Trail ends at old lookout tower and cabin on Cuyama Peak.

GPS: N34°45.24' W119°28.52'

CENTRAL MOUNTAINS #31

Potrero Seco Trail

Starting Point:	**California 33, 31 miles north of Ojai, 3.6 miles north of Pine Mountain Inn**
Finishing Point:	**Monte Arido**
Total Mileage:	**13.7 miles (one-way)**
Unpaved Mileage:	**13.7 miles**
Driving Time:	**1.5 hours (one-way)**
Elevation Range:	**4,700–5,600 feet**
Usually Open:	**Year-round, closed after rain or snow**
Best Time to Travel:	**Dry weather**
Difficulty Rating:	**3**
Scenic Rating:	**8**
Remoteness Rating:	**+1**

Special Attractions

- Lightly traveled, permit-only trail within Los Padres National Forest.
- Trail travels around the edge of Dick Smith Wilderness and Matilija Wilderness.
- Beautiful, winding ridge top trail.

Description

This trail sees a maximum of 10 vehicles a day, so your chances of meeting other travelers are slim. The trail is in good condition with a fairly smooth surface. The 3-rating is mainly for some moderately steep sections and the forest service's requirement for 4WD vehicles.

The trail leaves California 33 and immediately enters the permit area through a gate. The first couple of miles are roughly graded because they access private property. The trail then runs along the boundary of two separate wilderness areas, the Dick Smith Wilderness to the north and the Matilija Wilderness to the east. Hiking trails access both wilderness areas.

There is one forest service camping area near the start of the trail, immediately past private property at Potrero Seco. There are two sites, both with shade. Both have picnic tables and either a fire ring or BBQ.

Once past the camping area, the trail starts to climb onto the ridge top. When the trail passes the Don Victor Hiking Trail, the conditions of the permit require that 4WD be engaged. Seco Peak is on the left as the trail proceeds toward the Three Sisters, prominent rock formations that stand on either side of the trail.

Near vertical granite fins called the Three Sisters rise up along Potrero Seco Trail

From here the trail winds along open ridge tops, offering views down Diablo Canyon to the west and toward Matilija Canyon to the east. The vegetation is low scrub—California scrub oak, manzanita, and sagebrush. Animals that might be seen include the elusive bobcat, deer, and many different raptors, including the endangered California candor.

The trail finishes at a closure gate below Monte Arido. From here you must retrace your steps back to the entry point on California 33.

Permit Information

It is essential to obtain the free permit necessary to drive this trail prior to travel. This will provide you with the code to the combination lock on a gate before the area. The code is changed frequently. The maximum number of permits issued is 10 vehicles per day and is strictly enforced. Please adhere to the regulations available at Ojai Ranger Station so that this trail remains open to public use. Too many other, similar trails in Los Padres National Forest are limited to Administration Use Only and are not open to the public. Let's retain

Winding away from Potrero Seco along the ridge top

the access we have to this one. Permits can be obtained from:

Los Padres National Forest
Ojai Ranger District
1190 East Ojai Avenue
Ojai, CA 93023
(805) 646-4348

Call the Ojai office for permit availability between 8 A.M. and 4:30 P.M. Monday through Friday during winter months, and seven days a week during summer months. Reservations are made by phone only, but permits are available on a walk-in basis if there are some still available for that day. Reservations may be made up to 14 days prior to the date of use. During hunting season there is a lot of competition for permits; other times use can be very light. One vehicle permit is issued per person with a maximum of 4 people per vehicle. A Forest Adventure Pass is also required.

Permits are free and are valid for up to 3 days at any one time. Permits must be picked up by 10 A.M. the day of the trip or reservations will be canceled and released to others. One permit for up to 3 days will be issued per person in a 7-day period. After hours pickup can be arranged if desired.

Current Road Information

Los Padres National Forest
Ojai Ranger District
1190 East Ojai Avenue
Ojai, CA 93023
(805) 646-4348

Map References

BLM Cuyama
USFS Los Padres National Forest: Mt. Pinos, Ojai and Santa Barbara Ranger Districts
USGS 1:24,000 Rancho Nuevo Creek, Old Man Mt.
1:100,000 Cuyama
Maptech CD-ROM: San Luis Obispo/Los Padres National Forest
Southern & Central California Atlas & Gazetteer, p. 76
California Road & Recreation Atlas, p. 101

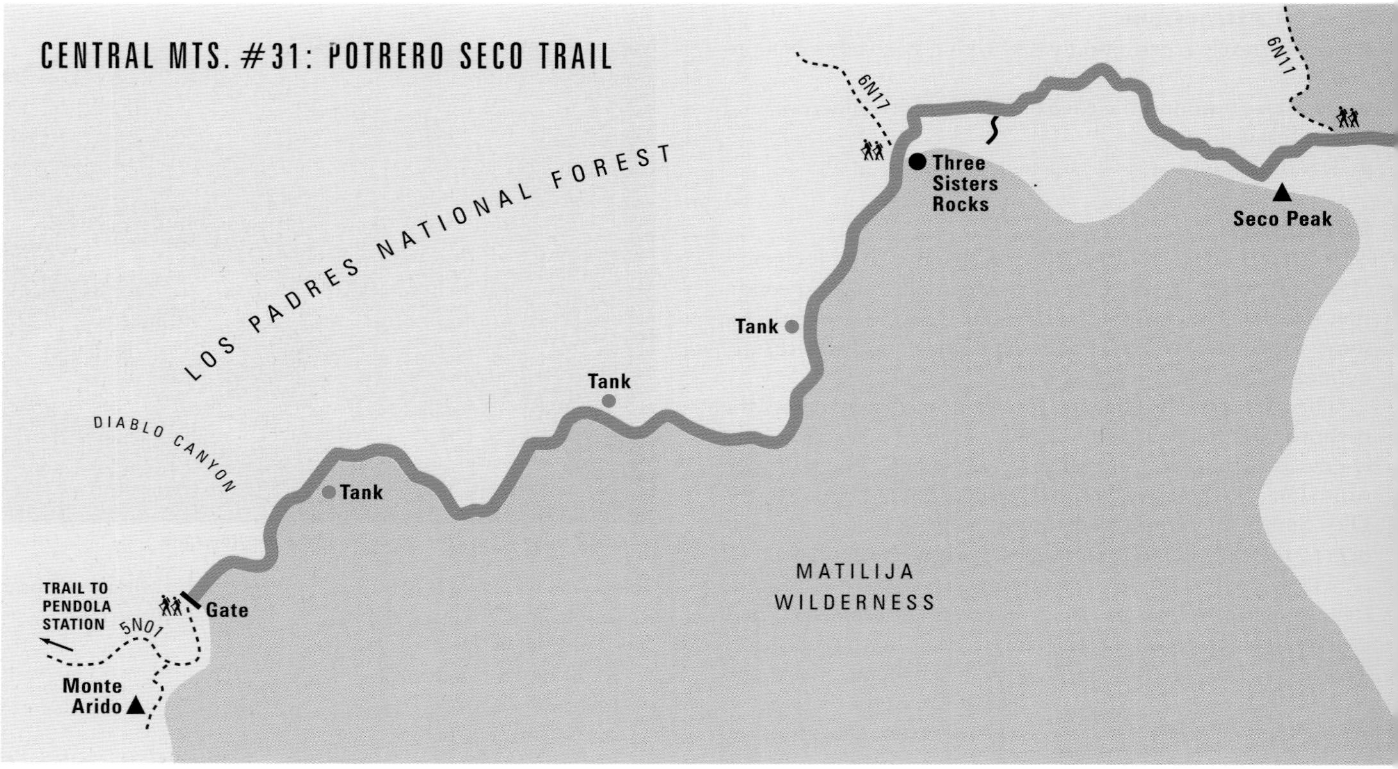

CENTRAL MTS. #31: POTRERO SECO TRAIL

LOS PADRES NATIONAL FOREST
6N17
6N11
Three Sisters Rocks
Seco Peak
Tank
Tank
Tank
DIABLO CANYON
MATILIJA WILDERNESS
TRAIL TO PENDOLA STATION
5N01
Gate
Monte Arido

Route Directions

▼ 0.0		From California 33, 31 miles north of Ojai and 3.6 miles north of Pine Mountain Inn, zero trip meter and turn west onto graded dirt road. The turn is opposite sign-posted road to Pine Mountain. Pass through closure gate using combination given to you with your permit.
		GPS: N34°38.95′ W119°23.08′
▼ 0.6	SO	Track on left.
		GPS: N34°38.50′ W119°23.18′
▼ 1.5	SO	Cattle guard.
▼ 2.1	SO	Cattle guard.
▼ 3.1	SO	Cattle guard. Entering Los Padres National Forest.
		GPS: N34°38.25′ W119°25.41′
▼ 3.3	SO	Track on right to Potrero Seco Campground.
		GPS: N34°38.27′ W119°25.56′
▼ 3.4	SO	Gate.
		GPS: N34°38.19′ W119°25.69′
▼ 4.7	SO	Hiking trail on right is Don Victor Trail (6N11), which enters the Dick Smith Wilderness. Zero trip meter at 4x4 only sign. 4WD must be engaged past this sign to comply with permit requirements.
		GPS: N34°37.89′ W119°26.44′
▼ 0.0		Continue to the south.
▼ 1.8	SO	Track on right.
▼ 2.4	SO	Faint track on left.
		GPS: N34°36.81′ W119°27.69′
▼ 3.2	SO	Track on right is 6N17 (closed to vehicles). Zero trip meter at Three Sisters Rocks.
		GPS: N34°36.33′ W119°27.84′
▼ 0.0		Continue to the southeast.
▼ 0.5	SO	Gate.
		GPS: N34°35.99′ W119°27.62′
▼ 1.1	SO	Game water tank on right.
		GPS: N34°35.59′ W119°27.37′
▼ 2.8	SO	Game water tank on right.
		GPS: N34°34.67′ W119°27.72′
▼ 4.7	SO	Game water tank below track on left.
		GPS: N34°33.58′ W119°28.35′
▼ 5.8		Trail ends at closure gate below Monte Arido. Track on right goes short distance to dam. Hiking trail 5N01, 0.2 miles south of the closure gate, goes to Pendola Station.
		GPS: N34°32.81′ W119°28.26′

Potrero Seco Trail follows ridgeline above the upper reaches of Agua Caliente Canyon

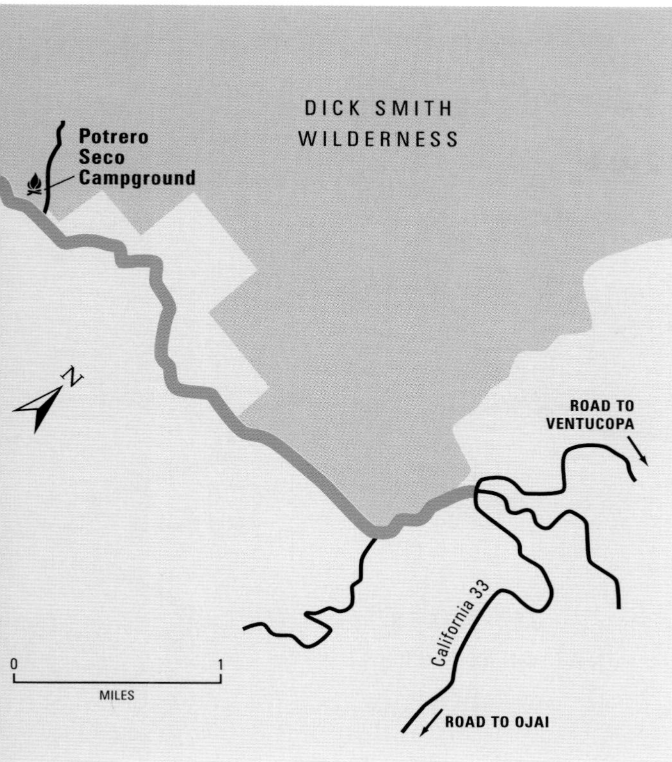

CENTRAL MOUNTAINS #32

Nordhoff Ridge Trail

Starting Point:	**Rose Valley Road, 3 miles east of California 33 at Lower Rose Lake**
Finishing Point:	**Nordhoff Peak/Sespe Wilderness boundary**
Total Mileage:	**28.8 miles (round-trip) including both spurs**
Unpaved Mileage:	**27.6 miles**
Driving Time:	**2 hours for both legs**
Elevation Range:	**4,600–5,100 feet**
Usually Open:	**Year-round**
Best Time to Travel:	**Dry weather**
Difficulty Rating:	**3 for Chief Peak spur, 4 for Nordhoff Peak spur**
Scenic Rating:	**9**
Remoteness Rating:	**+1**

Special Attractions

- Lightly traveled, permit-only trail within Los Padres National Forest.
- Excellent ocean views as well as views over Lion Canyon and the Sespe Wilderness.
- Lookout tower on Nordhoff Peak.
- Rose Valley Falls.
- Popular mountain bike route that can be combined with the Gridley Trail.

History

At one time, Nordhoff Peak and Nordhoff Ridge overlooked a town of the same name. R. G. Surdam established the town in 1874. The Germanic name came from Charles Nordhoff. A writer of renown in his day, Nordhoff had written favorably about the features within the Ojai Valley. His grandson, Charles B. Nordhoff, was also a writer. Charles co-authored with James N. Hall, the 1932 best-seller, *Mutiny on the Bounty.* In 1916, the town of Nordhoff changed its name to Ojai, a Chumash-derived word referring to the moon.

Narrow shelf road up to Nordhoff Ridge

Ojala, located at the foot of Nordhoff Ridge, was reported as having the smallest post office premises in the nation at the time. The tiny post office was reputed to be the size of a phone booth.

Nordhoff Ridge Trail becomes a hiking trail when it enters the Sespe Wilderness. At this point, it passes the end of the eye-catching Topatopa Bluff. This name, along with many others, is taken from a Chumash word of similar pronunciation. A rancheria (a native village or community) was noted as being located nearby in the upper reaches of the Ojai Valley. Indications are that the rancheria name may refer to a brushy place.

In 1947, the Sespe Condor Sanctuary was established to the east of the bluff. This refuge encompassed 53,000 acres, mainly within the southeastern corner of Los Padres National Forest. Except for two through corridors, public access was closed in an effort to protect the habitat of these magnificent birds.

In 1944, a P-51 aircraft crashed into the mountains below the Nordhoff Peak lookout tower. With the passing of time,

The trail runs out on a ridge—Lake Casitas is visible on clear days

natural re-vegetation, and official and unofficial salvaging, little evidence of the crash remains today.

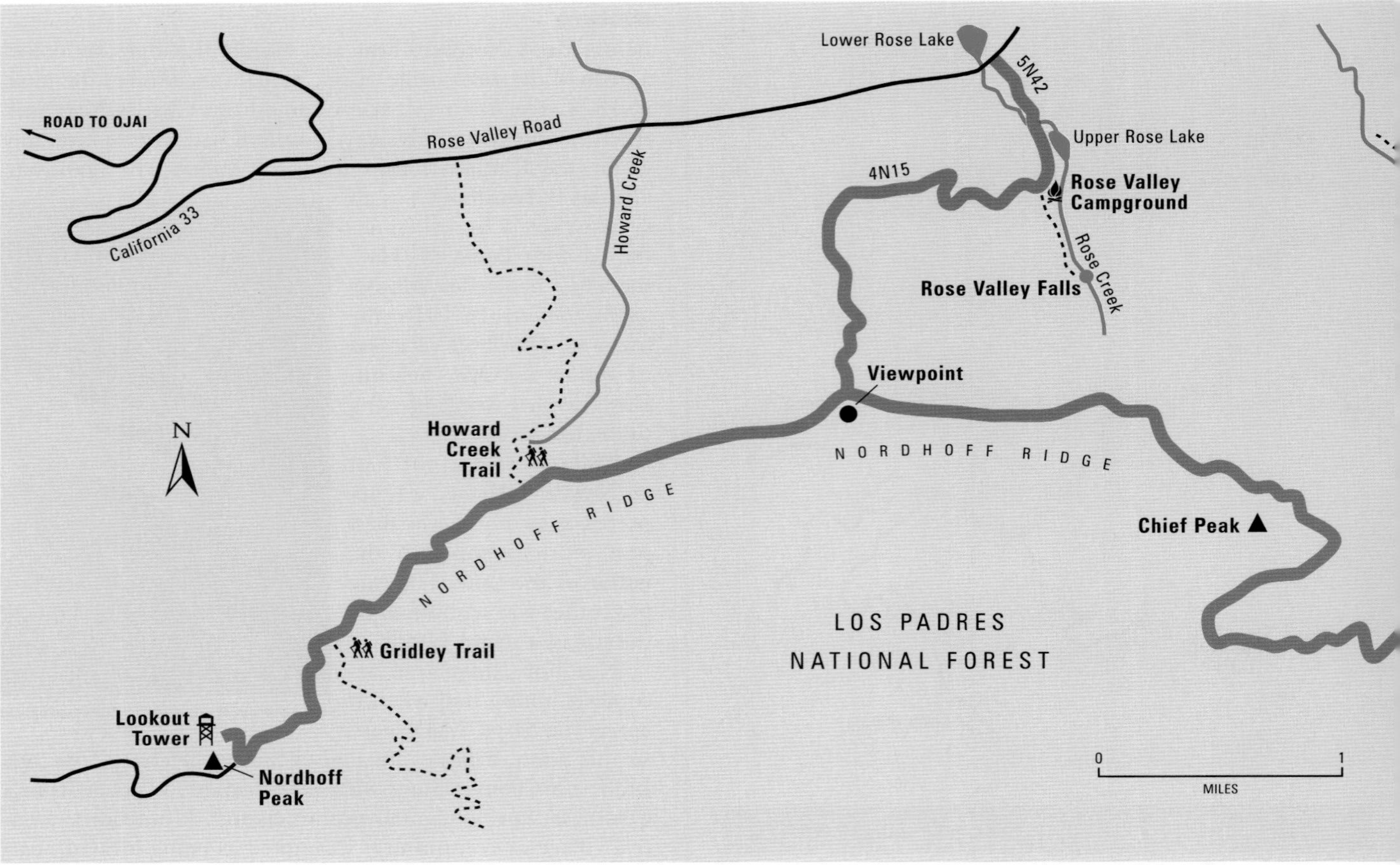

Description

This lightly traveled trail sees a maximum of 20 vehicles a day, often fewer. Your chances of meeting anyone, especially if you travel outside the hunting season, are remote. The trail leaves

Past Nordhoff Peak, the trail is less used and is overgrown with scrub vegetation

Rose Valley Road opposite Lower Rose Lake. It travels a short distance to the Rose Valley Campground and then leaves through the locked gate. From the campground, a valid permit is essential. A short, marked foot trail also leads off through the campground to the fern-covered Rose Valley Falls. It is a 10-minute walk to the base of the falls.

Once you're through the gate, the trail starts to climb steeply. The road was once paved, but has fallen into disrepair and is now a mix of paved patches and loose, scrabbly dirt. The forest service requires 4WD to be engaged for the surfaced parts of this climb, and for this reason will issue permits only to 4WD vehicles. The trail climbs up the steep spur to Nordhoff Ridge, where it forks along the top. Both trails are well worth the trip.

The first spur travels along Nordhoff Ridge and is rated 4 for difficulty, because of the loose, rough climb up to Nordhoff Peak. There is an excellent picnic and camping spot perched right on top of the ridge with views in all directions. Although it is very exposed, it is an excellent place to stop when the weather is good.

On top of Nordhoff Peak is an old metal lookout tower. It is possible to climb the tower for an even more elevated view of the coastline and inland valleys. The trail continues past the tower to hiking trail 23W09, which heads steeply down the valley to join Signal Road. Past the hiking trail, the vehicle trail is less used and brushy. It continues for approximately 2 miles along Nordhoff Ridge.

The second spur, which is rated a 3 for difficulty, winds

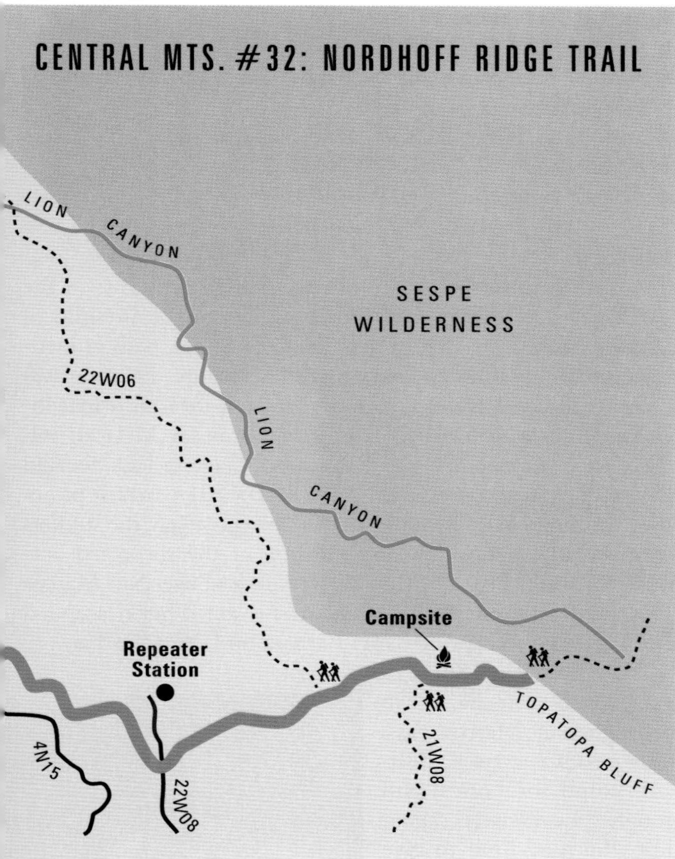

around the side of Chief Peak to finish at the boundary of the Sespe Wilderness. Like the spur along Nordhoff Ridge, there are panoramic views over the Pacific Coastline and Channel Islands National Park—the islands of Santa Cruz and Anacapa. This spur also offers views down into Lion Canyon and over toward the Sespe Wilderness, as well as views of Topatopa Bluff—a prominent striated ridge of mainly bare rock.

Permit Information

It is essential to obtain the free permit necessary to drive this trail prior to travel. This will provide you with the code to the combination lock on a gate before the area. The code is changed frequently. The maximum number of permits issued is limited to 20 vehicles per day and is strictly enforced. Please adhere to the regulations available at Ojai Ranger Station so that this trail remains open to public use. Too many other, similar trails in Los Padres National Forest are limited to Administration Use Only and are not open to the public. Let's retain the access we have to this one. Permits can be obtained from:

Los Padres National Forest
Ojai Ranger District
1190 East Ojai Avenue
Ojai, CA 93023
(805) 646-4348

Call the Ojai office for permit availability 8 A.M. to 4:30 P.M. Monday through Friday during winter months, and seven days a week during summer months. Reservations are made by phone only, but are available on a walk-in basis if there are some still available for that day. Reservations may be made up to 14 days prior to the date of use. During hunting season there is a lot of competition for permits; other times use can be very light. One vehicle permit is issued per person with a maximum of 4 people per vehicle. A Forest Adventure Pass is also required.

Permits are free and are valid for up to 3 days at any one time. Permits must be picked up by 10 A.M. on the day of the trip or reservations will be canceled and released to others. One permit for up to 3 days will be issued per person in a 7-day period. After hours pickup can be arranged if desired.

Current Road Information

Los Padres National Forest
Ojai Ranger District
1190 East Ojai Avenue
Ojai, CA 93023
(805) 646-4348

Map References

BLM Cuyama, Santa Barbara
USFS Los Padres National Forest: Mt. Pinos, Ojai and Santa Barbara Ranger Districts
USGS 1:24,000 Lion Canyon, Ojai, Santa Paula Peak
1:100,000 Cuyama, Santa Barbara
Maptech CD-ROM: San Luis Obispo/Los Padres National Forest; Ventura/Los Angeles/Orange County
Southern & Central California Atlas & Gazetteer, pp. 76, 77
California Road & Recreation Atlas, p. 102

Route Directions

▼ 0.0		From Rose Valley Road at Lower Rose Lake, 3 miles east of California 33, zero trip meter and turn southeast on the paved road 5N42 at the 4-way intersection. Intersection is unmarked. Lower Rose Lake is on the left. Rose Valley Road is 14 miles north of Ojai on California 33.
		GPS: N34°32.38' W119°11.11'
▼ 0.3	SO	Cross through Rose Creek on concrete ford.
▼ 0.5	SO	Rose Valley Campground. Road passes through campground.
		GPS: N34°32.01' W119°10.87'
▼ 0.6	BR	Bear right through campground and cross through creek. Then pass through closure gate onto 4N15. Permit and valid combination number required past this point. Zero trip meter.
		GPS: N34°31.93' W119°10.95'
▼ 0.0		Continue to the northwest on paved road.
▼ 2.1	TR	Cattle guard; then track on right is spur to Nordhoff Peak. Track on left is spur to Chief Peak. Viewpoint ahead. Turn right onto Nordhoff Peak Spur and zero trip meter.
		GPS: N34°31.14' W119°11.77'

Nordhoff Peak Spur

▼ 0.0		Continue to the southwest on Nordhoff Peak Spur from the T-intersection at the top of climb from Rose Valley Campground.
		GPS: N34°31.14' W119°11.77'
▼ 1.3	SO	Track on left goes around dam.
▼ 1.4	SO	Well-used track on right to campsite with picnic table and fire ring. Well-used track on left rejoins. Continue up the middle track.

		GPS: N34°30.86' W119°13.11'
▼ 1.6	SO	Howard Creek Trail on right for hikers, horses, and mountain bikes.
		GPS: N34°30.81' W119°13.24'
▼ 2.0	SO	Track on right is blocked.
▼ 2.7	SO	Gridley Trail on left for hikers, horses, and mountain bikes.
		GPS: N34°30.34' W119°13.97'
▼ 3.7	TR	Turn right to travel to the lookout tower.
		GPS: N34°29.85' W119°14.47'
▼ 3.9		Trail ends at lookout tower on Nordhoff Peak.
		GPS: N34°29.90' W119°14.47'

Chief Peak Spur

▼ 0.0		Continue to the east on Chief Peak Spur from the T-intersection at the top of climb from Rose Valley Campground.
		GPS: N34°31.14' W119°11.77'
▼ 1.1	SO	Dam on left.
▼ 2.0	SO	Chief Peak on right.
		GPS: N34°30.77' W119°09.96'
▼ 4.7	TL	Unmarked track ahead is a continuation of 4N15. Turn left onto unmarked trail 5N08. Zero trip meter.
		GPS: N34°30.03' W119°09.24'
▼ 0.0		Continue to the northeast.
▼ 1.2	SO	Track on right is 22W08 to Thacher School. Track on left goes to Repeater Station.
		GPS: N34°29.70' W119°08.43'
▼ 2.0	SO	Lion Canyon Hiking Trail (22W06) on left to Middle Lion Campground.
		GPS: N34°29.97' W119°07.70'
▼ 2.5	SO	Hiking trail 21W08 on right to Upper Ojai.
		GPS: N34°30.03' W119°07.27'
▼ 2.6	SO	Campsite on left with picnic table and fire ring.
▼ 3.1		Trail ends at boundary of the Sespe Wilderness.
		GPS: N34°30.01' W119°06.86'

CENTRAL MOUNTAINS #33

Big Caliente Spring Trail

Starting Point:	**California 154, 5.6 miles north of Santa Barbara**
Finishing Point:	**Big Caliente Hot Springs**
Total Mileage:	**28.9 miles (one-way), plus 5.6-mile spur to Little Caliente Hot Springs**
Unpaved Mileage:	**10.6 miles, plus 5.6-mile spur**
Driving Time:	**2.5 hours (one-way), including spur**
Elevation Range:	**400–3,600 feet**
Usually Open:	**Year-round**
Best Time to Travel:	**Year-round**
Difficulty Rating:	**1, 2 for spur to Little Caliente Hot Springs**
Scenic Rating:	**9**
Remoteness Rating:	**+0**

Special Attractions

- Painted Cave State Historic Park.
- Natural hot springs for soaking at Big and Little Caliente Hot Springs.
- Long ridge top trail above Santa Barbara.
- Access to Divide Peak OHV Trail.
- Birding along the Santa Ynez River.

History

This trail commences at the historic San Marcos Pass in the Santa Ynez Mountains. In 1846, soldiers of the Presidio of Santa Barbara went to great lengths to block the path of Lieutenant Colonel John C. Frémont and his troops. Frémont was en route to Los Angeles to support the push for California's independence from Mexico. Tales vary. Some say Mexican soldiers lay in wait to ambush Frémont at Gaviota Pass, located 20 miles west on the present route of US 101 where it passes over the Santa Ynez Mountains. Other reports say the soldiers were already in Los Angeles. Hearing of the suspected ambush, Frémont instead made his way up and over San Marcos Pass, guided by Benjamin Foxen and his son. They descended from the pass to capture Santa Barbara on Christmas Day.

By the late 1860s, a stagecoach route ran through San Marcos Pass. The pass was a steep, difficult climb for horses, and rough grooves were carved into the sandstone to give traction on the climb out of Santa Barbara. Horse teams were changed at the top before the stagecoaches proceeded down the north side of the Santa Ynez Mountains via Cold Spring Tavern. By the early 1890s, an improved toll road was constructed over the pass with fees so high that travelers and haulers thought it was daylight robbery. Genuine robberies were not uncommon on San Marcos Pass. There was also the danger of frightened horses getting away from the stagecoach driver on the steep terrain and overturning the coach.

Arroyo Burro Road, which is closed to vehicles to assist red-legged toad survival, is a pleasant hike

Though the large concrete bridge over Cold Spring Canyon (north of the pass) was constructed in the 1960s, it is still possible to get an insight about the original San Marcos Pass route. The old pass road, set below the more modern high bridge, passes the door of the Cold Spring Tavern. The tavern is still operating in its original buildings in the shade of the narrow oak-lined canyon. A nearby small cabin once housed a bottling plant for the natural spring water that was greatly valued by passing travelers.

The feast day of St. Barbara, a fourth-century woman beheaded by her father for converting to Christianity, is celebrated on December 4. On this date in 1602, Vizcaíno passed through the area and named the waters between the Channel Islands and the mainland Canal de Santa Bárbara. In 1782, this name was applied to the newly established Presidio de Santa Bárbara, now referred to as the birthplace of the town of Santa Barbara. On December 4, 1786, the site of the mission at Santa Barbara was declared by placing a cross at the location referred to as Pedregoso, meaning stony.

Santa Cruz Island, the largest of the visible islands offshore, had a number of names given to it over the centuries. In 1543, Juan Cabrillo called it San Sebastian. Vizcaíno, on his voyage of 1602, named it Isla de Gente Barbuda after some bearded people seen on the island. By the latter half of the eighteenth century it had become informally known as Santa Cruz, because a friar who had visited the island lost his cross-bearing staff there. A native found the staff for the friar, and the incident was well remembered until finally the name of the holy cross stuck. Santa Rosa, formerly Isla de San Lucas, and the other islands of this group also had a number of names over the years. Prior to the arrival of Europeans, the Chumash inhabited several of these islands. Santa Rosa was known as Wimat to the Chumash, San Miguel was Tukan, and Santa Cruz was Limu.

European diseases took their toll on the mainland tribal populations. The Tongva people of the Los Angeles region, the Humaliwu division of the Chumash, and the Tejon Chumash of the hinterland succumbed in great numbers to plagues of the white man. The same also happened on the islands. It is thought that the Limu islanders were the most resilient against disease.

Many of the island people were taken to the mainland to be used as labor for the construction of missions. Santa Barbara, Santa Ynez, and Purisimo were relocation centers for such people. The Limu fought to retain independence, but they too were drafted against their will into the workforce.

Today the islands of San Miguel, Santa Rosa, Santa Cruz, Anacapa, and Santa Barbara comprise Channel Islands National Park. Originally established as a national monument in 1938, the islands were classified as a national biosphere reserve in 1976, before gaining national park status in 1980.

As you take in the ocean views from high up along the aptly named Camino Cielo (Spanish for "Sky Road"), cast your eyes and mind some 95 miles south of the eastern end of Santa Cruz Island. Here is the lonely San Nicholas Island. Now try to imagine being stranded there for 18 years by yourself. This was the case for one native woman in the nineteenth century.

In 1835, Chumash living on San Nicholas were moved to the mainland to become part of the workforce building Spanish missions. Realizing that her baby was not on the ship, one woman jumped overboard in a fierce storm. The ship was not very sturdy, and Captain George Nidever did not return for her because he was worried about his ship weathering the storm.

Over the years, Captain Nidever made efforts to find the woman. The island is about 25 square miles in area, and although searchers found evidence of a human inhabitant, the woman always managed to elude them. For 18 years she lived alone, surviving on a diet of fish and edible plants. However, the persistent captain eventually found her. She was dressed in skins and huddled in a small shelter made of sagebrush. The only dialect she could speak was not comprehended by anyone, including local Indians, whose dialect had changed and evolved through contact with mainland tribes and Europeans. No evidence of the baby was ever found, and she was unable to tell her rescuers about her life over the past 18 years.

Little Caliente Spring—the upper level is hottest

Named Juana Maria by her guardians, she was housed in the Santa Barbara community. Sadly she died after only six or seven weeks; the abrupt change of diet was a likely cause. She was buried in the cemetery of the Santa Barbara Mission. The artifacts that she had brought with her from San Nicholas were made available for scientific study but were lost in the fires of San Francisco in the early twentieth century. Sometimes referred to as the lone woman, her time on the island was the inspiration behind the book *Island of the Blue Dolphins.*

Though it is also a naval reservation, the San Nicholas Island Archaeological District covers the entire island. It was recorded in 1984 as having 355 prehistoric sites listed throughout the island.

Description

Big Caliente and Little Caliente Springs are natural hot springs, located a short distance apart in beautiful natural settings. The springs, which are suitable for bathing, are reached

View from Blue Canyon Pass

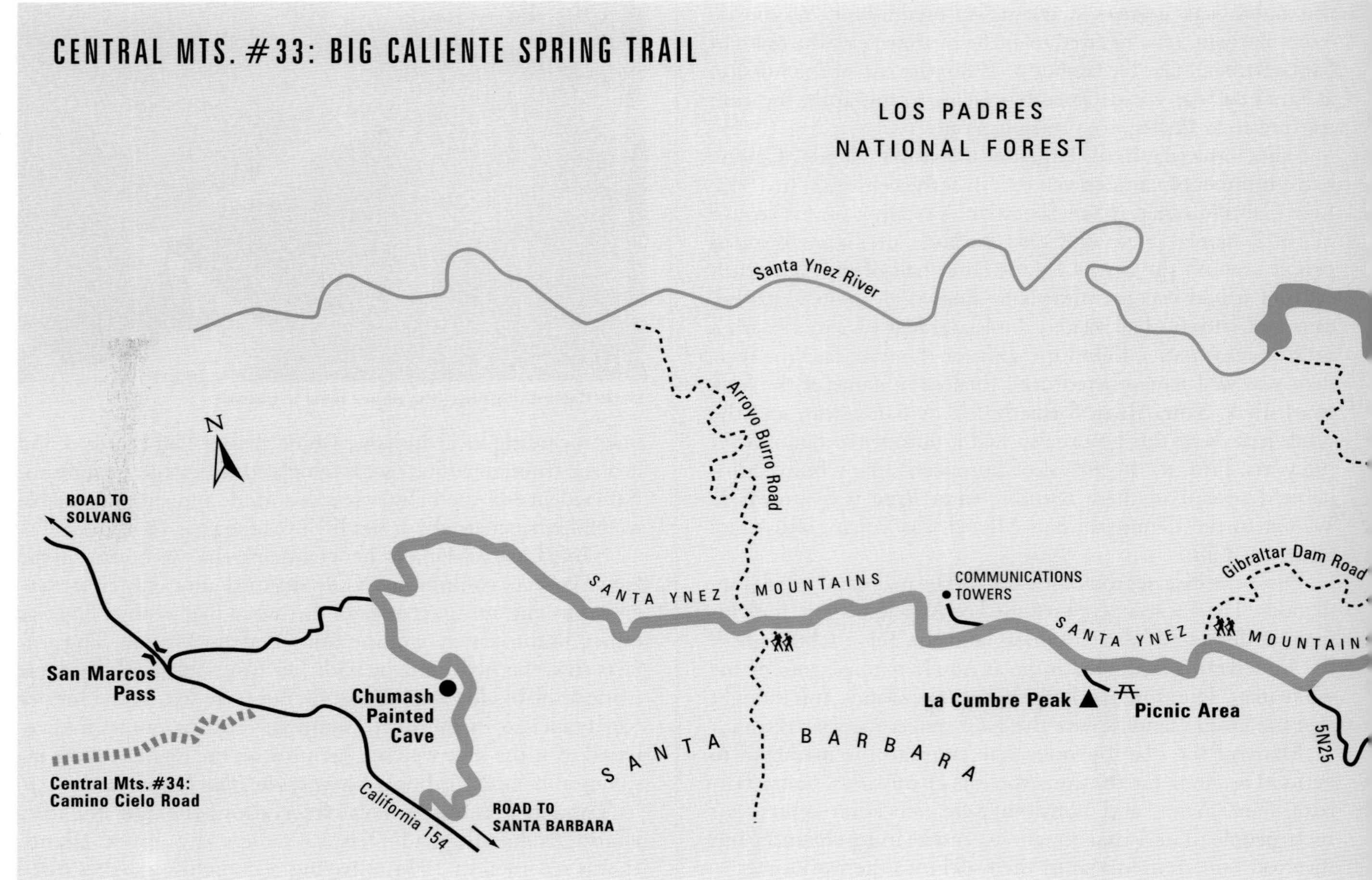

by a long and winding ridge top road that travels along the Santa Ynez Mountains.

There are plenty of interesting things along the way. Near the start of the trail is Chumash Painted Cave, a rock shelter lavishly decorated with rock art. A small sign on a tree points to the cave; the state historic park sign is farther along and hard to see in the forward direction of this trail. There is limited parking alongside the road, which is narrow and twisting at this point.

On a clear day you can see Santa Barbara below and the numerous oil-drilling platforms in the Pacific Ocean. The turnoff for Arroyo Burro Road enables you to travel to the campground and recreation area on the Santa Ynez River to the north. The road is currently closed at the lower end to protect the habitat of the red-legged toad.

On the main trail, the winding road travels along a narrow spine on top of the range and offers great views to the north and south. There are many turnouts for admiring the view. The trail passes the start of the Divide Peak OHV Route, for motorbikes and ATVs only, before starting the long descent to the Santa Ynez River. The ford through the river is concrete, and the water is normally very shallow. The national forest map shows Juncal Campground at this point, but the campground has been closed since May 2000 to protect the habitat of the red-legged toad. Those wishing to camp can proceed to the P-Bar Campground, where there are some pleasant open sites under large pine trees. No primitive camping is permitted along this route.

Birders have a chance to spot many species along the river. The endangered Bell's vireo, a small migratory bird, visits the Santa Ynez River. The southern spotted owl, black chinned hummingbird, hairy woodpecker, spotted sandpiper, and yellow-breasted chat are just some of the other species found here.

The trail divides at Pendola Guard Station. The main route continues for 2.5 miles to Big Caliente Spring. A parking area, pit toilet, and changing area are located at the end of the trail. Beside the parking area, there is a rectangular concrete tub about 3 feet deep for soaking—the water is warm to hot. The trail to Little Caliente Spring continues past the parking area to Caliente Debris Dam and Potrero Seco. This is for hikers only. A second spring is found only a short distance up the trail on the far side of the creek. The tub is built out of river rocks. No camping is permitted at the springs.

Debris dams were constructed by the forest service to trap debris from the Coyote Fire of September 1964 before it washed into Gibraltar Lake and reduced its capacity for water storage.

The trail to Little Caliente requires a high-clearance 2WD vehicle. The final section can be deeply rutted and is not suitable for passenger vehicles. They can, however, access the P-Bar Campground. Little Caliente Spring tends to be quieter than Big Caliente, and is set in a narrow creek valley. There are

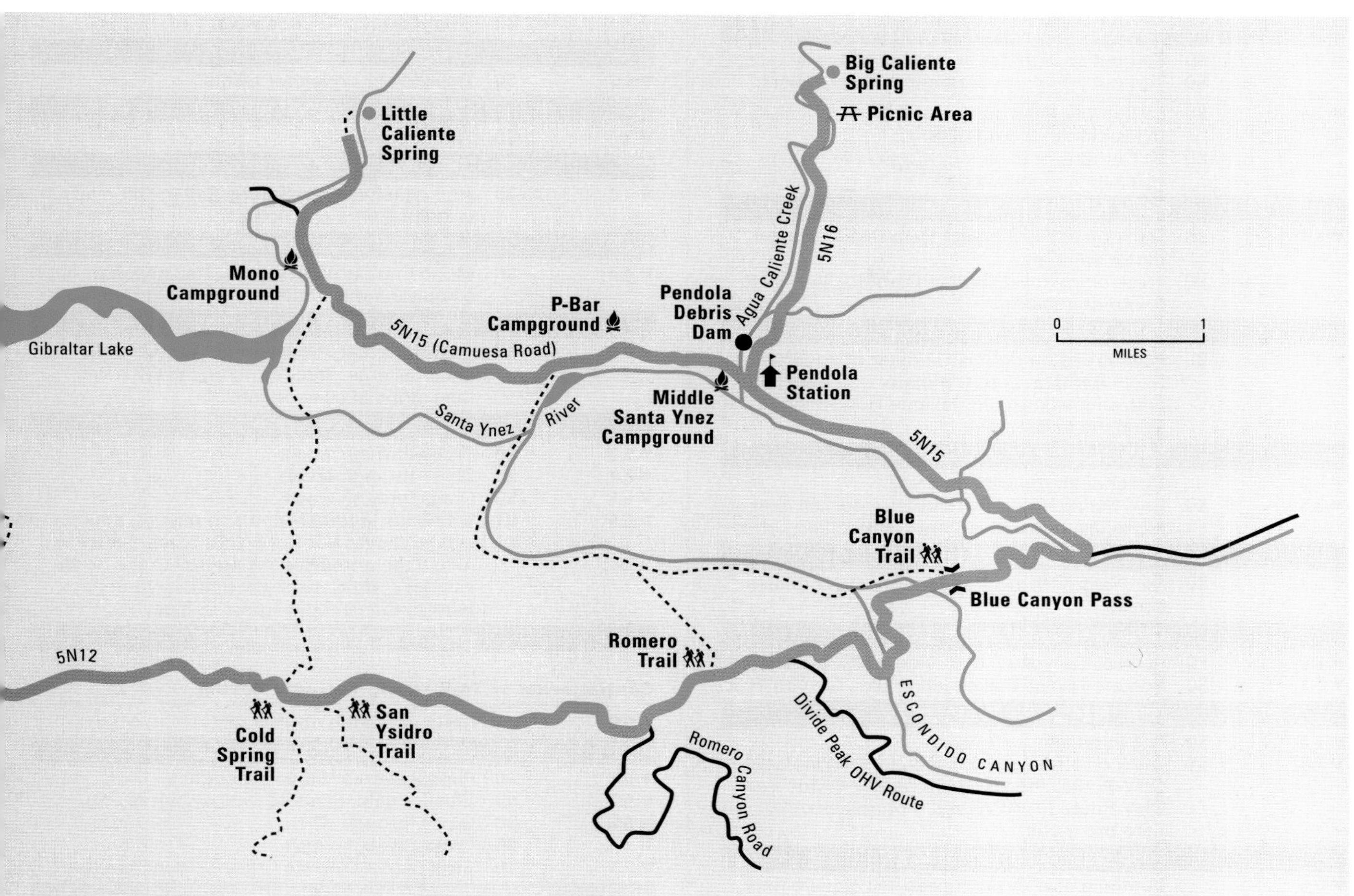

three soaking pools, set one above the other on the hillside; each holds two to four people. The water is hot and the view fabulous. The stone pools are well constructed and there are a couple of wooden platforms and benches for your clothes but no other facilities. The de facto dress code for both these springs is "clothing optional."

Current Road Information

Los Padres National Forest
Santa Barbara Ranger District
3505 Paradise Road
Santa Barbara, CA 93105
(805) 967-3481

Map References

BLM Santa Barbara, Cuyama
USFS Los Padres National Forest: Mt. Pinos, Ojai and Santa Barbara Ranger Districts
USGS 1:24,000 Goleta, San Marcos Pass, Little Pine Mt., Santa Barbara, Carpinteria, White Ledge Peak, Hildreth Peak
1:1100,000 Santa Barbara, Cuyama
Maptech CD-ROM: San Luis Obispo/Los Padres National Forest; Ventura/Los Angeles/Orange County
Southern & Central California Atlas & Gazetteer, pp. 89, 90, 76
California Road & Recreation Atlas, p. 101

Route Directions

Mileage		Directions
▼ 0.0		From California 154, 5.6 miles north of Pacific Coast Highway in Santa Barbara, zero trip meter and turn north on paved road at sign for Painted Cave Road.
3.2 ▲		Trail ends on California 154. Turn left for Santa Barbara.
		GPS: N34°29.48' W119°47.67'
▼ 1.9	SO	Chumash Painted Cave on left of paved road.
1.3 ▲	SO	Chumash Painted Cave on right of paved road.
		GPS: N34°30.25' W119°47.20'
▼ 3.2	TR	Turn sharp right onto unmarked paved road. Zero trip meter.
0.0 ▲		Continue to the east.
		GPS: N34°30.81' W119°47.76'
▼ 0.0		Continue to the northeast.
3.9 ▲	TL	Turn sharp left onto unmarked, paved road. Zero trip meter.
▼ 3.9	SO	Track on left is Arroyo Burro Road. Zero trip meter at sign. Hiking trail on right for hikers, horses, and mountain bikes.
0.0 ▲		Continue to the south.
		GPS: N34°30.31' W119°45.12'
▼ 0.0		Continue to the north.
4.7 ▲	SO	Track on right is Arroyo Burro Road. Zero trip meter at sign. Hiking trail on left for hikers, horses, and mountain bikes.
▼ 2.2	SO	Track on left to communications towers.
2.5 s	SO	Track on right to communications towers.

			GPS: N34°30.06' W119°43.42'
▼ 2.6		SO	Turnout on right for communications towers.
	2.1 ▲	SO	Turnout on left for communications towers.
▼ 2.9		SO	La Cumbre Peak on right. Picnic area is 0.25 miles behind locked gate.
	1.8 ▲	SO	La Cumbre Peak on left. Picnic area is 0.25 miles behind locked gate.
			GPS: N34°29.73' W119°42.80'
▼ 4.1		SO	Track on left is Gibraltar Dam Road—closed to motor vehicles.
	0.6 ▲	SO	Track on right is Gibraltar Dam Road—closed to motor vehicles.
			GPS: N34°29.78' W119°41.89'
▼ 4.7		BL	Paved road on right is Gibraltar Road (5N25) to Santa Barbara. Zero trip meter and bear left, following sign to Big Caliente Hot Spring.
	0.0 ▲		Continue to the west.
			GPS: N34°29.47' W119°41.36'
▼ 0.0			Continue to the east on 5N12.
▼ 3.5		SO	Cold Spring Hiking Trail crosses road. Left goes to Mono Campground and right to Mountain Drive.
			GPS: N34°29.06' W119°38.29'
▼ 3.7		SO	San Ysidro Hiking Trail on right to Mountain Drive.
			GPS: N34°29.01' W119°38.05'
▼ 6.5		SO	Romero Canyon on right. Trail is now graded dirt.
▼ 7.1		SO	Romero Hiking Trail on left to Blue Canyon Trail.
			GPS: N34°28.82' W119°35.25'
▼ 7.5		SO	Pull-in on left.
▼ 7.8		SO	Track on left to parking area for Divide Peak OHV Route; then track on right is Divide Peak OHV Route for ATVs and motorbikes only. Zero trip meter.
			GPS: N34°28.86' W119°34.61'
▼ 0.0			Continue east through seasonal closure gate.
▼ 1.1		SO	Cross over Escondido Canyon Creek.
			GPS: N34°28.62' W119°33.98'
▼ 2.3		SO	Cross over creek on bridge.
			GPS: N34°29.16' W119°33.56'
▼ 2.4		SO	Trail 26W12 on left for hikers and horses.
			GPS: N34°29.19' W119°33.52'
▼ 2.5		SO	Blue Canyon Pass.
			GPS: N34°29.18' W119°33.35'
▼ 3.8		SO	Cross over wash.
▼ 3.9		BL	Cross over Santa Ynez River on concrete ford; then bear left, following sign to Big Caliente Canyon. Zero trip meter.
			GPS: N34°29.20' W119°32.41'
▼ 0.0			Continue to the north on 5N15.
▼ 1.1		SO	Cross over wash on concrete ford.
			GPS: N34°29.76' W119°33.18'
▼ 2.9		TR	Graded road straight ahead is 5N15. Turn right onto 5N16, following sign to Caliente Hot Spring and zero trip meter.
			GPS: N34°30.50' W119°34.56'

Spur to Little Caliente Spring (Camuesa Road)

▼ 0.0		Continue to the northwest through closure gate and cross Agua Caliente Creek on concrete ford. Road is marked 5N15 to Little Caliente.
		GPS: N34°30.50' W119°34.56'
▼ 0.1	SO	Middle Santa Ynez Campground on left.
		GPS: N34°30.56' W119°34.66'
▼ 0.3	SO	Closure gate.
▼ 1.1	SO	P-Bar Campground on right.
		GPS: N34°30.88' W119°35.41'
▼ 1.7	SO	Trail 26W12 on left for hikers.
		GPS: N34°30.80' W119°35.98'
▼ 3.4	SO	Closure gate.
		GPS: N34°31.19' W119°37.26'
▼ 4.0	SO	Trail on left is Cold Spring Trail to Gibraltar Lake for hikers and horses.
		GPS: N34°31.48' W119°37.48'
▼ 4.4	SO	Mono Campground on left. Trail on left through campground is 5N15 for hikers and horses.
		GPS: N34°31.69' W119°37.61'
▼ 4.8	BR	Bear right onto smaller trail, following sign for Little Caliente. Track on left goes 0.2 miles then stops at closure gate.
		GPS: N34°31.98' W119°37.60'
▼ 5.3	SO	Cross through wash.
▼ 5.4	SO	Cross through creek.
▼ 5.5	SO	Cross through wash.
▼ 5.6	UT	Trail ends at turnaround and parking area for Little Caliente Hot Spring. To reach the spring, follow the unmarked hiking trail to the northeast for a short distance. Retrace your steps back to the Pendola Forest Station.
		GPS: N34°32.43' W119°37.16'

Continuation of Trail to Big Caliente Spring

▼ 0.0		Continue to the north.
		GPS: N34°30.50' W119°34.56'
▼ 0.1	SO	Pendola Forest Station on right.
▼ 0.3	SO	Closure gate. Pendola Debris Dam on left.
▼ 0.7	SO	Cross through wash.
▼ 1.5	SO	Cross through wash.
▼ 2.1	SO	Cross Agua Caliente Creek on concrete ford.
		GPS: N34°32.07' W119°33.75'
▼ 2.2	SO	Picnic area on right is Lower Caliente.
		GPS: N34°32.14' W119°33.74'
▼ 2.3	SO	Cross over Agua Caliente Creek on concrete ford.
▼ 2.5		Cross over Agua Caliente Creek on concrete ford. Then trail ends at Big Caliente Spring.
		GPS: N34°32.35' W119°33.83'

CENTRAL MOUNTAINS #34

Camino Cielo Road

Starting Point:	**California 154, 7 miles north of US 101**
Finishing Point:	**US 101 at Refugio State Beach**
Total Mileage:	**25.2 miles**
Unpaved Mileage:	**9.2 miles**
Driving Time:	**1.5 hours**
Elevation Range:	**100–4,200 feet**
Usually Open:	**Year-round**
Best Time to Travel:	**Year-round**
Difficulty Rating:	**2**
Scenic Rating:	**9**
Remoteness Rating:	**+0**

Special Attractions

- Gun club target shooting—open to the public.
- Extensive views of the Pacific Ocean and coastline.

History

Refugio Pass, at the western end of the trail, has many colorful stories attached to its surrounding area. In the 1850s, Don Nicholás Den was leased the College Ranch, Cañada de los Pinos, which was part of the Santa Inés Mission holdings north of the Santa Ynez Mountains. For the grazing rights, he paid the Catholic Church $3,000 a year. Den's wealth caught the eye of a disreputable character by the name of Jack Powers. Powers made plans to steal the thousand head of cattle that had been rounded up for sale to a dealer in Los Angeles. While Den was negotiating the sale in Los Angeles, Powers rode to the College Ranch and informed the majordomo that he had purchased the cattle and had come to take possession of them. The majordomo did not believe this outrageous tale but, realizing he was outnumbered by Powers' armed men, he quietly ordered the cattle to be released from their pen, thereby delaying attempts to remove them from the ranch.

The majordomo made his way to Den's house in Santa Barbara to relay the news. He was greeted by Den's foreman, an Irishman named Tom Meehan. Meehan wanted to take the law into his own hands and go after Powers and his gang himself. Den forbade this course of action and persuaded the sheriff to visit the College Ranch and oust Powers from his land. When the posse arrived, Powers realized that he was outnumbered. He left, but not before issuing many threats to both Den and Meehan.

The trail runs just below a ridge top in the Santa Ynez Mountains

Den returned to Los Angeles, leaving Meehan in charge of the ranch. Over the next few weeks, Meehan had several encounters with Powers and his gang but always managed to escape. Eventually, Meehan was forced to leave the ranch to secure more food and supplies. His intention was to ride over to Nuestra Señora del Refugio on the southern side of Refugio Pass. As he approached the pass, his horse spooked, and he came face to face with one of Powers men. Others approached and surrounded Meehan. He and his horse were gunned down without ever firing a shot in return.

A passing shepherd discovered Meehan's body trapped under his horse. He managed to tie him onto a burro and bring him back to nearby Dos Pueblos Ranch. Meehan's killers had gone straight to the sheriff claiming they had been ambushed and that they had acted in self-defense. Although it was obviously a lie, there was no way of proving it without a witness. Again, Don Nicholás refused to take the law into his own hands. However, two of Meehan's killers were quietly gunned down later by two of Den's ranch hands.

Camino Cielo Road offers views north toward the San Rafael Wilderness

In 1951, Refugio Pass was the scene of an aircraft crash. A Douglas DC-3C en route from Santa Maria to Santa Barbara did not maintain the sufficient minimum altitude of 4,000 feet and crashed into the mountain near the pass. All 19 passengers and 3 crew members onboard died in the accident.

Description

Camino Cielo (Spanish for "Sky Road") follows a ridge top path through the Santa Ynez Mountains, the closest range to the Pacific Ocean. The trail is initially a single-lane, paved road as it heads west from California 154 through a small group of houses to travel into Los Padres National Forest. Once past the popular Winchester Canyon Gun Club, which is open to the public when its gate is open, the road turns to uneven, roughly graded dirt. There are good views of Lake Cachuma to the north, with the San Rafael Wilderness behind. It winds down toward the head of Ellwood Canyon, gradually descending some switchbacks, before running around the head of the canyon. Ellwood Canyon opens directly to the ocean. From here, the trail travels mainly on the south side of the ridge, providing great views over the coastline, back to Santa Barbara, and west over the less populated state beach areas. Several drilling rigs can be seen out at sea.

The road services a series of communications towers along the ridge, so the area is well traveled. Although there are several trails, the forest service has been attempting to close many of the smaller trails. Please respect these closures and travel only on marked trails. Motorbike riders will find a couple of trails marked specifically for their use.

At Santa Ynez Peak, the trail reverts to a small, single-lane paved road as it descends toward Refugio Pass. It then becomes a wider road, finishing on US 101 at Refugio Beach State Park.

Current Road Information

Los Padres National Forest
Santa Barbara Ranger District
3505 Paradise Road
Santa Barbara, CA 93105
(805) 967-3481

Map References

BLM Santa Barbara, Santa Maria, Cuyama, Point Conception

USFS Los Padres National Forest: Mt. Pinos, Ojai and Santa Barbara Ranger Districts

USGS 1:24,000 San Marcos Pass, Lake Cachuma, Santa Ynez, Tajiguas
1:100,000 Santa Barbara, Santa Maria, Cuyama, Point Conception

Maptech CD-ROM: San Luis Obispo/Los Padres National Forest; Ventura/Los Angeles/Orange County

Southern & Central California Atlas & Gazetteer, pp. 75, 74, 88

California Road & Recreation Atlas, pp. 100, 101

Route Directions

▼ 0.0		From California 154, 7 miles north of US 101, 0.2 miles east of mile marker 25, zero trip meter and turn west on West Camino Cielo at sign. Road is initially paved.
3.8 ▲		Trail ends at T-intersection with California 154. Turn right for Santa Barbara.
		GPS: N34°30.26' W119°48.69'
▼ 0.1	SO	Cross over San Jose Creek on bridge.
3.7 ▲	SO	Cross over San Jose Creek on bridge.
▼ 0.2	BL	Bear left on Camino Cielo. Paved road on right is Kinevan Road.
3.6 ▲	BR	Bear right on Camino Cielo. Paved road on left is Kinevan Road.
		GPS: N34°30.27' W119°48.89'
▼ 0.6	SO	Paved road on left.
3.2 ▲	SO	Paved road on right.
▼ 1.4	SO	Road on left.
2.4 ▲	SO	Road on right.
▼ 3.8	SO	Winchester Canyon Gun Club (trap and skeet range) entrance on right. Public is welcome when gate is open. Zero trip meter.
0.0 ▲		Continue to the southeast.
		GPS: N34°30.34' W119°51.86'
▼ 0.0		Continue to the northwest.
7.8 ▲	SO	Winchester Canyon Gun Club (trap and skeet range) entrance on left. Public is welcome when open. Zero trip meter.
▼ 0.2	SO	Road turns to graded dirt.
7.6 ▲	SO	Road is now paved.
▼ 0.3	SO	View of Lake Cachuma on right.
7.5 ▲	SO	View of Lake Cachuma on left.
▼ 1.3	SO	Track on right through gate.
6.5 ▲	SO	Track on left through gate.
		GPS: N34°30.57' W119°52.61'
▼ 1.5	SO	Track on left under power lines.
6.3 ▲	SO	Track on right under power lines.
▼ 3.8	SO	Track on right.
4.0 ▲	SO	Track on left.
		GPS: N34°31.25' W119°54.68'
▼ 4.1	SO	Two tracks on right.
3.7 ▲	SO	Two tracks on left.
		GPS: N34°31.32' W119°54.96'
▼ 4.6	SO	Track on left.
3.2 ▲	SO	Track on right.
▼ 5.2	SO	Track on right.

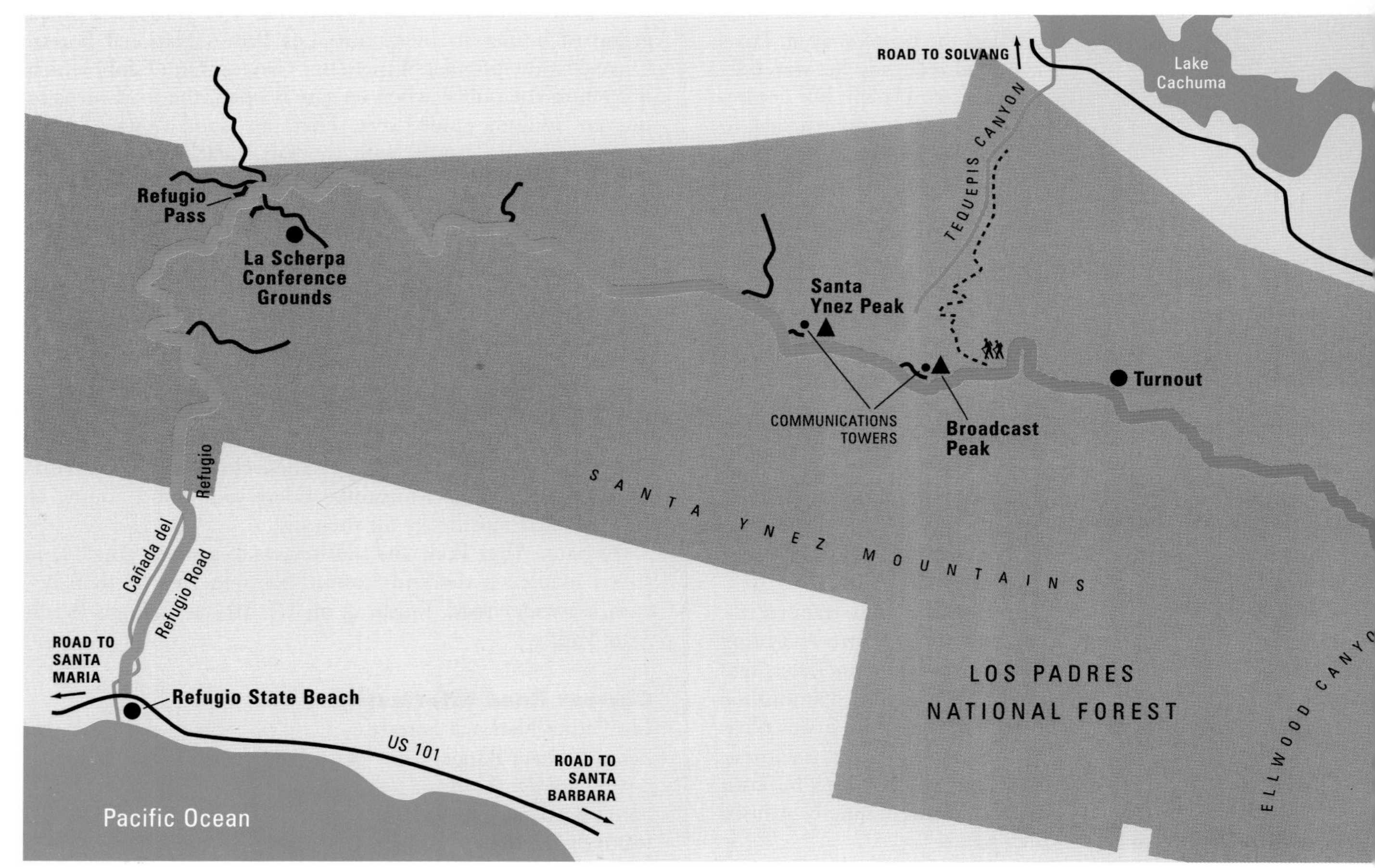

2.6 ▲	SO	Track on left.
▼ 5.3	SO	Turnout on right.
2.5 ▲	SO	Turnout on left.
		GPS: N34°31.64' W119°55.91'
▼ 5.8	SO	Track on right.
2.0 ▲	SO	Track on left.
▼ 5.9	SO	Turnout on left and track on left.
1.9 ▲	SO	Track on right and turnout on right.
▼ 6.7	SO	Track on right.
1.1 ▲	SO	Track on left.
▼ 6.9	SO	Trail on right for hikers, horses, and mountain bikes goes to Tequepis Canyon.
0.9 ▲	SO	Trail on left for hikers, horses, and mountain bikes goes to Tequepis Canyon.
		GPS: N34°31.60' W119°56.98'
▼ 7.8	BL	Well-used track on right goes to communications towers. Zero trip meter.
0.0 ▲		Continue to the southeast.
		GPS: N34°31.53' W119°57.82'
▼ 0.0		Continue to the west.
6.9 ▲	BR	Well-used track on left goes to communications towers. Zero trip meter.
▼ 0.5	SO	Track on right goes to communications towers.
6.4 ▲	BR	Track on left goes to communications towers.
		GPS: N34°31.58' W119°58.37'
▼ 1.2	SO	Road on right goes to communications tower.
5.7 ▲	BL	Road on left goes to communications tower.
		GPS: N34°31.68' W119°58.87'
▼ 1.6	SO	Paved road on right. Road is now paved.

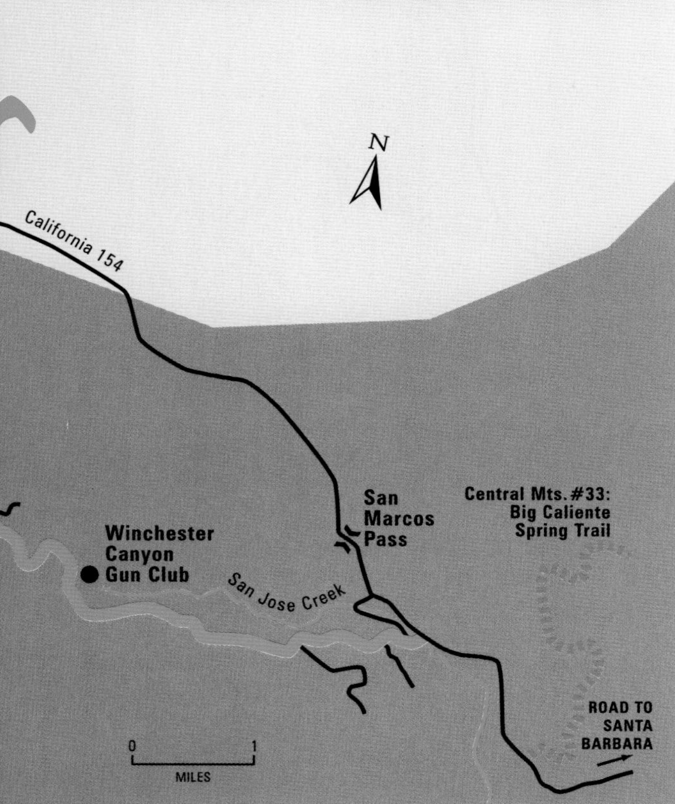

Ocean clouds blanket Camino Cielo Road near Santa Ynez Peak

5.3 ▲	BR	Paved road on left. Road is now graded dirt.
		GPS: N34°31.83' W119°59.33'
▼ 3.8	SO	Road on right goes into private property.
3.1 ▲	BL	Road on left goes into private property.
		GPS: N34°32.00' W120°01.44'
▼ 6.9	TL	Turn left on top of Refugio Pass, remaining on paved road. Two roads on right and entrance of La Scherpa Conference Grounds on left. Zero trip meter.
0.0 ▲		Continue to the east.
		GPS: N34°32.01' W120°03.67'
▼ 0.0		Continue to the south.
6.7 ▲	TR	Entrance of La Scherpa Conference Grounds on right; then turn right on top of Refugio Pass. Road continues ahead and second track on right. Zero trip meter.
▼ 0.9	SO	Cattle guard.
5.8 ▲	SO	Cattle guard.
▼ 2.2	SO	Cattle guard.
4.5 ▲	SO	Cattle guard.
▼ 3.3	SO	Track on left is private.
3.4 ▲	SO	Track on right is private.
		GPS: N34°30.75' W120°04.08'
▼ 3.6	SO	Cross over creek on bridge.
3.1 ▲	SO	Cross over creek on bridge.
▼ 3.7	SO	Cross over creek on bridge.
3.0 ▲	SO	Cross over creek on bridge.
▼ 3.8	SO	Cross over creek on bridge.
2.9 ▲	SO	Cross over creek on bridge.
▼ 3.9	SO	Cross over creek on bridge.
2.8 ▲	SO	Cross over creek on bridge.
▼ 5.0	SO	Cross over creek on bridge.
1.7 ▲	SO	Cross over creek on bridge.
		GPS: N34°29.47' W120°03.87'
▼ 6.4	SO	Cross over creek on bridge.
0.3 ▲	SO	Cross over creek on bridge.
▼ 6.5	SO	Cross over creek on bridge.
0.2 ▲	SO	Cross over creek on bridge.
▼ 6.7		Trail ends at intersection with US 101 at the Refugio State Beach exit. Refugio Beach is straight ahead. Enter freeway south for Santa Barbara or north for Santa Maria.
0.0 ▲		Trail commences on US 101 at Refugio State Beach exit. Exit freeway and proceed to the north side. Zero trip meter and then proceed north on paved, two-lane Refugio Road.
		GPS: N34°28.01' W120°04.07'

Miranda Pine Road

Starting Point:	**Central Mountains #37: Sierra Madre Road, 8.6 miles from California 166**
Finishing Point:	**Tepusquet Road, 5.6 miles north of Foxen Canyon Road**
Total Mileage:	**25 miles**
Unpaved Mileage:	**25 miles**
Driving Time:	**2 hours**
Elevation Range:	**1,000–3,800 feet**
Usually Open:	**April to November**
Best Time to Travel:	**Dry weather**
Difficulty Rating:	**2**
Scenic Rating:	**9**
Remoteness Rating:	**+0**

Special Attractions

- Alternative exit from Central Mountains #37: Sierra Madre Road.
- Long winding trail that includes both ridge top and canyon scenery.
- Many crossings of North Fork La Brea Creek.

Description

This trail can be combined with Central Mountains #37: Sierra Madre Road to make an easy loop that travels through a wide variety of beautiful scenery within Los Padres National Forest. The trail leaves Sierra Madre Road, 8.6 miles from California 166. The turn is unmarked but it is opposite the turn to Miranda Pine USFS Campground. This campground is small and very pretty, offering great views from its ridge top location.

The trail snakes above Kerry Canyon

From the outset, the trail descends a wide shelf road that runs down from the main backbone of the Sierra Madres. It travels through open vegetation of low shrubs, manzanitas, and the tall spikes of century plants (a type of yucca). The route wraps around Kerry Canyon and passes the Kerry Canyon Trail, a black-rated trail for motorbikes and non-motorized use. There is a good campsite at the intersection that is roomy with plenty of shade.

Short trail to Johnson Surprise Spring

The trail continues to descend as it runs below Treplett Mountain, giving good views out to the west. A second trail, this one suitable for 4WD vehicles, is Central Mountains #36: Buckhorn Ridge Trail—a more difficult, loose sandy trail that travels along the narrow Buckhorn Ridge. The main trail enters Smith Canyon before traveling alongside the pretty, rocky North Fork La Brea Creek, crossing it often.

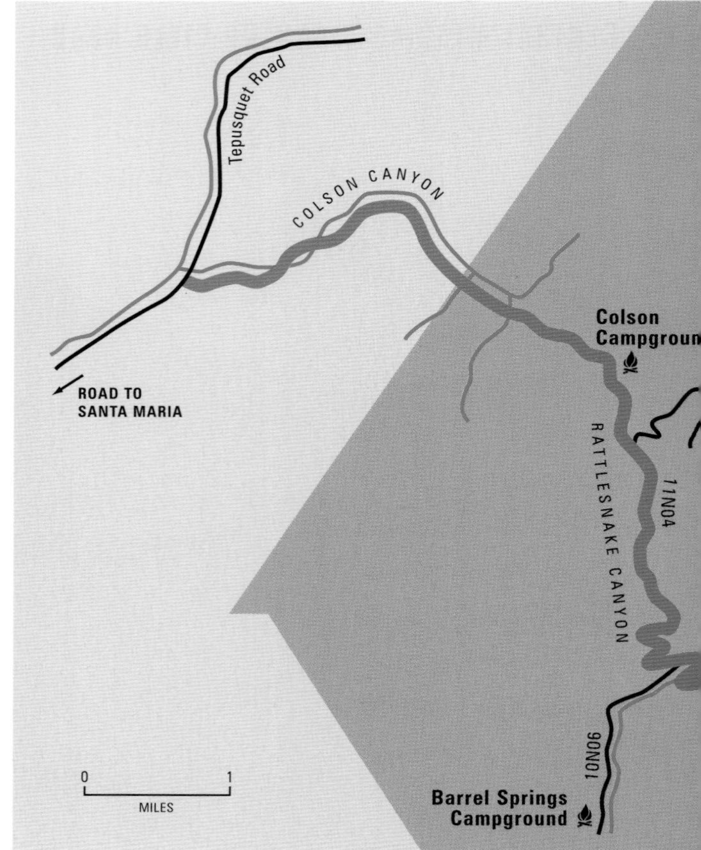

Leaving North Fork La Brea Creek, the route climbs up Rattlesnake Canyon, crossing a saddle and descending the western side of the tighter Colson Canyon. The Colson USFS Campground is located just over the western side of the saddle at the head of the canyon. The trail ends at the intersection with Tepusquet Road, 5.6 miles north of Foxen Canyon Road.

A Forest Adventure Pass is required to be displayed on all parked vehicles or if you are undertaking any recreational activities. The campgrounds do not require any additional fees.

Current Road Information

Los Padres National Forest
Santa Lucia Ranger District
1616 Carlotti Drive
Santa Maria, CA 93454
(805) 925-9538

Map References

BLM San Luis Obispo, Santa Maria
USFS Los Padres National Forest: Monterey and Santa Lucia Ranger Districts
USGS 1:24,000 Miranda Pine Mt., Manzanita Mt., Tepusquet Canyon
1:100,000 San Luis Obispo, Santa Maria
Maptech CD-ROM: San Luis Obispo/Los Padres National Forest
Southern & Central California Atlas & Gazetteer, pp. 60, 74
California Road & Recreation Atlas, p. 100

Route Directions

▼ 0.0		From Central Mountains #37: Sierra Madre Road, 8.6 miles from California 166, zero trip meter and turn south on graded dirt road. Turn is unmarked but is opposite the turn to Miranda Pine Campground. Immediately track on right to Miranda Pine Spring; then closure gate. Trail starts to descend along shelf road.
3.2 ▲		Trail passes through closure gate; then track on left to Miranda Pine Spring. Trail ends at intersection with Central Mountains #37: Sierra Madre Road, opposite the turn to Miranda Pine Campground. Turn left to exit to California 166; turn right to continue along Sierra Madre Road to exit via Central Mountains #38: Bates Canyon Trail.
		GPS: N35°01.95' W120°02.00'
▼ 1.4	SO	Cross through wash.
1.8 ▲	SO	Cross through wash.
▼ 3.2	SO	Campsite on left. Track on right is Kerry Canyon Trail to Pine Canyon Road #31 (30W02) for motorbikes only—rated black. Zero trip meter at sign.
0.0 ▲		Continue to the southeast.
		GPS: N35°01.36' W120°03.45'
▼ 0.0		Continue to the south.
5.8 ▲	SO	Campsite on right. Track on left is Kerry Canyon Trail to Pine Canyon Road #31 (30W02) for motorbikes only—rated black. Zero trip meter at sign.
▼ 0.1	SO	Kerry Canyon Trail on left goes to Lazy Camp.

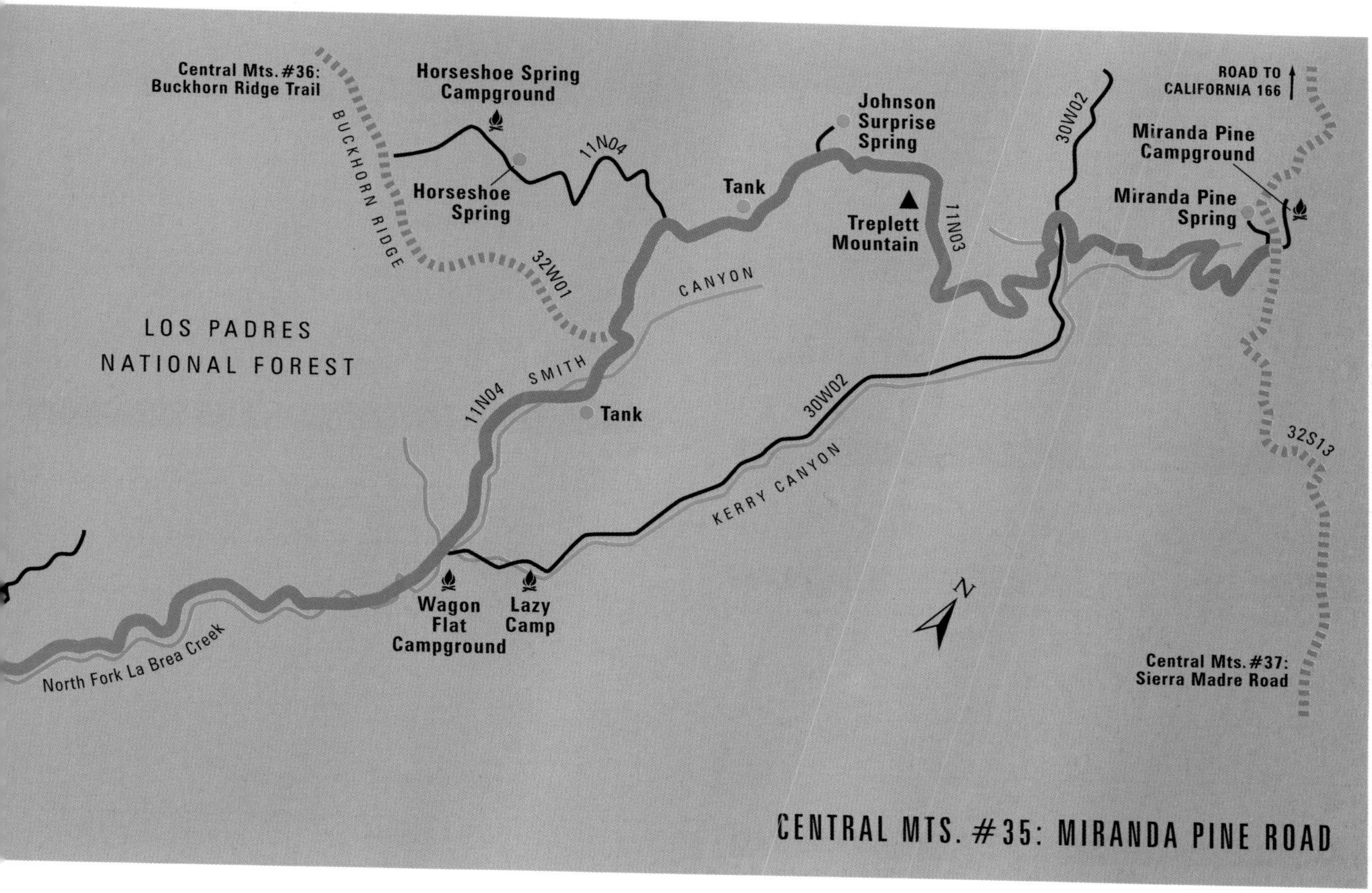

CENTRAL MTS. #35: MIRANDA PINE ROAD

5.7 ▲	SO	Kerry Canyon Trail on right goes to Lazy Camp.
		GPS: N35°01.28' W120°03.40'
▼ 0.3	SO	Cross through wash.
5.5 ▲	SO	Cross through wash.
▼ 4.4	SO	Track on right goes 0.4 miles to Johnson Surprise Spring.
1.4 ▲	BR	Track on left goes 0.4 miles to Johnson Surprise Spring.
		GPS: N35°00.78' W120°05.22'
▼ 5.1	SO	Tank on right.
0.7 ▲	SO	Tank on left.
		GPS: N35°00.26' W120°05.30'
▼ 5.8	TL	Turn sharp left; graded road 11N04 continues ahead to Horseshoe Spring Campground. Intersection is unmarked. Zero trip meter.
0.0 ▲		Continue to the southeast.
		GPS: N35°00.01' W120°05.83'
▼ 0.0		Continue to the southwest.
1.0 ▲	TR	Turn sharp right; graded road 11N04 continues ahead to Horseshoe Spring Campground. Intersection is unmarked. Zero trip meter.
▼ 1.0	SO	Small track on right; then Central Mountains #36: Buckhorn Ridge Trail on right at sign. Zero trip meter.
0.0 ▲		Continue to the north past small track on left.
		GPS: N34°59.22' W120°05.68'
▼ 0.0		Continue to the south.
7.2 ▲	SO	Central Mountains #36: Buckhorn Ridge Trail on left at sign. Zero trip meter.
▼ 0.8	SO	Cross through creek in Smith Canyon.
6.4 ▲	SO	Cross through creek in Smith Canyon.
▼ 0.9	SO	Tank on left.
6.3 ▲	SO	Tank on right.
		GPS: N34°58.84' W120°05.58'
▼ 1.0	SO	Cross through wash; then track on left.
6.2 ▲	SO	Track on right; then cross through wash.
▼ 1.7	SO	Closure gate.
5.5 ▲	SO	Closure gate.
▼ 2.3	SO	Gate; then cattle guard.
4.9 ▲	SO	Cattle guard; then gate.
		GPS: N34°57.71' W120°05.79'
▼ 2.5	SO	Cross through two washes.
4.7 ▲	SO	Cross through two washes.
▼ 2.6	SO	Kerry Canyon Trail on left; then cross through wash.
4.6 ▲	BL	Cross through wash; then Kerry Canyon Trail on right.
		GPS: N34°57.51' W120°05.81'
▼ 2.7	SO	Wagon Flat USFS Campground on left alongside North Fork La Brea Creek.
4.5 ▲	SO	Wagon Flat USFS Campground on right alongside North Fork La Brea Creek.
		GPS: N34°57.42' W120°05.82'
▼ 3.0	SO	Cross through North Fork La Brea Creek wash. There are many creek crossings in the next 4.2 miles.
4.2 ▲	SO	Cross through North Fork La Brea Creek wash for the last time.
▼ 4.7	SO	Faint track on right.
2.5 ▲	SO	Faint track on left.
▼ 6.0	SO	Faint track on right.
1.2 ▲	SO	Faint track on left.
		GPS: N34°55.68' W120°07.64'
▼ 7.0	SO	Cross through North Fork La Brea Creek wash.
0.2 ▲	SO	Cross through North Fork La Brea Creek wash.
▼ 7.1	SO	Cattle guard.
0.1 ▲	SO	Cattle guard.
		GPS: N34°55.14' W120°08.42'
▼ 7.2	TR	Turn right onto 11N04, following sign to Tepusquet Road. Track ahead is 10N06, which goes to Barrel Springs Campground and stops 0.5 miles afterwards. Zero trip meter.
0.0 ▲		Continue to the north.
		GPS: N34°55.05' W120°08.53'
▼ 0.0		Continue to the east and cross through North Fork La Brea Creek wash for the last time.
3.7 ▲	TL	Cross through North Fork La Brea Creek wash. There are many creek crossings in the next 4.2 miles. T-intersection. Track on right is 10N06, which goes to Barrel Springs Campground and stops 0.5 miles afterwards. Turn left onto 11N04, following sign to Miranda Pine Road. Zero trip meter.
▼ 0.2	SO	Track on right.
3.5 ▲	SO	Track on left.
		GPS: N34°55.16' W120°08.52'
▼ 3.1	SO	Gate; then cattle guard; then gated track on right.
0.6 ▲	SO	Gated track on left; then cattle guard; then gate.
		GPS: N34°56.03' W120°09.75'
▼ 3.5	SO	Track on left.
0.2 ▲	SO	Track on right.
		GPS: N34°56.26' W120°10.02'
▼ 3.7	SO	Track on right goes to Colson USFS Campground. Small sign at intersection. Zero trip meter.
0.0 ▲		Continue to the northeast.
		GPS: N34°56.31' W120°10.11'
▼ 0.0		Continue to the west.
4.1 ▲	SO	Track on left goes to Colson USFS Campground. Small sign at intersection. Zero trip meter.
▼ 1.3	SO	Cross over wash.
2.8 ▲	SO	Cross over wash.
▼ 1.5	SO	Cross through creek; then exit Los Padres National Forest at sign; then cross through creek again.
2.6 ▲	SO	Cross through creek; then enter Los Padres National Forest at sign; then cross through creek again.
		GPS: N34°56.34' W120°11.37'
▼ 1.7	SO	Cross through creek twice.
2.4 ▲	SO	Cross through creek twice.
▼ 2.0	SO	Cross through creek.
2.1 ▲	SO	Cross through creek.
▼ 2.2	SO	Cattle guard.
1.9 ▲	SO	Cattle guard.
▼ 2.9	SO	Cross through creek.
1.2 ▲	SO	Cross through creek.
▼ 3.1	SO	Cross through wash.
1.0 ▲	SO	Cross through wash.
▼ 3.2	SO	Cross through wash.
0.9 ▲	SO	Cross through wash.
▼ 3.3	SO	Track on left through gate.
0.8 ▲	BL	Track on right through gate.
▼ 3.8	SO	Cattle guard.
0.3 ▲	SO	Cattle guard.

▼ 4.0		SO	Cattle guard.
	0.1 ▲	SO	Cattle guard.
▼ 4.1			Trail ends at T-intersection with Tepusquet Road. Turn left for Santa Maria.
	0.0 ▲		Trail commences on Tepusquet Road, 5.6 miles north of Foxen Canyon Road. Zero trip meter and turn east over cattle guard onto Colson Canyon Road. Road crosses private property for first 3 miles.
			GPS: N34°55.43' W120°13.14'

CENTRAL MOUNTAINS #36

Buckhorn Ridge Trail

Starting Point:	**Central Mountains #35: Miranda Pine Road, 10 miles south of Central Mountains #37: Sierra Madre Road**
Finishing Point:	**Buckhorn Ridge**
Total Mileage:	**3.6 miles (one-way)**
Unpaved Mileage:	**3.6 miles**
Driving Time:	**1 hour (one-way)**
Elevation Range:	**1,800–2,400 feet**
Usually Open:	**Year-round**
Best Time to Travel:	**Dry weather**
Difficulty Rating:	**3**
Scenic Rating:	**9**
Remoteness Rating:	**+0**

Special Attractions

- Moderately challenging spur trail.
- Excellent wide ranging views over the Sierra Madre Range.
- Access to trails suitable for motorbikes and non-motorized use.

Description

Buckhorn Ridge Trail is a spur trail that runs in a northwest direction from the main Central Mountains #35: Miranda

Sections of Buckhorn Ridge Trail can be loose and slightly off-camber

The trail is seldom used and brushy, but it gives some good views

Pine Road. The trail is designated for 4WDs, ATVs, and motorbikes and undulates for 3.6 miles along the narrow Buckhorn Ridge. Views from the ridge are fantastic. To the north is Pine Canyon, with the Sierra Madre rising in the distance. To the south is Bear Canyon. Three trails for motorbikes and non-motorized recreation lead off from the main trail. These side trails are not designated for vehicles.

In recent times, brush threatened to obscure this beautiful ridge trail, but the track was widened in mid-2000 and is now suitable for wide vehicles for most of its length. The final 2 miles to the Los Padres National Forest boundary can be very brushy at times, and most people will probably prefer to turn back shortly after the intersection with the Bear Canyon Trail, which is the final point described in the directions.

The trail's main difficulty comes from steep climbs and descents, which, combined with the loose, low traction surface and occasional side slope, make this a moderately challenging trail. It should be avoided in wet weather.

Current Road Information

Los Padres National Forest
Santa Lucia Ranger District
1616 Carlotti Drive
Santa Maria, CA 93454
(805) 925-9538

Map References

BLM Santa Maria
USFS Los Padres National Forest: Monterey and Santa Lucia Ranger Districts
USGS 1:24,000 Manzanita Mt., Tepusquet Canyon
1:100,000 Santa Maria
Maptech CD-ROM: San Luis Obispo/Los Padres National Forest
Southern & Central California Atlas & Gazetteer, pp. 60, 74
California Road & Recreation Atlas, p. 100

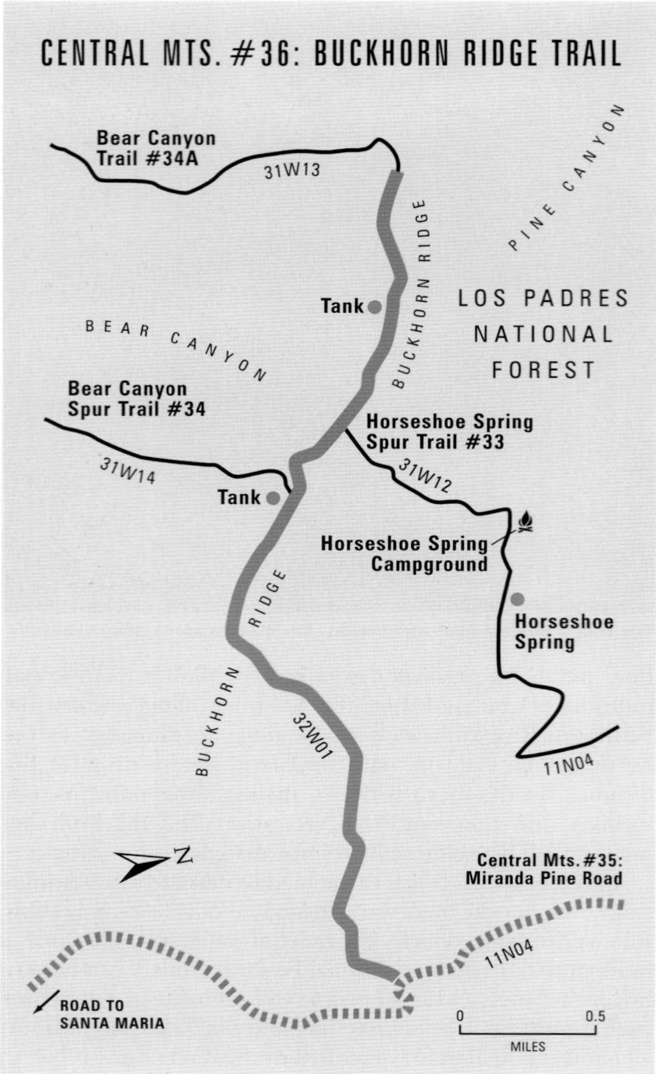

CENTRAL MTS. #36: BUCKHORN RIDGE TRAIL

Bear Canyon Trail #34A
31W13
PINE CANYON
BUCKHORN RIDGE
Tank
LOS PADRES NATIONAL FOREST
BEAR CANYON
Bear Canyon Spur Trail #34
Horseshoe Spring Spur Trail #33
31W14
31W12
Tank
Horseshoe Spring Campground
RIDGE
Horseshoe Spring
BUCKHORN
32W01
11N04
N
Central Mts. #35: Miranda Pine Road
11N04
ROAD TO SANTA MARIA
0
0.5
MILES

Route Directions

▼ 0.0		From Central Mountains #35: Miranda Pine Road, 10 miles south of Central Mountains #37: Sierra Madre Road, zero trip meter and turn southeast on small formed trail at sign for Buckhorn Ridge ORV Trail.
		GPS: N34°59.22' W120°05.68'
▼ 2.1	SO	Tank on left; then Bear Canyon Spur Trail #34 (31W14) on left for motorbikes only—rated black.
		GPS: N34°59.08' W120°07.44'
▼ 2.7	SO	Track on right is Horseshoe Spring Spur #33 (31W12) for motorbikes and non-motorized use—rated blue. Zero trip meter.
		GPS: N34°59.39' W120°07.89'
▼ 0.0		Continue to the northwest.
▼ 0.4	SO	Tank on left.
		GPS: N34°59.58' W120°08.24'
▼ 0.9		Track on left is Bear Canyon #34A (31W13) for motorbikes and non-motorized use—rated black. Trail continues past this point to national forest boundary, but it quickly becomes overgrown.
		GPS: N34°59.67' W120°08.74'

CENTRAL MOUNTAINS #37

Sierra Madre Road

Starting Point:	**California 166, 26.3 miles east of US 101**
Finishing Point:	**McPherson Peak**
Total Mileage:	**29.7 miles (one-way)**
Unpaved Mileage:	**29.7 miles**
Driving Time:	**3 hours (one-way)**
Elevation Range:	**1,400–5,900 feet**
Usually Open:	**Year-round**
Best Time to Travel:	**Dry weather**
Difficulty Rating:	**2**
Scenic Rating:	**8**
Remoteness Rating:	**+0**

Special Attractions

- Wildlife viewing—chance to see Tule elk and the California condors.
- Long, winding ridge trail with great views.
- Can be combined with Central Mountains #38: Bates Canyon Trail to make a loop back to California 166.

History

The name Sierra Madre (Spanish for "Mother Range") reflects the fact that this mountain range serves as a backbone from which other ranges branch off. The range was officially designated as the Sierra Madres in 1965.

The trail leaves from the Cuyama Valley, which is best known for the oil strikes of the 1940s and 1950s. The town of Cuyama was a company town established by the Richfield Oil Company to house its employees. In its heyday, Richfield's oil fields were the fifth most productive in California. The oil and gas industry still figures quite prominently in the valley and is a major local employer.

The beginning of this trail provides spectacular views of Cuyama Valley

The name Cuyama is pronounced "Kwee-ah-ma," though mispronunciations abound. The name is thought to have originated from the Chumash word for Valley of the Clams. This theory is supported by a deep layer of fossilized marine sediment that has been found throughout the valley. Dating back about 25 million years, this sediment includes remains of the *ostrea titan,* or huge oyster. The name Cuyama is documented as far back as 1843, as part of the name Arroyo Llamado de Cuyam.

Some of the earliest inhabitants of the valley were Chumash Indians, whose population reached about 20,000 before the arrival of the Spanish. The Chumash were hunter-gatherers who harvested pinyon nuts on the ridges and hunted antelopes, rabbits, and quails in the valley. They did not practice agriculture. The valley is home to cave and rock paintings that are approximately 500 to 800 years old.

'lease respect Native American istorical artifacts

It is not known what became of the Chumash Indians who made their homes in the valley. One persistent legend relates the tale of an unscrupulous trader, Alexis Godey. Godey took over land in the valley in the 1850s and appropriated government cattle intended for the Chumash. He sold the cattle to local miners and kept the profits for himself. Despite his mistreatment of the Chumash, he was still annoyed by their presence in the valley. Seeking to end his "problem," he invited all the local Chumash to a meal and fed them poisoned beans, sparing only one young girl whom he wanted for himself. This story is largely unsubstantiated and has been vigorously denied on several occasions, but it still persists in the oral tradition of present-day locals.

The first Europeans in the Cuyama Valley were the Spanish, who traveled north from Mexico. There were two large Mexican land grants in the Cuyama Valley. On the whole, Spanish ranches did not flourish in the region; no provision was made for the long periods of drought. The land soon became overgrazed and a number of the imported longhorn cattle were left to die.

Description

This long graded road runs along the ridge tops of the Sierra Madre for more than 30 miles to McPherson Peak. Along the way it passes many other peaks, including Timber Peak, Spoor Peak, Center Peak, and Peak Mountain.

There are only a few side trails that leave from this road. The San Rafael Wilderness is on the western side, which precludes vehicular access. The Cuyama River Valley is to the east, with a steep drop down from the range that limits potential exit points.

Central Mountains #35: Miranda Pine Road meanders down Kerry Canyon from Miranda Pine Campground

Ten miles from the start of the road is the small Miranda Pine Campground, located on top of the ridge. The open campground has a couple of tables, fire rings, and a pit toilet. A Forest Adventure Pass is required, but there is no other fee. Opposite the turn to the campground is a short spur to Miranda Pine Spring and one of the major exits from this area, Central Mountains #35: Miranda Pine Road.

The main trail continues along the ridge for another 22 miles, running underneath the row of peaks that make up the range. It passes the top of Central Mountains #38: Bates Canyon Trail, which can be used as an exit to California 166. There is a shady campsite just prior to this intersection, one of the few along the trail.

The final section of the trail forks, with one branch climbing up to the communications towers on McPherson Peak, and the other continuing to a locked gate on the edge of the San Rafael Wilderness. The trail beyond the gate is an administrative road; there is no public use. There is hiking access into the wilderness beyond this point, and the region contains a few examples of prehistoric rock art.

The area is used as part of the California condor recovery program. These massive birds can often be seen soaring above and are recognizable from underneath by numbered identification tags and a white triangle spreading over both wings. Do not approach or feed the condors; this will jeopardize their chances of remaining wild. Condors have also been known to approach humans and should be discouraged by yelling or clapping your hands loudly. The end of the trail is an excellent place for seeing these birds.

Current Road Information

Los Padres National Forest
Santa Lucia Ranger District
1616 Carlotti Drive
Santa Maria, CA 93454
(805) 925-9538

Map References

BLM San Luis Obispo, Cuyama
USFS Los Padres National Forest: Monterey and Santa Lucia Ranger Districts
USGS 1:24,000 Miranda Pine Mt., Manzanita Mt., Bates Canyon, Peak Mt.
1:100,000 San Luis Obispo, Cuyama
Maptech CD-ROM: San Luis Obispo/Los Padres National Forest
Southern & Central California Atlas & Gazetteer, pp. 60, 61, 75
California Road & Recreation Atlas, pp. 91, 100, 101

Route Directions

▼ 0.0			From California 166, 26.3 miles east of US 101, zero trip meter and turn southeast on graded dirt road at sign for Sierra Madre Road. Turn is sign-posted to McPherson Peak. Road is marked 32S13 and is 0.3 miles east of Central Mountains #39: Big Rocks Trail. Immediately cross cattle guard.
	4.9 ▲		Trail ends at intersection with California 166. Turn left for Santa Maria; turn right for Maricopa. Central Mountains #39: Big Rocks Trail is 0.3 miles to the west.
			GPS: N35°06.69' W120°05.41'
▼ 0.1		SO	Information board on right.
	4.8 ▲	SO	Information board on left.
▼ 0.5		SO	Cattle guard. Entering Los Padres National Forest.
	4.4 ▲	SO	Cattle guard. Leaving Los Padres National Forest.
▼ 2.0		SO	Cross over petroleum pipeline.
	2.9 ▲	SO	Cross over petroleum pipeline.
▼ 2.9		SO	Track on left.
	2.0 ▲	SO	Track on right.
▼ 3.2		SO	Track on right.
	1.7 ▲	SO	Track on left.
			GPS: N35°05.26' W120°04.17'
▼ 3.8		SO	Cattle guard.
	1.1 ▲	SO	Cattle guard.
▼ 4.9		SO	Track on right over rise is Old Sierra Madre Road, which goes 2.5 miles to a locked gate. Zero trip meter.
	0.0 ▲		Continue to the north.
			GPS: N35°04.29' W120°03.40'
▼ 0.0			Continue to the southeast.
	3.7 ▲	SO	Track on left over rise is Old Sierra Madre Road, which goes 2.5 miles to a locked gate. Zero trip meter.
▼ 0.2		SO	Track on left to tank.
	3.5 ▲	SO	Track on right to tank.
			GPS: N35°04.19' W120°03.21'
▼ 0.8		SO	Track on right.
	2.9 ▲	SO	Track on left.
▼ 2.4		SO	Track on left goes 0.3 miles to communications towers on Plowshare Peak.
	1.3 ▲	BL	Track on right goes 0.3 miles to communications towers on Plowshare Peak.
			GPS: N35°02.86' W120°02.23'
▼ 3.7		SO	Track on left goes 0.4 miles to Miranda Pine Campground. Two tracks on right—first goes 0.4 miles to Miranda Pine Spring, second goes through closure gate and is Central Mountains #35: Miranda Pine Road. Zero trip meter.
	0.0 ▲		Continue to the northwest.
			GPS: N35°01.95' W120°02.00'
▼ 0.0			Continue to the southeast.
	12.8 ▲	SO	Track on right goes 0.4 miles to Miranda Pine Campground. Two tracks on left-first goes through closure gate and is Central Mountains #35: Miranda Pine Road, second goes 0.4 miles to Miranda Pine Spring. Zero trip meter.
▼ 7.3		SO	Cattle guard.
	5.5 ▲	SO	Cattle guard.
			GPS: N34°58.04' W119°58.12'
▼ 10.8		SO	Two tracks on left up hill.
	2.0 ▲	SO	Two tracks on right up hill.
▼ 12.5		SO	Campsite on left.
	0.3 ▲	SO	Campsite on right.
			GPS: N34°55.14' W119°54.71'
▼ 12.8		SO	Graded road on left is Central Mountains #38: Bates Canyon Trail (11N01) to California 166. Zero trip meter.
	0.0		Continue to the west.
			GPS: N34°54.99' W119°54.47'
▼ 0.0			Continue to the southeast, remaining on 32S13 and following sign to McPherson Peak.
▼ 6.8		BR	Trail forks. Track to the left goes 0.8 miles to towers on McPherson Peak. Zero trip meter.
			GPS: N34°53.57' W119°49.04'

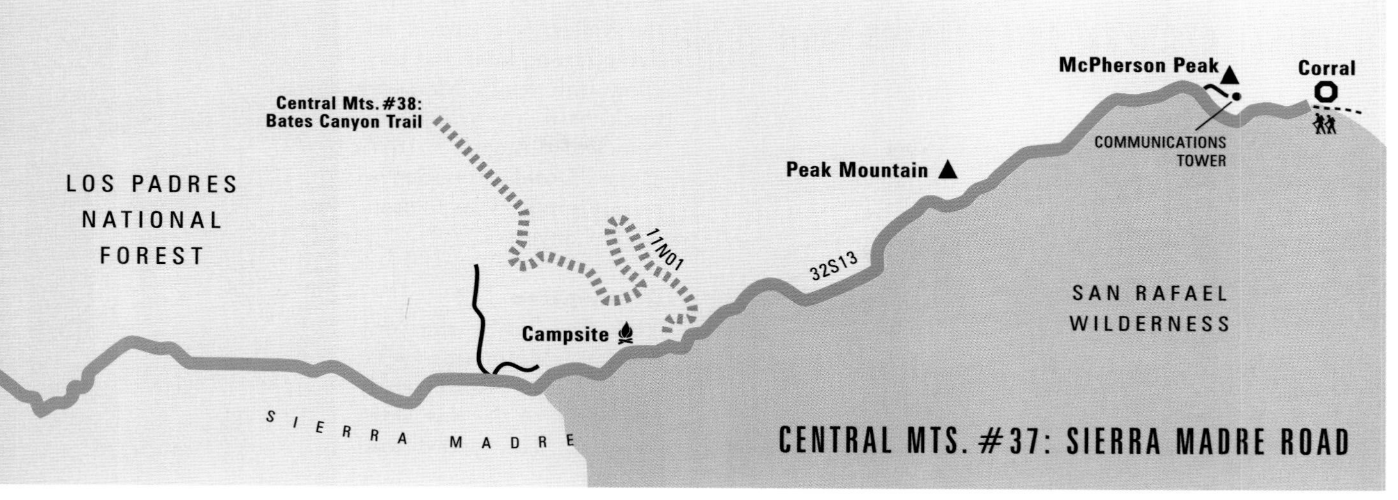

▼ 0.0	Continue to the east.
▼ 1.5	Vehicle trail ends at a corral and locked gate on the edge of the San Rafael Wilderness. Hikers and horses only past this point.
	GPS: N34°52.73' W119°48.33'

CENTRAL MOUNTAINS #38

Bates Canyon Trail

Starting Point:	**Central Mountains #37: Sierra Madre Road, 21.4 miles from California 166**
Finishing Point:	**California 166, 12.5 miles west of New Cuyama**
Total Mileage:	**11.9 miles**
Unpaved Mileage:	**7.2 miles**
Driving Time:	**1 hour**
Elevation Range:	**1,800–5,200 feet**
Usually Open:	**Year-round**
Best Time to Travel:	**Dry weather**
Difficulty Rating:	**2**
Scenic Rating:	**8**
Remoteness Rating:	**+0**

Special Attractions

- Alternative exit from the long Central Mountains #37: Sierra Madre Road.
- Winding descent into Bates Canyon.

History

The lower end of this trail travels along Cottonwood Canyon, which is the final resting place of one of the most famous pioneers in the region. In 1841, the Bartleson-Bidwell Party was heading west to settle in California. Sixty-nine men, women, and children left Missouri, but six months later only twenty-four of them had reached the San Joaquin Valley. Many were turned back by fierce weather and harsh conditions. Two of the survivors were Nancy Kelsey and her husband, Benjamin. Nancy became the first white woman to cross the Sierra Nevada into California.

Nancy's main claim to fame was that she was chosen to create the flag for the California Republic during the Bear Flag Revolt of 1846. Using a design created by William Todd, a nephew of Abraham Lincoln's, Nancy created the new flag from unbleached muslin and a strip torn from her red petticoat. Her creation is still the state flag of California, though the grizzly bear represented on it is now extinct in the state.

Nancy and Benjamin were keen travelers and were some of the first to stake mining claims in the Sierra Nevada foothills. Kelsey's Dry Diggings in El Dorado County is named after them, as is Kelsey Canyon in the Sierra Nevada. After Benjamin's death in 1888, Nancy received a government homestead plot of 160 acres in what is now Cotton-

The trail begins to wind slowly into Bates Canyon—a meandering descent of nearly 3,500 feet

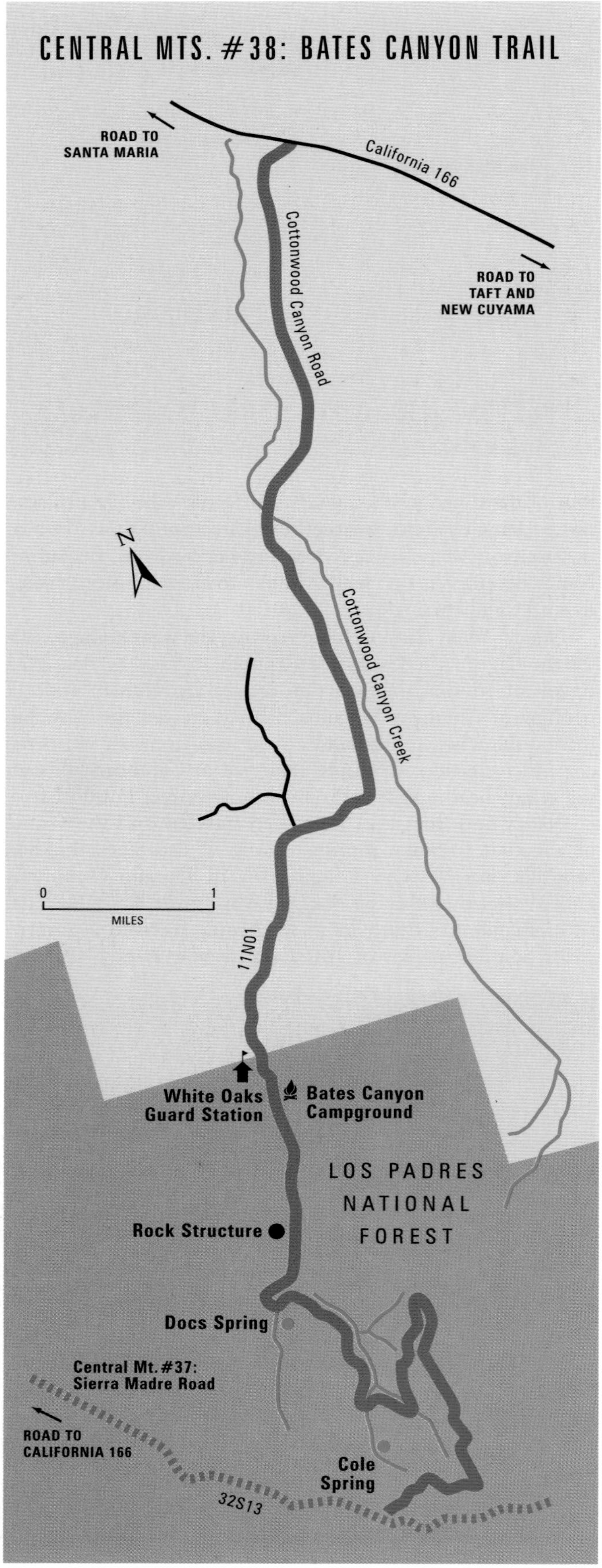

CENTRAL MTS. #38: BATES CANYON TRAIL

ROAD TO SANTA MARIA
California 166
ROAD TO TAFT AND NEW CUYAMA
Cottonwood Canyon Road
Cottonwood Canyon Creek
N
0 1
MILES
11N01
White Oaks Guard Station
Bates Canyon Campground
LOS PADRES NATIONAL FOREST
Rock Structure
Docs Spring
Central Mt. #37: Sierra Madre Road
ROAD TO CALIFORNIA 166
Cole Spring
32S13

wood Canyon in the Cuyama Valley. She earned her living raising hens and traveling into Santa Maria by buckboard to sell them. Nancy died August 9, 1896, at age 73, and was buried on private property in Cottonwood Canyon.

The old, steel-banded wooden tank c Cole Spring is well camoflagued beneath the canopy of oaks

Description

This trail leaves the long Central Mountains #37: Sierra Madre Road nearly two-thirds of the way along its route. The graded road immediately starts winding down some gentle switchbacks, passing Bates Peak, to drop into Bates Canyon. The deep gullies within the canyon hide a couple of springs that are visible beside the trail. Older topographical maps show campgrounds at these springs, but they no longer exist.

Close to the exit of Bates Canyon is the Bates Canyon USFS Campground. The open area has some shade and a couple of picnic tables and fire rings. A Forest Adventure Pass is required.

The trail exits the forest past the disused White Oaks Forest Station. The road past here was paved once, but has fallen into disrepair and is rougher than the graded dirt road above it. At Cottonwood Canyon, the road becomes paved and crosses private land, looking north to the Caliente Range, before it finishes on California 166.

Current Road Information

Los Padres National Forest
Santa Lucia Ranger District
1616 Carlotti Drive
Santa Maria, CA 93454
(805) 925-9538

Map References

BLM Cuyama, Taft
USFS Los Padres National Forest: Monterey and Santa Lucia Ranger Districts
USGS 1:24,000 Bates Canyon, Taylor Canyon
1:100,000 Cuyama, Taft
Maptech CD-ROM: San Luis Obispo/Los Padres National Forest
Southern & Central California Atlas & Gazetteer, pp. 75, 61
California Road & Recreation Atlas, p. 101

Route Directions

▼ 0.0	Trail commences on Central Mountains #37: Sierra Madre Road, 21.4 miles from California 166. Zero trip meter at sign for Bates Canyon Road and proceed southeast on roughly graded dirt road, following sign to California 166 through closure gate.

5.6 ▲ Trail finishes on Central Mountains #37: Sierra Madre Road. Turn right to exit to California 166; turn left to continue to the end of the trail.

GPS: N34°54.99′ W119°54.47′

▼ 2.8 SO Cross through wash.
2.8 ▲ SO Cross through wash.

GPS: N34°55.44′ W119°54.17′

▼ 3.1 SO Cross through wash; then Cole Spring on left.
2.5 ▲ SO Cole Spring on right; then cross through wash.

GPS: N34°55.55′ W119°54.47′

▼ 4.1 SO Cross through wash. Tank on left is Doc Spring.
1.5 ▲ SO Tank on right is Doc Spring. Cross through wash.

GPS: N34°56.17′ W119°54.81′

▼ 4.8 SO Stone structure on left.
0.8 ▲ SO Stone structure on right.

GPS: N34°56.55′ W119°54.56′

▼ 5.4 SO Closure gate.
0.2 ▲ SO Closure gate.

▼ 5.6 SO Bates Canyon USFS Campground on right. Zero trip meter.
0.0 ▲ Continue to the southeast.

GPS: N34°57.28′ W119°54.43′

▼ 0.0 Continue to the northwest.
6.3 ▲ BR Bates Canyon USFS Campground on left. Zero trip meter.

▼ 0.1 SO Track on left.
6.2 ▲ SO Track on right.

▼ 0.2 SO White Oaks Forest Service Station (now closed) on right and left. Leaving Los Padres National Forest.
6.1 ▲ SO White Oaks Forest Service Station (now closed) on right and left. Entering Los Padres National Forest.

GPS: N34°57.42′ W119°54.45′

▼ 0.7 SO Two cattle guards. Road was once paved but is breaking up and is mainly dirt.
5.6 ▲ SO Two cattle guards. Road is now graded dirt.

▼ 1.7 BR Bear right onto small paved road. Paved road on left.
4.6 ▲ BL Bear left at sign for Bates Canyon Road. Paved road on right.

GPS: N34°58.55′ W119°53.83′

▼ 2.1 TL Turn left onto Cottonwood Canyon Road. Private entrance ahead.
4.2 ▲ TR Turn right onto Foothill Road. Private entrance on left. Follow sign for Los Padres National Forest.

GPS: N34°58.62′ W119°53.34′

▼ 2.8 SO Cattle guard.
3.5 ▲ SO Cattle guard.

▼ 3.9 SO Cross through Cottonwood Canyon Creek on concrete ford.
2.4 ▲ SO Cross through Cottonwood Canyon Creek on concrete ford.

GPS: N35°00.22′ W119°53.41′

▼ 6.3 Cattle guard; then trail ends at T-intersection with California 166. Turn right for Maricopa; turn left for Santa Maria.
0.0 ▲ Trail starts on California 166, 12.5 miles west of New Cuyama and immediately west of mile marker 52. Zero trip meter and turn southwest on paved road sign-posted Cottonwood Canyon Road. Immediately cross cattle guard.

GPS: N35°02.07′ W119°52.56′

CENTRAL MOUNTAINS #39

Big Rocks Trail

Starting Point:	**California 166, 26 miles east of US 101**
Finishing Point:	**Central Mountains #42: Paradise Road at the western end**
Total Mileage:	**4.4 miles**
Unpaved Mileage:	**4.4 miles**
Driving Time:	**30 minutes**
Elevation Range:	**1,400–2,000 feet**
Usually Open:	**Year-round**
Best Time to Travel:	**Dry weather**
Difficulty Rating:	**2**
Scenic Rating:	**8**
Remoteness Rating:	**+0**

Special Attractions

- Wildlife viewing for Tule elk.
- Access to many challenging trails for 4WDs, ATVs, and motorbikes.

History

The area around Branch Creek is a habitat of the Tule elk. Although once plentiful in the central coast woodlands, these elk were driven to near extinction by 1850 because of loss of habitat. One herd in Kern County, the Tupman herd, was protected and has managed to survive. The herd thrived so well that farmers found them to be a nuisance, and some were relocated to other areas in California.

Tule elk were re-introduced into this area in 1983 with the transplant of 17 animals from the Tupman herd. The Tule elk, the smallest subspecies of elk in North America, are now thriving, with approximately 3,000 animals spread throughout 19 regions of the state.

Big Rocks are a striking feature along this easy trail

This pleasant trail hugs the wash, weaving through oaks beneath Big Rocks

Description

This short, roughly graded road forms the backbone for a network of trails within this region. However, the trail is attractive in its own right, running along a roughly graded dirt road from California 166. It crosses the Cuyama River and runs alongside Branch Creek into Los Padres National Forest. There is a network of side 4WD trails of varying standards that offer access to the more open ridge tops on either side of the valley.

The road is roughly graded and suitable for high-clearance 2WD vehicles in dry weather; in wet weather it is likely to be impassable for any vehicle. A couple of the steeper sections of the trail are paved in order to control erosion.

The trail passes alongside the Big Rocks, large outcroppings of conglomerate rocks that line the small valley. The trail continues on, passing a couple of very pleasant camping areas to finish at the boundary of private property.

A Forest Adventure Pass is required for all national forest recreation activities.

Current Road Information

Los Padres National Forest
Santa Lucia Ranger District
1616 Carlotti Drive
Santa Maria, CA 93454
(805) 925-9538

Map References

BLM San Luis Obispo
USFS Los Padres National Forest: Monterey and Santa Lucia Ranger Districts
USGS 1:24,000 Miranda Pine Mt., Branch Mt., Los Machos Hills
1:100,000 San Luis Obispo
Maptech CD-ROM: San Luis Obispo/Los Padres National Forest
Southern & Central California Atlas & Gazetteer, p. 60
California Road & Recreation Atlas, p. 91

Route Directions

▼ 0.0		From California 166, 26 miles east of US 101, zero trip meter and turn northwest on graded dirt road. Pass under the entrance of Rock Front Ranch and immediately bear left. There is no forest road marker on the highway.
1.9 ▲		Trail bears right and finishes on California 166. Turn left for Taft; turn right for US 101 and Santa Maria.
		GPS: N35°06.65' W120°05.68'
▼ 0.1	SO	Cross through Cuyama River on concrete ford.
1.8 ▲	SO	Cross through Cuyama River on concrete ford.
▼ 0.2	SO	Cattle guard.
1.7 ▲	SO	Cattle guard.
▼ 0.3	SO	Parking area and information board on left.
1.6 ▲	SO	Parking area and information board on right.
▼ 0.4	SO	Closure gate; then cross through wash.
1.5 ▲	SO	Cross through wash; then closure gate.
▼ 0.5	SO	Cattle guard.
1.4 ▲	SO	Cattle guard.
▼ 0.6	SO	Cross through wash.

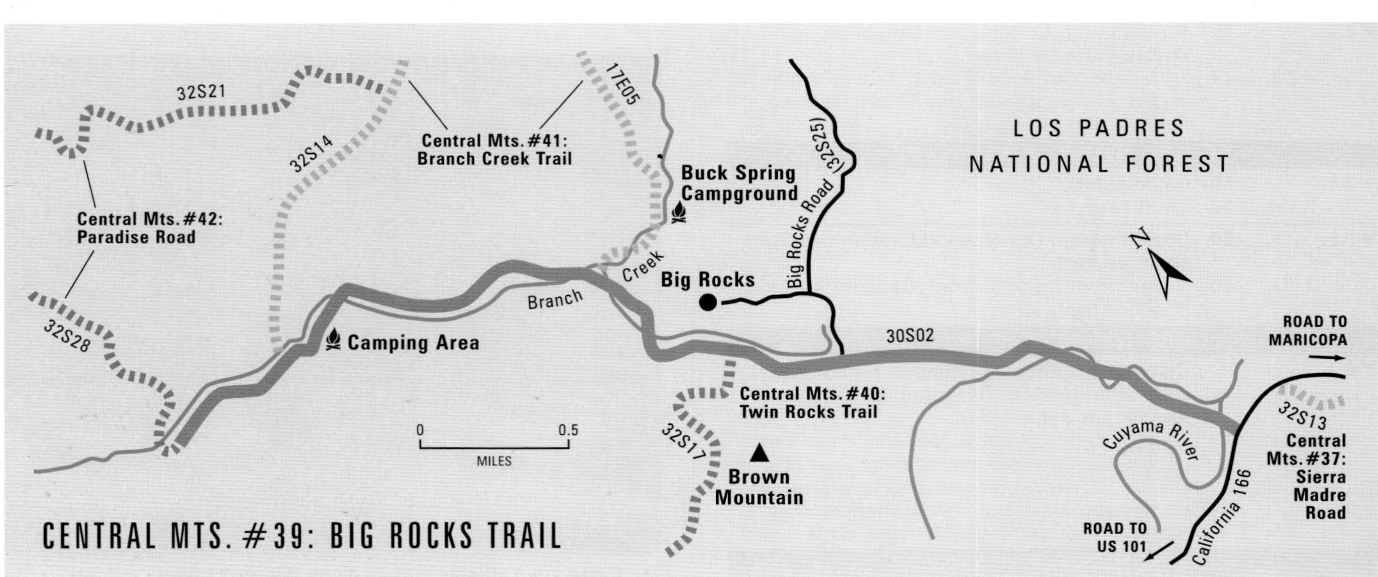

1.3 ▲ SO Cross through wash.

▼ 0.7 SO Cross through two washes. Road is paved as it climbs the hill.
1.2 ▲ SO Road is paved as it descends the hill. Cross through two washes.

▼ 1.5 BL Track on right is Big Rocks Road #28 (32S25) for 4WDs, ATVs, and motorbikes—rated black.
0.4 ▲ BR Track on left is Big Rocks Road #28 (32S25) for 4WDs, ATVs, and motorbikes—rated black.

GPS: N35°07.46′ W120°06.65′

▼ 1.9 BR Track on left is Central Mountains #40: Twin Rocks Trail, marked Twin Rocks Road #30 (32S17) for 4WDs, ATVs, and motorbikes—rated black. Zero trip meter.
0.0 ▲ Continue to the east.

GPS: N35°07.68′ W120°06.99′

▼ 0.0 Continue to the northwest.
0.7 ▲ BL Track on right is Central Mountains #40: Twin Rocks Trail, marked Twin Rocks Road #30 (32S17) for 4WDs, ATVs, and motorbikes-rated black. Zero trip meter.

▼ 0.4 SO Cross through wash.
0.3 ▲ SO Cross through wash.

▼ 0.6 SO Cross through wash.
0.1 ▲ SO Cross through wash.

▼ 0.7 SO Track on right is Central Mountains #41: Branch Creek Trail #27 (17E05) for 4WDs, ATVs, and motorbikes-rated blue. Zero trip meter.
0.0 ▲ Continue to the southwest.

GPS: N35°08.08′ W120°07.26′

▼ 0.0 Continue to the west and cross through wash.
1.4 ▲ SO Cross through wash; then track on left is other end of Central Mountains #41: Branch Creek Trail #27 (17E05) for 4WDs, ATVs, and motorbikes—rated blue. Zero trip meter.

▼ 0.1 SO Cross through wash.
1.3 ▲ SO Cross through wash.

▼ 0.2 SO Cross through wash.
1.2 ▲ SO Cross through wash.

▼ 0.3 SO Cattle guard.
1.1 ▲ SO Cattle guard.

▼ 0.6 SO Cross through wash. Trail crosses wash many times in next 0.8 miles.
0.8 ▲ SO Cross through wash.

▼ 1.2 SO Camping area on left.
0.2 ▲ SO Camping area on right.

GPS: N35°08.38′ W120°08.24′

▼ 1.4 SO Cattle guard; then track on right is other end of Central Mountains #41: Branch Creek Trail. Initially marked as 35 Canyon (32S14) for 4WDs, ATVs, and motorbikes—rated green. Zero trip meter.
0.0 ▲ Continue east and cross second cattle guard.

GPS: N35°08.35′ W120°08.42′

▼ 0.0 Continue to the southwest and cross second cattle guard.
0.4 ▲ SO Cattle guard; then track on left is Central Mountains #41: Branch Creek Trail. Initially marked as 35 Canyon (32S14) for 4WDs, ATVs, and motorbikes—rated green. Zero trip meter. Trail crosses wash many times in next 0.8 miles.

▼ 0.3 SO Cross through wash.
0.1 ▲ SO Cross through wash.

▼ 0.4 Cross through wash; then track on right is Central Mountains #42: Paradise Road, marked as Los Machos #25 (32S28) for 4WDs, ATVs, and motorbikes—rated green. Trail ends immediately past this intersection at a locked gate before private property.
0.0 ▲ Trail commences at the western end of Central Mountains #42: Paradise Road. Zero trip meter and turn northeast on graded dirt road. Trail to the west is blocked by a locked gate before private property.

GPS: N35°08.30′ W120°08.85′

CENTRAL MOUNTAINS #40

Twin Rocks Trail

Starting Point:	**Central Mountains #39: Big Rocks Trail, 1.9 miles north of California 166**
Finishing Point:	**Shaw Ridge**
Total Mileage:	**5.6 miles (one-way)**
Unpaved Mileage:	**5.6 miles**
Driving Time:	**45 minutes (one-way)**
Elevation Range:	**1,400–2,500 feet**
Usually Open:	**Year-round**
Best Time to Travel:	**Dry weather**
Difficulty Rating:	**6, 7 for last 0.7 miles**
Scenic Rating:	**9**
Remoteness Rating:	**+0**

Special Attractions

- Winding trail with a very steep grade.
- Views into the Cuyama River Valley.

History

There are some small pieces of private property in this section of Los Padres National Forest. One of them was settled in 1893 by John Logan, after whom Logan Ridge is named. It is likely that John worked on a nearby ranch and gained his

Big Rocks area seen from the steep climb up Twin Rocks Road

Descending the final part of this ridge trail

property through continuous occupation of the land, a common practice in those days.

Description

The trail leaves Central Mountains #39: Big Rocks Trail, the main backbone through this region of forest, and immediately starts to climb steeply, switchbacking its way out of the valley to the ridge tops. The trail is rated a 6 for difficulty because of the steepness of the grade and occasional low traction sections. The surface is generally smooth; it is not a rock crawling trail.

At the top of the first steep climb on Brown Mountain, a short spur trail leads off to a viewpoint over the Cuyama Valley. The mile-long spur leads down to a steeply sloping overlook that offers great views. The best view of the Twin Rocks is to the south from the spur trail.

The trail descends steeply to cross a creek before climbing again to run along Shaw Ridge. There are some steep sections, particularly after the trail passes the Shaw Ridge Trail sign. The final 0.6 miles of the trail jumps in difficulty to a 7 because of the extreme steepness and looseness of the trail. Traction is very poor. The trail ends at a Road Closed sign, so be prepared to return the way you came. Unless you are driving a suitably equipped vehicle to tackle the steepest section—lockers are advised—it is best to turn around at the point indicated in the route description. This will keep the difficulty level at a 6.

Current Road Information

Los Padres National Forest
Santa Lucia Ranger District
1616 Carlotti Drive
Santa Maria, CA 93454
(805) 925-9538

Map References

BLM San Luis Obispo
USFS Los Padres National Forest: Monterey and Santa Lucia Ranger Districts
USGS 1:24,000 Branch Mt., Miranda Pine Mt., Chimney Canyon, Los Machos Hills
1:100,000 San Luis Obispo
Maptech CD-ROM: San Luis Obispo/Los Padres National Forest
Southern & Central California Atlas & Gazetteer, p. 60
California Road & Recreation Atlas, p. 91

Route Directions

▼ 0.0	From Central Mountains #39: Big Rocks Trail, 1.9 miles north of California 166, zero trip meter and turn southeast on formed trail.

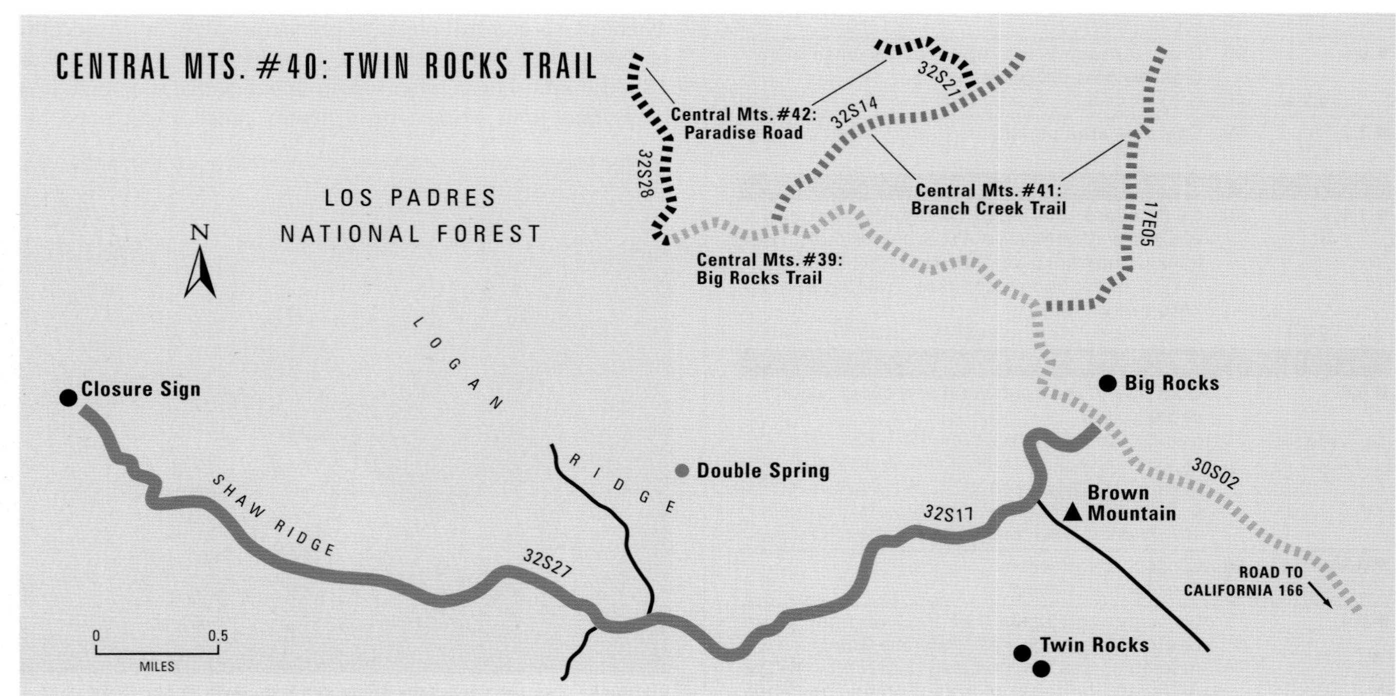

		Road is marked Twin Rocks Road #30 (32S17) for 4WDs, ATVs, and motorbikes-rated black.
		GPS: N35°07.68' W120°06.99'
▼ 0.2	SO	Turnout on right.
▼ 0.6	BR	Well-used, unmarked track on left goes 1 mile to a viewpoint with superb views over the Cuyama River Valley and Twin Rocks. Zero trip meter.
		GPS: N35°07.45' W120°07.25'
▼ 0.0		Continue to the southwest.
▼ 0.3	SO	Cattle guard.
▼ 0.6	SO	Track on right.
▼ 2.0	SO	Track on right leads into private property.
		GPS: N35°06.92' W120°09.00'
▼ 2.2	BR	Track on left; bear right onto trail marked Shaw Ridge #22 (32S27) for 4WDs, ATVs, and motorbikes-rated black. Zero trip meter.
		GPS: N35°06.91' W120°09.12'
▼ 0.0		Continue to the northwest.
▼ 2.1	SO	Trail increases in difficulty in 0.1 miles. Turn here if not equipped to tackle the steeper, looser 7-rated trail. This is the final turning point before the 7-rated section. It is a very tight turn.
		GPS: N35°07.34' W120°10.80'
▼ 2.3	SO	Trail becomes extremely steep as it descends from Shaw Ridge.
		GPS: N35°07.36' W120°11.10'
▼ 2.8		Trail ends at road closure sign.
		GPS: N35°07.70' W120°11.40'

CENTRAL MOUNTAINS #41

Branch Creek Trail

Starting Point:	**Central Mountains #39: Big Rocks Trail, 2.6 miles north of California 166**
Finishing Point:	**Central Mountains #39: Big Rocks Trail, 4 miles north of California 166**
Total Mileage:	**7.3 miles**
Unpaved Mileage:	**7.3 miles**
Driving Time:	**1.5 hours**
Elevation Range:	**1,400–2,400 feet**
Usually Open:	**Year-round**
Best Time to Travel:	**Dry weather**
Difficulty Rating:	**5**
Scenic Rating:	**8**
Remoteness Rating:	**+0**

Special Attractions

- Moderately challenging ridge top and canyon trail.
- Intersects with a number of other 4WD trails.

Description

This trail offers a moderately difficult loop from Central Mountains #39: Big Rocks Trail. Initially the trail is formed, passing through the forest service camping area at Buck Spring. This large open area has no marked sites, just a couple of tables and a fire ring. A Forest Adventure Pass is required, but there is no other fee.

Bear prints are easy to spot in the deep dust below Branch Mountain

The trail continues along Branch Creek for a short distance, before leaving the creek to climb steeply onto the ridge top. The grade is moderately steep, and the surface is even but loose. Branch Creek is seen down to the east through the low, scrubby vegetation. The moderately steep grade continues along the ridge tops. Panoramic views encompass the surrounding hills, and you will be able to see many of the other 4WD trails in the area.

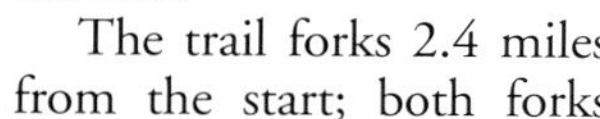

The trail forks 2.4 miles from the start; both forks become black-rated trails because of steep grades and deep, talcum powderlike surface that makes traction difficult. Travel is easier if following the forward route directions. Following the reverse directions forces you to climb up the loosest section. The final section joins the better-surfaced trail that runs along Thirtyfive Canyon to rejoin Big Rocks Road.

The soft surface makes it easy to see the tracks of animals that have walked along the trail. Look out for Tule elk tracks and the distinctive tracks of black bears.

Current Road Information

Los Padres National Forest
Santa Lucia Ranger District
1616 Carlotti Drive
Santa Maria, CA 93454
(805) 925-9538

Branch Creek Trail snakes its way along the ridge above Buck Spring

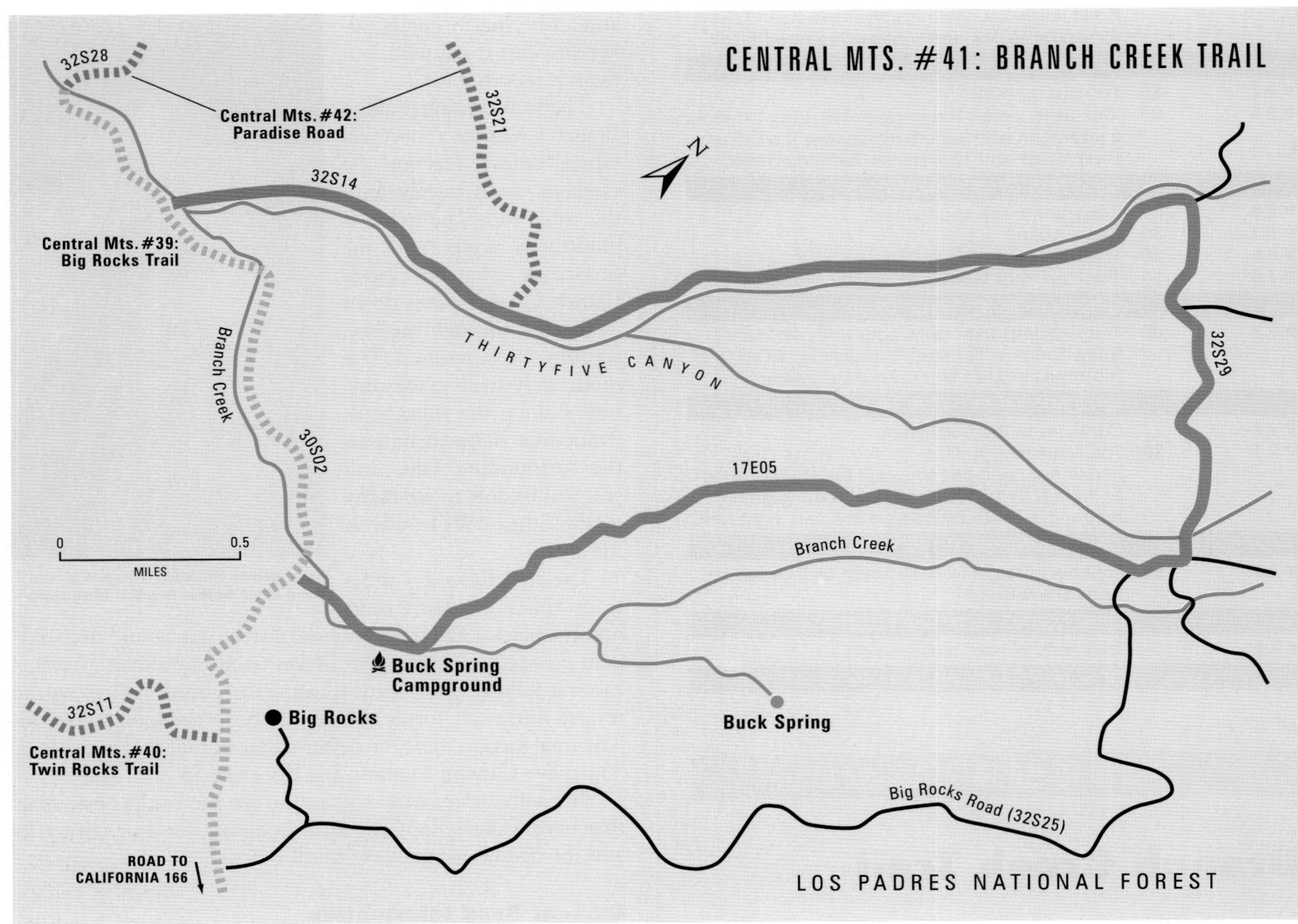

Map References

BLM San Luis Obispo
USFS Los Padres National Forest: Monterey and Santa Lucia Ranger Districts
USGS 1:24,000 Branch Mt., Los Machos Hills
1:100,000 San Luis Obispo
Maptech CD-ROM: San Luis Obispo/Los Padres National Forest
Southern & Central California Atlas & Gazetteer, p. 60
California Road & Recreation Atlas, p. 91

Route Directions

▼ 0.0 From Central Mountains #39: Big Rocks Trail, 2.6 miles north of California 166, zero trip meter and turn northeast on formed trail and cross cattle guard. Trail is marked as Branch Creek #27 (17E05) for 4WDs, ATVs, and motorbikes—rated blue. Trail crosses Branch Creek many times for next 0.5 miles.
2.6 ▲ Trail ends on Central Mountains #39: Big Rocks Trail. Turn left to exit to California 166.

GPS: N35°08.08' W120°07.26'

▼ 0.3 BL Buck Spring Campground on right.
2.3 ▲ BR Buck Spring Campground on left.

GPS: N35°08.09' W120°06.99'

▼ 0.5 BL Bear left, crossing Branch Creek. Trail climbs steeply up ridge. Track on right to Buck Spring.
2.1 ▲ BR End of descent. Bear right, crossing Branch Creek. Track on left to Buck Spring. Trail crosses Branch Creek many times for next 0.5 miles.

GPS: N35°08.23' W120°06.89'

▼ 2.6 BL Trail forks. Track on right is Big Rocks Road #28 (32S25) for 4WDs, ATVs, and motorbikes—rated black. Bear left onto Jack Spring Road #29 (32S29) and zero trip meter.
0.0 ▲ Continue to the southwest.

GPS: N35°09.63' W120°05.94'

▼ 0.0 Continue to the north.
3.5 ▲ SO Track on left is Big Rocks Road #28 (32S25) for 4WDs, ATVs, and motorbikes—rated black. Continue straight ahead on Branch Creek Road #27 (30S92, which is a different number than far end). Zero trip meter.

▼ 0.3 TL 4-way intersection. Track straight ahead goes to parking area and track on right goes to locked gate. Follow most-used trail.
3.2 ▲ TR 4-way intersection. Track straight ahead goes to locked gate and track on left goes to parking area. Follow most-used trail.

GPS: N35°09.79' W120°05.74'

▼ 1.2 SO Closed track on right.
2.3 ▲ SO Closed track on left. Route is now marked Jack Spring Road #29 (32S29)—rated black.

			GPS: N35°10.13′ W120°06.45′
▼ 1.6		TL	Well-used, unmarked track on right. Turn left and join roughly graded road.
	1.9 ▲	TR	Well-used, unmarked track ahead. Turn right onto smaller formed trail.
			GPS: N35°10.35′ W120°06.67′
▼ 1.9		SO	Cross over creek. Trail crosses creek many times for next 2.8 miles.
	1.6 ▲	SO	Cross over creek.
▼ 3.5		BL	Track on right is Central Mountains #42: Paradise Road (32S21) for 4WDs, ATVs, and motorbikes—rated green. Zero trip meter.
	0.0 ▲		Continue to the northeast.
			GPS: N35°08.85′ W120°07.53′
▼ 0.0			Continue to the south.
	1.2 ▲	BR	Track on left is Central Mountains #42: Paradise Road (32S21) for 4WDs, ATVs, and motorbikes—rated green. Zero trip meter.
▼ 1.2			Trail ends at T-intersection with Central Mountains #39: Big Rocks Trail. Turn right to continue along the trail; turn left to exit to California 166.
	0.0 ▲		Trail commences on Central Mountains #39: Big Rocks Trail, 4 miles from intersection with California 166. Zero trip meter and turn west on small graded road at sign for Thirtyfive Canyon (32S14) for 4WDs, ATVs, and motorbikes—rated green. Trail follows along creek in Thirtyfive Canyon, crossing it often for next 1.5 miles.
			GPS: N35°08.35′ W120°08.42′

CENTRAL MOUNTAINS #42

Paradise Road

Starting Point:	**End of Central Mountains #39: Big Rocks Trail, 4.4 miles from California 166**
Finishing Point:	**Central Mountains #41: Branch Creek Trail, 1.2 miles from northern intersection of Central Mountains #39: Big Rocks Trail**
Total Mileage:	**3.4 miles, plus 1.1-mile spur**
Unpaved Mileage:	**3.4 miles, plus 1.1-mile spur**
Driving Time:	**1 hour (including spur)**
Elevation Range:	**1,300–2,200 feet**
Usually Open:	**Year-round**
Best Time to Travel:	**Dry weather**
Difficulty Rating:	**3, optional 4-rated spur**
Scenic Rating:	**8**
Remoteness Rating:	**+0**

Special Attractions

- Loop trail from the main Central Mountains #39: Big Rocks Trail.
- Connects to a number of other 4WD trails in this region of Los Padres National Forest.
- Optional 4-rated spur trail.

Mature oaks dot the hillsides along Paradise Road

Description

This short trail follows one of the green-rated (easiest) trails through Los Padres National Forest. The trail describes a loop from the end of Central Mountains #39: Big Rocks Trail. It climbs to a saddle through open grasslands studded with mature oak trees. From the saddle, there is an optional 4-rated spur trail that climbs up the ridge away from the saddle and travels for just over a mile before finishing at the boundary of private property. This spur is more difficult because of the loose trail surface and steep grade. The main trail is 3-rated because of the rutted surface and some moderately steep climbs and descents.

The main trail descends to Paradise Camp, a national forest campground with two small sites along the creek. A Forest Adventure Pass is required to camp there, but no other fee is charged. From the camp, the trail follows through denser vegetation to finish on Central Mountains #41: Branch Creek Trail, 1.2 miles from the main Big Rocks Trail.

Current Road Information

Los Padres National Forest
Santa Lucia Ranger District
1616 Carlotti Drive
Santa Maria, CA 93454
(805) 925-9538

Map References

BLM San Luis Obispo
USFS Los Padres National Forest: Monterey and Santa Lucia Ranger Districts
USGS 1:24,000 Los Machos Hills
1:100,000 San Luis Obispo
Maptech CD-ROM: San Luis Obispo/Los Padres National Forest
Southern & Central California Atlas & Gazetteer, p. 60
California Road & Recreation Atlas, p. 91

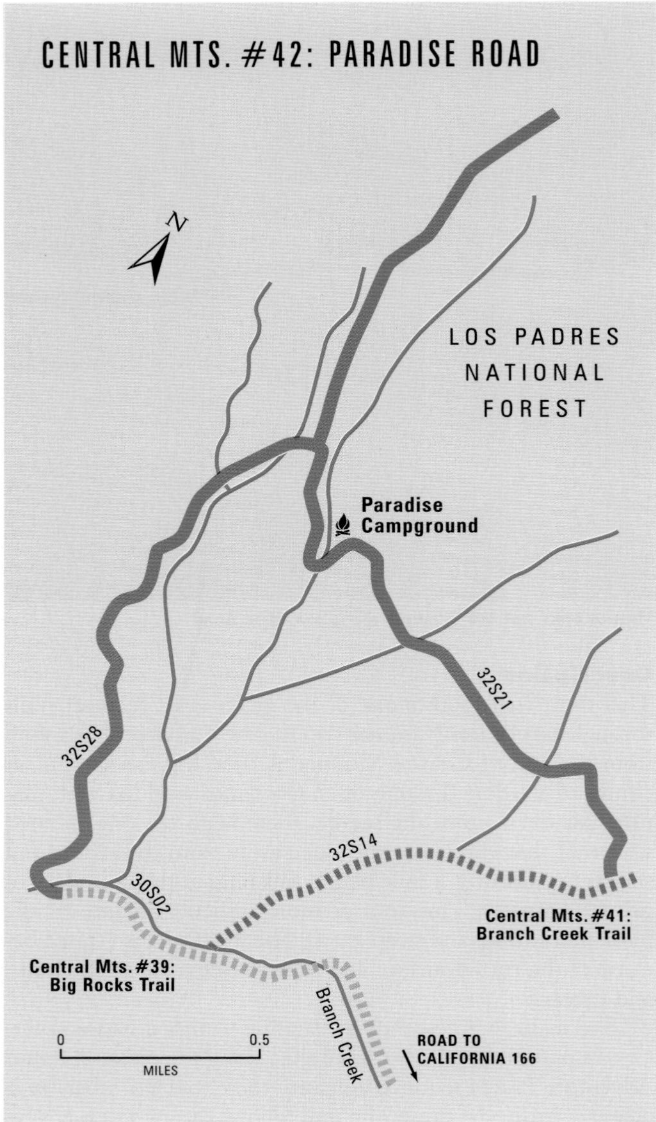

Route Directions

▼ 0.0		From the end of Central Mountains #39: Big Rocks Trail, 4.4 miles from California 166, zero trip meter and turn northwest over cattle guard onto formed trail. Trail is marked Los Machos #25 (32S28) for 4WDs, ATVs, and motorbikes—rated green.
1.6 ▲		Trail ends at end of Central Mountains #39: Big Rocks Trail. Turn left for California 166.
		GPS: N35°08.30' W120°08.85'
▼ 1.2	SO	Cross through wash.
0.4 ▲	SO	Cross through wash.
▼ 1.5	SO	Cross through wash.
0.1 ▲	SO	Cross through wash.
		GPS: N35°09.40' W120°08.82'
▼ 1.6	BR	Well-used unmarked track on left is start of spur trail that climbs ridge. Zero trip meter and join Paradise Road #26 (32S21) for 4WDs, ATVs, and motorbikes—rated green.
0.0 ▲		Continue to the west.
		GPS: N35°09.39' W120°08.76'

Ridge Top Spur

▼ 0.0		Proceed to the north. Immediately trail climbs ridge.
▼ 0.9	SO	Cattle guard.
▼ 1.1	UT	Spur ends at a locked gate into private property.
		GPS: N35°10.26' W120°08.59'

Continuation of Main Trail

▼ 0.0		Continue to the southeast.
1.8 ▲	BL	Well-used unmarked track on right is start of spur trail that climbs ridge. Zero trip meter and continue straight ahead.
		GPS: N35°09.39' W120°08.76'
▼ 0.3	BL	Paradise Campground on right and left; then cross over creek.
1.5 ▲	BR	Cross over creek; then Paradise Campground on right and left.
		GPS: N35°09.15' W120°08.62'
▼ 0.8	SO	Cross through wash.
1.0 ▲	SO	Cross through wash.
▼ 1.2	SO	Cross over wash.
0.6 ▲	SO	Cross over wash.
		GPS: N35°08.98' W120°07.89'
▼ 1.8		Trail ends on Central Mountains #41: Branch Creek Trail, 1.2 miles from the end. Turn right to exit via Central Mountains #39: Big Rocks Trail to California 166; turn left to continue along Branch Creek Trail.
0.0 ▲		Trail starts on Central Mountains #39: Branch Creek Trail, 1.2 miles from the northern end. Zero trip meter and turn southwest on formed trail marked Paradise Road #26 (32S21).
		GPS: N35°08.85' W120°07.53'

CENTRAL MOUNTAINS #43

Sand Highway

Starting Point:	**End of Pier Avenue, at the fee station**
Finishing Point:	**Gate to wilderness area**
Total Mileage:	**5.3 miles**
Unpaved Mileage:	**5.3 miles**
Driving Time:	**45 minutes**
Elevation Range:	**0–30 feet**
Usually Open:	**Year-round**
Best Time to Travel:	**Year-round**
Difficulty Rating:	**3**
Scenic Rating:	**9**
Remoteness Rating:	**+0**

Special Attractions

- Beautiful views over the dunes to the Pacific Ocean.
- Dunes offer a scenic challenge to all levels of off-highway enthusiasts.

Description

The Oceano Dunes State Vehicular Recreation Area is located at the end of Pier Avenue in Oceano. From California 1,

Barbeque Flats Camping Area

turn west onto Pier Avenue. After a couple of blocks the road will dead-end at the fee station for the recreation area. After paying a small fee, you are free to explore the beach and dunes to your heart's content. Although you can go anywhere your vehicle will take you in the recreation area, one route, called Sand Highway, has been marked with orange marker posts. This route follows along the shoreline at the start, before branching off into the dunes. Once in the dunes, orange signs mark the route about every tenth of a mile. The rolling course of Sand Highway is usually consistent, avoiding the major drops and ridgelines. However, the dunes are constantly changing shape, and drivers should approach drop-offs with caution.

A few campsites are scattered along the route. They are typically tucked beneath the dunes to provide some shelter from the ocean wind. There are a few roped areas for long-term RV camping along the shoreline. The trail ends at a gate and information board before the start of a hiking trail to Oso Flaco Lake. This wide-open area is a great place to park and take in the scenery. The natural area around freshwater Oso Flaco Lake was set up to protect plants and animals deemed threatened by the state and federal governments. The lake is also an annual refuge for migrating waterfowl.

As you drive along the sand, remember that it can be soft in some areas and quite hard in others. It is a good idea to avoid building up your speed on descents because there are often hard bottoms that will have your vehicle rocking like a seesaw. If you are having problems getting adequate traction, lower your tire pressure. There is a gas station nearby to refill them after you are finished on the dunes.

Current Road Information

Oceano Dunes SVRA District Office
576 Camino Mercado
Arroyo Grande, CA 93420
(805) 473-7230

Map References

BLM San Luis Obispo
USGS 1:24,000 Oceano
1:100,000 San Luis Obispo

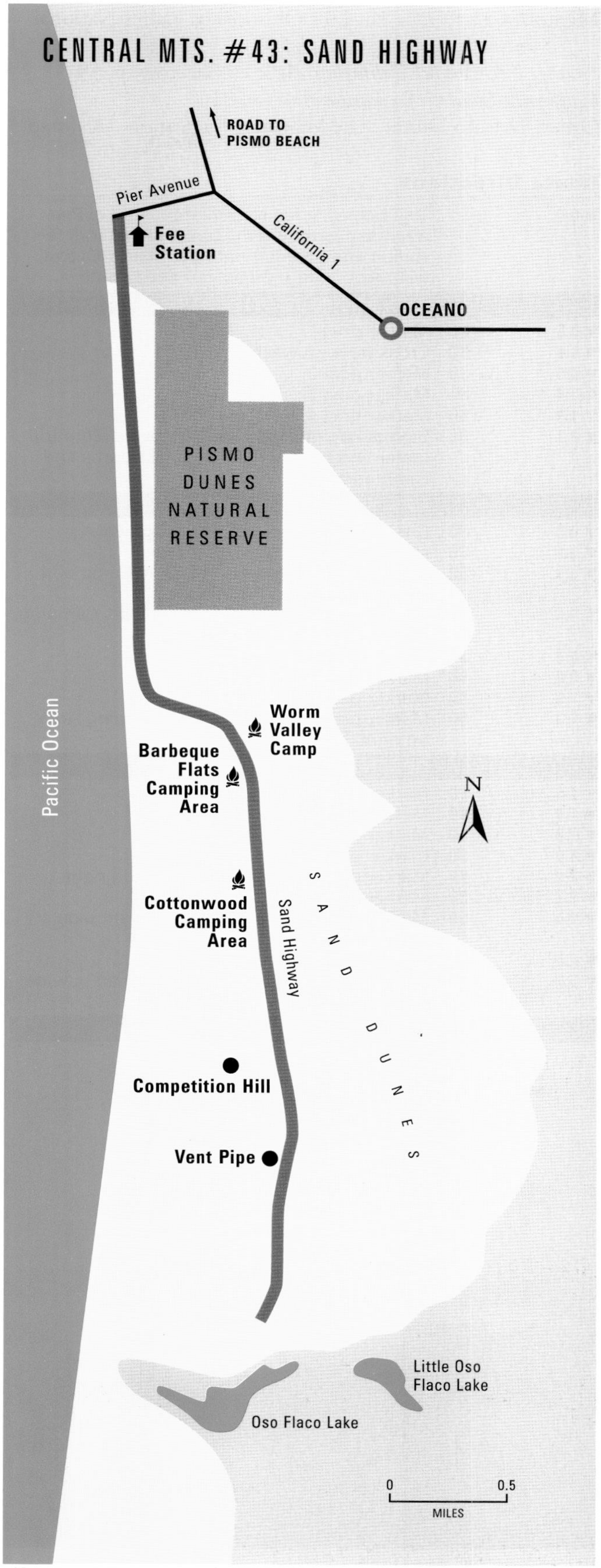

CENTRAL MTS. #43: SAND HIGHWAY

ROAD TO PISMO BEACH
Pier Avenue
California 1
Fee Station
OCEANO
PISMO DUNES NATURAL RESERVE
Pacific Ocean
Worm Valley Camp
Barbeque Flats Camping Area
Cottonwood Camping Area
Sand Highway
SAND DUNES
N
Competition Hill
Vent Pipe
Little Oso Flaco Lake
Oso Flaco Lake
0 0.5
MILES

Maptech CD-ROM: San Luis Obispo/Los Padres National Forest
Southern & Central California Atlas & Gazetteer, p. 59
California Road & Recreation Atlas, p. 91
Other: Oceano Dunes State Vehicular Recreation Area map

Route Directions

▼ 0.0		Trail begins at fee station at the end of Pier Avenue (fee required). Zero trip meter at fee station and bear left onto the beach. Ocean will be on your right as you head south.
		GPS: N35°00.33′ W120°37.79′
▼ 0.5	SO	Marker post 1.
▼ 0.6	SO	Cross through wash.
▼ 0.9	SO	Marker post 2.
▼ 1.4	SO	Marker post 3.
▼ 1.9	SO	Marker post 4.
▼ 2.1	BL	Sign at beginning of Sand Highway. Zero trip meter and bear left just past restrooms and camping area.
		GPS: N35°04.48′ W120°37.15′
▼ 0.0	SO	Continue southeast on Sand Highway.
▼ 0.1	SO	Marker post 10.
▼ 0.3	SO	Marker post 11 and Worm Valley Camp and restrooms.
▼ 0.4	SO	Marker post 12; then Barbeque Flats Camping Area on right.
▼ 0.6	SO	Marker post 13.
▼ 0.8	SO	Marker post 14.
▼ 1.0	SO	Marker post 15.
▼ 1.3	SO	Marker post 16; Cottonwood Camping Area on right.
		GPS: N36°03.63′ W120°37.14′
▼ 1.4	SO	Marker post 17.
▼ 1.6	SO	Marker post 18.
▼ 1.8	SO	Marker post 19.
▼ 1.9	SO	Marker post 20.
▼ 2.0	SO	Marker post 21. Competition Hill on right.
▼ 2.2	SO	Marker post 22.
▼ 2.5	SO	Marker post 24. There is a large vent pipe on the right.
▼ 2.6	SO	Marker post 25.
▼ 3.2		Trail ends at gate and hiking trailhead in wide, open area.
		GPS: N35°02.10′ W120°37.15′

Misty view over Oso Flaco Lake

CENTRAL MOUNTAINS #44

Pozo Road

Starting Point:	**California 58 (Carrisa Highway), 0.4 miles west of mile marker 35**
Finishing Point:	**Pozo Road at the Pozo Station**
Total Mileage:	**18.2 miles**
Unpaved Mileage:	**10.7 miles**
Driving Time:	**1 hour**
Elevation Range:	**1,400–2,800 feet**
Usually Open:	**Year-round**
Best Time to Travel:	**Dry weather**
Difficulty Rating:	**1**
Scenic Rating:	**8**
Remoteness Rating:	**+0**

Special Attractions

- Old Pozo stage stop, now the Pozo Saloon.
- Main route through the Pozo–La Panza OHV Area.

History

La Panza takes its name from early Spanish bear hunters and their baiting technique. These hunters used the paunch, or *la panza,* of a cow to attract bears. To the north of La Panza, Carnaza Creek refers to these same hunters; *carnaza* is animal meat with the skin still attached.

Grizzly bears, although now extinct in California, were noticed in great numbers by early expeditions through the region. Although they posed a significant danger, they were an essential part of the food supply for these expeditions.

In 1772, Spanish settlers experienced near famine conditions just two years after establishing the Presidio of Monterey. This period was made worse when supply ships, an essential part of the supply chain in Southern California, failed to arrive with provisions. The troops remembered that the men on Portolá's coastal expedition of 1769 had encountered many lean bears to the south, which were found to be very savory. In an attempt to alleviate the food shortage, the commander of the presidio, Pedro Fages, led a dozen troops south into the region surrounding today's San Luis Obispo in search of grizzlies. This venture has been referred to as one of the largest grizzly bear hunts of Southern California. Pack load after pack load of salted bear meat was shipped north to the starving Spaniards at Mission San Antonio de Padua and farther still to settlers at the Presidio of Monterey. Jerked grizzly meat became the order of the day for months, thus saving the Spanish from starvation. Father Junipero Serra, the head of the Presidio in Monterey, had one regret following this successful venture. Many of the soldiers had taken a liking to the region because of its plentiful food supply and friendly native maidens. Needless to say, many chose not to return to the mission.

In the 1860s, the settlement of Pozo had both a Wells Fargo stage stop and a pony express delivery stop. Built in 1858, the existing Pozo Saloon was once the stage stop. In 1878, there was a short-lived gold rush in the nearby canyons and a post office was opened shortly thereafter. Pozo, though taken to mean "well" in Spanish, also refers to a saucer-shaped depression. Pozo was chosen as the name for the post office because early settlers found the saucer-shaped valley to have water. Thus they were able to grow corn, beans, and other crops without needing to develop an irrigation system.

The Pozo Saloon was closed during Prohibition. However, it reopened its doors in 1967, and was run by a former sheriff of San Luis Obispo named Paul Merrick. The 12-foot-long mahogany bar in the main room was transported around Cape Horn in 1860 and was originally the bar in the Cosmopolitan Hotel in San Luis Obispo. The saloon is definitely worth a visit for one of its great burgers and a Pozo Martini—a draught beer with two green olives dropped into the glass.

San Miguel Mission records mention an Indian village to the north of this trail. The village bordered the Obispeño Chumash and Migueleño Salinan tribes and was called Camata. This village name has lingered on in the name of Camatta Creek, which flows away from this trail to the north.

Another descriptive name is witnessed as the trail passes over Pozo Summit. Here, an OHV trail called Las Chiches leads off to the north to climb up to a flat of the same name. *Las chiches* is Spanish for "the nipples."

Description

Together, Pozo and Redhill Roads form the main backbone through the Pozo–La Panza OHV Area, with many trails branching off from them. Pozo Road itself is suitable for passenger vehicles in dry weather and, like all the trails in this area, should be avoided when wet. Within Los Padres National Forest, a Forest Adventure Pass is required for all parked vehicles, as well as for any recreational activity.

Pozo Road leaves California 58 along a paved road as it enters Los Padres National Forest. The vegetation is open, consisting mainly of low shrubs. The area was burned severely by wildfire a few years ago. Central Mountains #45: Pine Mountain Road, a lovely blue-rated trail, leaves from La Panza Summit, before Pozo Road descends to the shaded La Panza Campground.

ozo Road running down toward La Panza Campground

Pozo Saloon

From here, the trail climbs along a wide shelf road, running around the Mariana Creek valley to Pozo Summit. Two difficult trails lead off from the summit—Pine Mountain Road and Las Chiches Trail. Both are black-rated trails that are suitable for 4WDs, ATVs, and motorbikes. The second section of the trail descends along Fraser Canyon to the trail's end at the old settlement of Pozo.

Current Road Information

Los Padres National Forest
Santa Lucia Ranger District
1616 Carlotti Drive
Santa Maria, CA 93454
(805) 925-9538

Map References

BLM San Luis Obispo
USFS Los Padres National Forest: Monterey and Santa Lucia Ranger Districts
USGS 1:24,000 Pozo Summit, La Panza Ranch, La Panza, Santa Margarita Lake
1:100,000 San Luis Obispo
Maptech CD-ROM: San Luis Obispo/Los Padres National Forest
Southern & Central California Atlas & Gazetteer, p. 60
California Road & Recreation Atlas, p. 91

Route Directions

▼ 0.0	From California 58 (Carrisa Highway), 0.4 miles west of mile marker 35, zero trip meter and turn southwest onto Pozo Road, sign-posted to Pozo. The road is initially paved.
5.7 ▲	Trail ends at T-intersection with California 58 (Carrisa Highway). Turn left for Santa

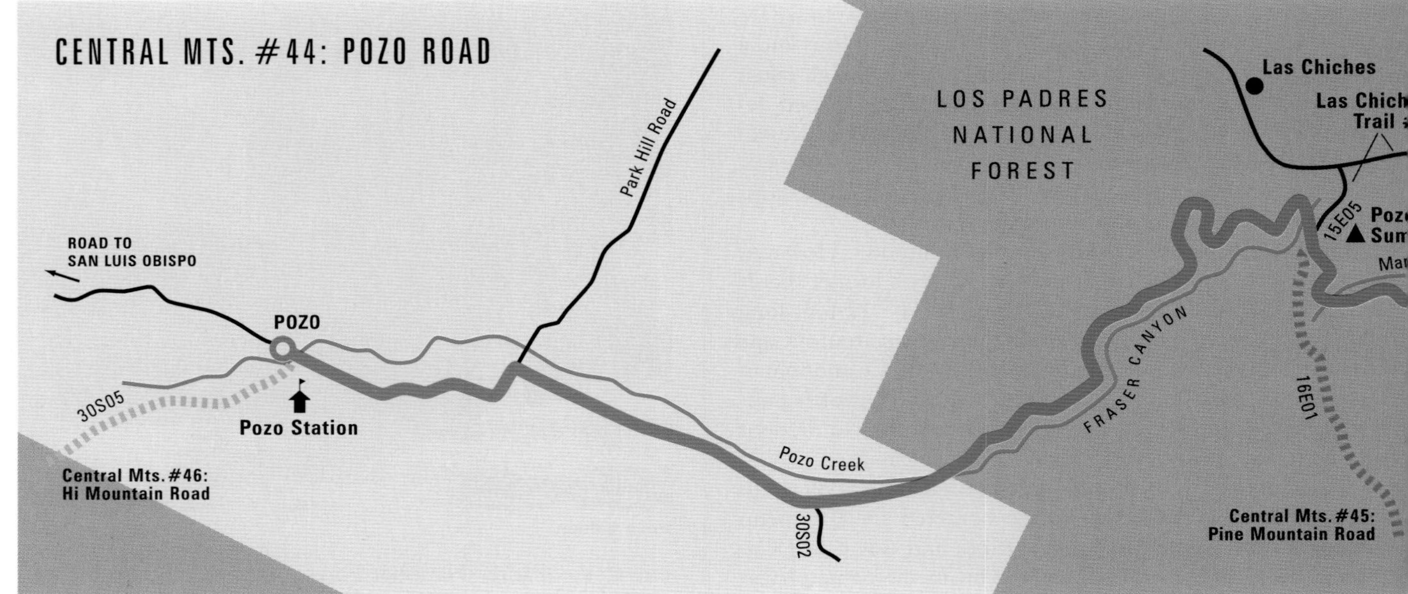

			Margarita; turn right for Taft and I-5.
			GPS: N35°23.20' W120°09.89'
▼ 1.4		SO	La Panza Fire Station on right.
	4.3 ▲	SO	La Panza Fire Station on left.
			GPS: N35°22.77' W120°11.27'
▼ 3.5		SO	Road turns to graded dirt.
	2.2 ▲	SO	Road is now paved.
▼ 5.1		SO	Entering Los Padres National Forest.
	0.6 ▲	SO	Leaving Los Padres National Forest.
			GPS: N35°21.47' W120°14.50'
▼ 5.7		SO	Central Mountains #45: Pine Mountain Road on left at information board at La Panza Summit. Zero trip meter.
	0.0 ▲		Continue to the northeast.
			GPS: N35°21.31' W120°15.06'
▼ 0.0			Continue to the west. Track on right is La Panza Bypass Trail #10A (16E12) for ATVs and motorbikes—rated blue.
	1.9 ▲	SO	Track on left is La Panza Bypass Trail #10A (16E12) for ATVs and motorbikes—rated blue. Then Central Mountains #45: Pine Mountain Road on right at information board at La Panza Summit. Zero trip meter.
▼ 1.3		SO	La Panza USFS Campground on right. Forest Adventure Pass required, no other fee.
	0.6 ▲	SO	La Panza USFS Campground on left. Forest Adventure Pass required, no other fee.
			GPS: N35°21.16' W120°15.93'
▼ 1.7		SO	Track on left.
	0.2 ▲	SO	Track on right.
▼ 1.9		BL	Track on right is Redhill Road (29S02), signposted to California 58. Zero trip meter.
	0.0 ▲		Continue to the southeast.
			GPS: N35°21.42' W120°16.48'
▼ 0.0			Continue to the southwest.
	2.6 ▲	BR	Track on left is Redhill Road (29S02), signposted to California 58. Zero trip meter.
▼ 0.1		SO	Turnout on right.
	2.5 ▲	SO	Turnout on left.
▼ 2.6		SO	Pozo Summit. Track on left is Central Mountains #45:Pine Mountain Road (16E01)—rated black. Route is recommended for travel in opposite direction. Track on right is Las Chiches Trail #5 (15E05) for 4WDs, ATVs, and motorbikes—rated black. Zero trip meter.
	0.0 ▲		Continue to the west.
			GPS: N35°20.85' W120°17.67'
▼ 0.0			Continue to the east.
	4.9 ▲	SO	Pozo Summit. Track on right is Centtral Mountains #45: Pine Mountain Trail Road (16E01)—rated black. Route is recommended for travel in opposite direction. Track on left is Las Chiches Trail #5 (15E05) for 4WDs, ATVs, and motorbikes-rated black. Zero trip meter.
▼ 4.0		SO	Cross over Fraser Creek on bridge; then two tracks on left. Information board on left. Leaving Los Padres National Forest. Road is now paved.
	0.9 ▲	SO	Entering Los Padres National Forest. Road turns to graded dirt. Information board on right and two tracks on right; then cross over Fraser Creek on bridge.
			GPS: N35°19.12' W120°18.83'
▼ 4.9		TR	Paved road on left is San Jose Avenales Road (30S02) to American Canyon Campground. Zero trip meter.
	0.0 ▲		Continue to the northeast, following sign to La Panza Campground.
			GPS: N35°18.64' W120°19.59'
▼ 0.0			Continue to the southwest.
	3.1 ▲	BL	Paved road on right is San Jose Avenales Road (30S02) to American Canyon Campground. Zero trip meter.
▼ 1.7		TL	T-intersection. Park Hill Road on right.
	1.4 ▲	TR	Turn right, remaining on Pozo Road. Park Hill Road continues straight ahead.
			GPS: N35°18.65' W120°21.40'
▼ 3.1			Trail ends in Pozo at the Pozo USFS Station on Pozo Road. Continue straight for San Luis Obispo. Turn left to commence Central Mountains #46: Hi Mountains Road.
	0.0 ▲		Trail commences in Pozo at the Pozo USFS Station on Pozo Road. Zero trip meter at Pozo Station and continue east on Pozo Road, following sign to La Panza Campground. Paved road on right is Central Mountains #46: Hi Mountains Trail.
			GPS: N35°18.23' W120°22.55'

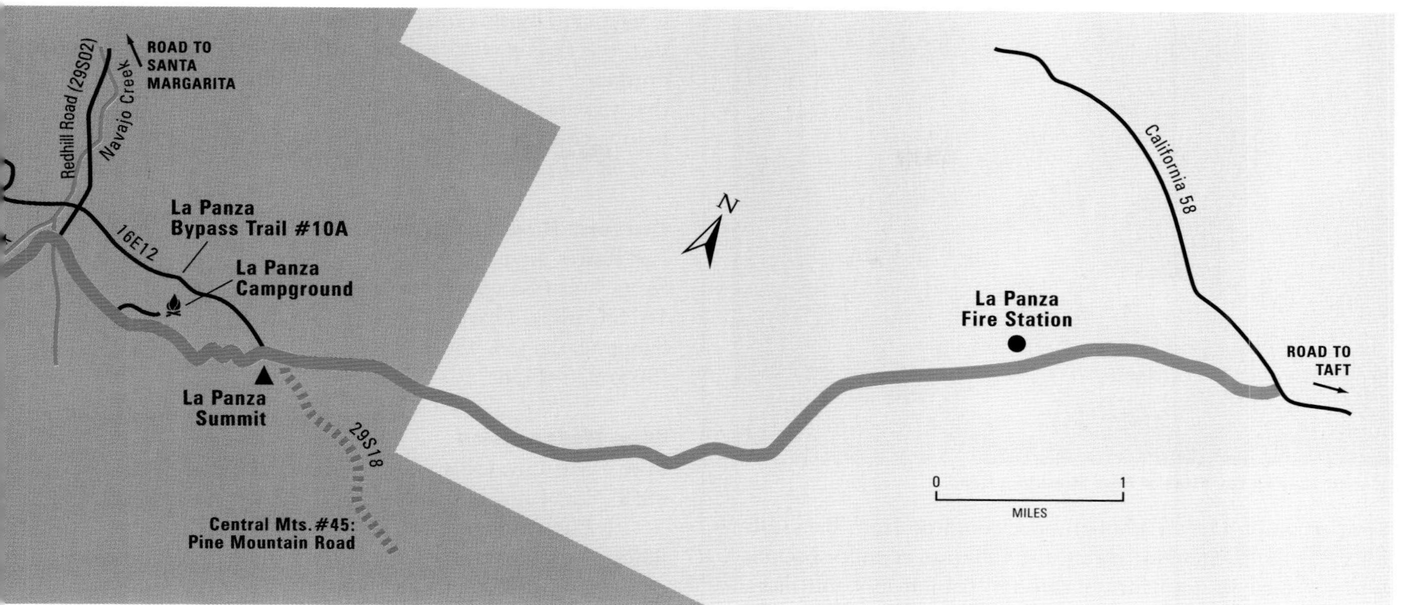

CENTRAL MOUNTAINS #45

Pine Mountain Road

Starting Point:	**Central Mountains #44: Pozo Road at La Panza Summit**
Finishing Point:	**Central Mountains #44: Pozo Road at Pozo Summit**
Total Mileage:	**8.8 miles**
Unpaved Mileage:	**8.8 miles**
Driving Time:	**1.5 hours (one-way) for 4-rated section.**
Elevation Range:	**2,000–3,600 feet**
Usually Open:	**Year-round**
Best Time to Travel:	**Dry weather only**
Difficulty Rating:	**4, with one short 9-rated descent; 6 for final 1.4 miles**
Scenic Rating:	**9**
Remoteness Rating:	**+0**

Special Attractions

- Chance to see the California condor in its native habitat.
- Very scenic ridge trail, with the option for an extremely difficult finale for modified vehicles.

Description

Pine Mountain Road (30S14, shown on some maps as 30S17) is one of the 4WD trails suitable for vehicles as well as ATVs and motorbikes within the Pozo–La Panza OHV Area. The route travels around the northern edge of the Machesna Mountain Wilderness, running for the most part along ridge tops, with spectacular views in all directions.

The trail starts by leaving the main backbone route through the region, Central Mountains #44: Pozo Road, 5.7 miles west of California 58. It heads southeast, following alongside the small Queen Bee Creek and passing two flowing springs and a couple of shady campsites along the creek. This section of the trail is suitable for high-clearance vehicles.

Once the route turns onto the steep Pine Mountain Road, a high-clearance 4WD is required. From this intersection, the trail climbs steadily, becoming steeper and rougher the higher it goes. The trail should not be attempted in wet weather because the surface becomes extremely greasy, which, combined with the narrow trail, makes for dangerous driving. The forest service will often close the trail in wet weather to avoid road damage. In dry weather the surface is uneven, with reasonable traction and a number of embedded rocks.

An observation point on the left of the trail over Castle Crag is located 0.6 miles from the turnoff onto Pine Mountain Road. From this point, you may see the California condor if you are lucky. It is the largest land bird of North America, with

Modified vehicles only! These steps are good at damaging vehicles

Easy shelf road at the start of Pine Mountain Road

a wingspan of 9 feet. Although once common from Baja California to the Pacific Northwest, the California condor population declined so dramatically through habitat loss and illegal shooting that it was put on the endangered species list in 1967. The Los Angeles and San Diego Zoos began a program in 1981 that successfully raised the threatened birds in captivity. The first birds were released back into the wild in 1992. There is now a secure population within Los Padres National Forest.

As the trail climbs higher, there are views over the La Panza Range to the north and the Machesna Mountain Wilderness to the south. Hikers can access the wilderness along an old vehicle trail.

The trail starts to descend at the top of Pine Mountain. The top of the mountain makes a good place to turn around if you are driving a stock 4WD vehicle or if you do not wish to tackle the more difficult trail ahead. It is possible to continue for 0.8 miles before the trail requires a heavily modified vehicle. The first portion of the descent is rated a 5 for difficulty and follows along a narrow, rough shelf road before reaching a national forest sign warning of the difficult road ahead. Only heavily modified, short-wheelbase vehicles should continue past here. A short, approximately 60-yard section of rock steps, each approximately 2 feet high and very rugged, follows the sign and is rated 9 for difficulty when approached in its entirety. Even modified vehicles with experienced drivers risk significant vehicle damage along this short section. If you continued to this point, you can turn around at the sign and view the steps from above.

Top of the steps on Pine Mountain

From the bottom of the steps, the trail continues to undulate steeply, with some steep loose sections to negotiate before it finishes on Pozo Summit. The final descent to Pozo Summit is steep and loose. From the bottom of the steps to Pozo Summit, the trail is rated a 6 for difficulty. The forest service recommends travel only from Queen Bee to Pozo Summit, so that vehicles descend the most difficult sections. The trail can be treated in the reverse direction as a 6-rated spur trail to the bottom of the steps.

Current Road Information

Los Padres National Forest
Santa Lucia Ranger District
1616 Carlotti Drive
Santa Maria, CA 93454
(805) 925-9538

Map References

BLM San Luis Obispo
USFS Los Padres National Forest: Monterey and Santa Lucia Ranger Districts
USGS 1:24,000 La Panza, Pozo Summit
1:100,000 San Luis Obispo
Maptech CD-ROM: San Luis Obispo/Los Padres National Forest
Southern & Central California Atlas & Gazetteer, p. 60
California Road & Recreation Atlas, p. 91

Route Directions

Mileage			Directions
▼ 0.0			Trail begins on Central Mountains #44: Pozo Road at La Panza Summit, 5.7 miles west of California 58. Zero trip meter at information board and turn east onto graded dirt road. There is no route name or number at the intersection.
	2.2 ▲		Trail ends on Central Mountains #44: Pozo Road at information board at La Panza Summit. Turn right for California 58.
			GPS: N35°21.31' W120°15.06'
▼ 0.1		SO	Closure gate.
	2.1 ▲	SO	Closure gate.
▼ 0.4		SO	Cattle guard; then track on left is Queen Bee Trail #9 (16E15) for ATVs and motorbikes—rated blue.
	1.8 ▲	SO	Track on right is Queen Bee Trail #9 (16E15) for ATVs and motorbikes—rated blue; then cattle guard.
			GPS: N35°21.17' W120°14.83'
▼ 0.5		SO	Track on right.
	1.7 ▲	SO	Track on left.
▼ 0.8		SO	Track on left.
	1.4 ▲	SO	Track on right.
▼ 0.9		SO	Queen Bee Spring on right.
	1.3 ▲	SO	Queen Bee Spring on left.
			GPS: N35°21.06' W120°14.41'
▼ 1.3		SO	Cross through wash.
	0.9 ▲	SO	Cross through wash.
▼ 1.5		SO	Track on left is Queen Bee Trail #9 (16E15) for ATVs and motorbikes—rated blue.
	0.7 ▲	SO	Track on right is Queen Bee Trail #9 (16E15) for ATVs and motorbikes—rated blue.
			GPS: N35°20.70' W120°13.91'
▼ 1.6		SO	Track on left.
	0.6 ▲	SO	Track on right.
▼ 1.7		SO	Cross through wash.

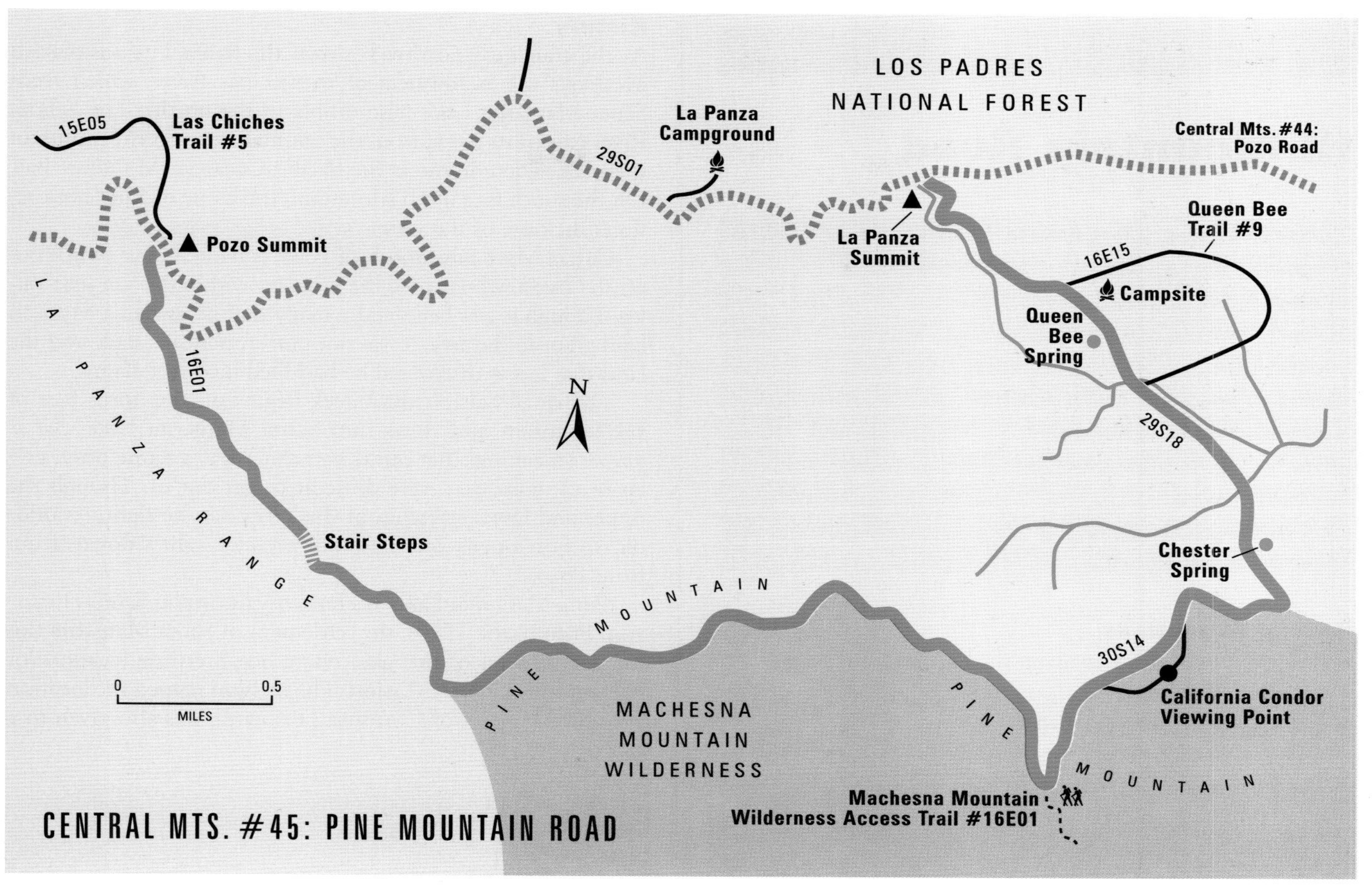

0.5 ▲	SO	Cross through wash.
▼ 1.8	SO	Track on left; then Chester Spring on right.
0.4 ▲	SO	Chester Spring on left; then track on right.
		GPS: N35°20.47′ W120°13.73′
▼ 2.2	BR	Bear right onto Pine Mountain Road #8 (30S14, called 30S17 on forest service map), and zero trip meter. Trail is suitable for 4WDs, ATVs, and motorbikes—rated green.
0.0 ▲		Continue to the northwest.
		GPS: N35°20.20′ W120°13.54′
▼ 0.0		Continue to the south.
4.4 ▲	BL	Bear left onto larger graded dirt road and zero trip meter.
▼ 0.6	SO	Track on left to viewpoint over Castle Crag and Machesna Mountain Wilderness (California condor viewing point).
3.8 ▲	BL	Track on right to viewpoint over Castle Crag and Machesna Mountain Wilderness (California condor viewing point).
		GPS: N35°20.11′ W120°13.91′
▼ 0.9	SO	Track on left.
3.5 ▲	SO	Track on right.
▼ 1.6	SO	Machesna Mountain Wilderness access trail 16E01 on left for hikers only. No trailhead parking.
2.8 ▲	SO	Machesna Mountain Wilderness access trail 16E01 on right for hikers only. No trailhead parking.
		GPS: N35°19.58′ W120°14.31′
▼ 4.1	SO	Track on right goes short distance to viewpoint.
0.3 ▲	SO	Track on left goes short distance to viewpoint.
		GPS: N35°19.81′ W120°16.16′
▼ 4.4	SO	Gated road on left goes into wilderness. Remain on Pine Mountain Trail #7—now rated black. Zero trip meter.
0.0 ▲		Continue to the northeast.
		GPS: N35°19.63′ W120°16.36′
▼ 0.0		Continue to the southwest.
2.2 ▲		Gated road on right goes into wilderness. Remain on Pine Mountain Trail #7—now rated green. Zero trip meter.
▼ 0.7	SO	Warning sign. Trail past this point has a difficulty rating of 9. The most difficult section of the trail, the stair steps, is immediately past the sign. The most difficult section is near the bottom and is not immediately visible.
1.5 ▲	SO	Warning sign and end of 9-rated section. Trail is now 4-rated.
		GPS: N35°19.93′ W120°16.91′
▼ 0.8		Bottom of the steps. Trail is now 6-rated.
1.4 ▲	SO	Trail past this point has a difficulty rating of 9. The most difficult section of the trail, the stair steps, is visible straight ahead.
		GPS: N35°20.00′ W120°16.99′
▼ 2.2		Trail ends on Central Mountains #44: Pozo Road at Pozo Summit. Turn left for Pozo; turn right for California 58. Ahead is Las Chiches Trail #5 (15E05) for 4WDs, ATVs, and motorbikes—rated black.
0.0 ▲		Trail commences on Central Mountains #44: Pozo Road at Pozo Summit. Zero trip meter and turn south on formed trail suitable for 4WDs, ATVs, and motorbikes—rated black.
		GPS: N35°20.85′ W120°17.67′

CENTRAL MOUNTAINS #46

Hi Mountain Road

Starting Point:	**Pozo Road at Pozo Station**
Finishing Point:	**Big Falls Hiking Trailhead**
Total Mileage:	**12.1 miles**
Unpaved Mileage:	**12 miles**
Driving Time:	**1 hour**
Elevation Range:	**1,400–3,000 feet**
Usually Open:	**Year-round**
Best Time to Travel:	**Dry weather**
Difficulty Rating:	**1**
Scenic Rating:	**8**
Remoteness Rating:	**+0**

Special Attractions

- Ridge top trail with views over the La Panza Range and Santa Lucia Wilderness.
- Hiking access into wilderness.

History

As the trail runs northwest down the Santa Lucia Range, it overlooks the headwaters of the Salinas River, which feeds Santa Margarita Lake (also visible to the north). The Salinas River gained its name from the salt marshes near the mouth of the river, where it enters the Pacific Ocean in Monterey Bay. On the south face of Hi Mountain, the name of Salt Creek reflects the taste of the water.

Garcia Mountain, south of Pozo, is named after Don Ynocento Garcia, who owned the property within the San Jose Valley. Though it was believed by many that he owned a Mexican land grant in the area, it was not until Americans took over the land that it was discovered he had filed incorrect claims.

The small Salsipuedes Creek begins on the north face of Hi Mountain and flows into Santa Margarita Lake. *Sal si puedes* (meaning, "get out if you can") was a name often given to canyons that were difficult to get out of. Though the upper and lower stretches of this creek can be tight, its middle section opens out into the broader valley downstream from Pozo.

Santa Margarita Lake was formerly known as Salinas Reservoir. Prior to the 1790s, the settlement of Santa Margarita (located northwest of the lake) was a hog-breeding location for the San Luis Obispo Mission. The mission named the location after St. Margaret of Cortona. This name was also given to a

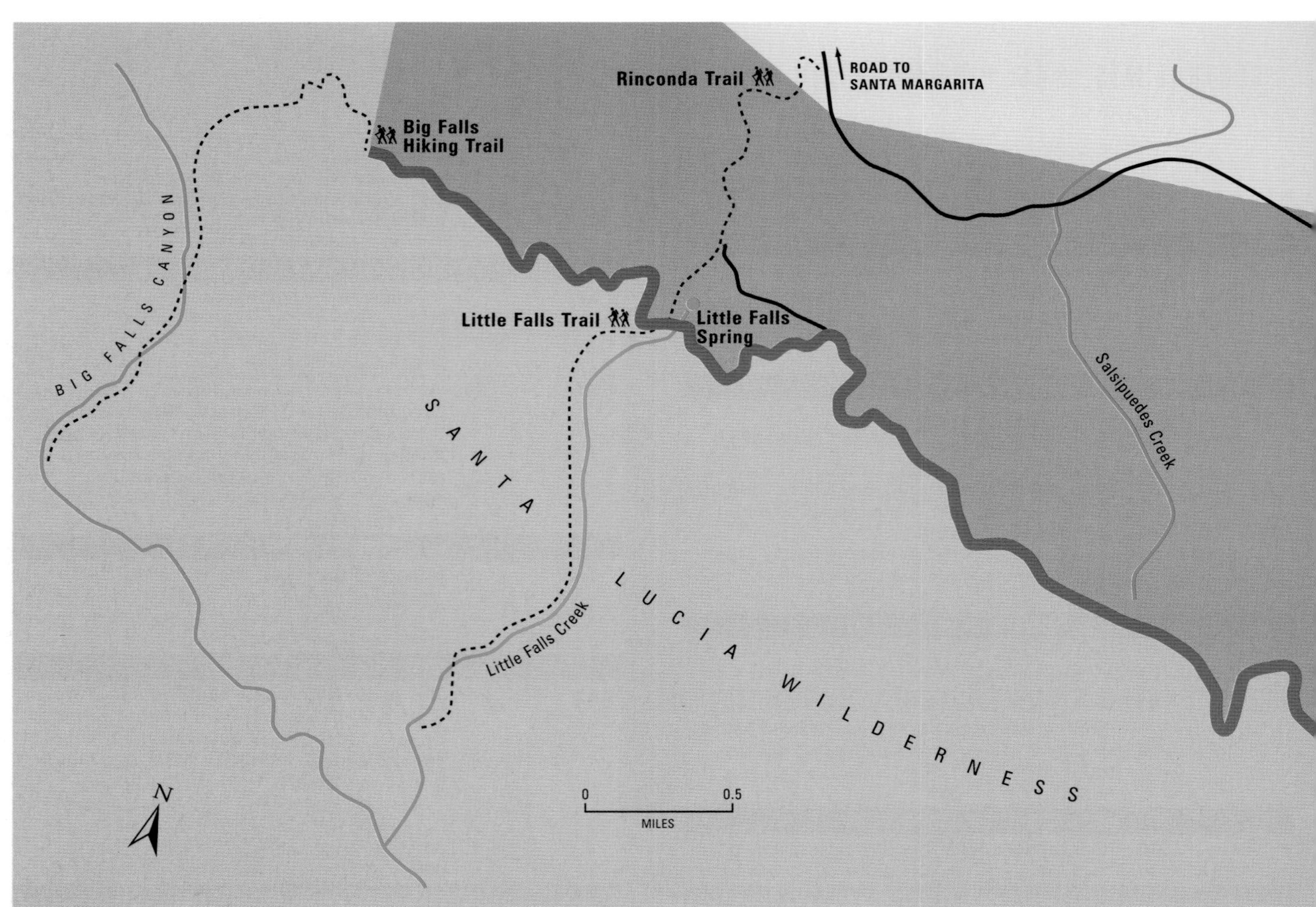

land grant in September of 1841 of nearly 18,000 acres on the western side of the Santa Lucia Range to Joaquin Estrada. It was patented 20 years later to Joaquin and is still evident on regional maps today.

After Mexico became independent from Spain in 1822, the padres began to lose control of their missions. Indian neophytes were released from the missions, and missionary lands became available as land grants. What was originally planned as a land-holding policy for an eventual return of mission lands to Indians turned into a large-scale sale of land to ranchers. The Santa Margarita Mission lands became known as El Rancho de Santa Margarita and were granted to Don Joaquin Estrada. Estrada was renowned for his lavish behavior, including throwing expensive celebrations for his guests. He was soon bought out by Martin Murphy, an Irish emigrant who was expanding his land holdings after he moved west in the mid-1840s. By the 1870s, the town was showing up on maps of the day, and it gained a post office by 1880. A small land boom hit the settlement in the late 1880s and early 1890s, with the arrival of the railroad from the north. Today, the Assistencia de Santa Margarita is merely ruins located on private land just northwest of Santa Margarita.

Another saint remembered in these mountains is Saint Lucy of Syracuse (whose feast day is celebrated by the Catholic church on December 13). The Sierra de Santa Lucia, or Santa Lucia Range, is named in her honor. The Hi Mountain Trail is situated near the southern end of the range, which runs all the way north to Carmel Bay. During the nineteenth century, the range was considered to run continuously as far south as the Santa Clara River at Ventura.

Hi Mountain Road travels below the ridge

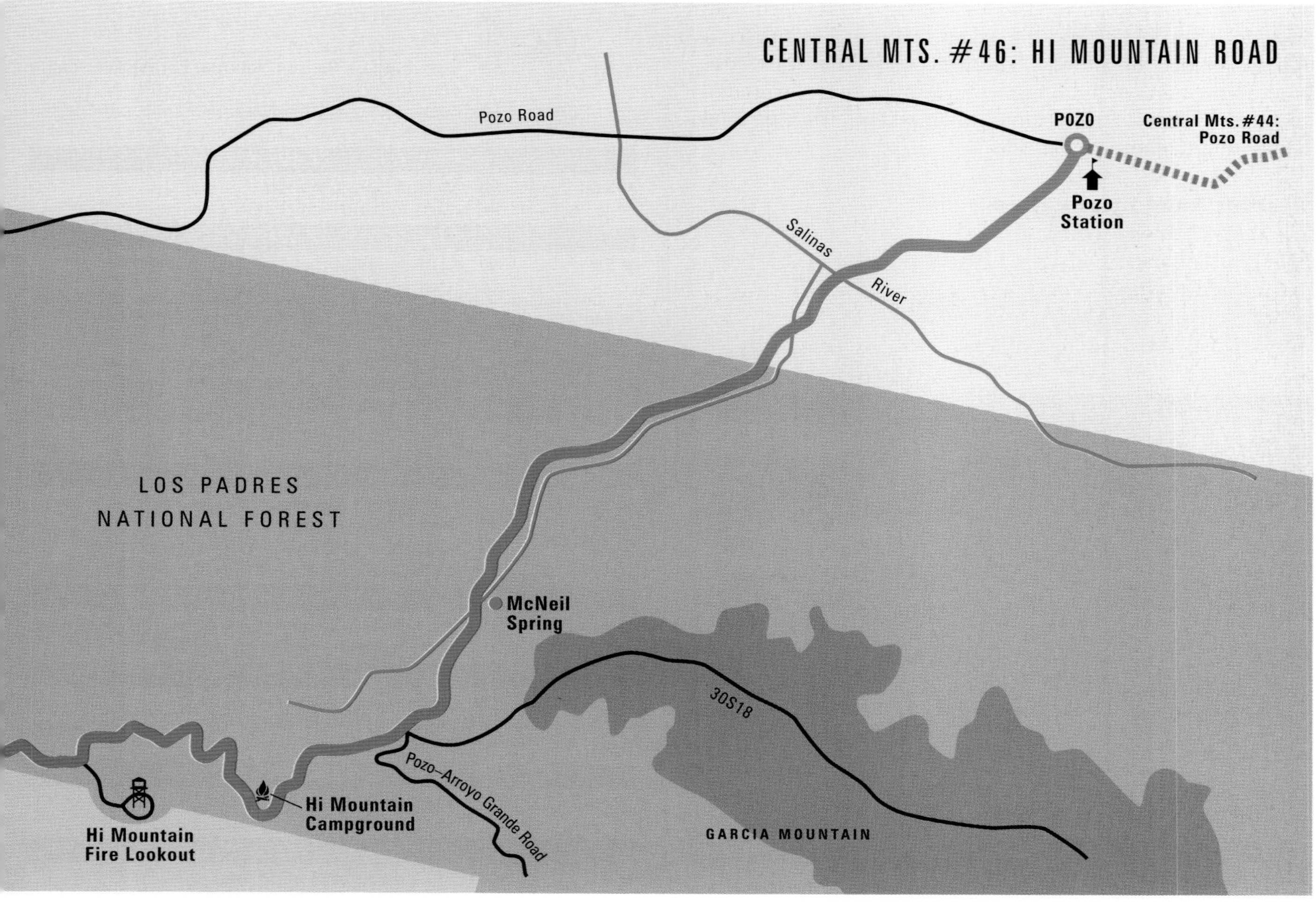

CENTRAL MTS. #46: HI MOUNTAIN ROAD

Pozo Road
POZO
Central Mts. #44: Pozo Road
Pozo Station
Salinas River
LOS PADRES NATIONAL FOREST
McNeil Spring
30S18
Pozo–Arroyo Grande Road
Hi Mountain Campground
Hi Mountain Fire Lookout
GARCIA MOUNTAIN

Description

Hi Mountain Road begins in Pozo and travels through the Los Padres National Forest to finish at the Big Falls Hiking Trailhead. Much of the easy graded road runs along a ridge top, offering stunning views in all directions.

Initially the trail passes through a short section of private property. A mile from the start, the trail crosses the Salinas River. The river crossing typically has water year-round, but it is normally shallow and should pose no difficulty to high-clearance vehicles under normal conditions.

From the intersection with Garcia Ridge Road, Hi Mountain Trail swings west and begins a long run along the ridge tops of the Santa Lucia Range. The La Panza Range is to the north of the ridge and the Santa Lucia Wilderness and Lopez Lake are to the south. The trail along Garcia Ridge is steep and rocky in places and is of a moderate to difficult standard.

The main trail passes the developed Hi Mountain Campground, which has pit toilets and a few shady camping spots. A mile and a half farther, you will come to a T-intersection with great views over Lopez Lake and the Santa Lucia Wilderness. A short spur trail to the left at this point leads to the abandoned fire lookout on Hi Mountain. You can climb up the tower for a glimpse of the breathtaking 360-degree views. A small outhouse near the tower tells of the meager and lonely life of a fire lookout.

Hi Mountain Road then follows along a wide shelf road with views to the left into the wilderness area. The surface is roughly graded all the way. The Rinconada Trail leaves this route to the north and drops steeply from the ridge to join Pozo Road. The trail finally comes to an end at a turning loop and hiking trailhead to Big Falls.

Current Road Information

Los Padres National Forest
Santa Lucia Ranger District
1616 Carlotti Drive
Santa Maria, CA 93454
(805) 925-9538

Year-round crossing of the Salinas River

Map References

BLM San Luis Obispo
USFS Los Padres National Forest: Monterey and Santa Lucia Ranger Districts
USGS 1:24,000 Santa Margarita Lake
1:100,000 San Luis Obispo
Maptech CD-ROM: San Luis Obispo/Los Padres National Forest
Southern & Central California Atlas & Gazetteer, pp. 60, 59
California Road & Recreation Atlas, p. 91

Route Directions

Mileage		Direction	
▼ 0.0			From the western end of Central Mountains #44: Pozo Road at the Pozo USFS Station, turn south on paved Hi Mountain Road and zero trip meter.
	3.5 ▲		Trail finishes in Pozo at the Pozo USFS Station. Turn left for Santa Margarita; turn right to continue along Central Mountains #44: Pozo Road.
			GPS: N35°18.23' W120°22.54'
▼ 0.1		SO	Closure gate.
	3.4 ▲	SO	Closure gate.
▼ 0.7		SO	Closure gate.
	2.8 ▲	SO	Closure gate.
▼ 1.0		SO	Cross through Salinas River.
	2.5 ▲	SO	Cross through Salinas River.
			GPS: N35°17.66' W120°23.30'
▼ 1.2		SO	Cross through wash.
	2.3 ▲	SO	Cross through wash.
▼ 1.5		SO	Entering Los Padres National Forest over cattle guard.
	2.0 ▲	SO	Leaving Los Padres National Forest over cattle guard.
			GPS: N35°17.24' W120°23.55'
▼ 2.8		SO	McNeil Spring on left.
	0.7 ▲	SO	McNeil Spring on right.
			GPS: N35°16.47' W120°24.25'
▼ 3.4		SO	Cattle guard.
	0.1 ▲	SO	Cattle guard.
▼ 3.5		TR	Track on left is Garcia Ridge Road #18 (30S18)—rated blue. Track ahead and to the left is Pozo–Arroyo Grande Road, which goes to Arroyo Grande Station and Lopez Lake. Zero trip meter and turn right, following sign to Hi Mountain Campground.
	0.0 ▲		Continue to the north.
			GPS: N35°15.98' W120°24.41'
▼ 0.0			Continue to the west.
▼ 0.5		SO	Water trough on left.
▼ 0.7		SO	Hi Mountain USFS Campground on right. Forest Adventure Pass required; no other fee.
			GPS: N35°15.66' W120°24.75'
▼ 2.2		BR	Track on left through gate goes to Hi Mountain Fire Lookout.
			GPS: N35°15.66' W120°25.76'
▼ 2.3		SO	Cattle guard.
▼ 2.5		SO	Viewpoint on left with views over Lopez Lake.
▼ 4.1		SO	Track on left to viewpoint.
			GPS: N35°15.96' W120°27.10'
▼ 4.9		SO	Track on right up hill. Viewpoint and campsite on left.
			GPS: N35°16.26' W120°27.60'
▼ 5.2		SO	Track on right in wide area.

		GPS: N35°16.38' W120°27.85'
▼ 5.7	SO	Faint track on left.
▼ 5.8	SO	Well-used track on right and faint track on left rejoins.
		GPS: N35°16.58' W120°28.11'
▼ 6.6	SO	Tank on right. Little Falls Spring on right.
▼ 6.7	SO	Rinconada Trail on right for hiking and horses only. Zero trip meter.
		GPS: N35°16.50' W120°28.68'
▼ 0.0		Continue to the southwest.
▼ 0.1	SO	Little Falls Trail on left into the Santa Lucia Wilderness and track on right.
		GPS: N35°16.47' W120°28.75'
▼ 0.4	SO	Two tracks on right.
▼ 1.9		Trail ends at Big Falls Hiking Trailhead. Hiking trail continues to the west down Big Falls Canyon.
		GPS: N35°16.82' W120°29.89'

CENTRAL MOUNTAINS #47

Parkfield Grade Trail

Starting Point:	**California 198, 9.5 miles southwest of Coalinga**
Finishing Point:	**Intersection of Cholame Road and Vineyard Canyon Road in Parkfield**
Total Mileage:	**18.4 miles**
Unpaved Mileage:	**10 miles**
Driving Time:	**1.25 hours**
Elevation Range:	**1,200–3,600 feet**
Usually Open:	**Year-round**
Best Time to Travel:	**Dry weather**
Difficulty Rating:	**1**
Scenic Rating:	**8**
Remoteness Rating:	**+0**

Special Attractions

- Meandering road that follows the Parkfield Grade.
- Views of Middle Mountain and Joaquin Canyon.

History

Parkfield was originally called Russelsville, but the post office denied the request for that name in 1883, forcing the occupants to choose a new one. Parkfield was chosen to reflect the parklike setting of the locality dotted with majestic oaks. The town is located in Cholame Valley, a name reputed to mean "evil people."

Parkfield, one of the few settlements in this remote region along the San Andreas Fault, was a center of seismic research between 1984 and 1992. Criteria were developed for predicting earthquakes and a system was designed to alert the public. In 1991, that system warned Parkfield of a possible earthquake predicted to reach a 6 on the Richter scale. Fortunately, nothing happened. The calculation was based on the fact that such earthquakes had been recorded in 1857, 1881, 1901, 1922, 1934, and lastly in 1966. Instrumentation remains to assist in the ongoing study of earthquakes in Parkfield.

The vista over Jacalitos Creek Valley typifies the landscape along the Parkfield Grade Trail

This trail crosses Jacalitos (Mexican Spanish for "Little Hut") Creek. It seems to have been named by surveyors who noticed a small hut during their work in the Jacalitos Hills to the east.

Description

This route passes through ranchland in the Cholame Hills south of Coalinga. The graded road is suitable for passenger vehicles in dry weather, but it is often impassable when wet. There are no public lands along the trail. Please respect the private property on either side of the road and remain on the designated county road.

The road turns to graded dirt after crossing Jacalitos Creek and climbs toward Gavilan Ridge. Traveling around the head of Castro Canyon, there are spectacular views over the oak-studded hills and rocky outcrops, back down into the Jacalitos Creek Valley. A prominent ridge of rocks can be seen that includes Church Rock, Eagle Rock, Wildcat Rock, and Swallow Rock. After crossing a saddle, the trail gradually descends toward Parkfield. The views are now to the west over the Cholame Creek Valley to the Cholame Hills on the far side.

The trail ends in the small settlement of Parkfield. According to a sign, the town is bustling with a population of 37 and is the self-proclaimed earthquake capital of the world.

Parkfield—earthquakes have been regularly reported here since 1857

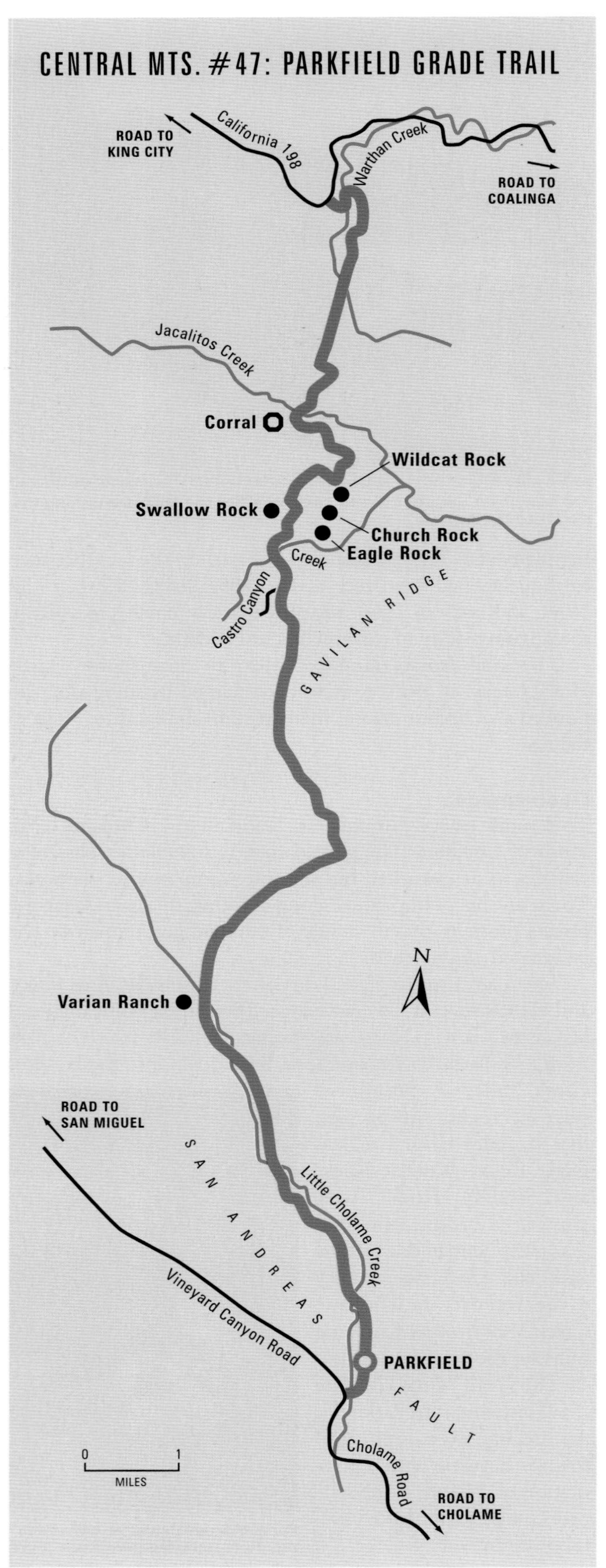

Current Road Information

BLM Hollister Field Office
20 Hamilton Court
Hollister, CA 95023
(831) 630-5000

Map References

BLM Coalinga, Paso Robles
USGS 1:24,000 Curry Mt., Parkfield
1:100,000 Coalinga, Paso Robles
Maptech CD-ROM: San Luis Obispo/Los Padres National Forest; Central Coast/Fresno
Southern & Central California Atlas & Gazetteer, pp. 34, 46
California Road & Recreation Atlas, p. 83

Route Directions

Mileage		Direction
▼ 0.0		From California 198, 9.5 miles southwest of Coalinga, zero trip meter and turn east on paved road marked Parkfield Grade.
3.4 ▲		Trail ends on California 198. Turn right for Coalinga.
		GPS: N36°04.92′ W120°28.79′
▼ 1.5	SO	Cross through Warthan Creek.
1.9 ▲	SO	Cross through Warthan Creek.
▼ 3.4	SO	Cross over Jacalitos Creek. Corral on right. Road becomes graded dirt. Zero trip meter.
0.0 ▲		Continue to the south.
		GPS: N36°02.91′ W120°28.64′
▼ 0.0		Continue to the northeast.
10.0 ▲	SO	Cross over Jacalitos Creek. Corral on left. Road is now paved. Zero trip meter.
▼ 1.1	SO	Wildcat Rock on left.
8.9 ▲	SO	Wildcat Rock on right.
		GPS: N36°02.44′ W120°28.11′
▼ 2.4	SO	Swallow Rock on right.
7.6 ▲	SO	Swallow Rock on left.
		GPS: N36°01.91′ W120°28.57′
▼ 2.5	SO	Cattle guard.
7.5 ▲	SO	Cattle guard.
▼ 3.0	SO	Cross over Castro Canyon Creek.
7.0 ▲	SO	Cross over Castro Canyon Creek.
		GPS: N36°01.53′ W120°28.69′
▼ 3.1	SO	Track on right into private property.
6.9 ▲	SO	Track on left into private property.
▼ 4.5	SO	Cattle guard.
5.5 ▲	SO	Cattle guard.
		GPS: N36°00.59′ W120°28.27′
▼ 6.0	SO	Cattle guard.
4.0 ▲	SO	Cattle guard.
▼ 9.2	SO	Track on right is marked Lake Track; then cattle guard.
0.8 ▲	SO	Cattle guard; then track on left is marked Lake Track.
		GPS: N35°57.87′ W120°28.40′
▼ 10.0	SO	Cross over Little Cholame Creek on bridge; then Varian Ranch on right. Road is now paved. Zero trip meter.
0.0 ▲		Continue to the northwest.
		GPS: N35°57.18′ W120°28.49′
▼ 0.0		Continue to the southeast.
5.0 ▲	SO	Road turns to graded dirt. Varian Ranch on left; then cross over Little Cholame Creek on bridge. Zero trip meter.

▼ 0.6		SO	Cross over Little Cholame Creek on bridge.
	4.4 ▲	SO	Cross over Little Cholame Creek on bridge.
▼ 1.9		SO	Cross over Little Cholame Creek on bridge.
	3.1 ▲	SO	Cross over Little Cholame Creek on bridge.
▼ 3.8		SO	Cross over Little Cholame Creek on bridge.
	1.2 ▲	SO	Cross over Little Cholame Creek on bridge.
			GPS: N35°54.60' W120°26.18'
▼ 4.5		SO	Entering Parkfield. Graded road on right and left is Park Street. Continue on paved road through town.
	0.5 ▲	SO	Leaving Parkfield. Graded road on right and left is Park Street. Continue on paved Parkfield-Coalinga Road.
▼ 5.0			Cross over Little Cholame Creek on bridge; then trail ends at intersection of Cholame Road and Vineyard Canyon Road. Turn left for Cholame; turn right for San Miguel.
	0.0 ▲		Trail commences at intersection of Cholame Road and Vineyard Canyon Road in Parkfield. Zero trip meter at intersection and turn east on paved Parkfield-Coalinga Road. Immediately cross over Little Cholame Creek on bridge.
			GPS: N35°53.72' W120°26.05'

CENTRAL MOUNTAINS #48

Willow Creek Road

Starting Point:	**California 1, just south of Willow Creek Campground**
Finishing Point:	**Central Mountains #49: South Coast Ridge Road, 14.3 miles from the northern end**
Total Mileage:	**7.4 miles, plus 1.9-mile spur to San Martin Top**
Unpaved Mileage:	**7.4 miles, plus 1.9-milespur**
Driving Time:	**45 minutes**
Elevation Range:	**100–3,200 feet**
Usually Open:	**Year-round**
Best Time to Travel:	**Year-round**
Difficulty Rating:	**1, 3 for spur trail**
Scenic Rating:	**9**
Remoteness Rating:	**+0**

Special Attractions

- Spur trail to San Martin Top.
- Spectacular views from high above the Pacific Ocean.

Description

Willow Creek Road starts off of California 1 and heads east into Los Padres National Forest. Just north of the trailhead is the Willow Creek USFS Campground. The campground, only a short walk from the ocean, has a number of sites with fire pits and bathroom facilities. You must have a Forest Adventure Pass and pay a fee to stay at the campground.

As you head out on Willow Creek Road, the trail climbs high above the Pacific Ocean. Within the first mile are a cou-

Willow Creek Road climbs high above the Pacific Ocean

ple of great spots from which to take in a breathtaking sunset. The trail enters the trees at 1.4 miles and continues to meander in and out of forested areas on a graded dirt road. The trail is relatively easygoing and passes a number of closed trails as well as some private property.

At the 3-way intersection, you can proceed southwest on a spur trail to San Martin Top. This trail rates more difficult than the main trail, and a high-clearance 4WD is required to negotiate some of the rutted sections. At the end of the spur is a primitive campsite with excellent views. Back at the 3-way intersection, the second trail leads 1.4 miles along a 2-rated track to Alder Creek Camp. This campground, set alongside Alder Creek, provides a beautiful, sheltered spot to pitch a tent. It is somewhat isolated, and you will most likely be the only one camping there. A narrow track leads out from the back of the campground, but it is very overgrown and not suitable for driving.

From the intersection, the main trail continues for 1.6 miles before coming to an end halfway along Central Mountains #49: South Coast Ridge Road.

On some maps, this trail is called Los Burros Road.

Current Road Information

Los Padres National Forest
Monterey Ranger District
406 South Mildred
King City, CA 93930
(831) 385-5434

Map References

BLM Cambria
USFS Los Padres National Forest: Monterey and Santa Lucia Ranger Districts
USGS 1:24,000 Cape San Martin
1:100,000 Cambria
Maptech CD-ROM: San Luis Obispo/Los Padres National Forest
Southern & Central California Atlas & Gazetteer, pp. 43, 44
California Road & Recreation Atlas, p. 82

Route Directions

▼ 0.0		Trail starts on California 1, just south of Willow Creek Campground, 1 mile north of gas station at Gorda. Turn northeast onto graded dirt road and immediately cross cattle guard. Zero trip meter and turn left onto Willow Creek Road (23S01). Track on right is private.
2.3 ▲		Turn right and cross cattle guard onto California 1. Track continues ahead. Turn left for Gorda; turn right for Big Sur.
		GPS: N35°53.15' W121°27.46'
▼ 0.4	SO	Parking area for hiking trail on left.
1.9 ▲	SO	Parking area for hiking trail on right.
▼ 1.7	SO	Cross over South Fork Willow Creek.
0.6 ▲	SO	Cross over South Fork Willow Creek.
▼ 2.0	SO	Viewpoint on left.
0.3 ▲	SO	Viewpoint on right.
▼ 2.3	SO	Willow Creek Hiking Trail on left. Zero trip meter.
0.0 ▲		Continue to northwest.
		GPS: N35°53.38' W121°26.25'
▼ 0.0		Continue to the southeast.
3.5 ▲	SO	Willow Creek Hiking Trail on right. Zero trip meter.
▼ 0.3	SO	Track on right goes short distance to campsite.
3.2 ▲	SO	Track on left goes short distance to campsite.
▼ 1.2	SO	Gated road on left.
2.3 ▲	SO	Gated road on right.
▼ 1.4	SO	Gated road on right.
2.1 ▲	SO	Gated road on left.
▼ 1.7	SO	Gated road on right.
1.8 ▲	SO	Gated road on left.
▼ 1.9	BR	Gated road on left.
1.6 ▲	SO	Gated road on right.
▼ 2.9	SO	Gated road on left.
0.6 ▲	SO	Gated road on right.
▼ 3.0	BL	Gated road on right.
0.5 ▲	SO	Gated road on left.
▼ 3.5	SO	Two tracks on right at sign for California 1, San Martin Top, and Alder Creek Camp. First track is spur to San Martin Top. Second track goes 1.4 miles to Alder Creek Camp. Zero trip meter and turn first right for San Martin Top.
0.0 ▲		Continue to the north on main trail.
		GPS: N35°53.12' W121°23.77'

Spur Trail to San Martin Top

▼ 0.0		Continue to the southwest toward San Martin Top.
▼ 0.6	SO	Track on left.
		GPS: N35°52.72' W121°24.17'
▼ 0.8	SO	Track on right.
▼ 1.0	SO	Gated road joins on left.
▼ 1.1	SO	Track on left rejoins almost immediately.
▼ 1.6	BR/SO	Trail forks on left; then track on left.
▼ 1.7	TL	Track straight ahead goes to campsite.
▼ 1.8	SO	Trail forks and rejoins at viewpoint.
▼ 1.9	UT	Viewpoint at San Martin Top. Turn around and retrace your route back to the main trail.
		GPS: N35°52.31' W121°25.20'

Continuation of Main Trail

▼ 0.0		Continue to the southeast.
1.6 ▲		Two tracks on left at sign for California 1, San Martin Top, and Alder Creek Camp. First track goes 1.4 miles to Alder Creek Camp. Second track is spur to San Martin Top. Zero trip meter and turn second left for San Martin Top.
		GPS: 35°53.12' W121°23.77'
▼ 0.1	SO	Gated road on right.
1.5 ▲	SO	Gated road on left.
▼ 0.2	SO	Gated road on right; then gated road on left.
1.4 ▲	BL/SO	Gated road splits off on right; then gated road on left.
▼ 0.7	SO	Gated road on left.
0.9 ▲	SO	Gated road on right.
▼ 0.8	SO	Track on left.
0.8 ▲	SO	Track on right.
▼ 1.6		Trail ends at Central Mountains #49: South Coast Ridge Road. Turn right to continue southeast along South Coast Ridge Road; turn left to follow South Coast Ridge Road to Nacimiento-Ferguson Road.
0.0 ▲		Trail starts on Central Mountains #49: South Coast Ridge Road, 14.3 miles from the northern end. Zero trip meter and head west on Willow Creek Road (23S01).
		GPS: N35°53.51' W121°22.42'

CENTRAL MOUNTAINS #49

South Coast Ridge Road

Starting Point:	**Nacimiento-Ferguson Road, 6.8 miles east of California 1**
Finishing Point:	**Gate before Fort Hunter Liggett**
Total Mileage:	**26.5 miles (one-way)**
Unpaved Mileage:	**26.1 miles**
Driving Time:	**2.5 hours (one-way)**
Elevation Range:	**2,200–3,400 feet**
Usually Open:	**Year-round**
Best Time to Travel:	**Year-round**
Difficulty Rating:	**2**
Scenic Rating:	**8**
Remoteness Rating:	**+1**

Special Attractions

- Long, scenic trail that follows a ridgeline on the Santa Lucia Range.
- Many backcountry hiking and camping opportunities along the trail.

Description

South Coast Ridge Road begins on Nacimiento-Ferguson Road and heads south along the boundary between Los Padres National Forest and Fort Hunter Liggett. As its name indicates, the road follows a ridgeline along the Santa Lucia Range for much of its length. It is one of the few roads in this part of the national forest that allows vehicle access. The early part of the trail follows along a shelf road with outstanding views to the west over the Pacific Ocean. The route then turns inland as you travel beneath Chalk Peak.

Trail meanders along the top of the Santa Lucia Range

The road is typically graded dirt; however it does wash out in places. At the time of research, there were still a number of bulldozed tracks that branch off the main trail and end shortly thereafter. Most of these were cut to fight a forest fire in 1999. The vegetation is in a state of regrowth and there are a number of barren, scarred areas with signs of new life springing up.

Trail follows along the ridge as a storm moves in

After you pass Central Mountains #48: Willow Creek Road, set beneath the shadows of Alder Peak, the trail standard drops slightly, mainly because it is less used. The trail from Willow Creek Road is no longer a through-road; rather, it ends at a gate before Fort Hunter Liggett. This last portion of the trail is typically used to access hiking trailheads into the Silver Peak Wilderness. A number of hiking opportunities and a particularly scenic backcountry camping spot can be found near the end of the trail.

Current Road Information

Los Padres National Forest
Monterey Ranger District
406 South Mildred
King City, CA 93930
(831) 385-5434

Map References

BLM Point Sur, Cambria
USFS Los Padres National Forest: Monterey and Santa Lucia Ranger Districts
USGS 1:24,000 Cone Peak, Cape San Martin, Alder Peak, Burro Mt., Burnett Peak
1:100,000 Point Sur, Cambria
Maptech CD-ROM: Central Coast/Fresno; San Luis Obispo/Los Padres National Forest
Southern & Central California Atlas & Gazetteer, pp. 31, 43, 44
California Road & Recreation Atlas, pp. 82, 90

Route Directions

▼ 0.0	Trail starts on Nacimiento-Ferguson Road at sign for South Coast Ridge Road (20S05). Turn is opposite the start of Central Mountains #50: Cone Peak Trail, 6.8 miles from California 1. Zero trip meter and turn southwest on graded dirt road.
6.5 ▲	Trail ends on Nacimiento-Ferguson Road, opposite the start of Central Mountains #50: Cone Peak Trail. Turn right for Fort Hunter Liggett; turn left for California 1.

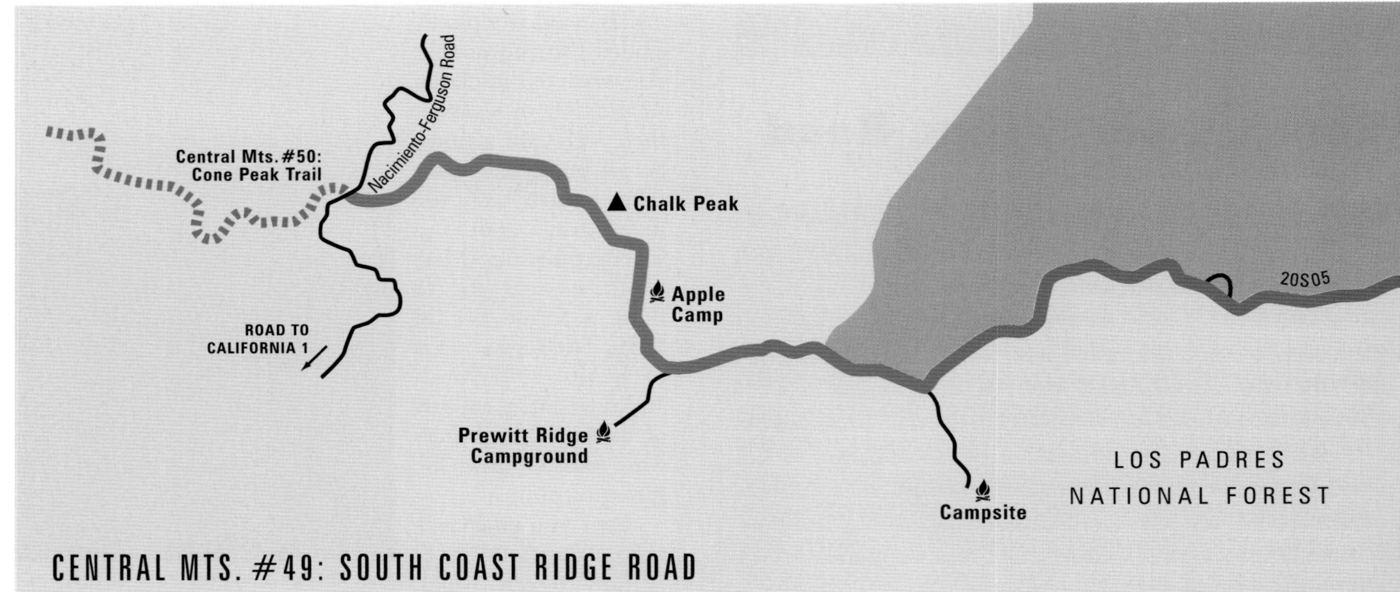

			GPS: N36°00.60′ W121°27.07′
▼ 0.5		SO	Restricted track on right.
	6.0 ▲	SO	Restricted track on left.
▼ 2.9		SO	Viewpoint on right over Pacific Ocean.
	3.6 ▲	SO	Viewpoint on left over Pacific Ocean.
▼ 3.5		SO	Apple Camp on left.
	3.0 ▲	SO	Apple Camp on right.
			GPS: N35°58.83′ W121°26.04′
▼ 3.9		SO	Private road on right.
	2.6 ▲	SO	Private road on left.
▼ 4.3		SO	Road to Prewitt Ridge Camp on right at sign.
	2.2 ▲	SO	Road to Prewitt Ridge Camp on left at sign.
			GPS: N35°58.30′ W121°26.40′
▼ 4.8		SO	Track on left.
	1.7 ▲	SO	Track on right.
▼ 5.4		SO	Track on right.
	1.1 ▲	SO	Track on left.
▼ 5.5		SO	Track on left.
	1.0 ▲	SO	Track on right.
▼ 6.5		SO	Track on right at wide intersection goes 0.2 miles to campsite before ending at a gate in 1.2 miles. Zero trip meter and continue along South Coast Ridge Road.
	0.0 ▲		Continue to the northwest.
			GPS: 35°57.04′ W121°25.23′
▼ 0.0			Continue to the southeast.
	7.8 ▲	SO	Track on left at wide intersection goes 0.2 miles to campsite before ending at a gate in 1.2 miles. Zero trip meter and continue along South Coast Ridge Road.
▼ 2.1		SO	Track on right and campsite on right.
	5.7 ▲	SO	Track on left and campsite on left.
▼ 2.8		SO	Track on right.
	5.0 ▲	SO	Track on left.
▼ 3.2		SO	Track splits off on left.
	4.6 ▲	SO	Track rejoins on right.
▼ 3.4		SO	Steep, loose track rejoins on left.
	4.4 ▲	SO	Steep, loose track splits off on right.
			GPS: N35°55.96′ W121°23.12′
▼ 5.0		SO	Trail forks and rejoins immediately.
	2.8 ▲	SO	Trail forks and rejoins immediately.
▼ 5.1		SO	Viewpoint on left.
	2.7 ▲	SO	Viewpoint on right.
▼ 5.4		SO	Trail forks and rejoins immediately.
	2.4 ▲	SO	Trail forks and rejoins immediately.
▼ 5.7		SO	Track on left at faded No Trespassing sign.
	2.1	SO	Track on right at faded No Trespassing sign.
▼ 7.8		SO	Central Mountains #48: Willow Creek Road on right. Zero trip meter.
	0.0 ▲		Continue to northeast on South Coast Ridge Road.
			GPS: N35°53.51′ W121°22.42′
▼ 0.0			Continue to the southeast toward Three Peaks and Lion Camps.
▼ 1.2		SO	Overlook on right and gated road on left.
			GPS: N35°52.80′ W121°22.18′
▼ 4.1		SO	Two tracks on right at sign. The first is gated and is the start of hiking trail to Lion Den Camp; the second goes a short distance to a viewpoint.
			GPS: N35°51.63′ W121°19.85′
▼ 4.3		SO	Salmon Creek Trailhead on right at sign.
			GPS: N35°51.44′ W121°19.61′
▼ 4.5		SO	Track on left.
▼ 6.3		BL	Sign for Three Peaks Camp (1.5 miles) and track on right. Zero trip meter.
			GPS: N35°50.75′ W121°18.16′
▼ 0.0			Continue to the southeast.
▼ 0.4		SO	Cross through wash.
▼ 0.8		SO	Hiking trailhead on right at tight switchback.
▼ 2.5		SO	Track on right leads to primitive campsite (0.1 miles); track on left.
▼ 2.6		SO	Track on left.
▼ 2.7		SO	Track on left.
▼ 2.8		SO	Track on left; then sign for Fort Hunter Liggett (3 miles).
▼ 5.6		BL	Track on right goes to locked gate in 0.4 miles.
			GPS: N35°49.42′ W121°13.79′
▼ 5.9			Trail ends at gate before Fort Hunter Liggett.
			GPS: N35°49.44′ W121°13.54′

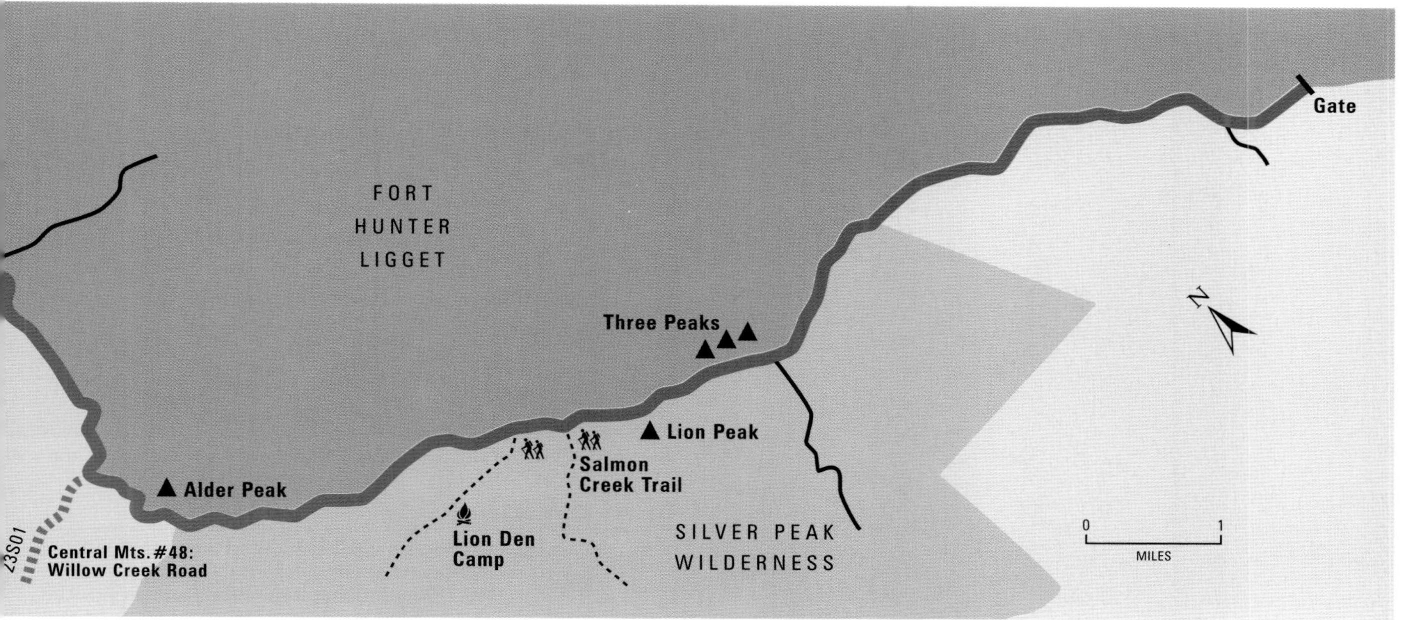

CENTRAL MOUNTAINS #50

Cone Peak Trail

Starting Point:	**Nacimiento-Ferguson Road, 6.8 miles east of California 1**
Finishing Point:	**Gate at the boundary of Ventana Wilderness**
Total Mileage:	**6.4 miles (one-way)**
Unpaved Mileage:	**6.4 miles**
Driving Time:	**30 minutes (one-way)**
Elevation Range:	**2,600–4,200 feet**
Usually Open:	**Spring to fall**
Best Time to Travel:	**Dry weather**
Difficulty Rating:	**1**
Scenic Rating:	**8**
Remoteness Rating:	**+0**

Special Attractions

- Hiking access into the Ventana Wilderness.
- Great views along a mild shelf road.

Description

Cone Peak Trail starts on paved Nacimiento-Ferguson Road—a very scenic road in its own right—and heads north into a corridor through the Ventana Wilderness. The trail immediately begins to climb along an easygoing, graded dirt road. Although it is an easy trail in dry weather, the road can become very slick when wet and can wash out in places. The bulk of the trail follows along a wide shelf road with ample passing places.

As you drive through the wilderness corridor, the trail passes a number of scenic overlooks that face across the valley to the Santa Lucia Range. Cone Peak comes in and out of view as you approach the closure gate at the trail's end.

Climbing the shelf road toward Cone Peak

Hikers often use this trail to reach the trailheads at the end of the road. Past the gate, the old vehicle trail continues to the northwest into the Ventana Wilderness. From there you can hike up to the top of Cone Peak or continue along North Coast Ridge Trail to connect with other trails and campsites in the more northerly parts of the wilderness area.

Current Road Information

Los Padres National Forest
Monterey Ranger District
406 South Mildred
King City, CA 93930
(831) 385-5434

Map References

BLM Point Sur
USFS Los Padres National Forest: Monterey and Santa Lucia Ranger Districts
USGS 1:24,000 Cone Peak
1:100,000 Point Sur
Maptech CD-ROM: Central Coast/Fresno
Southern & Central California Atlas & Gazetteer, p. 31
California Road & Recreation Atlas, p. 82

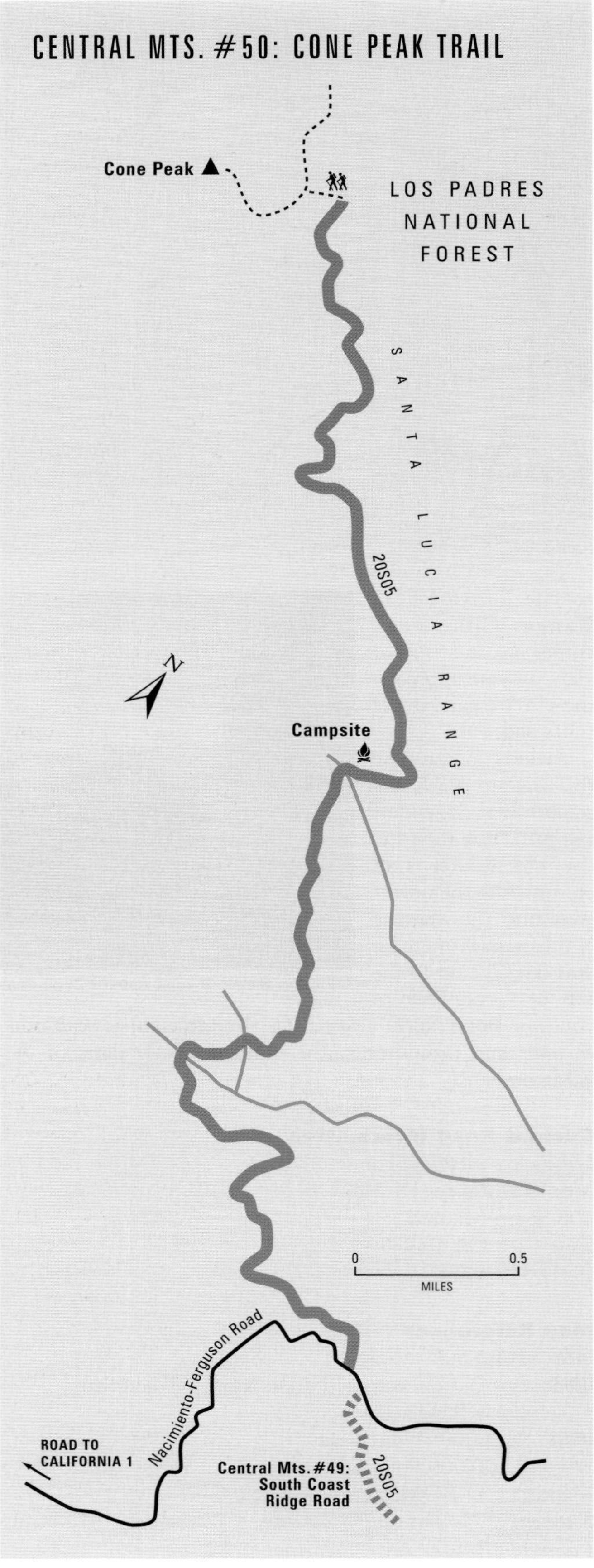

CENTRAL MTS. #50: CONE PEAK TRAIL

Cone Peak

LOS PADRES NATIONAL FOREST

SANTA LUCIA RANGE

20S05

Campsite

0 0.5 MILES

Nacimiento-Ferguson Road

ROAD TO CALIFORNIA 1

Central Mts. #49: South Coast Ridge Road

20S05

Spectacular view of the Santa Lucia Mountains from the end of the trail

Route Directions

▼ 0.0	TL	Trail starts on Nacimiento-Ferguson Road. Turn west at intersection. Central Mountains #49: South Coast Ridge Road starts opposite. Follow sign for Central Coast Ridge Road and immediately pass through seasonal closure gate. Zero trip meter.
		GPS: N36°00.61' W121°27.07'
▼ 0.5	SO	Track on right goes to overlook.
▼ 0.7	SO	Cross over creek.
▼ 1.9	SO	Cross over wash.
▼ 2.0	SO	Cross over wash.
▼ 2.4	SO	Cross over wash.
▼ 3.0	SO	Cross over wash.
▼ 3.6	SO	Saddle and campsite on left.
▼ 4.0	SO	Turnout on left at viewpoint.
▼ 4.7	SO	Track on right at viewpoint leads to campsite.
		GPS: N36°02.46' W121°28.64'
▼ 5.2	SO	Hiking and horseback riding trail on left.
▼ 6.4		Viewpoint on right. Trail ends at signs for hiking trails and campsites—North Coast Ridge Trail, Gamboa Trail, Arroyo Seco Trail, Lost Valley Connect, and Bee Camp Connect.
		GPS: N36°03.27' W121°29.34'

CENTRAL MOUNTAINS #51

Coast Road

Starting Point:	**California 1, 2.5 miles north of Big Sur**
Finishing Point:	**California 1, just north of Bixby Bridge**
Total Mileage:	**10.1 miles**
Unpaved Mileage:	**10.1 miles**
Driving Time:	**45 minutes**
Elevation Range:	**100–1,200 feet**
Usually Open:	**Year-round**
Best Time to Travel:	**Year-round**
Difficulty Rating:	**1**
Scenic Rating:	**9**
Remoteness Rating:	**+0**

Special Attractions

- Spectacular views over the Pacific Ocean.
- Pleasant, easygoing trail that travels through some of California's southernmost redwoods.

History

The Esselen were the first people to live in the mountainous coastal region south of Monterey. However, as Spanish missionaries made their way into the area, the Esselen culture began to disappear as many were baptized at the missions in Carmel and Monterey. Many scholars believe this period of assimilation to have occured around the 1840s.

As Spanish and Mexican development of the Monterey Peninsula spread, the rugged Santa Lucia Mountains were a physical boundary that defied settlement. Early settlers generally referred to the unknown terrain along the Santa Lucias as *el pais grande del sur* (Spanish for "the big country to the south"). It wasn't until the early 1850s that a few intrepid men decided to move in and attempt to survive in the Big Sur wilderness. George Davis is thought to have been the first American to homestead in the region. He built a cabin along the banks of the Big Sur River in what is now Pfeiffer Big Sur State Park (located south of this trail). Mexican governor Figueroa had given the Rancho El Sur land grant to Juan Bautista Alvarado in 1834. This grant, which extended from the Little Sur River south to Cooper Point, remained mostly unsettled until the 1850s, when Roger Cooper started to run cattle in the area. Slowly but surely, the next 20 years saw the arrival of a small number of settlers. William Brainard Post, Michael Pfeiffer, Charles Bixby, John Partington, and Eusebio Molera are a few of the settlers whose names linger on in many of the area's landforms and parks.

oast Road alternates between a shelf ad and forest trail

The coastline along the Big Sur region was just as treacherous as the terrain it bordered. In the early years of Spanish exploration, the ocean provided the only access to this area and it remained an important link to other parts of California throughout the nineteenth century. A number of shipwrecks along the coast demonstrated the need for a lighthouse. However, it still took sailors 11 years of lobbying to get money for the construction of the Point Sur Light Station. Between 1887 and 1889, a lighthouse was constructed on the huge rock of Point Sur, which juts more than 300 feet above the ocean.The lighthouse has changed hands a few times over the years. It was abandoned in 1974 and lay dormant for 10 years until it was taken over by the state parks department. Volunteers currently tend to the aging lighthouse and give guided tours of the facility.

Overlooking the meandering course of Coast Road

Near the end of this trail, the magnificent Bixby Bridge comes into view. Built in 1933, this bridge remains one of the world's highest single-span, concrete arch bridges. It stands about 285 above Bixby Creek and extends more than 700 feet in length. Its construction was a difficult and dangerous process. Access to the site entailed a number of hairpin turns and steep shelf roads. High winds against the arch's frames and high waves against its foundations posed additional problems. The bridge was named after early settler Charles Bixby. Bixby, a cousin of President James K. Polk's, ran a sawmill in the area and is credited with greatly improving the land. If you've ever seen the movie, *The Graduate,* you've seen a young, existential Dustin Hoffman speeding across the bridge in his famous red sports car.

Description

Coast Road begins and ends on California 1 and offers a great alternative to speeding down the Coast Highway. The trail begins 2.5 miles north of Big Sur, opposite the entrance to Andrew Molera State Park. It immediately begins to climb up a graded dirt road, passing through patches of thick trees and open ranchland. Along the early stretch of the trail, you can look west to see the highway, coast, and ocean. The views along this section are excellent and show just what you miss by staying on the main road.

The trail then goes through private property, passing a number of ranch access roads and private buildings. As it heads into the forested regions, the trail crosses Little Sur River before traveling along Sierra Creek. These wooded areas are on private property. Please respect landowners' rights and stay on the main trail.

As the trail winds along Mescal Ridge and heads back to the coast, it leaves the redwoods behind and travels on a shelf road through low shrubs. As the Bixby Bridge comes into view, the trail nears its end; it then descends to join California 1 at Division Knoll.

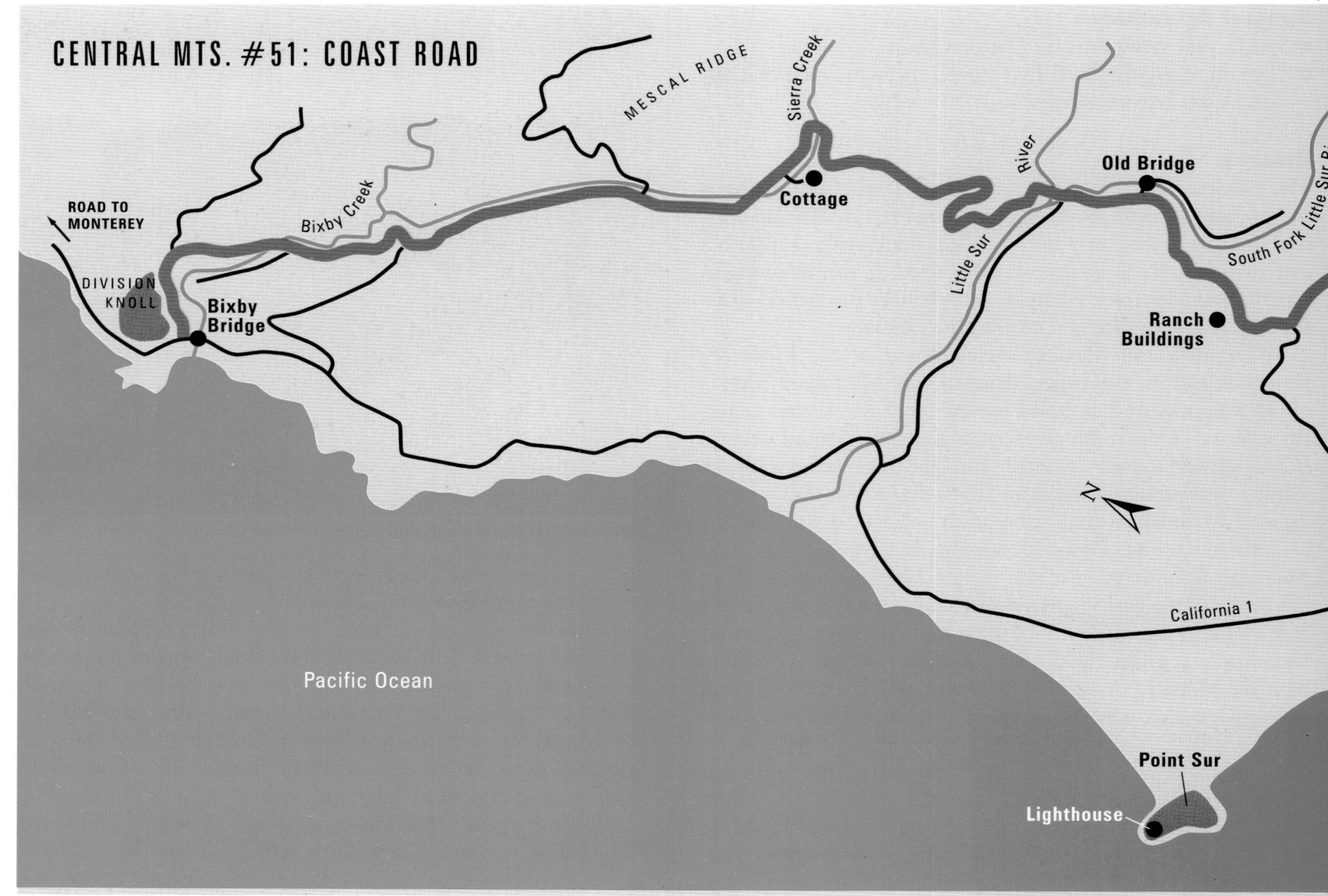

Current Road Information

BLM Hollister Field Office
20 Hamilton Court
Hollister, CA 95023
(831) 630-5000

Map References

BLM Point Sur
USGS 1:24,000 Big Sur, Point Sur
1:100,000 Point Sur
Maptech CD-ROM: Central Coast/Fresno
Southern & Central California Atlas & Gazetteer, pp. 31, 30
California Road & Recreation Atlas, p. 82

Route Directions

▼ 0.0		Trail starts off of California 1, 2.5 miles north of Big Sur. Turn northwest onto Coast Road. Entrance to Andrew Molera State Park is opposite. Zero trip meter.
6.9 ▲		Trail ends on California 1, opposite entrance to Andrew Molera State Park. Turn right for Monterey; turn left for Big Sur.
		GPS: N36°17.32′ W121°50.60′
▼ 0.2	SO	Two hiking trails on right.
6.7 ▲	SO	Two hiking trails on left.
▼ 0.7	SO	Cattle guard and private property sign. Next 6 miles is property of El Sur Ranch.
6.2 ▲	SO	Cattle guard.
▼ 2.3	SO	Gate on right.
4.6 ▲	SO	Gate on left.
▼ 2.8	SO	Cattle guard.
4.1 ▲	SO	Cattle guard.
▼ 3.1	SO	Gated ranch road on left.
3.8 ▲	SO	Gated ranch road on right.
▼ 3.4	SO	House and ranch buildings on left.
3.5 ▲	SO	House and ranch buildings on right.
▼ 4.1	SO	Old bridge on right on private property.
2.8 ▲	SO	Old bridge on left on private property.
▼ 4.5	SO	Gated road on left; then bridge over South Fork Little Sur River; then shed on left.
2.4 ▲	SO	Shed on right; then bridge over South Fork Little Sur River; then gated road on right.
▼ 4.6	SO	Gated road on right; then cross over Little Sur River on bridge.
2.3 ▲	SO	Cross over Little Sur River on bridge; then gated road on left.
▼ 5.7	SO	Cattle guard.
1.2 ▲	SO	Cattle guard.
▼ 6.3	SO	Gates on left and right.
0.6 ▲	SO	Gates on left and right.
▼ 6.6	SO	Cross over Sierra Creek.
0.3 ▲	SO	Cross over Sierra Creek.
		GPS: N36°20.71′ W121°51.89′

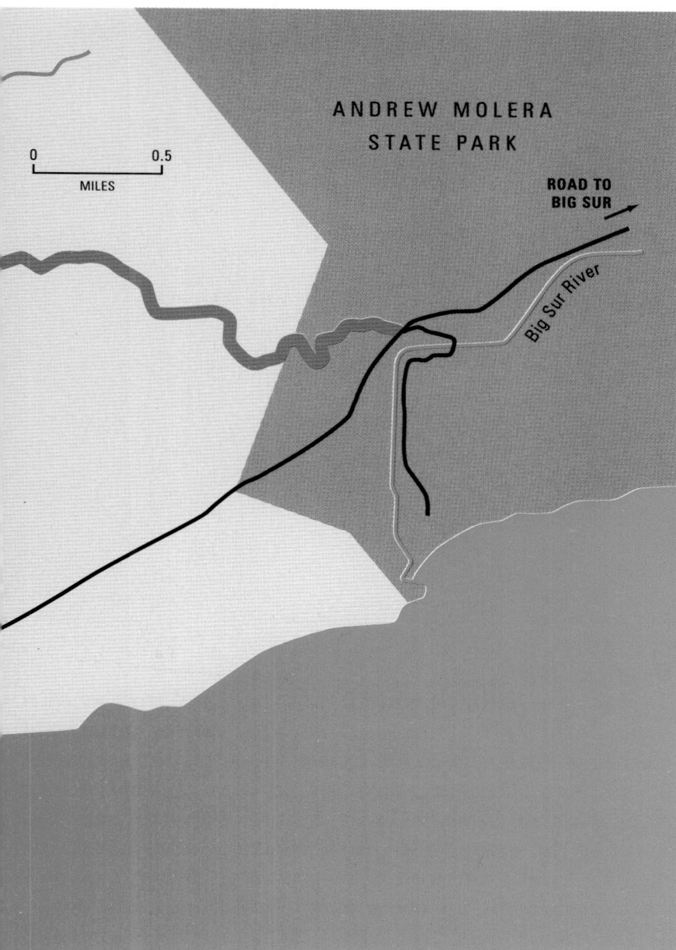

▼ 6.8		SO	Cottage on left below trail.
	0.1 ▲	SO	Cottage on right below trail.
▼ 6.9		SO	Cottage entrance on left. Zero trip meter.
	0.0 ▲		Continue to the northeast.
			GPS: N36°20.73' W121°52.17'
▼ 0.0		SO	Continue to the west.
	3.2 ▲	SO	Cottage entrance on right. Zero trip meter.
▼ 0.7		SO	Gated road on right.
	2.5 ▲	SO	Gated road on left.
▼ 1.7		SO	Gated road on left.
	1.5 ▲	SO	Gated road on right.
▼ 2.3		SO	Gated road on left; then cross over Bixby Creek on bridge; then private road on right.
	0.9 ▲	SO	Private road on left; then cross over Bixby Creek on bridge; then gated road on right.
▼ 2.4		SO	Gated road on left.
	0.8 ▲	SO	Gated road on right.
▼ 2.9		SO	Gated road on right. Views ahead to Bixby Bridge.
	0.3 ▲	SO	Gated road on left.
▼ 3.2		SO	Trail ends on California 1. Turn right for Monterey; turn left for Big Sur.
	0.0 ▲		Trail begins on California 1, just north of the Bixby Bridge. Zero trip meter and head west on Coast Road.
			GPS: N36°22.36' W121°54.09'

Tassajara Road

Starting Point:	**Tassajara Road, at Jamesburg**
Finishing Point:	**Tassajara Zen Mountain Center Monastery**
Total Mileage:	**13.6 miles (one-way)**
Unpaved Mileage:	**13.6 miles**
Driving Time:	**1 hour (one-way)**
Elevation Range:	**2,000–4,700 feet**
Usually Open:	**Year-round**
Best Time to Travel:	**May 1 to September 1**
Difficulty Rating:	**2**
Scenic Rating:	**8**
Remoteness Rating:	**+0**

Special Attractions

- Tassajara Hot Springs at the Tassajara Zen Mountain Center Monastery.
- Scenic route traveling through a vehicle corridor in the Ventana Wilderness.
- Numerous backcountry hiking trails.

History

The earliest inhabitants of the Carmel Valley near Tassajara Hot Springs are thought to have been members of the Esselen tribe. A pictograph depicting a series of hands has been found in a cave above the springs. The poet Robinson Jeffers used the pictograph as material for his poem "Hands."

Although some sources report the hot springs as being a tourist destination as early as the 1860s, a hotel was not established at the springs until 1904. Equipped with bathhouses, the

Cement catchment basins above Tassajara Hot Springs

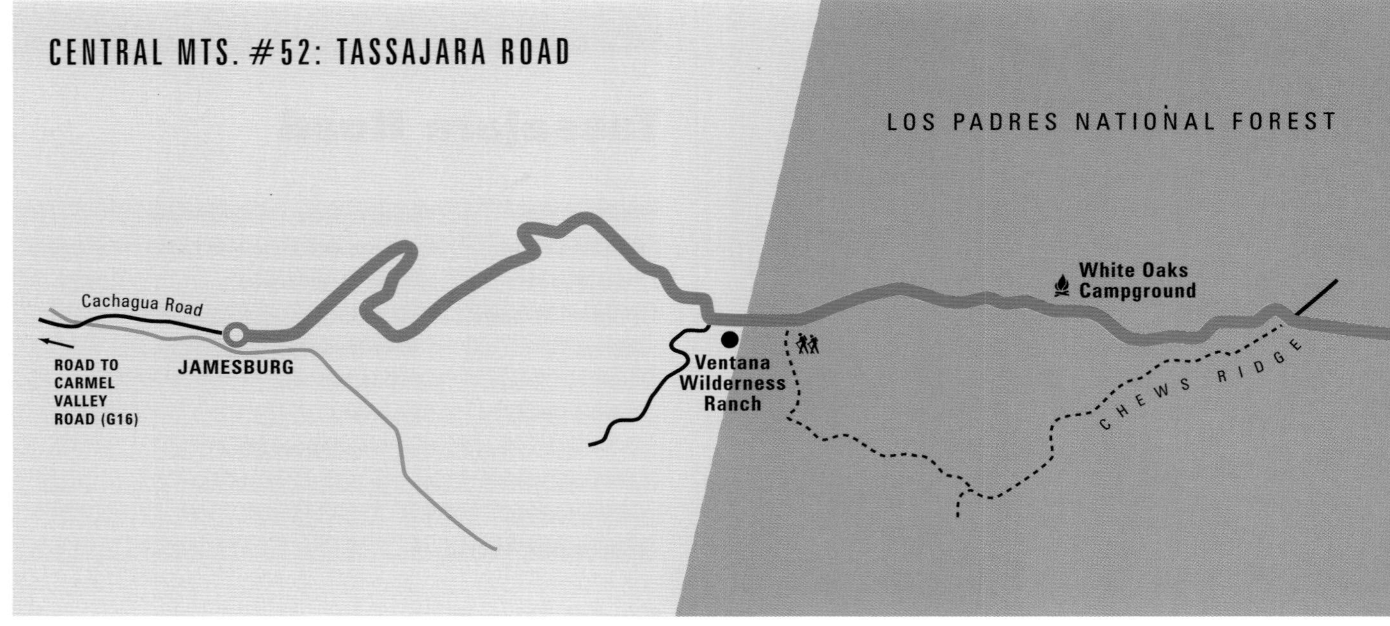

hotel operated until 1949, when it was destroyed by a fire. The area remained relatively quiet for about 20 years until the San Francisco Zen Center purchased the land and developed the Tassajara Zen Mountain Center.

Attracted by the serene mountain setting and the soothing waters of the hot springs, students of Buddhism can come and practice monastic traditions at the center all year. The monastery is open to visitors from May 1 to September 7 every year. During this time, you can reserve rooms and take part in the daily monastic life. Please call ahead; do not show up unannounced expecting to use the hot springs. Please respect the monastery's time of closure and do not approach the gates during the off-season.

Trail descends along shelf road below Black Butte

Description

To reach the starting point for Tassajara Road from Carmel Valley Road (G16), turn south onto the eastern entrance of Cachagua Road (signed for Tassajara Road). Follow signs for 2.9 miles to Jamesburg, staying right at the T about 1 mile along the road. When you see the Jamesburg snack bar, head south on the wide, graded dirt road along James Creek. For the first 3 miles, the road passes a number of private and/or gated roads. Only the major ones have been listed below.

The trail enters Los Padres National Forest after 3.3 miles, at the Ventana Wilderness Ranch. The ranch offers hiking and horseback expeditions of varying lengths into the Ventana Wilderness. The trail continues to climb onto Chews Ridge as it meanders along forested sections of shelf road. Once in the national forest, the trail passes a number of side roads that are either gated or peter out after a short distance. Up on the ridge, the trail passes two developed national forest campgrounds—White Oaks and China Camps. The Pine Ridge Hiking Trail heads off to the west from China Camp. Remember, if you plan to camp or park your vehicle and hike, you must have a Forest Adventure Pass from the forest service.

After traveling along Chews Ridge, the trail begins to descend along the west side of Black Butte, offering excellent views over the valley to the west. The trail descends sharply at this point; watch out for overheating brakes in the summer. Toward the end, the trail passes a couple hiking trailheads before coming to an end at the Tassajara Zen Mountain Center Monastery, located on the north side of Tassajara Creek.

Current Road Information

Los Padres National Forest
Monterey Ranger District
406 South Mildred
King City, CA 93930
(831) 385-5434

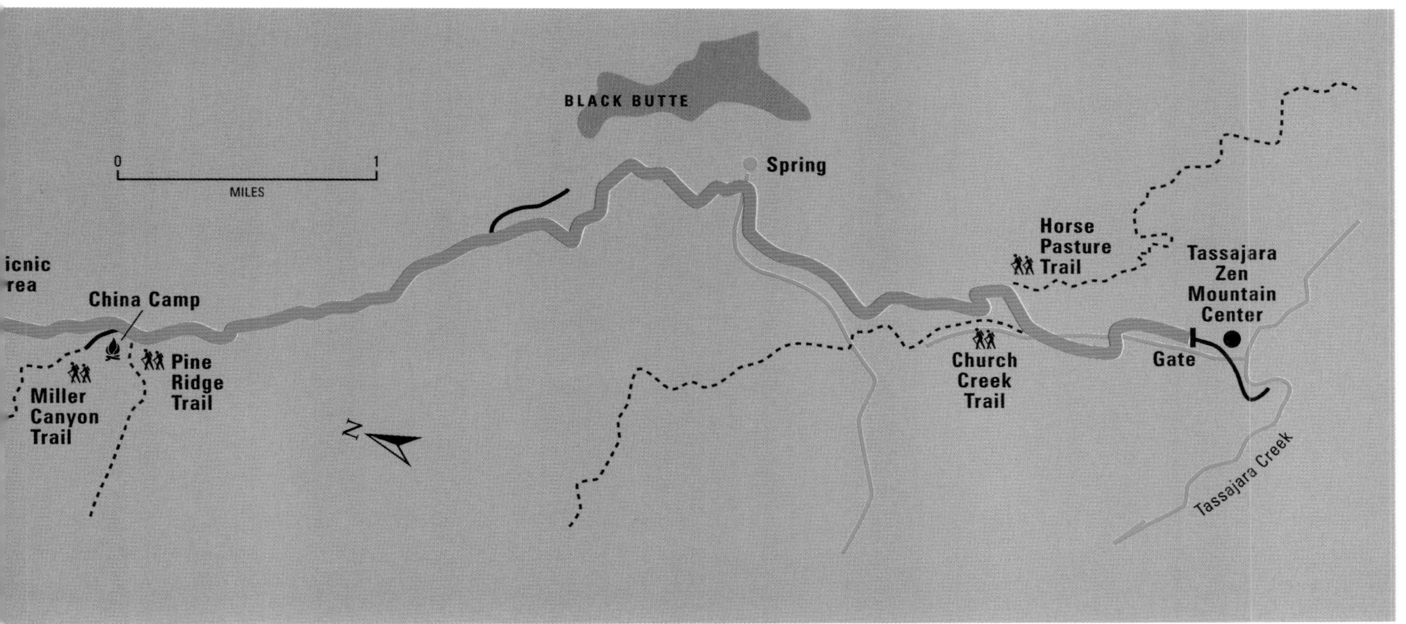

Map References

BLM Point Sur
USFS Los Padres National Forest: Monterey and Santa Lucia Ranger Districts
USGS 1:24,000 Chews Ridge, Tassajara Hot Springs
1:100,000 Point Sur
Maptech CD-ROM: Central Coast/Fresno
Southern & Central California Atlas & Gazetteer, p. 31
California Road & Recreation Atlas, p. 82

Route Directions

▼ 0.0		Trail starts in Jamesburg at sign for Tassajara Zen Mountain Center Monastery. Road turns from paved to graded dirt at this point. Head southeast past the Jamesburg snack bar. Zero trip meter.
		GPS: N36°22.13' W121°35.35'
▼ 0.3	SO	Private road on left.
▼ 1.6	SO	Private roads on left and right.
▼ 2.1	SO	Private road on left.
▼ 3.0	SO	Gated drive on right.
▼ 3.3	SO	Ventana Wilderness ranch on right; then cattle guard; then sign for Los Padres National Forest.
		GPS: N36°20.55' W121°34.79'
▼ 3.5	SO	Hiking trailhead on right (before second national forest sign).
▼ 4.7	SO	White Oaks Campground on left. Zero trip meter.
		GPS: N36°19.59' W121°34.44'
▼ 0.0	SO	Continue to the southwest.
▼ 0.7	SO	Cross through wash.
▼ 1.2	SO	Gated roads on left and right.
▼ 1.6	SO	Picnic area on right.
▼ 1.7	SO	Hiking trailhead on left.
▼ 2.7	SO	China Camp on right; then hiking trailhead on right.
		GPS: N36°17.72' W121°34.44'
▼ 3.5	SO	Tracks on left and right.
▼ 3.7	SO	Track on right.
▼ 4.3	SO	Track splits off on left.
▼ 5.9	SO	Spring and rusted-out tub on left.
		GPS: N36°15.78' W121°32.70'
▼ 6.7	SO	Viewpoint on right.
▼ 7.6	SO	Horse Pasture Trail for hiking and horseback riding on left.
▼ 7.9	SO	Church Creek Trail for hiking and horseback riding on right.
▼ 8.4	SO	Cross over wash.
▼ 8.8	SO	Cement buildings on left.
▼ 8.9	SO	Trail ends at sign for Tassajara Zen Mountain Center.
		GPS: N36°14.19' W121°32.92'

Side trail fromTassajara Road dead-ends shortly

Trails in the South Coast Region

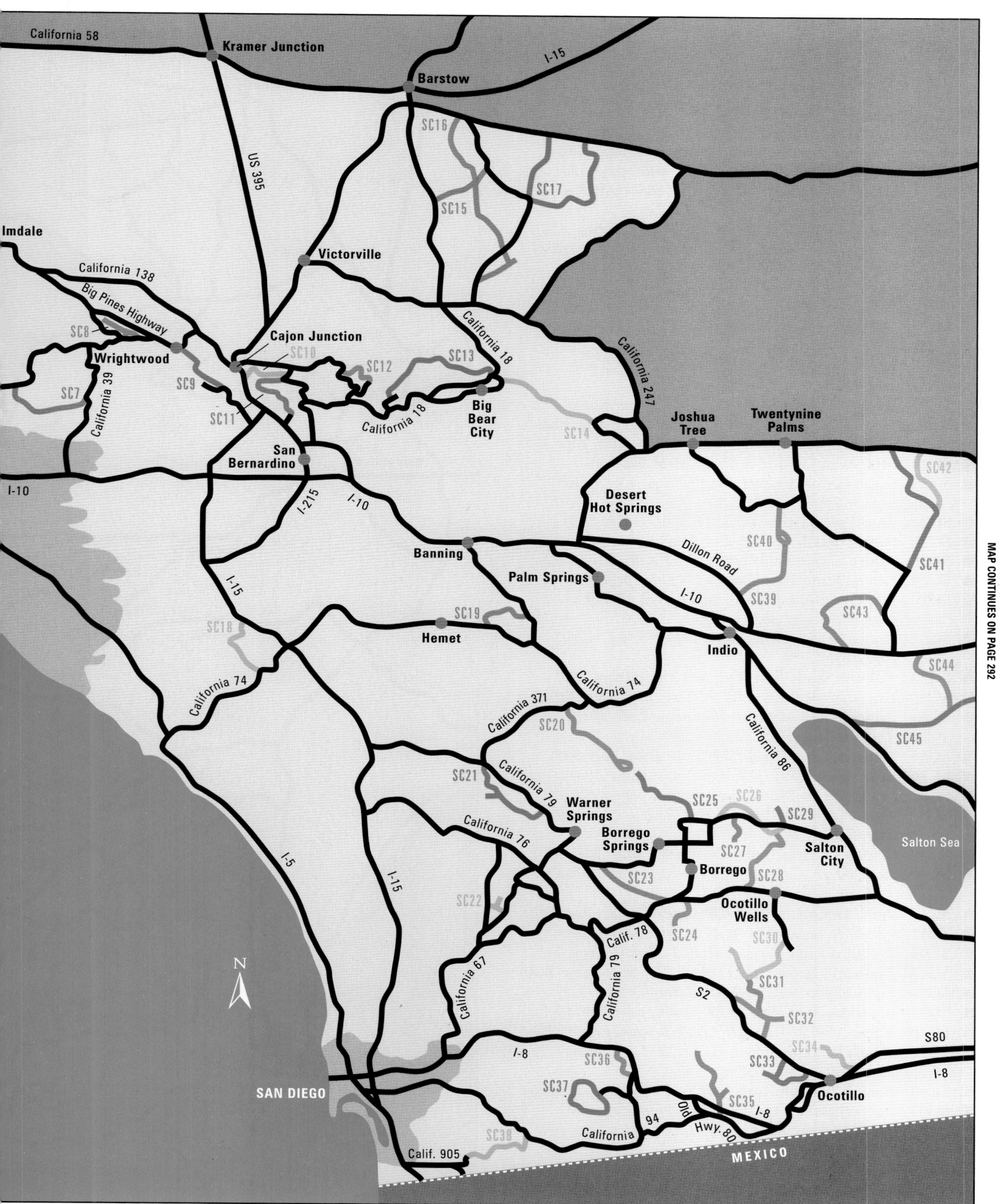

MAP CONTINUES ON PAGE 292

Trails in the South Coast Region

MAP CONTINUES ON PAGE 291

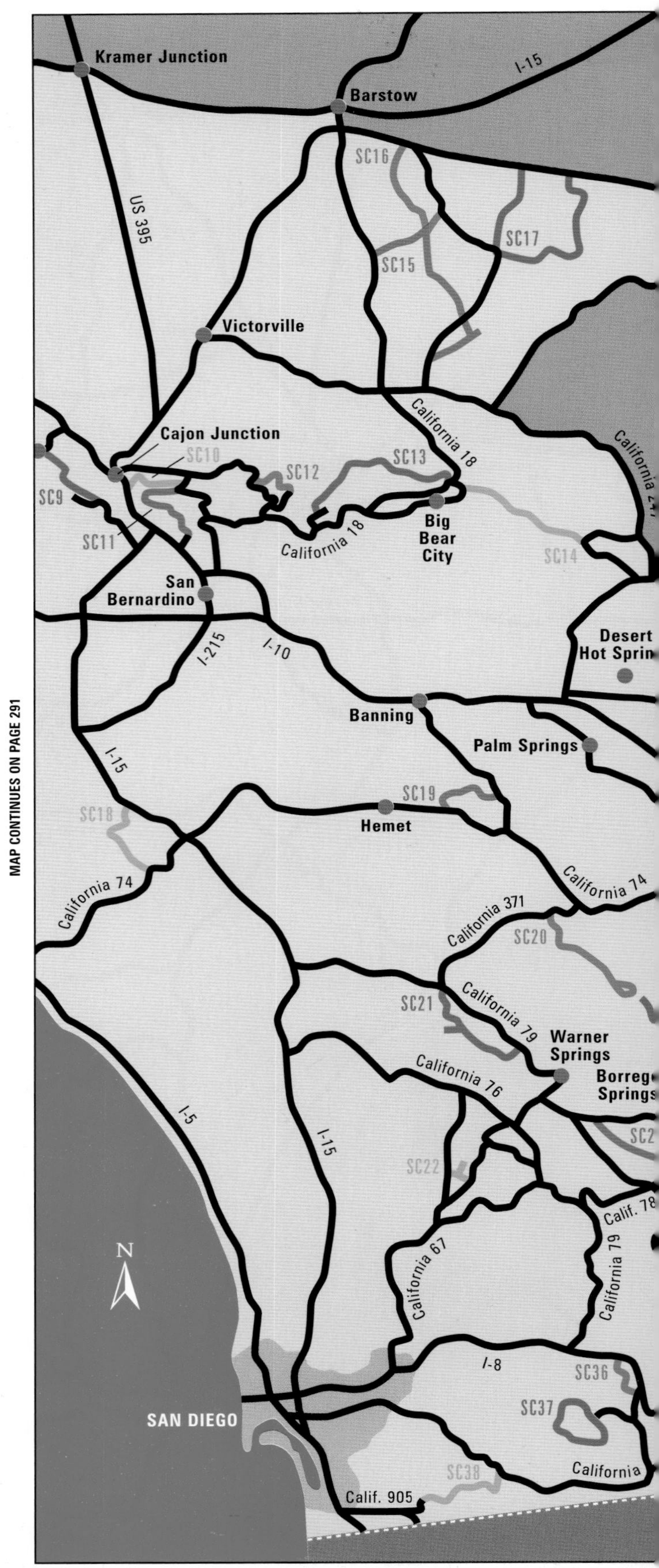

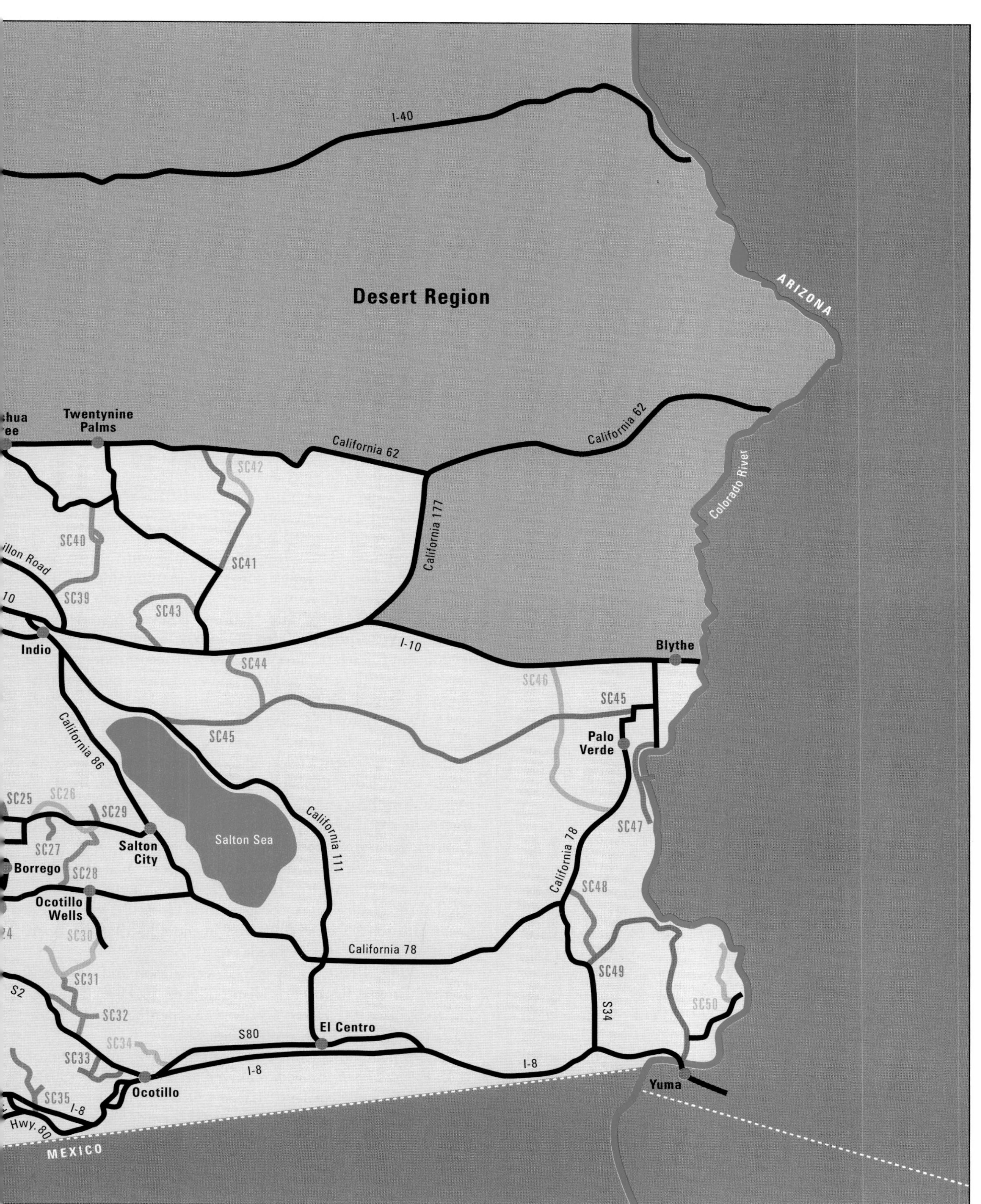

I-40
Desert Region
ARIZONA
Twentynine Palms
California 62
California 62
SC42
Colorado River
SC40
SC41
California 177
Dillon Road
10
SC39
SC43
Indio
I-10
Blythe
SC44
SC46
SC45
California 86
SC45
Palo Verde
SC25
SC26
SC29
California 111
SC47
California 78
Salton City
Salton Sea
SC27
Borrego
SC28
SC48
Ocotillo Wells
SC30
California 78
SC49
SC31
S2
SC50
SC32
S34
S80
El Centro
SC34
SC33
I-8
I-8
Ocotillo
Yuma
SC35
I-8
Hwy. 80
MEXICO

SOUTH COAST #1

Liebre Mountain Trail

Starting Point:	**California 138, 3.3 miles east of I-5**
Finishing Point:	**Lake Hughes Road, 0.4 miles south of intersection with Pine Canyon Road**
Total Mileage:	**29.3 miles**
Unpaved Mileage:	**24.1 miles**
Driving Time:	**3 hours**
Elevation Range:	**3,300–5,600 feet**
Usually Open:	**Year-round**
Best Time to Travel:	**Dry weather**
Difficulty Rating:	**2**
Scenic Rating:	**9**
Remoteness Rating:	**+0**

Special Attractions

- Trail travels a short section of the Old Ridge Route.
- Long, easy ridge trail traveling the top of Liebre Mountain.
- Hunting in season and backcountry camping.
- Panoramic views from the ridge.

History

This trail traverses the Old Ridge Route for a short distance, a historic trail that travels over Fort Tejon Pass from Castaic to the San Joaquin Valley. The route, first used in 1910, was an important trading link with Bakersfield and the communities beyond. It opened to the public five years later when the dirt road was sprayed with oil to help retain its form. The road proved so popular with traders and travelers that an even better standard was needed and further construction began around 1917 to upgrade the route to a concrete surface. By 1920, the wide central concrete strip of road surface we see today had extended up and over the pass.

Easy access up Liebre Mountain attracts game hunters to these rewarding slopes

If you try to travel the actual curve of this reinforced concrete surface today, you will find yourself getting dizzy at the wheel as the road snakes its way over the ridge. Now try to envision the lack of visibility around all those tight cuttings in the hillside and the concentration needed to guide a vehicle without power steering or power brakes over this route. Accidents were not uncommon, and the rising death rate associated with increased public usage became a growing concern for the California Highway Commission, which has been accountable for such highways since its inception in 1911. In an effort to reduce accidents, the commission directed that speed limit signs be posted and motorists be restricted to 15 miles per hour on the tight curves between Castaic School and Quail Lake. In the late 1920s, many of those blind corners were cut away and the asphalt side infills that are still visible today were added.

The Pacific Crest National Scenic Trail follows Liebre Mountain ridgeline

The commercial haunts that evolved along this old cliff-hanging route knew how to draw the weary traveler inside their doors. Many businesses sprang up; gas stations, restaurants, and hotels opened. Wild dancing establishments and gambling houses appeared. The latter attracted not only thirsty customers, but also the police intent on maintaining Prohibition. Premises with names such as Summit Cafe, Tumble Inn, Sandberg's Lodge, and National Forest Inn traded and faded from the early 1900s to the 1960s. Tumble Inn opened its doors in the 1920s, supplying gas and accommodations to motorists traveling the route. The foundations of this establishment are still visible.

In 1918, Harold Sandberg became the first postmaster at the post office he named after himself. In the 1920s, he opened the Sandberg Lodge. The three-story building was the largest resort along the Ridge Route and has also survived the longest. Sandberg's name lives on in the region, attached to the first peak that Liebre Mountain Trail passes as it twists and climbs away from the Old Ridge Route.

Descriptively named points along the way, such as Swede's Cut and Serpentine Drive, reflect the difficult terrain encountered during the route's construction. Horse-drawn graders and steam shovels were employed in the mid-1910s to open the 100-foot-high gap of Swede's Cut.

The Ridge Route finally gained recognition and was listed on the National Register of Historic Places in 1997. The listing recognized the efforts involved in opening up the trade route to the north from Los Angeles.

Liebre Mountain gained its name from a land grant of 1846 called *El paraje que llaman la Cueba de la Liebre* (Spanish for "the parcel of land that is called the burrow of the jackrabbit"). Edward F. Beale acquired the 48,000-acre Rancho La Liebre, although it was registered in his wife's name. Beale, who had resigned from the position of state superintendent of Indian affairs, was named a brigadier general in 1855. Together with his family, he moved into an adobe home to the north of Liebre Mountain, close to Tehachapi. A controversial character, Beale had used his position as superintendent to relocate many Native Americans, thus leaving "vacant" land that he was able to purchase for a minimal price from the government. Some parcels he obtained for as little as 5 cents an acre. In addition, the general consolidated five Mexican grants until his total holdings rose to nearly 300,000 acres. These grants included El Tejon Ranch, La Liebre, Castaic, Los Alamos, and Aqua Caliente.

Description

The long, scenic Liebre Mountain Trail follows a gentle, winding dirt road that travels along the ridge tops of Angeles National Forest.

The trail leaves California 138 at Quail Lake, a short distance from I-5. For the first few miles, the route follows the marked Old Ridge Route. This rough concrete road is now broken up and uneven in spots, but it provides an easy climb along a wide shelf road to the start of the dirt trail.

Liebre Mountain Trail is one of a series of identified vehicle routes within Angeles National Forest. It is marked as Back Country Discovery Trail #1 and is suitable for 4WD vehicles, ATVs, and motorbikes. The entire standard of the trail is such that a high-clearance 2WD vehicle will have no problems in dry weather.

The first section of dirt road snakes its way up to Sandberg Mountain, passing through open grassland and a scattering of oak trees. Many species of oak can be found on this ridge including canyon, valley, and interior live oak. Many of the oaks support clusters of parasitic mistletoe.

There are many tracks off the main trail as it runs along the ridge top. Most of these sidetracks end after a short distance at viewpoints or campsites. The Pacific Crest National Scenic Trail (reserved for nonmotorized use) crosses several times, its path roughly paralleling that of the vehicle trail.

Besides a number of undeveloped campsites, there are two national forest campgrounds along the trail—Bear and Sawmill. Both are open areas with tables and fire rings. A Forest Adventure Pass is required.

The trail finishes by dropping down from the ridge, heading toward Lake Hughes.

Current Road Information

Angeles National Forest
Saugus Ranger District
30800 Bouquet Canyon Road
Saugus, CA 91390
(661) 296-9710

Map References

BLM Lancaster
USFS Angeles National Forest
USGS 1:24,000 La Liebre Ranch, Liebre Mt., Burnt Peak, Lake Hughes
1:100,000 Lancaster
Maptech CD-ROM: Barstow/San Bernardino County
Southern & Central California Atlas & Gazetteer, p. 78
California Road & Recreation Atlas, pp. 102, 103

Route Directions

Mileage		Directions
▼ 0.0		From California 138, 3.3 miles east of I-5, zero trip meter and turn southeast on paved road at sign for Old Ridge Route. Turn is immediately southeast of Quail Lake and is marked N2. Remain on paved road.
5.2 ▲		Trail ends at T-intersection with California 138 at Quail Lake. Turn right for Lancaster; turn left for I-5 and Los Angeles.
		GPS: N34°45.89' W118°43.93'
▼ 2.1	SO	Entering Angeles National Forest.
3.1 ▲	SO	Leaving Angeles National Forest.
▼ 2.2	SO	4-way intersection. Paved road on left is Pine Canyon Road; paved road on right is Liebre Gulch Road. Continue straight ahead on paved road 8N04, following sign to Castaic via Old Ridge Road.
3.0 ▲	SO	4-way intersection. Paved road on right is Pine Canyon Road; paved road on left is Liebre Gulch Road. Continue straight ahead on paved road.
		GPS: N34°44.68' W118°42.72'
▼ 2.6	SO	Track on right.
2.6 ▲	SO	Track on left.
▼ 2.7	SO	Track on left.
2.5 ▲	SO	Track on right.
▼ 5.2	TL	Turn left onto graded dirt road 7N23, following sign to Sawmill USFS Campground, and zero trip meter. Road is suitable for 4WDs, ATVs, and motorbikes—rated green.
0.0 ▲		Continue to the north.
		GPS: N34°42.94' W118°42.60'
▼ 0.0		Continue to the northeast.
8.4 ▲	TR	T-intersection with paved Ridge Road. Zero trip meter.
▼ 0.6	BL	Track on right is 7N22. Remain on 7N23.
7.8 ▲	SO	Track on left is 7N22. Remain on 7N23.
		GPS: N34°43.05' W118°42.25'
▼ 0.8	SO	Turnout on left.
7.6 ▲	SO	Turnout on right.
▼ 3.1	SO	Track on left.
5.3 ▲	SO	Track on right.
▼ 3.5	SO	Small track on left.
4.9 ▲	SO	Small track on right.
▼ 3.7	SO	Small track on right.
4.7 ▲	SO	Small track on left.
▼ 3.9	SO	Track on left.
4.5 ▲	SO	Track on right.
		GPS: N34°43.62' W118°41.42'
▼ 4.3	SO	Two tracks on left.
4.1 ▲	SO	Two tracks on right.
▼ 4.6	SO	Gate.
3.8 ▲	SO	Gate.
▼ 5.3	SO	Small track on right.
3.1 ▲	SO	Small track on left.
▼ 5.5	SO	Track on right.
2.9 ▲	SO	Track on left.
▼ 5.8	SO	Viewpoint on right overlooking Pyramid Lake.
2.6 ▲	SO	Viewpoint on left overlooking Pyramid Lake.
		GPS: N34°43.13' W118°40.11'
▼ 5.9	SO	Track on right.
2.5 ▲	SO	Track on left.
▼ 6.1	SO	Track on right.
2.3 ▲	SO	Track on left.
		GPS: N34°43.06' W118°39.91'

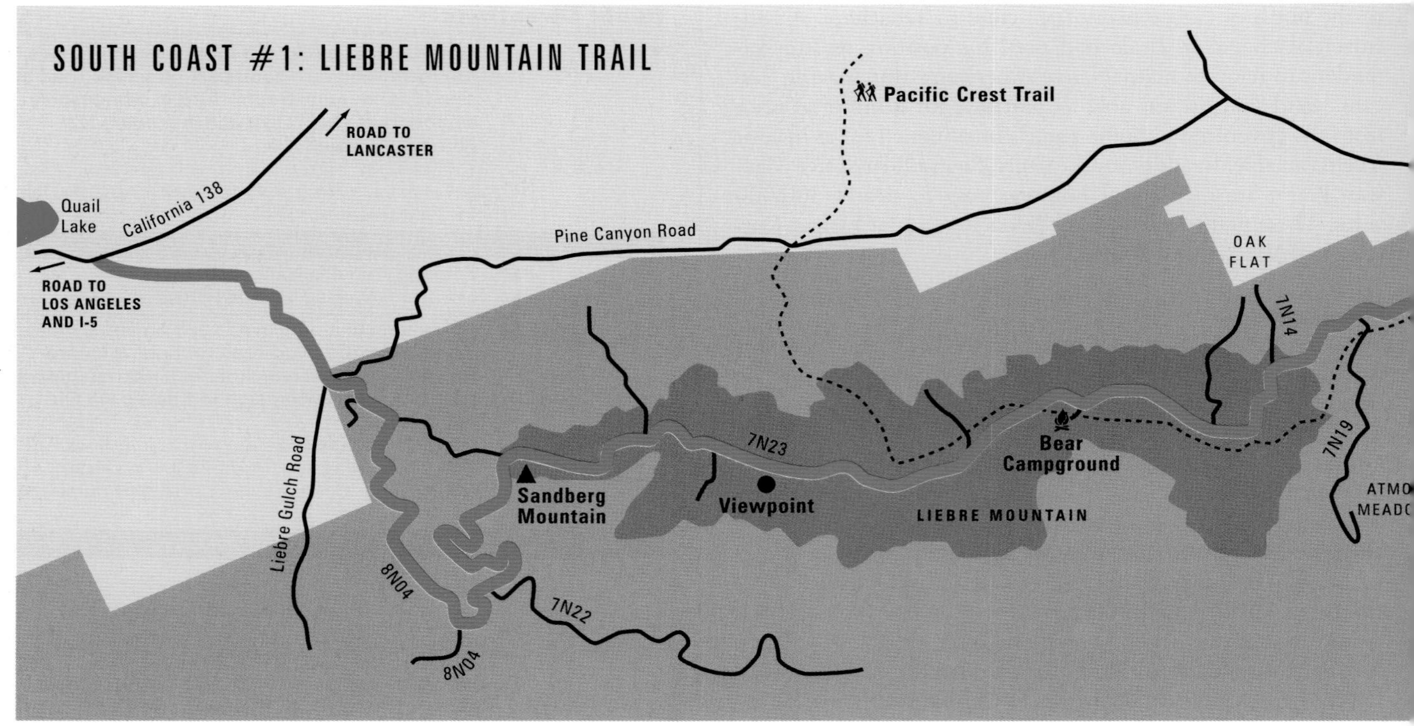

▼	▲		
▼ 6.2		SO	Track on right.
	2.2 ▲	SO	Track on left.
▼ 6.5		SO	Track on left to game water tank.
	1.9 ▲	SO	Track on right to game water tank.
			GPS: N34°42.90' W118°39.45'
▼ 6.8		SO	Track on left.
	1.6 ▲	SO	Track on right.
▼ 6.9		SO	Track on left.
	1.5 ▲	SO	Track on right.
▼ 7.2		SO	Track on right.
	1.2 ▲	SO	Track on left.
▼ 7.5		SO	Track on left.
	0.9 ▲	SO	Track on right.
▼ 8.1		SO	Pacific Crest National Scenic Trail, for hikers and horses, crosses main vehicle route.
	0.3 ▲	SO	Pacific Crest National Scenic Trail, for hikers and horses, crosses main vehicle route.
			GPS: N34°42.82' W118°38.08'
▼ 8.2		SO	Track on left to game water tank.
	0.2 ▲	SO	Track on right to game water tank.
▼ 8.4		SO	Track on right into Bear USFS Campground is 7N23E. Zero trip meter. Track on left.
	0.0 ▲		Continue to the northwest.
			GPS: N34°42.78' W118°37.84'
▼ 0.0			Continue to the east.
	2.0 ▲	SO	Track on left into Bear USFS Campground is 7N23E. Zero trip meter. Track on right.
▼ 1.0		SO	Well-used track on left.
	1.0 ▲	SO	Well-used track on right rejoins.
			GPS: N34°42.29' W118°36.99'
▼ 1.1		SO	Track on left rejoins.
	0.9 ▲	SO	Track on right.
▼ 1.2		SO	Track on right.
	0.8 ▲	SO	Track on left.
▼ 1.3		SO	Track on right.
	0.7 ▲	SO	Track on left.
▼ 2.0		BR	Track on left is 7N14 to Oak Flat. Zero trip meter.
	0.0 ▲		Continue to the northwest on 7N23.
			GPS: N34°42.52' W118°36.34'
▼ 0.0			Continue to the east on 7N23.
	4.2 ▲	SO	Track on right is 7N14 to Oak Flat. Zero trip meter.
▼ 1.0		SO	Track on right is 7N19 to Atmore Meadows. Continue straight ahead on 7N23. Pacific Crest National Scenic Trail follows Atmore Meadows Road.
	3.2 ▲	BR	Track on left is 7N19 to Atmore Meadows. Pacific Crest National Scenic Trail follows Atmore Meadows Road. Remain on 7N23, following sign to Old Ridge Route. Note that this sign is a bit misleading in the direction it points.
			GPS: N34°42.62' W118°35.62'
▼ 1.4		SO	Pacific Crest National Scenic Trail on left and right for hikers and horses only. No mountain bikes.
	2.8 ▲	SO	Pacific Crest National Scenic Trail on right and left for hikers and horses only. No mountain bikes.
			GPS: N34°42.54' W118°35.20'
▼ 2.7		SO	Track on left.
	1.5 ▲	SO	Track on right.
▼ 2.8		SO	Track on left into Sawmill USFS Campground is 7N23A.
	1.4 ▲	SO	Track on right into Sawmill USFS Campground is 7N23A.
			GPS: N34°42.01' W118°34.36'
▼ 2.9		SO	Pull-in on left.
	1.3 ▲	SO	Pull-in on right rejoins.
▼ 3.0		SO	Pull-in on left rejoins.
	1.2 ▲	SO	Pull-in on right.
▼ 3.6		SO	Track on right.
	0.6 ▲	SO	Track on left.
▼ 4.2		SO	Track on right is closed road to Burnt Peak communications site. Graded road on left is

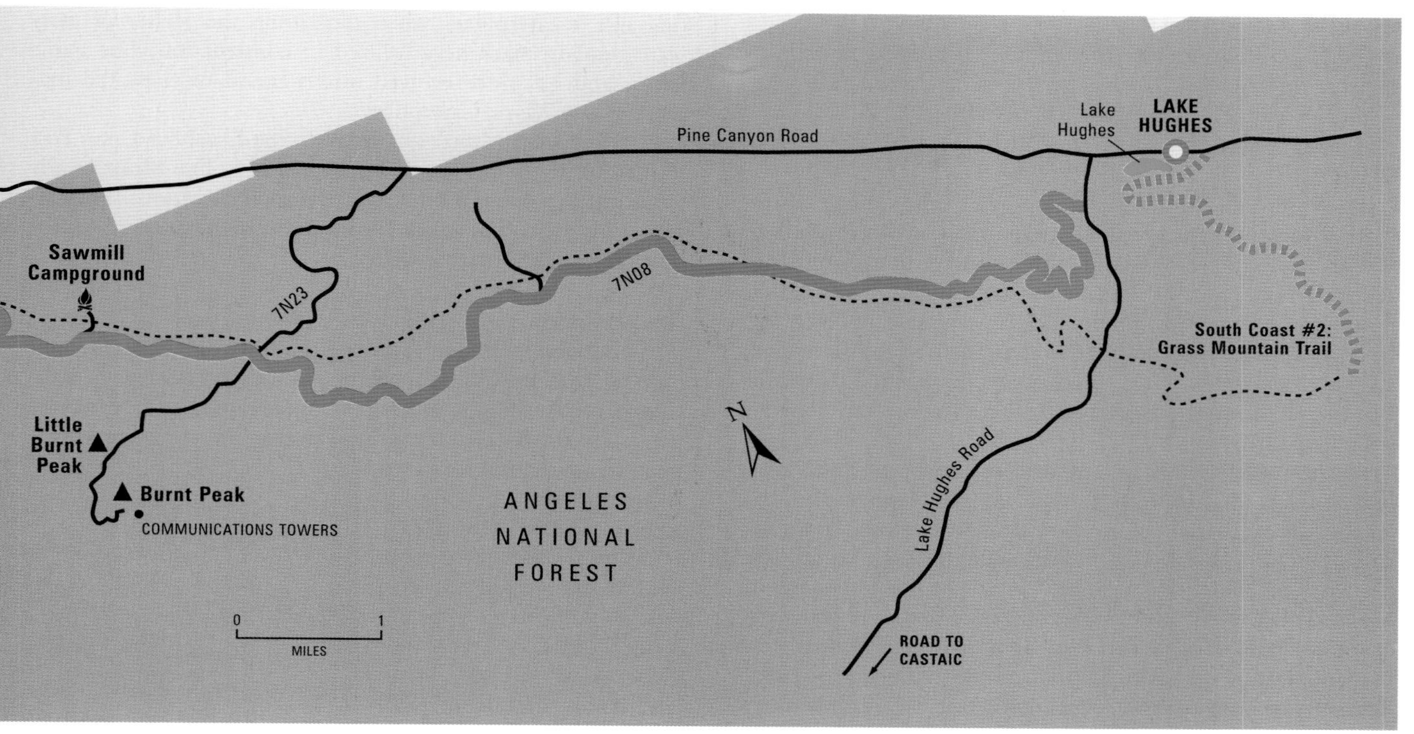

7N23 to Pine Canyon for 4WDs, ATVs, and motorbikes—rated green. Pacific Crest National Scenic Trail enters and leaves on the left. Zero trip meter and continue straight ahead on 7N08. Trail is suitable for 4WDs, ATVs, and motorbikes—rated green.

0.0 ▲ Continue to the northwest.

GPS: N34°41.50′ W118°33.23′

▼ 0.0 Continue to the southeast.

9.5 ▲ SO Track on left is closed road to Burnt Peak communications site. Graded road on right is 7N23 to Pine Canyon for 4WDs, ATVs, and motorbikes—rated green. Pacific Crest National Scenic Trail enters and leaves on the right. Zero trip meter and continue straight ahead on 7N23. Trail is suitable for 4WDs, ATVs, and motorbikes—rated green.

▼ 1.4 SO Track on left.

8.1 ▲ SO Track on right.

▼ 3.2 SO Track on left.

6.3 ▲ SO Track on right.

▼ 5.2 SO Pacific Crest National Scenic Trail on left and right.

4.3 ▲ SO Pacific Crest National Scenic Trail on left and right.

GPS: N34°40.81′ W118°29.59′

▼ 5.5 SO Small track on left.

4.0 ▲ SO Small track on right.

▼ 5.7 SO Track on left.

3.8 ▲ SO Track on right.

GPS: N34°40.53′ W118°29.14′

▼ 6.6 SO Pacific Crest National Scenic Trail runs alongside on the right.

2.9 ▲ SO Pacific Crest National Scenic Trail runs alongside on the left.

▼ 7.4 SO Track on left.

2.1 ▲ SO Track on right.

▼ 9.5 Trail ends at T-intersection with Lake Hughes Road. Turn left for Lake Hughes; turn right for Castaic.

0.0 ▲ Trail starts on Lake Hughes Road, 0.4 miles south of the intersection with Pine Canyon Road in Lake Hughes. Zero trip meter and turn west on graded dirt road 7N08, sign-posted as Maell Road to Burnt Peak. Road is suitable for 4WDs, ATVs, and motorbikes—rated green. Road is also marked as Back Country Discovery Trail #1.

GPS: N34°40.43′ W118°27.27′

SOUTH COAST #2

Grass Mountain Trail

Starting Point:	**Elizabeth Lake Road at Lake Hughes**
Finishing Point:	**Bouquet Canyon Road, 3.6 miles south of the intersection with Elizabeth Lake Road**
Total Mileage:	**18 miles, plus 0.8-mile spur to Grass Mountain**
Unpaved Mileage:	**18 miles, plus 0.8-mile spur**
Driving Time:	**1.5 hours**
Elevation Range:	**3,300-4,400 feet**
Usually Open:	**Year-round**
Best Time to Travel:	**Dry weather**
Difficulty Rating:	**2**
Scenic Rating:	**8**
Remoteness Rating:	**+0**

Special Attractions

- Ridge top views over Antelope Valley and Bouquet Lake.
- Easy winding trail that can be driven in conjunction with South Coast #1: Liebre Mountain Trail.

History

Grass Mountain Trail travels along the ridge above Munz Canyon, just west of Elizabeth Lake. The canyon carries the name of an early emigrant family who became prominent settlers in the region. The Munz family came from Bottighofen, Switzerland, where their ancestors had lived for several hundred years. John Munz immigrated to America in 1878 and made his way to Illinois, where he married Amalia Tischauser, also from Switzerland. Together they developed a successful farm.

In the mid-1890s they moved to the newly forming German and Swiss settlement of Palendale (or Palmenthal), California. The Lutheran colony would later be known as Palmdale. Here, the couple ran the Munz General Store until the drought of 1898 drove most settlers out of the young town. Munz managed to trade his store and its contents for 160 acres of undeveloped land at Elizabeth Lake. Though not great at ranching, John and his eight children slowly tamed the land. Amalia had died earlier during childbirth. Later, John became a justice of the peace. The naming of John Munz Camp recognized his services.

In the late 1800s, the Butterfield Stagecoach Trail passed through the Munz Ranch between Fairmont (located in Antelope Valley) and San Francisquito Canyon. The Los Angeles Aqueduct also passed by the Munz Ranch, and the Los Angeles Department of Water and Power set up its headquarters on the property for the duration of construction. William Mulholland got to know the property well, and it was here that he was said to have coined the phrase "behaving like a caterpillar" when describing the ability of early earthmoving machinery utilized in construction. The name stuck and has since evolved into a brand of respected machinery—CAT or Caterpillar.

West end of Grass Mountain approaching Lake Hughes

One of John Munz's children ran the Elizabeth Lakes Post Office from the old family home in 1914. The Munz family continued to develop the ranch over the generations. They also set up the Munz Lakes Resort and were pioneers in turkey farming in the Antelope Valley.

Description

Grass Mountain Trail travels along the range of hills on the west side of Antelope Valley, south of the small settlement of Lake Hughes. The roughly graded dirt road climbs away from the edge of town and wraps around the chaparral-covered ridge tops and valleys of Angeles National Forest. For 1.1 miles, the trail shares its route with South Coast #3: Tule Ridge Trail, before they diverge. Tule Ridge Trail travels down South Portal Canyon and Grass Mountain Trail wraps around the northeastern face of Grass Mountain.

Grass Mountain Trail sign

A short spur leads to the top of Grass Mountain, where there is a large open area ringed by large Coulter pines. The trail then descends to cross San Francisquito Canyon Road. The Green Valley Ranger Station is 0.8 miles to the south along San Francisquito Canyon Road.

The second part of the trail continues along the ridge top, passing the top of Spunky Canyon Road, and descends to finish on Bouquet Canyon Road. Bouquet Lake can be seen by looking south from the shelf road.

All of the trails around here may be closed sporadically for weather or fire-related concerns. Check with the forest service if in any doubt.

Current Road Information

Angeles National Forest
Saugus Ranger District
30800 Bouquet Canyon Road
Saugus, CA 91390
(661) 296-9710

Map References

BLM Lancaster
USFS Angeles National Forest
USGS 1:24,000 Lake Hughes, Del Sur, Sleepy Valley
1:100,000 Lancaster
Maptech CD-ROM: Barstow/San Bernardino County
Southern & Central California Atlas & Gazetteer, p. 78
California Road & Recreation Atlas, p. 103

Route Directions

Mileage		Directions
▼ 0.0		From Elizabeth Lake Road at Lake Hughes, 0.8 miles east of intersection with Lake Hughes Road, zero trip meter and turn south at sign for Back Country Discovery Trails #1. Cross over creek on bridge.
3.4 ▲		Cross over creek on bridge. Trail ends at T-intersection with Elizabeth Lake Road. Turn left to enter Lake Hughes; turn right for Palmdale.
		GPS: N34°40.46' W118°26.29'
▼ 0.1	BR	Bear right in front of Lake Hughes Community Center onto formed trail 7N05, suitable for 4WDs, ATVs, and motorbikes—rated green.
3.3 ▲	BL	Bear left in front of Lake Hughes Community Center toward paved road.
▼ 0.3	BL	Track on right and Lake Hughes on right. Remain on 7N05.
3.1 ▲	BR	Track on left and Lake Hughes on left. Remain on 7N05.
▼ 0.7	TL	Track on right.
2.7 ▲	TR	Track straight ahead.
		GPS: N34°40.44' W118°26.95'
▼ 1.3	SO	Small track on right.
2.1 ▲	SO	Small track on left.
▼ 1.8	SO	Track on left.
1.6 ▲	BL	Track on right.
▼ 2.6	SO	Track on left.
0.8 ▲	SO	Track on right.
▼ 3.4	TL	Turn left onto 7N01, sign-posted to Drinkwater Flat. Road is suitable for 4WDs, ATVs, and motorbikes—rated green. Graded road on left is South Coast #3: Tule Ridge Trail (7N01). Zero trip meter.
0.0 ▲		Continue to the northwest.
		GPS: N34°38.78' W118°25.91'
▼ 0.0		Continue to the east.
1.1 ▲	TR	Turn right onto 7N05, sign-posted to Lake Hughes. Road is suitable for 4WDs, ATVs, and motorbikes—rated green. Graded road straight ahead is South Coast #3: Tule Ridge Trail (7N01). Zero trip meter.
▼ 1.1	BL	Closed road on left is 7N02; then trail forks. Bear left onto 7N01. Road is suitable for 4WDs, ATVs, and motorbikes—rated green. Graded road on right is South Coast #3: Tule Ridge Trail (7N02). This road exits via South Portal Canyon. Pacific Crest National Scenic Trail crosses road and small track on left up ridge. Zero trip meter.
0.0 ▲		Continue to the west. Closed road on right is 7N02.
		GPS: N34°38.89' W118°24.95'
▼ 0.0		Continue to the northeast.
1.4 ▲	BR	Graded road on left is South Coast #3: Tule Ridge Trail (7N02). Pacific Crest National

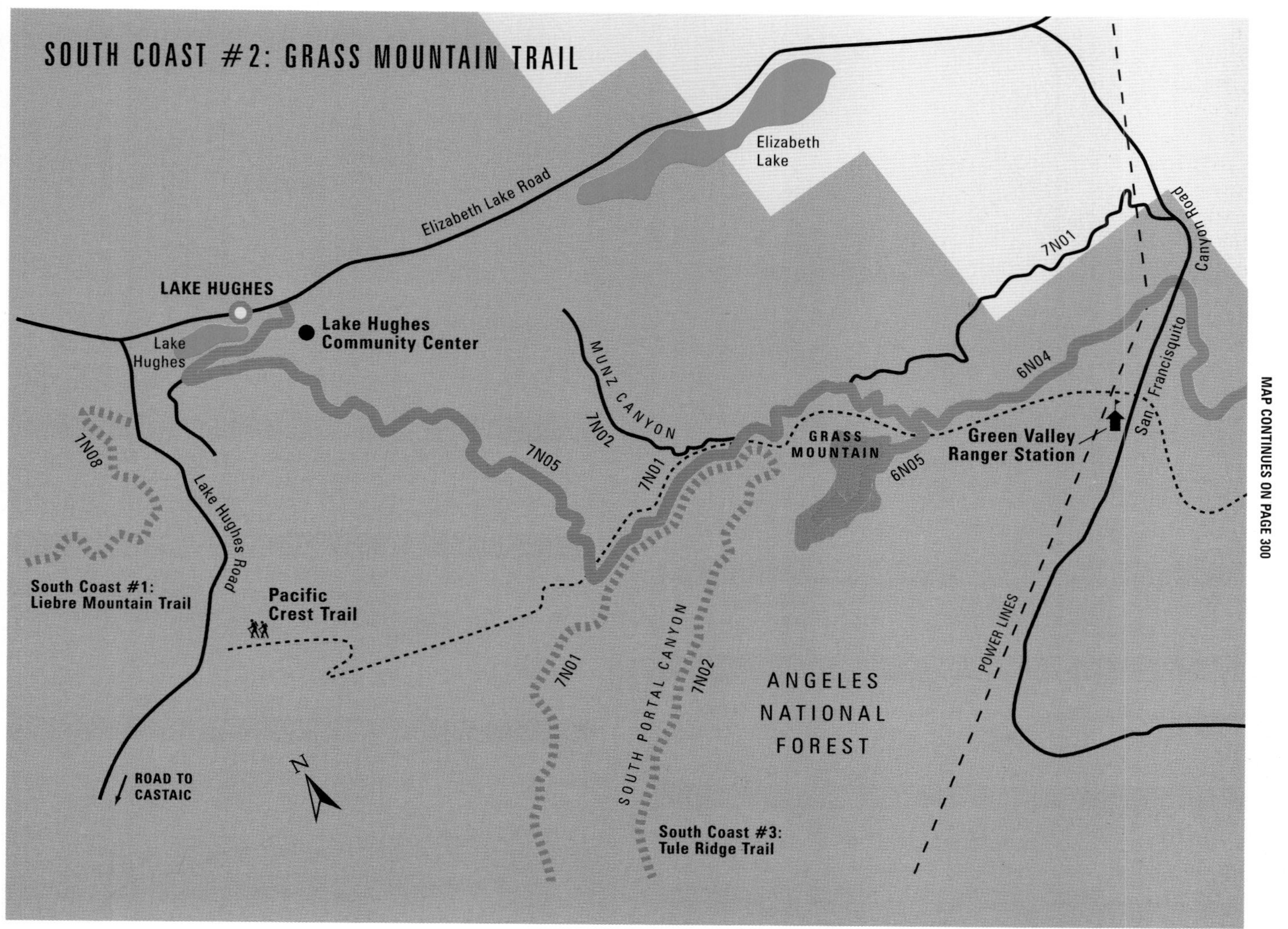

MAP CONTINUES ON PAGE 300

MAP CONTINUES ON PAGE 299

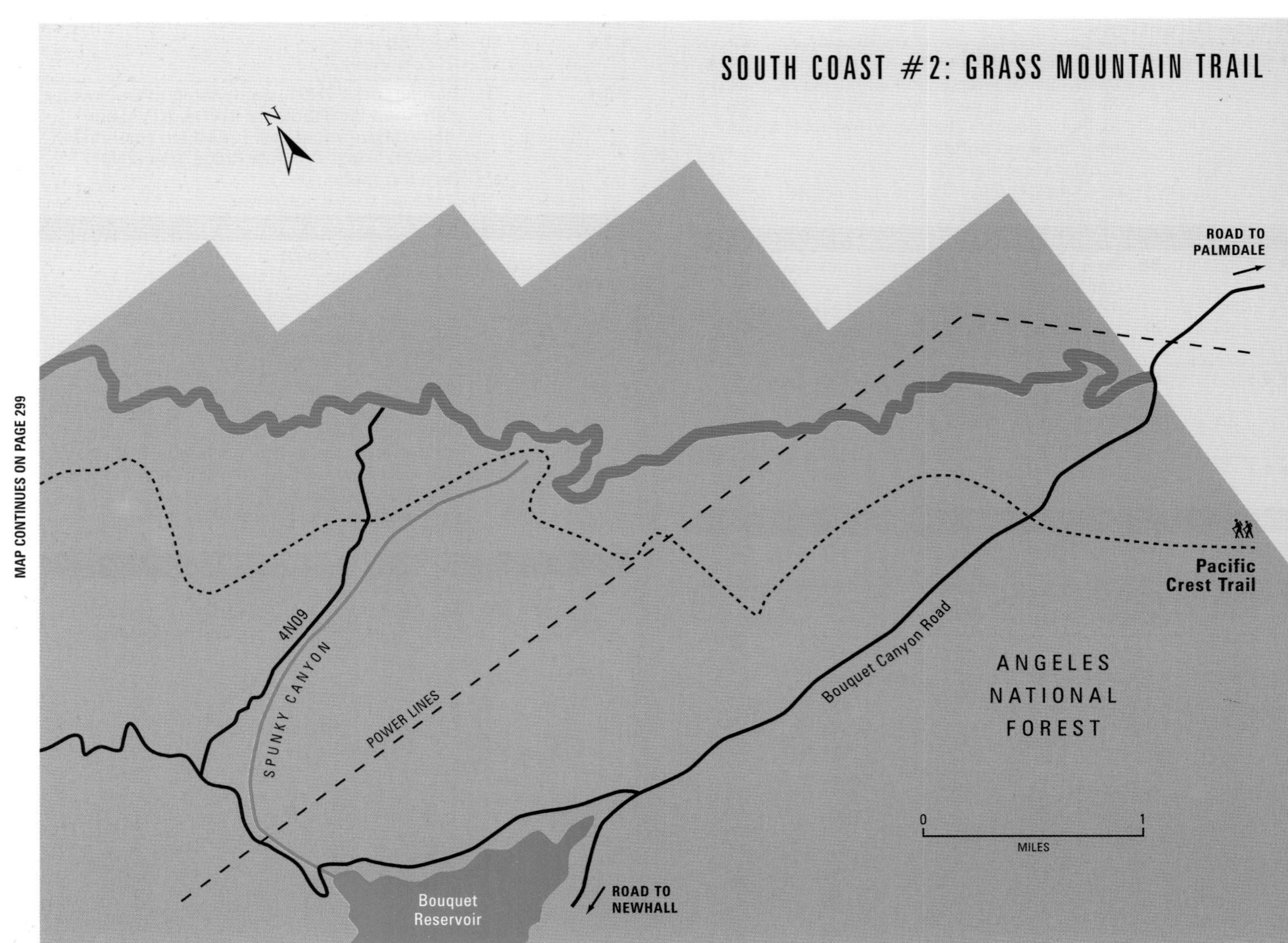

		Scenic Trail crosses road and small track on left up ridge. Bear right on 7N01, also suitable for 4WDs, ATVs, and motorbikes—rated green. Zero trip meter.
▼ 0.6	BR	Track on left is 7N01. Bear right onto 6N04, suitable for 4WDs, ATVs, and motorbikes—rated green. Pass through closure gate.
0.8 ▲	BL	Closure gate; then track on right is 7N01 for 4WDs, ATVs, and motorbikes—rated green. Bear left onto 7N01, suitable for 4WDs, ATVs, and motorbikes—rated green.
		GPS: N34°38.88′ W118°24.48′
▼ 1.4	TL	Graded road on right is spur to Grass Mountain (6N05). Zero trip meter.
0.0 ▲		Continue to the southwest.
		GPS: N34°38.54′ W118°24.21′

Grass Mountain Spur

▼ 0.0		Turn south onto 6N05.
▼ 0.1	SO	Pacific Crest National Scenic Trail crosses road.
		GPS: N34°38.47′ W118°24.22′
▼ 0.8		T-intersection. Left goes 0.1 miles to turnaround with views over South Portal Canyon and Tule Ridge. Right goes 0.1 miles to large open area with views over Antelope Canyon.
		GPS: N34°38.46′ W118°24.84′

Continuation of Main Trail

▼ 0.0		Continue to the north.
1.8 ▲	TR	Graded road ahead is spur to Grass Mountain (6N05). Zero trip meter.
		GPS: N34°38.54′ W118°24.21′
▼ 1.5	SO	Closure gate; then track on left and track on right under power lines.
0.3 ▲	SO	Track on left and track on right under power lines; then closure gate.
		GPS: N34°38.38′ W118°22.99′
▼ 1.8	SO	Track on left; then small trail on left is San Francisquito Bypass for ATVs and motorbikes—rated green. Cross over paved San Francisquito Canyon Road onto 6N04. Zero trip meter.
0.0 ▲		Continue to the west. Small trail on right is San Francisquito Bypass for ATVs and motorbikes—rated green; then track on right.
		GPS: N34°38.38′ W118°22.80′
▼ 0.0		Continue to the south.
4.1 ▲	SO	Cross over paved San Francisquito Canyon Road onto 6N04, following sign for Grass Mountain and Tule Ridge. Zero trip meter.
▼ 4.1	SO	Graded road 4N09 on right runs down Spunky Canyon and is suitable for 4WDs, ATVs, and motorbikes—rated green. Zero trip meter.

	0.0 ▲		Continue to the northwest on 6N041.
			GPS: N34°36.93′ W118°21.28′
▼ 0.0			Continue to the southeast on 6N041.
	6.2 ▲	SO	Graded road 4N09 on left runs down Spunky Canyon and is suitable for 4WDs, ATVs, and motorbikes—rated green. Zero trip meter.
▼ 2.7		SO	Track on left.
	3.5 ▲	SO	Track on right.
			GPS: N34°36.07′ W118°20.41′
▼ 3.5		SO	Track on left.
	2.7 ▲	SO	Track on right.
▼ 3.6		SO	Pass under power lines.
	2.6 ▲	SO	Pass under power lines.
			GPS: N34°35.79′ W118°19.66′
▼ 6.2			Trail ends at T-intersection with paved Bouquet Canyon Road. Turn right for Newhall; turn left for Palmdale.
	0.0 ▲		Trail commences on paved Bouquet Canyon Road, 3.6 miles south of Elizabeth Lake Road. Zero trip meter and turn northwest on graded dirt road 6N041, following sign for San Francisquito Canyon. Turn is beside the "Leaving Angeles National Forest" sign.
			GPS: N34°35.18′ W118°18.30′

SOUTH COAST #3

Tule Ridge Trail

Starting Point:	**San Francisquito Canyon Road, 6.6 miles south of the intersection with Elizabeth Lake Road**
Finishing Point:	**San Francisquito Canyon Road, 4.6 miles south of the intersection with Elizabeth Lake Road**
Total Mileage:	**14.5 miles**
Unpaved Mileage:	**14.5 miles**
Driving Time:	**1 hour**
Elevation Range:	**2,200–4,200 feet**
Usually Open:	**Year-round**
Best Time to Travel:	**Dry weather**
Difficulty Rating:	**2**
Scenic Rating:	**8**
Remoteness Rating:	**+0**

Special Attractions

- Varied trail encompassing canyon and ridge top scenery.
- Can be combined with South Coast #2: Grass Mountain Trail to form alternate routes.

History

San Francisquito Canyon was the scene of a horrific disaster back in 1928. Just two years after its construction, the Saint Francis Dam was thought to have sprung a leak. Word traveled fast that morning to inform authorities in Los Angeles of the fault in the dam wall. William Mulholland and his assistants rushed to the scene. Mulholland was the man responsible for bringing water from the Owens Valley on the eastern side of the Sierra Nevada to Los Angeles. Though not the actual engineer, he is credited with saving Los Angeles from droughts and enabling the city to grow without water restrictions. He is also seen by many residents in the Owens Valley as a water thief who threatened their survival.

Mature cottonwoods, sycamores, and oaks line the lower elevations of South Portal Canyon

Mulholland and his team inspected the dam, determined that it was safe, and returned home. At midnight, the dam wall gave way, loosing a wall of water the height of a 10-story building. The San Francisquito Canyon acted as a chute for the raging water, which destroyed many communities downstream and killed 385 people. A total of 7,900 acres of land was flooded.

The city of Los Angeles, recognizing the magnitude of the disas-

Tule Ridge Trail follows a shelf road down South Portal Canyon

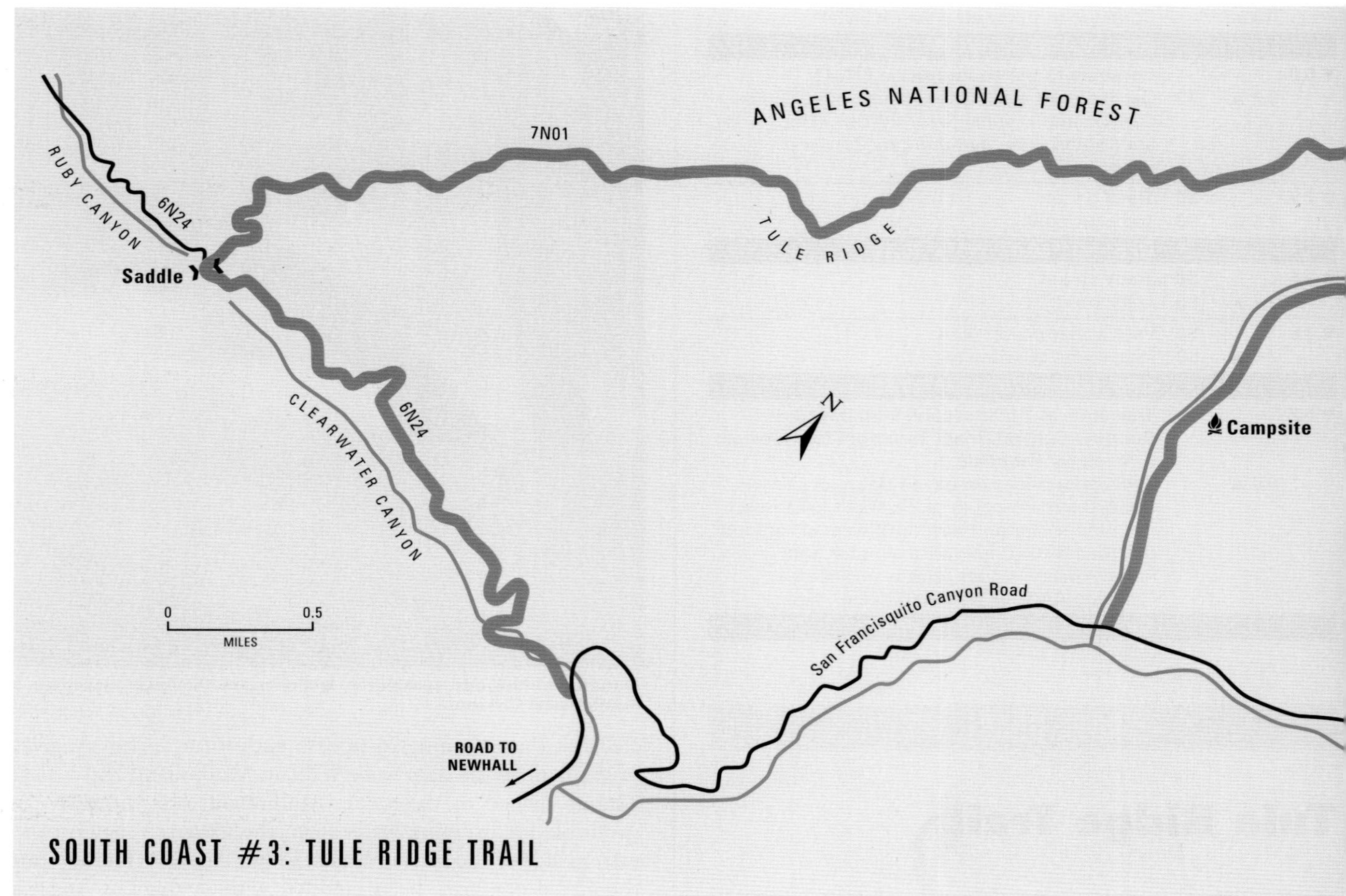

ter, immediately set aside $1 million to compensate and rehabilitate the land and its devastated people. Committees in Ventura and Los Angeles Counties organized to implement the assistance program. Some thought the leak was an act of sabotage by Owens Valley folk; others wanted Mulholland to take full blame. Not until recent years was it determined that an old, underlying landslide had weakened the dam.

Description

This trail runs up Clearwater Canyon to a saddle and travels along Tule Ridge before descending South Portal Canyon back to San Francisquito Canyon Road. Along the way, it offers a pleasant variety of canyon and ridge top scenery within Angeles National Forest.

Clearwater Canyon is narrow and the trail travels alongside the sycamore-lined creek before snaking its way up to the saddle. From the saddle, it travels along a wide shelf road, just below the top of Tule Ridge. There are views to the north into chaparral-lined South Tule Canyon. As the ridge top occasionally dips to a saddle, there are views to the south over South Portal Canyon and Grass Mountain (easily distinguished by its bald, grassy top).

For 1.1 miles, the trail intersects with South Coast #2: Grass Mountain Trail before diverging from it to travel down South Portal Canyon. There are a couple of pleasant campsites in the lower end of the canyon, near the workings of an old mine.

Trails in this region can be closed sporadically for weather or fire-related concerns. Check with the forest service if in any doubt.

Current Road Information

Angeles National Forest
Saugus Ranger District
30800 Bouquet Canyon Road
Saugus, CA 91390
(661) 296-9710

Map References

BLM Lancaster
USFS Angeles National Forest
USGS 1:24,000 Green Valley, Lake Hughes
1:100,000 Lancaster
Maptech CD-ROM: Barstow/San Bernardino County
Southern & Central California Atlas & Gazetteer, p. 78
California Road & Recreation Atlas, p. 103

Route Directions

▼ 0.0	From San Francisquito Canyon Road, 6.6 miles south of the intersection with Elizabeth Lake Road, zero trip meter and turn west on narrow graded dirt road, sign-posted Clearwater Canyon to Lake Hughes Road.

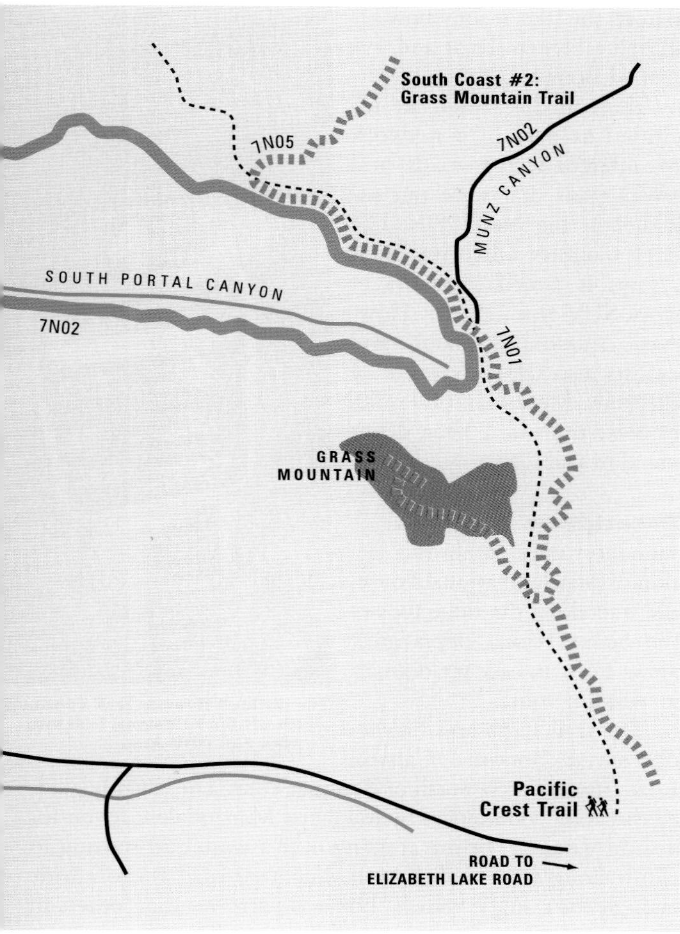

2.9 ▲ Trail ends at T-intersection with San Francisquito Canyon Road. Turn left for Elizabeth Lake Road; turn right for Newhall.

GPS: N34°35.45′ W118°27.49′

▼ 0.1 **SO** Track on right; then cross through wash.
2.8 ▲ **BR** Cross through wash; then track on left.

▼ 0.2 **SO** Cross through wash on concrete ford.
2.7 ▲ **SO** Cross through wash on concrete ford.

▼ 0.4 **SO** Cross through wash.
2.5 ▲ **SO** Cross through wash.

▼ 2.9 **TR** Saddle. Turn first right onto 7N01, which starts to climb up Tule Ridge. Second right is 6N24, which travels down Ruby Canyon. Track on left. Zero trip meter on saddle.
0.0 ▲ Continue to the northeast on 6N24.

GPS: N34°35.60′ W118°29.50′

▼ 0.0 Continue to the north on 7N01.
6.8 ▲ **TL** Saddle. Turn left onto 6N24, suitable for 4WDs, ATVs, and motorbikes—rated green. Track on right is also 6N24, which travels down Ruby Canyon. Track straight ahead. Trail starts to descend to Clearwater Canyon. Zero trip meter on saddle.

▼ 1.2 **SO** Track on right.
5.6 ▲ **BR** Track on left.

▼ 2.1 **SO** Saddle with views to the east and west. Bouquet Lake is visible on the right.
4.7 ▲ **SO** Saddle with views to the east and west. Bouquet Lake is visible on the left.

GPS: N34°36.68′ W118°28.66′

▼ 3.4 **SO** Views on right to Grass Mountain (with the bald top) and the trail ahead snaking down South Portal Canyon.
3.4 ▲ **SO** Views on left to Grass Mountain (with the bald top) and the trail behind snaking down South Portal Canyon.

GPS: N34°37.20′ W118°27.87′

▼ 6.8 **SO** Track on left is South Coast #2: Grass Mountain Trail (7N05) for 4WDs, ATVs, and motorbikes—rated green. Zero trip meter and continue on 7N01. Route now follows Grass Mountain Trail for the next 1.1 miles before diverging.
0.0 ▲ Continue to the northwest.

GPS: N34°38.78′ W118°25.91′

▼ 0.0 Continue to the east, following sign to Drinkwater Flat.
1.1 ▲ **BL** Track on right is South Coast #2: Grass Mountain Trail (7N05), which diverges at this point. Zero trip meter and bear left, remaining on 7N01. Trail starts to climb around Tule Ridge.

▼ 1.1 **BR** Closed road on left is 7N02; then trail forks. Bear right onto 7N02, suitable for 4WDs, ATVs, and motorbikes—rated green. Graded road on left is the continuation of South Coast #2: Grass Mountain Trail (7N01), which diverges at this point. Pacific Crest National Scenic Trail crosses road, and small track on left up ridge.
0.0 ▲ Continue to the west, closed road on right is 7N02.

GPS: N34°38.89′ W118°24.95′

▼ 0.0 Continue to the east.
3.7 ▲ **BL** Graded road on right is South Coast #2: Grass Mountain Trail (7N01) for 4WDs, ATVs, and motorbikes—rated green. Pacific Crest National Scenic Trail crosses road, and small track on right up ridge. Bear left on 7N02, which is also suitable for 4WDs, ATVs, and motorbikes—rated green. Route now follows Grass Mountain Trail for the next 1.1 miles before diverging. Zero trip meter.

▼ 2.1 **SO** Track on right crosses creek.
1.6 ▲ **SO** Track on left crosses creek.

GPS: N34°37.99′ W118°26.37′

▼ 2.9 **SO** Shady campsite on left.
0.8 ▲ **SO** Shady campsite on right.

▼ 3.0 **SO** Track on right over bridge is marked Back Country Discovery Trails #1A, suitable for ATVs and motorbikes only—rated blue. Remain on 7N02. Green-sticker vehicles permitted past this point.
0.7 ▲ **SO** Track on left over bridge is marked Back Country Discovery Trails #1A, suitable for ATVs and motorbikes only—rated blue. Remain on 7N02. Street legal vehicles only past this point.

GPS: N34°37.26′ W118°26.52′

▼ 3.7 Trail ends at T-intersection with San Francisquito Canyon Road. Turn right for Newhall; turn left for Lancaster.
0.0 ▲ Trail starts on paved San Francisquito Canyon Road, at mile marker 4.6, 2.9 miles south of Green Valley Ranger Station. Zero trip meter and turn northwest on graded dirt road, sign-posted to South Portal Canyon.

GPS: N34°36.70′ W118°26.21′

Sierra Pelona Trail

Starting Point:	**Bouquet Canyon Road, 7.4 miles southeast of intersection with Elizabeth Lake Road**
Finishing Point:	**Bouquet Canyon Road, 1.5 miles north of Texas Canyon USFS Ranger Station**
Total Mileage:	**14 miles**
Unpaved Mileage:	**14 miles**
Driving Time:	**1.5 hours**
Elevation Range:	**2,100–4,600 feet**
Usually Open:	**Year-round**
Best Time to Travel:	**Dry weather**
Difficulty Rating:	**2**
Scenic Rating:	**9**
Remoteness Rating:	**+0**

Special Attractions

- Trail commences near Bouquet Lake.
- Views over Bouquet Lake.
- Optional, more-difficult Rowher Trail accessible at several points.

History

Sierra pelona is Spanish for "bald mountain," an apt name for this grass-topped mountain range.

Bouquet Lake owes its name to something of a mix-up. A French sailor called Chari settled nearby and gave the name *el buque* (Spanish for "the ship") to the lake. When mapmakers named the lake, it somehow acquired a French flavor and was named Bouquet.

Bouquet Lake rests far below the trail

Trails in this region are included as part of a network of interconnected roads and 4WD trails that were put together in the mid-1980s. The Back Country Discovery Trails system is aimed primarily at stock SUV-type vehicles. However, equestrians, hikers, and cyclists also take advantage of the trails. More than 600 miles of these trails have been designated in California.

The difficult Rowher Trail continue south off Sierra Pelona Trail into Rowher Flat OHV Area

Description

Like most trails within this section of Angeles National Forest, the trail along the ridge tops of the Sierra Pelona offers great views from an easy yet dramatic, winding route.

The trail starts and finishes on paved Bouquet Canyon Road, immediately north of Bouquet Lake. The roughly graded dirt road commences by following Martindale Canyon for a short distance, before crossing over a wash and starting to climb along an easy shelf road. The shelf road is easily wide enough for a single vehicle, but it is narrower than others in the region and, at times, passing places are limited.

The more difficult Rowher Trail, a challenging run for experienced drivers only, can be accessed on many occasions as it crosses the trail described here. Less experienced drivers can follow shorter sections of the Rowher Trail without committing themselves to the entire trail. However, be warned that the entire Rowher Trail is indeed difficult and an articulate, modified vehicle is recommended. The northern end of Rowher Trail that leads off from Bouquet Lake is one of the more challenging sections, with very steep grades and rocky stretches that will test both the traction and wheel articulation of your vehicle. Excellent views over Bouquet Lake can be distracting on this steep incline.

The main Sierra Pelona Trail passes Artesian Spring and Willow Spring. The latter was once the site of a homestead. The trail continues to climb steadily to the site of the old Sierra Pelona Fire Lookout.

Once you are on top of the ridge, a dramatic spur trail leads off to the east to a viewpoint. This ridge top has many OHV trails leading off alongside it and crisscrossing the main route. The Rowher Flat OHV Area is to the south; it is the ultimate destination of the Rowher Trail. Although there are many sidetracks mentioned in the route directions, the main trail is the correct one for the most part, so navigation should not be a problem.

One of the easier sections of the Rowher Trail leads off to the site of the old fire lookout tower. The open area has a great view and a shady campsite under some large trees. Nothing remains of the tower.

From here, the trail continues along the Sierra Pelona Ridge before descending a narrow, steep shelf road back to Bouquet Canyon Road.

Trails here can be closed sporadically for weather or fire-related concerns. Check with the forest service if in any doubt.

Current Road Information

Angeles National Forest
Saugus Ranger District
30800 Bouquet Canyon Road
Saugus, CA 91390
(661) 296-9710

Map References

BLM Lancaster
USFS Angeles National Forest
USGS 1:24,000 Sleepy Valley, Green Valley
1:100,000 Lancaster
Maptech CD-ROM: Barstow/San Bernardino County
Southern & Central California Atlas & Gazetteer, p. 78
California Road & Recreation Atlas, p. 103

Route Directions

Mileage		Directions
▼ 0.0		From Bouquet Canyon Road, 6.9 miles south of intersection with Elizabeth Lake Road, zero trip meter and turn northeast on graded dirt road 6N08, suitable for 4WDs, ATVs, and motorbikes-rated green.
2.1 ▲		Trail ends on Bouquet Canyon Road. Turn right for Palmdale; turn left for Newhall.
		GPS: N34°34.80′ W118°22.07′
▼ 0.3	SO	Track on left through closure gate.
1.8 ▲	SO	Track on right through closure gate.
		GPS: N34°34.84′ W118°21.84′
▼ 0.9	SO	Cross through Martindale Canyon wash.
1.2 ▲	SO	Cross through Martindale Canyon wash.
▼ 2.1	SO	Rowher Trail crosses road, suitable for 4WDs, ATVs, and motorbikes—rated black. Zero trip meter.
0.0 ▲		Continue to the east.
		GPS: N34°34.55′ W118°21.94′
▼ 0.0		Continue to the southwest.
3.0 ▲	SO	Rowher Trail crosses road, suitable for 4WDs, ATVs, and motorbikes—rated black. Zero trip meter.
▼ 0.2	SO	Artesian Spring on right.
2.8 ▲	SO	Artesian Spring on left.
		GPS: N34°34.26′ W118°21.96′
▼ 0.6	SO	Track on right.
2.4 ▲	SO	Track on left.
▼ 0.9	SO	Rowher Trail crosses road.
2.1 ▲	SO	Rowher Trail crosses road.
		GPS: N34°34.25′ W118°21.77′
▼ 1.0	SO	Pull-in on right joins Rowher Trail.
2.0 ▲	SO	Pull-in on left joins Rowher Trail.
▼ 2.0	BL	Track on right.
1.0 ▲	SO	Track on left.
		GPS: N34°33.88′ W118°21.16′
▼ 2.6	BR	Well-used track on left. Bear right onto 6N07; then track on right up ridge.
0.4 ▲	BL	Track on left up ridge; then bear left onto 6N08. Well-used track straight ahead.
		GPS: N34°33.74′ W118°20.69′
▼ 2.8	SO	Rowher Trail crosses road.
0.2 ▲	SO	Rowher Trail crosses road.
		GPS: N34°33.65′ W118°20.79′
▼ 2.9	SO	Track on right.
0.1 ▲	SO	Track on left.
▼ 3.0	SO	Rowher Trail crosses road, marked as Back Country Discovery Trails 1A. Zero trip meter.
0.0 ▲		Continue to the northeast, remaining on 6N07.
		GPS: N34°33.68′ W118°20.93′
▼ 0.0		Continue to the west, remaining on 6N07.
0.2 ▲	SO	Rowher Trail crosses road, marked as Back Country Discovery Trails 1A. Zero trip meter.
▼ 0.2	BR	Rowher Trail enters and leaves on left. Site of the Sierra Pelona Fire Lookout is on the left (no tower remains). Zero trip meter.
0.0 ▲		Continue to the northeast on 6N07.
		GPS: N34°33.64′ W118°21.10′
▼ 0.0		Continue to the northwest on 6N07.
3.7 ▲	BL	Rowher Trail enters and leaves on right. Site of the Sierra Pelona Fire Lookout is on the right (no tower remains). Zero trip meter.
▼ 0.4	SO	Track on left and single-track trail on right.
3.3 ▲	SO	Track on right and single-track trail on left.
		GPS: N34°33.77′ W118°21.49′
▼ 0.5	SO	Rowher Trail on right.
3.2 ▲	SO	Rowher Trail on left.
		GPS: N34°33.83′ W118°21.52′
▼ 0.7	SO	Track on left.
3.0 ▲	SO	Track on right.
▼ 0.9	BR	Two tracks on left.
2.8 ▲	BL	Two tracks on right.
▼ 1.0	SO	Track on right and track on left.
2.7 ▲	SO	Track on left and track on right.
▼ 1.3	SO	Two tracks on right.
2.4 ▲	BR	Two tracks on left.
▼ 1.4	SO	Track on right and track on left.
2.3 ▲	SO	Track on right and track on left.
▼ 1.6	SO	Track on left; then track on right.
2.1 ▲	SO	Track on left; then track on right.
		GPS: N34°33.61′ W118°22.57′
▼ 1.7	BL	Two tracks on right.
2.0 ▲	BR	Two tracks on left.
▼ 2.0	SO	Track on right; then track on left.
1.7 ▲	SO	Track on right; then track on left.
▼ 2.1	SO	Track on left and track on right to small telecommunication antennas.
1.6 ▲	SO	Track on right and track on left to small telecommunication antennas.
		GPS: N34°33.37′ W118°22.92′
▼ 2.6	SO	Two tracks on right.
1.1 ▲	SO	Two tracks on left.
▼ 2.7	SO	Fall Trail crosses main route, suitable for ATVs and motorbikes only—rated black.
1.0 ▲	SO	Fall Trail crosses main route, suitable for ATVs and motorbikes only—rated black.
		GPS: N34°32.96′ W118°23.21′
▼ 3.6	SO	Track on right; then track on left.
0.1 ▲	SO	Track on right; then track on left.
▼ 3.7	BR	Small track on left; then graded road on left is 5N18 to Rowher Flat, suitable for 4WDs, ATVs, and motorbikes—rated green. Zero trip meter.
0.0 ▲		Continue to the north on 6N07 past small track on right.

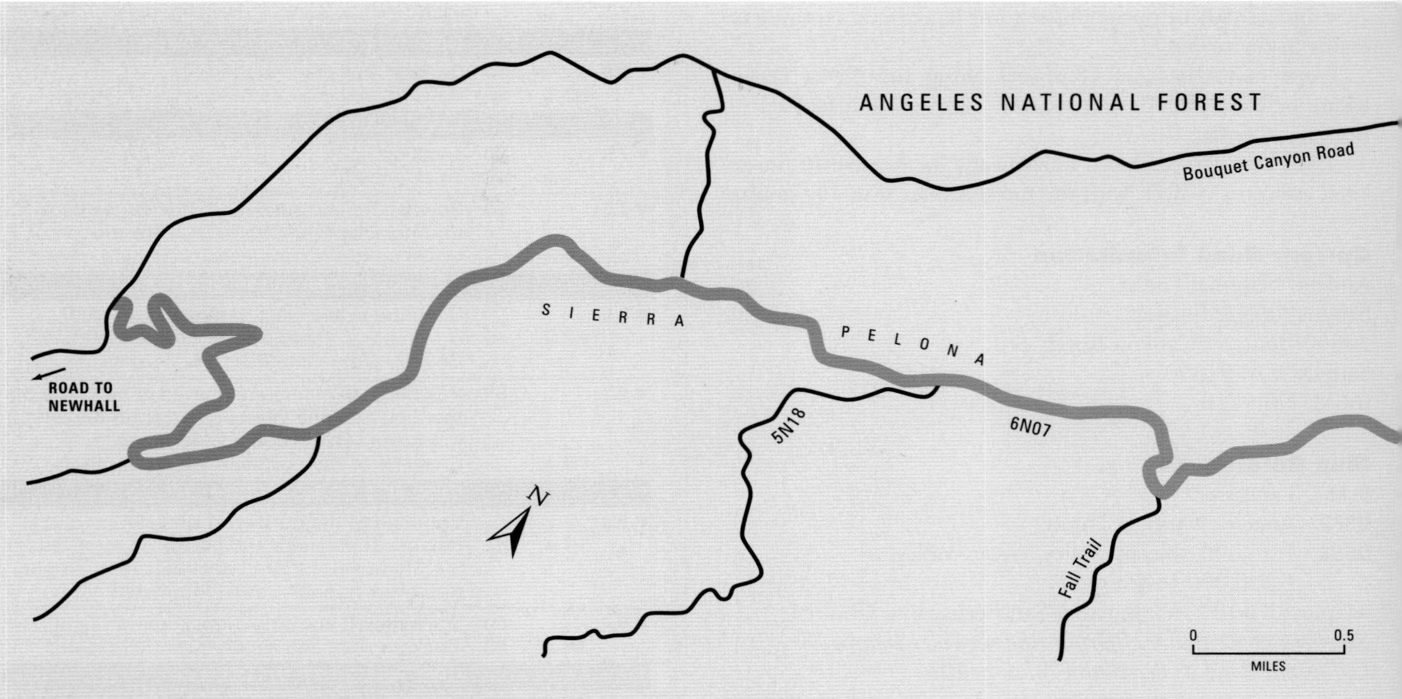

ANGELES NATIONAL FOREST

Bouquet Canyon Road

ROAD TO NEWHALL

SIERRA PELONA

5N18

6N07

Fall Trail

N

0 0.5 MILES

SOUTH COAST #4: SIERRA PELONA TRAIL

Mileage		Direction	Description
			GPS: N34°32.88′ W118°24.04′
▼ 0.0			Continue to the south on 6N07, following sign to Drinkwater Flat.
	5.0 ▲	BL	Graded road on right is 5N18 to Rowher Flat, suitable for 4WDs, ATVs, and motorbikes—rated green. Zero trip meter.
▼ 0.1		BL	Track on right.
	4.9 ▲	SO	Track on left.
▼ 0.3		SO	Track on right; then track on left.
	4.7 ▲	SO	Track on right; then track on left.
▼ 0.5		BR	Two tracks on left.
	4.5 ▲	BL	Two tracks on right.
			GPS: N34°32.70′ W118°24.47′
▼ 0.7		SO	Track on left. Track on right is Bouquet Trail to Drinkwater Flat, suitable for ATVs and motorbikes only—rated blue. Continue on 6N07.
	4.3 ▲	SO	Track on right. Track on left is Bouquet Trail to Drinkwater Flat, suitable for ATVs and motorbikes only—rated blue. Continue straight on 6N07.
			GPS: N34°32.70′ W118°24.70′
▼ 1.0		SO	Track on right.
	4.0 ▲	SO	Track on left.
▼ 1.2		BL	Two tracks on right.
	3.8 ▲	BR	Two tracks on left.
▼ 1.4		SO	Track on right.
	3.6 ▲	SO	Track on left.
▼ 1.7		SO	Track on left.
	3.3 ▲	BL	Track on right.
			GPS: N34°32.32′ W118°25.52′
▼ 2.0		SO	Track on right.
	3.0 ▲	SO	Track on left.
▼ 2.1		SO	Two tracks on right.
	2.9 ▲	SO	Two tracks on left.
▼ 2.3		SO	Track on right.
	2.7 ▲	SO	Track on left.
▼ 2.4		SO	Track on left.
	2.6 ▲	SO	Track on right.
▼ 2.6		SO	Two tracks on left.
	2.4 ▲	SO	Two tracks on right.
▼ 3.2		BR	Track on left at switchback goes to viewpoint.
	1.8 ▲	BL	Track on right at switchback goes to viewpoint.
			GPS: N34°31.24′ W118°26.10′
▼ 3.7		SO	Two tracks on right to pull-in.
	1.3 ▲	SO	Two tracks on left to pull-in.
▼ 5.0			Trail ends at intersection with paved Bouquet

The alternative Rowher Trail travels up steep, rocky, and rutted slopes

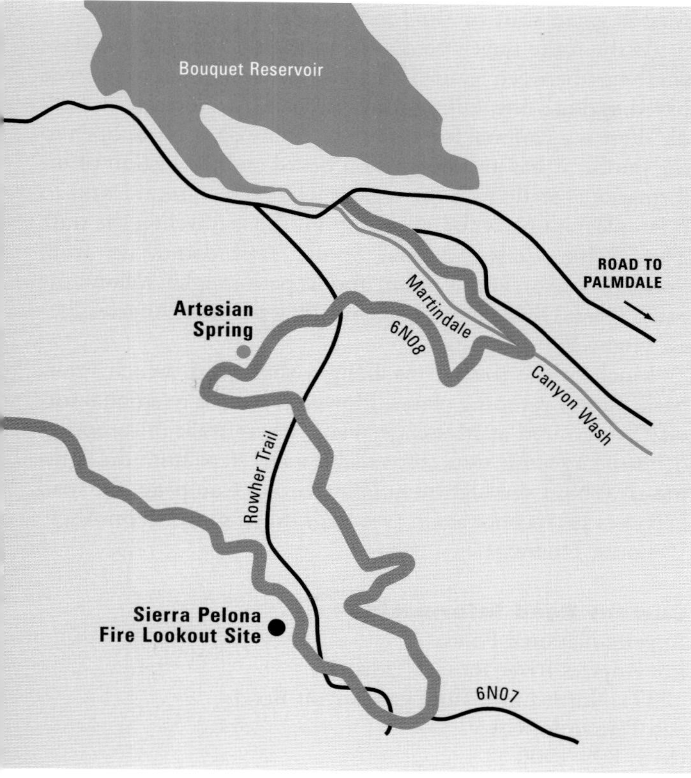

Canyon Road. Turn left for Newhall; turn right for Bouquet Lake and Palmdale.

0.0 ▲ Trail commences on Bouquet Canyon Road, 1.5 miles north of Texas Canyon Ranger Station. Zero trip meter and turn southeast on graded dirt road 6N07, suitable for 4WDs, ATVs, and motorbikes—rated green. Discovery point marker at intersection.

GPS: N34°31.64' W118°26.50'

SOUTH COAST #5

Santa Clara Divide Road

Starting Point:	**Sand Canyon Road, 6 miles south of California 14**
Finishing Point:	**Angeles Forest Highway, 10 miles south of California 14**
Total Mileage:	**30.5 miles**
Unpaved Mileage:	**15.5 miles**
Driving Time:	**2.5 hours**
Elevation Range:	**2,600–6,400 feet**
Usually Open:	**Year-round**
Best Time to Travel:	**Year-round**
Difficulty Rating:	**1**
Scenic Rating:	**9**
Remoteness Rating:	**+0**

Santa Clara Divide Road descends from Mount Snow with Soledad Canyon in the distance

Special Attractions

- Long ridge top trail within the San Gabriel Mountains suitable for passenger vehicles in dry weather.
- Intersects with other trails that lead down from the ridge.

History

Near the start of this trail, on top of Magic Mountain, is the site of a Nike ground-based supersonic anti-aircraft missile system that was installed during the Cold War. The missiles were deployed in a circular pattern around key industrial and military locations in the United States. In 1958, the Magic Mountain site was one of sixteen sites that protected an area of some 4,000 square miles around greater Los Angeles. The sites were equipped with two or three launching platforms, each with underground storage magazines, elevators, and four missile erectors. Each missile was enclosed in a self-contained launch area and stored underground. The missiles were brought to the surface via elevator and, once there, raised to an 85-degree angle for launch. They were guided by a ground-based system. The battery on Magic Mountain was closed in 1963, but the administration area was used until the early 1970s. On February 4, 1974, the military ordered all existing Nike batteries to be deactivated. The presence of the Nike battery on Magic Mountain is the reason for the paved road along the western section of the trail. There is no public vehicle access to the top of the mountain.

The Santa Clara Divide takes its name from the Santa Clara River, which it feeds to the north and east. The Gaspar de Portolá expedition of 1769 named the waterway while taking a rest day at the river on August 9, the Remembrance Day for Saint Clare of Assisi.

Stranded forty-niners who escaped death in Death Valley and the Mojave Desert passed to the north of this trail, down Soledad Canyon, to the waters of the Santa Clara River.

The sky above the Santa Clara Divide is a busy flight path that has seen more than its share of plane crashes. A B-13 aircraft crashed on Christmas Eve near Mount Gleason while

Manzanitas, granitic rock formations, and weathered pines typify the eastern end of this scenic trail

searching for a B-24 that had crashed two days earlier. In early 1951, a CAP Cessna 140 crashed while surveying the scene of the two earlier crashes.

At North Fork Campground is a well-used vehicle trail that heads off to the north under the power lines. This track crosses Mill Canyon, which was the scene of an airplane crash back in July 1960. A B-25 crashed while fighting fires in the lower reaches of Mill Canyon. All three crew members were killed and their bodies burned almost beyond recognition.

Several streams and creek beds in the region are habitat for the endangered arroyo toad. The small amphibian, found in Southern California and northwestern Baja California, depends on clear water and undisturbed stream banks to survive. Although it was once common to Central and Southern California, today it has lost more than 75 percent of its habitat. The OHV area at Little Rock is currently closed to protect the arroyo toad.

Description

Santa Clara Divide Road begins east of Santa Clarita on paved Sand Canyon Road. Initially, the road climbs along a single-lane, paved road toward Magic Mountain. There is no longer vehicle access to the top of the mountain; the road is gated shut by the forest service.

As the route travels across the top of the ridge, the surface alternates between graded dirt and sections that were once paved and are now falling into disrepair. At North Fork Saddle there is a national forest station. Although it is not open to the public, it has an information board and a selection of informational leaflets on the region. The picnic ground next to it is a pleasant place for a rest stop for those traveling the trail. The Pacific Crest National Scenic Trail comes up from Soledad Canyon at this point, and its path roughly follows the Santa Clara Divide Road to its finishing point on Angeles Forest Highway.

Much of the route runs along a shelf road, which limits backcountry camping places. However, there is a national forest campground at Messenger Flats, where walk-in campsites beneath large pine trees are available a few steps from the parking area. Near the Lightning Point Group Campsite, the road becomes paved once again as it leads down to finish on Angeles Forest Highway.

Current Road Information

Angeles National Forest
Los Angeles River Ranger District
12371 North Little Tujunga Canyon Road
San Fernando, CA 91342
(818) 899-1900

Map References

BLM Los Angeles
USFS Angeles National Forest
USGS 1:24,000 San Fernando, Sunland, Agua Dulce, Acton, Pacifico Mt., Condor Peak
1:100,000 Los Angeles
Maptech CD-ROM: Ventura/Los Angeles/Orange County
Southern & Central California Atlas & Gazetteer, pp. 92, 93
California Road & Recreation Atlas, p. 103

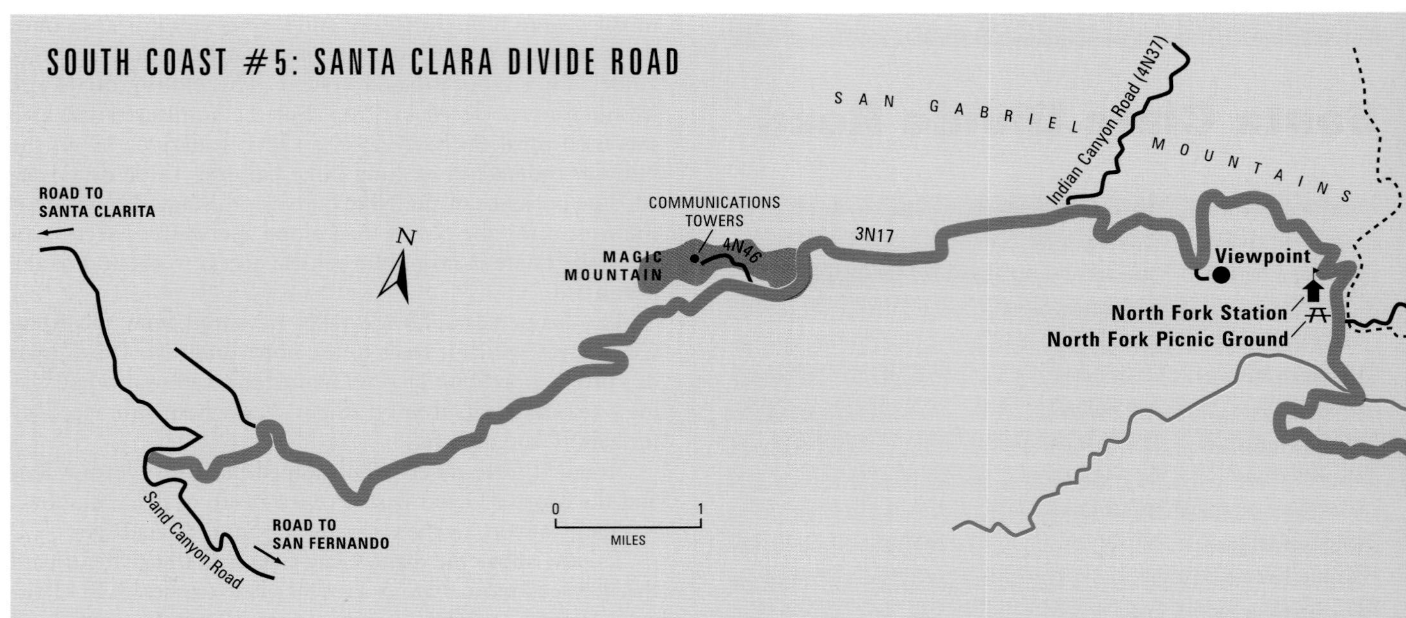

Route Directions

▼ 0.0		From Sand Canyon Road, 6 miles south of California 14, zero trip meter and turn southeast on paved Santa Clara Divide Road (3N17). There is a sign for Messenger Flats and Angeles Forest Highway after the turn.
6.2 ▲		Trail ends on Sand Canyon Road. Turn left for San Fernando; turn right for Santa Clarita.
		GPS: N34°21.65' W118°23.48'
▼ 1.2	SO	Track on left.
5.0 ▲	SO	Track on right.
▼ 4.7	SO	Pull-in on right.
1.5 ▲	SO	Pull-in on left.
▼ 6.2	BR	Bear right onto graded dirt road. Paved road through closure gate on left is 4N46 to telecommunications towers on Magic Mountain. This road is closed. Zero trip meter.
0.0 ▲		Continue to the west.
		GPS: N34°23.07' W118°19.30'
▼ 0.0		Continue to the east.
2.8 ▲	SO	Paved road through closure gate on right is 4N46 to telecommunications towers on Magic Mountain. This road is closed. Continue straight ahead and join paved road. Zero trip meter.
▼ 0.3	SO	Track on right.
2.5 ▲	SO	Track on left.
▼ 1.7	SO	Track on right.
1.1 ▲	SO	Track on left.
▼ 2.8	SO	Graded road on left is Indian Canyon Road (4N37) for 4WDs, ATVs, and motorbikes—rated green. Zero trip meter.
0.0 ▲		Continue to the southwest on 3N17, following sign to Sand Canyon Road.
		GPS: N34°23.75' W118°17.12'
▼ 0.0		Continue to the northeast on 3N17, following sign to Mount Gleason.
4.3 ▲	SO	Graded road on right is Indian Canyon Road (4N37) for 4WDs, ATVs, and motorbikes—rated green. Zero trip meter.
▼ 1.4	BL	Track on right to viewpoint.
2.9 ▲	BR	Track on left to viewpoint.
		GPS: N34°23.51' W118°16.11'
▼ 4.2	SO	North Fork USFS Station on right; then North Fork Picnic Ground on right. Pacific Crest National Scenic Trail on left.
0.1 ▲	SO	Pacific Crest National Scenic Trail on right. North Fork Picnic Ground on left; then North Fork USFS Station on left.
		GPS: N34°23.28' W118°15.11'
▼ 4.3	BR	Track on left is B.P.L. Road (4N32), which goes to Aliso Canyon Road for 4WDs, ATVs, and motorbikes—rated green. Zero trip meter.
0.0		Continue to the northwest on 3N17.
		GPS: N34°23.24' W118°15.06'
▼ 0.0		Continue to the southeast on 3N17, following sign to Angeles Forest Highway.
5.7 ▲	BL	Track on right is B.P.L. Road (4N32), which goes to Aliso Canyon Road for 4WDs, ATVs, and motorbikes—rated green. Zero trip meter.
▼ 0.7	SO	Cross through wash.
5.0 ▲	SO	Cross through wash.
▼ 1.4	SO	Pull-in on right.
4.3 ▲	SO	Pull-in on left.
		GPS: N34°22.65' W118°15.39'
▼ 3.5	SO	Track on left.
2.2 ▲	SO	Track on right.
		GPS: N34°22.73' W118°13.79'
▼ 4.5	SO	Pacific Crest National Scenic Trail on left.
1.2 ▲	SO	Pacific Crest National Scenic Trail on right.
		GPS: N34°22.75' W118°13.18'
▼ 5.7	SO	Graded road on left is Moody Canyon Road (4N33) for 4WDs, ATVs, and motorbikes—rated green. Zero trip meter.
0.0 ▲		Continue to the west on 3N17.
		GPS: N34°22.62' W118°12.35'
▼ 0.0		Continue to the southeast on 3N17.
2.3 ▲	SO	Graded road on right is Moody Canyon Road (4N33) for 4WDs, ATVs, and motorbikes—rated green. Zero trip meter.

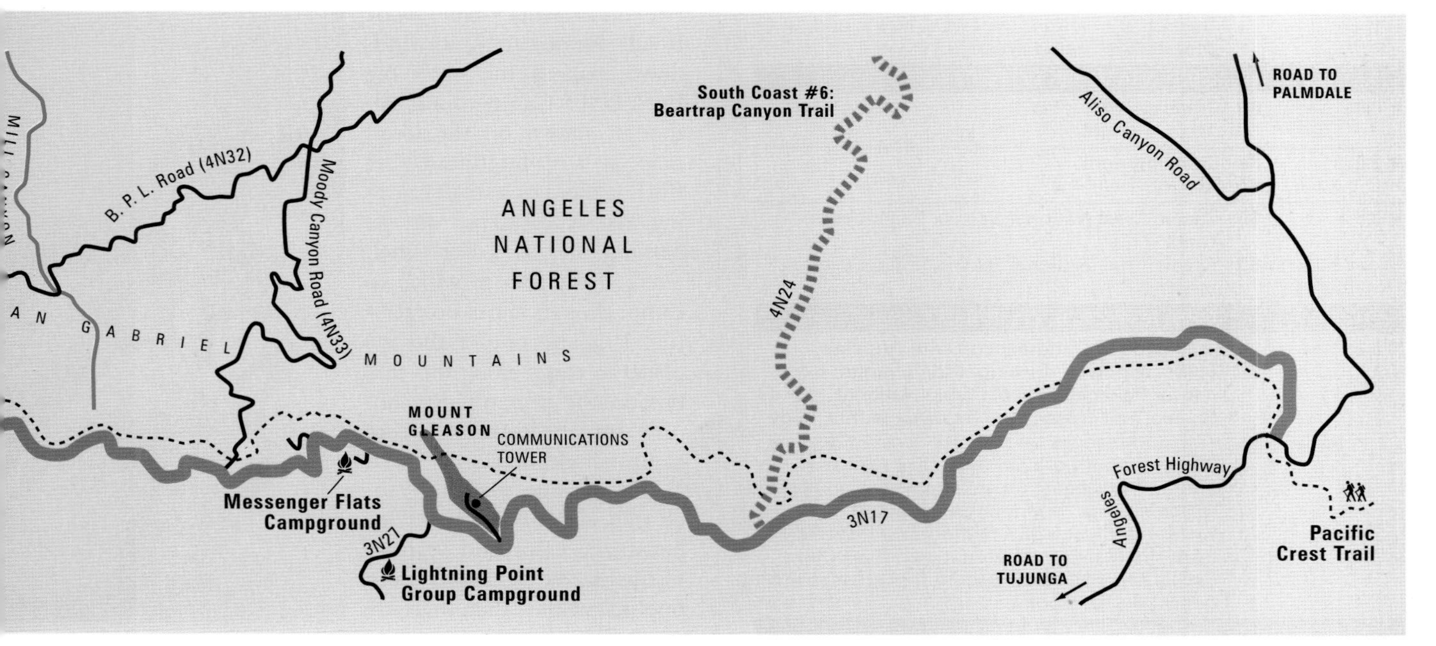

▼ 1.0		SO	Track on left is 3N17N.
	1.3 ▲	SO	Track on right is 3N17N.
			GPS: N34°22.87' W118°11.69'
▼ 1.4		BL	Track on right goes into Messenger Flats USFS Campground. Pacific Crest National Scenic Trail on left.
	0.9 ▲	SO	Track on left goes into Messenger Flats USFS Campground. Pacific Crest National Scenic Trail on right.
			GPS: N34°22.87' W118°11.37'
▼ 2.3		TL	Paved road on right is 3N27 to Lightning Point Group Campground. Turn left onto paved road. Zero trip meter.
	0.0 ▲		Continue to the north on 3N17.
			GPS: N34°22.47' W118°10.80'
▼ 0.0			Continue to the east.
	3.0 ▲	TR	Paved road on left is 3N27 to Lightning Point Group Campground. Turn right onto graded dirt road, following sign to Sand Canyon Road. Zero trip meter.
▼ 0.5		SO	Closed road on left; then communications tower on right.
	2.5 ▲	SO	Communications tower on left; then closed road on right. Follow sign to Messenger Flats Campground.
▼ 2.6		SO	Road turns to graded dirt.
	0.4 ▲	SO	Road is now paved.
▼ 3.0		SO	Join paved road and continue straight. Paved road on left goes to state prison camp. Zero trip meter.
	0.0 ▲		Continue to the west.
			GPS: N34°22.55' W118°08.87'
▼ 0.0			Continue to the east.
	6.2 ▲	BL	Bear left onto graded dirt road, following sign to North Fork Saddle Station. Paved road on right goes to state prison camp. Zero trip meter.
▼ 0.5		SO	Track on left.
	5.7 ▲	SO	Track on right.
			GPS: N34°22.52' W118°08.46'
▼ 0.6		SO	Track on left is South Coast #6: Beartrap Canyon Trail (4N24) for 4WDs, ATVs, and motorbikes—rated green.
	5.6 ▲	SO	Track on right is South Coast #6: Beartrap Canyon Trail (4N24) for 4WDs, ATVs, and motorbikes—rated green.
			GPS: N34°22.58' W118°08.41'
▼ 0.9		SO	Track on left.
	5.3 ▲	SO	Track on right.
▼ 2.0		SO	Track on right.
	4.2 ▲	SO	Track on left.
▼ 3.6		SO	Pacific Crest National Scenic Trail crosses road.
	2.6 ▲	SO	Pacific Crest National Scenic Trail crosses road.
			GPS: N34°23.76' W118°06.37'
▼ 6.2			Trail ends at T-intersection with Angeles Forest Highway. Turn right for Tujunga; turn left for Palmdale. Pacific Crest National Scenic Trail crosses the highway at this point.
	0.0 ▲		Trail commences on Angeles Forest Highway, 10 miles south of California 14. Zero trip meter and turn northeast on small paved road 3N17, following sign to Mount Gleason and Messenger Flat USFS Campground. Turn is opposite Mill Creek Summit Picnic Ground. Pacific Crest National Scenic Trail crosses the highway at this point.
			GPS: N34°23.52' W118°04.82'

SOUTH COAST #6

Beartrap Canyon Trail

Starting Point:	**South Coast #5: Santa Clara Divide Road, 5.6 miles west of intersection with Angeles Forest Highway**
Finishing Point:	**Aliso Canyon Road, 2.6 miles south of the intersection with Soledad Canyon Road**
Total Mileage:	**9.2 miles**
Unpaved Mileage:	**9.2 miles**
Driving Time:	**1 hour**
Elevation Range:	**3,100–5,700 feet**
Usually Open:	**Year-round**
Best Time to Travel:	**Year-round**
Difficulty Rating:	**2**
Scenic Rating:	**8**
Remoteness Rating:	**+0**

Special Attractions

- Alternative entry/exit point to South Coast #5: Santa Clara Divide Road.
- Popular with hunters and bird-watchers.

Description

This trail can be used as an alternative entry/exit point to the long South Coast #5: Santa Clara Divide Road, which runs along the ridge tops of the San Gabriel Mountains. Taking this trail as an alternative to the eastern end of Santa Clara Divide Road avoids nearly 6 miles of paved road and takes you north into Aliso Canyon.

The trail leaves from the ridge top, 5.6 miles from the eastern end of Santa Clara Divide Road. Immediately, it winds down, passing the small Big Buck USFS Campground. Although shown on the forest map as a campground, Big Buck is more of a small camping area. A few steps from the parking area is a very sheltered, shady area in which to camp, though it has no facilities. It is also one of the few places to camp along this trail because the ridge top does not offer much in the way of campsite selection.

View over Beartrap Canyon

The narrow, roughly graded trail winds down the ridge between Gleason and Beartrap Canyons. As it crosses from one side to the other, there are views down into both.

At approximately the halfway mark, a spur trail leads along a very narrow ridge for a short distance. Although this trail is there primarily to give access to power lines, it leads to an excellent viewpoint as well.

The trail ends in Aliso Canyon. The shortest way out, as shown on the national forest map, is closed off to public use. Instead, the trail follows alongside the power lines for a short distance before joining the paved road at the forest boundary.

The trail is normally open year-round, but may be closed for short periods because of heavy rain or snow.

Current Road Information

Angeles National Forest
Los Angeles River Ranger District
12371 North Little Tujunga Canyon Road
San Fernando, CA 91342
(818) 899-1900

Map References

BLM Los Angeles
USFS Angeles National Forest
USGS 1:24,000 Acton
1:100,000 Los Angeles
Maptech CD-ROM: Ventura/Los Angeles/Orange County
Southern & Central California Atlas & Gazetteer, p. 93
California Road & Recreation Atlas, p. 103

Route Directions

▼ 0.0		From South Coast #5: Santa Clara Divide Road, 5.6 miles west of the intersection with Angeles Forest Highway, zero trip meter and turn north onto graded dirt road 4N24. Road is suitable for 4WDs, ATVs, and motorbikes—rated green.
3.4 ▲		Trail ends on South Coast #5: Santa Clara Divide Road. Turn left to exit to Angeles Forest Highway; turn right to continue along Santa Clara Divide Road.
		GPS: N34°22.58′ W118°08.41′
▼ 0.2	BR	Track on left.
3.2 ▲	BL	Track on right.

Twisting down the chaparral-covered ridge to Beartrap Canyon

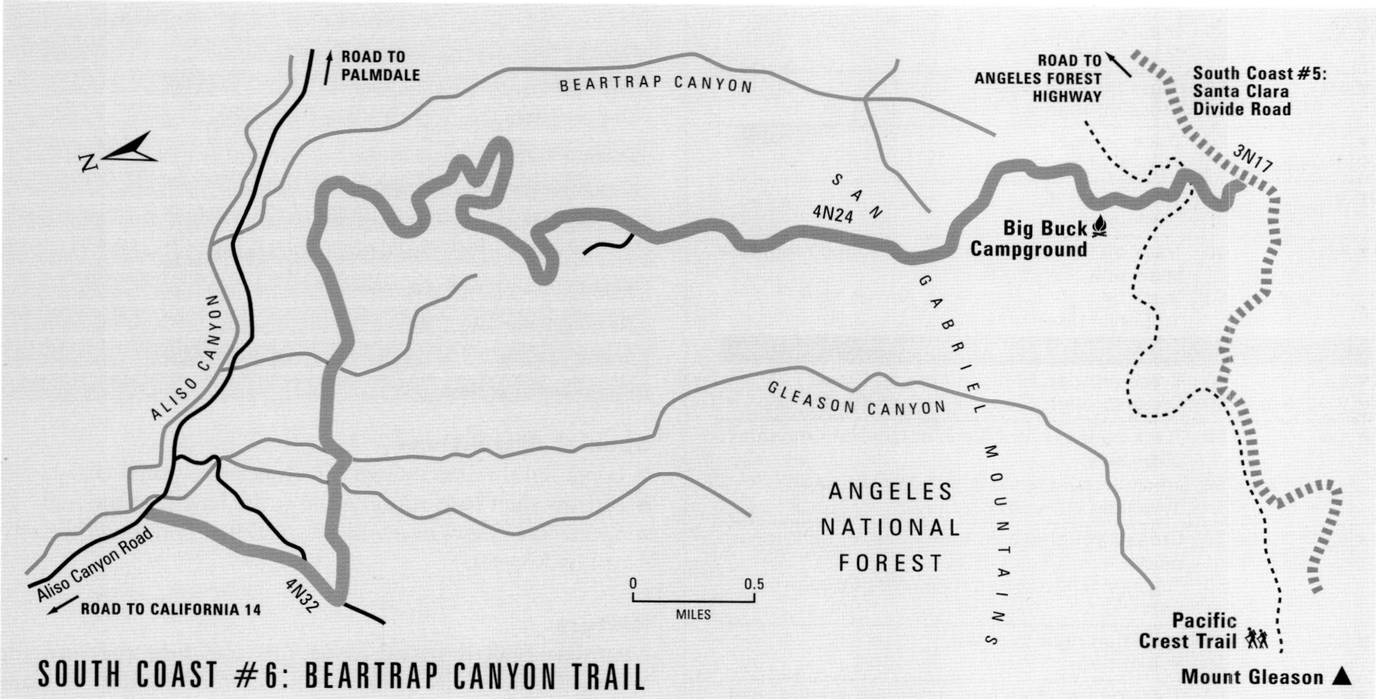

ROAD TO PALMDALE
BEARTRAP CANYON
ROAD TO ANGELES FOREST HIGHWAY
South Coast #5: Santa Clara Divide Road
3N17
4N24
SAN GABRIEL MOUNTAINS
Big Buck Campground
ALISO CANYON
GLEASON CANYON
ANGELES NATIONAL FOREST
Aliso Canyon Road
ROAD TO CALIFORNIA 14
4N32
0 0.5 MILES
Pacific Crest Trail
Mount Gleason

SOUTH COAST #6: BEARTRAP CANYON TRAIL

▼ 0.4		TL	Track ahead through gate; swing around to the left. Pacific Crest National Scenic Trail crosses road.
	3.0 ▲	TR	Track on left through gate; swing around to the right. Pacific Crest National Scenic Trail crosses road.
			GPS: N34°22.81' W118°08.33'
▼ 1.0		BR	Big Buck USFS Campground on left.
	2.4 ▲	BL	Big Buck USFS Campground on right.
			GPS: N34°23.12' W118°08.40'
▼ 1.9		SO	Track on left.
	1.5 ▲	SO	Track on right.
▼ 2.0		SO	Track on left.
	1.4 ▲	SO	Track on right.
▼ 2.4		SO	Track on left.
	1.0 ▲	SO	Track on right.
▼ 3.4		BR	Trail forks. Keep to the right, heading downhill. Track on left climbs ridge and travels 0.4 miles to a viewpoint. Zero trip meter.
	0.0 ▲		Continue to the southwest, crossing the saddle to travel around Beartrap Canyon.
			GPS: N34°24.72' W118°08.15'
▼ 0.0			Continue to the northeast.
	5.0 ▲	SO	Track on sharp right climbs ridge and travels 0.4 miles to a viewpoint. Zero trip meter.
▼ 1.0		SO	Track on left.
	4.0 ▲	SO	Track on right.
▼ 2.4		SO	Track on left.
	2.6 ▲	SO	Track on right.
			GPS: N34°25.56' W118°07.98'
▼ 3.0		SO	Cross through wash.
	2.0 ▲	SO	Cross through wash.
▼ 3.4		BL	Track on right.
	1.6 ▲	SO	Track on left.
▼ 3.5		SO	Track on right.
	1.5 ▲	BR	Track on left.
▼ 3.6		SO	Track on right.
	1.4 ▲	SO	Track on left.
▼ 3.7		SO	Track on right.
	1.3 ▲	SO	Track on left.
▼ 4.0		SO	Cross through wash.
	1.0 ▲	SO	Cross through wash.
▼ 4.1		SO	Track on right.
	0.9 ▲	SO	Track on left.
▼ 4.2		SO	Track on right.
	0.8 ▲	SO	Track on left.
▼ 4.4		SO	Track on left is for hikers, horses, and mountain bikes only.
	0.6 ▲	SO	Track on right is for hikers, horses, and mountain bikes only.
			GPS: N34°25.94' W118°08.87'
▼ 4.5		SO	Cross through Gleason Canyon Creek.
	0.5 ▲	SO	Cross through Gleason Canyon Creek.
▼ 4.6		SO	Track on left is for hikers, horses, and mountain bikes only.
	0.4 ▲	SO	Track on right is for hikers, horses, and mountain bikes only.
▼ 4.7		SO	Cross through wash; then track on right to pylon.
	0.3 ▲	SO	Track on left to pylon; then cross through wash.
▼ 4.8		SO	Pull-in on right to pylon.
	0.2 ▲	SO	Pull-in on left to pylon.
▼ 5.0		TR	Track on left; then turn right onto graded road 4N32. Road is suitable for 4WDs, ATVs, and motorbikes—rated green. Zero trip meter. Track straight ahead.
	0.0 ▲		Continue to the southeast.
			GPS: N34°26.05' W118°09.45'
▼ 0.0			Continue to the northeast.
	0.8 ▲	TL	Track on right; then turn left onto formed trail marked 4N24. Immediately track on right. Zero trip meter.
▼ 0.1		BL	Track on right.
	0.7 ▲	BR	Track on left.
▼ 0.3		SO	Track on right.
	0.5 ▲	SO	Track on left.
▼ 0.8			Trail ends at T-intersection with paved Aliso Canyon Road. Turn right for Palmdale; turn left for California 14.
	0.0 ▲		Trail commences on paved Aliso Canyon Road, 2.6 miles south of the intersection with Soledad Canyon Road. Zero trip meter and turn southwest onto unmarked graded dirt road. Turn is just south of the Angeles National Forest sign and is south of the marked turn for 4N23.
			GPS: N34°26.66' W118°09.01'

SOUTH COAST #7

Rincon-Shortcut OHV Route

Starting Point:	**San Gabriel Canyon Road (California 39), 0.2 miles north of the San Gabriel OHV Staging Area**
Finishing Point:	**California 2, 0.6 miles north of the intersection of Upper Big Tujunga Canyon Road**
Total Mileage:	**25.2 miles**
Unpaved Mileage:	**25.2 miles**
Driving Time:	**3 hours**
Elevation Range:	**1,600–4,900 feet**
Usually Open:	**Year-round; may be closed from time to time for safety reasons**
Best Time to Travel:	**Year-round**
Difficulty Rating:	**2**
Scenic Rating:	**10**
Remoteness Rating:	**+0**

Special Attractions

- Long, lightly used trail within Angeles National Forest.
- Narrow shelf road running the entire length of the trail.
- Spectacular views over Angeles National Forest and the city of Los Angeles.

History

Monrovia Peak is passed along this trail near the turn for Spring Camp. This peak's name commemorates William Monroe, a railroad engineer who, along with his associates, laid out the town of Monrovia near the southern base of this peak in 1886. Rankin Peak, just to the south of Spring Camp, was named after Edward Rankin, a Monrovia resident who frequented these mountains. The old truck trail east of these two peaks that winds down into Sawpit Canyon is called the Upper Clamshell Truck Trail. The Sawpit-Clamshell Fault is where the 1991 Sierra Madre earthquake was centered. Sawpit Canyon got its name because it was the location of a loggers' sawpit. One operator of the large crosscut saw would be positioned in the pit while the other was above. Together they provided the up and down thrust for the sawing action. Sawpit Canyon is attributed with being one of the major sources of the stones and timbers used in the construction of Mission San Gabriel Arcángel.

This region was popular with hunters from the developing settlement of Monrovia. Among them was Ben Overtuff, who built a wooden lodge close to Deer Park in 1905 and a stone lodge in 1911. Stone Cabin Flat is located southeast of Monrovia Peak.

Description

The Rincon-Shortcut OHV Route takes the traveler from the San Gabriel Canyon OHV Area along the crest of the San Gabriel Mountains in Angeles National Forest. All motorized-vehicle drivers need a USFS permit in order to travel the trail. The trail is popular with mountain bikers, who normally prefer to travel it in the reverse direction, as it is slightly more downhill. Camping is permitted along the trail, but suitable places are limited because of the shelf road. There is one campground along the trail with a few tables, fire rings, and a vault toilet. It is a mile hike from the main trail.

From the start, the trail climbs steadily around the edge of Rincon Canyon along a single-lane shelf road with sufficient passing places. It winds its way up the mountain as a roughly graded, easygoing shelf road. The trail is lined with holly oak and trumpet bush on the rocky walls. It travels over Pine Mountain and around the side of Monrovia Peak to descend toward the West Fork of the San Gabriel River. There is a concrete ford over the tree lined river. The trail starts to climb, once again following a shelf road to end on California 2.

The Rincon-Shortcut OHV Route climbs and twists its way out of San Gabriel Canyon

Permit Information

A permit to travel the Rincon-Shortcut OHV Route is essential. The free permits are valid for two weeks from the date of issue and include the necessary numbers for combination locks on the gates at either end of the trail. The combination numbers are changed on the first day of every month; if your permit spans the first of the month you will be issued both numbers. Permits are obtained on a walk-in basis from any of the following locations. A valid driver's license and vehicle details are required. A National Forest Adventure Pass is required if you plan to stop or camp along the trail but not if you are simply driving through.

Cogswell Reservoir is set far below the Rincon-Shortcut OHV Route in Angeles National Forest

San Gabriel River National Forest Office
110 North Wabash Avenue
Glendora, CA 91741
(626) 335-1251

Hours are 8 A.M. to 4:30 P.M. Monday to Friday; the office is closed on weekends and holidays.

The entrance station to the San Gabriel Recreation Area, at the mouth of San Gabriel Canyon, can issue the permits. Hours are 9 A.M. to 3:30 P.M. weekdays, 8 A.M. to 4 P.M. weekends and holidays.

The San Gabriel Canyon OHV Staging Area at the start of the trail can also issue permits but hours are limited to weekends only.

These hours are subject to change without notice and drivers are advised to contact the San Gabriel River Ranger District ahead of time to verify operating hours of their chosen location.

Current Road Information

Angeles National Forest
San Gabriel River Ranger District
110 North Wabash Avenue
Glendora, CA 91741
(626) 335-1251

Angeles National Forest
Los Angeles River Ranger District
12371 North Little Tuyunga Canyon Road
San Fernando, CA 91342
(818) 899-1900

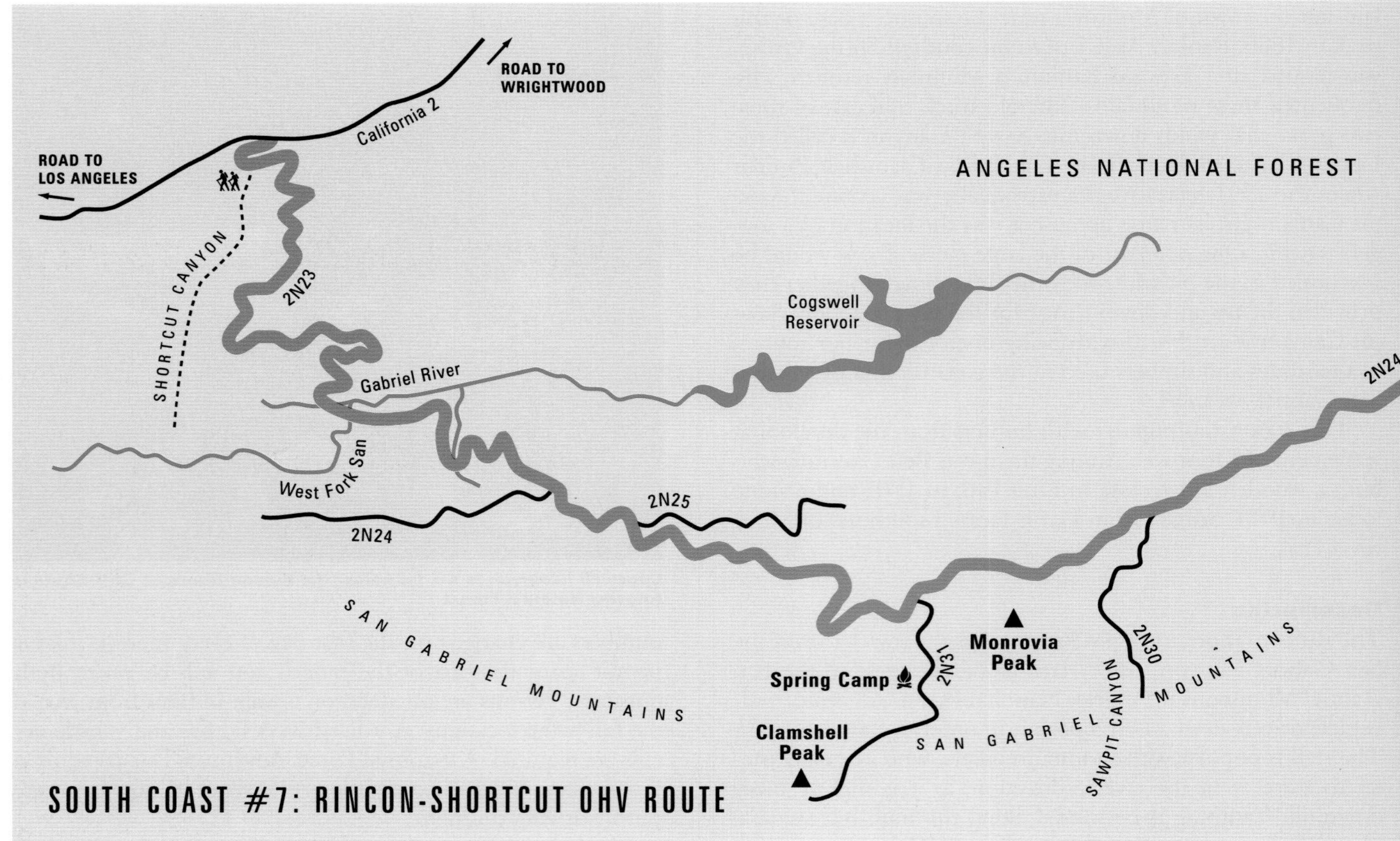

Map References

BLM San Bernardino, Los Angeles
USFS Angeles National Forest
USGS 1:24,000 Glendora, Azusa, Mt. Wilson, Chilao Flat
1:100,000 San Bernardino, Los Angeles
Maptech CD-ROM: Ventura/Los Angeles/Orange County
Southern & Central California Atlas & Gazetteer, pp. 94, 93
California Road & Recreation Atlas, p. 103

Route Directions

▼ 0.0			From San Gabriel Canyon Road (California 39), 11 miles from the entrance station at the mouth of the canyon and 0.2 miles north of the San Gabriel OHV Staging Area, zero trip meter and turn south onto graded dirt road 2N24 and immediately pass through gate. A valid permit is required past this point. Start of shelf road.
	7.7 ▲		Gate (combination number required); then trail ends at T-intersection with San Gabriel Canyon Road (California 39). Turn right for Los Angeles; turn left for Wrightwood.
			GPS: N34°14.28' W117°51.75'
▼ 3.7		SO	Turnout on right.
	4.0 ▲	SO	Turnout on left.
▼ 7.7		BL	Track on right is 2N2A, which goes a short distance to the radio towers on Pine Mountain. Zero trip meter.
	0.0 ▲		Continue to the south.
			GPS: N34°13.58' W117°54.50'
▼ 0.0			Continue to the northwest.
	4.8 ▲	BR	Track on left is 2N2A, which goes a short distance to the radio towers on Pine Mountain. Zero trip meter.
▼ 2.8		TR	Track on left is 2N30, closed to motor vehicles.
	2.0 ▲	TL	Track on right is 2N30, closed to motor vehicles.
			GPS: N34°13.17' W117°57.01'
▼ 3.5		SO	Trail follows alongside power lines. Trail stops climbing and starts to descend.
	1.3 ▲	SO	Trail leaves power lines. Trail stops climbing and starts to descend.
▼ 4.4		SO	Power line maintenance track on right.
	0.4 ▲	SO	Power line maintenance track on left.
▼ 4.8		SO	Track on left is 2N31, closed to vehicles. Spring USFS Camp is a mile down this road. Zero trip meter.
	0.0 ▲		Continue to the northeast.
			GPS: N34°13.02' W117°58.67'
▼ 0.0			Continue to the southwest.
	4.1 ▲	SO	Track on right is 2N31, closed to vehicles. Spring USFS Camp is a mile down this road. Zero trip meter.
▼ 0.3		TR	Track on left to viewpoint and campsite.
	3.8 ▲	TL	Track on right to viewpoint and campsite.
			GPS: N34°12.92' W117°58.88'
▼ 0.9		TR	Track on left.
	3.2 ▲	TL	Track on right.
▼ 3.2		SO	Track on right is 2N25, closed to motor vehicles. Continue straight ahead onto 2N24.
	0.9 ▲	BR	Track on left is 2N25, closed to motor vehicles. Bear right onto 2N23.
			GPS: N34°13.87' W118°00.33'

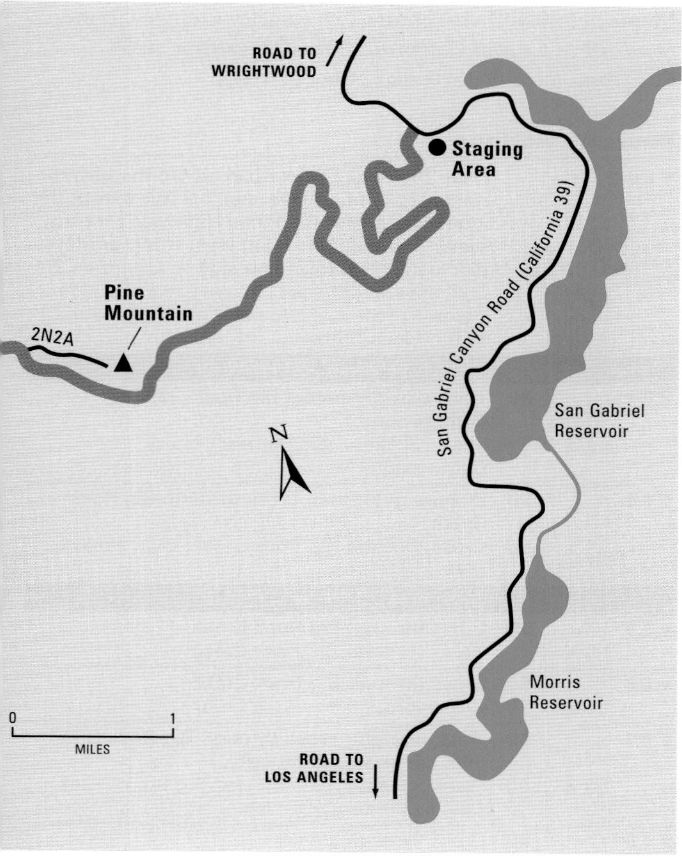

▼ 4.1	BR	Track on left is 2N24. Bear right onto 2N23 and zero trip meter.
0.0 ▲		Continue to the east.
		GPS: N34°14.11' W118°00.80'
▼ 0.0		Continue to the northwest.
8.6 ▲	SO	Track on right is 2N24. Continue straight ahead onto 2N24.
▼ 1.3	SO	Track on right.
7.3 ▲	SO	Track on left.
▼ 1.4	SO	Cross over creek.
7.2 ▲	SO	Cross over creek.
		GPS: N34°14.37' W118°01.42'
▼ 2.7	BL	Track on right.
5.9 ▲	BR	Track on left.
▼ 2.8	SO	Concrete ford over West Fork San Gabriel River. End of descent. Trail starts to climb.
5.8 ▲	SO	Concrete ford over West Fork San Gabriel River. End of descent. Trail starts to climb.
		GPS: N34°14.84' W118°01.96'
▼ 2.9	SO	Cross through wash.
5.7 ▲	SO	Cross through wash.
▼ 4.2	SO	Track on right is closed to motor vehicles.
4.4 ▲	SO	Track on left is closed to motor vehicles.
▼ 7.9	SO	Hiking trail joins vehicle trail on right.
0.7 ▲	SO	Hiking trail leaves vehicle trail on left.
▼ 8.0	SO	Hiking trail leaves vehicle trail on left.
0.6 ▲	SO	Hiking trail joins vehicle trail on right.
		GPS: N34°16.37' W118°02.03'
▼ 8.6		Gate (combination number required); then trail finishes at T-intersection with California 2. Turn left for Los Angeles; turn right for Wrightwood.
0.0 ▲		Trail commences on California 2, 0.6 miles north of the intersection of Upper Big Tujunga Canyon Road and 4.7 miles north of Los Angeles National Forest Red Box Station. Zero trip meter and turn southwest onto 2N23 and immediately pass through gate. A valid permit is required past this point. Trail is marked by a sign for Rincon/Shortcut Trail and Silver Moccasin Hiking and Equestrian Trail, 11W06. Start of shelf road.
		GPS: N34°16.41' W118°01.95'

SOUTH COAST #8

Pinyon Ridge Trail

Starting Point:	**Big Rock Creek Road at Camp Fenner**
Finishing Point:	**Big Pines Highway, 0.1 miles west of Mountain Oak Campground**
Total Mileage:	**7 miles, plus 3.8-mile spur along Pinyon Ridge**
Unpaved Mileage:	**7 miles, plus 3.8-mile spur**
Driving Time:	**1.5 hours**
Elevation Range:	**5,400–7,100 feet**
Usually Open:	**March to November**
Best Time to Travel:	**March to November**
Difficulty Rating:	**2**
Scenic Rating:	**9**
Remoteness Rating:	**+0**

Special Attractions

- Very pretty canyon along Big Rock Creek.
- Open ridge top along Pinyon Ridge.
- Access for other recreation opportunities—hiking, birding, and hunting in season.

Tenacious plant life clings to the mountainsides on Pinyon Ridge Trail

Pinyon pines are abundant once the trail reaches the ridge

Description

This trail travels a twisting route through Angeles National Forest. It commences along Big Rock Creek Road, 5.6 miles from the intersection with Big Pines Highway, outside Camp Fenner, where the road turns from paved to graded dirt. Note that Camp Fenner is a state prison facility, and there is no entry to forest road 4N55 through the prison camp, as the Angeles National Forest map appears to indicate.

The first 2 miles of the trail travel alongside Big Rock Creek, passing a national forest campground and ascending gradually up the valley. The roughly graded road crosses through the creek on many occasions before ascending to the saddle on California 2 at Vincent Gulch Divide. This is a popular hiking trailhead; the Pacific Crest National Scenic Trail crosses the road here and access to the High Desert National Recreation Trail is close by.

From Vincent Gulch Divide, the trail wraps around a shelf road, initially doubling back above Big Rock Creek. The major spur trail along the route leads off along Pinyon Ridge. The open grassy ridge is liberally scattered with the pinyon pines that give the ridge its name. There are some good campsites along this stretch and excellent views to the north and south from the ridge. The spur ends at a viewpoint overlooking Big Rock Creek and the Devils Punchbowl. A rewarding short hike from the end of the vehicle trail farther out along the ridge offers an even better view. This spur trail is extremely popular with deer hunters in season.

Back on the main trail, there are another few miles of pretty shelf road before the trail finishes on Big Pines Highway at Mountain Oak USFS Campground. For those wanting to travel slightly farther, a spur trail leads off from the very end of the main route and goes 1.4 miles through the pine forest before stopping.

Snow can close the trail during winter months, but it is often passable for longer than the stated times.

Current Road Information

Angeles National Forest
Saugus Ranger District
30800 Bouquet Canyon Road
Saugus, CA 91390
(661) 296-9710

Map References

BLM San Bernardino
USFS Angeles National Forest
USGS 1:24,000 Valyermo, Mescal Creek
1:100,000 San Bernardino
Maptech CD-ROM: Ventura/Los Angeles/Orange County
Southern & Central California Atlas & Gazetteer, p. 94
California Road & Recreation Atlas, p. 103

Route Directions

▼ 0.0			From Big Rock Creek Road where the paved road stops at Camp Fenner, 5.6 miles from the intersection with Big Pines Highway, zero trip meter and continue southwest along graded dirt road 4N11, following sign to California 2.
	2.0 ▲		Trail ends at the start of paved road outside Camp Fenner. Continue along the paved road to Big Pines Highway.
			GPS: N34°23.38' W117°46.49'
▼ 0.1		SO	Track on right enters Big Rock USFS Campground.
	1.9 ▲	SO	Track on left enters Big Rock USFS Campground.
▼ 0.4		SO	Closure gate; then cross through Big Rock Creek.
	1.6 ▲	SO	Cross through Big Rock Creek; then closure gate.
			GPS: N34°23.15' W117°46.35'
▼ 0.5		SO	Cross through Big Rock Creek.
	1.5 ▲	SO	Cross through Big Rock Creek.
▼ 0.6		SO	Cross through Big Rock Creek.
	1.4 ▲	SO	Cross through Big Rock Creek.
▼ 0.7		SO	Track on right; cross through Big Rock Creek; then second track on right.
	1.3 ▲	SO	Track on left; cross through Big Rock Creek; then second track on left.
▼ 1.0		SO	Cross through creek.

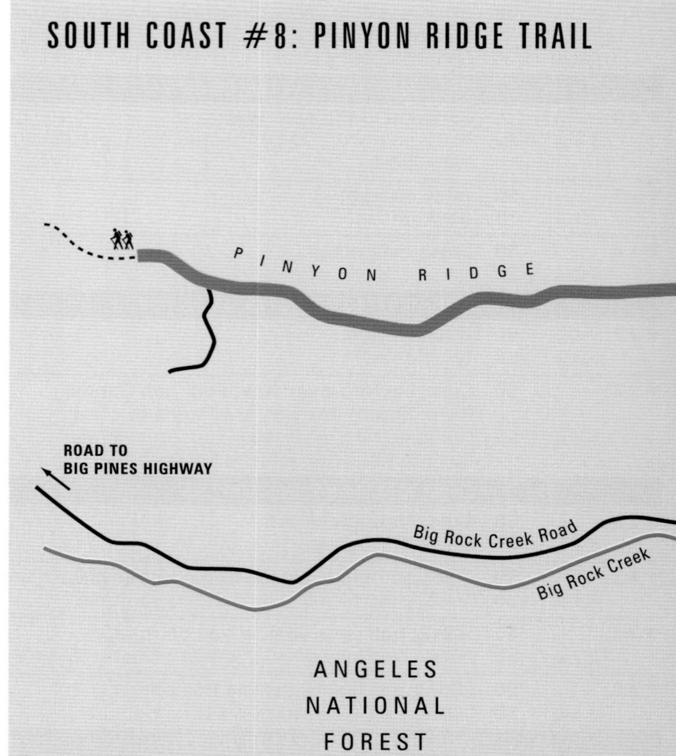

	1.0 ▲	SO	Cross through creek.
▼ 1.1		SO	Cross through creek.
	0.9 ▲	SO	Cross through creek.
▼ 2.0		TL	Trail reaches California 2 at Vincent Gulch Divide. Zero trip meter and turn sharp left (back on yourself) onto 3N26, following sign to Big Pines Highway. Pacific Crest National Scenic Trail crosses vehicle trail at this point.
	0.0 ▲		Continue to the northwest.
			GPS: N34°22.42′ W117°45.07′
▼ 0.0			Continue to the north through closure gate.
	2.7 ▲	TR	Closure gate; then trail reaches California 2 at Vincent Gulch Divide. Zero trip meter and turn sharp right (back on yourself) onto 4N11, following sign to Big Rock Campground. Pacific Crest National Scenic Trail crosses vehicle trail at this point.
▼ 0.9		BL	Graded road on right is 3N26 to Jackson Flat Group Campground. Bear left onto 4N12, following sign to Pinyon Ridge.
	1.8 ▲	TR	Graded road on left is 3N26 to Jackson Flat Group Campground.
			GPS: N34°23.02′ W117°45.43′
▼ 2.7		TR	T-intersection. Track on left is Pinyon Ridge spur (4N56). Remain on 4N12 and zero trip meter.
	0.0 ▲		Continue to the south.
			GPS: N34°23.54′ W117°45.08′

Pinyon Ridge Spur

▼ 0.0			From the intersection of 4N56 and 4N12, zero trip meter and turn west onto 4N56.
▼ 0.5		SO	Small track on right.
▼ 2.8		SO	Track on left to campsite.
			GPS: N34°24.37′ W117°47.65′
▼ 2.9		SO	Track on left rejoins.
▼ 3.3		SO	Track on left.
▼ 3.6		BR	Well-used track on left goes 0.4 miles along a narrow ridge to a turning place.
			GPS: N34°24.63′ W117°48.34′
▼ 3.8		UT	Road ends at a turnaround and viewpoint over Big Rock Creek wash and Devils Punchbowl County Park.
			GPS: N34°24.77′ W117°48.52′

Continuation of Main Trail

▼ 0.0			Continue to the east.
	2.3 ▲	TL	Track straight ahead is Pinyon Ridge spur (4N56). Remain on 4N12 and zero trip meter.
			GPS: N34°23.54′ W117°45.08′
▼ 0.6		SO	Cross over creek.
	1.7 ▲	SO	Cross over creek.
▼ 1.7		SO	Cross over creek.
	0.6 ▲	SO	Cross over creek.
▼ 2.1		SO	Closure gate.
	0.2 ▲	SO	Closure gate.
			GPS: N34°23.73′ W117°43.99′
▼ 2.2		SO	Track on right into private children's camp.
	0.1 ▲	BL	Track on left into private children's camp.
▼ 2.3			Track on right continues for an additional 1.4 miles. Trail finishes on paved Big Pines Highway, opposite Mountain Oak USFS Campground. Turn right for Wrightwood; turn left for Palmdale.
	0.0 ▲		Trail commences on Big Pines Highway, 0.1

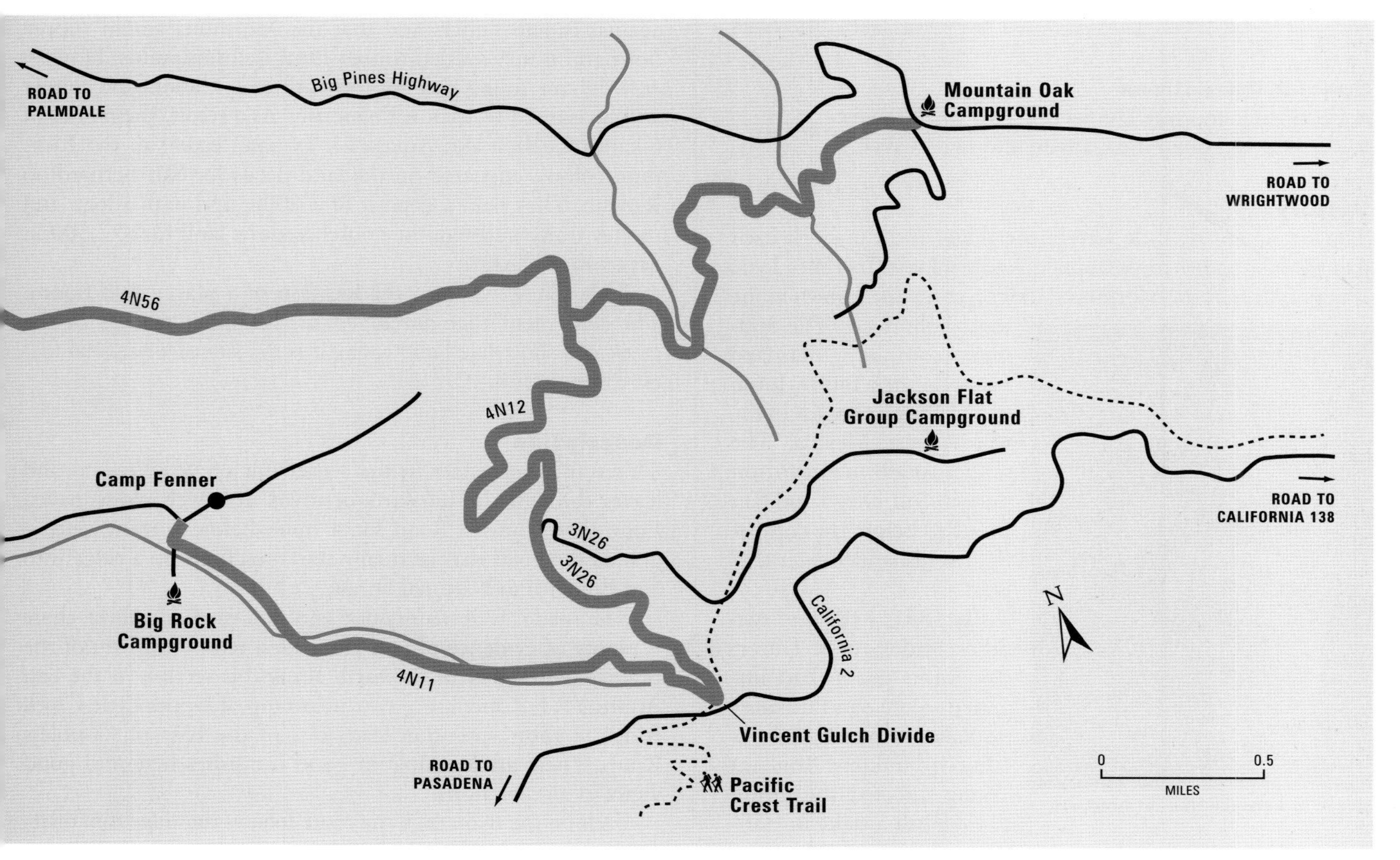

miles west of the entrance to Mountain Oak USFS Campground and 3 miles west of the intersection with Angeles Crest Highway (California 2). Zero trip meter and turn northwest on dirt road. Swing immediately right, leaving a track on your left, which travels 1.4 miles before stopping.

GPS: N34°23.67' W117°43.78'

SOUTH COAST #9

Upper Lytle Creek Ridge Trail

Starting Point:	**California 2 in Wrightwood**
Finishing Point:	**Lytle Creek Road, 1.5 miles north of the settlement of Scotland**
Total Mileage:	**16.5 miles**
Unpaved Mileage:	**12.3 miles**
Driving Time:	**1.5 hours**
Elevation Range:	**3,300–6,400 feet**
Usually Open:	**Year-round**
Best Time to Travel:	**Year-round**
Difficulty Rating:	**2**
Scenic Rating:	**8**
Remoteness Rating:	**+0**

Special Attractions

- Long ridge top trail connecting two small towns.
- Views over Lone Pine Canyon and Lytle Creek.

History

The settlement of Lytle Creek, the ridge, and the creek itself gained their names from Captain Andrew Lytle. In 1846, Lytle was an officer of the Mormon Battalion company known as the Iowa Volunteers. The 500-man company marched from Council Bluffs, Iowa, to San Diego to assist in the war against Mexico. The soldiers performed garrison duty in San Diego and San Luis Rey before the company was disbanded later that year.

Mistletoe in a spruce tree on Gobblers Knob

By 1851, Lytle and two other leaders of a Latter-day Saints group had migrated to the San Bernardino Valley to purchase land. Church President Brigham Young directed the group to establish a stake in California. Lytle's wagon train crossed what is now known as Cajon Pass, close to the vertical sandstone rock formations now known as Mormon Rocks. His group set up camp on the west side of the wide Cajon Wash, close to where Lytle Creek runs into the San Bernardino Valley. Thus the captain's name became linked to the creek.

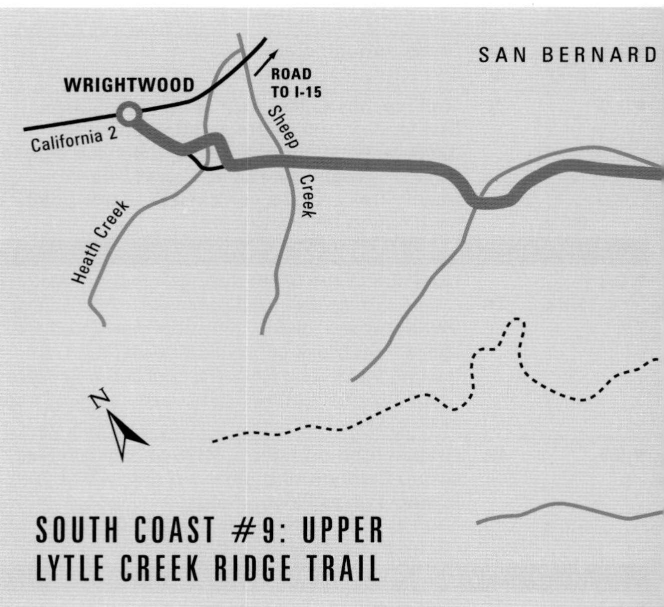

SOUTH COAST #9: UPPER LYTLE CREEK RIDGE TRAIL

Los Angeles residents welcomed the Mormon colony in San Bernardino Valley. They knew it would offer protection against Indian raiders and that the Mormons would supply flour and much-needed timber from the mountains. However, Brigham Young was not too enthusiastic about the colony and he refused to back it financially. As a result, the names of Charles C. Rich and Amasa M. Lyman, leaders of the Mormon colony, appeared on the land deeds for San Bernardino Rancho. They paid a deposit of $7,000, and with a loan and money from brethren, they purchased the land for $77,500 in September 1851.

Lytle Creek was also the location of a placer gold boom. The settlement that developed in the upper reaches of the creek was short-lived and today it is the site of a national forest campground.

Description

This trail commences in the settlement of Wrightwood and leaves through the outskirts of town. It travels along paved Lone Pine Canyon Road for 4 miles before turning onto a graded dirt road that gradually starts to climb up a ridge into San Bernardino National Forest.

The road is well maintained and well used. However, there is plenty of evidence of past landslides, reminding you of the precarious stability of the earth along this section of the San Andreas Rift Zone. Once you are on top of Upper Lytle Creek Ridge, a short spur trail leads out to the base of Gobblers Knob. There are a couple of good campsites here and good views in all directions.

Back on the main trail, the route follows the ridge top, offer-

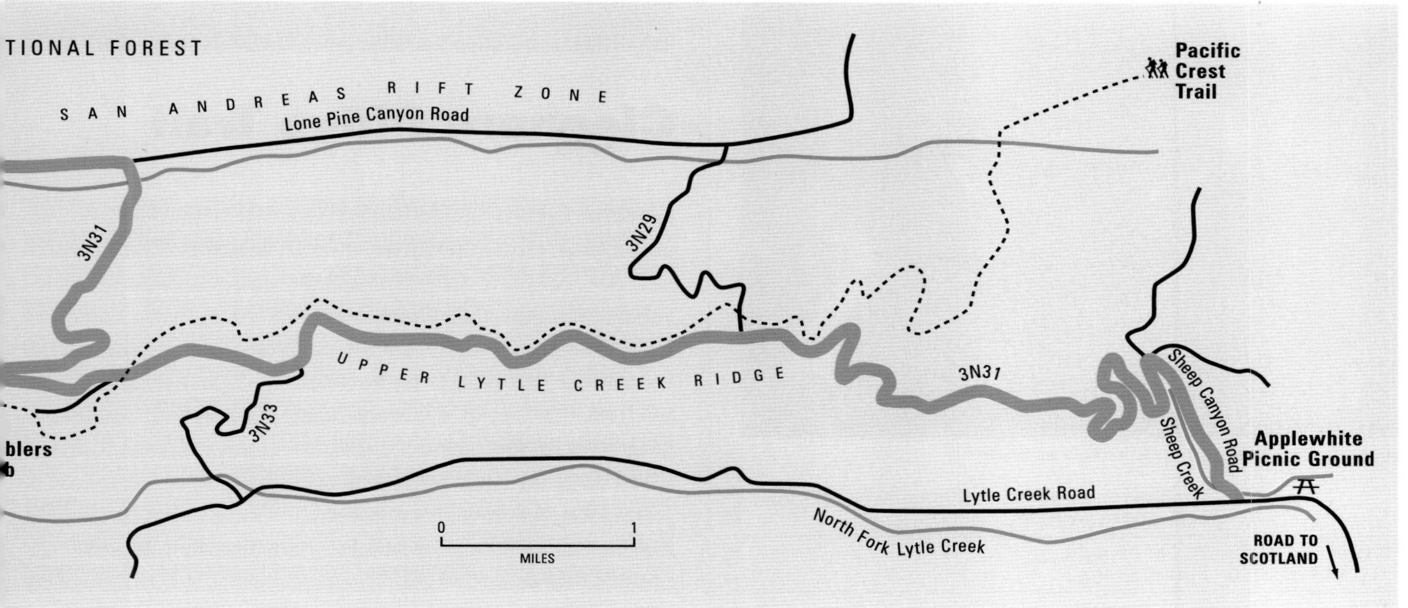

ing views into Lone Pine Canyon to the north and Lytle Creek to the south. The trail eventually drops down alongside Sheep Creek to exit to Lytle Creek Road, immediately west of Applewhite Picnic Ground, near the small settlement of Scotland.

Current Road Information

San Bernardino National Forest
Cajon Ranger District
1209 Lytle Creek Road
Lytle Creek, CA 92358
(909) 887-2576

Map References

BLM San Bernardino
USFS San Bernardino National Forest
USGS 1:24,000 Telegraph Peak, Cajon
1:100,000 San Bernardino
Maptech CD-ROM: Ventura/Los Angeles/Orange County
Southern & Central California Atlas & Gazetteer, p. 94
California Road & Recreation Atlas, p. 104

Route Directions

▼ 0.0		In Wrightwood, at the intersection of California 2 and Lone Pine Canyon Road, zero trip meter and turn south on paved Lone Pine Canyon Road. Remain on Lone Pine Canyon Road, ignoring turns to the left and right.
4.2 ▲		Trail ends in Wrightwood on California 2. Turn right for I-15; turn left for the main part of Wrightwood.
		GPS: N34°21.48′ W117°37.42′
▼ 0.3	TL	Turn left onto Thrush Street, following sign for Lone Pine Canyon Road.
3.9 ▲	TR	Turn right and rejoin main Lone Pine Canyon Road.
▼ 0.5	TR	Cross over Heath Creek; then turn right onto Heath Creek Drive, following signs for Lone Pine Canyon Road.
3.7 ▲	TL	Turn left onto Thrush Street, following signs for Lone Pine Canyon Road; then cross over Heath Creek.
▼ 0.7	TL	Turn left and rejoin Lone Pine Canyon Road. Remain on main road, ignoring residential streets to the right and left.
3.5 ▲	TR	Turn right onto Heath Creek Drive, following sign for Lone Pine Canyon Road.
		GPS: N34°21.03′ W117°37.15′
▼ 1.0	SO	Cross through Sheep Creek.
3.2 ▲	SO	Cross through Sheep Creek.
▼ 3.1	SO	Cross through wash.
1.1 ▲	SO	Cross through wash.
▼ 4.2	TR	Turn right on graded road 3N31, signed by a forest road marker, and zero trip meter.
0.0 ▲		Continue to the west.
		GPS: N34°19.55′ W117°34.10′
▼ 0.0		Continue to the south through closure gate.
3.8 ▲	TL	Closure gate; then turn left and join paved Lone Pine Canyon Road. Zero trip meter.
▼ 0.1	SO	Cross through wash.
3.7 ▲	SO	Cross through wash.
▼ 2.8	BL	Track on right goes 0.8 miles to viewpoint at the base of Gobblers Knob. End of shelf road. Gobblers Knob is on the right. Pacific Crest National Scenic Trail crosses road.
1.0 ▲	BR	Track on left goes 0.8 miles to a viewpoint at the base of Gobblers Knob. Start of shelf road. Gobblers Knob is on the left. Pacific Crest National Scenic Trail crosses road.
		GPS: N34°18.70′ W117°34.74′
▼ 3.0	SO	Track on left.
0.8 ▲	SO	Track on right.
▼ 3.1	SO	Small track on left.
0.7 ▲	SO	Small track on right.
▼ 3.5	SO	Track on left.
0.3 ▲	SO	Track on right.
▼ 3.8	SO	Graded road 3N33 on right goes to North Fork Lytle Creek. Zero trip meter.
0.0 ▲		Continue to the southwest.
		GPS: N34°18.34′ W117°33.88′
▼ 0.0		Continue to the northeast.

Upper Lytle Creek Ridge Trail is narrow at times

	2.8 ▲	SO	Graded road 3N33 on left goes to North Fork Lytle Creek. Zero trip meter.
▼ 1.1		SO	Pull-in on right.
	1.7 ▲	SO	Pull-in on left.
▼ 1.5		SO	Track on right.
	1.3 ▲	SO	Track on left.
▼ 2.2		SO	Track on right.
	0.6 ▲	SO	Track on left.
			GPS: N34°17.62' W117°32.31'
▼ 2.6		SO	Track on right and track on left.
	0.2 ▲	SO	Track on right and track on left.
▼ 2.8		SO	Unsigned track on left is 3N29. Zero trip meter.
	0.0 ▲		Continue to the west.
			GPS: N34°17.48' W117°31.72'
▼ 0.0			Continue to the southeast.
	4.7 ▲	SO	Unsigned track on right is 3N29. Zero trip meter.
▼ 1.8		SO	Pull-in on right.
	2.9 ▲	SO	Pull-in on left.
▼ 1.9		SO	Track on left; then track on right.
	2.8 ▲	SO	Track on left; then track on right.
▼ 2.6		SO	Track on right.
	2.1 ▲	SO	Track on left.
			GPS: N34°16.47' W117°30.55'
▼ 4.7		TR	Saddle. Turn sharp right at unmarked intersection toward Lytle Creek. Graded road on left and small track straight ahead. Zero trip meter.
	0.0 ▲		Continue to the southwest.
			GPS: N34°16.46' W117°29.90'
▼ 0.0			Continue to the southeast.
	1.0 ▲	TL	Saddle. Turn sharp left at unmarked intersection. Graded road ahead and small track on right. Zero trip meter.
▼ 0.7		SO	Track on right.
	0.3 ▲	SO	Track on left.
▼ 0.9		SO	Cross through Sheep Creek.
	0.1 ▲	SO	Cross through Sheep Creek.
▼ 1.0			Track on left to community center; then trail ends at T-intersection with paved Lytle Creek Road. Turn left for Scotland and I-15.
	0.0 ▲		Trail commences on paved Lytle Creek Road, 1.5 miles north of Scotland. Zero trip meter and turn northeast on graded dirt road marked Sheep Canyon Road to Lone Pine Canyon. Immediately bear left past road on right to community center. Turn is 0.1 miles west of Applewhite Picnic Ground.
			GPS: N34°15.69' W117°29.89'

SOUTH COAST #10

Cleghorn Ridge Trail

Starting Point:	**California 138, 1 mile south of the intersection with California 173 at Silverwood Lake**
Finishing Point:	**I-15, at Cajon exit**
Total Mileage:	**14.4 miles**
Unpaved Mileage:	**14.4 miles**
Driving Time:	**1.5 hours**
Elevation Range:	**3,000–5,300 feet**
Usually Open:	**Year-round**
Best Time to Travel:	**Dry weather**
Difficulty Rating:	**2, 4 to 8 for alternative route sections**
Scenic Rating:	**8**
Remoteness Rating:	**+0**

Special Attractions

- Choice of two trail standards following the same route—one easy, one moderate to very difficult.
- Ridge top trail giving views over Mount Baldy.
- Silverwood Lake.

History

Cleghorn Ridge Trail provides a good view over the historic Cajon Pass, which separates the San Bernardino and San Gabriel Mountains. The first European thought to have traveled over this pass was Fray Francisco Garcés, a Spanish missionary who came this way in 1776. Early settlers had a difficult time finding a way through these mountains. But by 1849, at the dawn of the gold rush, the rough route over Cajon Pass had gained popularity. Even so, passage was difficult. Wagons would often have to be lowered over the large rocks in their path. The name of the pass is a descriptive one; *cajon* is Spanish for a "box" or a "chest."

The smaller track that runs along Cleghorn Ridge is more difficult

In 1851, a group of Mormons crossed Cajon Pass en route to the San Bernardino Valley. The nearby formations called Mormon Rocks are named after these pioneers.

In the 1850s, a Los Angeles freight company improved the rough and dangerous wagon trail through Cajon Pass known as the Sanford Route. This remained the major wagon route until 1861, when

John Brown and his business associates built a much-improved toll road through Crowder Canyon to allow better access to the booming mining settlements in Holcomb Valley. The Cajon Pass Toll Road, with its manual boom gates at either end, remained in operation until 1881. After its negotiated franchise on the route ended that year, the road was free for all to travel. By 1885, survey engineer Fredrick Thomas Perris persuaded the Santa Fe Railroad Company to construct a railroad through Cajon Pass. The pass has been reshaped in a number of ways to facilitate different modes of traffic in generations since—one of these being a section of the famous Route 66 between Devore and Cajon Summit.

Cleghorn Ridge is named after Mathew Cleghorn and his son John, who operated a lumber business in the region in the 1870s.

Silverwood Lake has a number of recreation opportunities, including picnic areas accessible only by boat

Description

Cleghorn Ridge is an open ridge top that runs between Silverwood Lake and I-15. The trail is actually two separate trails that parallel each other and intersect frequently. The route mapped here is the easier of the two. The roughly graded dirt road is suitable for high-clearance 2WD vehicles in dry weather, even though it is rockier and lumpier than a lot of other 2-rated trails.

The 4WD trail that parallels the main route is a smaller formed trail that clings more tightly to the ridge tops. It intersects with the main trail many times along its length and varies from a 4 to an 8 difficulty rating. Most parts of the more rugged trail are easy to see from the graded road, so drivers can pick which sections and difficulty levels they wish to undertake. Generally speaking, the start of the trail is the easiest, with a 4 rating. Near the top of the ridge at Cleghorn Peak, the trail increases in difficulty to a 5 or 6 rating. Some sections, as the trail descends the far side, are rated 7 and 8 because of the extreme steepness and eroded loose surface of the trail. Even the easier sections of the parallel route will challenge the wheel articulation and placement of stock vehicles. It is best suited to smaller vehicles because of tight clearance between boulders and other obstacles along the way. The trail has been adopted by a local 4WD club, which performs basic trail maintenance.

Cleghorn Ridge Trail offers good views over Silverwood Lake, a popular recreation spot for camping, picnicking, boating, and fishing. There are quiet picnic areas around the lake that are accessible only by boat. The trail ends on I-15 at the Cajon exit, a few miles north of San Bernardino.

Current Road Information

San Bernardino National Forest
Cajon Ranger District
1209 Lytle Creek Road
Lytle Creek, CA 92358
(909) 887-2576

San Bernardino National Forest
Arrowhead Ranger District
PO Box 350
28104 Highway 18
Skyforest, CA 92385
(909) 337-2444

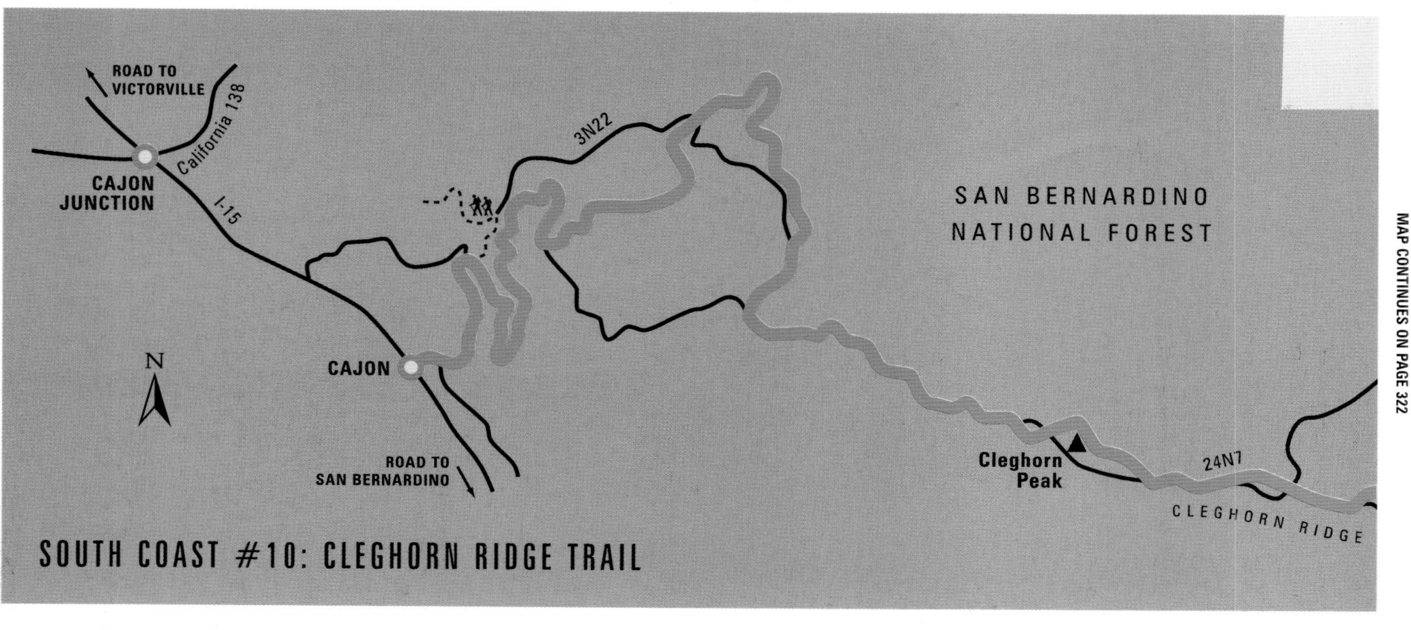

MAP CONTINUES ON PAGE 322

SOUTH COAST #10: CLEGHORN RIDGE TRAIL

MAP CONTINUES ON PAGE 321

Map References

BLM San Bernardino
USFS San Bernardino National Forest
USGS 1:24,000 Silverwood Lake, Cajon
1:100,000 San Bernardino
Maptech CD-ROM: Ventura/Los Angeles/Orange County
Southern & Central California Atlas & Gazetteer, pp. 94, 95
California Road & Recreation Atlas, p. 104

Route Directions

▼ 0.0		From California 138 at Silverwood Lake (mile marker 25), 1 mile south of California 173, zero trip meter and turn west on graded dirt road 2N47. Road is suitable for motorbikes, ATVs, and 4WDs—rated green. Trail is marked as 3N22.
10.6 ▲		Trail ends at T-intersection with paved California 138 at Silverwood Lake, which is directly opposite. Turn left for I-15 and Cajon Junction; turn right for Crestline.

The trail weaves its way down to Silverwood Lake

		GPS: N34°18.03′ W117°20.17′
▼ 0.3	SO	Small track on left.
10.3 ▲	SO	Small track on right.
▼ 0.8	SO	Two tracks on left. Track on right is start of alternate 4WD trail up ridge.
9.8 ▲	SO	Two tracks on right. Track on left is end of alternate 4WD route.
		GPS: N34°18.07′ W117°20.40′
▼ 1.2	SO	Track on right to pylon. Many tracks to the base of pylons.
9.4 ▲	SO	Track on left to pylon.
▼ 5.5	SO	Track on left and track on right.
5.1 ▲	SO	Track on left and track on right.
		GPS: N34°17.39′ W117°23.57′
▼ 5.6	SO	Track on right and track on left. Alternate 4WD trail is now 6-rated.
5.0 ▲	SO	Track on right and track on left.
▼ 7.1	SO	Track on left and track on right. Cleghorn Peak on left.
3.5 ▲	SO	Track on left and track on right. Cleghorn Peak on right.
		GPS: N34°17.65′ W117°24.80′
▼ 8.5	SO	Alternate tracks on left and right are more difficult.
2.1 ▲	SO	Alternate tracks on left and right are more difficult.
		GPS: N34°18.00′ W117°25.88′
▼ 10.6	SO	4WD trail on left. Track on right is 3N22 for 4WDs, ATVs, and motorbikes—rated green. Continue straight ahead on 2N47, signed to I-15, suitable for 4WDs, ATVs, and motorbikes—rated green. Zero trip meter.
0.0 ▲		Continue to the northeast.
		GPS: N34°18.74′ W117°26.23′
▼ 0.0		Continue to the southwest.
3.8 ▲	SO	4WD trail on right. Track on left is 3N22 for 4WDs, ATVs, and motorbikes—rated green. Continue straight ahead on 2N47, signed to Highway 138, suitable for 4WDs, ATVs, and motorbikes—rated green. Zero trip meter.
▼ 1.1	SO	Track on left.
2.7 ▲	SO	Track on right.

			GPS: N34°18.30′ W117°26.82′
▼ 1.5		BL	Track on right around pylon.
	2.3 ▲	BR	Track on left around pylon.
▼ 3.0		SO	Track on right is for hikers, horses, and mountain bikes.
	0.8 ▲	SO	Track on left is for hikers, horses, and mountain bikes.
			GPS: N34°18.28′ W117°27.11′
▼ 3.1		SO	Cross through wash; then track on right.
	0.7 ▲	SO	Track on left; then cross through wash.
▼ 3.8		SO	Closed track on left; then cattle guard. Trail ends at intersection with I-15 at Cajon. Turn north for Victorville; turn south for San Bernardino.
	0.0 ▲		Trail commences at Cajon exit on I-15. Exit freeway and proceed to the east side. Zero trip meter and head east along roughly graded dirt road. Cross cattle guard; then closed track on right. Trail is marked as 2N47 and is suitable for 4WDs, ATVs, and motorbikes—rated green.
			GPS: N34°17.97′ W117°27.36′

SOUTH COAST #11

Sugarpine Mountain Trail

Starting Point:	**Verdemont Drive and Palm Avenue, 1.2 miles north of US 215**
Finishing Point:	**California 138, 2.4 miles south of the intersection with California 173**
Total Mileage:	**17.1 miles**
Unpaved Mileage:	**16 miles**
Driving Time:	**2 hours**
Elevation Range:	**2,000–5,600 feet**
Usually Open:	**Year-round**
Best Time to Travel:	**Year-round**
Difficulty Rating:	**3**
Scenic Rating:	**9**
Remoteness Rating:	**+0**

Special Attractions

- Silverwood Lake State Recreation Area.
- Long, moderately difficult trail very close to Los Angeles.
- Trail passes through a variety of chaparral and forest vegetation.

History

The ascent to Monument Peak along this trail parallels the climb up nearby Waterman Canyon Road to the east. The original passable route up the rugged Waterman Canyon was constructed in 1852 for Mormon settlers in the San Bernardino Valley to use as a lumber road to access the tall trees of Seeley and Huston Flats. It was completed in just two and a half weeks, although nearly a thousand man-days of labor were used under the supervision of Captain Jefferson Hunt.

The climb along a narrow and twisty shelf road has limited passing places

Located at the mouth of Cajon Canyon, Muscupiabe Rancho was known to Serrano Indians as Amuscupiabit, which means “the place of little pines.” In 1843, Governor Manuel Micheltorena granted this land to Michael C. White.

Cajon Pass had originally been used as an entryway to the valley below by the Indians. Now it became their route for stealing settlers’ stock. Muscupiabe Rancho was established to guard this route and to try to stem the flow of stolen cattle. Michael White built a heavily fortified house close to the southern end of Sugarpine Mountain Trail in an effort to detect intruders and defend local settlers. White’s family remained only six weeks. Indians took their stock and White, unable to have any effect on the traffic through the pass, was forced to retreat only nine months after the establishment of his ranch.

On top of Monument Peak, a historical marker commemorates the Mohave Indian Trail that follows part of this route. It was placed there in 1931 by the San Bernardino Historical Society. The trail was also traveled by Fray Francisco Garcés in March 1776 and Jedediah S. Smith in November 1826.

Description

This moderate trail is only a short distance from San Bernardino, making it an easy day trip from the Los Angeles metropolitan area. The trail leaves US 215 through the com-

Silverwood Lake can be seen through trees along the trail

munity of Verdemont, and after a mile it leaves the paved road and continues along a narrow road into San Bernardino National Forest. The road is restricted to street legal vehicles only—no green-sticker vehicles. It immediately starts to climb into the mountains along a narrow, uneven shelf road. The surface gets a little rougher as it climbs around the West Fork of Devil Canyon.

After 5.9 miles, a very short spur trail leads to the top of Monument Peak and the historical marker commemorating the Mohave Trail. Immediately past the marker is a wonderful view over the San Bernardino Valley.

This trail is pleasant in fall, with the combination of deciduous and evergreen trees providing a beautiful contrast of color. As the trail runs along the ridge tops, there are clear views to the north over Silverwood Lake. It turns to the east below Cleghorn Ridge and runs down to finish in Silverwood Lake State Recreation Area. The final section of the trail is graded road and passes through some private property.

There is a large, shady campground and a couple group campsites at Silverwood Lake. The lake is a great place for a picnic or camp at the end of the trail. Other activities, such as swimming, fishing, and boating, are available at the lake.

Current Road Information

San Bernardino National Forest
Cajon Ranger District
1209 Lytle Creek Road
Lytle Creek, CA 92358
(909) 887-2576

San Bernardino National Forest
Arrowhead Ranger District
PO Box 350
28104 Highway 18
Skyforest, CA 92385
(909) 337-2444

Map References

BLM San Bernardino
USFS San Bernardino National Forest
USGS 1:24,000 San Bernardino North, Silverwood Lake, Cajon
1:100,000 San Bernardino
Maptech CD-ROM: Ventura/Los Angeles/Orange County
Southern & Central California Atlas & Gazetteer, p. 95
California Road & Recreation Atlas, p. 104

Route Directions

▼ 0.0			From the Verdemont exit on US 215, exit freeway and turn north. Proceed along Palm Avenue for 1.2 miles. Zero trip meter at paved Verdemont Drive on the right and continue north on Palm Avenue.
	5.9 ▲		Trail ends at intersection of Verdemont Drive and Palm Avenue. Continue straight ahead for 1.2 miles to reach US 215.
			GPS: N34°12.33' W117°21.08'
▼ 0.2		SO	Road turns to graded dirt. Continue through closure gate into San Bernardino National Forest. Road is marked as 2N49.
	5.7 ▲	SO	Closure gate. Exiting San Bernardino National Forest. Road is now paved.
			GPS: N34°12.52' W117°20.96'
▼ 1.5		BL	Two tracks on right.
	4.4 ▲	BR	Two tracks on left.
			GPS: N34°13.19' W117°20.33'
▼ 1.9		SO	Cross through wash.
	4.0 ▲	SO	Cross through wash.
▼ 5.4		SO	Saddle. Small track on right. Track on left goes 0.3 miles to viewpoint over San Bernardino Valley. Intersection is unmarked. End of shelf road.
	0.5 ▲	SO	Saddle. Small track on left rejoins. Track on right goes 0.3 miles to a viewpoint over San Bernardino Valley. Intersection is unmarked. Start of shelf road.

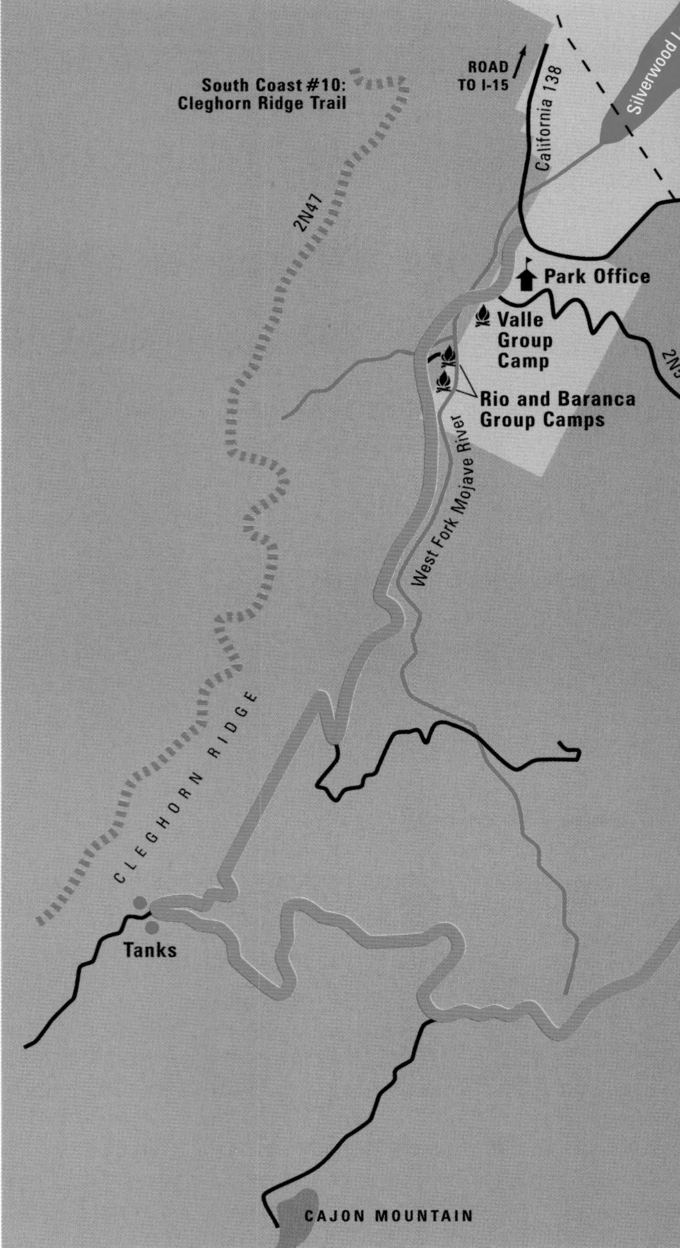

		GPS: N34°14.41′ W117°21.18′
▼ 5.6	SO	Track on right rejoins.
0.3 ▲	SO	Track on left.
▼ 5.9	BL	Track on right is 2N43. Zero trip meter.
0.0 ▲		Continue to the south.
		GPS: N34°14.75′ W117°21.14′
▼ 0.0		Continue to the north. Track on left goes short distance to the historical marker and viewpoint at the top of Monument Peak.
2.1 ▲	BR	Track on right goes short distance to historical marker and viewpoint at the top of Monument Peak. Track on left is 2N43. Zero trip meter.
▼ 0.1	SO	Track on right.
2.0 ▲	SO	Track on left.
▼ 0.5	SO	Track on right and track on left.
1.6 ▲	SO	Track on right and track on left.
▼ 0.8	SO	Track on left and track on right under power lines.
1.3 ▲	SO	Track on left and track on right under power lines.
		GPS: N34°15.08′ W117°21.56′
▼ 1.4	SO	Track on left is gated shut.
0.7 ▲	SO	Track on right is gated shut.
▼ 2.1	SO	Track on right through closure gate is 2N45. Zero trip meter.
0.0 ▲		Continue to the southeast.
		GPS: N34°15.68′ W117°22.19′
▼ 0.0		Continue to the north.
3.0 ▲	BR	Track on left through closure gate is 2N45. Zero trip meter.
▼ 0.9	SO	Two tracks on right.
2.1 ▲	SO	Two tracks on left.

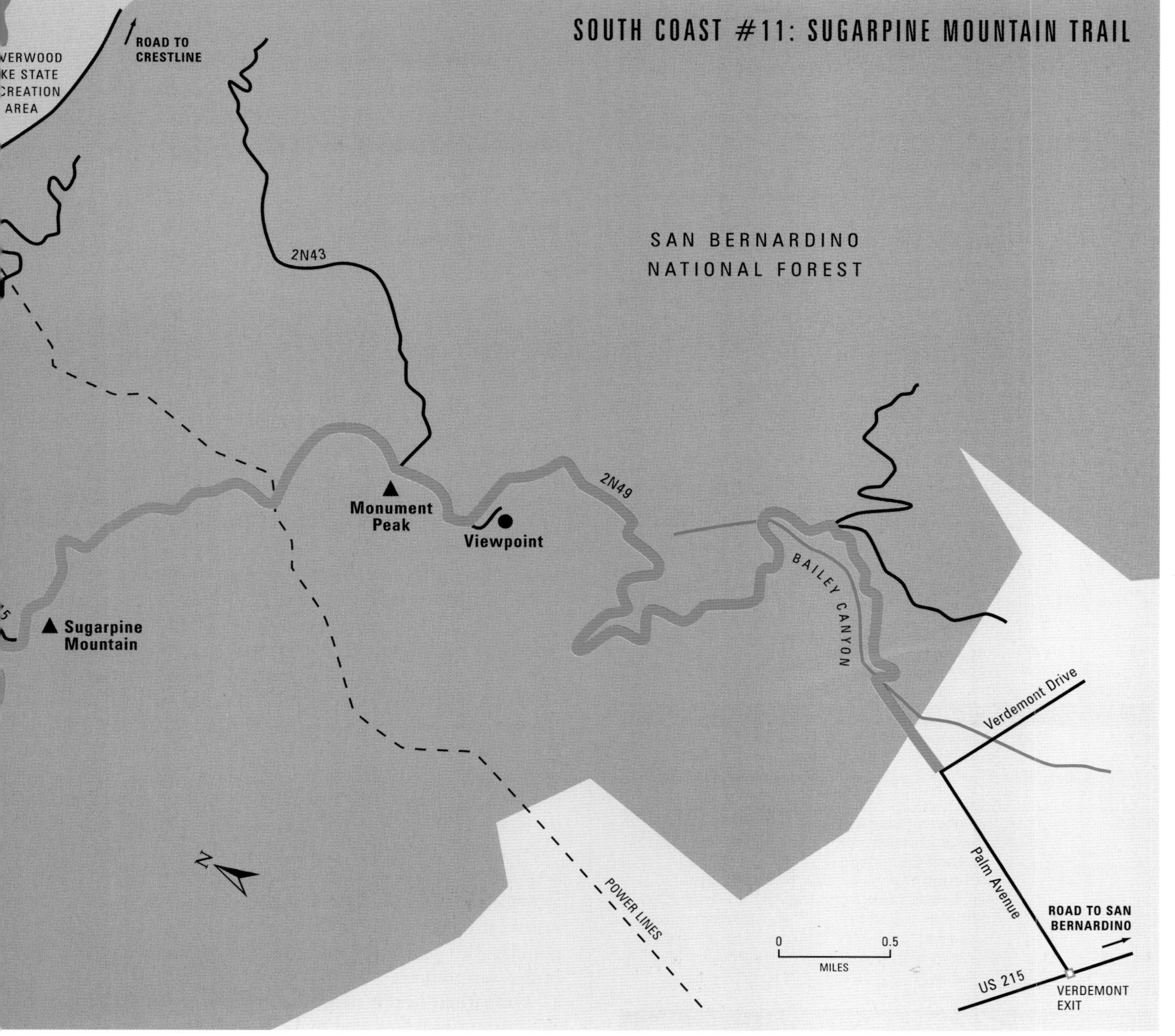

▼	▲		
▼ 1.9		SO	Turnout on left.
	1.1 ▲	SO	Turnout on right.
▼ 3.0		SO	Unmarked, well-used track on left goes to Cajon Mountain. Zero trip meter.
	0.0 ▲		Continue to the south.
			GPS: N34°16.24' W117°24.16'
▼ 0.0			Continue to the northwest.
	2.2 ▲	SO	Unmarked, well-used track on right goes to Cajon Mountain. Zero trip meter.
▼ 0.4		SO	Turnout on right.
	1.8 ▲	SO	Turnout on left.
▼ 1.0		SO	Track on right.
	1.2 ▲	SO	Track on left.
▼ 2.1		SO	Closure gate.
	0.1 ▲	SO	Closure gate.
▼ 2.2		TR	Track straight ahead. Two concrete tanks at intersection. Zero trip meter.
	0.0 ▲		Continue to the southeast.
			GPS: N34°17.20' W117°24.39'
▼ 0.0			Continue to the east.
	3.9 ▲	TL	Track straight ahead. Two concrete tanks at intersection. Zero trip meter.
▼ 1.5		BL	Graded road on right is private property.
	2.4 ▲	BR	Graded road on left is private property.
▼ 2.5		SO	Cross through creek.
	1.4 ▲	SO	Cross through creek.
▼ 3.0		SO	Road turns to paved.
	0.9 ▲	SO	Road turns to graded dirt and is marked as 2N49. Street legal vehicles only—no green-sticker vehicles.
			GPS: N34°17.22' W117°22.14'
▼ 3.2		SO	Paved road on right goes to Rio and Baranca Group Camps.
	0.7 ▲	SO	Paved road on left goes to Rio and Baranca Group Camps.
▼ 3.3		SO	Cross through wash on concrete ford.
	0.6 ▲	SO	Cross through wash on concrete ford.
▼ 3.4		SO	Cross through wash on concrete ford.
	0.5 ▲	SO	Cross through wash on concrete ford.
▼ 3.5		SO	Cross through wash on concrete ford; then paved road on right goes to Valle Group Camp; then cross through second wash on concrete ford.
	0.4 ▲	SO	Cross through wash on concrete ford; then paved road on left goes to Valle Group Camp; then cross through second wash on concrete ford.
▼ 3.6		SO	Track on right is 2N59.
	0.3 ▲	SO	Track on left is 2N59. Remain on paved road, following signs to group camps.
			GPS: N34°17.23' W117°21.60'
▼ 3.7		SO	Silverwood Lake State Recreation Area office on right.
	0.2 ▲	SO	Silverwood Lake State Recreation Area office on left.
▼ 3.9			Trail ends at intersection with California 138. Turn right for Crestline; turn left for Cajon Junction on I-15. Lake Campground is straight ahead.
	0.0 ▲		Trail commences on California 138 at Silverwood Lake State Recreation Area. Exit California 138 at the exit for Silverwood Lake State Recreation Area. Proceed to the south side and zero trip meter. Proceed west on paved road, following sign to group camp areas and the park office.
			GPS: N34°17.28' W117°21.31'

SOUTH COAST #12

Willow Creek Trail

Starting Point:	**California 173, 7 miles south of intersection with Arrowhead Lake Road**
Finishing Point:	**National forest boundary on Hook Creek Road, 3 miles from Cedar Glen**
Total Mileage:	**8.9 miles for more difficult route (slightly longer for easier option)**
Unpaved Mileage:	**8.9 miles**
Driving Time:	**2 hours**
Elevation Range:	**4,400–5,400 feet**
Usually Open:	**Year-round**
Best Time to Travel:	**Year-round**
Difficulty Rating:	**2/4**
Scenic Rating:	**7**
Remoteness Rating:	**+0**

Special Attractions

- Trail through a popular OHV area with a choice of an easy or moderately difficult route.
- Remains of Splinters Cabin.
- Access to hiking trailheads and fishing spots.

History

A major wildfire—the Willow Creek Fire—raged through the north side of Lake Arrowhead in the fall of 1999, burning 65,000 acres in 14 days. Twelve million dollars was spent fighting the fire, with a further $2 million allocated for restoration work. This trail travels through part of the burned area.

Splinters Cabin, a short distance from the main trail, was constructed in 1922 by Le Roy Raymond. In 1918, he visited the region on a fishing and camping trip with his brother and applied to build a cabin. His request wasn't granted until 1922. He hired a man to haul river rock up from the creek as well as the cement and pipe needed to build the foundation. The cabin has a river rock and cement base and originally had a wooden frame above it. The name of the cabin is credited to Le Roy's wife, who commented that everything he built seemed to be full of splinters. So Le Roy dedicated the cabin to her.

Just before the trail ends at Cedar Glen, it passes the junction of Little Bear Creek and Hooks Creek. The head of Little Bear Creek is close to Lake Arrowhead, which was originally called Little Bear Lake. The name Arrowhead was adopted because vegetation above the lake was shaped like an arrowhead. The formation seems to point downward to the warm springs at the foot of the mountain. These springs were popular with generations of Indians who refreshed themselves in the warm waters.

The earliest health resort at Arrowhead, Smith's Hygienic Sanatorium, was founded by Dr. David Noble Smith. Smith

Splinters Cabin

built an impressive two-story building above one of the springs.

Description

This trail follows one of the main routes through a popular OHV area in San Bernardino National Forest. Drivers can choose either an easy, roughly graded route or a more difficult route that encompasses portions of other 4WD trails in the region. One route is described here, but drivers will find it easy to combine portions of easier or more difficult routes as they wish.

The more difficult option travels on formed, weathered trails with some quite severe holes, ruts, and off-camber sections. Good wheel articulation is an advantage. Vehicles with less flexible suspensions will find themselves lifting wheels on occasion. These sections are rated blue in the OHV area.

The graded trail travels through the same scenery, burned over by the Willow Creek Fire in 1999. Recovery is slow and many large sections of the landscape are still blackened and bare.

Many trails within this area are suitable for different OHV use. Designated trails are clearly marked. Part of the trail travels within the Deep Creek area, which is for day use only and allows fishing access to Deep Creek.

One point of interest along the trail is the remains of Splinters Cabin. The cabin is located at the hiking trailhead that provides fishing access to the creek. The waist-high stone walls of the cabin are protected from the elements by a wooden ramada. Even though the original timber frame is gone, the cabin still has an enclosed feel to it. Splinters Cabin is a pleasant place for a picnic, with shady trees alongside the cabin. Brown and rainbow trout can be caught in the creek below.

The White Mountains are visible from the start of the trail

A short distance farther, a trail provides the only crossing of Deep Creek open to vehicles. The black-rated trail is extremely rocky and boulder-strewn for a couple of miles past the Deep Creek crossing. Rated an 8 for difficulty, it is recommended for vehicles with additional lift and good tires only. There is a risk of panel damage from the large boulders.

The trail finishes where the paved road leaves San Bernardino National Forest. From here it is only 3 miles to Cedar Glen.

Current Road Information

San Bernardino National Forest
Arrowhead Ranger District
PO Box 350
28104 Highway 18
Skyforest, CA 92385
(909) 337-2444

Map References

BLM San Bernardino
USFS San Bernardino National Forest
USGS 1:24,000 Lake Arrowhead
1:100,000 San Bernardino
Maptech CD-ROM: Ventura/Los Angeles/Orange County
Southern & Central California Atlas & Gazetteer, p. 95
California Road & Recreation Atlas, p. 104

Route Directions

▼ 0.0			From California 173, 7 miles south of the intersection with Arrowhead Lake Road, 9.5 miles north of Lake Arrowhead, zero trip meter and turn east onto graded dirt road marked Willow Creek Jeep Trail to Squit Ranch. Road is also marked 3N34 and is suitable for street legal 4WDs and motorbikes only—rated green.
	0.4 ▲		Trail ends at T-intersection with California 173. Turn left for Lake Arrowhead; turn right for Victorville.
			GPS: N34°18.01′ W117°12.26′
▼ 0.4		TL	Pinnacles Staging Area on right—parking area, picnic tables, and pit toilets. Graded road ahead is 3N34 for street legal vehicles only. Zero trip meter and turn left onto formed sandy trail 3N34, suitable for 4WDs, ATVs, and motorbikes—rated blue.
	0.0 ▲		Continue to the west.
			GPS: N34°17.88′ W117°11.92′
▼ 0.0			Continue to the northeast.
	2.9 ▲	TR	End of 4WD section. Pinnacles Staging Area is straight ahead—parking area, picnic tables, and pit toilets. Road on left is 3N34 for street legal vehicles only. Zero trip meter and turn right onto graded dirt road marked 3N34.
▼ 0.9		SO	Cross through wash.
	2.0 ▲	SO	Cross through wash.
▼ 1.0		BL	Graded road on right is 3N34. Bear left onto graded road, also 3N34—now rated green.
	1.9 ▲	BR	Graded road on left is 3N34. Bear right onto 3N34—now rated blue.
			GPS: N34°18.04′ W117°10.97′
▼ 1.1		SO	Cross through wash.

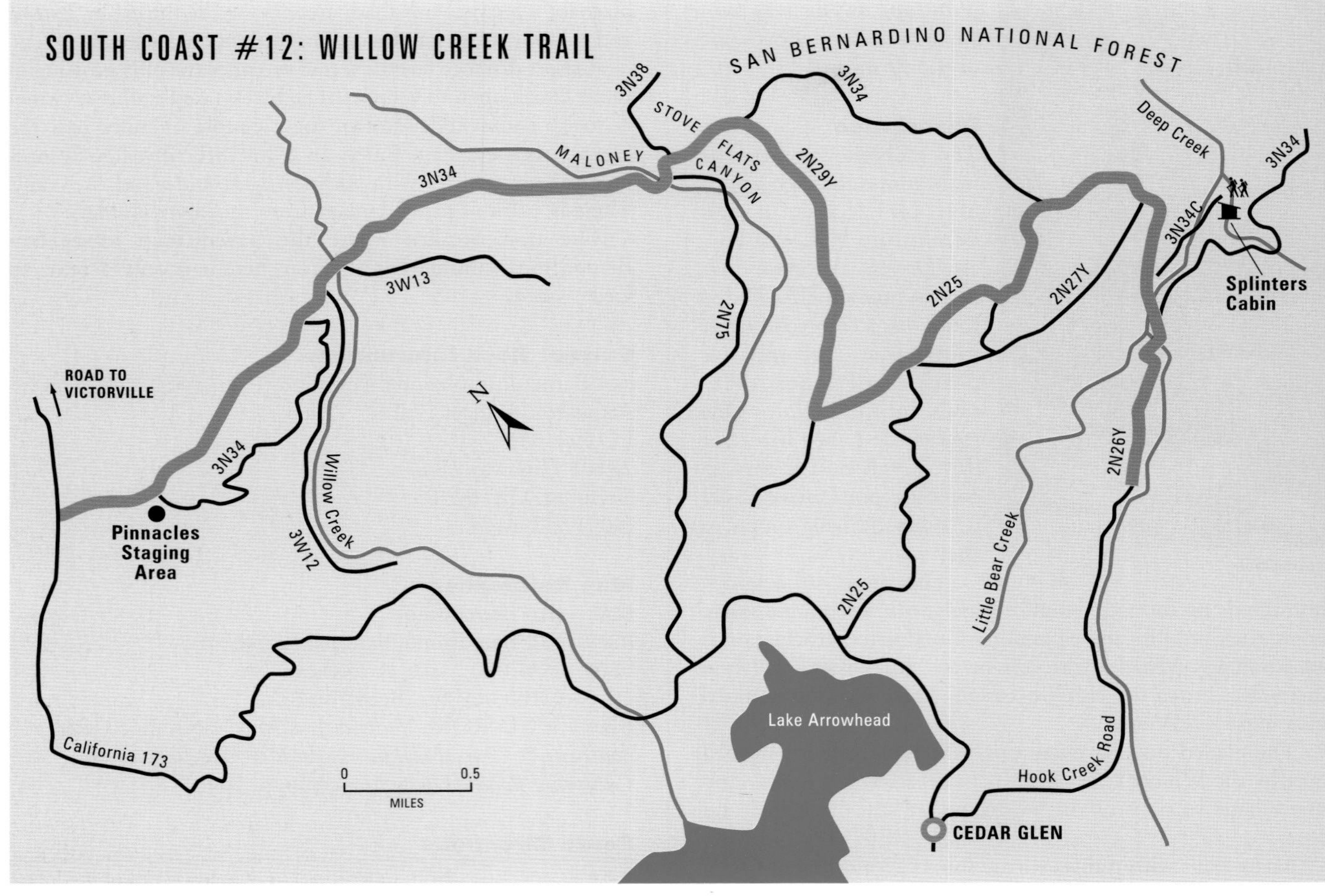

1.8 ▲ SO Cross through wash.

▼ 1.2 SO Trail on right is 3W12 for ATVs and motorbikes only—rated blue.

1.7 ▲ SO Trail on left is 3W12 for ATVs and motorbikes only—rated blue.

GPS: N34°18.08' W117°10.82'

▼ 1.3 SO Cross through Willow Creek; then trail on right is 3W13 for ATVs and motorbikes only—rated blue. Continue on 3N34—now rated blue.

1.6 ▲ SO Trail on left is 3W13 for ATVs and motorbikes only—rated blue. Continue on 3N34—now rated green—and cross through Willow Creek.

GPS: N34°18.09' W117°10.71'

▼ 2.6 SO Cross through wash.

0.3 ▲ SO Cross through wash.

▼ 2.8 SO Cross through wash.

0.1 ▲ SO Cross through wash.

▼ 2.9 TL Turn left, remaining on 3N34—now rated green. Track on right is 2N75 for street legal vehicles only. Zero trip meter. This is Maloney Canyon.

0.0 ▲ Continue to the west.

GPS: N34°17.59' W117°09.41'

▼ 0.0 Continue to the northwest.

3.6 ▲ TR Turn right, remaining on 3N34—now rated blue. Track straight ahead is 2N75 for street legal vehicles only. Zero trip meter. This is Maloney Canyon.

▼ 0.2 BR Stove Flats. Track on left is 3N38 for street legal vehicles only.

3.4 ▲ BL Stove Flats. Track on right is 3N38 for street legal vehicles only.

GPS: N34°17.67' W117°09.36'

▼ 0.5 SO Track on left is continuation of 3N34—rated green. Continue straight ahead on 2N29Y, suitable for 4WDs, ATVs, and motorbikes—rated blue.

3.1 ▲ SO Track on right is 3N34—rated green. Continue straight ahead and join 3N34, suitable for 4WDs, ATVs, and motorbikes—rated green.

GPS: N34°17.61' W117°09.03'

▼ 1.9 TL T-intersection. Turn left onto 2N28Y, suitable for 4WDs, ATVs, and motorbikes—rated blue. Track on right is also 2N28Y—rated blue.

1.7 ▲ TR Turn right onto 2N29Y, suitable for 4WDs, ATVs, and motorbikes—rated blue. Track straight ahead is continuation of 2N28Y—rated blue.

GPS: N34°16.64' W117°09.58'

▼ 2.2 BR Trail forks. Trail is rated blue to the left and black to the right.

1.4 ▲ SO Trail rejoins.

GPS: N34°16.58' W117°09.33'

▼ 2.3 SO Trail rejoins.

1.3 ▲ BL Trail forks. Trail is rated blue to the right and black to the left.

▼ 2.5 TL Graded road on left and right is 2N25, restricted to street legal vehicles. Track ahead is 2N27Y (marked to 3N34) for 4WDs, ATVs, and motorbikes—rated black.

1.1 ▲ TR Track on left is 2N27Y (marked to 3N34) for 4WDs, ATVs, and motorbikes—rated black.

Graded road 2N25 continues straight ahead. Turn right onto 2N28Y, suitable for 4WDs, ATVs, and motorbikes—rated blue.

GPS: N34°16.58′ W117°09.12′

▼ 3.0		SO	Track on right.
	0.6 ▲	SO	Track on left.
▼ 3.3		SO	Game water tank on left below trail.
	0.3 ▲	SO	Game water tank on right below trail.
▼ 3.6		TR	Turn right onto 3N34—rated green. Track on left is also 3N34—rated green. Information board at intersection. Zero trip meter.
	0.0 ▲		Continue to the southwest.

GPS: N34°16.72′ W117°08.26′

▼ 0.0			Continue to the east on 3N34, marked to Deep Creek-T6—rated green.
	1.1 ▲	BL	Bear left onto 2N25, suitable for street legal vehicles only. Track on right is continuation of 3N34. Information board at intersection. Zero trip meter.
▼ 0.5		SO	Track on left through gate; then cattle guard.
	0.6 ▲	SO	Cattle guard; then track on right through gate.
▼ 0.6		SO	Track on right is 2N27Y, which leads to 2N28Y, for 4WDs, ATVs, and motorbikes—rated black. Then track on left.
	0.5 ▲	SO	Track on right. Then track on left is 2N27Y, which leads to 2N28Y, for 4WDs, ATVs, and motorbikes—rated black.

GPS: N34°16.53′ W117°07.96′

▼ 0.8		SO	Closure gate.
	0.3 ▲	SO	Closure gate.
▼ 0.9		SO	Track on left is 3N34C, which goes through closure gate 0.5 miles to Splinters Trailhead. Trail PC2000 leads to Deep Creek and fishing access for hikers and horses only.
	0.2 ▲	BL	Track on right is 3N34C, which goes through closure gate 0.5 miles to Splinters Trailhead. Trail PC2000 leads to Deep Creek and fishing access for hikers and horses only.

GPS: N34°16.29′ W117°08.12′

▼ 1.0		SO	Trail on right is 2N27Y for ATVs and motorbikes only—rated blue; then cross over creek.
	0.1 ▲	SO	Cross over creek; then trail on left is 2N27Y for ATVs and motorbikes only—rated blue.
▼ 1.1		SO	Track on left is continuation of 3N34 to Deep Creek—rated green. Zero trip meter and continue straight ahead on 2N26Y, suitable for street legal vehicles only.
	0.0 ▲		Continue to the north.

GPS: N34°16.18′ W117°08.23′

▼ 0.0			Continue to the southwest.
	0.9 ▲	BL	Track on right is continuation of 3N34 to Deep Creek—rated green. Zero trip meter and bear left on 3N34—rated green.
▼ 0.1		SO	Cross over creek; then road turns to paved.
	0.8 ▲	SO	Cross over creek; road is now graded dirt.
▼ 0.9		SO	Leaving San Bernardino National Forest. Trail ends here. Continue 3 miles on paved road into Cedar Glen to join California 173.
	0.0 ▲		Trail commences at Cedar Glen. Turn off California 173 at the gas station onto Hook Creek Road. Remain on paved Hook Creek Road for 3 miles, ignoring turns to the right and left. At the national forest boundary, the road is marked by forest signs and is designated 2N26Y. Zero trip meter and continue to the northeast on paved road. Entering San Bernardino National Forest.

GPS: N34°15.77′ W117°08.75′

SOUTH COAST #13

Big Pine Flat Trail

Starting Point:	**Green Valley Lake Road, 2.5 miles north of California 18**
Finishing Point:	**California 18, 3 miles east of Big Bear City**
Total Mileage:	**26.6 miles**
Unpaved Mileage:	**25.4 miles**
Driving Time:	**3 hours**
Elevation Range:	**5,500–7,600 feet**
Usually Open:	**March to December**
Best Time to Travel:	**March to December**
Difficulty Rating:	**1**
Scenic Rating:	**9**
Remoteness Rating:	**+0**

Special Attractions

- Points of historic interest in and around Holcomb Valley.
- Excellent backcountry camping.
- Access to a network of graded dirt roads and off-road trails.

History

The eastern end of Big Pine Flat Trail, also known as Holcomb Valley Road, passes high above Baldwin Lake through the workings of the Gold Mountain Mine. Elias Jackson Baldwin owned this mine from 1860 to approximately 1900. Baldwin, known as "Lucky," had struck it rich in the Comstock Lode and was to become one of the biggest investors of the time. Set into the mountainside at his Gold Mountain Mine are the remains of a 40-stamp mill built in 1870 and destroyed by fire in 1876. The settlement that developed around the mine was

Beware, the ford through Holcomb Creek is subject to flash flooding

The juniper hangman's tree can still be seen in Holcomb Valley

known as Bairdstown, later to become Doble in recognition of Budd Doble, Lucky's son-in-law who managed the mine for a period.

The mine changed hands several times after the turn of the twentieth century, with the last attempts at extraction taking place around 1940. Baldwin was also a part investor in a 10-stamp mill in Bear Valley, which was not profitable. Lucky is remembered by the city named after him, Baldwin Park, located on one of the many ranchos he owned.

William Francis Holcomb was hunting in the Bear Valley region in 1859 when he discovered the rich gold region that bears his name. In no time, prospectors began working claims throughout the area. Prospecting in the area continued until the 1950s. The mining community of Belleville grew out of these busy times. The town was named for road builder Jed Van Dusen's daughter Belle, the first baby born in the new settlement. Belleville supported a typical saloon, known as Two Gun Bill's, a sawmill, and other businesses. At its peak the town had a population of nearly 1,500. At one stage Belleville competed for the San Bernardino County seat. The settlement did have a wild side, and the hangman's tree had its share of business. Each time someone was hanged from a limb of the tree, that limb was cut off. The number of missing branches can be seen from the trail. By 1880, the mines were not paying off enough to retain miners and the settlement soon became a ghost town. Nestled in the remnants of this settlement are remains often referred to as Pygmy Cabin. However, this structure is not the original cabin. The real Pygmy Cabin burned down in the 1980s.

Pygmy cabin in Holcomb Valley

Bear Valley was named by Benjamin D. Wilson, a hunter-trapper who was in this region in the 1840s. Originally from Tennessee, Wilson was traveling with a party from New Mexico in pursuit of Indian warriors when they surprised a group of grizzly bears by a lake. They caught 22 bears in the locale, quite a number even in those days. Afterward, the area became known as Bear Valley. The first reservoir built in Bear Valley established a reliable irrigation system for the citrus groves of Redlands in the 1880s. By 1890 it was necessary to construct an even larger dam. The "Big" in Big Bear Lake was adopted to distinguish Bear Lake from nearby Lake Arrowhead, which at the time was known as Little Bear Lake.

In 1994, the Devil Fire burned a large area in this region. In 1999, the Willow Creek Fire burned areas that had not yet recovered from the Devil Fire. A number of tracks within the fire-damaged area have been temporarily closed to vehicle access until regrowth stabilizes the region and encourages the return of wildlife.

Description

This long, easygoing trail follows a winding route through San Bernardino National Forest from Green Valley to Big Bear City. Along the way it passes through a variety of forest scenery and the historic Holcomb Valley. The trail leaves the paved road near Green Valley Lake and follows a graded dirt road around the side of the range before dropping down to cross through Crab Creek.

There are several excellent places to camp along this road. You can choose between the forest service campgrounds at Crab Creek and the very pretty Big Pine Flat, as well as many backcountry sites, either just off the main graded route or along one of the numerous side trails. The area is popular with all types of OHV enthusiasts, and there are lots of trails to explore, most of which do not appear on maps of the region. The trails use the green, blue, and black rating system and are clearly marked as to the type of OHVs that can use them. ATV owners should note that many of the roads and trails allow street legal vehicles only.

The route passes through the sites of Belleville and Holcomb Valley, and visitors can see the site of Two-Gun Bill's Saloon, the hangman's tree, and other remains of this historic area. An interpretive auto tour leaflet is available from the forest service; it covers the sites within the valley.

The trail finishes just west of Big Bear Lake on California 18, with expansive views over Baldwin Lake.

Current Road Information

San Bernardino National Forest
Big Bear Ranger District
PO Box 290
41397 North Shore Drive, Highway 38
Fawnskin, CA 92333
(909) 866-3437

Big Bear Visitor Center
PO Box 66
40971 North Shore Drive, Highway 38
Fawnskin, CA 92333
(909) 866-3437

Map References

BLM San Bernardino, Big Bear Lake
USFS San Bernardino National Forest
USGS 1:24,000 Keller Peak, Butler Peak, Fawnskin, Big Bear City
1:100,000 San Bernardino, Big Bear Lake
Maptech CD-ROM: Ventura/Los Angeles/Orange County; San Bernardino County/Mojave
Southern & Central California Atlas & Gazetteer, pp. 95, 96
California Road & Recreation Atlas, pp. 104, 105

Route Directions

Mileage		Directions
▼ 0.0		From Green Valley Lake Road, 2.5 miles north of California 18, zero trip meter and turn northeast on graded dirt road 3N16, sign-posted to Big Pine Flat.
3.8 ▲		Trail ends at T-intersection with paved Green Valley Lake Road. Turn left for Green Valley Lake; turn right for California 18.
		GPS: N34°14.01' W117°05.32'
▼ 0.2	SO	Track on left.
3.6 ▲	SO	Track on right.
▼ 0.8	SO	Track on right through gate.
3.0 ▲	SO	Track on left through gate.
▼ 1.8	SO	Track on right is 2N90 for street legal vehicles only; then second track on right. Third track on right is 2N12X for ATVs and motorbikes only.
2.0 ▲	SO	Track on left is 2N12X for ATVs and motorbikes only; then second track on left. Third track on left is 2N90 for street legal vehicles only.
		GPS: N34°14.82' W117°05.15'
▼ 2.2	BR	Track on left is 3N16Q, which goes 0.25 miles to a locked gate.
1.6 ▲	SO	Track on right is 3N16Q, which goes 0.25 miles to a locked gate.
		GPS: N34°14.88' W117°05.47'
▼ 3.1	SO	Track on right.
0.7 ▲	SO	Track on left.
▼ 3.4	SO	Track on left; then road becomes paved.
0.4 ▲	SO	Road becomes graded dirt; then track on right.
▼ 3.7	SO	Cross through Crab Creek on concrete ford.
0.1 ▲	SO	Cross through Crab Creek on concrete ford.
		GPS: N34°15.55' W117°05.00'
▼ 3.8	TR	Graded road ahead is 3N34 to Crab Flats USFS Campground. Remain on 3N16, suitable for 4WDs, ATVs, and motorbikes—rated green. Zero trip meter.
0.0 ▲		Continue to the southeast on 3N16.
		GPS: N34°15.64' W117°05.02'
▼ 0.0		Continue to the east. Trail on right is 2W12 for ATVs and motorbikes—rated blue.
4.8 ▲	TL	Trail on left is 2W12 for ATVs and motorbikes—rated blue. Graded road on right is 3N34 to Crab Flats USFS Campground. Zero trip meter.
▼ 0.2	SO	Road turns to graded dirt.
4.6 ▲	SO	Road becomes paved.
▼ 0.4	SO	Campsite on left.
4.4 ▲	SO	Campsite on right.
▼ 1.1	SO	Small track on left.
3.7 ▲	SO	Small track on right.
▼ 2.4	SO	Cross through wash. Road is now paved.
2.4 ▲	SO	Cross through wash. Road is now graded dirt.
▼ 2.7	SO	Pacific Crest National Scenic Trail crosses road. Track on right goes to 3N14 for street legal 4WDs and motorbikes only—rated black; then cross through Holcomb Creek.
2.1 ▲	SO	Cross through Holcomb Creek; then track on left goes to 3N14 for street legal 4WDs and motorbikes only—rated black. Pacific Crest National Scenic Trail crosses road.
		GPS: N34°16.53' W117°03.00'
▼ 3.0	SO	Road turns to graded dirt.
1.8 ▲	SO	Road is now paved.
▼ 3.9	SO	Track on right.
0.9 ▲	SO	Track on left.
▼ 4.8	SO	Track on right is 2N06X, which goes to 3N93, for street legal 4WDs and motorbikes only—rated black. Zero trip meter.
0.0 ▲		Continue to the west.
		GPS: N34°17.36' W117°02.12'
▼ 0.0		Continue to the northeast.
3.2 ▲	SO	Track on left is 2N06X, which goes to 3N93, for street legal 4WDs and motorbikes only—rated black. Zero trip meter.
▼ 1.7	SO	Track on right is 3N97.
1.5 ▲	SO	Track on left is 3N97.
		GPS: N34°18.12' W117°01.21'
▼ 2.8	SO	Track on left.
0.4 ▲	SO	Track on right.
▼ 2.9	SO	Track on right.
0.3 ▲	SO	Track on left.
▼ 3.1	SO	Track on right.
0.1 ▲	SO	Track on left.
▼ 3.2	SO	Graded roads on right and left are both 3N14—rated green. To the right is for street legal vehicles only; to the left is for 4WDs, ATVs, and motorbikes. Big Pine Flat USFS Campground on left. Zero trip meter.
0.0 ▲		Continue to the southwest.
		GPS: N34°19.19' W117°00.57'
▼ 0.0		Continue to the northeast on graded dirt 3N16.
6.2 ▲	SO	Graded roads on right and left are both 3N14—rated green. To the right is for 4WDs, ATVs, and motorbikes; to the left is for street legal vehicles only. Big Pine Flat USFS Campground on right. Zero trip meter.
▼ 0.1	SO	Track on left is 3N11 for 4WDs, ATVs, and motorbikes—rated green. Track is temporarily gated to allow revegetation, but is open to hikers and horses.
6.1 ▲	SO	Track on right is 3N11 for 4WDs, ATVs, and motorbikes—rated green. Track is temporarily gated to allow revegetation, but is open to hikers and horses.
▼ 0.6	SO	Track on right.
5.6 ▲	SO	Track on left.
▼ 0.7	SO	Track on left is 3N03Y—temporarily closed to allow revegetation after wildfire.
5.5 ▲	SO	Track on right is 3N03Y—temporarily closed to allow revegetation after wildfire.
▼ 1.2	SO	Track on right.
5.0 ▲	SO	Track on left.

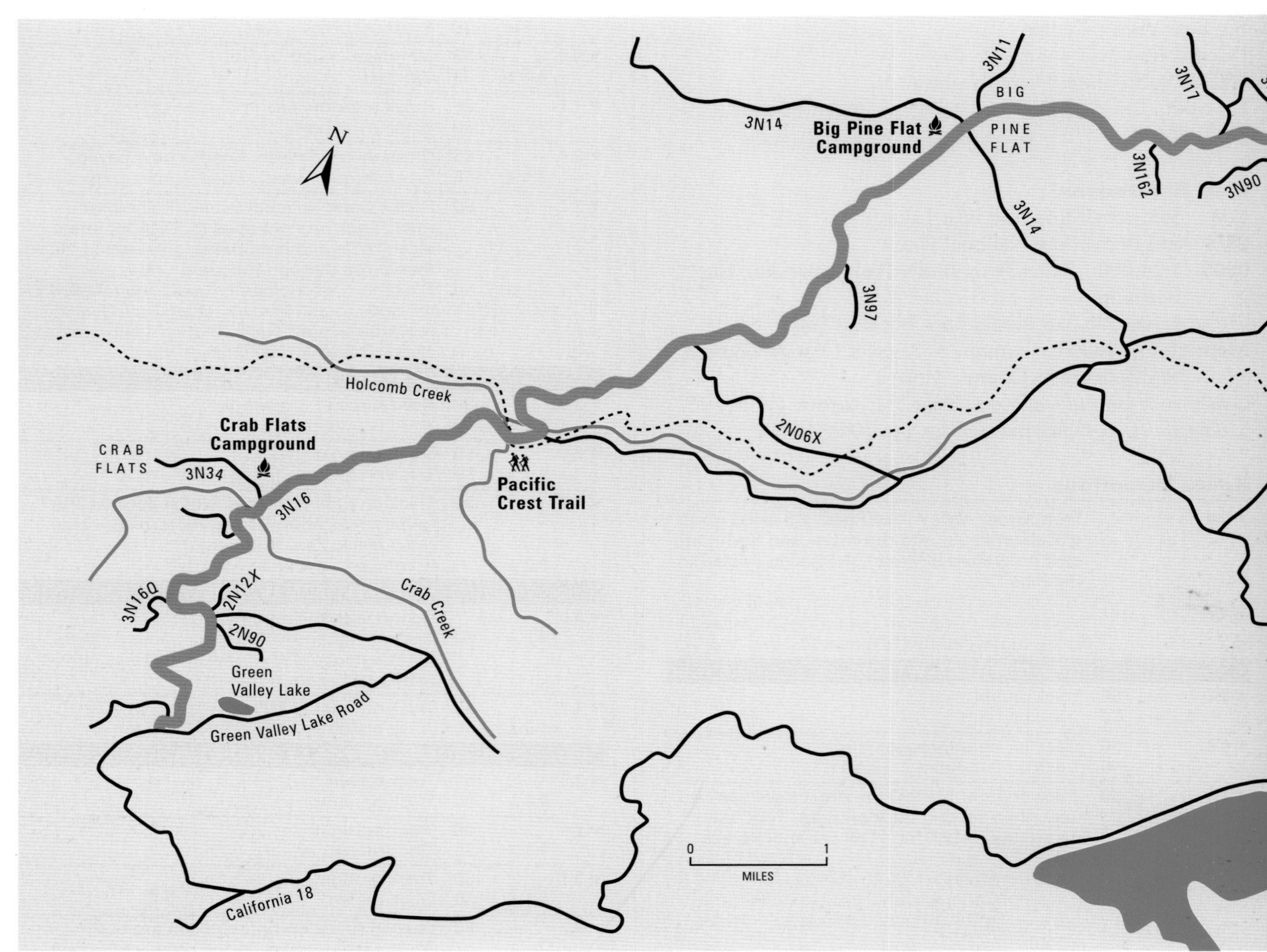

▼ 1.6		SO	Track on right is 3N16L.
	4.6 ▲	SO	Track on left is 3N16L.
			GPS: N34°19.44' W116°59.18'
▼ 1.9		SO	Track on right.
	4.3 ▲	SO	Track on left.
▼ 2.3		SO	Track on left is 3N17—temporarily closed to allow revegetation after wildfire.
	3.9 ▲	SO	Track on right is 3N17—temporarily closed to allow revegetation after wildfire.
			GPS: N34°19.54' W116°58.64'
▼ 2.6		SO	Track on right.
	3.6 ▲	SO	Track on left.
▼ 2.7		SO	Track on right.
	3.5 ▲	SO	Track on left.
▼ 2.9		SO	Track on right is 3N90.
	3.3 ▲	SO	Track on left is 3N90.
			GPS: N34°19.60' W116°58.08'
▼ 3.4		SO	Track on left is 3N17, which goes to White Mountain, for 4WDs, ATVs, and motorbikes—rated black. Track is temporarily closed to allow revegetation after wildfire. Also hiking trail on left and track on right to diggings.
	2.8 ▲	SO	Track on right is 3N17, which goes to White Mountain, for 4WDs, ATVs, and motorbikes—rated black. Track is temporarily closed to allow revegetation after wildfire. Also hiking trail on right and track on left to diggings.
			GPS: N34°19.67' W116°57.58'
▼ 3.6		SO	Track on left.
	2.6 ▲	SO	Track on right.
▼ 4.2		SO	Track on right is 3N89.
	2.0 ▲	SO	Track on left is 3N89.
			GPS: N34°19.18' W116°57.12'
▼ 4.6		SO	Graded dirt road on left and right; then track on right.
	1.6 ▲	SO	Track on left; then graded dirt road on left and right.
▼ 4.9		SO	Track on left.
	1.3 ▲	SO	Track on right.
▼ 5.5		SO	Large tailings heap on right.
	0.7 ▲	SO	Large tailings heap on left.
			GPS: N34°18.82' W116°56.10'
▼ 5.7		SO	Track on left is 3N54.
	0.5 ▲	BL	Track on right is 3N54.
			GPS: N34°18.82' W116°55.84'
▼ 5.8		SO	Track on right is 3N08 for street legal vehicles—rated blue.
	0.4 ▲	SO	Track on left is 3N08 for street legal vehicles—rated blue.

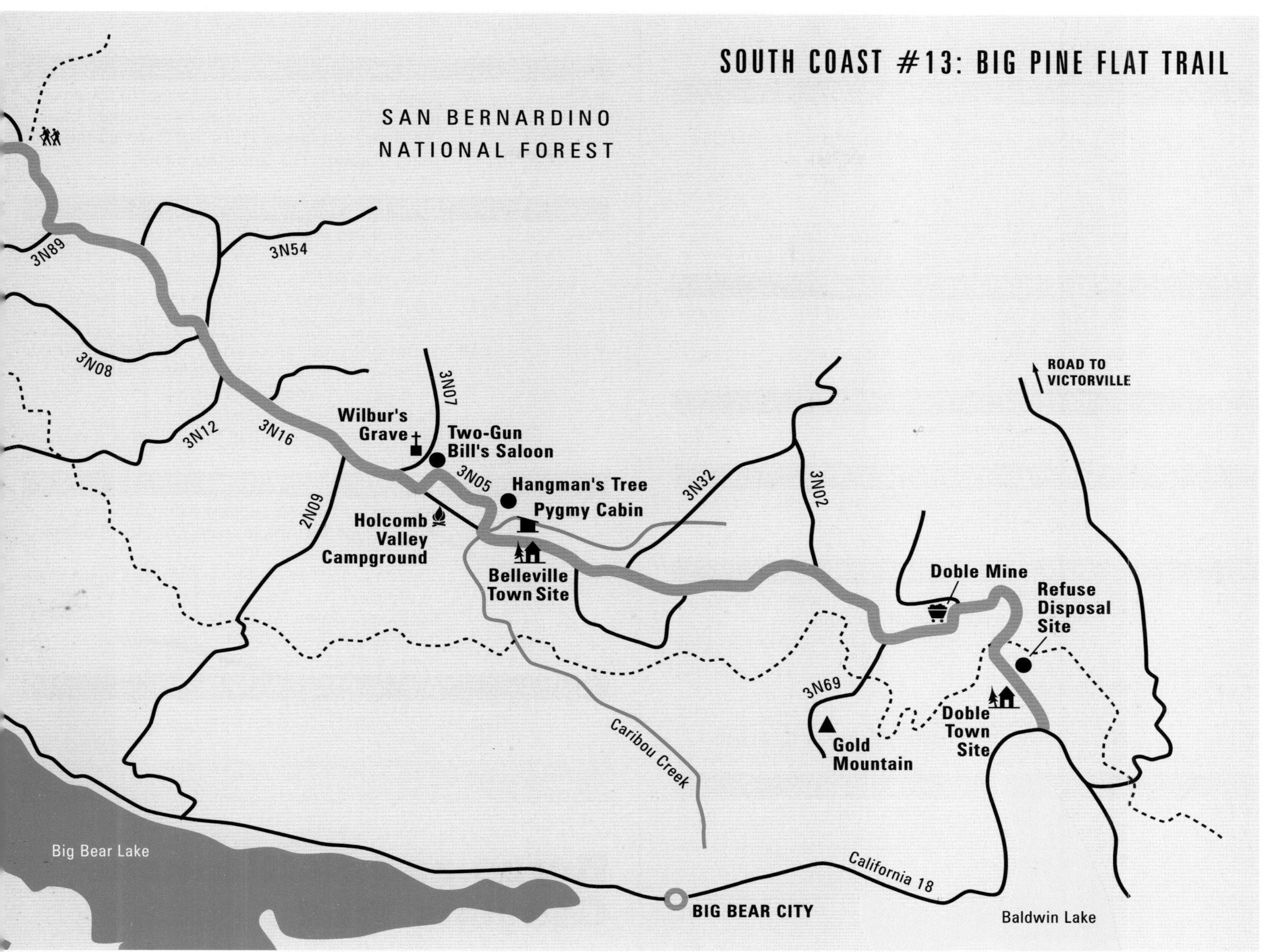

			GPS: N34°18.77′ W116°55.84′
▼ 6.0		SO	Track on left is 3N16H; then track on right.
	0.2 ▲	SO	Track on left; then track on right is 3N16H.
▼ 6.2		SO	Graded road on right is 3N12. Zero trip meter and continue on 3N16, following sign to Holcomb Valley Campground.
	0.0 ▲		Continue to the west.
			GPS: N34°18.57′ W116°55.59′
▼ 0.0			Continue to the east.
	1.1 ▲	SO	Graded road on left is 3N12. Zero trip meter and continue on 3N16, following sign to Big Pine Flat Campground.
▼ 0.1		SO	Track on left.
	1.0 ▲	SO	Track on right.
▼ 0.2		SO	Two tracks on left.
	0.9 ▲	SO	Two tracks on right.
▼ 0.4		SO	Two tracks on left.
	0.7 ▲	SO	Two tracks on right.
▼ 0.5		SO	Track on left.
	0.6 ▲	SO	Track on right.
▼ 0.9		SO	Two tracks on left; then track on left is 3N10; then track on right.
	0.2 ▲	SO	Track on left; then track on right is 3N10; then two tracks on right.

			GPS: N34°18.38′ W116°54.67′
▼ 1.1		TL	Turn left, remaining on 3N16 and following the sign to Holcomb Valley Campground. Graded road straight ahead is 2N09, which goes to California 38. Zero trip meter.
	0.0 ▲		Continue to the north.
			GPS: N34°18.28′ W116°54.55′
▼ 0.0			Continue to the east.
	0.7 ▲	TR	T-intersection. Graded road on left is 2N09, which goes to California 38. Turn right, remaining on 3N16 and following the sign to Big Pine Flat. Zero trip meter.
▼ 0.1		SO	Track on left.
	0.6 ▲	SO	Track on right.
▼ 0.2		SO	Track on left; then track on right.
	0.5 ▲	SO	Track on left; then track on right.
▼ 0.4		BR	Track on left is 3N07, which goes 0.2 miles to Wilbur's Grave and farther to Arctic Canyon. Follow sign to Holcomb Valley.
	0.3 ▲	BL	Track on right is 3N07, which goes 0.2 miles to Wilbur's Grave and farther to Arctic Canyon.
			GPS: N34°18.21′ W116°54.13′
▼ 0.7		TL	Turn left onto 3N05 to Holcomb Valley and the site of Belleville. Road 3N16 continues straight

ahead to Holcomb Valley Campground. Zero trip meter.

0.0 ▲ Continue to the west.

GPS: N34°18.16' W116°53.91'

▼ 0.0 Continue to the north.

5.2 ▲ TR T-intersection with 3N16. Zero trip meter and rejoin 3N16.

▼ 0.1 SO Track on right.

5.1 ▲ SO Track on left.

▼ 0.3 SO Site of Two-Gun Bill's Saloon on left.

4.9 ▲ SO Site of Two-Gun Bill's Saloon on right.

GPS: N34°18.34' W116°53.84'

▼ 0.7 SO Site of Jonathan Tibbett's Grasshopper Quartz Mill on left.

4.5 ▲ SO Site of Jonathan Tibbet's Grasshopper Quartz Mill on right.

GPS: N34°18.22' W116°53.78'

▼ 0.8 SO Hangman's tree on left.

4.4 ▲ SO Hangman's tree on right.

GPS: N34°18.18' W116°53.33'

▼ 1.0 TL Turn left, rejoining 3N16, sign-posted as the Gold Fever Trail.

4.2 ▲ TR Turn right onto 3N05.

GPS: N34°18.02' W116°53.40'

▼ 1.1 SO Cross through Caribou Creek; then diggings on left at marker. Track on right.

4.1 ▲ SO Track on left. Diggings on right at marker; then cross through Caribou Creek.

▼ 1.2 SO Track on right.

4.0 ▲ SO Track on left.

▼ 1.4 SO Pygmy Cabin on left at Belleville town site.

3.8 ▲ SO Pygmy Cabin on right at Belleville town site.

GPS: N34°18.07' W116°53.07'

▼ 1.5 SO Track on right is 3N16B.

3.7 ▲ SO Track on left is 3N16B.

▼ 1.7 SO Track on right.

3.5 ▲ SO Track on left.

▼ 1.9 SO Track on right.

3.3 ▲ SO Track on left.

▼ 2.1 SO Track on left.

3.1 ▲ SO Track on right.

▼ 2.2 SO Track on left is 3N32; then track on right is 3N76.

3.0 ▲ SO Track on left is 3N76; then track on right is 3N32.

GPS: N34°17.96' W116°52.24'

▼ 2.7 SO Track on right is 3N79.

2.5 ▲ SO Track on left is 3N79.

▼ 3.2 SO Track on right is 3N16A.

2.0 ▲ SO Track on left is 3N16A.

GPS: N34°18.11' W116°51.24'

▼ 3.6 SO Faint track on right and faint track on left.

1.6 ▲ SO Faint track on right and faint track on left.

▼ 3.7 SO Track on left is 3N02.

1.5 ▲ SO Track on right is 3N02.

GPS: N34°18.30' W116°50.78'

▼ 4.5 BL Track on right is 3N69 to Gold Mountain for street legal 4WDs and motorbikes only—rated black.

0.7 ▲ BR Track on left is 3N69 to Gold Mountain for street legal 4WDs and motorbikes only—rated black.

GPS: N34°17.95' W116°50.18'

▼ 5.0 SO Remains of Doble Mine on left and wooden loading hopper on right.

0.2 ▲ SO Remains of Doble Mine on right and wooden loading hopper on left.

GPS: N34°18.17' W116°49.71'

▼ 5.2 TR Track on left is 3N61 to California 18 for street legal 4WDs and motorbikes only—rated blue. Track straight ahead. Turn right, remaining on main graded road. Zero trip meter.

0.0 ▲ Continue to the east.

GPS: N34°18.28' W116°49.74'

▼ 0.0 Continue to the south.

1.6 ▲ TL Track on right. Track straight ahead is 3N61 to California 18 for street legal 4WDs and motorbikes only—rated blue. Turn left, remaining on main graded road. Zero trip meter.

▼ 0.7 TR Turn right onto paved road. San Bernardino County Refuse Disposal Site is on the left.

0.9 ▲ TL Turn left onto roughly graded dirt road immediately before entrance to San Bernardino County Refuse Disposal Site. Road is marked 3N16.

GPS: N34°18.22' W116°49.31'

▼ 1.6 Trail ends at T-intersection with California 18. Turn left for Victorville; turn right for Big Bear City.

0.0 ▲ Trail commences on California 18, 3 miles east of Big Bear City. Zero trip meter and turn northwest on paved Holcomb Valley Road, following sign for Holcomb Valley. Turn is 0.1 miles east of mile marker 58.

GPS: N34°17.63' W116°48.78'

SOUTH COAST #14

Burns and Rattlesnake Canyons Trail

Starting Point:	**4-way intersection of Pioneertown Road, Pipes Canyon Road, and Rimrock Road, 7.3 miles northwest of Yucca Valley**
Finishing Point:	**Baldwin Lake Road, 4 miles east of Big Bear Park**
Total Mileage:	**20.4 miles**
Unpaved Mileage:	**18.3 miles**
Driving Time:	**3 hours**
Elevation Range:	**4,300–7,000 feet**
Usually Open:	**May to November**
Best Time to Travel:	**May to November, dry weather**
Difficulty Rating:	**2**
Scenic Rating:	**9**
Remoteness Rating:	**+0**

Special Attractions

- Easy trail through Joshua tree forest.
- Rugged and scenic Rattlesnake Canyon.
- Access to a network of 4WD trails of varying standards.
- Remains of the Rose Mine.

History

Situated near the start of this trail, Pioneertown was built in 1946 specifically as a movie set, mainly for Westerns, and was used as the backdrop for such movies as *Annie Oakley, Range Rider*, and *Buffalo Bill*. Actors lived at Pioneertown while filming. Roy Rogers was one of the better-known investors in Pioneertown.

The Rose Mine was the most profitable gold mine in the San Bernardino Mountains, producing nearly 100 times as much gold per ton of ore than the better-known Gold Mountain Mine. Opening in 1887 as the Homestake Mine, it became the Rose Mine in 1898 and operated until 1906.

San Francisco millionaire Elias J. "Lucky" Baldwin established the settlement of Baldwin at the end of the Holcomb Valley gold rush. He constructed a 40-stamp mill at Gold Mountain. The town of Bairdstown sprang up to support the mill, but the gold wasn't as high a grade as first thought and the mill closed down after only seven months. It burned down in 1876.

In 1900, Baldwin and a new associate, J. R. DeLaMar, opened a second mill on the hill above the original site. Using cyanide, they extracted enough gold from the low-grade ore to turn a modest profit. This mill operated until 1903.

Description

This easy trail travels from high desert at Yucca Valley through two spectacular canyons to the pine forests around Big Bear City. The trail commences a short distance from Yucca Valley, along Pioneertown Road. The old, privately-owned movie sets are still there. Once through the small community of Rimrock, the road becomes roughly graded dirt as it enters Burns Canyon. The surface is sandy, but high-clearance 2WDs will have no problems under normal conditions. Burns Canyon Road has several different routes, and traffic operates as a one-way system in the divided sections of trail. Unless otherwise stated, keep to the right at any division of the main trail; the trail will rejoin in a short distance.

A "Welcome" at Burn's Cabin

The first few miles of the trail pass through a mix of BLM and private land, and there are many houses scattered on the boulder-strewn hillsides. Tracks on either side that obviously lead to private property have not been mentioned in the route directions unless there is the possibility of confusion.

The trail climbs out of Burns Canyon and descends gradually to cross the head of Rattlesnake Canyon. There are many Joshua trees growing at elevations as high as 6,000 feet that mix with the juniper trees of the higher elevations. This is a rarely-seen vegetation mix.

Joshua trees are abundant along the trail as high as 6,000 feet

One of the most spectacular sections of the trail is the shelf road that runs along Rattlesnake Canyon. The trail is lumpy with embedded rocks, but it has a good, firm surface, and there are ample passing places.

Those looking to camp will find several sites with good views and some shade between Rattlesnake Canyon and the Rose Mine. The Rose Mine makes a pleasant stopping place midway along the trail. Several tailings heaps and the stone foundations of the mill remain. The workings extend for a couple of miles in each direction.

The trail follows forest road 2N02, which swings to the north to climb toward Big Bear Lake. You will need to ford Arrastre Creek along this section, but it is normally shallow and is unlikely to cause any difficulty. The trail finishes on Baldwin Lake Road, 4 miles east of Big Bear Park.

Current Road Information

San Bernardino National Forest
Big Bear Ranger District
PO Box 290
41397 North Shore Drive, Highway 38
Fawnskin, CA 92333
(909) 866-3437

Big Bear Visitor Center
PO Box 66
40971 North Shore Drive, Highway 38
Fawnskin, CA 92333
(909) 866-3437

Map References

BLM Palm Springs
USFS San Bernardino National Forest
USGS 1:24,000 Rimrock, Onyx Peak, Rattlesnake Canyon, Big Bear City
1:100,000 Palm Springs
Maptech CD-ROM: San Diego/Joshua Tree
Southern & Central California Atlas & Gazetteer, pp. 97, 96
California Road & Recreation Atlas, p. 105

Route Directions

Mileage		Direction
▼ 0.0		From California 62 at Yucca Valley, turn northwest on Pioneertown Road. Remain on the paved road and pass the Pioneertown movie set on right after 3.9 miles. Continue to the 7.3-mile mark and a major 4-way intersection with Pipes Canyon Road, Pioneertown Road, and Rimrock Road. Zero trip meter at 4-way intersection and continue straight ahead (west) on Rimrock Road. There is a sign at the intersection for Pipes Canyon Preserve to the north, down Pipes Canyon Road. Remain on paved road, ignoring turns to the right and left into private property.
7.9 ▲		Trail ends at 4-way intersection with Pipes Canyon Road, Rimrock Road, and Pioneertown Road. Continue straight ahead (east) on Pioneertown Road for 7.3 miles to reach Yucca Valley and California 62. Pioneertown is passed on the left after 3.4 miles.
		GPS: N34°10.92' W116°32.11'
▼ 1.3	TL	Turn left onto paved Burns Canyon Road and enter community of Rimrock.
6.6 ▲	TR	Turn right onto paved Rimrock Road.
		GPS: N34°11.88' W116°32.71'
▼ 2.1	SO	Road turns to graded dirt. Enter Burns Canyon.
5.8 ▲	SO	Road turns to paved and enters community of Rimrock. Remain on paved road, ignoring turns to the left and right into private property.
▼ 3.2	SO	Small stone and concrete ruins on left. Enter line of wash. Many wash crossings for next 1.1 miles.
4.7 ▲	SO	Exit line of wash. Small stone and concrete ruins on right.
		GPS: N34°12.21' W116°34.59'
▼ 3.9	SO	Homestead ruin on right near Burns Spring.
4.0 ▲	SO	Homestead ruin on left near Burns Spring.
▼ 4.3	BR	Part of one-way system. Keep right; trail rejoins almost immediately. Trail exits line of wash.
3.6 ▲	BR	Part of one-way system. Keep right; trail rejoins almost immediately. Road enters line of Burns Canyon Wash. Many wash crossings for next 1.1 miles.
▼ 4.7	SO	Cross through wash.
3.2 ▲	SO	Cross through wash.
▼ 5.2	SO	Track on right.
2.7 ▲	SO	Track on left.
▼ 5.5	SO	Track on right.
2.4 ▲	SO	Track on left.
		GPS: N34°12.84' W116°36.63'
▼ 5.8	SO	Track on right.
2.1 ▲	SO	Track on left.
▼ 6.2	SO	Track on right.
1.7 ▲	SO	Track on left.
▼ 6.3	SO	Cross through Antelope Creek.
1.6 ▲	SO	Cross through Antelope Creek.
▼ 6.5	BL	Well-used track on right.
1.4 ▲	BR	Well-used track on left.
		GPS: N34°13.49' W116°37.23'
▼ 6.7	SO	Track on right is Deer Road; then track on left.
1.2 ▲	SO	Track on right; then track on left is Deer Road.
▼ 6.9	SO	Track on left.
1.0 ▲	SO	Track on right.
▼ 7.0	SO	Track on right.
0.9 ▲	SO	Track on left.
		GPS: N34°13.55' W116°37.76'
▼ 7.2	SO	Track on left and track on right.

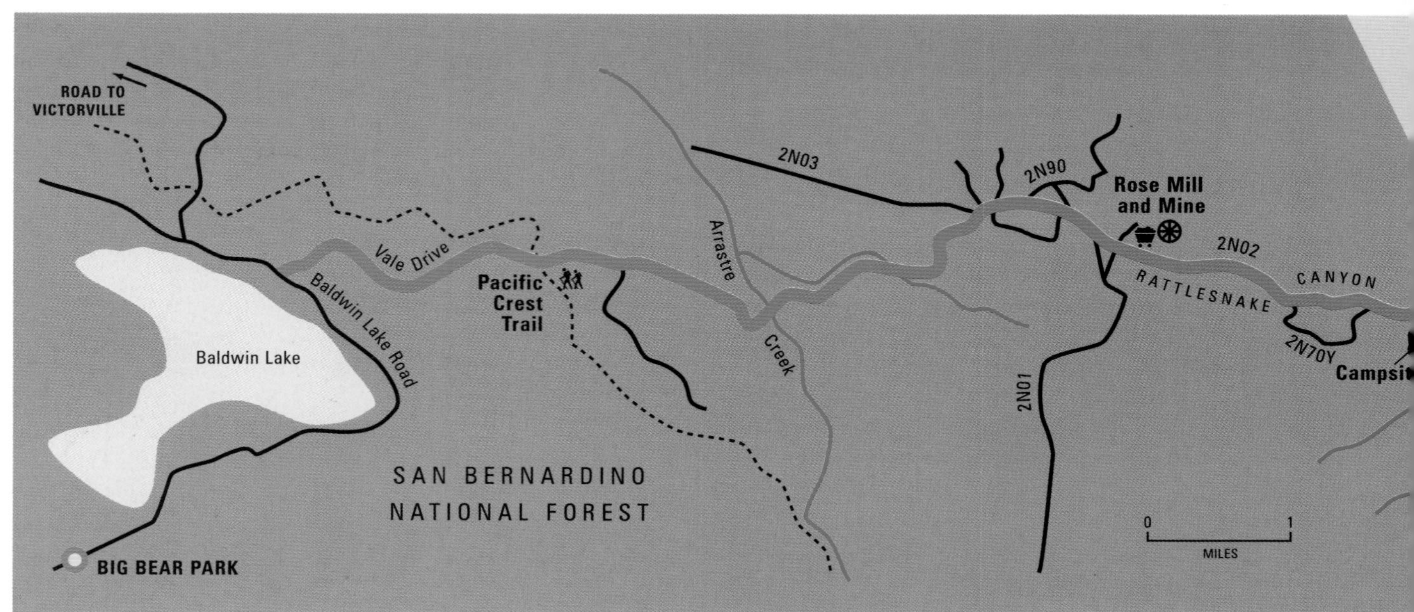

0.7 ▲ SO Track on left and track on right.

▼ 7.5 TR T-intersection. Remain on public road.
0.4 ▲ TL Trail continues straight ahead. Remain on public road.

▼ 7.9 TL 4-way intersection. Follow wooden sign for Big Bear and zero trip meter.
0.0 ▲ Continue to the south.

GPS: N34°13.93' W116°38.28'

▼ 0.0 Continue to the west.
2.1 ▲ TR 4-way intersection. Follow wooden sign for Yucca Valley and Rimrock and zero trip meter.

▼ 0.3 BL Small track on left; then well-used track on right. Bear left onto the marked 2N02.
1.8 ▲ SO Well-used track on left; then small track on right.

GPS: N34°14.01' W116°38.61'

▼ 0.6 SO Enter San Bernardino National Forest.
1.5 ▲ SO Exit San Bernardino National Forest.

▼ 0.9 SO Track on right.
1.2 ▲ SO Track on left.

▼ 1.2 SO Two tracks on left and track on right on saddle.
0.9 ▲ SO Two tracks on right and track on left on saddle.

▼ 1.4 SO Cross through wash; then track on left.
0.7 ▲ SO Track on right; then cross through wash.

▼ 1.5 SO Track on left to mine.
0.6 ▲ SO Track on right to mine.

▼ 1.9 SO Track on left; then track on right.
0.2 ▲ SO Track on left; then track on right.

▼ 2.1 BR Campsite on left; then track on left is 2N61Y—rated black for 4WDs and rated blue for ATVs and motorbikes. Remain on 2N02, marked to Cactus Flat, suitable for 4WDs, ATVs, and motorbikes—rated green. Zero trip meter.
0.0 ▲ Continue to the north.

GPS: N34°13.64' W116°40.24'

▼ 0.0 Continue to the southwest.
2.5 ▲ SO Track on right is 2N61Y—rated black for 4WDs and rated blue for ATVs and motorbikes. Remain on 2N02, marked to Cactus Flat. Zero trip meter.

▼ 0.4 BR Track on left is 2N70Y, which is a loop to 2N02 for 4WDs, ATVs, and motorbikes—rated black. Start of shelf road along Rattlesnake Canyon.
2.1 ▲ SO Track on right is 2N70Y, which is a loop to 2N02 for 4WDs, ATVs, and motorbikes—rated black. End of shelf road.

GPS: N34°13.75' W116°40.56'

▼ 1.4 SO Track on left is 2N70Y, which is a loop to 2N02.
1.1 ▲ BL Track on right is 2N70Y, which is a loop to 2N02.

GPS: N34°14.17' W116°41.23'

▼ 1.9 BL Track on right.
0.6 ▲ SO Track on left.

▼ 2.0 SO Track on left.
0.5 ▲ SO Track on right.

▼ 2.2 SO Rose Mine and mill site on right. Stone foundations of mill and tailings on right. Many tracks on right and left to mining works for the next 0.3 miles.
0.3 ▲ SO Rose Mine and mill site on left. Stone foundations of mill and tailings on left.

GPS: N34°14.58' W116°41.88'

▼ 2.5 SO 4-way intersection. Track on left is 2N01. Zero trip meter and continue straight ahead on marked 2N02.
0.0 ▲ Continue to the southeast.

GPS: N34°14.78' W116°42.12'

▼ 0.0 Continue to the northwest.
1.1 ▲ SO 4-way intersection. Track on right is 2N01. Zero trip meter and continue on 2N02. Many tracks on right and left to mining works for the next 0.3 miles.

▼ 0.1 SO Track on left joins 2N61Y for 4WDs, ATVs, and motorbikes—rated green.
1.0 ▲ SO Track on right joins 2N61Y for 4WDs, ATVs, and motorbikes—rated green.

▼ 0.2 SO Track on left to adit.
0.9 ▲ SO Track on right to adit.

GPS: N34°15.00' W116°42.27'

▼ 0.4 SO Track on right; then track on left.

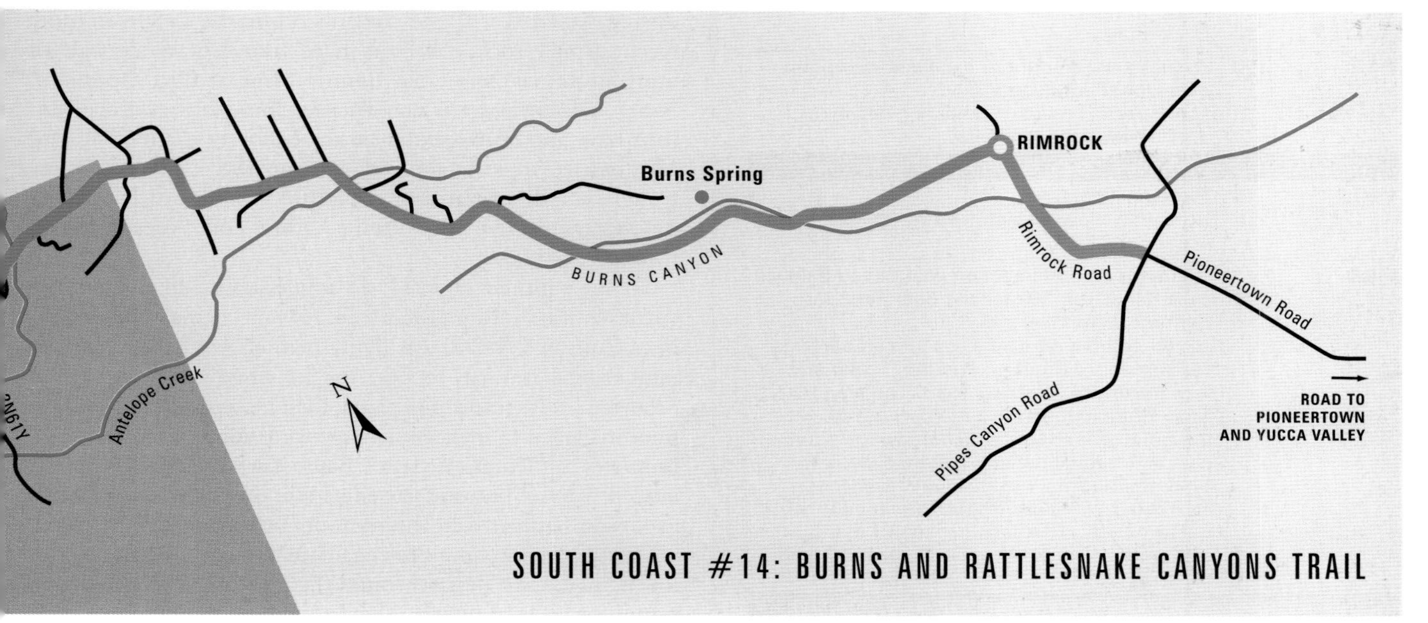

	0.7 ▲	SO	Track on right; then track on left.
▼ 0.7		SO	Track on right is 2N90.
	0.4 ▲	BR	Track on left is 2N90.
▼ 0.8		SO	Track on right.
	0.3 ▲	SO	Track on left.
▼ 1.0		SO	Track on left and track on right.
	0.1 ▲	SO	Track on left and track on right.
▼ 1.1		TL	4-way intersection on saddle. Zero trip meter and turn left, remaining on 2N02. Track ahead is 2N03 for 4WDs, ATVs, and motorbikes—rated green.
	0.0 ▲		Continue to the east.
			GPS: N34°15.37' W116°42.96'
▼ 0.0			Continue to the northwest.
	6.8 ▲	TR	4-way intersection on saddle. Zero trip meter and turn right, remaining on 2N02 for 4WDs, ATVs, and motorbikes—rated green. Track on left is 2N03 for 4WDs, ATVs, and motorbikes—rated green.
▼ 0.5		SO	Track on left.
	6.3 ▲	SO	Track on right.
▼ 0.9		SO	Track on left.
	5.9 ▲	SO	Track on right.
▼ 1.0		SO	Cross through wash.
	5.8 ▲	SO	Cross through wash.
▼ 2.2		SO	Cross through Arrastre Creek.
	4.6 ▲	SO	Cross through Arrastre Creek.
			GPS: N34°15.33' W116°44.61'
▼ 2.6		SO	Track on left.
	4.2 ▲	SO	Track on right.
▼ 3.6		SO	Track on left.
	3.2 ▲	SO	Track on right.
▼ 4.0		SO	Track on right.
	2.8 ▲	SO	Track on left.
▼ 4.1		SO	Pacific Crest National Scenic Trail crosses.
	2.7 ▲	SO	Pacific Crest National Scenic Trail crosses.
			GPS: N34°16.16' W116°46.02'
▼ 5.2		SO	Track on left.
	1.6 ▲	SO	Track on right.
▼ 5.6		SO	Track on left.
	1.2 ▲	SO	Track on right.
▼ 6.1		SO	Track on right.
	0.7 ▲	SO	Track on left.
▼ 6.2		SO	Three tracks on right to excellent viewpoint over Upper Johnson Valley.
	0.6 ▲	SO	Three tracks on left to excellent viewpoint over Upper Johnson Valley.
			GPS: N34°16.88' W116°47.24'
▼ 6.7		TR	T-intersection.
	0.1 ▲	TL	Turn left, following sign for Arrastre Shooting Areas and 2N02.
▼ 6.8			Trail ends at T-intersection with paved Baldwin Lake Road. Turn left for Big Bear Park; turn right for Victorville.
	0.0 ▲		To reach the start of the trail, take California 38 east out of Big Bear Park for 1 mile and turn northeast on Shay Road. The sign for Shay Road can be hard to spot, but it is at the point where California 38 swings southeast and intersects with Greenspot Road. Shay Road turns into Baldwin Lake Road. Proceed 3.2 miles from the intersection with California 38; then zero trip meter and turn east on graded dirt Vale Drive, also marked 2N02.
			GPS: N34°16.77' W116°47.78'

SOUTH COAST #15

Ord Mountains Trail

Starting Point:	**Intersection of Harrod Road and Camp Rock Road, 3.9 miles north of California 247**
Finishing Point:	**Barstow Road (California 247) at mile marker 63, 15 miles south of I-40**
Total Mileage:	**29.7 miles, plus 1.2-mile spur to Yucca Rings**
Unpaved Mileage:	**29.7 miles, plus 1.2-mile spur**
Driving Time:	**2.5 hours**
Elevation Range:	**3,000–4,600 feet**
Usually Open:	**Year-round**
Best Time to Travel:	**Year-round**
Difficulty Rating:	**3**
Scenic Rating:	**8**
Remoteness Rating:	**+0**

Special Attractions

- Upper Johnson Valley Yucca Rings Preserve Area of Critical Environmental Concern.
- Stoddard Valley and Johnson Valley OHV Open Areas.
- Rock climbing area at Sawtooth Canyon (New Jacks City).

History

The Ord Mountains were named for Major General E. O. C. Ord of Civil War fame. The gold mining district was established around 1870, though it was not a big producer at the time. Many mines can be seen across the mountainsides. Names such as Azucar, Gold Brick, Grandview, Ord Belt, Red Hill, and Alarm drew prospectors from near and far. Some mines, including the White Dollar, extracted tungsten during World War II and continued into the 1950s. In more recent times, rock collectors have found black crystals of mottramite near the Gold Banner Mine at Ord Mountain. Some well-formed chrysocolla pseudomorphs and chalcanthite have also been found near the Modesta Claim. The Ord Mountains region, located within the Bristol-Barstow trough, is a diverse area of rocks and minerals. It is bisected by the major Lenwood Fault. Other fault lines also run through the region.

In the summer of 1957, an unusual aircraft incident occurred in the vicinity of this trail. A twin-engine Western Airlines Convair CV-240 was flying high above the Ord Mountains from Las Vegas to Los Angeles when a large explosion occurred in the rear of the plane. Despite great difficulties, the pilot managed to make an emergency landing just a few minutes later at George Air Force Base near Adelanto. The plane landed with all but one passenger still on board. It seems the explosion happened in the restroom at the rear of the plane, where the one missing passenger was thought to be. The following day, a search party found the missing passenger's body, minus a couple of fingers, high in the Ord Mountains. Criminal investigations revealed the man had purchased two life insurance policies just hours before boarding the plane.

Description

The Ord Mountain Route Network links the Stoddard Valley and Johnson Valley OHV Areas with a series of marked trails. No cross-country travel is permitted within the area; vehicles must remain on marked trails. However, there is an extensive network of marked trails for 4WDs, ATVs, and motorbikes to explore. This route traverses the region from south to north, passing highly scenic areas and interesting features along the way.

The well-used, sand trail leaves Camp Rock Road and runs up the gently sloping, creosote-covered terrain. A number of large and spectacular granite boulders and outcrops are passed as the trail enters the Johnson Valley OHV Area.

The trail passes yucca rings in the Upper Johnson Valley Yucca Rings Preserve. The rings are a short distance from the main route along a spur trail. The rings of Mojave yuccas have diameters of as much as 20 feet and are composed of as many as 130 stalks. They are extremely rare, and the oldest are thought be at least 2,100 years old. The main area of the preserve is fenced, but it is easy to see some fine examples from the fence line. Smaller examples can be found outside the fenced area to the left of the trail.

The trail crosses graded dirt Camp Rock Road before winding its way through the Cinnamon Hills Restoration Area on the eastern edge of the Ord Mountain Route Network. This area of multicolored hills and granite boulders is a great place for photographers wanting some unusual shots of Mojave Desert scenery. Although it is not clearly marked, no camping is allowed within the Cinnamon Hills in order to protect the desert tortoise. Some individual sites are posted with No Camping signs, but the entire area at the north end of Tyler Valley is off limits to campers as well. Outside of this area, camping is permitted within 50 feet of the road in previously used areas. There are plenty of pretty sites to choose from.

Old yucca rings catch the eye in Upper Johnson Valley

A closer look reveals a rock climber in a white T-shirt at Stoddard Ridge

The trail skirts the edge of Ericksen Dry Lake in Tyler Valley before exiting to the north, passing west of Ord Mountain. It intersects with South Coast #16: Daggett Wash Trail before swinging west and following a series of small formed trails that leads past the remains of the Anita Mine (only tailings and blocked-in adits remain). The trail joins a graded pipeline road and follows it out to end on California 247, 15 miles south of Barstow.

Opposite the finishing point of the trail, a graded road goes 1.7 miles to a popular and challenging rock climbing area. This area, shown on maps as Stoddard Ridge, is called Sawtooth Canyon by the Bureau of Land Management. Many rock climbers refer to the area as New Jacks City. This internationally renowned area offers climbs to suit all abilities, including some of the toughest and most technically challenging climbs anywhere. However, it is also a prime nesting habitat for prairie falcons and golden eagles. Rock climbing may be restricted in the future during nesting season. For the sake of the birds, the BLM requests that you not climb in the area between mid-February and June.

Current Road Information

Bureau of Land Management
Barstow Field Office
2601 Barstow Road
Barstow, CA 92311
(760) 252-6000

Map References

BLM Newberry Springs
USGS 1:24,000 Grand View Mine, Fry Mt., Ord Mt., West Ord Mt.
1:100,000 Newberry Springs
Maptech CD-ROM: San Bernardino County/Mojave
Southern & Central California Atlas & Gazetteer, p. 82
California Road & Recreation Atlas, p. 105

Route Directions

▼ 0.0			Trail starts at the intersection of Harrod Road and Camp Rock Road, 3.9 miles north of California 247. Turn northeast on paved Camp Rock Road, following sign to Johnson Valley OHV Area; then immediately turn east onto wide, graded Granite Road and zero trip meter.
	6.7 ▲		Trail ends at the intersection of Harrod Road and Camp Rock Road. Turn left on Camp Rock Road for California 247 and the Lucerne Valley; turn right on Camp Rock Road for Barstow.
			GPS: N34°30.10' W116°51.39'
▼ 0.5		SO	Track on right and track on left.
	6.2 ▲	SO	Track on right and track on left.
▼ 1.0		SO	Track on left and track on right.
	5.7 ▲	SO	Track on left and track on right.
▼ 1.9		BL	Bear left and follow under power lines. Two tracks on right. Trail enters Johnson Valley OHV Area at sign; then track on left. Many tracks on left and right within OHV area. Only major ones are mentioned in the directions.
	4.8 ▲	BR	Track on right; then bear right, leaving power lines and Johnson Valley OHV Area. Two tracks on left.
			GPS: N34°30.08' W116°49.34'
▼ 4.8		BR	5-way intersection. Bear first right onto Squaw Bush Road.
	1.9 ▲	BL	5-way intersection. Bear first left and continue under power lines.
			GPS: N34°30.94' W116°46.42'
▼ 5.0		TL	Turn left onto Firethorn Road.
	1.7 ▲	TR	Turn right onto Squaw Bush Road.
▼ 5.1		TR	Turn right at 4-way intersection, continuing under power lines.
	1.6 ▲	TL	Turn left at 4-way intersection away from power lines.
			GPS: N34°31.01' W116°46.18'
▼ 6.7		TL	4-way intersection. Turn left away from power lines and zero trip meter. Straight ahead is the spur to Upper Johnson Valley Yucca Rings Preserve.
	0.0 ▲		Continue to the southwest.
			GPS: N34°31.46' W116°44.52'

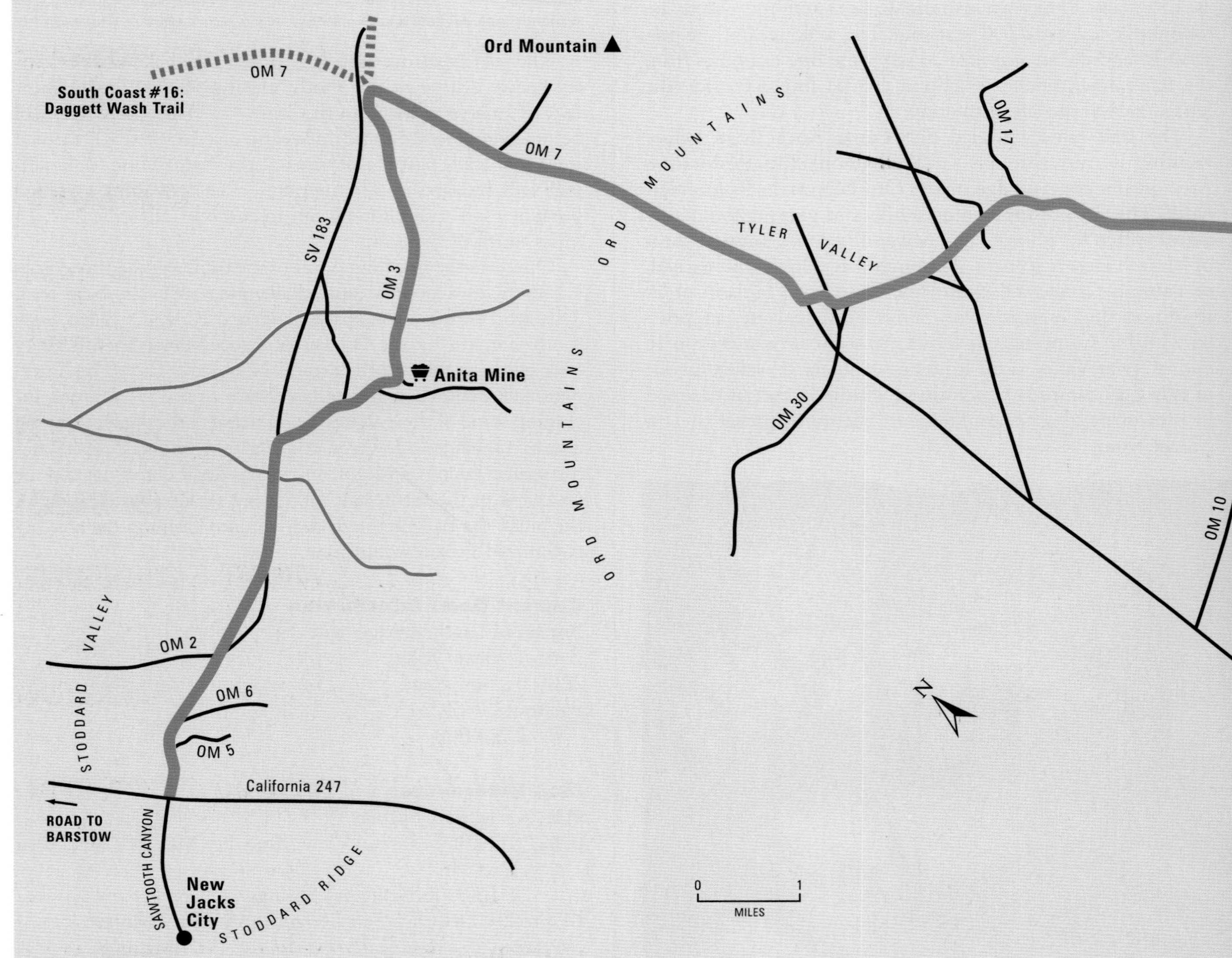

Spur to Yucca Rings

Mileage	Reverse	Dir.	Directions
▼ 0.0			Proceed northeast on graded road, remaining alongside power lines.
▼ 0.6		SO	Cross through wash.
▼ 1.2			Upper Johnson Valley Yucca Rings Preserve on right.
			GPS: N34°32.02′ W116°43.43′

Continuation of Main Trail

Mileage	Reverse	Dir.	Directions
▼ 0.0			Continue to the northwest.
	3.4 ▲	TR	4-way intersection. Turn right, following alongside power lines, and zero trip meter. To the left is the spur to Upper Johnson Valley Yucca Rings Preserve.
			GPS: N34°31.46′ W116°44.52′
▼ 2.1		SO	Anderson Dry Lake on right.
	1.3 ▲	SO	Anderson Dry Lake on left.
▼ 3.0		BR	Bear right and cross through wash on concrete ford.
	0.4 ▲	BR	Bear right and cross through wash on concrete ford.
			GPS: N34°33.57′ W116°46.42′
▼ 3.4		TL	Turn left onto graded dirt Camp Rock Road at information board for Johnson Valley OHV Area. Leaving OHV area. Zero trip meter.
	0.0 ▲		Continue to the southeast and enter OHV area. Many tracks on left and right within the OHV area. Only major ones are mentioned in the directions.
			GPS: N34°33.68′ W116°46.90′
▼ 0.0			Continue to the southwest.
	5.2 ▲	TR	Turn right onto well-used formed trail at information board for Johnson Valley OHV Area. Zero trip meter.
▼ 0.1		TR	Turn sharp right on formed trail marked OM 30, suitable for 4WDs, ATVs, and motorbikes.
	5.1 ▲	TL	Turn sharp left onto graded dirt Camp Rock Road.
			GPS: N34°33.67′ W116°46.88′
▼ 1.9		SO	Track on right and track on left under power lines is OM 10.
	3.3 ▲	SO	Track on right and track on left under power lines is OM 10.
			GPS: N34°35.25′ W116°47.21′
▼ 4.2		SO	Track on right is OM 17.
	1.0 ▲	SO	Track on left is OM 17.
			GPS: N34°37.13′ W116°48.12′
▼ 4.7		SO	Unmarked track on left and track on right.
	0.5 ▲	SO	Unmarked track on right and track on left.
▼ 5.2		SO	Track on left and track on right along gas pipeline. Zero trip meter.
	0.0 ▲		Continue to the east.
			GPS: N34°37.45′ W116°49.01′
▼ 0.0			Continue to the west.
	6.3 ▲	SO	Track on left and track on right along gas pipeline. Zero trip meter.
▼ 0.4		SO	Unmarked graded road on left.
	5.9 ▲	BL	Unmarked graded road on right.
▼ 0.6		SO	Two unmarked tracks on right at south end of Tyler Valley.
	5.7 ▲	SO	Two unmarked tracks on left at south end of Tyler Valley.
			GPS: N34°37.67′ W116°49.52′
▼ 1.1		BR	Marked track on left is continuation of OM 30.
	5.2 ▲	SO	Marked track on right is continuation of OM 30.
			GPS: N34°38.00′ W116°50.01′
▼ 1.2		BR	Bear right across Tyler Valley onto OM 7.
	5.1 ▲	BL	Bear left onto OM 30.
			GPS: N34°38.06′ W116°50.07′
▼ 1.3		BL	Bear left onto smaller formed trail, marked OM 7 to SV 183; then immediately bear right.
	5.0 ▲	BR	Track on right; then bear right onto larger, roughly graded road marked OM 7.
			GPS: N34°38.15′ W116°50.04′
▼ 1.6		TR	T-intersection along pipeline road.
	4.7 ▲	TL	Turn left away from pipeline, following open route sign.
			GPS: N34°38.30′ W116°50.20′
▼ 2.0		SO	Track on right into private property.
	4.3 ▲	BR	Track on left into private property.
▼ 3.7		SO	Exiting Tyler Valley.
	2.6 ▲	SO	Entering Tyler Valley.
▼ 5.0		SO	Track on right.
	1.3 ▲	SO	Track on left.
			GPS: N34°41.24′ W116°50.36′
▼ 5.5		SO	Entrance to private property on right.

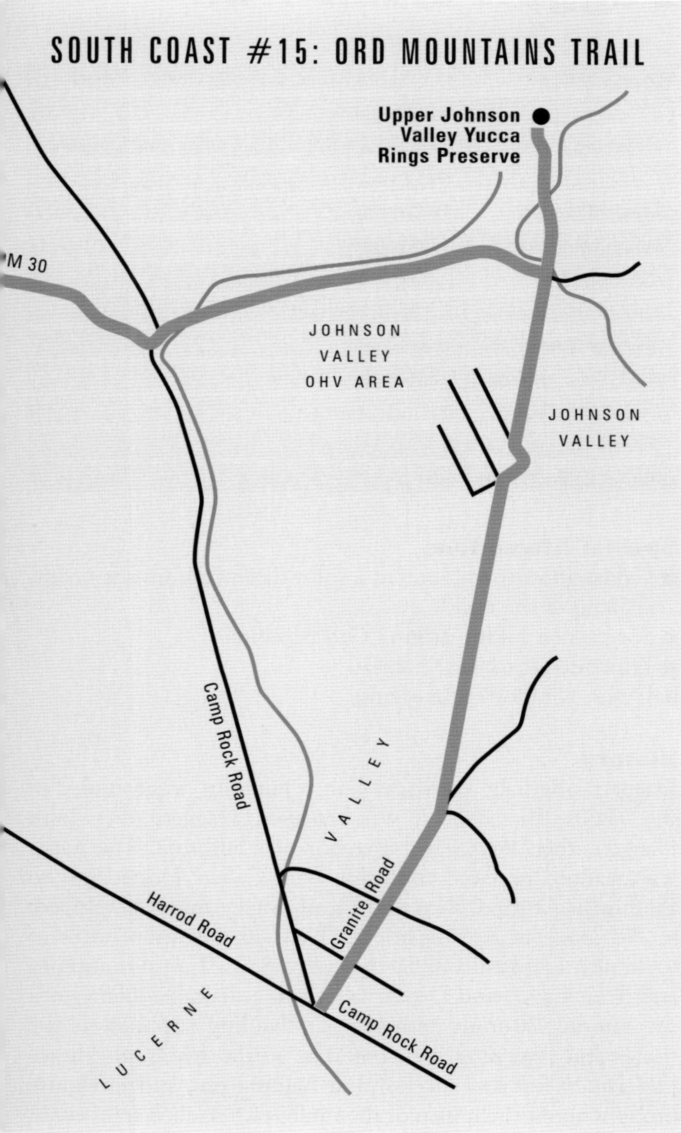

SOUTH COAST #15: ORD MOUNTAINS TRAIL

Upper Johnson Valley Yucca Rings Preserve
OM 30
JOHNSON VALLEY OHV AREA
JOHNSON VALLEY
Camp Rock Road
VALLEY
Granite Road
Harrod Road
Camp Rock Road
LUCERNE

	0.8 ▲	SO	Entrance to private property on left.
▼ 6.3		TL	4-way intersection with South Coast #16: Daggett Wash Trail (SV 183 and OM 7), which is straight ahead and to the right. Zero trip meter and turn left onto SV 183 along pipeline. OM 7 continues straight ahead.
	0.0 ▲		Continue to the south.
			GPS: N34°42.46' W116°50.35'
▼ 0.0			Continue to the west.
	4.4 ▲	TR	4-way intersection with South Coast #16: Daggett Wash Trail (OM 7 and SV 183), which is straight ahead and to the left. Zero trip meter and turn right onto SV 183 away from pipeline. SV 183 continues straight ahead.
▼ 0.2		TL	Turn left onto small, formed trail marked OM 3.
	4.2 ▲	TR	T-intersection with pipeline road (SV 183).
			GPS: N34°42.36' W116°50.57'
▼ 2.3		SO	Small track on left and small track on right.
	2.1 ▲	SO	Small track on left and small track on right.
			GPS: N34°41.23' W116°52.24'
▼ 2.6		SO	Cross through wash.
	1.8 ▲	SO	Cross through wash.
▼ 2.8		SO	Enter wash.
	1.6 ▲	SO	Exit wash.
▼ 2.9		SO	Exit wash.
	1.5 ▲	SO	Enter wash.
▼ 3.0		SO	Anita Mine on left.
	1.4 ▲	SO	Anita Mine on right.
			GPS: N34°40.95' W116°52.85'
▼ 3.1		SO	Unmarked track on left.
	1.3 ▲	SO	Unmarked track on right.
▼ 3.4		SO	Unmarked track on left.
	1.0 ▲	BL	Unmarked track on right.
			GPS: N34°41.08' W116°53.16'
▼ 3.8		SO	Unmarked track on right.
	0.6 ▲	BR	Unmarked track on left.
▼ 4.4		TL	T-intersection with pipeline road (SV 183). Zero trip meter.
	0.0 ▲		Continue to the east.
			GPS: N34°41.59' W116°54.11'
▼ 0.0			Continue to the southwest.
	3.7 ▲	TR	Turn right onto small trail marked OM 3 and zero trip meter.
▼ 0.1		SO	Cross through wash. Many wash crossings for next 3.6 miles.
	3.6 ▲	SO	Cross through wash. End of wash crossings.
▼ 1.1		SO	Track on left is OM 2.
	2.6 ▲	SO	Track on right is OM 2.
			GPS: N34°41.19' W116°55.22'
▼ 1.5		SO	Cattle guard; then cross through wash. Track on left up wash is OM 2.
	2.2 ▲	SO	Cross through wash. Track on right up wash is OM 2; then cattle guard.
			GPS: N34°41.15' W116°55.57'
▼ 1.7		SO	Pass through fence line.
	2.0 ▲	SO	Pass through fence line.
▼ 2.2		SO	Unmarked track on left. Track on right is OM 2.
	1.5 ▲	SO	Unmarked track on right. Track on left is OM 2.
			GPS: N34°41.12' W116°56.37'
▼ 3.0		SO	Track on left up wash is OM 6.
	0.7 ▲	SO	Track on right up wash is OM 6.
			GPS: N34°41.14' W116°57.25'
▼ 3.2		SO	Track on left is OM 5.
	0.5 ▲	SO	Track on right is OM 5.
			GPS: N34°41.09' W116°57.41'
▼ 3.7			Trail ends at paved Barstow Road (California 247), 15 miles south of I-40. Turn right for Barstow; turn left for Lucerne Valley. Dirt road opposite goes 1.7 miles to the popular rock climbing area of Sawtooth Canyon (New Jacks City).
	0.0 ▲		Trail starts on Barstow Road (California 247), 15 miles south of I-40, at mile marker 63. Zero trip meter and turn northeast on graded dirt pipeline road, marked as an open route. Graded road opposite also follows pipeline. Many wash crossings for the first 3.6 miles. Dirt road opposite the start of the trail goes 1.7 miles west to the popular rock climbing area of Sawtooth Canyon (New Jacks City).
			GPS: N34°40.86' W116°57.92'

SOUTH COAST #16

Daggett Wash Trail

Starting Point:	**Pendleton Road, 0.2 miles west of I-40 and Daggett**
Finishing Point:	**Camp Rock Road, 10.1 miles south of I-40 and Daggett**
Total Mileage:	**15.3 miles**
Unpaved Mileage:	**14.9 miles**
Driving Time:	**2 hours**
Elevation Range:	**2,100–4,200 feet**
Usually Open:	**Year-round**
Best Time to Travel:	**September to June**
Difficulty Rating:	**3**
Scenic Rating:	**8**
Remoteness Rating:	**+0**

Special Attractions

- Calico ghost town, located a short distance from the northern end of the trail.
- Spectacular hiking around Ord Mountain.
- Prime desert tortoise habitat.
- Desert wildflowers in spring.

History

Daggett, originally known as Calico Junction, was founded in the 1860s. In 1883, it was renamed Daggett after John Daggett, then lieutenant governor of California. The name was changed to avoid confusion with Calico, located just to the north. As the Calico and Death Valley mines developed, so did Daggett. A 10-stamp mill was in operation north of town near Elephant Hill by the early 1880s. Transportation to and from Calico and Death Valley was a major problem until the famous 20-mule teams began hauling supplies to the mines and returning with ore. The steam-driven workhorse *Old Dinah* was less successful at hauling ore, and its failure brought about the return of the mule team. Calico went on to be the driving force behind Daggett. When railroads were

Daggett Ridge rises up from the edge of Daggett Wash

built, transportation costs fell from $2 per ton to less than 20 cents per ton.

By the early 1900s, Daggett had a lumberyard, restaurants, three saloons, and several stores. The Stone Hotel had been constructed in the early 1870s. John Muir, the famous writer, conservationist, and founder of the Sierra Club in 1892, stayed at the Stone Hotel on occasion. His younger daughter, Helen, married Buel Funk, a resident of Daggett who had moved to the Mojave Desert for health reasons. In 1914, Muir developed pneumonia while visiting their ranch at Daggett. His daughter found him almost delirious and summoned a doctor from Los Angeles. Muir was placed on the next westbound train for Los Angeles, but he died within a few hours of his arrival at the hospital.

Born in 1838 in Dunbar, Scotland, Muir died at the age of 76 on Christmas Eve. His wife had passed away in 1905; their estate, approaching $200,000, was left to their daughters. Helen and Buel went on to build a red-tiled mansion surrounded by a grove of palm trees. Known as Casa Desierto, it was the most lavish construction in the entire area.

Like the Newberry and Rodman Mountains to the northwest, the Ord Mountains were inhabited by people for thousands of years. Some of their petroglyphs still adorn the mountains.

Miners turned to the land to survive when their dreams of gold in the Ord Mountains did not pay off. One such couple, the Willises, took up residence near some petroglyphs on Ord Mountain, with the belief that they may have been located at a spring (as is often the case with petroglyphs). Sure enough, they dug down only 20 feet and struck water. They set up a shack and cleared the land of rocks, slowly creating their own work of art in rock on Ord Mountain. The combination of old and new stonework is now the subject of archaeological studies in the area.

Description

The Daggett Wash Trail connects I-40 to South Coast #15: Ord Mountains Trail. It provides an alternative exit to the north and allows for a more exotic route through the spectacular and remote Ord Mountains.

The trail starts at Daggett on I-40 and travels south, quickly joining Daggett Wash as it leads into the Ord Mountains. The trail passes along the east side of Daggett Ridge, which looms up alongside the trail. This is a good area in which to see endangered desert tortoises. The best chance of seeing one of these elusive animals is in spring, when they come out to feed on new growth. Daggett Ridge offers excellent remote area hiking, and the wildflower viewing is particularly good in spring.

The trail connects with South Coast #15: Ord Mountains Trail below the summit of Ord Mountain. A spur leads up the side of the mountain toward communications towers. However, you have to hike the final stretch to the top of the ridge. The remains of several privately-owned mines can be seen in the valley below and are best reached by foot.

The trail finishes on wide, graded Camp Rock Road. This road is used at all hours by mining trucks.

Within the Ord Mountains area, vehicle travel is permitted only on routes marked as "open." Trails not marked specifically as open for vehicle travel should be considered closed. A map of open routes is available from the BLM office in Barstow. Some unmarked trails are mentioned in the directions below; this is purely for navigational purposes—no trail should be considered open unless designated as such.

Current Road Information

Bureau of Land Management
Barstow Field Office
2601 Barstow Road
Barstow, CA 92311
(760) 252-6000

Map References

BLM Newberry Springs
USGS 1:24,000 Daggett, Mineola, Ord Mt.
1:100,000 Newberry Springs
Maptech CD-ROM: San Bernardino County/Mojave
Southern & Central California Atlas & Gazetteer, p. 82
California Road & Recreation Atlas, p. 105

Old mining sites around Ord Mountain are best investigated on foot

Route Directions

Mileage		Directions
▼ 0.0		From I-40 at Daggett, proceed to the south side of the freeway and turn right (west) on Pendleton Road. Proceed west for 0.2 miles; then zero trip meter and turn southwest on graded dirt Ord Mountain Road.
3.0 ▲		Trail ends at T-intersection with paved Pendleton Road. Turn right for 0.2 miles to access I-40 at Daggett. Calico ghost town is a short distance north of I-40 from this intersection.
		GPS: N34°51.29' W116°53.61'
▼ 0.4	SO	Track on left and track on right alongside power lines. Trail is now formed dirt.
2.6 ▲	SO	Track on left and track on right alongside power lines. Road is now graded.
▼ 1.3	SO	Track on left and track on right alongside power lines.
1.7 ▲	SO	Track on left and track on right alongside power lines.
		GPS: N34°50.34' W116°54.39'
▼ 1.7	BR	Track on left.
1.3 ▲	SO	Track on right.
		GPS: N34°50.03' W116°54.50'
▼ 2.3	SO	Enter line of wash.
0.7 ▲	SO	Exit line of wash.
▼ 2.4	SO	Trail visible running parallel on right. Continue up wash.
0.6 ▲	SO	Trail visible running parallel on left. Keep to the right.
▼ 2.6	SO	Track on right.
0.4 ▲	BR	Track on left.
		GPS: N34°49.23' W116°54.78'
▼ 3.0	SO	Graded road on right and left along power lines. Zero trip meter and continue straight ahead on OM 4 in line of wash.
0.0 ▲		Continue to the north in Daggett Wash.
		GPS: N34°48.85' W116°54.84'
▼ 0.0		Continue to the south in Daggett Wash.
9.6 ▲	SO	Graded road on right and left along power lines. Zero trip meter and continue straight ahead on trail in line of Daggett Wash.
▼ 3.4	SO	Cattle guard.
6.2 ▲	SO	Cattle guard.
		GPS: N34°46.29' W116°53.79'
▼ 3.7	SO	Unmarked track on right up side wash.
5.9 ▲	SO	Unmarked track on left up side wash.
		GPS: N34°46.02' W116°53.54'
▼ 5.6	SO	Exit line of wash, remaining on marked OM 4.
4.0 ▲	SO	Enter line of Daggett Wash, remaining on open route.
		GPS: N34°45.29' W116°51.91'
▼ 7.2	SO	Cross through wash.
2.4 ▲	SO	Cross through wash.
▼ 7.4	SO	Cross through wash.
2.2 ▲	SO	Cross through wash.
▼ 7.6	SO	Cross through wash.
2.0 ▲	SO	Cross through wash.
▼ 7.9	SO	Cross through wash.
1.7 ▲	SO	Cross through wash.
▼ 8.6	TR	T-intersection with marked trail OM 7. Turn right onto OM 7 along gas pipeline.
1.0 ▲	TL	Turn left onto small marked trail OM 4, leaving gas pipeline.
		GPS: N34°43.29' W116°50.54'
▼ 8.7	SO	Cross through wash; then unmarked track on right.
0.9 ▲	SO	Unmarked track on left; then cross through wash.
▼ 9.5	SO	Graded road on left and track on right.
0.1 ▲	SO	Graded road on right and track on left.
▼ 9.6	TL	4-way intersection. Track straight ahead and track on right are South Coast #15: Ord Mountains Trail, marked SV 183 to the right. Zero trip meter and turn left onto SV 183 along gas pipeline

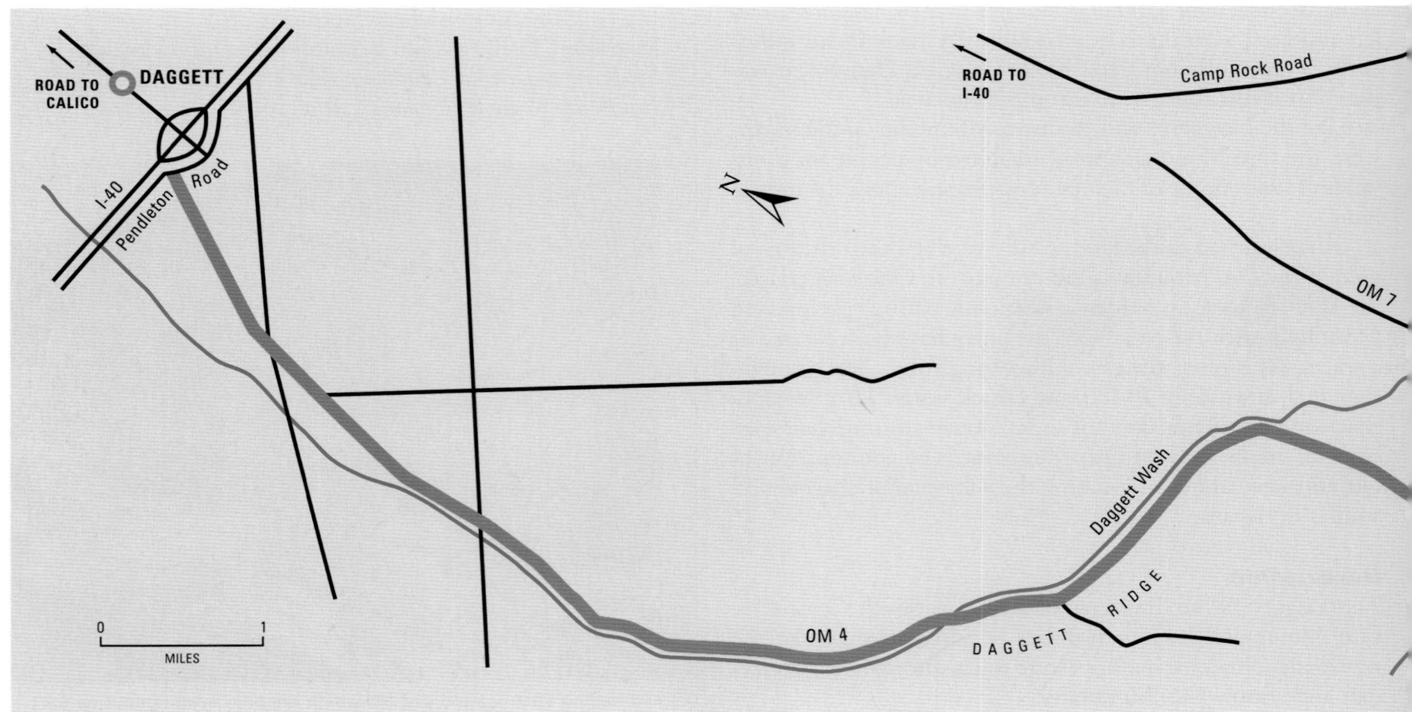

0.0 ▲ Continue to the north.

GPS: N34°42.46' W116°50.35'

▼ 0.0 Continue to the northeast.

0.8 ▲ TR 4-way intersection. Track straight ahead and track on left are South Coast #15: Ord Mountains Trail, marked SV 183. Zero trip meter and turn right onto OM 7.

▼ 0.4 SO Unmarked track on left.

0.4 ▲ SO Unmarked track on right.

▼ 0.8 TL 4-way intersection. Zero trip meter and turn left onto SV 183 detour, which is also OJ 208. Pipeline road continues ahead. To the right, open route leads 0.9 miles to locked gate, viewpoint over mines, and the start of a hiking trail up Ord Mountain—no mountain bikes permitted.

0.0 ▲ Continue to the west.

GPS: N34°42.74' W116°49.54'

▼ 0.0 Continue to the northwest.

1.9 ▲ TR 4-way intersection. Zero trip meter and turn right onto OM 7 along gas pipeline. Pipeline road continues on the left. Track straight ahead leads 0.9 miles to locked gate, viewpoint over mines, and the start of a hiking trail up Ord Mountain—no mountain bikes permitted.

▼ 0.4 SO Unmarked track on right to tanks.

1.5 ▲ SO Unmarked track on left to tanks.

▼ 1.3 BL Unmarked track on right. Remain on SV 183 detour.

0.6 ▲ SO Unmarked track on left. Remain on SV 183 detour.

▼ 1.9 Trail finishes at T-intersection with Camp Rock Road, 10.1 miles south of I-40. Turn left to exit to I-40; turn right to intersect with South Coast #17: Rodman Mountains Trail.

0.0 ▲ Trail commences on Camp Road Road, 10.1 miles south of I-40 at Daggett. Zero trip meter and turn southeast on well-used formed trail, sign-posted as Ord Mountain Road (OJ 208 and SV 183 detour).

GPS: N34°44.30' W116°49.26'

SOUTH COAST #16: DAGGETT WASH TRAIL

SOUTH COAST #17

Rodman Mountains Trail

Starting Point:	**National Trails Highway (old Route 66), 3 miles east of the Fort Cady exit on I-40**
Finishing Point:	**National Trails Highway (old Route 66), 2 miles west of the Fort Cady exit on I-40**
Total Mileage:	**34.8 miles, plus 2.2-mile spur**
Unpaved Mileage:	**33.9 miles, plus 2.2-mile spur**
Driving Time:	**4.5 hours**
Elevation Range:	**1,800–5,200 feet**
Usually Open:	**Year-round**
Best Time to Travel:	**Year-round**
Difficulty Rating:	**3**
Scenic Rating:	**8**
Remoteness Rating:	**+1**

Special Attractions

- Trail travels a vehicle corridor through the Rodman Mountains Wilderness.
- Extensive petrolgyphs on the edge of the Rodman Mountains Wilderness.
- Lightly traveled trail offers a remote desert experience.
- Chance to see raptors—particularly prairie falcons and golden eagles.
- Bagdad Cafe, setting of the movie of the same name.

History

Newberry Springs, located near the start and finish of this trail, was a town that relied on passing trade almost from its beginning. The Mojave Trail passed to the north of today's settlement and was a trading route for Indians before it became a vehicle trail. For thousands of years, people traveled between the coastal and Colorado River tribes, exchanging various items of value. They used water from the Mojave River near Newberry Springs, known in mission days as Rio de los Animas (Spanish for "River of the Spirits").

Surprise Tank Petroglyphs, in the Rodman Mountains, are estimated by archaeologists to be more than 11,000 years old. The Vanyume Indians, members of the Serrano tribe, roamed this region in hunter-gatherer groups. Potential water points became more and more important for these people as the lush landscape became more arid. Their shamans are attributed with creating the supernatural images found on the patina boulders at Surprise Tank.

The rugged Newberry Mountains north of Kane Wash also provided refuge for early inhabitants of the region. The Newberry and Schuilling Caves are two locations in the mountains that are the subjects of archaeological study.

The Mojave Trail was also used for many illicit activities, from horse theft to Indian slave trading. As the price of beaver pelts declined, trappers joined Indians in stealing horses from the Spanish. Other natives were marched along the trail to be

The pumps are dry at Dry Creek Station on old Route 66

sold to the California missions. Newberry Springs may have been a stop off and exchange point because of its abundant grass and reliable water supply.

The Mojave Trail saw even more traffic during the gold rush of 1849. Parties from Salt Lake City often got lost while taking shortcuts to the West Coast and were attacked by Indians when they broke into small groups. Sticking to the well-used trail was an emigrant party's best bet.

Freight and mail companies also began to use the trail. Because of its good water supply, Newberry Springs was chosen as the site of Fort Cady. A horse- and camel-mounted cavalry unit was based there to protect travelers from attacking Paiute and Chemehuevi. By 1868, the last of the Indians were relocated to reservations. This opened the region to white settlers who catered to prospectors and travelers.

Calico, situated to the north, became quite important because it supplied mine workers with farm produce. The railroad construction of the 1880s took away much of the passing trade. Yet Newberry Springs was still important, supplying water for all the railroad tanks as far east as Essex. In the early days, the locality had been known simply as Water.

Prospectors were busy in the Rodman Mountains in the 1880s, as well as along Iron Ridge to the south of this trail. Names like Silver Bell, Silver Cliffs, Bessemer, and Tiptop Mines still appear on maps. Tiptop, now within the boundaries of the Marine Corps Air Ground Combat Center to the east of this trail, was originally a silver mine that went on to produce high grade copper in the late 1890s. The mine produced such good returns on its ore that, unlike many, the owners could afford to ship it around the globe to Swansea, Wales, for reduction.

In the 1950s, a large vein of iron ore was found to the south of this trail on Iron Ridge above Kaiser Steel's Bessemer Iron Mine. Farther east lies the Bagdad Chase Mine, which was established in the 1890s by John Suter, a road master with the Santa Fe Railroad. The mine went through troubled times, but still became one of San Bernardino County's most famous gold mines.

Highway construction was the next major event to hit Newberry Springs, and again, passing trade was the lifeline of the community. The Depression saw many people working and living off the land. With its good water supply, Newberry Springs remained popular. The town also supplied moonshine whiskey to Los Angeles. After the Depression, local businesses thrived again as travelers along Route 66 filled their restaurants and stores. The gas rationing of World War II reduced the number of tourists along Route 66, but increased military activity made up for it. By the end of the war, travelers returned once again. Newberry, as it was known then, slowly grew to support several local businesses, including a number of classic restaurants and motels. All seemed well again until construction of I-40 in the 1960s took passing trade away from Newberry Springs. The town's population became too small to support the number of businesses, and many commercial buildings were boarded up, never to reopen. Though interest in Old Route 66 continues to grow, local establishments are slow to risk opening for fear of another crippling blow.

Bagdad Cafe, at the western end of this trail, was formerly known as Sidewinder Cafe. It was featured in *Bagdad Cafe,* an offbeat comedy about mismatched characters transforming a forgotten motel into a desert oasis. The name stuck, and the cafe still attracts quite a following.

Today, Newberry Springs residents enjoy quiet times. Many of the travelers along Route 66 are retired people driving RVs along the same route that some traveled decades ago to escape the dust bowls of the Midwest.

Description

The Rodman Mountains Trail makes a pleasant excursion from the town of Barstow and passes through some spectacular and remote high desert scenery. The trail leaves I-40 at the Fort Cady exit, 5 miles east of Newberry Springs. It follows a pipeline road, crossing the bajada, to reach the start of the vehicle corridor that travels north-south through the Rodman Mountains Wilderness. The Rodman Mountains are a dramatic series of ridges and valleys, the result of earthquake activity many years ago. The area is composed of vol-

Box Canyon exits north to the Mojave Valley

canic basalt and lava rock; a lava flow cuts through the region.

The vehicle corridor travels through the jagged rocks of Box Canyon. This is a good place to look for bighorn sheep that frequent the area. Other wildlife that can be seen includes raptors, which breed in the region. In particular, keep an eye out for prairie falcons and golden eagles.

Exiting the vehicle corridor, the trail travels along the northern edge of the Johnson Valley OHV Area. This popular open area covers a wide valley to the south. The Rodman Mountains route swings north, remaining on the southern edge of the wilderness area. Some spectacular petroglyphs can be found a short distance from the trail. They are etched into the dark volcanic basalt above a small gully and are well worth the slight detour. To find them, park where indicated in the route directions and climb above the fence line to view the petroglyphs. There are many different patterns and animal shapes to be seen. The coordinates of the petroglyphs are GPS: N34°40.40' W116°35.61'.

A second spur leads into the Rodman Mountains Area of Critical Environmental Concern, where a small fenced area of desert pavement contains several small intaglios and rock patterns arranged on the flat surface. Curious hikers can find other petroglyphs in the region. Remember not to touch or disturb the petroglyphs in any way.

The route then joins wide, graded Camp Rock Road, which serves as the access road for a quarry. Mine trucks use this road at all times, so watch for fast-moving vehicles. A worthwhile spur from this section runs along a graded road up to communications towers. It is an easy drive up a wide shelf road to the towers. From the top there are far-reaching views to the south over Johnson Valley and to the north over the Mojave Valley.

The trail then swings north up Troy Road to complete the loop back to I-40. Troy Road is rough in places, and travels part of the way in a loose, gravelly wash. The scenery in this canyon is as rugged and spectacular as any in the region. For the most part, Troy Road is easy to navigate because it travels along the well-defined SV 183, the SV 183 detour, and a small graded road along a gas pipeline. However, the section of road immediately before it that drops down the final wash to the north, back to National Trails Highway, can be confusing. The route leaves the defined road and travels on a small, unmarked trail in the wash. Geography and landmarks in the wash can change after storms. This intersection comes at the junction of two canyons. Proceed north down the canyon toward the Mojave Valley. Do not go south into the other large canyon that can be seen at this point.

The trail finishes on National Trails Highway, 0.1 miles east of the famous Bagdad Cafe. This very friendly cafe is open seven days a week from 6 A.M. and serves a hearty breakfast—just the thing before heading off on the trail.

Current Road Information

Bureau of Land Management
Barstow Field Office
2601 Barstow Road
Barstow, CA 92311
(760) 252-6000

Map References

BLM Newberry Springs
USGS 1:24,000 Troy Lake, Silver Bell Mine, Camp Rock Mine, Newberry Springs
1:100,000 Newberry Springs
Maptech CD-ROM: San Bernardino County/Mojave
Southern & Central California Atlas & Gazetteer, pp. 83, 82
California Road & Recreation Atlas, p. 105

Route Directions

Mileage		Direction	Description
▼ 0.0			From I-40, 5 miles east of Newberry Springs, take the Fort Cady exit and proceed to the south side of the freeway. Turn east on paved National Trails Highway (old Route 66) and zero trip meter. Proceed east for 3 miles and then turn south on formed dirt trail sign-posted to Belangeri Ranch. Zero trip meter. Trail follows alongside power poles.
	3.4 ▲		Trail ends at T-intersection with paved National Trails Highway (old Route 66). The closest exit to I-40 is to turn left.
			GPS: N34°48.24' W116°33.39'
▼ 0.7		SO	Track on left is Eagle Way Road.
	2.7 ▲	SO	Track on right is Eagle Way Road.
▼ 1.0		SO	Track on right.
	2.4 ▲	SO	Track on left.
▼ 1.6		SO	Track on right and track on left at pipeline valves.
	1.8 ▲	SO	Track on left and track on right at pipeline valves.
▼ 1.9		TL	T-intersection with pipeline road.
	1.5 ▲	TR	Turn right, away from pipeline road.
			GPS: N34°46.54' W116°33.39'
▼ 2.3		SO	Cross through wash.
	1.1 ▲	SO	Cross through wash.
▼ 3.4		TR	Turn right up line of wash onto marked trail, OJ 295, suitable for 4WDs, ATVs, and motorbikes. Zero trip meter.
	0.0 ▲		Continue to the west.
			GPS: N34°46.62' W116°31.75'
▼ 0.0			Continue south on OJ 295.
	8.8 ▲	TL	Turn left out of line of wash onto roughly graded pipeline road. Zero trip meter.
▼ 1.0		SO	Enter vehicle corridor. Rodman Mountains Wilderness is on either side of the trail. Remain on main trail.
	7.8 ▲	SO	Exit Rodman Mountains Wilderness.
▼ 2.4		SO	Enter Box Canyon.
	6.4 ▲	SO	Exit Box Canyon.
▼ 5.7		SO	Exit Box Canyon.
	3.1 ▲	SO	Enter Box Canyon.
▼ 7.6		SO	Exit line of wash.
	1.2 ▲	SO	Enter line of wash.
▼ 8.3		SO	Exit vehicle corridor through Rodman Mountains Wilderness.
	0.5 ▲	SO	Enter vehicle corridor through Rodman Mountains Wilderness.
▼ 8.8		TR	4-way intersection under major power lines. Track on left is Powerline Road. Track straight ahead enters Johnson Valley OHV Area and goes to Soggy Dry Lake. Zero trip meter and turn right onto Camp Road. There is a sign-post at the intersection.
	0.0 ▲		Continue to the north.
			GPS: N34°39.41' W116°33.07'

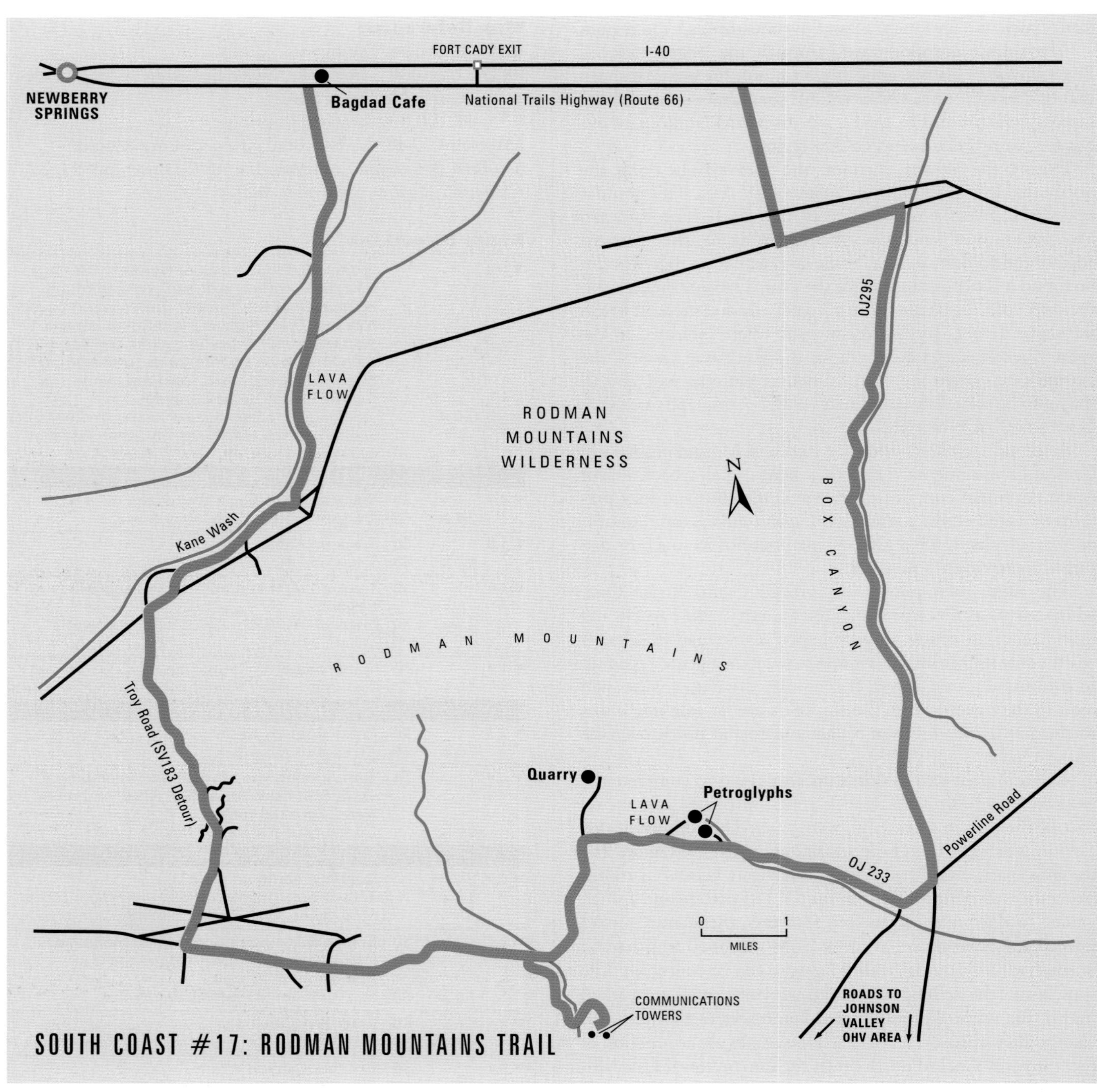

SOUTH COAST #17: RODMAN MOUNTAINS TRAIL

▼ 0.0			Continue to the southwest along power lines.
	2.8 ▲	TL	4-way intersection under power lines. Track straight ahead is Powerline Road. Track on right enters Johnson Valley OHV Area and goes to Soggy Dry Lake. Zero trip meter and turn left onto OJ 295 at marker post.
▼ 0.5		TR	Track on left goes into Johnson Valley OHV Area. Turn right onto formed trail, marked OJ 233, leaving power lines.
	2.3 ▲	TL	Turn left on formed trail along power lines. Track straight ahead enters Johnson Valley OHV Area.
			GPS: N34°39.25′ W116°33.49′
▼ 1.2		SO	Enter line of wash.
	1.6 ▲	SO	Exit line of wash.
▼ 2.7		SO	Exit line of wash.
	0.1 ▲	SO	Enter line of wash.
▼ 2.8		BL	Track on right goes 0.2 miles to large area of petroglyphs. Zero trip meter.
	0.0 ▲		Continue to the east.
			GPS: N34°40.25′ W116°35.54′
▼ 0.0			Continue to the west.
	1.9 ▲	BR	Track on left goes 0.2 miles to large area of petroglyphs. Zero trip meter.
▼ 0.8		BL	Well-used track on right enters Rodman Mountains ACEC and travels 0.6 miles to fenced intaglios at coordinates GPS: N34°40.64′ W116°35.85′.

1.1 ▲ BR Well-used track on left enters Rodman Mountains ACEC and travels 0.6 miles to fenced intaglios at coordinates GPS: N34°40.64' W116°35.85'.

GPS: N34°40.48' W116°36.31'

▼ 1.0 SO Track on right.
0.9 ▲ SO Track on left.

GPS: N34°40.49' W116°36.44'

▼ 1.1 SO Trail passes alongside small basalt lava flow. Petroglyphs can be found along the flow.
0.8 ▲ SO Trail passes alongside small basalt lava flow. Petroglyphs can be found along the flow.

GPS: N34°40.49' W116°36.49'

▼ 1.2 SO Track on right.
0.7 ▲ SO Track on left.

▼ 1.9 TL T-intersection with wide graded road. Track on right goes into active quarry. Zero trip meter.
0.0 ▲ Continue to the east.

GPS: N34°40.64' W116°37.26'

▼ 0.0 Continue to the south.
2.0 ▲ TR Turn right onto well-used formed trail marked OJ 233. Straight ahead goes into active quarry. Zero trip meter.

▼ 2.0 SO Track on left is spur trail to communications towers and a panoramic view to the north and south over Johnson Valley. Zero trip meter.
0.0 ▲ Continue to the east.

GPS: N34°39.57' W116°38.35'

Spur to Communications Towers

▼ 0.0 Proceed to the southeast up small graded trail.
▼ 0.3 SO Enter line of wash
▼ 0.4 SO Track on right up side wash.
▼ 1.2 SO Exit line of wash and start to climb shelf road.
▼ 2.1 BR Communications tower on left. End of climb.
▼ 2.2 UT Spur ends at communications towers and viewpoint.

GPS: N34°38.63' W116°37.62'

Continuation of Main Trail

▼ 0.0 Continue to the west.
3.9 ▲ SO Track on right is spur trail to communications towers and a panoramic view to the north and south over Johnson Valley. Zero trip meter.

GPS: N34°39.57' W116°38.35'

▼ 0.8 SO Road turns to graded dirt.
3.1 ▲ SO Road turns to formed trail.

▼ 1.8 SO Track on right.
2.1 ▲ SO Track on left.

▼ 2.3 SO Track on left and track on right to well.
1.6 ▲ SO Track on right and track on left to well.

GPS: N34°39.84' W116°40.71'

▼ 2.9 TR Track on left goes to Camp Rock Road and Anderson Dry Lake. Continue straight ahead, following sign to I-15. Turn right immediately past the sign onto unmarked formed trail.
1.0 ▲ TL Turn left onto wide graded road.

GPS: N34°40.02' W116°41.36'

▼ 3.9 TR Turn right onto SV 183 detour (Troy Road) at sign. Camp Rock Road is ahead and to the left. SV 183 detour also goes straight ahead. Zero trip meter.
0.0 ▲ Continue to the east.

GPS: N34°40.35' W116°42.39'

▼ 0.0 Continue to the north.
4.5 ▲ TL 4-way intersection with wide graded Camp Rock Road and Troy Road. Zero trip meter and turn left, following sign for I-15. Road is marked as not maintained. Camp Rock Road is ahead and to the right. SV 183 detour continues to the right.

▼ 0.3 SO Track on right and track on left.
4.2 ▲ SO Track on right and track on left.

▼ 0.4 SO Track on right and track on left.
4.1 ▲ SO Track on right and track on left.

▼ 1.0 SO Track on right.
3.5 ▲ SO Track on left.

▼ 1.3 SO Track on right.
3.2 ▲ SO Track on left.

▼ 1.5 BL Two tracks on right.
3.0 ▲ BR Two tracks on left.

GPS: N34°41.58' W116°41.68'

▼ 1.6 SO Two tracks on left.
2.9 ▲ SO Two tracks on right.

▼ 1.9 BL Well-used track on right. Enter down wash.
2.6 ▲ SO Well-used track on left. Exit wash.

GPS: N34°41.90' W116°41.77'

▼ 4.5 TR Turn right at 4-way intersection onto graded road alongside gas pipeline, following the marker for SV 183. Zero trip meter.
0.0 ▲ Continue to the south along wash up side canyon.

GPS: N34°44.04' W116°41.95'

▼ 0.0 Continue to the northeast, leaving the wash, along graded road down main canyon.
2.1 ▲ TL 4-way intersection. Turn left, leaving pipeline road onto formed trail up wash. Follow marker for SV 183 detour and zero trip meter.

▼ 0.2 SO Cross through wash. Graded road on left down wash.
1.9 ▲ SO Cross through wash. Graded road on right down wash.

▼ 0.4 SO Cross through wash.
1.7 ▲ SO Cross through wash.

▼ 0.5 TL Turn left onto unmarked graded road, leaving pipeline road.
1.6 ▲ TR T-intersection. Turn right and join pipeline road.

▼ 0.7 TR T-intersection. Track on left goes to Kane Springs.
1.4 ▲ TL Turn left onto graded road. Track straight ahead goes to Kane Springs.

GPS: N34°44.35' W116°41.39'

▼ 1.5 SO Graded road on right.
0.6 ▲ BR Graded road on left follows pipeline.

▼ 1.7 SO Enter line of wash.
0.4 ▲ SO Exit line of wash.

▼ 1.9 SO Pass through fence line.
0.2 ▲ SO Pass through fence line.

▼ 2.1 TL Turn left onto small formed trail at 4-way intersection, leaving graded road, and zero trip meter. Track on left can be easily missed in this direction because of washout realignment.
0.0 ▲ Continue to the west.

GPS: N34°44.80' W116°39.95'

▼ 0.0 Continue to the north.
5.4 ▲ TR 4-way intersection with small graded roads. Turn right and zero trip meter. This intersection is not how it appears on most maps because of washout realignment.

▼ 0.1 TR Turn right at T-intersection in wash and travel

			down wash. This intersection is also easy to miss.
	5.3 ▲	TL	Turn left (southeast) out of main wash, heading toward side canyon. This intersection is easy to miss in this direction. If you miss this turn, you will meet a fence line after a short distance that blocks the main wash.
			GPS: N34°44.88′ W116°39.98′
▼ 0.3		SO	Exit canyon. Remain in wash.
	5.1 ▲	BR	Trail enters canyon. Keep to the right in wash.
▼ 1.0		SO	Trail travels alongside lava flow.
	4.4 ▲	SO	Trail travels alongside lava flow.
▼ 1.3		SO	Exit line of wash.
	4.1 ▲	SO	Enter line of wash.
▼ 2.9		SO	Cross through wash. Track on right in wash.
	2.5 ▲	SO	Cross through wash. Track on left in wash.
▼ 3.1		SO	Enter wash.
	2.3 ▲	SO	Exit wash.
▼ 3.2		SO	Exit wash and continue straight ahead on graded road that joins from the left.
	2.2 ▲	BL	Bear left onto smaller track up wash. Graded road continues to the right.
			GPS: N34°47.35′ W116°39.01′
▼ 4.5		SO	Graded road on right. Road is now paved.
	0.9 ▲	SO	Graded road on left. Road turns to graded dirt.
▼ 5.4			Trail ends on National Trails Highway (old Route 66). Turn right to pass Bagdad Cafe (0.1 miles down the road on the left) and to exit to I-40; turn left for Newberry Springs.
	0.0 ▲		From I-40 at the Fort Cady exit, proceed to the south side of the freeway and almost immediately turn west onto National Trails Highway (old Route 66). Zero trip meter. After 1.9 miles, Bagdad Cafe is on the right. After 2.0 miles from the freeway exit, zero trip meter and turn south on paved Poniente Drive. Continue south on paved road, ignoring turns to the left and right.
			GPS: N34°49.19′ W116°38.66′

SOUTH COAST #18

Main Divide Road

Starting Point:	**Ortega Highway (California 74) at Riverside County mile marker 5.5, 21 miles east of San Juan Capistrano**
Finishing Point:	**Knabe Road, 0.5 miles south of the I-15 exit at El Cerrito**
Total Mileage:	**28.3 miles**
Unpaved Mileage:	**24.4 miles**
Driving Time:	**3.5 hours**
Elevation Range:	**1,000–5,300 feet**
Usually Open:	**Year-round**
Best Time to Travel:	**Dry weather**
Difficulty Rating:	**3**
Scenic Rating:	**9**
Remoteness Rating:	**+0**

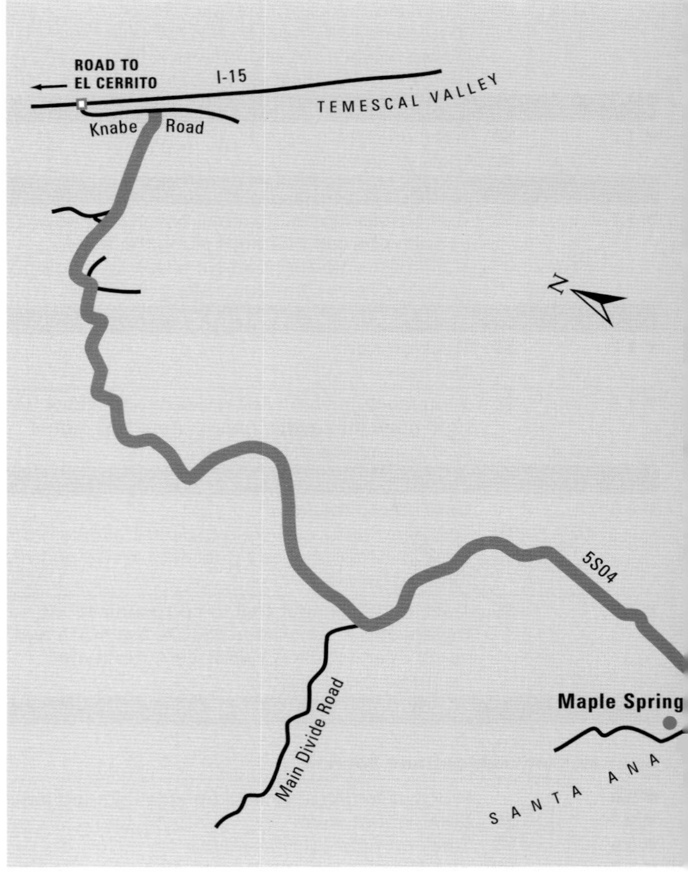

Special Attractions

- Long ridge top trail that makes an easy day trip from Los Angeles and San Diego.
- Access to many hiking, mountain biking, and horseback riding trails.
- Highest point in Orange County—Santiago Peak (5,687 feet).

History

The Holy Jim Hiking Trail, which connects to Main Divide Road, is named for Jim Smith, a beekeeper who lived in the North Fork of Trabuco Canyon in the 1870s. Jim got the nickname "Cussin' Jim" for his foul mouth. When the canyon was first mapped, surveyors chose the name "Holy Jim" as opposed to "Cussin' Jim." Remains of his residence can still be seen in the Holy Jim Recreation Site.

Description

Main Divide Road travels along the ridge tops of the Santa Ana Mountains within Cleveland National Forest. The trail leaves Ortega Highway and immediately starts to climb steadily, passing Blue Jay USFS Campground. This is the only campground along the trail. The ridge top trail means there are no suitable campsites along the way, so Blue Jay is the best place for campers.

The trail climbs steadily through the low shrub vegetation of manzanita and sugarbush toward the first of the peaks along the way—Trabuco Peak. Although narrow for

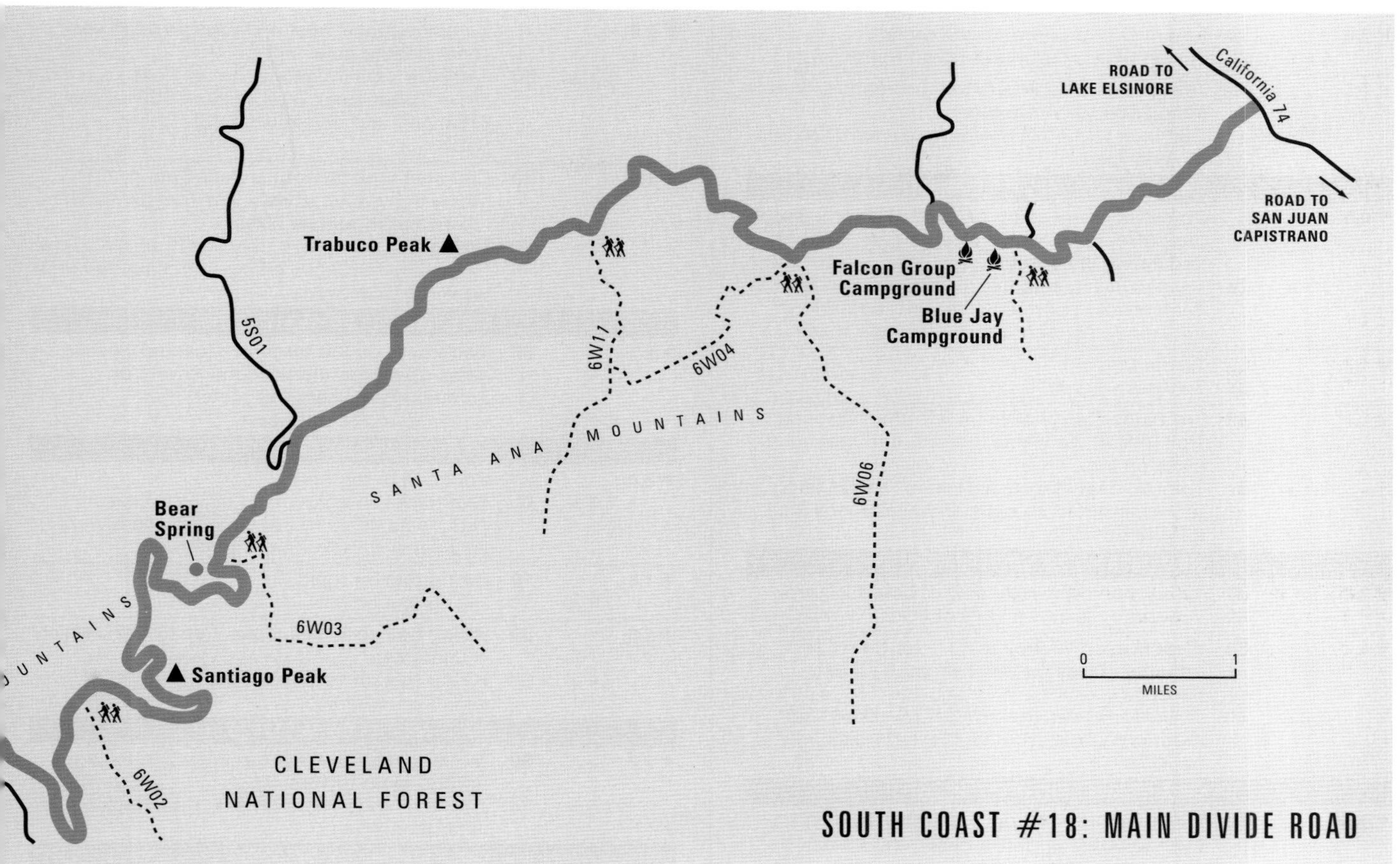

much of its length, the trail is mainly easygoing. Some of the climbs are rough with a loose, uneven surface, but they are suitable for any stock high-clearance 4WD. The trail follows along a shelf road for most of its length, and there are sufficient passing places. There are many small alternate trails that crisscross the main route. These have not been mentioned in the route directions unless they are likely to confuse the navigator.

As the trail starts to climb, Lake Elsinore can be seen to the east, 2,000 feet below in the Temescal Valley. Farther along the trail the views encompass Mission Viejo, the Joaquin Hills, and on a clear day Santa Catalina Island. To the east is Lake Mathews.

There are many opportunities for hikers, horseback riders, and mountain bikers along this trail. One of the most popular is the Holy Jim Trail, a moderate to strenuous trail that leaves from Bear Spring.

North of the radio towers on Santiago Peak, the trail standard improves because it is the normal access route to the towers.

A National Forest Adventure Pass is required for this trail if you intend to stop along the way.

Current Road Information

Cleveland National Forest
Trabuco Ranger District
1147 East 6th Street
Corona, CA 92879
(909) 736-1811

Map References

BLM Santa Ana
USFS Cleveland National Forest
USGS 1:24,000 Alberhill, Santiago Peak, Corona South
1:100,000 Santa Ana
Maptech CD-ROM: Ventura/Los Angeles/Orange County
Southern & Central California Atlas & Gazetteer, pp. 105, 104
California Road & Recreation Atlas, p. 110

Route Directions

▼ 0.0		From Ortega Highway (California 74) at Riverside County mile marker 5.5, 21 miles east of San Juan Capistrano, turn west on paved road and zero trip meter. The road is unmarked, but there is a sign for Los Pinos Camp at the start.
3.3 ▲		Trail ends on paved Ortega Highway (California 74). Turn left for Lake Elsinore; turn right for San Juan Capistrano.
		GPS: N33°38.24′ W117°25.28′
▼ 1.7	TR	T-intersection. Follow marker for 6S05, Long Canyon.
1.6 ▲	TL	Turn left onto paved road. Paved road also continues ahead.
		GPS: N33°38.81′ W117°26.66′
▼ 2.4	SO	Track on right and hiking trailhead on left; then Blue Jay USFS Campground on left.
0.9 ▲	SO	Blue Jay USFS Campground on right; then track on left and hiking trailhead on right.
		GPS: N33°39.14′ W117°26.85′

▼	▲		
▼ 2.9		SO	Falcon Group Campground on left.
	0.4 ▲	SO	Falcon Group Campground on right.
▼ 3.3		TL	Turn sharp left onto graded dirt road marked N Main 3S04. Zero trip meter.
	0.0 ▲		Continue to the southeast on paved road. End of shelf road.
			GPS: N33°39.74' W117°26.83'
▼ 0.0			Continue to the south on graded dirt road and pass through seasonal closure gate. Start of undulating shelf road.
	7.3 ▲	TR	Seasonal closure gate; then turn sharp right at T-intersection onto small paved road, following sign for campgrounds. Zero trip meter.
▼ 1.3		SO	Turnout on left.
	6.0 ▲	BL	Turnout on right.
▼ 1.7		BR	Los Pinos Trail (6W06) on left; then Trabuco Trail (6W04) for hikers, horses, and mountain bikes on left.
	5.6 ▲	BL	Trabuco Trail (6W04) for hikers, horses, and mountain bikes on right; then Los Pinos Trail (6W06) on right.
			GPS: N33°40.29' W117°27.56'
▼ 2.2		SO	Turnout on right with view of Lake Elsinore.
	5.1 ▲	SO	Turnout on left with view of Lake Elsinore.
▼ 4.2		SO	West Horsethief Trail (6W11) for hikers and mountain bikes on left. Limited trailhead parking.
	3.1 ▲	SO	West Horsethief Trail (6W11) for hikers and mountain bikes on right. Limited trailhead parking.
			GPS: N33°41.38' W117°27.91'
▼ 7.3		SO	Well-used track on right is Indian Truck Trail, marked 5S01. Zero trip meter and continue straight ahead on 3S04.
	0.0 ▲		Continue to the east.
			GPS: N33°42.47' W117°30.03'

Main Divide Road starts to climb through low vegetation in the Santa Ana Mountains

▼	▲		
▼ 0.0			Continue to the west and pass through seasonal closure gate.
	4.3 ▲	SO	Seasonal closure gate; then well-used track on left is Indian Truck Trail, marked 5S01. Zero trip meter and continue straight ahead on 3S04.
▼ 1.5		SO	Concrete tank on right is Bear Spring; then hiking trail on left is Holy Jim Trail (6W03) for hikers and mountain bikes.
	2.8 ▲	SO	Hiking trail on right is Holy Jim Trail (6W03) for hikers and mountain bikes; then concrete tank on left is Bear Spring.
			GPS: N33°42.64' W117°31.09'
▼ 4.3		BR	Two tracks on left through seasonal closure gates go to communications towers on Santiago Peak. Zero trip meter.
	0.0 ▲		Continue to the northeast.
			GPS: N33°42.69' W117°31.90'
▼ 0.0			Continue to the north.
	4.3 ▲	BL	Two tracks straight ahead through seasonal closure gates go to communications towers on Santiago Peak. Zero trip meter.
▼ 1.8		SO	Hiking trail on right.
	2.5 ▲	SO	Hiking trail on left.
▼ 1.9		SO	Hiking trail on left is Joplin Trail (6W02), which is unmarked.
	2.4 ▲	SO	Hiking trail on right is Joplin Trail (6W02), which is unmarked.
			GPS: N33°43.04' W117°32.36'
▼ 2.8		SO	Track on right at large turnout; then track on right to radio towers.
	1.5 ▲	SO	Track on left to radio towers; then track on left at large turnout.
			GPS: N33°42.81' W117°33.11'
▼ 2.9		SO	Track on left to radio towers.
	1.4 ▲	SO	Track on right to radio towers.
▼ 4.3		BR	Well-used track on left is Maple Springs Road and Harding Road. Bear right onto 5S04 at the small marker and zero trip meter. Small track on right climbs hill.
	0.0 ▲		Continue to the south.
			GPS: N33°43.73' W117°32.77'
▼ 0.0			Continue to the east.
	3.3 ▲	BL	Small track on left climbs hill. Bear left, remaining on Main Divide Road. Well-used track on right is Maple Springs Road and Harding Road. Zero trip meter.
▼ 2.7		SO	Pass under power lines.
	0.6 ▲	SO	Pass under power lines.
▼ 3.3		TR	Well-used, unmarked trail straight ahead is continuation of Main Divide. Turn right onto unmarked Bedford Road and zero trip meter.
	0.0 ▲		Continue to the southeast.
			GPS: N33°45.74' W117°32.99'
▼ 0.0			Continue to the northeast.
	5.8 ▲	TL	Well-used, unmarked trail on right is Main Divide Road northbound. Turn left onto unmarked Main Divide Road southbound and zero trip meter.
▼ 3.8		SO	Seasonal closure gate.
	2.0 ▲	SO	Seasonal closure gate.
			GPS: N33°47.81' W117°31.83'
▼ 3.9		SO	Track on right.
	1.9 ▲	SO	Track on left.
▼ 4.0		SO	Track on right.
	1.8 ▲	SO	Track on left.

▼ 4.1		SO	Track on right.
	1.7 ▲	SO	Track on left.
▼ 4.3		SO	Two tracks on right and track on left. Remain on main trail.
	1.5 ▲	SO	Two tracks on left and track on right. Remain on main trail.
			GPS: N33°47.95' W117°31.55'
▼ 4.6		SO	Track on left is private entrance; then pass beside private property.
	1.2 ▲	SO	Private property on right; then track on right is private entrance.
			GPS: N33°48.10' W117°31.40'
▼ 4.8		SO	Track on left.
	1.0 ▲	SO	Track on right.
▼ 4.9		SO	Track on left.
	0.9 ▲	SO	Track on right.
▼ 5.0		SO	Track on left.
	0.8 ▲	SO	Track on right.
▼ 5.1		SO	Gate.
	0.7 ▲	SO	Gate.
▼ 5.2		SO	Road becomes paved.
	0.6 ▲	SO	Road turns to graded dirt.
▼ 5.3		SO	Small paved road on right.
	0.5 ▲	SO	Small paved road on left.
▼ 5.6		SO	Small paved road on right and left.
	0.2 ▲	SO	Small paved road on right and left.
▼ 5.8			Trail ends at T-intersection with Knabe Road. Turn left for El Cerrito and entrance to I-15.
	0.0 ▲		Trail commences on Knabe Road, 0.5 miles south of I-15 exit at El Cerrito. Exit I-15 at Weirick Road exit, south of El Cerrito, and proceed to the west side. Immediately turn south on Knabe Road. Proceed 0.5 miles; then zero trip meter and turn west on small, unmarked paved road.
			GPS: N33°48.01' W117°30.20'

SOUTH COAST #19

Bee Canyon to Pine Cove Road

Starting Point:	**California 74, opposite Riverside County mile marker 49.25, 4 miles east of Fairview Avenue in Valle Vista**
Finishing Point:	**California 243 in Pine Cove**
Total Mileage:	**15.5 miles**
Unpaved Mileage:	**15 miles**
Driving Time:	**1.5 hours**
Elevation Range:	**2,000–6,200 feet**
Usually Open:	**May to November, dry weather only**
Best Time to Travel:	**May to November**
Difficulty Rating:	**2**
Scenic Rating:	**9**
Remoteness Rating:	**+0**

The trail climbs high above Bee Canyon

Special Attractions

- Easy trail through a variety of vegetation zones determined by elevation.
- Pleasant backcountry camping near Pine Cove.

History

Hemet, near the start of this trail, is thought to have gotten its name from a derivative of hemmett (Scandinavian for "home"). The area was originally inhabited by Cahuilla Indians before it was taken over by Mission San Luis Rey in the early 1800s for cattle ranching. After the missions were disbanded by the Mexican government, the land was given to José Antonia Estudillo in 1842. The town itself dates back to 1879, with the first post office opening in 1895. Water was a primary reason for the town's development, with a masonry dam constructed in the San Jacinto Mountains and the formation of the Lake Hemet Water Company. With water available, future development in the region was possible and agriculture became an important industry. Crops included olives, walnuts, apricots, and citrus fruits.

Near Pine Cove, a historical marker commemorates the important experiments by Albert Abraham Michelson, a Polish scientist who attempted to ascertain the speed of light. Michelson, born in Strzelno, Prussia, in 1852, immigrated to America in 1855 with his parents. He attended the United States Naval Academy and served as a science instructor at the academy after graduation. He took various academic positions in universities around the country and overseas before being appointed professor and the first head of the department of physics at the new University of Chicago, a position he held until his retirement in 1929.

Michelson began work on the speed of light in 1878 using homemade apparatus. In 1882, he announced the velocity of light to be 299,853 km/second, a value that remained unchallenged for many years.

Mount Wilson was the scene of one of his definitive experiments. The U.S. Coast and Geodetic Survey had determined the distance between Mount Wilson and Mount San Antonio (also know as Old Baldy) to be 35,385.53 meters (116,135.3

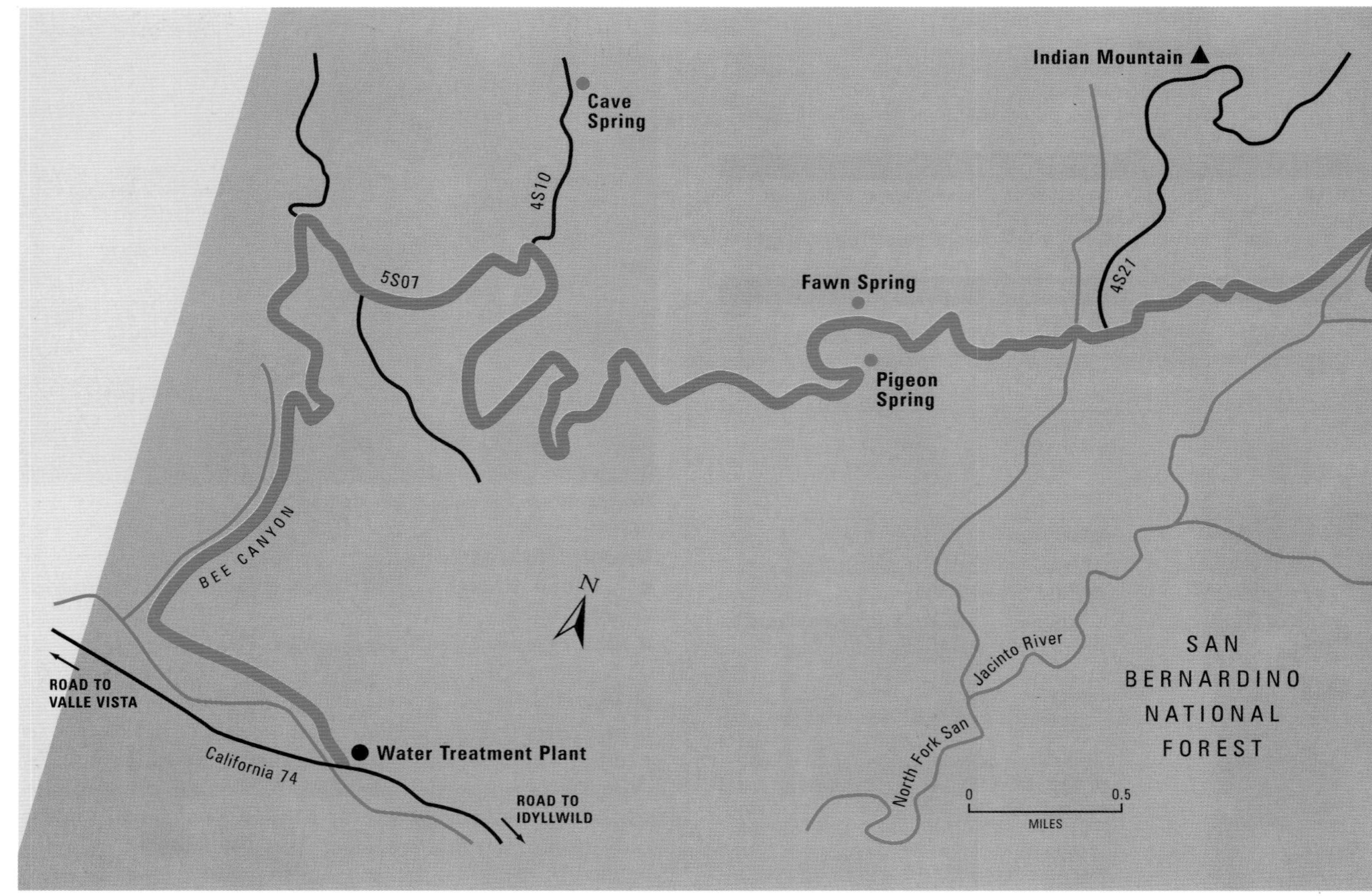

feet, nearly 22 miles), which was accurate to within 3 millimeters. The first two years of Michelson's experiment, begun in 1924, was spent checking equipment and measurements. The experiment was based on light traveling from Mount Wilson to Mount San Antonio and being reflected back again. It was repeated several times under different conditions and with various refinements to the instrumentation, and a reading was obtained, which is accurate within 0.006 percent of the modern value.

The North Fork San Jacinto River is a cool oasis in an arid environment

Description

This easy trail takes a high-clearance vehicle from California 74 near Hemet along a spectacular shelf road to Pine Cove, passing through a variety of vegetation zones. The trail commences by running in a wash line through the dry Bee Canyon. The powder-fine sand is soft, but in dry weather is normally passable without 4WD. In wet weather this trail is likely to be gated closed by the forest service.

Climbing steadily out of Bee Canyon, the trail travels along a shelf road through low shrubby vegetation. There are excellent views back over the South Fork of the San Jacinto River Valley and the citrus groves to Hemet. The trail is roughly graded along its length and climbs steadily toward Indian Mountain. The Indian Mountain Trail, a moderate to difficult 4WD trail, leaves to the north. Continue climbing along the main trail, entering the pine, oak, and cypress forest near Pine Cove.

There are some excellent backcountry campsites along this final section, but they are snatched up quickly on summer weekends. The trail ends in Pine Cove on California 243.

Current Road Information

San Bernardino National Forest
San Jacinto Ranger District
PO Box 518
54270 Pinecrest Street
Idyllwild, CA 92549
(909) 659-2117

Map References

BLM Palm Springs
USFS San Bernardino National Forest

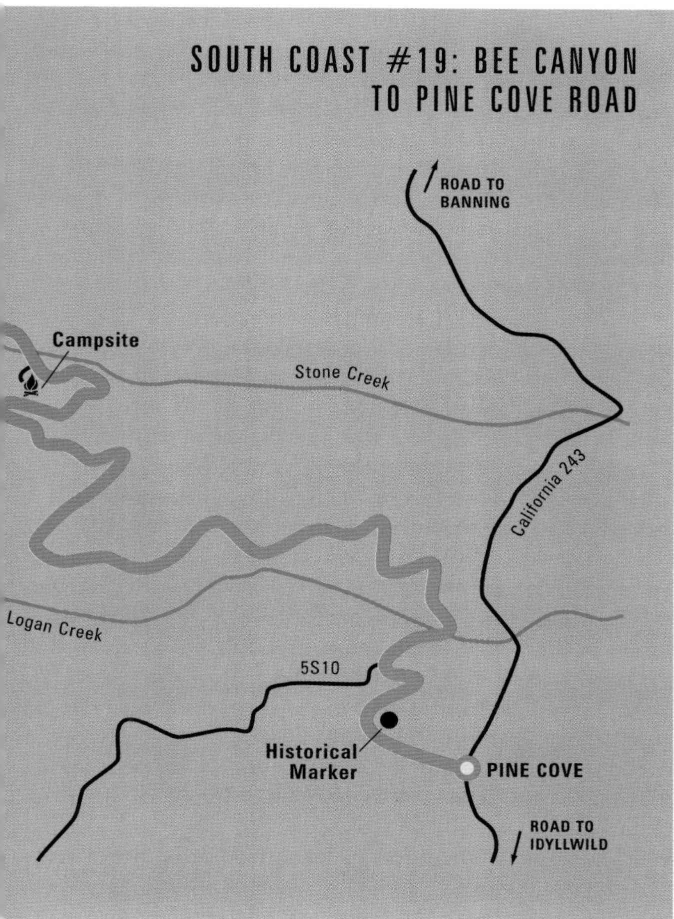

USGS 1:24,000 Blackburn Canyon, Lake Fulmor, San Jacinto Peak
1:100,000 Palm Springs
Maptech CD-ROM: San Diego/Joshua Tree
Southern & Central California Atlas & Gazetteer, p. 106
California Road & Recreation Atlas, p. 111

Route Directions

▼ 0.0		From California 74, opposite Riverside County mile marker 49.25, 4 miles east of Fairview Avenue in Valle Vista, zero trip meter and turn west on unmarked graded dirt road. Immediately there is a turn to the right. Remain on wider graded dirt road. Water treatment plant on right. Remain on main graded trail for next 0.9 miles, ignoring tracks on right and left into private property.
4.0 ▲		Water treatment plant on left; then trail ends on California 74. Turn right for Valle Vista; turn left for Idyllwild.
		GPS: N33°44.22' W116°49.43'
▼ 0.9	SO	Enter line of wash in Bee Canyon. Seasonal closure gate. Trail is now marked 5S07.
3.1 ▲	SO	Seasonal closure gate; then exit Bee Canyon. Remain on main graded road for next 0.9 miles, ignoring tracks on right and left into private property.
▼ 1.8	SO	Exit line of wash and climb out of Bee Canyon up shelf road.
2.2 ▲	SO	End of shelf road. Enter line of wash in Bee Canyon.
		GPS: N33°45.24' W116°50.01'
▼ 2.5	SO	End of shelf road.
1.5 ▲	SO	Start of shelf road. Start to descend to Bee Canyon.
▼ 2.9	BR	Turnout on left and track on left.
1.1 ▲	BL	Track on right and turnout on right.
		GPS: N33°45.74' W116°50.11'
▼ 3.3	SO	Track on right.
0.7 ▲	SO	Track on left.
▼ 3.7	SO	Seasonal closure gate.
0.3 ▲	SO	Seasonal closure gate.
▼ 4.0	BR	Well-used, unmarked track on left is 4S10 to Cave Spring. Zero trip meter.
0.0 ▲		Continue to the southeast.
		GPS: N33°45.79' W116°49.33'
▼ 0.0		Continue to the north and pass through seasonal closure gate.
4.9 ▲	BL	Seasonal closure gate; then well-used track on right is 4S10 to Cave Spring. Zero trip meter.
▼ 0.2	SO	Start of shelf road.
4.7 ▲	SO	End of shelf road.
▼ 2.8	SO	End of shelf road.
2.1 ▲	SO	Start of shelf road.
▼ 3.2	SO	Pigeon Spring on right.
1.7 ▲	SO	Pigeon Spring on left.
		GPS: N33°45.74' W116°48.11'
▼ 3.8	SO	Fawn Spring on left. Start of shelf road.
1.1 ▲	SO	End of shelf road. Fawn Spring on right.
		GPS: N33°45.89' W116°47.99'
▼ 4.8	SO	Cross through wash.
0.1 ▲	SO	Cross through wash.
▼ 4.9	SO	Track on left is Indian Mountain Trail (4S21) for 4WDs, ATVs, and motorbikes—rated blue. Zero trip meter.
0.0 ▲		Continue to the south on 5S09.
		GPS: N33°46.05' W116°47.32'
▼ 0.0		Continue to the northeast on the marked 5S09.
6.6 ▲	SO	Track on right is Indian Mountain Trail (4S21) for 4WDs, ATVs, and motorbikes—rated blue. Zero trip meter.
▼ 1.1	SO	Cross over North Fork San Jacinto River.
5.5 ▲	SO	Cross over North Fork San Jacinto River.
		GPS: N33°46.53' W116°46.56'
▼ 1.8	SO	Cross over Stone Creek; then track on right to campsite.
4.8 ▲	SO	Track on left to campsite; then cross over Stone Creek.
		GPS: N33°46.29' W116°46.03'
▼ 1.9	SO	Track on left to campsite.
4.7 ▲	SO	Track on right to campsite.
▼ 3.6	SO	Track on right. End of shelf road.
3.0 ▲	SO	Start of shelf road. Track on left.
▼ 4.7	SO	Track on left.
1.9 ▲	SO	Track on right.
▼ 5.4	SO	Track on left.
1.2 ▲	BL	Track on right.
▼ 5.5	SO	Cross over Logan Creek.
1.1 ▲	SO	Cross over Logan Creek.
		GPS: N33°45.84' W116°44.45'
▼ 5.6	SO	Seasonal closure gate.
1.0 ▲	SO	Seasonal closure gate.
▼ 5.7	BL	Track on right is 5S10.
0.9 ▲	BR	Track on left is 5S10. Remain on marked 5S09.
		GPS: N33°45.76' W116°44.60'

▼ 6.0		TR	4-way intersection. Turn right onto Pine Cove Road.
	0.6 ▲	TL	4-way intersection.
▼ 6.1		SO	Road is now paved. Remain on Pine Cove Road, ignoring turns to the right and left for next 0.5 miles.
	0.5 ▲	SO	Road is now graded dirt.
▼ 6.2		SO	Speed of light experiment historical marker on left on the corner of Green Craig Drive.
	0.4 ▲	SO	Speed of light experiment historical marker on right on the corner of Green Craig Drive.
▼ 6.6			Trail ends at T-intersection with California 243 in Pine Cove. Turn right for Idyllwild; turn left for Banning.
	0.0 ▲		Trail starts on California 243 at Pine Cove, 3 miles north of Idyllwild. Zero trip meter and turn west on paved Pine Cove Road. Turn is at the Pine Cove Market. Remain on paved Pine Cove Road for next 0.5 miles, ignoring turns to the right and left.
			GPS: N33°45.49' W116°44.28'

SOUTH COAST #20

North Coyote Canyon Trail

Starting Point:	**California 371, 1 mile east of Anza**
Finishing Point:	**Bailey's Cabin, Coyote Canyon**
Total Mileage:	**15.9 miles (one-way)**
Unpaved Mileage:	**9.6 miles**
Driving Time:	**2.5 hours (one-way)**
Elevation Range:	**2,400–4,200 feet**
Usually Open:	**Year-round**
Best Time to Travel:	**October 1 to May 31**
Difficulty Rating:	**7**
Scenic Rating:	**9**
Remoteness Rating:	**+0**

Special Attractions

- Bailey's Cabin.
- Challenging section of trail along Turkey Grade.
- Remote desert habitat of Coyote Canyon and peninsular bighorn sheep habitat.
- Access for hikers to travel the full length of the canyon.
- Juan Bautista de Anza Expedition route of 1774.

History

Juan Bautista de Anza opened up the first European route through this region in 1774 under orders from Spain to colonize Alta California before other countries, such as Russia, beat them to it. His route took him through Coyote Canyon to Nance Canyon, and over San Carlos Pass on the edge of Terwilliger Valley. This pleasant valley was a change from the harshness of the desert below and a transition point for those who followed. Here, the expedition could rely on fodder for weary animals and rest after the long climb into the mountains. Upon his arrival at this memorable location March 15, de Anza named the passage El Puerto Real de San Carlos, "The Royal Mountain Pass of Saint Charles." From here the expedition made its way northeast via today's Hemet and on to Mission San Gabriel (the fourth mission of Alta California) on the edge of today's Los Angeles. The passage of Anza's expedition has left its mark on the land in many ways. A pictograph in North Coyote Canyon depicts a human figure on horseback and a man carrying a cross, presumably alluding to de Anza's expedition of 1774.

Interpretations vary about the nature of life for indigenous groups at these missions. Were Indians simply offered food, blankets, and clothing by the missionary padres in return for converting to Christianity and working at the missions? Or were they displaced people who lost the use of their land, only to become enslaved neophites who were beaten when they tried to escape or revolt? One Indian, Toypurina of the Jachivit rancheria close to the San Gabriel Mission, was labeled a rebel savage in a 1785 plot to remove the padres. Jailed for two years while awaiting sentence, she was exiled to the San Carlos Borromeo Mission in Carmel, cut off from her family. A mural of this young woman's plight stands far from this trail at the Metrolink stop in Baldwin Park, the region where, as a child in the Los Angeles foothills, she witnessed many of her people being lured into captivity.

The Cahuilla people lived in this region for generations. Their language belonged to the Takic branch of the Uto-Aztecan group. Inhabitants of the ancient village near the Terwilliger Valley, known as Paui, were alarmed at the arrival of the second de Anza expedition in 1775 with its multitude of men, women, and animals. The Cahuilla used a similar route to descend into Coyote Canyon. The trail continued to be used into the twentieth century. The Cahuilla Reservation at the start of this trail was established by executive order in December 1875.

Start of the long descent down Coyote Canyon

In later years, Judge Terwilliger moved from the Banning district to take up land in the region of this trail, leaving his name attached to Terwilliger Valley. Anza Valley sits to the north of Terwilliger, encompassing the settlement of Anza.

From as early as 1921, Riverside County officials sought to access Borrego Springs by pushing a major road down Coyote Canyon. Doc Beaty, a local figure of Truckhaven Trail (featured on page 372) fame and the owner of a ranch in Coyote Canyon, was brought in to consult on a possible route down the canyon. The proposal needed the approval of

ailey's Cabin, near the northern end of the trail

San Diego County. However, the county dragged its feet on any roadwork in the Borrego Valley and the project never got off the ground. It did resurface as late as the 1970s.

In 1967, two border patrol officers fell victim to felons trafficking illegal substances in the region. The officers were operating a traffic check nearby along California 79, a recognized route for trafficking narcotics and undocumented aliens. While searching a vehicle that was found to contain marijuana, they were overpowered by the occupants of a second vehicle. Their bodies were found a few days later in a cabin on Bailey's Ranch, close to the northern end of this trail.

The Baileys were early settlers in the area. James Bailey had struck gold in the Julian area and stayed on to settle there. His family ran cattle in Borrego Valley. In 1940, the Larner brothers built a cabin in Fig Tree Valley, at the southern end of this trail. They used the stone cabin as a line cabin. Howard Bailey, James's son, frequented the cabin with his stock over the years. Howard and his wife, Lola, left the cabin and funds to the state park when Howard passed away in the mid-1970s.

Description

Coyote Canyon is a wide, deep canyon along the San Jacinto Fault, one of the major branches of the San Andreas Fault. These are two of Southern California's most active faults. Coyote Canyon separates the Santa Rosa Mountains to the north from the San Ysidro Mountains to the south. For eight months of the year hikers, horseback riders, and mountain bikers can traverse the full length of the canyon. Vehicles cannot access the middle section of the canyon, the fragile riparian area between Upper Willows and Lower Willows. However, the rough trail into the canyon and the magnificent scenery and desert solitude to be found within the Anza-Borrego Desert State Park make the northern section of the canyon alone a worthwhile trip.

This middle section of Coyote Canyon is closed to everyone, including hikers, between June 1 and September 30 to protect the habitat of the rare peninsular bighorn sheep. The closure allows them unimpeded access to waterholes in the hot summer months. Coyote Canyon is also home to many reptile and bird species, including the Bell's vireo.

The start of the trail follows paved roads through housing subdivisions in the Terwilliger Valley before turning off onto a dirt trail that leads to the park boundary. There are no signs directing you to the park until you are almost at the boundary.

Once away from the houses, the trail turns into a rough, lumpy formed trail. It crests a saddle close to San Carlos Pass and gradually starts to descend. There are views in all directions, but the predominant view is into the wide chasm of Coyote Canyon to the south. The trail descends Anza Ridge along a shelf road known as the Turkey Grade, a rough road cut by the Civilian Conservation Corps in 1933. This is the major difficulty encountered along the trail. The shelf road is ample width for one vehicle, but the roughness of the trail and the instability of the surface mean there is only one practical line to pick your way through for most of its length. Passing places are very limited. Take extra care close to the edge; the ground is unstable and especially loose after rain. Large boulders, deep holes, uneven camber, and loose surfaces will challenge the wheel articulation and clearance of most vehicles. Additional vehicle clearance and large tires will help, as will the absence of low-hanging brush bars, underbody spare tires, and sidesteps. The difficulty increases the closer you get to the bottom. Water runoff tends to follow the line of the trail and the two stretches on either side of the final switchback are the roughest and most uneven, reaching a difficulty rating of 7. The trail only receives maintenance from passing trail users, and conditions can change rapidly in this remote region. In particular, drivers who attempt the trail in October, immediately after its reopening each year, should be prepared for altered conditions.

The descent along Turkey Grade in Coyote Canyon is quite rocky

Once down in the canyon, the trail standard becomes easier. The sandy trail winds along, crossing Tule Canyon to enter the main Coyote Canyon. The sand can be deep enough to require lower tire pressure. The main trail through the wash can become rearranged after every rainstorm. It can be hard to pick the correct route on occasion, in particular the start of the loop through Fig Tree Valley to Bailey's Cabin.

The final section of the trail is a short loop past Bailey's Cabin, which is very sturdy and kept in good order. Overnight use of the cabin is permitted; of course, be sure to leave it in better condition than you found it.

The trail passes beside a fence, which marks the end of the vehicle route, and loops back in the wash to rejoin the main

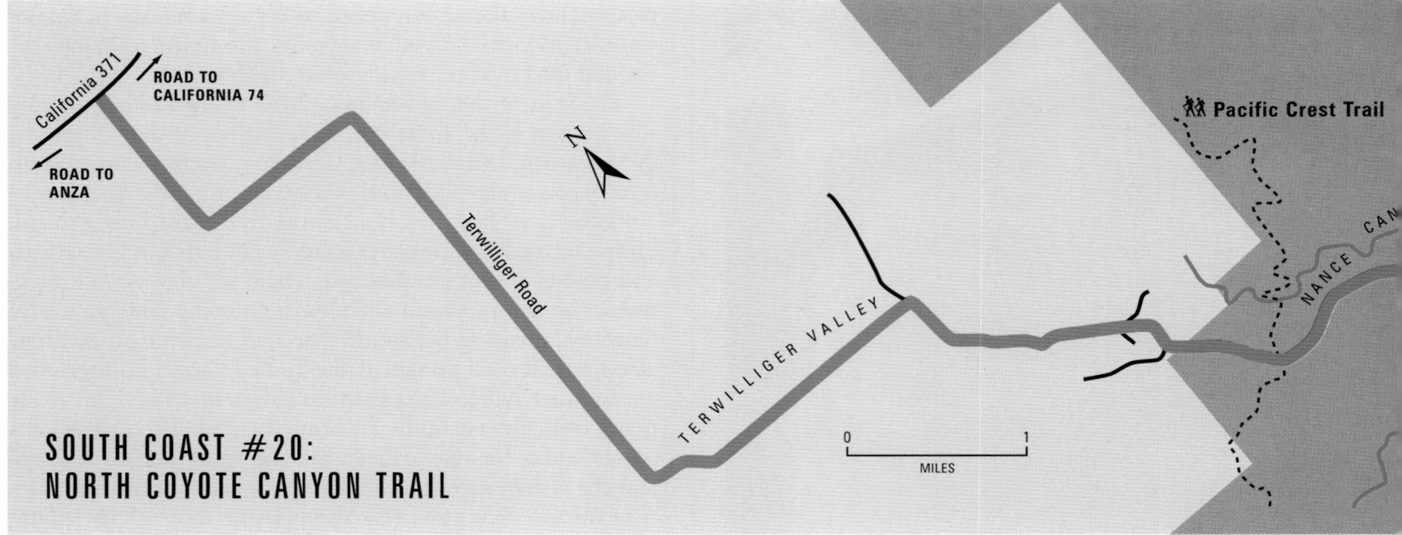

trail. Exit the way you came, climbing back up Turkey Grade.

Backcountry camping is allowed in the park, but there are only a couple of suitable spots along this trail. No camping is permitted south of the vehicle trail in the fragile area between Upper Willows and Lower Willows.

Current Road Information

Anza-Borrego Desert State Park
200 Palm Canyon Drive
Borrego Springs, CA 92004
(760) 767-5311

Map References

BLM Palm Springs, Borrego Valley
USFS Cleveland National Forest
USGS 1:24,000 Anza, Bucksnort Mt., Beauty Mt.
1:100,000 Palm Springs, Borrego Valley
Maptech CD-ROM: San Diego/Joshua Tree
Southern & Central California Atlas & Gazetteer, pp. 106, 114, 115
California Road & Recreation Atlas, p. 111
Other: Tom Harrison Maps—San Diego Backcountry Recreation map

Route Directions

▼ 0.0		From California 371, 1 mile east of Anza, zero trip meter and turn south on the paved Terwilliger Road, also known as Kirby Road at this point. Remain on paved road.
		GPS: N33°33.31′ W116°38.86′
▼ 4.5	TL	Turn left onto paved Coyote Canyon Road and zero trip meter.
		GPS: N33°30.05′ W116°37.80′
▼ 0.0		Continue to the east.
▼ 1.8	TR	T-intersection. Remain on Coyote Canyon Road, which is now graded dirt.
		GPS: N33°29.94′ W116°35.99′
▼ 2.2	SO	Graded road on right and left on saddle.
▼ 2.9	SO	Track on right.
▼ 3.1	SO	Road splits into three. Continue straight ahead down the middle road, remaining outside of fence line.
		GPS: N33°29.19′ W116°35.16′
▼ 3.4	TL	Turn left, following sign for Anza-Borrego Desert State Park. Ahead is private property. Zero trip meter.
		GPS: N33°28.97′ W116°35.03′
▼ 0.0		Continue to the east.
▼ 0.1	SO	Entering Anza-Borrego Desert State Park at gate.
		GPS: N33°28.89′ W116°34.90′
▼ 0.3	SO	Track on left.
▼ 0.7	SO	Pacific Crest National Scenic Trail, for hikers and horses, crosses the trail.
		GPS: N33°28.60′ W116°34.58′
▼ 1.6	SO	Turnout on right.
		GPS: N33°28.55′ W116°33.72′
▼ 2.0	SO	Turnout on left. Start to descend the steep Turkey Grade.
▼ 3.1	SO	End of descent.
		GPS: N33°28.27′ W116°32.95′
▼ 3.2	SO	Cross through Tule Canyon Wash.
▼ 3.4	SO	Enter line of Coyote Canyon Wash.
▼ 3.5	TR	Faint track on left up Coyote Canyon Wash.
		GPS: N33°28.18′ W116°32.54′
▼ 4.2	SO	Small track on right.
▼ 5.2	BR	Track on left in wash is end of loop. Bear right into Fig Tree Valley, away from the wash, and zero trip meter. This intersection is easy to miss.
		GPS: N33°27.10′ W116°31.41′
▼ 0.0		Continue to the south and exit line of wash.
▼ 0.8	SO	Track on right leads up Alder Canyon. Follow sign to Borrego.
		GPS: N33°26.39′ W116°31.39′
▼ 1.1	SO	Cross through wash.
▼ 1.6	SO	Corral and Bailey's Cabin on right.
		GPS: N33°26.44′ W116°30.68′
▼ 1.8	SO	Cross over Coyote Canyon Wash.
▼ 1.9	BL	Entrance to the south part of Coyote Canyon for hikers, horses, and mountain bikes. Bear left up wash.
		GPS: N33°26.72′ W116°30.67′
▼ 2.8		End of loop. Return the way you came.
		GPS: N33°27.10′ W116°31.41′

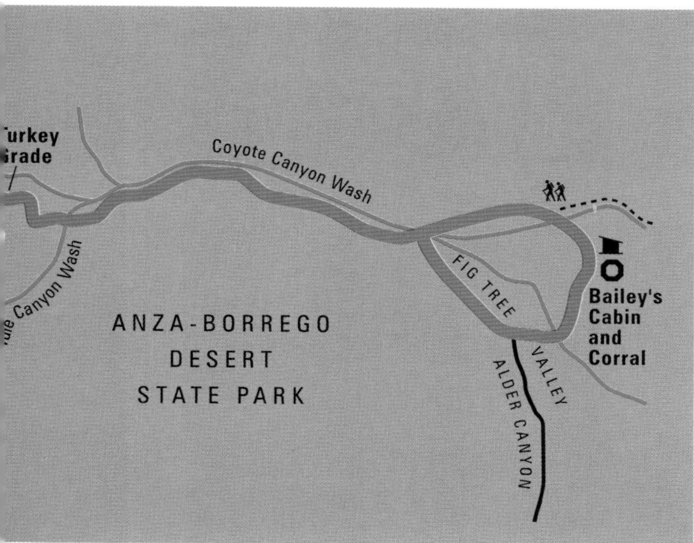

SOUTH COAST #21

Palomar Divide Road

Starting Point:	**California 79, 0.4 miles east of the intersection with California 371 and Aguanga**
Finishing Point:	**California 79, 12.7 miles east of the intersection of California 371**
Total Mileage:	**22.1 miles, plus 1-mile spur to High Point Lookout**
Unpaved Mileage:	**17.4 miles, plus 1-mile spur**
Driving Time:	**3.5 hours**
Elevation Range:	**2,000–5,700 feet**
Usually Open:	**Year-round**
Best Time to Travel:	**Dry weather**
Difficulty Rating:	**3**
Scenic Rating:	**9**
Remoteness Rating:	**+0**

Special Attractions

- 360-degree views from High Point Lookout.
- Long winding shelf and ridge road.
- Remains of the Ware Mine.

History

Mount Palomar, like the Palomar Divide, is named after the Spanish word meaning "dove" or "pigeon." Both species of bird are found in the region.

In 1928, the International Education Board, which was endowed by the Rockefeller Foundation, donated $6 million for the construction of a 200-inch reflecting telescope and related buildings. At the time, it was the largest in the world. Mount Palomar was chosen as the location because of its elevation and clear skies.

Snow-capped San Bernardino Mountains glimmer in the sunlight

The Pyrex dish that formed the main part of the telescope was manufactured in 1935 by Corning Glass Works in New York. The dish, which took nearly two years to fire, was eventually shipped to Pasadena, arriving at the California Institute of Technology in 1936. The final grinding of the dish was done there.

World War II interrupted the polishing of the dish, but the finished mirror was trucked from Pasadena to Mount Palomar in 1947. Its first image was recorded in 1949. The observatory remains on the mountain, but it is closed to the public. The telescope is no longer the largest in the world, and its location is becoming less ideal as light pollution from the ever-growing surrounding cities presents more and more interference.

Oak Grove Stage Station, set below the trail to the east, was one of the stops of the Butterfield Stage, which carried mail from St. Louis, Missouri, to San Francisco. The first stage passed the Oak Grove Stage Station on October 6, 1858.

Description

Palomar Divide Road is close enough to Los Angeles and San Diego to make an easy and scenic day trip from either metropolitan area. The trail leaves from California 79, which runs east out of the Temecula Valley. It leaves just east of Aguanga, down a road that initially appears to be a private entrance to an RV resort. However, the dirt road heads off to the south at the resort entrance, initially passing through private property before entering Cleveland National Forest.

The trail starts to climb along a well-used shelf road, steadily increasing elevation until it reaches the high point of the

The high-altitude Mendenhall Valley was a popular summer retreat for Native Americans and is now favored by motorbikers

trail at High Point Lookout (6,140 feet) on Mount Palomar. Views along the ridge and shelf road are spectacular in all directions. As you climb in the forward direction, Cottonwood Creek is to the west with Dameron Valley to the east.

Midway along the trail, a spur leads off through a shady grove of large oak trees to the High Point Lookout. Vehicle access to the lookout is restricted these days, but it is a very pleasant short hike from the gate to the tower, which is visible above you. It is possible to climb partway up the tower, but access to the very top is blocked. There are 360-degree views from the tower. On a clear day it is possible to see the Pacific Ocean.

From the tower, the trail continues along the Palomar Divide, undulating along the ridges of Palomar Mountain and Aguanga Mountain. It travels mainly through chaparral as it gradually descends to rejoin California 79.

The remains of the Ware Mine can be found immediately before the trail descends in earnest. A large, and now roofless, stone building can be seen, as well as the remains of some diggings.

Current Road Information

Cleveland National Forest
Palomar Ranger District
1634 Black Canyon Road
Ramona, CA 92065
(760) 788-0250

Map References

BLM Borrego Valley
USFS Cleveland National Forest
USGS 1:24,000 Aguanga, Palomar Observatory, Warner Springs
1:100,000 Borrego Valley
Maptech CD-ROM: San Diego/Joshua Tree
Southern & Central California Atlas & Gazetteer, p. 114
California Road & Recreation Atlas, p. 111

Route Directions

▼ 0.0		From California 79, 0.4 miles east of the intersection of California 371 at Aguanga, zero trip meter and turn south on paved road. The road is also the entrance to an RV resort. There is a brown forest service marker for 8S05 immediately west of the turn.
3.0 ▲		Trail ends on California 79, immediately east of Aguanga. Turn left for Temecula; turn right for Warner Springs.
		GPS: N33°26.42' W116°51.38'
▼ 0.4	SO	Paved road on right goes into RV resort. Trail turns to graded dirt.
2.6 ▲	SO	Paved road on left goes into RV resort. Trail is now paved.
▼ 0.5	SO	Cross through the wide Temecula Creek. Remain on main trail for next 1 mile. Initially the road passes through private property.

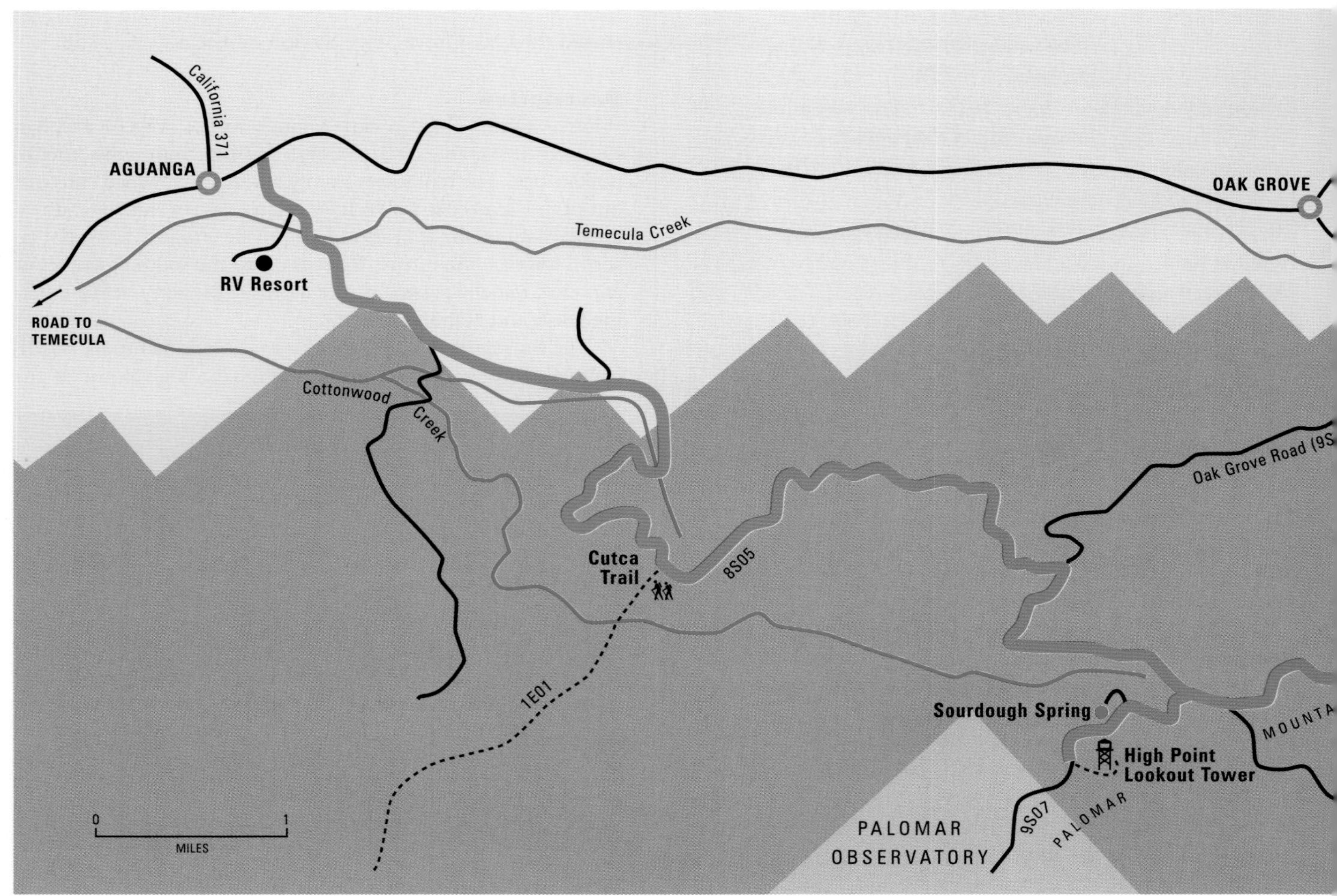

▼	▲		
			Tracks on right and left lead to private property.
	2.5 ▲	SO	Cross through the wide Temecula Creek.
▼ 1.5		SO	Track on right.
	1.5 ▲	SO	Track on left. Road passes through private property. Remain on main trail for next 1 mile. Tracks on right and left lead to private property.
▼ 2.6		SO	Track on left. Start of shelf road.
	0.4 ▲	SO	End of shelf road. Track on right.
			GPS: N33°24.59' W116°50.77'
▼ 3.0		SO	Closure gate. Zero trip meter.
	0.0 ▲		Continue to the northeast.
			GPS: N33°24.35' W116°50.69'
▼ 0.0			Continue to the southwest.
	6.0 ▲	SO	Closure gate. Zero trip meter.
▼ 0.4		SO	Cross through creek.
	5.6 ▲	SO	Cross through creek.
▼ 2.2		SO	Cutca Hiking Trail (1E01) on right goes to Agua Tibia Wilderness and Dripping Springs. Parking on left.
	3.8 ▲	SO	Cutca Hiking Trail (1E01) on left goes to Agua Tibia Wilderness and Dripping Springs. Parking on right.
			GPS: N33°23.78' W116°51.24'
▼ 6.0		TR	Closure gate; then T-intersection with Oak Grove Road (9S09). Zero trip meter and turn right onto 9S09.
	0.0 ▲		Continue to the west.
			GPS: N33°22.58' W116°49.56'
▼ 0.0			Continue to the south.
	1.8 ▲	TL	Turn left onto 8S05 at marker. Oak Grove Road (9S09) continues straight ahead. Zero trip meter.
▼ 0.3		SO	Turnout on right.
	1.5 ▲	SO	Turnout on left.
▼ 0.7		SO	Cattle guard.
	1.1 ▲	SO	Cattle guard.
▼ 1.8		SO	Palomar Divide Road (9S07) on right is the spur to High Point Lookout. Zero trip meter and proceed south, also on Palomar Divide Road (9S07). End of shelf road.
	0.0 ▲		Continue to the north along shelf road.
			GPS: N33°21.76' W116°49.54'

Spur to High Point Lookout

▼		
▼ 0.0		Proceed to the northwest on Palomar Divide Road (9S07).
▼ 0.1	SO	Track on left.
▼ 0.5	TL	Track straight ahead goes to Sourdough Spring. Spring is on right below main trail after turn.
		GPS: N33°21.92' W116°49.92'
▼ 1.0	UT	Track on left goes to High Point Lookout and is closed to vehicles. It is a short hike to the top. The road continues past this point for 0.3 miles to Palomar Observatory property. There is no access to the observatory.
		GPS: N33°21.89' W116°50.25'

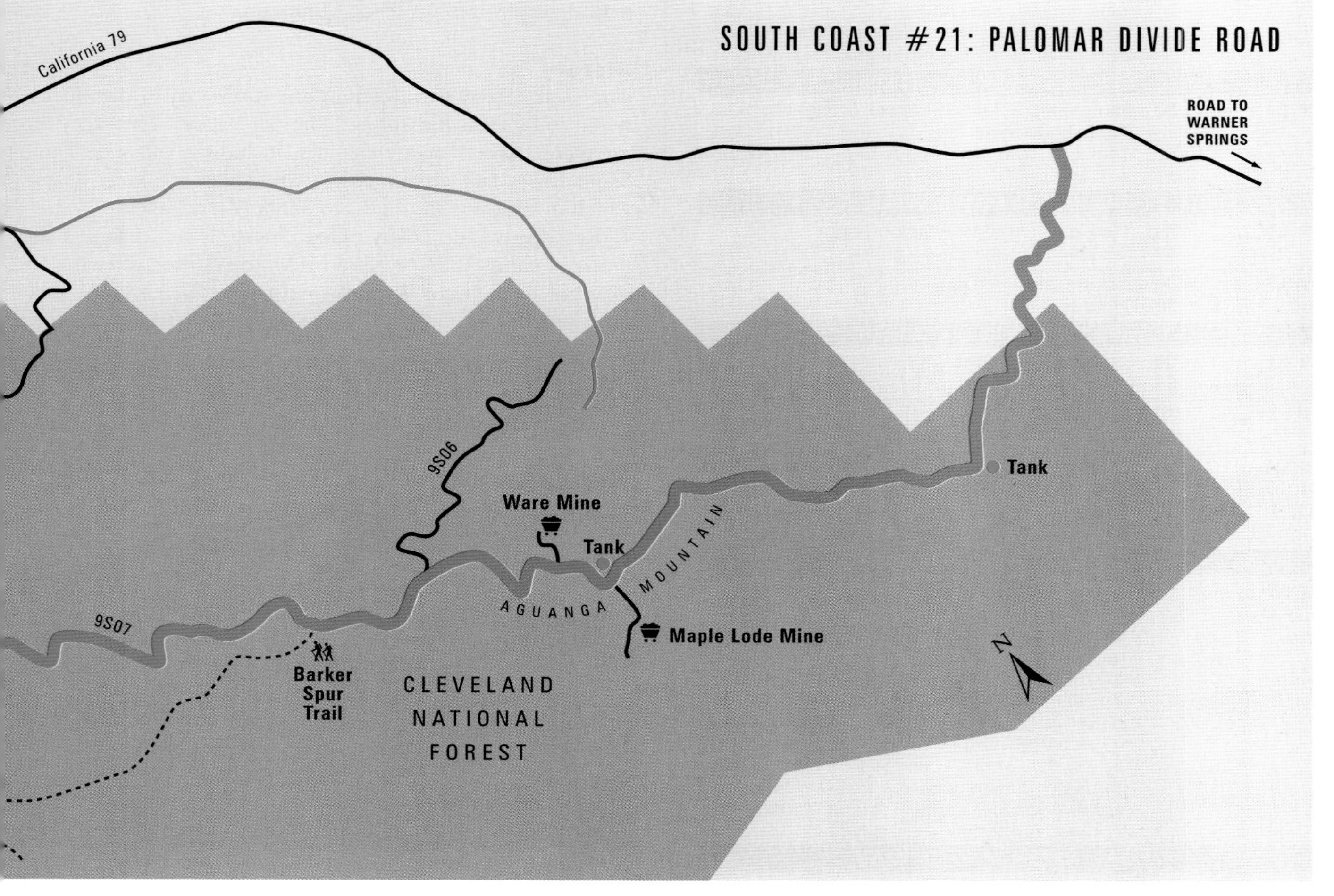

Continuation of Main Trail

▼ 0.0			Continue to the south.
	4.4 ▲	SO	Track on left is continuation of Palomar Divide Road (9S07) and is the spur to High Point Lookout. Zero trip meter and proceed north onto Oak Grove Road (9S09).
			GPS: N33°21.76' W116°49.54'
▼ 0.2		SO	Track on right.
	4.2 ▲	SO	Track on left.
▼ 0.6		SO	Game tank on left.
	3.8 ▲	SO	Game tank on right.
▼ 3.1		SO	Cattle guard.
	1.3 ▲	SO	Cattle guard.
▼ 3.3		SO	Game tank on right. Shelf road starts.
	1.1 ▲	SO	End of shelf road. Game tank on left.
▼ 3.7		SO	Barker Spur Hiking Trail on right at information board.
	0.7 ▲	SO	Barker Spur Hiking Trail on left at information board.
			GPS: N33°20.38' W116°47.23'
▼ 4.4		BR	Cattle guard; then trail forks. Graded road on left is 9S06, which is closed a short distance from the start. Remain on 9S07 and zero trip meter.
	0.0 ▲		Continue to the southwest over cattle guard.
			GPS: N33°20.22' W116°46.66'
▼ 0.0			Continue to the east.
	6.9 ▲	SO	Graded road on right is 9S06. Remain on 9S07 and zero trip meter.
▼ 1.1		SO	Track on left goes 0.1 miles to Ware Mine ruins. Road is now paved.
	5.8 ▲	SO	Track on right goes 0.1 miles to Ware Mine ruins. Road turns to graded dirt.
			GPS: N33°19.89' W116°46.06'
▼ 1.4		SO	Game tank on left; then track on right to Maple Lode Mine.
	5.5 ▲	SO	Track on left to Maple Lode Mine; then game tank on right.
			GPS: N33°19.64' W116°45.92'
▼ 3.3		SO	Track on right. Game tank on right.
	3.6 ▲	SO	Track on left. Game tank on left.
▼ 3.7		SO	Closure gate.
	3.2 ▲	SO	Closure gate.
			GPS: N33°19.10' W116°44.30'
▼ 4.1		SO	Game tank on right.
	2.8 ▲	SO	Game tank on left.
▼ 5.3		SO	Track on right.
	1.6 ▲	SO	Track on left.
▼ 5.4		SO	Exiting Cleveland National Forest at sign. Road turns to graded dirt. End of shelf road.
	1.5 ▲	SO	Entering Cleveland National Forest at sign. Road is now paved. Start of shelf road.
			GPS: N33°19.31' W116°43.23'
▼ 6.9			Private track on left; then closure gate. Trail ends at intersection with California 79. Turn left for Temecula; turn right for Warner Springs.
	0.0 ▲		Trail commences on California 79, 0.1 miles east of San Diego County mile marker 42 and 12.7 miles east of the intersection with California 371. Zero trip meter and turn south on graded dirt Palomar Divide Road (9S07). Immediately after the turn is a forest sign for High Point Lookout, as well as a route marker. Pass through closure gate; then track on right to private property.
			GPS: N33°19.86' W116°42.50'

SOUTH COAST #22

Santa Ysabel Creek Trail

Starting Point:	**Black Canyon Road, 7.5 miles north of California 78 and Ramona**
Finishing Point:	**Lusardi Pamo Road, 6.2 miles north of California 78 and Ramona**
Total Mileage:	**5 miles, plus 3.1-mile spur up Black Mountain**
Unpaved Mileage:	**5 miles, plus 3.1-mile spur**
Driving Time:	**1.5 hours (including spur)**
Elevation Range:	**1,000–2,800**
Usually Open:	**Year-round**
Best Time to Travel:	**Dry weather**
Difficulty Rating:	**2, spur is 3-rated**
Scenic Rating:	**8**
Remoteness Rating:	**+0**

Special Attractions

- Easy loop north of the town of Ramona.
- Views along Santa Ysabel Creek from the shelf road.
- Rough spur trail up Black Mountain.

History

The small, pretty town of Ramona is situated in the area referred to by local Indians as "The Big Valley." The valley has undergone several name changes, including Valley de Pamo Santa Maria, which means "Warm Valley of Saint Mary," which in turn was shortened to Santa Maria Valley.

Ramona was originally called Nuevo. It was renamed Ramona in either 1884 or 1886 by Milton Santee, after the Indian girl in the book *Ramona*, written by Helen Hunt Jackson. Jackson named her character after her friend Ramona

Black Canyon Road Bridge is near the start of the trail

Wolf, the wife of the storekeeper at Temecula.

Jackson was born in 1830 and became a passionate advocate for Indian rights. In 1881, her book *A Century of Dishonor* told the sad story of the Ponca Indians in South Dakota, and she used it as a basis to lobby the federal government for reform of its Indian policies. She arrived in California in 1881, in response to an invitation to write about Native Americans for *Century Magazine*. She was appointed as a special federal agent to visit Indians living at the missions and to locate public lands that could be turned into Indian reservations. Her novel, *Ramona*, was written during this time.

Jackson did not live to see her suggestions for reform come to fruition; she died in 1885, but various reform groups continued her work; the Act for the Relief of the Mission Indians in the State of California was finally passed in January 1891.

Ramona briefly lost its name to a new division of Los Angeles County, but regained it in 1895 when the division closed. The present town of Ramona has retained the name ever since.

To this day, the Ramona Pageant is the state's oldest continuing outdoor drama. Begun in 1920 and based around Jackson's best-selling novel, it is hosted in the natural open-air amphitheater known as the Ramona Bowl near Hemet. The bowl has been improved over the years, with a museum being added in 1952.

Another Spanish name in the region is Santa Ysabel Creek, named in connection with the settlement of Santa Ysabel, near Julian. Ysabel is the older form of Isabel and is commonly thought to refer to Isabella of Portugal, daughter of the King of Aragon. Santa Ysabel has maintained a chapel since 1924, and is a place of worship for Native Americans from five local reservations. The site also has a small museum and a Native American burial ground.

Description

This short trail leaves Black Canyon Road from Ramona and follows a winding shelf road that runs high above Santa Ysabel Creek. The road is suitable for high-clearance 2WD vehicles in dry weather. There are a couple of pleasant options for hikers here; a hiking trail heads off near the start of the vehicle trail and travels along Black Canyon Creek. The creek flows for much of the year and there are a couple of turnout points under giant shady oak trees that make a lovely place for picnicking and relaxing.

The easygoing shelf road along Santa Ysabel Creek is wide enough for a single vehicle and has sufficient passing places. On a saddle, the spur trail up Black Mountain departs to the north. This stretch is rougher and more lumpy with uneven sections and embedded rocks, making 4WD preferable. The old Black Mountain Truck Trail, as it was called, is closed to vehicles after 3 miles. Hikers, horses, and mountain bikes can continue around the gate to the top of the peak.

The main trail descends gradually to Lusardi Pamo Road. From here it is 6 miles back to Ramona.

This trail is likely to be gated shut by the forest service during or after wet weather. Check ahead with the ranger station in Ramona if there is any doubt. A National Forest Adventure Pass is required. No camping is permitted along this trail.

Santa Ysabel Creek Trail runs above Black Canyon

Current Road Information

Cleveland National Forest
Palomar Ranger District
1634 Black Canyon Road
Ramona, CA 92065
(706) 788-0250

Map References

BLM Borrego Valley
USFS Cleveland National Forest
USGS 1:24,000 Ramona, Mesa Grande
1:100,000 Borrego Valley
Maptech CD-ROM: San Diego/Joshua Tree
Southern & Central California Atlas & Gazetteer, p. 114
California Road & Recreation Atlas, p. 116

Route Directions

▼ 0.0		Trail commences on Black Canyon Road, 7.5 miles north of Ramona and 0.2 miles north of the Black Canyon Road Bridge. Zero trip meter and turn west on graded dirt road 12S07 through closure gate. Intersection is unmarked but well used.
3.5 ▲		Trail finishes at T-intersection with Black Canyon Road. Turn right for California 78 and Ramona.
		GPS: N33°07.44′ W116°48.07′
▼ 0.3	BL	Black Canyon Hiking Trailhead on right. Bear left and cross through Black Canyon Creek on concrete ford.
3.2 ▲	BR	Cross through Black Canyon Creek on concrete ford. Bear right past Black Canyon Hiking Trailhead on left.
		GPS: N33°07.61′ W116°48.15′
▼ 1.3	SO	Track on left; then cattle guard.
2.2 ▲	SO	Cattle guard; then track on right.
▼ 2.9	SO	Closure gate.
0.6 ▲	SO	Closure gate.
		GPS: N33°08.00′ W116°49.98′
▼ 3.0	SO	Track on left.
0.5 ▲	SO	Track on right.
▼ 3.2	SO	Cross through creek.
0.3 ▲	SO	Cross through creek.
▼ 3.5	SO	Track on right is spur up Black Mountain,

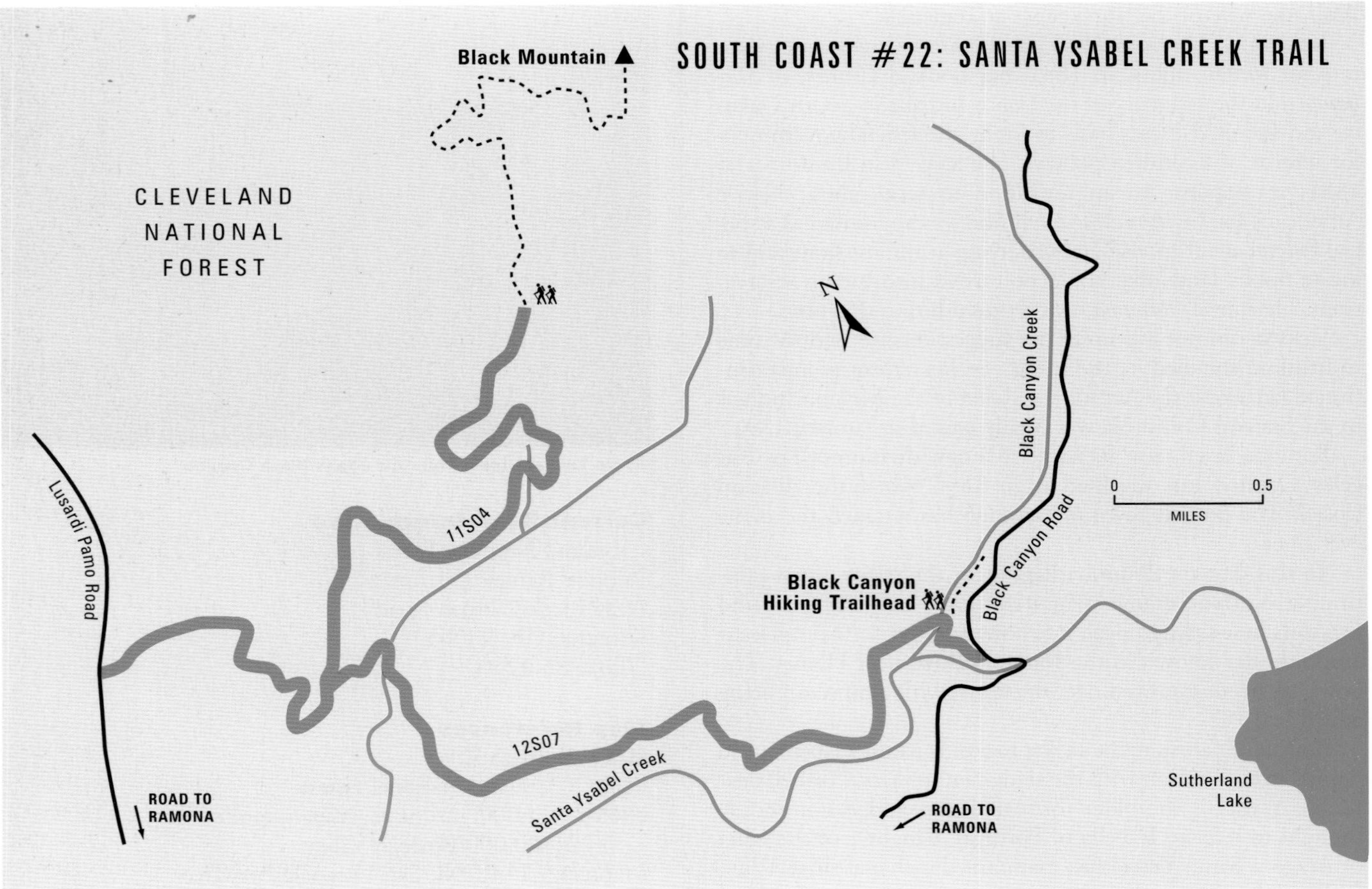

SOUTH COAST #22: SANTA YSABEL CREEK TRAIL

Black Mountain
CLEVELAND NATIONAL FOREST
Black Canyon Creek
Black Canyon Road
Lusardi Pamo Road
11S04
12S07
Santa Ysabel Creek
Black Canyon Hiking Trailhead
ROAD TO RAMONA
ROAD TO RAMONA
Sutherland Lake
0 0.5 MILES

		marked 11S04. Zero trip meter and continue straight ahead on 12S07.
0.0 ▲		Continue to the northeast.

GPS: N33°08.13' W116°50.23'

Spur up Black Mountain

▼ 0.0		Proceed to the north up shelf road.
▼ 0.1	SO	Closure gate.
▼ 0.6	SO	Cattle guard.
▼ 1.6	SO	Cross through creek.
▼ 2.9	SO	Cattle guard.
▼ 3.1	UT	Vehicle trail ends at information board. Road to the top is closed to vehicles. It is 2.4 miles (one-way) to the top of Black Mountain. Track on left goes 0.1 miles to overlook.

Fording Black Canyon Creek

GPS: N33°08.98' W116°49.09'

Continuation of Main Trail

▼ 0.0		Continue to the south.
1.5 ▲	BR	Track on left is spur up Black Mountain, marked 11S04. Zero trip meter and continue straight ahead on 12S07.

GPS: N33°08.13' W116°50.23'

▼ 0.2	SO	Track on left.
1.3 ▲	SO	Track on right.
▼ 0.8	SO	Cattle guard.
0.7 ▲	SO	Cattle guard.
▼ 1.5		Cattle guard and closure gate; then trail ends at T-intersection with graded dirt Lusardi Pamo Road. To reach Ramona, turn left and proceed south for 5.4 miles; then swing right and pass Elm Road on the left. Continue for 0.7 miles more to join California 78, north of Ramona.
0.0 ▲		From California 78, 3.8 miles north of Ramona, turn east on Haverford Road and proceed for 6.2 miles. (Haverford Road becomes graded dirt Lusardi Pamo Road.) Trail starts on Lusardi Pamo Road, 6.2 miles from California 78. Zero trip meter and turn east on graded dirt road at the national forest marker. Immediately pass through closure gate and cattle guard.

GPS: N33°08.43' W116°50.95'

SOUTH COAST #23

Grapevine Canyon Trail

Starting Point:	**Montezuma Valley Road (S22), 2.7 miles east of the intersection with San Felipe Road (S2)**
Finishing Point:	**Yaqui Pass Road (S3), 0.1 miles north of California 78**
Total Mileage:	**13.6 miles**
Unpaved Mileage:	**13.6 miles**
Driving Time:	**1.5 hours**
Elevation Range:	**1,400–4,000 feet**
Usually Open:	**Year-round**
Best Time to Travel:	**October to June**
Difficulty Rating:	**3**
Scenic Rating:	**9**
Remoteness Rating:	**+0**

Special Attractions

- Birding at historic Yaqui Well.
- Moderate-standard, historic trail within Anza-Borrego Desert State Park.
- Wide variety of succulents and Colorado Desert plant life.

History

Grapevine Canyon Trail follows one of the earliest routes used to reach the Borrego Valley region from the west. The valley initially attracted a number of homesteaders, but the advent of World War I led to a population decline in the area. By 1920, returning veterans homesteaded in the region because of government incentives.

Automobiles and highways were opening up many rural regions across the nation. In 1922, the earliest automobile route into the valley was constructed down the San Felipe Valley and through Sentenac Canyon. This new route took a lot of traffic off the older Grapevine Canyon route to the north of the San Felipe Hills. Grapevine had been a harder route to ascend and descend; now many avoided it and the trail fell into disuse. The canyon gained its named from the wild grapes that early travelers found along the canyon.

The new auto route followed an earlier trail constructed in 1872 by the McCain brothers, early ranchers associated with the Butterfield Stagecoach Line. Their trail gave access to Yaqui Well at the eastern end of Grapevine Canyon. Ranchers Paul and Pete Sentenac used the well to water large cattle herds in winter. They also constructed a cabin at the well. Paul filed a claim in 1883 on the nearby canyon that still bears the family name.

Before the arrival of European settlers in this part of Southern California, Kumeyaay Indians frequented this region. The territorial boundary between the northern and southern bands of Kumeyaay lay close to the wash line of San Felipe Creek. Some used Yaqui Well as a winter camp where they could gather and process food from the surrounding region.

The walls of Grapevine Canyon are covered with granite boulders

In the latter part of 1929, San Diego County established its first prison road camp, referred to as an honor farm, close to Yaqui Well. Officials at the primitive camp had tamarisk trees planted around it to offer some basic shelter in this remote location. Today, Tamarisk Grove Ranger Station and Camp can be found at the western end of Grapevine Canyon Trail. Prisoners used hand tools to carve the first roadbed along the south side of San Felipe Creek. By 1933, this primitive route became a state highway. It is known today as California 78.

Description

Grapevine Canyon is a narrow, sometimes sandy trail that runs between the Volcan Mountains and Grapevine Hills into Anza-Borrego Desert State Park. The start of the trail passes through private property off S22. The road is posted on either side, and there is currently de facto access on Grapevine Canyon Road. Please respect the property and avoid straying from the road. This access, although well known and used, is not always certain. Should it change in the future, the only access to the west end of Grapevine Canyon will be from S22 via the rougher Jasper Trail.

The road is roughly graded as far as the state park boundary, at which point it turns into a small, formed trail that follows the line of Grapevine Canyon Wash. To the north are the Grapevine Hills and to the south the trail runs along the boundary of the Grapevine Mountains Wilderness. The

Ocotillos, chollas, and agaves flourish at Yaqui Flat

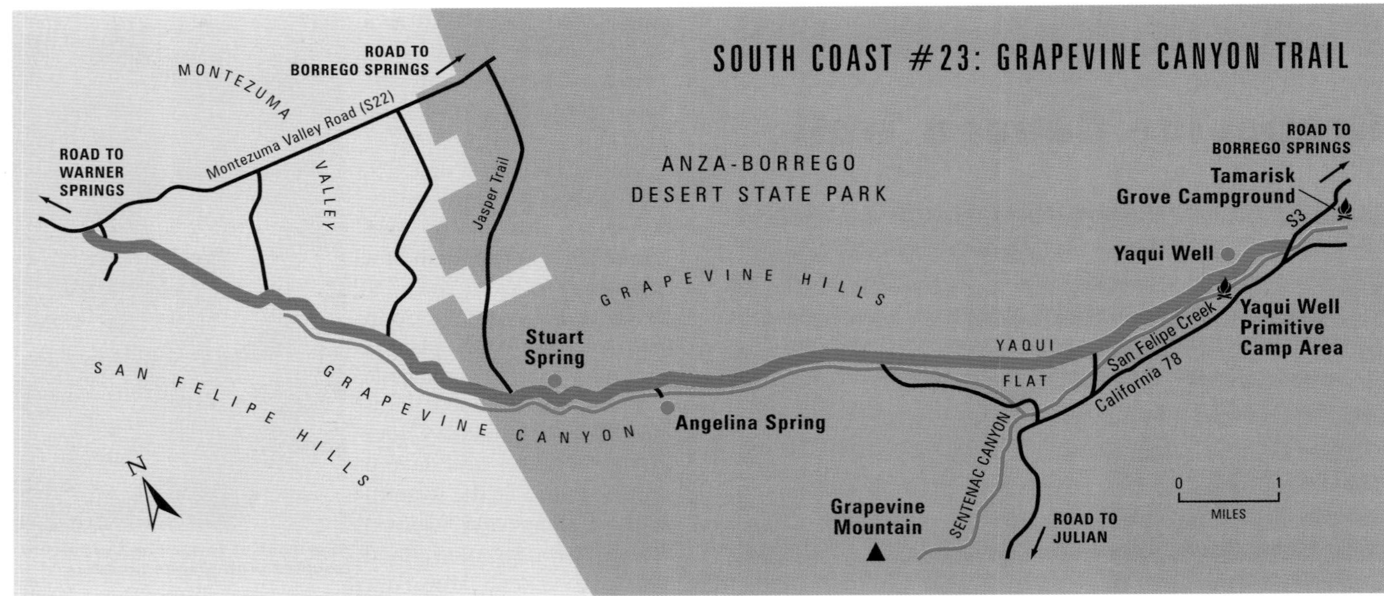

wash is vegetated with buckhorn cholla, sugarbush, and creosote bush. As the trail gradually descends there are good views to the southeast over the Pinyon and Whale Peak Mountains.

The trail passes Stuart Spring, which flows into a small trough, and close to Angelina Spring. A major fork in the trail takes you across Yaqui Flat toward Yaqui Well. Turning right at this fork will take you out to California 78. Across Yaqui Flat the trail undulates across the bajada, passing through dense stands of succulents—buckhorn and cane cholla, prickly pear, beavertail cactus, and fishhook barrel cactus.

One of the park's undeveloped campgrounds is located close to Yaqui Well. There are pit toilets but no other facilities and no fee. Campsites are semishaded alongside San Felipe Creek Wash.

Yaqui Well is a few steps away from the trail. The well is surrounded by ironwood trees, many of which are covered with parasitic mistletoe. Birders will enjoy looking for western bluebirds, roadrunners, cactus wrens, and hummingbirds.

The trail finishes on Yaqui Pass Road (S3) immediately south of the developed Tamarisk Grove Campground. There are shady developed sites and even showers. A daily fee is charged. The Cactus Loop Walk and the Yaqui Well self-guided trail start opposite the campground. These gentle, short walks offer a good insight into the area's vegetation and desert life.

Current Road Information

Anza-Borrego Desert State Park
200 Palm Canyon Drive
Borrego Springs, CA 92004
(760) 767-5311

Map References

BLM Borrego Valley
USFS Cleveland National Forest
USGS 1:24,000 Ranchita, Tubb Canyon
1:100,000 Borrego Valley
Maptech CD-ROM: San Diego/Joshua Tree
Southern & Central California Atlas & Gazetteer, p. 115
California Road & Recreation Atlas, p. 117
Other: Tom Harrison Maps—San Diego Backcountry Recreation map, Earthwalk Press—Anza-Borrego Desert Region Recreation map, Wilderness Press—Map of the Anza-Borrego Desert Region

Route Directions

Mileage		Directions
▼ 0.0		From Montezuma Valley Road (S22), 2.7 miles east of the intersection with San Felipe Road (S2), zero trip meter and turn south through metal gate marked Vista Irrigation District. Pass through gate and bear left, following the power lines. Trail passes through private property for the first 4.7 miles. Remain on main trail, ignoring property entrances to the left and right.
3.5 ▲		Trail ends on Montezuma Valley Road (S22). Turn right for Borrego Springs; turn left for Warner Springs.
		GPS: N33°12.75' W116°33.83'
▼ 0.2	BR	Track on left.
3.3 ▲	SO	Track on right.
▼ 0.4	SO	Track on right.
3.1 ▲	SO	Track on left.
▼ 1.4	SO	Track on right.
2.1 ▲	SO	Track on left.
▼ 2.1	TR	T-intersection with well-used dirt road.
1.4 ▲	TL	Turn left, following small sign for Grapevine Canyon Road.
		GPS: N33°11.56' W116°32.41'
▼ 3.2	SO	Track on left.
0.3 ▲	SO	Track on right.
▼ 3.4	SO	Track on left.
0.1 ▲	SO	Track on right.
▼ 3.5	SO	Track on left is alternate exit to S22. Zero trip meter.
0.0 ▲		Continue to the west along power lines.
		GPS: N33°10.76' W116°31.51'
▼ 0.0		Continue to the east along power lines.
1.7 ▲	SO	Track on right is alternate exit to S22. Zero trip meter.

▼ 0.4	BL	Bear left, following small sign to state park. Private property on right.
1.3 ▲	BR	Private property on left.
▼ 0.5	SO	Concrete foundations on right.
1.2 ▲	SO	Concrete foundations on left.
		GPS: N33°10.40' W116°31.33'
▼ 1.2	SO	Enter Anza-Borrego Desert State Park at sign. Trail now travels in line of wash.
0.5 ▲	SO	Exit Anza-Borrego Desert State Park at sign. Exit line of wash.
		GPS: N33°10.02' W116°30.92'
▼ 1.7	SO	Track on left is Jasper Trail, marked by a post. Zero trip meter.
0.0 ▲		Continue to the west.
		GPS: N33°09.83' W116°30.59'
▼ 0.0		Continue to the east.
4.2 ▲	SO	Track on right is Jasper Trail, marked by a post. Zero trip meter.
▼ 0.3	SO	Stuart Spring on left.
3.9 ▲	SO	Stuart Spring on right.
		GPS: N33°09.76' W116°30.36'
▼ 1.5	TL	T-intersection. Right goes 0.1 miles to Angelina Spring. Turn left and exit line of wash.
2.7 ▲	TR	Straight ahead goes 0.1 miles to Angelina Spring. Turn right and enter line of wash.
		GPS: N33°09.44' W116°29.24'
▼ 2.3	SO	Enter line of wash.
1.9 ▲	SO	Exit line of wash.
▼ 4.2	BL	Bear left, following marker post for Yaqui Well. Straight ahead is a shorter exit to California 78. Zero trip meter.
0.0 ▲		Continue to the west, entering up line of wash.
		GPS: N33°08.75' W116°26.87'
▼ 0.0		Continue to the northeast, exiting line of wash.
4.2 ▲	BR	Track on left rejoins California 78. Zero trip meter and turn right, following marker for Grapevine Trail.
▼ 2.0	SO	Well-used track on right.
2.2 ▲	SO	Well-used track on left.
▼ 2.6	SO	Cross through two washes. Trail crosses many small washes for next 1.3 miles.
1.6 ▲	SO	Cross through two washes.
▼ 3.5	SO	Entering Yaqui Well Primitive Camp Area. Track on right.
0.7 ▲	SO	Track on left. Exiting Yaqui Well Primitive Camp Area.
		GPS: N33°08.24' W116°23.41'
▼ 3.6	SO	Yaqui Well on left, a short distance up the foot trail.
0.6 ▲	SO	Yaqui Well on right, a short distance up the foot trail.
		GPS: N33°08.26' W116°23.28'
▼ 3.9	SO	Exit Yaqui Well Primitive Camp Area. Enter line of wash.
0.3 ▲	SO	Enter Yaqui Well Primitive Camp Area. Exit line of wash. Trail crosses many small washes for next 1.3 miles.
▼ 4.2		Trail ends on Yaqui Pass Road (S3). Turn left for Borrego Springs; turn right to join California 78 for Julian.
0.0 ▲		Trail commences on Yaqui Pass Road (S3), 0.1 miles north of California 78 and 12 miles south of Borrego Springs. Zero trip meter and turn west up wash at the sign for Yaqui Well Camp.
		GPS: N33°08.20' W116°22.70'

SOUTH COAST #24

Mine Wash Trail

Starting Point:	**California 78, 2.7 miles east of Yaqui Pass Road (S3)**
Finishing Point:	**Mine Wash**
Total Mileage:	**4.5 miles (one-way)**
Unpaved Mileage:	**4.5 miles**
Driving Time:	**30 minutes (one-way)**
Elevation Range:	**1,200–2,600 feet**
Usually Open:	**Year-round**
Best Time to Travel:	**October to June**
Difficulty Rating:	**2**
Scenic Rating:	**8**
Remoteness Rating:	**+0**

Special Attractions

- Kumeyaay village site.
- Scenic, easy canyon of Mine Wash.

History

The Kumeyaay Indians, early inhabitants of the region, spent winters here. The Cahuilla, another indigenous group, lived just to the northeast. Both groups may have shared this picturesque desert valley. Yaqui Well, a short distance to the northwest on South Coast #23: Grapevine Canyon Trail, was a campsite for those who gathered and partially processed food, after which they returned to their winter village in Mine Wash. Additional food processing took place at the village, as can be witnessed by the many bedrock mortar holes and worked stone surfaces at the ancient site. A Kumeyaay village site is set on the boulder-strewn hillside on the east side of the trail. Grinding stones, mortar holes, and the shallow caves used for shelter can be seen. However, the complete tale behind these early inhabitants' lifestyle is not always evident.

Native Americans made winter camps in Mine Wash and processed their foods in these mortar beds

Spanish expeditions, such as the one led by Juan Bautista de Anza in 1774, passed close to this

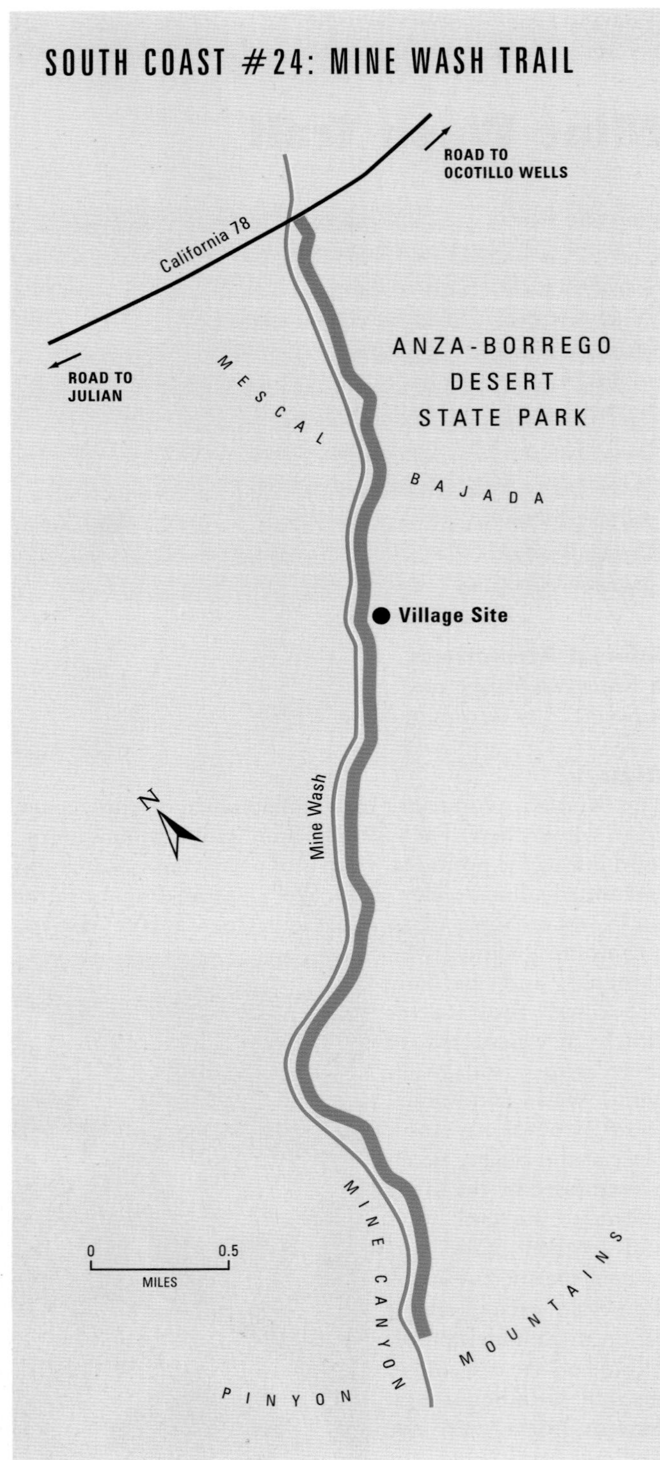

valley. Settlers from the East, prospectors, and many others brought change to these remote parts. Native groups encountered disease and suppression as incoming settlers took hold of the land. Newcomers had little time to absorb the knowledge of the indigenous groups they confronted. In turn, Indians were reluctant to relate the wealth of knowledge and experience gained throughout many generations on the land.

Description

This short spur trail heads south of California 78 up Mescal Bajada to enter into the rugged and beautiful Mine Canyon, which penetrates into the Pinyon Mountains. The hard-to-spot entrance to the trail is signed with a park marker. The trail travels south, up the loose sandy wash through abundant succulents scattered across the alluvial fan.

Crossing the sandy Mescal Bajada toward Mine Wash

After 1.5 miles, an information board marks the site of the ancient Indian village. Hike the few steps into the large tumbled-boulder landscape and take a few minutes to look around. Evidence of flat rocks used as grinding stones and shallow rock shelters among the boulders can be seen.

Past the village site, the trail winds its way up Mine Wash into the canyon. The surface is sandy, but it is normally passable by a high-clearance 2WD vehicle. The trail travels another 3 miles up the canyon before ending at a turnaround point. Hikers can continue up the canyon. Observant hikers will spot additional large granite boulders that have been used as grinding surfaces.

Current Road Information

Anza-Borrego Desert State Park
200 Palm Canyon Drive
Borrego Springs, CA 92004
(760) 767-5311

Map References

BLM Borrego Valley
USFS Cleveland National Forest
USGS 1:24,000 Borrego Sink, Whale Peak
1:100,000 Borrego Valley
Maptech CD-ROM: San Diego/Joshua Tree
Southern & Central California Atlas & Gazetteer, p. 115
California Road & Recreation Atlas, p. 117
Other: Tom Harrison Maps—San Diego Backcountry Recreation map, Earthwalk Press—Anza-Borrego Desert Region Recreation map, Wilderness Press—Map of the Anza-Borrego Desert Region

Route Directions

▼ 0.0		From California 78, 2.7 miles east of the intersection with Yaqui Pass Road (S3), zero trip meter and turn south on formed dirt road. There is a small park sign for Mine Wash at the intersection. Trail enters line of wash.
		GPS: N33°07.97' W116°19.99'
▼ 1.5	SO	Site of the Kumeyaay village on left.

		GPS: N33°06.77' W116°20.66'
▼ 3.8	SO	Track on right is a turnout. Hike a short distance up this canyon to see more Native American grinding stones.
		GPS: N33°05.28' W116°21.83'
▼ 4.0	SO	Enter Mine Canyon.
▼ 4.5		Trail ends at a turnaround point. No vehicles or horses beyond this point.
		GPS: N33°04.74' W116°22.10'

SOUTH COAST #25

South Coyote Canyon Trail

Starting Point:	**DiGiorgio Road, 7.6 miles north of Borrego Springs**
Finishing Point:	**Middle Willows, Coyote Canyon**
Total Mileage:	**13.2 miles (one-way)**
Unpaved Mileage:	**13.2 miles**
Driving Time:	**2.5 hours (one-way)**
Elevation Range:	**700–1,800 feet**
Usually Open:	**October 1 to May 31**
Best Time to Travel:	**October 1 to May 31**
Difficulty Rating:	**6**
Scenic Rating:	**10**
Remoteness Rating:	**+0**

Special Attractions

- Challenging historic trail to the southern end of the beautiful Coyote Canyon.
- Access to many trails suitable for hikers and horseback riders.
- Prolific and varied succulents in the Desert Gardens.
- Primitive camping at Sheep Canyon.
- Juan Bautista de Anza expedition route of 1774 and 1775.

History

South Coyote Canyon Trail travels up the canyon wash, passing close to a campsite of the second Juan Bautista de Anza expedition in 1775. The campsite was chosen because it had a suitable water source for the expedition; hand-dug wells produced enough water for nearly 800 head of stock and more than 200 people. In time, the area became known as Borrego Sink.

Juan Bautista de Anza first passed through the Borrego Valley in March 1774, on his first route-finding mission to the new Spanish settlements in California. Santa Catarina Springs was their campsite on March 14, 1774. They reached the spring on the feast day of Saint Catherine and, following tradition, named the spring after the saint. Fray Francisco Garcés carved words in a willow tree near the spring recounting the difficulties they were having with the natives.

Even though the route was partially known on Anza's second journey in 1775, conditions were just as difficult. The expedition, from Tubac in what was then Sonora, Mexico, (now part of Arizona), would take five and a half months to reach Alta California. The winter was harsh that year, and many expedition members suffered, including Gertrudis Rivas, an expectant mother. The expedition battled its way across the Yuha Desert through winter snows, following San Felipe Creek through the Borrego Badlands before heading up the daunting Coyote Canyon. Gertrudis went into labor on Christmas Eve near Middle Willows Spring, just north of Collins Valley past the end of the vehicle trail. She gave birth to a son whom she named named Salvador, meaning "savior" in Spanish. The child's name lives on in Salvador Canyon on the northwest side of Collins Valley.

Set in the heart of Coyote Canyon, Collins Valley was named just after the turn of the twentieth century for a squatter named Collins. He took the opportunity to jump claim on an earlier homesteader's property.

The Galleta Meadows Estate marker near the start of this trail commemorates Sebastian Tarabal, a Cochimi Indian of Baja California who guided Juan Bautista de Anza on his first expedition through the difficult region.

Rancho De Anza is bypassed these days as the trail enters the first narrows of the canyon. This was one of the earliest farming claims on the old trail, just north of the El Vado historical marker. *El vado* means a shallow part of a river, effectively a ford.

Doc Beaty, one of the colorful settlers of the Borrego Valley region, had tried his hand at many things: horse breaking, breaking unheard-of records in Wild West shows in Los Angeles, and mining. In 1913, he set about establishing a farm in Coyote Canyon with his family. He went on to become an important figure in the development of old Borrego. In 1927, he sold his valuable 1,000 Palms Ranch, so named because of the many palms upstream in Salvador Canyon. In 1936, the property sold again and was renamed Rancho De Anza by the

The second crossing of Coyote Creek

new owner, A. A. Burnand Jr. Burnand also became a figurehead in Borrego Springs as a founding member of the Borrego Land Development Company.

Description

Coyote Canyon runs from Anza to Borrego Springs and offers two separate vehicle trails, one from the north and one from the south. Of the two, the southern approach is more popular with hikers and four-wheelers. It is also slightly easier, although a rough half-mile section will test any vehicle. For eight months of the year, hikers, horses, and mountain bikers can connect the two trails via a 3-mile section of the canyon between Middle and Upper Willows. Between June 1 and September 30 each year, Coyote Canyon is closed to all users to protect water sources for the rare peninsular bighorn sheep. A seasonal closure gate after Second Crossing restricts users during this time.

The trail leaves from Borrego Springs to the north, passing the historical marker commemorating Sebastian Tarabal. It passes the graded road to Vern Whitaker Horse Camp before leaving the citrus groves behind and entering Anza-Borrego Desert State Park up a formed, sandy trail. There are three crossings of Coyote Creek; the first is usually dry, the others normally have year-round water that may be up to 24 inches deep. Conventional vehicles can generally handle the trail as far as Second Crossing but should not attempt to cross.

Evidence of early human activity is revealed by grinding stones around the spring

You can view abundant succulents at the Desert Gardens. The gardens make a pleasant spot for a picnic. Two small tables have been set among the ocotillos, cane chollas, teddy bear chollas, creosote bushes, beaver tails, and prickly pear cacti. Many hiking and horse trails leave from along this trail and access other remote corners of the park.

Second Crossing is approximately 100 yards long, with a moderately soft bottom. It is often the deepest of the three crossings, but a slow steady approach in a high-clearance 4WD will normally be trouble free. Do not attempt this if the creek is in flood or appears unusually deep.

The notoriously difficult stretch of trail comes a short distance after Third Crossing. The trail ascends a steep, rocky pinch that consists of loose, fist-size rocks and large embedded boulders. Careful wheel placement and a spotter to help select the best line and watch the undercarriage are a big advantage. However, with a careful experienced driver at the wheel and a bit of care, most stock SUVs will make the ascent. Good tires with sturdy sidewalls are also an advantage to help minimize the risk of flats from sharp rocks. This is the 6-rated section of the trail, and it extends for half a mile. The first 200 yards are the worst; park at the base of the climb and scout ahead on foot to be sure you want to tackle it. This is not a safe place to back down should you change your mind. It is difficult to pass on this section, so if you see oncoming vehicles, wait for them to finish their descent before you head up.

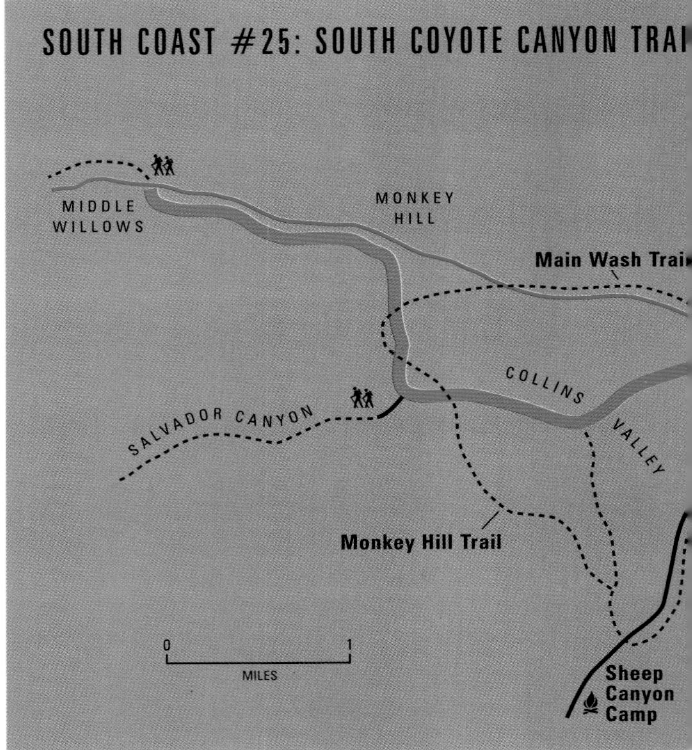

Once at the saddle, looking north into Collins Valley, the difficult part of the trail is over—although you do have to return the way you came. The trail reverts to a smooth, sandy surface as it descends into Collins Valley. A trail to the east leads a short distance to a historical marker at the site of Juan Bautista de Anza's camp near Santa Catarina Springs. The springs can be seen from the trail a short distance farther. The green growth and trees of the marshy area around the springs stands out clearly in the drier surroundings. The springs are a major source of Coyote Canyon's year-round water supply and attract many species of birds and other animals. The springs themselves cover a large area and are the largest single natural water supply in San Diego County.

The trail forks in a short distance. To the left leads around an alternate, slightly longer loop around Sheep Canyon, which passes a primitive camping area with a few picnic tables and pit toilets but no other facilities. There is no fee. Looking farther up the canyon from the camping area, you can see an area of fan palms. The Indian Canyon–Cougar Canyon trail for hikers and horses also leads off from near the campground. This trail passes an Indian sweat lodge as well as grinding stones.

The main trail continues through Collins Valley before it swings past the entrance to Salvador Canyon, where there are

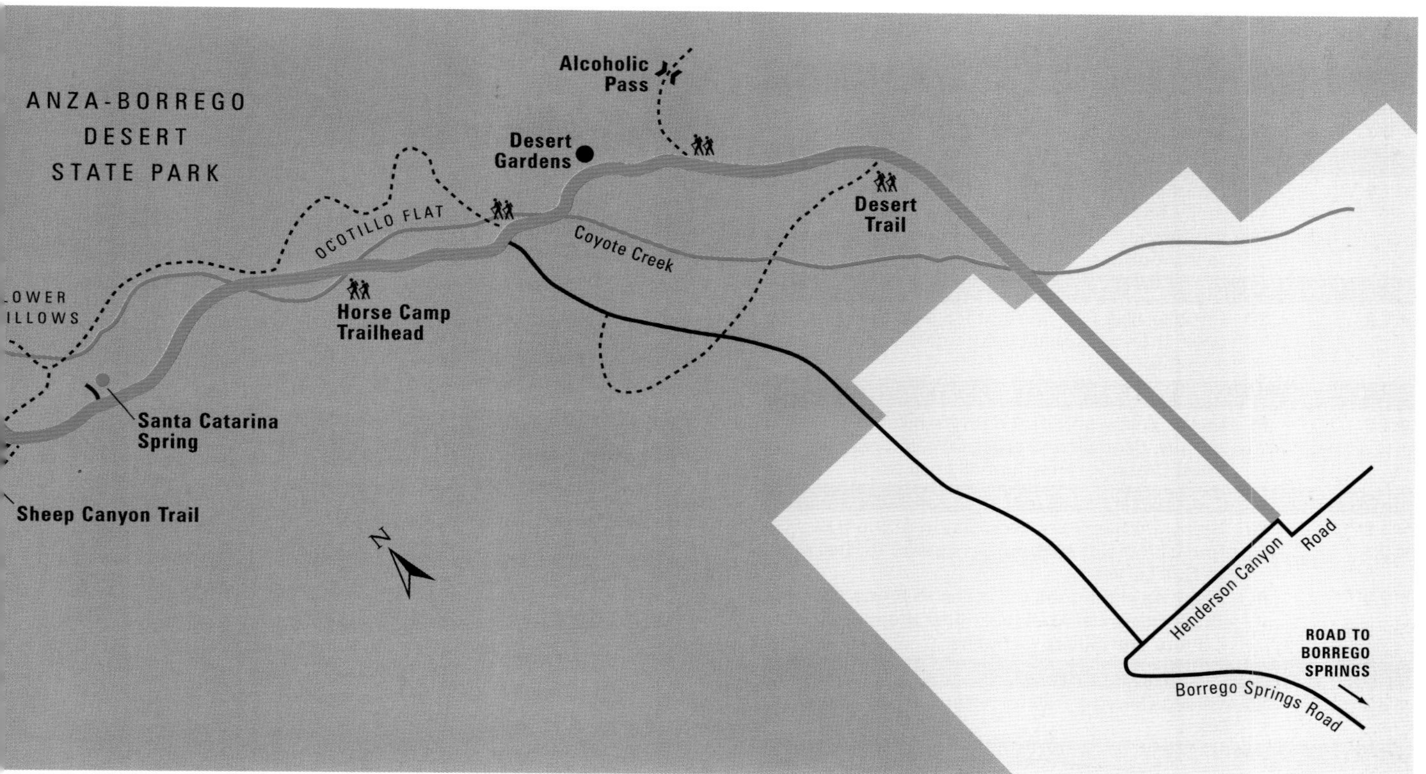

more fan palms, and drops into Coyote Creek. The trail here is lumpy and uneven, but even though it is slow going, it will not cause any difficulty to anyone who has made it this far. Water flows in this section of Coyote Creek for most of the year. The trail ends at the closure gate just south of Middle Willows, where a keen eye will find the mortar beds of Indian camps from a time long past.

The trail is best suited for small and midsize SUVs because of a couple spots where there is tight clearance between large boulders. Good clearance and tires, and an absence of side steps and low-hanging brush bars, are a definite advantage.

Current Road Information

Anza-Borrego Desert State Park
200 Palm Canyon Drive
Borrego Springs, CA 92004
(760) 767-5311

Map References

BLM Borrego Valley
USFS Cleveland National Forest
USGS 1:24,000 Borrego Palm Canyon, Collins Valley, Clark Lake
1:100,000 Borrego Valley
Maptech CD-ROM: San Diego/Joshua Tree
Southern & Central California Atlas & Gazetteer, p. 115
California Road & Recreation Atlas, p. 111
Other: Tom Harrison Maps—San Diego Backcountry Recreation map, Earthwalk Press—Anza-Borrego Desert Region Recreation map, Wilderness Press—Map of the Anza-Borrego Desert Region

Route Directions

▼ 0.0		From Christmas Circle in Borrego Springs, zero trip meter and turn north on Borrego Springs Road. After 2.9 miles, the Galleta Meadows Estate historical marker will be on the right. Swing right 0.3 miles after the marker and join Henderson Canyon Road. After the turn, a dirt road to the left goes to Vern Whitaker Horse Camp. Continue east on Henderson Canyon Road for 4.4 miles to the T-intersection with DiGiorgio Road and zero trip meter. Turn left and proceed north on DiGiorgio Road.
		GPS: N33°18.08′ W116°21.96′
▼ 1.6	SO	Graded road on right. Road turns to a formed dirt trail. Continue straight ahead, following the marker for Coyote Canyon.
		GPS: N33°19.52′ W116°22.01′
▼ 1.8	SO	Entering Anza-Borrego Desert State Park.
		GPS: N33°19.66′ W116°22.01′
▼ 3.0	SO	Desert Trail on left for hikers and horses only (no dogs allowed).
		GPS: N33°20.70′ W116°22.10′
▼ 4.1	SO	Alcoholic Pass Hiking Trail on right.
		GPS: N33°21.18′ W116°22.97′
▼ 4.7	SO	Desert Gardens plaque on right and couple of benches and picnic tables.
		GPS: N33°21.53′ W116°23.48′
▼ 5.0	SO	Cross through Coyote Creek. This is First Crossing and is often dry.
		GPS: N33°21.48′ W116°23.79′
▼ 5.3	SO	Ocotillo Trail for hikers and horses on right.
		GPS: N33°21.55′ W116°24.01′

▼ 5.4	BR	Track on left at Anza's Overland Expedition Marker. Zero trip meter.
		GPS: N33°21.51' W116°24.08'
▼ 0.0		Continue to the west.
▼ 0.9	SO	Trailhead on left to Horse Trail Camp.
		GPS: N33°21.93' W116°24.89'
▼ 1.0	BR	Second Crossing of Coyote Creek. This normally has water. The trail enters the creek at the Second Crossing marker and bears around to the right.
		GPS: N33°21.94' W116°24.92'
▼ 1.3	SO	Ocotillo Flat Trail on right for hikers and horses only; then seasonal closure gate (closed June 1 to Sept. 30).
		GPS: N33°22.12' W116°25.21'
▼ 1.5	BL	Lower Willows Trail on right for hikers and horses only. Bear left and cross Coyote Creek at Third Crossing. This normally has water.
		GPS: N33°22.28' W116°25.36'
▼ 1.8	SO	Start of difficult 6-rated section of the trail.
▼ 2.3	SO	End of difficult section. Trail starts to descend to Collins Valley.
▼ 2.6	BL	Track on right goes 0.3 miles to Santa Catarina State Historical Marker. Follow the marker to Coyote and Sheep Canyons.
		GPS: N33°22.21' W116°26.35'
▼ 3.2	SO	Sheep Canyon Trail for hikers and horses on left.
		GPS: N33°22.32' W116°26.90'
▼ 3.3	BR	Track on left is alternate longer loop via Sheep Canyon Camp. Zero trip meter and follow the marker to Middle Willows.
		GPS: N33°22.45' W116°26.90'
▼ 0.0		Continue to the north. Lower Willows Trail for hikers and horses is on the right just after the intersection. Santa Catarina Springs is visible to the right (south of the trail), marked by palms and abundant growth. Juan Bautista de Anza Historic Trail parallels the main trail at this point.
▼ 1.2	BR	Track on left is end of loop through Sheep Canyon. Zero trip meter and follow the marker to Middle Willows.
		GPS: N33°22.94' W116°27.74'
▼ 0.0		Continue to the northwest.
▼ 0.9	SO	Monkey Hill Trail, for hikers and horses only, crosses the main route. To the left it goes to Sheep Canyon Camp.
		GPS: N33°23.56' W116°28.17'
▼ 1.1	TR	T-intersection. Track on left goes 0.25 miles to the start of a hiking trail into Salvador Canyon. Turn right and pass through fence line.
		GPS: N33°23.66' W116°28.34'
▼ 1.3	SO	Monkey Hill Trail crosses the main route.
▼ 1.7	SO	Track on left is Monkey Hill Trail. Track on right is Main Wash Trail, for hikers and horses only. Trail now enters the line of Coyote Canyon Wash.
		GPS: N33°24.00' W116°28.03'
▼ 3.3		Trail ends just south of Middle Willows at the start of the hiking trail through Upper Willows that connects with South Coast #20: North Coyote Canyon Trail. Hikers, equestrians, and mountain bikers can connect through but vehicles are prohibited. Retrace your steps back to Borrego Springs.
		GPS: N33°25.23' W116°28.54'

SOUTH COAST #26

Truckhaven Trail

Starting Point:	**Borrego-Salton Seaway (S22), 9 miles east of Borrego Springs**
Finishing Point:	**Borrego-Salton Seaway (S22), 18.5 miles east of Borrego Springs**
Total Mileage:	**11.3 miles**
Unpaved Mileage:	**11.3 miles**
Driving Time:	**1.25 hours**
Elevation Range:	**600–1,000 feet**
Usually Open:	**Year-round**
Best Time to Travel:	**October to June**
Difficulty Rating:	**5 (detour around the washout rates a 7 and is the only way around)**
Scenic Rating:	**8**
Remoteness Rating:	**+0**

Special Attractions

- Historic route of the Truckhaven Grade.
- Scenic Cannonball, Arroyo Salado, and North Fork Arroyo Salado Canyons.

History

The western end of Truckhaven Trail crosses the vast Clark Valley south of Clark Dry Lake. The lake is named after Fred and Frank Clark, who lived just northwest in the Anza settlement. The brothers were among the earliest cattlemen to reside in the Borrego Valley region; they established a well and camp at the dry lake in the 1890s.

In the early 1940s the lake at the foot of the 8,000-foot-high Santa Rosa Mountains was part of a bombing range established by the military, which set up a training base in the quiet Borrego Valley.

From the earliest days of modern settlement to the 1940s, Borrego Springs was a remote settlement without paved roads, telephones, or an electricity supply system. Over the years, Borrego Valley attracted many farmers, who tried their hands at growing alfalfa, dates, tomatoes, and pecans. Some tried hog and turkey farming. Not all survived. Water wells were drilled and talk of joining San Diego County in a venture to construct a pipeline from the Imperial Valley irrigation canals brought hope to early settlers. A reliable route to outside markets where they could sell their produce was of prime interest to growers. Brawley, to the south, was the supply town for early homesteaders but reaching it involved an arduous journey that took at least two and a half days by horse and wagon. The primitive Julian–Kane Springs Road that headed southwest from town was not opened until 1925.

The community-funded Truckhaven Trail became an all-important route to the east. The road joined California 99, the predecessor of today's California 86, at a gas station called Truckhaven. This basic road was built with money and labor contributions from locals because San Diego County was not forthcoming with funds. Doc Beaty, an early settler, was instrumental in the road's creation, dragging a mule-drawn scraper through the badlands to the Truckhaven gas station to create the first rough road. Funds were received from the few businesses that might gain from the road, including the Truckhaven Cafe. Private individuals gave funds whenever possible; others worked voluntarily through sweltering heat. Many men did pick and shovel work while women helped set up and cook at the road construction camps.

The road, completed in 1930 at a cost of $750, angled down through the deep badland washes, climbing out in the same fashion. It was not a route for speedy travel, and trucks and autos took their time weaving through the weathered landscape.

In 1968, the Borrego-Salton Seaway was dedicated. This larger-scale, paved road follows Doc's route closely, and sections of the old trail remain. Since World War II, the old route has been popular with people in 4WDs who wish to sample the rugged badlands terrain rather than travel the faster blacktop.

Description

Truckhaven Trail has changed little from the sandy grade realized by Beaty in the late 1920s. Much of the original route has been paved to form S22, and other sections cross private property. But there are sections, including this 11-mile trail, that are open and accessible to hikers and private vehicles. Most of the trail is 3-rated because of the deep loose sand, but the stretch between the intersections with South Coast #28: Arroyo Salado Trail and South Coast #29: Calcite Mine Trail is predominantly 5-rated. In addition, the original incline out of North Fork Arroyo Salado Wash has subsided. A detour is in place, but it involves a short pinch that is very steep and difficult, with a twist at the top. Whether you are climbing or descending, the loose, flaking surface offers little in the way of traction. This pinch is rated a 7 for difficulty in reverse and an 8 in the forward direction because there is a possibility of damaging the sides of your vehicle if you slip sideways on the loose surface.

Truckhaven Trail descends to the North Fork of Arroyo Salado Wash

The sandy trail bears away from S22 at an acute angle, heading toward the Santa Rosa Mountains. It is easygoing through undulating scenery, crossing the wide, sandy Inspiration Point Wash and Fonts Point Wash. The normally dry Clark Lake is visible to the northwest in Clark Valley.

The trail joins paved S22 for 2.9 miles before turning off south of the paved road to travel down Arroyo Salado Wash. There is a popular primitive camping area 0.3 miles from the paved road; it has fire rings and a pit toilet but no other facilities.

Approaching the dry Clark Lake below Coyote Mountain

The trail enters down the very scenic Arroyo Salado Wash and winds through a red-walled canyon along the sandy wash. After traveling 2.2 miles from S22, the trail turns into a side wash. The Arroyo Salado Trail continues down Arroyo Salado Wash from this point. This intersection is unmarked, small, and very easy to miss. Once you have made the turn, the side canyon opens up, and you will see the formed trail leading out of the wash. If you see this, you will know you are traveling the correct route.

The trail climbs over a saddle before descending North Fork Arroyo Salado Wash. There is a trail marker at the intersection with the wash. A short distance later, the trail turns sharp left to exit the wash. This is the site of the washout. The coordinates given in the route directions are the coordinates of the correct turn. Should the proper trail still be washed out, the alternate exit up the loose pinch is immediately upstream on the left.

Once out of the wash, the trail is 5-rated as it undulates in and out of the deep badland canyons. This section has some loose, eroded, and low-traction climbs to negotiate. There are some narrow bits where the trail is sliding down the shelf road. After Cannonball Canyon, a tributary of the North Fork Arroyo Salado Wash, the trail reverts to an easy, sandy trail that rejoins S22 opposite the start of the difficult South Coast #29: Calcite Mine Trail.

The Truckhaven Trail is not to be confused with the Truckhaven Hills, an area of difficult 4WD trails immediately west of Salton City.

Current Road Information

Anza-Borrego Desert State Park
200 Palm Canyon Drive
Borrego Springs, CA 92004
(760) 767-5311

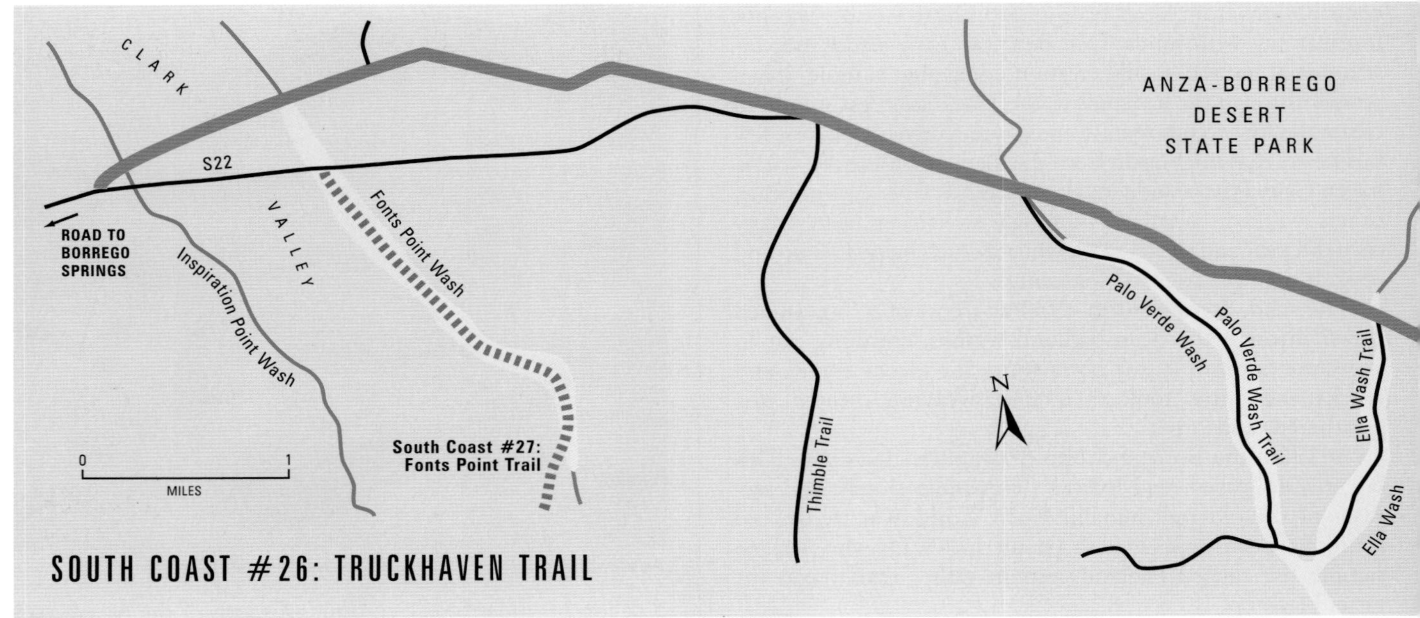

Map References

BLM Borrego Valley
USGS 1:24,000 Clark Lake, Fonts Point, Seventeen Palms
1:100,000 Borrego Valley
Maptech CD-ROM: San Diego/Joshua Tree
Southern & Central California Atlas & Gazetteer, pp. 115, 116
California Road & Recreation Atlas, p. 117
Other: Tom Harrison Maps—San Diego Backcountry Recreation map, Earthwalk Press—Anza-Borrego Desert Region Recreation map, Wilderness Press—Map of the Anza-Borrego Desert Region

Route Directions

▼ 0.0		From Borrego Salton Seaway (S22), 0.7 miles east of mile marker 29 and 9 miles east of Borrego Springs, zero trip meter and turn northeast on unmarked trail running at an acute angle to S22.
3.7 ▲		Trail ends at S22. Turn right for Borrego Springs; turn left for Salton City.
		GPS: N33°18.22' W116°15.47'

Rugged sandstone walls of North Fork Arroyo Salado Wash

▼ 0.2	SO	Cross through Inspiration Point Wash. Tracks on right and left up and down wash. Clark Lake visible on left.
3.5 ▲	SO	Cross through Inspiration Point Wash. Tracks on right and left up and down wash. Clark Lake visible on right.
▼ 1.0	SO	Cross through wide Fonts Point Wash.
2.7 ▲	SO	Cross through wide Fonts Point Wash.
		GPS: N33°18.47' W116°14.50'
▼ 1.4	SO	Well-used track on left.
2.3 ▲	SO	Well-used track on right.
		GPS: N33°18.59' W116°14.03'
▼ 1.5	SO	Entering Anza-Borrego Desert State Park. Trail is now designated Truckhaven Trail.
2.2 ▲	SO	Exiting Anza-Borrego Desert State Park. Trail is now designated Truckhaven Trail.
▼ 3.2	SO	Cross through wash.
0.5 ▲	SO	Cross through wash.
▼ 3.3	SO	Cross through wash.
0.4 ▲	SO	Cross through wash.
▼ 3.7	TL	Turn left onto S22. Thimble Trail is opposite. Zero trip meter.
0.0 ▲		Continue to the northwest on formed trail.
		GPS: N33°18.17' W116°11.84'
▼ 0.0		Continue to the southeast on paved road.
2.9 ▲	TR	Turn right onto sandy, formed Truckhaven Trail at trail marker. Turn is opposite Thimble Trail and is 0.1 miles west of mile marker 32.
▼ 1.0	SO	Palo Verde Wash Trail on right.
1.9 ▲	SO	Palo Verde Wash Trail on left.
▼ 2.8	SO	Ella Wash Trail on right.
0.1 ▲	SO	Ella Wash Trail on left.
▼ 2.9	TR	Turn right on formed sandy trail, marked Arroyo Salado, and zero trip meter. The turn is 0.8 miles west of mile marker 34.
0.0 ▲		Continue to the west on paved road.
		GPS: N33°16.98' W116°09.09'
▼ 0.0		Continue to the southeast on formed trail.
2.2 ▲	TL	Turn left onto paved S22 and zero trip meter.
▼ 0.3	SO	Track on right enters Arroyo Salado Primitive Camp Area.

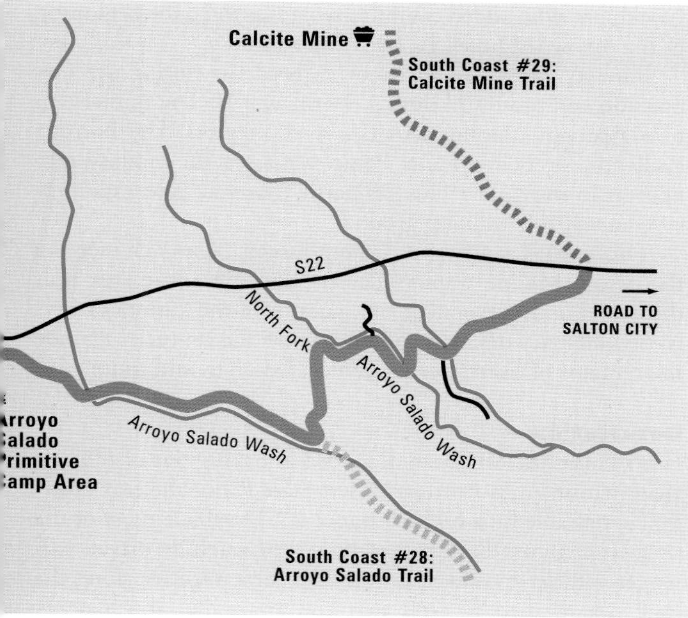

1.9 ▲ SO Track on left enters Arroyo Salado Primitive Camp Area.

▼ 0.4 SO Track on left.
1.8 ▲ SO Track on right.

▼ 0.5 SO Track on left.
1.7 ▲ BL Track on right.

▼ 0.6 SO Enter down Arroyo Salado Wash.
1.6 ▲ SO Exit Arroyo Salado Wash.

▼ 1.6 SO Exit Arroyo Salado Wash.
0.6 ▲ SO Enter up Arroyo Salado Wash.

▼ 2.2 TL Turn left up unmarked Truckhaven Trail and zero trip meter. South Coast #28: Arroyo Salado Trail on right. Intersection is easy to miss in this direction.
0.0 ▲ Continue to the northwest up wash.

GPS: N33°16.23' W116°07.15'

▼ 0.0 Continue to the north up side canyon.
1.2 ▲ TR Turn right up Arroyo Salado Wash and zero trip meter. South Coast #28: Arroyo Salado Trail on left.

▼ 0.1 BR Bear right out of wash.
1.1 ▲ SO Join wash in the side canyon.

▼ 0.5 SO Drop down toward North Fork Arroyo Salado Wash.
0.7 ▲ SO End of climb out of North Fork Arroyo Salado Wash

GPS: N33°16.59' W116°07.09'

▼ 0.6 TR Turn right down North Fork Arroyo Salado Wash, following Truckhaven Trail marker. Track on left up wash.
0.6 ▲ TL Track continues in wash. Turn left and climb out of wash, following Truckhaven Trail marker.

GPS: N33°16.67' W116°07.11'

▼ 0.9 SO Track on left up side wash.
0.3 ▲ SO Track on right up side wash.

▼ 1.2 TL Turn left, up and out of the wash. The official road is washed out and impassable; there is a difficult loose, alternate route immediately upstream before the main trail junction. It is very difficult in this direction because of the loose surface. Care is needed on this ascent at a tight twist on top of the short rise. Zero trip meter.
0.0 ▲ Continue to the northwest.

GPS: N33°16.49' W116°06.68'

▼ 0.0 Continue to the north.
1.3 ▲ TR Turn right up North Fork Arroyo Salado Wash and zero trip meter. The official route is washed out and impassable; there is a difficult loose, alternate route to the right immediately before the main trail junction. Care is needed on this short descent. It is easy to damage side panels in the narrow cut on all but well-prepared short-wheelbase vehicles.

▼ 0.1 SO Top of rise.
1.2 ▲ SO Top of rise.

▼ 0.2 SO Cross through wash.
1.1 ▲ SO Cross through wash; then climb out of canyon.

▼ 0.4 TL Track on right down wash. Follow the marker for S22 and climb out of wash.
0.9 ▲ TR Track straight ahead down wash. Follow the marker for Truckhaven Trail.

GPS: N33°16.56' W116°06.44'

▼ 0.6 SO End of climb from wash. Track on right is generally easier; then cross through wash.
0.7 ▲ SO Cross through wash. Two exits from wash—left-hand one is generally easier. Trail starts to descend to cross wash.

▼ 0.7 SO Track on right.
0.6 ▲ SO Track on left.

▼ 1.3 Trail ends on Borrego-Salton Seaway (S22), opposite the start of South Coast #29: Calcite Mine Trail. Turn left for Borrego Springs; turn right for Salton City.
0.0 ▲ Trail commences on Borrego-Salton Seaway (S22), 18.5 miles east of Borrego Springs. Zero trip meter and turn southwest on formed sandy trail. There is an information board and marker for the Truckhaven Trail at intersection. The turn is 0.3 miles west of a prominent telecommunications tower, 0.2 miles east of mile marker 38, and opposite the start of South Coast #29: Calcite Mine Trail.

GPS: N33°16.86' W116°05.73'

SOUTH COAST #27

Fonts Point Trail

Starting Point:	**Borrego-Salton Seaway (S22), 0.5 miles west of mile marker 30, 10.1 miles east of Borrego Springs**
Finishing Point:	**Fonts Point**
Total Mileage:	**4.1 miles (one-way)**
Unpaved Mileage:	**4.1 miles**
Driving Time:	**30 minutes (one-way)**
Elevation Range:	**800–1,200 feet**
Usually Open:	**Year-round**
Best Time to Travel:	**October to June**
Difficulty Rating:	**2**
Scenic Rating:	**9**
Remoteness Rating:	**+0**

Fonts Point Wash drains north toward Clark Lake

Special Attractions

- Exceptional view of the Borrego Badlands and the Borrego Valley from Fonts Point.
- Interesting, sandy trail up Fonts Point Wash.

History

Fonts Point is named after Father Pedro Font, a chaplain who traveled with Juan Bautista de Anza. Anza was the Spanish explorer who traveled through the Borrego Badlands in 1774 and 1775 to the developing network of missions in Alta California. Font kept a diary of his travels and referred to the view of the badlands as the "sweepings of the earth."

Fonts Point overlooks the Borrego Badlands with the Pinyon Mountains beyond

In the 1930s, a West Coast real estate developer named Dana Burks saw both tourism and agricultural opportunities in the desert location of Borrego Valley. About 6 miles southwest of Fonts Point, Burks constructed a Spanish-style adobe dwelling and envisioned a community that would peak during winter and encourage desert farming in the surrounding valley. The Depression of the 1930s may have been the downfall of Burks's vision. By the late 1930s, Burks had sold his adobe to the Crickmers, who added cabins to what was to be the beginning of the renowned hotel, La Casa Del Zorro.

Borrego Valley lost many of its residents during the Depression and more still during World War II. The military, in turn, brought training activities to the region. The Borrego Badlands, set below Fonts Point, was used for military maneuvers in the early 1940s. Its harsh, mazelike landscape provided a valuable training ground.

This eroded landscape is the remnant of a river meeting the ocean. Marine waters once covered the entire area near the outlet of a major river, an ancestor of the Colorado River. Sedimentary deposits laid down over the centuries include the remains of bears, horses, camels, beaches, and more.

Description

Fonts Point has long been described as having one of the best views within Anza-Borrego Desert State Park. The easy sandy trail is passable by a high-clearance 2WD vehicle most of the time. It can even be traversed by a very carefully driven passenger vehicle. However, if you take these vehicles along the trail, you need to be extra alert and aware that you may get stuck in soft sand.

The trail leaves S22 up the wide, sandy Fonts Point Wash. It is easy to follow; although there are a couple of forks in the trail, they all rejoin within a short distance. The only side trail is the Short Wash 4WD Trail.

The trail finishes in a loop that passes below Fonts Point. It is a few steps up to the viewpoint, high over the Borrego Badlands. From here you can see the convoluted washes and eroded canyons of the badlands, Vallecito Mountains, the Borrego Valley with the green oasis of Borrego Springs, the Peninsular Range, Borrego Buttes, and Pinyon Mountains.

This is one of the most popular and spectacular views in the Anza-Borrego Desert State Park. The sedimentary rocks that make up the viewpoint range in age from 250 million to 4 million years old.

Current Road Information

Anza-Borrego Desert State Park
200 Palm Canyon Drive
Borrego Springs, CA 92004
(760) 767-5311

Map References

BLM Borrego Valley
USGS 1:24,000 Fonts Point
1:100,000 Borrego Valley
Maptech CD-ROM: San Diego/Joshua Tree
Southern & Central California Atlas & Gazetteer, p. 115
California Road & Recreation Atlas, p. 117
Other: Tom Harrison Maps—San Diego Backcountry Recreation map, Earthwalk Press—Anza-Borrego Desert Region Recreation map, Wilderness Press—Map of the Anza-Borrego Desert Region

Route Directions

▼ 0.0 From Borrego-Salton Seaway (S22), 0.5 miles west of mile marker 30 and 10.1 miles east of

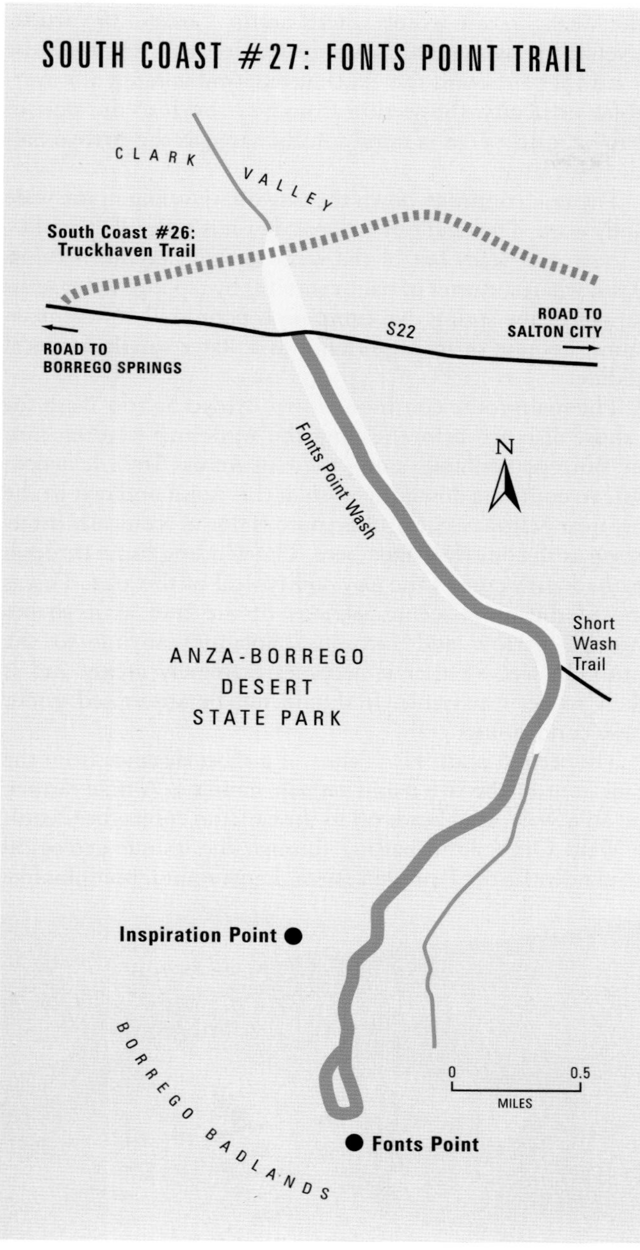

		Borrego Springs, zero trip meter and turn south at the sign for Fonts Point onto a sandy trail running up Fonts Point Wash.
		GPS: N33°18.21′ W116°14.29′
▼ 0.1	SO	Information board on left.
▼ 1.7	SO	Track on left is Short Wash Trail.
		GPS: N33°17.06′ W116°13.24′
▼ 3.3	SO	Exit Fonts Point Wash.
▼ 3.5	BL	Start of one-way loop.
		GPS: N33°15.69′ W116°13.99′
▼ 3.8	SO	Parking area for Fonts Point. Fonts Point is a short hike to the east. Marker is visible from parking area. Continue around the loop.
		GPS: N33°15.47′ W116°13.96′
▼ 4.1	TL	End of loop. Turn left to exit the way you came.
		GPS: N33°15.69′ W116°13.99′

SOUTH COAST #28

Arroyo Salado Trail

Starting Point:	**South Coast #26: Truckhaven Trail, 2.2 miles south of S22**
Finishing Point:	**California 78, 2.8 miles west of the ranger station at Ocotillo Wells**
Total Mileage:	**14.1 miles**
Unpaved Mileage:	**14.1 miles**
Driving Time:	**2.5 hours**
Elevation Range:	**300–800 feet**
Usually Open:	**Year-round**
Best Time to Travel:	**October to June, dry weather**
Difficulty Rating:	**3**
Scenic Rating:	**9**
Remoteness Rating:	**+1**

Special Attractions

- Seventeen Palms Oasis and the prospector's post office.
- Beautiful Arroyo Salado and other Borrego Badlands scenery.
- The Pumpkin Patch—round concretions a short distance from the main trail.
- Ocotillo Wells OHV Area.

History

Arroyo Salado Trail takes the traveler through impressive examples of the Borrego Badlands. The badlands evolved over millions of years to the barren, twisted landscape you see today. Sandstone, claystone, and mudstone have trapped fossil life-forms for today's observant traveler to see.

This maze of a landscape was a challenge for all who dared to traverse it. Juan Bautista de Anza's expedition, which opened up the trail to Alta California in the 1770s, followed the flow of the San Felipe Creek upstream in a northeasterly direction. The historic expedition's route is crossed along this scenic trail.

Seventeen Palms, an excellent bird habitat

Like Mexican colonists, early European prospectors in the area quickly realized that water was nearly as valuable as gold. The Seventeen Palms mailbox along this trail seems to have evolved

The Prospector's Post Office at Seventeen Palms now has a visitors book

from those pioneering days. The water in the spring was unreliable, so travelers left extra water for the next passers-by in large glass jars hidden under the palms. People started to leave notes attached to the jars for delivery to old Borrego and elsewhere. Travelers passing through the badlands would oblige, taking the notes for delivery while collecting what would possibly be their last supply of water before following the near invisible track through the badlands. The practice stuck and the "prospector's post office" is still there, although nowadays it is a sturdy wooden box jammed between the two central palm trees. Today, travelers write notes and their thoughts on the landscape in the visitors book in the box.

The palms, seventeen of them when noted by European explorers, are native to the desert Southwest. Their scientific name is *Washingtonia filifera.* Nearby is another little oasis called Five Palms, although now only four trees remain standing.

As Borrego Valley attracted more growers to the desert, building a route to outside markets became more and more urgent. Doc Beaty, an early pioneer in the valley, promoted the construction of what became known as the Truckhaven Trail (featured on page 372). Branching off to the east from Arroyo Salado in its route through the Borrego Badlands, Truckhaven Trail headed for the Salton Sea. Arroyo Salado Trail departs from the Truckhaven Trail at the location of Beaty's Icebox. While working on the trail in this inhospitable terrain and sweltering conditions, the men preserved their food in a cool, natural cave in the wash line at the junction. The icebox is no longer there, having been obliterated over time.

Description

Arroyo Salado cuts a deep swath into the hills of the barren, friable Borrego Badlands that comprise much of the center section of Anza-Borrego Desert State Park. The trail is a very pretty one, running in the shallow multihued Arroyo Salado Wash and then the equally colorful badlands.

The trail commences part of the way down Arroyo Salado Wash, at the point where South Coast #26: Truckhaven Trail swings northeast up a side wash. It should be noted that although the Truckhaven Trail is rated a 5 overall for difficulty, the section from S22 south to the start of Arroyo Salado Trail is rated a 3, the same as the Arroyo Salado Trail itself.

The trail continues down the canyon, traveling in the wide sandy wash. The sand can be loose, but it is generally passable. A short spur leads out of the wash to visit Seventeen Palms Oasis, where a cluster of palms survives by tapping water seeping out of the spring. No camping is permitted at Seventeen Palms, because of its importance as a water supply for local wildlife.

The main route continues down Arroyo Salado Wash for a short distance before leaving the wash and heading into the Borrego Badlands along the Cut Across Trail. It is possible to continue down the wash at this point and exit to the east near Salton Sea, but this route is not as scenically interesting as the one described here. The winding route through the badlands crosses the clay soil typical of the area. This is one of the most scenic sections of the trail as it snakes through narrow and tortuous badlands canyons to the south. In wet weather it becomes extremely greasy and is likely to be impassable. It should not be attempted under these conditions.

The second oasis, Five Palms, is a short distance from the trail. Four of the five palms remain standing. A mile farther, the Tule Wash Trail heads off to the east and enters the Ocotillo Wells OHV Area, passing through the unique geological area known as the Pumpkin Patch. Large round, pumpkinlike

Sedimentary uplift is apparent as you pass through Buttes Canyon

concretions are scattered over the area.

The trail leaves the badlands, passing to the south toward Borrego Mountain. It crosses many wide sandy washes, traveling a short distance down Bank Wash. Many tracks leave this section of the trail and head south into Ocotillo Wells OHV Area.

The widest wash is the San Felipe Wash, the route of Juan Bautista de Anza's expedition. Navigation can be a little confusing here—the intersection is not marked, but the route heads slightly upstream and joins the Buttes Pass Trail. Buttes Pass is the gap between West Butte and East Butte of Borrego Mountain. The high-walled canyon is both rugged and beautiful. The trail exits the canyon and heads south toward California 78. Hawk Canyon near the exit is the most beautiful of all, and it is worth the short detour to drive to its end. This is a popular primitive camping spot, but be wary of camping close to the wash.

The trail finishes on California 78, 2.8 miles west of the ranger station at Ocotillo Wells. Campers will be pleased to find coin-operated showers at the ranger station. The trail is not completely shown on topographical maps of the region.

Current Road Information

Anza-Borrego Desert State Park
200 Palm Canyon Drive
Borrego Springs, CA 92004
(760) 767-5311

Map References

BLM Borrego Valley
USGS 1:24,000 Seventeen Palms, Shell Reef, Borrego Mt.
1:100,000 Borrego Valley
Maptech CD-ROM: San Diego/Joshua Tree
Southern & Central California Atlas & Gazetteer, pp. 116, 115
California Road & Recreation Atlas, p. 117
Other: Tom Harrison Maps—San Diego Backcountry Recreation map, Earthwalk Press—Anza-Borrego Desert Region Recreation map, Wilderness Press—Map of the Anza-Borrego Desert Region

Route Directions

▼ 0.0 From South Coast #26: Truckhaven Trail, 2.2 miles south of S22, past the Arroyo Salado Primitive Camping Area, at the point where Truckhaven Trail swings up the side wash, zero trip meter and continue southeast in the wide, sandy Arroyo Salado Wash. This intersection can be difficult to distinguish; a GPS unit will greatly assist. Trail is running alongside Desert Oasis Wilderness boundary on the right.

1.6 ▲ Trail ends at the intersection with South Coast #26: Truckhaven Trail. This intersection can be difficult to distinguish; a GPS unit will greatly assist. Turn right to exit via the difficult section of Truckhaven Trail to S22; continue straight ahead to exit via the easier section of the trail and the Arroyo Salado Primitive Camping Area.

GPS: N33°16.23' W116°07.15'

▼ 1.3 BR Major fork in wash. Bear right to pass the end of the side trip to Seventeen Palms.

0.3 ▲ SO Track on right.

GPS: N33°15.34' W116°06.48'

▼ 1.4 SO Track on right goes 0.2 miles to Seventeen Palms Oasis. Intersection is unmarked.

0.2 ▲ SO Track on left goes 0.2 miles to Seventeen Palms Oasis. Intersection is unmarked.

GPS: N33°15.26' W116°06.43'

▼ 1.6 TR Fork rejoins on left. Trail continues down Arroyo Salado Wash. Zero trip meter and turn out of wash, following marker for Five Palms.

0.0 ▲ Continue to the west.

GPS: N33°15.22' W116°06.27'

▼ 0.0 Continue to the southeast. Immediately, small track on right.

1.3 ▲ TL Small track on left; then T-intersection with wide sandy Arroyo Salado Wash. Zero trip meter and turn left up wash, remaining close to the left-hand side of wash.

▼ 0.4 SO Five Palms. Five Palms Spring on right. Follow marker for Cut Across Trail. Trail is in line of wash.

0.9 ▲ BR Five Palms. Five Palms Spring on left. Follow marker for Seventeen Palms and Arroyo Salado.

GPS: N33°14.93' W116°06.27'

▼ 1.3 TR Turn right, following marker for Cut Across Trail. To the left is Tule Wash and the Pumpkin Patch. Zero trip meter.

0.0 ▲ Continue to the northwest.

GPS: N33°14.39' W116°05.85'

▼ 0.0 Continue to the southwest.

3.1 ▲ TL Turn left, following marker for Five Palms. Straight ahead is Tule Wash and the Pumpkin Patch. Zero trip meter.

▼ 0.9 SO Track on right goes to Una Palma.

2.2 ▲ SO Track on left goes to Una Palma.

GPS: N33°14.69' W116°06.66'

▼ 1.4 BL Bear left out of line of wash.

1.7 ▲ BR Bear right down wash.

GPS: N33°14.71' W116°07.15'

▼ 1.7 SO Cross through wide Basin Wash. Track on left down wash.

1.4 ▲ SO Cross through wide Basin Wash. Track on right down wash.

GPS: N33°14.67' W116°07.38'

▼ 2.0 SO Cross through wash.

1.1 ▲ SO Cross through wash.

▼ 2.1 SO Enter down Bank Wash.

1.0 ▲ SO Exit Bank Wash.

▼ 3.1 BR Leaving Anza-Borrego Desert State Park; then bear right, leaving Bank Wash. Track on left down wash. Zero trip meter.

0.0 ▲ Continue to the north up Bank Wash. Entering Borrego Badlands.

GPS: N33°13.64' W116°07.82'

▼ 0.0 Continue to the southwest out of wash, following marker for Cut Across Trail. Trail now leaves Borrego Badlands.

4.6 ▲ BL Entering Anza-Borrego Desert State Park. Bear left, remaining on Cut Across Trail. Track on right down Bank Wash.

▼ 0.7 SO Track on left is Anopheles Wash. Remain on Cut Across Trail.

3.9 ▲ SO Track on right is Anopheles Wash. Remain on Cut Across Trail.

GPS: N33°13.26' W116°08.42'

▼ 0.8 SO Track on left is Pack Rat Wash.

3.8 ▲ SO Track on right is Pack Rat Wash.

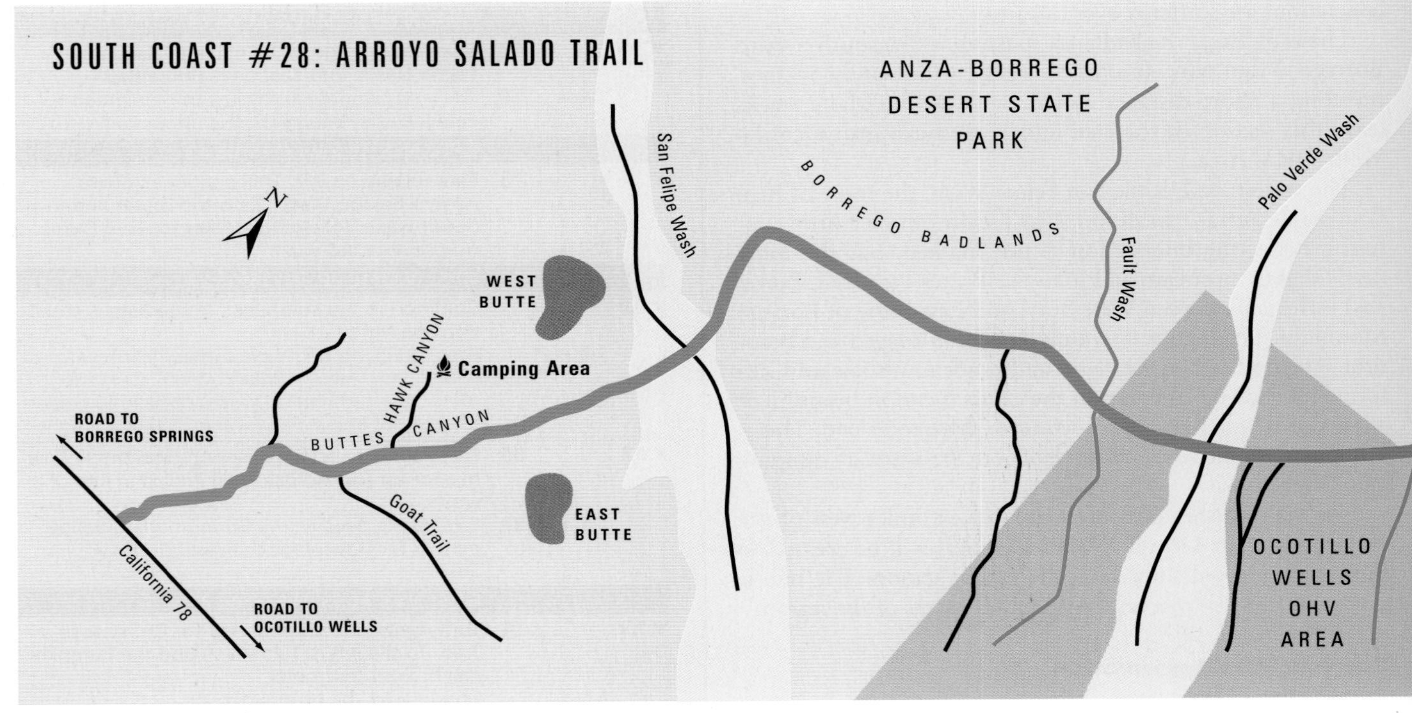

▼ 1.1 SO Cross through Palo Verde East Wash. Track on right and left up and down wash. End of Desert Oasis Wilderness boundary on right.

3.5 ▲ SO Cross through Palo Verde East Wash. Track on right and left up and down wash. Desert Oasis Wilderness boundary starts on left.

▼ 1.2 SO Cross through Palo Verde Wash. Track on right enters Anza-Borrego Desert State Park. Track on left enters Ocotillo Wells OHV Area.

3.4 ▲ SO Cross through Palo Verde Wash. Track on left enters Anza-Borrego Desert State Park. Track on right enters Ocotillo Wells OHV Area.

GPS: N33°13.05′ W116°08.83′

▼ 1.6 SO Cross through the wide Fault Wash. Track on left and track on right up and down wash. Exit wash and enter Anza-Borrego Desert State Park.

3.0 ▲ SO Exit Anza-Borrego Desert State Park; then cross through the wide Fault Wash. Track on left and track on right up and down wash.

GPS: N33°12.94′ W116°09.35′

▼ 2.3 SO Track on left is Military Wash.

2.3 ▲ SO Track on right is Military Wash.

GPS: N33°12.90′ W116°09.98′

▼ 3.8 BL Bear left down Third Wash.

0.8 ▲ BR Bear right and exit wash.

GPS: N33°12.55′ W116°11.45′

▼ 4.5 BR Edge of the very wide San Felipe Wash. Intersection is unmarked. Bear right slightly up wash, heading for far side of wash.

0.1 ▲ BL Bear left out of San Felipe Wash, heading northwest up side wash (Third Wash). Intersection is unmarked.

GPS: N33°11.98′ W116°11.24′

▼ 4.6 BL Bear left out of wash onto unmarked, well-used trail and zero trip meter.

0.0 ▲ Continue to the northeast across the wash.

GPS: N33°11.91′ W116°10.28′

▼ 0.0 Continue to the southwest out of wash.

3.5 ▲ BR Edge of the very wide San Felipe Wash. Intersection is unmarked. Bear right slightly down wash, heading for far side of wash. Zero trip meter.

▼ 0.5 SO Enter up line of wash.

3.0 ▲ SO Exit line of wash.

▼ 0.9 SO Entering Buttes Canyon.

2.6 ▲ SO Exit Buttes Canyon.

▼ 1.4 SO Track on left.

2.1 ▲ SO Track on right.

▼ 1.7 BL Well-used track on right goes 0.4 miles into primitive camping area up Hawk Canyon. Bear left, exiting canyon and line of wash.

1.8 ▲ SO Well-used track on left goes 0.4 miles into primitive camping area up Hawk Canyon. Bear right, entering down line of wash and entering Buttes Canyon.

GPS: N33°10.66′ W116°12.12′

▼ 2.1 BR Track on left is Goat Trail. Follow sign for Buttes Pass and Highway 78.

1.4 ▲ BL Track on right is Goat Trail.

GPS: N33°10.39′ W116°12.32′

▼ 2.6 TL T-intersection. Follow marker to Highway 78. To the right is Borrego Mountain Wash.

0.9 ▲ TR Straight ahead is Borrego Mountain Wash. Follow marker to Buttes Pass.

GPS: N33°10.27′ W116°12.74′

▼ 3.4 BR Track on left joins California 78.

0.1 ▲ SO Track on right rejoins California 78.

▼ 3.5 Trail ends on California 78. Turn left for Ocotillo Wells; turn right for Borrego Springs.

0.0 ▲ Trail starts on California 78, 2.8 miles west of ranger station at Ocotillo Wells and 0.3 miles west of mile marker 87.5. Zero trip meter and turn north on well-used sandy trail. If approaching from the west, there is a sign for Buttes Pass immediately before the turn.

GPS: N33°09.53′ W116°13.08′

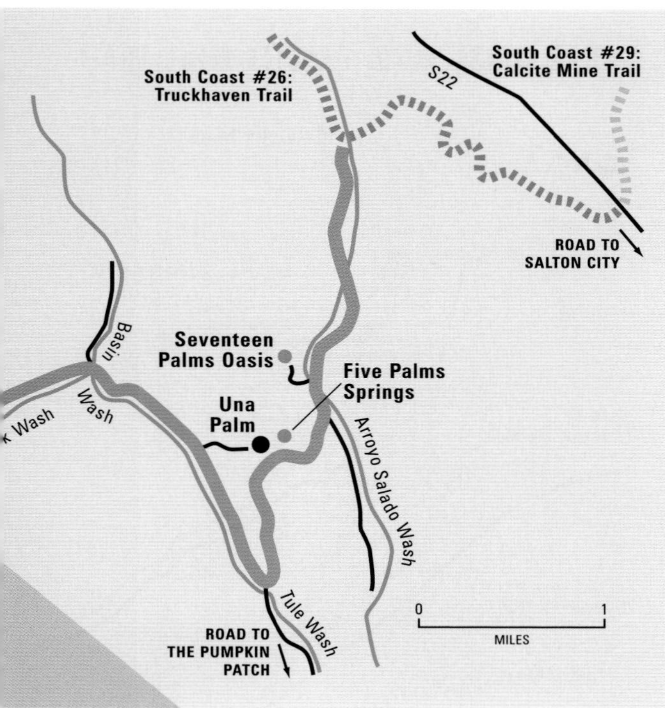

SOUTH COAST #29

Calcite Mine Trail

Starting Point:	**Borrego-Salton Seaway (S22), 18.5 miles east of Borrego Springs**
Finishing Point:	**Calcite Mine**
Total Mileage:	**1.9 miles (one-way)**
Unpaved Mileage:	**1.9 miles**
Driving Time:	**45 minutes (one-way)**
Elevation Range:	**600–1,100 feet**
Usually Open:	**Year-round**
Best Time to Travel:	**October to June**
Difficulty Rating:	**7**
Scenic Rating:	**9**
Remoteness Rating:	**+0**

Special Attractions

- Panoramic view from the Salton Sea to northern Mexico.
- Challenging short trail requiring an excellent stock vehicle and an experienced driver.
- Calcite crystals and the remains of the Calcite Mine.

History

During World War II, the U.S. government commissioned specialists to inspect calcite deposits found in the wind- and water-carved sandstone region around this trail. The high quality of the calcite crystals resulted in the development of the Calcite Mine for wartime use. Optical grade crystals were processed for use in gun sights and rocket launchers. The Polaroid Corporation bought the mine from owners Hilton and Gary Hazen and employed several dozen men to mine the crystals. The vertical shafts the company dug on the southern end of the Santa Rosa Mountains are clearly visible from the peak of this trail. A synthetic replacement for calcite was eventually developed, but the narrow, open shafts continued to be mined for collectors.

Calcite crystals line the walls of old mining cuts

Calcite Mine Trail ascends a twisted route through an ancient landscape composed of Canebrake conglomerate. These weathered, rounded rock shapes are the solidified remnants of an earlier landscape in which rivers once washed sediments into an ancient sea.

Description

Although short, Calcite Mine Trail is a challenging trail for high-clearance 4WD vehicles, mountain bikes, and hikers. The trail leaves S22, 18.5 miles east of Borrego Springs. Keep an eye out for the information board that marks the start of the trail, which descends to cross through the south fork of Palm Wash, climbing out the other side on a narrow shelf road. Sections of this wartime road are beginning to wash away, leaving a narrow path for vehicles around the natural erosion.

The trail then runs along the ridge top, offering good views south toward Mexico. The difficult section of the trail starts 0.9 miles from the start. Deep, uneven sections need to be straddled, and careful wheel placement is necessary to avoid dropping into them or catching your undercarriage on rocks. The clay surface is very greasy when wet, and the trail

Climbing the ledge trail above Palm Wash en route to Calcite Mine

should be avoided after rain. The deep sediment walls of Palm Wash are below you as the trail climbs a rough shelf road. The trail becomes more difficult after crossing through Palm Wash; there are large embedded boulders to climb. Extra vehicle undercarriage clearance and stamina on foot or mountain bike are advantages here. Be sure to use a spotter to watch vehicle underbody clearance; it can be a little deceptive in spots. Hiking up or down Palm Wash from the old Calcite Mine trail crossing takes you into a wonderland of narrow, slotlike canyons.

The trail ends at the Calcite Mine area, on a flat turnaround that offers a wonderful view toward Mexico. Climbing many of the wind-pocked Canebrake conglomerate rocks will give a great view to the east over the Salton Sea. The workings of the mine are all around you. The large, deep trenches still contain some beautiful calcite crystals, which can be admired in place. Collecting is prohibited within the state park. The closest trenches are on top of the rise to the north of the flat area.

Current Road Information

Anza-Borrego Desert State Park
200 Palm Canyon Drive
Borrego Springs, CA 92004
(760) 767-5311

Map References

BLM Borrego Valley
USGS 1:24,000 Seventeen Palms
1:100,000 Borrego Valley
Maptech CD-ROM: San Diego/Joshua Tree
Southern & Central California Atlas & Gazetteer, p. 116
Other: Tom Harrison Maps—San Diego Backcountry Recreation map, Earthwalk Press—Anza-Borrego Desert Region Recreation map, Wilderness Press—Map of the Anza-Borrego Desert Region

Wind-eroded Canebrake conglomerate cliffs at the southern end of the Santa Rosa Mountains

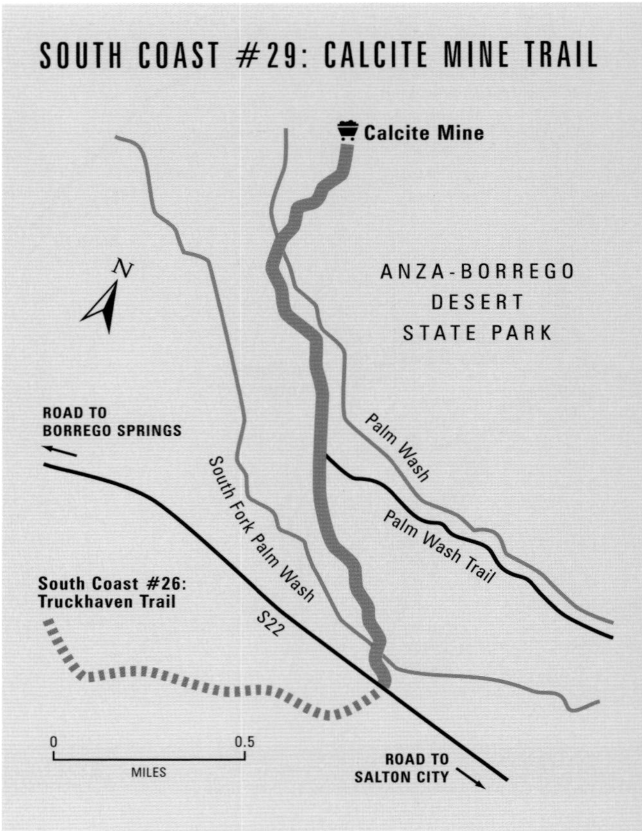

Route Directions

▼ 0.0		From S22, 18.5 miles east of Borrego Springs, zero trip meter and turn northwest on formed dirt trail. There is an information board about the Calcite Mine at the intersection and a marker for Calcite Mine Area. The turn is 0.3 miles west of a prominent telecommunications tower, 0.2 miles east of mile marker 38 and opposite the start of South Coast #26: Truckhaven Trail. This trail immediately descends along shelf road toward wash.
		GPS: N33°16.86' W116°05.74'
▼ 0.1	SO	Cross through South Fork Palm Wash. Track on left and track on right up and down wash. Climb out of the wash along shelf road, following the marker for Calcite Mine.
		GPS: N33°16.95' W116°05.81'
▼ 0.3	SO	End of shelf road.
▼ 0.7	SO	Track on right is Palm Wash Trail. Continue straight ahead, following the marker to Calcite Mine.
		GPS: N33°17.25' W116°06.19'
▼ 0.9	SO	Start of difficult section. Shelf road resumes.
		GPS: N33°17.43' W116°06.32'
▼ 1.4	SO	Cross through head of Palm Wash.
		GPS: N33°17.66' W116°06.61'
▼ 1.8	SO	Entering Calcite Mine Area.
▼ 1.9		Trail ends on a wide turnaround at the Calcite Mine.
		GPS: N33°17.94' W116°06.54'

Fish Creek–Sandstone Canyon Trail

Starting Point:	**Split Mountain Road, 8 miles south of California 78 and Ocotillo Wells**
Finishing Point:	**Sandstone Canyon**
Total Mileage:	**14.3 miles (one-way)**
Unpaved Mileage:	**14.3 miles**
Driving Time:	**1.5 hours (one-way)**
Elevation Range:	**300–1,900 feet**
Usually Open:	**Year-round**
Best Time to Travel:	**October to June, dry weather**
Difficulty Rating:	**3**
Scenic Rating:	**10**
Remoteness Rating:	**+0**

Special Attractions

- Fossilized marine reefs in the Split Mountain Fault Zone.
- Beautiful narrow Sandstone Canyon and Fish Creek Canyon.
- Wind Caves Hiking Trail.

History

The geologic history in this region is interesting and abundant; Fish Creek holds its share of that history. Some 20 million years ago in the desert region we explore today, a predecessor of the Colorado River flowed into an earlier version of the Gulf of California. Ancient mollusk beds are evident once you travel south of the tight canyon in Fish Creek as it cuts through the Split Mountain Fault Zone. These marine reefs appear as a dark, uplifted layer on the west side of the canyon. They have been appropriately named Fossil Reef. Pectens, fish, and oyster shells were left behind as the sea retreated with the uplift of the land.

Split Mountain is just what its name suggest—a single layer of eroded sediment from the Vallecito Mountains that has experienced a combination of floodwater erosion and earthquake movement. Several million years ago, massive pressure caused the squeezing and buckling effect on the sandstone rocks we see exposed along the eroded fault line, which is the course of today's Fish Creek. One of these buckled formations, along an old trail just south of Fish Creek Canyon, is aptly called the Elephants Knees.

ossilized oyster shells embedded in he ancient reef along Fish Creek Wash

Approximately 3 miles northwest of the canyon is a group of unusual trees called *Bursera microphylla.* They are more commonly known as elephant trees because their trunks have a folded skin look. The Kumeyaay and Cahuilla people who frequented this region for generations kept the location of these rare trees a secret. They believed that potions made from the trees provided powerful strength to those who took them, a resource worth preserving for their own use.

Description

The combination of Fish Creek and Sandstone Canyon offers a varied and very beautiful drive within Anza-Borrego Desert State Park. The trail commences on Split Mountain Road, 8 miles south of Ocotillo Wells. The intersection is marked for the Fish Creek Area and travels up the sandy Fish Creek Wash right from the start. After 1.4 miles, the primitive Fish Creek Camp area is reached. Set above the wash, the area has plenty of cleared spaces for campsites, but no facilities other than a pit toilet. There is no fee. Campers are advised to select a site here; once in the canyon there are no places to camp out of the wash.

Sedimentary layers clearly show the uplift that took place along the Split Mountain Fault Zone

After the campsite, the trail enters Fish Creek Canyon, traveling through the gap in Split Mountain along the fault zone. Keep a careful eye out for the many fossilized mollusk shells to be found embedded in the wall of the canyon and fallen boulders. Remember that collecting within the park is prohibited by law, so look, enjoy, and then leave them for others to appreciate.

As Fish Creek Canyon widens, the trail continues as a lovely easygoing drive along the sandy wash in the canyon. Forks in the trail, unless noted in the route directions, normally rejoin after a very short distance. Use your judgment and pick the best route. The Wind Caves Hiking Trail leads 1.5 miles to the natural sandstone sculptures of the Wind Caves.

The end of the one-way South Coast #31: Arroyo Seco del Diablo Trail is passed. This trail can only be driven from

The 8-rated section of the trail is very narrow, necessitating manuevering around and over granite boulders

south to north because of a difficult drop-off near the north end.

The trail swings south into the marked Sandstone Canyon and almost immediately enters a narrow, extremely twisty, red-walled sandstone canyon. The bottom is sandy, and the trail winds a tortuous route through the narrow gap. At times it is barely wider than your vehicle.

The route described here ends at a turnaround point in the canyon suited to most SUVs. The trail does continue, but immediately becomes extremely narrow, forcing the majority of SUVs to ride the sheer walls of the canyon with their tire rims. Past this point, the vehicle trail jumps to an 8-rating for difficulty, with large boulders and rocky challenges for smaller vehicles, mountain bikes, and hikers.

Current Road Information

Anza-Borrego Desert State Park
200 Palm Canyon Drive
Borrego Springs, CA 92004
(760) 767-5311

Map References

BLM Borrego Valley, El Cajon
USGS 1:24,000 Borrego Mt. SE, Carrizo Mt. NE, Arroyo Tapiado
1:100,000 Borrego Valley, El Cajon
Maptech CD-ROM: San Diego/Joshua Tree
Southern & Central California Atlas & Gazetteer, pp. 116, 124, 123
California Road & Recreation Atlas, p. 117
Other: Tom Harrison Maps—San Diego Backcountry Recreation map, Earthwalk Press—Anza-Borrego Desert Region Recreation map, Wilderness Press—Map of the Anza-Borrego Desert Region

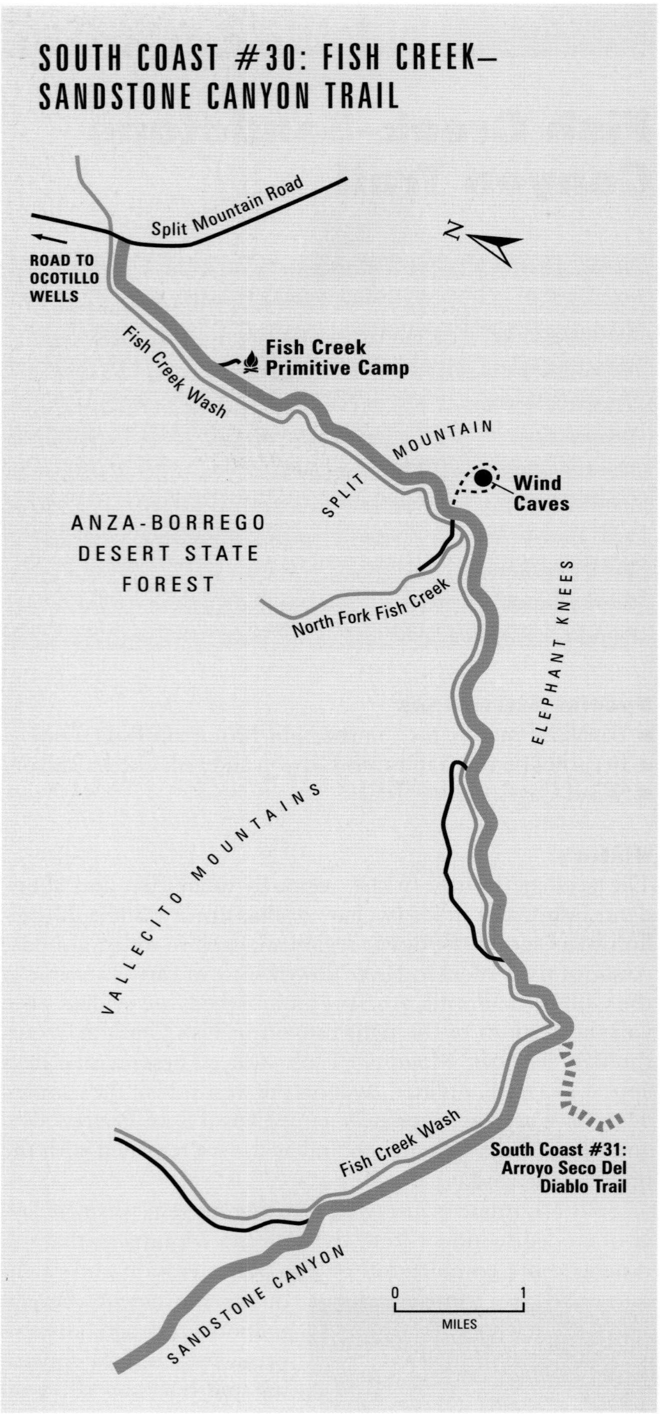

Route Directions

▼ 0.0 From Split Mountain Road, 8 miles south of California 78 at Ocotillo Wells, zero trip meter and turn southwest up Fish Creek, following the sign for Fish Creek Area. Road follows the wide, sandy wash.
4.0 ▲ Trail ends at intersection with Split Mountain Road. Turn left for Ocotillo Wells and California 78; turn right for Ocotillo and I-8.

GPS: N33°02.38′ W116°05.76′

▼ 1.4 **SO** Track on left enters Fish Creek Primitive Camp.
2.6 ▲ **SO** Track on right enters Fish Creek Primitive Camp.

GPS: N33°01.45′ W116°06.57′

▼ 1.5 **SO** Entering Fish Creek Canyon.
2.5 ▲ **SO** Exiting Fish Creek Canyon.

▼ 3.5 **SO** Information board on left.
0.5 ▲ **SO** Information board on right.

GPS: N32°59.89′ W116°06.91′

▼ 4.0 **SO** Wind Caves Hiking Trail on left; then track on right up side wash is North Fork Fish Creek. Zero trip meter at intersection.
0.0 ▲ Continue to the northwest and pass Wind Caves Hiking Trail on right.

GPS: N32°59.56′ W116°07.05′

▼ 0.0 Continue to the southeast.

SOUTH COAST #30: FISH CREEK–SANDSTONE CANYON TRAIL

	2.5 ▲	SO	Track on left up side wash is North Fork Fish Creek. Zero trip meter at intersection.
▼ 0.3		SO	Information board on left for Fossil Reef.
	2.2 ▲	SO	Information board on right for Fossil Reef.
▼ 2.5		SO	Track on right is Loop Wash. Zero trip meter. This is an alternate loop to the main trail.
	0.0 ▲		Continue to the east.
			GPS: N32°58.88' W116°08.97'
▼ 0.0			Continue to the southwest.
	1.6 ▲	SO	Track on left is Loop Wash rejoining.
▼ 1.6		SO	Track on right is Loop Wash rejoining. Zero trip meter.
	0.0 ▲		Continue to the northeast.
			GPS: N32°58.24' W116°10.29'
▼ 0.0			Continue to the south.
	1.0 ▲	BR	Track on left is Loop Wash. Zero trip meter. This is an alternate loop to the main trail.
▼ 1.0		SO	Track on left is South Coast #31: Arroyo Seco del Diablo Trail. Zero trip meter and continue in Fish Creek Wash.
	0.0 ▲		Continue to the east.
			GPS: N32°57.63' W116°10.68'
▼ 0.0			Continue to the northwest.
	2.8 ▲	SO	Track on right is South Coast #31: Arroyo Seco del Diablo Trail. Zero trip meter and continue in Fish Creek Wash.
▼ 2.8		TL	Track continues straight ahead up Fish Creek Wash. Zero trip meter and turn left at the sign for Sandstone Canyon.
			GPS: N32°58.77' W116°12.81'
▼ 0.0			Continue to the south.
▼ 1.0		SO	Enter Sandstone Canyon narrows.
▼ 2.4			Turnaround point. Trail past this point becomes a very difficult, 8-rated trail and is best suited for small vehicles.
			GPS: N32°59.63' W116°14.49'

SOUTH COAST #31

Arroyo Seco del Diablo Trail

Starting Point:	**South Coast #32: Vallecito Wash Trail, 5.3 miles from S2 via Canyon sin Nombre**
Finishing Point:	**South Coast #30: Fish Creek–Sandstone Canyon Trail, 9.1 miles from Split Mountain Road**
Total Mileage:	**8.2 miles (one-way)**
Unpaved Mileage:	**8.2 miles**
Driving Time:	**1 hour (one-way)**
Elevation Range:	**600–1,100 feet**
Usually Open:	**Year-round**
Best Time to Travel:	**October to June**
Difficulty Rating:	**5**
Scenic Rating:	**9**
Remoteness Rating:	**+1**

Arroyo Seco del Diablo cuts a tortuous path through the Carrizo Badlands

Special Attractions

- Challenging Diablo Drop Off.
- Twisting canyon of Arroyo Seco del Diablo through the Carrizo Badlands.

History

Arroyo Seco del Diablo (Spanish for "Devil's Dry Wash") lies in the midst of the Carrizo Badlands, part of an alluvial fan from the ancestral Colorado River. This ancient river emptied into the Gulf of California as a delta outlet. Arroyo Seco del Diablo has cut through the hardened sandstone concretions carried downstream from afar to create the deep-sided canyon this trail follows today. To the west of the trail is Arroyo Tapiado. Its Spanish name refers to the muddy, walled-in effect the dry river bed gives as it cuts through the alluvial fan of yesteryear. Diablo Drop Off, on the northeastern rim of Middle Mesa, sits high above the deep eroded path carved by massive floodwaters millions of years ago, forming the basis for the ever deepening Fish Creek. This northbound, one-way section of the trail takes the traveler off the rim within the ancient delta, down into the eroded path that followed the Fish Creek fault line.

Description

The state park service and various guidebooks about the region list this trail as being one-way-only because of the steep, challenging Diablo Drop Off located near Fish Creek. Although it does not look particularly difficult as you stand at the top and look down, the loose sand makes it difficult to impossible for a vehicle to return up the drop-off.

The trail leaves the easier route along Vallecito Wash 1.1 miles west of the intersection with Canyon sin Nombre. It travels up Arroyo Seco del Diablo, a side wash of Vallecito Canyon. For most of the way it twists within this sandstone canyon, traveling in the sandy wash. The loose and fragile walls of the canyon mean that rock and sand falls are common, and you are likely to have to climb over fallen debris. On windy days, dust and sand pour off the canyon walls like miniature waterfalls.

After 6 miles, the trail exits the top of the canyon and travels across Middle Mesa toward Diablo Drop Off. An overlook at the top of the drop-off provides excellent views over the Fish

The Vallecito Mountains rise above the Carrizo Badlands

Creek region and the Vallecito Mountains. There are some good campsites here, although they have no shade and can be extremely windy.

The Diablo Drop Off is made up of two descents with a break in the middle. The first is loose sand with a twist in the middle, and, although it is steep, it is unlikely to cause anyone any problems descending. The second part of the drop-off is more difficult; a narrow slot with large steps and wheel ruts drops to a small creek that feeds into Fish Creek. Careful wheel placement is necessary to avoid dropping into the deep ruts and holes. This descent is short and most high-clearance 4WDs with an experienced driver at the wheel will manage it. Larger or longer vehicles are the most likely to risk catching their rears as they descend the steep drop. Larger vehicles may wish to consider walking the short distance down to view this section before starting the descent from Middle Mesa. Once down off Middle Mesa, you are committed to continuing down the more difficult drop-off. This section should not be attempted in wet weather. Moisture can turn the trail surface into a slick bed, making it difficult to stay out of the ruts.

Once you are in the narrow creek, there is a short distance of rocky creek bed and some boulders to climb over before the trail ends on South Coast #30: Fish Creek–Sandstone Canyon Trail.

Current Road Information

Anza-Borrego Desert State Park
200 Palm Canyon Drive
Borrego Springs, CA 92004
(760) 767-5311

Map References

BLM El Cajon
USGS 1:24,000 Arroyo Tapiado
1:100,000 El Cajon
Maptech CD-ROM: San Diego/Joshua Tree
Southern & Central California Atlas & Gazetteer, p. 123
California Road & Recreation Atlas, p. 117
Other: Tom Harrison Maps—San Diego Backcountry Recreation map

Route Directions

▼ 0.0	From South Coast #32: Vallecito Wash Trail, 5.3 miles from S2 via Canyon sin Nombre, 1.1 miles west of the intersection of Canyon sin Nombre and Carrizo Creek wash, zero trip meter and turn north up formed sandy trail marked Arroyo Seco del Diablo.

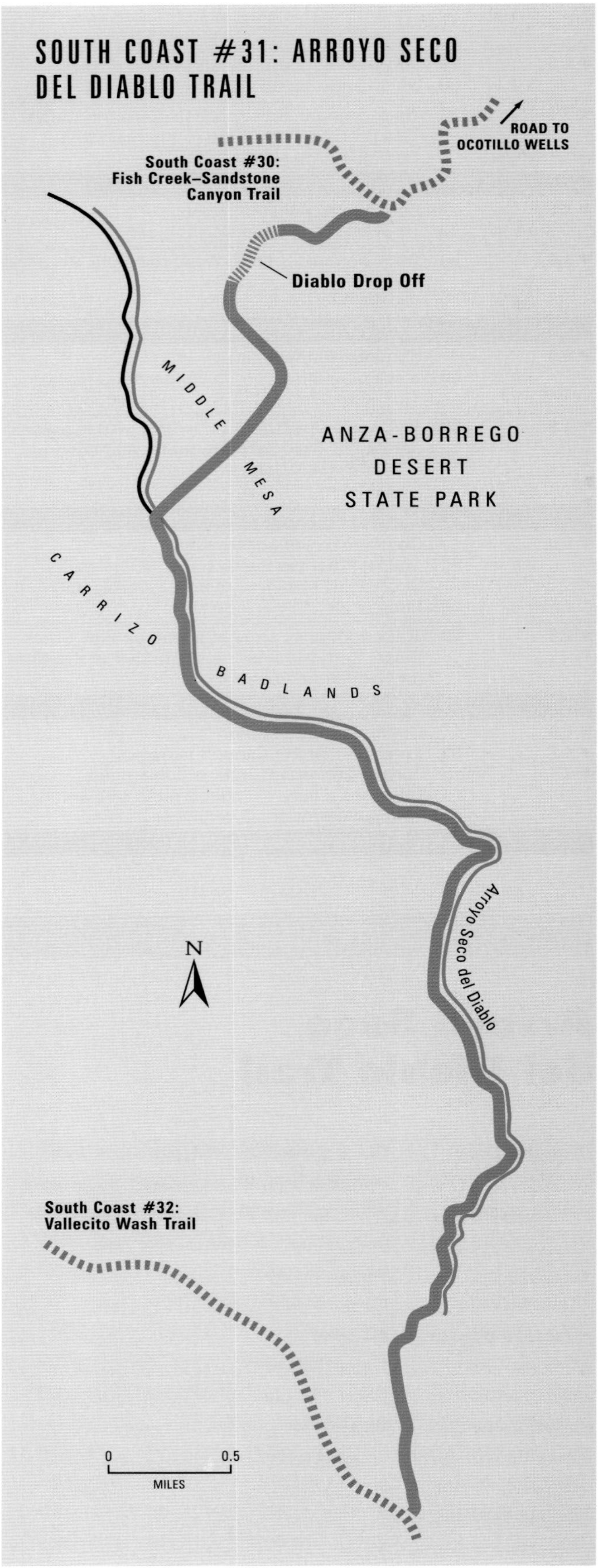

SOUTH COAST #31: ARROYO SECO DEL DIABLO TRAIL

ROAD TO OCOTILLO WELLS
South Coast #30: Fish Creek–Sandstone Canyon Trail
Diablo Drop Off
MIDDLE MESA
ANZA-BORREGO DESERT STATE PARK
CARRIZO BADLANDS
Arroyo Seco del Diablo
N
South Coast #32: Vallecito Wash Trail
0 0.5
MILES

		GPS: N32°52.94' W116°09.50'
▼ 0.8	SO	Enter Arroyo Seco del Diablo Canyon.
▼ 6.0	SO	Exit canyon, but remain in wash.
▼ 6.1	TR	Track continues ahead in the wash. Turn right out of wash, following marker for Fish Creek. Zero trip meter.
		GPS: N32°56.34' W116°11.36'
▼ 0.0		Continue to the northeast.
▼ 0.9	SO	Track on right to overlook.
		GPS: N32°57.05' W116°11.01'
▼ 1.3	BR	Top of Diablo Drop Off. Trail drops steeply from Middle Mesa.
		GPS: N32°57.29' W116°11.22'
▼ 1.4	SO	Cross through wash. Bottom of first drop-off after long sandy descent.
▼ 1.5	SO	Second drop-off.
		GPS: N32°57.47' W116°11.19'
▼ 1.6	BR	Bottom of Diablo Drop Off. Bear right down wash.
		GPS: N32°57.48' W116°11.14'
▼ 2.1		Trail ends at T-intersection with South Coast #30: Fish Creek–Sandstone Canyon Trail. Turn left to visit Sandstone Canyon; turn right to exit to Split Mountain Road and Ocotillo Wells.
		GPS: N32°57.63' W116°10.68'

SOUTH COAST #32

Vallecito Wash Trail

Starting Point:	**Sweeney Pass Road (S2), 13 miles north of Ocotillo**
Finishing Point:	**Sweeney Pass Road (S2), 21.3 miles north of Ocotillo and 4.3 miles south of Agua Caliente State Park**
Total Mileage:	**11 miles, plus 2.9-mile spur to Carrizo Stage Station**
Unpaved Mileage:	**11 miles, plus 2.9-mile spur**
Driving Time:	**1.5 hours**
Elevation Range:	**500–1,200 feet**
Usually Open:	**Year-round**
Best Time to Travel:	**October to June, dry weather**
Difficulty Rating:	**3**
Scenic Rating:	**8**
Remoteness Rating:	**+0**

Special Attractions

- Spectacular geology within Canyon sin Nombre.
- Site of the Carrizo Stage Station.
- Wide, easy trail along the sandy Vallecito Wash.

History

For thousands of years, the course of Vallecito Wash has been a refuge and trail for many native and immigrant Americans. Generations of Kumeyaay people camped at the springs along the earthquake fault at Vallecito and Agua Caliente. Early explorers passed through this way en route to the Pacific Coast to avoid the lower desert lands to the east. The Mormon Battalion of 1847 passed through to join Kearny's army in the war between the United States and Mexico; they carved through Box Canyon at the north end of the valley to enable their wagons to pass freely. Their remarkable trail was named the Southern Emigrant Trail. A section of their trail would later become the mail route between San Antonio and San Diego operated by James Birch. This less than satisfactory service was nicknamed the Jackass Mail because six mules towed a coach, which seldom ran on time.

The original sod building just north of this trail at Vallecito (Spanish for "little valley") was extended by the Lassator family in 1852. The Lassators had moved west from the Carolinas and offered supplies and hospitality to many passing travelers, before they moved on to Green Valley in the mid-1850s. Andrew Lassator remained at the staging station with three other men; together they operated this major stopping point for the Jackass Mail.

Vallecito Wash Trail also follows a section of the 2,800-mile-long Butterfield Overland Stage route between St. Louis and San Francisco. Butterfield bought out Birch's Jackass Mail and improved the service along this section of the long stage route. The death-defying journey of the late 1850s took passengers and mail up to 24 days to complete. At times passengers had no option but to walk and even push their stagecoach through the more difficult sections. One such section lies to the north of Carrizo Valley and is referred to as Foot and Walker Pass.

Stagecoaches passing through the Carrizo Badlands initially had to travel from Vallecito Stage Station, at the western end of Vallecito Valley, all the way to Carrizo Stage Station at the eastern end of this trail, a distance of about 20 miles. In time, a station was established midway at Palm Spring just off the western end of this trail.

Varied geology in Canyon sin Nombre provides an insight into folding and faulting in the Carrizo Badlands

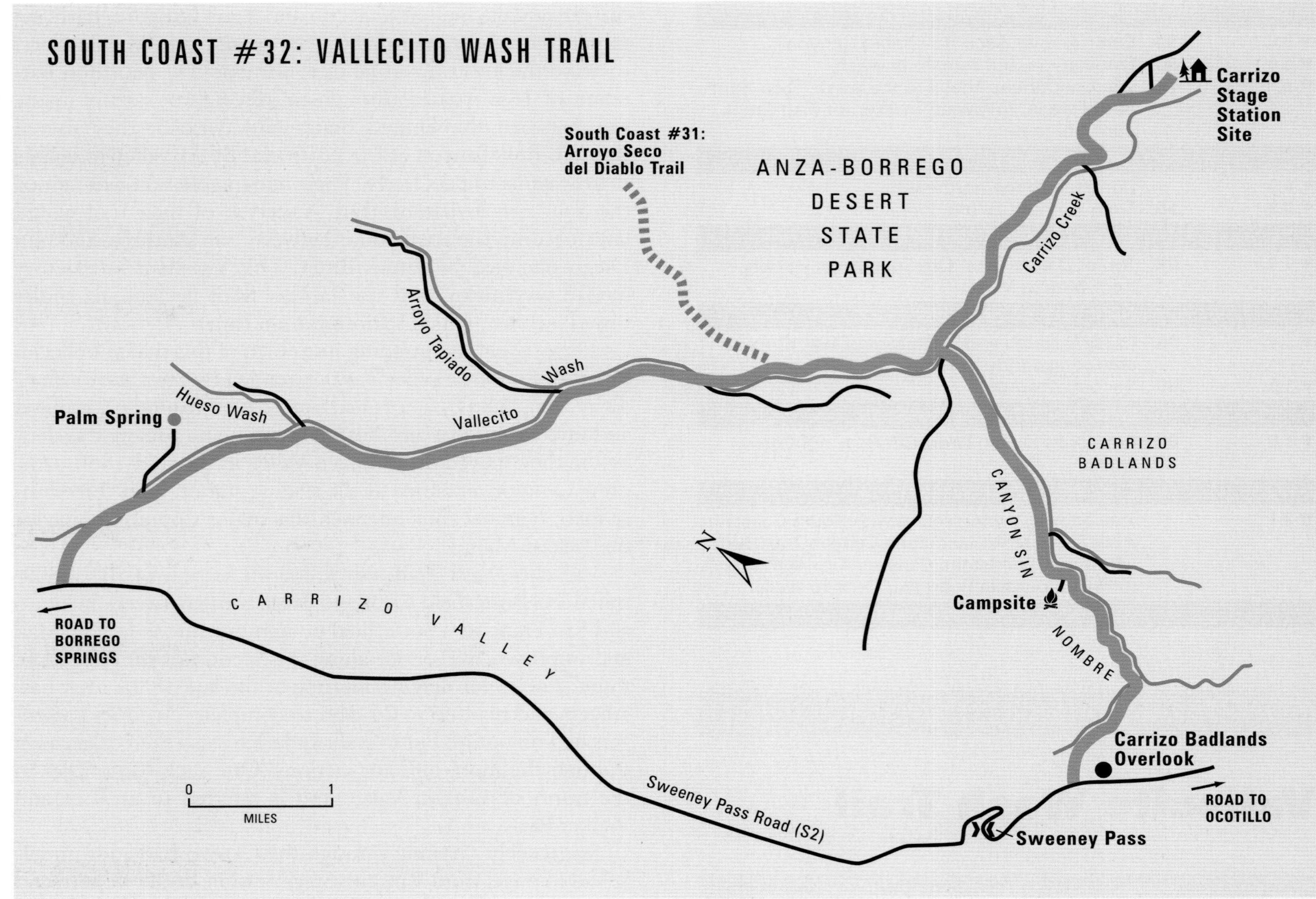

Butterfield always warned his passengers before they purchased tickets that he could not guarantee their personal safety because of the presence of Indians along this tortuous route to the West Coast. The Butterfield Overland Stage route operated until the outbreak of the Civil War in 1861, when it was replaced by a route via Salt Lake City and Sacramento. (This southerly route passed through the contested territories of Arizona and New Mexico, thereby reducing passenger safety even further.)

More than 10,000 military troops were enlisted in the California Volunteers during the Civil War, so the stage stations lived on as supply stations. Vallecito was finally abandoned in 1877. In 1879, James Mason, the Jackass Mail's earliest stagecoach driver, took up private ownership of the abandoned Vallecito Stage Station.

Description

Vallecito Wash Trail travels two very different washes: the narrow, twisty Canyon sin Nombre (Spanish for "No Name Canyon") and the wide, sandy Vallecito Wash.

The trail leaves S2 near the Carrizo Badlands Overlook—a turnout from the highway that offers a spectacular view of this beautiful region. Immediately, the trail drops into the sandy wash, where it stays until the end. Canyon sin Nombre is a geologist's paradise. The folded layers of uplifted sediment can be seen clearly in the canyon walls, and there are many narrow, slotlike canyons that can be explored on foot.

Exiting the canyon, the route continues in the sandy wash as it heads down to join the wide swath of Vallecito Wash. There are many forks in the wash, but most rejoin after a short distance; generally the most-used trail is the correct one.

At the T-intersection with Vallecito Wash, a spur trail leads up the wash to the site of the old Carrizo Stage Station. This spur travels along Carrizo Creek through a narrow, marshy area. Wider vehicles will find it slightly brushy, and the creek often flows along the surface.

There is a maze of tracks once you exit the wash. Some lead to a couple of good sheltered campsites by a natural rock wall. However, it is possible to follow the tracks through close to the site of the Carrizo Stage Station.

The main trail continues down the sandy wash, passing the start of South Coast #31: Arroyo Seco del Diablo Trail, to Fish Creek. Other sandy wash tracks invite exploration to the north. The trail passes the turn to Palm Spring before finishing back on S2. The Agua Caliente Hot Springs are a short distance to the north, at a county park. There is a pleasant campground there, but campers should note that the springs are for use in the daytime only and close at 5:30 P.M. each day. The campground is open from Labor Day to Memorial Day and a fee is charged.

Current Road Information

Anza-Borrego Desert State Park
200 Palm Canyon Drive
Borrego Springs, CA 92004
(760) 767-5311

Map References

BLM El Cajon
USGS 1:24,000 Sweeney Pass, Arroyo Tapiado, Carrizo Mt. NE
1:100,000 El Cajon
Maptech CD-ROM: San Diego/Joshua Tree
Southern & Central California Atlas & Gazetteer, pp. 123, 124
California Road & Recreation Atlas, p. 117
Other: Tom Harrison Maps—San Diego Backcountry Recreation map

Route Directions

▼ 0.0		From Sweeney Pass Road (S2), 13 miles north of Ocotillo, 0.6 miles northwest of mile marker 52, and 0.1 miles northwest of Carrizo Badlands Overlook, zero trip meter and turn northeast on well-used formed trail, marked Canyon sin Nombre.
4.2 ▲		Trail ends on S2. Turn right for Julian and Borrego Springs; turn left for Ocotillo and I-8.
		GPS: N32°49.80′ W116°10.16′
▼ 0.3	BR	Bear right down Canyon sin Nombre wash.
3.9 ▲	BL	Bear left out of wash.
▼ 0.9	SO	Entering Canyon sin Nombre.
3.3 ▲	SO	Exit canyon.
		GPS: N32°50.01′ W116°09.32′
▼ 1.9	SO	Track on right.
2.3 ▲	BL	Track on left.
		GPS: N32°50.60′ W116°09.20′
▼ 2.3	SO	Track on left to campsite.
1.9 ▲	SO	Track on right to campsite.
▼ 2.7	SO	Track on right up side wash. Exit canyon.
1.5 ▲	SO	Enter Canyon sin Nombre. Track on left up side wash.
		GPS: N32°51.08′ W116°08.97′
▼ 3.8	BL	Bear left down left side of wash, track continues straight ahead. If you miss this turn you will meet Vallecito Wash a short distance east of the proper point.
0.4 ▲	SO	Track on left down wash.
		GPS: N32°52.05′ W116°08.60′
▼ 4.2	TL	Track on left; then T-intersection with wide, sandy Vallecito Wash. To the right is the spur to Carrizo Stage Station site. Zero trip meter and turn left up the main wash, past the marker for Vallecito Canyon.
0.0 ▲		Continue to the south.
		GPS: N32°52.39′ W116°08.60′

Spur to Carrizo Stage Station Site

▼ 0.0		Proceed to the east. Second entrance to Canyon sin Nombre on right.
▼ 0.9	SO	Trail enters narrow reedy area, which can have running water and can be soft.
		GPS: N32°52.59′ W116°07.77′
▼ 1.4	BL	Trail forks out of wash and rejoins later. This can be brushy. Stay in river course or sandy track.
▼ 1.7	BL	Track on right; then bear left out of creek.
		GPS: N32°52.64′ W116°06.97′
▼ 1.9	BR	Track on left; then cross through wash; then bear right past track on left.
▼ 2.0	SO	Track on left. Cross through wash; then second track on left.
▼ 2.3	TR	Track continues straight ahead.
		GPS: N32°52.75′ W116°06.44′
▼ 2.6	SO	Track on left; then old shelter and scattered machinery.
		GPS: N32°52.58′ W116°06.17′
▼ 2.9	UT	Trail ends at small hillock a short distance north of the stage station site.
		GPS: N32°52.62′ W116°06.02′

Continuation of Main Trail

▼ 0.0		Continue to the west.
1.1 ▲	TR	Trail continues straight ahead in wash and is the start of spur to Carrizo Stage Station site. Zero trip meter and turn right out of wash at the marker for Canyon sin Nombre. Immediately there is a track on right up similar wash.
		GPS: N32°52.39′ W116°08.60′
▼ 1.1	BL	Track on right is South Coast #31: Arroyo Seco del Diablo Trail. Zero trip meter and continue in Vallecito Wash.
0.0 ▲		Continue to the southeast.
		GPS: N32°52.94′ W116°09.50′
▼ 0.0		Continue to the northwest.
5.7 ▲	BR	Track on left is South Coast #31: Arroyo Seco del Diablo Trail. Zero trip meter and continue in Vallecito Wash.
▼ 0.6	BR	Track on left in wash—keep right along the edge.
5.1 ▲	SO	Track on right in wash—keep left along the edge.
		GPS: N32°53.28′ W116°10.04′
▼ 1.4	BL	Track on right up wash is Arroyo Tapiado, marked by a sign. Remain in Vallecito Wash.
4.3 ▲	BR	Track on left up wash is Arroyo Tapiado, marked by a sign. Remain in Vallecito Wash.
		GPS: N32°53.69′ W116°10.70′
▼ 3.2	SO	Track on right to sheltered campsite out of wash.
2.5 ▲	SO	Track on left to sheltered campsite out of wash.
▼ 3.4	BL	Track on right is Hueso Wash, marked with a sign.
2.3 ▲	SO	Track on left is Hueso Wash, marked with a sign.
		GPS: N32°54.58′ W116°12.33′
▼ 4.7	SO	Track on right out of wash goes to Palm Spring, marked with sign.
1.0 ▲	SO	Track on left out of wash goes to Palm Spring, marked with a sign.
		GPS: N32°54.96′ W116°13.55′
▼ 5.1	SO	Track on right.
0.6 ▲	SO	Track on left.
▼ 5.4	BL	Bear left out of wash.
0.3 ▲	BR	Bear right down wash.
▼ 5.7		Trail ends on Sweeney Pass Road (S2). Turn right for Borrego Springs; turn left for Ocotillo and I-8.
0.0 ▲		Trail starts on Sweeney Pass Road (S2), immediately south of mile marker 43, 21.3 miles north of Ocotillo, and 4.3 miles south of Agua Caliente County Park. Zero trip meter and turn north on formed sandy trail, marked Palm Spring.
		GPS: N32°54.92′ W116°14.39′

Dos Cabezas Road

Starting Point:	**Imperial Highway (S2), 4 miles northwest of Ocotillo**
Finishing Point:	**Imperial Highway (S2), 8.4 miles northwest of Ocotillo**
Total Mileage:	**10.9 miles, plus 2.2-mile spur**
Unpaved Mileage:	**10.9 miles, plus 2.2-mile spur**
Driving Time:	**1 hour**
Elevation Range:	**700–1,700 feet**
Usually Open:	**Year-round**
Best Time to Travel:	**October to June**
Difficulty Rating:	**3**
Scenic Rating:	**8**
Remoteness Rating:	**+0**

Special Attractions

- The historic Carrizo Gorge Railroad, now a popular hiking, horse, and mountain bike trail.
- Excellent backcountry camping.
- Remote, easy-to-follow trail through Colorado Desert vegetation.

History

The name Dos Cabezas recurs throughout the Southwest, from mines to town sites. In this case, Dos Cabezas refers to a rock formation that resembles two heads, or at least one monkey face and a head. The formation was referred to as Dos Cabezas (Spanish for "Two Heads") by Mexican railroad construction workers, and the name became an obvious choice for the railroad siding a couple miles away.

The construction of the San Diego & Arizona Eastern Railroad was a feat that many considered impossible, given the gigantic granite boulders perched on steep mountainsides along the proposed route. The railroad was the first to connect San Diego with the Colorado River and took close to 12 years to complete. Pushed through in 1919, the project cost nearly $19 million (not only was it an engineering feat, but a financial feat, too). Fourteen trestles and twenty-one tunnels were constructed around the edge of the Jacumba Mountains as the railroad progressed less than 11 miles over an elevation range of nearly 4,000 feet. Goat Canyon trestle at Tunnel Fifteen spur was one of the classic wooden trestles along the Carrizo Gorge stretch.

Indians constructed shelters from ocotillo branches, which are abundant in the Colorado Desert

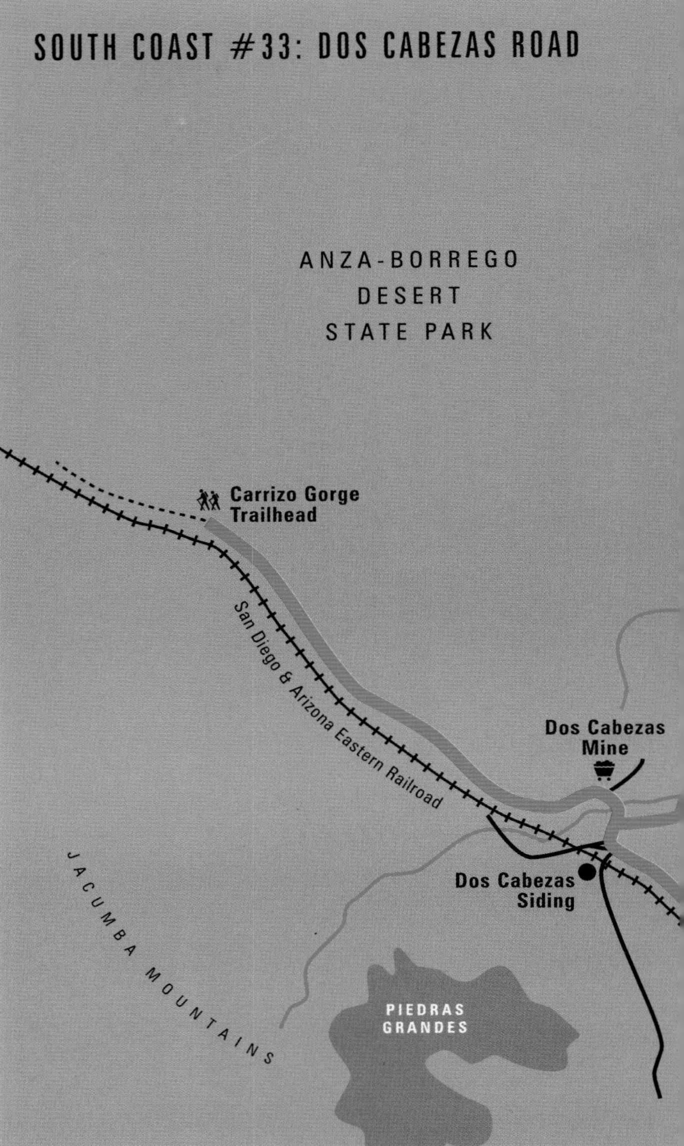

The railroad followed on the heels of the agricultural boom in the Imperial Valley. Growers now had an efficient way to get their produce to the San Diego market and port. When construction of the line commenced in 1907, the population of San Diego was approximately 35,000. By the time the railroad was up and running in 1919, the population had roughly doubled and the pressure was on to meet growing market demands. Now came the challenging task of keeping this "Impossible Railroad" open. Avalanches, floods, and fires were just a few of the natural disasters encountered throughout the railroad's existence. Sabotage was suspected on other occasions. Repair crews were kept busy on this infamous route that suffered regular closures. The railroad ended passenger service in the early 1950s because of competition with automobiles, but freight service continued.

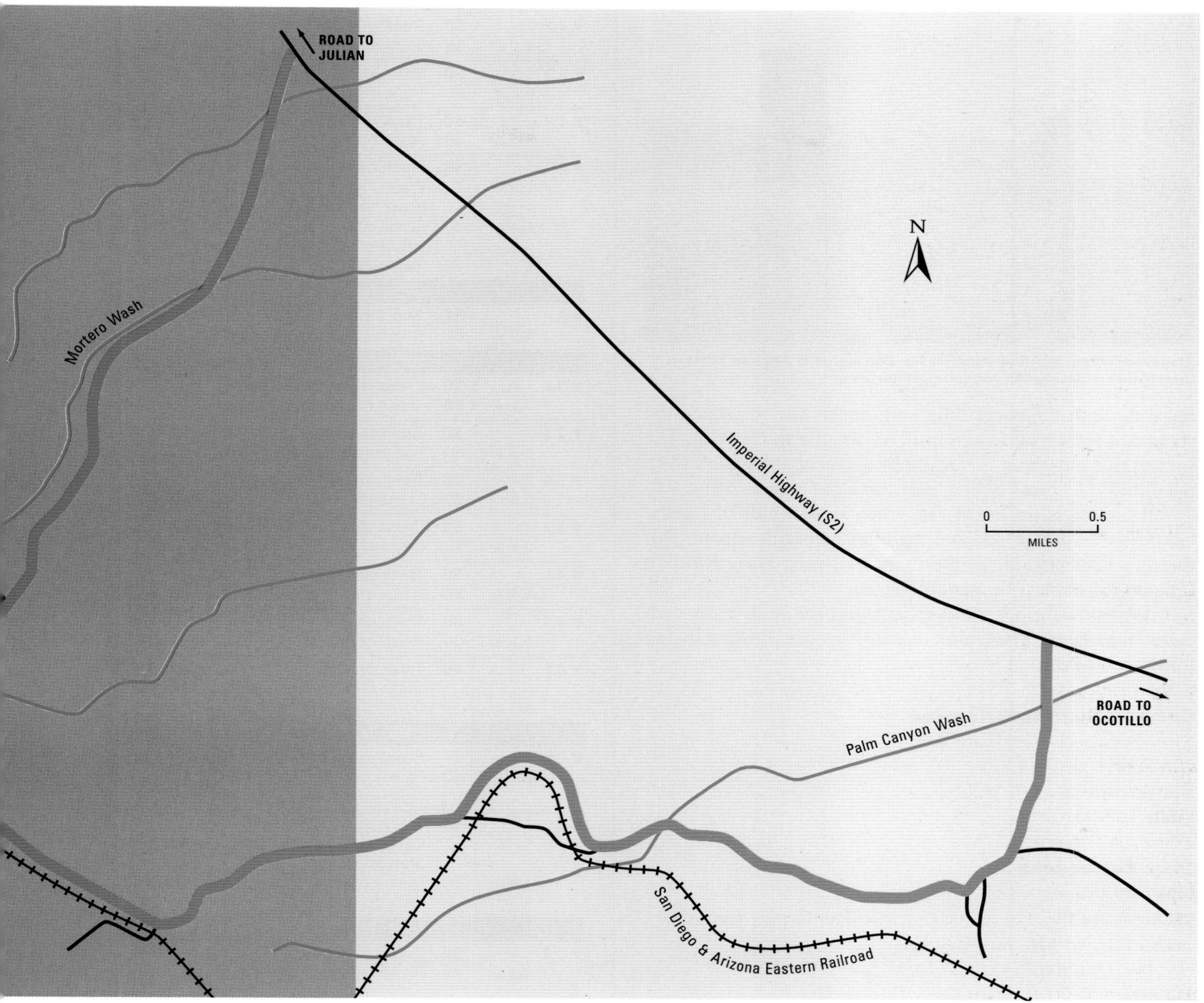

Mother Nature dealt a crushing blow in 1976 in the form of Tropical Storm Kathleen, which closed the line until 1981. The following year, another storm closed the line for a period. By 1984, high repair costs and downtime were such crippling factors that the line closed for good.

Attempts at operating tourist trains through this spectacular landscape continue to fail. Although companies are swamped with bookings, the high cost of operation and difficulties associated with safety assurance prove to be insurmountable obstacles.

The Jacumba Mountains, through which this section of the railroad and trail pass, gained their name from a Native American rancheria in the region. According to early Spanish reports, the village was named Jacom, which is thought to mean "hut by the water." The present-day town of Jacumba, located along the railroad to the southwest of Dos Cabezas, lies immediately north of the international border with Mexico. The town, one of the oldest inhabited sites in San Diego County, further developed as the railroad pushed through these challenging mountains. Old Jacumba House was the original center of the town.

Description

Dos Cabezas Trail describes an arc from the paved Imperial Highway northwest of Ocotillo and runs along the bajada near the base of the Jacumba Mountains. The route travels along easy-to-follow, sandy formed trails through the wide valley between the Jacumba Mountains to the west and the Coyote Mountains to the east. Colorado Desert vegetation is stunning, particularly in spring when the ocotillos are flowering, adding their brilliant flags of orange to the landscape.

The trail follows part of the route of the San Diego & Arizona Eastern Railroad. A highlight of the rail route is the section that runs through the deep cut of Carrizo Gorge. The grade is not accessible to vehicles, but hikers, horseback riders, and mountain bikers will enjoy the winding, dramatic 11-mile

Dos Cabezas Siding, the final stop on the San Diego & Arizona Eastern Railroad before entering the rugged Carrizo Gorge

route through the gorge. Plans are under way to reopen the gorge as a tourist railroad, but it is currently in disrepair. The start of the gorge trail is reached by a spur that leads off from the old Dos Cabezas Siding, past the Dos Cabezas Mine.

The siding is set below the stone-colored hills of Piedras Grandes. A concrete pad and the old water tank remain. Past the Dos Cabezas Siding, the main trail runs along Mortero Canyon to return to Imperial Highway.

Campers will find many spots along the trail, most with panoramic views. These sites typically provide limited shelter from wind or sun.

Current Road Information

Anza-Borrego Desert State Park
200 Palm Canyon Drive
Borrego Springs, CA 92004
(760) 767-5311

Map References

BLM El Cajon
USGS 1:24,000 Carrizo Mt., In-Ko-Pah Gorge, Jacumba, Carrizo Mt., Sweeney Pass
1:100,000 El Cajon
Maptech CD-ROM: San Diego/Joshua Tree
Southern & Central California Atlas & Gazetteer, pp. 124, 123
California Road & Recreation Atlas, p. 117

Route Directions

▼ 0.0		From Imperial Highway (S2), 4 miles northwest of Ocotillo, zero trip meter and turn south on well-used, formed dirt road at marker for Dos Cabezas Road.
4.5 ▲		Trail ends on Imperial Highway (S2). Turn right for Ocotillo and I-8; turn left for Julian.
		GPS: N32°45.23' W116°02.84'
▼ 0.3	SO	Cross through Palm Canyon Wash. Track on right and track on left up and down wash.
4.2 ▲	SO	Cross through Palm Canyon Wash. Track on right and track on left up and down wash.
▼ 0.8	SO	Cross through wash.
3.7 ▲	SO	Cross through wash.
▼ 1.0	SO	Track on left.
3.5 ▲	BL	Track on right.
		GPS: N32°44.32' W116°03.04'
▼ 1.2	SO	Track on left.
3.3 ▲	SO	Second entrance to track on right.
▼ 1.3	SO	Second entrance to track on left.
3.2 ▲	BL	Track on right.
▼ 1.8	SO	Track on left.
2.7 ▲	SO	Track on right.
▼ 2.7	SO	Track on left; then cross through Palm Canyon Wash. Track on left and track on right up and down wash.
1.8 ▲	SO	Cross through Palm Canyon Wash. Track on left and track on right up and down wash; then track on right.
		GPS: N32°44.42' W116°04.67'
▼ 3.0	BR	Two tracks on left. Remain on main trail.
1.5 ▲	BL	Two tracks on right. Remain on main trail.
		GPS: N32°44.34' W116°04.97'
▼ 3.1	SO	Cross through wash.
1.4 ▲	SO	Cross through wash.
▼ 3.3	SO	Two tracks on right.
1.2 ▲	SO	Two tracks on left.
▼ 3.6	SO	Track on left; then cross through wash.
0.9 ▲	SO	Cross through wash; then track on right.
▼ 3.7	SO	Cross through wash.
0.8 ▲	SO	Cross through wash.
▼ 4.1	SO	Track on left.
0.4 ▲	SO	Track on right.
▼ 4.4	SO	Track on left.
0.1 ▲	SO	Track on right.
▼ 4.5	SO	Track on right; then enter Anza-Borrego Desert State Park at sign. Zero trip meter.
0.0 ▲		Continue to the northeast. Track on left.
		GPS: N32°44.32' W116°06.13'
▼ 0.0		Continue to the southwest.
2.4 ▲	SO	Leaving Anza-Borrego Desert State Park at sign, entering BLM land. Zero trip meter.
▼ 1.0	TR	Track on left crosses rail line and goes to Dos Cabezas Primitive Camp Area. Turn right alongside railroad.
1.4 ▲	TL	Turn left away from railroad. Track on right goes to Dos Cabezas Primitive Camp Area.
		GPS: N32°44.07' W116°07.15'
▼ 1.4	SO	Cross through wash.
1.0 ▲	SO	Cross through wash.

Granite boulders in a striking desert landscape above Mortero Canyon

▼ 1.6	SO	Cross through wash.
0.8 ▲	SO	Cross through wash.
▼ 2.4	TR	Dos Cabezas Siding—loading point and water tank remain. Track on left over railroad and track straight ahead. Dos Cabezas Mine is visible to the right. Zero trip meter and turn right toward mine.
0.0 ▲		Continue to the east.
		GPS: N32°44.78' W116°08.34'

Spur to Carrizo Gorge Railroad

▼ 0.0		From Dos Cabezas Siding, continue on the main trail north for 0.1 miles; then take second track on left, leading toward Dos Cabezas Mine. Zero trip meter at the turn.
▼ 0.1	SO	Cross through wash.
▼ 0.3	TL	Turn left through workings of the Dos Cabezas Mine. Track on right.
		GPS: N32°44.99' W116°08.33'
▼ 0.5	BR	Track on left. Bear right alongside railroad.
▼ 0.6	SO	Track on right.
		GPS: N32°44.97' W116°08.75'
▼ 1.1	SO	Track on left.
▼ 1.4	SO	Cross through wash.
▼ 1.5	SO	Cross through wash.
▼ 2.2	UT	Spur ends at turnaround and parking area at the start of hiking, horse, and mountain bike trail into Carrizo Gorge. Vehicles can turn sharp right here, drop into the wash, and continue to explore further vehicle tracks within the region.
		GPS: N32°45.94' W116°09.93'

Continuation of Main Trail

▼ 0.0		Continue to the north.
4.0 ▲	TL	Dos Cabezas Siding—loading point and water tank remain. Track straight ahead over the railroad and track on right. Zero trip meter and turn left alongside railroad.
		GPS: N32°44.78' W116°08.34'
▼ 0.1	BR	Track on left; then second track on left is start of spur to Carrizo Gorge. Remain on main trail.
3.9 ▲	BL	Track on right is start of spur to Carrizo Gorge; then second track on right. Remain on main trail leading toward Dos Cabezas Siding.
		GPS: N32°44.89' W116°08.29'
▼ 0.4	SO	Cross through wash.
3.6 ▲	SO	Cross through wash.
▼ 0.8	SO	Track on left.
3.2 ▲	SO	Track on right.
▼ 1.5	BR	Bear right down Mortero Wash.
2.5 ▲	BL	Bear left out of wash.
		GPS: N32°45.68' W116°07.69'
▼ 3.7	SO	Start to cross multichanneled wash.
0.3 ▲	SO	Exit wash crossing.
▼ 3.9	SO	Exit wash crossing.
0.1 ▲	SO	Start to cross multichanneled wash.
▼ 4.0		Trail ends on Imperial Highway (S2). Turn right for Ocotillo and I-8; turn left for Julian.
0.0 ▲		Trail commences on Imperial Highway (S2), 8.4 miles northwest of Ocotillo and 0.8 miles east of mile marker 55. Zero trip meter and turn south on formed, well-used sandy trail. There is a notice board at the start of the trail and a marker post for Mortero Wash. The trail opposite is marked North Mortero Wash.
		GPS: N32°47.57' W116°06.40'

SOUTH COAST #34

Painted Gorge–Carrizo Mountain Trail

Starting Point:	**S80, 5 miles west of Plaster City and 4 miles east of Ocotillo**
Finishing Point:	**Carrizo Mountain**
Total Mileage:	**8.9 miles (one-way)**
Unpaved Mileage:	**8.9 miles**
Driving Time:	**1.5 hours (one-way)**
Elevation Range:	**200–2,100 feet**
Usually Open:	**Year-round**
Best Time to Travel:	**October to June, dry weather**
Difficulty Rating:	**5**
Scenic Rating:	**9**
Remoteness Rating:	**+1**

Special Attractions

- Multihued Rainbow Canyon.
- The Plaster City OHV Area and a network of old mining trails to explore on Carrizo Mountain.
- Commanding views from Carrizo Mountain over the Salton Sea, Yuha Basin, and into Mexico.

History

Painted Gorge got its name from the colored sections of vertical sandstone blocks within the gorge. Metallic oxides and sulfides have introduced red, blue, and green staining to parts of the narrow gorge. Nearby Fossil Canyon, set within the Coyote Mountains, exposes a geologic history dating back some 50 million years. It contains a record of marine life from a time when a sea covered the region. Fossilized remains of clams, coral, cone shells, barnacles, and turret shells paint an ancient seabed picture in this dry desert landscape.

At the end of the trail, Carrizo Mountain sits high above

Looking south from Carrizo Mountain over the Yuha Desert

the colorful shapes of the Carrizo Badlands and the edge of the Coyote Mountains. Wind and rain have carved these mountains to create caverns and shapes in the sandstone. Many small mining remains are scattered over the side of the mountain; most of these mines extracted silica.

Climbing the highest hiking-only trail on top of Carrizo Mountain in a northwesterly direction offers rewarding views over Carrizo Wash. The wash is closed to the public, having once been a military target-practice zone. In the late 1850s, Butterfield Overland stagecoaches traveled along the line of the wash far below, carrying mail and passengers on a tortuous route from St. Louis to San Francisco. One of several dozen stage stations along this exhausting route was the Carrizo Stage Station, northwest of the peak near Carrizo Wash. With so much of the Butterfield route through the Carrizo Badlands and across the Yuha Desert visible from this one point, it is easy to see why so many stations were established. Water, a momentary rest for the desert-weary passengers, a quick meal, and a change of horses were needed for the stage line to fulfill its transportation contract.

Carrizo is a Spanish word meaning "reed grass." This reed was found to give a sweet taste to the water found in its vicinity. Native Americans used the reed as a sweetener for less palatable waters.

Plaster City, near the start of this trail, is the nation's largest manufacturing plant of gypsum wallboards. Today, there is only the plant; workers drive in from nearby towns. Originally there was a settlement with worker housing and a school.

Description

Painted Gorge truly lives up to its name—a multihued canyon of vibrant colors contained in the rocks that form its walls. The trail leaves S80 between Plaster City and Ocotillo. The road is marked with an informal sign immediately west of the sign for the Plaster City West Staging Area. Initially, it is a well-used graded road that serves as access for Painted Gorge Estates. Entering public lands, the graded road becomes a formed trail that passes through a wide open area and then swings west, dropping into the sandy wash of Painted Canyon and almost immediately entering the canyon.

The trail through the canyon is sandy and twisty as it winds its way into the Coyote Mountains. Embedded rocks litter the wash, but the difficulty of the trail comes not in this section but the following one, as the trail climbs high up Carrizo Mountain. After 1.4 miles, the trail swings out of the wash and starts to climb a well-used shelf road out of the canyon. If you remain in the wash at this point, you will reach a dead end in 0.2 miles.

Painted Gorge cuts deep within the Coyote Mountains

The shelf road climbs steeply. The surface is loose in places and the road is narrow, limited to single vehicle width for most of its length. Passing places are limited. As you climb, Painted Gorge unfolds beneath you. Beyond the gorge to the south are the Yuha Basin and Mexico.

The trails on Carrizo Mountain were put through for mining, and there are many of them to explore. There are some good backcountry campsites, most of which have excellent views. The trail described below leads through the network of trails to a viewpoint near the summit of Carrizo Mountain. Other trails lead to equally good spots, although care must be taken on the extremely narrow, rough shelf roads. The final 0.9 miles of the trail is the most challenging, with embedded rocks, loose surfaces, and a very narrow shelf road. There is enough room to turn around at the end.

Current Road Information

Bureau of Land Management
El Centro Field Office
1661 South Fourth Street
El Centro, CA 92243
(760) 337-4400

Map References

BLM El Centro, El Cajon
USGS 1:24,000 Painted Gorge, Carrizo Mt.
1:100,000 El Centro, El Cajon
Maptech CD-ROM: San Diego/Joshua Tree
Southern & Central California Atlas & Gazetteer, p. 124
California Road & Recreation Atlas, p. 117

Route Directions

Mileage		Directions
▼ 0.0		From S80, 5 miles west of Plaster City and 4 miles east of Ocotillo, zero trip meter and turn northwest on graded dirt road marked Painted Gorge Road. The turn is at the sign for leaving Plaster City Open OHV Area.
3.3 ▲		Trail ends on S80. Turn right for Ocotillo and I-8; turn left for El Centro and I-8.
		GPS: N32°45.76' W115°55.84'
▼ 0.1	SO	Track on left and track on right. Private property tracks on left and right for next 2 miles. Remain on main graded road.
3.2 ▲	SO	Track on left and track on right.
▼ 0.5	SO	Cross through the wide, multichanneled Coyote Wash.
2.8 ▲	SO	Cross through the wide, multichanneled Coyote Wash
▼ 1.1	SO	Cross through wash.
2.2 ▲	SO	Cross through wash.
▼ 1.3	BL	Graded road on right. Follow sign for Painted Gorge Road.
2.0 ▲	SO	Graded road on left.
		GPS: N32°46.74' W115°56.38'

▼ 2.1		SO	Cross through wash.
	1.2 ▲	SO	Cross through wash. Private property tracks on left and right for next 2 miles. Remain on main graded road.
▼ 2.3		SO	Track on left and track on right under power lines. Plaster City OHV Area is on the right. Many small vehicle and ATV tracks on right for next 1 mile. Remain on main trail.
	1.0 ▲	SO	Track on left and track on right under power lines. Plaster City OHV Area is on the left.
▼ 2.4		SO	Enter line of wash.
	0.9 ▲	SO	Exit line of wash.
▼ 3.3		BR	Graded road on left at sign for Imperial County Gravel Pit. Zero trip meter.
	0.0 ▲		Continue to the south and enter line of wash. Many small vehicle and ATV tracks on right for next 1 mile. Remain on main trail.
			GPS: N32°47.88′ W115°57.58′
▼ 0.0			Continue to the northeast and exit line of wash.
	1.4 ▲	SO	Graded road on right at sign for Imperial County Gravel Pit. Zero trip meter.
▼ 0.1		SO	Track on left.
	1.3 ▲	SO	Track on right.
▼ 0.3		SO	Track on left.
	1.1 ▲	SO	Track on right.
▼ 0.6		SO	Enter line of wash.
	0.8 ▲	SO	Exit line of wash.
▼ 1.2		BR	Track on left continues up wash. Exit line of wash.
	0.2 ▲	BL	Track on right up wash. Enter line of wash.
			GPS: N32°48.67′ W115°58.30′
▼ 1.3		SO	Track on right.
	0.1 ▲	SO	Track on left.
▼ 1.4		SO	Trail crosses open wide area. Zero trip meter. Track on right down wash.
	0.0 ▲	SO	Continue to the southeast.
			GPS: N32°48.82′ W115°58.33′
▼ 0.0			Continue to the northwest.
▼ 0.1		SO	Enter up wash.
▼ 0.3		SO	Track on right down wash. Continue up wash. Entering Painted Gorge.
			GPS: N32°48.86′ W115°58.55′
▼ 1.4		BR	Track straight ahead continues in wash for 0.2 miles before finishing. Bear right out of wash along shelf road.
			GPS: N32°48.59′ W115°59.55′
▼ 1.7		SO	Campsite on right and track on right.
			GPS: N32°48.58′ W115°59.74′
▼ 2.0		BR	Small track on left.
▼ 2.1		SO	Cross through wash.
			GPS: N32°48.63′ W116°00.08′
▼ 3.3		TL	Well-used track on left; then turn left onto second track on left.
			GPS: N32°49.08′ W116°00.23′
▼ 4.2			Trail ends at a turnaround high on Carrizo Mountain.
			GPS: N32°49.48′ W116°00.76′

SOUTH COAST #35

McCain Valley Road

Starting Point:	**Old Highway 80, 6.2 miles northwest of Jacumba, 0.5 miles northwest of mile marker 29**
Finishing Point:	**Boundary of the Sawtooth Mountains Wilderness**
Total Mileage:	**14 miles (one-way), plus 1.9-mile spur to Sacatone Overlook**
Unpaved Mileage:	**14 miles, plus 1.9-mile spur**
Driving Time:	**1.75 hours (one-way)**
Elevation Range:	**3,100–4,500 feet**
Usually Open:	**Year-round**
Best Time to Travel:	**October to June**
Difficulty Rating:	**1**
Scenic Rating:	**8**
Remoteness Rating:	**+0**

Special Attractions

- Sacatone Overlook with views over Carrizo Gorge to the historic San Diego & Arizona Eastern Railroad trestles.
- Beautiful, boulder-strewn landscape and access to Sawtooth Mountains Wilderness.
- Lark Canyon OHV Area for motorbikes.
- Carrizo Scenic Overlook with views deep into the Carrizo Gorge.

History

The McCain family name became attached to the valley just east of this trail in 1852, when George McCain took up homesteading and cattle grazing in the region. McCain had traveled from Texas in a covered wagon (also referred to as a prairie schooner) in search of new territory. Descendants of his remain in the area to this day. The McCain Valley Resource Conservation Area was established in 1963 to provide a mixture of wildlife, recreation, and livestock areas.

Earlier inhabitants of this region were the Kumeyaay (also called the Diegueno). They were hunters and agriculturists who lived in a wetter landscape than we know today. As conditions became more arid, they learned to plant corn, squash, and beans near natural springs, summer thunderstorm catchment basins, and the Colorado River during its flood periods. The *San Diego Herald* of June 1851 reported considerable numbers of these Indians in McCain Valley. The Kumeyaay were reported as being a kindly group of Indians. Several had visited white settlements, and some even spoke a little Spanish.

Granite boulders at the approach to Lost Valley

By the 1870s, they were losing ground to new settlers in Southern California. Many native groups were scattered; some worked for the new settlers in return for goods and food, while others moved to the Capitan Grande Indian Reservation, north of today's Alpine. The Sequoya League and Indian Rights Association highlighted the plight of Indians in this region, pressuring the Bureau of Indian Affairs to allocate reservations for these disbanded groups. The outcome was the establishment of the Manzanita, Cuyapaipe, and La Poste Indian Reservations, all of which border McCain Valley Road.

Cuyapaipe (sometimes spelled *Cuyapaipa*) means "leaning rock" in the native tongue. The reservation was established in 1875 and is located just east of the end of this trail. The Guyapipe people lived in the vicinity of the Laguna Mountains. *La Posta* (Spanish for "stagecoach express") was the name of a staging station in Cameron Valley, located east along Old Highway 80. La Posta was an important stopping point for the San Diego to Yuma stagecoaches south of the Laguna Mountains. The In-Ko-Pah Mountains, across which this trail climbs, were named after the eastern mountain people, or, as the Kumeyaay called them, the *enyaak 'iipay.*

The Sacatone Overlook, takes in views of the "Impossible Railroad" through Carrizo Gorge. Against all odds, the San Diego & Arizona Eastern Railroad was constructed in the 1910s down the narrows of the canyon. Some railroad boxcars were left hanging off the side of this spectacular gorge. The Spanish word *sacatone* refers to a bunch-type grass that grows in alkaline soils and is used as feed for cattle in desert regions.

Description

McCain Valley Road is a well-maintained, graded trail that accesses Lark Canyon OHV Area, the Cottonwood Recreation Site, and the Sawtooth Mountains Wilderness. Along the way, it passes two stunning viewpoints over the Carrizo Gorge area and travels through a magnificent undulating landscape, strewn with giant granite boulders.

The trail is accessed from Old Highway 80, at the settlement of Boulevard, northwest of Jacumba. There is no freeway exit from I-8 directly to McCain Valley Road, but it is only a short distance in either direction along Old Highway 80 to the freeway. The road is clearly marked to McCain Valley and Lark Canyon OHV Area.

The paved road turns to graded dirt as it enters the McCain Valley Conservation Area and immediately starts to travel through the striking, boulder-strewn landscape. The views along the trail are wide and open. A worthwhile side trip is the short spur to Sacatone Overlook. This leads to a view over the Carrizo Gorge and the famous railroad trestles of the San Diego & Arizona Eastern Railroad. The line is currently closed, but the trail is popular with hikers, horseback riders, and mountain bikers. It can be accessed from South Coast #33: Dos Cabezas Trail.

Lark Canyon OHV Area is for motorbikes only. A network of small trails crisscrosses the region. There is pleasant, shady camping at the recreation site (fee charged). A second overlook into the Carrizo Gorge region encompasses the badlands as well as the canyon area.

The trail ends a short distance past the Cottonwood Recreation Site at the edge of the Sawtooth Mountains Wilderness. Hikers and horseback riders can continue into the wilderness. Cottonwood Recreation Site has many shady creekside campsites and is popular on weekends (fee charged).

Camping along this trail is limited to the developed sites

Sacatone Overlook offers views into Carrizo Gorge

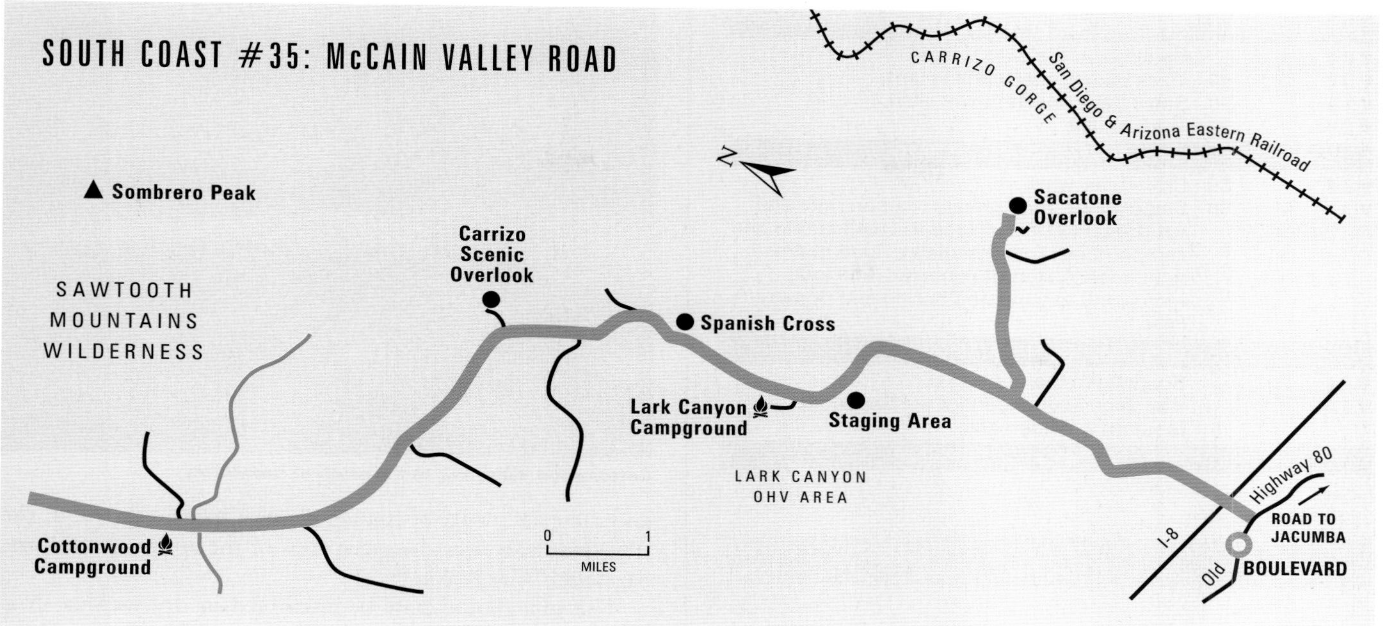

at Cottonwood Recreation Site and Lark Canyon Recreation Site. Although maps show an exit to the south via the Manzanita Indian Reservation, it is currently blocked.

Current Road Information

Bureau of Land Management
El Centro Field Office
1661 South Fourth Street
El Centro, CA 92243
(760) 337-4400

Map References

BLM El Cajon
USFS Cleveland National Forest
USGS 1:24,000 Live Oak Springs, Sombrero Peak
1:100,000 El Cajon
Maptech CD-ROM: San Diego/Joshua Tree
Southern & Central California Atlas & Gazetteer, p. 123
California Road & Recreation Atlas, p. 117
Other: Tom Harrison Maps—San Diego Backcountry Recreation map

Route Directions

▼ 0.0 From Old Highway 80 at Boulevard, 6.2 miles northwest of Jacumba and 0.5 miles northwest of mile marker 29, zero trip meter and turn north on paved road sign-posted to McCain Valley and Lark Canyon OHV Area.

GPS: N32°39.80' W116°15.56'

▼ 0.4 SO Pass under freeway. Remain on paved road.
▼ 2.4 SO Cattle guard. Road turns to graded dirt. Entering McCain Valley Conservation Area at sign.

GPS: N32°41.75' W116°15.52'

▼ 2.5 SO Track on right.
▼ 2.8 SO Graded road on right is the spur to Sacatone Overlook. Zero trip meter.

GPS: N32°42.07' W116°15.47'

Spur to Sacatone Overlook

▼ 0.0 Proceed to the northeast, following sign to Sacatone Lookout.
▼ 0.1 SO Cattle guard.
▼ 0.7 SO Track on right.
▼ 1.5 SO Track on right.

GPS: N32°42.76' W116°14.16'

▼ 1.8 BL Well-used track on right; then cross over wash; then track on left.
▼ 1.9 Spur ends at Sacatone Overlook, with views over Carrizo Gorge, the San Diego & Arizona Eastern Railroad, and its famous trestles.

GPS: N32°42.82' W116°13.75'

Continuation of Main Trail

▼ 0.0 Continue to the north.

GPS: N32°42.07' W116°15.47'

▼ 0.2 SO Track on left.
▼ 1.5 SO Cattle guard.
▼ 1.6 SO Lark Canyon OHV Area boundary on left.
▼ 1.7 SO Track on left into Lark Canyon OHV Area; then cattle guard.

GPS: N32°43.42' W116°15.71'

▼ 2.1 SO Lark Canyon OHV Staging Area on left.

GPS: N32°43.43' W116°16.12'

▼ 2.4 SO Track on left enters Lark Canyon Recreation Site Campground (fee charged). Zero trip meter.

GPS: N32°43.66' W116°16.33'

▼ 0.0 Continue to the northwest.
▼ 0.2 SO Track on left also goes to Lark Canyon Recreation Site Campground.
▼ 0.3 SO Cattle guard.
▼ 1.4 SO Spanish cross carved low into boulder on right.
▼ 1.9 SO Track on right to viewpoint.

GPS: N32°45.27' W116°16.29'

▼ 2.3 SO Track on left.
▼ 2.6 SO Track on left.
▼ 3.3 SO Track on right goes 0.2 miles to Carrizo Scenic Overlook. Zero trip meter.

		GPS: N32°46.27′ W116°16.98′
▼ 0.0		Continue to the west.
▼ 0.4	SO	Track on left; then cattle guard.
▼ 1.5	SO	Small track on left down wash.
▼ 2.9	SO	Track on left.
		GPS: N32°47.19′ W116°19.76′
▼ 3.8	SO	Cross over wash.
▼ 3.9	SO	Cattle guard; then graded road on right and left goes into Cottonwood Recreation Site and campground. Zero trip meter. Road to the right goes to start of Peppered Trail (non-motorized) to Peppered Spring and Sombrero Peak.
		GPS: N32°48.01′ W116°20.25′
▼ 0.0		Continue to the northwest.
▼ 1.6		Trail ends at boundary of the Sawtooth Mountains Wilderness.
		GPS: N32°49.41′ W116°20.66′

SOUTH COAST #36

Bear Valley Road

Starting Point:	**Buckman Springs Road (S1), 1 mile south of I-8**
Finishing Point:	**I-8, at the Pine Valley exit**
Total Mileage:	**8.2 miles**
Unpaved Mileage:	**8.2 miles**
Driving Time:	**1 hour**
Elevation Range:	**3,200–4,600 feet**
Usually Open:	**Year-round**
Best Time to Travel:	**Dry weather**
Difficulty Rating:	**3**
Scenic Rating:	**8**
Remoteness Rating:	**+0**

Special Attractions

- Ridge top trail in Cleveland National Forest that travels over Fuzz, Sage, and Wire Peaks.
- Easy day trip from San Diego.

History

Near the southern end of the trail, Buckman Springs and Buckman Peak were named for Amos Buckman, who settled in the valley in the late 1860s. Buckman owned a large block of land in the region, including the springs.

Description

This ridge top trail is conveniently located within day-trip distance of San Diego. It offers fantastic views of the Cottonwood Valley to the east and Bear Valley to the west. The trail leaves less than a mile south of I-8 at the Buckman Springs Road exit and immediately enters Cleveland National Forest through a gate. It starts to climb a shelf road onto the ridge. The shelf road is more than wide enough for a single vehicle,

Cottonwood Valley lies to the south of Bear Valley

and there are plenty of passing places. Once on the ridge, the trail undulates over the green tops of the aptly named Fuzz, Sage, and Wire Peaks.

The trail should only be attempted in dry weather. It is likely to be gated closed by the forest service when wet. Deep ruts in the trail and the uneven surface make it difficult to travel when wet. The trail descends to finish at Pine Valley, immediately south of the I-8 freeway exit.

A National Forest Adventure Pass is required for all recreational activities within Cleveland National Forest.

Current Road Information

Cleveland National Forest
Descanso Ranger District
3348 Alpine Boulevard
Alpine, CA 91901
(619) 445-6235

Map References

BLM El Cajon
USFS Cleveland National Forest
USGS 1:24,000 Cameron Corners, Morena Reservoir, Descanso
1:100,000 El Cajon
Maptech CD-ROM: San Diego/Joshua Tree
Southern & Central California Atlas & Gazetteer, p. 123
California Road & Recreation Atlas, p. 117
Other: Tom Harrison Maps—San Diego Backcountry Recreation map

Route Directions

▼ 0.0		Take the Buckman Springs Road (S1) southbound exit from I-8 and proceed to the south side of the freeway. Cross over Old Highway 80 and continue south on Buckman Springs Road for 1 mile, following the sign to Morena Lake County Park. Zero trip meter and turn west on formed dirt trail, marked 16S12. Immediately pass through a gate. Track on left after gate.
	8.2 ▲	Track on right; then pass through gate. Trail finishes on Buckman Springs Road (S1). Turn left for I-8 and Pine Valley; turn right for Morena Village and Campo.

		GPS: N32°44.92' W116°29.59'
▼ 0.1	SO	Track on left.
8.1 ▲	SO	Track on right.
▼ 0.3	SO	Track on left and track on right.
7.9 ▲	SO	Track on right and track on left.
▼ 0.6	SO	Start of shelf road and ascent.
7.6 ▲	SO	End of shelf road and descent.
▼ 0.8	SO	Gate.
7.4 ▲	SO	Gate.
		GPS: N32°45.12' W116°30.16'
▼ 1.3	SO	Gate.
6.9 ▲	SO	Gate.
▼ 1.7	SO	Track on left is Long Valley Road (16S14). This is Mount Fuzz. End of shelf road.
6.5 ▲	SO	Track on right is Long Valley Road (16S14). This is Mount Fuzz. Start to descend along shelf road.
		GPS: N32°45.56' W116°30.40'
▼ 2.1	SO	Concrete pad on right; then track on right.
6.1 ▲	SO	Track on left; then concrete pad on left.
▼ 4.4	SO	Track on right.
3.8 ▲	SO	Track on left.
		GPS: N32°47.54' W116°30.47'
▼ 4.5	SO	Track on right.
3.7 ▲	SO	Track on left.
▼ 4.7	SO	Track on left.
3.5 ▲	SO	Track on right.
▼ 4.8	SO	Track on right.
3.4 ▲	SO	Track on left.
▼ 6.3	SO	Track on right.
1.9 ▲	SO	Track on left.
▼ 8.1	SO	Gate.
0.1 ▲	SO	Gate.
		GPS: N32°48.94' W116°31.90'
▼ 8.2		Cattle guard; then trail ends on the south side of I-8 at Pine Valley.
0.0 ▲		From I-8 at the Pine Valley exit, proceed to the south side of the freeway and zero trip meter at cattle guard. Head south onto formed dirt trail.
		GPS: N32°48.98' W116°31.92'

SOUTH COAST #37

Los Pinos Trail

Starting Point:	**Corral Canyon Road, at Four Corners Trailhead, 5.6 miles west of Buckman Springs Road**
Finishing Point:	**Corral Canyon Road, at Four Corners Trailhead, 5.6 miles west of Buckman Springs Road**
Total Mileage:	**18.6 miles**
Unpaved Mileage:	**17.7 miles**
Driving Time:	**3 hours**
Elevation Range:	**2,800–4,900 feet**
Usually Open:	**Year-round**
Best Time to Travel:	**Dry weather**
Difficulty Rating:	**5**
Scenic Rating:	**9**
Remoteness Rating:	**+0**

Special Attractions

- Loop trail through a spectacular granite boulder landscape.
- Lake Morena County Park and lake access.
- Corral Canyon OHV Area.

History

The first occupants of the Los Pinos region were coastal and desert Indian tribes, such as the Luiseño and the Cahuilla, who roamed the ranges and plains living on the abundant vegetation and game.

In 1769, Junípero Serra established the first California mission in San Diego, under the direction of the Spanish govern-

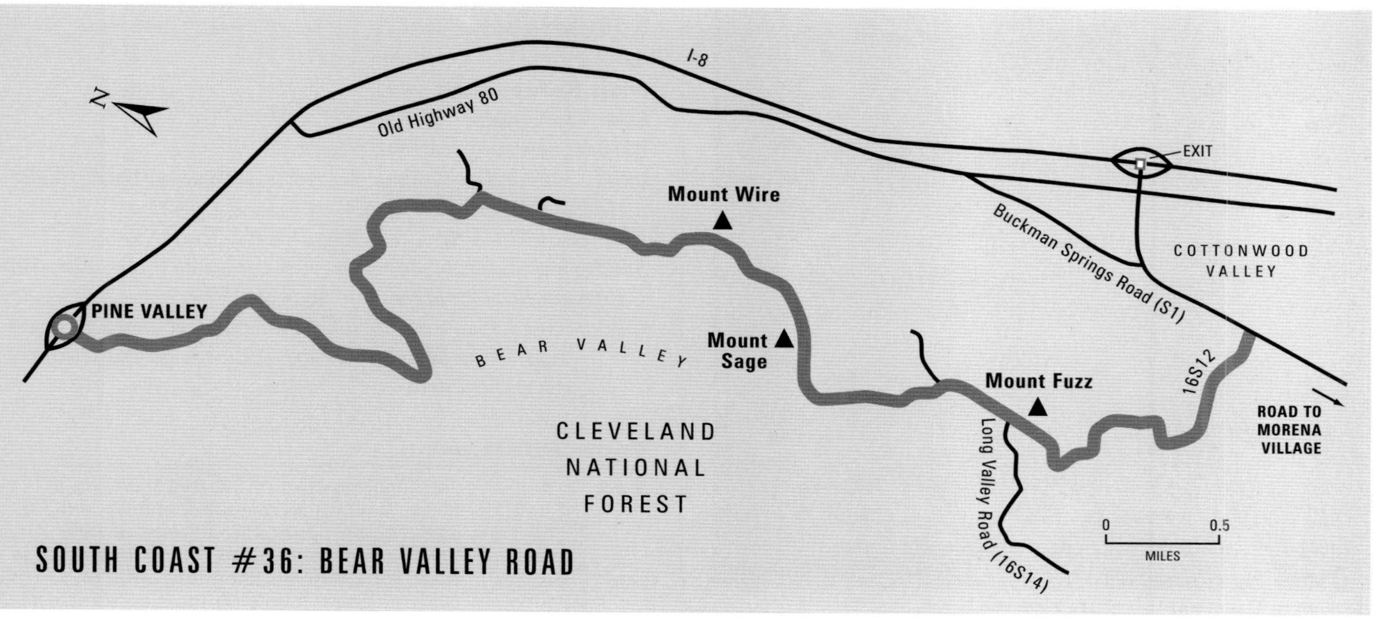

Espinoza Trail runs below the face of Corte Madera Mountain

ment. To the north of Espinosa Creek is Corte Madera Mountain. The mountain's name is Spanish for "a place where wood is cut." This region, now in Cleveland National Forest, supplied much of the timber used to build many of the California missions.

Before European settlement, Native Americans regularly burned brushlands to keep the land fertile and in balance. During the 1800s, much of the land was parceled into land grants to use for ranching. Subsequent overgrazing and timber cutting heavily taxed the land, which has never fully recovered.

The name "Morena" is applied to several features in the region, the most prominent of which is Lake Morena. Morena was also applied to a siding along the Santa Fe Railroad in the 1900s. Although *morena* means "brown" in Spanish, it was also a fairly common family name, and the features of the region are more likely to have been named after early settlers.

Description
Los Pinos Trail is a designated 4WD route that loops around granite boulders near Corral Canyon OHV Area and Lake Morena. The 5-rating for the trail comes from the section that follows the Espinoza Trail; the remainder of the trail rates a 3 for difficulty.

Corte Madera Mountain rises above Espinosa Creek

The loop starts and finishes at the Four Corners Trailhead on the edge of the OHV area. The trail can be traveled in either direction. It starts by climbing up Los Pinos Mountain, following an uneven shelf road to the fire lookout on top. The tower is not used anymore because aerial surveillance has replaced the old lookout system. There is no access to the tower, but the view from the top of the mountain is worth the short detour.

The main trail descends Los Pinos Mountain to a saddle, where it swings to the west onto the smaller Espinoza Trail, which runs down alongside Espinosa Creek. (On the BLM map the trail is spelled with a "z" and the creek with an "s.") This section of the loop can be very rough and uneven and is slow going as it heads down the valley. There are a couple of tricky descents before you reach the creek and an off-camber squeeze between two large boulders. Watch your side panels as you tilt.

Exiting from Espinosa Creek, the trail becomes an easier, roughly graded road again as it wraps around the eastern boundary of the Pine Creek Wilderness. Traveling through Skye Valley, it then passes between the northern boundary of the Hauser Wilderness and the southern boundary of the Corral Canyon OHV Area.

A short, rough spur trail leads 0.8 miles to Lake Morena, finishing at a turnaround at the dam. There is no exit this way.

The main trail passes Bobcat Meadows Campground and the start of several trails that lead into the OHV area—some are suitable for 4WD vehicles, although they are twisty and best suited to smaller vehicles. The loop ends back where it started at the Four Corners Trailhead.

Current Road Information
Cleveland National Forest
Descanso Ranger District
3348 Alpine Boulevard
Alpine, CA 91901
(619) 445-6235

Map References
BLM El Cajon
USFS Cleveland National Forest
USGS 1:24,000 Morena Reservoir, Descanso, Barrett Lake
1:100,000 El Cajon
Maptech CD-ROM: San Diego/Joshua Tree
Southern & Central California Atlas & Gazetteer, pp. 122, 123
California Road & Recreation Atlas, p. 117
Other: Corral Canyon Open OHV Area (free national forest map), Tom Harrison Maps—San Diego Backcountry Recreation map

Route Directions
▼ 0.0	To reach the start of the trail traveling in either forward or reverse direction, exit I-8 at Buckman Springs Road (east of Pine Valley). Proceed south on Buckman Springs Road for 3.2 miles; then turn west on Corral Canyon Road, following the sign for Corral

Canyon OHV Area. Remain on this road for 5.6 miles to the Four Corners Trailhead and staging area. Zero trip meter and turn northwest on formed dirt trail, marked Los Pinos 16S17. Wrangler and Corral Trails, for ATVs and motorbikes only, start from this trailhead. Corral Canyon Road continues to the west.

2.3 ▲ Trail finishes back at Four Corners Trailhead and staging area. Exit via Corral Canyon Road.

GPS: N32°43.50′ W116°33.50′

▼ 0.3 SO Gate. Start of shelf road.
2.0 ▲ SO Gate. End of shelf road.

▼ 2.3 SO Track on right goes 0.3 miles to Los Pinos Fire Lookout. Zero trip meter.
0.0 ▲ Continue to the south.

GPS: N32°44.16′ W116°34.71′

▼ 0.0 Continue to the northwest.
1.8 ▲ SO Track on left goes 0.3 miles to Los Pinos Fire Lookout. Zero trip meter.

▼ 1.0 TR Track on left is Spur Meadow Cycle Trail for hikers, horses, mountain bikes, motorbikes, and ATVs less than 40 inches wide.
0.8 ▲ TL Track straight ahead is Spur Meadow Cycle Trail for hikers, horses, mountain bikes, motorbikes, and ATVs less than 40 inches wide.

GPS: N32°44.49′ W116°34.87′

▼ 1.8 TL 4-way intersection on saddle. Hiking and horse trail on right; straight ahead goes to private property. Zero trip meter and turn left onto Espinoza Trail, marked by a forest marker.
0.0 ▲ Continue to the southwest.

GPS: N32°44.85′ W116°34.48′

▼ 0.0 Continue to the west.
3.0 ▲ TR 4-way intersection on saddle. Track on left goes to private property; straight ahead is for hikers and horses only. Zero trip meter and start to climb shelf road.

▼ 0.8 SO Tanks on left; then trail drops down to cross creek.
2.2 ▲ SO Trail rises up from creek; then tanks on right.

GPS: N32°45.01′ W116°35.15′

▼ 1.8 SO Cross through wash; then squeeze between two large boulders.
1.2 ▲ SO Squeeze between two large boulders; then cross through wash.

GPS: N32°45.10′ W116°36.10′

▼ 2.3 SO Track on left is turnout only.
0.7 ▲ SO Track on right is turnout only.

▼ 2.5 SO Cross through Espinosa Creek.
0.5 ▲ SO Cross through Espinosa Creek.

GPS: N32°45.19′ W116°36.70′

▼ 2.6 SO Tank on left.
0.4 ▲ SO Tank on right.

▼ 2.8 SO Cross through creek twice.
0.2 ▲ SO Cross through creek twice.

▼ 2.9 SO Cross through creek.
0.1 ▲ SO Cross through creek.

▼ 3.0 TL T-intersection. Track on right goes into private property. Zero trip meter and turn left onto Corte Madera Road.
0.0 ▲ Continue to the east.

GPS: N32°45.25′ W116°37.13′

▼ 0.0 Continue to the southwest and cross through creek.
3.9 ▲ TR Cross through creek; then track straight ahead goes into private property. Zero trip meter and turn right onto Espinoza Trail at the forest marker.

Seen from high above on Los Pinos Trail, Lake Morena is popular with anglers and boaters

▼ 0.9 SO Turnout on right.
3.0 ▲ SO Turnout on left.

▼ 2.3 BL Camping area on right and track on right; then cross through wash.
1.6 ▲ BR Cross through wash; then track on left and camping area on left.

GPS: N32°43.63′ W116°37.21′

▼ 3.5 SO Track on left.
0.4 ▲ SO Track on right rejoins.

GPS: N32°43.08′ W116°36.85′

▼ 3.6 SO Track on left rejoins.
0.3 ▲ SO Track on right.

▼ 3.7 SO Cross through wash.
0.2 ▲ SO Cross through wash.

▼ 3.8 SO Two tracks on left.
0.1 ▲ SO Two tracks on right.

▼ 3.9 TL T-intersection. Right goes to locked gate. Zero trip meter.
0.0 ▲ Continue to the north.

GPS: N32°42.92′ W116°36.87′

▼ 0.0 Continue to the east.
1.8 ▲ TR Straight ahead goes to locked gate. Zero trip meter.

▼ 0.1 SO Two tracks on left and two tracks on right.
1.7 ▲ SO Two tracks on left and two tracks on right.

▼ 0.4 BL Track on right.
1.4 ▲ BR Track on left.

▼ 0.8 SO Track on right is private.
1.0 ▲ SO Track on left is private.

▼ 0.9 SO Track on right.
0.9 ▲ SO Track on left.

▼ 1.0 SO Track on right.
0.8 ▲ SO Track on left.

▼ 1.1 SO Track on right.
0.7 ▲ SO Track on left.

▼ 1.2 SO Track on right.
0.6 ▲ BR Track on left.

GPS: N32°42.36′ W116°36.39′

▼ 1.3 SO Track on right.
0.5 ▲ SO Track on left.

▼ 1.5 SO Track on right.

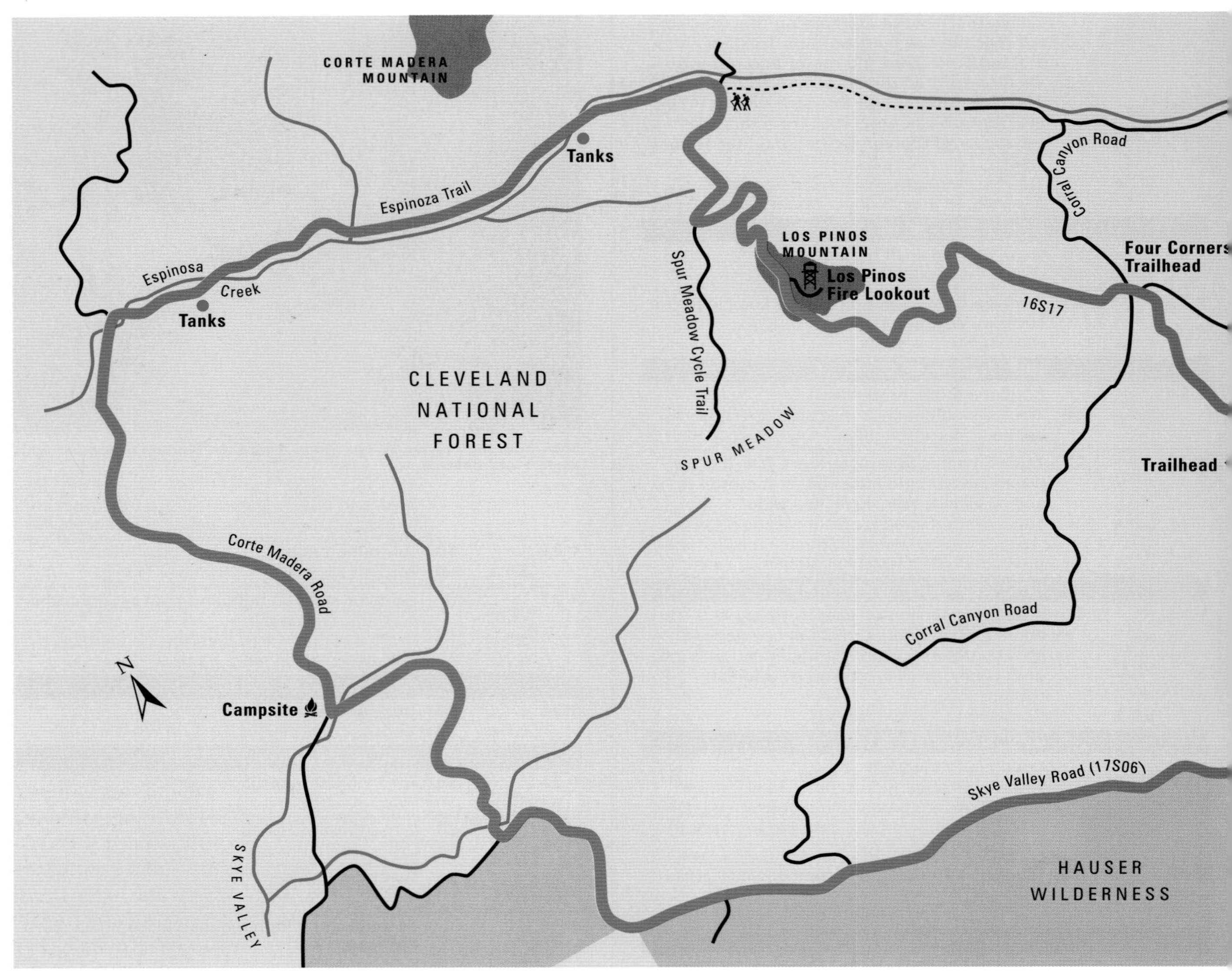

	0.3 ▲	SO	Track on left.
▼ 1.8		BR	Graded road on left is Corral Canyon Road. Bear right onto Skye Valley Road (17S06) and zero trip meter. Intersection is unmarked.
	0.0 ▲		Continue to the south.
			GPS: N32°42.22' W116°35.78'
▼ 0.0			Continue to the east.
	2.8 ▲	SO	Graded road on right is Corral Canyon Road. Zero trip meter. Intersection is unmarked.
▼ 2.0		SO	Two tracks on left.
	0.8 ▲	SO	Two tracks on right.
▼ 2.1		SO	Track on right.
	0.7 ▲	SO	Track on left.
▼ 2.7		SO	Track on left.
	0.1 ▲	SO	Track on right.
			GPS: N32°41.59' W116°33.21'
▼ 2.8		BL	Track on right goes through gate for 0.8 miles to Lake Morena Dam. There is no exit this way. Zero trip meter.
	0.0 ▲		Continue to the west.
			GPS: N32°41.57' W116°33.11'
▼ 0.0			Continue to the northwest.
	3.0 ▲	BR	Track on left goes through gate for 0.8 miles to Lake Morena Dam. There is no exit this way. Zero trip meter.
▼ 0.2		SO	Track on left is Greenhorn Trail for ATVs and motorbikes only.
	2.8 ▲	SO	Track on right is Greenhorn Trail for ATVs and motorbikes only.
			GPS: N32°41.74' W116°33.08'
▼ 1.0		SO	Track on left is Greenhorn Trail.
	2.0 ▲	SO	Track on right is Greenhorn Trail.
			GPS: N32°42.06' W116°32.95'
▼ 1.3		SO	Track on left is Bronco Peak Trail for 4WDs, ATVs, and motorbikes.
	1.7 ▲	SO	Track on right is Bronco Peak Trail for 4WDs, ATVs, and motorbikes.
			GPS: N32°42.29' W116°32.98'
▼ 1.6		SO	Track on left.
	1.4 ▲	SO	Track on right.
			GPS: N32°42.51' W116°33.11'
▼ 2.1		SO	Graded road on right leads into Bobcat Meadow Campground. Wrangler and Bobcat Trails for ATVs and motorbikes, Sodbuster Trail for motorbikes, and Sidewinder Trail for

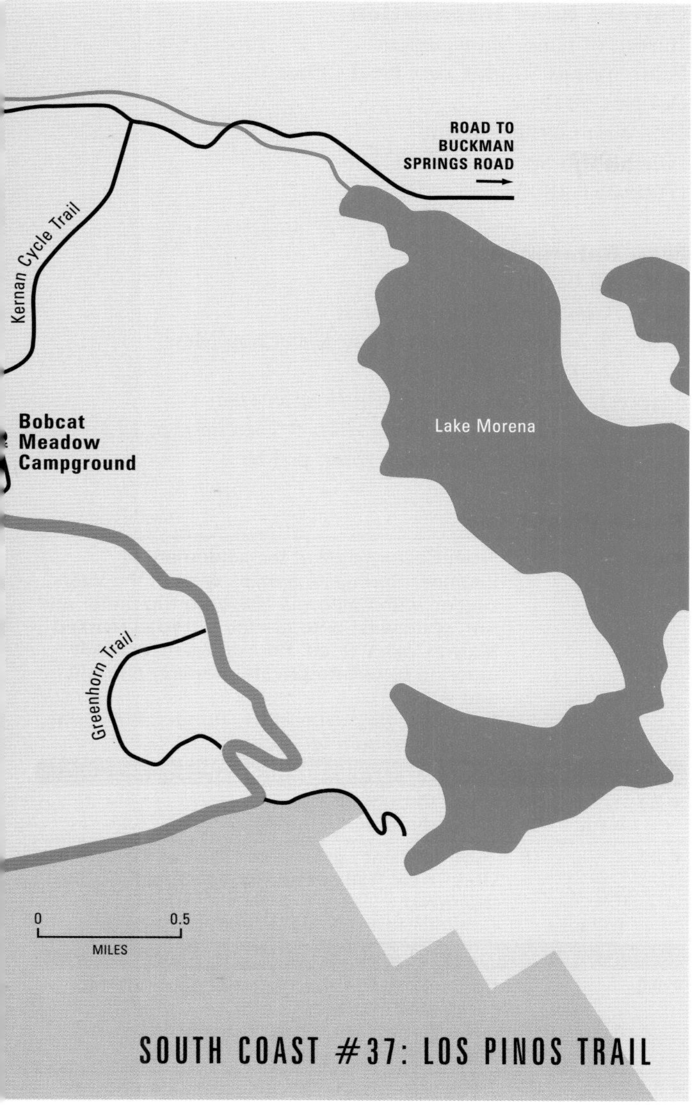

ROAD TO BUCKMAN SPRINGS ROAD

Kernan Cycle Trail

Bobcat Meadow Campground

Lake Morena

Greenhorn Trail

0 0.5 MILES

SOUTH COAST #37: LOS PINOS TRAIL

4WDs, ATVs, and motorbikes lead off on the left at information board. Trail is now paved.

0.9 ▲ SO Graded road on left leads into Bobcat Meadow Campground. Wrangler and Bobcat Trails for ATVs and motorbikes, Sodbuster Trail for motorbikes, and Sidewinder Trail for 4WDs, ATVs, and motorbikes lead off on the right at information board. Trail turns to dirt.

GPS: N32°42.75′ W116°33.46′

▼ 2.5 SO Sidewinder Trail for 4WDs, ATVs, and motorbikes on left.

0.5 ▲ SO Sidewinder Trail for 4WDs, ATVs, and motorbikes on right.

▼ 3.0 Kernan Cycle Trail for vehicles less than 40 inches wide on right; then trail finishes back at the Four Corners Trailhead and staging area. Turn right to exit via Corral Canyon Road.

0.0 ▲ See start of forward directions for the same starting point in reverse. Trail commences at the Four Corners Trailhead. Zero trip meter and turn southeast on small paved road; then Kernan Cycle Trail for vehicles less than 40 inches wide on left.

GPS: N32°43.50′ W116°33.50′

SOUTH COAST #38

Otay Mountain Truck Trail

Starting Point:	**California 94 at Engineer Springs, 8.5 miles west of the intersection with California 188**
Finishing Point:	**Alta Road, 2.4 miles north of the intersection of Otay Mesa Road and California 905**
Total Mileage:	**16.2 miles**
Unpaved Mileage:	**16.2 miles**
Driving Time:	**2 hours**
Elevation Range:	**700–3,400 feet**
Usually Open:	**Year-round**
Best Time to Travel:	**Year-round**
Difficulty Rating:	**2**
Scenic Rating:	**9**
Remoteness Rating:	**+0**

Special Attractions

- Easy scenic trail that can be traveled in most weather.
- Views over the international border, San Diego Bay, and the San Ysidro Mountains.

History

The name Otay may be attributed to one of two cultures. It comes from either the Kumeyaay word *etaay,* meaning "big," or the Spanish word *otero* (pronounced oh-TAY-roh) meaning "hill" or "height." An Indian rancheria called Otai is on records as early as 1775. The name transmuted into Otay shortly thereafter, first being used in this form for two land grants in 1829 and 1846. The valley had a post office for a brief period beginning in 1870.

The tiny settlement of Dulzura sits along Dulzura Creek near the start of the trail. Its name comes from the Spanish word for "sweetness." In 1869, there was a booming honey industry, which was introduced to the area by John S. Harbison. When the post office was established in 1887 and a name was needed for the settlement, Dulzura was suggested by a local lover of wildflowers. Honey Bee Ranch and Road can be found just north of Dulzura.

This trail traverses the Otay Mountain Wilderness, established by President Clinton in December 1999 to protect this mountain ecosystem.

Mirrors are on many of the blind bends along the trail to assist in seeing oncoming traffic

Views of Mexico, just 3 miles to the south of Otay Mountain Truck Trail

The area is a habitat for 20 sensitive plant and animal species, including the endangered quino checkerspot butterfly and the only known population of Mexican flannel bush. Be sure to travel only on marked trails while in the wilderness area.

The Otay Mountain Truck Trail was upgraded in 1997 at the request of the U.S. Border Patrol, which actively patrols this route known for smuggling people and drugs across the international border.

Otay Mesa was the site of the first heavier-than-air flight, made in 1883 by John Joseph Montgomery. Montgomery continued to be a pioneer in aircraft and flight until his death in 1911 from a glider accident near Evergreen in Santa Clara County.

Description

Otay Mountain Truck Trail is a well-maintained road that winds over the ridge tops of the San Ysidro Mountains. The trail is well used by the U.S. Border Patrol, which takes advantage of its ridge top views and turnouts to maintain an active presence near the international border. Expect to see their distinctive white and green vehicles along this trail. Although camping is not prohibited, you can expect a very disturbed night if you camp here.

The trail follows a narrow shelf road for almost its entire length. The surface of the road is very smooth, but there are frequent blind corners and limited passing places. Mirrors have been placed on many of these corners to assist drivers in avoiding unexpected encounters on these bends.

From the top of the ridge you can see south into Mexico, northwest to the Jamul Mountains, northeast to Lyons Peak, and east to Tecate Peak. At Doghouse Junction, the major intersection on the trail, a second well-maintained trail leads down the ridge to the north. Other side trails lead mainly to observation points used by the border patrol.

The trail finishes a short distance north of Otay Mesa Road. If traveling the trail in reverse, be aware that the trail is not marked and can be difficult to spot.

Otay Mountain is popular with hang gliders and paragliders, particularly in the winter and late spring.

Current Road Information

Bureau of Land Management
Palm Springs South Coast Field Office
PO Box 581260
690 West Garnet Avenue
North Palm Springs, CA 92258
(760) 251-4800

Map References

BLM El Cajon
USFS Cleveland National Forest
USGS 1:24,000 Dulzura, Otay Mt., Otay Mesa
1:100,000 El Cajon
Maptech CD-ROM: San Diego/Joshua Tree
Southern & Central California Atlas & Gazetteer, p. 122
California Road & Recreation Atlas, p. 116

Route Directions

▼ 0.0		From California 94 at the settlement of Engineer Springs, 8.5 miles west of the intersection with California 188, zero trip meter and turn southwest onto graded dirt road marked Marron Valley Road. Remain on main road, ignoring turns into private property on right and left.
2.5 ▲		Trail ends on California 94. Turn left for Spring Valley; turn right for Tecate.
		GPS: N32°37.88' W116°45.79'
▼ 2.1	SO	Cross through creek.
0.4 ▲	SO	Cross through creek.
▼ 2.5	TR	Turn right onto graded dirt road at the sign for Otay Truck Trail and Doghouse Junction. Zero trip meter.
0.0 ▲		Continue to the north. End of shelf road.
		GPS: N32°36.04' W116°46.16'
▼ 0.0		Continue to the west through gate. Start to climb shelf road.
6.0 ▲	TL	Pass through gate; then T-intersection with Marron Valley Road. Zero trip meter.
▼ 0.7	SO	Track on left and track on right along power lines.
5.3 ▲	SO	Track on left and track on right along power lines.
▼ 1.1	SO	Gate.
4.9 ▲	SO	Gate.
▼ 1.2	BL	Track on right.
4.8 ▲	BR	Track on left.
		GPS: N32°36.75' W116°46.88'
▼ 1.9	SO	Entering Otay Mountain Wilderness.
4.1 ▲	SO	Exiting Otay Mountain Wilderness.
		GPS: N32°36.68' W116°47.29'
▼ 2.1	SO	Track on right and track on left. Tank on right.
3.9 ▲	SO	Tank on left. Track on right and track on left.
		GPS: N32°36.66' W116°47.49'
▼ 2.7	SO	Track on left.
3.3 ▲	SO	Track on right.
▼ 4.5	SO	Track on left opposite turnout.
1.5 ▲	SO	Track on right opposite turnout.
		GPS: N32°36.10' W116°49.14'
▼ 5.4	SO	Track on left is for administrative use only.
0.6 ▲	SO	Track on right is for administrative use only.
▼ 6.0	SO	Doghouse Junction. Intersection is unmarked. Track on right to telecommunications towers;

then Minniewawa Truck Trail descends north side of ridge. Zero trip meter and continue on Otay Truck Trail.

0.0 ▲ Continue to the southeast.

GPS: N32°36.02' W116°50.46'

▼ 0.0 Continue to the southwest past track on right.

5.0 ▲ SO Track on left; then Doghouse Junction. Intersection is unmarked. Track on left is the Minniewawa Truck Trail, which descends north side of ridge; then track on left to telecommunications towers. Zero trip meter and continue on Otay Truck Trail.

▼ 0.2 SO Track on right.

4.8 ▲ SO Track on left.

▼ 0.6 SO Track on right to telecommunications tower.

4.4 ▲ SO Track on left to telecommunications tower.

▼ 1.3 BL Two tracks on right at tank.

3.7 ▲ BR Two tracks on left at tank.

GPS: N32°35.20' W116°51.16'

▼ 1.7 SO Track on right.

3.3 ▲ SO Track on left.

▼ 1.8 SO Track on left at tank.

3.2 ▲ SO Track on right at tank.

GPS: N32°34.89' W116°50.96'

▼ 2.3 SO Track on left.

2.7 ▲ SO Track on right.

▼ 2.9 SO Two tracks on left.

2.1 ▲ SO Two tracks on right.

▼ 3.1 SO Track on left.

1.9 ▲ SO Track on right.

▼ 3.4 SO Track on right.

1.6 ▲ SO Track on left.

▼ 3.9 SO Track on left is for authorized vehicles only.

1.1 ▲ SO Track on right is for authorized vehicles only.

▼ 4.4 SO Track on left.

0.6 ▲ SO Track on right.

▼ 5.0 SO Exiting Otay Mountain Wilderness at sign. Zero trip meter.

0.0 ▲ Continue to the east.

GPS: N32°34.49' W116°53.16'

▼ 0.0 Continue to the west.

2.7 ▲ SO Entering Otay Mountain Wilderness at sign. Zero trip meter.

▼ 0.2 SO Track on right.

2.5 ▲ SO Track on left.

▼ 0.4 SO Graded road on left. Exiting Otay Mountain Cooperative Land and Wildlife Management Area at sign.

2.3 ▲ SO Graded road on right. Entering Otay Mountain Cooperative Land and Wildlife Management Area at sign.

▼ 1.2 SO Track on left.

1.5 ▲ SO Track on right.

▼ 1.6 SO Gate.

1.1 ▲ SO Gate.

▼ 1.8 SO Graded road on left.

0.9 ▲ SO Graded road on right.

GPS: N32°34.76' W116°54.53'

▼ 2.3 SO End of shelf road. Track on right.

0.4 ▲ SO Track on left. Start of shelf road.

▼ 2.6 BR Graded road on left; then track on left and track on right.

0.1 ▲ BL Track on left and track on right; then graded road on right.

▼ 2.7 Trail ends at T-intersection with paved Alta

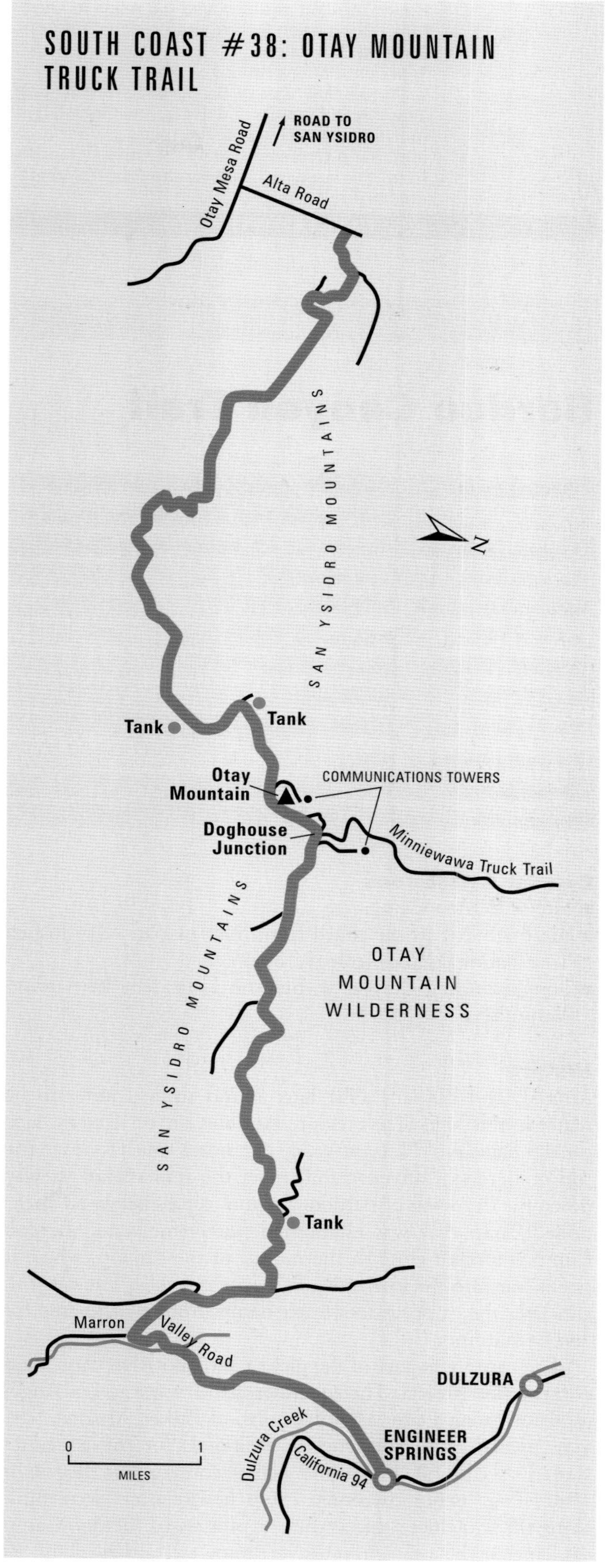

Road. Turn left and proceed 0.8 miles to Otay Mesa Road; then turn right to reach California 905 and San Ysidro.

0.0 ▲ Trail commences on paved road. From California 905, east of San Ysidro, turn east on Otay Mesa Road for 1.6 miles; then turn left (north) up Alta Road for 0.8 miles. Zero trip meter and turn east up rise on small unmarked road. The road is paved for the first 100 yards before turning to graded dirt.

GPS: N32°34.82' W116°55.09'

SOUTH COAST #39

Berdoo Canyon Trail

Starting Point:	**South Coast #40: Joshua Tree National Park Geology Tour, 7.9 miles from the start**
Finishing Point:	**Dillon Road, 6.3 miles northwest of I-10**
Total Mileage:	**14.9 miles**
Unpaved Mileage:	**14.9 miles**
Driving Time:	**2 hours**
Elevation Range:	**900–4,400 feet**
Usually Open:	**Year-round**
Best Time to Travel:	**October to June**
Difficulty Rating:	**4**
Scenic Rating:	**8**
Remoteness Rating:	**+0**

Special Attractions

- Site of Berdoo Camp.
- Alternate exit to the south from South Coast #40: Joshua Tree National Park Geology Tour.
- Long, winding canyon within the Little San Bernardino Mountains.

History

Animals and humans alike have found surface water to be scarce in this high desert region. Berdoo Canyon Trail ascends the dry bajadas of Pleasant Valley as it heads south to reach the top of Berdoo Canyon. From here, the trail snakes its way down the dry wash of Berdoo Canyon to pass below an abandoned camp that was established purely for water. Berdoo Camp is located close to the mouth of the canyon, where it opens out into the lowlands of Coachella Valley. The canyon, and later the camp, gained their names from a nickname for San Bernardino.

The camp was part of the giant Colorado River Aqueduct construction project. The aqueduct carries water to Los Angeles from Parker Dam, 15 miles north of Parker, Arizona. Survey, research, and construction proposals for the aqueduct started as early as 1923, and actual construction began in 1932. Four major divisional camp headquarters were built along the aqueduct route as the line progressed. Berdoo Camp was one of the more impressive camps established along its

Berdoo Canyon Trail has some uneven sections as it climbs the bajada

route. It was headquarters for the tunnel section under the Little San Bernardino Mountains and the area known as the East Coachella Tunnel Division. This engineering feat consisted of several tunnel sections that stretched more than 18 miles. The section immediately under Berdoo Camp was just over 5 miles long and 2,000 feet beneath the surface.

Berdoo Camp had a hospital that slowly expanded to accommodate 35 inpatients. Though many thousands of construction workers had occasion to visit the new hospital for varying degrees of injury, the safety record of the project was reportedly quite good for the period. Workers lived in dormitories at the camp, meals were served in the mess hall, and there was also a store on site. By late 1936 the short-lived hospital was out of business as most of the construction was finished. The majority of the camp was vacated about a year later; a lot of the temporary structures were sold off, uprooted, and recycled for use elsewhere. All that remains of the camp today are concrete pads, walls, roadways, and a vast tiered area on the mountainside that represents what was once a hive of burrowing activity. Throughout the course of the project, 35,000 men were employed. Construction was completed by late 1939.

By 1941, the fruit-growing industry in Coachella Valley was benefiting from the aqueduct as water was made available for citrus, raisin, and date growers. Many nearby settlements, such as Skye Valley to the northwest of this trail, got their start as a result of this major construction project. Dillon Road, at the westerly end of this trail, was just one of several roads established to access work sites.

Description

Berdoo Canyon Trail travels down the sandy, winding Berdoo Canyon through the Little San Bernardino Mountains, connecting South Coast #40: Joshua Tree National Park Geology Tour to Dillon Road. The trail leaves from the one-way loop of the geology tour. If driving the trail in reverse, you must turn left at the end of the trail to complete the loop in the required direction.

The trail initially travels south across sandy Pleasant Valley toward the Little San Bernardino Mountains, gradually ascending the bajada to enter the mouth of Berdoo Canyon. The slope's surface is easily rearranged by rainfall. This section is often uneven, with ruts and loose sand.

The route enters the canyon and remains in the wash for most of the way. The high-walled canyon has relatively little vegetation between its striking, pale-colored rock walls. The route through the mountains is twisty and dramatic. This region may appear deserted to the casual eye, but it is really habitat for a variety of life. Woodrats make their nests under overhanging boulders. Coyotes and birds of prey are frequently seen as well.

The trail is mainly easygoing, but a couple of rough, rocky sections that require careful wheel placement give the trail its 4-rating. Navigation is very easy as there are few turnoffs. The couple of places where the trail forks in the wash rejoin almost immediately.

The lower end of the trail passes near the site of Berdoo Camp. The concrete shells of the old buildings remain on a flat area slightly above the canyon at this point. The trail then joins the old paved road that served the camp to lead out of Berdoo Canyon.

No camping is allowed in the national park outside of the developed campgrounds.

Current Road Information

Joshua Tree National Park
74485 National Park Drive
Twentynine Palms, CA 92277
(760) 367-5500

Map References

BLM Palm Springs
USGS 1:24,000 Malapai Hill, Rockhouse Canyon, West Berdoo Canyon
1:100,000 Palm Springs
Maptech CD-ROM: San Diego/Joshua Tree
Southern & Central California Atlas & Gazetteer, pp. 108, 107
California Road & Recreation Atlas, p. 112
Trails Illustrated, Joshua Tree National Park (226)
Other: Tom Harrison Maps—Joshua Tree National Park Recreation map, Joshua Tree National Park Service map

Route Directions

Mileage		Direction	Description
▼ 0.0			Trail commences on South Coast #40: Joshua Tree National Park Geology Tour, 7.9 miles from the start. Zero trip meter and turn southeast on formed sandy trail at the signpost for Berdoo Canyon.
	5.0 ▲		Trail finishes on South Coast #40: Joshua Tree National Park Geology Tour, on the one-way loop section. Turn left to finish the loop and exit to Park Boulevard and Twentynine Palms.
			GPS: N33°54.62' W116°03.40'
▼ 3.3		BR	Closed vehicle trail on left is open to hikers and horses.
	1.7 ▲	BL	Closed vehicle trail on right is open to hikers and horses.
			GPS: N33°51.78' W116°02.60'
▼ 4.5		SO	Cross through wash.
	0.5 ▲	SO	Cross through wash.
▼ 5.0		SO	Track on left is off-limits to motor vehicles, but open to hikers and horses. Zero trip meter.
	0.0 ▲		Continue to the north. Exit line of wash.
			GPS: N33°50.59' W116°03.46'
▼ 0.0			Continue to the south. Enter line of wash into Berdoo Canyon.
	6.9 ▲	SO	Track on right is off-limits to motor vehicles, but open to hikers and horses. Zero trip meter.
▼ 1.1		SO	Enter Berdoo Canyon.
	5.8 ▲	SO	Exit Berdoo Canyon.
▼ 5.5		SO	Track on right up side canyon.
	1.4 ▲	SO	Track on left up side canyon.
			GPS: N33°50.15' W116°07.80'
▼ 6.2		SO	Exiting Joshua Tree National Park at sign.

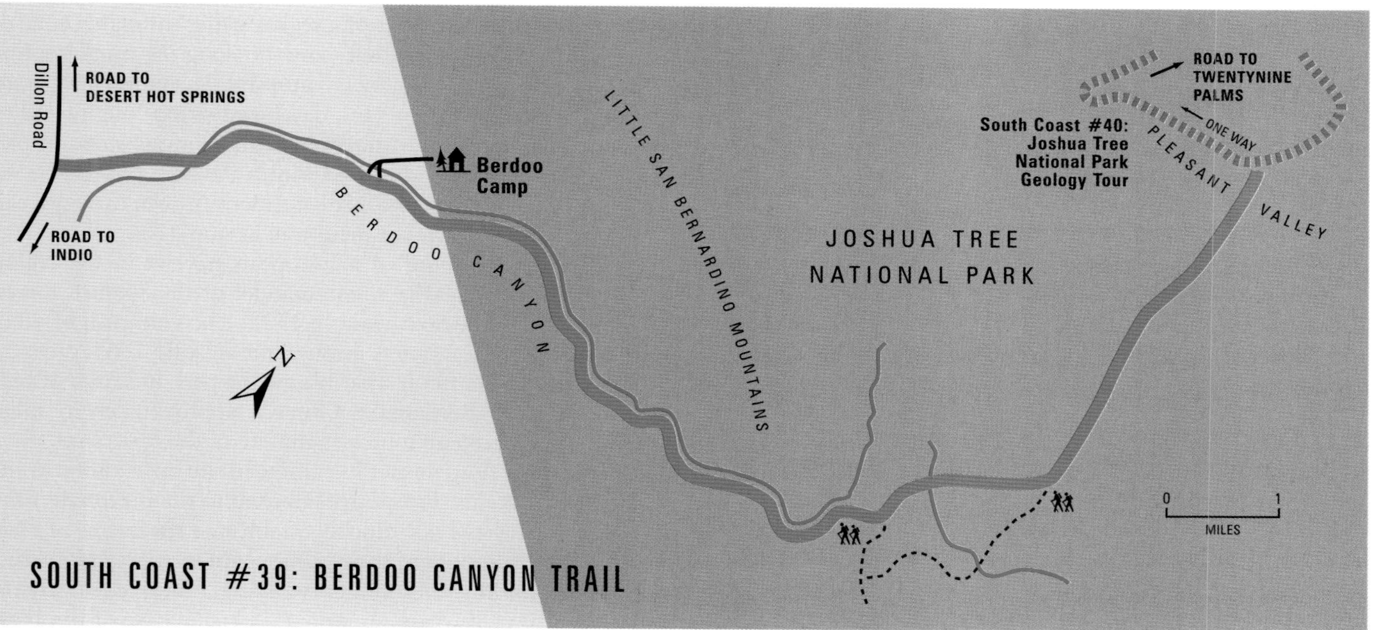

	0.7 ▲	SO	Entering Joshua Tree National Park at sign.
			GPS: N33°49.84' W116°08.25'
▼ 6.3		SO	Track on right into quarry and track on left.
	0.6 ▲	SO	Track on left into quarry and track on right.
▼ 6.8		SO	Track on right.
	0.1 ▲	SO	Track on left.
			GPS: N33°49.73' W116°08.84'
▼ 6.9		SO	Track on right climbs out of canyon to Berdoo Camp. Zero trip meter. Aqueduct runs underground in a tunnel near this point.
	0.0 ▲		Continue to the east.
			GPS: N33°49.70' W116°08.94'
▼ 0.0			Continue to the southwest.
	3.0 ▲	BR	Track on left climbs out of canyon to Berdoo Camp. Zero trip meter. Aqueduct runs underground in a tunnel near this point.
▼ 0.3		SO	Cross over old paved road that served the camp. Remain in the wash.
	2.7 ▲	SO	Cross over old paved road that served the camp. Remain in the wash.
			GPS: N33°49.63' W116°09.18'
▼ 0.6		SO	Paved road on left.
	2.4 ▲	BL	Paved road on right.
▼ 1.8		SO	Exit Berdoo Canyon and exit wash. Remain on paved road.
	1.2 ▲	SO	Enter Berdoo Canyon up wash.
			GPS: N33°48.76' W116°10.23'
▼ 3.0			Trail ends at T-intersection with Dillon Road. Turn right for Desert Hot Springs; turn left for Indio.
	0.0 ▲		Trail commences at the intersection of paved Dillon Road and Berdoo Canyon, 6.3 miles northwest of I-10 and north of Indio. Zero trip meter and turn northeast on the paved road, marked Berdoo Canyon on a white post.
			GPS: N33°47.99' W116°11.09'

SOUTH COAST #40

Joshua Tree National Park Geology Tour

Starting Point:	**Park Boulevard (also known as Loop Road), 1.6 miles west of Jumbo Rocks Campground**
Finishing Point:	**Pleasant Valley**
Total Mileage:	**11.5 miles**
Unpaved Mileage:	**11.5 miles**
Driving Time:	**2 hours**
Elevation Range:	**3,300–4,600 feet**
Usually Open:	**Year-round**
Best Time to Travel:	**October to June**
Difficulty Rating:	**2**
Scenic Rating:	**9**
Remoteness Rating:	**+0**

Ranchers' tank from the early 1900s at Squaw Tank

Special Attractions

- National park service self-guided auto tour.
- Many geologic features passed along the trail.
- Bouldering among the monzogranite inselbergs.

History

While the Joshua Tree Geology Tour takes the traveler along a short course in ancient landscape evolution, it is accurate to say that human evolution has also occurred in the area for a shorter, less obvious time span.

The date of man's earliest visit to this region is difficult to pinpoint. The Paleo-Indian period seems the most accurate to date. Crafted projectiles possibly used for game hunting are believed to date back close to 9000 B.C. Archaeological evidence of the later Middle to Late Archaic Era has also been found, revealing man's presence around A.D. 1100. A greater quantity of evidence dates to the more recent Chemehuevi, Cahuilla, and Serrano peoples. Their pictographs, petroglyphs, and bedrock mortar work areas indicate a culture in tune with the limitations of a region going through a time of desertification. Squaw Tank (stop #9 along the tour) is a fine example of a Native American campsite. The mortars worn into the bedrock near the tank developed over a long period of time, possibly up to a thousand years. Various stone implements were used to grind seed within the deep pockets we see today. Some petroglyphs, Native American rock carvings, can be seen farther down the main trail at stop #10.

The earliest record of a European traveler in the region comes from Pedro Fages, commander of the Spanish forces, who explored the Southwest in 1772. The gold rush of 1849 brought the next travelers through the area. By 1865, prospectors were closing in on what is now the park in search of hidden treasures. Rattlesnake Canyon, approximately 6 miles north of the geology tour, was the site of the first claim.

Mining activity began in earnest in the early 1880s in the Pinto Mountains. Prospectors flocked to the Pintos after the first gold strike. They quickly established the towns of Dale and New Dale close to their mines. Miners spread out across the surrounding mountains, working hundreds of claims over the next 50 years. At stop #12, at the base of the Hexie Mountains, several diggings from mining activities around the turn of the twentieth century are clearly visible. Hikers will notice many such diggings along the face of the mountain that overlooks the aptly named Pleasant Valley. The old Fried Liver Wash wagon trail, now a hiking trail, leads down Pleasant Valley past more such mining remains in the Hexie Mountains.

Three miles east of Malapai Hill, the Lost Horse Mountains rise up to the west of the valley floor. The Lost Horse Mine, located in these high-desert mountains, was discovered in 1893 by "Dutch Frank" Diebold. The miner was attempting to retrieve his lost horse, which had in fact been stolen by local rustlers known as the McHaney Gang. Diebold eventually got his horse back and moved on, finding a rich gold vein the same day. He named his find the Lost Horse Mine. The mine traded hands several times in a short period. One of its less reputable owners disappeared from his desert cabin. His desiccated corpse was found months later; he had run out of food while making one of his regular treks for supplies. A later owner, Jep Ryan from Banning, developed the mine into one of the biggest in the area. The mine had an impressive 10-stamp mill built on the hillside and it produced gold valued at more than $300,000 before closing in the early 1900s. The mountains just west of the start of this trail are called the Ryan Mountains.

Cattle grazing was brought to this region in the 1880s and continued to the 1940s. One character of note was Bill Keys, a Russian immigrant turned miner, cowboy, and sheriff. He worked hard from 1910 until his death in 1969 to develop his model ranch just north of this trail. He also operated a mine called Hidden Gold Mine. His impressive property, called the Desert Queen Ranch, is now part of Joshua Tree National Park and is listed on the National Register of Historic Places. Visitors to the property must make reservations ahead of time.

The park was originally established as Joshua Tree National Monument in 1936. In 1994 it became a National Park and gained more than 200,000 acres.

Monzogranite in the foreground has weathered faster than the black basalt Malapai Hill in the distance

Description

The scenery in Joshua Tree National Park is truly spectacular. High rock inselbergs, large piles of granite boulders, beautiful cactus gardens, and occasional California junipers growing along moist wash lines make for contrast and interest along the trail.

The geology auto tour takes visitors through Joshua Tree National Park along a scenic back road that travels past many spectacular geologic features. The trail leaves from paved Park Boulevard, west of Jumbo Rocks Campground. The first few miles of the trail are deemed suitable for passenger vehicles, but as the road descends toward Pleasant Valley, uneven ground and sandy surfaces make driving a passenger vehicle inadvisable.

California Riding and Hiking Trail crosses the Geology Tour

The stops, with the exception of Auto Tour Stop #10, are well marked. The marker post for #10 was missing at the time of driving, but a careful eye and a GPS unit will help locate the petroglyphs. A descriptive park brochure available from the visitor center offers valuable insights into features along the way.

The trail ends in a one-way loop that passes over a small dry lakebed in Pleasant Valley and past the start of South Coast #39: Berdoo Canyon Trail, which offers a moderately difficult exit to the south. The Little San Bernardino Mountains rise up behind Pleasant Valley.

The trail is the starting point for many backcountry hikes. One popular route leaves from the mines in Pleasant Valley and travels up Fried Liver Wash to the Silver Bell Mine. Another popular activity is bouldering; one recommended site is the area around Squaw Tank (stop #9).

Current Road Information

Joshua Tree National Park
74485 National Park Drive
Twentynine Palms, CA 92277
(760) 367-5500

Map References

BLM Big Bear Lake, Palm Springs
USGS 1:24,000 Queen Mt., Malapai Hill
1:100,000 Big Bear Lake, Palm Springs
Maptech CD-ROM: San Bernardino County/Mojave; San Diego/Joshua Tree
Southern & Central California Atlas & Gazetteer, pp. 98, 108
California Road & Recreation Atlas, p. 112
Trails Illustrated, Joshua Tree National Park (226)
Other: Tom Harrison Maps—Joshua Tree National Park Recreation map, Joshua Tree National Park Service map

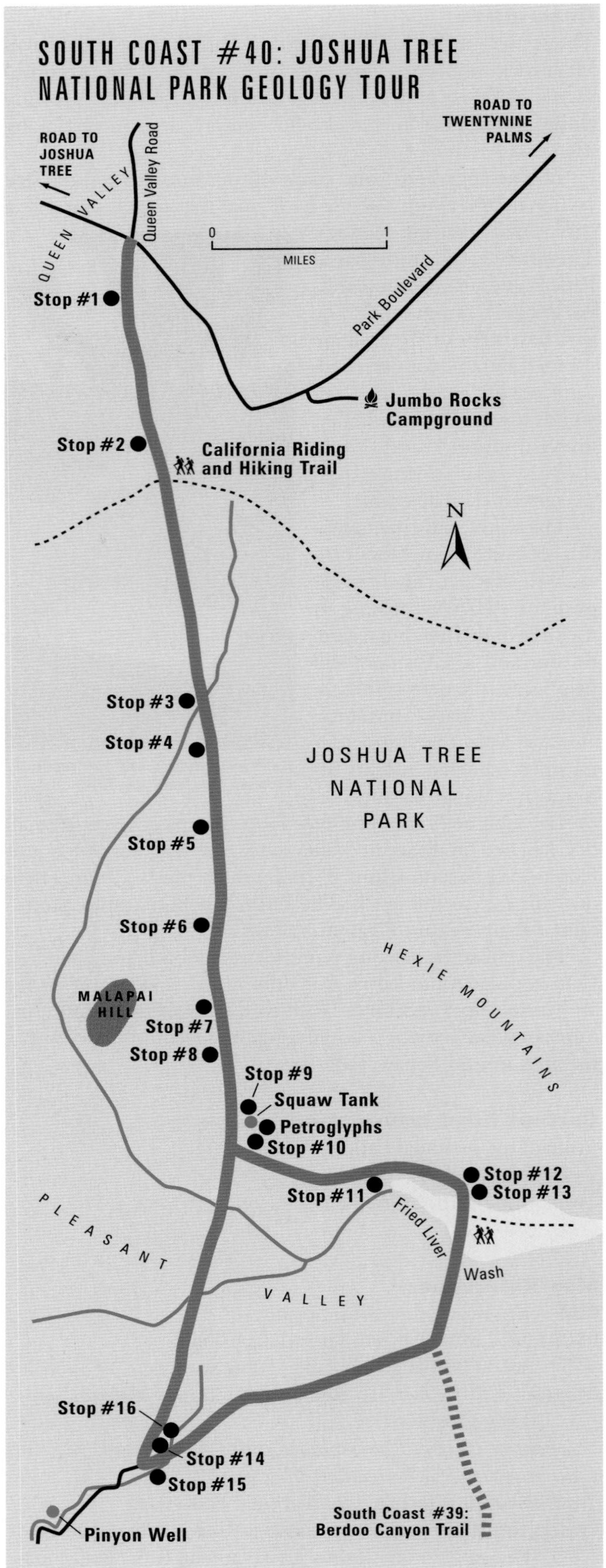

Route Directions

▼ 0.0		From Park Boulevard (also known as Loop Road), 5.5 miles west of the intersection with Pinto Basin Road (also known as El Dorado Mine Road) and 1.6 miles west of Jumbo Rocks Campground, zero trip meter and turn south on the graded dirt road, sign-posted for the Geology Tour. The area is for day use only; no overnight camping.
5.6 ▲		Trail ends at intersection with paved Park Boulevard, opposite the graded dirt Queen Valley Road. Turn left for Joshua Tree; turn right for Twentynine Palms.
		GPS: N34°00.36' W116°05.05'
▼ 0.4	SO	Turnout on right is Auto Tour Stop #1—Why A Valley?
5.2 ▲	SO	Turnout on left is Auto Tour Stop #1—Why A Valley?
		GPS: N34°00.05' W116°05.08'
▼ 1.2	SO	Turnout on right is Auto Tour Stop #2—A Raindrop Divides.
4.4 ▲	SO	Turnout on left is Auto Tour Stop #2—A Raindrop Divides.
		GPS: N33°59.35' W116°04.97'
▼ 1.5	SO	Hiking trailhead on left for the California Riding and Hiking Trail, which crosses the road at this point.
4.1 ▲	SO	Hiking trailhead on right for the California Riding and Hiking Trail, which crosses the road at this point.
		GPS: N33°59.12' W116°04.88'
▼ 2.8	SO	Turnout on right is Auto Tour Stop #3—Nature's Gutter; then cross through wash.
2.8 ▲	SO	Cross through wash; then turnout on left is Auto Tour Stop #3—Nature's Gutter.
		GPS: N33°57.97' W116°04.69'
▼ 3.1	SO	Turnout on right is Auto Tour Stop #4—Old Erosional Level.
2.5 ▲	SO	Turnout on left is Auto Tour Stop #4—Old Erosional Level.
		GPS: N33°57.71' W116°04.64'
▼ 3.6	SO	Turnout on right is Auto Tour Stop #5—Rock Piles. Road is not recommended for passenger vehicles past this point.
2.0 ▲	SO	Turnout on left is Auto Tour Stop #5—Rock Piles. Road standard improves past this point.
		GPS: N33°57.31' W116°04.63'
▼ 4.2	SO	Turnout on right is Auto Tour Stop #6—Rock Sculpture.
1.4 ▲	SO	Turnout on left is Auto Tour Stop #6—Rock Sculpture.
		GPS: N33°56.78' W116°04.63'
▼ 4.6	SO	Turnout on right is Auto Tour Stop #7—Malapai Hill.
1.0 ▲	SO	Turnout on left is Auto Tour Stop #7—Malapai Hill.
		GPS: N33°56.39' W116°04.63'
▼ 5.1	SO	Turnout on right is Auto Tour Stop #8—Alluvial Fans and Badlands.
0.5 ▲	SO	Turnout on left is Auto Tour Stop #8—Alluvial Fans and Badlands.
		GPS: N33°56.11' W116°04.58'
▼ 5.5	SO	Turnout on left is Auto Tour Stop #9—Squaw Tank.
0.1 ▲	SO	Turnout on right is Auto Tour Stop #9—Squaw Tank.
		GPS: N33°55.76' W116°04.54'
▼ 5.6	SO	Trail now enters one-way loop. Track on right is end of one-way system. Zero trip meter and begin loop.

0.0 ▲		Continue to the north.
		GPS: N33°55.65′ W116°04.56′
▼ 0.0		Continue to the southeast.
▼ 0.1	SO	Slight turnout on left is Auto Tour Stop #10—Pleasant Valley (marker post may be missing). Turnout is where the dark rocks first come down close to the road. Petroglyphs can be seen on the rocks, approximately 150 feet to the left.
		GPS: N33°55.60′ W116°04.48′
▼ 0.8	SO	Turnout on right is Auto Tour Stop #11—Debris Flows.
		GPS: N33°55.49′ W116°03.74′
▼ 1.3	SO	Turnout on left is Auto Tour Stop #12—Mines.
		GPS: N33°55.41′ W116°03.20′
▼ 1.4	SO	Turnout on left is Auto Tour Stop #13—Dry Lake.
		GPS: N33°55.35′ W116°03.20′
▼ 2.3	BR	Track on left is South Coast #39: Berdoo Canyon Trail, marked by a sign. Zero trip meter and bear right, remaining on the auto tour.
		GPS: N33°54.62′ W116°03.40′
▼ 0.0		Continue to the southwest.
▼ 1.6	SO	Enter wash; then Auto Tour Stop #14—Pinto Gneiss on right.
		GPS: N33°54.09′ W116°05.05′
▼ 1.7	BR	Auto Tour Stop #15—Pinyon Well Junction on left. Bear right and exit wash.
		GPS: N33°54.06′ W116°05.10′
▼ 1.8	SO	Turnout on right is Auto Tour Stop #16—Panoramic View.
		GPS: N33°54.15′ W116°05.07′
▼ 2.8	SO	Cross through wash.
▼ 3.3	SO	Cross through wash.
▼ 3.6		Trail ends back at the start of the loop. Turn left to exit the way you entered to Park Boulevard; turn right to exit via Berdoo Canyon.
		GPS: N33°55.65′ W116°04.56′

SOUTH COAST #41

Old Dale Road

Starting Point:	**Pinto Basin Road (also known as El Dorado Mine Road), 6 miles north of Cottonwood Campground**
Finishing Point:	**California 62 at Old Dale, 14 miles east of Twentynine Palms**
Total Mileage:	**25.8 miles, plus 1.1-mile spur to Duplex Mine**
Unpaved Mileage:	**25.8 miles, plus 1.1-mile spur**
Driving Time:	**3 hours**
Elevation Range:	**1,300–2,500 feet**
Usually Open:	**Year-round**
Best Time to Travel:	**Year-round**
Difficulty Rating:	**4**
Scenic Rating:	**8**
Remoteness Rating:	**+0**

Mission Well in Pinto Basin was once the location of a shallow lake where Native Americans found abundant food sources

Special Attractions

- Dale Mining District.
- Rough trail partly within Joshua Tree National Park that travels through the transition zone between the Colorado and Mojave Deserts.
- Desert wildflowers in spring.

History

In the early 1880s, Old Dale, located at the northern end of this trail, was the site of the earliest mining in what would become the Dale Mining District. Originally called Dale, the town was supplied with water from diggings at Dale Lake, a dry lake about 5 miles northeast where a deep well produced water. Prospectors arrived when word of a gold discovery got out. They quickly spread out across the region, ever hopeful of striking it rich.

By 1885, the Virginia Dale Mine had been established 4 miles southwest of Dale. The mine was quite successful, operating until the turn of the century. The nearby Supply Mine was a big producer after the turn of the century. It was such a good moneymaker that the town of Dale relocated closer to it, taking on the name New Dale. From then on the original Dale was called Old Dale. The new town was closer to the mountains and southeast of the Virginia Dale Mine. The site can be visited along South Coast #42: Brooklyn Mine Trail.

Another mine, the Golden Egg, suggests quite a good find. Set on the mountainside above San Bernardino Wash and below Old Dale Road, it was active from the 1940s to the 1970s. A German immigrant named Carl Schappel worked the gold mine until his death in the 1970s. The adit, very narrow in places, followed a fault line into the mountain for several hundred feet. Schappel used small ore carts to carry ore through the narrow tunnel. The remains of an earlier mill are set above the canyon of San Bernardino Wash.

Carl Schappel's cabin burned down New Year's Eve, 1962. The Marine Corps came to his aid by constructing an impressive replacement cabin in just one day. Arsonists burned his

Late winter flowers dot the landscape of Pinto Basin as a snowstorm approaches

cabin in the 1990s, some 20 years after his death, when mining had resumed at the Golden Egg.

As the main trail continues south toward Pinto Wash, the Sunset and Mission Mines are on the left among the craggy mountains. The mines were active in the 1930s. An old arrastra is located beside a latter-day mill on the floor of Pinto Wash. A well was dug to obtain water for miners working at the early structure.

The Mission Mill was built in 1934, and it too gained a new well, Mission Well, which went to a depth of 449 feet. This was also the location of the Sunrise Mill and Well. Miners from the surrounding region used both facilities. The main corrugated iron tank at Mission Mill has recently been dislodged from its old hilltop perch to expose its circular concrete base. This is now used as a helicopter landing pad. The Mission Mine reflects the pattern of many mines in the Dale Mining District, going through periods of activity and rest. This particular mine operated sporadically into the late 1990s.

Description

Two deserts meet in Joshua Tree National Park, the Colorado and the Mojave. This trail crosses the Colorado Desert section of the park, traveling through the spectacular and varied veg-

Misson Mill site in Pinto Basin

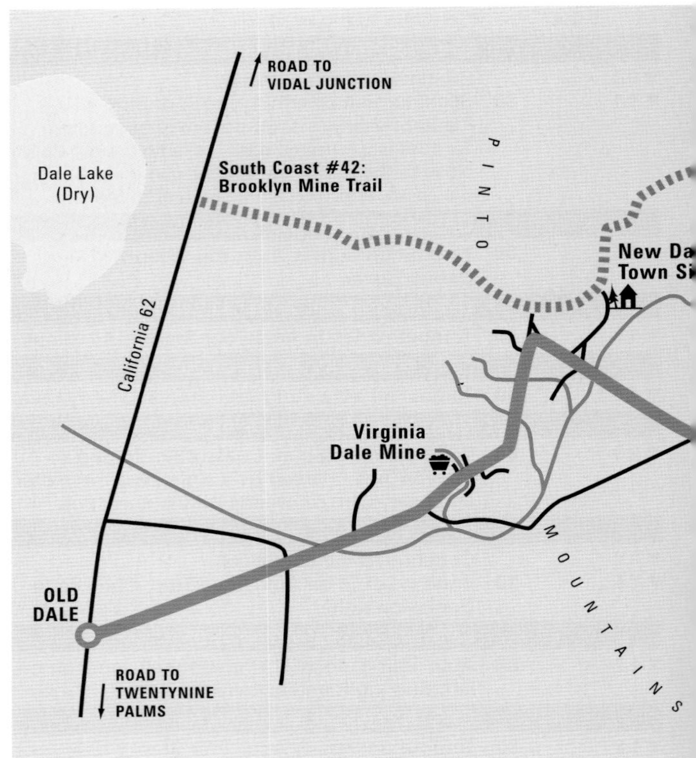

etation of Pinto Basin before entering the transition zone between the two deserts, where the distinct vegetations merge. The Colorado Desert, the hotter and drier of the two, has an abundance of cacti, chollas, ocotillos, and hardy ironwood trees. The Mojave Desert, the smallest of the five North American deserts, is famous for its Joshua trees.

The trail leaves paved Pinto Basin Road 6 miles north of the Cottonwood Visitor Center. Black Eagle Road also leaves from the same intersection; both roads are well marked. For the first 10 miles, the trail travels across a sandy bajada, descending gradually toward the base of the Pinto Mountains. This area, particularly around the washes, can be a sea of color in spring as the cacti and seasonal wildflowers bloom. Each year is different, though, because the amount of flowers depends on winter rainfall.

The trail passes Mission Well and, almost immediately afterward, the Mission Mill site. Little remains at either site. The rugged South Coast #42: Brooklyn Mine Trail leaves to the east as the road starts to climb into the Pinto Mountains, exiting Joshua Tree National Park and leaving the Colorado Desert in the basin below. This is where the trail earns its 4 rating for difficulty; the climb around the shelf road is narrow and uneven in places, with some large embedded rocks that vehicles must negotiate. However, a high-clearance 4WD with good tires should have no difficulty under normal conditions.

There are many mining remains scattered throughout the Pinto Mountains, and many small side trails invite further exploration. This route stays on the main formed trail. One spur leads over a dramatic ridge top to the Duplex Mine site high on the ridge. Little remains of the mine, but

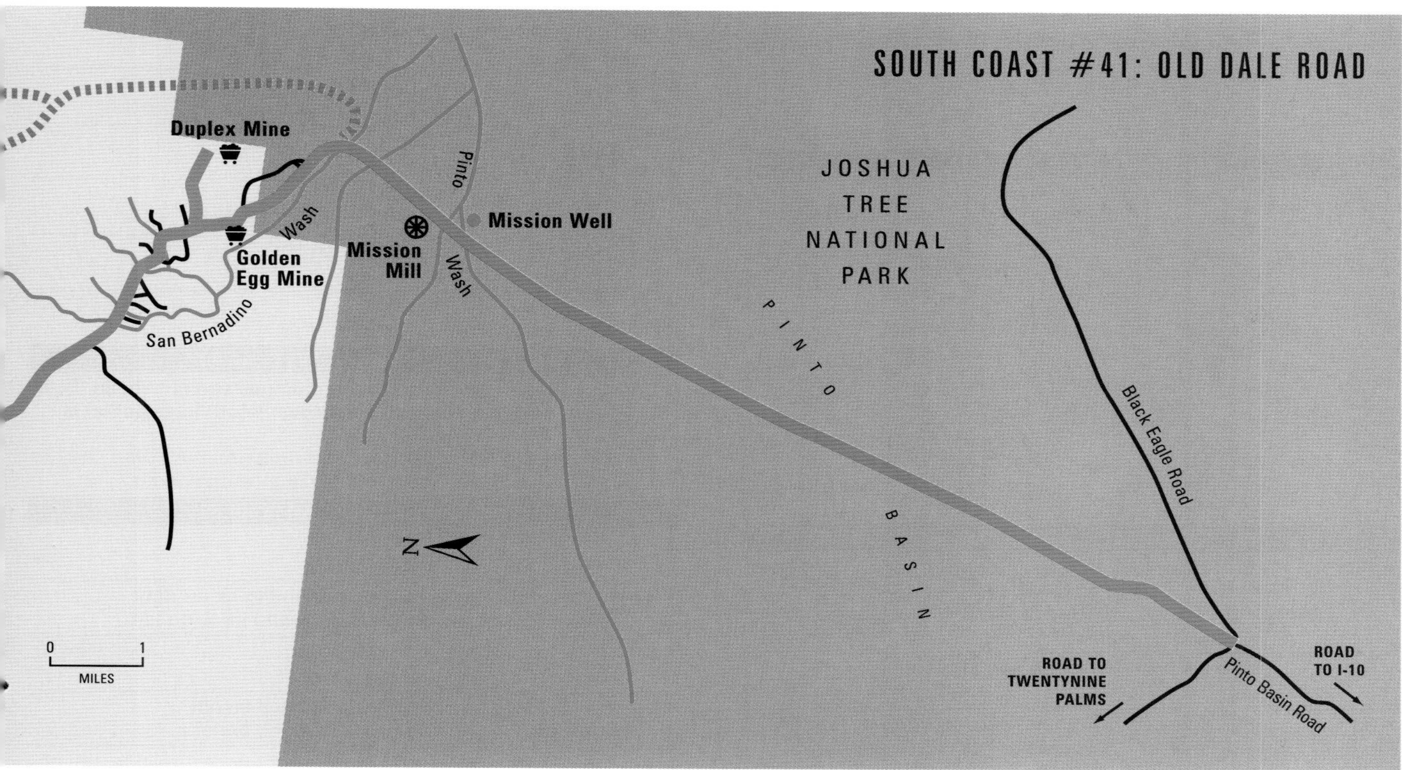

the short spur is worth the trip for the views alone. From the spur, you can look east into Pinto Basin and south back into Joshua Tree National Park.

The main route then joins Gold Crown Road, passing close to the site of New Dale. Nothing remains except piles of cans that mark the site. The trail becomes wider and easier going again as it descends to finish on California 62 at the small settlement of Old Dale.

Note that no camping is allowed within Joshua Tree National Park along this trail. However, there is a developed campground at the visitor center in Cottonwood Canyon. There is an entry fee to Joshua Tree National Park.

Current Road Information

Joshua Tree National Park
74485 National Park Drive
Twentynine Palms, CA 92277
(760) 367-5500

Bureau of Land Management
Palm Springs South Coast Field Office
PO Box 581260
690 West Garnet Avenue
North Palm Springs, CA 92258
(760) 251-4800

Map References

BLM Eagle Mts., Sheep Hole Mts.
USGS 1:24,000 Porcupine Wash, Conejo Well, San Bernardino Wash, New Dale, Humbug Mt.
1:100,000 Eagle Mts., Sheep Hole Mts.

Maptech CD-ROM: San Diego/Joshua Tree; San Bernardino County/Mojave
Southern & Central California Atlas & Gazetteer, pp. 108, 109, 98
California Road & Recreation Atlas, p. 112
Trails Illustrated, Joshua Tree National Park (226)
Other: Tom Harrison Maps—Joshua Tree National Park Recreation map, Joshua Tree National Park Service map

Route Directions

▼ 0.0		From Pinto Basin Road (also known as El Dorado Mine Road) in Joshua Tree National Park, 6 miles north of Cottonwood Campground and 13 miles north of I-10, zero trip meter and turn northeast on Old Dale Road. The start of this road is also the start of Black Eagle Road, which leaves from the same point, immediately on the right. There is a sign for both roads at the intersection.
11.5 ▲		Black Eagle Road on left, then trail ends at intersection with paved Pinto Basin Road. Turn left for I-10; turn right for Twentynine Palms.
		GPS: N33°49.68' W115°45.50'
▼ 0.7	SO	Cross through wash.
10.8 ▲	SO	Cross through wash.
▼ 9.8	SO	Mission Well on right.
1.7 ▲	SO	Mission Well on left.
		GPS: N33°57.43' W115°41.69'
▼ 9.9	SO	Cross through wide wash.
1.6 ▲	SO	Cross through wide wash.
▼ 10.1	SO	Parking on left at site of Mission Mill.
1.4 ▲	SO	Parking on right at site of Mission Mill.
		GPS: N33°57.65' W115°41.49'
▼ 10.9	SO	Cross through wide wash.
0.6 ▲	SO	Cross through wide wash.

▼ Mileage	▲ Mileage	Direction	Description
▼ 11.4		SO	Cross through San Bernardino Wash.
	0.1 ▲	SO	Cross through San Bernardino Wash.
▼ 11.5		SO	Track on right is South Coast #42: Brooklyn Mine Trail. Zero trip meter at sign.
	0.0 ▲		Continue to the south.
			GPS: N33°58.60' W115°40.82'
▼ 0.0			Continue to the north.
	2.2 ▲	SO	Track on left is South Coast #42: Brooklyn Mine Trail. Zero trip meter at sign.
▼ 0.4		SO	Track on right.
	1.8 ▲	SO	Second entrance to track on left.
▼ 0.5		SO	Second entrance to track on right.
	1.7 ▲	SO	Track on left.
▼ 0.8		SO	Trail starts to climb into Pinto Mountains.
	1.4 ▲	SO	Trail enters Pinto Basin.
▼ 1.2		SO	Leaving Joshua Tree National Park at sign.
	1.0 ▲	SO	Entering Joshua Tree National Park at sign (entry fee). No camping permitted past this point.
			GPS: N33°59.27' W115°41.64'
▼ 1.3		SO	Track on right; then second track on right into remains of small cabin.
	0.9 ▲	SO	Track on left into remains of small cabin; then second track on left.
▼ 1.6		SO	Track on left to Golden Egg Mine.
	0.6 ▲	SO	Track on right to Golden Egg Mine.
▼ 2.2		BL	Track on right; then second track on right is spur to Duplex Mine. Zero trip meter.
	0.0 ▲		Continue to the southeast.
			GPS: N33°59.79' W115°41.92'

Spur to Duplex Mine

▼ Mileage	▲ Mileage	Direction	Description
▼ 0.0			Proceed down the hill to the north.
▼ 0.2		SO	Shaft on left.
▼ 0.6		BR	Track on left on crest.
			GPS: N33°59.84' W115°41.35'
▼ 1.1		UT	Spur ends at Duplex Mine—shaft and some concrete footings remain. The mine is still posted as an active mining claim but is not restricted in any way.
			GPS: N33°59.71' W115°41.09'

Continuation of Main Trail

▼ Mileage	▲ Mileage	Direction	Description
▼ 0.0			Continue to the northwest.
	5.9 ▲	BR	Track on left is spur to Duplex Mine; then second track on left. Zero trip meter.
			GPS: N33°59.79' W115°41.92'
▼ 0.1		SO	Cross through wash; then track on left and track on right.
	5.8 ▲	SO	Track on left and track on right; then cross through wash.
			GPS: N33°59.88' W115°42.02'
▼ 0.4		BR	Track on right; then cross through wash.
	5.5 ▲	BL	Cross through wash; then track on left.
			GPS: N34°00.05' W115°42.08'
▼ 0.6		SO	Track on left.
	5.3 ▲	SO	Track on right.
▼ 0.7		SO	Track on right and track on left.
	5.2 ▲	SO	Track on left and track on right.
▼ 0.9		SO	Cross through wash; then track on left.
	5.0 ▲	SO	Track on right; then cross through wash.
			GPS: N34°00.25' W115°42.52'
▼ 1.0		SO	Track on right; then track on left.
	4.9 ▲	SO	Track on right; then track on left.
▼ 1.2		SO	Track on left.
	4.7 ▲	SO	Track on right.
▼ 1.3		SO	Track on left; then cross through wash.
	4.6 ▲	SO	Cross through wash; then track on right.
▼ 1.6		SO	Track on left.
	4.3 ▲	SO	Track on right.
▼ 1.7		SO	Track on left.
	4.2 ▲	SO	Track on right.
▼ 1.9		SO	Well-used track on left.
	4.0 ▲	BL	Well-used track on right.
▼ 3.2		SO	Track on left.
	2.7 ▲	SO	Track on right.
			GPS: N34°01.45' W115°44.40'
▼ 3.8		BR	Well-used track continues straight ahead. Bear right onto Gold Crown Road. Intersection is unmarked.
	2.1 ▲	BL	Well-used track on right. Bear left onto Old Dale Road. Intersection is unmarked.
			GPS: N34°01.88' W115°44.69'
▼ 4.4		SO	Track on right.
	1.5 ▲	SO	Track on left.
▼ 5.0		SO	Small track on left and track on right.
	0.9 ▲	SO	Small track on right and track on left.
▼ 5.1		SO	Cross through wash.
	0.8 ▲	SO	Cross through wash.
▼ 5.3		SO	Track on right and track on left.
	0.6 ▲	SO	Track on right and track on left.
▼ 5.4		SO	Well-used track on right goes 1 mile to site of New Dale.
	0.5 ▲	BR	Well-used track on left goes 1 mile to site of New Dale.
			GPS: N34°03.19' W115°43.91'
▼ 5.8		BL	Well-used track on right.
	0.1 ▲	BR	Well-used track on left.
			GPS: N34°03.51' W115°43.72'
▼ 5.9		BL	Well-used track on right. Zero trip meter.
	0.0 ▲		Continue to the southeast.
			GPS: N34°03.58' W115°43.75'
▼ 0.0			Continue to the west.
	6.2 ▲	BR	Well-used track on left. Bear right onto well-used track at stone marker for Vail Mining Co. Zero trip meter.
▼ 0.2		SO	Track on right.
	6.0 ▲	SO	Track on left.
▼ 0.3		SO	Cross through wash; then track on right.
	5.9 ▲	SO	Track on left; then cross through wash.
▼ 0.5		SO	Cross through wash; then track on right.
	5.7 ▲	SO	Track on left; then cross through wash.
▼ 0.8		SO	Track on right; then cross through wash.
	5.4 ▲	SO	Cross through wash; then track on left.
▼ 0.9		SO	Track on right.
	5.3 ▲	SO	Track on left.
▼ 1.1		SO	Cross through wash.
	5.1 ▲	SO	Cross through wash.
▼ 1.2		SO	Several tracks on left and right at mines.
	5.0 ▲	SO	Several tracks on left and right at mines.
			GPS: N34°03.69' W115°45.06'
▼ 1.4		SO	Cross through wash; then track on right.
	4.8 ▲	SO	Track on left; then cross through wash.
▼ 1.5		SO	Track on left and adit on right.
	4.7 ▲	SO	Track on right and adit on left.
▼ 1.6		SO	Track on left and track on right.
	4.6 ▲	SO	Track on left and track on right.

▼ 1.7		SO	Track on left and track on right to Virginia Dale Mine.
	4.5 ▲	SO	Track on right and track on left to Virginia Dale Mine.
			GPS: N34°04.02′ W115°45.37′
▼ 1.8		SO	Cross over wash; then two tracks on right.
	4.4 ▲	SO	Two tracks on left; then cross over wash.
▼ 2.2		SO	Track on left and track on right.
	4.0 ▲	SO	Track on left and track on right.
▼ 2.3		SO	Track on right; then track on left.
	3.9 ▲	SO	Track on right; then track on left.
▼ 2.4		SO	Track on left.
	3.8 ▲	BL	Track on right.
▼ 2.5		SO	Track on left.
	3.7 ▲	SO	Track on right.
▼ 3.2		SO	Track on right.
	3.0 ▲	SO	Track on left.
▼ 3.5		SO	Cross through wide wash.
	2.7 ▲	SO	Cross through wide wash.
▼ 3.8		SO	Track on right and track on left.
	2.4 ▲	SO	Track on right and track on left.
▼ 4.8		SO	Track on right and track on left.
	1.4 ▲	SO	Track on right and track on left.
▼ 6.2			Trail ends at T-intersection with paved California 62 at the settlement of Old Dale. Turn left for Twentynine Palms; turn right for Vidal Junction.
	0.0 ▲		Trail commences on California 62, 14 miles east of Twentynine Palms and 0.5 miles east of mile marker 48, at the settlement of Old Dale. Zero trip meter and turn southeast on wide dirt road marked Gold Crown Road.
			GPS: N34°07.33′ W115°47.64′

SOUTH COAST #42

Brooklyn Mine Trail

Starting Point:	**California 62, 4.8 miles east of Gold Crown Road, 18.8 miles east of Twentynine Palms**
Finishing Point:	**South Coast #41: Old Dale Road, 11.5 miles northeast of Pinto Basin Road**
Total Mileage:	**12.3 miles, plus 1.2-mile spur to Brooklyn Mine**
Unpaved Mileage:	**12.3 miles, plus 1.2-mile spur**
Driving Time:	**3.5 hours**
Elevation Range:	**1,200–2,500 feet**
Usually Open:	**Year-round**
Best Time to Travel:	**October to June**
Difficulty Rating:	**6**
Scenic Rating:	**9**
Remoteness Rating:	**+1**

Special Attractions

- Challenging trail through the rugged Pinto Mountains.
- Extensive remains of the Brooklyn and other mines.

History

Brooklyn Mine Trail traverses the Pinto Mountains along a route that developed as mining took place from the late 1800s to the mid-1900s. Digging in this region was quite intense. Names such as the Lorman, Carlyle, Supply, Ivanhoe, O.K., Gold Standard, Los Angeles, Gold Rose, Rose of Peru, Moose, Goldenrod, and of course Brooklyn Mine popped up as prospectors searched the rocky mountainsides near this trail.

The Supply Mine, near the northern end of the trail, was one of the district's more prominent gold mines during the 1910s; it occupied an area of 350 acres and supported a town of more than 2,000 people. The old town of Dale to the north was moved closer to the Supply Mine and renamed New Dale to avoid unnecessary travel for miners between work and home. By 1920, the Supply Mine was exhausted and residents moved on. Some concrete foundations of the old mine buildings can still be seen.

Supply Mine was the biggest producing mine of Dale Mining District

The Carlyle Mine, about 1 mile east of the trail, is set on the side of a mountain. Activity occurred here in varying degrees from shortly after the turn of the century to the 1930s. The shafts within the mountain are extremely deep and some tunnels are up to 2,550 feet long. Ore cars followed intricate routes within the tunnels, finally making their way down the mountainside to a mill at the base of the mountain.

Another big producer along this trail was the O.K. Mine, set in the Pinto Mountains just southeast of New Dale. It was operated sporadically well into the twentieth century.

The Iron Age Mine, 3 miles to the east of this trail, was an impressive iron mine operated from the 1930s to the 1960s. Resourceful miners used diesel and cow manure as explosives. As with many mines of the World War II era, the War Department was one of its big customers.

The Brooklyn Mine was discovered in 1893, though it was not fully operational until the turn of the century. Cyanide leaching tanks were installed, and the mine remained active until about 1915. It continued to operate at a lower level until the 1930s. A 3-stamp mill served the Brooklyn Mine and the nearby Los Angeles Mine, which also remained in operation in the 1930s.

Artifact collectors and people who have a low regard for the mines and Mother Nature have contributed to the slow decline of the historic mining ruins that lie within these once bustling desert mountains. Please leave all artifacts in place for future generations to enjoy. Take extreme care if exploring the old remains. The area is riddled with unstable ground and hidden shafts.

Description

The Brooklyn Mine Trail is short, but extremely slow going for most of its 12 miles. The trail's difficulty rating of 6 does not apply to the whole trail, but even the easier parts at the start and finish are rough going, with embedded rocks and an uneven trail surface.

The trail leaves California 62 up a sandy wash, but quickly becomes a well-used formed trail that leads across the bajada into the Pinto Mountains up a V-shaped valley. Once the trail starts to climb along the narrow rough shelf road, the difficulty quickly increases. There are no passing places for nearly a mile, and the trail has a number of fist-size rocks that make traction difficult. Add some narrow sections where erosion has reduced the road to a scant vehicle width, some large embedded rocks to climb over, and tight clearance, and you will see how the trail earns its difficulty rating. Drivers will need to watch side panels along this trail. There are a couple of sections where a climb over boulders will tilt your vehicle toward the large rocks on the opposite side of the trail. Some of these rocks bear marks of vehicle paint, showing where others were not so careful. Wide vehicles will need to take special care. Use a spotter to help with wheel placement and watch side panels when necessary.

The trail eases off as it passes beside the first of the many mines. However, there are sporadic rocky climbs and difficult 6-rated sections all along the trail until it enters Joshua Tree National Park at the far end.

The remains of the Supply Mine are on a saddle; a brick ruin stands to the west of the trail. On the east side, concrete foundations set in a line were most probably the bases of the miners' cottages.

The trail passes through the site of New Dale and close to South Coast #41: Old Dale Road, an easier route through the Pinto Mountains than this one. Little remains of New Dale these days—only piles of tin cans and some rubble mark the site.

The narrow, rocky shelf road winds up the creosote-lined canyon into the Pinto Mountains north of the New Dale town site

The trail continues through the Pinto Mountains before descending to enter a rubble-filled wash. The spur to the Brooklyn Mine leads up the wash, passing beside the Gold Rose, the Rose of Peru, and Los Angeles Mines, before continuing to the Brooklyn Mine. All of these mines have remains that are both substantial and photogenic. The climb out of the wash to the Los Angeles and Brooklyn Mines requires care. Again, it has a very loose, low-traction surface, with uneven camber and large embedded rocks to catch the unwary.

The trail finishes by continuing down the same wash to cross a bajada, before joining South Coast #41: Old Dale Road, north of the site of Mission Well.

Current Road Information

Joshua Tree National Park
74485 National Park Drive
Twentynine Palms, CA 92277
(760) 367-5500

Bureau of Land Management
Palm Springs South Coast Field Office
PO Box 581260
690 West Garnet Avenue
North Palm Springs, CA 92258
(760) 251-4800

Map References

BLM Sheep Hole Mts., Eagle Mts.
USGS 1:24,000 New Dale, San Bernardino Wash
1:100,000 Sheep Hole Mts., Eagle Mts.
Maptech CD-ROM: San Diego/Joshua Tree; San Bernardino County/Mojave
Southern & Central California Atlas & Gazetteer, pp. 98, 99, 109
California Road & Recreation Atlas, p. 112
Trails Illustrated, Joshua Tree National Park (226)
Other: Tom Harrison Maps—Joshua Tree National Park Recreation map, Joshua Tree National Park Service map (trail not marked on this map)

Route Directions

▼ 0.0		From California 62, 4.8 miles east of Gold Crown Road and 0.4 miles east of mile marker 53, zero trip meter and turn south up wide, sandy wash. The intersection is unmarked, but tire tracks can be seen traveling up the wash. The Pinto Mountains are straight ahead.
3.5 ▲		Trail ends on California 62. Turn left for Twentynine Palms; turn right for Vidal Junction.
		GPS: N34°06.82' W115°42.57'
▼ 0.1	BL	Bear left, remaining in line of wash.
3.4 ▲	SO	Remain in sandy wash.
▼ 0.6	SO	Exit line of wash.
2.9 ▲	SO	Enter line of wash.
▼ 0.8	SO	Small track on left and small track on right.
2.7 ▲	SO	Small track on left and small track on right.
		GPS: N34°06.13' W115°42.67'
▼ 1.4	SO	Track on left.

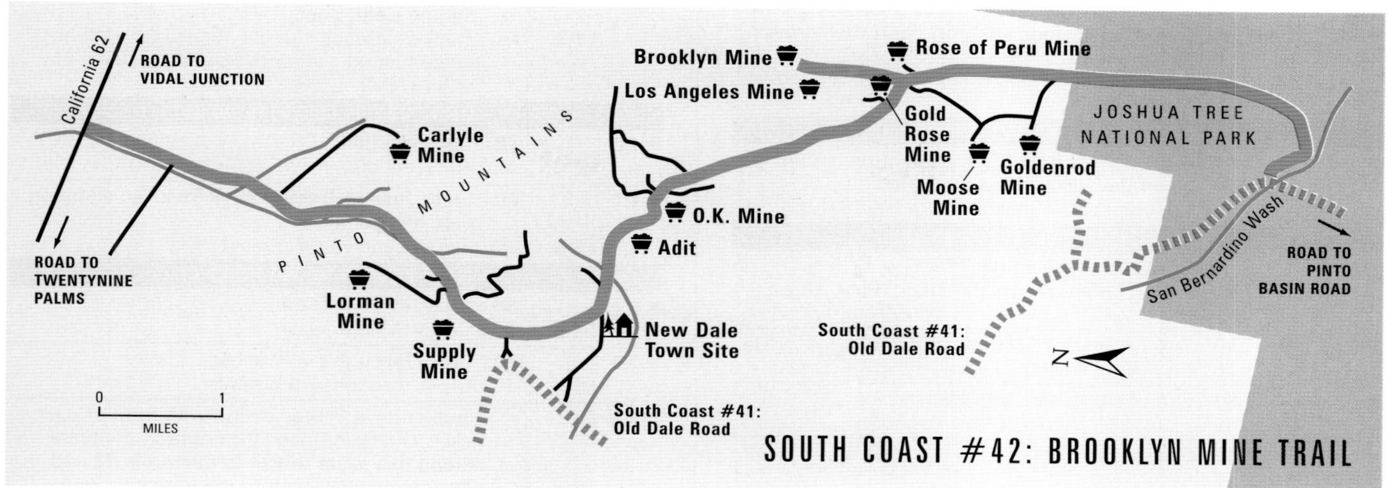

2.1 ▲ SO Track on right.

▼ 1.5 SO Cross through wash.
2.0 ▲ SO Cross through wash.

▼ 1.6 BR Well-used track on left. Bear right toward pass in Pinto Mountains.
1.9 ▲ SO Well-used track on right.

GPS: N34°05.45' W115°42.78'

▼ 1.8 SO Enter line of wash.
1.7 ▲ SO Exit line of wash.

▼ 1.9 SO Small track on right.
1.6 ▲ SO Small track on left.

▼ 2.2 SO Exit line of wash.
1.3 ▲ SO Enter line of wash.

GPS: N34°04.94' W115°42.80'

▼ 2.5 SO Start of shelf road up canyon.
1.0 ▲ SO Descent along shelf road ends.

GPS: N34°04.73' W115°42.74'

▼ 2.9 SO Cross through wash.
0.6 ▲ SO Cross through wash.

GPS: N34°04.42' W115°42.89'

▼ 3.3 SO End of climb up shelf road. Track on right.
0.2 ▲ BR Track on left. Start to descend down shelf road.

GPS: N34°04.13' W115°43.08'

▼ 3.4 BL Two tracks on right to Lorman Mine.
0.1 ▲ BR Two tracks on left to Lorman Mine.

▼ 3.5 SO Remains of Supply Mine on saddle, brick ruin on right, and concrete footings on left. Zero trip meter. Track on left on saddle climbs to mines.
0.0 ▲ Continue to the northeast.

GPS: N34°04.04' W115°43.23'

▼ 0.0 Continue to the southwest past track on right to Supply Mine.
2.9 ▲ SO Track on left to Supply Mine; then remains of Supply Mine on saddle, brick ruin on left, and concrete footings on right. Track on right on saddle climbs to mines. Zero trip meter.

▼ 0.1 BL Track forks and rejoins almost immediately (left is easier).
2.8 ▲ SO Track forks and rejoins almost immediately (right is easier).

▼ 0.2 SO Track on right.
2.7 ▲ SO Track on left.

▼ 0.6 BL Well-used track on right goes to South Coast #41: Old Dale Road.
2.3 ▲ SO Well-used track on left goes to South Coast #41: Old Dale Road.

GPS: N34°03.59' W115°43.50'

▼ 0.7 SO Cross through wash.
2.2 ▲ SO Cross through wash.

▼ 0.8 SO Cross through wash.
2.1 ▲ SO Cross through wash.

▼ 1.1 SO Cross through wash.
1.8 ▲ SO Cross through wash.

▼ 1.3 SO Cross through wash.
1.6 ▲ SO Cross through wash.

▼ 1.5 TL Track on right. Turn left onto well-used, unmarked formed trail; then track on right at site of New Dale.
1.4 ▲ BR Track on left at site of New Dale; then track on left. Turn right onto well-used, unmarked formed trail.

GPS: N34°02.97' W115°43.08'

▼ 1.6 SO Track on left; then enter wash.
1.3 ▲ SO Exit wash; then track on right.

▼ 1.7 SO Exit wash.
1.2 ▲ SO Enter wash.

▼ 1.9 BR Track on left enters wash. Bear right up shelf road past old Vail Mining Company sign.
1.0 ▲ SO Track on right at old Vail Mining Company sign enters wash. End of shelf road.

GPS: N34°02.99' W115°42.57'

▼ 2.2 SO Adit on right.
0.7 ▲ SO Adit on left.

▼ 2.4 BL End of shelf road. Scattered mining remains. O.K. Mine on right.
0.5 ▲ BR Scattered mining remains. O.K. Mine on left. Start of shelf road.

GPS: N34°02.75' W115°42.20'

▼ 2.5 BR Track on left.
0.4 ▲ SO Track on right.

▼ 2.6 SO Two tracks on left and two tracks on right. Continue straight, heading slightly downhill to the east. Mine workings and buildings on both sides of the trail.
0.3 ▲ SO Two tracks on left and two tracks on right. Continue to the west. Mine workings and buildings on both sides of the trail.

GPS: N34°02.74' W115°42.05'

▼ 2.7 SO Track on left; then cross through wash.
0.2 ▲ SO Cross through wash; then track on right.

▼ 2.8 SO Track on left; then shaft on right; then cross through wash.
0.1 ▲ BL Cross through wash; then bear left immediately after shaft.

GPS: N34°02.63' W115°41.87'

▼ 2.9 SO Track on left. Bear right, joining track running down the valley. Zero trip meter.
0.0 ▲ Continue to the northwest.

GPS: N34°02.56' W115°41.83'

▼ 0.0 Continue to the south.
2.0 ▲ BL Track continues straight ahead. Bear left on unmarked track toward shaft. Zero trip meter.

▼ 0.1 SO Trail begins to descend shelf road.
1.9 ▲ SO End of shelf road.

▼ 0.8 SO End of shelf road. Enter wash.
1.2 ▲ SO Exit wash. Start to climb shelf road.

▼ 1.1 SO Exit wash.
0.9 ▲ SO Enter wash.

▼ 1.3 SO Cross through wash.
0.7 ▲ SO Cross through wash.

▼ 1.6 SO Cross through wash.
0.4 ▲ SO Cross through wash.

▼ 1.8 SO Cross through wash; then small track on left to mine; then cross through wash.
0.2 ▲ SO Cross through wash; then small track on right to mine; then cross through wash.

GPS: N34°01.31' W115°40.84'

▼ 1.9 SO Enter wash.
0.1 ▲ SO Exit wash.

▼ 2.0 TR Faint track on right down wash. Bearing left at this point is the start of spur to Brooklyn Mine. This intersection is extremely indistinct and easy to miss. Zero trip meter.
0.0 ▲ Continue to the southwest.

GPS: N34°01.22' W115°40.68'

Spur to Brooklyn Mine

▼ 0.0 Proceed to the northeast.

GPS: N34°01.22' W115°40.68'

▼ 0.3 SO Remains of Gold Rose Mine on left. Rose of Peru Mine on right of wash. Small track on right.

GPS: N34°01.39' W115°40.64'

▼ 0.4 SO Ruins on left and two tracks on right.
▼ 0.5 SO Track on right; then track on left.

GPS: N34°01.57' W115°40.62'

▼ 0.6 SO Exit wash and start to climb shelf road; track on left.

GPS: N34°01.64' W115°40.64'

▼ 0.8 SO Los Angeles Mine shafts around mountainside on left.
▼ 1.2 UT Spur ends at the ruin below Brooklyn Mine.

GPS: N34°02.13' W115°40.71'

Continuation of Main Trail

▼ 0.0 Continue to the south and immediately bear left past track on right.
3.9 ▲ TL Track on left; then trail continues ahead in the wash and is the start of the spur to the Brooklyn Mine. Turn left toward the left-hand edge of the wash and zero trip meter. This intersection is extremely indistinct and easy to miss.

GPS: N34°01.22' W115°40.68'

▼ 0.2 TR Bear left out of wash; then T-intersection on top of rise. Turn right at the white mining claim post.
3.7 ▲ TL Track continues straight ahead. Turn left at the white mining claim post and drop down to enter wash.

GPS: N34°01.08' W115°40.55'

▼ 1.2 SO Track on right.
2.7 ▲ BR Track on left.

▼ 1.4 SO Enter Joshua Tree National Park. No camping past this point.
2.5 ▲ SO Exit Joshua Tree National Park.

GPS: N34°00.10' W115°40.33'

▼ 2.7 SO Cross through wash.
1.2 ▲ SO Cross through wash.

▼ 2.9 SO Cross through two washes.
1.0 ▲ SO Cross through two washes.

▼ 3.9 Trail ends at T-intersection with South Coast #41: Old Dale Road. Turn right to continue along this route to exit to California 62 and Twentynine Palms; turn left to exit to Pinto Basin Road and I-10.
0.0 ▲ Trail commences on South Coast #41: Old Dale Road, 11.5 miles northeast of Pinto Basin Road (also called El Dorado Mine Road on some maps). Zero trip meter at wooden sign for Brooklyn Mine Jeep Trail and turn southeast on well-used formed trail.

GPS: N33°58.60' W115°40.82'

SOUTH COAST #43

Pinkham Canyon Trail

Starting Point:	**Pinto Basin Road (also known as El Dorado Mine Road), opposite Cottonwood Visitor Center**
Finishing Point:	**I-10 at frontage road exit, 17 miles east of Indio**
Total Mileage:	**21.5 miles**
Unpaved Mileage:	**21.5 miles**
Driving Time:	**2.5 hours**
Elevation Range:	**1,400–3,400 feet**
Usually Open:	**Year-round**
Best Time to Travel:	**October to June**
Difficulty Rating:	**3**
Scenic Rating:	**8**
Remoteness Rating:	**+1**

Special Attractions

- Trail crosses the transition zone between the Colorado and Mojave Deserts.
- Sandy canyon trail within Joshua Tree National Park.

History

The northeasterly end of Pinkham Canyon Trail ascends the upper reaches of Smoke Tree Wash, so named for the grayish-green smoke trees that grow in the line of the wash. Smoke

Tree Wash is part of the catchment area that drains northwest into the vast Pinto Basin, north of the Eagle Mountains. The name Pinto is a reminder of early inhabitants of the region, the Pinto people. However, the basin was named for the varied, speckled array of colors in the Pinto and Eagle Mountains that surround the massive basin. *Pinto,* like the namesake horse, is Spanish for "speckled" or "mottled."

The Pinto Basin is lower in elevation than the western end of Joshua Tree National Park. It represents a fine example of the Colorado Desert—a drier, lower elevation, hotter desert than the western section of the park, which is part of the higher landscape of the Mojave Desert. In the Mojave, the yucca has evolved as a representative plant of the wetter, cooler climatic conditions of that area. In the lower Pinto region, the creosote is king of the plants, as can be seen when dropping from Smoke Tree Wash into the creosote-lined bajadas of Pinto Basin.

The Pinto people were some of the earliest inhabitants of the Southwest. They roamed the Pinto Valley and used its river as a food-gathering source. The Pinto Valley has evolved to support the plant life we see today. Evidence of habitation has been left behind as rock art scattered throughout the region on patina rocks.

Prospectors arrived in this area long after Pinto Valley became a dry basin. They observed the shape of the peak near Cottonwood Spring at the northeastern end of this trail. Thinking it resembled the rolling curves of an elephant's back, they named the peak and their gold mine Mastodon. The mine, active from the 1910s to 1930s, was just southeast of today's Cottonwood Visitor Center near the base of Mastodon Peak. Shafts and some ruins remain. Moorten's Mill and Winona Mill were also located in this region.

Miners used trickling water at Cottonwood Spring for their mills. Teamsters, who took supplies from Mecca to the mines in the Pinto Mountains, also made use of the water source.

The Cahuilla Indians who roamed this region for many generations knew where to find water in these desert mountains. They camped at this spring and left bedrock mortar marks in nearby rocks.

Description

Pinkham Canyon is an easy to moderate 4WD trail within Joshua Tree National Park. Park fees are applicable. The trail leaves opposite the Cottonwood Visitor Center, which is an excellent place to gather park information, inquire about road conditions, or stroll through the native plant garden trying to identify the vegetation commonly found within the park.

The trail is initially graded to provide access to a park service road, before becoming a single-width, formed trail. It is well used and easy to follow as it crosses a gently sloping bajada and winds through abundant stands of Mojave yuccas toward a gap in the Cottonwood Mountains. The prominent peak to the north is Monument Mountain.

The trail enters Pinkham Canyon Wash, leaving the Cottonwood Mountains to the south. The surface is loose and sandy in spots, but under normal conditions it is an easy route for a high-clearance 4WD.

Navigation is easy within the canyon. There is only one side trail—the well-marked trail down Thermal Canyon. Pinkham Canyon is not particularly deep or narrow, but it is extremely pretty, and the drive adds a beautiful new dimension to the wide-ranging park views that most visitors to Joshua Tree National Park experience.

Starting to descend Pinkham Canyon Trail through the Cottonwood Mountains of the Colorado Desert

The trail exits close to I-10 and follows along a graded road to the freeway entrance.

Current Road Information

Joshua Tree National Park
74485 National Park Drive
Twentynine Palms, CA 92277
(760) 367-5500

Map References

BLM Eagle Mts.
USGS 1:24,000 Cottonwood Spring, Porcupine Wash, Washington Wash, Cottonwood Basin
1:100,000 Eagle Mts.
Maptech CD-ROM: San Diego/Joshua Tree
Southern & Central California Atlas & Gazetteer, p. 108
California Road & Recreation Atlas, p. 112
Trails Illustrated, Joshua Tree National Park (226)
Other: Tom Harrison Maps—Joshua Tree National Park Recreation map, Joshua Tree National Park Service map

Route Directions

▼ 0.0 From Pinto Basin Road (also known as El Dorado Mine Road) in Joshua Tree National Park, 7 miles north of I-10 and opposite the Cottonwood Visitor Center, zero trip meter and turn northwest on the sandy Pinkham Canyon Jeep Trail. The road is marked for Pinkham Canyon and I-10 immediately after the turn.

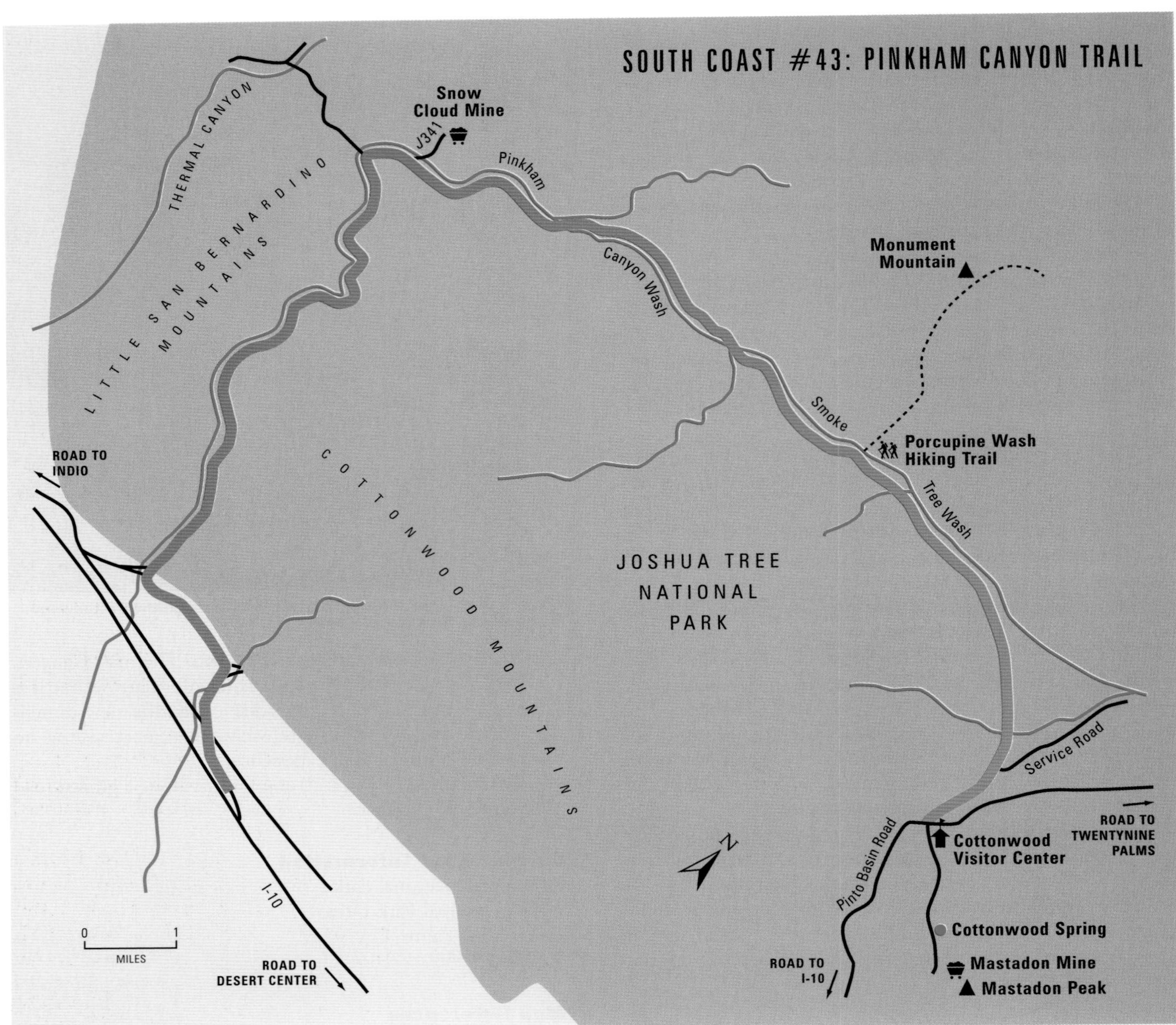

12.0 ▲ Trail ends on Pinto Basin Road opposite the Cottonwood Visitor Center. Turn left for Twentynine Palms; turn right for I-10.

GPS: N33°44.88′ W115°49.45′

▼ 1.0 BL Service road ahead at gate. Follow sign for Pinkham Canyon.
11.0 ▲ BR Service road on left at gate.

GPS: N33°45.74′ W115°49.35′

▼ 1.2 SO Cross through wash.
10.8 ▲ SO Cross through wash.

▼ 3.9 SO Cross through wash.
8.1 ▲ SO Cross through wash.

▼ 4.9 SO Porcupine Wash Hiking Trail on right is marked with post 44.
7.1 ▲ SO Porcupine Wash Hiking Trail on left is marked with post 44.

GPS: N33°46.91′ W115°52.99′

▼ 6.9 SO Enter down wash.
5.1 ▲ SO Exit wash.

GPS: N33°46.75′ W115°54.99′

▼ 8.9 BL Wash joins on right (closed to vehicles).
3.1 ▲ BR Wash joins on left (closed to vehicles).

GPS: N33°46.61′ W115°56.96′

▼ 11.3 SO Track on right goes toward Snow Cloud Mine and is marked J 341 for 4WDs, ATVs, and motorbikes. The marker is hard to spot.
0.7 ▲ SO Track on left goes toward Snow Cloud Mine and is marked J 341 for 4WDs, ATVs, and motorbikes. The marker is hard to spot.

GPS: N33°45.82′ W115°58.98′

▼ 12.0 TL Track on right goes to Thermal Canyon. Zero trip meter and turn left, following sign for Pinkham Canyon.
0.0 ▲ Continue to the north.

GPS: N33°45.48′ W115°59.53′

▼ 0.0 Continue to the southeast.
6.5 ▲ TR Track on left goes to Thermal Canyon. Zero

			trip meter and turn right, following sign for Pinkham Canyon.
▼ 3.7		SO	Exiting Pinkham Canyon, which starts to widen out.
	2.8 ▲	SO	Entering Pinkham Canyon.
▼ 5.4		SO	Exit wash, but remain in line of wash.
	1.1 ▲	SO	Enter wash.
▼ 6.0		SO	Exit line of wash.
	0.5 ▲	SO	Enter line of wash.
			GPS: N33°41.56' W115°57.64'
▼ 6.3		TL	Leaving Joshua Tree National Park at sign; then cross through wash; then track straight ahead.
	0.2 ▲	BR	Track on left; then cross through wash. Entering Joshua Tree National Park at sign for Pinkham Canyon Back Country Road.
			GPS: N33°41.24' W115°57.63'
▼ 6.5		TL	T-intersection with graded dirt road, marked by a marker post for Pinkham Canyon Trail. Zero trip meter.
	0.0 ▲		Continue to the northwest.
			GPS: N33°41.13' W115°57.56'
▼ 0.0			Continue to the east.
	3.0 ▲	TR	Turn right onto small formed trail, marked Pinkham Canyon Trail, and zero trip meter.
▼ 0.2		SO	Track on left.
	2.8 ▲	SO	Track on right.
▼ 0.6		SO	Track on left.
	2.4 ▲	SO	Track on right.
▼ 0.9		SO	Track on left.
	2.1 ▲	SO	Track on right.
▼ 1.2		SO	Track on left.
	1.8 ▲	SO	Track on right.
▼ 1.4		BR	Track on left. Bear right toward freeway at marker post for Pinkham Canyon.
	1.6 ▲	BL	Track on right. Bear left at marker post for Pinkham Canyon.
			GPS: N33°41.07' W115°56.12'
▼ 1.7		SO	Cross through wash.
	1.3 ▲	SO	Cross through wash.
▼ 2.1		SO	Track on left and track on right under power lines.
	0.9 ▲	SO	Track on left and track on right under power lines.
			GPS: N33°40.48' W115°55.76'
▼ 2.9		SO	Track on left.
	0.1 ▲	BL	Track on right.
▼ 3.0			Trail ends at freeway junction on I-10. Proceed eastbound for Joshua Tree National Park and Desert Center, westbound for Indio.
	0.0 ▲		Trail commences at frontage road exit of I-10, which is 6 miles west of the Cottonwood Exit for Joshua Tree National Park. Westbound traffic on I-10: Exit at frontage road and proceed 0.3 miles to the west. Immediately before the road swings left and passes under freeway, zero trip meter and turn right (west) onto small graded dirt road, marked Pinkham Canyon Trail. There is a notice board at the intersection. Eastbound traffic on I-10: Exit at frontage road and turn right (west) along paved road for 0.4 miles. Pass under freeway and immediately turn left (west) onto small graded dirt road, marked Pinkham Canyon Trail. Zero trip meter. There is a notice board at the intersection.
			GPS: N33°40.26' W115°55.01'

SOUTH COAST #44

Red Canyon Trail

Starting Point:	**I-10, at the Chiriaco Summit exit**
Finishing Point:	**South Coast #45: Bradshaw Trail, 21 miles from the western end at North Shore**
Total Mileage:	**13.8 miles**
Unpaved Mileage:	**12.7 miles**
Driving Time:	**2 hours**
Elevation Range:	**1,400–2,200 feet**
Usually Open:	**Year-round**
Best Time to Travel:	**October to June**
Difficulty Rating:	**4**
Scenic Rating:	**9**
Remoteness Rating:	**+1**

Special Attractions

- The General George S. Patton Memorial Museum at Chiriaco Summit.
- Spectacular narrow ridge top trail above Red Canyon.
- Alternative exit point from South Coast #45: Bradshaw Trail.

History

The northern end of Red Canyon Trail leads off from Chiriaco Summit at the foot of the Eagle Mountains. The summit's name comes from Joseph and Rosie Chiriaco, who established a gas station and store here in 1933.

Chiriaco Summit is also the location of the General George S. Patton Memorial Museum. The museum is close to the original entrance of Camp Young, headquarters for Patton's Desert Training Center (DTC), established in 1942. The museum, opened in 1988, offers an insight into what life was like for the 1 million troops who trained in this harsh desert environment, preparing to fight the Nazis in the North African deserts.

General George S. Patton is honored at a military museum at the start of Red Canyon Trail

Camp Young was one of eleven such desert army camps across California, Arizona, and Nevada. Together the collection of camps occupied an area of 18,000 square miles, making it the largest military and maneuver area in the world. Patton chose these particular sites after several weeks of flying, driving, and horseback riding over vast areas of desert in all three states. He said the locations chosen were "desolate and remote," a perfect training ground for combat in North Africa. The other camps included in the DTC were Camp Coxcomb, Camp Iron Mountain, Camp Granite, Camp Essex, Camp Ibis, Camp Hyder, Camp Horn, Camp Laguna, Camp Pilot Knob, and Camp Bouse.

Patton was unfamiliar with the desert and was assisted by Roy Chapman Andrews, an explorer who had made many expeditions into the Gobi Desert for the American Museum of Natural History in New York. Conditions were primitive at the camps, because their sole purpose was field training. Tent life was the norm. Patton also lived at the Camp Young, though he had been offered accommodations not too far west at Indio. His wife, Beatrice, stayed at a nearby ranch. Beatrice donated a piano to the troops for entertainment purposes; it can be seen at the museum.

A small runway, Shavers Army Airfield, was built west of Camp Young. From late 1943 to January 1944, Camp Young's mission changed from that of headquarters for a training center to being the headquarters for Preparation of army units for Overseas Movement, referred to as POM.

By March 16, 1944, the War Department declared all camps and ranges as surplus. The 3,228-acre Camp Young was relinquished to the Department of the Interior in January 1947.

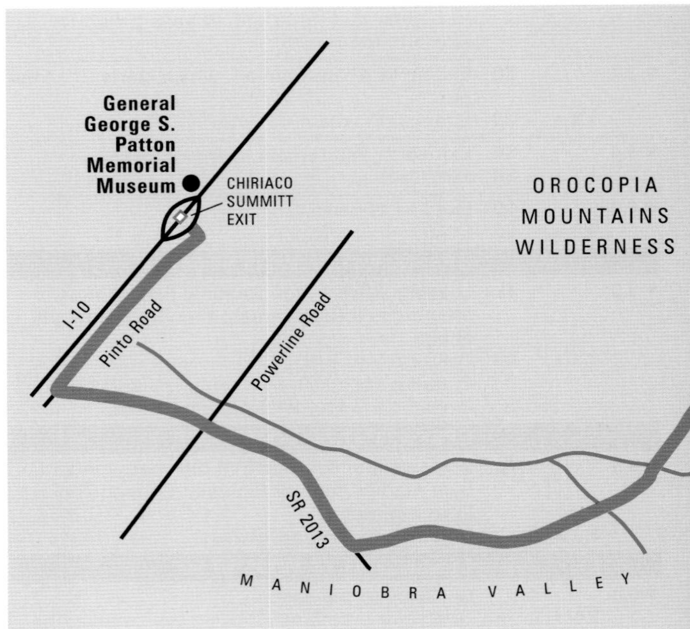

Description

Red Canyon Trail follows a well-marked, spectacular route that runs high above Red Canyon. Much of the trail winds along the top of an extremely narrow spine before descending to meet South Coast #45: Bradshaw Trail at Salt Creek Wash.

The trail leaves I-10 at the Chiriaco Summit exit near the General George S. Patton Memorial Museum. The museum is open daily except on Christmas and Thanksgiving.

The route leaves paved Pinto Road to travel along a well-used sandy trail that passes along the wide Maniobra Valley. This section is easygoing, although as you advance, the trail crosses many small washes and the deep gully at the head of Red Canyon. From here, the trail runs close to the rim as it travels a vehicle corridor through the Orocopia Mountains Wilderness. There are many viewpoints over Red Canyon, which becomes deeper and more rugged the closer it gets to Salt Creek.

Red Canyon Trail follows a vehicle corridor through the scenic Orocopia Mountains Wilderness

The trail surface is smooth, although there are some steep sections. The trail undulates along the ridge top, which is extremely narrow in places with dizzying drops on both sides. There are many blind crests along the trail and care should be taken when approaching them; many of them hide abrupt changes of direction, and there is little margin for error.

The trail drops down gradually to cross Salt Creek Wash, before finishing on South Coast #45: Bradshaw Trail. Red Canyon Trail is maintained under the Adopt-a-Trail program.

Current Road Information

Bureau of Land Management
Palm Springs South Coast Field Office
PO Box 581260
690 West Garnet Avenue
North Palm Springs, CA 92258
(760) 251-4800

Map References

BLM Eagle Mts.
USGS 1:24,000 Hayfield, Red Canyon, East of Red Canyon
1:100,000 Eagle Mts.
Maptech CD-ROM: San Diego/Joshua Tree
Southern & Central California Atlas & Gazetteer, pp. 108, 109
California Road & Recreation Atlas, p. 112

Route Directions

▼ 0.0	From I-10, at the Chiriaco Summit exit, 4 miles east of the Joshua Tree National Park exit, proceed to the south side of the freeway and zero trip meter at the notice board. Turn right (west) along the paved frontage road, marked Pinto

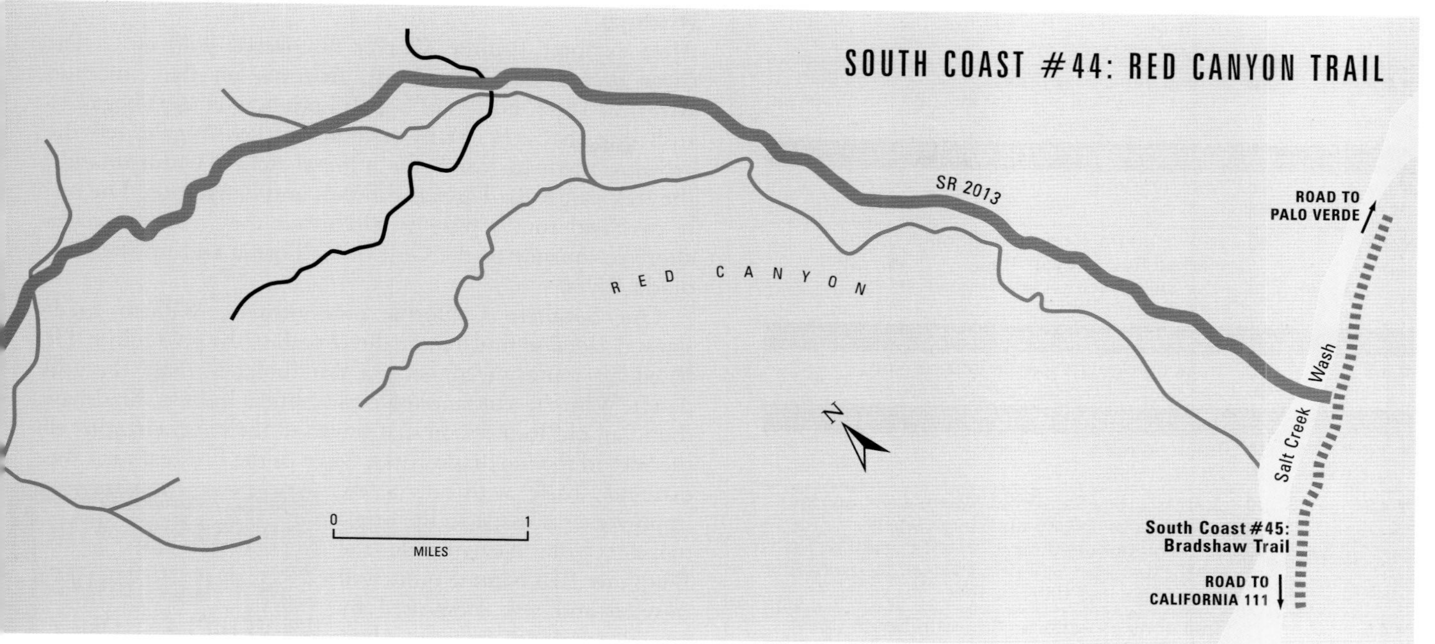

			Road. The General George S. Patton Memorial Museum is on the north side of the freeway.
	1.1 ▲		Trail ends on I-10 at Chiriaco Summit. Proceed eastbound for Desert Center, westbound for Indio. The General George S. Patton Memorial Museum is on the north side of the freeway.
			GPS: N33°39.53' W115°43.37'
▼ 1.1		TL	Turn left onto formed trail, marked Red Canyon Trail (SR 2013), and zero trip meter. There is a notice board at the intersection.
	0.0 ▲		Continue to the east.
			GPS: N33°39.51' W115°44.57'
▼ 0.0			Continue to the southeast.
	2.4 ▲	TR	T-intersection with paved Pinto Road. Zero trip meter and turn right alongside the freeway.
▼ 0.1		SO	Track on right and track on left alongside power lines.
	2.3 ▲	SO	Track on right and track on left alongside power lines.
▼ 0.8		SO	Track on right and track on left under power lines is marked Powerline Road.
	1.6 ▲	SO	Track on right and track on left under power lines is marked Powerline Road.
▼ 1.5		SO	Two tracks on left.
	0.9 ▲	SO	Two tracks on right.
▼ 1.6		SO	Two tracks on left.
	0.8 ▲	SO	Two tracks on right.
▼ 1.8		BL	Track on right. Follow marker for Red Canyon Trail.
	0.6 ▲	SO	Track on left. Follow marker for Red Canyon Trail.
			GPS: N33°38.04' W115°44.08'
▼ 2.1		BL	Bear left past track on right, following marker for Red Canyon Trail. Then track on left.
	0.3 ▲	SO	Track on right; then track on left. Follow marker for Red Canyon Trail.
			GPS: N33°37.82' W115°43.76'
▼ 2.4		SO	Entering vehicle corridor through the Orocopia Mountains Wilderness. Zero trip meter at sign.
	0.0 ▲		Continue to the northwest.
			GPS: N33°37.69' W115°43.63'
▼ 0.0			Continue to the southeast.
	5.8 ▲	SO	Leaving vehicle corridor. Zero trip meter at sign.
▼ 0.8		SO	Cross through wash; then closed trail on right and left.
	5.0 ▲	SO	Closed trail on right and left; then cross through wash.
▼ 1.1		SO	Cross through wide wash.
	4.7 ▲	SO	Cross through wide wash.
▼ 2.2		BL	Enter wash.
	3.6 ▲	BR	Exit wash.
			GPS: N33°37.49' W115°41.49'
▼ 2.7		SO	Exit wash.
	3.1 ▲	SO	Enter wash.
▼ 2.9		BL	Closed road on right goes to small mine site. Trail crosses many small washes for next 1.2 miles.
	2.9 ▲	BR	Closed road on left goes to small mine site. End of small washes.
			GPS: N33°37.29' W115°40.89'
▼ 4.1		SO	Enter wash.
	1.7 ▲	SO	Exit wash. Trail crosses many small washes for next 1.2 miles.
			GPS: N33°37.06' W115°39.81'
▼ 4.2		BL	Bear left and exit wash.
	1.6 ▲	BR	Bear right up wash.
▼ 5.1		TL	Drop down and swing sharp left up wash.
	0.7 ▲	TR	Turn right and climb out of wash.
			GPS: N33°36.66' W115°38.97'
▼ 5.2		TR	Turn right and climb out of wash.
	0.6 ▲	TL	Drop down and swing sharp left down wash.
▼ 5.8		BL	Well-used track on right goes 0.1 miles to an overlook above Red Canyon. Bear left, remaining on the marked Red Canyon Trail and zero trip meter.
	0.0 ▲		Continue to the north.
			GPS: N33°36.29' W115°38.70'
▼ 0.0			Continue to the southeast.
	4.5 ▲	BR	Well-used track on left goes 0.1 miles to an overlook above Red Canyon. Bear right,

remaining on the marked Red Canyon Trail and zero trip meter.

▼ 0.2	SO	Exiting vehicle corridor.
4.3 ▲	SO	Entering vehicle corridor through the Orocopia Mountains Wilderness.
		GPS: N33°36.17' W115°38.53'
▼ 0.9	BL	Track on right.
3.6 ▲	BR	Track on left.
▼ 2.6	SO	Well-used track on right. Remain on the marked Red Canyon Trail.
1.9 ▲	SO	Well-used track on left. Remain on the marked Red Canyon Trail.
		GPS: N33°34.36' W115°37.62'
▼ 3.5	SO	Track on right descends into canyon.
1.0 ▲	SO	Track on left descends into canyon.
		GPS: N33°33.71' W115°37.39'
▼ 3.6	SO	Track on right.
0.9 ▲	SO	Track on left.
▼ 4.3	SO	Start to cross Salt Creek Wash; track on right and track on left up and down wash.
0.2 ▲	SO	Track on right and track on left up and down wash; then exit Salt Creek Wash, following the marker for Red Canyon Trail.
▼ 4.5		Trail ends at T-intersection with South Coast #45: Bradshaw Trail. Turn right for North Shore and California 111; turn left to travel the Bradshaw Trail to Palo Verde.
0.0 ▲		Trail commences on South Coast #45: Bradshaw Trail, 21 miles from the western end at North Shore. Zero trip meter and turn northwest at the marker post for Red Canyon Trail. Note that there are two marker posts for Red Canyon Trail. This post is the eastern-most one, which also designates the trail as SR 2013.
		GPS: N33°32.90' W115°37.12'

SOUTH COAST #45

Bradshaw Trail

Starting Point:	**California 78, 5 miles north of Palo Verde**
Finishing Point:	**California 111 at North Shore**
Total Mileage:	**79.4 miles**
Unpaved Mileage:	**77.8 miles**
Driving Time:	**4 hours**
Elevation Range:	**0–2,600 feet**
Usually Open:	**Year-round**
Best Time to Travel:	**October to June**
Difficulty Rating:	**2**
Scenic Rating:	**8**
Remoteness Rating:	**+1**

Special Attractions

- Long historic route of William Bradshaw's Trail.
- Rockhounding in the Chuckwalla Mountains.
- Mule Mountains Long-Term Visitor Area.
- Salton Sea.

History

After explorer Pauline Weaver discovered gold at La Paz (near present-day Ehrenburg, Arizona, on the Colorado River) in 1862, hordes of hopeful rainbow-chasers began to rush into that area. Many residents of Los Angeles left the growing town to search for mineral riches. Unfortunately, the trek east to La Paz was difficult and dangerous. The only overland routes were so circuitous that many travelers chose to journey to the Gulf of California and up the Colorado River.

One Southern California outdoorsman, William Bradshaw, decided to find a more direct path to the gold mines. He based his route on connecting waterholes through the arid desert. With the assistance of local Cahuilla Indians, Bradshaw found an old Indian trail that traversed the harsh environs all the way to the Colorado River. Most of the finished road was extremely basic, with only a few improvements made to the original dirt path. Nevertheless, the Bradshaw Trail became quite well traveled and was soon used by several stagecoach lines as well as the U.S. Postal Service.

The Bradshaw Trail, established in 1862, took the lives of many gold rush travelers

Water holes such as Wiley Well, Indian Well, Chuckwalla Well, Tabaseca Tanks, Dos Palmas, Indian Wells, Agua Caliente, and Whitewater Well were essential to travelers on this challenging journey between Los Angeles and La Paz.

The Cahuilla may have been the only native people to install wells in this area. Indian Well is a classic example of the Indians' determination to access a deep hidden seep. Entry to the well was through a natural tunnel that dropped far below the surface. Cahuilla women carved steps in order to reach the water level. Wells such as this were known to reach about 30 feet below the surface.

Use of Bradshaw's desert road gradually slowed as the La Paz mines dried up and the Southern Pacific Railroad (see page 66) connected nearby Yuma to Los Angeles, but the trail still makes for a pleasant backcountry drive. (For more information on the historic Bradshaw Trail see page 62.)

Description

The Bradshaw Trail closely follows William Bradshaw's historic route that connected the rich mines at La Paz, Arizona, to San Bernardino, California. It also served as a trade route to and from the Colorado River.

This trail travels from Palo Verde, on the Colorado River, to the shores of the Salton Sea, a large inland body of water. The road is graded along its length, and in dry weather is normally suitable for high-clearance 2WD vehicles. However, some sections of loose sand, particularly in Salt Creek near the western end of the trail, are better tackled with a 4WD. Passenger vehicles should not attempt the route west of the intersection with South Coast #46: Milpitas Wash Road at Wiley Well Campground.

Initially, the trail leaves California 78 and travels west to cross over Palo Verde Mesa on its way toward the Mule Mountains. It crosses through the Mule Mountains Long-Term Visitor Area (LTVA), which is popular with snowbirds in winter. With a permit, RV drivers are permitted to camp between September 15 and April 15. The Wiley Well Campground caters to these long-term users as well as short-term visitors.

West of Wiley Well, the trail is looser and rougher, crossing many shallow washes as it winds its way along the south side of the Chuckwalla Mountains. Most of the Chuckwalla Mountains are now encompassed in wilderness areas, although a few vehicle corridors penetrate the range. These mountains are popular with rock hounds, who search for agate, jasper, and chalcedony.

A long section of the trail follows the northern boundary of the Chocolate Mountains Aerial Gunnery Range. This military zone is used for live-fire exercises, and there is no public admittance. The area is well marked so there is little chance of accidentally straying into the range. A few tracks do lead into the range. Major ones have been mentioned for navigation purposes only; they are not intended for public travel. This section of the trail is one of the most beautiful. The trail crosses the wide Chuckwalla Bench with the Chuckwalla and Orocopia Mountains to the north and the Chocolate Mountains to the south. The vegetation is a profusion of yucca, cholla, ocotillo, sagebrush, and creosote bush.

The trail drops to the sandy Salt Creek Wash in a shallow canyon close to the Eagle Mountain Railroad, which once served the mines north of I-10. It passes the south end of South Coast #44: Red Canyon Trail. Note that there are two trails, both marked Red Canyon and only a short distance apart.

The Bradshaw Trail then exits via the Coachella Canal to the settlement of North Shore and the Salton Sea.

Current Road Information

Bureau of Land Management
Palm Springs South Coast Field Office
PO Box 581260
690 West Garnet Avenue
North Palm Springs, CA 92258
(760) 251-4800

Map References

BLM Trigo Mts., Blythe, Salton Sea, Eagle Mts.
USGS 1:24,000 Palo Verde, Thumb Peak, Roosevelt Mine, Wiley Well, Little Chuckwalla Mt., Chuckwalla Spring, Augustine Pass, Pilot Mt., Iris Pass, Red Cloud Canyon, East of Red Canyon, Red Canyon, Orocopia Canyon, Mortmar
1:100,000 Trigo Mts., Blythe, Salton Sea, Eagle Mts.
Maptech CD-ROM: San Diego/Joshua Tree
Southern & Central California Atlas & Gazetteer, pp. 119, 118, 117, 109, 108
California Road & Recreation Atlas, pp. 114, 113, 112

The disused railroad trestle crosses above Salt Creek Wash

Route Directions

Mileage		Description
▼ 0.0		From California 78, 5 miles north of Palo Verde, and 0.3 miles north of mile marker 5, zero trip meter and turn west on paved road marked The Bradshaw Trail. Cross over irrigation channel.
3.1 ▲		Trail ends on California 78. Turn right for Palo Verde; turn left for Blythe.
		GPS: N33°29.67' W114°42.60'
▼ 1.0	SO	Road on left. Road is now graded dirt.
2.1 ▲	SO	Road on right. Road is now paved.
▼ 1.9	SO	Cross over Hodges Drain; then two tracks on left and track on right.
1.2 ▲	SO	Two tracks on right and track on left; then cross over Hodges Drain.
▼ 2.8	SO	Track on left and track on right under power lines.
0.3 ▲	SO	Track on right and track on left under power lines.
▼ 3.1	BL	Graded road on right goes to Hodge Mine. Bear left onto SR 301, marked as Bradshaw Trail, Back Country Byway. Zero trip meter.
0.0 ▲		Continue to the northeast.
		GPS: N33°29.60' W114°45.82'
▼ 0.0		Continue to the southwest.
7.5 ▲	SO	Graded road on left goes to Hodge Mine. Continue straight ahead on graded dirt road and zero trip meter.
▼ 0.9	SO	Track on left and track on right.
6.6 ▲	SO	Track on left and track on right.
▼ 1.2	SO	Track on left; then second track on left into quarry.
6.3 ▲	SO	Track on right; then second track on right into quarry.
▼ 1.3	SO	Cross through wash.
6.2 ▲	SO	Cross through wash.
▼ 1.4	SO	Track on right under power lines.
6.1 ▲	SO	Track on left under power lines.
		GPS: N33°29.54' W114°47.37'
▼ 1.7	SO	Enter wash.
5.8 ▲	SO	Exit wash.
▼ 1.9	SO	Exit wash.
5.6 ▲	SO	Enter wash.

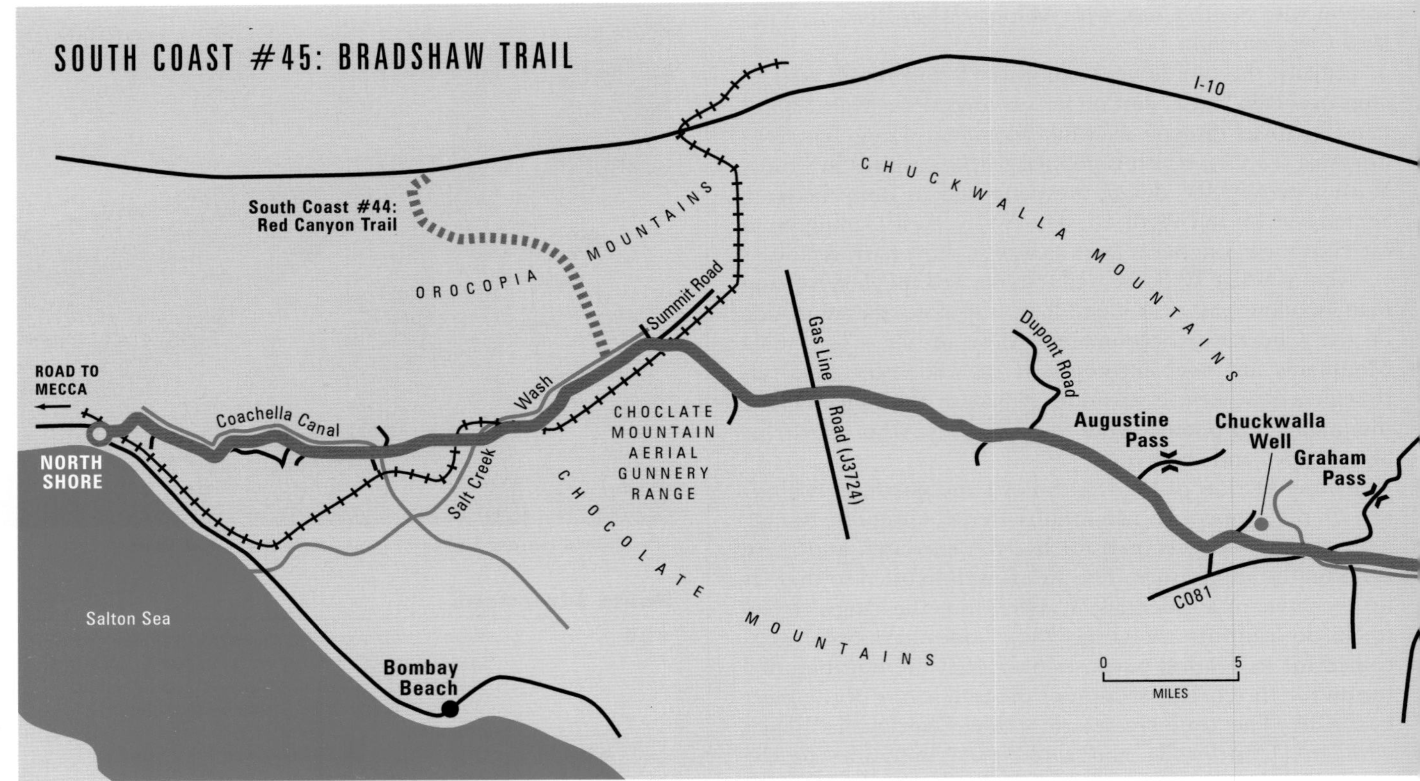

Mileage	Reverse	Direction	Description
▼ 3.4		SO	Track on right to Roosevelt Mine in the Mule Mountains.
	4.1 ▲	SO	Track on left to Roosevelt Mine in the Mule Mountains.
			GPS: N33°29.79' W114°49.39'
▼ 3.5		SO	Enter wash.
	4.0 ▲	SO	Exit wash.
▼ 4.2		SO	Exit wash.
	3.3 ▲	SO	Enter wash.
▼ 4.6		SO	Cross through wash.
	2.9 ▲	SO	Cross through wash.
▼ 4.7		SO	Track on right. Passing through the Mule Mountains.
	2.8 ▲	SO	Track on left. Passing through the Mule Mountains.
▼ 4.9		SO	Track on left.
	2.6 ▲	SO	Track on right.
▼ 5.1		SO	Enter Mule Mountains Long-Term Visitor Area.
	2.4 ▲	SO	Exit Mule Mountains Long-Term Visitor Area.
			GPS: N33°30.09' W114°51.10'
▼ 6.2		SO	Cross through wash.
	1.3 ▲	SO	Cross through wash.
▼ 7.5		SO	Graded road on right and left is South Coast #46: Milpitas Wash Road (Wiley's Well Road, M 058). Wiley Well Campground is 0.2 miles to the north along this road. Zero trip meter.
	0.0 ▲		Continue to the northeast.
			GPS: N33°29.60' W114°53.38'
▼ 0.0			Continue to the southwest.
	4.6 ▲	SO	Graded road on right and left is South Coast #46: Milpitas Wash Road (Wiley's Well Road, M 058). Wiley Well Campground is 0.2 miles to the north along this road. Zero trip meter.
▼ 0.2		SO	Exit Mule Mountains Long-Term Visitor Area at sign; then cross through wash.
	4.4 ▲	SO	Cross through wash; then enter Mule Mountains Long-Term Visitor Area at sign.
▼ 0.4		SO	Track on right.
	4.2 ▲	SO	Track on left.
▼ 3.8		SO	Track on right.
	0.8 ▲	SO	Track on left.
			GPS: N33°28.36' W114°56.99'
▼ 4.6		SO	Track on right and information board on right. Little Chuckwalla Mountains Wilderness boundary is on right of road. Zero trip meter.
	0.0 ▲		Continue to the northeast.
			GPS: N33°28.05' W114°57.79'
▼ 0.0			Continue to the south.
	3.5 ▲	SO	Track on left and information board on left. Wilderness boundary ends. Zero trip meter.
▼ 1.8		SO	Cross through wash.
	1.7 ▲	SO	Cross through wash.
▼ 2.7		SO	Cross through wash.
	0.8 ▲	SO	Cross through wash.
▼ 3.0		SO	Cross through wash.
	0.5 ▲	SO	Cross through wash.
			GPS: N33°26.85' W115°00.55'
▼ 3.1		SO	Trail now follows under power lines.
	0.4 ▲	SO	Trail leaves power lines.
▼ 3.5		SO	Track on left is Ashley Flats. Zero trip meter at marker post.
	0.0 ▲		Continue to the east.
			GPS: N33°26.60' W115°01.02'
▼ 0.0			Continue to the west and cross through wash.
	9.8 ▲	SO	Cross through wash; then track on right is Ashley Flats. Zero trip meter at marker post.
▼ 0.5		SO	Wilderness boundary finishes on right.
	9.3 ▲	SO	Little Chuckwalla Mountains Wilderness boundary starts on left.

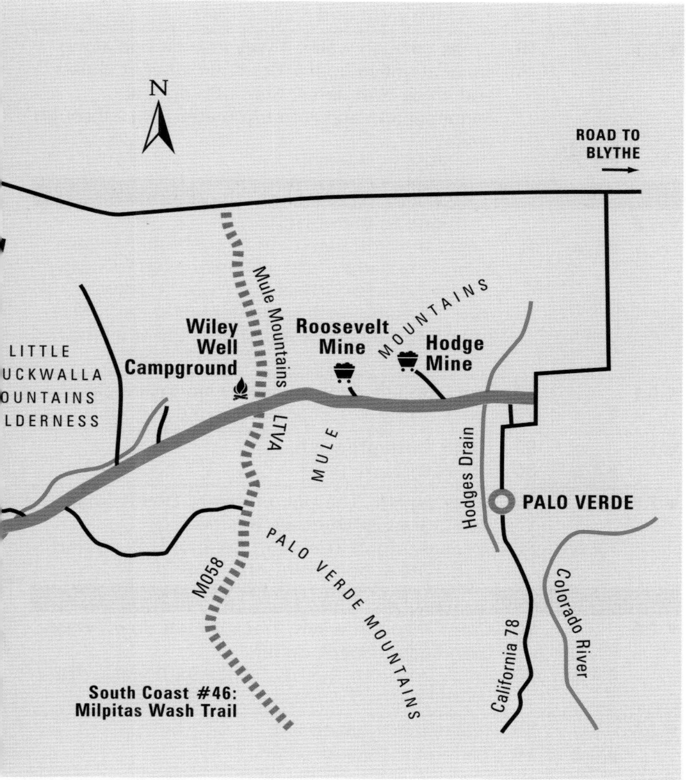

▼ 1.1 SO Start to cross through wide wash.
8.7 ▲ SO Exit wash.

▼ 1.3 SO Exit wash.
8.5 ▲ SO Start to cross through wide wash.

▼ 1.4 SO Track on right. Remain on marked Bradshaw Trail.
8.4 ▲ SO Track on left. Remain on marked Bradshaw Trail.

GPS: N33°26.11′ W115°02.43′

▼ 1.9 SO Enter line of wash.
7.9 ▲ SO Exit line of wash.

▼ 2.4 SO Exit line of wash.
7.4 ▲ SO Enter line of wash.

▼ 2.7 SO Track on left and track on right to power line.
7.1 ▲ SO Track on left and track on right to power line.

▼ 2.9 SO Little Chuckwalla Mountains Wilderness boundary on right.
6.9 ▲ SO Little Chuckwalla Mountains Wilderness boundary ends on left.

GPS: N33°25.70′ W115°03.86′

▼ 3.3 SO Track on right. Wilderness boundary ends on right.
6.5 ▲ SO Track on left. Little Chuckwalla Mountains Wilderness boundary on left.

▼ 3.9 SO Cross through wash.
5.9 ▲ SO Cross through wash.

▼ 4.2 SO Cross through wash.
5.6 ▲ SO Cross through wash.

▼ 4.6 SO Track on left; then cross through wash.
5.2 ▲ SO Cross through wash; then track on right.

GPS: N33°24.72′ W115°05.16′

▼ 5.6 SO Track on left.
4.2 ▲ SO Track on right.

▼ 6.6 SO Little Chuckwalla Mountains Wilderness boundary on right.
3.2 ▲ SO Wilderness boundary ends on left.

GPS: N33°24.92′ W115°07.22′

▼ 8.5 SO Track on left.
1.3 ▲ SO Track on right.

▼ 9.6 SO Wilderness boundary ends on right.
0.2 ▲ SO Little Chuckwalla Mountains Wilderness boundary starts on left.

▼ 9.8 TL T-intersection with graded road. To the right is Graham Pass Road. Remain on marked Bradshaw Trail and zero trip meter. There is a notice board at the intersection.
0.0 ▲ Continue to the southeast.

GPS: N33°25.42′ W115°10.29′

▼ 0.0 Continue to the west.
3.1 ▲ TR Graded road ahead is Graham Pass Road. Turn right, remaining on marked Bradshaw Trail, and zero trip meter. There is a notice board at the intersection.

▼ 0.1 SO Cross through wash.
3.0 ▲ SO Cross through wash.

▼ 0.2 SO Track on left is C 081.
2.9 ▲ SO Track on right is C 081.

▼ 0.9 SO Cross through wash.
2.2 ▲ SO Cross through wash.

▼ 2.2 SO Live bombing area boundary on left. Keep out!
0.9 ▲ SO Live bombing area boundary on right. Keep out!

GPS: N33°25.79′ W115°12.58′

▼ 3.1 SO Track on right at notice board is Chuckwalla Trail. Zero trip meter.
0.0 ▲ Continue to the southeast.

GPS: N33°26.23′ W115°13.40′

▼ 0.0 Continue to the west.
5.4 ▲ SO Track on left at notice board is Chuckwalla Trail. Zero trip meter.

▼ 0.1 SO Track on right.
5.3 ▲ SO Track on left.

▼ 1.2 SO Track on left.
4.2 ▲ SO Track on right.

▼ 5.4 SO Track on right at notice board is Augustine Pass Road. Zero trip meter.
0.0 ▲ Continue to the southeast.

GPS: N33°28.29′ W115°17.40′

▼ 0.0 Continue to the west.
4.5 ▲ SO Track on left at notice board is Augustine Pass Road. Zero trip meter.

▼ 2.6 SO Track on right.
1.9 ▲ SO Track on left.

▼ 4.5 SO Track on right at notice board is Dupont Road (C 117). Zero trip meter.
0.0 ▲ Continue to the east.

GPS: N33°29.96′ W115°21.63′

▼ 0.0 Continue to the west.
8.0 ▲ SO Track on left at notice board is Dupont Road (C 117). Zero trip meter.

▼ 0.3 SO Track on right.
7.7 ▲ SO Track on left.

▼ 1.1 SO Track on left enters gunnery. Small track on right.
6.9 ▲ SO Track on right enters gunnery. Small track on left.

▼ 7.8 SO Small track on right.
0.2 ▲ SO Small track on left.

▼ 8.0 SO Track on left and track on right under power lines is marked Gas Line Road, J 3724. Zero trip meter.

0.0 ▲ Continue to the east.

GPS: N33°31.71' W115°29.40'

▼ 0.0 Continue to the west.
6.9 ▲ SO Track on left and track on right under power lines is marked Gas Line Road, J 3724. Zero trip meter.

▼ 3.4 SO Track on left enters gunnery.
3.5 ▲ SO Track on right enters gunnery.

▼ 6.9 TL Track on left; then cross over railroad; then 4-way intersection. Turn left, remaining on the marked Bradshaw Trail, and zero trip meter. Small track ahead and track on right is Summit Road (C 041). Notice board at intersection.
0.0 ▲ Continue to the southeast and cross over railroad; then track on right.

GPS: N33°33.74' W115°35.30'

▼ 0.0 Continue to the southwest.
2.0 ▲ TR 4-way intersection. Small track on left and track straight ahead is Summit Road (C 041). Turn right, remaining on the marked Bradshaw Trail, and zero trip meter.

▼ 0.9 SO Track on right down wash.
1.1 ▲ SO Track on left down wash.

▼ 1.0 SO Track on right is Amy's Wash Road.
1.0 ▲ SO Track on left is Amy's Wash Road.

GPS: N33°33.31' W115°36.22'

▼ 2.0 SO Track on right is South Coast #44: Red Canyon Trail (S 2013). Zero trip meter.
0.0 ▲ Continue to the northeast.

GPS: N33°32.90' W115°37.12'

▼ 0.0 Continue to the southwest.
6.0 ▲ SO Track on left is South Coast #44: Red Canyon Trail (S 2013). Zero trip meter.

▼ 0.4 SO Track on right goes to Red Canyon.
5.6 ▲ SO Track on left goes to Red Canyon.

▼ 1.7 SO Enter line of Salt Creek Wash.
4.3 ▲ SO Exit line of Salt Creek Wash.

▼ 4.0 SO Pass under old railroad trestle; then track on left.
2.0 ▲ SO Track on right; then pass under old railroad trestle.

GPS: N33°31.06' W115°40.60'

▼ 5.2 SO Track on right.
0.8 ▲ SO Track on left.

▼ 5.5 SO Exit Salt Creek Wash to the right.
0.5 ▲ SO Enter up line of Salt Creek Wash.

▼ 5.7 SO Track on right.
0.3 ▲ SO Track on left.

▼ 5.8 SO Track on right.
0.2 ▲ SO Track on left.

▼ 6.0 SO Track on left enters gunnery; then rise up to cross over railroad embankment. Zero trip meter at railroad crossing.
0.0 ▲ Continue to the northeast.

GPS: N33°30.73' W115°42.73'

▼ 0.0 Continue to the southwest.
3.1 ▲ SO Rise up to cross over railroad embankment; then track on right enters gunnery. Zero trip meter at railroad crossing.

▼ 0.2 SO Track on right and track on left.
2.9 ▲ SO Track on right and track on left.

▼ 1.1 SO Track on right.
2.0 ▲ SO Track on left.

GPS: N33°30.65' W115°43.84'

▼ 2.8 SO Track on right and track on left.
0.3 ▲ SO Track on right and track on left.

▼ 3.1 TR Cross through wash. 4-way intersection along canal at notice board. Continue straight ahead and cross over canal; then turn right at T-intersection and zero trip meter. Cross through wash.
0.0 ▲ Continue to the east.

GPS: N33°30.35' W115°45.95'

▼ 0.0 Continue to the north.
9.5 ▲ TL Cross through wash. Road continues ahead alongside canal. Turn left over canal toward notice board and zero trip meter. Continue straight ahead at 4-way intersection at notice board. Road is now marked as the Bradshaw Trail.

▼ 0.1 SO Track on left. Start to follow alongside canal.
9.4 ▲ SO Track on right. Canal is now underground.

▼ 1.1 SO Cross through wash.
8.4 ▲ SO Cross through wash.

▼ 1.9 SO Track on left. The palm trees of Dos Palmas ACEC are visible down this trail.
7.6 ▲ SO Track on right. The palm trees of Dos Palmas ACEC are visible down this trail.

GPS: N33°30.62' W115°47.80'

▼ 2.6 SO Cross through wash. Track on left down wash; then second track on left.
6.9 ▲ SO Track on right; then cross through wash. Track on right down wash.

▼ 3.5 SO Well-used track on left.
6.0 ▲ SO Well-used track on right.

▼ 3.6 SO Cross through wash; then track on left.
5.9 ▲ SO Track on right; then cross through wash.

▼ 4.1 SO Cross through wash, track on left down wash.
5.4 ▲ SO Cross through wash, track on right down wash.

▼ 5.6 SO Cross through wash, track on right up wash.
3.9 ▲ SO Cross through wash, track on left up wash.

GPS: N33°31.22' W115°51.54'

▼ 6.1 SO Track on left.
3.4 ▲ SO Track on right.

▼ 7.6 SO Graded road on left.
1.9 ▲ SO Graded road on right.

▼ 8.3 SO Track on left, track on right crosses canal.
1.2 ▲ SO Track on right, track on left crosses canal.

▼ 9.0 SO Graded road on left.
0.5 ▲ SO Graded road on right.

GPS: N33°31.52' W115°54.42'

▼ 9.5 SO Cross through wash. Small track on left. Track on right past information board is Meccacopia Trail (SR 1811). Zero trip meter.
0.0 ▲ Continue to the southeast.

GPS: N33°31.96' W115°54.73'

▼ 0.0 Continue to the northwest.
2.4 ▲ SO Cross through wash. Small track on right. Track on left past information board is Meccacopia Trail (SR 1811). Zero trip meter.

▼ 0.5 TL Cross through wash, track on right up wash. Turn left down wash.
1.9 ▲ TR Track straight ahead crosses canal, graded road on right and left along canal. Turn right along western side of canal.

GPS: N33°32.25' W115°55.08'

▼ 0.7 SO Track on left and track on right.
1.7 ▲ SO Track on left and track on right.

▼ 0.9 SO Track on right.
1.5 ▲ SO Track on left.

▼ 1.4	TR	Track on right and track on left along power lines; then turn right onto paved road. Trail continues ahead.
1.0 ▲	TL	Turn left onto unmarked, formed sandy trail immediately before power lines. Cross over paved road before a sharp right-hand bend. Then track on right and track on left along power lines.
		GPS: N33°31.53' W115°55.62'
▼ 1.6	SO	Paved road on right is Sea View Way. Continue straight ahead on 72nd Avenue.
0.8 ▲	SO	Paved road on left is Sea View Way. Continue straight ahead on 72nd Avenue.
▼ 2.0	TR	Turn right onto Commerce Street.
0.4 ▲	TL	Turn left onto 72nd Avenue.
▼ 2.2	TL	4-way intersection. Turn left onto Bay Drive.
0.2 ▲	TR	4-way intersection. Turn right onto Vander Veer Road.
		GPS: N33°31.70' W115°56.31'
▼ 2.4		Cross over railroad; then trail ends at the intersection with California 111 in North Shore. Turn right for Mecca; turn left for Bombay Beach.
0.0 ▲		Trail commences on California 111 in North Shore. Zero trip meter and turn northeast onto paved Bay Drive at sign. The turn is 9 miles south of Mecca.
		GPS: N33°31.64' W115°56.43'

SOUTH COAST #46

Milpitas Wash Road

Starting Point:	**I-10 at Wiley Well Road exit**
Finishing Point:	**California 78, 12 miles south of Palo Verde**
Total Mileage:	**28.8 miles**
Unpaved Mileage:	**26.2 miles**
Driving Time:	**1.5 hours**
Elevation Range:	**400–800 feet**
Usually Open:	**Year-round**
Best Time to Travel:	**October to June**
Difficulty Rating:	**2**
Scenic Rating:	**8**
Remoteness Rating:	**+0**

Special Attractions

- Mule Mountains Long-Term Visitor Area.
- Rockhounding for geodes and fire agate.
- Easy trail through a remote area.

History

South Coast #45: Bradshaw Trail crosses Milpitas Wash Road near the northern end of the road and Wiley Well, just west of the rugged Mule Mountains. The Bradshaw Trail developed as the overland route taken by West Coast miners on their way to the gold rush at La Paz, on the banks of the Colorado River near today's Ehrenburg, Arizona.

Wiley Well Campground caters to long-term winter residents and short-term camping visitors

The desert trail, researched and promoted by William Bradshaw in 1862, was far from a golden road. Deep sand, volcanic rock, boulder-strewn washes, and long hot stretches with limited water made it a difficult road to travel. The secret to the success of Bradshaw's trail was that it connected one waterhole to the next.

Wiley Well was one such waterhole along the treacherous route, though this particular well was not established until 1863. It was the first watering point for travelers heading west from the Palo Verde Valley. It also served as a much-needed resting place to shake off the dust after the climb through the Mule Mountains.

Farther south, Milpitas Wash Road passes the southern end of the Mule Mountains near the Opal Hill Mine. The owner, Howard Fisher, originally from Brawley (at the northern end of Imperial Valley), went gold prospecting in Alaska. He eventually returned to the warmer Colorado Desert, most likely for wealth, climate, or love of his homeland.

The Butterfield Stage Route passed this way in the 1860s, after leaving the Palo Verde Valley and traveling through a low pass in the Mule Mountains. One of Butterfield's stagecoach drivers returned with magnificent geodes from this area. Native Americans had known about the location for years, using some of the rocks as tools. The stagecoach driver related the general location of his findings to his son Joel Hauser. Years later, Joel scoured the region, finally discovering what is now called the Hauser Geode Beds. These beds, located just west of the trail, hold a slice of history within. You may also be fortunate enough to see petrified palm roots that were once part of an ancient, lush landscape.

Description

Milpitas Wash Road is a long, easygoing trail that passes close to two popular rockhounding areas, as well as the Mule Mountains Long-Term Visitor Area.

The trail leaves I-10 at the Wiley Well Road exit. The first couple miles are paved. Once the trail passes the state prison, it becomes a smooth graded road. The trail then enters the Mule Mountains Long-Term Visitor Area, where recreational

Mesquite trees and other plantlife hug the wash lines at the north end of the Palo Verde Mountains

vehicle owners may camp for the winter with an appropriate permit. Wiley Well Campground mainly attracts long-term visitors, but short-term and overnight campers are welcome as well.

From I-10 as far as the campground, the road is well graded and smooth enough to cater to large RVs. Past the intersection with South Coast #45: Bradshaw Trail at the campground, the road becomes slightly rougher, though still graded. A carefully driven passenger vehicle should be able to negotiate the road in dry weather, but RVs might prefer to return the way they came.

A track to the east leads to the privately owned Opal Hill Mine. This area is open to the public for a small fee. The second rockhounding area is the Hauser Geode Beds, located a short distance west of the trail. These beds offer rock hounds the chance to hunt for geodes that, when cracked open, may reveal hollow, crystal-filled interiors. The two turns to the geode beds are well marked.

The trail continues to the south, wrapping around the edge of the Palo Verde Mountains Wilderness. It crosses many shallow washes and can be slightly sandy in spots, but poses no real difficulty.

The trail finishes on California 78. It is marked on some maps as Wiley Well Road.

Current Road Information

Bureau of Land Management
Palm Springs South Coast Field Office
PO Box 581260
690 West Garnet Avenue
North Palm Springs, CA 92258
(760) 251-4800

Bureau of Land Management
El Centro Field Office
1661 South Fourth Street
El Centro, CA 92243
(760) 337-4400

Map References

BLM Blythe, Trigo Mts.
USGS 1:24,000 Hopkins Well, Wiley Well, West of Palo Verde Peak, Palo Verde Peak
1:100,000 Blythe, Trigo Mts.
Maptech CD-ROM: San Diego/Joshua Tree
Southern & Central California Atlas & Gazetteer, pp. 110, 118, 119
California Road & Recreation Atlas, p. 113

Route Directions

▼ 0.0			From the Wiley Well exit on I-10, proceed to the south side of the freeway and zero trip meter. Head south and remain on paved road.
	2.6 ▲		Trail ends at Wiley Well exit on I-10. Take the freeway west for Indio, east for Blythe.
			GPS: N33°36.40' W114°54.06'
▼ 2.6		SO	Paved road turns right into state prison. Continue south, following the sign to Wiley Well Campground. Road turns to graded dirt. Zero trip meter.
	0.0 ▲		Continue to the north.
			GPS: N33°34.20' W114°53.84'
▼ 0.0			Continue to the south.
	5.7 ▲	SO	Paved road on left into state prison. Zero trip meter and continue to the north. Road is now paved.
▼ 1.0		SO	Track on right.
	4.7 ▲	SO	Track on left.
▼ 1.8		SO	Information board on right; then cross through wash.
	3.9 ▲	SO	Cross through wash; then information board on left.
▼ 2.9		SO	Track on right.
	2.8 ▲	SO	Track on left.
▼ 4.5		SO	Enter Mule Mountains Long-Term Visitor Area.

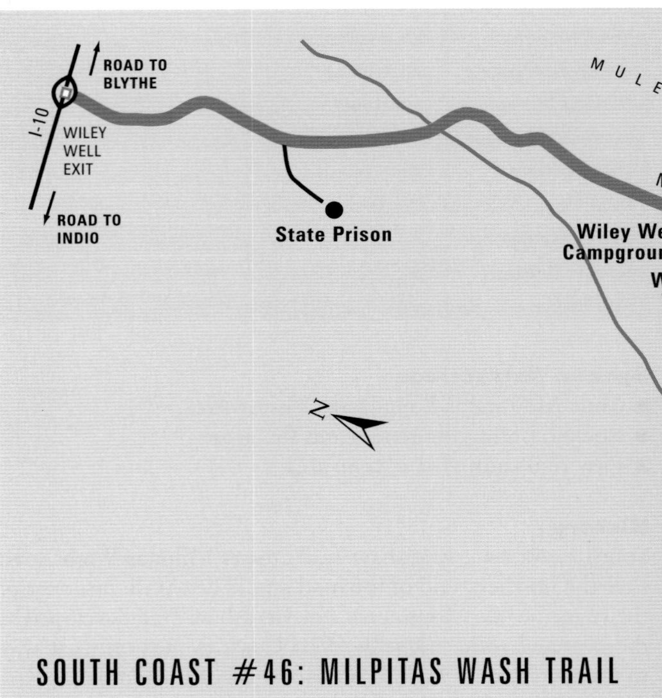

1.2 ▲ SO Exit Mule Mountains Long-Term Visitor Area.

GPS: N33°30.46′ W114°53.11′

▼ 5.5 SO Wiley Well Campground on right, for long- and short-term use.

0.2 ▲ SO Wiley Well Campground on left, for long- and short-term use.

GPS: N33°29.61′ W114°53.21′

▼ 5.7 SO Graded road on right and left is South Coast #45: Bradshaw Trail. Zero trip meter and continue straight ahead.

0.0 ▲ Continue to the north.

GPS: N33°29.60′ W114°53.38′

▼ 0.0 Continue to the south.

2.8 ▲ SO Graded road on right and left is South Coast #45: Bradshaw Trail. Zero trip meter and continue straight ahead.

▼ 0.2 SO Track on left and track on right under power lines.

2.6 ▲ SO Track on left and track on right under power lines.

▼ 0.8 SO Track on right.

2.0 ▲ SO Track on left.

▼ 1.3 SO RV dump station on right. Many tracks on left and right to camping areas for the next 1.8 miles.

1.5 ▲ SO RV dump station on left.

▼ 2.8 SO Track on left goes 2 miles to the Opal Hill Mine, which is open to the public for a small fee. Zero trip meter.

0.0 ▲ Continue to the northwest.

GPS: N33°26.99′ W114°53.57′

▼ 0.0 Continue to the south.

1.5 ▲ SO Track on right goes 2 miles to the Opal Hill Mine, which is open to the public for a small fee. Zero trip meter.

▼ 0.3 SO Graded road on right goes into Coon Hollow Campground, for long- and short-term camping; then track on left.

1.2 ▲ SO Track on right; then graded road on left goes into Coon Hollow Campground, for long- and short-term camping. Many tracks on left and right to camping areas for the next 1.8 miles.

GPS: N33°26.73′ W114°53.65′

▼ 0.8 SO Exit the Mule Mountains Long-Term Visitor Area. Track on right is M 042. Palo Verde Mountains Wilderness now starts on the left.

0.7 ▲ SO Leaving Palo Verde Mountains Wilderness. Enter Mule Mountains Long-Term Visitor Area. Track on left is M 042.

▼ 1.5 SO Track on right is signed to the Hauser Geode Beds Area. Entering Imperial County. Zero trip meter.

0.0 ▲ Continue to the north.

GPS: N33°25.79′ W114°54.14′

▼ 0.0 Continue to the south.

6.2 ▲ SO Track on left is signed to the Hauser Geode Beds Area. Entering Riverside County. Zero trip meter.

▼ 0.3 SO Second entrance of spur to Hauser Geode Beds on right.

5.9 ▲ SO Track on left goes to the Hauser Geode Beds.

▼ 0.8 SO Track on right.

5.4 ▲ SO Track on left.

▼ 0.9 SO Cross through wash.

5.3 ▲ SO Cross through wash.

▼ 1.0 SO Cross through wash.

5.2 ▲ SO Cross through wash.

▼ 1.3 SO Cross through wash.

4.9 ▲ SO Cross through wash.

▼ 1.6 SO Cross through wash.

4.6 ▲ SO Cross through wash.

▼ 2.2 SO Cross through wash; then track on right.

4.0 ▲ SO Track on left; then cross through wash.

GPS: N33°24.01′ W114°54.50′

▼ 2.7 SO Track on right.

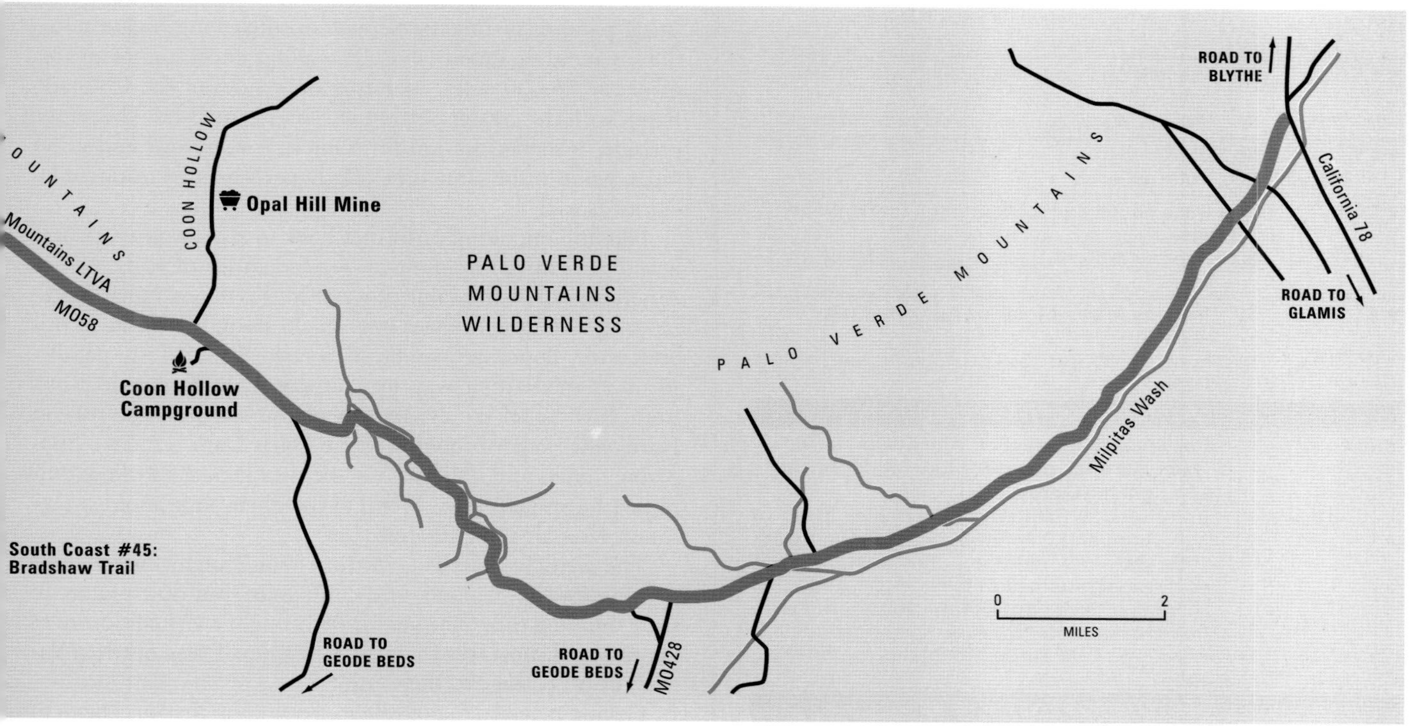

3.5 ▲	SO	Track on left.
▼ 2.8	SO	Track on right; then cross through wash.
3.4 ▲	SO	Cross through wash; then track on left.
▼ 3.2	SO	Track on right.
3.0 ▲	SO	Track on left.
▼ 3.4	SO	Cross through wash.
2.8 ▲	SO	Cross through wash.
▼ 3.5	SO	Cross through wash.
2.7 ▲	SO	Cross through wash.
▼ 3.6	SO	Cross through two washes.
2.6 ▲	SO	Cross through two washes.
▼ 3.7	SO	Cross through wash.
2.5 ▲	SO	Cross through wash.
▼ 4.7	SO	Cross through wash.
1.5 ▲	SO	Cross through wash.
▼ 5.5	SO	Track on right.
0.7 ▲	SO	Track on left.
		GPS: N33°21.79' W114°55.24'
▼ 6.2	SO	Track on right is M 0428, sign-posted to the Hauser Geode Beds Area. Zero trip meter.
0.0 ▲		Continue to the northwest.
		GPS: N33°21.33' W114°54.90'
▼ 0.0		Continue to the southeast.
10.0 ▲	SO	Track on left is M 0428, sign-posted to the Hauser Geode Beds Area. Zero trip meter.
▼ 1.2	SO	Track on right.
8.8 ▲	SO	Track on left.
▼ 1.4	SO	Cross through wash.
8.6 ▲	SO	Cross through wash.
▼ 1.6	SO	Cross through wash.
8.4 ▲	SO	Cross through wash.
▼ 1.8	SO	Palo Verde Mountains Wilderness ends on left; then track on left.
8.2 ▲	SO	Track on right; then Palo Verde Mountains Wilderness starts on right.
		GPS: N33°20.06' W114°53.89'
▼ 3.1	SO	Cross through wash. Trail crosses through many small washes for next 6.9 miles.
6.9 ▲	SO	Cross through wash.
▼ 6.5	SO	Milpitas Wash is running alongside on the right.
3.5 ▲	SO	Milpitas Wash is running alongside on the left.
▼ 8.5	SO	Track on left.
1.5 ▲	SO	Track on right.
▼ 8.6	SO	Track on left and track on right under power lines.
1.4 ▲	SO	Track on left and track on right under power lines.
▼ 9.1	SO	Track on left and track on right are both M 0611.
0.9 ▲	SO	Track on left and track on right are both M 0611.
		GPS: N33°17.00' W114°47.62'
▼ 10.0		Trail ends at intersection with California 78. There is a track opposite. Turn left for Blythe; turn right for Glamis.
0.0 ▲		Trail starts on California 78, 12 miles south of Palo Verde and 0.4 miles south of mile marker 69. Zero trip meter and turn west on graded dirt road, marked Milpitas Wash Road. There is a track opposite the start of the trail. Trail crosses many washes for the next 6.9 miles. The Palo Verde Mountains are on the right.
		GPS: N33°16.97' W114°46.68'

Cibola Wildlife Refuge Trail

Starting Point:	**Neighbour's Boulevard, 6 miles south of California 78, 0.1 miles north of Cibola Bridge**
Finishing Point:	**River Road (in Arizona), 7.7 miles south of Cibola Bridge and the start of the trail**
Total Mileage:	**21 miles**
Unpaved Mileage:	**21 miles**
Driving Time:	**1.5 hours**
Elevation Range:	**200–300 feet**
Usually Open:	**Year-round**
Best Time to Travel:	**Year-round**
Difficulty Rating:	**1**
Scenic Rating:	**9**
Remoteness Rating:	**+0**

Special Attractions

- One of the few trails alongside the Colorado River.
- Wildlife watching for waterfowl and deer.
- Hunting, fishing, and boating in season.
- Flat, easygoing trail for mountain bikes.

History

The Cibola National Wildlife Refuge was established in 1964 to provide a wetland habitat that would accommodate the existing patterns of migratory birds on their long flights across the surrounding desert lands. The refuge encompasses an area of nearly 16,000 acres, spanning both sides of the Colorado River, with the greater portion on the Arizona side. The refuge provides a stable location for wintering waterfowl and other birds, while at the same time offering excellent recreational facilities as well.

Like the migrating birds that flock to this location, people have been enticed by the river for thousands of years. Native Americans knew the value of water in this desert valley. Regular camps and pilgrimages were made along the banks of this once wide, flooding river. From as early as the 1850s, paddle-steamers made their way up and down the Colorado River from Port Isabel (at the mouth of the river) all the way to Hardyville (located roughly where Davis Dam is today). Supplying miners and settlers along the river kept the shallow-bottomed steamboats busy. Wood to fuel their boilers sold at premium rates all along the river.

The arrival of railroads in the 1870s brought heavy competition for the steamers, and companies shut down many of their shipping runs. The year 1909 brought a virtual closure to the river transport system when the Laguna Dam, north of Yuma, cut off passage to the south.

Having played a major role in developing the San Diego to

Yuma stage road, U.S. government surveyor Oliver P. Calloway was very familiar with this southern section of the Colorado River. Calloway could see great potential in the Cibola region—a wide, well-watered alluvial valley set between the Trigo Mountains in Arizona and the Palo Verde Mountains (as they were later to be named) in California. Calloway convinced Thomas Blythe, a speculator from San Francisco, that the riverside location had immense potential.

By the late 1870s, Blythe had acquired a large tract of land in the region of today's Palo Verde, mainly toward the northern end of the valley. Water rights were established in 1877, and Blythe proceeded to construct the first diversion canal off the Colorado River in an effort to colonize the Colorado Desert. Blythe died of a heart attack in San Francisco, without seeing his dream come to fruition. His assets were frozen after his death, and no further work was completed.

In 1904, ranchers Frank Murphy and Ed Williams took on the task. They attracted the interest of the Hobson Brothers and formed the Palo Verde Land and Water Company. Water was flowing, agriculture was under way, and settlers began to move in.

A heavy silt load was always a problem for the Palo Verde diversion system, but construction of the Hoover Dam in 1935 alleviated this problem to a great extent. The dam effectively captured the silt and released clearer water, thereby reducing the overall silt load for the district. As with many diversion systems, this one has had its problems over the decades. Temporary weirs that were built to raise falling water levels during the 1940s have been replaced with more permanent such structures. Additional dams, levees, and drains were installed in the mid-1950s, further improving the potential of this valuable agricultural valley.

Small communities have developed along the Colorado River

For generations, Palo Verde has attracted many full- and part-time residents, not all of them associated with the local agricultural industry. Those interested in water-based activities, birders, hunters, and fishermen have found the Palo Verde pace of life and the neighboring wildlife refuge to be an oasis in the Colorado Desert.

Description

This mainly graded dirt road is usually suitable for passenger vehicles in dry weather. It travels alongside the Colorado River for miles and is an easygoing route for mountain bikers. Part of the trail crosses into Arizona, where it follows the more recently dredged channel of the Colorado River. The state line remains along the old channel.

Crossing into Arizona over the old Colorado River channel on right

Two dirt roads parallel the river. This route mainly travels directly along the riverbank on the smaller one. A slightly larger dirt road travels along the top of the embankment above the river. This route takes the riverside trail where possible, looping back for a short distance along the embankment road to return to Cibola.

The trail leaves immediately north of the Cibola Bridge and drops down to the riverside trail. Thick patches of arrow weed border the road in many places, but there are excellent river panoramas and fishing spots all along its length. Tamarisk (salt cedar), originally introduced to control riverbank erosion, is now a constant problem. Efforts are continually under way to control this fast-growing exotic plant and restore native cottonwoods, willows, and mesquites.

The route passes through the Oxbow Recreation Area, where there is a riverside camping area suitable for RVs and a boat launch. Oxbow Lagoon also offers more secluded campsites. There is a fee for day use and camping in the recreation area, but if you simply drive through without stopping you do not have to pay the user fee. Stopping, picnicking, fishing, or any other recreational activity requires the daily fee. The fee station is located at the campground.

Camping and campfires are not permitted inside the refuge, and there are also seasonal restrictions on the use of motor vehicles and boating within certain areas to protect waterfowl. Hunting and fishing are permitted in season, but please check with the Cibola National Wildlife Refuge for exact dates and locations. Boating is allowed in the main, dry cut channel of the Colorado River. Canoes and kayaks are allowed on the old river channel, although there are seasonal restrictions on some bodies of water. Fishing is permitted anywhere in the refuge if you have a Colorado River Fishing stamp. State seasons and dates vary. Anglers can fish for large-mouthed bass, small-mouthed bass, striped bass, channel catfish, flathead catfish, crappie, sunfish, and tilapia. Hunting for wildfowl is permitted on a limited basis; a lottery is held at 4:30 A.M. daily during hunting season. In addition, hunting for deer, cottontail rabbit, quail, goose, duck, coot, mourning dove, and gallinule is permitted in season with the appropriate permits.

The trail loops back to the embankment road just north of Walters Camp. Traveling the embankment road lets visitors appreciate the mountains on either side of the river. The trail finishes at the paved River Road, south of Cibola, in Arizona.

Another worthwhile drive a short distance from the end of the trail in Arizona is the 4-mile, graded dirt Canada Goose Drive. This short drive, which leaves from the Cibola National Wildlife Refuge Visitor Center, is particularly good in winter, when there are many wintering waterfowl in the area, particularly Canada geese and sandhill cranes. The stands of salt cedar along the drive harbor small birds such as doves and meadowlarks.

The drive runs through alfalfa fields that have been planted for the express purpose of providing feed for wintering waterfowl. This has the dual purpose of keeping the birds on the refuge and making it less likely that they will damage farmers' crops by foraging on surrounding farms.

Note that the 1:24,000 topographical maps do not show the new channel of the river and most maps do not show the track alongside the river.

Current Road Information

Cibola National Wildlife Refuge
Route 2, Box 138
66600 Cibola Lake Road
Cibola, AZ 85328-9801
(520) 857-3253

Map References

BLM Trigo Mts.
USGS 1:24,000 Palo Verde, Cibola, Picacho NW
1:100,000 Trigo Mts.
Maptech CD-ROM: San Diego/Joshua Tree
Southern & Central California Atlas & Gazetteer, p. 119
California Road & Recreation Atlas, p. 114
Other: Cibola National Wildlife Refuge map

Route Directions

Mileage		Direction
▼ 0.0		From California 78, 7 miles south of I-10, zero trip meter and proceed south on Neighbour's Boulevard for 6 miles. Bear right, leaving paved road to your left. Then, after 0.1 miles more, zero trip meter and turn west on unmarked, wide graded dirt road. The turn is 0.1 miles north of the Cibola Bridge.
4.4 ▲		Trail ends on Neighbour's Boulevard. Turn right to cross the river into Arizona; turn left for Blythe.
		GPS: N33°24.95' W114°39.42'
▼ 0.2	TL	Turn left onto unmarked, smaller formed trail.
4.2 ▲	TR	Turn right onto wide, graded road.
		GPS: N33°24.95' W114°39.59'
▼ 0.3	TR	Track on left is closed. Turn right onto graded trail along riverbank.
4.1 ▲	TL	Turn left away from river. Track ahead is closed.
▼ 1.1	SO	Track on right.
3.3 ▲	SO	Track on left.
▼ 1.7	SO	Track on right to lagoon.
2.7 ▲	SO	Track on left to lagoon.
		GPS: N33°24.98' W114°41.20'
▼ 2.4	SO	Small lagoon on right.
2.0 ▲	SO	Small lagoon on left.
▼ 3.0	TR	Pull-in and camp area on left.
1.4 ▲	TL	Pull-in and camp area on right.
▼ 3.1	TL	T-intersection with graded embankment road; then track on right.
1.3 ▲	TR	Track on left; then turn right onto smaller trail, away from embankment road.
		GPS: N33°24.34' W114°42.34'
▼ 3.2	TL	Track on right; then turn left on smaller trail, away from embankment road.
1.2 ▲	TR	T-intersection with wider, graded embankment road; then immediately track on left.
		GPS: N33°24.22' W114°42.44'
▼ 3.3	TR	Turn right onto riverside track.
1.1 ▲	TL	Turn left away from river.
▼ 3.9	SO	Track on right.
0.5 ▲	SO	Track on left.
▼ 4.2	SO	Pass under road bridge.
0.2 ▲	SO	Pass under road bridge.
		GPS: N33°23.42' W114°42.62'
▼ 4.3	TR	Turn right, away from river. Track ahead leads into camping area.
0.1 ▲	TL	Turn left along river trail. Track on right leads into camping area.
▼ 4.4	TL	T-intersection with embankment road and small track straight ahead into camping area at Oxbow Lagoon. Turn left along embankment road. To the right accesses the bridge on Baseline Road, which crosses the river into Arizona and goes to Cibola National Wildlife Refuge Headquarters. Zero trip meter.
0.0 ▲		Continue to the east.
		GPS: N33°23.38' W114°42.72'
▼ 0.0		Continue to the south.
3.9 ▲	TR	Small track on left to camping area at Oxbow Lagoon. Ahead accesses the bridge on Baseline Road, which crosses the river into Arizona and goes to Cibola National Wildlife Refuge Headquarters. Turn right at sign for recreation area and zero trip meter.
▼ 0.1	SO	Graded road on right joins California 78.
3.8 ▲	SO	Graded road on left joins California 78.
▼ 0.2	TL	Turn left into Oxbow Recreation Area. Trail is now marked as #175. Immediately on the left is a camping area, boat launching ramp, and fee station.
3.7 ▲	TR	Oxbow Recreation Area on right—camping area, boat launching ramp, and fee station. Then T-intersection with graded embankment road.
		GPS: N33°23.23' W114°42.71'
▼ 0.3	TR	Turn right along riverbank. Camping area on left.
3.6 ▲	TL	Turn left away from riverbank. Camping area straight ahead.
▼ 1.0	BR	Track on right; then track on left goes 0.3 miles along small groin. Head away from river.
2.9 ▲	SO	Track on right goes 0.3 miles along small groin. Track on left.
		GPS: N33°22.61' W114°42.45'
▼ 1.7	SO	Track on right.
2.2 ▲	SO	Track on left.
▼ 2.9	SO	Track on right.
1.0 ▲	SO	Track on left.
▼ 3.1	SO	Entering Cibola National Wildlife Refuge at sign. No camping or fires past this point.

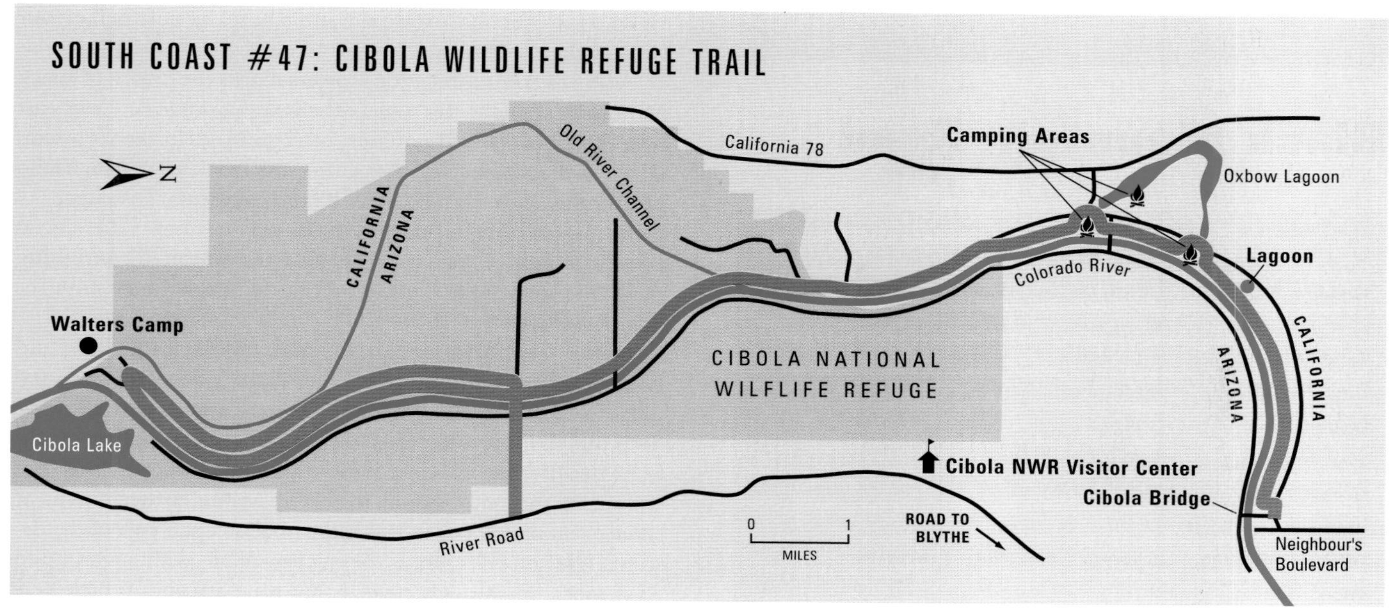

0.8 ▲ SO Leaving Cibola National Wildlife Refuge at sign.

GPS: N33°20.87′ W114°41.94′

▼ 3.2 SO Track on right.
0.7 ▲ SO Track on left.

▼ 3.9 SO Entering Arizona at state line sign. Zero trip meter.
0.0 ▲ Continue to the north.

GPS: N33°20.14′ W114°42.03′

▼ 0.0 Continue to the south.
7.0 ▲ SO Entering California at state line sign. Zero trip meter.

▼ 0.1 SO Track on right.
6.9 ▲ SO Track on left.

▼ 1.4 SO Track on right.
5.6 ▲ SO Track on left.

▼ 2.6 SO Pass under bridge.
4.4 ▲ SO Pass under bridge.

GPS: N33°18.20′ W114°40.70′

▼ 2.8 SO Track on right.
4.2 ▲ SO Track on left.

▼ 5.1 SO Entering Zone III of Cibola National Wildlife Refuge. Vehicle travel is permitted through here between September 6 and March 14 only. Fishing, hiking, and picnicking are permitted outside these dates.
1.9 ▲ SO Exiting Zone III of Cibola National Wildlife Refuge.

GPS: N33°16.01′ W114°40.10′

▼ 6.4 SO Track on right.
0.6 ▲ SO Track on left.

▼ 7.0 TR Track straight ahead continues 0.8 miles to a point overlooking Walters Camp. Zero trip meter.
0.0 ▲ Continue to the northeast.

GPS: N33°14.71′ W114°40.76′

▼ 0.0 Continue to the west.
4.5 ▲ TL Turn left onto the river trail. Track on right goes 0.8 miles to a point overlooking Walters Camp. Zero trip meter.

▼ 0.2 TR Turn right onto embankment road. Straight ahead goes 0.3 miles to a point on the old river course opposite Walters Camp.
4.3 ▲ TL T-intersection. Right goes 0.3 miles to a point on the old river course opposite Walters Camp.

▼ 0.8 SO Track on left and track on right.
3.7 ▲ SO Track on left and track on right.

▼ 2.9 SO Hiking trail on left.
1.6 ▲ SO Hiking trail on right.

▼ 4.3 SO Track on right.
0.2 ▲ SO Track on left.

▼ 4.5 TR 4-way intersection. Zero trip meter and turn right toward bridge.
0.0 ▲ Continue to the south.

GPS: N33°18.19′ W114°40.84′

▼ 0.0 Continue to the east.
1.2 ▲ TL 4-way intersection. Zero trip meter and turn left along embankment.

▼ 0.1 SO Start to cross over Colorado River on bridge.
1.1 ▲ SO Exit bridge (still in Arizona).

▼ 0.2 SO Exit bridge (still in Arizona); then track on right.
1.0 ▲ SO Track on left; then start to cross over Colorado River on bridge.

▼ 0.3 SO Embankment road on left and right.
0.9 ▲ SO Embankment road on left and right.

▼ 0.5 SO Cattle guard. Leaving Cibola National Wildlife Refuge.
0.7 ▲ SO Cattle guard. Entering Cibola National Wildlife Refuge.

GPS: N33°18.20′ W114°40.27′

▼ 1.0 SO Track on right goes into Farm Unit II—Goose Hunting Area.
0.2 ▲ SO Track on left goes into Farm Unit II—Goose Hunting Area.

▼ 1.2 Trail ends at intersection with paved River Road. Turn right for Cibola Lake; turn left for Cibola NWR Visitor Center and Blythe. Straight ahead is Trail #194.
0.0 ▲ Trail commences in Arizona on paved River Road, 7.7 miles south of the state line at Cibola Bridge and the northern end of the trail, and 4.1 miles south of Cibola NWR Visitor Center. Zero trip meter and turn west at sign for Island Unit Road. Trail #194 is opposite (to the east).

GPS: N33°18.20′ W114°39.50′

Black Mountain Road

Starting Point:	**California 78, 2.8 miles north of the intersection with Ogilby Road (S34)**
Finishing Point:	**South Coast #49: Indian Pass Road, 0.8 miles east of Ogilby Road (S34)**
Total Mileage:	**15.5 miles**
Unpaved Mileage:	**10.9 miles**
Driving Time:	**2 hours**
Elevation Range:	**600–2,000 feet**
Usually Open:	**Year-round**
Best Time to Travel:	**October to June**
Difficulty Rating:	**6 forward direction, 7 reverse**
Scenic Rating:	**9**
Remoteness Rating:	**+0**

Special Attractions

- Panoramic view of the multihued Chocolate Mountains from Black Mountain.
- Challenging descent from Black Mountain for experienced drivers.
- Trail is suitable for passenger vehicles in the forward direction as far as the top of Black Mountain.

Description

Black Mountain Road really has something for everyone. Drivers of passenger vehicles will enjoy the easy graded dirt and paved road to the top of Black Mountain. Experienced drivers in high-clearance 4WDs will relish the challenge of the very steep and loose descent from the south side of the mountain. Really enthusiastic drivers might like to tackle the trail in reverse, climbing up to Black Mountain from the south on a loose and low-traction hill where the angle of the rutted slope reaches 35 degrees in places.

Black Mountain Road descends 1,600 feet to the valley below

The trail leaves California 78 at a marked intersection and follows a graded dirt road across undulating terrain to the base of Black Mountain. The road becomes a single-lane paved road as it starts to climb up the northern flank of the mountain. It travels through fields of black volcanic boulders and rocks that shine with the desert patina. Occasional ocotillos, chollas, and creosote bushes add splashes of green to the landscape. There are good views west over the Imperial Sand Dunes as you make your way up the mountain.

A line of communications towers marks the crown of Black Mountain. Behind the towers there are panoramic views east over the Chocolate Mountains, with glimpses of the Colorado River and Arizona. To the south are the Cargo Muchacho Mountains with Picacho Peak to the southeast. Passenger vehicles should turn around here. In dry weather, experienced drivers of high-clearance 4WDs have the option of continuing down the steep and challenging trail to South Coast #49: Indian Pass Road.

South of Black Mountain, the trail turns to formed dirt and immediately starts to descend. The descent becomes steep 0.6 miles from the towers. The surface is loose and eroded, allowing deep ruts to form along the trail. Conditions can change quickly, especially after rain. It can be difficult to climb back up this section of the trail, should it be impassable farther down, or should you decide not to tackle the final, steepest part of the descent. The last 0.2 miles is the steepest of all, with angles up to 35 degrees. We strongly suggest that you park your vehicle here and hike down the trail far enough to view the final steep descent and check that the trail is passable. These few minutes could save you an expensive recovery bill or even injury.

From the base of the descent, the trail travels across a bajada, crossing many small washes as it follows alongside small power lines to South Coast #49: Indian Pass Road.

Current Road Information

Bureau of Land Management
Yuma Field Office
2555 East Gila Ridge Road
Yuma, AZ 85365
(520) 317-3200

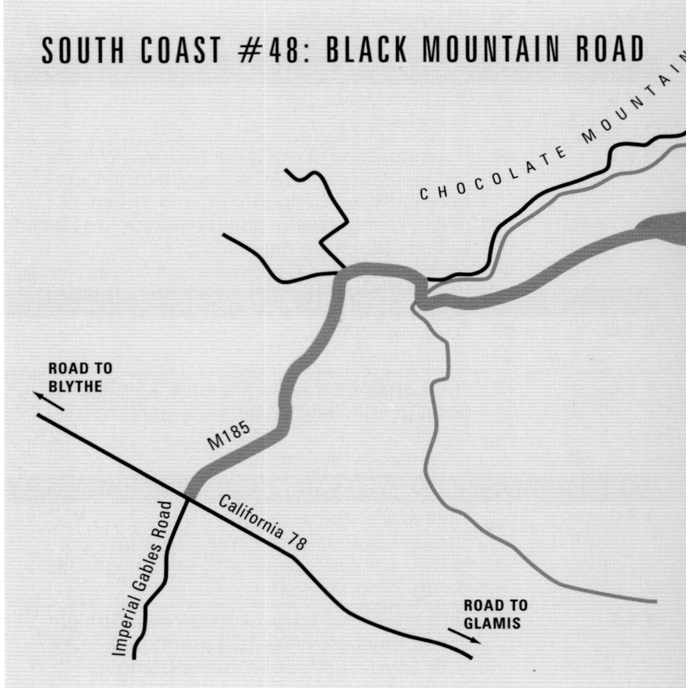

Map References

BLM Yuma, Trigo Mts.
USGS 1:24,000 Ninemile Wash, Quartz Peak, Hedges
1:100,000 Yuma, Trigo Mts.
Maptech CD-ROM: San Diego/Joshua Tree
Southern & Central California Atlas & Gazetteer, pp. 118, 126
California Road & Recreation Atlas, p. 119

Route Directions

▼ 0.0		From California 78, 2.8 miles north of the intersection with Ogilby Road (S34) and 0.3 miles north of mile marker 55, zero trip meter and turn east on graded dirt road at the sign for Black Mountain Road, marked M185. The road is suitable for 4WDs, ATVs, and motorbikes. Imperial Gables Road is opposite.
2.6 ▲		Trail ends at the intersection with California 78. Turn left for Glamis; turn right for Blythe. Imperial Gables Road is opposite.
		GPS: N33°07.28' W114°53.14'
▼ 2.1	BR	Two tracks on left. Remain on graded road.
0.5 ▲	BL	Two tracks on right. Remain on graded road.
		GPS: N33°06.44' W114°51.38'
▼ 2.6	SO	Small track on left through leveled open area. Zero trip meter.
0.0 ▲		Continue to the northeast.
		GPS: N33°06.03' W114°51.37'
▼ 0.0		Continue to the southwest and cross through wash. Road is now paved.
4.6 ▲	SO	Cross through wash. Road is now graded dirt. Small track on right through leveled open area. Zero trip meter.
▼ 0.2	SO	Cross through wash on concrete ford.
4.4 ▲	SO	Cross through wash on concrete ford.
▼ 2.1	SO	Track on left.
2.5 ▲	SO	Track on right.
		GPS: N33°04.58' W114°50.92'

The old mining region around Julian Wash is visible from Black Mountain

▼ 3.8	SO	Track on left.
0.8 ▲	SO	Track on right.
▼ 3.9	SO	Top of Black Mountain. Communications towers start on left.
0.7 ▲	SO	Top of Black Mountain. Last of the communications towers.
▼ 4.5	BL	Descend to flat open area; then bear left onto graded dirt road that follows power lines to the southeast.
0.1 ▲	BR	At the flat area at the start of the communications towers, head uphill and to the right toward the rest of the towers.
▼ 4.6	BR	Track on left goes to final communications tower. Zero trip meter and bear right, descending from Black Mountain under the small power line.
0.0 ▲		Continue to the north.
		GPS: N33°03.06' W114°49.60'

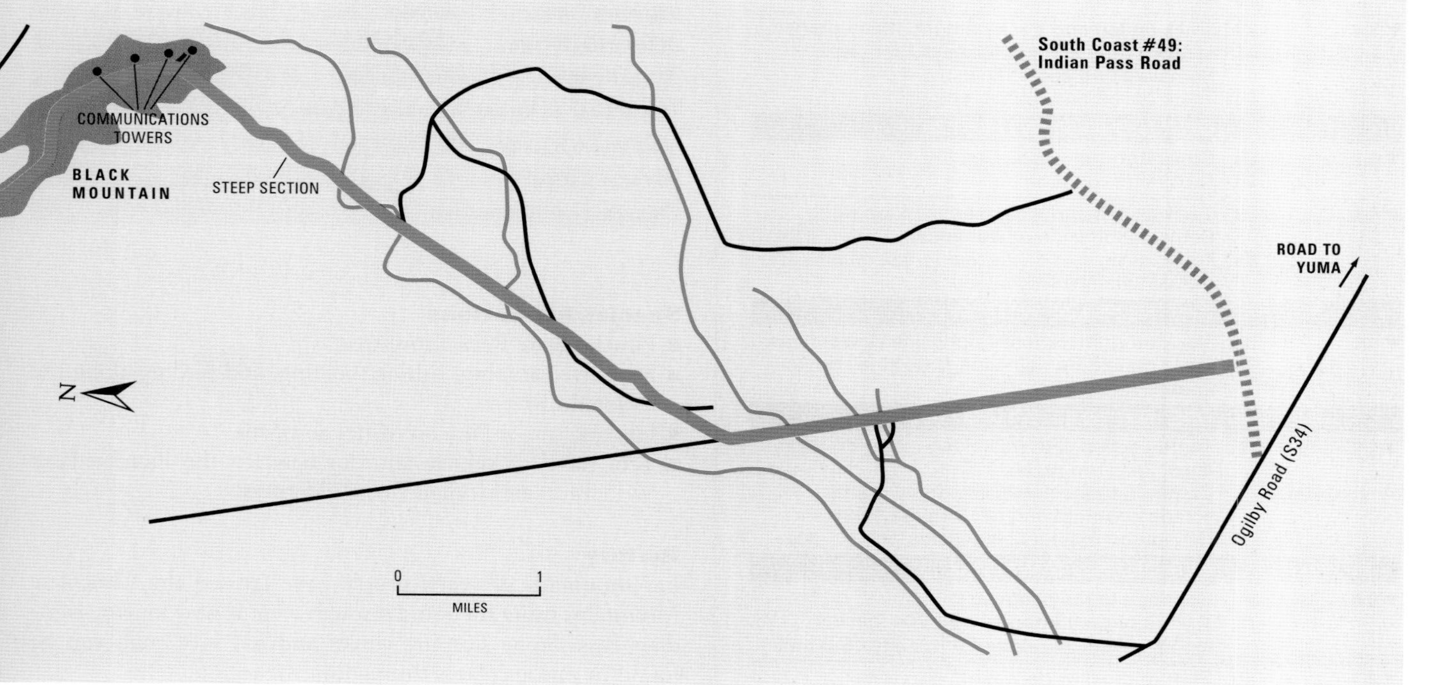

▼ 0.0			Continue to the southwest.
	4.9 ▲	BL	Track on right goes to the first of the communications towers. Zero trip meter and bear left toward the top of Black Mountain.
▼ 0.6		BR	Track on left; road swings away from power lines. Start of steep descent.
	4.3 ▲	BL	Track on right; road now follows power lines. End of steep ascent.
			GPS: N33°02.62' W114°49.94'
▼ 0.7		SO	Track on left to power lines.
	4.2 ▲	SO	Track on right to power lines.
▼ 0.8		SO	Track on right and track on left.
	4.1 ▲	SO	Track on right and track on left.
▼ 1.0		SO	Steepest part of descent.
	3.9 ▲	SO	End of steepest section. Trail continues to climb steeply.
			GPS: N33°02.34' W114°50.15'
▼ 1.2		SO	End of descent. Trail rejoins small power lines.
	3.7 ▲	SO	Start of climb. Trail leaves power lines.
			GPS: N33°02.23' W114°50.24'
▼ 1.5		SO	Cross through wash. Many wash crossings for the next 0.6 miles.
	3.4 ▲	SO	Cross through wash.
▼ 1.9		SO	Cross through wash, remaining alongside power lines. Track on left goes down wash, away from power lines.
	3.0 ▲	SO	Track on right goes down wash, away from power lines. Cross through wash.
			GPS: N33°01.74' W114°50.55'
▼ 2.1		SO	Track on left up wash; then track on left and track on right.
	2.8 ▲	SO	Track on left and track on right; then track on right up wash. Many wash crossings for next 0.6 miles.
▼ 2.8		SO	Cross through wash.
	2.1 ▲	SO	Cross through wash.
▼ 3.0		SO	Cross through wash.
	1.9 ▲	SO	Cross through wash.
▼ 3.3		SO	Cross through wash.
	1.6 ▲	SO	Cross through wash.
▼ 3.4		SO	Track on left and track on right. Many grader scrapes right and left for next 1.5 miles. Remain along power lines.
	1.5 ▲	SO	Track on left and track on right.
			GPS: N33°00.60' W114°51.36'
▼ 3.9		SO	Cross through wash.
	1.0 ▲	SO	Cross through wash.
▼ 4.4		SO	Track on left and well-used track on right. Remain alongside power lines.
	0.5 ▲	BR	Track on right and well-used track on left. Remain alongside power lines.
			GPS: N32°59.86' W114°51.87'
▼ 4.6		BL	Track on right. Remain alongside power lines.
	0.3 ▲	SO	Track on left. Remain alongside small power lines.
			GPS: N32°59.68' W114°52.00'
▼ 4.9		TL	T-intersection with trail along larger power lines. Zero trip meter.
	0.0 ▲		Continue to the northeast. Many grader scrapes on right and left for next 1.5 miles. Remain on main trail alongside power lines.
			GPS: N32°59.45' W114°52.05'
▼ 0.0			Continue to the southeast.
	3.4 ▲	TR	Turn right on unmarked trail that follows alongside smaller power lines. Zero trip meter.
▼ 0.1		SO	Start to cross wide wash.
	3.3 ▲	SO	Exit wash.
▼ 0.4		SO	Exit wash.
	3.0 ▲	SO	Start to cross wide wash.
▼ 0.8		SO	Cross through wash. Trail crosses many washes for next 2.6 miles.
	2.6 ▲	SO	Cross through wash.
▼ 0.9		SO	Track on right; then cross through wash.
	2.5 ▲	SO	Cross through wash; then track on left.
▼ 1.0		SO	Two entrances to track on right.
	2.4 ▲	SO	Two entrances to track on left.
▼ 1.3		SO	Track on right.
	2.1 ▲	BL	Track on left.
▼ 3.4			Trail ends at intersection with South Coast #49: Indian Pass Road (A 272). Turn right to exit to Ogilby Road (S34); turn left to continue along Indian Pass Road over Indian Pass to Picacho State Recreation Area.
	0.0 ▲		Trail commences on South Coast #49: Indian Pass Road, 0.8 miles east of Ogilby Road (S34). Zero trip meter and turn northwest on unmarked dirt road that travels alongside power lines. Trail crosses many washes for next 2.6 miles.
			GPS: N32°56.47' W114°51.22'

SOUTH COAST #49

Indian Pass Road

Starting Point:	**Ogilby Road (S34), 11.3 miles south of California 78**
Finishing Point:	**Winterhaven Road, 0.3 miles north of I-8**
Total Mileage:	**43.4 miles**
Unpaved Mileage:	**39.2 miles**
Driving Time:	**4 hours**
Elevation Range:	**100–1,100 feet**
Usually Open:	**Year-round**
Best Time to Travel:	**October to June**
Difficulty Rating:	**3**
Scenic Rating:	**10**
Remoteness Rating:	**+0**

Special Attractions

- Picacho State Recreation Area.
- Primitive camping, fishing, boating, and birding along the Colorado River.
- Historic site of Picacho Mines and Mill.
- Trail travels a vehicle corridor between the Picacho Peak Wilderness and Indian Pass Wilderness.

History

For thousands of years, people have crossed the Chocolate Mountains using the route through what is now known as Indian Pass. Stone sleeping circles and old foot trails can be found in various places throughout the region.

The Colorado River drifts past the site of Hoge Ranch, Arizona

One of the first of many steamboats to ply the waters of the Colorado River was the *Uncle Sam,* which left Fort Yuma in 1852 under the command of James Turnbell. Other steamers were quick to follow. The boats supplied prospectors, settlers, and military personnel to the north and returned with passengers and ore. The stretch of river from the Gulf of California to the Virgin River (a distance of nearly 600 miles) became a transportation route opening up various settlements along its twisting path. (See page 63 for more information on the Colorado River steamboat trade.)

The Picacho Mine is located along the southern approach to Indian Pass Road. Although a Native American may have been the first to discover the location, José Maria Mendivil of Sonora, Mexico, first discovered gold and staked a claim in 1852. The mine received the name Picacho (Spanish for "peak") from a landmark to the west—a spiraling peak, distinctive from afar. Mendivil sold his claims and homesteaded by the Colorado River near the influx of Picacho Wash. He laid out a town, calling it El Rio, and named the streets after his daughters.

David Neahr, who operated a store in Yuma, was drawn to the mine by prospectors who purchased goods with gold. He invested in the mine and constructed a mill by the river to process ore. Neahr also built the Yuma prison. In the early 1880s, financial strains forced Neahr to sell his interests in Picacho to Dr. DeWitt Jayne. When Jayne died, a group of investors took over and formed the Picacho Gold Mining Company. The company sold out after a short time to Stephen W. Dorsay and associates, who established the California King Gold Mines. Dorsay actively promoted the location, attracting many speculators to invest in the mine. A 450-ton stamp mill was constructed next to Neahr's smaller mill, and a railroad was built to connect it with the mine. The Gold Dream Mining Company and the California Queen Mining Company were other companies in operation around the boom time.

Mendivil sold lots at El Rio, which was eventually renamed Picacho because of the mine's influence. Shortly after the turn of the twentieth century, Picacho bustled with a population nearing 2,500. Nearly 700 men worked at the mines and mills, with payroll figures regularly approaching $40,000 a month.

By the late 1870s, railroads arrived in the lower Colorado River region and had an adverse effect on the paddlewheel service along the river. However, Picacho Landing was still a regular destination. Steamboats running out of Picacho kept woodcutters busy with a consistent demand for fuel. Picacho's saloons were also busy, as were the three schools and town stores. Wells Fargo ran a regular service to the riverside town. It is estimated that nearly $15 million worth of ore was sent downriver to Yuma from the mines at Picacho.

Although the Picacho mines, mills, and merchants were in full swing at the turn of the century, a series of events brought about the demise of the town. Dorsay had sold out just after the turn of the century, thinking he had drawn as many investors as possible. Around 1905, there was an explosion at the mine. There were no injuries, but it was a major setback in production. Two weeks later, the railroad connection between the mine and mill was washed out in a heavy downpour, further interrupting output and eating into profits. Next the value of ore depreciated. The final blow to large-scale operations came in 1909 with the construction of the Laguna Dam, 9 miles north of Yuma. This meant that steamers could no longer reach Picacho from Yuma. By 1910, only small-time miners were left, and Picacho was slowly fading away. The mines were not exhausted by any means, but larger companies could no longer keep up with their payments. Most went bankrupt. Mendivil moved his home to Yuma, where he died at the age of 78.

In 1938, construction of the Imperial Dam, 4 miles to the north of Laguna Dam, effectively raised the water level by 20 feet, flooding the remnants of the Picacho town site. The ruins of Neahr's Mill remain to this day. In the 1960s the Picacho town site was turned into a recreational site.

Some mining activity took place in the 1930s, but all activity ceased at the onset of World War II. Alfred Dallago of the Picacho Development Corporation took control of the main mine in 1971. By 1984, modern mining techniques brought life back to the mines, which are currently leased to Chemgold, Inc. The small cemetery beside the Picacho Mine was almost completely washed away at the turn of the twenty-first century. Just a tiny section remains.

Sunset over Taylor Lake

Description

Indian Pass Road is an alternate route into the very beautiful Picacho State Recreation Area. The trail starts on Ogilby Road (S34) and follows a graded road up the bajada toward Indian Pass in the Chocolate Mountains. From the start of the trail, the distinctive, rugged butte of Picacho Peak is visible directly to the east, with the Cargo Muchacho Mountains to the south.

Two wilderness areas border the road after a few miles —Picacho Peak Wilderness to the south and Indian Pass Wilderness to the north. The Picacho Peak Wilderness is composed of a range of dark-colored mountains, of which the 1,400-foot Mica Peak is the tallest, and a region of jagged peaks, spires, and wide sandy washes. Undulating bench lands, dissected by deep, narrow arroyos, complete the wilderness area, which provides a habitat for the Colorado River toad, Great Plains toad, and tree lizard. These species survive here because of the proximity of the Colorado River. Other animals that can be seen are Yuma king snakes, desert bighorn sheep, mule deer, desert tortoises, and a healthy population of wild burros. Indian Pass Wilderness encompasses part of the vast Chocolate Mountains, a twisting maze of multicolored canyons and rocky washes.

East of Indian Pass, the trail descends to Gavilan Wash; it remains in the wash all the way to Picacho State Recreation Area. Loose and soft in places, the wash is normally an easy run for a high-clearance 4WD vehicle.

Visitors entering the recreation area are required to pay a nominal day use fee. This includes those just driving through without stopping. The primitive and developed camping areas require an additional fee. A short distance into the park, a graded road to the left leads to the primitive campsites of Outpost Camp and 4-S Beach. There are two sites at each with picnic tables and a pit toilet, but no other facilities.

Continuing on the main trail, the roughly graded road passes through Bear Wash and a small area of badlands very close to the Colorado River. There are many overlooks and river views along this section of trail. A lovely primitive campsite can be found at Taylor Lake, an inlet on the Colorado River. There are four sites here with good river views. Campers should note that the boat-in campsites mentioned in the route directions are not for vehicle-based camping. Use one of the primitive campsites mentioned or the main developed campground. Past Taylor Lake, the trail is graded all the way to Winterhaven and is normally suitable for passenger vehicles in dry weather.

The recreation area has boat launching facilities, a small general store with limited hours, and a ranger station. One short, worthwhile hiking trail is the self-guided walk to Picacho Mills. Leaving the recreation area, the graded road exits from the south end of the Chocolate Mountains, passing the distinctively shaped Picacho Peak and the Picacho Mine.

The trail crosses through the Fort Yuma Indian Reservation and over the All American Canal to finish on US 8 in Winterhaven, immediately across the state line from Yuma, Arizona.

Current Road Information

Bureau of Land Management
Yuma Field Office
2555 East Gila Ridge Road
Yuma, AZ 85365
(520) 317-3200

Map References

BLM Trigo Mts., Yuma
USGS 1:24,000 Hedges, Quartz Peak, Picacho SW, Picacho, Picacho Peak, Araz, Bard, Yuma East, Yuma West
1:100,000 Trigo Mts., Yuma
Maptech CD-ROM: San Diego/Joshua Tree
Southern & Central California Atlas & Gazetteer, pp. 126, 127, 119
California Road & Recreation Atlas, p. 119

Route Directions

▼ 0.0		From Ogilby Road, 11.3 miles south of California 78, zero trip meter and turn east on wide, graded dirt Indian Pass Road (S272, on some maps this is shown as A272). The road has a stop sign but is unmarked and is opposite a smaller road that leads through a wide area of desert pavement. Many small tracks on right and left for next 6.4 miles.
8.2 ▲		Trail finishes on Ogilby Road (S34). Turn right for California 78 and Blythe; turn left for I-8 and Yuma.
		GPS: N32°56.29' W114°52.07'
▼ 0.8	SO	Track on right and track on left under power lines. Track on left is South Coast #48: Black Mountain Road.
7.4 ▲	SO	Track on left and track on right under power lines. Track on right is South Coast #48: Black Mountain Road.
		GPS: N32°56.47' W114°51.22'
▼ 1.6	SO	Cross through wash; then track on right.
6.6 ▲	SO	Track on left; then cross through wash.
▼ 2.2	SO	Track on left.
6.0 ▲	SO	Track on right.
▼ 2.5	SO	Track on left.
5.7 ▲	SO	Track on right.
▼ 3.6	SO	Track on right.
4.6 ▲	SO	Track on left.
▼ 4.3	SO	Cross through wash.
3.9 ▲	SO	Cross through wash.
▼ 5.5	SO	Track on right.
2.7 ▲	SO	Track on left.
		GPS: N32°59.32' W114°47.78'
▼ 6.4	SO	Picacho Peak Wilderness starts on right.
1.8 ▲	SO	Picacho Peak Wilderness ends on left. Many small tracks on left and right for next 6.4 miles.
		GPS: N32°59.94' W114°47.30'
▼ 6.7	SO	Cross through wash.
1.5 ▲	SO	Cross through wash.
▼ 7.8	SO	Indian Pass Wilderness starts on left.
0.4 ▲	SO	Indian Pass Wilderness finishes on right.
		GPS: N33°00.88' W114°46.50'
▼ 8.2	SO	Indian Pass. Zero trip meter at information board.
0.0 ▲		Continue to the south on wide, graded dirt road.

GPS: N33°01.23′ W114°46.39′

▼ 0.0 Continue to the northwest and start to descend. Trail becomes rougher.

6.5 ▲ SO End of ascent at Indian Pass. Zero trip meter at information board.

▼ 0.2 SO Cross through wash.

6.3 ▲ SO Cross through wash and start to ascend.

▼ 0.5 BR Enter Gavilan Wash down canyon.

6.0 ▲ BL Exit Gavilan Wash and canyon.

GPS: N33°01.52′ W114°46.14′

▼ 3.6 SO Track on left up side wash goes 0.1 miles to mine diggings.

2.9 ▲ SO Track on right up side wash goes 0.1 miles to mine diggings.

GPS: N33°02.02′ W114°43.29′

▼ 4.0 SO Concrete foundations on top of mesa on left. Canyon becomes wider.

2.5 ▲ SO Concrete foundations on top of mesa on right. Canyon becomes narrower.

GPS: N33°02.13′ W114°42.80′

▼ 5.8 SO Enter Picacho State Recreation Area at sign (fee required for driving through).

0.7 ▲ SO Exit Picacho State Recreation Area at sign.

GPS: N33°02.72′ W114°41.42′

▼ 6.5 BR Self-registration point for park use. Track on left goes 1.5 miles to Outpost Camp and 4-S Beach Camp. Zero trip meter. Exit line of wash.

0.0 ▲ Continue to the southwest, following sign to Ogilby. Trail leaves Colorado River and enters line of wash.

GPS: N33°03.10′ W114°40.93′

▼ 0.0 Continue to the east. Trail now follows close to the Colorado River.

5.3 ▲ BL Self-registration point for park use. Track on right goes 1.5 miles to Outpost Camp and 4-S Beach Camp. Zero trip meter.

▼ 1.5 SO Carrizo Wash Hiking Trail on right goes approximately 2 miles to Carrizo Falls.

3.8 ▲ SO Carrizo Wash Hiking Trail on left goes approximately 2 miles to Carrizo Falls.

GPS: N33°02.21′ W114°40.40′

▼ 1.7 SO Track on left to overlook over river. Carrizo Boat-In Camp is below (no vehicle-based camping).

3.6 ▲ SO Track on right to overlook over river. Carrizo Boat-In Camp is below (no vehicle-based camping).

GPS: N33°02.17′ W114°40.21′

▼ 2.3 SO Closure gate; then enter Bear Canyon up wash.

3.0 ▲ SO Exit Bear Canyon; then closure gate.

GPS: N33°01.90′ W114°39.77′

▼ 2.9 SO Exit wash.

2.4 ▲ SO Enter wash.

▼ 3.0 BL Track on right up Bear Canyon Wash.

2.3 ▲ BR Track on left up Bear Canyon Wash.

GPS: N33°01.37′ W114°39.75′

▼ 3.2 SO Exit Bear Canyon. Enter line of wash.

2.1 ▲ SO Exit line of wash. Enter Bear Canyon.

▼ 4.1 SO Track on left goes to Paddlewheeler Boat-In Camp (no vehicle-based camping).

1.2 ▲ SO Track on right goes to Paddlewheeler Boat-In Camp (no vehicle-based camping).

GPS: N33°02.01′ W114°39.20′

▼ 4.4 SO Exit line of wash.

0.9 ▲ SO Enter line of wash.

▼ 5.3 SO Track on left goes to Taylor Lake Primitive Camp Area. Zero trip meter.

0.0 ▲ Continue to the northwest.

GPS: N33°01.75′ W114°38.26′

▼ 0.0 Continue to the southeast.

2.0 ▲ SO Track on right goes to Taylor Lake Primitive Camp Area. Zero trip meter.

▼ 0.5 SO Cross through wash; then enter White Wash.

1.5 ▲ SO Exit White Wash; then cross through wash.

▼ 0.9 SO Exit White Wash.

1.1 ▲ SO Enter White Wash.

▼ 1.3 SO Hiking trail on left.

0.7 ▲ SO Hiking trail on right.

GPS: N33°01.07′ W114°37.39′

▼ 1.4 SO Hiking trail on left.

0.6 ▲ SO Hiking trail on right.

▼ 1.5 SO Track on left goes into Main Campground.

0.5 ▲ SO Second entrance to Main Campground on right. Continue straight ahead, following sign to Taylor Lake.

▼ 1.6 SO Second entrance to Main Campground on left. Red Rock Canyon Hiking Trail on right. Cross through wash.

0.4 ▲ SO Cross through wash. Track on right goes to Main Campground. Red Rock Canyon Hiking Trail on left.

GPS: N33°01.08′ W114°37.16′

▼ 2.0 TR T-intersection. Track on left goes short distance to Main Campground, store, and the self-guided hiking trail to Picacho Stamp Mill. Small track ahead goes to river overlook. Follow sign for Winterhaven and pass fee station. Zero trip meter.

0.0 ▲ Continue to the west.

GPS: N33°01.11′ W114°36.86′

▼ 0.0 Continue to the south.

4.0 ▲ TL Small track on right goes to river overlook. Graded road ahead goes short distance to Main Campground, store, and the self-guided hiking trail to Picacho Stamp Mill. Zero trip meter and turn left on graded road.

▼ 0.7 SO Exit Picacho State Recreation Area. Trail enters line of wash.

3.3 ▲ SO Enter Picacho State Recreation Area (fee required for driving through).

GPS: N33°00.49′ W114°37.15′

▼ 1.3 SO Track on left up wash.

2.7 ▲ SO Track on right up wash.

▼ 1.8 SO Track on left.

2.2 ▲ SO Track on right.

▼ 2.0 SO Track on right is A 278, marked with a brown marker post.

2.0 ▲ SO Track on left is A 278, marked with a brown marker post.

GPS: N32°59.61′ W114°38.00′

▼ 3.5 SO Exit line of wash.

0.5 ▲ SO Enter line of wash.

▼ 3.6 SO Historical marker for Picacho Mines on left.

0.4 ▲ SO Historical marker for Picacho Mines on right.

GPS: N32°58.31′ W114°38.06′

▼ 3.7 SO Track on left.

0.3 ▲ SO Track on right.

▼ 4.0 SO Track on right goes into the active Picacho Mines. An information board and historical marker are a short distance to the right. This is

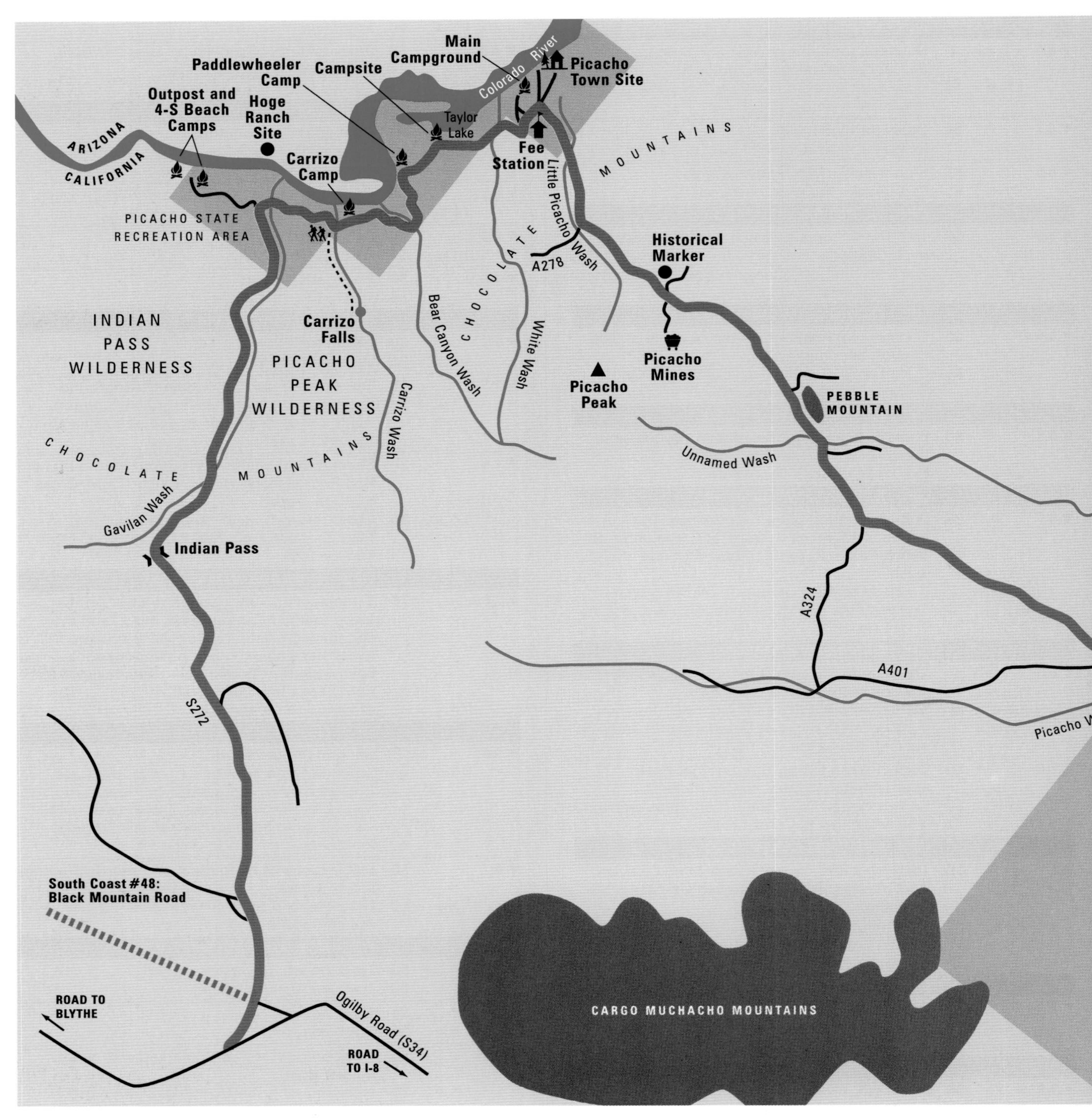

			also the location of the Picacho Cemetery (mainly washed out). Zero trip meter.
	0.0 ▲		Continue to the west.
			GPS: N32°58.01′ W114°38.11′
▼ 0.0			Continue to the east.
	9.7 ▲	BR	Track on left goes into the active Picacho Mines. An information board and historical marker are a short distance to the right. This is also the location of the Picacho Cemetery (mainly washed out). Zero trip meter.
▼ 0.3		SO	Cross through wash.
	9.4 ▲	SO	Cross through wash.
▼ 0.9		SO	Cross through wash.
	8.8 ▲	SO	Cross through wash.
▼ 1.2		SO	Cross through wash.
	8.5 ▲	SO	Cross through wash.
▼ 2.0		SO	Cross through wash.
	7.7 ▲	SO	Cross through wash.
▼ 2.5		SO	Track on left.
	7.2 ▲	SO	Track on right.
			GPS: N32°55.97′ W114°38.28′

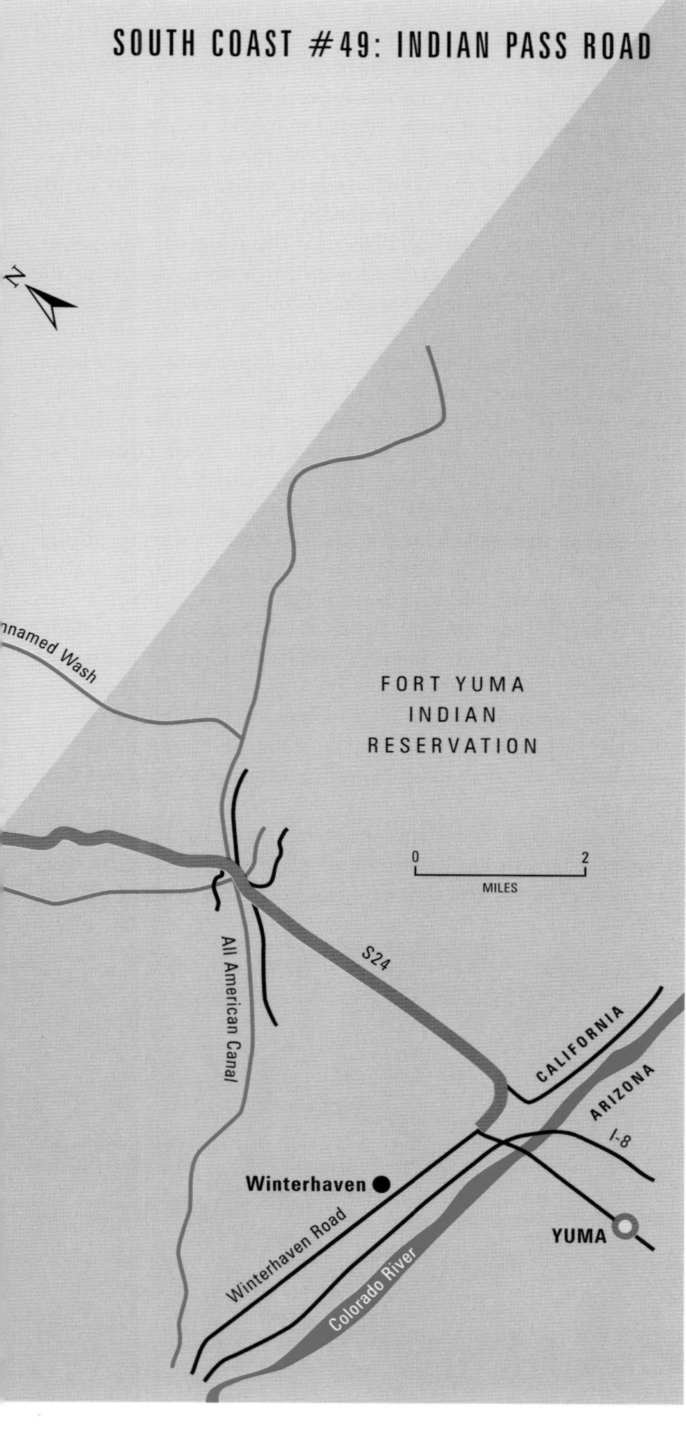

▼	▲		
▼ 3.5		BR	Cross through Unnamed Wash. Track on left down wash. Trail now crosses many washes for the next 3 miles.
	6.2 ▲	BL	Cross through Unnamed Wash. Track on right down wash.
			GPS: N32°55.16′ W114°38.50′
▼ 3.9		SO	Track on right.
	5.8 ▲	SO	Track on left.
▼ 5.0		SO	Track on right is A 324, marked by a brown marker post a short distance back from the intersection.
	4.7 ▲	SO	Track on left is A 324, marked by a brown marker post a short distance back from the intersection.
			GPS: N32°54.20′ W114°39.18′
▼ 6.5		SO	Track on left.
	3.2 ▲	SO	Track on right. There are many wash crossings for the next 3 miles.
▼ 7.8		SO	Start to cross through wide wash.
	1.9 ▲	SO	Exit wash.
▼ 8.0		SO	Exit wash.
	1.7 ▲	SO	Start to cross through wide wash.
▼ 9.7		SO	Graded road on right is A 401. Zero trip meter.
	0.0 ▲		Continue to the northwest on A 481, following sign for Picacho State Recreation Area.
			GPS: N32°50.17′ W114°38.40′
▼ 0.0			Continue to the southeast on A 481.
	3.1 ▲	BR	Graded road on left is A 401. Zero trip meter.
▼ 0.1		SO	Track on left and track on right under power lines.
	3.0 ▲	SO	Track on left and track on right under power lines.
▼ 0.2		SO	Enter Fort Yuma Indian Reservation.
	2.9 ▲	SO	Exit Fort Yuma Indian Reservation.
▼ 2.9		SO	Track on right.
	0.2 ▲	SO	Track on left.
▼ 3.0		SO	Track on left along canal.
	0.1 ▲	SO	Track on right along canal.
▼ 3.1		TR	Cross over All American Canal on bridge; then turn right past track on left along canal. Zero trip meter.
	0.0 ▲		Continue to the northwest.
			GPS: N32°47.83′ W114°36.74′
▼ 0.0			Continue to the southwest and cross over Picacho Wash on bridge; then track on left.
	4.6 ▲	TL	Track on right; then cross over Picacho Wash on bridge; then track continues straight ahead alongside canal. Zero trip meter and cross over All American Canal on bridge, following sign for Picacho State Recreation Area.
▼ 0.2		BL	Two small tracks on left; then track on right. Bear left, following graded dirt road.
	4.4 ▲	BR	Track on left; then two small tracks on right. Continue on graded dirt road alongside canal.
▼ 0.4		SO	Track on right; then road becomes paved. Road on left is White Road. Remain on paved Picacho Road for the next 4.2 miles.
	4.2 ▲	SO	White Road on right. Road turns to graded dirt; then track on left.
▼ 4.4		TR	Turn right, remaining on S24.
	0.2 ▲	TL	Turn left, remaining on S24 and following signs for Picacho.
			GPS: N32°44.14′ W114°37.36′
▼ 4.6			Trail ends at intersection of S24 and US 8 (Winterhaven Drive), north of the I-8 freeway intersection and immediately west of Colorado River and Arizona state line. Turn right for Winterhaven; turn left for Yuma, AZ.
	0.0 ▲		From US 8 in Yuma, AZ, at the Arizona state line on the Colorado River, proceed into California. Cross over I-8 freeway and proceed 0.3 miles. Turn right onto paved S24, following sign for Picacho State Recreation Area. Zero trip meter and proceed east on paved road. Road is traveling through the Fort Yuma Indian Reservation.
			GPS: N32°44.18′ W114°37.57′

Ferguson Lake Road

Starting Point:	**Imperial Dam Road, 0.4 miles west of the California state line**
Finishing Point:	**Ferguson Lake**
Total Mileage:	**13.4 miles (one-way)**
Unpaved Mileage:	**13.4 miles**
Driving Time:	**1.25 hours (one-way)**
Elevation Range:	**200–500 feet**
Usually Open:	**Year-round**
Best Time to Travel:	**October to June**
Difficulty Rating:	**1**
Scenic Rating:	**9**
Remoteness Rating:	**+0**

Special Attractions

- Birding, fishing, and picnicking at Ferguson Lake.
- The Imperial Long-Term Visitor Area.

History

The southern end of Ferguson Lake Road heads away from the Colorado River just inside the California state line. The All American Canal passes under the trail at this point, near the start of its long journey west to irrigate the enormous market gardens of the Imperial Valley. The canal is fed by the Colorado River at the Imperial Dam, less than a mile to the north of the trail's start. The dam was constructed in 1938 to harness the flow and energy of the Colorado. Laguna Dam, just 4 miles to the south, had been built 21 years earlier. However, developers saw an opportunity to construct an even mightier dam upstream that would provide additional irrigation flow and safeguard the lowlands of the South Gila Valley for habitation, or as they put it, "reclaiming the Colorado Desert."

The distinctive shape of Castle Dome, Arizona, looms beyond Martinez Lake

Just as with the county and valley name, the name "Imperial" was chosen by leading members of the Colorado Development Company in the early 1900s. Chaffey, Heher, and Holt all felt that calling the region the Colorado Desert, correct though it was, might not attract settlers to this developing valley. They named their land promotion company the Imperial Land Company and the valley the Imperial Valley, thinking the name would prove more attractive to investors and settlers.

The earliest canal water from the Yuma area was flowing by 1901. Natural obstacles forced the canal through Mexico, nearly 60 miles to the south, before returning north to the Imperial Valley. Yet the partnership was not always easy to handle. The machinery available by the time the All American Canal was constructed allowed for a route that kept the canal north of the international border, making it an "all American canal."

The Chaffey brothers had previous experience in irrigation and land development, both locally and overseas. The communities of Etiwanda and Ontario, at the foothills of the San Gabriel Mountains, had both gained from their efforts. The two brothers had also helped transform the desert community of Mildura in Victoria, Australia, into an intense agricultural region in 1886. Mildura sits in a remote setting, similar to that of Yuma. The Murray River, Australia's longest river, flows through the Mildura region. But the water was not harnessed until the Chaffey brothers introduced their water pumps and irrigation systems. Today, Mildura is a thriving agricultural community.

Towns such as Holtville, El Centro, Calexico, and Imperial appeared and flourished in what had been desert bajadas before the arrival of irrigation channels from the Colorado River.

Constructing the large Imperial Dam in 1938 had its drawbacks upstream. Settlements such as old Picacho, once the river port for the nearby Picacho Mines, were inundat-

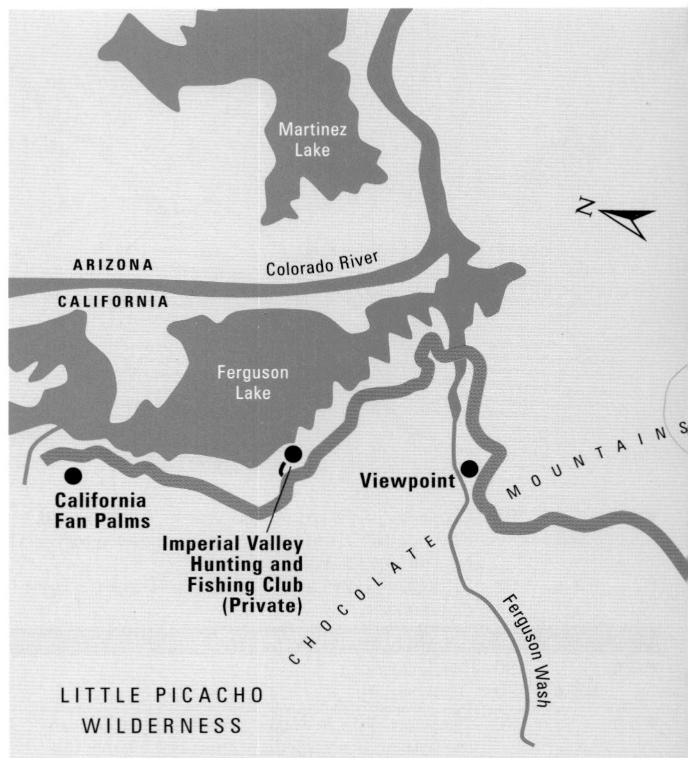

Ferguson Lake is a quiet place for anglers

ed by rising waters. At the same time, larger areas of water provided greater recreational opportunities.

The northern end of Ferguson Lake Road terminates just south of the Imperial National Wildlife Refuge (INWR). This refuge was established in 1941 to safeguard an area where native animal and plant life could exist without too much human interference. The extensive refuge, some 25,000 acres, spans both sides of the Colorado River as far north as Walker Lake (near Walter Camp), where it abuts the Cibola National Wildlife Refuge. The INWR is further complemented by its location alongside the Picacho State Recreation Area, which was established in the 1960s and encompasses the old town site of Picacho.

Description

Ferguson Lake Road passes through the Imperial Long-Term Visitor Area, a popular spot for winter RV parking (permit required). The road as far as the visitor area is normally smooth and well graded to cater to large, low-clearance vehicles. There are many small sidetracks in this area that lead to flat areas of desert pavement for parking.

Past the RV area, the trail is slightly less maintained, but many passenger vehicles easily make the trip to Ferguson Lake. The road dips down to cross the deep cut of Senator Wash before winding through the lower end of the Chocolate Mountains, traveling partly in the wash and partly across open ridge tops. A viewpoint 5 miles past the RV area gives a panoramic view of Ferguson Lake, the Castle Dome Mountains in Arizona, and the Chocolate Mountains in California.

There are no facilities at Ferguson Lake. A couple of small, pull-in campsites overlooking the lake make a pleasant rest stop, whether for a picnic or for camping overnight. There is no concrete boat ramp, but there are a couple of places where it is possible to put a boat into the water. The trail ends at a turnaround close to the lake. Retrace your steps to exit. There is no exit through the Imperial NWR to the north.

Note that there is public access to the start of this trail through the Yuma Military Proving Ground (in Arizona) from US 95, along the road sign-posted to Imperial Dam.

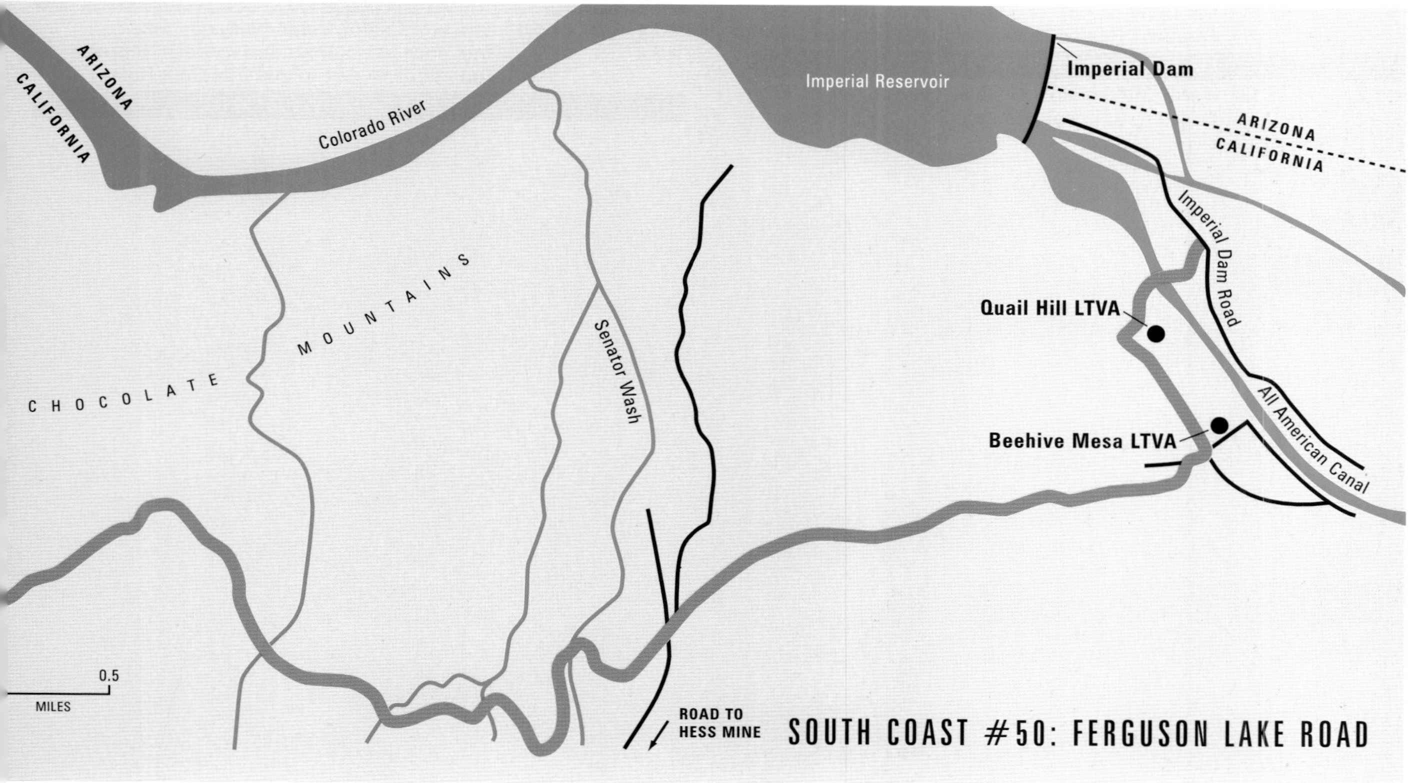

ARIZONA
CALIFORNIA
Colorado River
Imperial Reservoir
Imperial Dam
ARIZONA
CALIFORNIA
Imperial Dam Road
CHOCOLATE MOUNTAINS
Senator Wash
Quail Hill LTVA
Beehive Mesa LTVA
All American Canal
0.5
MILES
ROAD TO HESS MINE

SOUTH COAST #50: FERGUSON LAKE ROAD

Current Road Information

Bureau of Land Management
Yuma Field Office
2555 East Gila Ridge Road
Yuma, AZ 85365
(520) 317-3200

Imperial National Wildlife Refuge
PO Box 72217
Red Cloud Mine Road
Martinez Lake
Yuma, AZ 85365
(520) 783-3371

Map References

BLM Yuma
USGS 1:24,000 Laguna Dam, Imperial Reservoir, Little Picacho Peak
1:100,000 Yuma
Maptech CD-ROM: San Diego/Joshua Tree
Southern & Central California Atlas & Gazetteer, p. 127
California Road & Recreation Atlas, p. 119

Route Directions

▼ 0.0 Trail commences on northern end of Imperial Dam Road, 0.4 miles west of the California state line and 13 miles north of the intersection with Picacho Road (along Ross Road via Bard). Zero trip meter and turn northwest on paved Ferguson Road, following sign for Ferguson Lake.

GPS: N32°52.24' W114°28.48'

▼ 0.5 TL Entering Imperial Dam Recreation Area. Quail Hill LTVA on left. Then turn left on paved Ferguson Road, following sign to Ferguson Lake.

GPS: N32°52.50' W114°28.91'

▼ 1.2 TR 4-way intersection. Beehive Mesa LTVA on left. Paved road continues straight ahead. Follow sign to Ferguson Lake. Road turns to graded dirt. Immediately bear left past RV area. Many tracks on left and right into RV parking areas for the next 3.1 miles.

GPS: N32°52.14' W114°29.42'

▼ 3.8 SO Graded road on right; then wide track on left to Hess Mine and track on right. No marker at the intersection.

GPS: N32°54.11' W114°30.70'

▼ 4.3 SO Cross through deep Senator Wash.
▼ 4.7 SO Graded road on right enters fee area. Zero trip meter.

GPS: N32°54.47' W114°31.15'

▼ 0.0 Continue to the west, following sign to Ferguson Lake.
▼ 0.1 SO Little Picacho Wilderness begins on left.
▼ 0.5 SO Cross through wash.
▼ 1.0 SO Cross through wash.
▼ 1.6 SO Track on right; then cross through wash. Trail now crosses many washes for the next 7.1 miles.
▼ 1.7 SO Track on right.

GPS: N32°55.66' W114°30.92'

▼ 4.6 SO Track on right.

GPS: N32°57.59' W114°30.57'

▼ 5.1 SO Viewpoint on left over Ferguson Lake, Colorado River, and Fishers Landing.

GPS: N32°57.87' W114°30.40'

▼ 5.8 SO Two tracks on right.
▼ 5.9 SO Start to cross Ferguson Wash.
▼ 6.1 BL Exit wash. Track on right goes down to Ferguson Lake. Zero trip meter.

GPS: N32°58.14' W114°29.81'

▼ 0.0 Continue to the north.
▼ 1.1 BL Graded road on right goes into Imperial Valley Hunting and Fishing Club (members only).

GPS: N32°58.63' W114°30.55'

▼ 2.4 SO Grove of California fan palms on left.
▼ 2.6 Trail ends at a turnaround in wash. Retrace your steps to exit to Imperial Dam Road.

GPS: N32°59.58' W114°30.63'

The Desert Region

Trails in the Desert Region

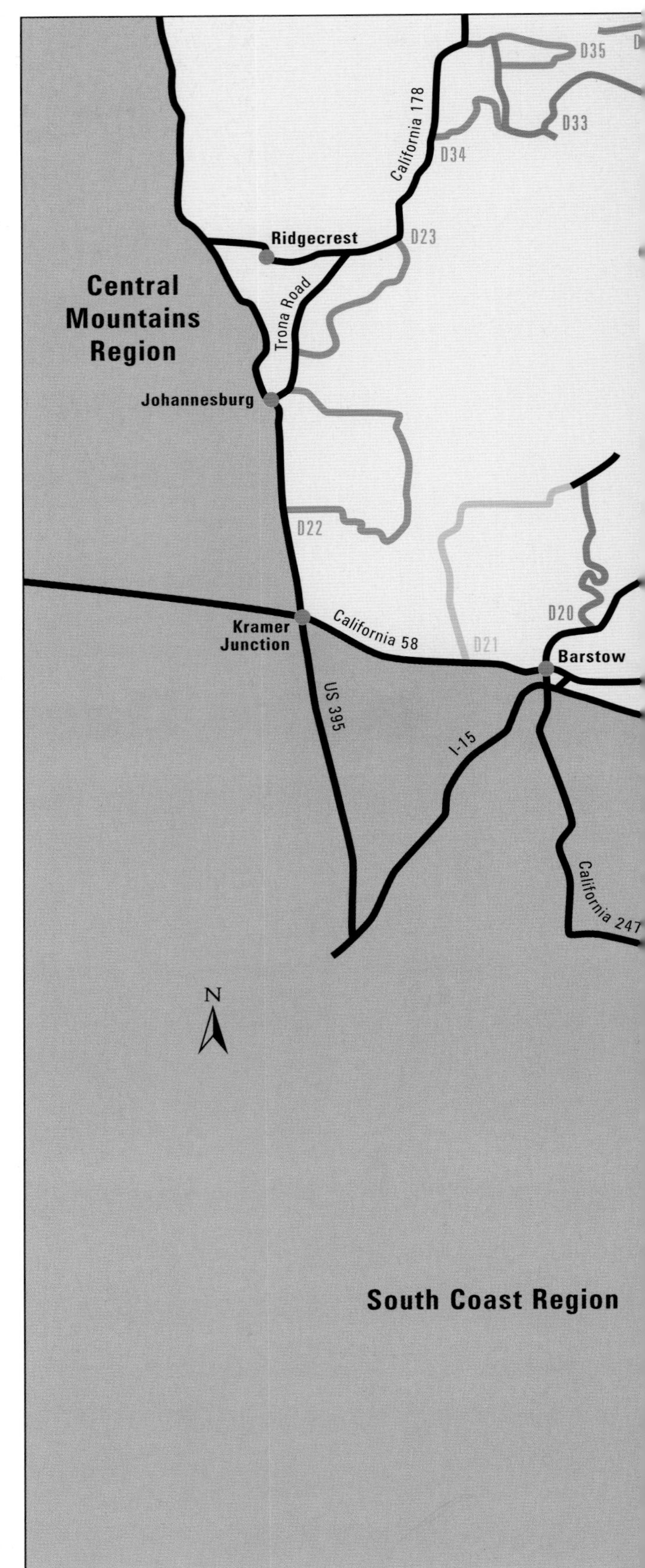

MAP CONTINUES ON PAGE 451

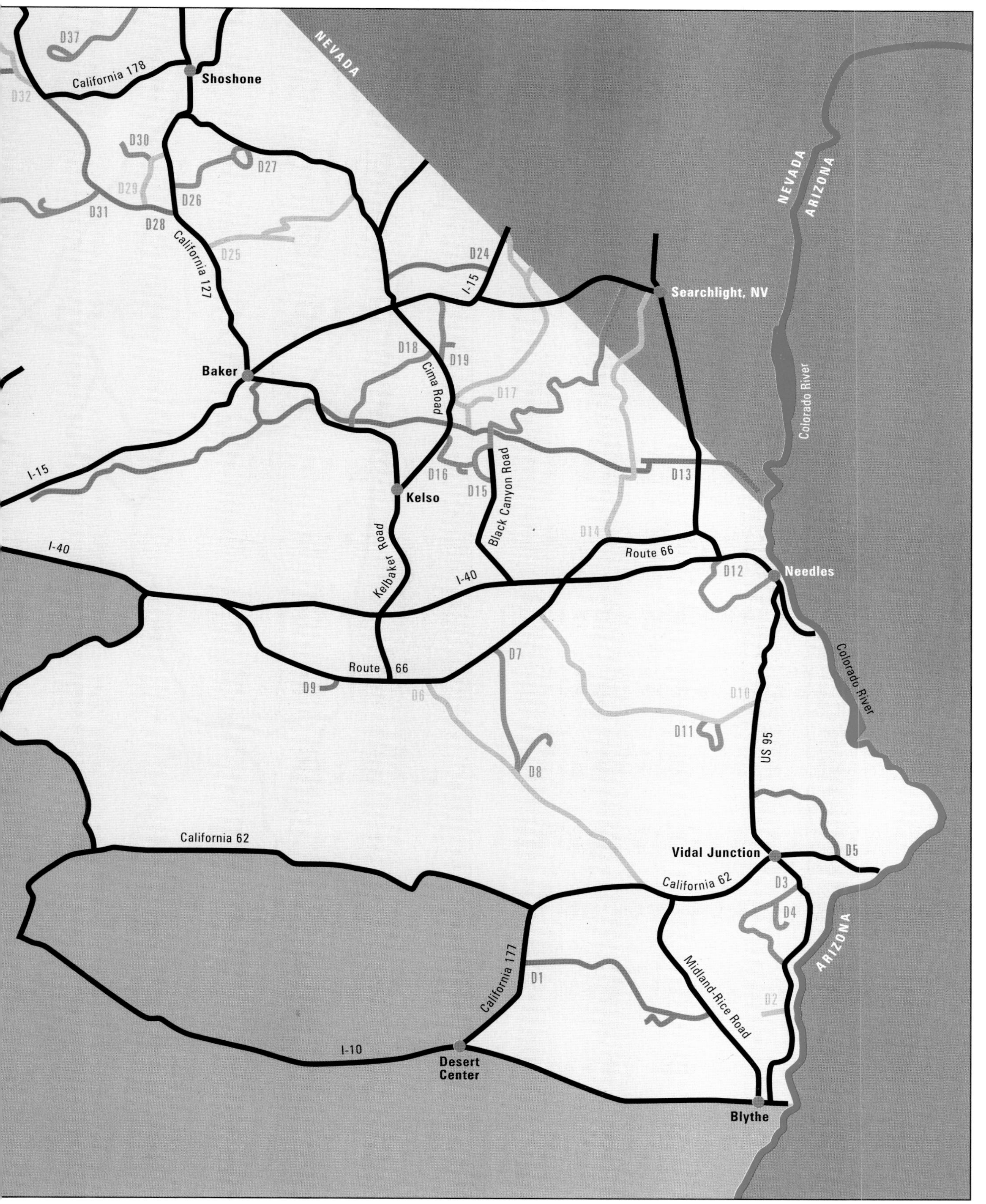

Trails in the Desert Region

- D12 Eagle Pass Trail *(DR: 3; 23.4 miles; page 484)*
- D13 Mojave Road *(DR: 4; 128.6 miles; page 487)*
- D14 East Lanfair Valley Trail *(DR: 4; 49.1 miles; page 501)*
- D15 New York Mountains Trail *(DR: 2; 62.1 miles; page 507)*
- D16 Macedonia Canyon Trail *(DR: 3; 8.1 miles; page 512)*
- D17 Nipton Desert Road *(DR: 2; 41.4 miles; page 514)*
- D18 Cima Dome Trail *(DR: 2; 19.4 miles; page 519)*
- D19 Ivanpah Mountains Trail *(DR: 3; 12.8 miles; page 522)*
- D20 Starbright Trail *(DR: 3; 29.1 miles; page 524)*
- D21 Black Canyon Road *(DR: 3; 35.4 miles; page 529)*
- D22 Grass Valley Trail *(DR: 3; 50.6 miles; page 534)*
- D23 Trona Pinnacles Trail *(DR: 3; 24.6 miles; page 538)*
- D24 Colosseum Gorge Trail *(DR: 3; 18.4 miles; page 541)*
- D25 Kingston Wash Trail *(DR: 3; 30 miles; page 545)*
- D26 Sperry Wash Route *(DR: 4; 18.6 miles; page 547)*
- D27 Alexander Hills Trail *(DR: 4; 6.4 miles; page 551)*
- D28 Harry Wade Exit Route *(DR: 2; 30.5 miles; page 553)*
- D29 Ibex Dunes Trail *(DR: 3; 13.5 miles; page 555)*
- D30 Ibex Spring Road *(DR: 3; 7.8 miles; page 557)*
- D31 Owlshead Mountains Trail *(DR: 2; 28.7 miles; page 560)*
- D32 Death Valley West Side Road *(DR: 1; 34.2 miles; page 562)*
- D33 Mengel Pass Trail *(DR: 4; 50.1 miles; page 565)*
- D34 Slate Range Trail *(DR: 3; 13.9 miles; page 570)*
- D35 Pleasant Canyon Loop Trail *(DR: 7; 23.5 miles; page 573)*
- D36 Johnson Canyon Trail *(DR: 3; 10 miles; page 579)*
- D37 Deadman Pass Trail *(DR: 3; 27.5 miles; page 580)*
- D38 Echo Canyon Trail *(DR: 3; 9.1 miles; page 583)*
- D39 Funeral Range Trail *(DR: 6; 25.4 miles; page 585)*
- D40 Titus Canyon Trail *(DR: 2; 25.4 miles; page 588)*
- D41 Chloride City Trail *(DR: 3; 15.4 miles; page 590)*
- D42 Cottonwood Canyon Trail *(DR: 3; 17.4 miles; page 594)*
- D43 Skidoo Road *(DR: 2; 8.7 miles; page 596)*
- D44 Darwin Falls Trail *(DR: 3; 12.1 miles; page 598)*
- D45 Cactus Flat Road *(DR: 3; 23.5 miles; page 602)*
- D46 Saline Valley Road *(DR: 2; 91.4 miles; page 605)*
- D47 Cerro Gordo Road *(DR: 2; 23.7 miles; page 611)*
- D48 Swansea–Cerro Gordo Road *(DR: 5; 23 miles; page 614)*
- D49 Hidden Valley Road *(DR: 2; 28.5 miles; page 618)*
- D50 Lippincott Mine Road *(DR: 4; 8 miles; page 621)*
- D51 Racetrack Road *(DR: 2; 30.5 miles; page 623)*

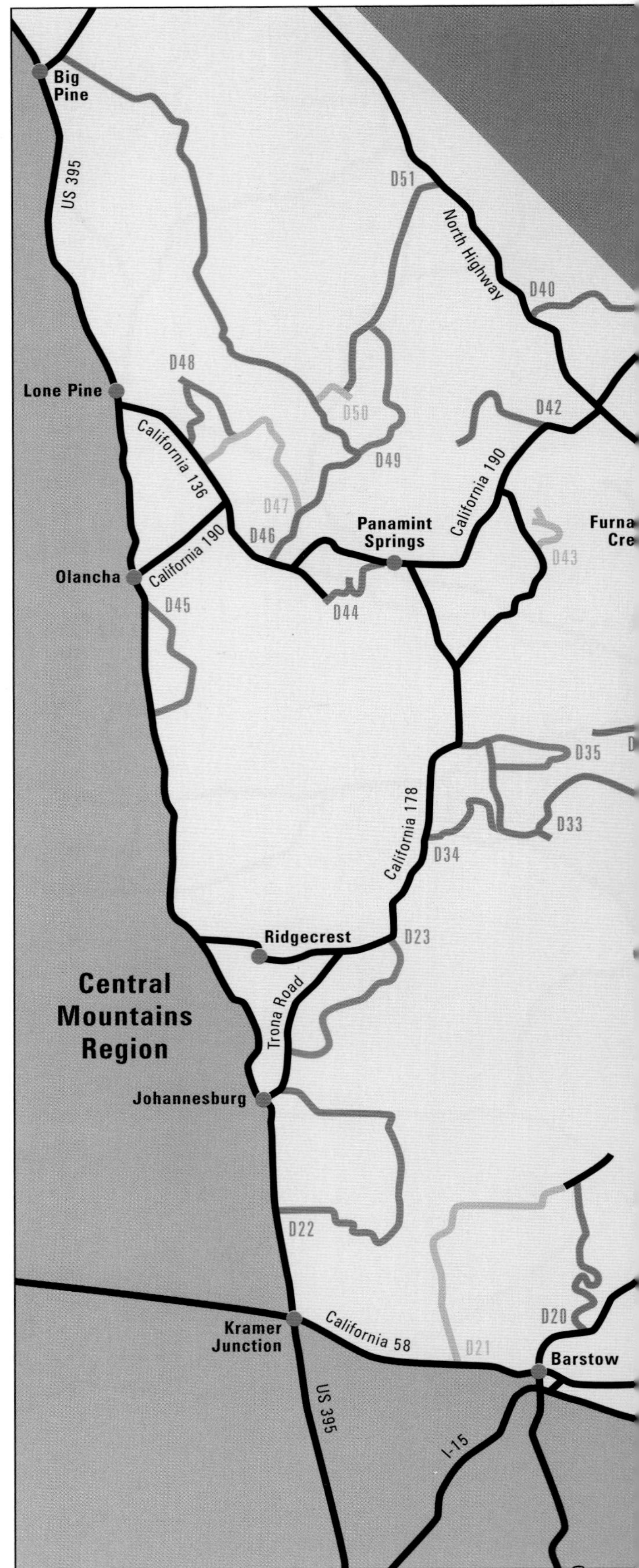

MAP CONTINUES ON PAGE 449

Palen Pass Trail

Starting Point:	**Desert Center-Rice Road (California 177), 9.7 miles south of the intersection with California 62**
Finishing Point:	**Midland-Rice Road, 17.7 miles north of I-10**
Total Mileage:	**33.8 miles, plus 0.9-mile spur**
Unpaved Mileage:	**33.8 miles, plus 0.9-mile spur**
Driving Time:	**3 hours**
Elevation Range:	**600–1,600 feet**
Usually Open:	**Year-round**
Best Time to Travel:	**October to June**
Difficulty Rating:	**3**
Scenic Rating:	**8**
Remoteness Rating:	**+1**

Special Attractions

- Trail travels a vehicle corridor through the Palen-McCoy Wilderness.
- Remains of the Arlington and Black Jack Mines.
- Midland Long-Term Visitor Area, located a short distance from the trail.

History

In the late 1800s, an Irish miner named Matthew Palen prospected the mountains of this remote desert region. His name has been attached to the wide valley at the western end of this trail as well as the pass between the Granite and Palen Mountains.

Camp Coxcomb is at the western end of Palen Pass Trail. The camp was part of General George Patton's Desert Training Center (DTC), later called the California-Arizona Maneuver Area (CAMA), established in the spring of 1942. The camp was one of 11 that spanned a combined area of nearly 18,000 square miles in California, Nevada, and Arizona. The camps, set in a harsh desert environment, were chosen to train troops for action in the same conditions they would face in North Africa during World War II. CAMA was declared surplus in March 1944, when the last troops were deployed and cleanup began. Hundreds of duds were located and destroyed onsite. However, because only a limited number of troops were available, an extensive search could not be undertaken. Although cleanups have occurred since then, the CAMA locations generally have surface clearance only. The public is advised not to dig below the surface and to report finding any duds.

Inca Siding

Rock enclosures on the west side of Palen Pass are left over from World War II training exercises

Palen Pass was a site used by troops from the DTC to stage practice ambushes. Divisions would carry out maneuvers against fortified positions at Palen Pass. These exercises could go on for up to four days at a time, in temperatures reaching as high as 130 degrees. They taught soldiers the importance of depending on the regiment for much needed supplies. A division could not last in such a harsh setting without water, gas, and rations. Water supplies were kept at a minimum to continually test the troops. When hiking in this region, you will likely encounter several small stone enclosures left over from these training maneuvers.

The McCoy Mountains, along the south side of this trail, were named after the operator of a local government trading post, Bill McCoy. His store was in Ehrenburg, on the Arizona side of the Colorado River. The McCoy Mountains were the site of a lost placer mine in the late 1800s. An old Papago chief, named Papuan, and his Mojave wife would always pay for goods with gold. The couple bought so much that it was estimated McCoy had acquired more than $70,000 from them. The Mojave woman had known of a gold mine in the McCoy Mountains in the 1860s, prior to meeting her husband. Together they would slip away from their camp by the Colorado River, always returning from the McCoy Mountains with gold in hand. They were known to share their treasure with other Indians, who would also shop at McCoy's trading post. Though questioned and followed by would-be claim jumpers, the chief and his wife were artists when it came to evading detection. They never revealed the location of the gold.

The Palen-McCoy Wilderness was established in 1994, encompassing 270,629 acres. Ironwood trees are predominant as you travel down the sandy wash east of Palen Pass. This forest is one of the most lush ironwood forests in California's desert. The name of the trees reflects the dense nature of the wood, which Native Americans used for tools and weapons. Seeds were part of their staple diet. Ironwoods are found in other harsh environments, such as the hot deserts of Australia; the wood is so heavy it sinks in water.

Description

Palen Pass Trail follows the marked Palen Pass Road and Arlington Mine Road. The route is marked by white posts with the road's name. Most intersections and points where there is a chance for confusion have such markers, so navigation is easy.

The trail leaves California 177 south of its intersection with California 62. It travels in a plumb line up the bajada toward the pale, jagged peaks of the mountain ranges of the Palen-McCoy Wilderness. There are many shallow wash crossings along this route; they have not been mentioned in the route directions because they are so numerous. Along the bajada, the trail traverses areas of loose, deep sand. It enters a vehicle corridor within the wilderness; vehicle travel is not permitted off the formed trail. As the trail begins the gradual ascent toward the pass, it becomes a rough formed road. The trail's difficulty rating of 3 is based upon this section on the west side of the pass. The uneven surface makes a high-clearance 4WD preferable.

Approaching Palen Pass from the west

Palen Pass is a gentle rise between the Granite Mountains to the north and the Palen Mountains to the south. The Granite Mountains are a popular hiking destination. The ranges are pale in color, with jagged peaks and sparse vegetation. Tailings heaps and long cuts indicate past strip-mining endeavors along the trail.

On the east side of the pass, the route joins Arlington Mine Road. This wider, once-graded road makes for easier travel. However, it can be rough in places, and gullies and sand traps can catch the unwary. The trail descends a wide valley, with the Little Maria Mountains to the north and the McCoy Mountains to the south; both ranges rise abruptly from the broad valley floor.

East of Palen Pass, ironwoods, mesquites, and palo verdes provide habitat for coyotes, bobcats, kit foxes, gray foxes, kangaroo rats, and mountain lions.

The Arlington and Black Jack Mines are reached by a short spur. Trails within the mine areas can be confusing because they weave around many diggings, large pits, and adits over 30 feet tall. Many of these trails are unsafe or washed away. Be careful when exploring the area, whether on foot or in a vehicle.

The trail continues along the wide valley, passing the railroad siding at Inca on the Atchison, Topeka & Santa Fe Railroad, before finishing northwest of Blythe on Midland-Rice Road. A short distance south of the end of the trail is the Midland Long-Term Visitor Area, a BLM-managed area that caters to winter RV visitors. They are permitted to stop within the area between September and April with the appropriate permit. Although not as popular as Quartzsite, Arizona, the area still attracts many winter visitors.

Current Road Information

Bureau of Land Management
Palm Springs South Coast Field Office
PO Box 581260
690 West Garnet Avenue
North Palm Springs, CA 92258
(760) 251-4800

Map References

BLM Eagle Mts., Blythe
USGS 1:24,000 West of Palen Pass, Palen Pass, Arlington Mine, Little Maria Mt., Inca, Big Maria Mt. SW
1:100,000 Eagle Mts., Blythe
Maptech CD-ROM: San Diego/Joshua Tree
Southern & Central California Atlas & Gazetteer, pp. 110, 111
California Road & Recreation Atlas, p. 113

Route Directions

▼ 0.0			From Desert Center-Rice Road (California 177) at mile marker 17, 9.7 miles south of the intersection with California 62, zero trip meter and turn east on Palen Pass Road (shown on some maps as P 172). The road is marked with a BLM route marker as Palen Pass Road. There is a historical marker on the road opposite.
	1.7 ▲		Trail finishes on Desert Center-Rice Road (California 177). Turn left for Desert Center; turn right for Vidal Junction.
			GPS: N33°54.49' W115°14.82'
▼ 1.0		BR	Trail forks, left track can be sandier.
	0.7 ▲	SO	Trail rejoins.
▼ 1.2		SO	Trail rejoins.
	0.5 ▲	BL	Trail forks, right track can be sandier.
▼ 1.7		SO	Track on left and right is marked as Palen Dunes Drive by a marker post. Zero trip meter and continue into the vehicle corridor through the Palen-McCoy Wilderness.
	0.0 ▲		Continue to the west.
			GPS: N33°54.58' W115°12.96'
▼ 0.0			Continue to the east.

7.9 ▲ SO Track on left and right is marked as Palen Dunes Drive by a marker post. Zero trip meter and leave vehicle corridor.

▼ 6.7 SO Trail deviates around a large washout. Follow marker posts.
1.2 ▲ SO Trail deviates around a large washout. Follow marker posts.

GPS: N33°54.19' W115°05.89'

▼ 7.1 BL Track on right gives wilderness access for foot and horse travel only.
0.8 ▲ BR Track on left gives wilderness access for foot and horse travel only.

GPS: N33°54.17' W115°05.54'

▼ 7.9 BR Track on left gives wilderness access for foot and horse travel only. Zero trip meter at sign.
0.0 ▲ Continue to the south.

GPS: N33°54.76' W115°05.21'

▼ 0.0 Continue to the east and cross through wash.
3.1 ▲ BL Cross through wash; then track on right gives wilderness access for foot and horse travel only. Zero trip meter at sign.

▼ 0.1 SO Track on left gives wilderness access for foot and horse travel only.
3.0 ▲ SO Track on right gives wilderness access for foot and horse travel only.

▼ 0.2 SO Track on right.
2.9 ▲ SO Track on left.

▼ 0.3 SO Start to cross through wide wash.
2.8 ▲ SO Exit wide wash crossing.

▼ 0.4 SO Exit wide wash crossing and wilderness corridor.
2.7 ▲ SO Enter vehicle corridor through the Palen-McCoy Wilderness and start to cross through wide wash.

▼ 0.7 SO High above the trail on the left are small rock enclosures.
2.4 ▲ SO High above the trail on the right are small rock enclosures.

GPS: N33°54.82' W115°04.61'

▼ 0.8 SO Five small stone ruins on left.
2.3 ▲ SO Five small stone ruins on right.

GPS: N33°54.86' W115°04.58'

▼ 0.9 SO Enter wash.
2.2 ▲ SO Exit wash.

▼ 1.1 SO Exit wash.
2.0 ▲ SO Enter wash.

▼ 1.4 SO Track on left; then cross through wash.
1.7 ▲ SO Cross through wash; then track on right.

▼ 1.5 SO Track on left; then track on right into mining area.
1.6 ▲ SO Track on left into mining area; then track on right.

GPS: N33°54.94' W115°03.81'

▼ 1.9 SO Cross through two washes.
1.2 ▲ SO Cross through two washes.

▼ 2.1 SO Enter wash.
1.0 ▲ SO Exit wash.

▼ 2.2 SO Exit wash.
0.9 ▲ SO Enter wash.

▼ 2.3 SO Palen Pass. Many small tracks on left and right to mines for the next 0.7 miles.
0.8 ▲ SO Palen Pass.

GPS: N33°55.23' W115°03.17'

▼ 2.4 SO Enter down wash. Track on left.
0.7 ▲ SO Track on right. Exit wash.

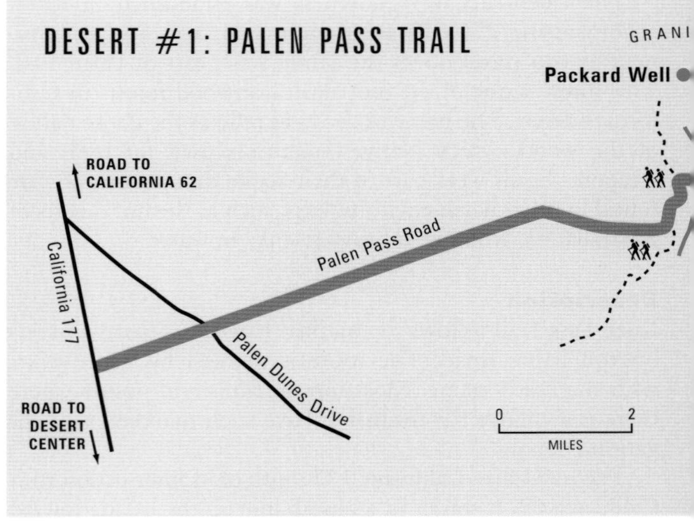

▼ 2.7 SO Track on right.
0.4 ▲ SO Track on left.

▼ 2.9 SO Exit wash.
0.2 ▲ SO Enter wash.

▼ 3.0 SO Track on right; then cross through wash.
0.1 ▲ SO Cross through wash; then track on left. Many small tracks on left and right to mines for the next 0.7 miles.

▼ 3.1 TR Turn right onto Arlington Mine Road and zero trip meter at marker post. Wide track on left goes to Packard Well.
0.0 ▲ Continue to the southwest.

GPS: N33°55.37' W115°02.35'

▼ 0.0 Continue to the east.
9.4 ▲ TL Turn left onto Palen Pass Road and zero trip meter at marker post. Wide track ahead goes to Packard Well.

▼ 0.1 SO Track on left.
9.3 ▲ SO Track on right.

▼ 0.7 SO Cross through wash.
8.7 ▲ SO Cross through wash.

▼ 1.8 SO Track on left.
7.6 ▲ SO Track on right.

GPS: N33°54.86' W115°00.54'

▼ 3.0 SO Track on right.
6.4 ▲ SO Track on left.

▼ 3.1 SO Cross through wash.
6.3 ▲ SO Cross through wash.

GPS: N33°54.06' W114°59.58'

▼ 3.4 SO Track on right.
6.0 ▲ SO Track on left.

▼ 8.2 SO Cross through wash.
1.2 ▲ SO Cross through wash.

GPS: N33°50.26' W114°57.01'

▼ 8.3 SO Graded track on left. Continue on Arlington Mine Road.
1.1 ▲ SO Graded track on right. Continue on Arlington Mine Road.

GPS: N33°50.23' W114°56.92

▼ 9.1 SO Track on left in wash. Continue on Arlington Mine Road.
0.3 ▲ SO Track on right in wash. Continue on Arlington Mine Road.

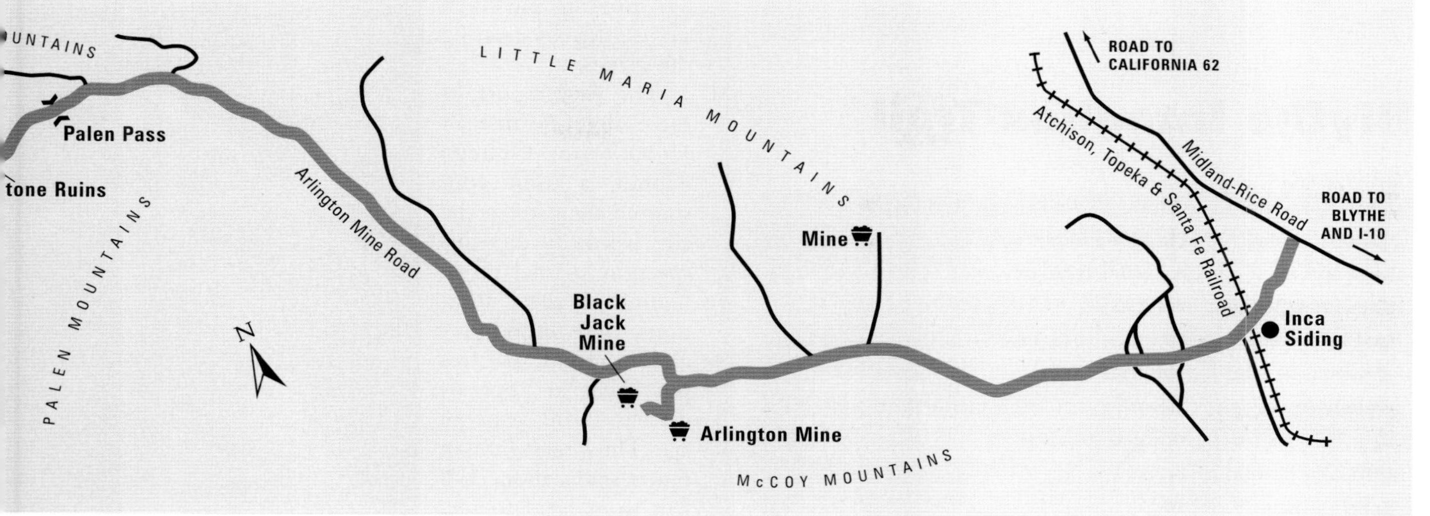

▼ 9.4 BL Well-used track on right. Zero trip meter at Arlington Mine Road marker.
0.0 ▲ Continue to the west.

GPS: N33°49.71' W114°55.98'

▼ 0.0 Continue to the northeast.
1.4 ▲ BR Well-used track on left. Zero trip meter at Arlington Mine Road marker.

▼ 0.3 SO Track on right.
1.1 ▲ SO Track on left.

▼ 1.0 SO Track on left.
0.3 ▲ SO Track on right.

▼ 1.2 SO Track on right.
0.2 ▲ SO Track on left.

▼ 1.4 BL Well-used track on right is spur to Arlington and Black Jack Mines. Zero trip meter at marker post.
0.0 ▲ Continue to the northwest.

GPS: N33°49.30' W114°54.87'

Spur to Arlington and Black Jack Mines

▼ 0.0 Proceed to the southwest.
▼ 0.1 BL Track on right.
▼ 0.4 BR Track on left; then track on left and track on right.

GPS: N33°49.03' W114°55.09'

▼ 0.5 TR Track on left. Straight ahead goes 0.1 miles to Arlington Mine pit. Turn right; then track on left goes into Arlington Mine pit.

GPS: N33°48.96' W114°55.13'

▼ 0.8 SO Track on left to adit.
▼ 0.9 UT Large adit of the Black Jack Mine on left. Track on right descends to loading hopper. Road ahead is extremely rough and will stop most vehicles in a short distance. Hiking is recommended.

GPS: N33°49.00' W114°55.46'

Continuation of Main Trail

▼ 0.0 Continue to the northeast.
3.3 ▲ BR Well-used track on left is the spur to Arlington and Black Jack Mines. Zero trip meter at marker post.

GPS: N33°49.30' W114°54.87'

▼ 2.1 SO Track on left.
1.2 ▲ SO Track on right.

▼ 2.9 SO Wide formed road on left.
0.4 ▲ SO Wide formed road on right.

GPS: N33°49.07' W114°51.84'

▼ 3.3 SO Graded road on left goes to mine. Zero trip meter at route marker.
0.0 ▲ Continue to the west.

GPS: N33°48.98' W114°51.41'

▼ 0.0 Continue to the east.
7.0 ▲ BL Graded road on right goes to mine. Zero trip meter at route marker.

▼ 0.4 SO Track on right and track on left.
6.6 ▲ SO Track on left and track on right.

▼ 2.5 SO Track on left.
4.5 ▲ SO Track on right.

▼ 3.3 SO Track on left.
3.7 ▲ SO Track on right.

▼ 4.2 SO Track on right and track on left.
2.8 ▲ SO Track on left and track on right.

GPS: N33°47.90' W114°47.10'

▼ 4.9 BL Graded road on right. Continue on Arlington Mine Road.
2.1 ▲ SO Graded road on left. Continue on Arlington Mine Road.

▼ 5.0 SO Track on left.
2.0 ▲ SO Track on right.

▼ 5.2 BL Track on right. Bear left toward railroad crossing.
1.8 ▲ BR Track on left. Bear right away from railroad.

GPS: N33°47.97' W114°46.03'

▼ 5.4 SO Cross over railroad at Inca Siding.
1.6 ▲ SO Cross over railroad at Inca Siding.

GPS: N33°48.09' W114°45.94'

▼ 7.0 Trail ends at T-intersection with paved Midland-Rice Road. Small formed road opposite. Turn left for Rice Siding and California 62; turn right for I-10 and Blythe.
0.0 ▲ Trail commences on paved Midland-Rice Road, 17.7 miles north of I-40 and the Lovekin Boulevard exit in Blythe. (Lovekin Boulevard becomes Midland-Rice Road.) Zero trip meter and turn southwest on wide, graded dirt road, marked Arlington Mine Road by a BLM marker post. There is a notice board at the intersection and a formed road opposite.

GPS: N33°49.05' W114°44.85'

DESERT #2

Blythe Intaglios Trail

Starting Point:	**US 95, 15.3 miles north of Blythe**
Finishing Point:	**Big Maria Mountains**
Total Mileage:	**4.0 miles (one-way)**
Unpaved Mileage:	**4.0 miles**
Driving Time:	**45 minutes (one-way)**
Elevation Range:	**300–1,000 feet**
Usually Open:	**Year-round**
Best Time to Travel:	**October to June**
Difficulty Rating:	**3**
Scenic Rating:	**10**
Remoteness Rating:	**+0**

Special Attractions

- Blythe intaglios.
- Narrow ridge top trail into the Big Maria Mountains.
- Varied vegetation and views over the Colorado River and Big Maria Mountains.

History

Paleo-Indians roamed the Colorado River region for thousands of years before the arrival of Euro-Americans. Records of these peoples' histories appear in many forms across the landscape. One of the more striking is the collection of intaglios (in-TAL-yos) situated north of Blythe. Giant human and animal figures are etched into the desert surface high above the riverbed, alongside geometrical shapes. All of the figures are bare areas on the stony hillside, with outlines made by moving patinaed stones, thereby creating the shapes.

This ridge top trail offers splendid views into the Big Maria Mountains

Blythe intaglio—human figure

The first report of these figures came in 1930 from George Palmer, a pilot who spotted them from the air. Upon further inspection, a total of six figures in three locations were found; archaeological studies put them at approximately 1,100 years of age. The largest human figure spans about 170 feet from head to toe. Creations such as these in the United States are seldom seen and have only been found in Arizona and California. Though it is not always possible, the best way to view these intaglios is from the air.

Theories and tales about the figures' meaning or purpose have evolved throughout the years. Local Mojave and Quechan say the human figures represent Mastamho, the creator of life, and the animals represent Hatakulya, a part-lion part-person who helped at the time of creation. Religious ceremonies honoring Mastamho occurred at this location.

Pilgrimages were held along the banks of the Colorado River, with ceremonies at points such as this. The southern end of the river was referred to as the Land of the Dead. As the pilgrimage moved north, it celebrated the actions of mythic beings that were represented by intaglios along the way. When the pilgrimage reached the northern end of the great river, it was said to have entered into the Place of Creation.

Other interpretations associate the figures with astronomy, religious lore, and territorial markers. One controversial author, Erich Von Daniken, put forward the theory that God was an astronaut from outer space in a number of books from the late 1960s to the present. He based his theory on the abundance of these giant figures worldwide.

Description

The Blythe intaglios are excellent examples of ancient desert art. This short trail leaves US 95 north of Blythe and passes alongside the figures. The trail is fenced on either side within the intaglio area. A couple of small parking areas mark the start of short hiking trails to the intaglios. Human figures, an animal believed to be part horse, and spiral and circular shapes can be seen.

Past the intaglio area, the trail is less used and unmarked. It follows a formed trail toward the Big Maria Mountains.

At the 1.7-mile mark, the route turns down a side trail. This turn is easily missed, but if you continue straight ahead at this point, the trail continues only 0.6 miles before being blocked by the Big Maria Mountains Wilderness.

The trail crosses a wide wash, then ascends to a ridge top.

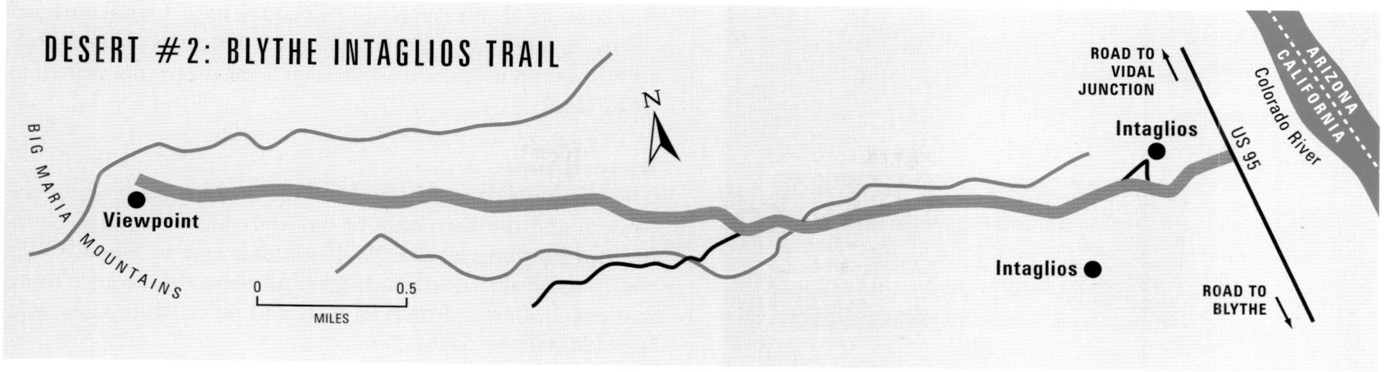

It runs along the narrow spine of the ridge, overlooking a deep wash on either side. The views are dramatic. Ahead are the pale and sandy Big Maria Mountains and behind are the Colorado River and Arizona. The vegetation is varied. Ocotillos, small barrel cacti, creosote bushes, and beavertail cacti sparsely cover the slopes, but they stand out dramatically against the pale rocks.

The trail finishes at the end of the ridge, where the rugged terrain of the Big Maria Mountains will draw avid hikers farther.

Current Road Information

Bureau of Land Management
Needles Field Office
101 West Spikes Road
Needles, CA 92363
(760) 326-7000

Map References

BLM Blythe
USGS 1:24,000 Big Maria Mt. SE
1:100,000 Blythe
Maptech CD-ROM: San Diego/Joshua Tree
Southern & Central California Atlas & Gazetteer, p. 111
California Road & Recreation Atlas, p. 114

Route Directions

▼ 0.0		From US 95, 15.3 miles north of Blythe, zero trip meter and turn west on road #52 at the BLM sign for Blythe Intaglios. The road is designated as suitable for 4WDs, ATVs, and motorbikes.
		GPS: N33°48.00' W114°31.62'
▼ 0.1	SO	Track on left and track on right under power lines is road #53 for 4WDs, ATVs, and motorbikes. Continue straight ahead and enter the site of the Blythe Intaglios. Please remain on the established road.
▼ 0.4	SO	Parking area on right and short walk to two fenced areas containing a horse and a circular shape in one and a human figure in the other.
▼ 0.7	SO	Parking area on right and short walk to fenced area containing a human figure.
		GPS: N33°47.95' W114°32.29'
▼ 1.0	SO	Leaving intaglio area.
		GPS: N33°48.00' W114°32.61'
▼ 1.4	BR	Well-used track on left.
		GPS: N33°48.01' W114°33.07'
▼ 1.5	SO	Cross through wash.
▼ 1.7	TR	Track continues straight ahead to the edge of the Big Maria Mountains Wilderness. Turn right on unmarked track and cross through wash.
		GPS: N33°48.04' W114°33.34'
▼ 3.9	SO	Track on left to mine. Track on right descends to wash.
		GPS: N33°48.51' W114°35.31'
▼ 4.0		Spur ends at a viewpoint of the mountains at the end of the ridge.
		GPS: N33°48.52' W114°35.38'

DESERT #3

Blythe-Vidal Old Road

Starting Point:	**US 95 at Vidal, 6.1 miles south of the intersection with California 62**
Finishing Point:	**US 95, immediately south of mile marker 24.5**
Total Mileage:	**22.2 miles**
Unpaved Mileage:	**22.2 miles**
Driving Time:	**2 hours**
Elevation Range:	**400–1,400 feet**
Usually Open:	**Year-round**
Best Time to Travel:	**October to June**
Difficulty Rating:	**4**
Scenic Rating:	**8**
Remoteness Rating:	**+1**

Special Attractions

- Historic old road between Blythe and Vidal.
- Road passes between two wilderness areas.

History

The old Blythe-Vidal Road reminds travelers how early routes through desert terrain developed. The old road followed the path of least resistance, traversing the gently sloping, sandy bajadas where possible and weaving a path through the more jagged interiors. No earthmoving machinery was available to

The rerouted road now travels north up Big Wash

remove obstacles or fill in washes. The trail skirts the high craggy peaks of the Riverside Mountains between Blythe and Vidal, two early settlements close to the Colorado River. The original trail followed the course of Big Wash and was somewhat less circuitous than today's realigned route. Passage along the river was not always possible because floods would erode any evidence of a trail.

In 1882, Thomas Blythe took measures to curb the periodic flooding of the Colorado River, harness its waters, and avail of the exposed alluvial valley. A diversion channel was constructed and Blythe attended the ceremonious final blasting into the Colorado River in the fall of 1882. Before this, the river was up to 5 miles wide in places. The final cut was the intake point for Blythe's diversion channel. The diversion opened up land for development and settlement. Blythe appointed George Irish, a 28-year-old Englishman, to oversee his project. Blythe spent more than $80,000 to clear the land, setting up an irrigation scheme that covered an area of 40,000 acres, including a 40-acre farm actively experimenting with various crops. Blythe was enthusiastic about developing an empire on the Colorado. Fort Yuma lay just 90 miles downstream, prospectors were working the riverside mountains, settlers were coming west, and he could see the need for development.

Unfortunately, Blythe never got to see his "empire on the Colorado." He suffered a heart attack and died in San Francisco. His project fell by the wayside after his death. However, his name survives in the city that developed on the banks of the Colorado River.

The wide expanse of Rice Valley slopes to the northwest of this trail. The sandy valley and old army air base have taken their names from the Rice Siding on the floor of the valley. The siding got its name in the 1910s from Guy R. Rice, a chief engineer of the California Southern Railroad. Later, a World War II training facility was located in the heart of the valley. General George Patton conducted training maneuvers in the vicinity in 1942, choosing many such desolate locations to prepare for combat in North Africa. The only reminders of this base are shell casings, a large concrete pad, and scattered debris. A 1994 report indicates that 1,000 acres of unexploded ordnance sites were suspected on what is now designated as BLM land.

Description

The Blythe-Vidal Old Road follows a sandy path along the western and southern edge of the Riverside Mountains, starting and finishing on US 95. The trail is easy to follow. Once you find the unmarked starting point, there are adequate route markers, both BLM marker posts and older white signs, and few side trails to confuse you.

The trail's main difficulty is very loose, very deep sand along much of its length. One particularly deep stretch is the 1.1-mile section that travels within a tributary of Big Wash. Apart from the sand, there are many steep entries to and exits from washes; good tires will help gain traction on the often scrabbly surface.

The trail leaves sleepy Vidal, and travels southwest along a loose, sandy surface, crossing Vidal Wash and traveling across Vidal Valley toward the Riverside Mountains. The difficult Desert #4: Gold Rice Mine Trail leaves this route and makes an adventurous detour for experienced drivers or mountain bikers.

The old road continues on the smaller trail, skirting the edge of the Riverside Mountains Wilderness. It travels along a tributary of Big Wash for a short distance; this section has some of the deepest sand along the entire trail. Exiting the wash, the trail follows alongside power lines through a vehicle corridor with wilderness on both sides. Sections here can be rough and uneven, and a few steeper pinches on the low-traction surface may pose a slight challenge to some. Leaving the vehicle corridor, the trail swings east along the southern side of the Riverside Mountains Wilderness toward the Colorado River. Navigation can be a challenge because the trail is often faint. Pay close attention to the route to avoid inadvertently entering the wilderness. There are more marker posts along this section to aid route finding, but it is still easy to lose your way, especially in some of the wide, tangled washes where boulders, disturbed surfaces, and vegetation conspire to hide the true route.

For the most part, though, the trail is well used and easy to follow. It ends back at US 95, opposite the Colorado River. Part of the original Blythe-Vidal Old Road is now enclosed within the wilderness. This route follows the more modern detour around these areas.

Long sections of deep sand bogged down early travelers

Current Road Information

Bureau of Land Management
Needles Field Office
101 West Spikes Road
Needles, CA 92363
(760) 326-7000

Map References

BLM Parker, Blythe
USGS 1:24,000 Vidal, Grommet, Big Maria Mt. NW, Big Maria Mt. NE,
1:100,000 Parker, Blythe
Maptech CD-ROM: San Bernardino County/Mojave; San Diego/Joshua Tree
Southern & Central California Atlas & Gazetteer, pp. 101, 111
California Road & Recreation Atlas, p. 114

Route Directions

▼ 0.0 From the intersection of California 62 and US 95 at Vidal Junction (west of Parker, AZ), continue southeast on US 95 for 6 miles to Vidal. Cross over railroad and proceed 0.1 miles south. Turn southwest onto an unmarked small, formed, single-track trail. The turn is opposite the sign for Main Street, but it is not the wider road that runs perpendicular to US 95. It is the smaller trail leading off at an angle to the southwest. Zero trip meter.
3.7 ▲ Trail ends at US 95 at Vidal. Turn right for Blythe; turn left for Vidal Junction.

GPS: N34°07.13' W114°30.56'

▼ 0.2 SO Cross through wash.
3.5 ▲ SO Cross through wash.

▼ 0.3 SO Cross through wash.
3.4 ▲ SO Cross through wash.

▼ 0.4 SO Cross through wash.
3.3 ▲ SO Cross through wash.

▼ 0.6 SO Road is now marked Blythe-Vidal Old Road.
3.1 ▲ SO Marker post for Blythe-Vidal Old Road.

▼ 0.8 SO Start to cross through wide Vidal Wash.
2.9 ▲ SO Exit wash crossing.

▼ 1.0 SO Exit wash crossing.
2.7 ▲ SO Start to cross through wide Vidal Wash.

▼ 2.9 SO Pass under power lines, remaining on Blythe-Vidal Old Road.
0.8 ▲ SO Pass under power lines, remaining on Blythe-Vidal Old Road.

GPS: N34°05.07' W114°32.46'

▼ 3.4 BR Small track on left.
0.3 ▲ SO Small track on right.

GPS: N34°04.67' W114°32.77'

▼ 3.7 SO Track on left is Desert #4: Gold Rice Mine Trail. Also track on right. Zero trip meter and continue straight ahead on Blythe-Vidal Road. There is a large concrete block at the intersection used as a direction marker.
0.0 ▲ Continue to the northeast.

GPS: N34°04.49' W114°32.93'

▼ 0.0 Continue to the southwest.
5.2 ▲ SO Track on right is Desert #4: Gold Rice Mine Trail. Also track on left. Zero trip meter and continue straight ahead on Blythe-Vidal Road. There is a large concrete block at the intersection used as a direction marker.

▼ 3.1 SO Cross through wash.
2.1 ▲ SO Cross through wash.

▼ 3.9 SO Cross through wash.
1.3 ▲ SO Cross through wash.

GPS: N34°01.97' W114°35.73'

▼ 5.2 TR Enter a tributary of Big Wash and turn sharp right up wash, following marker for Blythe-Vidal Road. The wash forms the wilderness boundary (now on your left). Remain in wash for next 1.1 miles. Zero trip meter.
0.0 ▲ Continue to the north.

GPS: N34°01.35' W114°36.35'

▼ 0.0 Continue to the northwest up the wash.
3.9 ▲ TL Exit tributary of Big Wash, turning sharp left and climbing out of the wash, following marker for Blythe-Vidal Road. Leaving wilderness boundary. Zero trip meter.

▼ 1.1 TL Turn left out of wash alongside power lines. Trail enters a vehicle corridor through the wilderness.
2.8 ▲ TR Turn right down wash, away from power lines, following the Blythe-Vidal Road trail markers. Trail now has wilderness on the right. Remain in wash for the next 1.1 miles.

GPS: N34°01.70' W114°37.25'

▼ 1.5 SO Cross through wash.
2.4 ▲ SO Cross through wash.

▼ 2.2 SO Cross through wash.
1.7 ▲ SO Cross through wash.

▼ 2.4 SO Cross through wide wash.
1.5 ▲ SO Cross through wide wash.

▼ 3.4 SO Cross through two washes.
0.5 ▲ SO Cross through two washes.

▼ 3.7 SO Cross through wash.
0.2 ▲ SO Cross through wash.

▼ 3.8 SO Cross through wash.
0.1 ▲ SO Cross through wash.

▼ 3.9 TL Turn left onto formed trail, away from power lines, following the marker for Blythe-Vidal Road. Zero trip meter.
0.0 ▲ Continue to the north.

GPS: N33°59.79' W114°38.88'

▼ 0.0 Continue to the southeast.
4.8 ▲ TR Turn right onto formed trail under power lines, following the marker for Blythe-Vidal Road. Zero trip meter. The wilderness boundary is on the right.

▼ 0.1 SO Cross through two washes.
4.7 ▲ SO Cross through two washes.

▼ 0.4 BL Track on right. Follow route marker and cross through wash.
4.4 ▲ BR Cross through wash; then track on left. Follow route marker.

▼ 1.2 BL Track on right.
3.6 ▲ SO Track on left.

GPS: N33°59.09' W114°38.24'

▼ 1.8 BL Track on right. Follow marker for Blythe-Vidal Old Road.
3.0 ▲ SO Track on left. Follow marker for Blythe-Vidal Old Road.

▼ 2.0 TL Drop down and turn left up wash.
2.8 ▲ TR Turn right and exit wash at route marker.

GPS: N34°58.98' W114°37.50'

▼ 2.1 BR Bear right, exiting wash at route marker. Track on left also leaves wash.
2.7 ▲ TL Enter wash and turn left down wash. Track ahead exits wash.

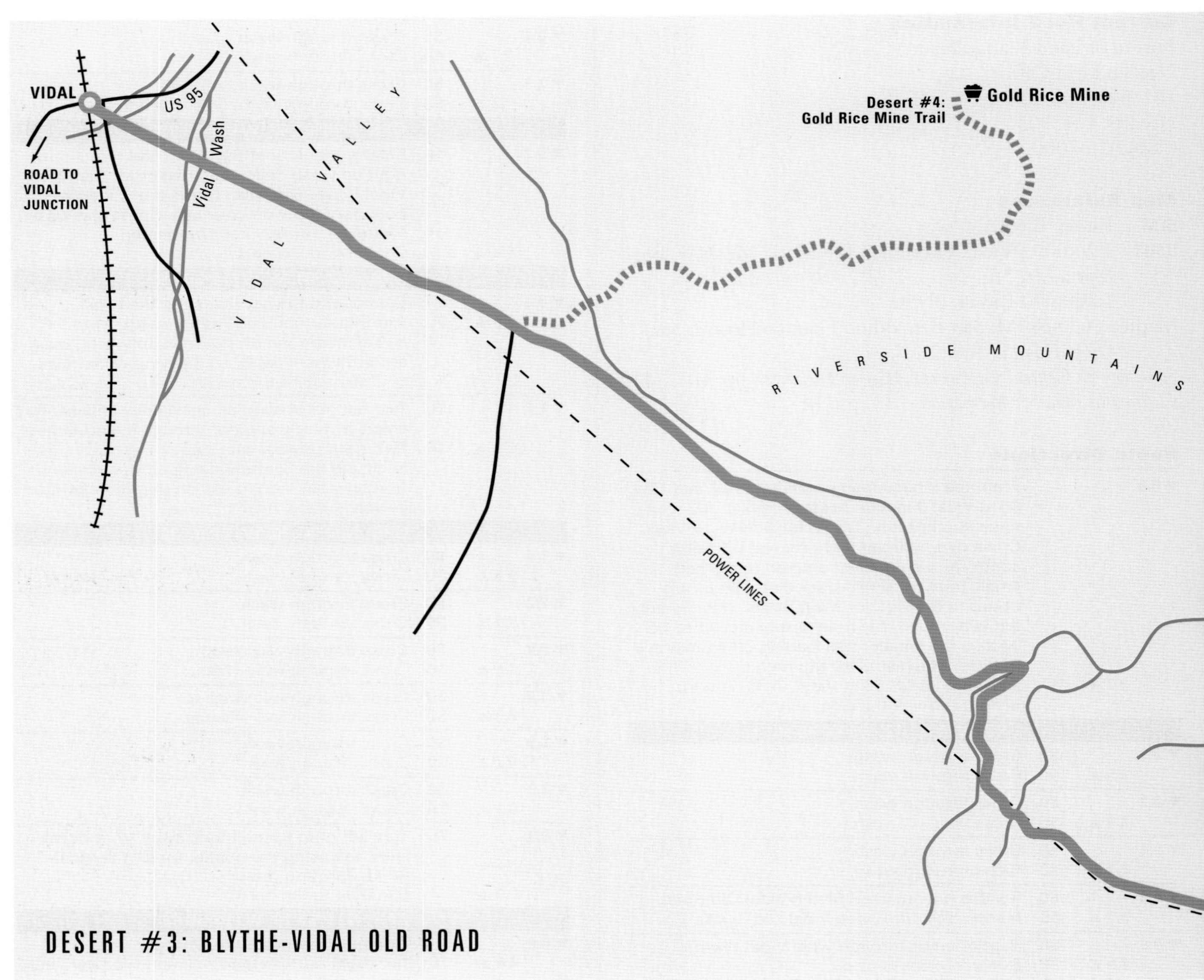

Mileage	Direction	Description
▼ 3.1	BR	Bear right, following route marker. This intersection is faint and easily missed. Trail now heads across a wide area of desert pavement and is indistinct. Watch for route markers.
1.7 ▲	SO	Continue straight ahead at trail marker.
		GPS: N33°58.65′ W114°36.59′
▼ 3.7	SO	Cross through wash.
1.1 ▲	SO	Cross through wash.
▼ 3.8	SO	Cross through two washes.
1.0 ▲	SO	Cross through two washes. Trail now heads across a wide area of desert pavement and is indistinct. Watch for route markers.
		GPS: N33°58.49′ W114°36.02′
▼ 3.9	SO	Start to cross through wide wash.
0.9 ▲	SO	Exit wide wash.
▼ 4.0	BR	Exit wash and bear right to cross through another wash.
0.8 ▲	BL	Cross through wash; then bear left and start to cross through wide wash. Wilderness boundary is on right. Be sure you don't inadvertently enter the wilderness area.
		GPS: N33°58.62′ W114°35.94′
▼ 4.1	SO	Cross through two washes.
0.7 ▲	SO	Cross through two washes.
▼ 4.2	SO	Cross through wash.
0.6 ▲	SO	Cross through wash.
▼ 4.3	SO	Track on left.
0.5 ▲	SO	Track on right.
▼ 4.8	BR	Bear right, remaining on Blythe-Vidal Road. Track on left is for foot and horse travel only and enters the wilderness. Zero trip meter at wilderness access sign.
0.0 ▲		Continue to the west.
		GPS: N33°58.48′ W114°35.38′
▼ 0.0		Continue to the southeast.
4.6 ▲	BL	Bear left, remaining on Blythe-Vidal Road. Track on right is for foot and horse travel only and enters the wilderness. Zero trip meter at wilderness access sign. Trail now follows along wilderness boundary on the right.
▼ 1.5	SO	Cross through wash.
3.1 ▲	SO	Cross through wash.

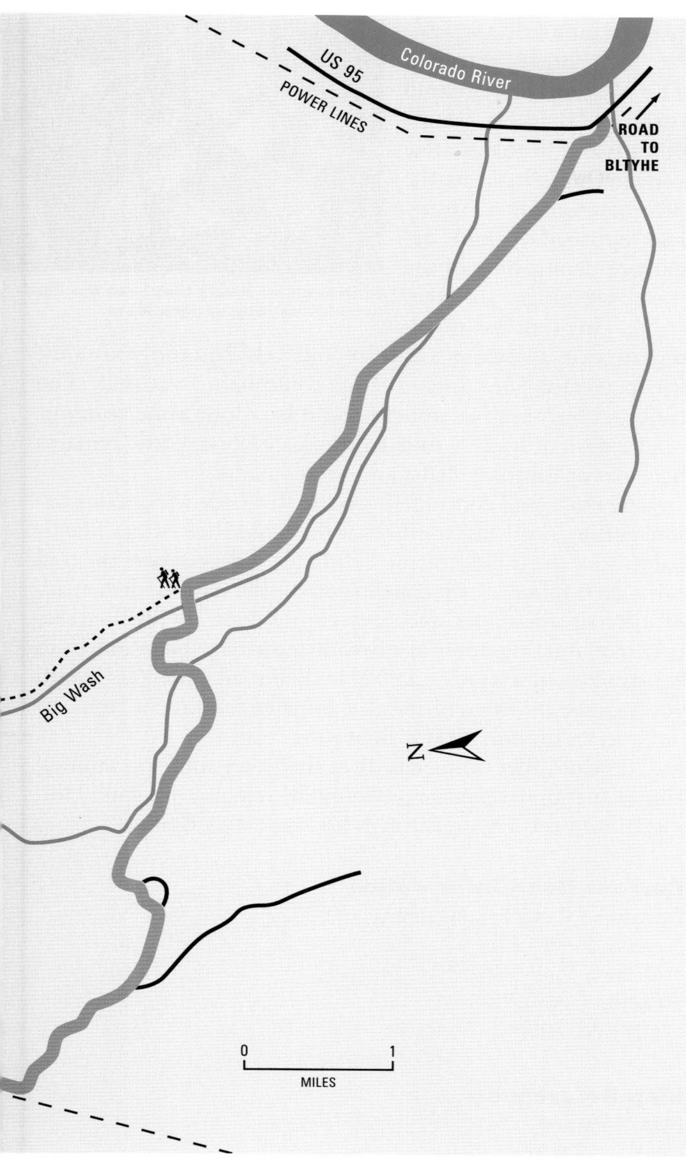

▼ 2.1	SO	Cross through Big Wash.
2.5 ▲	SO	Cross through Big Wash.
		GPS: N33°57.20′ W114°33.94′
▼ 2.2	SO	Trail moves away from wilderness boundary on left; then cross through wash. Track on right and track on left up and down wash.
2.4 ▲	SO	Cross through wash. Track on right and track on left up and down wash. Riverside Mountains Wilderness boundary is now on right of trail.
		GPS: N33°57.09′ W114°33.85′
▼ 2.9	SO	Cross through wash. Track on left and track on right up and down wash.
1.7 ▲	SO	Cross through wash. Track on left and track on right up and down wash.
▼ 3.1	BR	Track on left; then cross through wash.
1.5 ▲	SO	Cross through wash; then track on right. Continue on Blythe-Vidal Road.
▼ 3.3	SO	Track on left.
1.3 ▲	SO	Track on right.
▼ 3.7	SO	Track on left.
0.9 ▲	SO	Track on right.
▼ 3.8	BL	Well-used track on right. Bear left toward Colorado River.
0.8 ▲	BR	Well-used track on left. Follow marker for Blythe-Vidal Road.
		GPS: N33°56.06′ W114°32.96′
▼ 4.0	BR	Track on left.
0.6 ▲	SO	Track on right.
▼ 4.1	BR	Track on left.
0.5 ▲	SO	Track on right.
▼ 4.3	TR	T-intersection along power lines.
0.3 ▲	TL	Turn left away from power lines at marker for Blythe-Vidal Road.
		GPS: N33°55.78′ W114°32.49′
▼ 4.4	BL	Descend steeply into large sandy wash.
0.2 ▲	SO	End of climb out of wash. Continue alongside power lines.
▼ 4.5	TL	Turn left down wash toward Colorado River.
0.1 ▲	TR	Turn right and climb high embankment out of wash alongside power lines.
▼ 4.6		Trail ends at US 95. Turn left for California 62 and Parker, AZ; turn right for Blythe.
0.0 ▲		Trail commences on US 95, 9 miles south of Wilson Road and immediately south of mile marker 24.5. Zero trip meter and turn southwest up wide sandy wash. Track is unmarked.
		GPS: N33°55.63′ W114°32.36′

DESERT #4

Gold Rice Mine Trail

Starting Point:	**Desert #3: Blythe-Vidal Old Road, 3.7 miles south of US 95**
Finishing Point:	**Gold Rice Mine**
Total Mileage:	**6.2 miles (one-way)**
Unpaved Mileage:	**6.2 miles**
Driving Time:	**1.5 hours (one-way)**
Elevation Range:	**900–1,200 feet**
Usually Open:	**Year-round**
Best Time to Travel:	**October to June**
Difficulty Rating:	**6**
Scenic Rating:	**8**
Remoteness Rating:	**+1**

Special Attractions

- Remains of the Gold Rice and Jean Mines.
- Trail travels a vehicle corridor within the Riverside Mountains Wilderness.
- Remote and challenging trail for stock vehicles and mountain bikes.

History

The famous lawman Wyatt Earp frequented the nearby settlements of Vidal, on the Atchison, Topeka & Santa Fe Railroad, and Earp, on the Colorado River. Earp was born in Illinois in 1848 and gradually moved west as opportunities arose in the

1870s. He developed a reputation as a fearless frontier lawman in places such as Prescott, Arizona, and Wichita and Dodge City, Kansas. He may also be remembered as a survivor of the gunfight at the O.K. Corral in Tombstone, Arizona. His addiction for mining and a spot of gambling took him and his wife, Josie, to many gold mining camps throughout the Southwest.

Between 1897 and 1902, the couple operated a saloon in Alaska at the peak of the Klondike gold rush. Even though it was a very profitable period for them, they decided to return to the Southwest to mining boom towns. Wyatt prospected heavily at the base of the mountains around Vidal, establishing a home in the town. He discovered gold and copper veins on many claims, although his investments from earlier ventures proved sufficient for both him and his wife. They spent the hot summers in the Hollywood area, befriending many movie stars. They would return to work their claims in the cooler winter months. Wyatt Earp passed away in Los Angeles in 1929 at the age of 80. Josie survived him by 15 years.

The mines in this region are important roosting sites for bats. Field studies of bats in California and Arizona go back to the 1860s. Studies in the 1950s and 1960s showed that banded bats, found in mines close to this trail, were from as far away as eastern Arizona. Bats usually roost in small crevices, such as small drill holes found in mining tunnels. As more bats join in, they tend to cluster around the location of the first group in the drill holes, even though they are less protected and sheltered on the walls of the mine.

Description

Gold Rice Mine Trail travels along a roughly formed trail through a vehicle corridor in the Riverside Mountains Wilderness. The first couple of miles are easygoing, but the farther along the trail, the tougher it becomes. Much of the trail travels along a very narrow shelf road that is barely wide enough for a full size vehicle to venture through. The roughness of the trail surface further compounds the problem. The surface offers little in the way of traction at times, and approaches and departures from some of the wash crossings are very steep. This trail has no alternate exit, so be confident in your vehicle's and your ability to retrace your steps before committing yourself. The trail sees little traffic, so help could be a long time coming.

The rugged Riverside Mountains challenged early road builders

Broken chisel heads testify to the hardness of the rock at Jean Mine

A side trail leads 1 mile to the Jean Mine. Little remains here except for three shafts and some tailings.

The main trail continues into the Riverside Mountains before curling northeast to finish at the Gold Rice Mine. The final mile of the trail is the most difficult. This is where the trail earns its 6 rating. Rock crawling along the narrow shelf road, off-camber side slopes, and steep climbs make up the final section. An amazing amount of work must have been put in to construct such a sturdy and stable shelf road. Along its length you can see evidence of the dry stone embankment supporting it as it contours its way above the wash.

The Gold Rice Mine has three shafts, an adit, and tailings. Concrete foundations are probably the remains of a mill. Hiking around this region is rough but very rewarding.

Current Road Information

Bureau of Land Management
Needles Field Office
101 West Spikes Road
Needles, CA 92363
(760) 326-7000

Map References

BLM Parker
USGS 1:24,000 Vidal
1:100,000 Parker
Maptech CD-ROM: San Bernardino County/Mojave
Southern & Central California Atlas & Gazetteer, p. 101
California Road & Recreation Atlas, p. 114

Route Directions

▼ 0.0		From Desert #3: Blythe-Vidal Old Road, 3.7 miles from the northern end at Vidal, zero trip meter at the large concrete block marker and proceed east on well-used, unmarked trail. Riverside Mountains Wilderness starts on the right at the intersection.
		GPS: N34°04.49' W114°32.93'
▼ 0.1	TR	Turn right on sandy trail and pass "Riverside Mountains Wilderness Area Ahead" sign.
▼ 0.6	SO	Cross through wide wash.
▼ 1.0	SO	Cross through wide wash.
▼ 2.1	SO	Unmarked track on left goes 1 mile to the Jean Mine. Zero trip meter. This short track is rated 6 for difficulty because of steep entrances and exits at gullies and off-camber sections.

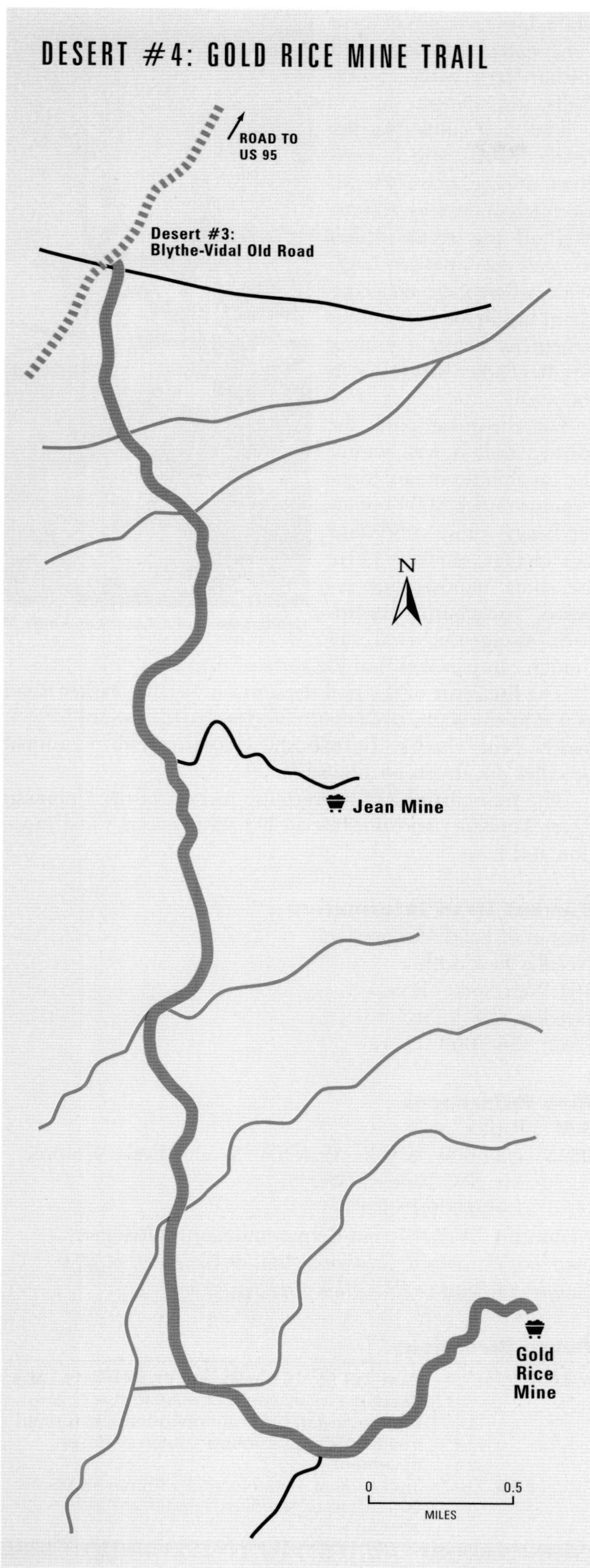

		GPS: N34°02.93' W114°32.69'
▼ 0.0		Continue to the southeast on main trail.
▼ 1.1	SO	Cross through wash.
▼ 1.7	SO	Cross through two washes.
▼ 1.8	SO	Cross through wash.
▼ 2.2	SO	Start to cross through wide wash.
▼ 2.3	SO	Exit wash crossing.
▼ 2.5	BL	Drop down to enter wash and bear left up wash.
		GPS: N34°00.97' W114°32.61'
▼ 2.6	BR	Exit wash to the right.
▼ 2.8	SO	Cross through wash.
▼ 3.0	TL	T-intersection. Zero trip meter and turn left, heading uphill.
		GPS: N34°00.77' W114°32.16'
▼ 0.0		Continue to the northeast.
▼ 0.9	SO	Cross over wash on rocky waterfall.
▼ 1.1		Trail ends at the Gold Rice Mine.
		GPS: N34°01.19' W114°31.39'

DESERT #5

Whipple Mountains Trail

Starting Point:	**US 95, 15.9 miles south of Havasu Lake Road**
Finishing Point:	**California 62, 7 miles west of Earp**
Total Mileage:	**23.4 miles**
Unpaved Mileage:	**23.4 miles**
Driving Time:	**3.5 hours**
Elevation Range:	**800–2,000**
Usually Open:	**Year-round**
Best Time to Travel:	**October to June**
Difficulty Rating:	**3**
Scenic Rating:	**8**
Remoteness Rating:	**+1**

Special Attractions

- Remains of many old mining camps.
- Rockhounding for chalcedony.
- Remote, easy-to-follow desert trail, popular with ATVs and 4WDs.

History

As a lieutenant in the Corps of U.S. Topographical Engineers, Amiel W. Whipple assisted in the early exploration of California. In 1853, Whipple's expedition left Fort Smith, Arkansas, with a party of about 70 men. Whipple's group was one of several survey parties sent out to find a route for a transcontinental railroad. The epic journey, which ran close to the thirty-fifth parallel, ultimately took the survey party to Los Angeles. The journey was difficult, and it tested all the men involved. By the time the explorers reached the Colorado River, most of their wagons had been abandoned.

The Mojave guided the expedition through the Colorado

River region. The group might not have made it across the river without this assistance. After crossing the river, the expedition suffered its only casualty; Paiute Indians killed one of the herders who had fallen behind with the stock.

Although a more northerly route was chosen for the first transcontinental railroad, the expedition successfully mapped a lot of previously unknown territory. In 1856, federal funding was used to improve the Whipple Trail. The Atchison, Topeka & Santa Fe Railroad would eventually follow much of Whipple's route from Albuquerque, New Mexico, to California.

The rugged Whipple Mountains were the scene of gold mining during the Southwest's early prospecting days. The remoteness of the mountains that bear the lieutenant's name, combined with the harsh weather of this locality, kept many from entering the region. Although several mines can be seen along this trail, the mountains have remained relatively undisturbed by people. The American Eagle Mine, also known as the New American Mine, was discovered in 1875 and produced copper and gold. The Whipple Mining District was further developed in the 1930s and early 1940s. Native gold was found in several mines along with oxidized copper and iron minerals. The gold was found in narrow quartz veins that ran through gneiss and metamorphic rocks of the Precambrian era.

Description

The trail through the Whipple Mountains runs between US 95 and the Colorado River. It passes through some remote desert areas that are more reminiscent of Arizona than California.

The trail leaves US 95 along a well-used, but unmarked, trail. There is a marker post for the Heritage Trail 1 mile to the north of the trail's beginning. The Heritage Trail joins the route described below, but it is seldom used and overgrown in places. Most vehicles seem to follow the route described here.

The route travels over desert pavement toward the prominent Pyramid Butte. It then wraps around the butte to the east. Many small trails leave from the main route in this region. Some of them access popular rockhounding areas to the north, where it is possible to find chalcedony. The pale-colored rock is easy to see against the darker desert pavement. It will take a bit of hunting, though, to find the more prized chalcedony roses.

Blue copper rock at the Gold Standard Mine

As you get farther along the trail, there are fewer side trails and the major intersections are well marked. Spur trails lead off a short distance to the Gold Hill Mine and the Gold Standard Mine. Little remains of these mines except some collapsed timber structures, adits, shafts, and tailings.

Headframe at the American Eagle Mine

The trail joins Needles Parker Road, which runs down a loose, gravelly wash for much of the way. A short loop off this section takes you past the American Eagle Mine, where there are a couple of headframes and other structures, before rejoining Needles Parker Road back in the wash.

For the most part, the formed trail is well within the capabilities of any high-clearance stock SUV, but after heavy rains, conditions can change quickly. There are some remote, but exposed, backcountry campsites along the trail, although campers will find the surfaces uneven.

The final part of the trail remains on Needles Parker Road as it exits the wash, crossing the sloping bajada toward US 95. Teddy bear chollas, brittlebush, creosote, and occasional ocotillos dot the stony alluvial fan.

The trail crosses an underground section of the Colorado River Aqueduct and finishes on US 95 between Vidal Junction and Earp.

Current Road Information

Bureau of Land Management
Needles Field Office
101 West Spikes Road
Needles, CA 92363
(760) 326-7000

Map References

BLM Parker
USGS 1:24,000 Savahia Peak SW, Savahia Peak, Whipple Mt. SW, Parker NW
1:100,000 Parker
Maptech CD-ROM: San Bernardino County/Mojave
Southern & Central California Atlas & Gazetteer, p. 101
California Road & Recreation Atlas, p. 115

Route Directions

▼ 0.0	From US 95, 15.9 miles south of Havasu Lake Road, 0.1 miles south of mile marker 2, zero trip meter and turn east on unmarked formed trail that leaves across a stretch of desert pavement.
8.0 ▲	Trail ends at T-intersection with paved US 95. Turn right for Needles; turn left for Vidal Junction.

GPS: N34°19.21' W114°39.11'

▼ 1.3	SO	Pyramid Butte is the taller of the two hills on the right.
6.7 ▲	SO	Pyramid Butte is the taller of the two hills on the left.
▼ 1.7	BR	Faint track straight ahead and to the left. Bear right and proceed along the north face of Pyramid Butte.
6.3 ▲	BL	Faint track straight ahead and to the right. Bear left and proceed around the west side of Pyramid Butte.
		GPS: N34°19.91' W114°37.81'
▼ 2.0	BL	Track on right. Follow Heritage Trail mile marker 587.2. Pyramid Butte is immediately south of the trail.
6.0 ▲	SO	Track on left. Pyramid Butte is immediately south of the trail.
		GPS: N34°19.95' W114°37.45'
▼ 2.2	BR	Small track on left. There is a rockhounding area for chalcedony to the north along this trail.
5.8 ▲	SO	Small track on right. There is a rockhounding area for chalcedony to the north along this trail.
▼ 2.3	SO	Small track on right.
5.7 ▲	SO	Small track on left.
▼ 2.4	SO	Cross through wash.
5.6 ▲	SO	Cross through wash.
▼ 2.8	SO	Small track on left.
5.2 ▲	SO	Small track on right.
▼ 3.1	SO	Well-used track on right.
4.9 ▲	BR	Well-used track on left.
		GPS: N34°19.71' W114°36.40'
▼ 3.4	SO	Cross through wash. Many wash crossings for the next 2.9 miles.
4.6 ▲	SO	Cross through wash.
▼ 6.3	SO	Cross through wash.
1.7 ▲	SO	Cross through wash. Many wash crossings for the next 2.9 miles.
		GPS: N34°20.29' W114°33.92'
▼ 7.2	SO	Well-used track on left.
0.8 ▲	SO	Well-used track on right.
		GPS: N34°19.86' W114°33.16'
▼ 8.0	TL	T-intersection. Track on left is Heritage Trail, suitable for 4WDs, ATVs, and motorbikes. Track on right, which goes 0.2 miles to the Gold Hill Mine, is suitable for 4WDs, ATVs, and motorbikes. Zero trip meter and turn left, following marker for the Heritage Trail.
0.0 ▲		Continue to the northwest.
		GPS: N34°19.22' W114°32.89'
▼ 0.0		Continue to the northeast.
1.2 ▲	TR	Track ahead, which goes 0.2 miles to the Gold Hill Mine, is suitable for 4WDs, ATVs, and motorbikes. Zero trip meter and turn right onto unmarked, well-used trail.
▼ 0.2	SO	Cross through wash.
1.0 ▲	SO	Cross through wash.
▼ 0.3	SO	Diggings on left.
0.9 ▲	SO	Diggings on right.
		GPS: N34°19.03' W114°32.70'
▼ 0.5	SO	Cross through wash.
0.7 ▲	SO	Cross through wash.
▼ 0.6	SO	Enter wash.
0.6 ▲	SO	Exit wash.
▼ 0.7	BR	Small track on left out of wash. Exit wash.
0.5 ▲	BL	Small track on right out of wash. Enter wash.
		GPS: N34°19.11' W114°32.46'
▼ 1.0	SO	Cross through wash.
0.2 ▲	SO	Cross through wash.
▼ 1.2	BL	Track straight ahead, which goes 1.6 miles to the Gold Standard Mine, is suitable for 4WDs, ATVs, and motorbikes. Zero trip meter and bear left. Remain on the marked Heritage Trail.
0.0 ▲		Continue to the west.
		GPS: N34°18.87' W114°32.05'
▼ 0.0		Continue to the northeast.
1.7 ▲	BR	Track on left, which goes 1.6 miles to the Gold Standard Mine, is suitable for 4WDs, ATVs, and motorbikes. Zero trip meter and bear right on well-used, unmarked trail.
▼ 0.1	SO	Start to cross through wide wash.
1.6 ▲	SO	Exit wide wash.
▼ 0.3	SO	Exit wash crossing. Track on right joins trail to the Gold Standard Mine; then cross through wash.
1.4 ▲	BR	Cross through wash; then track on left joins the trail to the Gold Standard Mine. Start to cross through wide wash.
		GPS: N34°18.96' W114°31.81'
▼ 0.8	SO	Cross through wash.
0.9 ▲	SO	Cross through wash.
▼ 1.0	SO	Cross through wash.
0.7 ▲	SO	Cross through wash.
▼ 1.2	SO	Cross through wash.
0.5 ▲	SO	Cross through wash.
▼ 1.7	TR	T-intersection with trail in the wash. It is marked as Needles Parker Road to the right and left, suitable for 4WDs, ATVs, and motorbikes. It is also marked as the Heritage Trail to the left. Small trail straight ahead, exiting wash. Zero trip meter and turn right onto Needles Parker Road, traveling up the wash.
0.0 ▲		Continue to the west.
		GPS: N34°18.93' W114°30.58'
▼ 0.0		Continue to the southeast.

Approaches to washes can change frequently after storms

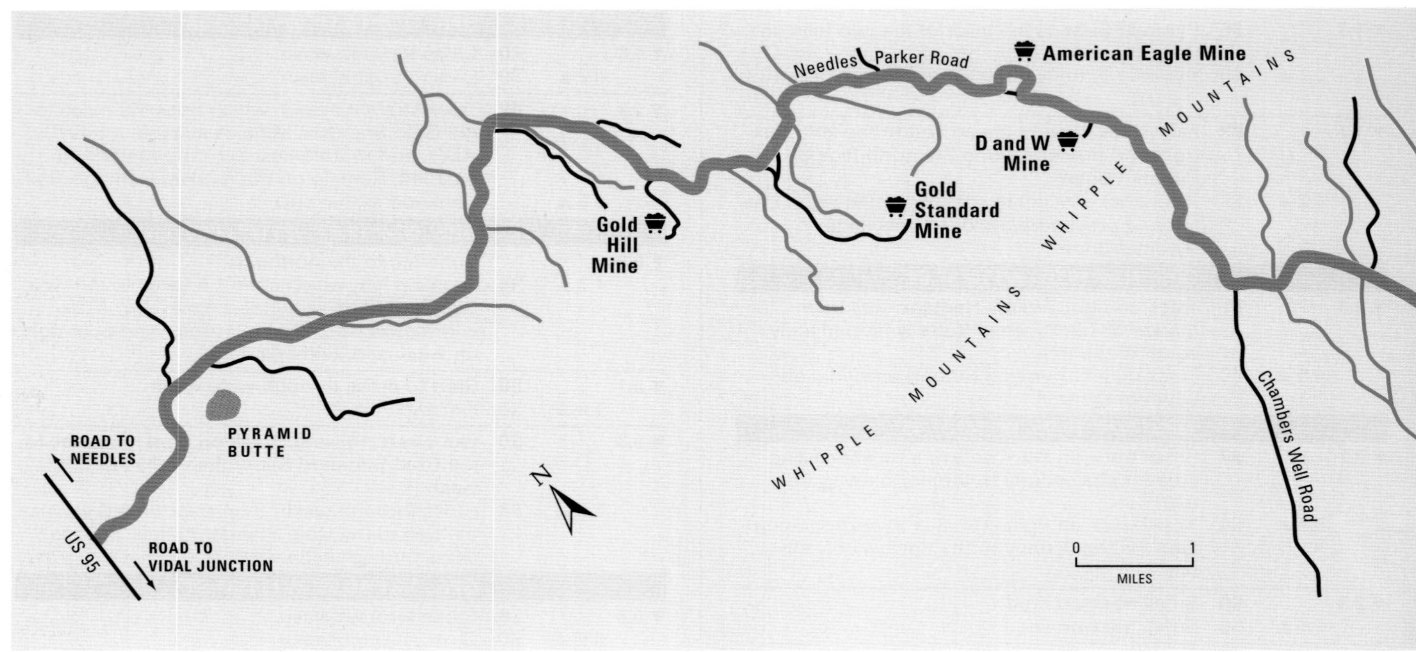

	1.2 ▲	TL	Needles Parker Road continues ahead in the wash at the marker. It is also now signed for the Heritage Trail, suitable for 4WDs, ATVs, and motorbikes. Small track on right out of wash and well-used formed trail on left out of wash. Zero trip enter and turn left onto unmarked, well-used, formed trail exiting the wash.
▼ 1.1		SO	Exit wash.
	0.1 ▲	SO	Enter down wash.
▼ 1.2		TL	Needles Parker Road continues ahead in wash. Turn left away from wash, following marker for the American Eagle Mine. Trail is suitable for 4WDs, ATVs, and motorbikes. Zero trip meter.
	0.0 ▲		Continue to the northwest.
			GPS: N34°18.32′ W114°29.75′
▼ 0.0			Continue to the northeast.
	3.5 ▲	TR	T-intersection with Needles Parker Road, running in the wash. Turn right to rejoin this road and zero trip meter.
▼ 0.2		SO	Track on right.
	3.3 ▲	SO	Track on left.
▼ 0.3		SO	American Eagle Mine on left. Headframe and concrete foundations remain.
	3.2 ▲	SO	American Eagle Mine on right. Headframe and concrete foundations remain.
			GPS: N34°18.35′ W114°29.59′
▼ 0.4		TR	Track ahead goes to white wooden headframe and shed. Turn right down wash.
	3.1 ▲	TL	Track on right goes to white wooden headframe and shed. Turn left out of wash.
▼ 0.7		TL	T-intersection with Needles Parker Road. Turn left down wash, rejoining this road.
	2.8 ▲	TR	Turn right up unmarked trail in side wash to loop past the American Eagle Mine. Needles Parker Road continues ahead.
			GPS: N34°18.20′ W114°29.70′
▼ 1.3		SO	Track on left.
	2.2 ▲	SO	Track on right.
▼ 1.4		SO	Track on right is D and W Mine Track, suitable for 4WDs, ATVs, and motorbikes.
	2.1 ▲	SO	Track on left is D and W Mine Track, suitable for 4WDs, ATVs, and motorbikes.
			GPS: N34°17.72′ W114°29.25′
▼ 3.4		SO	Exit wash to the left.
	0.1 ▲	SO	Enter up wash.
▼ 3.5		BL	Track on right is Chambers Well Road, suitable for 4WDs, ATVs, and motorbikes. Zero trip meter and remain on marked Needles Parker Road.
	0.0 ▲		Continue to the north.
			GPS: N34°16.08′ W114°29.07′
▼ 0.0			Continue to the southeast.
	5.5 ▲	SO	Track on left is Chambers Well Road, suitable for 4WDs, ATVs, and motorbikes. Zero trip meter and remain on marked Needles Parker Road.
▼ 0.3		SO	Cross through wash.
	5.2 ▲	SO	Cross through wash.
▼ 0.4		SO	Cross through wash.
	5.1 ▲	SO	Cross through wash.
▼ 1.3		SO	Cross through wash; then track on left.
	4.2 ▲	SO	Track on right; then cross through wash.
▼ 1.4		SO	Cross through wash.
	4.1 ▲	SO	Cross through wash.
▼ 3.0		SO	Cross through wash.
	2.5 ▲	SO	Cross through wash.
			GPS: N34°14.15′ W114°27.15′
▼ 3.5		SO	Cross through wash.
	2.0 ▲	SO	Cross through wash.
▼ 3.8		SO	Enter wash.
	1.7 ▲	SO	Exit wash.
▼ 3.9		SO	Exit wash.
	1.6 ▲	SO	Enter wash.
▼ 4.1		SO	Cross through wash. Many wash crossings for the next 1.4 miles.
	1.4 ▲	SO	Cross through wash.
▼ 4.8		SO	Leaving Whipple Mountains Wilderness boundary on left.
	0.7 ▲	SO	Whipple Mountains Wilderness boundary now on right.
▼ 5.0		SO	Small track on left.

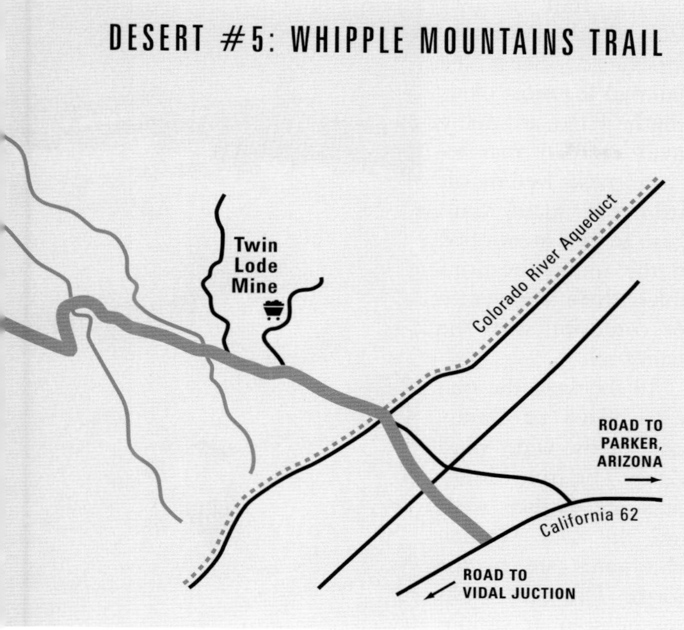

	0.5 ▲	SO	Small track on right.
			GPS: N34°13.46′ W114°25.98′
▼ 5.2		SO	Track on left.
	0.3 ▲	SO	Track on right.
▼ 5.3		SO	Cross through wide wash.
	0.2 ▲	SO	Cross through wide wash.
▼ 5.5		SO	Unmarked, well-used track on left goes 0.8 miles to Twin Lode Mine and wilderness boundary. Zero trip meter.
	0.0 ▲		Continue to the northwest. Many wash crossings for the next 1.4 miles.
			GPS: N34°13.09′ W114°25.59′
▼ 0.0			Continue to the southeast.
	2.3 ▲	BL	Unmarked, well-used track on right goes 0.8 miles to Twin Lode Mine and wilderness boundary. Bear left on unmarked trail and zero trip meter.
▼ 0.7		BL	Track on right.
	1.6 ▲	SO	Track on left.
▼ 0.9		SO	Cross over graded water pipeline road, remaining on small formed trail; then track on left.
	1.4 ▲	SO	Track on right; then cross over graded water pipeline road, remaining on small formed trail.
			GPS: N34°12.41′ W114°25.05′
▼ 1.0		SO	Small track on left.
	1.3 ▲	BR	Small track on right.
▼ 1.6		SO	Track on left and track on right is pipeline road.
	0.7 ▲	SO	Track on left and track on right is pipeline road.
▼ 2.3			Trail ends at intersection with California 62. Turn right for Vidal Junction; turn left for Parker, AZ.
	0.0 ▲		Trail commences on California 62, 7 miles west of Earp, which is immediately on the California side of the Colorado River. Trail is 0.1 miles west of mile marker 135. Zero trip meter and turn north on well-used, unmarked formed trail.
			GPS: N34°11.12′ W114°24.95′

DESERT #6

Cadiz Road

Starting Point:	**California 62 at the Freda Railroad Siding, 23 miles west of Vidal Junction**
Finishing Point:	**National Trails Highway (Route 66) at Chambless**
Total Mileage:	**47.1 miles**
Unpaved Mileage:	**42.8 miles**
Driving Time:	**2 hours**
Elevation Range:	**600–1,400 feet**
Usually Open:	**Year-round**
Best Time to Travel:	**September to June**
Difficulty Rating:	**1**
Scenic Rating:	**8**
Remoteness Rating:	**+1**

Special Attractions

- Cadiz Dunes Wilderness sand dunes.
- Marble Mountain Fossil Beds Area of Critical Environmental Concern.
- Broad, sweeping views of the Ward and Cadiz Valleys and the old salt works.

History

The Atlantic & Pacific Railroad constructed the line through Cadiz at the northern end of this trail in 1883. The company also named the location. The names of the railroad sidings across this section of the Mojave Desert run alphabetically from the east—Amboy, Bristol, (Saltus Siding came later), Cadiz, Danby, Essex, Fenner, Goffs, and Homer. The line eventually became part of the Atchison, Topeka & Santa Fe Railroad.

Just northwest of Cadiz Siding is an old marble quarry noted for its unusual fossils. The quarry site now known as Marble Mountain Fossil Beds has a fossil of one of the earliest known animals, called trilobites, to have a skeleton and eyes. When the dry Bristol Lake was part of an ancient Cambrian sea, it was habitat for a number of creatures, including trilobites. These animals were small marine crustaceans somewhat like today's horseshoe crabs. The fragile nature of the fossils makes the discovery and observation of a complete trilobite quite difficult. Some may be fortunate enough to see tiny specks that are thought to be trilobite eggs.

The Calevanto marble mine at the fossil beds was worked from 1937 to 1939. Marble from the quarry was used in the San Francisco Customs House and the Oxnard and Gardena post offices.

Bristol and Cadiz Lakes (west of this trail) are dried-out basins, remains of a wet period some time in the past. Weathering of the surrounding mountains lined the lakebeds with salts, mainly calcium chloride and sodium. The evaporation of the waters over time has encrusted the lakebeds with concentrated salts. These salts have been collected in both lakes at different times. Bristol has produced so much that a railroad siding was named Saltus in 1915.

The dry lake area is noted for chloride mining operations, which have been ongoing since the early part of the twentieth century. Trenches are dug on the lakebed, filled with a brine solution pumped from wells, then allowed to concentrate by evaporation. Calcium chloride is shipped as a liquid concentrate for the agricultural industry. The other product, sodium chloride, is used for table salt and is an essential chemical in many industrial processes.

Midway along the trail, at Chubbuck, are the remains of several large limestone mines and quarries that operated in the 1920s. The equipment used in these mines was freighted in by the Sugar Lime Rock Company, which ran the Baxter and Ballardi claim north of Baxter. When the Baxter mines closed down, the equipment was moved to Chubbuck.

Bristol Lake has fooled many a lost traveler or wishful prospector in the summer (or even winter) heat. The enormous dry lake develops spectacular mirages. Visions of water seem to shimmer at the base of the rugged Bullion Mountains.

Description

Cadiz Road is a wide graded road that links California 62 with the National Trails Highway (Route 66). The road is sandy and loose along its length, and suitable for a carefully driven passenger vehicle in dry weather. Patches of loose sand, gullies, and occasional washouts may make some drivers wish for a high-clearance vehicle. The road may be impassable when wet, even to a 4WD vehicle, because the deep sand traps turn to greasy mud. The road is often washboardy from low maintenance.

Explosives bunker at the Chubbuck Mines

The trail follows alongside the Atchison, Topeka & Santa Fe Railroad for most of its length. There are many small railroad maintenance tracks leading off from the main trail; these are not mentioned in the route directions unless there is a chance for confusion with the main trail.

To the west, the trail offers views of Danby Lake in the wide Ward Valley. The Iron Mountains are farther west, and the Old Woman Mountains are to the north. The salt works can be seen at various points along the way.

Sodium and calcium chloride processing works at the dry Danby Lake

The Cadiz Dunes can be reached by a 5-mile spur trail. Hikers can continue to explore farther into the wilderness area.

Current Road Information

Bureau of Land Management
Needles Field Office
101 West Spikes Road
Needles, CA 92363
(760) 326-7000

Map References

BLM Amboy, Sheep Hole Mts., Parker
USGS 1:24,000 Arica Mt., Sablon, Danby Lake, East of Milligan, Milligan, Chubbuck, Cadiz Lake NE, Cadiz Lake NW, Cadiz Summit, Cadiz
1:100,000 Amboy, Sheep Hole Mts., Parker
Maptech CD-ROM: San Bernardino County/Mojave
Southern & Central California Atlas & Gazetteer, pp. 100, 99, 85
California Road & Recreation Atlas, pp. 107, 113

Route Directions

▼ 0.0		From California 62 at the Freda Railroad Siding, 23 miles west of Vidal Junction and 0.7 miles west of mile marker 103, zero trip meter and turn north on graded dirt road. The road is unsigned, but has a yellow "Not maintained by San Bernardino County" sign at the start. If approaching from the east, the sign is immediately before a left-hand bend.
13.8 ▲		Trail ends on California 62 at Freda Railroad Siding. Turn left for Vidal Junction and Parker, AZ; turn right for Twentynine Palms.
		GPS: N34°06.42' W114°55.90'
▼ 0.6	SO	Cross through wash. Atchison, Topeka & Santa Fe Railroad joins on the right.
13.2 ▲	SO	Railroad tracks leave on the left.

▼ 1.4	SO	Cross through wash.
12.4 ▲	SO	Cross through wash.
▼ 2.6	SO	Cross through wash.
11.2 ▲	SO	Cross through wash.
		GPS: N34°08.24' W114°57.47
▼ 3.5	SO	Cross through wash.
10.3 ▲	SO	Cross through wash.
▼ 4.2	SO	Cross through wash.
9.6 ▲	SO	Cross through wash.
		GPS: N34°09.37' W114°58.57'
▼ 5.1	SO	Cross through wash.
8.7 ▲	SO	Cross through wash.
▼ 6.1	SO	Cross through wash.
7.7 ▲	SO	Cross through wash.
▼ 6.7	SO	Cross through wash.
7.1 ▲	SO	Cross through wash.
▼ 7.6	SO	Cross through wash.
6.2 ▲	SO	Cross through wash.
▼ 9.4	SO	Track on right.
4.4 ▲	SO	Track on left.
		GPS: N34°12.74' W115°02.49'
▼ 10.5	SO	Track on right.
3.3 ▲	SO	Track on left.
▼ 11.2	SO	Cross through wash.
2.6 ▲	SO	Cross through wash.
▼ 11.6	SO	Cross through wash.
2.2 ▲	SO	Cross through wash.
▼ 12.6	SO	Graded road on left and graded road on right along pipeline.
1.2 ▲	SO	Graded road on left and graded road on right along pipeline.
		GPS: N34°14.40' W115°05.14'
▼ 13.8	SO	Graded road on left and graded road on right under power lines. Left goes 8 miles to California 62; right goes 50 miles to I-40. Zero trip meter.
0.0 ▲		Continue to the southeast.
		GPS: N34°15.06' W115°06.19'
▼ 0.0		Continue to the northwest and cross through wash. Road is now marked as Cadiz Road
4.2 ▲	SO	Cross through wash; then graded road on left and graded road on right under power lines. Right goes 8 miles to California 62; left goes 50 miles to I-40. Zero trip meter.
▼ 2.9	SO	Graded road on left under power lines and graded road on right; then entrance into dry lake mining operations on right.
1.3 ▲	SO	Entrance into dry lake mining operations on left; then road on left. Road on right under power lines.
		GPS: N34°16.56' W115°08.73'
▼ 3.0	SO	Track on left.
1.2 ▲	SO	Track on right.
▼ 3.4	SO	Cross through wash.
0.8 ▲	SO	Cross through wash.
▼ 3.9	SO	Track on left.
0.3 ▲	SO	Track on right.
▼ 4.1	SO	Milligan Siding on right at small sign.
0.1 ▲	SO	Milligan Siding on left at small sign.
		GPS: N34°16.59' W115°10.08'
▼ 4.2	SO	Wide graded road on left. Road on right crosses railroad. Zero trip meter.
0.0 ▲		Continue to the east.
		GPS: N34°16.60' W115°10.20'
▼ 0.0		Continue to the west.

9.1 ▲	SO	Wide graded road on right. Road on left crosses railroad. Zero trip meter.
▼ 0.2	SO	Cross through wash; then track on right along railroad.
8.9 ▲	SO	Track on left along railroad; then cross through wash.
▼ 1.4	SO	Graded road on left.
7.7 ▲	SO	Graded road on right.
		GPS: N34°16.71' W115°11.60'
▼ 3.3	SO	Cross through wash.
5.8 ▲	SO	Cross through wash.
▼ 4.2	SO	Cross through wash.
4.9 ▲	SO	Cross through wash.
▼ 6.3	SO	Cross through wash.
2.8 ▲	SO	Cross through wash.
▼ 7.2	SO	Cross through wash.
1.9 ▲	SO	Cross through wash.
▼ 7.7	SO	Cross through wash.
1.4 ▲	SO	Cross through wash.
▼ 8.3	SO	Graded road on left goes 1 mile to mine and workings.
0.8 ▲	SO	Graded road on right goes 1 mile to mine and workings.
		GPS: N34°21.26' W115°16.68'
▼ 9.1	SO	Track on left; then cross through wash; then track on right is Desert #7: Skeleton Pass Road, which leaves at an angle and crosses the railroad. Marker for the trail is set back from Cadiz Road. Zero trip meter.
0.0 ▲		Continue to the southeast and cross through wash; then track on right.
		GPS: N34°21.84' W115°17.14'
▼ 0.0		Continue to the northwest.
7.3 ▲	SO	Track on left is Desert #7: Skeleton Pass Road, which leaves at an acute angle and crosses the railroad. Marker for the trail is set back from Cadiz Road. Zero trip meter.
▼ 0.5	SO	Cross through wash.
6.8 ▲	SO	Cross through wash.
▼ 0.8	SO	Track on right follows alongside rail line.
6.5 ▲	SO	Track on left follows alongside rail line.
▼ 1.4	SO	Track on right follows alongside rail line.
5.9 ▲	SO	Track on left follows alongside rail line.
▼ 1.6	SO	Cross through wash.
5.7 ▲	SO	Cross through wash.
▼ 1.7	SO	Track on left leads toward Cadiz Lake along edge of the Cadiz Dunes Wilderness.
5.6 ▲	SO	Track on right leads toward Cadiz Lake along edge of the Cadiz Dunes Wilderness.
		GPS: N34°22.92' W115°18.42'
▼ 2.0	SO	Cross through wash.
5.3 ▲	SO	Cross through wash.
▼ 2.9	SO	Track on right.
4.4 ▲	SO	Track on left.
▼ 4.1	SO	Track on right.
3.2 ▲	SO	Track on left.
▼ 4.3	SO	Cross through wash.
3.0 ▲	SO	Cross through wash.
▼ 5.7	SO	Track on right.
1.6 ▲	SO	Track on left.
▼ 6.0	SO	Track on right.
1.3 ▲	SO	Track on left.
▼ 6.7	SO	Cross through wash.
0.6 ▲	SO	Cross through wash.
		GPS: N34°25.40' W115°23.12'

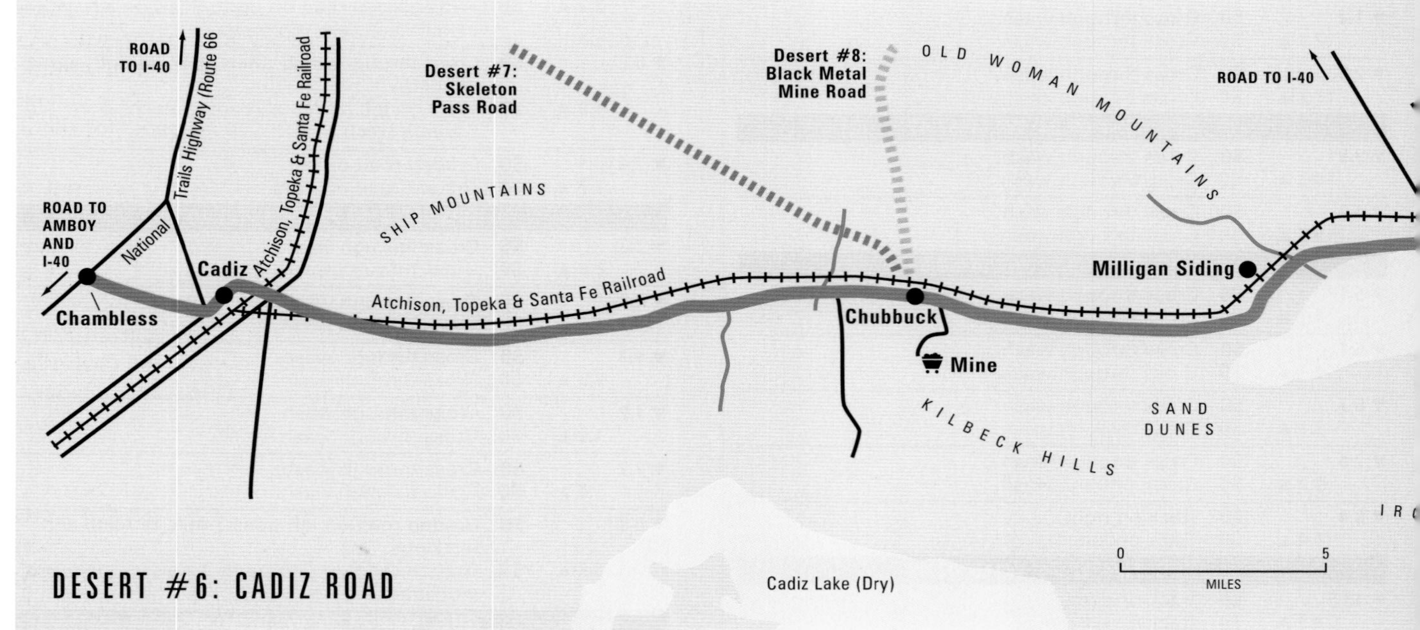

▼ 7.3		SO	Well-used track on left is CZ 332, which leads to the edge of the Cadiz Dunes and is suitable for 4WDs, ATVs, and motorbikes. Zero trip meter.
	0.0 ▲		Continue to the southeast.
			GPS: N34°25.61' W115°23.53'
▼ 0.0			Continue to the northwest.
	6.4 ▲	SO	Well-used track on right is CZ 332, which leads to the edge of the Cadiz Dunes and is suitable for 4WDs, ATVs, and motorbikes. Zero trip meter.
▼ 0.4		SO	Cross through wash.
	6.0 ▲	SO	Cross through wash.
▼ 1.0		SO	Track on right.
	5.4 ▲	SO	Track on left.
▼ 1.3		SO	Cross through wash.
	5.1 ▲	SO	Cross through wash.
▼ 1.9		SO	Track on right.
	4.5 ▲	SO	Track on left.
▼ 2.1		SO	Cross through wash.
	4.3 ▲	SO	Cross through wash.
▼ 2.7		SO	Cross through wash.
	3.7 ▲	SO	Cross through wash.
▼ 2.9		SO	Cross through wash.
	3.5 ▲	SO	Cross through wash.
▼ 3.5		SO	Cross through wash.
	2.9 ▲	SO	Cross through wash.
▼ 4.7		SO	Cross through wash.
	1.7 ▲	SO	Cross through wash.
			GPS: N34°28.41' W115°27.43'
▼ 5.3		SO	Cross through wash.
	1.1 ▲	SO	Cross through wash.
▼ 6.0		SO	Track on left to pipeline works and track on right; then cross through wash.
	0.4 ▲	SO	Cross through wash; then track on right to pipeline works and track on left.
▼ 6.2		SO	Cadiz Pump Station on left.
	0.2 ▲	SO	Cadiz Pump Station on right.
			GPS: N34°29.32' W115°28.45'
▼ 6.4		BR	Graded road on left; then track on right and track on left along rail line. Cross over rail line and zero trip meter.
	0.0 ▲		Continue to the south. Track on left and track on right along rail line; then bear left past graded road on right.
			GPS: N34°29.50' W115°28.58'
▼ 0.0			Continue to the north. Track on left and track on right along rail line.
	6.3 ▲	BL	Track on right and track on left along rail line. Cross over rail line and zero trip meter.
▼ 0.1		SO	Track on right.
	6.2 ▲	SO	Track on left.
▼ 1.5		SO	Track on left.
	4.8 ▲	SO	Track on right.
▼ 2.0		SO	Cadiz. Graded road on left. Graded road on right goes along rail line to Danby. Cross over railroad. Two tracks on left and two tracks on right. Road is now paved. Remain on paved road, ignoring tracks on right and left.
	4.3 ▲	SO	Cadiz. Road turns to graded dirt. Two tracks on left and two tracks on right. Cross over the Atchison, Topeka & Santa Fe Railroad. Graded road on left goes along rail line to Danby. Graded road on right.
			GPS: N34°31.10' W115°29.59'
▼ 2.3		SO	Track on right goes to Marble Mountain Fossil Beds ACEC.
	4.0 ▲	SO	Track on left goes to Marble Mountain Fossil Beds ACEC.
			GPS: N34°31.29' W115°29.73'
▼ 3.2		TR	Road on left goes to Cadiz Siding.
	3.1 ▲	TL	Road straight ahead goes to Cadiz Siding.
▼ 6.3			Trail ends on National Trails Highway (Route 66) at Chambless. Turn right for I-40; turn left for Amboy.
	0.0 ▲		Trail commences on National Trails Highway (Route 66) at Chambless, 11.2 miles west of Amboy. Zero trip meter and turn southeast on paved Cadiz Road at sign.
			GPS: N34°33.71' W115°32.59'

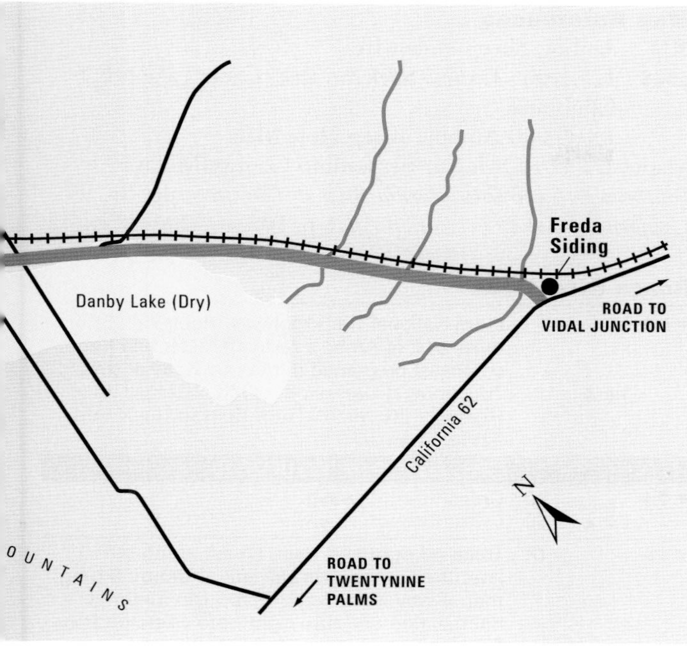

DESERT #7

Skeleton Pass Road

Starting Point:	**National Trails Highway (Route 66), 23.5 miles east of Amboy**
Finishing Point:	**Desert #6: Cadiz Road, 20 miles south of Chambless**
Total Mileage:	**20.3 miles**
Unpaved Mileage:	**20.3 miles**
Driving Time:	**1.5 hours**
Elevation Range:	**1,100–1,600 feet**
Usually Open:	**Year-round**
Best Time to Travel:	**September to June**
Difficulty Rating:	**2**
Scenic Rating:	**8**
Remoteness Rating:	**+1**

Special Attractions

- Rockhounding for opalite in the Ship Mountains.
- Views of the rugged Old Woman Mountains and Cadiz Valley.

History

The ruins at the Danby intersection on Route 66 are all that remains of the old Justice Court building, gas station, and garage from the 1930s. The famous Route 66 was a long strip of tarmac that stretched a total 2,278 miles from Chicago to Santa Monica. Migrants from the Dust Bowl packed up their jalopies and headed west in search of opportunity. Some fell by the wayside, because conditions were harsh for automobiles of the day. Small business enterprises along Route 66 offered support to those who failed. For some migrants who were down to their last resources, this meant selling their automobiles to buy food. Weather conditions and elevation changes made progress along this route almost impossible for the ill-prepared.

In 1926, the nation adopted a numbered route system, thus bringing Route 66 to life. By 1936, Route 66 was completely paved. The road was decommissioned 49 years later when major sections of the route were replaced, relocated, renamed, and updated.

The Vulcan Mine, just over a mile west of Skeleton Pass in the Ship Mountains, was a gold and copper mine established in 1898. Close by are the remains of the Ship Mountain Mine, an old iron mine.

Description

Skeleton Pass Road is a roughly graded dirt road that travels from National Trails Highway (Route 66) to join the wider, graded dirt road in Cadiz Valley. Along the way, it travels down the wide, sloping bajada between the jagged peaks of the Old Woman Mountains and the Ship Mountains, passing through a varied landscape vegetated with creosote bush and cactus.

Rockhounding areas in the Ship Mountains containing the multicolored opalite can be reached from this trail. The trail borders the Old Woman Mountains Wilderness on its western edge. It is easygoing in dry weather and suitable for high-clearance 2WD vehicles.

Current Road Information

Bureau of Land Management
Needles Field Office
101 West Spikes Road
Needles, CA 92363
(760) 326-7000

Trains still pass by Danby Siding but do not stop anymore

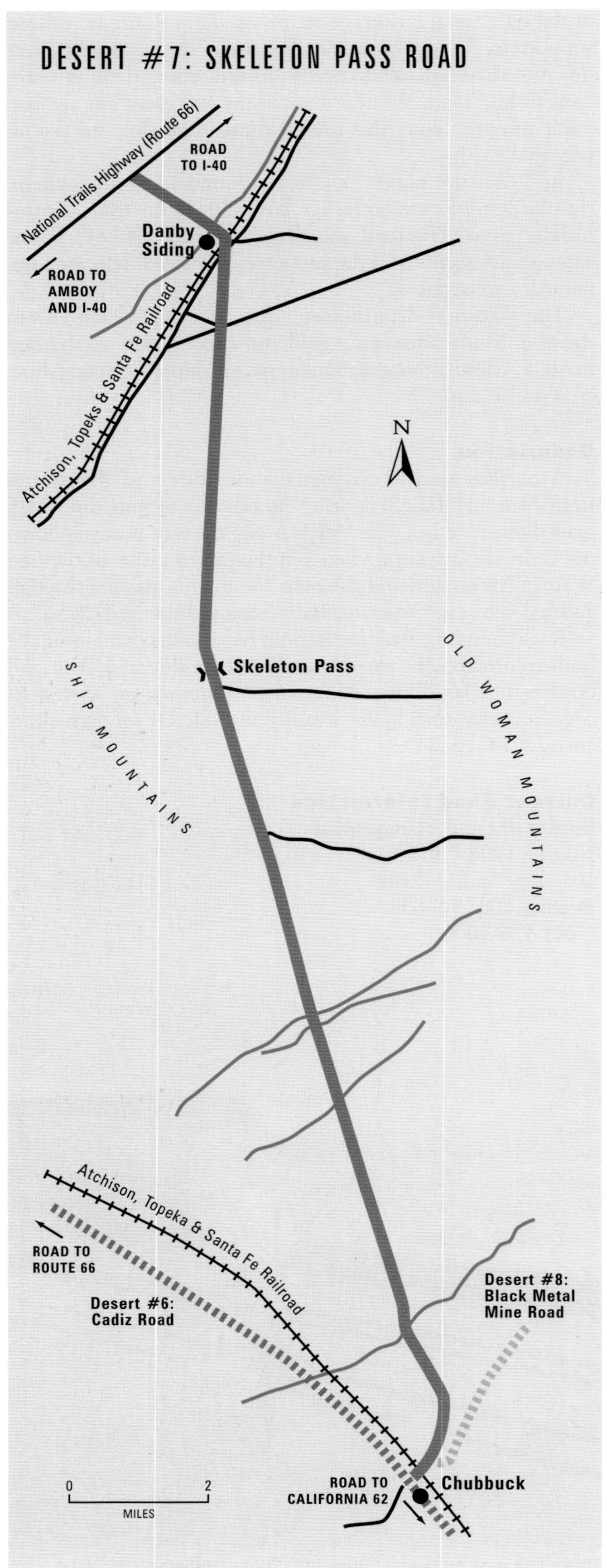

Map References

BLM Amboy, Sheep Hole Mts.
USGS 1:24,000 Danby, Skeleton Pass, Cadiz Lake NE, Chubbuck
1:100,000 Amboy, Sheep Hole Mts.
Maptech CD-ROM: San Bernardino County/Mojave
Southern & Central California Atlas & Gazetteer, pp. 85, 99
California Road & Recreation Atlas, p. 107

Route Directions

▼ 0.0		From National Trails Highway (Route 66), 23.5 miles east of Amboy, zero trip meter and turn southeast on graded dirt Danby Road at sign.
1.6 ▲		Trail ends at Danby on paved National Trails Highway (Route 66). Turn right for I-40; turn left for Amboy.
		GPS: N34°38.92′ W115°22.19′
▼ 1.4	SO	Cross through wash.
0.2 ▲	SO	Cross through wash.
▼ 1.6	TR	Track on right and track on left along rail line; then cross over rail line at Danby Siding; then 4-way intersection. Zero trip meter at intersection and turn right onto Skeleton Pass Road, which is marked by a BLM marker and is suitable for 4WDs, ATVs, and motorbikes.
0.0 ▲		Continue to the northwest. Track on left and track on right along rail line.
		GPS: N34°38.11′ W115°20.65′
▼ 0.0		Continue to the south. Track on right follows rail line.
5.1 ▲	TL	Track on left follows rail line; then 4-way intersection. This is Danby Siding. Zero trip meter. Turn left and cross over rail line.
▼ 1.3	SO	Two tracks on right and two tracks on left along pipeline.
3.8 ▲	SO	Two tracks on right and two tracks on left along pipeline.
▼ 5.1	SO	Pipeline works on left. Track on left and track on right along pipeline. Zero trip meter and continue straight ahead, following sign to Skeleton Pass. Route is now a small, formed trail. The Old Woman Mountains Wilderness is now on the left of the trail.
0.0 ▲		Continue to the north. The Old Woman Mountains Wilderness is no longer on the right.
		GPS: N34°33.48′ W115°20.93′
▼ 0.0		Continue to the south and cross through wash.
1.5 ▲	SO	Cross through wash; then pipeline works on right. Track on right and track on left along pipeline. Zero trip meter and continue straight ahead, following sign to Danby. Road is now wide and graded.
▼ 1.2	SO	Pass through the gap of Skeleton Pass. Ship Mountains are to the right (west).
0.3 ▲	SO	Pass through the gap of Skeleton Pass. Ship Mountains are to the left (west).
▼ 1.5	SO	Track on left travels along a vehicle corridor up Carbonate Gulch into the Old Woman Mountains Wilderness. Zero trip meter.
0.0 ▲		Continue to the north.
		GPS: N34°32.17′ W115°20.67′
▼ 0.0		Continue to the south.
2.2 ▲	SO	Track on right travels along a vehicle corridor up Carbonate Gulch into the Old Woman Mountains Wilderness. Zero trip meter.
▼ 2.2	SO	Track on left travels a vehicle corridor into the Old Woman Mountains Wilderness to

0.0 ▲		private property. Zero trip meter. Continue to the north.
		GPS: N34°30.24' W115°19.94'
▼ 0.0		Continue to the south.
9.9 ▲	SO	Track on right travels a vehicle corridor into the Old Woman Mountains Wilderness to private property. Zero trip meter.
▼ 1.2	SO	Cross through wash.
8.7 ▲	SO	Cross through wash.
▼ 2.6	SO	Start to cross through two washes.
7.3 ▲	SO	Exit washes.
		GPS: N34°27.95' W115°19.11'
▼ 2.7	SO	Exit washes.
7.2 ▲	SO	Start to cross through two washes.
▼ 4.0	SO	Cross through wash.
5.9 ▲	SO	Cross through wash.
▼ 4.1	SO	Cross through wash.
5.8 ▲	SO	Cross through wash.
▼ 7.5	SO	Cross through wash.
2.4 ▲	SO	Cross through wash.
		GPS: N34°23.73' W115°17.50'
▼ 9.8	SO	Track on left is Desert #8: Black Metal Mine Road, suitable for 4WDs, ATVs, and motorbikes.
0.1 ▲	BL	Track on right is Desert #8: Black Metal Mine Road, suitable for 4WDs, ATVs, and motorbikes.
		GPS: N34°21.93' W115°17.13'
▼ 9.9		Cross over railroad; then track on right. Trail finishes on graded dirt Desert #6: Cadiz Road. Track straight ahead.
0.0 ▲		Trail commences on graded dirt Desert #6: Cadiz Road, 20 miles south of Chambless. Zero trip meter and turn north on well-used formed trail, marked with a brown post as Skeleton Pass Road, suitable for 4WDs, ATVs, and motorbikes. The marker is set back from Cadiz Road. Immediately track on left; then cross over railroad.
		GPS: N34°21.84' W115°17.15'

DESERT #8

Black Metal Mine Road

Starting Point:	**Desert #7: Skeleton Pass Road at Chubbuck, 0.1 miles from southern end at Desert #6: Cadiz Road**
Finishing Point:	**Black Metal Mine**
Total Mileage:	**7.1 miles**
Unpaved Mileage:	**7.1 miles**
Driving Time:	**30 minutes**
Elevation Range:	**1,100–2,700 feet**
Usually Open:	**Year-round**
Best Time to Travel:	**September to May**
Difficulty Rating:	**3**
Scenic Rating:	**8**
Remoteness Rating:	**+1**

Special Attractions

- Remains of the Black Metal Mine.
- Route travels a vehicle corridor into the Old Woman Mountains Wilderness.
- General location where the Old Woman Meteorite was found in 1975.

History

The Black Metal Mine lies at the southern end of the Old Woman Mountains, a little traveled part of the Mojave Desert. In 1975, three prospectors roaming the surrounding mountains made an unusual find. They noticed a boulder that did not match any of the surrounding rocks on the mountainside and were instantly drawn to it. Further investigation suggested the boulder might in fact be a valuable meteorite. So the prospectors filed a mining claim on the site, which was within BLM jurisdiction. Unfortunately for the prospectors, meteorites are not locatable minerals under the definition of mining laws. In fact, any meteorite that lands on federal property is considered an item of national scientific interest. The Smithsonian Institution in Washington, D.C., was now the official organization concerned with this rare find. The rock was dubbed the Old Woman Meteorite after the location in which it was found.

Caution! The timber-lined shaft of Black Metal Mine is deep

A meteoroid is a mass of rock or metal traveling in space. When one enters the earth's atmosphere, it is referred to as a meteor. The earth's gravity forces it to travel at high speeds, causing friction with the atmosphere, and resulting in extremely high temperatures. Most meteors burn up on entry and may be seen at night as a streak in the sky. Those that survive entry to land on the earth's surface are referred to as meteorites; most end up as tiny particles the size of a grain of sand. More than 90 percent of meteorites are made up of stone that blends well among other rocks. A few (as low as 6 percent) meteorites are made up of iron and nickel. These are easily spotted because they stand out from surrounding rocks.

The Old Woman Meteorite definitely stood out among the surrounding rocks, and a site inspection of the boulder by Dr. Roy Clarke of the Smithsonian Institution confirmed that it was an iron meteorite. The task of removing it from this remote desert mountain range was beyond the capabilities of any earthmoving machinery. So the U.S. Marine Corps was brought in to assess the possibility of moving it. Special equipment was lowered by helicopter, and an experienced rigging team managed to place an extra heavy-duty webbed netting

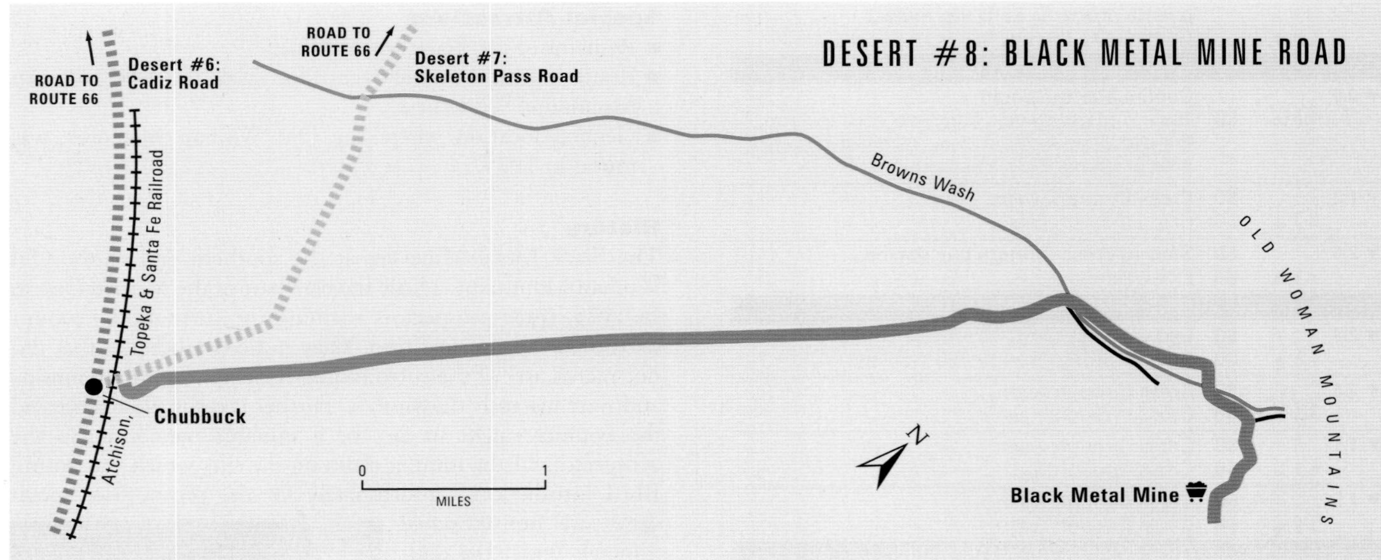

around the three-ton meteorite. A Marine Heavy Helicopter Squadron helicopter then airlifted the meteorite to a truck for transport to Barstow.

The Old Woman Meteorite was taken to the Smithsonian for further research and display. It was determined the meteorite consisted of two previously known metals that had never been seen together before, thereby making this a rare find indeed.

Two copies of the Old Woman Meteorite have been made. One moves around the nation for public display; the other can usually be seen at the Barstow BLM office. The original is on permanent display at the California Desert Information Center in Barstow, where children love to test the meteorite's strong magnetism with demonstrational magnets. The Old Woman Meteorite is the second largest meteorite ever found in the United States.

Remains of the Black Metal Mine

Description

The Black Metal Mine is reached via a vehicle corridor through the Old Woman Mountains Wilderness. The trail is fairly short, and its only difficulty comes from the deep, loose sand in Browns Wash. The trail is a spur that begins near the intersection of Desert #6: Cadiz Road and Desert #7: Skeleton Pass Road. It crosses a sandy bajada, climbing gradually toward the mountains before entering Browns Wash. The trail travels through a wider valley before leaving the wash to finish at the Black Metal Mine. The remains of an old cabin, a deep timber-lined shaft, and a wooden loading hopper can be seen at the mine site.

The mountains are home to bighorn sheep and desert tortoises, and the area is an important habitat for many species of raptors.

Current Road Information

Bureau of Land Management
Needles Field Office
101 West Spikes Road
Needles, CA 92363
(760) 326-7000

Map References

BLM Sheep Hole Mts.
USGS 1:24,000 Chubbuck, Cadiz Lake NE, Sheep Camp Spring
1:100,000 Sheep Hole Mts.
Maptech CD-ROM: San Bernardino County/Mojave
Southern & Central California Atlas & Gazetteer, pp. 99, 100
California Road & Recreation Atlas, p. 107

Route Directions

▼ 0.0	From Desert #7: Skeleton Pass Road at Chubbuck, 0.1 miles north of the intersection with Desert #6: Cadiz Road, zero trip meter

and turn northeast on formed dirt trail marked with a brown route marker as Black Metal Mine Road. Trail is suitable for 4WDs, ATVs, and motorbikes.

GPS: N34°21.93′ W115°14.13′

▼ 5.0	SO	Enter line of Browns Wash. Track on right up wash.
		GPS: N34°25.66′ W115°14.06′
▼ 5.3	SO	Track forks and immediately rejoins.
▼ 6.3	BR	Bear right across main wash. Track on left continues up wash.
		GPS: N34°25.99′ W115°12.84′
▼ 6.5	BR	Track on right; then track on left; then bear right in front of old wooden post and exit wash.
		GPS: N34°25.86′ W115°12.65′
▼ 6.6	SO	Track on right.
▼ 6.9	BL	Trail passes through remains of the Black Metal Mine—old cabin on right and various wooden structures.
		GPS: N34°25.61′ W115°12.61′
▼ 7.1		Trail ends at a saddle that overlooks the next valley in the Old Woman Mountains.
		GPS: N34°25.48′ W115°12.46′

DESERT #9

Amboy Crater Road

Starting Point:	**National Trails Highway (Route 66), 1.7 miles west of Amboy, 1.1 miles west of intersection with Amboy Road**
Finishing Point:	**Amboy Crater**
Total Mileage:	**1.7 miles (one-way)**
Unpaved Mileage:	**1.7 miles**
Driving Time:	**30 minutes**
Elevation Range:	**700 feet**
Usually Open:	**Year-round**
Best Time to Travel:	**September to June**
Difficulty Rating:	**4**
Scenic Rating:	**9**
Remoteness Rating:	**+0**

Special Attractions

- The volcanic cone of Amboy Crater.
- Spectacular hiking trail to the crater rim.

History

Amboy Crater, one of the younger cinder cones in the region, measures 250 feet high and approximately 1,500 feet in diameter. Cinder cones are formed by explosive volcanic eruptions that can last from a few short weeks to years. The volcanos produce lava that can burst through the side or base of a cone because the cone's walls are too fragile to contain the pooling lava. Amboy Crater shows signs of lava having escaped from the base. The western side of the cone seems to have floated away with the lava.

Medicine wheel in the lava flow en route to Amboy Crater

Basalt lava flows around Amboy Crater have a mixture of forms, some are aa surfaces and others are smoother sections called pahoehoe. Both terms are Hawaiian, where people are well and truly versed in volcanic eruptions. The temperature of a lava flow determines whether it will have a rough or smooth finish. More steam within a flow will yield a smoother pahoehoe surface.

Radiocarbon dating has not been carried out at this cone. Carbon dating is usually performed on wood that has been caught in an eruption; with no wood to examine, no answer can be given. Recent observations and estimates by geologists suggest that the volcano is anywhere from 500 to 6,000 years old. Earlier estimates dated the age between 50,000 to 100,000 years old.

Medicine wheels, such as the one pictured above, were made by Indians to mark sacred spaces. Ceremonies were held in and around them because they were thought to hold great power.

Amboy Siding is located at the northern end of the salt-encrusted Bristol Lake. The settlement was established with the construction of the Atlantic & Pacific Railroad in 1883. Though little happened in this remote location, it was strate-

Amboy Crater rises abruptly above the surrounding lava flow

The walls of Amboy Crater stand high above the Mojave Desert floor

gically placed on what was to become the famous Route 66. In the 1930s, Buster Burris and his partner Roy opened a service station at this railroad siding and old road junction. The town flourished to support a school, café, motel, and major repair shop. These services catered to the increasing traffic of the 1940s. Amboy's population neared 100 at its peak in the late 1940s.

The town's days were numbered with the construction of Interstate 40. The new and faster highway took passing motor trade to the north, leaving Amboy a quiet, forgotten little town. Amboy faded; property was hard to sell, and some people ended up walking away from their properties. Burris stuck with the vanishing railroad settlement, whether or not by choice is hard to say. He ended up owning most of the nearly abandoned settlement.

A reawakening of interest in classic travel routes across the nation, in particular old Route 66 (also referred to as National Trails Highway), has brought attention to many small abandoned towns along quiet stretches of the route. In the late 1990s, Burris finally sold out to a duo from the East Coast. White and his partner Wilson are slowly returning a 1940s atmosphere to this once important desert crossroads. Many people are starting to appreciate the remote feeling of this gas station and motel in the depths of the sweltering Mojave Desert.

Description

This very short trail travels to the base of the towering, black cinder cone of Amboy Crater. The first 0.7 miles of the trail can be tackled by a carefully driven passenger vehicle, but it is rough and slow going with embedded black lava rock.

Past a small parking area, the trail is marked for 4WD vehicles only; passenger vehicles should stop here. The trail continues to twist and snake its way to the base of the cone. The embedded lava rock makes for a rough ride and is very hard on tires. However the trail is not technically difficult. It is marked sporadically with brown route markers, which are useful because the trail is often indistinct and a couple of incorrect trails can confuse the navigator.

The trail wraps around the cone for a short distance before finishing at the start of a hiking trail that climbs to the crater, passing through a wide opening in the wall to climb an additional 144 feet to the narrow rim. The hike is not recommended on windy days because the path at the top is extremely narrow. This loose climb offers the reward of panoramic views over the Cadiz Valley and Bristol Mountains. Allow one to two hours for the round-trip hike if you park your vehicle at the start of the 4WD section. Note that the trail going straight up the north rim of the crater is being reclaimed; it should not be attempted.

Current Road Information

Bureau of Land Management
Needles Field Office
101 West Spikes Road
Needles, CA 92363
(760) 326-7000

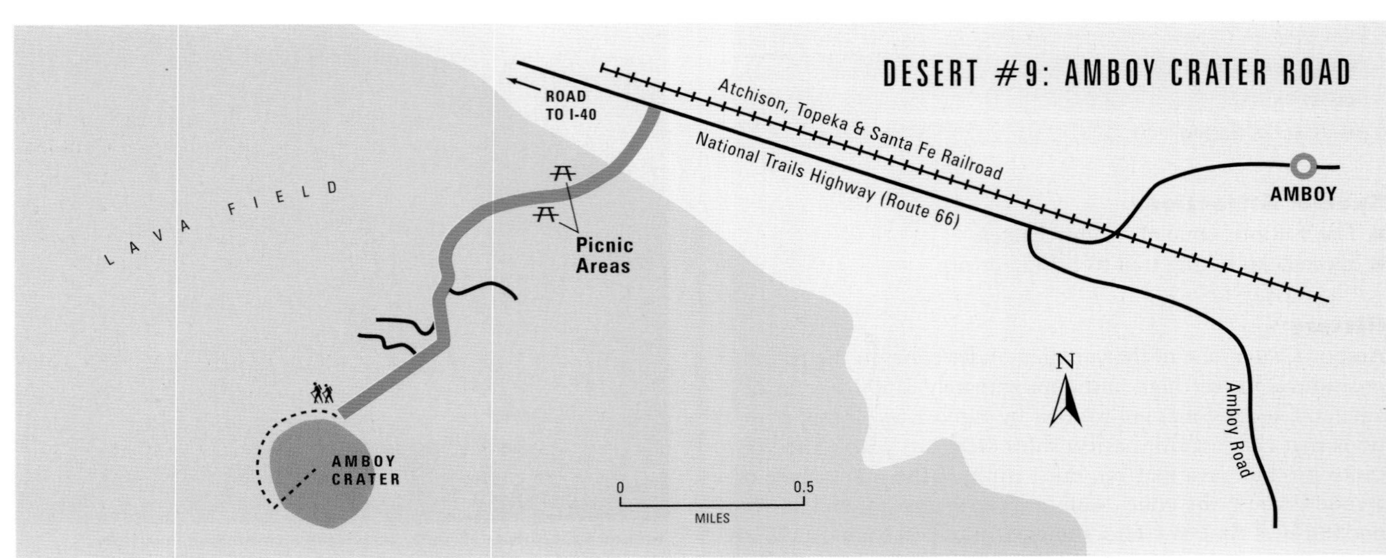

Map References

BLM Amboy
USGS 1:24,000 Amboy Crater
1:100,000 Amboy
Maptech CD-ROM: San Bernardino County/Mojave
Southern & Central California Atlas & Gazetteer, p. 84
California Road & Recreation Atlas, p. 106

Route Directions

▼ 0.0		Trail commences on National Trails Highway (Route 66) 1.7 miles west of Amboy, 1.1 miles west of the intersection with Amboy Road. Zero trip meter and turn south on formed trail at BLM sign for Amboy Crater National Natural Landmark.
		GPS: N34°33.61' W115°46.43'
▼ 0.3	SO	Picnic table on right.
▼ 0.5	SO	Picnic table and information board on left.
		GPS: N34°33.40' W115°46.76'
▼ 0.7	BL	Bear left, following sign for crater. Trail is marked 4x4 only past this point for 4WDs, ATVs, and motorbikes.
		GPS: N34°33.39' W115°46.91'
▼ 1.0	SO	Track on left.
		GPS: N34°33.19' W115°47.03'
▼ 1.2	BL	Track on right.
▼ 1.3	SO	Trail crosses flat desert pavement. In reverse this point is marked with a brown exit marker.
		GPS: N34°33.02' W115°47.03'
▼ 1.4	TL	Track on right.
		GPS: N34°32.99' W115°47.11'
▼ 1.6	BR	Trail forks and immediately rejoins.
▼ 1.7		Trail ends at the base of Amboy Crater. Return the way you came. A hiking trail begins here and wraps around the base before climbing to the crater.
		GPS: N34°32.86' W115°47.33'

DESERT #10

Sunflower Spring Road

Starting Point:	**National Trails Highway (Route 66) at Essex, 6 miles south of I-40**
Finishing Point:	**US 95, 23 miles south of Needles**
Total Mileage:	**45 miles, plus 1.7-mile spur to Golden Fleece Mine**
Unpaved Mileage:	**45 miles, plus 1.7-mile spur**
Driving Time:	**6 hours**
Elevation Range:	**1,400–3,400 feet**
Usually Open:	**Year-round**
Best Time to Travel:	**October to June**
Difficulty Rating:	**4**
Scenic Rating:	**10**
Remoteness Rating:	**+2**

Granite outcroppings near Painted Rock Wash

Special Attractions

- Long, exceedingly remote trail passing the boundaries of four wilderness areas.
- Trail follows a section of the East Mojave Heritage Trail.
- Chalcedony roses and agate on either side of Turtle Mountain Road.
- Old Woman Statue.

History

Camp Essex was located just north of Essex, between the Clipper and the Piute Mountains, at the northern end of this trail. The camp spanned both sides of Essex Road and covered an area of more than 31,000 acres. Interstate 40 runs through the northern section of the old camp. The rest area on Interstate 40 occupies the old garrison area.

Camp Essex was acquired as a Desert Training Center in 1943. The camp included the area previously occupied by Camp Clipper, which had been established in 1942. Clipper was occupied by the 33rd Infantry Division from March 28 to July 17, 1943. Camp Clipper, located in the western section of the newer camp, was abandoned when Camp Essex was completed. The new camp was active from November 1943 to January 1944. It was declared surplus in March 1944. A 500,000-gallon water tank was the only permanent structure. An airstrip occupying 85 acres was also constructed. It was used by spotter planes and routine flights. All other structures were temporary.

In May 1944, more than 300 Italian prisoners of war were given the task of removing artillery duds from the ranges. However, a clean bill of health in regards to unexploded rounds may never occur. Time has eroded most traces of the camp's layout and most of the leftovers seem to be bullets rather than bombs. Surface activity is all that is allowed in the area nowadays.

The trail leaves Essex and heads south into the Old Woman Mountains. These rugged mountains got their name from a rock formation close to Sunflower Spring. When viewed side-on, the formation somewhat resembles an old woman bent over a wash tub. Several mines are visible in the Old Woman Mountains. The Blue Bugle Mine consisted of eight claims, including the Florence claim, and was on the north side of the mountain range in the Danby Mining District. Three quartz veins were worked to depths of 160 feet. Ore was processed north of Lancaster at Rosamond that assayed at $50 per ton. The Florence claim reportedly returned up to $200 per ton in gold.

Description

Sunflower Spring Road is a long, very remote trail with sweeping desert vistas, hiking access into four wilderness areas, and the solitude of the east Mojave Desert. The trail borders the Piute Mountains Wilderness, Old Woman Mountains Wilderness, Turtle Mountains Wilderness, and Stepladder Mountains Wilderness, making it an excellent trail for hikers who wish to explore these remote areas on foot.

The trail leaves the small settlement of Essex a few miles south of I-40 on Route 66. Gas is available at the freeway exit at Fenner. For the first few miles, the wide, though unmaintained, road is used to service a pipeline's workings. It travels in a broad, flat valley with the Old Woman Mountains to the south, the Little Piute Mountains to the southeast, and the Piute Mountains to the east.

Once past the pipeline workings, the trail follows a small, sandy formed road that skirts the eastern boundary of the Old Woman Mountains Wilderness. A short spur travels 1.7 miles in a vehicle corridor into the wilderness, passing the workings of the Golden Fleece Mine to finish at a spot with views down Willow Springs Canyon.

The trail continues south, joining the East Mojave Heritage Trail. It descends gradually, twisting its way along the eastern bajada of the Old Woman Mountains and crossing many deep and sandy washes. The approaches to some of these washes can be steep and eroded. Some will test a vehicle's wheel articulation and traction. This spectacular area of desert vegetation is one of the most scenic sections along the trail.

Near Sunflower Wash, the distinctive, conically shaped Pilot Peak can be seen to the east. Beyond it are distant views to the Stepladder Mountains. Old Woman Statue can be seen to the west. The rock shape resembles a cloaked and stooping old woman.

The trail now gradually descends a long and gently sloping, sandy bajada down to the broad Ward Valley. This section has some of the loosest and deepest sand on the trail. In the forward direction, it is not too bad, but heading uphill in the reverse direction, the sand can quickly bog a vehicle down. The yuccas along the edge of the Old Woman Mountains disappear and the valley floor becomes covered with creosote bush and little else. The eastern side of the valley, as you ascend into the Turtle Mountains, has a firmer surface.

Loose, deep sand in Ward Valley

Shaft of the Golden Fleece Mine

The trail enters a vehicle corridor between the Stepladder Mountains Wilderness on the left and the Turtle Mountains Wilderness on the right. The jagged peaks of the Turtle Mountains rise up to the south, and as you crest a slight rise, the Chemehuevi Mountains and Whipple Mountains are visible to the east. Looking back to the west you can see over Ward Valley to the Old Woman Mountains.

The trail continues as a rough, well-used formed trail as it passes both ends of Desert #11: Lost Arch Inn Trail, which loops farther into the Turtle Mountains. Staghorn chollas and ocotillos can now be seen among the creosote bush. They give a brilliant display in the spring.

The final 10 miles of the route follow the wider, formed Turtle Mountain Road. This is often washboardy and has loose sand, particularly where it crosses the wide Chemehuevi Wash, a short distance before it ends at US 95. Rock hounds may like to hunt for agate and chalcedony roses in the washes and along Turtle Mountain Road.

Campers will find plenty of sites along this trail. A nice spot near the end of the trail is situated in the trees at Chemehuevi Wash. The best and most scenic spots are in the Turtle Mountains and at the southern end of Sunflower Spring Road. Campers will notice that all the spots tend to be rocky.

Current Road Information

Bureau of Land Management
Needles Field Office
101 West Spikes Road
Needles, CA 92363
(760) 326-7000

Map References

BLM Amboy, Sheep Hole Mts., Parker, Needles
USGS 1:24,000 Essex, Old Woman Statue, Painted Rock Wash, Wilhelm Spring, West of Mohawk Spring, Mohawk Spring, Savahia Peak NW, Snaggletooth
1:100,000 Amboy, Sheep Hole Mts., Parker, Needles
Maptech CD-ROM: San Bernardino County/Mojave
Southern & Central California Atlas & Gazetteer, pp. 86, 100, 101, 87
California Road & Recreation Atlas, pp. 107, 115

Route Directions

▼ 0.0		At Essex, 6 miles south of the Fenner exit on I-40, zero trip meter at the intersection of Essex Road and National Trails Highway (Route 66). Turn southeast on graded dirt road, alongside the Essex Post Office.
4.6 ▲		Trail ends on National Trails Highway (Route 66) at Essex. Continue straight ahead for I-40; turn right for Fenner.
		GPS: N34°44.10′ W115°14.69′
▼ 0.1	SO	Cross over rail line.
4.5 ▲	SO	Cross over rail line.
▼ 0.2	SO	Track on left and right; then cattle guard.
4.4 ▲	SO	Cattle guard; then track on left and right.
▼ 4.6	SO	Track on left and track on right is gas pipeline road. Zero trip meter.
0.0 ▲		Continue to the northwest.
		GPS: N34°40.87′ W115°11.50′
▼ 0.0		Continue to the southeast.
3.9 ▲	SO	Track on left and track on right is gas pipeline road. Zero trip meter.
▼ 1.0	SO	Track on left and track on right is gas pipeline road. Pipeline valves at intersection.
2.9 ▲	SO	Track on left and track on right is gas pipeline road. Pipeline valves at intersection.
		GPS: N34°40.16′ W115°10.78′
▼ 1.5	SO	Track on left and track on right is gas pipeline road. Trail ahead is now marked with a brown route marker as Sunflower Spring Road, suitable for 4WDs, ATVs, and motorbikes.
2.4 ▲	SO	Track on left and track on right is gas pipeline road.
		GPS: N34°39.83′ W115°10.44′
▼ 2.2	BR	Well-used track on left.
1.7 ▲	SO	Well-used track on right.
		GPS: N34°39.31′ W115°10.02′
▼ 2.5	SO	Cross through the three channels of Carson Wash.
1.4 ▲	SO	Cross through the three channels of Carson Wash.
▼ 3.7	SO	Track on left.
0.2 ▲	SO	Track on right.
		GPS: N34°37.99′ W115°09.94′
▼ 3.9	SO	Well-used track on right is spur to Golden Fleece Mine. Intersection is unmarked. Zero trip meter.
0.0 ▲		Continue to the northwest.
		GPS: N34°37.75′ W115°09.86′

Spur to Golden Fleece Mine

▼ 0.0		Proceed to the southwest.
▼ 0.1	SO	Track on left rejoins main trail.
▼ 0.3	SO	Cross through Honeymoon Wash.
		GPS: N34°37.62′ W115°10.06′
▼ 0.6	SO	Diggings of the Golden Fleece Mine on right and left; then cross through wash.
		GPS: N34°37.48′ W115°10.28′
▼ 1.4	BR	Bear right onto smaller trail. Track on left goes to gate—foot and horse travel only past the gate into the Old Woman Mountains Wilderness.
		GPS: N34°36.98′ W115°10.85′
▼ 1.7	UT	Spur ends at a tight turnaround below the hill. Views into Willow Springs Canyon.
		GPS: N34°37.03′ W115°11.05′

Continuation of Main Trail

▼ 0.0		Continue to the southeast.
2.6 ▲	SO	Well-used track on left is spur to Golden Fleece Mine. Intersection is unmarked. Zero trip meter.
		GPS: N34°37.75′ W115°09.86′
▼ 0.1	BL	Small track on right joins spur trail. Track straight ahead goes to well.
2.5 ▲	SO	Track on sharp left goes to well. Small track on left joins spur trail.
▼ 0.2	SO	Track on right to well.
2.4 ▲	SO	Track on left to well.
▼ 0.3	SO	Cross through wash.
2.3 ▲	SO	Cross through wash.
▼ 0.4	BL	Track on right to well.
2.2 ▲	BR	Track on left to well.
		GPS: N34°37.49′ W115°09.56′
▼ 0.5	SO	Cross through wash.
2.1 ▲	SO	Cross through wash.
▼ 0.6	SO	Cross through wash.
2.0 ▲	SO	Cross through wash.
▼ 1.0	SO	Cross through Carson Wash; then well-used track on left.
1.6 ▲	BL	Well-used track on right; then cross through Carson Wash.
		GPS: N34°37.33′ W115°09.06′
▼ 1.2	SO	Enter wash.
1.4 ▲	SO	Exit wash.
▼ 1.3	SO	Exit wash.
1.3 ▲	SO	Enter wash.
▼ 1.4	SO	Cross through wash.
1.2 ▲	SO	Cross through wash.
▼ 1.5	SO	Trail forks and immediately rejoins.
1.1 ▲	SO	Trail forks and immediately rejoins.
▼ 2.6	BR	Track on left and ahead is marked with a brown route marker as East Mojave Heritage Trail, suitable for 4WDs, ATVs, and motorbikes. Sunflower Spring Road is ahead. Zero trip meter.
0.0 ▲		Continue to the west.
		GPS: N34°36.66′ W115°07.77′
▼ 0.0		Continue to the east.
4.2 ▲	SO	Track on right is marked with a brown route marker as East Mojave Heritage Trail, suitable for 4WDs, ATVs, and motorbikes. Sunflower Spring Road is straight ahead. Zero trip meter.
▼ 0.1	SO	Cross through wash.
4.1 ▲	SO	Cross through wash.
▼ 0.6	SO	Small track on left.
3.6 ▲	SO	Small track on right.
▼ 0.9	SO	Cross through wash.
3.3 ▲	SO	Cross through wash.
▼ 1.0	SO	Cross through wash.
3.2 ▲	SO	Cross through wash.
		GPS: N34°36.05′ W115°07.04′
▼ 1.1	SO	Track on left.
3.1 ▲	SO	Track on right.
▼ 1.2	SO	Old vehicle trail on right enters wilderness and goes 0.1 miles to the Copper King Mine—foot and horse travel only. Track on left.
3.0 ▲	SO	Old vehicle trail on left enters wilderness and goes 0.1 miles to the Copper King Mine—foot and horse travel only. Track on right.
		GPS: N34°35.89′ W115°07.06′
▼ 1.4	SO	Cross through wash.

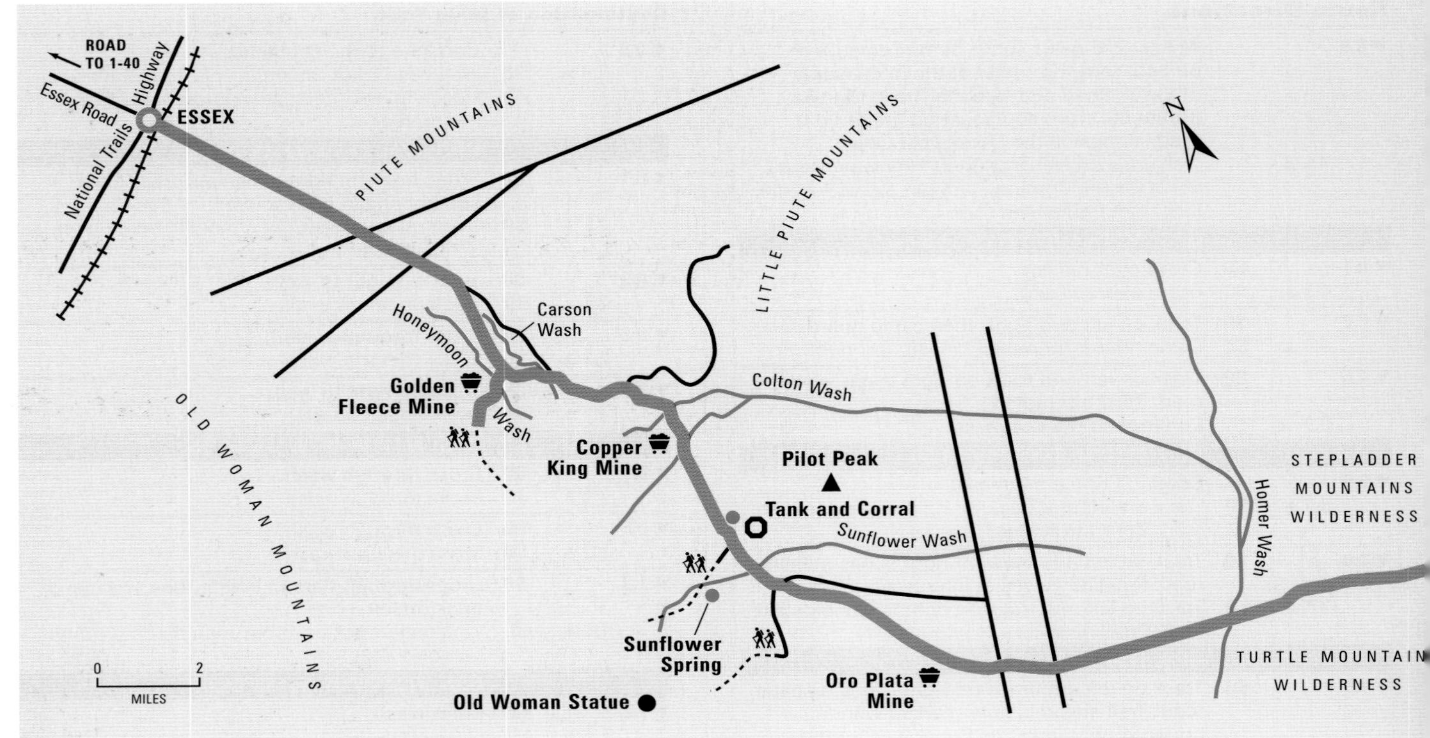

Mileage		Direction
2.8 ▲	SO	Cross through wash.
▼ 1.6	BR	Track on left.
2.6 ▲	SO	Track on right.
▼ 1.7	SO	Track on left.
2.5 ▲	SO	Track on right.
▼ 1.8	SO	Cross through deep Colton Wash.
2.4 ▲	SO	Cross through deep Colton Wash.
		GPS: N34°35.46' W115°07.05'
▼ 3.8	SO	Cross through wash.
0.4 ▲	SO	Cross through wash.
▼ 3.9	SO	Well and corral on left.
0.3 ▲	SO	Well and corral on right.
		GPS: N34°33.57' W115°06.92'
▼ 4.1	SO	Cross through wash.
0.1 ▲	SO	Cross through wash.
▼ 4.2	SO	Track on left. Track on right goes 0.5 miles to a slightly closer view of Old Woman Statue. Hikers and horses can continue past this point on the old vehicle trail. Zero trip meter.
0.0 ▲		Continue to the north.
		GPS: N34°33.30' W115°06.89'
▼ 0.0		Continue to the south.
1.1 ▲	SO	Track on right. Track on left goes 0.5 miles to a slightly closer view of Old Woman Statue. Hikers and horses can continue past this point on the old vehicle trail. Zero trip meter.
▼ 0.5	SO	Campsite on right; then start to cross through wide Sunflower Wash.
0.6 ▲	SO	Exit wide wash crossing; then campsite on left.
▼ 0.6	SO	Exit wide wash crossing.
0.5 ▲	SO	Start to cross through wide Sunflower Wash.
		GPS: N34°32.83' W115°06.76'
▼ 1.0	BR	Track on left.
0.1 ▲	SO	Track on right.
▼ 1.1	BL	Closure gate on right; then track on right travels 3 miles to the start of a hiking trail toward Old Woman Statue and good bouldering opportunities in a natural rock amphitheater. Zero trip meter.
0.0 ▲		Continue to the northwest past closure gate on left.
		GPS: N34°32.48' W115°06.51'
▼ 0.0		Continue to the southeast.
4.8 ▲	BR	Track on left travels 3 miles to the start of a hiking trail toward Old Woman Statue and good bouldering opportunities in a natural rock amphitheater. Zero trip meter.
▼ 0.2	BR	Track on sharp left is East Mojave Heritage Trail; then second track on left.
4.6 ▲	BL	Track on right; then second track on right is East Mojave Heritage Trail.
		GPS: N34°32.40' W115°06.29'
▼ 3.3	SO	Cross through wash.
1.5 ▲	SO	Cross through wash.
▼ 3.4	SO	Cross through wash. Track on left down wash.
1.4 ▲	SO	Cross through wash. Track on right down wash.
▼ 3.8	SO	Oro Plata Mine workings on right.
1.0 ▲	SO	Oro Plata Mine workings on left.
		GPS: N34°30.10' W115°03.71'
▼ 4.0	SO	Cross through wash.
0.8 ▲	SO	Cross through wash.
▼ 4.7	SO	Track on right.
0.1 ▲	SO	Track on left.
▼ 4.8	TL	T-intersection with graded road under power lines. Zero trip meter and follow along power lines.
0.0 ▲		Continue to the southwest away from power lines.
		GPS: N34°29.75' W115°02.79'

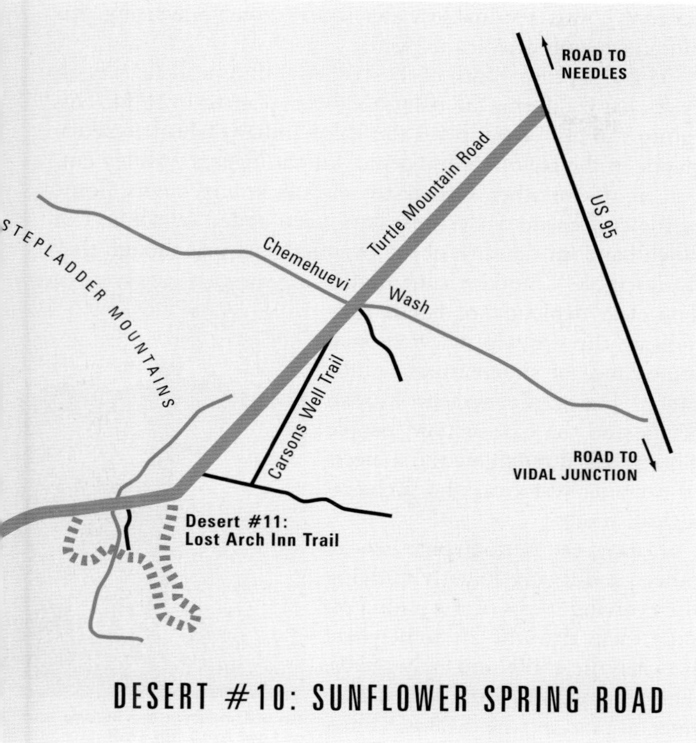

DESERT #10: SUNFLOWER SPRING ROAD

Mileage		Directions
▼ 0.0		Continue to the north.
11.6 ▲	TR	Turn right onto smaller, formed trail marked East Mojave Heritage Trail and zero trip meter.
▼ 0.1	TR	Small track on left. Turn right onto smaller, formed trail marked East Mojave Heritage Trail and leave power lines.
11.5 ▲	TL	Small track ahead. Turn left onto graded road under power lines.
		GPS: N34°29.81′ W115°02.76′
▼ 1.2	SO	Cross through wash; then track on left and track on right. Start of Turtle Mountains Wilderness on right.
10.4 ▲	SO	Track on right and track on left; then cross through wash. End of Turtle Mountains Wilderness on left.
		GPS: N34°29.30′ W115°01.71′
▼ 4.6	SO	Cross through Homer Wash.
7.0 ▲	SO	Cross through Homer Wash.
		GPS: N34°28.96′ W114°58.05′
▼ 5.8	SO	Start of the Stepladder Mountains Wilderness on left. Trail now enters a vehicle corridor between the two wilderness areas.
5.8 ▲	SO	Exit vehicle corridor between the wilderness areas. Turtle Mountains Wilderness is on the left.
		GPS: N34°28.92′ W114°56.79′
▼ 6.0	SO	Cross through wash.
5.6 ▲	SO	Cross through wash.
▼ 6.5	SO	Cross through wash.
5.1 ▲	SO	Cross through wash.
▼ 7.3	SO	Cross through wash.
4.3 ▲	SO	Cross through wash.
▼ 7.7	SO	Cross through wash.
3.9 ▲	SO	Cross through wash.
▼ 8.3	SO	Cross through wash.
3.3 ▲	SO	Cross through wash.
▼ 9.9	SO	Cross through wash.
1.7 ▲	SO	Cross through wash.
▼ 10.4	SO	Saddle. Ruins of a stone chimney on left. Views ahead over the Chemehuevi Valley and the Whipple Mountains.
1.2 ▲	SO	Saddle. Ruins of a stone chimney on right. Views ahead over Ward Valley and the Old Woman Mountains.
		GPS: N34°28.69′ W114°52.11′
▼ 11.6	SO	Track on right is western end of Desert #11: Lost Arch Inn Trail. There is a mailbox on a post at the intersection, but it is otherwise unmarked. Zero trip meter.
0.0 ▲		Continue to the west.
		GPS: N34°28.52′ W114°50.83′
▼ 0.0		Continue to the east.
2.0 ▲	BR	Track on left is western end of Desert #11: Lost Arch Inn Trail. There is a mailbox on a post at the intersection, but it is otherwise unmarked. Zero trip meter.
▼ 0.6	SO	Cross through wash.
1.4 ▲	SO	Cross through wash.
▼ 0.9	SO	Track on right.
1.1 ▲	SO	Track on left.
▼ 2.0	TL	Cross through wash; then T-intersection. To the right is marked Lost Arch Inn, suitable for 4WDs, ATVs, and motorbikes. This is the eastern end of Desert #11: Lost Arch Inn Trail. To the left is the continuation of the East Mojave Heritage Trail. Zero trip meter and remain on the East Mojave Heritage Trail.
0.0 ▲		Continue to the northwest.
		GPS: N34°28.12′ W114°48.79′
▼ 0.0		Continue to the northeast.
10.2 ▲	TR	Turn right onto formed trail and cross through wash, remaining on the marked East Mojave Heritage Trail. Ahead is marked Lost Arch Inn, suitable for 4WDs, ATVs, and motorbikes. This is the eastern end of Desert #11: Lost Arch Inn Trail. Zero trip meter.
▼ 0.5	SO	Track on right.
9.7 ▲	SO	Track on left.
▼ 4.3	SO	Track on right is Carsons Well Trail, suitable for 4WDs, ATVs, and motorbikes.
5.9 ▲	SO	Track on left is Carsons Well Trail, suitable for 4WDs, ATVs, and motorbikes.
		GPS: N34°29.77′ W114°44.57′
▼ 5.0	SO	Track on right; then cross through wide, sandy Chemehuevi Wash.
5.2 ▲	SO	Cross through wide, sandy Chemehuevi Wash; then track on left.
		GPS: N34°30.05′ W114°43.85′
▼ 5.2	SO	Cross through wash.
5.0 ▲	SO	Cross through wash.
▼ 10.2		Trail ends at T-intersection with US 95. Turn left for Needles; turn right for Vidal Junction.
0.0 ▲		Trail commences on US 95, 1.6 miles south of the intersection with Havasu Lake Road, 23 miles south of Needles, and 0.4 miles south of mile marker 36. Zero trip meter and turn southwest on wide dirt road, marked with a white post as Turtle Mountain Road. Road is also marked with a brown BLM route marker as East Mojave Heritage Trail, suitable for 4WDs, ATVs, and motorbikes.
		GPS: N34°32.01′ W114°38.82′

DESERT #11

Lost Arch Inn Trail

Starting Point:	**Desert #10: Sunflower Spring Road, 10.2 miles west of US 95**
Finishing Point:	**Desert #10: Sunflower Spring Road, 12.2 miles west of US 95**
Total Mileage:	**7.7 miles**
Unpaved Mileage:	**7.7 miles**
Driving Time:	**1 hour**
Elevation Range:	**1,600–2,000 feet**
Usually Open:	**Year-round**
Best Time to Travel:	**October to May**
Difficulty Rating:	**3**
Scenic Rating:	**8**
Remoteness Rating:	**+0**

Special Attractions

- Rockhounding for opalite, chalcedony roses, agate, and jasper.
- Lost Arch Inn cabins.
- Hiking trail to Mohawk Spring petroglyph.
- Can be combined with Desert #10: Sunflower Spring Road.

History

Mohawk Spring, located about half a mile east of this trail, was a known water source to the Indians who roamed the region. Though the spring is hardly a trickle these days, it was once an important camp in the dry, rugged Turtle Mountains. The meaning behind the unusual abstract petroglyph near the spring is unclear. Prospectors sought out the spring because it was a valuable water source when traversing this difficult region of volcanic spires.

Rugged and unusual rock formations form a dramatic backdrop for Buckhorn chollas along the trail

Mopah Spring, south of the Lost Arch Inn near the Mopah Peaks, has California fan palms that were planted in 1924. This spring was also a camp for the Palco-Indians who left petroglyphs in the region. Some depict human figures possibly embracing one another. Others are abstract arrangements. Some of the concentric circles may have been added by soldiers or ranch hands at the turn of the twentieth century, though they do resemble Chumash sun motifs. The clear depiction of hands may indicate the site was of ceremonial importance or supernatural significance. The entire ancient Mopah Range and the Chemehuevi people who passed through are the subjects of ongoing historical and archaeological studies.

An old mailbox marks one end of Lost Arch Inn Trail

Dating the petroglyphs, like all others, is difficult. Experts studying the evolving stages of the patina on such rocks date the art somewhere between the 1500s and early 1800s. The Chemehuevi were forced into reservations in the 1880s. Their population may have rarely exceeded 1,000 because the harsh environment could not support great numbers. A census taken in 1902 of the people on the Chemehuevi Reservation counted just 32.

By the late 1800s, ranchers were adding their own creations to the rocky region. Then came the prospectors' additions in the early 1900s. World War II brought General George Patton and his troops to the region, and an airstrip was constructed. Bullets can still be found on the mountainside.

The name of the inn comes from its association with the Lost Arch Mine, which produced lode gold. The cabins at Lost Arch Inn were the home of Charley Brown and his mining partner, Jesse Craik. The two men prospected for gold and silver in the northern section of the Turtle Mountains for many years. These cabins were their home from 1922 to 1948. Although they are referred to as an inn, these cabins are barely standing.

Description

This trail describes a loop, starting and finishing near the eastern end of Desert #10: Sunflower Spring Road. The start of the trail is marked with a brown route marker. The trail follows a well-used, formed trail as far as the two old cabins known as the Lost Arch Inn. The cabins are in fair condition; one is timber, the other corrugated iron, and they stand side by side on a slight rise in the desert.

Access as far as the cabins is easy. They can normally be reached in a high-clearance 2WD vehicle. There is one wash crossing that may need some care depending on how eroded it is after recent rains. Past the cabin, the trail is smaller and a high-clearance 4WD is recommended. One wash crossing in particular is eroded and lumpy; it requires good clearance and wheel articulation.

The trail sees much less use past the cabins as it follows along the edge of the wilderness boundary. The hiking trails to Carsons Well and Mohawk Spring are just off the vehicle route.

The vehicle route is very quiet, and the traveler is rewarded with good views of the Turtle Mountains. The trail passes through a popular rockhounding area, where opalite, chalcedony roses, agate, and jasper can be found. These rocks are most common in the washes below Mohawk Spring.

Navigation can be a little confusing along this part of the trail. The signs stop just after the cabins and there are many small unmarked trails to choose from. Many of the side trails rejoin after a short distance. A GPS unit is very helpful along this section.

Campers will find some good remote sites, although those using tents will find it very rocky.

The trail ends back on Desert #10: Sunflower Spring Road at an old mailbox that now serves as a drop off point for travelers' messages. How the mailbox got there is a mystery; maybe it served as a drop off point for miners' mail or maybe it was just placed there for messages.

Current Road Information

Bureau of Land Management
Needles Field Office
101 West Spikes Road
Needles, CA 92363
(760) 326-7000

Map References

BLM Parker
USGS 1:24,000 Mohawk Spring
1:100,000 Parker
Maptech CD-ROM: San Bernardino County/Mojave
Southern & Central California Atlas & Gazetteer, p. 100
California Road & Recreation Atlas, p. 107

Route Directions

▼ 0.0			From Desert #10: Sunflower Spring Road, 10.2 miles from the easterly end at US 95, zero trip meter and turn southwest on formed trail marked Lost Arch Inn, suitable for 4WDs, ATVs, and motorbikes. Sunflower Spring Road bears northwest at this point.
	2.6 ▲		Trail ends at intersection with Desert #10: Sunflower Spring Road. Turn left to continue along this trail to Essex; continue straight ahead to exit 10.2 miles to US 95.
			GPS: N34°28.12' W114°48.79'
▼ 1.0		SO	Cross through wash.
	1.5 ▲	SO	Cross through wash.
▼ 1.1		BL	Well-used track on right. Remain on Lost Arch Inn Trail and cross through wash.
	1.5 ▲	SO	Cross through wash; then well-used track on left.
			GPS: N34°27.37' W114°49.52'
▼ 1.4		SO	Track on left.
	1.2 ▲	SO	Track on right.
▼ 1.9		SO	Track on left.
	0.7 ▲	SO	Track on right.

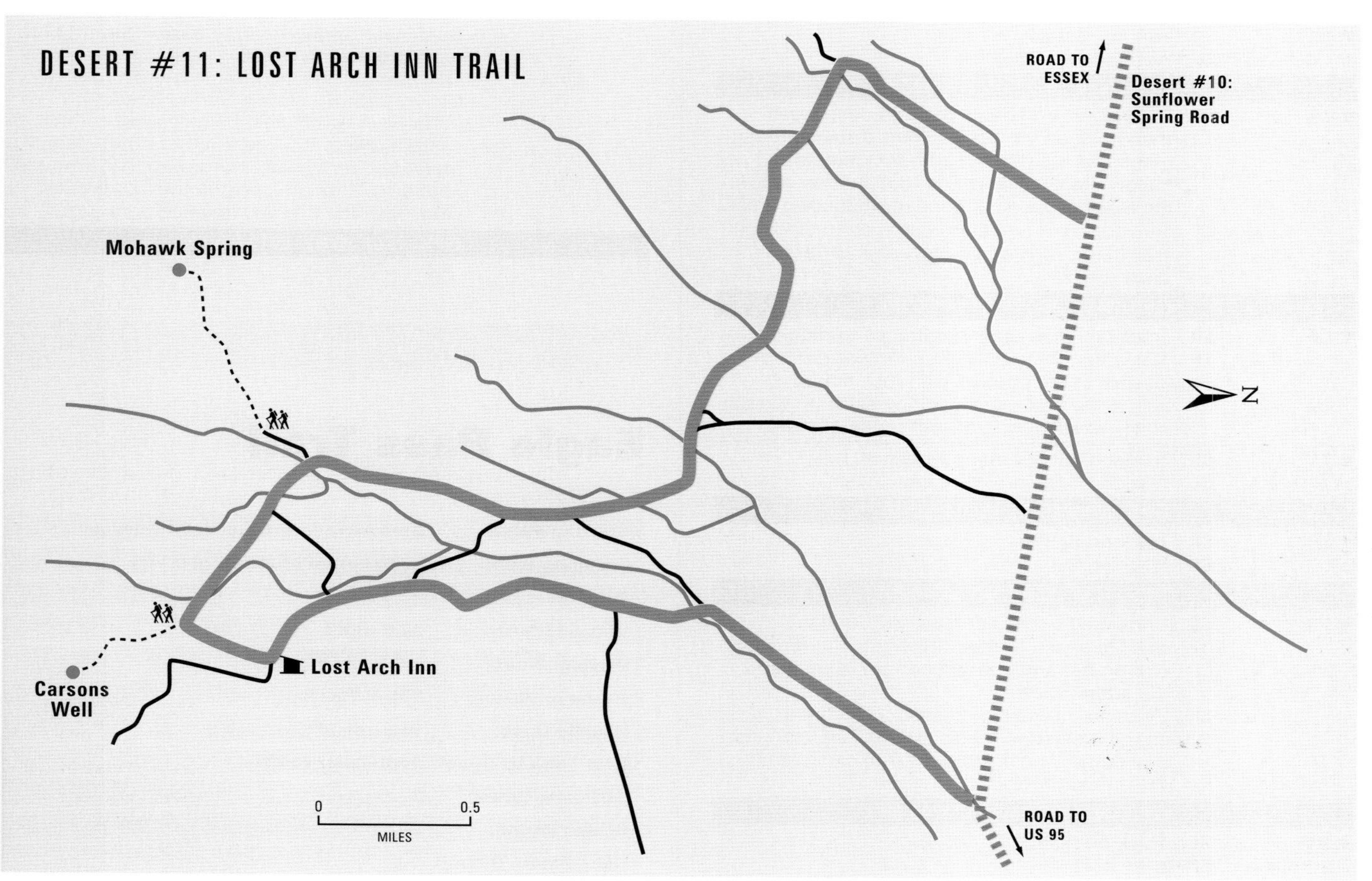

▼	▲		
▼ 2.0		SO	Track on left.
	0.6 ▲	SO	Track on right.
▼ 2.1		SO	Track on right; then cross through wash.
	0.5 ▲	BR	Cross through wash; then trail forks. Track on left.
			GPS: N34°26.52′ W114°49.66′
▼ 2.3		SO	Track on left; then cross through wash; then track on right.
	0.3 ▲	BR	Track on left; then cross through wash; then track on right.
▼ 2.5		SO	Track on left to concrete foundations.
	0.1 ▲	SO	Track on right to concrete foundations.
▼ 2.6		TR	Two cabins on left—one timber and one corrugated iron—are Lost Arch Inn. Small track straight ahead goes a short distance to the wilderness boundary. Zero trip meter and turn right, following the trail marker for Carsons Well.
	0.0 ▲		Continue to the west.
			GPS: N34°26.14′ W114°49.41′
▼ 0.0			Continue to the south.
	5.1 ▲	TL	Two cabins ahead—one timber and one corrugated iron—are Lost Arch Inn. Small track on right goes a short distance to the wilderness boundary. Zero trip meter and turn left onto well-used, unmarked trail.
▼ 0.3		TR	Well-used track on left goes 0.1 miles to Carsons Well Trail for hikers and horses only.
	4.8 ▲	TL	Well-used track straight ahead goes 0.1 miles to Carsons Well Trail for hikers and horses only.
			GPS: N34°25.86′ W114°49.54′
▼ 0.4		SO	Enter down line of wash. Trail continues to the northwest and looks somewhat less used.
	4.7 ▲	SO	Exit line of wash.
▼ 0.8		SO	Well-used track on right.
	4.3 ▲	SO	Well-used track on left.
			GPS: N34°26.13′ W114°49.94′
▼ 0.9		SO	Drop down and cross through deep wash; then track on left goes a short distance to diggings that are popular with rock hounds. Follow the small wash on foot southwest from the diggings for other good rockhounding areas.
	4.2 ▲	SO	Track on right is second entrance to diggings. Trail then drops down and crosses through deep wash.
			GPS: N34°26.17′ W114°50.00′
▼ 1.0		SO	Track on left is second entrance to diggings.
	4.1 ▲	SO	Track on right goes a short distance to diggings that are popular with rock hounds. Follow the small wash southwest from the diggings for other good rockhounding areas.
▼ 1.1		BR	Track on left into mine workings.
	4.0 ▲	BL	Track on right into mine workings.
			GPS: N34°26.28′ W114°50.10′
▼ 1.7		SO	Track on right.
	3.4 ▲	BR	Track on left.
			GPS: N34°26.83′ W114°49.87′
▼ 1.9		SO	Unmarked 5-way intersection. Continue straight ahead to the northwest. The remains of a timber and corrugated iron cabin are at the intersection.
	3.2 ▲	SO	Unmarked 5-way intersection. Continue straight ahead to the southeast. The remains of a timber and corrugated iron cabin are at the intersection.
			GPS: N34°26.96′ W114°49.89′
▼ 2.1		BL	Track on right.
	3.0 ▲	SO	Track on left.
▼ 2.2		SO	Cross through wash.
	2.9 ▲	SO	Cross through wash.
▼ 2.4		SO	Cross through wash.
	2.7 ▲	SO	Cross through wash.
▼ 2.6		SO	Well-used track on right; then second track on right.
	2.5 ▲	SO	Track on left; then second well-used track on left.
			GPS: N34°27.37′ W114°50.17′
▼ 2.7		SO	Cross through wash.
	2.4 ▲	SO	Cross through wash.
▼ 3.1		SO	Cross through wash.
	2.0 ▲	SO	Cross through wash.
▼ 3.2		SO	Track on right.
	1.9 ▲	BR	Track on left.
▼ 3.3		SO	Cross through wash.
	1.8 ▲	SO	Cross through wash.
▼ 4.0		SO	Cross through wide wash.
	1.1 ▲	SO	Cross through wide wash.
▼ 4.1		TR	Climb short wash embankment and turn right. To the left and straight ahead is the Turtle Mountains Wilderness boundary.
	1.0 ▲	TL	To the right and straight ahead is the Turtle Mountains Wilderness boundary. Turn left at small stone cairn in open area of desert pavement and descend to a wash. Intersection is easily missed in this direction.
			GPS: N34°27.84′ W114°51.45′
▼ 4.7		SO	Cross through wash.
	0.4 ▲	SO	Cross through wash.
▼ 5.1			Trail ends at T-intersection with Desert #10: Sunflower Spring Road at the mailbox. Trail is unmarked. Turn left to continue along Sunflower Spring Road to Essex; turn right to exit northeast to US 95.
	0.0 ▲		Trail commences near the eastern end of Desert #10: Sunflower Spring Road, 12.1 miles from US 95 and 1.9 miles west of the eastern end of the Lost Arch Inn Trail. Zero trip meter and turn south on formed trail. There is an old mailbox on a post at the intersection. Otherwise the trail is unmarked.
			GPS: N34°28.52′ W114°50.83′

DESERT #12

Eagle Pass Trail

Starting Point:	**Broadway, in the center of Needles**
Finishing Point:	**Intersection of US 95 and I-40**
Total Mileage:	**23.4 miles**
Unpaved Mileage:	**22.9 miles**
Driving Time:	**2.5 hours**
Elevation Range:	**500–2,200 feet**
Usually Open:	**Year-round**
Best Time to Travel:	**September to May**
Difficulty Rating:	**3**
Scenic Rating:	**8**
Remoteness Rating:	**+1**

Special Attractions

- Rockhounding for jasper.
- Trail is part of the East Mojave Heritage Trail.
- Remote trail traveling along desert washes.

History

Needles was established in 1869 as a port on the Colorado River. Native Americans, Spanish explorers, and the arrival of the railroad were influences that led to the town's development.

The Mojave have lived in the valley by the Colorado River for generations. Their trails, petroglyphs, pictographs, and mortise-working areas are evidence of their long residence in this area. Spanish padre Francisco Garcés passed through the site of Needles guided by the Mojave in 1776. Their trail followed alongside the river at this point. Fur trapper Jedediah Smith also used this trail in 1826. He was the first American to make a crossing of the Colorado River at what was later to be named Needles.

In the mid to late 1800s, steamboats plied the river, carrying passengers and freight. Needles developed as a supply center for mining prospectors and settlers in the region. By 1883, the Atlantic & Pacific Railroad had established a station on the Arizona side of the river. Later that year, they transferred operations to the California side, stating that it better suited their needs as a future division depot. The railroad soon replaced the steamboats.

The name Needles was derived from peaks near the town. Early railroad survey crews mentioned these prominent features, to the east and south of the locality, as a reference point. The name seemed appropriate when the post office was established in 1869.

Canyon walls close in as you approach Eagle Pass

Needles flourished as the railroad depot grew in importance. Soon highways brought automobiles and, like many desert locations, spawned a multitude of motels and restaurants. The ornate two-story Garces Building by the railroad resembles a Southern mansion, inviting all who pass by on the expanding railroad network. Today, the mansion awaits restoration. It was part of a series of Harvey Houses that were built along the Santa Fe Railroad system from Chicago to Los Angeles. These welcoming houses provided meals to rail passengers and crews along their long journey to the West Coast.

Early bridges were quite often washed away in floods. Dams and dredging on the Colorado River in the 1950s allowed more control of the river. This encouraged agriculture and further development of the town. Less flooding meant a more stable embankment and vegetation. It also made the river water clearer, which attracted recreationists. The river has since become one of the city's biggest attractions.

Eagle Peak sits on the northwest side of Eagle Pass

Description

Eagle Pass is an easy loop trail from Needles that can be done in half a day. The loop follows part of the long East Mojave Heritage Trail, the full length of which is no longer open to vehicle travel.

The trail leaves from the center of Needles and almost immediately travels along a loose, gravelly trail toward the Sacramento Mountains. It enters a canyon that climbs gently toward Eagle Pass. The towering bulk of Eagle Peak is immediately to the north. The vegetation is a mixture of sage, smoke trees, Mojave yuccas, chollas, and barrel cacti.

From Eagle Pass, the trail enters Crestview Wash and travels mainly in the line of the wash. One short stretch swings onto the ridge to cross a section of desert pavement that is studded with teddy bear chollas. The route can be hard to see along this section, but small cairns mark the way.

The trail's difficulty rating comes from the loose, soft wash beds that can make travel slow. In addition, there is one rocky descent over a shallow waterfall that requires careful wheel placement to ensure that your vehicle's underbody is not scraped on unforgiving rock. However, this section is extremely short.

The trail continues along Crestview Wash to join a pipeline road that runs alongside I-40. It finishes a short distance later at the intersection of US 95 and I-40.

Current Road Information

Bureau of Land Management
Needles Field Office
101 West Spikes Road
Needles, CA 92363
(760) 326-7000

Map References

BLM Needles
USGS 1:24,000 Needles, Needles SW, Flattop Mt., Bannock
1:100,000 Needles
Maptech CD-ROM: San Bernardino County/Mojave
Southern & Central California Atlas & Gazetteer, pp. 87, 86
California Road & Recreation Atlas, p. 115

Route Directions

▼ 0.0		From the main street, Broadway, in Needles, zero trip meter and turn southwest on L Street. Pass under the freeway (I-40) and immediately turn right onto paved Eagle Pass Road.
6.7 ▲		Turn left onto L Street and pass under freeway (I-40). Trail ends at the intersection with Broadway in the center of Needles.
		GPS: N34°50.52' W114°36.68'
▼ 0.5	SO	Road turns to roughly graded dirt. Cross over embankment.
6.2 ▲	SO	Cross over embankment. Road is now paved.
▼ 0.6	BL	Cross through wash; then bear left (west) up main trail. Small track on right.
6.1 ▲	SO	Small track on left. Cross through wash; then head east toward embankment.
		GPS: N34°50.67' W114°37.16'
▼ 0.7	SO	Two tracks on right. Remain on main trail.
6.0 ▲	SO	Two tracks on left. Remain on main trail.
▼ 1.2	SO	Track on left and track on right.
5.5 ▲	SO	Track on left and track on right.
		GPS: N34°50.43' W114°37.69'
▼ 1.9	SO	Cross through wash. Track on left in wash.
4.8 ▲	SO	Cross through wash. Track on right in wash.
▼ 2.3	SO	Track on left.
4.4 ▲	SO	Track on right.
▼ 3.4	SO	Track on right.
3.3 ▲	SO	Track on left.
		GPS: N34°48.90' W114°39.25
▼ 6.6	SO	Track on left.
0.1 ▲	SO	Track on right.
▼ 6.7	SO	Track on left on top of embankment. Zero trip meter.
0.0 ▲		Continue to the east.
		GPS: N34°47.08' W114°41.93'
▼ 0.0		Continue to the west.
3.6 ▲	SO	Track on right on top of embankment. Zero trip meter.

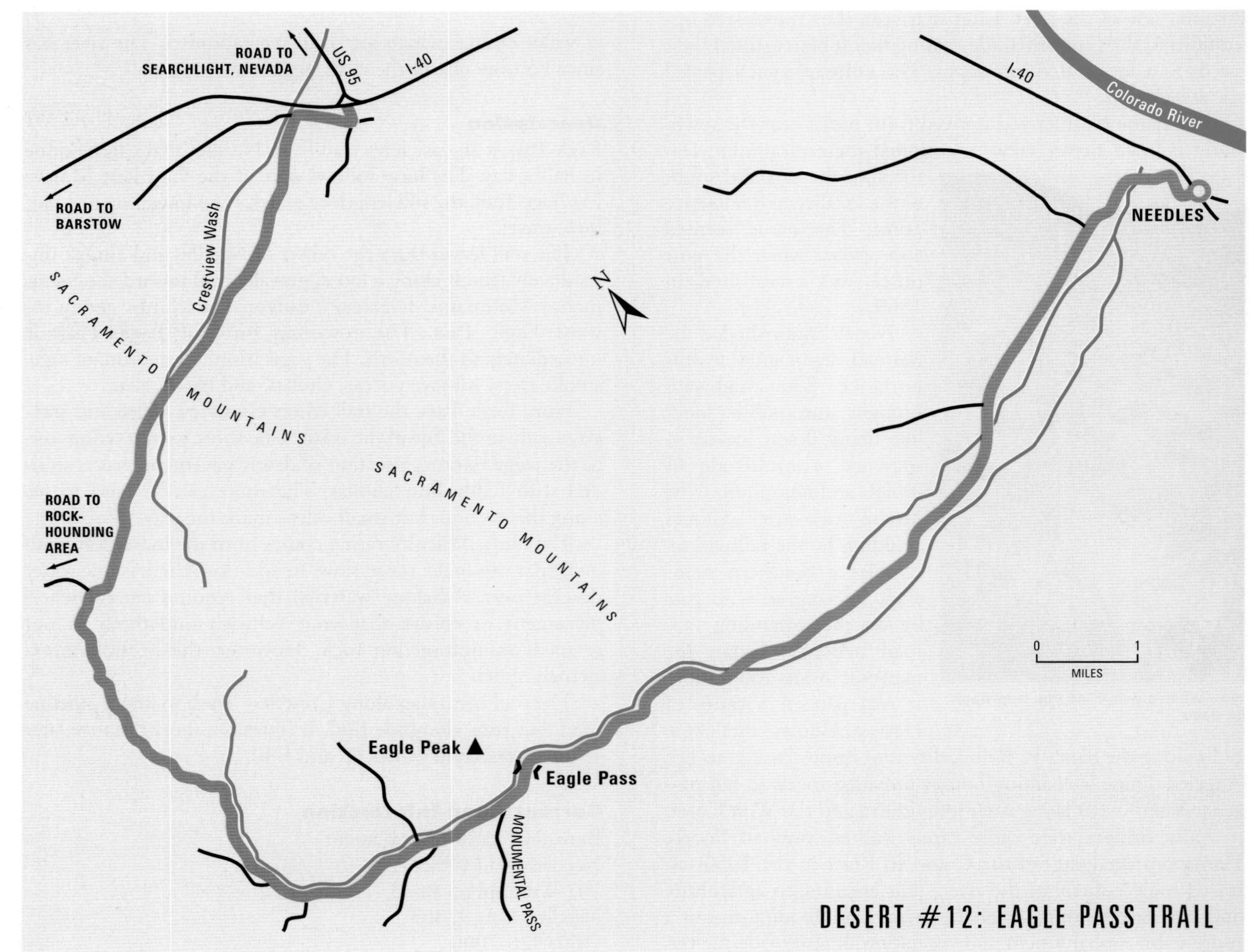

▼ 0.1 SO Track on left.
3.5 ▲ SO Track on right.

▼ 0.2 SO Cross over embankment. Track on left on top of embankment. Enter line of wash up canyon.
3.4 ▲ SO Exit line of wash and canyon. Cross over embankment. Track on right on top of embankment.

▼ 1.4 SO Track on right; then second track on right into mine diggings.
2.2 ▲ SO Track on left into mine diggings; then second track on left.

GPS: N34°46.92' W114°43.35'

▼ 2.3 SO Track on left.
1.3 ▲ SO Track on right.

▼ 2.6 SO Track on right.
1.0 ▲ SO Track on left.

▼ 3.3 SO Eagle Pass. The pass is not at the top, but in a narrow section of the canyon. Exit canyon.
0.3 ▲ SO Eagle Pass. The pass is not at the top, but in a narrow section of the canyon. Enter canyon.

GPS: N34°46.31' W114°44.90'

▼ 3.6 BR Well-used track on left is Monumental Pass, suitable for 4WDs, ATVs, and motorbikes. Zero trip meter and continue onto Crestview Wash, marked as suitable for 4WDs, ATVs, and motorbikes.
0.0 ▲ Continue to the north.

GPS: N34°46.19' W114°45.14'

▼ 0.0 Continue to the southwest.
6.8 ▲ SO Well-used track on right is Monumental Pass, suitable for 4WDs, ATVs, and motorbikes. Zero trip meter and continue straight ahead toward Eagle Pass.

▼ 0.3 BR Track on left.
6.5 ▲ SO Track on right.

▼ 0.8 SO Track on left out of wash.
6.0 ▲ SO Track on right out of wash.

GPS: N34°45.95' W114°45.94'

▼ 0.9 BL Track on right up wash.
5.9 ▲ SO Second entrance to track on left up wash.

GPS: N34°45.97' W114°46.03'

▼ 1.0 SO Second entrance to track on right.
5.8 ▲ BR Track on left.

▼ 2.2 BR Track on left up wash. Follow sign for Crestview Wash.
4.6 ▲ BL Bear left down main wash. Track on right up wash.

GPS: N34°45.68' W114°47.31'

▼ 2.6 SO Well-used track on left up side wash. Continue in main wash.
4.2 ▲ SO Well-used track on right up side wash. Continue in main wash.

GPS: N34°45.90' W114°47.66'

▼ 2.9 BL Trail skirts the rise of a shallow waterfall in the wash; then track on right. Remain in wash.
3.9 ▲ SO Track on left; then trail skirts the rise of a shallow waterfall in the wash. Remain in wash.

▼ 3.7 BL Bear left steeply out of wash.
3.1 ▲ BR Drop down and bear right in wash.

GPS: N34°46.66' W114°47.96'

▼ 4.3 SO Enter down line of Crestview Wash.
2.5 ▲ SO Exit line of wash.

GPS: N34°47.00' W114°48.40'

▼ 6.8 TR Small track on left; then track on left up side wash goes approximately 3 miles to a rockhounding area. Turn right, continuing down main wash, and zero trip meter.
0.0 ▲ Continue to the southwest, small track on right.

GPS: N34°48.79' W114°48.93'

▼ 0.0 Continue to the east.
6.3 ▲ TL Track on right up side wash goes approximately 3 miles to a rockhounding area. Turn left, continuing up main wash, and zero trip meter.

▼ 0.4 BR Bear right out of wash, following trail marker.
5.9 ▲ BL Bear left up wash.

GPS: N34°48.97' W114°48.64'

▼ 0.5 SO Enter down wash.
5.8 ▲ BR Bear right out of wash.

▼ 0.6 BR Rocky descent; then bear right down main wash.
5.7 ▲ BL Bear left out of wash up rocky ascent, following trail marker.

GPS: N34°49.07' W114°48.54'

▼ 3.4 BL Track on right.
2.9 ▲ SO Track on left.

GPS: N34°51.12' W114°47.04'

▼ 5.5 TR T-intersection with the pipeline road. Turn right alongside freeway; then track on left passes under freeway. Leave wash.
0.8 ▲ TL Track on right passes under freeway; then turn left onto formed trail up wash, marked Crestview Wash, suitable for 4WDs, ATVs, and motorbikes.

GPS: N34°52.69' W114°45.89'

▼ 6.2 TL 4-way intersection. Track straight ahead and to the right.
0.1 ▲ TR Turn sharp right at 4-way intersection. Track on left and graded road straight ahead.

GPS: N34°52.54' W114°45.25'

▼ 6.3 Trail ends at US 95 exit on the south side of I-40. Searchlight and Las Vegas are straight ahead on US 95. Take I-40 eastbound for Needles, westbound for Barstow.
0.0 ▲ Trail commences at the intersection of US 95 and I-40 at the freeway exit, 9 miles west of Needles. Proceed to the south side of the freeway, zero trip meter, and head south on graded dirt road.

GPS: N34°52.64' W114°45.26'

DESERT #13

Mojave Road

Starting Point:	**Needles Highway, NV, 0.7 miles north of California-Nevada state line**
Finishing Point:	**I-15, at the Harvard Road exit, 24 miles east of Barstow**
Total Mileage:	**128.6 miles**
Unpaved Mileage:	**123.5 miles**
Driving Time:	**2 days minimum, 3 or more preferably**
Elevation Range:	**900–5,200 feet**
Usually Open:	**Year-round**
Best Time to Travel:	**October to May**
Difficulty Rating:	**4 (the majority is rated 2 or 3)**
Scenic Rating:	**10**
Remoteness Rating:	**+1**

Special Attractions

- Historic Mojave Road route, including the sites of Fort Piute, The Caves, Rock Spring, Triangle Intaglios, and more.
- Unparalleled variety of Mojave Desert scenery and natural attractions, including Soda Lake and Afton Canyon.

History

The Mojave Trail was once a trade route used by various Indian cultures between the Colorado River and the Pacific Ocean. Rock Spring was a crucial link in a chain of desert springs that allowed early inhabitants to cross the Mojave Desert.

In 1854, Army Engineer Lieutenant Amiel W. Whipple led an exploration party along the Mojave Trail, seeking a transcontinental train route along the thirty-fifth parallel. He named Rock Spring and other features along the way for navigating purposes. Whipple saw an old Chemehuevi crop of corn and melons at what was later to become Fort Piute (also known as Fort Pah-Ute).

In 1857, the U.S. War Department hired explorer Edward Fitzgerald Beale and his camels to survey and establish a wagon road from New Mexico to the banks of the Colorado River. Although not required by his contract, Beale pushed farther west along the Mojave Trail and established a route through this part of California.

During the 1860s, five army posts were established approximately a day's ride apart, spanning the Mojave Desert from Camp Cady near Barstow to Fort Mohave on the Colorado River. Never officially established as a fort, Pah-Ute Creek, as it was commonly called, did house a small number of troops from November 17, 1867, to May 3, 1868. As many as 18 enlisted men from Company D, Ninth U.S. Infantry served at the remote hot spot. The small fort still stands on a low rise above Piute Spring wash, its thick stone walls having stood the test of time. A rock corral of a later date is also at the site.

Little Cowhole Mountain rises above the aptly named Soda Lake

Camp Rock Spring was established on December 20, 1866. It provided mail carriers and travelers safe escort across the desert, a dangerous and difficult task for all concerned in this remote area. Harsh conditions meant that Camp Rock Spring had one of the highest desertion rates of any army post. Its remote location made it very difficult to get adequate food, supplies, water, and medical attention. Rationing was strict. Lack of fresh foods led to outbreaks of scurvy. Morale was low and there was little to do at times. When the mail route was moved, the army post was no longer needed and its soldiers were moved to other duties. The camp was closed on January 2, 1868.

Farther east, Marl Spring was originally called Pozos de San Juan de Dios (Spanish for "Wells of St. John of God"). On March 8, 1776, Fray Francisco Garcés rested there and named the wells while on his journey from Mission San Xavier del Bac in Tucson, Arizona, to Mission San Gabriel, in present-day Los Angeles. Garcés passed by the spring on his return journey, resting there again on May 22 of the same year.

Mojave Road was an important route for the people of Los Angeles because it linked the town with Prescott, Arizona, a prominent settlement at that time. However, by 1883 the road became obsolete because of the completion of the Southern Pacific Railroad from Needles, on the Colorado River, to Mojave. The railroad intersected with the old Mojave Trail at Barstow.

In 1894, the Rock Spring Land and Cattle Company, later known as Ox Ranch, controlled most of the area's water. Battles erupted between homesteaders and ranchers over water rights. The last gunfight over water rights occurred at Government Holes in 1925. A hired hand named Bill Robertson, who was good with his gun, was positioned at the holes to protect the ranchers' water. An ex-hired hand named Matt Burts, also good with a gun, was passing by when his car radiator needed a top-up. According to witnesses in the car, conversation between the two men seemed pleasant. However, the end result was a shootout at a cabin near the holes. Both men died.

From the 1910s to 1940, many families were attracted to the Lanfair area by land available under homestead laws and a wetter than average weather period. Farming seemed feasible to the newcomers, and many acres were cleared for agricultural purposes. However, the difficulties of farming in this extreme environment drove many away with little return for their years of hard labor improving the lands and building cabins. Many moved out without fulfilling the homestead requirements that would allow them to patent the land. If they were lucky, they would sell their improvements to the next hopeful homesteader. Many such cleared areas are passed along Mojave Road with little regeneration occurring in places.

Though snow is not always associated with the eastern Mojave region, the winter of 1937 was certainly a reminder of how isolated this region is when extreme weather strikes. Ed Clark and his daughter Clara were homesteaders near the Grotto Hills, just north of Mojave Road in Lanfair Valley. Snow began piling up around their home forcing the Clarks to sit out the bad weather with only a little food. Their Model-T truck could not cope with the depth of snow, and they were unable to get to Needles to purchase their monthly supplies. The Clarks battled to survive freezing temperatures in their small cabin. They ate chicken feed when their food ran out. Fortunately for them, Al Mosher and Alan Cane arrived from the Providence Ranch in Round Valley. They had battled the deep snow for hours, digging and ramming the deep wall of snow with their 1928 Chevy truck to rescue the Clarks. Ranchers lost many heads of cattle in the snowstorm. In one instance, some 50 head were trapped in a box canyon where they all perished.

Only 12 years later an even worse snowstorm stranded homesteaders in drifts that were 5 to 12 feet deep in places. Winds reportedly reached 40 miles an hour, driving the powder-dry snow up and over ranchers' homes. Air Force flights over the region reported seeing few buildings, just white drifting snow. Some folks communicated with air rescue by writing OK in the snow. Plowing attempts were futile with snowdrifts repacking roads within a half hour of clearing them. Black Canyon Road disappeared as blowing snow filled the canyon to the top, leaving it impassable for six weeks.

Borax mining in Death Valley required a better transportation system than the famed 20-mule teams that hauled borax to market in the late 1800s. This resulted in the construction of the Tonopah & Tidewater Railroad from Ludlow to Sperry, and later on to Beatty, Nevada. The railroad was constructed across the wide flats of Soda Lake and Silver Lake in 1906. The line was laid directly on the floor of the dry lakebeds. In 1922, Silver Lake filled to a depth of nearly 3 feet. The railroad, which had already been raised in 1915 because of rising waters, was abandoned and rerouted for 5 miles along the eastern shore. Sailboats completed the picture on Silver Lake that year.

Mojave Indians lived at Soda Springs on the western shore of Soda Lake for at least 7,000 years. At the end of World War II, Zzyzx Mineral Springs was developed as a resort. The 200-mile trip from Los Angeles to the popular resort was quite a distance in the days of gasoline rationing. Doc Springer established his reputation by providing good food and many activities, such as swimming, hiking, horseback riding, shuffle board, and hunting for Indian artifacts (in the days before this was illegal). Electricity for the resort was supplied by World War II surplus diesel generators. Most of the food was grown on site and rabbits were raised for their meat. In the 1960s, Doc Springer's health products came under scrutiny, and he was accused of misleading the public about the quality of his health foods.

Afton Canyon, also known as Cave Canyon for a time, offered early travelers refuge in its caves. The canyon is the result of massive erosion combined with possible faulting. Prehistoric Lake Manix covered an immense area of more than 200 square miles, mainly along the course of the Mojave River, and connected the Cronese Lakes with Soda Lake and Silver Lake. The drainage of the prehistoric lake seems to have been the force behind the deep, rapid erosion of Afton Canyon. It may have been triggered by an earthquake, which would account for the offset layers in the canyon.

Afton Caves were an important way station on the old government road between Soda Springs and Fort Cady, where travelers could get supplies and protection from Indians. The Caves, a series of deep rock shelters, were used by Indians before the arrival of Euro-Americans. At least one of the caves is large enough to shelter wagons.

The Arbuckle Mine, later known as the Cliffside Mine, found high on the south side of Afton Canyon, mined magnesite for use in steel mills and smelters during World War I.

Description

Mojave Road is a long, extremely remote trail for 4WD vehicles that generally follows the historic route of the Mojave Trail. The trail can be traveled in two long days, though it is best to allow three days so you have time to explore the many points of interest along the way. It is best suited for people intending to camp. Although accommodations are available at Laughlin, NV, Baker, and Barstow, they require long detours from the trail.

Large Joshua trees in the Lanfair Valley

Camping is allowed almost anywhere. There are developed campgrounds a short distance from the trail at Hole-in-the-Wall and Mid Hills within the Mojave National Preserve. In addition, primitive camping is allowed anywhere that has been previously used as a campsite.

The beginning of Mojave Road is on the banks of the Colorado River in the Fort Mohave Indian Reservation opposite the site of Fort Mohave, Arizona. However, the road is partially blocked by agriculture on the Indian reservation. For ease of access, the route described here starts 3 miles from the river on Needles Highway.

The trail is marked along its length by cairns that were placed by the Friends of the Mojave Road. The forward (westbound) route directions describe the cairns as on the right; in the reverse (eastbound) direction, they are on the left. The cairns are placed at every intersection, but some are hard to spot and they should not be relied upon. In the Rasor OHV Area, they are absent from many intersections. In addition, some sections are marked by BLM trail markers.

The overall difficulty rating for the trail is a 4. However the majority of the trail is easier, only rating a 2 or a 3 for difficulty. Even these easier sections require 4WD to negotiate the loose, deep sand.

The trail leaves Needles Highway and travels up a wash to-

Stone cabin alongside the trail is on private property

ward the Dead Mountains. The trail surface for this section is generally loose sand interspersed with rocky sections. The trail crosses through the Dead Mountains, descending into the shallow Piute Valley on the western side. After crossing US 95, the trail gradually ascends toward the Piute Range. The original route past Fort Piute is blocked to vehicle travel by a wilderness area. A short, rough spur leads 1.9 miles to the old fort. Stone walls remain and there are some good, primitive campsites scattered around the fort. Piute Spring is a short distance upstream, accessible by the Fort Piute/Piute Spring Loop Hiking Corridor.

Half a mile before you reach the fort, the remains of a stone cabin and corral are alongside the wash below the trail. Hike down to view the cabin and take particular note of the corner stones; they have small rock art designs etched into them.

The main trail crests the Piute Range before descending into the Lanfair Valley. Mojave Road is not the commonly traveled route in this area; graded roads parallel much of the rougher, eroded trail. Longer vehicles will need to take extra care along this section. Deep gullies and moguls make it easy to catch a rear overhang or lift a wheel. Parts of this section reach a 4 rating for difficulty.

The Lanfair Valley has abundant and beautiful Mojave Desert vegetation. Joshua trees, the signature plant of the Mojave Desert, mingle with Mojave yuccas, chollas, greasewoods, and prickly pears.

The historic military site of Rock Spring is close to the deep, sandy Watson Wash, one of the many sections of loose, deep sand along the trail. A few stone walls remain at Camp Rock Spring. The spring is a short distance farther up the canyon. It is surrounded by numerous petroglyphs, many of which are faint.

Another important historic site is Government Holes. Today, there is a well and a corral at the site; a tank still bears the markings of the Ox Cattle Company. A short distance west of Government Holes, the trail rejoins Cedar Canyon Road and follows it to the intersection with paved Kelso-Cima Road.

West of Kelso-Cima Road, the trail skirts the edge of the Marl Mountains, passing close to Marl Spring. This section of trail resembles a roller coaster as it undulates over moguls to cross Aikens Mine Road, part of Desert #18: Cima Dome Trail.

West of Cima Dome Trail, the route follows along Willow Wash. The sand here can be deep, and you may need to lower tire pressures. The trail rounds Seventeen Mile Point and travels in a plumb line down to the dry Soda Lake, which can be seen almost shimmering in the desert heat, far below in the valley at the foot of the Soda Mountains.

In wet weather, or immediately after rain, the trail across Soda Lake can be impassable. The thick gooey mud quickly clogs tire treads and bogs down vehicles. On the flat lakebed, there is nothing to winch off, and it can be hard to get out of trouble. Exercise caution and be prepared to turn back and take the alternate route via Baker to the north. After crossing the fence line through Volunteer Gate, there is a short section of deep, rutty sand traps. This can be difficult both in very dry and very wet weather. The track leading north from Volunteer Gate is the alternate way around Soda Lake. It travels to Baker, avoiding the soft surface of the lakebed. From Baker you can take I-15 westbound for 11 miles and then travel south on Rasor Road for 5.1 miles to rejoin Mojave Road.

The trail across Soda Lake is marked by green stakes as well as occasional cairns. There are several deep channels that cut across the otherwise flat surface, so resist the temptation to speed. Remain close to the green posts to minimize tire tracks across this fragile area. Some sections of the lakebed can be muddy at any time of year. Midway across the lake is the Travelers or Government Cairn. Over the years, many travelers have added to this large cairn.

The far side of the lake is marked by The Granites, large granite boulders near the old Tonopah & Tidewater Railroad grade that make a pleasant place to camp. The site of Zzyzx (pronounced ZIE-zix) can be seen to the north, marked by palm trees and other splashes of green. The site, which has had an interesting history over the years, is now a desert center. Note that there is no through road from Mojave Road through Zzyzx to I-15.

The mud of Soda Lake is very caustic to vehicles. It is a good idea to wash your vehicle thoroughly as soon as possible after completing this trail. Don't forget about the underbody.

Mojave Road passes through the Rasor OHV Area. There are many small tracks to the right and left through the open area. This is one of the hardest sections to navigate. After the shallow, rocky Shaw Pass, the road drops into the sand dunes area of the Mojave River floodplain. Some of the deepest sand along the trail is encountered here; vehicles will need to lower tire pressures. From Shaw Pass to Basin Road, the trail is rated a 4 for difficulty. The road is poorly marked, and the large number of ever-shifting trails means it is impossible to give precise directions. The major trail intersections are noted. There are a few cairns along this section as well. Try to remain on the main trail, heading generally west-southwest in the forward direction. It is helpful to set the GPS GoTo feature to the coordinates on graded dirt Basin Road. If traveling the road in reverse it is even more difficult. There are several well-used trails that fork away from the correct one at a shallow angle. The coordinates for Shaw Pass are helpful to use as the GoTo point.

You will inevitably cross Basin Road at some point if you head generally west. If you do not see the well-used trail leading off from the west side, which is marked with a cairn, it is simple enough to scout up and down the road for a short distance until you find it.

West of Basin Road is one of the most dramatic sections of the trail. It descends through the narrow Afton Canyon. The Mojave River is crossed several times here. For most of the year there is a few inches of water in the channel, but there are two crossings near the lower end that usually have depths of a couple feet.

The road shares the canyon with a railroad, at times running right alongside the tracks. The canyon walls are narrow and brightly colored. The BLM has designated the route an Open Route, and it is marked with marker posts.

The Caves, an important stopping point along Mojave Road, are no longer accessible by vehicle. It is a short hike through the tamarisk to the caves. The river crossing at this point is one of two that can be deeper than normal. If in doubt, check the depth before proceeding.

The Afton Canyon BLM Campground is a popular overnight stop. Rock hounds are particularly fond of this spot because it is a good place to look for agate, calcite, chalcedony, and jasper in the nearby washes. Pyramid Canyon is a good spot, and so is under the railroad trestle opposite the campground. The campground has picnic tables and fire rings; there are shade ramadas over the picnic tables. A fee is charged for overnight camping, but day use is free.

Past the campground, the trail enters the Mojave River channel. The sand here is also deep and loose. A worthwhile detour is to take the side trail and short hike that leads on top of a mesa alongside the wash. The short scramble to the top of the mesa is rewarded by approximately 20 triangular shaped intaglios—etchings made into the desert pavement. Do not walk on the intaglios, as this will damage them.

The Mojave Road continues in the wash before turning up Manix Canyon to exit to the graded road at Manix, and then on to the intersection with I-15.

Current Road Information

Mojave National Preserve
PO Box 241
72157 Baker Boulevard
Baker, CA 92309
(760) 733-4040

Bureau of Land Management
Needles Field Office
101 West Spikes Road
Needles, CA 92363
(760) 326-7000

Map References

BLM Davis Dam, Ivanpah, Soda Mts., Newberry Springs
USGS 1:24,000 Mt. Manchester, East of Homer Mt., Homer Mt., Signal Hill, Hackberry Mt., Grotto Hills, Pinto Valley, Mid Hills, Cima, Marl Mt., Indian Spring, Seventeenmile Point, Soda Lake North, Soda Lake South, Crucero Hill, Cave Mt., Dunn, Hidden Valley West, Manix, Harvard Hill
1:100,000 Davis Dam, Ivanpah, Soda Mts., Newberry Springs
Maptech CD-ROM: San Bernardino County/Mojave
Southern & Central California Atlas & Gazetteer, pp. 73, 72, 71, 70, 69, 82
Nevada Atlas & Gazetteer, p. 72
California Road & Recreation Atlas, pp. 99, 98, 97, 96, 105
Trails Illustrated, Mojave National Preserve (256)

Route Directions

Mileage		Directions
▼ 0.0		From Needles Highway in Nevada, 0.7 miles north of the California state line, zero trip meter and turn southwest on formed sandy trail leading up a wide wash. A short distance off the highway is a Mojave Road trail marker, designating the trail suitable for 4WDs, ATVs, and motorbikes.
5.4 ▲		Trail ends on Needles Highway. Turn right for Needles; turn left for Laughlin, NV.
		GPS: N35°03.08' W114°40.57'
▼ 0.4	SO	Pass under power lines; track on right and left.
5.0 ▲	SO	Pass under power lines; track on right and left.
▼ 0.5	SO	Track on left.
4.9 ▲	SO	Track on right.
▼ 0.8	BL	Track on left; then enter main line of wash. Two tracks on right down wash.
4.6 ▲	BR	Exit main line of wash. Two tracks on left down wash. Track on right.
		GPS: N35°03.33' W114°41.31'
▼ 1.3	SO	Track on left.
4.1 ▲	SO	Track on right.
▼ 1.6	BR	Well-used track on left. Bear right under power lines.
3.8 ▲	SO	Track on right. Leave power lines.
		GPS: N35°03.58' W114°42.10'
▼ 1.7	SO	Track on right.
3.7 ▲	SO	Track on left.
▼ 1.8	BR	Track on right; then bear right past track on left and track straight ahead.
3.6 ▲	SO	Two tracks on right; then track on left.
		GPS: N35°03.79' W114°42.23'
▼ 2.0	SO	Track on left.
3.4 ▲	SO	Track on right.
▼ 2.1	BR	Track on left continues up wash. Follow Mojave Road trail marker; then track on left.
3.3 ▲	SO	Track on right; then second track on right up wash. There is a Mojave Road trail marker at this intersection.
		GPS: N35°03.95' W114°42.32'
▼ 2.6	SO	Track on left.
2.8 ▲	SO	Track on right.
▼ 2.7	SO	Track on left.
2.7 ▲	SO	Track on right.
▼ 2.9	BL	Track on right. Follow Mojave Road trail marker away from power lines.

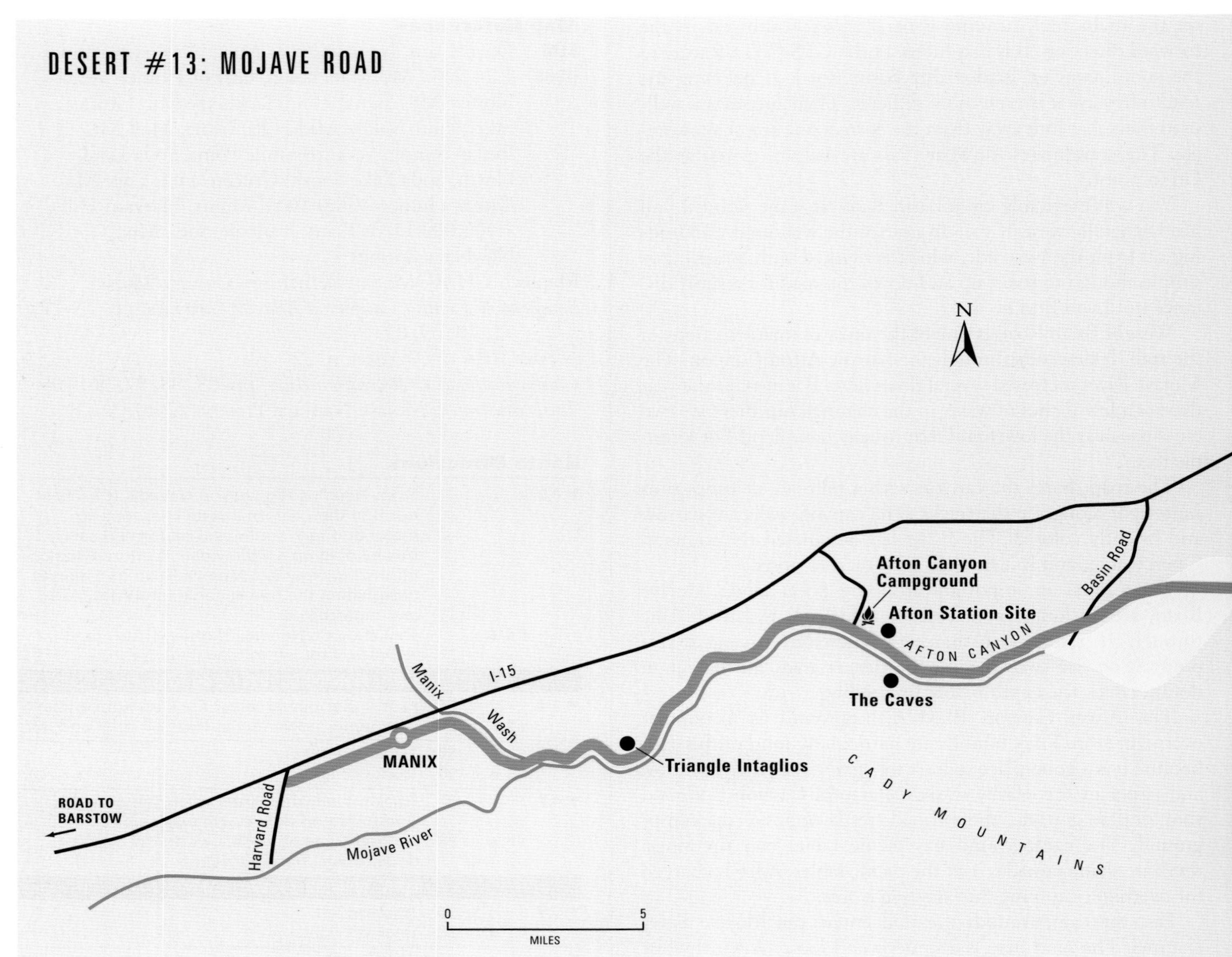

	2.5 ▲	SO	Track on left. Continue alongside power lines.
			GPS: N35°04.61' W114°42.84'
▼ 3.2		SO	Small track on left.
	2.2 ▲	SO	Small track on right.
▼ 3.3		TR	Track on left. Turn right, remaining on main trail up wash.
	2.1 ▲	TL	Track straight ahead. Turn left, remaining on main trail away from wash.
			GPS: N35°04.37' W114°43.07'
▼ 5.1		BR	Track on left.
	0.3 ▲	SO	Track on right.
			GPS: N35°05.55' W114°44.22'
▼ 5.4		SO	Staggered intersection under power lines. Follow Mojave Road marker. Well-used track on left and right. Zero trip meter.
	0.0 ▲		Continue to the east.
			GPS: N35°05.81' W114°44.45'
▼ 0.0			Continue to the west.
	5.3 ▲	SO	Staggered intersection under power lines. There is a Mojave Road marker at the intersection. Well-used track on left and right. Zero trip meter.
▼ 0.9		BR	Well-used track on right; then immediately bear right, following Mojave Road marker. Well-used track on left.
	4.4 ▲	BR	Well-used track on right; then immediately bear right past well-used track on left.
			GPS: N35°06.23' W114°45.29'
▼ 2.1		SO	Enter San Bernardino County, CA. State line is unmarked.
	3.2 ▲	SO	Enter Clark County, NV. State line is unmarked.
▼ 2.2		BL	Well-used track on right. Exit line of wash.
	3.1 ▲	BR	Well-used track on left. Enter line of wash.
			GPS: N35°06.90' W114°46.40'
▼ 2.4		SO	Track on right.
	2.9 ▲	SO	Track on left.
▼ 2.8		SO	Track on right and track on left; then cross through wash.
	2.5 ▲	SO	Cross through wash; then track on left and track on right.
▼ 2.9		SO	Cross Von Schmidt Boundary of 1873.
	2.4 ▲	SO	Cross Von Schmidt Boundary of 1873.
▼ 4.7		SO	Road on right into private property; then track on left.
	0.6 ▲	SO	Track on right; then road on left into private property.
			GPS: N35°06.76' W114°49.03'

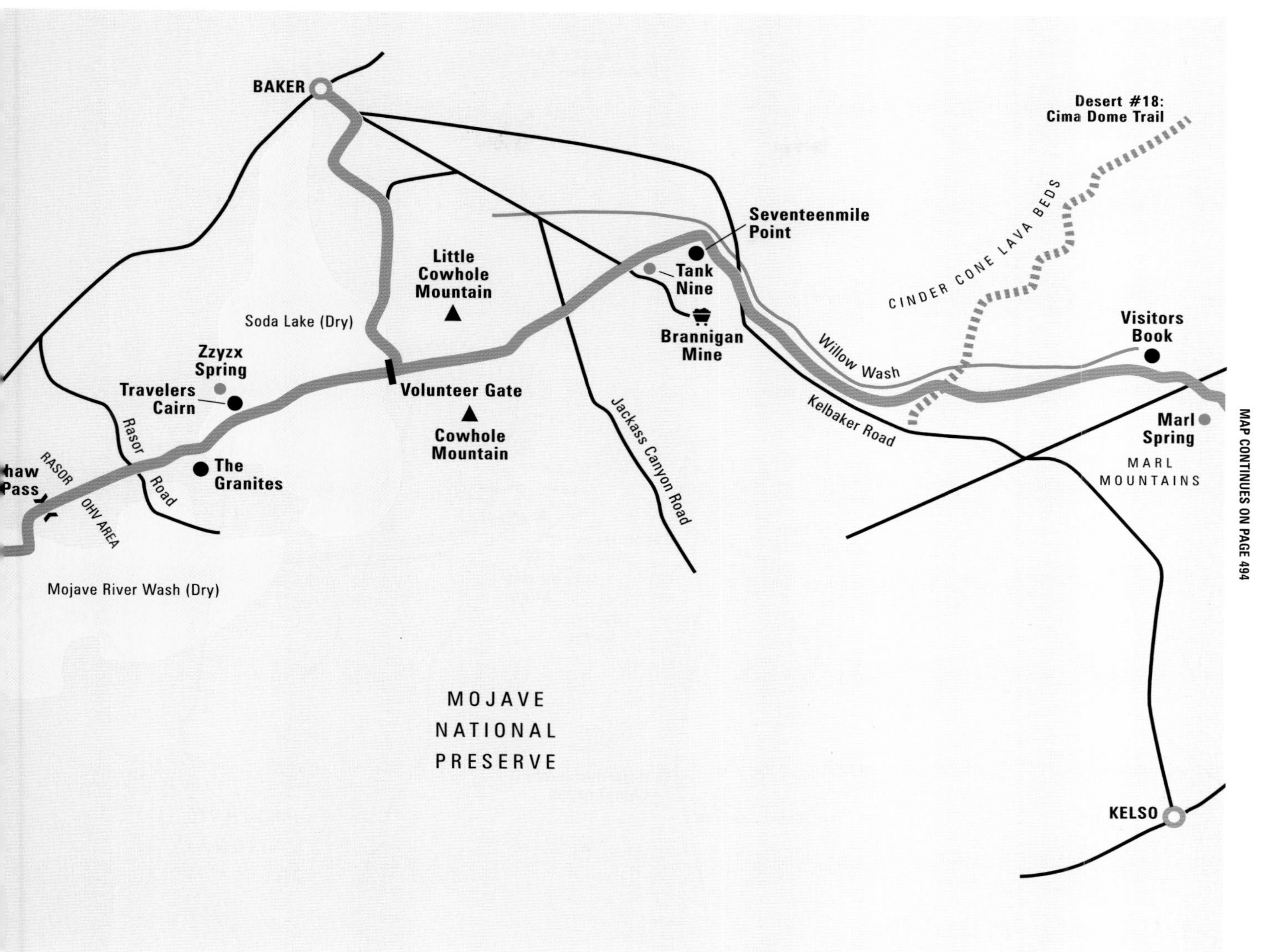

▼ 4.8	SO	Track on right.
0.5 ▲	SO	Track on left.
▼ 5.3	SO	Track on right; then intersection with US 95. Zero trip meter and cross paved highway onto formed trail on the west side. If anyone wants to join the trail at this point, this intersection is 0.1 miles south of mile marker 76 and 4.4 miles south of California-Nevada state line.
0.0 ▲		Continue to the east. Immediately track on left.
		GPS: N35°06.77′ W114°49.70′
▼ 0.0		Continue to the west.
6.9 ▲	SO	Intersection with US 95. Zero trip meter and cross paved highway onto graded road on east side. If anyone wants to join the trail at this point, this intersection is 0.1 miles south of mile marker 76 and 4.4 miles south of California-Nevada state line.
▼ 0.8	SO	Track on right; then cattle guard.
6.1 ▲	SO	Cattle guard; then track on left.
		GPS: N35°06.78′ W114°50.62′
▼ 1.6	SO	Small track on left.
5.3 ▲	SO	Small track on right.
▼ 2.1	SO	Start to cross through wide wash.
4.8 ▲	SO	Exit wash crossing.
		GPS: N35°06.77′ W114°52.05′
▼ 2.2	SO	Exit wash crossing.
4.7 ▲	SO	Start to cross through wide wash.
▼ 2.3	SO	Cross through Piute Wash.
4.6 ▲	SO	Cross through Piute Wash.
▼ 2.5	SO	Track on left and track on right.
4.4 ▲	SO	Track on left and track on right.
		GPS: N35°06.77′ W114°52.47′
▼ 4.0	SO	Small track on right and benchmark on left.
2.9 ▲	SO	Small track on left and benchmark on right.
		GPS: N35°06.82′ W114°54.14′
▼ 4.6	SO	Cross through wash.
2.3 ▲	SO	Cross through wash.
▼ 4.8	SO	Cross through wash.
2.1 ▲	SO	Cross through wash.
▼ 5.8	SO	Track on left and track on right.
1.1 ▲	SO	Track on left and track on right.
		GPS: N35°06.74′ W114°56.12′
▼ 6.9	TL	Turn left onto graded road alongside power lines. Track ahead is spur to Fort Piute. Zero trip meter.

MAP CONTINUES ON PAGE 493

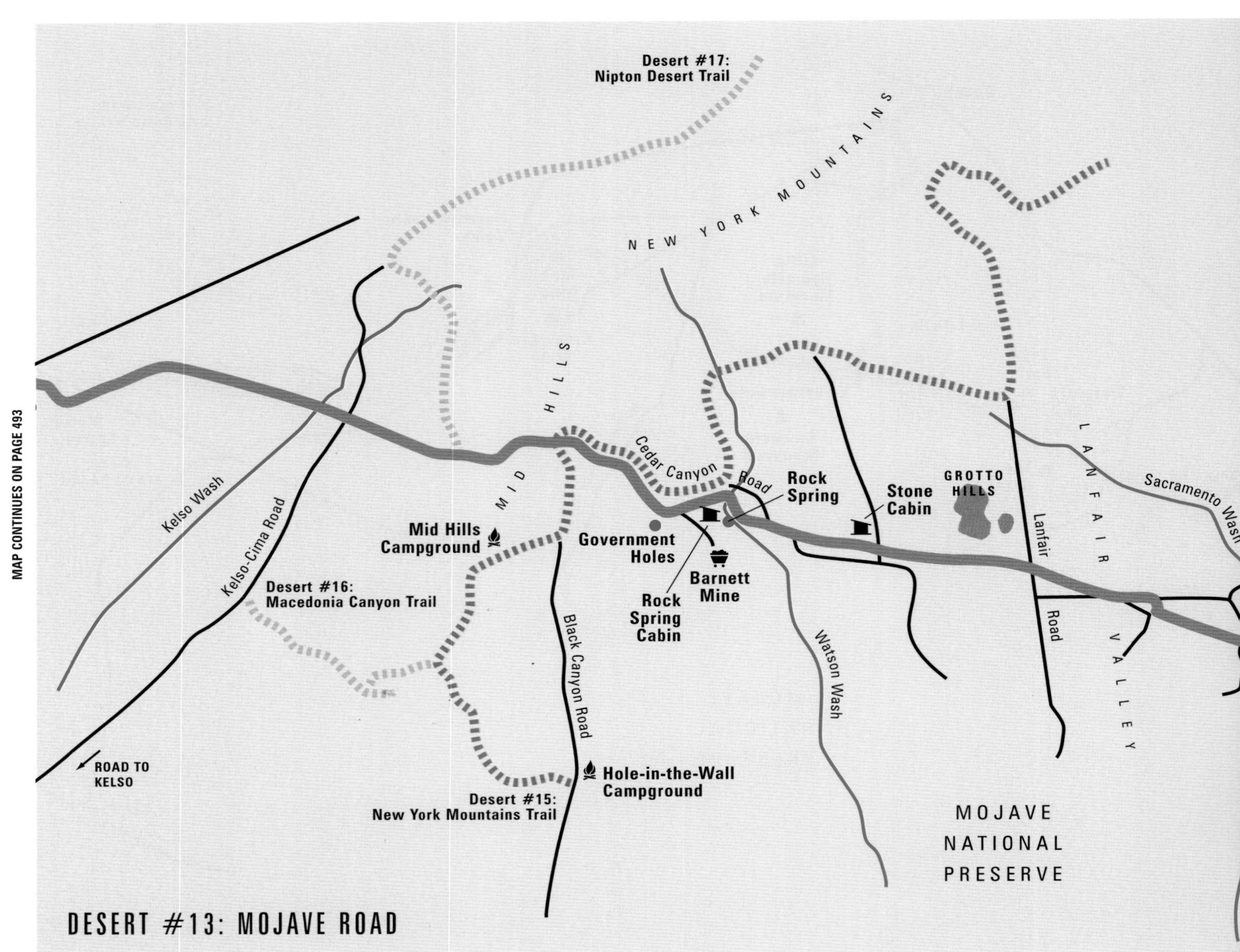

	0.0 ▲		Continue to the northeast on formed trail.
			GPS: N35°06.73' W114°57.20'

Spur to Fort Piute

▼ 0.0			Continue to the southwest.
▼ 1.1		SO	Campsite on left and track on right.
			GPS: N35°06.83' W114°58.23'
▼ 1.4		SO	Old corral on left and old stone house.
			GPS: N35°06.84' W114°58.55'
▼ 1.8		SO	Campsite on left; then site of Fort Piute on right. A plaque marks the site.
			GPS: N35°06.87' W114°59.05'
▼ 1.9		UT	Spur ends just downstream from the spring. Hiking trail continues past this point.
			GPS: N35°06.86' W114°59.10'

Continuation of Main Trail

▼ 0.0			Continue to the south on graded road.
	1.4 ▲	TR	Turn right onto formed trail, leaving power lines behind. Track on left is spur to Fort Piute. Zero trip meter.
			GPS: N35°06.73' W114°57.20'
▼ 0.5		SO	Cross through wash.
	0.9 ▲	SO	Cross through wash.
▼ 0.9		SO	Track on left and track on right to tank.
	0.5 ▲	SO	Track on right and track on left to tank.
▼ 1.1		SO	Cross through wash.
	0.3 ▲	SO	Cross through wash.
▼ 1.4		TR	4-way intersection. Turn right, leaving power lines. Zero trip meter.
	0.0 ▲		Continue to the north alongside power lines.
			GPS: N35°05.47' W114°57.26'
▼ 0.0			Continue to the west, away from power lines.
	3.8 ▲	TL	4-way intersection. Turn left and follow alongside power lines. Zero trip meter.
▼ 2.3		SO	Cross through wash.
	1.5 ▲	SO	Cross through wash.
▼ 3.7		SO	Cresting ridge of the Piute Range.
	0.1 ▲	SO	Cresting ridge of the Piute Range.
▼ 3.8		TR	Cattle guard; then turn right onto graded road. Track straight ahead is Desert #14: East Lanfair Valley Trail, which joins Mojave Road at this point. Zero trip meter.

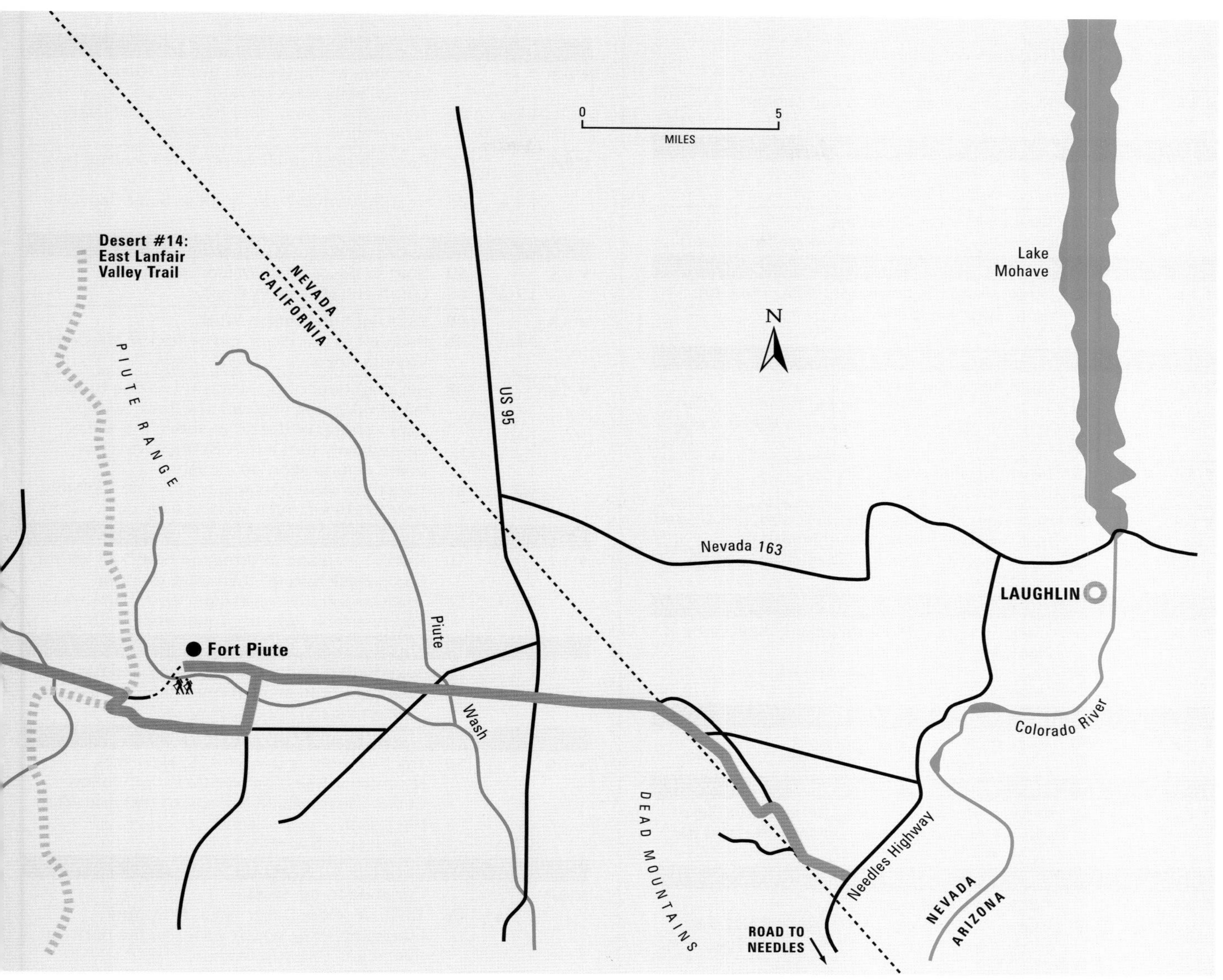

Mileage		Description
0.0 ▲		Continue to the east.
		GPS: N35°05.68′ W115°01.11′
▼ 0.0		Continue to the northeast.
0.5 ▲	TL	T-intersection. Turn left over cattle guard. Zero trip meter. Track on right is Desert #14: East Lanfair Valley Trail, which leaves Mojave Road at this point.
▼ 0.5	TL	4-way intersection. Track on right joins Fort Piute/Piute Spring Loop Hiking Corridor. Ahead is Desert #14: East Lanfair Valley Trail, which leaves Mojave Road at this point. Zero trip meter.
0.0 ▲		Continue to the south.
		GPS: N35°05.98′ W115°00.78′
▼ 0.0		Continue to the west.
6.8 ▲	TR	4-way intersection. Track ahead joins Fort Piute/Piute Spring Loop Hiking Corridor. Track on left is Desert #14: East Lanfair Valley Trail, which joins Mojave Road at this point. Zero trip meter.
▼ 0.8	SO	Cross through wash.
6.0 ▲	SO	Cross through wash.
▼ 1.9	SO	Faint track on right.
4.9 ▲	SO	Faint track on left.
▼ 2.0	SO	Cross through Sacramento Wash.
4.8 ▲	SO	Cross through Sacramento Wash.
		GPS: N35°06.35′ W115°02.88′
▼ 2.2	BL	Well-used graded track on left; then tank on right. Immediately bear left past track on right.
4.6 ▲	BL	Track on left; then tank on left. Bear left, leaving well-used graded track on right.
		GPS: N35°06.43′ W115°03°11′
▼ 3.1	SO	Track on right and track on left.
3.7 ▲	SO	Track on left and track on right.
		GPS: N35°06.64′ W115°04.08′
▼ 4.0	SO	Cross through wash.
2.8 ▲	SO	Cross through wash.
▼ 4.1	SO	Track on left and track on right.
2.7 ▲	SO	Track on left and track on right.
▼ 4.5	SO	4-way intersection with graded road. Remain on formed trail.
2.3 ▲	SO	4-way intersection with graded road. Remain on formed trail.
		GPS: N35°06.88′ W115°05.59′
▼ 4.9	SO	Cross through wash.

1.9 ▲ SO Cross through wash.

▼ 5.3 SO Dip; then cross through wash.
1.5 ▲ SO Cross through wash; then dip.

▼ 5.8 SO Track on right to old bus and shelter.
1.0 ▲ SO Track on left to old bus and shelter.

GPS: N35°07.13' W115°06.88'

▼ 6.0 SO Track on right and track on left.
0.8 ▲ SO Track on right and track on left.

▼ 6.6 TR T-intersection at fence line.
0.2 ▲ TL Leave fence. Track continues straight ahead.

GPS: N35°07.34' W115°07.72'

▼ 6.8 TL T-intersection at corner of fence. Track on right. Zero trip meter.
0.0 ▲ Continue to the south.

GPS: N35°07.58' W115°07.71'

▼ 0.0 Continue to the west.
3.3 ▲ TR Turn right at corner of fence, remaining alongside fence line. Track continues ahead. Zero trip meter.

▼ 0.6 SO Cross through wash.
2.7 ▲ SO Cross through wash.

▼ 0.9 BR Bear right at cairns onto well-used, but eroded trail. Track continues along fence line.
2.4 ▲ SO Track on right at cairns. Continue alongside fence line.

GPS: N35°07.60' W115°08.72'

▼ 1.6 BR Track on right; then immediately bear right at cairn past track on left.
1.7 ▲ BR Track on right; then immediately bear right at cairn past track on left.

GPS: N35°07.78' W115°09.39'

▼ 2.0 SO Track on left and track on right.
1.3 ▲ SO Track on left and track on right.

GPS: N35°07.89' W115°09.86'

▼ 3.3 SO Cross over wide, graded Lanfair Road. Zero trip meter and continue on small formed trail.
0.0 ▲ Continue to the east.

GPS: N35°08.32' W115°11.16'

▼ 0.0 Continue to the west.
6.7 ▲ SO Cross over wide, graded Lanfair Road. Zero trip meter and continue on small formed trail.

▼ 1.3 SO Cross through wash. Grotto Hills are on the right.
5.4 ▲ SO Cross through wash. Grotto Hills are on the left.

▼ 1.7 SO Track on right.
5.0 ▲ SO Track on left.

▼ 1.9 SO Graded road on right and left.
4.8 ▲ SO Graded road on right and left.

GPS: N35°08.37' W115°13.19'

▼ 2.0 SO Cross through wash.
4.7 ▲ SO Cross through wash.

▼ 3.8 SO Well-used track on right and left.
2.9 ▲ SO Well-used track on right and left.

GPS: N35°08.40' W115°15.30'

▼ 3.9 SO Track on right to stone cabin on private property.
2.8 ▲ SO Track on left to stone cabin on private property.

GPS: N35°08.41' W115°15.40'

▼ 5.9 SO Dam on left.
0.8 ▲ SO Dam on right.

▼ 6.3 SO Cross through wash. Track on right and track on left up and down wash.
0.4 ▲ SO Cross through wash. Track on left and track on right up and down wash.

▼ 6.7 BR Bear right onto wide, graded Cedar Canyon Road. Zero trip meter.
0.0 ▲ Continue to the northeast.

GPS: N35°08.74' W115°18.47'

▼ 0.0 Continue to the west on graded road. Immediately track on right.
1.6 ▲ BL Track on left; then bear left onto well-used, formed trail and zero trip meter.

▼ 0.4 BL Bear left onto small, formed trail marked by a cairn.
1.2 ▲ BR Bear right onto wide, graded Cedar Canyon Road.

GPS: N35°08.85' W115°18.84'

▼ 0.5 SO Start to descend to Watson Wash.
1.1 ▲ SO Climb out of Watson Wash.

▼ 0.8 BR Bear right up Watson Wash.
0.8 ▲ BL Bear left out of wash and climb toward Cedar Canyon Road.

▼ 1.3 BR Bear right out of main wash. Looking to the left at this point you can see Rock Spring Cabin on top of the ridge above the wash. Immediately turn left. A BLM information board can be seen on the left.
0.3 ▲ BL Turn right at T-intersection; then immediately bear left down main Watson Wash.

GPS: N35°09.18' W115°19.60'

▼ 1.4 SO Parking area and information board on left for Camp Rock Spring; then track on right.
0.2 ▲ BR Track on left; then parking area and information board on right for Camp Rock Spring.

GPS: N35°09.20' W115°19.63'

▼ 1.5 TL Join graded Cedar Canyon Road and turn left.
0.1 ▲ TR Turn right onto small formed trail down Watson Wash.

GPS: N35°09.37' W115°19.74'

▼ 1.6 SO Track on right is Desert #15: New York Mountains Trail. The two trails both follow Cedar Canyon Road for a short distance. Zero trip meter.
0.0 ▲ Continue to the east.

GPS: N35°09.43' W115°19.90'

▼ 0.0 Continue to the west.
2.2 ▲ SO Track on left is Desert #15: New York Mountains Trail, which leaves to the north at this point. Zero trip meter.

▼ 0.1 BL Bear left onto smaller graded road. The intersection is unmarked.
2.1 ▲ SO Join wide, graded Cedar Canyon Road.

GPS: N35°09.39' W115°20.08'

▼ 0.3 SO 4-way intersection. Track on left goes to old stone cabin above Rock Spring; then second track on left.
1.8 ▲ SO Track on right; then 4-way intersection. Track on right goes to old stone cabin above Rock Spring.

GPS: N35°09.33' W115°20.15'

▼ 0.7 SO Cross through wash.
1.5 ▲ SO Cross through wash.

GPS: N35°09.23' W115°20.57'

▼ 1.1 SO Track on left.
1.1 ▲ SO Track on right.

▼ 1.4 BL Track on right. Track on left goes to the Barnett Mine; then second track on right.
0.8 ▲ SO Track on left. Track on right goes to the Barnett Mine; then second track on left.

▼ 1.6 SO Track on left.
0.6 ▲ SO Track on right.

▼ 1.7 TR Track on left is private road. Well, tank, and corral at Government Holes.

0.5 ▲	TL	Track on right is private road. Well, tank, and corral at Government Holes.
		GPS: N35°08.84' W115°21.50'
▼ 1.8	BL	Pass through two wire gates; then bear left past small track on right.
0.4 ▲	BR	Small track on left; then bear right and pass through two wire gates.
▼ 1.9	BL	Track on right.
0.3 ▲	BR	Track on left.
▼ 2.1	SO	Cross through wash.
0.1 ▲	SO	Cross through wash.
▼ 2.2	TL	T-intersection with wide graded Cedar Canyon Road. Zero trip meter.
0.0 ▲		Continue to the southeast.
		GPS: N35°09.18' W115°21.68'
▼ 0.0		Continue to the west.
3.3 ▲	TR	Turn right onto small formed trail, leaving Cedar Canyon Road. Intersection is unmarked. Zero trip meter.
▼ 0.1	SO	Track on right.
3.2 ▲	SO	Track on left.
▼ 0.3	SO	Track on right; then cattle guard.
3.0 ▲	SO	Cattle guard; then track on left.
▼ 0.7	SO	Track on right.
2.6 ▲	SO	Track on left.
▼ 1.7	SO	Track on right; then cattle guard; then second track on right.
1.6 ▲	SO	Track on left; then cattle guard; then second track on left.
▼ 2.4	SO	Track on right.
0.9 ▲	SO	Track on left.
▼ 3.3	SO	Graded road on left is continuation of Desert #15: New York Mountains Trail, which diverges from Mojave Road and follows Black Canyon Road. Zero trip meter.
0.0 ▲		Continue to the northeast.
		GPS: N35°10.45' W115°24.65'
▼ 0.0		Continue to the southwest.
2.8 ▲	SO	Graded road on right is Desert #15: New York Mountains Trail, which joins Mojave Road at this point. Road on right is marked Black Canyon Road. Zero trip meter. Desert #15: New York Mountains Trail now follows Mojave Road for a short distance.
▼ 0.3	SO	Cross through wash.
2.5 ▲	SO	Cross through wash.
▼ 1.3	SO	Pipeline track on left and right.
1.5 ▲	SO	Pipeline track on left and right.
▼ 2.0	SO	Cross through wash.
0.8 ▲	SO	Cross through wash.
▼ 2.2	SO	Track on right joins pipeline road.
0.6 ▲	SO	Track on left joins pipeline road.
▼ 2.7	SO	Track on right.
0.1 ▲	SO	Track on left.
▼ 2.8	SO	Track on right is Desert #17: Nipton Desert Road. Zero trip meter.
0.0 ▲		Continue to the east.
		GPS: N35°09.83' W115°27.41'
▼ 0.0		Continue to the west.
2.9 ▲	SO	Track on left is Desert #17: Nipton Desert Road. Zero trip meter.
▼ 0.3	SO	Track on left.
2.6 ▲	SO	Track on right.
▼ 0.9	SO	Road is paved.
2.0 ▲	SO	Road turns to graded dirt.
▼ 2.2	SO	Track on left.
0.7 ▲	SO	Track on right.
▼ 2.9	SO	Cattle guard; then cross over railroad tracks. Then cross over paved Kelso-Cima Road. There is a historical marker at the intersection. Zero trip meter.
0.0 ▲		Continue to the east on paved road, following sign to Providence Mountain State Recreation Area. Cross over railroad tracks; then cattle guard.
		GPS: N35°10.57' W115°30.48'
▼ 0.0		Continue to the west on formed trail and cross cattle guard.
7.9 ▲	SO	Cattle guard; then cross over paved Kelso-Cima Road. There is a historical marker at the intersection. Zero trip meter.
▼ 0.1	SO	Cattle guard.
7.8 ▲	SO	Cattle guard.
▼ 0.4	SO	Start to cross through the many-channeled Kelso Wash.
7.5 ▲	SO	End of wash crossings.
▼ 0.8	SO	End of wash crossings.
7.1 ▲	SO	Start to cross through the many-channeled Kelso Wash.
▼ 2.2	SO	Cross through wash.
5.7 ▲	SO	Cross through wash.
		GPS: N35°10.71' W115°31.28'
▼ 4.5	SO	Track on left.
3.4 ▲	SO	Track on right.
▼ 5.1	BL	Track on right.
2.8 ▲	BR	Track on left.
		GPS: N35°11.32' W115°35.97'
▼ 5.9	SO	Track on left.
2.0 ▲	SO	Track on right.
▼ 7.1	SO	Track on left and track on right along power line.
0.8 ▲	SO	Track on left and track on right along power line.
		GPS: N35°10.51' W115°37.99'
▼ 7.9	TR	Track on left goes 0.1 miles to Marl Spring. Zero trip meter.
0.0 ▲		Continue to the northeast
		GPS: N35°10.20' W115°38.77'
▼ 0.0		Continue to the north.
3.2 ▲	TL	T-intersection. Track on right goes 0.1 miles to Marl Spring. Zero trip meter.
▼ 0.1	SO	Stone foundations on left.
3.1 ▲	SO	Stone foundations on right.
		GPS: N35°10.24' W115°38.77'
▼ 1.5	SO	Track on left and track on right under power lines.
1.7 ▲	SO	Track on left and track on right under power lines.
		GPS: N35°11.00' W115°39.79'
▼ 3.2	SO	Mojave Road visitors book on right on a metal post. Zero trip meter.
0.0 ▲		Continue to the northeast.
		GPS: N35°11.12' W115°41.52'
▼ 0.0		Continue to the southwest.
4.8 ▲	SO	Mojave Road visitors book on left on a metal post. Zero trip meter.
▼ 0.2	SO	Cattle guard.
4.6 ▲	SO	Cattle guard.
▼ 0.5	SO	Cattle guard.
4.3 ▲	SO	Cattle guard.
		GPS: N35°11.01' W115°42.06'

▼ 4.8 SO Trail crosses graded dirt Aikens Mine Road, part of Desert #18: Cima Dome Trail. Zero trip meter.
0.0 ▲ Continue to the east

GPS: N35°10.38' W115°46.61'

▼ 0.0 Continue to the west.
6.2 ▲ SO Trail crosses graded dirt Aikens Mine Road, part of Desert #18: Cima Dome Trail. Zero trip meter.

▼ 0.3 SO Enter line of Willow Wash.
5.9 ▲ SO Exit line of Willow Wash.

▼ 1.2 BL Trail forks, but rejoins in a short distance.
5.0 ▲ BR Trail forks, but rejoins in a short distance.

GPS: N35°09.84' W115°47.73'

▼ 2.7 SO Track on left and track on right.
3.5 ▲ SO Track on left and track on right.

GPS: N35°10.13' W115°49.24'

▼ 4.7 SO Track on right and track on left.
1.5 ▲ SO Track on left and track on right.

GPS: N35°11.07' W115°51.04'

▼ 6.2 SO Cross over paved Kelbaker Road and zero trip meter. Intersection has small cairns marking it. Baker, which has fuel, food, and accommodations, is approximately 14 miles to the right.
0.0 ▲ Continue to the southeast.

GPS: N35°11.94' W115°52.29'

▼ 0.0 Continue to the northwest.
6.0 ▲ SO Cross over paved Kelbaker Road and zero trip meter. Intersection has small cairns marking it. Baker, which has fuel, food, and accommodations, is approximately 14 miles to the left.

▼ 1.2 SO Track on left.
4.8 ▲ SO Track on right.

▼ 2.0 SO Track on right.
4.0 ▲ BR Track on left.

▼ 2.4 SO Exit line of wash.
3.6 ▲ SO Enter line of wash.

▼ 3.7 SO Tank Nine—few scattered remains.
2.3 ▲ SO Tank Nine—few scattered remains.

GPS: N35°12.50' W115°55.12'

▼ 3.8 SO Track on left to Brannigan Mine and track on right.
2.2 ▲ SO Track on right to Brannigan Mine and track on left.

▼ 6.0 SO Track on left and track on right at old tank is Jackass Canyon Road (also referred to as Kelso Road on some maps). Zero trip meter.
0.0 ▲ Continue to the northeast.

GPS: N35°11.21' W115°57.18'

▼ 0.0 Continue to the southwest.
4.6 ▲ SO Track on left and track on right at old tank is Jackass Canyon Road (also referred to as Kelso Road on some maps). Zero trip meter.

▼ 2.0 SO Well-used track on right.
2.6 ▲ BR Well-used track on left.

GPS: N35°10.15' W115°58.94'

▼ 2.6 SO Track on left and track on right.
2.0 ▲ SO Track on left and track on right.

▼ 2.7 SO Track on right.
1.9 ▲ SO Track on left.

▼ 3.0 SO Well-used track on left. Cowhole Mountain on left and Little Cowhole Mountain on right.
1.6 ▲ SO Well-used track on right. Cowhole Mountain on right and Little Cowhole Mountain on left.

GPS: N35°09.83' W115°59.92'

▼ 3.6 SO Two tracks on right.
1.0 ▲ BR Two tracks on left.

GPS: N35°09.71' W116°00.58'

▼ 3.7 SO Well-used road on left.
0.9 ▲ BL Well-used road on right.

GPS: N35°09.69' W115°00.67'

▼ 3.8 BL Well-used road on right.
0.8 ▲ SO Well-used road on left.

▼ 4.0 BL Track on right.
0.6 ▲ SO Track on left.

▼ 4.3 SO Track on right.
0.3 ▲ SO Track on left.

▼ 4.6 SO Well-used track on right is alternate exit to Baker, should Soda Lake be impassable. Zero trip meter. Cross cattle guard and pass through Volunteer Gate.
0.0 ▲ Continue to the northeast.

GPS: N35°09.48' W116°01.65'

Alternate Exit via Baker (Avoids Soda Lake)

▼ 0.0 From the east side of Volunteer Gate, on the eastern edge of Soda Lake, zero trip meter and proceed northeast on well-used track.
7.6 ▲ Trail joins Mojave Road. Turn right to cross Soda Lake; turn left for Kelbaker Road.

▼ 0.4 BL Bear left after corral. Track on right and mine on right.
7.2 ▲ BR Bear right at corral. Track on left and mine on left.

GPS: N35°09.76' W116°01.79'

▼ 0.6 SO Start to cross dry bed of Soda Lake. This trail stays close to the edge.
7.0 ▲ SO Exit lakebed.

▼ 1.3 SO Exit lakebed. Fence line is now on left.
6.3 ▲ SO Start to cross dry bed of Soda Lake. This trail stays close to the edge.

GPS: N35°10.48' W116°02.29'

▼ 2.8 SO Well-used track on left and track on right.
4.8 ▲ SO Well-used track on right and track on left.

GPS: N35°11.81' W116°02.30'

▼ 3.4 SO Cross through wash.
4.2 ▲ SO Cross through wash.

▼ 3.9 SO 4-way intersection with graded road.
3.7 ▲ SO 4-way intersection with graded road.

GPS: N35°12.85' W116°02.29'

▼ 4.1 SO Cross through wash.
3.5 ▲ SO Cross through wash.

▼ 4.5 SO Cross through wash.
3.1 ▲ SO Cross through wash.

▼ 4.6 BL Track on right.
3.0 ▲ SO Track on left.

GPS: N35°13.45' W116°02.34'

▼ 4.7 SO Track on right; then wire gate.
2.9 ▲ SO Wire gate; then track on left.

▼ 5.5 SO Cross through wash.
2.1 ▲ SO Cross through wash.

▼ 5.7 SO Track on right along fence line. Continue straight ahead with fence on right.
1.9 ▲ SO Track on left along fence line. Leave fence line.

▼ 6.0 SO Track on left.
1.6 ▲ SO Track on right.

▼ 6.2 SO Graded road on right into works area. Join graded road heading toward Baker.
1.4 ▲ BR Bear right onto smaller graded road. Road on left goes into works area.

GPS: N35°14.14′ W116°03.73′

▼ 6.4 SO Track on left.
1.2 ▲ SO Track on right.

▼ 6.8 SO Track on left and track on right along pipeline.
0.8 ▲ SO Track on left and track on right along pipeline.

▼ 7.6 TL Turn left onto paved Kelbaker Road. Zero trip meter.
0.0 ▲ Continue to the south.

GPS: N35°15.40′ W116°03.42′

▼ 0.0 Continue to the west.
0.8 ▲ TR Turn right onto wide graded road. Zero trip meter.

▼ 0.8 Exit route finishes at east side of I-15 on the edge of Baker. Proceed 11 miles west on I-15 to Rasor Road exit. Continue south on Rasor Road for 5.1 miles to rejoin Mojave Road west of Soda Lake. Mojave Road cannot be accessed via Zzyzx Spring (also called Soda Spring).
0.0 Alternate route around Soda Lake starts in Baker at the east side of I-15 at the Kelbaker Road exit. Zero trip meter and proceed east on paved Kelbaker Road.

GPS: N35°15.74′ W116°04.28′

Continuation of Main Trail

▼ 0.0 Continue to the southwest.
5.9 ▲ SO Cattle guard and Volunteer Gate; then well-used track on left is alternate exit to Baker. Zero trip meter.

GPS: N35°09.48′ W116°01.65′

▼ 0.3 SO Start to cross Soda Lake bed.
5.6 ▲ SO Leave Soda Lake bed.

GPS: N35°08.87′ W116°03.67′

▼ 2.9 SO Cross through channel.
3.0 ▲ SO Cross through channel.

GPS: N35°08.54′ W116°04.35′

▼ 3.1 SO Cross through channel.
2.8 ▲ SO Cross through channel.

GPS: N35°08.45′ W116°04.52′

▼ 3.4 SO Cross through channel.
2.5 ▲ SO Cross through channel.

▼ 4.3 SO Travelers or Government Cairn—large cairn in the middle of Soda Lake. Zzyzx Spring can be seen surrounded by palm trees behind the monument to the north.
1.6 ▲ SO Travelers or Government Cairn—large cairn in the middle of Soda Lake. Zzyzx Spring can be seen surrounded by palm trees behind the monument to the north.

GPS: N35°07.85′ W116°05.67′

▼ 5.6 BR Bear right at The Granites.
0.3 ▲ BL Bear left at The Granites and proceed across the lakebed.

GPS: N35°07.12′ W116°06.66′

▼ 5.9 SO Track on right goes toward Zzyzx but does not go through to connect to I-15. Track on left is the Tonopah & Tidewater Railroad grade. Exit Soda Lake. Zero trip meter.
0.0 ▲ Continue to the east.

GPS: N35°07.24′ W116°06.87′

▼ 0.0 Continue to the southwest.
1.8 ▲ BR Track on left goes toward Zzyzx but does not go through to I-15. Track on right is the Tonopah & Tidewater Railroad grade. Zero trip meter and start to cross Soda Lake bed.

▼ 0.9 BL Entering Rasor OHV Area at sign; then track on right. Many small tracks on right and left for the next 10.9 miles; only major ones are mentioned. Remain on main trail.
0.9 ▲ SO Track on left; then leaving Rasor OHV Area at sign.

GPS: N35°06.85′ W116°07.60′

▼ 1.8 SO Cross over graded dirt Rasor Road and zero trip meter. I-15 is 5.1 miles to the right. There is gas at the freeway exit.
0.0 ▲ Continue to the northeast.

GPS: N35°06.52′ W116°08.57′

▼ 0.0 Continue to the southwest.
10.0 ▲ SO Cross over graded dirt Rasor Road and zero trip meter. I-15 is 5.1 miles to the left. There is gas at the freeway exit.

▼ 2.1 SO Cross through wash.
7.9 ▲ SO Cross through wash.

▼ 2.3 SO Shaw Pass.
7.7 ▲ SO Shaw Pass.

GPS: N35°05.61′ W116°10.65′

▼ 2.4 SO Start to cross Mojave River floodplain.
7.6 ▲ SO Exit Mojave River floodplain.

▼ 2.5 TL 4-way intersection. Turn left, keeping cairns on your right.
7.5 ▲ TR 4-way intersection. Turn right, keeping cairns on your left.

GPS: N35°05.43′ W116°10.87′

▼ 3.3 SO Entering extremely soft, loose sand.
6.7 ▲ SO Exiting the worst of the soft sand.

▼ 3.5 SO Track on left and track on right. Continue to the southwest, keeping cairns on your right.
6.5 ▲ SO Track on left and track on right. Continue to the northeast, keeping cairns on your left.

GPS: N35°04.58′ W116°10.78′

▼ 3.8 SO Track on left.
6.2 ▲ BL Track on right.

GPS: N35°04.51′ W116°11.11′

▼ 8.6 SO Track on left.
1.4 ▲ SO Track on right.

GPS: N35°03.92′ W116°16.03′

▼ 10.0 SO Trail crosses graded dirt Basin Road. I-15 is 3.6 miles to the right. Continue straight ahead and zero trip meter. Leaving Rasor OHV Area. Intersection is marked by cairns.
0.0 ▲ Continue to the east and enter Rasor OHV Area. Many small tracks on right and left for the next 10.9 miles. Keep cairns on left and remain on main trail.

GPS: N35°03.10′ W116°17.17′

▼ 0.0 Continue to the west.
6.7 ▲ SO Trail crosses graded dirt Basin Road. I-15 is 3.6 miles to the left. Continue straight ahead and zero trip meter. Intersection is marked by cairns.

▼ 0.2 SO Ford through the Mojave River.
6.5 ▲ SO Ford through the Mojave River.

GPS: N35°03.09′ W116°17.34′

▼ 0.6 SO Track on right to mine remains.
6.1 ▲ SO Track on left to mine remains.

GPS: N35°02.92′ W116°17.76′

▼ 0.9 SO Track on right to mine. Mining remains on right.
5.8 ▲ BR Track on left to mine. Mining remains on left.

GPS: N35°02.78′ W116°18.09′

▼ 1.0 TR Ford through Mojave River; then turn right.
5.7 ▲ TL Turn left; then ford through the Mojave River.

▼ 1.2 SO Ford through Mojave River.
5.5 ▲ SO Ford through Mojave River.

▼ 1.5 SO Track on left and track on right. Ford through the Mojave River; then pass under railroad bridge and enter the start of Afton Canyon. The route is marked by BLM open route markers past this point.
5.2 ▲ SO Pass under railroad bridge and exit Afton Canyon. Ford through the Mojave River; then track on left and track on right.

GPS: N35°02.55′ W116°18.50′

▼ 1.6 SO Track on left and track on right.
5.1 ▲ SO Track on left and track on right.

▼ 2.1 SO Canyon walls start to narrow. Many crossings of the Mojave River channel for the next 4.6 miles.
4.6 ▲ SO Canyon starts to widen. End of the many crossings of the Mojave River channel.

▼ 4.9 SO Track on left.
1.8 ▲ SO Track on right.

▼ 5.0 TL T-intersection with track alongside rail line. Turn left along rail line.
1.7 ▲ TR Turn right away from rail line.

GPS: N35°01.56′ W116°21.55′

▼ 5.4 SO Pull-in on left. Trail is now directly alongside rail line.
1.3 ▲ SO Pull-in on right.

▼ 5.6 SO Ford through the Mojave River. This ford can often be quite deep. The Caves are a 0.5-mile hike to the left. If the growth is low, The Caves can be seen from the road on the northern side of the curve.
1.1 ▲ SO Ford through the Mojave River. This ford can often be quite deep. The Caves are a 0.5-mile hike to the right. If the growth is low, The Caves can be seen from the road on the northern side of the curve.

GPS: N35°01.88′ W116°21.98′

▼ 6.5 BR Bear right away from rail line. Site of Afton Station.
0.2 ▲ SO Join rail line. Site of Afton Station.

▼ 6.6 SO Ford through the Mojave River. This crossing can be quite deep.
0.1 ▲ SO Ford through the Mojave River. This crossing can be quite deep.

▼ 6.7 SO Afton Canyon BLM Campground on right—fee charged. Zero trip meter. Exit Afton Canyon.
0.0 ▲ Continue to the east alongside railroad line and enter Afton Canyon. Many crossings of the Mojave River channel for the next 4.6 miles.

GPS: N35°02.27′ W116°23.00′

▼ 0.0 Continue to the west along graded road.
8.0 ▲ SO Afton Canyon BLM Campground on left—fee charged. Zero trip meter.

▼ 0.3 SO Track on left.
7.7 ▲ SO Track on right.

▼ 0.5 SO Afton Canyon Group Camping Area on left.
7.5 ▲ SO Afton Canyon Group Camping Area on right.

GPS: N35°02.46′ W116°23.38′

▼ 0.7 TL Turn sharp left onto smaller, graded dirt road, following sign for Mojave Road.
7.3 ▲ TR Turn right and join the wide graded dirt road, following sign for Afton Canyon.

GPS: N35°02.49′ W116°23.58′

▼ 0.8 SO Pass under rail line. Track on right and track on left along rail line; then pass through gate into wildlife viewing area. Enter Mojave River wash.
7.2 ▲ SO Pass through gate, exiting the Mojave River wash and wildlife viewing area. Track on right and track on left along rail line; then pass under rail line.

▼ 7.1 SO Track on left.
0.9 ▲ SO Track on right.

GPS: N34°59.79′ W116°28.47′

▼ 8.0 SO Track on right is spur to the Triangle Intaglios. Intersection is marked by a cairn with a railroad sleeper placed vertically in the middle of it. Zero trip meter.
0.0 ▲ Continue to the northeast.

GPS: N34°59.13′ W116°28.78′

Spur to Triangle Intaglios

▼ 0.0 Proceed to the west.
▼ 0.2 SO Track on left and track on right.
▼ 0.3 UT Turning circle. Park here and hike to the top of the mesa above the Mojave River wash, up the small gully to the southeast of the parking area. The intaglios are protected by a barrier on top of the mesa. There are approximately 20 intaglios. The largest are 10 feet long and 6 feet wide. All are triangular in shape.

GPS: N34°59.23′ W116°29.08′

Continuation of Main Trail

▼ 0.0 Continue to the southwest.
7.5 ▲ SO Track on left is spur to the Triangle Intaglios. Intersection is marked by a cairn with a railroad sleeper placed vertically in the middle of it. Zero trip meter.

GPS: N34°59.13′ W116°28.78′

▼ 3.9 BR Track swings west up Manix Wash, leaving the Mojave River wash.
3.6 ▲ BL Track swings northeast down Mojave River wash, leaving Manix Wash.

GPS: N34°58.46′ W116°32.32′

▼ 4.6 SO Track on right.
2.9 ▲ SO Track on left.

▼ 5.4 SO Track on left and track on right. Pass under power lines.
2.1 ▲ SO Track on left and track on right. Pass under power lines.

GPS: N34°59.21′ W116°33.54′

▼ 5.9 SO Exit Manix Wash.
1.6 ▲ SO Enter down Manix Wash.

▼ 6.0 SO Pass through wire gate.
1.5 ▲ SO Pass through wire gate.

GPS: N34°59.40′ W116°34.16′

▼ 6.1 BR Track on left.
1.4 ▲ SO Track on right.

▼ 6.3 SO Track on left.
1.2 ▲ BL Track on right.

▼ 7.1 SO Track on right along rail line. Continue along rail line.
0.4 ▲ BR Track continues along rail line. Bear right, leaving the rail line.

GPS: N34°59.04′ W116°35.31′

▼ 7.4 TR 4-way intersection with graded dirt Alvord Mountain Road. Turn right and cross over rail line. This is Manix.
0.1 ▲ TL Cross over rail line and immediately turn left,

running alongside the rail line. This is Manix.

GPS: N34°58.90' W116°35°62'

▼ 7.5		TL	T-intersection with paved Yermo Road. Zero trip meter.
	0.0 ▲		Continue to the southeast.

GPS: N34°58.93' W116°35.65'

▼ 0.0			Continue to the southwest, remaining on paved road.
	3.1 ▲	TR	Turn right onto graded dirt Alvord Mountain Road and zero trip meter.
▼ 3.1			Trail ends at intersection of Yermo Road and Harvard Road, on the south side of I-15 at the Harvard Road exit.
	0.0 ▲		Trail commences at the Harvard Road exit of I-15, 24 miles east of Barstow. Proceed to the south side of the freeway at the intersection of Harvard Road and Yermo Road. Zero trip meter and proceed northeast on paved Yermo Road. Remain on paved road.

GPS: N34°57.64' W116°38.63'

DESERT #14

East Lanfair Valley Trail

Starting Point:	**Route 66 at Goffs**
Finishing Point:	**Nevada 164, 1.1 miles west of intersection with US 95 in Searchlight, NV**
Total Mileage:	**49.1 miles**
Unpaved Mileage:	**48.3 miles**
Driving Time:	**5.5 hours**
Elevation Range:	**2,600–4,500 feet**
Usually Open:	**Year-round**
Best Time to Travel:	**September to May**
Difficulty Rating:	**4**
Scenic Rating:	**9**
Remoteness Rating:	**+1**

Special Attractions

- Extensive remains of the Leiser Ray Mine.
- Remote, lightly traveled trail within the Mojave National Preserve.
- Piute Gorge.
- Intersects with historic Desert #13: Mojave Road.

History

Many nineteenth-century opportunists who pushed west through the much-avoided desert regions were mining prospectors. Travelers had no real intention of settling the harsh deserts and were wary of the problems associated with Indians who frequented the regions.

Searchlight, Nevada, at the northern end of this trail, was an important camp during the early development of this region. Mineral deposits were promising. Summit Springs, located 3.5 miles east of Searchlight, was the district name and location marker for claims in the area. The earliest working

Mill foundations at the Leiser Ray Mine

mines here were the Red Iron Claim and the Bowland Tunnels. In 1896 and 1897, John C. Swickard located and claimed the Golden Treasure and Copper King Mines, which were to become part of the Quartette Mining Company, the largest gold producer in Searchlight. On January 4, 1898, Mr. Colton and A. E. Moore located the Searchlight Claim, after which the mining district and camp were eventually named. The district produced gold, silver, copper, and lead. At the Quartette Mine, just south of this trail in Searchlight, ore values averaged $3.80 per ton for the first 100 feet. However, down at 700 feet, some ore assayed at $1,335.00 per ton. The Quartette's shaft went to 1,167 feet, and the length of the workings totaled 5.5 miles. Lumber and stone supports were used throughout.

The greatest mining activity in Searchlight took place between 1902 and 1916. There were more than 300 mining claims in 1906. A brief boom occurred in the early 1930s with a high-grade strike at the Cyrus Noble Mine. From 1902 to 1959, 246,997 ounces of gold were extracted from lode mines and 26 ounces from placer mines.

In 1902, the Quartette built a 20-stamp mill on the Colorado River with a 12-mile narrow gauge railroad connecting it to the mine site. The railroad also carried passengers from the mine to steamboats on the Colorado River. In 1906, the mill was moved to the mine site and the rails were sold. In the Searchlight District, water flooded the shafts around the 250-foot depth, which provided ample water for onsite processing. During a down time in 1904, the Duplex alone accumulated 350,000 gallons of water in its shaft. After 1906, the Quartette had enough water to operate a 40-stamp mill at the mine. It was one of the first mills in Nevada to use cyanide processing. The Quartette Mill burned down in 1913.

Searchlight became more connected with the outside world in 1907. Trains were already operating from Goffs to Barnwell when the Atchison, Topeka & Santa Fe linked Barnwell and Searchlight in April 1907. At its peak, daily railroad services operated from Goffs, north up Lanfair Valley, to Barnwell. From there trains continued to Searchlight

The original Goffs Schoolhouse is now a regional museum

every day except Sundays. This line operated until 1924.

Searchlight's other main industry was cattle ranching. Two roundups a year took place—one in spring to get new calves for branding and the other in fall to separate animals for sale. In the 1920s, the Kennedy family's ranching endeavors extended from Hole-in-the-Wall in the eastern Mojave Desert to the Newberry Mountains and Cottonwood Island.

Goffs was one of several locations used as a military training camp during World War II. Military units spent three months here before other units arrived for training. General Patton thought this vast region accommodated the need for realistic maneuvers. Goffs was a hive of activity during the war years. Troops and vehicles obliterated almost everything in their paths. Only lines of stones were visible between tents and roadways, some of which remain to this day. A visit to the restored Goffs Schoolhouse, with its unusual architecture and its information on life in the California desert over the centuries, will answer almost any question that may occur to travelers along this trail.

The Lanfair Valley was named in 1910 for Ernest Lanfair, a merchant from Searchlight who used his real estate connections to exploit the valley. He constructed a windmill to pump water in this seemingly dry valley and sold many acres to hopeful homesteaders. Whether he added water when would-be buyers appeared is debatable. However, the impression was that the land held water not far below the surface and thus the land sold.

Description

East Lanfair Valley Trail crosses the Mojave National Preserve in a south to north direction, intersecting with Desert #13: Mojave Road, which travels east to west. The small formed trail is well defined for most of its length as it travels from Goffs, California, to Searchlight, Nevada.

The trail begins in Goffs and immediately passes the historic Goffs Schoolhouse, recently renovated and open to the public on occasion. Once the trail enters the Mojave National Preserve, it turns off onto a small, sandy trail that travels north toward the prominent Signal Hill.

One interesting feature along the trail is the remains of the Leiser Ray Mine. Several diggings, concrete foundations, and stone walls remain. The trail north of the mine is lightly used. Many travelers swing east at this point, but the trail described here continues north, following wash lines and ridges to intersect with Desert #13: Mojave Road. The two trails follow the same route for 0.5 miles before Mojave Road continues west and East Lanfair Valley Trail continues north.

The Piute Range is now the dominant feature on the eastern side. A short spur leads 0.6 miles to the western end of the Fort Piute/Piute Spring Hiking Corridor. This hiking trail connects with Fort Piute on the eastern side of the ridge. It is a moderately strenuous but rewarding hike. The vehicle turnaround at the end of the spur offers a panoramic view of the Piute Range and the vast Lanfair Valley.

The main trail continues north and skirts Piute Gorge. There are some excellent campsites on the rim of the gorge, but they have no shade and no windbreaks. However, the view more than makes up for the exposure.

Past the gorge, the trail is lightly used as it winds through abundant vegetation. Tight twists and turns make for slow travel. The trail emerges onto a small graded road at the southern end of the New York Mountains. It then turns east, following the formed trail through the Castle Mountains into Nevada. The trail here is well defined but rocky and eroded in places; it is the 4-rated section of the trail. The remainder of the trail is rated 2 to 3 for difficulty. The latter part of the trail meanders along washes and among large boulders past some of the most spectacular scenery along its length.

The trail crosses into Nevada at Stray Cow Well. The state line is marked by a white post, but no sign. From here, it follows a variety of rough trails down the bajada toward Searchlight. The final section follows the old railroad grade. Sections along this part of the trail are very moguled; wheel articulation and side tilt angles will be tested along this stretch.

Piute Gorge

Current Road Information

Mojave National Preserve
PO Box 241
72157 Baker Boulevard
Baker, CA 92309
(760) 733-4040

Map References

BLM Amboy, Ivanpah, Davis Dam
USGS 1:24,000 Goffs, Signal Hill, East of Grotto Hills, Hart Peak, Tenmile Well, Hopps Well, Searchlight (NV)
1:100,000 Amboy, Ivanpah, Davis Dam
Maptech CD-ROM: San Bernardino County/Mojave
Southern & Central California Atlas & Gazetteer, pp. 86, 72
Nevada Atlas & Gazetteer, p. 72
California Road & Recreation Atlas, pp. 98, 107
Trails Illustrated, Mojave National Preserve (256)

Route Directions

▼ 0.0 From National Trails Highway (Route 66) at the north side of the railroad crossing in Goffs, turn north on paved Lanfair Road and zero trip meter.
3.3 ▲ Trail ends on National Trails Highway (Route 66) in Goffs. Turn left for US 95 and Needles; turn right for Fenner and I-40.

GPS: N34°55.18' W115°03.89'

▼ 0.1 SO Goffs Schoolhouse on left.
3.2 ▲ SO Goffs Schoolhouse on right.

▼ 0.4 SO Cattle guard.
2.9 ▲ SO Cattle guard.

▼ 0.7 SO Entering Mojave National Preserve.
2.6 ▲ SO Leaving Mojave National Preserve.

GPS: N34°55.74' W115°04.20'

▼ 0.8 TR Turn right off paved road onto small formed trail. There is a track opposite to the left. Immediately track on right.
2.5 ▲ TL Track on left; then turn left and join paved Lanfair Road. There is a track straight ahead.

GPS: N34°55.77' W115°04.22'

▼ 1.7 TL Turn left onto formed trail. There is a cairn at the intersection. Track continues ahead.
1.6 ▲ TR T-intersection. Turn right onto formed trail. There is a cairn at the intersection.

GPS: N34°56.41' W115°03.54'

▼ 2.8 SO Small track on right.
0.5 ▲ SO Small track on left.

▼ 3.3 SO Track on right and track on left under power lines. Zero trip meter and continue straight ahead on formed trail.
0.0 ▲ Continue to the south.

GPS: N34°57.71' W115°03.21'

▼ 0.0 Continue to the north.
4.7 ▲ SO Track on right and track on left under power lines. Zero trip meter and continue straight ahead on formed trail.

▼ 0.5 SO Cross through wash.
4.2 ▲ SO Cross through wash.

▼ 0.6 SO Cross through Sacramento Wash.
4.1 ▲ SO Cross through Sacramento Wash.

▼ 0.7 SO Cross through wash.
4.0 ▲ SO Cross through wash.

▼ 2.6 SO Track on left to US Arbor Mine.
2.1 ▲ SO Track on right to US Arbor Mine.

GPS: N34°59.81' W115°02.19'

▼ 2.8 SO Small track on left.
1.9 ▲ SO Small track on right.

▼ 3.5 SO Small track on left.
1.2 ▲ SO Small track on right.

▼ 3.6 SO Small track on right.
1.1 ▲ SO Small track on left.

▼ 3.7 SO Track on left.
1.0 ▲ SO Track on right.

▼ 3.9 SO Track on right; then cross through wash.
0.8 ▲ SO Cross through wash; then track on left.

GPS: N35°00.99' W115°01.89'

▼ 4.1 SO Cross through wash.
0.6 ▲ SO Cross through wash.

▼ 4.4 BL Bear left up wash.
0.3 ▲ BR Bear right out of wash.

▼ 4.6 SO Track on right into Leiser Ray Mine. Concrete foundations and diggings on right; then track on left and track on right.
0.1 ▲ SO Track on left and track on right; then track on left into Leiser Ray Mine. Concrete foundations and diggings on left.

GPS: N35°01.52' W115°02.03'

▼ 4.7 TL T-intersection in front of second set of concrete foundations. Track on right into mine. Zero trip meter.
0.0 ▲ Continue to the southwest.

GPS: N35°01.63' W115°02.00'

▼ 0.0 Continue to the northwest past track on left.
5.6 ▲ TR Track on right; then turn right in front of concrete foundations of the Leiser Ray Mine. Track straight ahead goes into mine. Zero trip meter.

▼ 0.1 SO Track on right; then enter wash.
5.5 ▲ SO Exit wash; then track on left.

▼ 0.2 SO Well-used track on right out of wash marked by cairn. Remain in wash.
5.4 ▲ SO Well-used track on left out of wash marked by cairn. Remain in wash.

GPS: N35°01.75' W115°02.05'

▼ 0.7 SO Exit wash.
4.9 ▲ SO Enter down wash.

▼ 0.9 SO Track on right to diggings.
4.7 ▲ SO Track on left to diggings.

GPS: N35°02.19' W115°02.55'

▼ 1.7 SO Small track on right.
3.9 ▲ SO Small track on left.

▼ 1.8 SO Track on right to diggings. Billie Mountain is on the left.
3.8 ▲ SO Track on left to diggings. Billie Mountain is on the right.

GPS: N35°02.89' W115°02.76'

▼ 2.0 SO Track on left at diggings.
3.6 ▲ SO Track on right at diggings.

▼ 2.1 SO Track on right.
3.5 ▲ BR Track on left.

▼ 2.3 SO Cross through wash.
3.3 ▲ SO Cross through wash.

▼ 2.4 SO Track on left.
3.2 ▲ SO Track on right.

▼ 2.8 SO Track on right.
2.8 ▲ SO Track on left.

GPS: N35°03.76' W115°02.85'

▼ 3.1 SO Cross through wide Sacramento Wash.

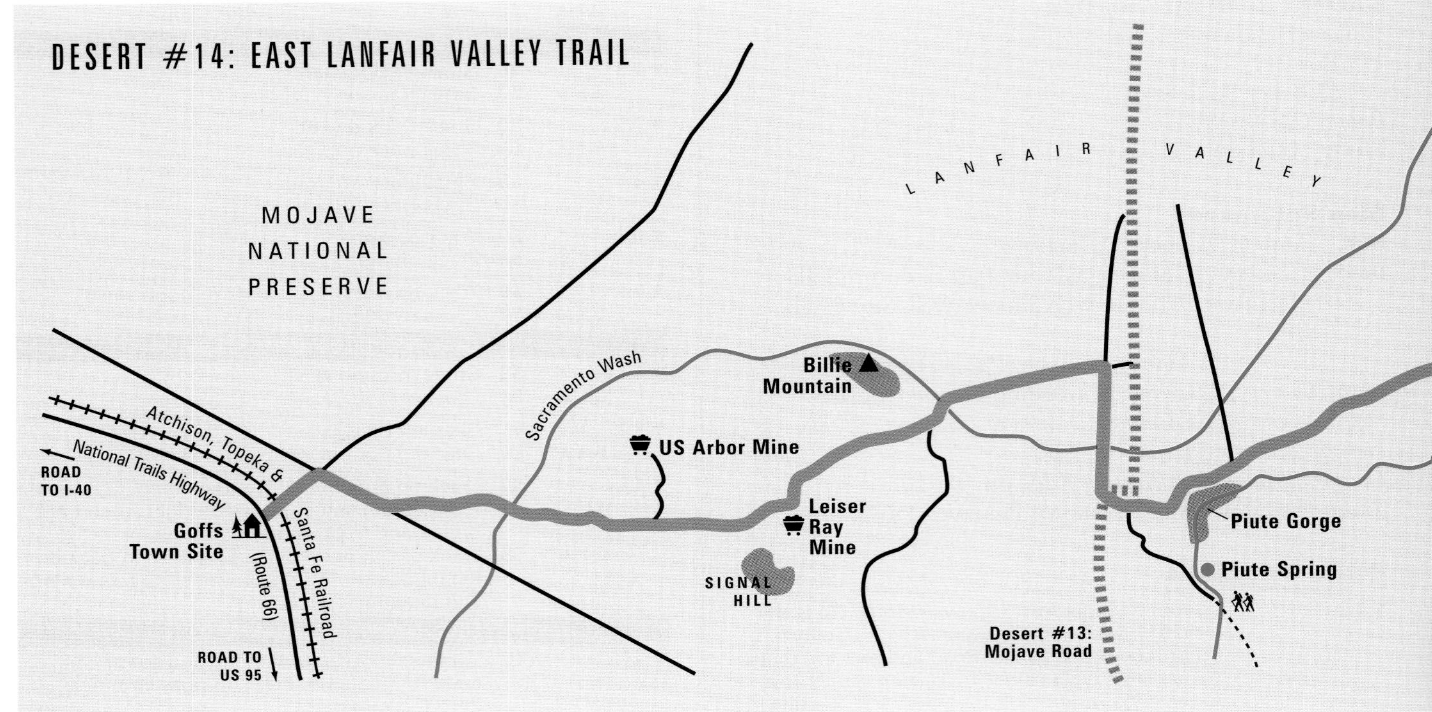

	2.5 ▲	SO	Cross through wide Sacramento Wash.
			GPS: N35°03.99′ W115°03.09′
▼ 3.4		SO	Water tank on left.
	2.2 ▲	SO	Water tank on right.
			GPS: N35°04.22′ W115°03.18′
▼ 4.7		SO	Cattle guard.
	0.9 ▲	SO	Cattle guard.
▼ 5.6		TR	4-way intersection with graded road. Zero trip meter.
	0.0 ▲		Continue to the southeast.
			GPS: N35°06.19′ W115°03.06′
▼ 0.0			Continue to the northeast.
	2.4 ▲	TL	4-way intersection. Zero trip meter and turn onto smaller, graded trail. Intersection is unmarked.
▼ 0.4		SO	Cross through Sacramento Wash.
	2.0 ▲	SO	Cross through Sacramento Wash.
▼ 1.3		SO	Cross through wash.
	1.1 ▲	SO	Cross through wash.
▼ 1.9		TL	Intersection with Desert #13: Mojave Road, which is straight ahead over cattle guard and to the left. Turn left, joining Mojave Road.
	0.5 ▲	TR	T-intersection. Track on left over cattle guard is continuation of Desert #13: Mojave Road. Turn right, leaving Mojave Road.
			GPS: N35°05.68′ W115°01.11′
▼ 2.4		SO	4-way intersection. Track on right is a short spur that goes 0.6 miles to the top of Piute Hill and the start of Fort Piute/Piute Spring Hiking Corridor. Intersection is marked by stone cairns. Track on left is continuation of Desert #13: Mojave Road, which leaves East Lanfair Valley Trail at this point. Zero trip meter.
	0.0 ▲		Continue to the south.
			GPS: N35°05.98′ W115°00.78′
▼ 0.0			Continue to the north.
	9.9 ▲	SO	4-way intersection. Track on left is a short spur that goes 0.6 miles to the top of Piute Hill and the Fort Piute/Piute Spring Hiking Corridor. Track on right is Desert #13: Mojave Road, which joins East Lanfair Valley Trail at this point. Intersection is marked by stone cairns. Zero trip meter.
▼ 0.3		SO	Corral on left.
	9.6 ▲	SO	Corral on right.
▼ 0.6		BL	Track on right on the edge of Piute Gorge.
	9.3 ▲	SO	Second entrance to track on left.
▼ 0.7		SO	Second entrance to track on right.
	9.2 ▲	BR	Track on left on the edge of Piute Gorge.
			GPS: N35°06.55′ W115°00.56′
▼ 0.9		SO	Campsite on right on the edge of Piute Gorge. Viewpoint over gorge.
	9.0 ▲	SO	Campsite on left on the edge of Piute Gorge. Viewpoint over gorge.
▼ 1.4		SO	Track on right.
	8.5 ▲	SO	Track on left.
▼ 1.9		SO	Track on right.
	8.0 ▲	SO	Track on left.
▼ 2.0		BR	Well-used track on left.
	7.9 ▲	SO	Well-used track on right.
			GPS: N35°07.49′ W115°01.00′
▼ 2.9		SO	Track on right.
	7.0 ▲	SO	Track on left.
▼ 3.0		SO	Track on right.
	6.9 ▲	SO	Track on left.
▼ 3.2		SO	Well-used track on right.
	6.7 ▲	SO	Well-used track on left.
			GPS: N35°08.52′ W115°01.23′
▼ 5.3		SO	Pass through wire gate.
	4.6 ▲	SO	Pass through wire gate.
			GPS: N35°10.29′ W115°01.78′
▼ 8.1		BR	Track on left. Bear right to pass alongside dam.
	1.8 ▲	SO	Track on right rejoins.
			GPS: N35°12.70′ W115°02.28′
▼ 8.4		SO	Track on left rejoins.

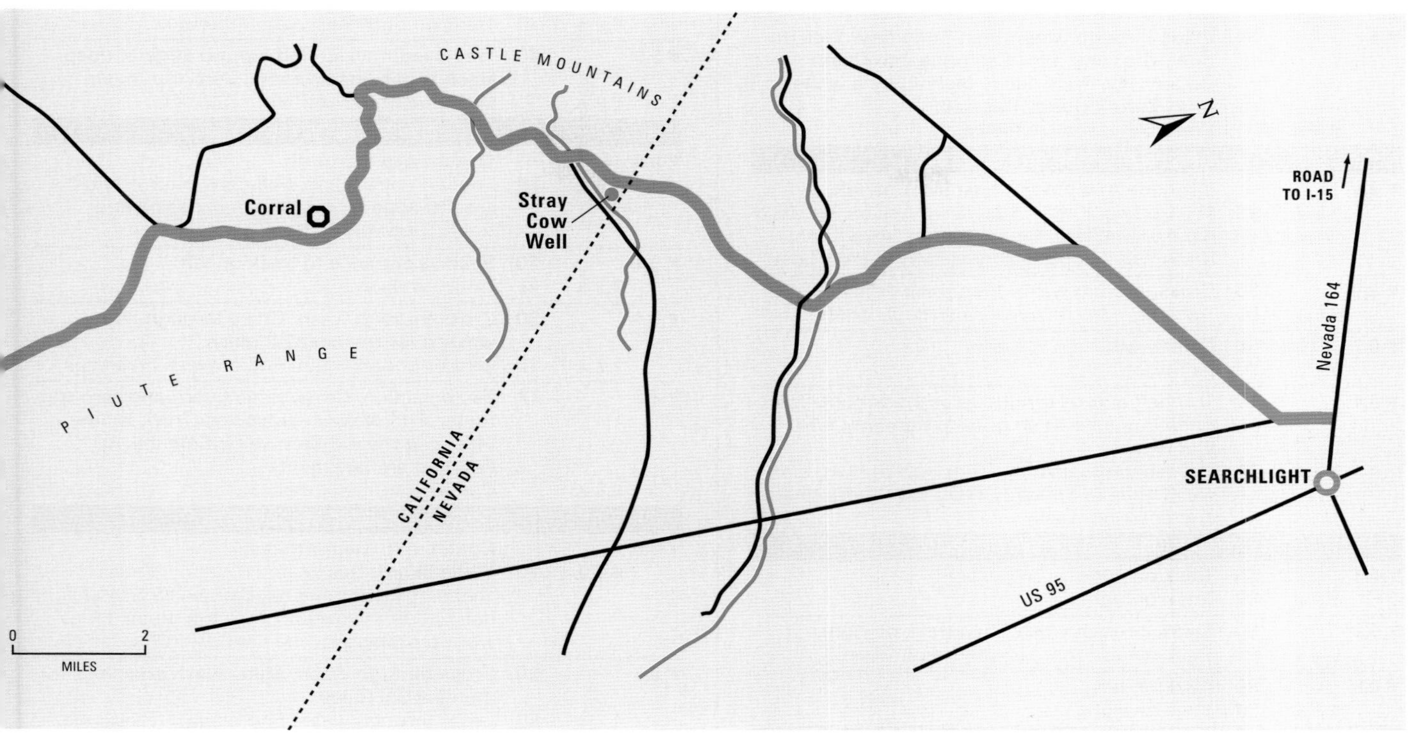

1.5 ▲ BL Track on right. Bear left to pass alongside dam.

▼ 9.9 TR 4-way intersection with well-used trail. Intersection is unmarked. Zero trip meter.
0.0 ▲ Continue to the southeast, entering Lanfair Valley.

GPS: N35°13.72' W115°03.60'

▼ 0.0 Continue to the northeast, leaving Lanfair Valley.
5.2 ▲ TL 4-way intersection with well-used trail. Intersection is unmarked. Zero trip meter.

▼ 1.2 SO Pass through wire gate.
4.0 ▲ SO Pass through wire gate.

GPS: N35°14.68' W115°03.21'

▼ 2.5 SO Corral on left.
2.7 ▲ SO Corral on right.

GPS: N35°15.85' W115°02.82'

▼ 2.9 SO Cross through wash.
2.3 ▲ SO Cross through wash.

▼ 3.1 SO Track on right.
2.1 ▲ BR Track on left.

GPS: N35°16.29' W115°03.08'

▼ 3.5 SO Cross through wash.
1.7 ▲ SO Cross through wash.

▼ 3.6 SO Cross through wash.
1.6 ▲ SO Cross through wash.

▼ 5.2 TR T-intersection with well-used track. Intersection is unmarked. Zero trip meter. There is no access to the left through the large open pit mine of the Viceroy Company. Some of the old Hart mines are accessible from this point. No vehicle access onto tracks running northwest up the Castle Mountain ridge.
0.0 ▲ Continue to the northeast.

GPS: N35°16.68' W115°05.02'

▼ 0.0 Continue to the north.
5.2 ▲ TL Turn left onto unmarked, small formed trail and zero trip meter. There is no access straight ahead through the large open pit mine of the Viceroy Company. Some of the old Hart mines are accessible from this point. No vehicle access onto the tracks running northwest up the Castle Mountain ridge.

▼ 0.3 SO Track on left.
4.9 ▲ SO Track on right.

▼ 1.9 SO Track on left.
3.3 ▲ SO Track on right.

GPS: N35°18.00' W115°04.33'

▼ 2.0 SO Cross through wash.
3.2 ▲ SO Cross through wash.

▼ 2.4 BL Track on right.
2.8 ▲ BR Track on left.

GPS: N35°18.17' W115°03.85'

▼ 2.6 TL T-intersection with track in wash.
2.6 ▲ TR Turn right out of wash. Track continues down wash.

GPS: N35°18.16' W115°03.65'

▼ 3.0 SO Exit line of wash.
2.2 ▲ SO Enter down line of wash.

▼ 3.4 SO Enter down line of wash.
1.8 ▲ SO Exit line of wash.

▼ 4.6 BL Bear left out of wash.
0.6 ▲ BR Bear right and enter line of wash.

▼ 4.7 SO Pass through wire gate; then cross through wash.
0.5 ▲ SO Cross through wash; then pass through wire gate.

GPS: N35°19.55' W115°02.70'

▼ 4.8 BR Bear right down wash.
0.4 ▲ BL Bear left out of wash.

▼ 4.9 BL Bear left up second wash. Track on right down wash.
0.3 ▲ BR Bear right up second wash. Track on left down wash.

GPS: N35°19.63' W115°02.58'

▼ 5.0 SO Exit wash.
0.2 ▲ SO Enter wash.

Mileage	Dir.	Description
▼ 5.2	SO	Cross through wash; then Stray Cow Well on right. Crossing from California into Clark County, NV. State line is marked by a white post. Zero trip meter at well.
0.0 ▲		Continue to the southeast.
		GPS: N35°19.88' W115°02.60'
▼ 0.0		Continue to the north past track on left.
5.6 ▲	SO	Track on right; then Stray Cow Well on left. Zero trip meter at well. Crossing from Nevada into California. State line is marked by a white post.
▼ 0.1	SO	Cross through wash; then track on left.
5.5 ▲	BL	Track on right; then cross through wash.
▼ 0.2	SO	Enter wash.
5.4 ▲	SO	Exit wash.
▼ 0.4	TL	Turn left and bear right up embankment. Track on left up side wash goes to Kennedy Well. Exit wash.
5.2 ▲	TR	Descend embankment. Track on right up side wash goes to Kennedy Well; then turn right and enter up wash.
		GPS: N35°20.18' W115°02.40'
▼ 0.5	SO	Track on left.
5.1 ▲	SO	Track on right.
▼ 0.6	SO	Cross through wash; then track on right.
5.0 ▲	SO	Track on left; then cross through wash.
▼ 0.9	SO	Track on left.
4.7 ▲	SO	Track on right.
		GPS: N35°20.47' W115°02.32'
▼ 1.2	SO	Enter wash.
4.4 ▲	SO	Exit wash.
▼ 1.5	SO	Entering Limited Use Area at sign. Trail is marked a designated route.
4.1 ▲	SO	Exiting Limited Use Area at sign.
		GPS: N35°20.70' W115°01.75'
▼ 1.7	SO	Track on left to game tank.
3.9 ▲	SO	Track on right to game tank.
▼ 1.8	SO	Track on left to game tank.
3.8 ▲	SO	Track on right to game tank.
▼ 1.9	BL	Track on right is designated route.
3.7 ▲	BR	Track on left is designated route.
		GPS: N35°20.77' W115°01.24'
▼ 2.0	SO	Cross through wide wash.
3.6 ▲	SO	Cross through wide wash.
▼ 2.4	SO	Cross through wide wash.
3.2 ▲	SO	Cross through wide wash.
▼ 3.1	SO	Cross through wide wash. Designated route on right and left up and down wash.
2.5 ▲	SO	Cross through wide wash. Designated route on left and right up and down wash.
		GPS: N35°21.49' W115°00.29'
▼ 3.3	SO	Cross through wash.
2.3 ▲	SO	Cross through wash.
▼ 3.4	SO	Track on left is designated route.
2.2 ▲	SO	Track on right is designated route.
▼ 3.9	SO	Cross through wash; then track on left.
1.7 ▲	SO	Track on right; then cross through wash.
▼ 4.0	SO	Track on right is designated route.
1.6 ▲	SO	Track on left is designated route.
		GPS: N35°21.99' W114°59.90'
▼ 4.5	SO	Track on left to game tank.
1.1 ▲	SO	Second track on right to game tank.
▼ 4.6	SO	Second track on left to game tank.
1.0 ▲	SO	Track on right to game tank.
▼ 4.7	SO	Track on left is designated route.
0.9 ▲	SO	Track on right is designated route.
▼ 5.6	SO	Well-used track on left around edge of deep wash is designated route. Zero trip meter.
0.0 ▲		Continue to the south.
		GPS: N35°23.38' W115°00.56'
▼ 0.0		Continue to the north.
2.6 ▲	SO	Second entrance to well-used track on right around edge of deep wash is designated route. Zero trip meter.
▼ 0.1	SO	Second entrance to track on left.
2.5 ▲	BL	Track on right.
▼ 0.4	SO	Cross through wash. Cross through many washes for the next 2.2 miles.
2.2 ▲	SO	Cross through wash. End of wash crossings.
▼ 2.6	TR	T-intersection. Cross cattle guard and zero trip meter. End of wash crossings. Track is now following the old Barnwell & Searchlight Railroad embankment.
0.0 ▲		Continue to the southeast.
		GPS: N35°25.58' W114°59.78'
▼ 0.0		Continue to the northeast.
4.6 ▲	TL	Cattle guard. Designated route continues ahead, following the old Barnwell & Searchlight Railroad embankment. Zero trip meter. Many wash crossings for the next 2.2 miles.
▼ 0.4	SO	Cross through wash. Many wash crossings for the next 3.5 miles.
4.2 ▲	SO	Cross through wash. End of wash crossings.
▼ 0.8	BL	Cross through wash; then track on right goes to well.
3.8 ▲	SO	Track on left goes to well; then cross through wash.
		GPS: N35°26.01' W114°59.06'
▼ 1.0	SO	Track on left and track on right at wash.
3.6 ▲	SO	Track on left and track on right at wash.
▼ 1.2	SO	Cattle guard.
3.4 ▲	SO	Cattle guard.
▼ 3.0	SO	Track on left.
1.6 ▲	SO	Track on right.
▼ 3.9	TL	5-way intersection under power lines. Turn second left onto graded road under power lines. Old railroad embankment continues straight ahead, but is not used as a roadway past this point. End of wash crossings.
0.7 ▲	TR	5-way intersection. Turn second right onto formed trail that runs along old Barnwell & Searchlight Railroad embankment. Old railroad embankment continues to the left but is not used as a roadway. Many wash crossings for the next 3.5 miles.
		GPS: N35°27.62' W114°56.33'
▼ 4.3	SO	Track on left. Track on right is pipeline road. Continue straight ahead and cross cattle guard; then track on right and track on left.
0.3 ▲	BR	Track on right and track on left; then cattle guard; then road splits three ways. Bear slightly right, taking the middle trail and keeping the power lines on your right.
		GPS: N35°27.98' W114°56.26'
▼ 4.6		Track on left and right; then trail ends at intersection with paved Nevada 164. Turn right for Searchlight; turn left for Nipton, CA, and I-15.
0.0 ▲		Trail commences on paved Nevada 164, 1.1 miles west of intersection with US 95 in Searchlight. Zero trip meter and turn south on graded dirt road immediately before power lines. Immediately track on left and track on right.
		GPS: N35°28.19' W114°56.24'

DESERT #15

New York Mountains Trail

Starting Point:	**Nevada 164, 6.9 miles west of Searchlight, NV**
Finishing Point:	**Black Canyon Road, 0.2 miles south of the turn to Hole-in-the-Wall Visitor Center**
Total Mileage:	**62.1 miles**
Unpaved Mileage:	**62.1 miles**
Driving Time:	**5 hours**
Elevation Range:	**4,000–5,600 feet**
Usually Open:	**Year-round**
Best Time to Travel:	**September to May**
Difficulty Rating:	**2**
Scenic Rating:	**9**
Remoteness Rating:	**+0**

Special Attractions

- Town site of Hart.
- Joshua tree forest in the Mojave National Preserve.
- Access to hiking trails through oak forest in the New York Mountains, a rarity in the Mojave Desert.
- Camp Rock Spring and Government Holes on Desert #13: Mojave Road.

History

Barnwell, formerly known as Manvel, was founded in 1893 at the foot of the New York Mountains. The Nevada Southern Railway Company was expected to construct a line north from Goffs. With this in mind, speculators moved in and established Manvel; six months later the railroad showed up. The new town was named after Allen Manvel, president of the Santa Fe Railroad. It became an important staging terminal for goods headed to Eldorado, Goodsprings, and the Ivanpah district. By the late 1890s freight teams were busy hauling goods from the railroad terminal at Manvel to Searchlight, Nevada.

Manvel supported two stores, a blacksmith, a butcher shop, saloons, and a small school. By 1902 the railroad company, which was now named California Eastern, had extended the line north to Ivanpah. This extension somewhat reduced the need for Manvel as a terminal. However, Searchlight continued to boom and stages and freight wagons kept Manvel thriving as a shipping depot. The town's name was changed to Barnwell in 1907. By 1908, the need for improved transportation in and out of Searchlight brought about the construction of the Barnwell & Searchlight Railroad, and the decline of Barnwell.

The Santa Fe Railroad engaged the services of the only doctor in this region and appointed him to Barnwell. Although Dr. Haenszel lived in Searchlight, where most of his patients were, his appointment was to the smaller town of Barnwell because he was licensed to practice in California. In fact, the doctor covered a large area of desert, about 40 to 50 miles in radius, tending to miners and ranchers. No one complained that Nevada did not recognize his California license. Dr. Haenszel accepted this position because his own ill health forced him to live in a dry climate. He had been confined to bed for years with tuberculosis, but he managed to keep up to date with his evolving profession while his wife tended to his needs.

The railroad station at Searchlight was quite substantial for its time, with living quarters on the first floor for the agent and his family. During its peak period, trains ran to Goffs daily except Sundays. A cattle loading ramp and a turntable for the tall-stack locomotive were installed. By 1923 the Santa Fe Railroad abandoned the line. Today, nothing but the concrete foundations of a tank and the railroad berm remain at the Searchlight Station.

Searchlight has experienced three eras since its founding in the 1890s. Initially, the town catered to ranchers and miners, which like many Wild West towns faded with the dwindling minerals in the region. The town lost the railroad and most of its residents by the end of this period in the 1920s.

Searchlight was revived between 1933 and 1935 with the construction of the Hoover Dam. Entertainment venues that were shunned, both in Boulder City and Las Vegas, flourished in Searchlight. Most of the workers had automobiles, and roads were improved by this time. Searchlight became an escape from the construction site, and workers could spend their money with few questions asked. Bordellos became big business in Searchlight. Associated crime and unscrupulous characters were attracted to the town. It was not until the late 1950s that Clark County authorities managed to curtail illegal businesses. The eventual closure and burning of the most prominent premises, El Rey, signaled the end of the world's oldest profession in Searchlight. Most of the old street frontages from the town's mining days were lost to fires as time passed.

The completion of US 95 from Needles to Las Vegas in the

Ox Ranch tank

Stone chimney at the town site of Hart

1950s brought the next wave of people to Searchlight. This time it was travelers and tourists. Filling stations appeared on the main road through town, with restaurants and motels following close behind. The new main street developed perpendicular to the old one. Traffic en route to Cottonwood Landing, on the Colorado River, brought many tourists to Searchlight as well. Some passing travelers decided that the fine climate, elevation, access to the river, desert attractions, and proximity to Las Vegas were enough reason to remain. Retirees filled the new streets with their trailers, bringing more activity than had been seen in the town in decades. A casino in the town center started operating in the late 1970s and has been one of the town's major employers.

In December 1907, Jim Hart and the Hitt brothers, Bert and Clark, discovered gold-bearing ore of rich proportions in the Castle Mountains. Hart sprang to life east of Manvel and immediately boomed. By April of the following year, the town had a hotel, post office, and stores that supported a population of several hundred. A newspaper ran from 1908 to 1909. The town apparently had neither a church nor a school.

Three mine names stood out, the Oro Belle, Jumbo, and Big Chief. Ore was transported 3.5 miles northwest to Hitt Siding on the Barnwell & Searchlight Railroad for processing in Searchlight. The Big Chief Mine eventually had its own mill. Hart seemed to have everything but liquor, apparently because liquor licenses were unavailable. Within a number of months, the high-grade ore dwindled and the attraction of Hart receded. The post office remained until 1915.

Joshua trees grow in front of the Castle Mountains

Silence returned to the Castle Mountains until 1984, when the mines reopened to make a profit using modern techniques. More than half a million ounces of gold had been extracted by the Viceroy Company by the mid-1990s.

The Walking Box Ranch, at the start of this trail in Nevada, was owned by silent-movie actress Clara Bow and her actor husband, Rex Bell. The ranch became headquarters for the Viceroy's mining operations for several years. The ranch, one of the earliest in the eastern Mojave region, has been listed on the National Register of Historic Places and has been restored to its former 1930s glory.

Description

This trail runs from Searchlight, Nevada, to Desert #13: Mojave Road, which it joins for a short distance before continuing south. The standard is much easier than Mojave Road, being predominantly rough, graded dirt road, with some sections of easy formed trail. Unlike Mojave Road, which requires a 4WD vehicle, New York Mountains Trail can be driven in a high-clearance 2WD in dry weather. In wet weather or snow, it is likely to be impassable.

The trail commences along Walking Box Ranch Road, passing the ranch once owned by Clara Bow and Rex Bell. It follows their wide, graded dirt access road through a Joshua tree forest on the north side of the Castle Mountains. This access road is not accurately represented on maps. A short distance before an open pit mine, a spur leads to the site of Hart. A historical marker marks the site, which is now in the shadow of the modern open pit mine. A large chimney and wooden headframe are all that remains of the town. The coordinates of Hart town site are GPS: N35°17.18' W115°06.53'.

The main trail swings around the open pit mine, following a roughly graded road along the Barnwell & Searchlight Railroad grade for a short distance. At the small settlement of Barnwell, the trail joins the wide, graded Ivanpah Road, traveling south into the Mojave National Preserve near the old grade of the Ivanpah to Goffs railroad. It then turns off onto the smaller New York Mountains Road at a corral and water tank that still bear the mark of the Ox Cattle Company, once the major ranching interest in this region.

New York Mountains Road winds along the face of the jumbled range. A spur leads a short distance north up Caruthers Canyon, past a balanced rock toward some mines high on the mountainside. The mountains offer excellent hiking opportunities through oak forests that are left over from a time when the whole region was lush with vegetation. This is a beautiful canyon and well worth the slight detour.

The trail runs along Cedar Canyon Road for a short distance, following the course of Mojave Road, before it turns south along Black Canyon Road. The trail follows around the scenic loop of Wild Horse Canyon Road. The blocky mountains and wide valleys along this section make for some of the best scenery in the preserve. The trail finishes at the developed Hole-in-the-Wall Campground and Visitor Center.

Current Road Information

Mojave National Preserve
PO Box 241
72157 Baker Boulevard
Baker, CA 92309
(760) 733-4040

Map References

BLM Mesquite Lake, Ivanpah
USGS 1:24,000 Hopps Well, Hart Peak, Castle Peaks, Grotto Hills, Pinto Valley, Mid Hills, Columbia Mt.
1:100,000 Mesquite Lake, Ivanpah
Maptech CD-ROM: San Bernardino County/Mojave
Southern & Central California Atlas & Gazetteer, pp. 71, 72
Nevada Atlas & Gazetteer, p. 72
California Road & Recreation Atlas, p. 98
Trails Illustrated, Mojave National Preserve (256)

Route Directions

Mileage		Direction
▼ 0.0		From Nevada 164, 6.9 miles west of Searchlight, 0.4 miles west of mile marker 12, zero trip meter and turn south on graded dirt Walking Box Ranch Road at sign. The road is also marked as a BLM designated route.
7.5 ▲		Trail ends at T-intersection with Nevada 164. Turn right for Searchlight, NV; turn left for Nipton, CA.
		GPS: N35°30.02′ W115°02.12′
▼ 0.2	SO	Designated route on left and right.
7.3 ▲	SO	Designated route on left and right.
▼ 0.7	BR	Entrance to Walking Box Ranch on left.
6.8 ▲	BL	Entrance to Walking Box Ranch on right.
▼ 1.1	SO	Track on left.
6.4 ▲	SO	Track on right.
▼ 3.0	SO	Track on right; then corral on left.
4.5 ▲	SO	Corral on right; then track on left.
		GPS: N35°27.44′ W115°03.26′
▼ 5.0	SO	Cross over wash.
2.5 ▲	SO	Cross over wash.
▼ 7.5	SO	Designated route on left, opposite corral on right. Zero trip meter.
0.0 ▲		Continue to the north.
		GPS: N35°23.84′ W115°05.08′
▼ 0.0		Continue to the south.
8.7 ▲	SO	Designated route on right, opposite corral on left. Zero trip meter.
▼ 1.1	SO	Designated route on left.
7.6 ▲	SO	Designated route on right.
▼ 2.1	SO	Small track on right; then cross through wash.
6.6 ▲	SO	Cross through wash; then small track on left.
▼ 3.3	SO	Track on left and track on right.
5.4 ▲	SO	Track on left and track on right.
		GPS: N35°21.33′ W115°06.20′
▼ 3.8	SO	Track on right.
4.9 ▲	SO	Track on left.
▼ 3.9	SO	Track on right and track on left.
4.8 ▲	SO	Track on left and track on right.
▼ 4.1	SO	Track on left.
4.6 ▲	SO	Track on right.
▼ 4.7	SO	Track on left.
4.0 ▲	SO	Track on right.
▼ 5.5	SO	Track on left.
3.2 ▲	SO	Track on right.
▼ 6.0	SO	Track on left.
2.7 ▲	SO	Track on right.
▼ 6.1	SO	Cattle guard.
2.6 ▲	SO	Cattle guard.
		GPS: N35°19.08′ W115°06.54′
▼ 7.5	SO	Track on right. Track on left goes past corral.
1.2 ▲	SO	Track on left. Track on right goes past corral.
		GPS: N35°18.00′ W115°07.33′
▼ 7.7	SO	Cattle guard.
1.0 ▲	SO	Cattle guard.
▼ 8.3	SO	Track on left.
0.4 ▲	SO	Track on right.
▼ 8.7	SO	Graded road on left and right. Intersection is unmarked, but there are stop signs on each side track. Zero trip meter. Road on left goes 1.2 miles to Hart town site.
0.0 ▲		Continue to the north.
		GPS: N35°16.92′ W115°07.14′
▼ 0.0		Continue to the southeast.
8.2 ▲	SO	Graded road on left and right. Intersection is unmarked, but there are stop signs on each side track. Zero trip meter. Road on right goes 1.2 miles to Hart town site.
▼ 0.3	TR	Turn sharp right onto graded road at water tank. Immediately small track on left. Workings of the open pit mine and buildings are visible ahead.
7.9 ▲	TL	Small track on right; then turn sharp left onto graded road at water tank. Workings of the open pit mine and buildings are visible ahead.
		GPS: N35°16.66′ W115°07.13′
▼ 0.4	SO	Cross through wash.
7.8 ▲	SO	Cross through wash.
▼ 0.7	SO	Nursery on left provides native plants for revegetation of the mine.
7.5 ▲	SO	Nursery on right provides native plants for revegetation of the mine.
▼ 1.4	SO	Graded road on right; then cattle guard.
6.8 ▲	BR	Cattle guard; then graded road on left.
		GPS: N35°17.37′ W115°07.91′
▼ 1.5	SO	Track on right.
6.7 ▲	SO	Track on left.
▼ 1.8	SO	Track on right and well #15 on left.
6.4 ▲	SO	Track on left and well #15 on right.
▼ 2.1	SO	Track on right.
6.1 ▲	SO	Track on left.
▼ 2.2	SO	Track on right at well #24.
6.0 ▲	SO	Track on left at well #24.
▼ 2.6	SO	Track on right.
5.6 ▲	SO	Track on left.
▼ 3.1	SO	Track on right.
5.1 ▲	SO	Track on left.
		GPS: N35°17.98′ W115°09.60′
▼ 3.6	BL	Track on right is the Barnwell & Searchlight Railroad grade. Trail now joins the railroad grade.
4.6 ▲	BR	Track on left is continuation of railroad grade. Bear right away from the grade.
		GPS: N35°17.95′ W115°10.01′
▼ 5.4	SO	Track on right.
2.8 ▲	SO	Track on left.
▼ 5.5	SO	Cross through wash.
2.7 ▲	SO	Cross through wash.
▼ 5.8	SO	Track on left.

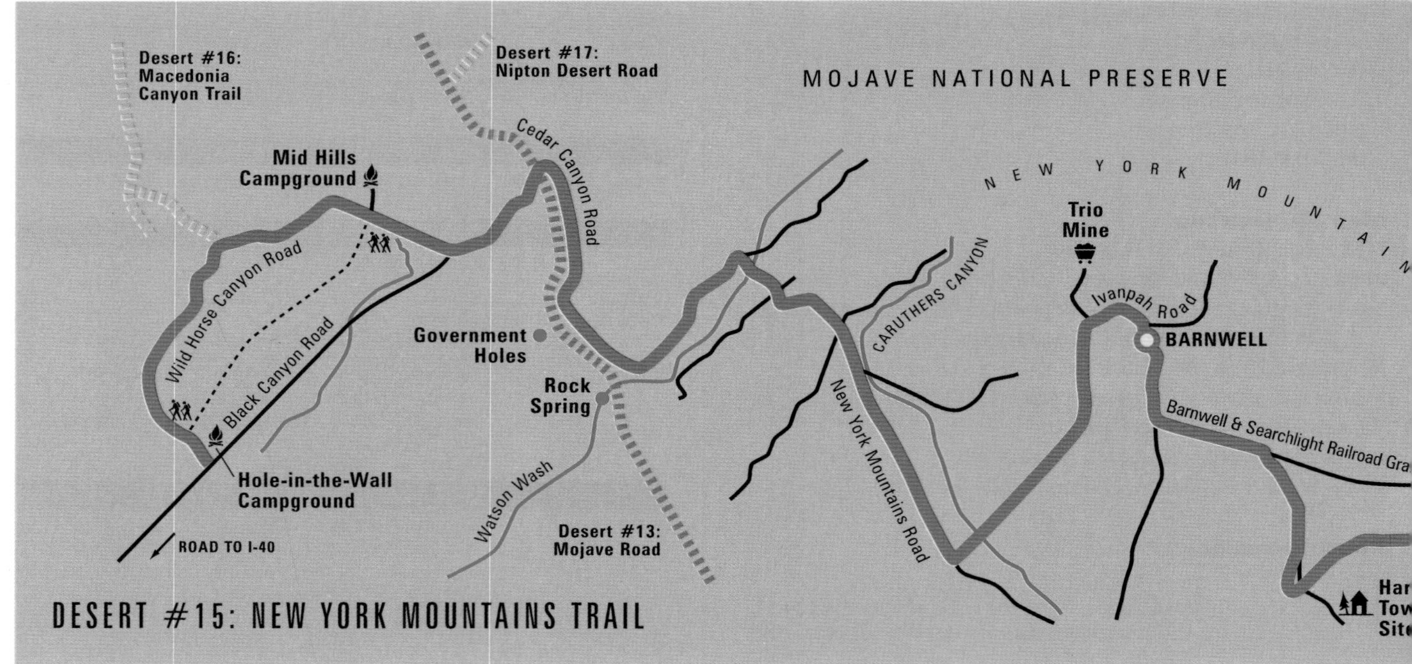

▼	▲		
	2.4 ▲	SO	Track on right.
			GPS: N35°16.69′ W115°11.97′
▼ 6.1		SO	Track on left.
	2.1 ▲	SO	Track on right.
▼ 7.5		SO	Well and tank on left.
	0.7 ▲	SO	Well and tank on right.
			GPS: N35°17.34′ W115°13.44′
▼ 7.6		SO	Track on right to corral and well.
	0.6 ▲	SO	Track on left to corral and well.
▼ 7.8		SO	Well on left.
	0.4 ▲	SO	Well on right.
▼ 8.1		SO	Cross through wash at Barnwell. Private property on left and right.
	0.1 ▲	SO	Leaving Barnwell. Cross through wash.
▼ 8.2		TL	T-intersection with graded Ivanpah Road. Zero trip meter.
	0.0 ▲		Continue to the southeast alongside the Barnwell & Searchlight Railroad grade.
			GPS: N35°17.56′ W115°14.15′
▼ 0.0			Continue to the southwest.
	7.1 ▲	TR	Turn right onto graded Hart Mine Road. Zero trip meter. This is the site of Barnwell. Private property on left and right.
▼ 0.1		SO	Cross through wash.
	7.0 ▲	SO	Cross through wash.
▼ 0.9		SO	Track on left.
	6.2 ▲	SO	Track on right.
▼ 1.2		SO	Track on right goes to Trio Mine.
	5.9 ▲	SO	Track on left goes to Trio Mine.
			GPS: N35°16.79′ W115°14.81′
▼ 2.5		SO	Cattle guard.
	4.6 ▲	SO	Cattle guard.
▼ 4.0		SO	Cross through wash.
	3.1 ▲	SO	Cross through wash.
▼ 4.1		SO	Railroad grade enters on left.
	3.0 ▲	SO	Railroad grade leaves on right.
▼ 4.3		SO	Cross through wash; then track on right.
	2.8 ▲	SO	Track on left; then cross through wash.
▼ 4.6		SO	Track on right.
	2.5 ▲	SO	Track on left.
▼ 5.1		SO	Cross through wash.
	2.0 ▲	SO	Cross through wash.
▼ 5.3		SO	Cross through wash.
	1.8 ▲	SO	Cross through wash.
▼ 5.7		SO	Cross through wash.
	1.4 ▲	SO	Cross through wash.
▼ 6.6		SO	Track on left.
	0.5 ▲	SO	Track on right.
▼ 6.8		SO	Track on right.
	0.3 ▲	SO	Track on left.
▼ 7.1		TR	Gate; then turn right onto the smaller, graded road marked New York Mountains Road. Zero trip meter. Turn is opposite a well and corral.
	0.0 ▲		Continue to the northwest and pass through gate, following close to the old railroad grade.
			GPS: N35°12.18′ W115°12.11′
▼ 0.0			Continue to the west, leaving the railroad route, and pass through wire gate.
	5.4 ▲	TL	Wire gate; then turn left onto wider, graded road marked Ivanpah Road. Zero trip meter. Turn is opposite a well and corral.
▼ 0.9		SO	Track on right.
	4.5 ▲	SO	Track on left.
▼ 3.0		SO	Track on right and track on left. Crossing Ross Horse Pasture.
	2.4 ▲	SO	Track on right and track on left. Crossing Ross Horse Pasture.
			GPS: N35°12.62′ W115°15.32′
▼ 4.3		SO	Cattle guard.
	1.1 ▲	SO	Cattle guard.
▼ 4.7		BL	Well-used track on right.
	0.7 ▲	BR	Well-used track on left.
			GPS: N35°12.90′ W115°17.07′
▼ 5.4		SO	4-way intersection. Track on right travels 2 miles toward Caruthers Canyon. Zero trip meter. Intersection is unmarked.
	0.0 ▲		Continue to the northeast.

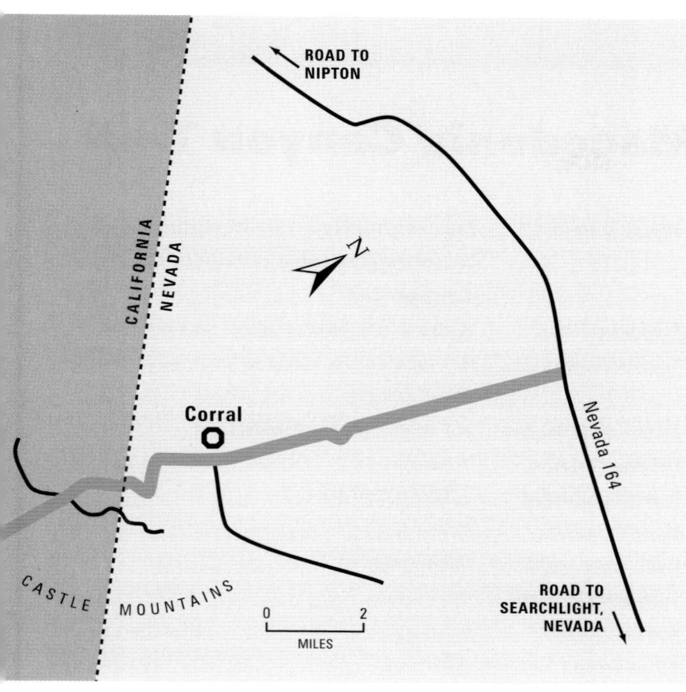

GPS: N35°13.04' W115°17.82'

▼	▲		
▼ 0.0			Continue to the southwest.
	3.0 ▲	SO	4-way intersection. Track on left travels 2 miles toward Caruthers Canyon. Zero trip meter. Intersection is unmarked.
▼ 0.3		SO	Track on left to mine.
	2.7 ▲	SO	Track on right to mine.
▼ 0.4		SO	Track on right and track on left.
	2.6 ▲	SO	Track on right and track on left.
▼ 0.5		BL	Track on right.
	2.5 ▲	BR	Track on left.

GPS: N35°13.03' W115°18.36'

▼	▲		
▼ 0.9		SO	Track on right and track on left.
	2.1 ▲	SO	Track on right and track on left.
▼ 1.5		SO	Track on left.
	1.5 ▲	SO	Track on right.
▼ 1.9		SO	Well-used track on left and track on right.
	1.1 ▲	SO	Well-used track on right and track on left.

GPS: N35°12.45' W115°19.33'

▼	▲		
▼ 2.4		BL	Track on right.
	0.6 ▲	BR	Track on left.
▼ 2.7		SO	Track on left.
	0.3 ▲	SO	Track on right.
▼ 2.9		SO	Cross through Watson Wash.
	0.1 ▲	SO	Cross through Watson Wash.

GPS: N35°12.30' W115°20.40'

▼	▲		
▼ 3.0		TL	T-intersection. Track on right goes into Fourth of July Canyon. Zero trip meter.
	0.0 ▲		Continue to the northeast.

GPS: N35°12.30' W115°20.49'

▼	▲		
▼ 0.0			Continue to the southeast.
	3.5 ▲	TR	Track straight ahead goes into Fourth of July Canyon. Zero trip meter.
▼ 0.1		SO	Track on right.
	3.4 ▲	BR	Track on left.
▼ 0.6		SO	Small track on left.
	2.9 ▲	SO	Small track on right.
▼ 1.1		SO	Track on right through wire gate.
	2.4 ▲	SO	Track on left through wire gate.
▼ 1.3		SO	Track on right; then Pinto Mountain on right.
	2.2 ▲	SO	Pinto Mountain on left; then track on left.
▼ 3.4		SO	Cross through wash; then pipeline crosses track.
	0.1 ▲	SO	Pipeline crosses track; then cross through wash.
▼ 3.5		TR	T-intersection with wide, graded Cedar Canyon Road. Trail briefly joins Desert #13: Mojave Road.
	0.0 ▲		Continue to the north.

GPS: N35°09.43' W115°19.90'

▼	▲		
▼ 0.0			Continue to the west.
	1.7 ▲	TL	Turn left onto smaller graded road and bear slightly right. Trail leaves Desert #13: Mojave Road.
▼ 0.1		SO	Track on left is Desert #13: Mojave Road, which leaves Cedar Canyon Road at this point.
	1.6 ▲	SO	Track on right is Desert #13: Mojave Road, which briefly joins Cedar Canyon Road at this point.
▼ 0.3		SO	Track on left.
	1.4 ▲	SO	Track on right.
▼ 0.5		SO	Track on right.
	1.2 ▲	SO	Track on left.
▼ 1.0		SO	Track on right.
	0.7 ▲	SO	Track on left.
▼ 1.7		SO	Track on left is Desert #13: Mojave Road, which rejoins New York Mountains Trail at this point. Zero trip meter.
	0.0 ▲		Continue to the east.

GPS: N35°09.18' W115°21.68'

▼	▲		
▼ 0.0			Continue to the west.
	3.3 ▲	BL	Track on right is Desert #13: Mojave Road, which leaves New York Mountains Trail at this point. Zero trip meter.
▼ 0.1		SO	Track on right.
	3.2 ▲	SO	Track on left.
▼ 0.3		SO	Track on right; then cattle guard.
	3.0 ▲	SO	Cattle guard; then track on left.
▼ 0.7		SO	Track on right.
	2.6 ▲	SO	Track on left.
▼ 1.7		SO	Track on right; then cattle guard; then second track on right.
	1.6 ▲	SO	Track on left; then cattle guard; then second track on left.
▼ 2.4		SO	Track on right.
	0.9 ▲	SO	Track on left.
▼ 3.3		TL	Turn left onto graded dirt Black Canyon Road, following sign for Hole-in-the Wall Campground and Mitchell Caverns. Zero trip meter. Desert #13: Mojave Road continues straight ahead at this point.
	0.0 ▲		Continue to the northeast.

GPS: N35°10.45' W115°24.65'

▼	▲		
▼ 0.0			Continue to the southeast and cross through wash.
	2.7 ▲	TR	Cross through wash; then T-intersection with graded Cedar Canyon Road. Zero trip meter. Trail now follows Desert #13: Mojave Road for a short distance.
▼ 0.8		SO	Track on left.
	1.9 ▲	SO	Track on right.
▼ 2.4		SO	Track on right to Hollman Well.
	0.3 ▲	SO	Track on left to Hollman Well.

GPS: N35°08.43' W115°24.10'

▼ 2.5		SO	Corral and track on right.
	0.2 ▲	SO	Corral and track on left.
▼ 2.7		TR	Turn right onto wide, graded dirt Wild Horse Canyon Road, following the sign to Mid Hills Campground. Zero trip meter.
	0.0 ▲		Continue to the north.
			GPS: N 35°08.19' W115°24.10'
▼ 0.0			Continue to the west.
	5.4 ▲	TL	T-intersection with graded dirt Black Canyon Road. Zero trip meter and turn left, following the sign to Kelso Dunes.
▼ 1.5		SO	Cross through wash.
	3.9 ▲	SO	Cross through wash.
▼ 1.9		SO	Well on left. Hiking and horse trailhead for the Mid Hills to Hole-in-the-Wall Trail. Graded road on right goes into Mid Hills NPS Campground (fee charged).
	3.5 ▲	SO	Well on right. Hiking and horse trailhead for the Mid Hills to Hole-in-the-Wall Trail. Graded road on left goes into Mid Hills NPS Campground (fee charged).
			GPS: N35°07.40' W115°25.93'
▼ 2.6		SO	Two tracks on right.
	2.8 ▲	SO	Two tracks on left.
▼ 2.7		SO	Cattle guard.
	2.7 ▲	SO	Cattle guard.
▼ 3.8		SO	Track on left.
	1.6 ▲	SO	Track on right.
▼ 5.4		SO	Track on right is Desert #16: Macedonia Canyon Trail, marked by a post. Zero trip meter.
	0.0 ▲		Continue to the north.
			GPS: N35°04.73' W115°27.35'
▼ 0.0			Continue to the south.
	5.6 ▲	SO	Track on left is Desert #16: Macedonia Canyon Trail, marked by a post. Zero trip meter.
▼ 0.9		SO	Track on right to Willow Well; then cattle guard.
	4.7 ▲	SO	Cattle guard; then track on left to Willow Well.
▼ 1.5		SO	Track on right and track on left.
	4.1 ▲	SO	Track on left and track on right.
▼ 2.5		SO	Track on left.
	3.1 ▲	SO	Track on right.
▼ 4.6		SO	Hiking and horse trailhead on left for Mid Hills to Hole-in-the-Wall Trail.
	1.0 ▲	SO	Hiking and horse trailhead on right for Mid Hills to Hole-in-the-Wall Trail.
			GPS: N35°02.21' W115°24.41'
▼ 5.0		SO	Track on left; then cattle guard.
	0.6 ▲	SO	Cattle guard; then track on right.
▼ 5.1		SO	Track on left.
	0.5 ▲	SO	Track on right.
▼ 5.5		SO	Cross through wash.
	0.1 ▲	SO	Cross through wash.
▼ 5.6			Trail ends on paved Black Canyon Road, 0.2 miles south of the turn to Hole-in-the-Wall NPS Visitor Center and Campground (fee charged). Turn right for Mitchell Caverns and I-40; turn left to return to Cedar Canyon Road and Cima.
	0.0 ▲		Trail commences on paved Black Canyon Road, 0.2 miles south of the turn to Hole -in-the-Wall NPS Visitor Center and Campground (fee charged), approximately 21 miles north of Essex Road exit of I-40. Zero trip meter and turn west on wide graded Wild Horse Canyon Road, marked with a post.
			GPS: N35°02.31' W115°23.34'

DESERT #16

Macedonia Canyon Trail

Starting Point:	**Desert #15: New York Mountains Trail, 5.6 miles northwest of Hole-in-the-Wall Campground**
Finishing Point:	**Kelso-Cima Road, 8 miles south of Cima**
Total Mileage:	**8.1 miles, plus 1.9-mile spur to Columbia Mine**
Unpaved Mileage:	**8.1 miles, plus 1.9-mile spur**
Driving Time:	**1 hour**
Elevation Range:	**3,100–5,000 feet**
Usually Open:	**Year-round**
Best Time to Travel:	**September to June**
Difficulty Rating:	**3**
Scenic Rating:	**8**
Remoteness Rating:	**+0**

Special Attractions

- Can be combined with Desert #15: New York Mountains Trail to exit to the west.
- Long trail in a spectacular canyon.
- Remains of the Columbia Mine.

History

The workings of the Columbia Mine include a shaft reaching a depth of 380 feet. The mine was worked around the turn of the twentieth century and a 5-stamp mill operated on site. The gneiss vein followed layers of dense, dark gray quartz and orthoclase. Records from the mid-1920s show the Columbia ores yielded 35 ounces of silver and 0.28 ounces of gold per ton.

Several copper mines were started in this region with promising content at surface level. However, none paid well enough to continue digging beyond a few feet. Many of these small excavations can be seen around Columbia Mountain.

Remains of the Columbia Mine dugout

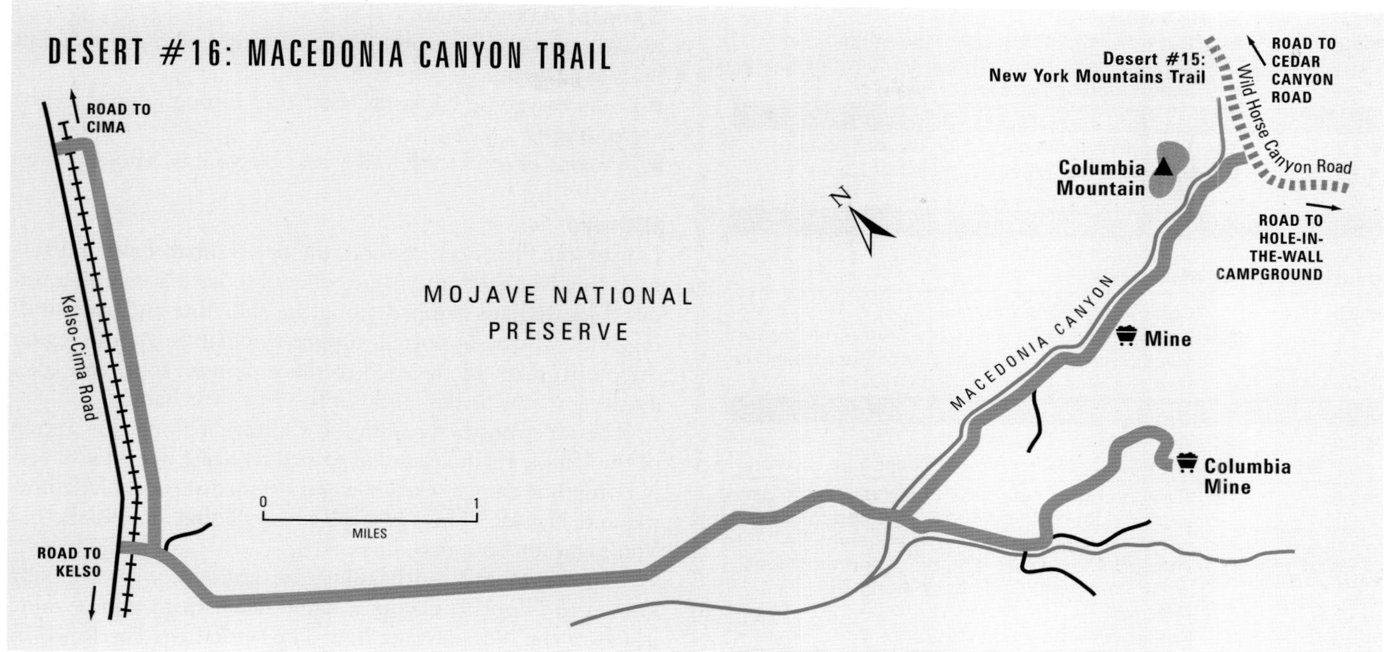

Description

Macedonia Canyon Trail is a sandy trail that connects the southern end of Desert #15: New York Mountains Trail with Kelso-Cima Road. The trail is well marked at the start. It immediately drops down into the loose, gravelly wash of Macedonia Canyon and descends steadily between the high walls of the canyon, before spilling out onto the bajada that leads down to Kelso Wash.

As the trail leaves Macedonia Canyon, a spur leads 1.9 miles to the remains of the Columbia Mine that are scattered around the hillside.

The trail officially ends by heading straight out to Kelso-Cima Road. However this route passes under the rail line at a point where there is insufficient clearance for most vehicles: approximately 6 feet, 4 inches (this clearance may change with build-up of sand). Taller vehicles will need to bear north alongside the rail line to exit at a point 2 miles farther north, where there is greater clearance, approximately 7 feet, 4 inches. Whichever exit you chose, watch your roofline carefully to avoid damage.

Current Road Information

Mojave National Preserve
PO Box 241
72157 Baker Boulevard
Baker, CA 92309
(760) 733-4040

Map References

BLM Ivanpah
USGS 1:24,000 Columbia Mt., Hayden, Cima
1:100,000 Ivanpah
Maptech CD-ROM: San Bernardino County/Mojave
Southern & Central California Atlas & Gazetteer, p. 71
California Road & Recreation Atlas, p. 97
Trails Illustrated, Mojave National Preserve (256)

Route Directions

▼ 0.0		From graded dirt Wild Horse Canyon Road (part of Desert #15: New York Mountains Trail), 5.6 miles northwest of Hole-in-the-Wall Campground, zero trip meter and turn northwest onto formed Macedonia Canyon Trail and immediately pass through wire gate.
2.5 ▲		Trail ends at T-intersection with graded dirt Wild Horse Canyon Road (part of Desert #15: New York Mountains Trail). Turn right for Hole-in-the-Wall Campground; turn left to exit to Cedar Canyon Road.
		GPS: N35°04.73' W115°27.35'
▼ 0.1	SO	Enter line of wash.
2.4 ▲	SO	Exit line of wash.
▼ 1.1	SO	Mine on left.
1.4 ▲	SO	Mine on right.
		GPS: N35°04.52' W115°28.39'
▼ 1.5	SO	Track on left. Exit Macedonia Canyon.
1.0 ▲	SO	Track on right. Enter Macedonia Canyon.
▼ 2.5	TR	T-intersection. Turn right and exit wash. Track on left is spur to Columbia Mine. Zero trip meter. There is a wooden marker for Macedonia Canyon Wash Road at the intersection.
0.0 ▲		Continue to the northeast.
		GPS: N35°04.37' W115°29.88'

Spur to Columbia Mine

▼ 0.0		Proceed southeast.
▼ 0.1	SO	Track on right.
▼ 0.2	SO	Enter up wash. Track on right down wash.
▼ 0.6	BR	Track on left. Bear right in wash.
		GPS: N35°03.95' W115°29.46'
▼ 0.7	SO	Track on right.
▼ 0.8	TL	Turn left and exit wash. Track continues in wash.
		GPS: N35°03.89' W115°29.32'
▼ 0.9	BR	Bear right up wash.
▼ 1.0	SO	Gate.
		GPS: N35°04.03' W115°29.20'

▼ 1.6		SO	Exit wash.
▼ 1.7		BL	Track on right. Columbia Mine remains on left—concrete foundations, old machinery, and timber loading hoppers.
			GPS: N35°03.98' W115°28.56'
▼ 1.8		SO	Track on right rejoins; then dugout on left.
▼ 1.9		UT	Spur ends at adit and remains of Columbia Mine.
			GPS: N35°03.88' W115°28.57'

Continuation of Main Trail

▼ 0.0			Continue to the northwest.
	3.6 ▲	TL	Turn left and enter wash at wooden marker for Macedonia Canyon Wash Road. Track ahead is spur to Columbia Mine. Zero trip meter.
			GPS: N35°04.37' W115°29.88'
▼ 3.5		SO	Wire gate.
	0.1 ▲	SO	Wire gate. Trail is marked Macedonia Canyon.
▼ 3.6		TR	Track on right; then pass under rail line to exit to paved Kelso-Cima Road. This underpass is very low, approximately 6'4" in height. Tall vehicles should zero trip meter and turn right along unmarked small track alongside railroad.
	0.0 ▲		Continue to the southeast.
			GPS: N35°06.05' W115°32.97'
▼ 0.0			Continue to the northeast alongside rail line.
	2.0 ▲	TL	Turn left onto formed trail away from rail line. To the right is the exit to Kelso-Cima Road for shorter vehicles. Zero trip meter.
▼ 2.0			Turn left and pass under rail line. Trail finishes on paved Kelso-Cima Road. Turn right for Cima; turn left for Kelso.
	0.0 ▲		Trail commences on Kelso-Cima Road, 8 miles south of Cima and 3.6 miles south of the intersection with Black Canyon Road. Zero trip meter and turn east. Pass under rail line; then immediately turn right (south) and follow alongside rail line on formed sandy trail.
			GPS: N35°07.60' W115°32.04'

DESERT #17

Nipton Desert Road

Starting Point:	**I-15 at Primm, NV**
Finishing Point:	**Desert #13: Mojave Road, 2.8 miles southwest of intersection with Black Canyon Road**
Total Mileage:	**41.4 miles, plus spurs**
Unpaved Mileage:	**41.4 miles, plus spurs**
Driving Time:	**4 hours**
Elevation Range:	**2,600–4,500 feet**
Usually Open:	**Year-round**
Best Time to Travel:	**September to June**
Difficulty Rating:	**2**
Scenic Rating:	**8**
Remoteness Rating:	**+0**

Special Attractions

- Old railroad sidings and the San Pedro, Los Angeles & Salt Lake Railroad.
- Long, easygoing Mojave Desert trail through dense Joshua tree forests.
- Remains of the Death Valley and Lucy Gray Mines.

History

During the Pleistocene period, the dry Ivanpah Lake and surrounding Ivanpah Valley were believed to have been under water. Paleo-Indians camped along the shoreline and surrounding hills, which supported juniper woodlands. As the region dried out, plant life receded to the mountain tops, and lake-dwelling toads, turtles, and pupfish lost their habitat.

The most northerly siding in California along this stretch of the Union Pacific Railroad gained its name like a lot of early borderline camps. Calada is a shortened version of California and Nevada. The Calada Railway Siding sits on the old Von Schmidt Boundary line of 1873.

Nipton, to the south along the railroad, was originally known as Nippeno Camp, a name taken from a local mine just over the Nevada state line. The settlement developed in the 1870s at the intersection of two trade routes where freight wagon drivers camped en route to nearby mines. The developing camp gained additional trade on February 9, 1905, when the first train arrived on the newly constructed San Pedro, Los Angeles & Salt Lake Railroad.

The name was changed to Nipton when the San Pedro, Los Angeles & Salt Lake merged with the Union Pacific around 1910. A regular stagecoach and freight service ran from the railroad to Searchlight, Nevada. Construction of the Hotel Nipton was completed by 1910, during the local mining boom. For many years, the depot was a cattle loading station for several local ranches, including one of the earliest, the Yates Ranch, whose headquarters were at Valley Wells on the west side of the Ivanpah Mountains. Other notable ranches included the Walking Box and Rock Springs Land and Cattle Company. The town became a supply center for the Clark Mining District. It was also a social center for the widely dispersed population of the region, supporting a school, post office, and several small businesses.

In the 1920s, the nearby Walking Box Ranch, just inside the Nevada border, was purchased by the famous Hollywood silent movie stars, Clara Bow and her husband, Rex Bell. They ran cattle on the ranch and herded them to the Nipton Siding when shipping them to market. Clara entertained a number of Hollywood guests, who availed themselves of the Nipton Hotel's hospitality. A car service dropped houseguests off at the stylish Walking Box Ranch headquarters en route to Searchlight, Nevada.

The small settlement of Nipton endured boom and bust times over the following decades and by the early 1950s, the railroad station was abandoned and Nipton became just another siding along the long desert railroad.

During the mid-1980s, large-scale mining at the nearby Old Hart, Morning Star, and Colosseum Mines brought life back to the Nipton Hotel and store, somewhat of a return to the boom of early Nippeno Camp. By the turn of the twenty-first century, Nipton was no longer totally reliant on fluctuating mining activities. The small settlement has estab-

Nipton Trading Post

lished itself as a remote destination, where travelers can relax and sample the untamed desert.

The name Ivanpah comes from the Chemehuevi word *aav-impa,* which means white clay water, sometimes called sweet water. Ivanpah was the earliest settlement and boomtown in the eastern Mojave region as a result of mining activities in 1870. At its peak, the town's population approached 500, mainly miners. Though the camp came and went by the close of the nineteenth century, the name lingered and was attached to a nearby railroad station.

Thomas Place, near the southern end of the trail, gained its name from Lewis and his brother "Wimpy" Thomas, who used the cabin there.

Description

Nipton Desert Road follows what is now the Union Pacific Railroad for the majority of its length. Commencing next to the state line in Primm, Nevada, the trail heads out along the desert trails to the east. Once it reaches the railroad, the trail swings south, following the roughly graded road that parallels the rail line. It passes the sidings that once served trains along the old San Pedro, Los Angeles & Salt Lake Railroad. The sidings are now little more than names on the map.

The small settlement of Nipton, California, survives more than a century after it blossomed in this remote desert area. Nipton currently has a general store, hotel, and cantina. There is no gas available. Continuing south along the railroad into the Mojave National Preserve, the trail becomes formed and narrow before rejoining the graded road approaching Ivanpah Siding. This section of the trail offers stunning views of the New York Mountains, and passes through a dense forest of Joshua trees, yuccas, and other desert vegetation.

The remains of the Death Valley Mine are close to Cima. A spur trail leads 5.6 miles into the Mid Hills to some mining remains. Death Valley Mine is posted as no trespassing, but the trail passes the gate and offers a good view of the old buildings.

The main trail continues south on a small formed trail, passing the Thomas Place well and tank to finish on the graded dirt Cedar Canyon Road, part of Desert #13: Mojave Road.

Current Road Information

Mojave National Preserve
PO Box 241
72157 Baker Boulevard
Baker, CA 92309
(760) 733-4040

Map References

BLM Mesquite Lake, Ivanpah
USGS 1:24,000 Ivanpah Lake, Desert, Nipton, Ivanpah, Joshua, Mid Hills
1:100,000 Mesquite Lake, Ivanpah
Maptech CD-ROM: San Bernardino County/Mojave
Southern & Central California Atlas & Gazetteer, pp. 57, 71
California Road & Recreation Atlas, p. 98
Trails Illustrated, Mojave National Preserve (256)

Route Directions

▼ 0.0			Trail commences at Primm, NV, on the east side of I-15. Zero trip meter and continue east on the paved Underpass Road.
	1.6 ▲		Trail ends in Primm, NV, on the east side of I-15.
			GPS: N35°36.75' W115°23.23'
▼ 0.1		SO	Stoplight.
	1.5 ▲	SO	Stoplight.
▼ 0.2		TR	Turn right onto unmarked paved road immediately before RV park.
	1.4 ▲	TL	T-intersection with Underpass Road.
			GPS: N35°36.78' W115°23.00'
▼ 0.3		TL	Turn left at the end of the paved road onto graded dirt road under power lines.
	1.3 ▲	TR	Turn right onto paved road on the outskirts of Primm.
			GPS: N35°36.58' W115°22.92'
▼ 0.7		TR	4-way intersection under power lines. Turn right and follow along fence line.
	0.9 ▲	TL	4-way intersection under power lines.
			GPS: N35°36.72' W115°22.74'
▼ 0.9		TL	Turn left away from the fence line on well-used, formed trail.
	0.7 ▲	TR	T-intersection. Turn right along fence line.
			GPS: N35°36.51' W115°22.73'
▼ 1.3		SO	Track on left and track on right; then second track on left and track on right.
	0.3 ▲	SO	Track on left and track on right; then second track on left and track on right.
▼ 1.5		SO	Track on left.
	0.1 ▲	SO	Track on right.
▼ 1.6		TR	T-intersection with track alongside railroad. Zero trip meter.
	0.0 ▲		Continue to the northwest. Immediately track on left.
			GPS: N35°36.12' W115°22.13'
▼ 0.0			Continue to the south.
	6.4 ▲	TL	Turn left onto well-used trail away from railroad and zero trip meter.
▼ 0.3		SO	Cross through wash.
	6.1 ▲	SO	Cross through wash.
▼ 0.4		SO	Cattle guard.
	6.0 ▲	SO	Cattle guard.
			GPS: N35°35.76' W115°22.20'
▼ 0.6		SO	Cross through wash; then track on right; then

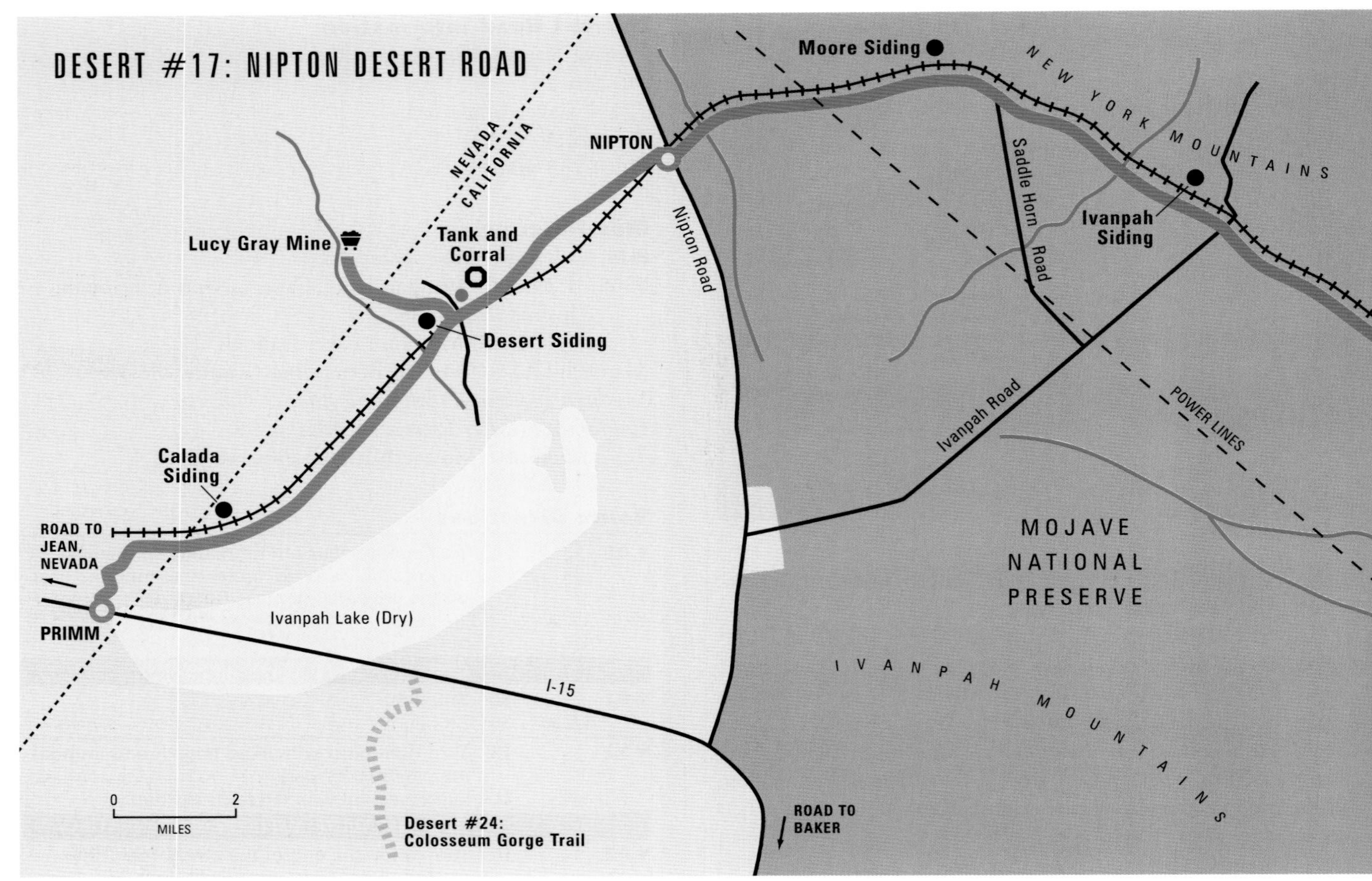

		California state line at cattle guard. Entering San Bernardino County, CA.
5.8 ▲	SO	Cattle guard at the Nevada state line. Entering Clark County, NV. Track on left; then cross through wash.
		GPS: N35°35.50' W115°22.24'
▼ 1.0	SO	Cross through wash.
5.4 ▲	SO	Cross through wash.
▼ 1.6	SO	Site of Calada Railway Siding.
4.8 ▲	SO	Site of Calada Railway Siding.
		GPS: N35°34.69' W115°22.16'
▼ 1.8	SO	Cross through wash. Track on left up wash under bridge.
4.6 ▲	SO	Cross through wash. Track on right up wash under bridge.
▼ 2.1	SO	Cross through wash.
4.3 ▲	SO	Cross through wash.
▼ 2.4	SO	Cross through wash; then track on right.
4.0 ▲	SO	Track on left; then cross through wash.
▼ 3.0	SO	Cross through wash.
3.4 ▲	SO	Cross through wash.
▼ 3.4	SO	Cross through wash.
3.0 ▲	SO	Cross through wash.
▼ 3.8	BR	Maintenance track on left.
2.6 ▲	SO	Maintenance track on right.
		GPS: N35°32.97' W115°20.88'
▼ 3.9	SO	Cross through wash.
2.5 ▲	SO	Cross through wash.
▼ 4.0	SO	Maintenance track on left.
2.4 ▲	BL	Maintenance track on right.
▼ 4.8	SO	Cross through wash.
1.6 ▲	SO	Cross through wash.
▼ 5.2	SO	Cross through wash.
1.2 ▲	SO	Cross through wash.
▼ 5.6	SO	Track on right.
0.8 ▲	SO	Track on left.
▼ 5.7	SO	Cross through wash; then track on right.
0.7 ▲	SO	Track on left; then cross through wash.
▼ 6.3	SO	Desert Siding. There is a private house and a water tower.
0.1 ▲	SO	Desert Siding. There is a private house and a water tower.
		GPS: N35°31.35' W115°18.94'
▼ 6.4	TL	Track on right is a dead end. Track continues ahead on west side of railroad. Turn left and pass under rail line; then turn immediately right and continue south on the east side of the line. Track on left. Track straight ahead is the spur to the Lucy Gray Mine. Zero trip meter under rail line.
0.0 ▲		Continue to the northwest.
		GPS: N35°31.28' W115°18.85'

Spur to Lucy Gray Mine

▼ 0.0		Continue to the northeast from the railroad bridge and cross cattle guard. Immediately track on right.
▼ 0.6	BR	Track on left.
		GPS: N35°31.70' W115°18.52'
▼ 1.1	SO	Enter up line of wash.

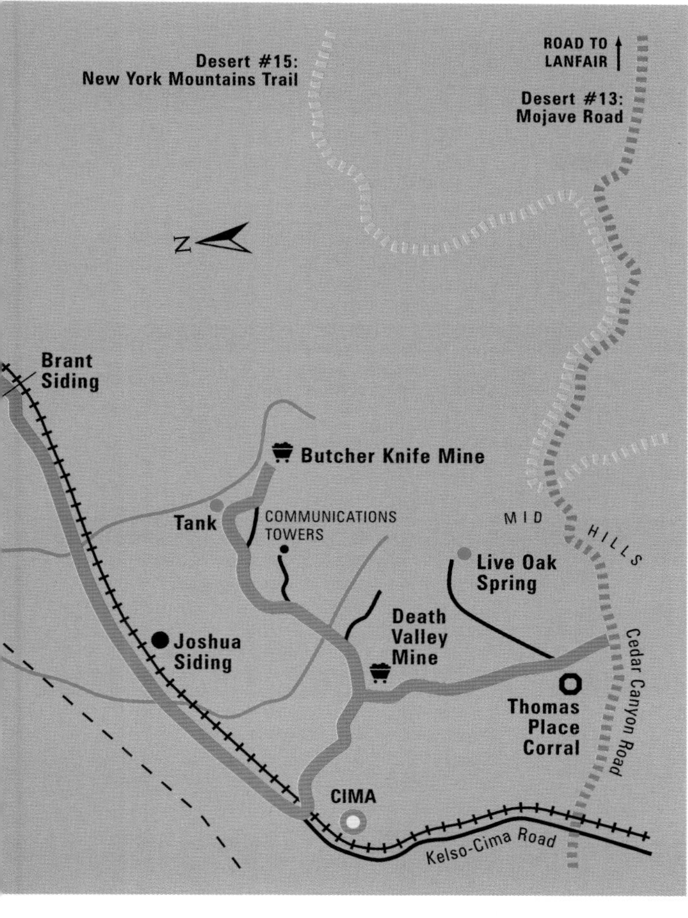

▼ 1.5 SO Cross state line (unmarked) back into Nevada.

GPS: N35°32.46' W115°18.08'

▼ 1.6 SO Enter wash at mouth of canyon into Lucy Gray Mountains.

▼ 1.8 BR Track on left.

GPS: N35°32.64' W115°17.90'

▼ 2.1 BR Mine on left; then bear right up wash past track on left.

GPS: N35°32.68' W115°17.58'

▼ 2.2 Bear left out of wash. Small mines are scattered around the hillside, including the Lucy Gray.

GPS: N35°32.70' W115°17.43'

Continuation of Main Trail

▼ 0.0 Continue to the southeast. Road is now paved.
4.3 ▲ TR Track on right is the spur to the Lucy Gray Mine. Track straight ahead. Turn left and pass under rail line. Zero trip meter. Turn second right on west side of rail line onto roughly graded road that remains below the railroad tracks. Track straight ahead is a dead end.

GPS: N35°31.28' W115°18.85'

▼ 0.2 SO Corral and tank on left.
4.1 ▲ SO Corral and tank on right.

▼ 0.8 BL Track on right. Remain on paved road and cross cattle guard. Railroad leaves on right.
3.5 ▲ BR Cattle guard. Track on left. Remain on paved road. Trail runs alongside the Union Pacific Railroad.

▼ 3.0 SO Cattle guard; then track on right.
1.3 ▲ SO Track on left; then cattle guard.

▼ 3.2 SO Track on right.
1.1 ▲ SO Track on left.

▼ 3.3 SO Track on left.
1.0 ▲ SO Track on right.

▼ 3.7 SO Track on right. Railroad rejoins on right.
0.6 ▲ SO Track on left. Railroad leaves on left.

▼ 4.3 TR Turn right onto paved Nipton Road at Nipton and cross over railroad. Zero trip meter.
0.0 ▲ Continue to the northwest.

GPS: N35°28.03' W115°16.29'

▼ 0.0 Continue to the southeast.
5.5 ▲ TL Cross over railroad and turn left onto small paved road, marked Nipton Desert Road. Zero trip meter.

▼ 0.1 TL Turn left onto graded dirt road running on the west side of the railroad. The road is marked Nipton-Moore Road.
5.4 ▲ TR Turn right onto the paved Nipton Road at Nipton.

GPS: N35°28.00' W115°16.35'

▼ 0.4 SO Cross through wash.
5.1 ▲ SO Cross through wash.

▼ 0.8 SO Cross through wash.
4.7 ▲ SO Cross through wash.

▼ 1.2 SO Cross through wash.
4.3 ▲ SO Cross through wash.

▼ 1.6 SO Cross through wash.
3.9 ▲ SO Cross through wash.

▼ 2.2 SO Cross through wash. Track on left up wash.
3.3 ▲ SO Cross through wash. Track on right up wash.

GPS: N35°26.26' W115°15.65'

▼ 2.6 SO Cross through wash; then track on right along power lines.
2.9 ▲ SO Track on left along power lines; then cross through wash.

▼ 3.1 SO Cross through wash.
2.4 ▲ SO Cross through wash.

▼ 3.4 SO Cross through wash.
2.1 ▲ SO Cross through wash.

▼ 3.7 SO Cross through wash.
1.8 ▲ SO Cross through wash.

▼ 4.1 SO Cross through wash.
1.4 ▲ SO Cross through wash.

▼ 4.4 SO Moore Siding on left.
1.1 ▲ SO Moore Siding on right.

GPS: N35°24.28' W115°15.49'

▼ 4.5 SO Cross through wash.
1.0 ▲ SO Cross through wash.

▼ 5.5 BL Graded road on right over cattle guard is Saddle Horn Road. Zero trip meter.
0.0 ▲ Continue to the northeast alongside railroad.

GPS: N35°23.36' W115°15.84'

▼ 0.0 Continue to the southwest alongside railroad.
4.4 ▲ SO Graded road on left over cattle guard is Saddle Horn Road. Zero trip meter.

▼ 0.1 SO Cross through wash.
4.3 ▲ SO Cross through wash.

▼ 0.6 SO Cross through wash.
3.8 ▲ SO Cross through wash.

Mileage		Description
▼ 1.4	SO	Cross over wash.
3.0 ▲	SO	Cross over wash.
▼ 2.5	BR	Cross through wash. Track on left up wash. Then track on left.
1.9 ▲	SO	Track on right; then cross through wash. Track on right up wash.
		GPS: N35°21.63' W115°17.59'
▼ 3.1	SO	Cross through wash.
1.3 ▲	SO	Cross through wash.
▼ 3.4	TR	Turn right alongside railroad; maintenance track on left.
1.0 ▲	TL	Turn left away from railroad; maintenance track straight ahead.
		GPS: N35°21.01' W115°18.13'
▼ 3.6	SO	Track on left.
0.8 ▲	BL	Track on right.
▼ 3.7	SO	Cross through wash. Ivanpah Siding on left.
0.7 ▲	SO	Ivanpah Siding on right. Cross through wash.
▼ 4.4	SO	Cross over paved Ivanpah Road and continue straight ahead on west side of railroad. Zero trip meter.
0.0 ▲		Continue to the northeast.
		GPS: N35°20.30' W115°18.76'
▼ 0.0		Continue to the southwest.
4.5 ▲	SO	Cross over paved Ivanpah Road and continue straight ahead. Zero trip meter.
▼ 0.1	SO	Cross through wash.
4.4 ▲	SO	Cross through wash.
▼ 0.6	BL	Cattle guard; then track on right.
3.9 ▲	SO	Track on left; then cattle guard.
▼ 1.3	SO	Cross through wash.
3.2 ▲	SO	Cross through wash.
▼ 2.0	SO	Cross through wash.
2.5 ▲	SO	Cross through wash.
▼ 2.4	SO	Track on right.
2.1 ▲	SO	Track on left.
▼ 2.8	BL	Track on right is marked as Lawler Lane.
1.7 ▲	SO	Track on left is marked as Lawler Lane.
		GPS: N35°18.50' W115°20.87'
▼ 3.3	SO	Cross through wash.
1.2 ▲	SO	Cross through wash.
▼ 4.4	SO	Wire gate on left at the start of track alongside railroad.
0.1 ▲	SO	Wire gate on right at the start of track alongside railroad.
		GPS: N35°17.53' W115°22.23'
▼ 4.5	BR	Wire gate on left at the start of track alongside railroad. Leave railroad. Trail is now smaller and formed. This is Brant Siding. Zero trip meter.
0.0 ▲		Continue to the north.
		GPS: N35°17.50' W115°22.32'
▼ 0.0		Continue to the west.
6.5 ▲	BL	Wire gate on right at the start of track alongside railroad. Bear left alongside railroad. Trail is now wider and roughly graded. This is Brant Siding. Zero trip meter.
▼ 0.2	SO	Cross through wash.
6.3 ▲	SO	Cross through wash.
▼ 0.4	SO	Small track on left.
6.1 ▲	SO	Small track on right.
▼ 0.9	SO	Cross through wash.
5.6 ▲	SO	Cross through wash.
▼ 1.2	SO	Track on left; then cross through wash.
5.3 ▲	SO	Cross through wash; then track on right.
▼ 1.5	SO	Cross through wash.
5.0 ▲	SO	Cross through wash.
▼ 2.1	SO	Track on right.
4.4 ▲	BR	Track on left.
		GPS: N35°17.12' W115°24.30'
▼ 2.6	SO	Cross through wash.
3.9 ▲	SO	Cross through wash.
▼ 3.5	SO	Cross through wash.
3.0 ▲	SO	Cross through wash.
▼ 4.2	SO	Cross through wash; then Joshua Siding on left.
2.3 ▲	SO	Joshua Siding on right; then cross through wash.
		GPS: N35°16.47' W115°26.51'
▼ 4.8	SO	Cross through wash.
1.7 ▲	SO	Cross through wash.
▼ 4.9	SO	Cross through wash.
1.6 ▲	SO	Cross through wash.
▼ 5.3	SO	Cross through wash.
1.2 ▲	SO	Cross through wash.
		GPS: N35°16.01' W115°27.58'
▼ 6.5	SO	Pass through wire gate; then cross through wash; then pass through second wire gate onto road alongside railroad. Zero trip meter between gates.
0.0 ▲		Continue to the north.
		GPS: N35°15.27' W115°28.68'
▼ 0.0		Continue to the south.
1.6 ▲	BL	Pass through wire gate; then cross through wash; then bear left and pass through second wire gate onto small formed trail. Gate on right continues alongside railroad. Zero trip meter between gates.
▼ 0.1	BR	Bear right onto graded road below railroad.
1.5 ▲	SO	Track on right.
▼ 0.6	SO	Track on left; then cross through wash.
1.0 ▲	BL	Cross through wash; then track on right.
▼ 1.6	TL	Turn left and cross over railroad. Immediately road on right and track on left. Zero trip meter. Turning right at this point takes you immediately out to paved Kelso-Cima Road at Cima.
0.0 ▲		Continue to the northeast.
		GPS: N35°14.26' W115°29.86'
▼ 0.0		Continue to the southeast.
2.3 ▲	TR	Road on left and track on right; then cross over railroad and turn right alongside railroad. Zero trip meter. Continuing straight at this point takes you immediately out to paved Kelso-Cima Road at Cima.
▼ 0.6	SO	Cattle guard.
1.7 ▲	SO	Cattle guard.
▼ 1.8	SO	Cross through wash.
0.5 ▲	SO	Cross through wash.
▼ 2.3	BR	Bear right onto smaller trail. Track on left is spur to the Death Valley and Butcher Knife Mines. The mines are posted as private property. Zero trip meter.
0.0 ▲		Continue to the northwest.
		GPS: N35°13.42' W115°27.87'

Spur to Death Valley and Butcher Knife Mines

Mileage		Description
▼ 0.0		Continue to the east.
▼ 0.2	BL	Death Valley Mine on right.
		GPS: N35°13.33' W115°27.71'
▼ 0.9	SO	Track on right.
		GPS: N35°13.50' W115°26.90'

▼ 1.7	BL	Track on right goes to communications towers.
▼ 1.9	SO	Cross through wash; then track on right.
▼ 3.8	SO	Corral and tank on left.
		GPS: N35°14.92′ W115°24.58′
▼ 4.5	TL	Track continues straight ahead.
		GPS: N35°14.42′ W115°24.30′
▼ 5.1	SO	Cross through wash.
▼ 5.3	TR	Track continues straight ahead.
		GPS: N35°14.31′ W115°23.49′
▼ 5.6		Trail ends at the Butcher Knife Mine—timber-lined shaft and tailings.
		GPS: N35°14.26′ W115°23.45′

Continuation of Main Trail

▼ 0.0			Continue to the south.
	3.2 ▲	SO	Track on right is spur to Death Valley and Butcher Knife Mines. The mines are posted as private property. Zero trip meter.
			GPS: N35°13.42′ W115°27.87′
▼ 0.3		SO	Cross through wash.
	2.9 ▲	SO	Cross through wash.
▼ 0.4		SO	Mine workings on left.
	2.8 ▲	SO	Mine workings on right.
			GPS: N35°13.11′ W115°27.89′
▼ 0.7		SO	Cross through wash.
	2.5 ▲	SO	Cross through wash.
▼ 1.5		SO	Cross through wash.
	1.7 ▲	SO	Cross through wash.
▼ 1.9		SO	Cross through wash.
	1.3 ▲	SO	Cross through wash.
▼ 2.2		SO	Cross through two washes.
	1.0 ▲	SO	Cross through two washes.
▼ 3.2		BR	4-way intersection. Track on sharp left goes to Live Oak Spring. Zero trip meter and bear right toward the corral.
	0.0 ▲		Continue to the northwest.
			GPS: N35°10.60′ W115°27.68′
▼ 0.0			Continue to the south.
	1.1 ▲	BL	4-way intersection. Track straight ahead goes to Live Oak Spring. Zero trip meter and bear left, rejoining main trail.
▼ 0.1		TL	Turn left in front of Thomas Place corral, tank, and cabin.
	1.0 ▲	TR	Thomas Place corral, tank, and cabin ahead.
			GPS: N35°10.54′ W115°27.73′
▼ 0.2		TR	Turn right to rejoin main trail.
	0.9 ▲	TL	Turn left toward corral and tank.
▼ 0.9		SO	Track on left.
	0.2 ▲	SO	Track on right.
▼ 1.0		BR	Track on left and track straight ahead.
	0.1 ▲	BL	Track on right and track straight ahead.
▼ 1.1			Trail ends at intersection with graded dirt Cedar Canyon Road, part of Desert #13: Mojave Road. Turn left to travel the road to Lanfair; turn right to exit to Cima and the Kelso-Cima Road.
	0.0 ▲		Trail commences on graded dirt Cedar Canyon Road, part of Desert #13: Mojave Road, 2.8 miles southwest of intersection with Black Canyon Road and 2.9 miles southeast of intersection with Kelso-Cima Road. Zero trip meter and turn north on unmarked, well-used formed trail that runs alongside a fence line.
			GPS: N35°09.83′ W115°27.41′

DESERT #18

Cima Dome Trail

Starting Point:	**Cima Road, 10 miles south of I-15, 1.2 miles northwest of the Teutonia Peak Hiking Trailhead**
Finishing Point:	**Kelbaker Road, 19 miles southeast of Baker**
Total Mileage:	**19.4 miles**
Unpaved Mileage:	**19.4 miles**
Driving Time:	**1.5 hours**
Elevation Range:	**3,200–5,100 feet**
Usually Open:	**Year-round**
Best Time to Travel:	**September to May**
Difficulty Rating:	**2**
Scenic Rating:	**8**
Remoteness Rating:	**+1**

Special Attractions

- Cima Dome and Cinder Cones.
- Views from Cima Dome over the Mojave Desert to the Kingston Range.
- Excellent example of a dense Joshua tree forest.

History

Cima Dome is an almost perfectly rounded landform consisting of quartz monzonite. Because of its immense size, its symmetrical shape is not always apparent at close range. A study of a topographical map shows how evenly the circular contour lines are spaced. Geologists describe this landform as a molten mass that stopped rising well before it reached the earth's surface, a feature referred to as a batholith. The massive dome rises as high as 1,500 feet above the surrounding desert area and supports one of the most striking Joshua tree forests in the Southwest. Cima (Spanish for "summit") Dome is approximately 10 miles in diameter and covers nearly 75 square miles. The name Cima was adopted by the nearby Union Pacific Railroad station in 1907.

Tall Joshua trees along Cima Road

Farther southwest along this trail are many small cinder cones. Some eruptions occurred 7 million years ago; the most recent was around 10,000 years ago. Lava spewed during violent eruptions cooled almost instantly, capturing bubbles of gas within. Eruptions continued for a long period of time, slowly developing the high cinder cones we see along the

Valley View Ranch in the winter

trail today. There are 53 vents and over 60 flows spread across this lava landscape.

The cinder cones near Black Tank Wash are the site of several cinder mines. The Valco cinder sites were discovered in 1954 and the nearby Red Beauty in 1955. Although a lot of mining activity occurred—screening plants were established on-site and roads were built to truck the material out—the mining claims were declared void by the BLM in the 1980s. The case was tied up in court for years before it was declared that the claims lacked marketability; they were not able to turn a profit when operating in the 1950s, and on these grounds should have been discontinued.

Description

The trail commences on Cima Road, a short distance from the popular hiking trailhead to Teutonia Peak in the Mojave National Preserve. Initially the trail is a graded dirt road that leads to the active Valley View Ranch. The trail passes through the middle of the ranch's yards, so be aware that there may be people and animals around. Past the ranch, the trail becomes a well-used, formed sandy trail. It runs high along the north face of Cima Dome. The elevation gives excellent views to the north over Shadow Valley toward the Clark Range and the distant Kingston Range.

The trail passes by a series of water tanks, corrals, and extensive Joshua tree forests. Desert #13: Mojave Road intersects this trail near Willow Wash, which provides an excellent example of the shapes lava may take as it cools. The trail then joins a roughly graded road and travels through the cinder pit of the Aikens Mine before descending the north slope to finish on paved Kelbaker Road.

Current Road Information

Mojave National Preserve
PO Box 241
72157 Baker Boulevard
Baker, CA 92309
(760) 733-4040

Map References

BLM Ivanpah
USGS 1:24,000 Cima Dome, Cow Cave, Marl Mt., Indian Spring
1:100,000 Ivanpah
Maptech CD-ROM: San Bernardino County/Mojave
Southern & Central California Atlas & Gazetteer, pp. 71, 70
California Road & Recreation Atlas, p. 97
Trails Illustrated, Mojave National Preserve (256)

Route Directions

Mileage		Direction
▼ 0.0		From Cima Road, 10 miles south of I-15 and 1.2 miles northwest of Teutonia Peak Hiking Trailhead, zero trip meter and turn southwest on small graded dirt road. There is a sign for Valley View Ranch at the intersection.
6.0 ▲		Trail ends at T-intersection with paved Cima Road. Turn right for Cima; turn left for I-15.
		GPS: N35°20.01' W115°33.50'
▼ 1.6	BL	Bear left of main shed. Track on right.
4.4 ▲	BR	Bear right of main shed; then track on left.
		GPS: N35°19.19' W115°34.93'
▼ 1.7	SO	4-way intersection. Proceed through the Valley View Ranch yard, leaving the homestead on left. Track on right. Proceed southwest and follow formed trail, marked with BLM post SH 433 for 4WDs, ATVs, and motorbikes.
4.3 ▲	SO	Track on left; then 4-way intersection. Continue straight, leaving homestead on right. Proceed northeast through the Valley View Ranch yard.
		GPS: N35°19.16' W115°34°98'
▼ 2.3	SO	Track on left.
3.7 ▲	BL	Track on right.
▼ 6.0	SO	Corral and tank on right, track on right. Zero trip meter at corral. This is Water Tank No. 1.
0.0 ▲		Continue to the northeast.
		GPS: N35°18.09' W115°39.67'

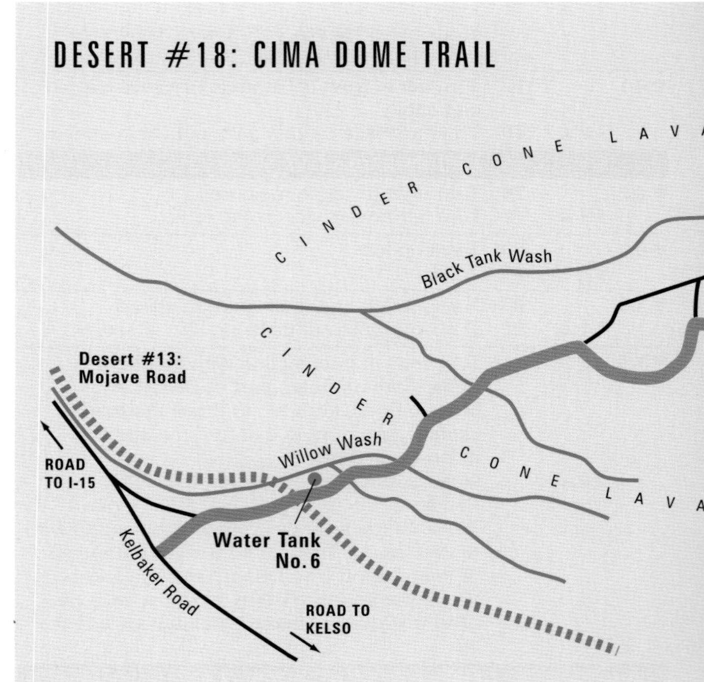

▼ 0.0			Continue to the southwest.
	5.3 ▲	SO	Corral and tank on left, track on left. Zero trip meter at corral. This is Water Tank No. 1.
▼ 1.8		SO	Track on left and track on right along power poles. Continue through gate, keeping corral on your right. This is Water Tank No. 2.
	3.5 ▲	SO	Pass through gate, corral on left. This is Water Tank No. 2. Track on left and track on right along power poles.
			GPS: N35°16.91′ W115°40.94′
▼ 2.2		SO	Well-used track on right.
	3.1 ▲	BR	Well-used track on left.
			GPS: N35°16.57′ W115°41.30′
▼ 3.5		SO	Track on left.
	1.8 ▲	SO	Track on right.
▼ 3.6		SO	Track on right, corral and well on left. This is Water Tank No. 3.
	1.7 ▲	SO	Track on left, corral and well on right. This is Water Tank No. 3.
			GPS: N35°15.84′ W115°42.54′
▼ 4.2		SO	Cross through wash.
	1.1 ▲	SO	Cross through wash.
▼ 5.3		SO	Track on right. Zero trip meter.
	0.0 ▲		Continue to the northeast.
			GPS: N35°14.81′ W115°43.82′
▼ 0.0			Continue to the southwest.
	6.7 ▲	SO	Track on left. Zero trip meter.
▼ 1.2		BR	Pass cinder pit works on left.
	5.5 ▲	BL	Pass cinder pit works on right.
			GPS: N35°13.92′ W115°43.51′
▼ 1.3		SO	Cattle guard. Exit cinder pit area.
	5.4 ▲	SO	Cattle guard. Enter cinder pit area.
▼ 2.2		SO	Track on right.
	4.5 ▲	BR	Track on left.
▼ 3.5		BL	Well-used track on right.
	3.2 ▲	SO	Well-used track on left.
			GPS: N35°12.69′ W115°44.94′
▼ 3.8		SO	Well-used track on right.
	2.9 ▲	BR	Well-used track on left.
▼ 4.2		SO	Track on right.
	2.5 ▲	SO	Track on left.
▼ 4.6		SO	Cross through wash.
	2.1 ▲	SO	Cross through wash.
▼ 5.2		SO	Track on right onto cinder cone.
	1.5 ▲	SO	Track on left onto cinder cone.
			GPS: N35°11.52′ W115°45.98′
▼ 5.3		SO	Track on right.
	1.4 ▲	SO	Track on left.
▼ 5.6		SO	Cross through Willow Wash.
	1.1 ▲	SO	Cross through Willow Wash.
▼ 5.7		SO	Cross through wash.
	1.0 ▲	SO	Cross through wash.
▼ 5.9		SO	Cross through wash.
	0.8 ▲	SO	Cross through wash.
▼ 6.0		SO	Cross through wash.
	0.7 ▲	SO	Cross through wash.
▼ 6.4		SO	Water Tank No. 6 on right.
	0.3 ▲	SO	Water Tank No. 6 on left.
▼ 6.5		SO	Corral on right.
	0.2 ▲	SO	Corral on left.
▼ 6.6		SO	Track on right to corral.
	0.1 ▲	BR	Track on left to corral.
▼ 6.7		SO	Track on right and track on left is Desert #13: Mojave Road. Cairns mark the intersection. Zero trip meter.
	0.0 ▲		Continue to the north.
			GPS: N35°10.38′ W115°46.61′
▼ 0.0			Continue to the south.
	1.4 ▲	SO	Track on right and track on left is Desert #13: Mojave Road. Cairns mark the intersection. Zero trip meter.
▼ 0.9		SO	Track on right.
	0.5 ▲	SO	Track on left.
▼ 1.4			Trail ends at intersection with paved Kelbaker

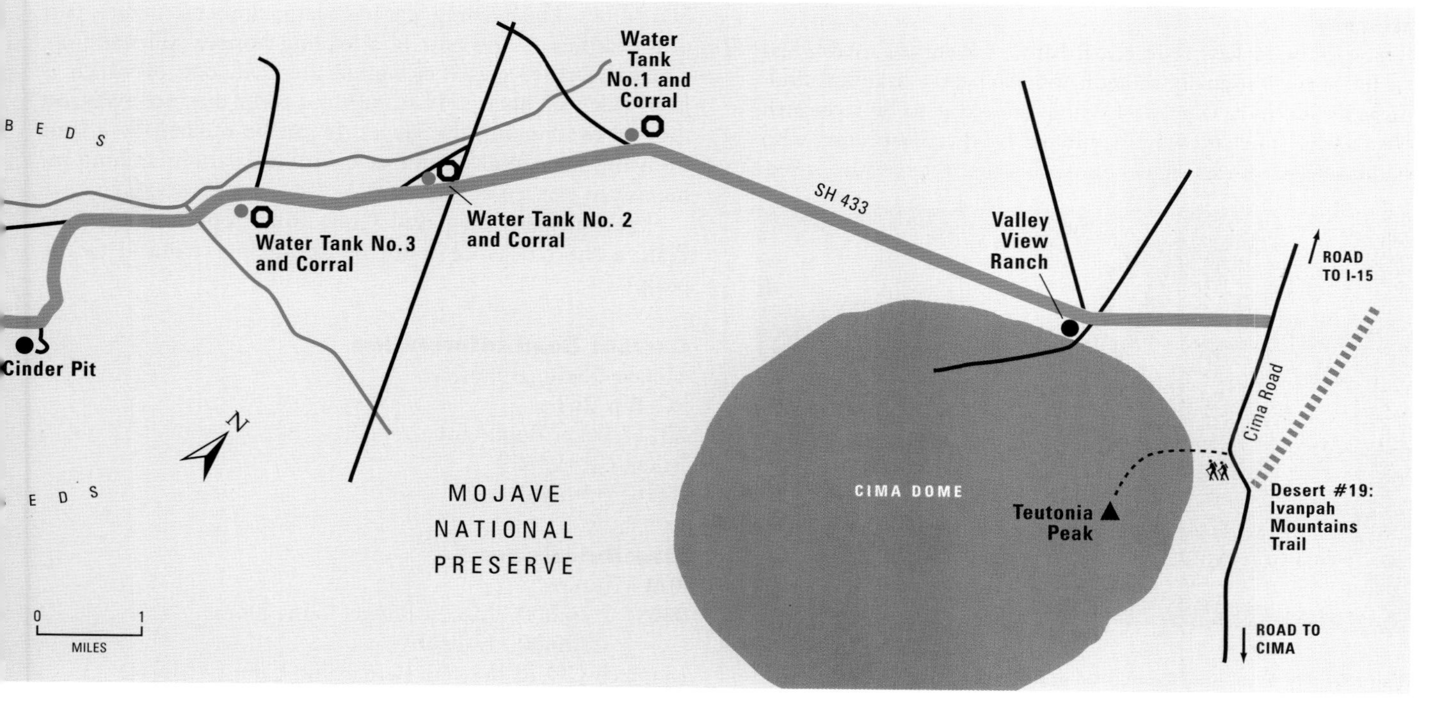

Road. Turn left for Kelso; turn right for Baker and I-15.

0.0 ▲ Trail starts on paved Kelbaker Road, 19 miles southeast of Baker. Zero trip meter and turn north on graded dirt road. Old sign for Aikens Mine Road at intersection and a small track opposite.

GPS: N35°09.32' W115°47.38'

DESERT #19

Ivanpah Mountains Trail

Starting Point:	**I-15, Bailey Road exit at Mountain Pass**
Finishing Point:	**Cima Road, 11.7 miles south of I-15**
Total Mileage:	**12.8 miles, plus 1.5-mile spur to Riley's Camp**
Unpaved Mileage:	**12 miles, plus 1.5-mile spur**
Driving Time:	**3 hours**
Elevation Range:	**4,500–5,400 feet**
Usually Open:	**Year-round**
Best Time to Travel:	**September to May**
Difficulty Rating:	**3**
Scenic Rating:	**9**
Remoteness Rating:	**+0**

Special Attractions

- Dinosaur trackway.
- Remains of Evening Star Mine and Riley's Camp.
- Lightly traveled Mojave Desert trail.

History

The Mountain Pass Rare Earth Mine, which was established in 1949, was originally thought to have been a uranium find. Tests by the U.S. Bureau of Mines proved it to be rare earth bastnaesite. The site was abandoned by the prospectors who had found it with a Geiger counter because the ore was useless at the time. Molycorp soon took an interest in the site and set about finding a market for its ore. Though it took 20 years to attract a market, the metals are now sought after for use in glass manufacturing, television tubes, microwave ovens, and as a coloring agent to control the index of glass refraction.

The northern end of this trail climbs slowly around the Mescal Range south of I-15. The southern face of this range contains a unit of cross-bedded arenitic sandstone, possibly reaching to a depth of more than 600 feet. Imprinted in the sandstone are the only dinosaur tracks to have been discovered in California. The prints, made when dinosaurs walked the soft mud and sediments that are now hardened rock, measure 2 to 4 inches in diameter and are difficult to find. Guided tours can be arranged through the Needles BLM Field Office.

Riley's Camp was a mining camp worked by John Riley Bembery, whose grave can be found a short distance from the site. Bembery spent many years prospecting in the Mojave Desert. On his death in 1984, the camp was ceded to the government and is now preserved by Bembery's friends.

Evening Star Mill truck now located along I-15 at Halloran Summit

Description

Ivanpah Mountains Trail takes a winding route through the rugged Ivanpah Mountains, which sit between I-15 and the Mojave National Preserve. The trail heads south from I-15, traveling along a small, roughly graded dirt road into the Mescal Range. It climbs steadily to a saddle before descending along the southern side into Piute Valley.

A prominent peak to the southwest is Kokoweef Peak, which is actively mined. The trail skirts the edge of the Dinosaur Trackway Area of Critical Environmental Concern, where dinosaur prints in the sandstone are preserved for posterity.

Continuing into Piute Valley, the trail passes through many Joshua trees near the remains of the Silverado and Evening Star Mines. The Evening Star has a large timber structure, part of a headframe, and part of a loading hopper still standing. There are three graves alongside the trail, one of which is John Riley Bembery's. His camp is a short distance away, on the rise overlooking the graves. It can be reached by a spur from the main trail. A timber cabin and various mining remains can be seen at the camp.

The trail ends on paved Cima Road, opposite Teutonia Peak, a short distance south of the hiking trailhead to the peak.

Current Road Information

Mojave National Preserve
PO Box 241
72157 Baker Boulevard
Baker, CA 92309
(760) 733-4040

Map References

BLM Ivanpah
USGS 1:24,000 Mescal Range, Cima Dome
1:100,000 Ivanpah
Maptech CD-ROM: San Bernardino County/Mojave

Southern & Central California Atlas & Gazetteer, p. 71
California Road & Recreation Atlas, p. 97
Trails Illustrated, Mojave National Preserve (256)

Route Directions

▼ 0.0			From I-15 at the Bailey Road exit (also called Mountain Pass), 14.8 miles west of Primm, NV, proceed to the south side of the freeway and zero trip meter at cattle guard. Immediately turn left on paved road and head east alongside the freeway.
	3.7 ▲		Turn right and proceed north to I-15 at the Bailey Road exit (also called Mountain Pass).
			GPS: N35°28.02′ W115°31.66′
▼ 0.8		SO	Road turns to graded dirt and swings away from freeway. Cross through wash; then track on left and track on right.
	2.9 ▲	SO	Track on left and track on right; then cross through wash. Road is now paved and runs alongside the freeway.
▼ 1.0		SO	Track on left.
	2.7 ▲	SO	Track on right.
▼ 1.2		SO	Corral on right; then two tracks on right.
	2.5 ▲	SO	Two tracks on left; then corral on left.
			GPS: N35°27.63′ W115°30.97′
▼ 1.4		SO	Track on right.
	2.3 ▲	SO	Track on left.
▼ 1.6		SO	Track on left.
	2.1 ▲	SO	Track on right.
▼ 1.9		SO	Two tracks on right.
	1.8 ▲	SO	Two tracks on left.
▼ 2.7		SO	Track on left; then track on right.
	1.0 ▲	SO	Track on left; then track on right.
			GPS: N35°26.69′ W115°30.11′
▼ 2.9		BR	Bear right past graded road on left; then track on right.
	0.8 ▲	SO	Track on left; then graded road on right.
			GPS: N35°26.53′ W115°30.29′
▼ 3.7		BR	Track on right; then graded road on left goes 1 mile to an active mine on Kokoweef Peak. Track on right. Bear right on graded road and zero trip meter.
	0.0 ▲		Continue to the north past track on left.
			GPS: N35°26.00′ W115°30.78′
▼ 0.0			Continue to the south.
	5.2 ▲	SO	Graded road on right goes 1 mile to an active mine on Kokoweef Peak. Track on left. Zero trip meter.
▼ 0.5		BL	Graded road on right goes to Iron Horse Mine and Blue Buzzard Mine.
	4.7 ▲	BR	Graded road on left goes to Iron Horse Mine and Blue Buzzard Mine.
			GPS: N35°25.56′ W115°31.06′
▼ 0.7		SO	Tank on left.
	4.5 ▲	SO	Tank on right.
▼ 0.8		SO	Cross over runway.
	4.4 ▲	SO	Cross over runway.
▼ 0.9		BR	Track on left.
	4.3 ▲	BL	Track on right.
▼ 1.3		TL	4-way intersection. Tank ahead. Graded road on right and track straight ahead. Turn left on formed trail.
	3.9 ▲	TR	4-way intersection. Tank on left. Track straight ahead and track on left. Turn right on graded road.

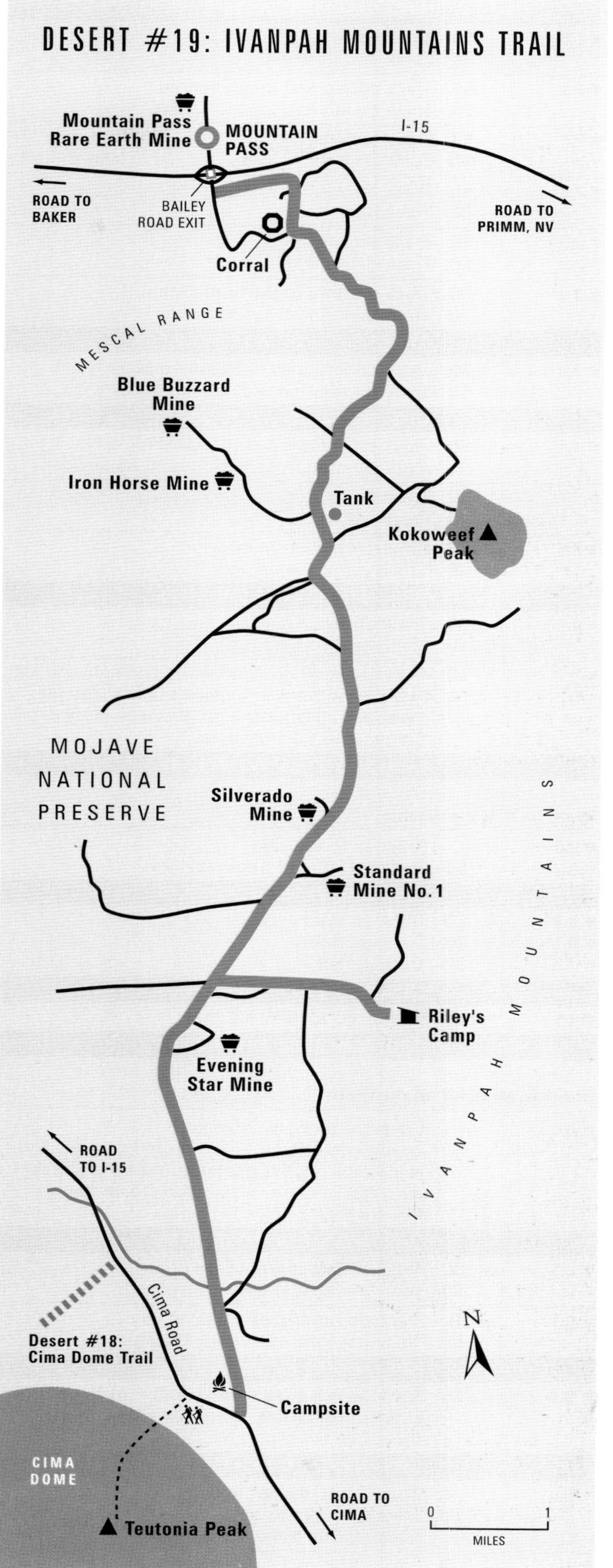

		GPS: N35°24.96' W115°31.16'
▼ 1.6	SO	Track on left.
3.6 ▲	SO	Track on right.
▼ 2.1	SO	Track on left and track on right.
3.1 ▲	SO	Track on left and track on right.
▼ 2.5	SO	Track on left.
2.7 ▲	SO	Track on right.
▼ 2.8	BL	Track on right.
2.4 ▲	BR	Track on left.
▼ 3.3	SO	Track on left.
1.9 ▲	SO	Track on right.
▼ 3.5	SO	Track on right to Silverado Mine.
1.7 ▲	SO	Track on left to Silverado Mine.
		GPS: N35°23.14' W115°31.27'
▼ 3.9	SO	Track on left goes to Standard Mine No. 1.
1.3 ▲	SO	Track on right goes to Standard Mine No. 1.
		GPS: N35°22.88' W115°31.54'
▼ 4.1	SO	Track on left goes to Standard Mine No. 1.
1.1 ▲	BL	Track on right goes to Standard Mine No. 1.
▼ 4.4	SO	Track on right.
0.8 ▲	SO	Track on left.
▼ 4.6	SO	Small cemetery on left.
0.6 ▲	SO	Small cemetery on right.
		GPS: N35°22.41' W115°31.99'
▼ 4.9	SO	Track on left.
0.3 ▲	SO	Track on right.
▼ 5.2	SO	4-way intersection. Graded road on right and left; to the left is the spur to Riley's Camp. Zero trip meter and continue straight ahead on formed trail.
0.0 ▲		Continue to the northeast.
		GPS: N35°21.98' W115°32.38'

Spur to Riley's Camp

▼ 0.0		Proceed to the east.
▼ 0.2	SO	Track on left and track on right.
		GPS: N35°21.95' W115°32.15'
▼ 0.4	SO	Track on right.
▼ 0.7	SO	Track on right.
▼ 1.2	BR	Track on left.
		GPS: N35°21.77' W115°31.06'
▼ 1.5	UT	Spur ends at Riley's Camp.
		GPS: N35°21.62' W115°30.92'

Continuation of Main Trail

▼ 0.0		Continue to the southwest.
0.4 ▲	SO	4-way intersection. Graded road on right and left; to the right is the spur to Riley's Camp. Zero trip meter and continue straight ahead on formed trail.
		GPS: N35°21.98' W115°32.38'
▼ 0.1	SO	Track on left and track on right.
0.3 ▲	SO	Track on left and track on right.
▼ 0.3	TL	Track on right; then track on left.
0.1 ▲	BR	Track on right; then track on left.
		GPS: N35°21.82' W115°32.58'
▼ 0.4	SO	Track on left goes 0.8 miles to remains of the Evening Star Mine. Zero trip meter.
0.0 ▲		Continue to the northeast.
		GPS: N35°21.71' W115°32.68'
▼ 0.0		Continue to the southwest.
3.5 ▲	SO	Track on right goes 0.8 miles to remains of the Evening Star Mine. Zero trip meter.
▼ 0.3	SO	Cross through wash; then track on left.
3.2 ▲	SO	Track on right; then cross through wash.
▼ 0.8	SO	Track on left.
2.7 ▲	SO	Track on right.
▼ 1.1	SO	Track on left.
2.4 ▲	SO	Track on right.
▼ 1.7	SO	Cross through wash.
1.8 ▲	SO	Cross through wash.
▼ 2.3	SO	Cross through wash. Track on left up wash.
1.2 ▲	SO	Cross through wash. Track on right up wash.
		GPS: N35°19.72' W115°32.70'
▼ 2.5	SO	Track on left.
1.0 ▲	BL	Track on right.
		GPS: N35°19.55' W115°32.66'
▼ 3.1	SO	Campsite on right in shelter of large granite boulders.
0.4 ▲	SO	Campsite on left in shelter of large granite boulders.
		GPS: N35°19.00' W115°32.61'
▼ 3.5		Trail ends on paved Cima Road, opposite Teutonia Peak. Turn right for I-15; turn left for Cima.
0.0 ▲		Trail commences on paved Cima Road, 11.7 miles south of I-15. Zero trip meter and turn northwest on formed dirt trail. Intersection is unmarked, but it is opposite Teutonia Peak and 0.6 miles south of Teutonia Peak Hiking Trailhead.
		GPS: N35°18.67' W115°32.58'

DESERT #20

Starbright Trail

Starting Point:	**Irwin Road, 9.5 miles northeast of Barstow**
Finishing Point:	**Goldstone Road (C332), 28.5 miles north of Barstow**
Total Mileage:	**29.1 miles**
Unpaved Mileage:	**29.1 miles**
Driving Time:	**3 hours**
Elevation Range:	**2,300–3,900 feet**
Usually Open:	**Year-round**
Best Time to Travel:	**September to May**
Difficulty Rating:	**3**
Scenic Rating:	**8**
Remoteness Rating:	**+1**

Special Attractions

- Remains of the Starbright Mine.
- Views of the Superior Valley.
- Trail ends close to the site of Goldstone.
- Can be combined with Desert #21: Black Canyon Road to form a loop from Barstow.

History

Rainbow Basin lies east of this trail in the unattractive sounding Mud Hills. This area provides a fossil link to the mammals that once roamed this region about 15 million years ago, when

This small stone cabin sits in a wash

the surrounding landscape was more lush and a shallow lake provided ample water. Giant pigs, camels, and bears frequented the region during the middle Miocene time and their bones have been found here. Sedimentary rocks of many colors, such as green, brown, red, and white, are present in the basin, hence the name. The rocks within Rainbow Basin have been folded and faulted over the years. The area was designated a national landmark in 1972.

Goldstone, near the northern end of this trail, was a hive of mining activity in 1881. Goldstone had been quiet for many decades when in 1958, it was chosen by the U.S. Army Ordnance Corps, Jet Propulsion Laboratory division, as the site for a ground-based, deep-space communication station. The reason behind Goldstone's selection was that it had no radio reception, or, as officials put it, it was an environment as free from radio noise as possible. NASA currently leases this quiet part of the Mojave Desert from the U.S. Army. The area is part of NASA's Deep Space Network (DSN). This network supports interplanetary spacecraft missions and a select number of earth orbiting missions. The network currently consists of three listening locations around the world. The other two facilities are not quite as quiet as old Goldstone. They are in Madrid, Spain, and Canberra, Australia.

In 1826, fur trapper Jedediah Smith may have been the first American to have met the Indians living in this region of the Mojave Desert. Many others followed, traveling the Old Spanish Trail between Santa Fe and the pueblo of Los Angeles. The old trail passed east of the Starbright Trail, close to the southeast boundary of the Fort Irwin Military Reservation. Bitter Spring, located just inside the boundary, was a popular camping spot along the trail. Kit Carson and Captain John C. Frémont traveled the Fort Irwin region in 1844 and established an official camp at Bitter Spring. Despite difficulties with Indians, the camp developed into a trading center as settlers and prospectors moved into the region. The camp was situated along the main Los Angeles to Salt Lake City route and trading boomed. The army constructed a stone fort above Bitter Spring in 1846, in an effort to gain control of the Fort Irwin region during the Indian Wars.

In the late 1880s, mining as far away as Death Valley contributed to the development of this crossroads settlement, resulting in the establishment of the nearby town of Barstow. By 1940 the Mojave Anti-Aircraft Range was established, encompassing old Fort Irwin. This military reservation covered an area of approximately 1,000 square miles and has had several roles over the years. Though deactivated at times and placed on basic maintenance status, the Fort Irwin National Training Center continues to serve as a major training center. To that end, it is safest to remain outside the reservation and not attempt to visit any of the historical locations mentioned that are within the range.

China Lake, to the north of this trail, became a research, development, test, and evaluation (RDT&E) site in 1943. By 1967, it was classed as a Naval Weapons Center. The site covers an area of more than 1 million acres and is used for the development and testing of air weapons and associated aircraft systems. Everything from air to surface missiles used in the Gulf War to demonstrating the technology of the Lunar Soft Landing Vehicle has occurred on the site. Again, for safety and security reasons, do not enter this site.

Description

This trail takes a circuitous route through the mountains and hills north of Barstow, twisting through the hills to finish near the boundary of the military reservation. Along the way, the trail travels past mining remains, along dry washes, on ridge tops that offer panoramic views of the sweeping Superior Valley, and past the dry beds of Coyote and Superior Lakes.

Navigation is very difficult along the trail. The trails are typically small, formed, and unmarked. Intersections are often confusing. A GPS unit will be invaluable here. A short time putting the route coordinates in will make navigation through the maze of unmarked trails much easier.

The rolling Mud Hills

The trail commences on paved Irwin Road, which leads northeast from Barstow. There is also a Fort Irwin Road that intersects with Irwin Road; the two roads should not be confused. Initially, the trail follows a graded dirt road before peeling off into the network of small trails. Many of the trails in this region are dead ends that branch into the mountains and either stop at a mining claim or just peter out.

The trail crosses the northern end of the Calico Mountains before swinging north to pass the remains of the Starbright Mine. There is a cabin at the site, as well as the wooden remains of an old loading hopper, numerous diggings, shafts, and tailings heaps.

The trail swings north, running through the sandy, creosote covered flats to intersect with Goldstone Road at the end of the trail. The site of Goldstone is a short distance to the north. The military reservation is located north of the finishing point. From the end of the trail, there are excellent views north and west into Superior Valley and the smooth surface of Superior Lake's bed.

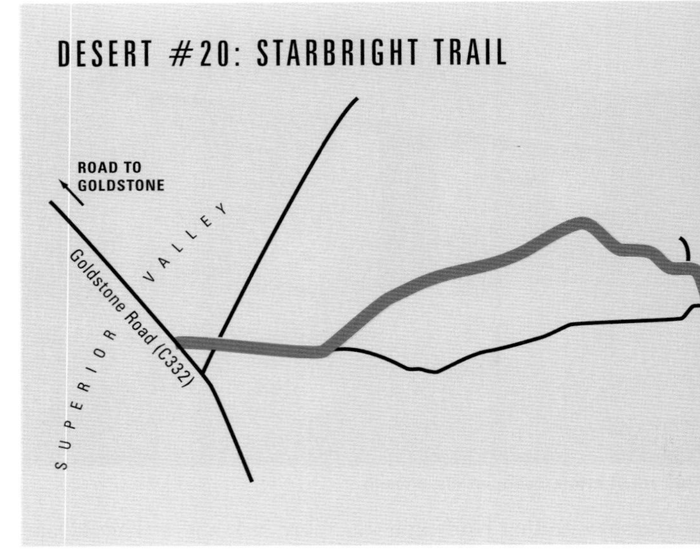

Current Road Information

Bureau of Land Management
Needles Field Office
101 West Spikes Road
Needles, CA 92363
(760) 326-7000

Map References

BLM Soda Mts.
USGS 1:24,000 Nebo, Lane Mt., Williams Well, Goldstone
1:100,000 Soda Mts.
Maptech CD-ROM: San Bernardino County/Mojave
Southern & Central California Atlas & Gazetteer, p. 68
California Road & Recreation Atlas, pp. 95, 105

Route Directions

Mileage		Direction	Description
▼ 0.0			From Irwin Road, 9.5 miles northeast of Barstow, zero trip meter and turn northwest on unmarked, formed dirt trail. Turn is 0.4 miles west of the major intersection of Irwin Road and Fort Irwin Road and is opposite the marked, paved road—Kolath Place.
	6.3 ▲		Trail ends on Irwin Road. Turn right for Barstow.
			GPS: N34°59.97′ W116°56.15′
▼ 0.6		SO	Track on left.
	5.7 ▲	SO	Track on right.
▼ 1.0		SO	Track on left.
	5.3 ▲	SO	Track on right.
▼ 1.3		SO	Track on right.
	5.0 ▲	SO	Track on left.
▼ 1.6		BR	Track on left.
	4.7 ▲	SO	Track on right.
			GPS: N35°01.18′ W116°57.01′
▼ 1.8		SO	Track on left.
	4.5 ▲	BL	Track on right.
▼ 1.9		SO	Well-used track on right.
	4.4 ▲	BR	Well-used track on left.
			GPS: N35°01.43′ W116°57.15′
▼ 2.1		SO	Track on right; then track on left.
	4.2 ▲	SO	Track on right; then track on left.
▼ 2.3		SO	Track on left.
	4.0 ▲	SO	Track on right.
▼ 2.4		TR	Turn sharp right before power lines; then track on left. Many tracks on left to transmission pylons ahead.
	3.9 ▲	TL	Track on right; then turn sharp left before reaching power lines.
			GPS: N35°01.59′ W116°57.57′
▼ 2.5		SO	Track on right.
	3.8 ▲	SO	Track on left.
▼ 3.7		BR	Well-used track on left.
	2.6 ▲	SO	Well-used track on right.
			GPS: N35°02.39′ W116°56.50′
▼ 3.8		SO	Graded road on right and left.
	2.5 ▲	SO	Graded road on right and left.
			GPS: N35°02.45′ W116°56.44′
▼ 4.5		SO	Track on left.
	1.8 ▲	SO	Track on right.
▼ 5.0		SO	Stone enclosure on right.
	1.3 ▲	SO	Stone enclosure on left.
			GPS: N35°03.13′ W116°55.46′
▼ 5.2		SO	Track on left.
	1.1 ▲	SO	Track on right.
▼ 6.0		SO	Track on left; then track on right.
	0.3 ▲	SO	Track on left; then track on right.
			GPS: N35°03.60′ W116°54.65′
▼ 6.3		TL	T-intersection with road along small power lines. Zero trip meter.
	0.0 ▲		Continue to the southwest. Many dead-end tracks to pylons ahead.
			GPS: N35°03.83′ W116°54.47′
▼ 0.0			Continue to the northwest and cross through many deep washes for the next 0.9 miles.
	4.1 ▲	TR	End of wash crossings. Track continues straight ahead. Turn away from the small power lines and zero trip meter.
▼ 0.3		SO	Track on left and faint track on right.
	3.8 ▲	SO	Track on left and faint track on right.
▼ 0.9		TL	T-intersection with track in wash under small power line. Proceed up the wash.
	3.2 ▲	TR	Turn right out of wash. Cross through many

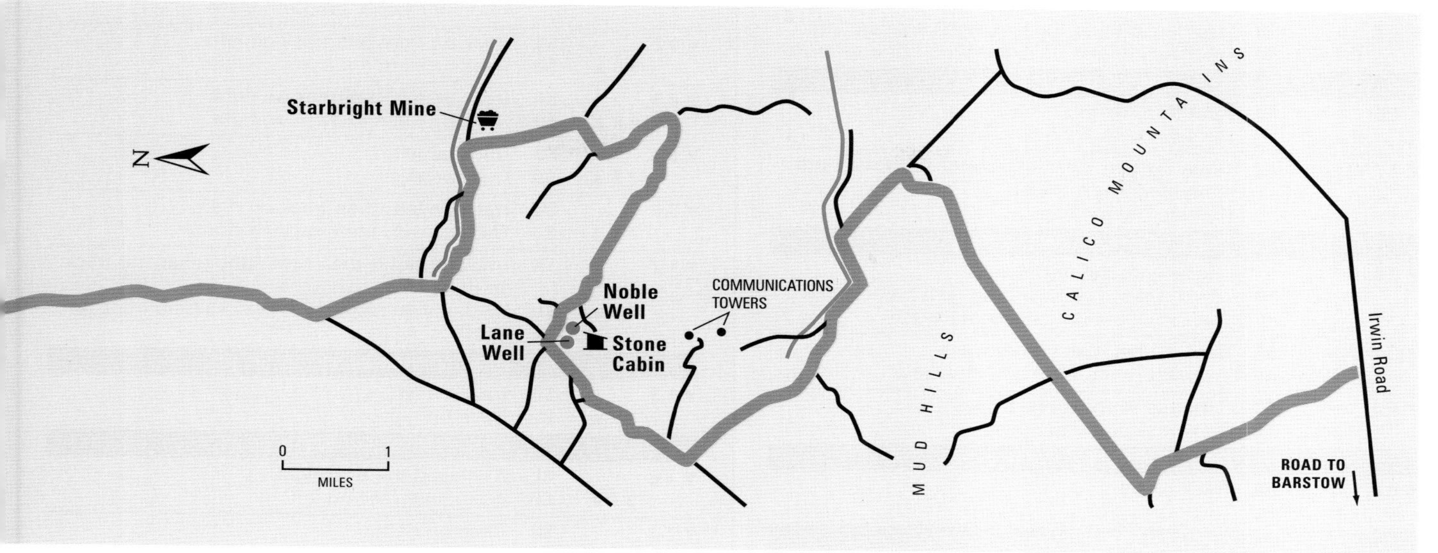

deep washes for the next 0.9 miles.

GPS: N35°04.31' W116°55.18'

▼ 1.5 SO Track on left.
2.6 ▲ SO Track on right.

▼ 1.6 SO Track on left.
2.5 ▲ SO Track on right.

▼ 1.8 TL Track on left and track on right. Turn away from the power lines up side wash.
2.3 ▲ TR Track on left and track on right. Follow along power lines down main wash.

GPS: N35°04.35' W116°55.96'

▼ 2.1 BR Small track on left.
2.0 ▲ BL Small track on right.

▼ 2.4 BR Fork in wash.
1.7 ▲ BL Fork in wash.

GPS: N35°04.44' W116°56.60'

▼ 2.7 SO Small track on right.
1.4 ▲ SO Small track on left.

▼ 2.9 SO Exit wash.
1.2 ▲ SO Enter wash.

▼ 3.0 SO Saddle. Track on right and track on left at saddle.
1.1 ▲ SO Saddle. Track on right and track on left at saddle.

GPS: N35°04.84' W116°56.99'

▼ 3.4 SO Track on left and track on right.
0.7 ▲ SO Track on right and track on left.

▼ 3.9 TR T-intersection with well-used formed trail.
0.2 ▲ TL Turn left onto well-used formed trail.

GPS: N35°05.39' W116°57.61'

▼ 4.0 SO Road is now small, single-lane paved.
0.1 ▲ SO Road is now formed dirt.

▼ 4.1 BL Bear left onto formed dirt trail. Paved road continues to the right to communication towers, but is blocked by a locked gate. Zero trip meter.
0.0 ▲ Continue to the south.

GPS: N35°05.56' W116°57.47'

▼ 0.0 Continue to the north.
2.1 ▲ SO Continue on small, single-lane paved road. Paved road on left continues to communications towers, but is blocked by a locked gate. Zero trip meter.

▼ 0.3 BL Track on right.
1.8 ▲ BR Track on left.

GPS: N35°05.80' W116°57.31'

▼ 0.4 BR Track on left.
1.7 ▲ BL Track on right.

▼ 0.7 BR Track on left.
1.4 ▲ BL Track on right.

▼ 0.9 SO Track on right and track on left.
1.2 ▲ SO Track on right and track on left.

GPS: N35°06.22' W116°57.07'

▼ 1.3 SO Track on left.
0.8 ▲ BL Track on right.

GPS: N35°06.46' W116°56.74'

▼ 1.6 TR 4-way intersection.
0.5 ▲ TL 4-way intersection.

GPS: N35°06.59' W116°56.54'

▼ 1.7 SO Track on left. Remain in line of wash.
0.4 ▲ SO Track on right. Remain in line of wash.

▼ 1.8 SO Track on left.
0.3 ▲ SO Track on right.

▼ 1.9 SO Lane Well behind fence on right.
0.2 ▲ SO Lane Well behind fence on left.

GPS: N35°06.51' W116°56.23'

▼ 2.0 SO Mine shaft behind fence on left; then track on left; then track on right; then concrete tank on right.
0.1 ▲ BL Concrete tank on left; then track on left; then track on right; then mine shaft behind fence on right.

GPS: N35°06.49' W116°56.18'

▼ 2.1 BL Track on right goes 0.2 miles to stone cabin at Noble Well. Zero trip meter.
0.0 ▲ Continue to the northwest.

GPS: N35°06.42' W116°56.15'

▼ 0.0 Continue to the east and start to head down canyon.
2.2 ▲ BR Track on left goes 0.2 miles to stone cabin at Noble Well. Exit canyon. Zero trip meter.

▼ 1.0 SO Track on left.
1.2 ▲ SO Track on right.

▼ 1.3 SO Track on left.
0.9 ▲ SO Track on right.

▼ Mileage	▲ Mileage	Direction	Description
▼ 1.8		SO	Track on left and track on right. Exit canyon.
	0.4 ▲	SO	Track on left and track on right. Enter canyon.
			GPS: N35°05.83′ W116°54.51′
▼ 2.0		SO	Faint track on left.
	0.2 ▲	SO	Faint track on right.
▼ 2.2		TL	T-intersection. Zero trip meter. Track on right continues down wash.
	0.0 ▲		Continue to the west.
			GPS: N35°05.76′ W116°54.03′
▼ 0.0			Continue to the northwest.
	1.2 ▲	TR	Turn right out of wash and zero trip meter. Track on left continues down wash.
▼ 0.1		BR	Track on left. Exit line of wash.
	1.1 ▲	SO	Track on right. Enter line of wash.
▼ 0.4		SO	Concrete foundations on right.
	0.8 ▲	SO	Concrete foundations on left.
			GPS: N35°06.02′ W116°54.24′
▼ 0.8		BR	Track on left.
	0.4 ▲	BL	Track on right.
			GPS: N35°06.31′ W116°54.56′
▼ 1.2		TL	Well-used track on right. Zero trip meter.
	0.0 ▲		Continue to the southwest.
			GPS: N35°06.49′ W116°54.24′
▼ 0.0			Continue to the northwest.
	2.9 ▲	TR	Well-used track on left. Zero trip meter.
▼ 0.5		SO	Exit wash. Track on left to mine.
	2.4 ▲	SO	Track on right to mine. Enter wash.
			GPS: N35°06.90′ W116°54.42′
▼ 0.6		SO	Enter wash.
	2.3 ▲	SO	Exit wash.
▼ 0.8		SO	Exit wash.
	2.1 ▲	SO	Enter wash.
▼ 1.0		SO	Small track on left.
	1.9 ▲	SO	Small track on right.
▼ 1.2		SO	4-way intersection. Cabin ruin on left. Continue past mine hopper of the Starbright Mine.
	1.7 ▲	SO	Pass mine hopper of the Starbright Mine; then 4-way intersection. Cabin ruin on right.
			GPS: N35°07.39′ W116°54.51′
▼ 1.3		TL	T-intersection with track in wash. Turn left up wash.
	1.6 ▲	TR	Track continues straight ahead. Turn right out of wash.
			GPS: N35°07.45′ W116°54.51′
▼ 1.7		BL	Track on right up side wash.
	1.2 ▲	SO	Track on left up side wash.
			GPS: N35°07.36′ W116°55.01′
▼ 1.8		SO	Track on left.
	1.1 ▲	SO	Track on right.
▼ 2.2		BR	Track on left up side wash.
	0.7 ▲	BL	Track on right up side wash.
			GPS: N35°07.31′ W116°55.44′
▼ 2.4		SO	Track on left.
	0.5 ▲	SO	Track on right.
▼ 2.8		SO	Track on left into diggings.
	0.1 ▲	SO	Track on right into diggings.
▼ 2.9		TR	4-way intersection. Track on left and track on right. Exit wash. Zero trip meter.
	0.0 ▲		Continue to the east.
			GPS: N35°07.55′ W116°56.03′
▼ 0.0			Continue to the northeast.
	5.2 ▲	TL	4-way intersection. Track on right and track on left. Enter wash. Zero trip meter.
▼ 0.2		SO	Track on right and track on left.
	5.0 ▲	SO	Track on right and track on left.
▼ 0.6		SO	Track on left and track on right.
	4.6 ▲	SO	Track on left and track on right.
▼ 0.7		SO	Track on left.
	4.5 ▲	SO	Track on right.
▼ 0.9		SO	Track on left; then track on right.
	4.3 ▲	SO	Track on left; then track on right.
▼ 1.2		TR	Track on right; then turn right at second track on right.
	4.0 ▲	TL	Track continues ahead; then second track on left.
			GPS: N35°08.49′ W116°56.42′
▼ 1.3		SO	Track on left.
	3.9 ▲	BL	Track on right.
			GPS: N35°08.58′ W116°56.41′
▼ 1.6		BL	Well-used track on right.
	3.6 ▲	SO	Well-used track on left.
▼ 1.7		SO	Track on right.
	3.5 ▲	SO	Track on left.
▼ 2.1		SO	Enter wash. Track on right down wash.
	3.1 ▲	SO	Track on left down wash. Exit wash.
			GPS: N35°09.14′ W116°56.25′
▼ 2.5		SO	Track on right.
	2.7 ▲	SO	Track on left.
▼ 4.2		SO	Exit out top of wash.
	1.0 ▲	SO	Enter wash.
▼ 4.8		BR	Well-used track on left.
	0.4 ▲	SO	Well-used track on right.
			GPS: N35°11.53′ W116°56.73′
▼ 5.2		TL	4-way intersection. Zero trip meter.
	0.0 ▲		Continue to the southwest.
			GPS: N35°11.67′ W116°56.38′
▼ 0.0			Continue to the north.
	5.1 ▲	TR	4-way intersection. Zero trip meter.
▼ 0.1		SO	Track on right.
	5.0 ▲	SO	Track on left.
▼ 1.5		SO	Track on right.
	3.6 ▲	SO	Track on left.
			GPS: N35°12.93′ W116°56.16′
▼ 3.8		TR	Well-used track on left.
	1.4 ▲	BL	Well-used track on right.
			GPS: N35°14.65′ 116°57.45′
▼ 4.7		SO	Track on left and track on right. Concrete foundations on left.
	0.4 ▲	SO	Track on left and track on right. Concrete foundations on right.
▼ 4.8		SO	Track on left and track on right.
	0.3 ▲	SO	Track on left and track on right.
			GPS: N35°15.55′ W116°57.45′
▼ 5.1			Trail ends at T-intersection with graded dirt Goldstone Road (C332), on the edge of Superior Valley. Turn left to return to Barstow, passing the start of Desert #21: Black Canyon Road after 2.9 miles.
	0.0 ▲		Trail starts on graded dirt Goldstone Road (C332), 22.4 miles north of the intersection of Copper City Road (Goldstone Road turns into Copper City Road to the south) and Irwin Road, 2.9 miles northeast of the intersection of Goldstone Road and Desert #21: Black Canyon Road. Zero trip meter and turn south on formed trail. Intersection is unmarked.
			GPS: N35°15.92′ W116°57.45′

DESERT #21

Black Canyon Road

Starting Point:	**Goldstone Road (C332), 2.9 miles southwest of the northern end of Desert #20: Starbright Trail**
Finishing Point:	**California 58 at Hinkley, 7 miles west of Barstow**
Total Mileage:	**35.4 miles**
Unpaved Mileage:	**34 miles**
Driving Time:	**2.5 hours**
Elevation Range:	**2,000–3,100 feet**
Usually Open:	**Year-round**
Best Time to Travel:	**September to May (dry weather only)**
Difficulty Rating:	**3**
Scenic Rating:	**10**
Remoteness Rating:	**+1**

Special Attractions

- Land sailing on the dry bed of Superior Lake.
- Numerous petroglyphs in Inscription Canyon and Black Canyon.
- Rockhounding for opal and jasper at Opal Mountain.
- Can be combined with Desert #20: Starbright Trail to form a loop from Barstow.
- Birding at Harper Dry Lake.

History

The northern end of this trail crosses the wide expanse of the dry Superior Lake. The lake depression is along the route to the old mining settlement of Copper City, which was active around the turn of the twentieth century. The town is approximately 7 miles inside the boundary of China Lake Naval Weapons Center.

By 1904, there were several mining claims in operation around Copper City, part of the Morrow Mining District. The state mineralogist reports that the Union Development Company (out of Boston) owned the Juanita Mine and 141 surrounding claims. Some shafts were more than 200 feet deep. By 1917, updated maps showed Copper City as ruins. Lower levels of mining activity prevailed at some of the claims until the early 1920s.

Long before the establishment of Copper City, generations of Indians camped in the region. The remains of regular camps can be seen in Black Canyon, where hundreds of petroglyphs adorn the volcanic canyon walls. Pot shards show that campfires blackened some of the already heavily patinaed rocks. Another campsite lies farther north along the trail. Inscription Canyon has thousands of petroglyphs that can set the imagination on fire. Paleo-Indians spent an enormous amount of time here, recording events, sightings, and beliefs on the surrounding landscape. Though no dates are available to tell us when these rock engravings were made, people are thought to have inhabited the California desert as early as 10,000 to 12,000 years ago.

Inscription Canyon petroglyph

In 1906, the first law was introduced to protect the artifacts of our ancestors. Since then, many improved laws have been passed to stem the removal of cultural items from their original locations, where they have the most relevant meaning and offer the greatest insight on how people lived in an earlier landscape.

The silver boom of 1873 in the Panamint Range led to the development of many roads through the region. Wells Fargo, the major stage company of the time, refused to travel to Panamint City because of its general lawlessness and the risk of holdups. So mine owners there banded together and formed their own company. They shaped their silver into 500-pound half balls that were too heavy to carry off on horseback. The route they took traveled down Black Canyon, where a stage station was set up as an overnight stopping point with wells used for water. Aaron Lane, a trader on the Mojave River, was responsible for pushing the route through Black Canyon.

The initials found partway down the canyon, low on the boulders, are those of A. Tillman, a teamster who regularly traveled the Black Canyon route. His signature can be found at other places within the region as well.

Scouts Cove is located in a side canyon between the main trail down Black Canyon and Opal Mountain. It was the site of an opal mining camp in the early 1900s. Miners carved their homes in the tufa rock at the site of the mines, which were financed by the Tiffany Company of New York.

J. W. Robinson chose the eastern side of Harper Lake as the spot for his camp in 1869. Recent rains had enhanced the pastures, and he thought the area would be good to ranch. An-

Expansive view north over Superior Lake

A strong wind whips up dust on the edge of Harper Lake

other early settler, J. D. Harper, left his name permanently attached to the lake. By 1872, Harper's homesteading work was improved upon to develop the first real known ranch in the region. C. S. Black arrived and constructed an adobe home that catered to stagecoach passengers. He made improvements to the ranch when time permitted. Black's ranch and stage station became known as Grant's Station, a valued service in this remote locality.

Around the same time, Anglo pioneers were settling around the Mojave River in the Barstow region to the southeast and prospectors were venturing into the mountain ranges to the north. The Searles brothers discovered borax at their namesake lake in 1863, though mining activity did not get under way for about 10 years. The Death Valley borax sites were established by the mid-1870s. Ed Stiles established a route for his mule teams from the Eagle Borax Works in Death Valley, over Wingate Pass, south via Granite Wells and Black's Ranch, and on to Daggett.

Harper Lake has long been an important refuge for birds migrating through this arid region. The lake's wetlands have diminished over the last century, yet the remaining marshes continue to attract waterfowl, wetland birds, shorebirds, and birds of prey. Animals such as jack rabbits, coyotes, and bobcats live well in this environment. The desert horned lizard and the zebratail can also be seen here. Measures have been taken to retain the disappearing water supply in order to help maintain the marshland and associated wildlife. In the late 1990s, the BLM installed a well with an irrigation system to provide an ongoing water source for this desert oasis.

Many birders come to the lake to try to spot the many species that can be seen here. Virginia rails, short-eared owls, and American bitterns can be found in the marshes. Great blue herons, white pelicans, snowy egrets, and ibises can be seen on the ponds. Killdeer, snowy and mountain plover, and American avocets can be found on the mud flats. The general area also supports a large population of raptors.

South of Harper Lake lies the settlement of Hinkley (originally spelled Hinckley). The town was named after the son of D. C. Henderson (of Barstow) when the railroad was constructed in 1882. Hinkley was the setting for the movie *Erin Brockovitch,* starring Julia Roberts. The movie is based on a real-life story of the battle against a large corporation that was contaminating local water supplies and causing cancers and other related illnesses in the people of the town.

Description

Black Canyon Road has a number of interesting features spread along its length. It can be combined with Desert #20: Starbright Trail to create a full day's excursion from Barstow. The graded dirt Indian Spring Road can be used as a fast entry point to the northern end of the trail.

The trail leaves Goldstone Road and heads west, crossing the dry lakebed of Superior Lake. The lake is often used for land yachts. Its perfectly flat, smooth surface makes for ideal conditions when dry. Land yachting is not exactly new to the desert; it has been enjoyed since the turn of the twentieth century. In wet weather, the lakebed quickly turns to mire and should be avoided. The trail leads across the lake, intersecting with other trails in the middle. Please remain on the main route and travel in a straight line from shore to shore. Motorized vehicle use off the designated trail line is not permitted. The trail is faint, so it helps to set the coordinates of the exit point into your GPS unit to use as a GoTo point.

Once away from Superior Lake, the trail joins graded Copper City Road for a short distance before entering the Black Canyon Area of Critical Environmental Concern. The entrance to the short, shallow Inscription Canyon is passed next. Park at the barrier and take the short hike into the canyon to see some excellent petroglyphs scattered on the dark lava boulders within the canyon. A few faint red-ochre pictographs can be seen if you look carefully.

The vehicle trail continues alongside a lava flow for the next mile. There are many more petroglyphs to be seen, including the well-known Birdman Petroglyph.

The trail then enters into the sandy Black Canyon wash. A well-used but rough trail leads east to the popular rockhounding area of Opal Mountain, where it is still possible to find opal and jasper. This trail also leads to the location of the old opal camp of Scouts Cove. Past this turn the trail enters the twisting Black Canyon, traveling in a sandy wash. The canyon is a good place to view wildflowers in spring. More petroglyphs can be found in the canyon, as well as one of the Tillman signatures (low on the rock wall). This particular one says, "A. Tillman S.F. July 1874."

Once out of the canyon, the trail swings south toward the flat, dry Harper Lake. A keen eye may be able to spot some white-colored chalcedony on the flats north of the lake. The section of trail that crosses Harper Lake should definitely be avoided when wet. The soft lakebed can quickly turn to quagmire, and it is extremely easy for a vehicle to bog down. The trail across the lake is hard to follow, being faint in places and covered with sagebrush. Keep a close eye on the trail so you don't inadvertently stray from the correct route.

South of the lake, the trail is sandy as it passes beside the well at Black's Ranch. It continues to the south over sandy, undulating ground to finish in Hinkley.

There is some good primitive camping to be found at the northern end of the trail, though it is very exposed with no shelter from wind or sun. Alternatively, the developed BLM campground at Owl Canyon is a short distance from the southern end of the trail.

Current Road Information

Bureau of Land Management
Ridgecrest Field Office
300 South Richmond Road
Ridgecrest, CA 93555
(760) 384-5400

Map References

BLM Cuddeback Lake, Soda Mts.
USGS 1:24,000 Superior Lake, Opal Mt., Bird Spring, Lockhart, Water Valley, Hinkley
1:100,000 Cuddeback Lake, Soda Mts.
Maptech CD-ROM: Barstow/San Bernardino County; San Bernardino County/Mojave
Southern & Central California Atlas & Gazetteer, pp. 67, 81
California Road & Recreation Atlas, pp. 95, 104

Route Directions

Mileage		Direction
▼ 0.0		From Goldstone Road, 19.5 miles north of the intersection of Copper City Road (Goldstone Road turns into Copper City Road to the south) and Irwin Road, 2.9 miles southwest of the intersection of Goldstone Road and Desert #20: Starbright Trail, zero trip meter and turn southwest at unmarked intersection on the edge of Superior Lake (dry). There is a brown BLM marker post at the intersection, but no trail number.
4.4 ▲		Trail ends at intersection with Goldstone Road. Turn sharp right for Barstow; turn left to continue to Desert #20: Starbright Trail.
		GPS: N35°14.81′ W117°00.12′
▼ 0.2	SO	Track on left and track on right. Start to cross Superior Lake.
4.2 ▲	SO	Track on left and track on right. Exit Superior Lake.
▼ 1.1	SO	Track on left and track on right.
3.3 ▲	SO	Track on left and track on right.
		GPS: N35°14.42′ W117°01.31′
▼ 1.6	SO	Well-used track on left is Indian Springs Road.
2.8 ▲	SO	Well-used track on right is Indian Springs Road.
		GPS: N35°14.29′ W117°01.75′
▼ 2.5	SO	Exit lakebed. There is a brown BLM marker post at the exit.
1.9 ▲	SO	Start to cross Superior Lake. There is a brown BLM marker post at this point.
		GPS: N35°14.16′ W117°02.66′
▼ 2.6	SO	Start to cross small dry lake.
1.8 ▲	SO	Exit lake.
▼ 2.7	SO	Track on left.
1.7 ▲	SO	Track on right.
▼ 2.8	SO	Exit lake.
1.6 ▲	SO	Start to cross small dry lake.
▼ 4.0	TL	Turn left onto graded dirt Old Copper City Road (C2617). Stone foundations opposite are Curtis Well. Small track to well.
0.4 ▲	TR	Turn right onto formed trail C332, marked for 4WDs, ATVs, and motorbikes. Stone foundations opposite are Curtis Well.
		GPS: N35°13.09′ W117°03.65′
▼ 4.4	TR	Turn right onto graded dirt Copper City Road (EF 373) and zero trip meter. Copper City Road also continues to the left. Small track straight ahead.
0.0 ▲		Continue to the northwest.
		GPS: N35°12.84′ W117°03.42′
▼ 0.0		Continue to the west.
7.8 ▲	TL	Turn left onto graded dirt Old Copper City Road (C2617) and zero trip meter. Copper City Road continues straight ahead. Small track on right.
▼ 0.3	SO	Track on left.
7.5 ▲	SO	Track on right.
▼ 0.4	SO	Track on right.
7.4 ▲	SO	Track on left.
▼ 1.4	SO	Graded road continues on right. Track on left and track straight ahead. Continue straight ahead on smaller trail.
6.4 ▲	SO	Graded road on left and track straight ahead. Track on right. Continue straight ahead, joining graded road.
		GPS: N35°12.85′ W117°04.79′
▼ 1.8	SO	Track on left and track on right.
6.0 ▲	SO	Track on left and track on right.
▼ 2.6	SO	Track on left and track on right.
5.2 ▲	SO	Track on left and track on right.
		GPS: N35°12.86′ W117°06.21′
▼ 4.4	SO	Track on left.
3.4 ▲	SO	Track on right.
▼ 4.7	SO	Track on right.
3.1 ▲	BR	Track on left.
		GPS: N35°12.98′ W117°08.45′
▼ 6.1	SO	Track on left.
1.7 ▲	SO	Track on right.
▼ 6.3	SO	Enter Black Mountains ACEC at sign.
1.5 ▲	SO	Exit Black Mountains ACEC at sign.
		GPS: N35°12.30′ W117°09.95′
▼ 7.0	BL	Track on right.
0.8 ▲	SO	Track on left.
		GPS: N35°12.21′ W117°10.71′
▼ 7.5	SO	Track on left.
0.3 ▲	SO	Track on right.
▼ 7.8	TR	T-intersection in front of wooden barrier at Inscription Canyon petroglyphs. Zero trip meter.
0.0 ▲		Continue to the east.
		GPS: N35°11.91′ W117°11.55′
▼ 0.0		Continue to the north. There are petroglyphs on the boulders to the left for the next mile.
3.5 ▲	TL	Turn left in front of wooden barrier at Inscription Canyon petroglyphs. Zero trip meter. Track continues straight ahead.
▼ 0.2	BL	Track on right.
3.3 ▲	SO	Track on left.
▼ 0.7	SO	Track on right.
2.8 ▲	BR	Track on left.
		GPS: N35°12.41′ W117°11.96′
▼ 0.8	SO	Two tracks on right.
2.7 ▲	SO	Two tracks on left. There are petroglyphs on the boulders to the right for most of the next mile.
▼ 1.6	SO	Track on left.

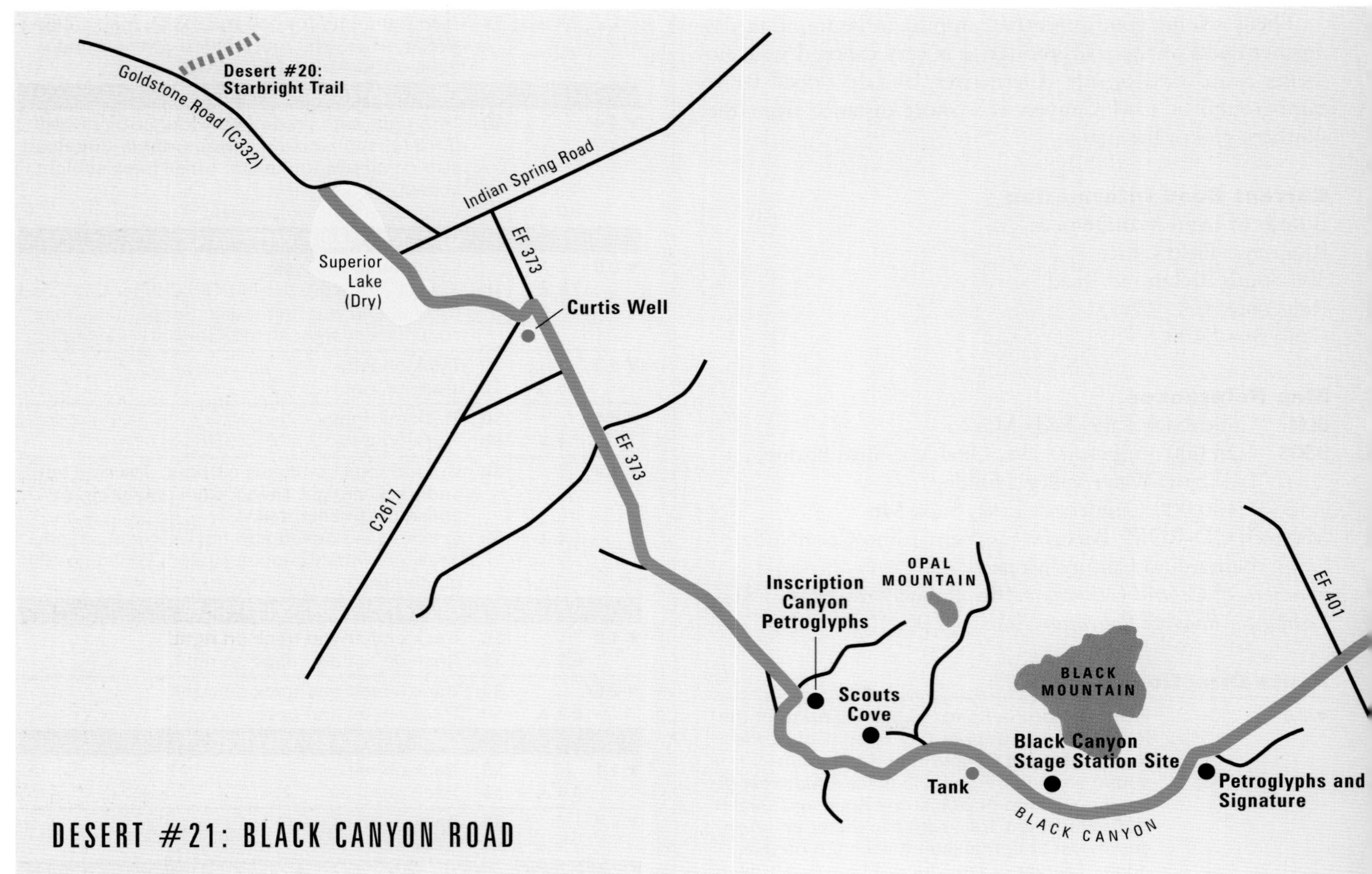

	1.9 ▲	SO	Track on right.
▼ 1.9		SO	Track on right.
	1.6 ▲	SO	Track on left.
▼ 2.3		SO	4-way intersection. Small caves on right. Trail forks a few times but all rejoin quickly. Enter line of wash.
	1.2 ▲	SO	4-way intersection. Small caves on left. Exit line of wash.
			GPS: N35°11.52′ W117°13.07′
▼ 2.7		SO	Well-used track on right.
	0.8 ▲	BR	Well-used track on left.
			GPS: N35°11.22′ W117°13.31′
▼ 2.8		BR	Bear right to pass mine adit.
	0.7 ▲	SO	Rejoin main trail.
▼ 2.9		SO	Track on left rejoins and is marked EF 373.
	0.6 ▲	BL	Track on right is marked EF 373. Bear left past mine adit on C283.
			GPS: N35°11.03′ W117°13.31′
▼ 3.2		SO	Track on left to mine.
	0.3 ▲	BL	Track on right to mine.
▼ 3.5		SO	Track on left goes approximately 4 miles to Opal Mountain rockhounding area and Scouts Cove. Zero trip meter.
	0.0 ▲		Continue to the north. Trail forks a few times but all rejoin quickly.
			GPS: N35°10.57′ W117°13.29′
▼ 0.0			Continue to the south.
	5.2 ▲	SO	Track on right goes approximately 4 miles to Opal Mountain rockhounding area and Scouts Cove. Zero trip meter.
▼ 0.9		SO	Stone tank and well on right. Entering Black Canyon.
	4.3 ▲	SO	Stone tank and well on left. Exiting Black Canyon.
			GPS: N35°10.00′ W117°13.87′
▼ 1.7		SO	Track on right.
	3.5 ▲	SO	Track on left.
▼ 2.5		SO	Site of Black Canyon Stage Station—little remains.
	2.7 ▲	SO	Site of Black Canyon Stage Station—little remains.
			GPS: N35°09.50′ W117°14.89′
▼ 3.2		SO	Track on right.
	2.0 ▲	SO	Track on left.
			GPS: N35°08.66′ W117°15.56′
▼ 4.9		SO	Petroglyphs and Tillman signature on right. There are also petroglyphs on the left, marked by a sign.
	0.3 ▲	SO	Petroglyphs on right, marked by a sign; then petroglyphs and Tillman signature on left.
			GPS: N35°07.35′ W117°15.30′
▼ 5.2		TL	Trail exits canyon. Turn left at unmarked intersection in wash. Harper Lake can be seen on the left. Track continues straight ahead.
	0.0 ▲		Continue to the northeast.
			GPS: N35°07.22′ W117°15.33′
▼ 0.0			Continue to the south.
	2.5 ▲	TR	Turn right at T-intersection in wash and enter Black Canyon.

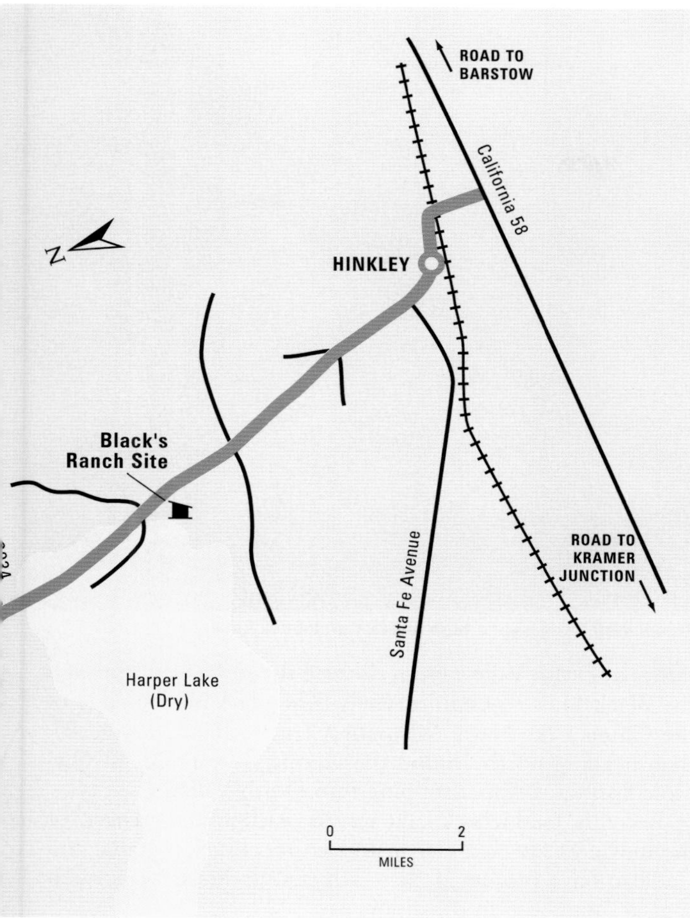

▼ 0.5 SO Exit line of wash.
2.0 ▲ SO Enter line of wash.

▼ 1.0 SO Exit Black Mountains ACEC at sign.
1.5 ▲ SO Enter Black Mountains ACEC at sign.

GPS: N35°06.37′ W117°15.12′

▼ 2.5 SO Well-used track on left and right is EF 401. Intersection is unmarked. Zero trip meter.
0.0 ▲ Continue to the northwest.

GPS: N35°04.98′ W117°14.80′

▼ 0.0 Continue to the southeast.
4.8 ▲ SO Well-used track on right and left is EF 401. Intersection is unmarked. Zero trip meter.

▼ 1.0 SO Track on left and track on right.
3.8 ▲ SO Track on left and track on right.

▼ 1.5 SO Track on left and track on right.
3.3 ▲ SO Track on left and track on right.

GPS: N35°03.63′ W117°14.49′

▼ 1.8 SO Unmarked track on left is C034.
3.0 ▲ SO Unmarked track on right is C034.

GPS: N35°03.35′ W117°14.34′

▼ 2.2 SO Start to cross edge of Harper Lake.
2.6 ▲ SO Exiting Harper Lake.

GPS: N35°03.05′ W117°14.24′

▼ 4.5 SO Exiting Harper Lake
0.3 ▲ SO Start to cross edge of Harper Lake.

GPS: N35°01.30′ W117°13.80′

▼ 4.7 SO Track on right; then track on left.
0.1 ▲ BR Track on right; then track on left.

GPS: N35°01.09′ W117°13.71′

▼ 4.8 SO Pass through wire gate. Well on right at Black's Ranch. Zero trip meter at gate.
0.0 ▲ Continue to the north.

GPS: N35°01.04′ W117°13.68′

▼ 0.0 Continue to the south. Track on right through fence.
7.2 ▲ SO Track on left; then well on left at Black's Ranch. Pass through wire gate and zero trip meter.

▼ 0.3 SO Track on right.
6.9 ▲ BR Track on left.

▼ 1.0 SO Cattle guard; then track on right along fence line.
6.2 ▲ SO Track on left along fence line; then cattle guard.

▼ 1.5 TL T-intersection with formed dirt road along power lines, immediately west of cattle guard.
5.7 ▲ TR Cattle guard; then immediately turn right on unmarked, small formed trail and leave power lines.

GPS: N34°59.72′ W117°13.42′

▼ 1.6 TR Turn right onto small formed trail and leave power lines. Small track opposite.
5.6 ▲ TL T-intersection with formed dirt road along power lines. Small track straight ahead.

GPS: N34°59.71′ W117°13.35′

▼ 2.5 SO Track on left.
4.7 ▲ SO Track on right.

▼ 3.0 SO Track on left.
4.2 ▲ SO Track on right.

▼ 3.3 SO Track on left and track on right.
3.9 ▲ SO Track on left and track on right.

GPS: N34°58.27′ W117°12.87′

▼ 3.8 SO Track on right; then track on left.
3.4 ▲ SO Track on right; then track on left.

▼ 3.9 BR Track on left.
3.3 ▲ SO Track on right.

▼ 4.1 SO Track on right.
3.1 ▲ SO Track on left.

GPS: N34°57.59′ W117°12.60′

▼ 4.4 SO Track on right.
2.8 ▲ BR Track on left.

▼ 4.7 SO Track on left and track on right; then track on left.
2.5 ▲ SO Track on right; then track on left and track on right.

▼ 5.1 SO Track on left and track on right.
2.1 ▲ SO Track on left and track on right.

▼ 5.2 TL Track on left; then T-intersection with wide graded Santa Fe Avenue. Intersection is unmarked. Then graded road on left.
2.0 ▲ TR Graded road on right; then immediately turn right on unmarked formed trail on left-hand bend. Proceed northwest. Intersection is unmarked. Immediately track on right.

GPS: N34°56.60′ W117°12.28′

▼ 5.6 SO Graded road on left and right.
1.6 ▲ SO Graded road on left and right.

▼ 5.7 SO Track on right.
1.5 ▲ SO Track on left.

▼ 5.8 SO Road on right is Almeda Street. Continue on Santa Fe Avenue alongside railroad. Road is now paved.
1.4 ▲ SO Road on left is Almeda Street. Road bears away from the railroad and turns to graded dirt.

GPS: N34°56.15′ W117°11.97′

▼ 6.4	TR	Turn right onto Hinkley Road and cross over railroad.
0.8 ▲	TL	Cross over railroad and immediately turn left on Santa Fe Avenue.
		GPS: N34°56.00′ W117°11.30′
▼ 7.2		Trail ends on California 58, 7 miles west of Barstow. Turn left for Barstow; turn right for Kramer Junction.
0.0 ▲		Trail commences on California 58 at Hinkley, 7 miles west of Barstow. Zero trip meter and turn north on paved Hinkley Road, following sign for Hinkley.
		GPS: N34°55.32′ W117°11.29′

DESERT #22

Grass Valley Trail

Starting Point:	**Trona Road, 1.3 miles north of intersection with US 395 at Johannesburg**
Finishing Point:	**US 395, 13.4 miles north of Kramer Junction**
Total Mileage:	**50.6 miles**
Unpaved Mileage:	**50.6 miles**
Driving Time:	**3.5 hours**
Elevation Range:	**2,300–3,800 feet**
Usually Open:	**Year-round**
Best Time to Travel:	**Year-round**
Difficulty Rating:	**3**
Scenic Rating:	**9**
Remoteness Rating:	**+1**

Special Attractions

- Steam Well Petroglyphs.
- Remote and rugged high desert scenery along a seldom traveled trail.
- Trail travels a vehicle corridor through the Grass Valley Wilderness.

History

The dry Cuddeback Lake lies in a shallow depression south of Almond Mountain along the northern end of this quiet trail. The lake's name comes from a local prospector named John Cuddeback, who hauled ore in team wagons from the mines at Randsburg south to the railroad siding at Kramer Junction. The famed 20-mule teams were a familiar sight in the east-west direction across the dusty depression of Cuddeback Lake. The teams (which actually consisted of 18 mules and 2 horses) pulled up to 30-ton loads in gigantic wagons. Two of these wagons generally carried ore plus an additional 500-gallon water tank. It was no easy task for man or beast to trek across the long straight stretch to Mojave, nearly 50 miles to the southeast. Blackwater Well was a welcome sight to teamsters returning northeast to the borax

Steam Well Petroglyphs high above Cuddeback Lake

mines in Death Valley. From the well the route went through the Black Hills to Granite Wells (nowadays on the edge of the China Lake Naval Weapons Center Mojave Range B), then heading north around the Granite Mountains to Owl Hole Springs, before dropping into Death Valley.

Recently, Cuddeback Lake was the background scenery for the movie *Desert Son*. Car manufacturers Buick, Mazda, and Cadillac have promoted their vehicles at the dry lake with rugged mountains in the distance.

Fremont Peak, a landmark known to many travelers in the northern Mojave region, was named for the famed explorer John C. Frémont. The name was also given to the railroad siding just west of the peak, along the railroad extension from Four Corners (Kramer Junction) to Johannesburg. Construction of the railroad was prompted by the discovery of huge gold deposits at the Yellow Aster Mine on what became known as Rand Mountain. The Randsburg and Johannesburg region boomed; some thought it would be another Comstock. Machinery needed to be installed at the mines, ore needed to be transported out to the mill, and the railroad was up and running by January 1898.

By June of the same year, Barstow had a 50-stamp mill and was receiving ore from the Yellow Aster Mine via the Randsburg Railroad, as it was called. The Barstow mill closed in 1901 because two mills with a total of 130 stamps were operating at Randsburg. Water was piped from Garlock to keep the mills running. By 1904 there were more than 10 miles of tunnels in the Yellow Aster Mine. By 1905 Atolia was producing tungsten, and the mill in Barstow was revived and converted to process the mine's ore.

Silver was the next boom for this desert community. Kelly Silver Mine at the base of Red Mountain (near the northern end of this trail) was discovered in 1919. The claim owner had recently passed away so his son sold out for $15,000. The mine went on to produce more than $7 million worth of silver in its first four years of operation.

Description

This long easygoing trail would be suitable for high-clearance 2WD vehicles in dry weather if it wasn't for a rough, uneven section through the Gravel Hills. A high-clearance 2WD, or even a carefully driven passenger vehicle, can access the Steam Well Petroglyphs from Trona Road in dry weather. Beyond the petroglyphs, 4WD is preferred.

The long trail leaves Trona Road a short distance north of US 395 and Johannesburg. Initially it passes alongside Red Mountain, following the well-used, formed trail. After 3.9 miles, a sign on the north side of the trail marks the start of a short hiking trail to the Steam Well Petroglyphs. Park your vehicle beside the sign and head approximately 0.4 miles along the old vehicle trail before bearing left to visit the petroglyphs. Unfortunately, the images have been extensively vandalized; people have removed parts of the rock face to get them out. However, they are still worth a visit. The coordinates of the petroglyphs are GPS: N35°23.38' W117°32.42'.

Past Steam Well the trail is marked on some maps as Granite Well Road. To the south, the wide dry expanse of Cuddeback Lake can be seen. The trail crosses through a 2-mile swath of an air force gunnery range impact area. This is not marked on the ground, and it might be wise to exercise some caution.

The trail turns sharply to the south near Blackwater Well and travels through a vehicle corridor that traverses the Grass Valley Wilderness. This is one of the most scenic sections of the trail, with rugged hills rising up from wide valley vistas. Cuddeback Lake can be seen lower down to the west at this point.

One poignant feature along the trail is the motorbike memorial, found to the south of the wilderness area. An old motorbike stands partially buried in the desert next to memorial markers for three friends, all avid desert rats.

The next major scenic area is the Granite Hills. This is the roughest section of the trail as it passes along a wash and through tight canyons in the low granitic hills. Much of this area is posted as private property. Please respect the landowners' rights and remain on the main trail.

The circuitous route joins the roughly graded Lockhart Road for a short distance before swinging west again to pass along the southern face of Fremont Peak. This section of the route can be slightly brushy. The road widens again for the final straight shoot that crosses the old Randsburg Railroad embankment at Fremont Siding, before joining US 395 north of Kramer Junction.

Motorbike memorial to three men who frequented and loved this region

Current Road Information

Bureau of Land Management
Ridgecrest Field Office
300 South Richmond Road
Ridgecrest, CA 93555
(760) 384-5400

Map References

BLM Cuddeback Lake
USGS 1:24,000 Klinker Mt., Red Mt., Cuddeback Lake, Blackwater Well, Bird Spring, Fremont Peak, Boron NE
1:100,000 Cuddeback Lake
Maptech CD-ROM: Barstow/San Bernardino County
Southern & Central California Atlas & Gazetteer, pp. 66, 67
California Road & Recreation Atlas, p. 95

Route Directions

▼ 0.0			From Trona Road, 1.3 miles north of intersection with US 395 at Johannesburg, zero trip meter and turn northeast onto formed trail RM 1444 for 4WDs, ATVs, and motorbikes. There is a brown marker post slightly after the turn.
	3.9 ▲		Trail ends on Trona Road. Turn right for Trona; turn left for US 395 and Johannesburg.
			GPS: N35°22.94' W117°36.45'
▼ 0.2		SO	Track on right.
	3.7 ▲	SO	Track on left.
▼ 0.4		SO	Pipeline track on right and left; then second track on left. Red Mountain is on the right.
	3.5 ▲	SO	Track on right; then pipeline track on left and right. Red Mountain is on the left.
▼ 0.6		SO	Track on right.
	3.3 ▲	SO	Track on left.
▼ 0.7		SO	Track on right.
	3.2 ▲	SO	Track on left.
▼ 1.5		SO	Track on left.
	2.4 ▲	SO	Track on right.
▼ 1.6		SO	Two tracks on left.
	2.3 ▲	SO	Two tracks on right.
			GPS: N35°23.31' W117°34.69'
▼ 1.7		BL	Bear left, remaining on RM 1444, past two tracks on right.
	2.2 ▲	SO	Track on left; then second track on left. Remain on RM 1444.
▼ 1.9		SO	Track on right and track on left.
	2.0 ▲	SO	Track on left and track on right.
▼ 2.1		BL	Track on right.
	1.8 ▲	SO	Track on left.
			GPS: N35°23.21' W117°34.16'
▼ 2.2		SO	Track on left and track on right.
	1.7 ▲	SO	Track on left and track on right.
▼ 2.4		SO	Two tracks on right.
	1.5 ▲	SO	Two tracks on left.
▼ 2.6		SO	Track on right into mine workings and track on left.
	1.3 ▲	SO	Track on left into mine workings and track on right.

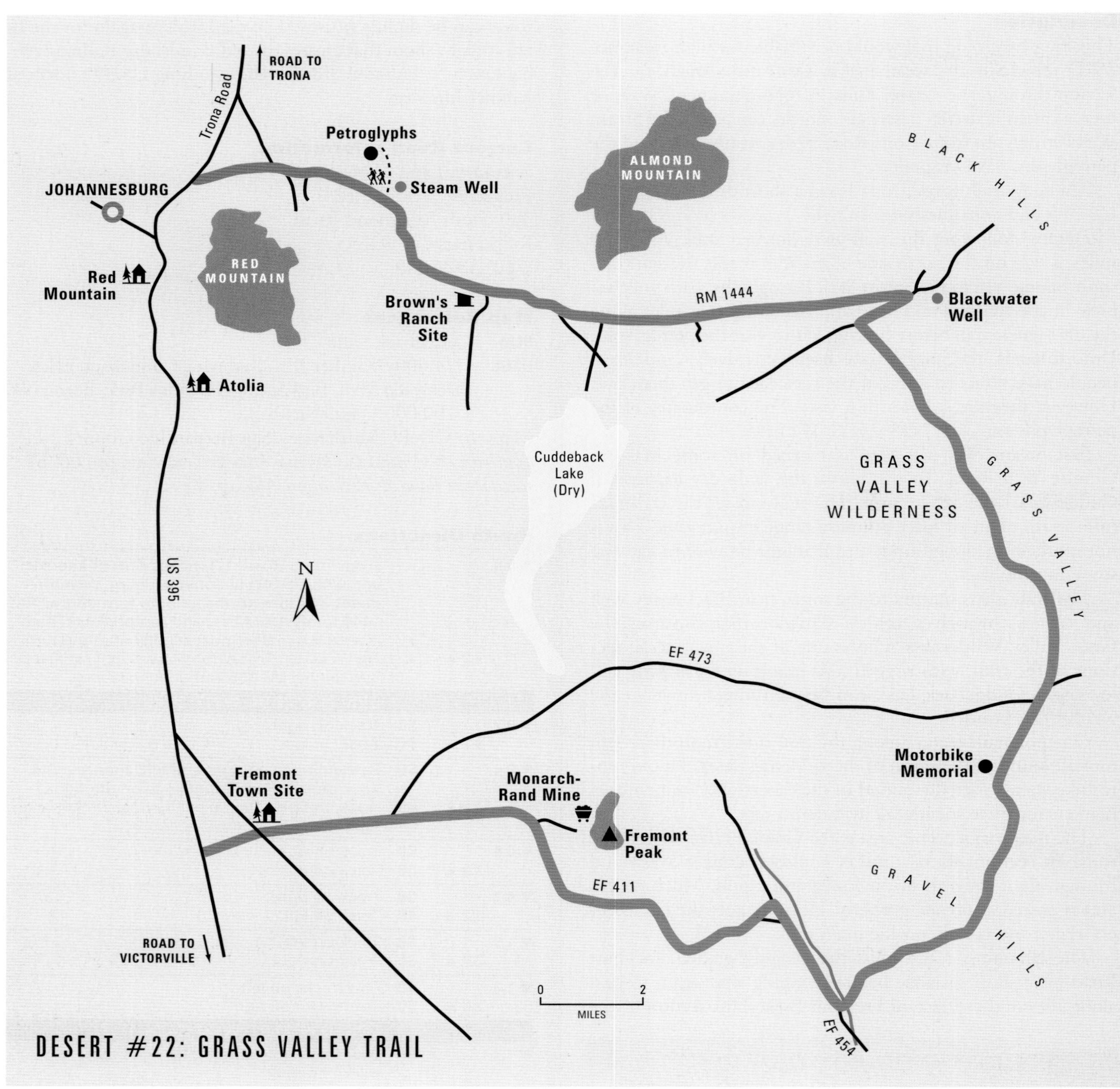

			GPS: N35°23.23' W117°33.69'
▼ 3.9		SO	Pull-in on left and sign for Steam Well Archaeological District and Golden Valley Wilderness. Zero trip meter.
	0.0 ▲		Continue to the northwest.
			GPS: N35°22.82' W117°32.36'
▼ 0.0			Continue to the southeast.
	5.8 ▲	SO	Pull-in on right and sign for Steam Well Archaeological District and Golden Valley Wilderness. Zero trip meter.
▼ 1.7		SO	Track on right.
	4.1 ▲	SO	Track on left.
			GPS: N35°21.57' W117°31.40'
▼ 2.7		SO	Track on right.
	3.1 ▲	SO	Track on left.
▼ 3.0		SO	Track on right in large cleared area in creosote with concrete foundations at the intersection. This is the site of Brown's Ranch.
	2.8 ▲	SO	Track on left in large cleared area in creosote with concrete foundations at the intersection. This is the site of Brown's Ranch. Remain on marked RM 1444.
			GPS: N35°21.22' W117°30.07'
▼ 4.2		BL	Track on right.
	1.6 ▲	SO	Track on left.
▼ 5.2		SO	Track on right.
	0.6 ▲	SO	Track on left.
▼ 5.8		SO	Track on right; then cattle guard underneath

old ranch entrance. Zero trip meter.
0.0 ▲ Continue to the southwest.

GPS: N35°20.74' W117°27.15'

▼ 0.0 Continue to the northeast.
5.5 ▲ SO Cattle guard underneath old ranch entrance; then track on left. Zero trip meter.

▼ 0.7 SO Track on left.
4.8 ▲ SO Track on right.

▼ 1.3 SO Track on right to tanks.
4.2 ▲ SO Track on left to tanks.

GPS: N35°20.84' W117°25.77'

▼ 1.7 SO Track on left.
3.8 ▲ SO Track on right.

▼ 1.9 SO Small track on right.
3.6 ▲ SO Small track on left.

▼ 2.4 SO Track on left and track on right.
3.1 ▲ SO Track on left and track on right. Remain on marked RM 1444.

▼ 5.5 TR Turn sharp right in front of gate. Track on left and track straight ahead through gate. Zero trip meter.
0.0 ▲ Continue to the west.

GPS: N35°21.37' W117°21.16'

▼ 0.0 Continue to the southwest.
1.3 ▲ TL Turn sharp left in front of gate. Track straight ahead and track on right through gate. Zero trip meter.

▼ 1.3 TL Turn left on unmarked, well-used trail and enter vehicle corridor through Grass Valley Wilderness. Track continues straight ahead. Zero trip meter.
0.0 ▲ Continue to the northeast.

GPS: N35°20.86' W117°22.39'

▼ 0.0 Continue to the southeast past Grass Valley Wilderness sign.
8.9 ▲ TR T-intersection. Exit vehicle corridor through Grass Valley Wilderness. Zero trip meter.

▼ 3.2 SO Pass through wire gate.
5.7 ▲ SO Pass through wire gate.

GPS: N35°18.89' W117°20.23'

▼ 5.5 SO Track on left and track on right. Pass through wire gate.
3.4 ▲ SO Pass through wire gate. Track on left and track on right.

GPS: N35°17.06' W117°19.18'

▼ 8.9 TR T-intersection with EF 473. Exit vehicle corridor through Grass Valley Wilderness. Zero trip meter.
0.0 ▲ Continue to the north.

GPS: N35°14.55' W117°17.98'

▼ 0.0 Continue to the southwest.
9.2 ▲ TL Turn left onto well-used trail and enter vehicle corridor through the Grass Valley Wilderness. Zero trip meter. There is a sign at the intersection for Grass Valley Wilderness.

▼ 0.3 SO Two tracks on left into mine workings.
8.9 ▲ SO Two tracks on right into mine workings.

▼ 0.4 SO Track on left.
8.8 ▲ BL Track on right.

▼ 0.6 TL Turn left onto unmarked, well-used trail. There is a large Joshua tree and a sign for the Grass Valley Wilderness at the intersection.
8.6 ▲ TR T-intersection with EF 473. There is a large Joshua tree and a sign for the Grass Valley Wilderness at the intersection.

GPS: N35°14.18' W117°18.37'

▼ 2.0 BR Trail forks. Track on left.
7.2 ▲ SO Track on right rejoins.

▼ 2.1 TL Motorbike memorial. Turn left at the motorbike. Track straight ahead and track on right.
7.1 ▲ TR Motorbike memorial. Turn right at the motorbike. Track straight ahead and track on left.

GPS: N35°12.95' W117°18.99'

▼ 2.2 SO Track on left rejoins.
7.0 ▲ BL Track on right.

▼ 2.4 SO Enter down line of wash.
6.8 ▲ SO Exit line of wash.

▼ 9.1 BL Cross through wash, bearing slightly left down the wash; then immediately exit wash to the right.
0.1 ▲ BR Cross through wash, bearing slightly left up the wash; then almost immediately bear right on small, unmarked formed trail up side wash. There is a private property warning at the start of the trail. Remain on main trail through restricted area.

GPS: N35°08.67' W117°22.18'

▼ 9.2 TR Cross over old graded Lockhart Road; then turn right onto unmarked, roughly graded Lockhart Road (EF 454). Zero trip meter.
0.0 ▲ Continue to the northeast up side wash.

GPS: N35°08.65' W117°22.22'

▼ 0.0 Continue to the northwest.
2.4 ▲ TL Turn left off graded road onto small unmarked trail. Cross old graded Lockhart Road; then bear left up wash. Zero trip meter.

▼ 1.0 SO Track on right. Road is now roughly formed.
1.4 ▲ SO Track on left.

▼ 2.0 SO Track on left.
0.4 ▲ SO Track on right.

▼ 2.4 TL Turn sharp left onto well-used formed trail marked 411. Zero trip meter.
0.0 ▲ Continue to the southeast.

GPS: N35°10.55' W117°23.63'

▼ 0.0 Continue to the south.
6.8 ▲ TL Turn sharp right onto unmarked, well-used trail. There is a marker for the trail you are leaving (411) at the intersection. Zero trip meter.

▼ 0.5 BR Well-used track on left joins.
6.3 ▲ BL Track on right.

GPS: N35°10.25' W117°23.93'

▼ 1.5 BL Track on right.
5.3 ▲ BR Track on left.

GPS: N35°09.85' W117°24.84'

▼ 3.2 SO Cross through wash. Tracks on left and right up and down wash.
3.6 ▲ SO Cross through wash. Tracks on left and right up and down wash.

GPS: N35°10.33' W117°26.06'

▼ 3.3 TL T-intersection.
3.5 ▲ TR Track continues straight ahead.

GPS: N35°10.39' W117°26.11'

▼ 4.3 SO Track on left.
2.5 ▲ SO Track on right.

GPS: N35°10.49' W117°27.22'

▼ 6.8 TL T-intersection with formed trail. Zero trip meter. To the right goes 1 mile to the Monarch-Rand Mine. There is a marker for EF 411 at the intersection pointing back the way you came.
0.0 ▲ Continue to the south.

GPS: N35°11.86' W117°28.68'

▼ 0.0			Continue to the west.
	6.8 ▲	TR	Turn right onto formed trail marked EF 411. Track ahead goes 1 mile to the Monarch-Rand Mine. Zero trip meter.
▼ 0.4		BL	Track on right.
	6.4 ▲	SO	Track on left.
			GPS: N35°11.97' W117°29.07'
▼ 0.6		SO	Two tracks on right.
	6.2 ▲	BR	Two tracks on left.
▼ 1.6		SO	Track on left and track on right.
	5.2 ▲	SO	Track on right and track on left.
▼ 2.6		SO	Track on left and track on right.
	4.2 ▲	SO	Track on left and track on right.
			GPS: N35°11.81' W117°31.41'
▼ 3.0		SO	Join larger graded Cuddeback Road (EF 473).
	3.8 ▲	BR	Bear right onto smaller formed road EF 411, marked by brown marker post.
			GPS: N35°11.78' W117°31.76'
▼ 3.8		SO	Track on left.
	3.0 ▲	SO	Track on right.
▼ 5.2		SO	Track on left.
	1.6 ▲	SO	Track on right.
▼ 5.5		SO	Track on left and track on right; then second track on left and track on right. This is the site of Fremont on the old Randsburg Railroad grade.
	1.3 ▲	SO	Track on left and track on right; then second track on left and track on right. This is the site of Fremont on the old Randsburg Railroad grade.
			GPS: N35°11.50' W117°34.57'
▼ 6.8			Trail ends at T-intersection with paved US 395. Turn left for Victorville; turn right for Randsburg.
	0.0 ▲		Trail commences on US 395, 13.4 miles north of Kramer Junction. Zero trip meter and turn northeast on graded dirt road. Immediately cross over pipeline road; then track on left. Continue straight ahead, following the brown marker post for Fremont Road (EF 411).
			GPS: N35°11.08' W117°35.65'

DESERT #23

Trona Pinnacles Trail

Starting Point:	**California 178, 1.8 miles south of Trona**
Finishing Point:	**Trona Road, 6 miles south of the intersection with Searles Station Cut Off Road**
Total Mileage:	**24.6 miles**
Unpaved Mileage:	**24.6 miles**
Driving Time:	**2 hours**
Elevation Range:	**1,600–3,900 feet**
Usually Open:	**Year-round**
Best Time to Travel:	**October to May**
Difficulty Rating:	**3**
Scenic Rating:	**9**
Remoteness Rating:	**+0**

Special Attractions

- Trona Pinnacles.
- Spangler Hills OHV Area.

History

The Trona Pinnacles are enormous tufa (calcium carbonate) towers, deposited by algal precipitation near carbonate-enriched springs on the lake floor of Searles Lake between 130,000 and 35,000 years ago. The lake reached depths approaching 600 feet at times and spilled into Panamint Valley through the Slate Range to the east. The land was lush and tropical at that stage. Some sections of the early shoreline are visible as horizontal bands to the northwest of the pinnacles. There are more than 500 tufa spires over an area of approximately 13 square miles. Some reach as high as 140 feet above the surrounding lakebed. The formations were known as Cathedral City to early travelers.

The Trona Pinnacles were designated as a National Natural Landmark in 1986. The dramatic scenery has been used as the backdrop for many movies, including *Star Trek V: The Final Frontier, Dinosaur,* and *Pitch Black.* The 2001 remake of *Planet of the Apes* was also filmed here.

John and Dennis Searles discovered borax at their namesake lake in 1863 and saline production began about 10 years later. The once tropical lake is now a mix of mud and sand to the northeast of this trail. The 12-square-mile area contains disseminated salt crystals to an average depth of 70 feet. Salts exist at lesser depths over a broad area around the lakebed. Potassium salt, boric acid, borax, lithium carbonate, bromine, and phosphoric acid are in near pure form, requiring little processing at the on-site plant. The town name Trona refers to a mineral consisting of sodium carbonate and bicarbonate.

Two different wagon routes were used by the Searles brothers to haul the borax they produced to the railroad at Mojave. The southern route passed west of the Trona Pinnacles to Searles freight station at Garden City. This is now the route of the current railroad. The western route traveled through Salt Wells Canyon (Poison Canyon, part of today's California 178) to a dry station 1 mile from the head of the canyon, to Garden City where the routes joined. It then continued through Garlock to Mojave.

The American Trona Corporation was formed in 1913 and found that the local mule haulage company, Rinaldi and Clark, cost too much money and took too much time. A more efficient transportation method was needed. The corporation struggled to finance its own railroad that stretched more than 30 miles up Teagle Wash to reach the Southern Pacific line. The trains were running by 1916 and still run to this day.

The Spangler brothers, Tony and Rea, worked a small, low-paying gold mine just west of the military road near Teagle Wash. Their house, close to the tamarisks growing near the railroad, was also the site of the Spangler water tower used by the old Trona Railroad steam engines.

Description

As you approach the Trona Pinnacles, you may find that they look familiar. This surreal landscape of gray spires and rocky

***Planet of the Apes* movie set at the Trona Pinnacles**

pinnacles has been used as the setting for the alien planetscape in many science fiction films.

The well-marked graded road heads off from California 178, south of the borax town of Trona. The road is dusty as it leads directly toward the pinnacles, which are visible a few miles away. There is a network of small tracks around the pinnacles that lead off from the main trail. The entire pinnacles area is best avoided when wet, because it can turn into a quagmire that will impound the most capable of vehicles. There are no official campgrounds here, but primitive camping is permitted.

The trail continues past the pinnacles as a well-used formed trail. Several miles southwest of the pinnacles, you will cross a paved road. This road is part of the China Lake Naval Weapons Center; there is no public access along this road! You are permitted to cross the road, remaining on RM 143, but not to exit along this road.

The trail follows the roughly graded RM 143 for a short distance before turning off onto the smaller 7A trail. This trail has very loose, deep sand as it climbs along the wash through scattered Joshua trees in the Summit Range.

The final section of the trail runs alongside the Spangler Hills OHV Area, where there are many trails and open areas suitable for a wide variety of off-road vehicles. To the south is the Golden Valley Wilderness, encompassing the rugged Lava Mountains. This area is more suited to remote hiking and horseback riding. The trail exits the mountains to finish on Trona Road, north of Red Mountain.

Trona Pinnacles

Current Road Information

Bureau of Land Management
Ridgecrest Field Office
300 South Richmond Road
Ridgecrest, CA 93555
(760) 384-5400

Map References

BLM Ridgecrest, Cuddeback Lake
USGS 1:24,000 Westend, Spangler Hills East, West of Black Hills, Klinker Mt.
1:100,000 Ridgecrest, Cuddeback Lake
Maptech CD-ROM: Barstow/San Bernardino County
Southern & Central California Atlas & Gazetteer, pp. 53, 52, 66
California Road & Recreation Atlas, p. 95

Route Directions

Mileage		Direction	Description
▼ 0.0			From California 178, 1.8 miles south of Trona, zero trip meter and turn southeast on graded dirt road at the sign for Trona Pinnacles. The road is marked RM 143, suitable for 4WDs, ATVs, and motorbikes.
	4.1 ▲		Trail ends on California 178. Turn right for Trona; turn left for Ridgecrest.
			GPS: N35°40.89' W117°23.44'
▼ 0.5		SO	Track on right; then cross through wash.
	3.6 ▲	SO	Cross through wash; then track on left.
▼ 0.6		BR	Graded road on left. Follow sign for RM 143; then track on right.
	3.5 ▲	SO	Track on left; then graded road on right. Follow sign for RM 143.
			GPS: N35°40.68' W117°22.92'
▼ 1.1		SO	Track on right.
	3.0 ▲	SO	Track on left.
▼ 1.2		SO	Track on right; then cross over railroad.
	2.9 ▲	SO	Cross over railroad; then track on left.
			GPS: N35°40.12' W117°22.75'
▼ 3.3		SO	Track on right.
	0.8 ▲	SO	Track on left.
▼ 3.9		SO	Track on right.
	0.2 ▲	SO	Track on left.
▼ 4.0		SO	Track on right; then entering the Trona Pinnacles at sign.
	0.1 ▲	SO	Leaving the Trona Pinnacles; then track on left.
			GPS: N35°37.70' W117°22.69'
▼ 4.1		SO	Well-used track on left goes into the pinnacles. Zero trip meter.
	0.0 ▲		Continue to the north.
			GPS: N35°37.56' W117°22.70'
▼ 0.0			Continue to the south and immediately second track on left into pinnacles. Remain on RM 143.
	1.1 ▲	SO	Track on right into the pinnacles; then second track on right after rise. Zero trip meter at second track on right.
▼ 0.6		SO	Track on left.
	0.5 ▲	SO	Track on right.
▼ 1.0		SO	Track on left.
	0.1 ▲	SO	Track on right.
▼ 1.1		BR	Graded road on left into pinnacles. Zero trip meter.
	0.0 ▲		Continue to the northwest.
			GPS: N35°36.65' W117°22.55'

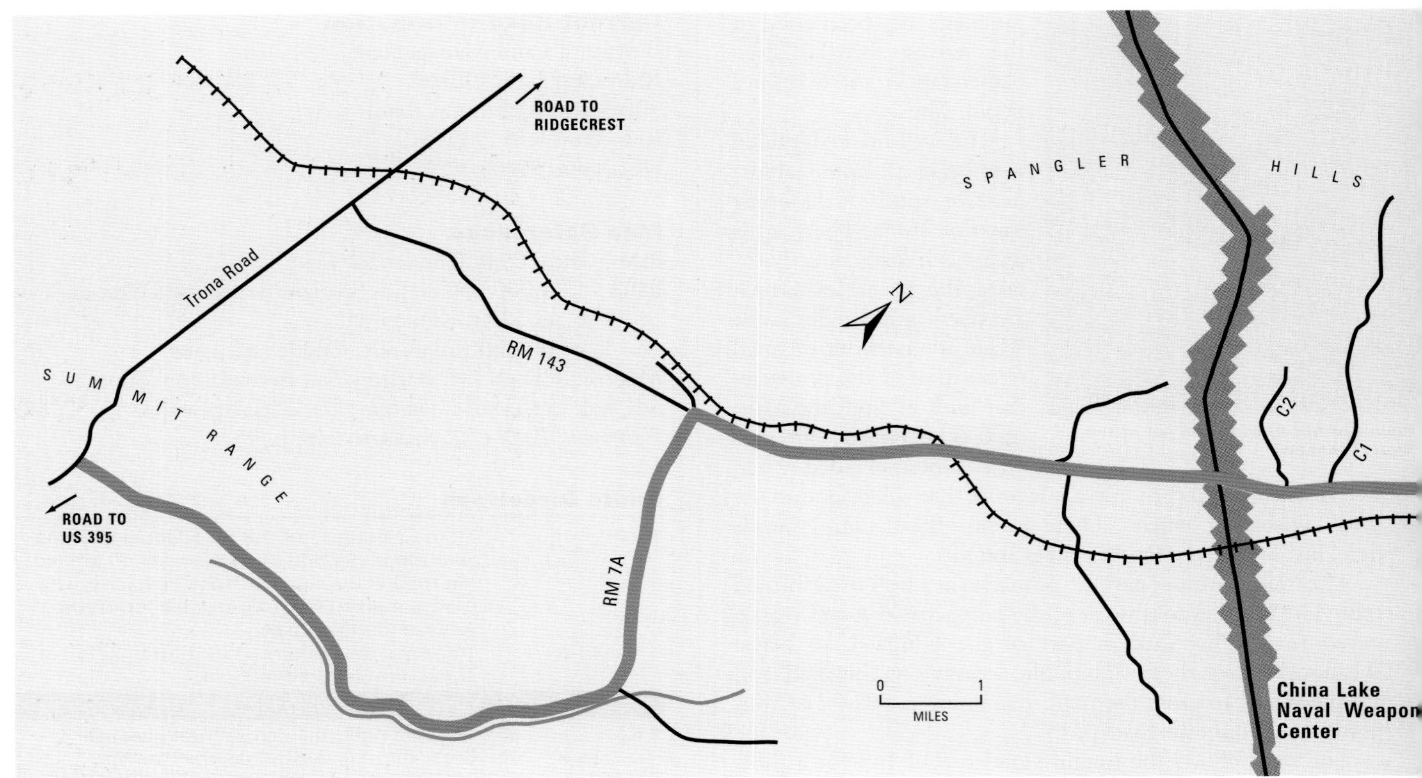

▼ 0.0			Continue to the south.
	4.7 ▲	BL	Graded road on right into pinnacles. Zero trip meter.
▼ 0.2		SO	Cross over railroad track.
	4.5 ▲	SO	Cross over railroad track.
▼ 0.4		SO	Track on left.
	4.3 ▲	SO	Track on right.
▼ 0.5		SO	Track on left.
	4.2 ▲	SO	Track on right.
▼ 0.8		SO	Track on left.
	3.9 ▲	SO	Track on right.
▼ 1.4		BL	Trail forks. Well-used track on right.
	3.3 ▲	SO	Well-used track on left.
			GPS: N35°35.97′ W117°23.59′
▼ 2.0		SO	Faint track on left.
	2.7 ▲	SO	Faint track on right.
▼ 2.1		SO	Track on right.
	2.6 ▲	BR	Track on left.
▼ 3.6		SO	Track on right is marked C1.
	1.1 ▲	SO	Track on left is marked C1.
			GPS: N35°34.89′ W117°25.57′
▼ 4.1		SO	Track on right.
	0.6 ▲	SO	Track on left.
▼ 4.2		SO	Track on right is marked C2.
	0.5 ▲	SO	Track on left is marked C2.
			GPS: N35°34.44′ W117°26.09′
▼ 4.7		SO	Track on right; then trail crosses paved road, which is government property—no public vehicles allowed. Zero trip meter and continue on RM 143.
	0.0 ▲		Continue to the northeast, following sign to the Trona Pinnacles; then track on left.
			GPS: N35°34.22′ W117°26.52′
▼ 0.0			Continue to the southwest.
	2.7 ▲	SO	Trail crosses paved road, which is government property—no public vehicles allowed. Zero trip meter and continue on RM 143.
▼ 0.2		SO	Cross through wash.
	2.5 ▲	SO	Cross through wash.
▼ 0.7		SO	Track on left and track on right.
	2.0 ▲	SO	Track on left and track on right.
▼ 1.0		SO	Cross through wash.
	1.7 ▲	SO	Cross through wash.
▼ 1.4		SO	Small track on left and small track on right.
	1.3 ▲	SO	Small track on left and small track on right.
▼ 1.7		SO	Small track on left and small track on right.
	1.0 ▲	SO	Small track on left and small track on right.
▼ 1.9		SO	Track on right.
	0.8 ▲	SO	Track on left.
▼ 2.7		SO	Track on right; then cross over railroad and zero trip meter.
	0.0 ▲		Continue to the northeast past track on left.
			GPS: N35°32.74′ W117°28.75′
▼ 0.0			Continue to the southwest. Track on left and track on right.
	2.5 ▲	SO	Track on left and track on right; then cross over railroad. Zero trip meter.
▼ 1.0		SO	Cross through wash.
	1.5 ▲	SO	Cross through wash.
▼ 1.2		SO	Track on right and track on left.
	1.3 ▲	SO	Track on right and track on left.
			GPS: N35°31.94′ W117°29.71′
▼ 1.3		SO	Track on left. Remain on RM 143.
	1.2 ▲	BL	Track on right. Remain on RM 143.
▼ 1.8		SO	Track on right and small track on left.
	0.7 ▲	SO	Track on left and small track on right.
▼ 2.5		TL	4-way intersection. Unmarked track on right,

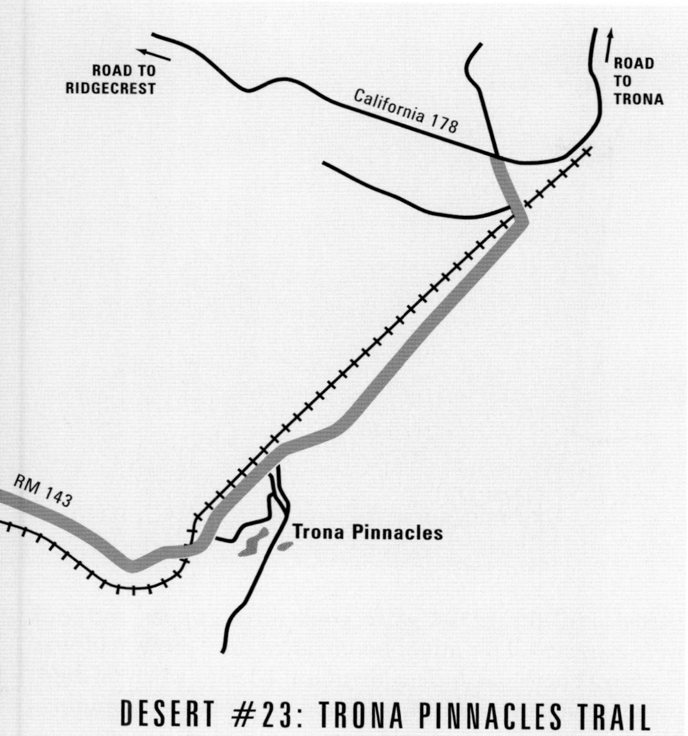

Mileage	Direction	Description
		track on left is RM 7A, and RM 143 continues straight ahead. Zero trip meter and turn onto RM 7A at the marker post.
0.0 ▲		Continue to the northeast.
		GPS: N35°31.45' W117°30.95'
▼ 0.0		Continue to the southeast. Trail is marked as both RM 7 and RM 7A.
3.0 ▲	TR	4-way intersection. RM 143 on left and on right and track straight ahead. Zero trip meter and turn right onto RM 143 at the marker post. Trail is marked as suitable for 4WDs, ATVs, and motorbikes.
▼ 0.5	SO	Track on left.
2.5 ▲	SO	Track on right.
▼ 1.5	BL	Track on right.
1.5 ▲	SO	Track on left.
▼ 1.6	SO	Track on left and track on right. Remain on RM 7A.
1.4 ▲	SO	Track on left and track on right. Remain on RM 7A.
		GPS: N35°30.20' W117°30.19'
▼ 1.9	SO	Faint track on left and faint track on right.
1.1 ▲	SO	Faint track on left and faint track on right.
▼ 2.0	SO	Motorbike trail crosses on left and right.
1.0 ▲	SO	Motorbike trail crosses on left and right.
▼ 3.0	TR	Turn right into wash, remaining on RM 7A. Track on left down wash and track straight ahead. Zero trip meter.
0.0 ▲		Continue to the northwest.
		GPS: N35°29.17' W117°29.35'
▼ 0.0		Continue to the south.
6.5 ▲	TL	Turn left out of wash at the marker, remaining on RM 7A. Track on right and track straight ahead in wash. Zero trip meter.
▼ 1.3	BL	Track on right; then second track on right is marked RM 1127.
5.2 ▲	SO	Track on left is marked RM 1127; then second entrance to track on left.
		GPS: N35°28.20' W117°30.07'
▼ 2.7	SO	Second entrance to track on right.
3.8 ▲	SO	Track on left.
		GPS: N35°27.53' W117°31.23'
▼ 3.6	SO	Small track on right.
2.9 ▲	SO	Small track on left.
▼ 4.3	SO	Track on right.
2.2 ▲	SO	Track on left.
▼ 4.5	SO	Top of rise. Trail exits wash. Track on right.
2.0 ▲	SO	Top of rise. Track on left. Trail ahead is now marked RM 7A for 4WDs, ATVs, and motorbikes. Trail enters down wash.
		GPS: N35°27.73' W117°33.07'
▼ 4.9	SO	Track on right.
1.6 ▲	SO	Track on left.
▼ 5.1	SO	Trail enters line of wash. Track on right.
1.4 ▲	BR	Track on left. Trail leaves line of wash.
▼ 5.2	SO	Track on right.
1.3 ▲	SO	Track on left.
▼ 5.8	SO	Track on left; then track on right.
0.7 ▲	SO	Track on left; then track on right.
▼ 5.9	SO	Track on right is C2.
0.6 ▲	BR	Track on left is C2.
▼ 6.2	SO	Track on left and track on right follow pipelines.
0.3 ▲	SO	Track on right and track on left follow pipeline.
▼ 6.5		Trail finishes at Trona Road. Turn right for Ridgecrest; turn left for Red Mountain and US 395.
0.0 ▲		From Trona Road, 4.5 miles south of the railroad and 6 miles south of the intersection with Searles Station Cut Off Road, zero trip meter and turn northeast on formed trail that travels up a wide, sandy wash. There is a small track opposite and a sign for BLM Limited Use Area, but no signposts. Track is called Savoy Road on some maps. Immediately, track on left is marked C2 and main trail is marked C2. Proceed straight ahead in wash on C2.
		GPS: N35°27.28' W117°35.08'

DESERT #24

Colosseum Gorge Trail

Starting Point:	**I-15 at Yates Well Road exit, 5 miles southwest of Primm, NV**
Finishing Point:	**Kingston Road, 6.5 miles north of I-15**
Total Mileage:	**18.4 miles**
Unpaved Mileage:	**18.4 miles**
Driving Time:	**2.5 hours**
Elevation Range:	**2,800–5,500 feet**
Usually Open:	**Year-round**
Best Time to Travel:	**September to June**
Difficulty Rating:	**3**
Scenic Rating:	**8**
Remoteness Rating:	**+0**

Special Attractions

- Dry Ivanpah Lake, popular place for land yachting.
- Clark Mountain Range and Mojave Desert scenery within the Mojave National Preserve.

History

The Chemehuevi, Mojave, and Paiute frequented the Clark Mountain region for many generations. Evidence of their turquoise mining was reported as early as 1898. Pottery shards, tools, and thousands of petroglyphs were found for quite some distance around the mines.

Clark Mountain is a notable landmark from afar; it is the highest mountain in the eastern Mojave region. The peak, which is to the south of this trail, reaches 7,929 feet. The mountain was formed from a series of thrust faults, and it was named after an early day miner, Senator William A. Clark, the copper king of Montana.

With the end of the war with Mexico and the ceding of these lands to the United States in 1848, there was a slow influx of surveyors, prospectors, and settlers in the region. Mineral deposits looked promising and the Clark Mining District was established in 1865. In 1869, the Paiute Company of California found silver deposits in the Clark Mountains (which may have been originally spelled Clarke). The first town in this remote region, old Ivanpah on the eastern side of Clark Mountain, had a population of about 500 people who were mainly workers at the mines. A supply route from the mines, through Crescent Springs in Nevada, to a steamboat landing at Cottonwood Island on the Colorado River developed. Though some activity occurred at the Colosseum Mine in the 1860s, no major development occurred until the 1930s, when gold, silver, copper, and lead were extracted. This minor boom lasted until the World War II years. There was little activity until 1986, when an Australian company built a mill and began serious mining. Nearly 7,000 ounces of gold were produced each month until 1993. Since its closing in the 1990s, millions of dollars of reclamation work has been undertaken at the site.

The large open pit of the Colosseum Mine

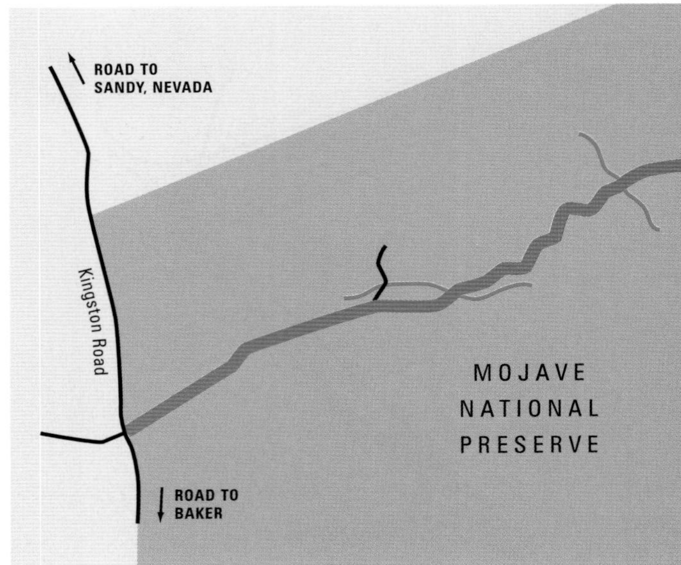

The Yates Ranch was one of the earliest cattle grazing ventures to work this eastern Mojave region in the 1880s. The name is remembered at the eastern end of this trail in the form of Yates Well Road. The well is now used by the Primm Valley Golf Club for irrigation. The Yates Ranch headquarters were on the western side of Clark Mountain at Valley Wells, which is to the north of Valley Wells Rest Area on present-day I-15.

Midway along the trail is old Greene's Cabin. The timber cabin was owned by the Greene family from 1900 to 1920. It was divided into a couple distinct areas. Mr. and Mrs. Greene used the western end of the cabin as their quarters; the middle section was the kitchen where Mrs. Greene cooked for miners who worked at the Greenes' gold mines to the north of the old cabin.

Description

Colosseum Gorge runs up the eastern side of the Clark Mountain Range from I-15, southwest of the casino town of Primm, Nevada. The trail turns off the paved road at the Primm Valley Golf Club, and travels along a graded dirt road up the gently sloping bajada toward the bulk of Clark Mountain. The bajada is vegetated with creosote bush, Mojave yuccas, chollas, and sagebrush. The trail enters Colosseum Gorge and climbs a wide, rough shelf road along the side of the gorge. The road used to serve the Colosseum open pit mine at the top of the saddle, so it was once wide enough for mining trucks, but it is now eroding and somewhat rough. At the top of the gorge is the open pit mine, which is currently not in use. It is posted and there is no access. Mining works in the area are being revegetated.

DESERT #24: COLOSSEUM GORGE TRAIL

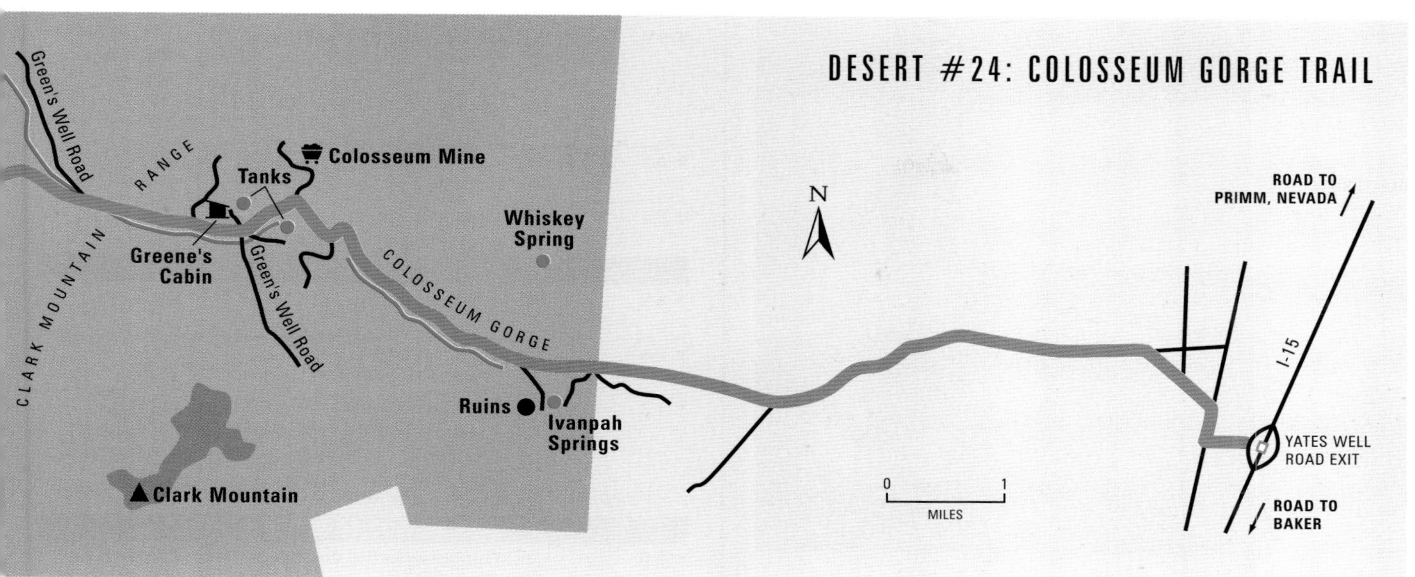

The trail descends the far side of the gorge on Green's Well Road along a smaller trail, running in or alongside the wash for the first 1.9 miles. Greene's Cabin can be found beside the wash.

The trail then swings out of the wash to follow a smaller formed trail that winds over the undulating slopes of the Clark Mountain Range, through a variety of vegetation, which on the west side of the range includes Joshua trees.

The trail finishes far below on paved Kingston Road.

Current Road Information

Mojave National Preserve
PO Box 241
72157 Baker Boulevard
Baker, CA 92309
(760) 733-4040

Map References

BLM Mesquite Lake
USGS 1:24,000 Ivanpah Lake, Clark Mt., Pachalka Spring
1:100,000 Mesquite Lake
Maptech CD-ROM: San Bernardino County/Mojave
Southern & Central California Atlas & Gazeteer, pp. 56, 57
California Road & Recreation Atlas, p. 97

Route Directions

Mileage		Directions
▼ 0.0		From I-15 at the Yates Well Road exit, 5 miles southwest of Primm and the Nevada state line, proceed to the west side of the freeway and zero trip meter. Proceed west on paved road.
1.0 ▲		Trail finishes at I-15. Proceed east for Primm, NV, west for Baker.
		GPS: N35°32.46' W115°25.25'
▼ 0.4	TR	Turn right at T-intersection onto paved road, following sign for Primm Valley Golf Club.
0.6 ▲	TL	Turn left onto unmarked paved road.
▼ 0.7	TL	Turn left on paved road. Road straight ahead goes into Primm Valley Golf Club.
0.3 ▲	TR	Turn right on paved road. Road on left goes into Primm Valley Golf Club.
		GPS: N35°32.75' W115°25.64'
▼ 1.0	BL	Bear left onto graded dirt road. Two paved roads on right. Intersection is unmarked. Zero trip meter.
0.0 ▲		Continue to the south on paved road.
		GPS: N35°32.90' W115°25.91'
▼ 0.0		Continue to the north on graded dirt road.
8.3 ▲	BR	Bear right onto paved road. Two paved roads on left. Intersection is unmarked. Zero trip meter.
▼ 0.4	BL	Bear left along power lines. Graded road on right.
7.9 ▲	BR	Bear right leaving power lines. Graded road on left.
		GPS: N35°33.16' W115°26.22'
▼ 0.9	SO	Track on left at pump on left.
7.4 ▲	SO	Track on right at pump on right.
▼ 1.4	SO	Track on right and track on left along power lines. Leave power lines.
6.9 ▲	SO	Track on right and track on left along power lines. Continue alongside power lines.
▼ 3.7	SO	Well-used track on left.
4.6 ▲	SO	Well-used track on right.
		GPS: N35°32.55' W115°29.60'
▼ 5.0	BR	Two tracks on left, second of which goes to Ivanpah Springs; then enter Mojave National Preserve. The preserve has no sign, just a marker.
3.3 ▲	SO	Exit Mojave National Preserve. There is no sign, just a marker at the boundary. Two tracks on right, first of which goes to Ivanpah Springs.
		GPS: N35°32.69' W115°31.07'
▼ 5.1	SO	Cross through wash. Track on right at wash goes toward Whiskey Spring, and track on left up wash. Trail gradually starts to ascend Colosseum Gorge.
3.2 ▲	SO	Track on right up wash. Cross through wash. Track on left at wash goes toward Whiskey Spring. Trail levels out.
▼ 5.5	SO	Cross through wash.

Old timber cabin in Colosseum Gorge

2.8 ▲ SO Cross through wash.

▼ 5.7 SO Memorial marker on right.
2.6 ▲ SO Memorial marker on left.

GPS: N35°32.77′ W115°31.87′

▼ 5.8 SO Track on left toward stone ruins.
2.5 ▲ SO Track on right toward stone ruins.

GPS: N35°32.78′ W115°31.93′

▼ 6.2 SO Track on left goes into wash. Trail starts to climb wide shelf road up Colosseum Gorge.
2.1 ▲ SO Track on right goes into wash. End of shelf road.

▼ 7.8 SO Cross over Colosseum Gorge Wash.
0.5 ▲ SO Cross over Colosseum Gorge Wash.

▼ 7.9 SO Well-used track on left goes into area of old mine workings.
0.4 ▲ SO Well-used track on right goes into area of old mine workings.

GPS: N35°33.55′ W115°33.62′

▼ 8.1 SO Tank on right.
0.2 ▲ SO Tank on left.

▼ 8.3 TL Turn left onto well-used, smaller trail. Track on right goes 0.4 miles to Colosseum Mine. Zero trip meter.
0.0 ▲ Continue to the east.

GPS: N35°33.86′ W115°34.01′

▼ 0.0 Continue to the southwest and enter line of wash.
0.6 ▲ TR Turn right and exit line of wash onto larger, roughly graded road. Track on left goes 0.4 miles to Colosseum Mine. Zero trip meter.

▼ 0.2 SO Tank on left and two tracks on right.
0.4 ▲ SO Tank on right and two tracks on left.

GPS: N35°33.76′ W115°34.22′

▼ 0.5 SO Small tank on right.
0.1 ▲ SO Small tank on left.

GPS: N35°33.61′ W115°34.41′

▼ 0.6 SO 5-way intersection. Two tracks on left and track on right. Second track on left is Green's Well Road, Public Bypass Route. Zero trip meter.
0.0 ▲ Continue to the north.

GPS: N35°33.55′ W115°34.48′

▼ 0.0 Continue to the southwest.
1.3 ▲ SO 5-way intersection. Two tracks on right and track on left. First track on right is marked Green's Well Road, Public Bypass Route. Zero trip meter.

▼ 0.1 SO Concrete footings on right.
1.2 ▲ SO Concrete footings on left.

▼ 0.4 SO Greene's Cabin on right.
0.9 ▲ SO Greene's Cabin on left.

GPS: N35°33.60′ W115°34.82′

▼ 0.5 SO Track on right.
0.8 ▲ SO Track on left.

▼ 0.6 SO Track on left.
0.7 ▲ SO Track on right.

▼ 1.3 BL Bear left out of wash on well-used track. Green's Well Road continues ahead in wash. Intersection is unmarked but there is a metal post opposite the turn. Zero trip meter.
0.0 ▲ Continue to the east.

GPS: N35°33.74′ W115°35.78′

▼ 0.0 Continue to the west on smaller formed trail.
7.2 ▲ BR Bear right up wash, joining Green's Well Road, which also continues to the left down wash. Intersection is unmarked but there is a metal post opposite the turn.

▼ 0.1 BR Well-used track on left.
7.1 ▲ SO Well-used track on right.

▼ 1.7 SO Cross through wash.
5.5 ▲ SO Cross through wash.

▼ 1.8 SO Cross through wash.
5.4 ▲ SO Cross through wash.

▼ 2.2 SO Wire gate.
5.0 ▲ SO Wire gate.

GPS: N35°33.66′ W115°38.06′

▼ 2.5 SO Cross through wash.
4.7 ▲ SO Cross through wash.

▼ 2.8 SO Cross through wash.
4.4 ▲ SO Cross through wash.

▼ 3.3 SO Cross through wash.
3.9 ▲ SO Cross through wash.

▼ 3.7 SO Cross through wash.
3.5 ▲ SO Cross through wash.

▼ 3.9 SO Cross through wash.
3.3 ▲ SO Cross through wash.

▼ 4.1 SO Cross through wash.
3.1 ▲ SO Cross through wash.

▼ 4.5 SO Cross through wash.
2.7 ▲ SO Cross through wash.

▼ 5.4 SO Track on right.
1.8 ▲ BR Track on left.

GPS: N35°32.54′ W115°40.64′

▼ 6.1 SO Track on right.
1.1 ▲ SO Track on left.

▼ 7.2 Trail ends at intersection with paved Kingston Road. Turn left for I-15 and Baker; turn right for Sandy, NV. There is a small track opposite.
0.0 ▲ Trail commences on Kingston Road, 6.5 miles north of the Excelsior Mine Road exit on I-15, 5.7 miles south of the intersection of Kingston Road and Excelsior Mine Road. Zero trip meter and turn northeast on well-used formed trail, which leads straight toward the Clark Mountain Range. Intersection is unmarked but there is a small track opposite.

GPS: N35°31.63′ W115°42.27′

DESERT #25

Kingston Wash Trail

Starting Point:	**Excelsior Mine Road, 8.6 miles north of the intersection with Kingston Road**
Finishing Point:	**California 127, opposite the site of Renoville**
Total Mileage:	**30 miles, plus 6.1-mile spur to Crusty Bunny Ranch**
Unpaved Mileage:	**30 miles, plus 6.1-mile spur**
Driving Time:	**4 hours (including spur)**
Elevation Range:	**700–3,600**
Usually Open:	**Year-round**
Best Time to Travel:	**September to June**
Difficulty Rating:	**3**
Scenic Rating:	**8**
Remoteness Rating:	**+1**

Special Attractions

- Long, remote desert wash trail that travels a vehicle corridor in the Kingston Range Wilderness.
- The Crusty Bunny Ranch cabin.

History

The settlement of Kingston, located just inside the California border, was homesteaded in the early 1920s. Dry farming was attempted throughout the valley, but the short growing season made efforts unprofitable. A post office was opened in 1924, and a school was established as well. Vineyards were ambitiously planted and bootlegging took place during Prohibition. Homesteaders had little choice during the Depression but to try and survive on their Kingston properties. A community hall was erected, a small library was established, and one store catered to the small settlement. When options opened up after the Depression, homesteaders slowly left their lands. The post office's closure in 1938 signaled the end of Kingston.

Kingston Wash formed part of a trail that was used by Indians, and later Spanish and American travelers. The Kingston Range was a welcome relief from the Mojave Desert for all who passed this way. Horsethief Spring, to the north of Kingston Peak, was a reliable watering point for herds of horses being traded along the Old Spanish Trail, which ran north of the mountains. The spring was also used to hide stolen horses.

At the western end of the trail lies the remote site of Valjean, a small settlement along the Tonopah & Tidewater Railroad. The railroad was constructed between 1905 and 1907, stretching from Ludlow, California, to Beatty, Nevada. This section of railroad operated on a schedule that was meant to prevent two trains from colliding. Yet in August 1929, two men were killed in a 15-car train accident south of Valjean. Nothing had been spotted on the line ahead and it seemed the train had simply crashed for no reason, killing the engineer and fireman. Like most railroads, this route was monitored regularly for line damage. However, there had been no foot patrol of the particular 2.5-mile-long section where the accident occurred. An official inquiry concluded that a rainstorm in the Silurian Hills to the south of this trail caused a localized flash flood that eroded a section of bridge. The damage was most likely undetectable from the engine car. Even if the displaced rail lines had been noticed by the engineer, it was doubtful the train could have stopped in time.

The Silurian Hills gained their name from the Silurian (Paleozoic) rocks found within.

Operating a railroad through such a harsh environment combined with a fluctuating freight market ultimately proved unprofitable. An application to close the route was lodged in 1938. The last train traveled the scenic route some time in 1940.

Description

Kingston Wash Trail is a recognized OHV access route through the remote Kingston Range Wilderness. It is lightly traveled and offers a remote, high desert experience for vehicle-based travelers.

The trail commences on Excelsior Mine Road, some 27 miles southeast of Tecopa via Tecopa Pass. The BLM has marked the trail with route markers. However, they are sporadic in places and should not be relied upon.

The trail travels along the southern edge of the Kingston Range, undulating across the bajada before entering a small wash line that gradually descends to join the wide channel of Kingston Wash. Within Kingston Wash, the trail can be difficult to see. Vehicles often take different routes. The constant rearrangement of boulders and vegetation within the wash makes it difficult to give precise directions. As long as you remain within the main wash channel it is unlikely that you will go wrong. You may need a bit of scouting to

Kingston Spring

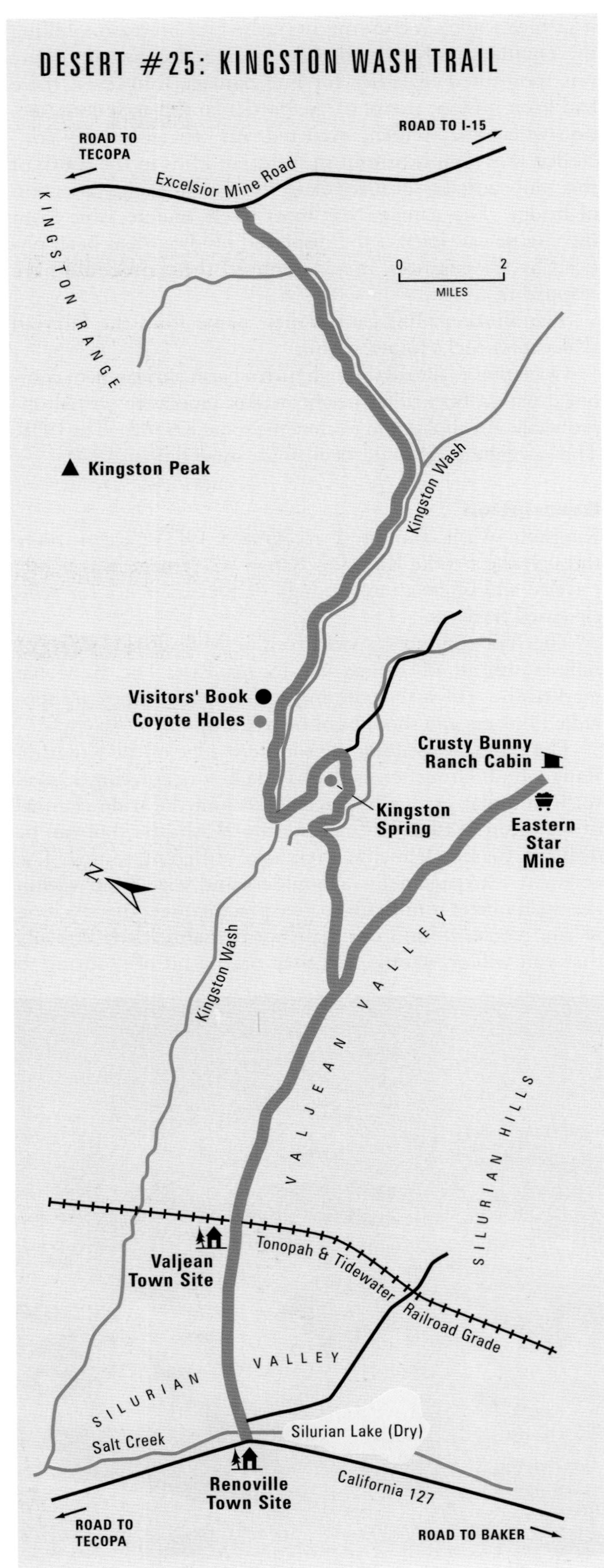

find the best route for your vehicle. Outside the wash channel is the Kingston Range Wilderness, where vehicle travel is prohibited.

The trail passes two springs. The first, Coyote Holes, is in the main wash channel. The second, Kingston Spring, is found after the trail has left the main wash.

A well-used spur trail goes 6.1 miles to the Crusty Bunny Ranch, where an old cabin is available on a first-come first-served basis to passing travelers. It is furnished and in generally good order. If you use the cabin, make sure you leave it in better condition than you found it. As always, when entering old premises be aware of the danger of hantavirus (see page 13).

From the Crusty Bunny Ranch spur the trail runs along the open Valjean Valley, crossing the old Tonopah & Tidewater Railroad grade and passing the site of Valjean. Nothing remains at the site except a few piles of rusty cans. The trail ends at the intersection with California 127, opposite the unmarked site of Renoville.

The route is marked as D171 on some maps, but not on the marker posts along the route.

Current Road Information

Bureau of Land Management
Needles Field Office
101 West Spikes Road
Needles, CA 92363
(760) 326-7000

Map References

BLM Mesquite Lake, Owlshead Mts.
USGS 1:24,000 East of Kingston Peak, Kingston Peak, Kingston Spring, Silurian Hills, Silurian Lake
1:100,000 Mesquite Lake, Owlshead Mts.
Maptech CD-ROM: Barstow/San Bernardino County; San Bernardino County/Mojave
Southern & Central California Atlas & Gazetteer, pp. 55, 56
California Road & Recreation Atlas, p. 97

Route Directions

Mileage		Directions
▼ 0.0		From Excelsior Mine Road, 8.6 miles north of the intersection with Kingston Road, zero trip meter and turn west on well-used, formed trail. A marker post at the start gives the name of the trail and indicates its suitability for 4WDs, ATVs, and motorbikes.
6.5 ▲		Trail ends at intersection with paved Excelsior Mine Road. Turn left for Tecopa; turn right for I-15 and Baker.
		GPS: N35°43.00' W115°48.25'
▼ 1.5	SO	Cross through wash.
5.0 ▲	SO	Cross through wash.
▼ 2.1	SO	Pass through wire gate.
4.4 ▲	SO	Pass through wire gate.
		GPS: N35°41.31' W115°49.17'
▼ 2.3	SO	Enter line of wash.
4.2 ▲	SO	Exit line of wash.
▼ 2.4	BR	Bear right down main wash.
4.1 ▲	BL	Bear left out of main wash.
▼ 6.5	BR	Bear right and enter main channel of Kingston

Wash. Zero trip meter. There is no vehicle travel to the left up Kingston Wash.
0.0 ▲ Continue to the north up side wash.

GPS: N35°38.31' W115°51.84'

▼ 0.0 Continue to the west down Kingston Wash.
5.3 ▲ BL Bear left out of main channel of Kingston Wash, following directional marker into a smaller side wash. Vehicles cannot continue in the main Kingston Wash past this point. Zero trip meter.

▼ 5.3 SO Old wire corral on right. Rock pile and visitor's book contained in a box on the right is marked Box 2. Zero trip meter.
0.0 ▲ Continue to the northeast.

GPS: N35°38.48' W115°57.30'

▼ 0.0 Continue to the southwest.
2.2 ▲ SO Old wire corral on left. Rock pile and visitor's book contained in a box on the left is marked Box 2. Zero trip meter.

▼ 0.2 SO Coyote Holes on right.
2.0 ▲ SO Coyote Holes on left.

GPS: N35°38.45' W115°57.50'

▼ 0.8 SO Adit on left in high embankment.
1.4 ▲ SO Adit on right in high embankment.

GPS: N35°38.20' W115°58.13'

▼ 2.2 BL Follow directional marker out of main Kingston Wash into a smaller side wash. Vehicles cannot continue in Kingston Wash past this point. Zero trip meter.
0.0 ▲ Continue to the northeast up Kingston Wash.

GPS: N35°37.73' W115°59.44'

▼ 0.0 Continue to the east up smaller side wash.
6.9 ▲ BR Bear right up main Kingston Wash and zero trip meter. Vehicles cannot travel down the wash to left.

▼ 1.4 SO Leave main wash and bear right.
5.5 ▲ SO Bear left into wash.

▼ 1.8 SO Bear right out of line of wash.
5.1 ▲ SO Bear left and enter line of wash.

▼ 1.9 BR Kingston Spring on right.
5.0 ▲ BL Bear left and pass Kingston Spring on left.

GPS: N35°37.22' W115°57.73'

▼ 2.0 SO Cross through wash.
4.9 ▲ SO Cross through wash.

▼ 2.5 SO Enter wash.
4.4 ▲ SO Exit wash.

▼ 3.5 BL Bear left out of wash following directional marker.
3.4 ▲ BR Bear right up wash.

GPS: N35°36.94' W115°59.23'

▼ 3.7 SO Cross through wide wash.
3.2 ▲ SO Cross through wide wash.

▼ 4.1 SO Cross through wash. Trail crosses many small washes for the next 2.8 miles.
2.8 ▲ SO Cross through wash. End of wash crossings.

▼ 6.9 SO Well-used track on left is spur to Crusty Bunny Ranch cabin. Zero trip meter and follow marker to Hwy 127.
0.0 ▲ Continue to the northeast. Trail crosses many small washes for the next 2.8 miles.

GPS: N35°35.45' W116°02.18'

Spur to the Crusty Bunny Ranch Cabin

▼ 0.0 Bear east on well-used, formed trail.
▼ 0.5 SO Cross through wash. Many small wash crossings for next 0.4 miles.
▼ 0.9 SO End of wash crossings.
▼ 4.3 SO Enter wash.
▼ 6.1 UT Mine workings of the Eastern Star Mine on right; then Crusty Bunny Ranch cabin.

GPS: N35°33.97' W115°56.11'

Continuation of Main Trail

▼ 0.0 Continue to the west into Valjean Valley.
9.1 ▲ BL Well-used track on right is spur to Crusty Bunny Ranch cabin. Zero trip meter.

GPS: N35°35.45' W116°02.18'

▼ 0.5 SO Enter line of wash.
8.6 ▲ SO Exit line of wash.

▼ 4.8 SO Cross over old Tonopah & Tidewater Railroad grade. Track on left and right along railroad corridor is for vehicle use through the wilderness. Site of Valjean is immediately past intersection on right—nothing remains. Trail exits line of wash and crosses bajada.
4.3 ▲ SO Trail enters line of wash. Site of Valjean on left—nothing remains. Then cross over old Tonopah & Tidewater Railroad grade. Track on left and right along railroad corridor is for vehicle use through the wilderness.

GPS: N35°35.14' W116°07.37'

▼ 8.8 SO Track on left.
0.3 ▲ SO Track on right.

GPS: N35°33.40' W118°11.10'

▼ 8.9 SO Cross through Salt Creek.
0.2 ▲ SO Cross through Salt Creek.

▼ 9.1 Trail ends at T-intersection with California 127, opposite the unmarked site of Renoville. Turn left for Baker; turn right for Tecopa.
0.0 ▲ Trail commences on California 127, opposite the unmarked site of Renoville, 23 miles north of Baker. Zero trip meter and turn north at unmarked intersection onto wide formed trail. The turn is 0.1 miles southeast of mile marker 21.5 and 0.6 miles southeast of an emergency phone.

GPS: N35°33.20' W116°11.32'

DESERT #26

Sperry Wash Route

Starting Point:	**California 127, at the entrance to the Dumont Dunes**
Finishing Point:	**Furnace Creek Road, 9 miles southeast of Tecopa**
Total Mileage:	**18.6 miles**
Unpaved Mileage:	**15.8 miles**
Driving Time:	**2.5 hours**
Elevation Range:	**500–2,300 feet**
Usually Open:	**Year-round**
Best Time to Travel:	**September to May**
Difficulty Rating:	**4**
Scenic Rating:	**9**
Remoteness Rating:	**+0**

Special Attractions

- Dumont Dunes OHV Area.
- Historic Sperry town site.
- Many crossings of the Amargosa River.

History

The Dumont Dunes were created approximately 18,000 years ago by the drying of Lake Manly, in Death Valley, and Lake Dumont, in Silurian Valley. Sand was blown around and deposited here by local prevailing winds. The main dune area is 4 miles long, 1 mile wide, with a high point about 450 feet above the desert floor. The total volume of sand is estimated at 7 billion cubic feet. Studies of aerial photographs taken in the summer of 1953 compared to similar photos taken in 1978 indicate that the Dumont Dunes had advanced a distance of 1.8 miles to the northeast. This translates into an expansion of approximately 40-odd feet per year over the 25-year period. The dunes crossed and almost obliterated the old Tonopah & Tidewater Railroad easement.

The Tonopah & Tidewater Railroad was constructed through the Amargosa Desert from 1905 to 1907. Much of the roadbed was built up with tailings from the borax mill in Death Valley, which gave the grade a white appearance as it snaked its way up the Amargosa River. Trestles as long as 500 feet and deep cuts were necessary to enter the canyon. Tent camps were erected in the wide wash to house and feed the railroad construction gang. Heat drove many of the workers away; some would spray others with water as they worked in the stifling heat. They would then switch to take a turn at the pick and shovel. Lack of materials, a dwindling workforce, and temperatures reportedly reaching as high as 140 degrees Fahrenheit forced the abandonment of further construction during the summer of 1906. Construction of the railroad had been estimated at $3 million. However, the Amargosa River section pushed the project way over budget. Later calculations show that construction of the railroad up the Amargosa River cost more than $40,000 per mile! The first train service between Ludlow and Sperry ran in February 1907. Originally, the line was planned to stretch from the shipping port near Los Angeles to Tonopah, Nevada, but only the middle section was ever completed. Hence, the line was referred to as "the railroad with no beginning and no end."

Dumont Dunes

Even after completion, the railroad was seldom out of the red. Flash floods commonly required major repairs. The last train ran in 1940, and the track was carefully dismantled two years later and shipped to Egypt for use in World War II.

The eastern end of the trail finishes at the intersection with Furnace Creek Road at what was once called Lower Noonday Camp, close to the Western Talc Mine. The foundations of the camp can still be seen near the edge of the creek. An old graveyard is on the north side of Furnace Creek at Tecopa Pass. The pass marks the southern end of the Nopah Range. The Tonopah & Tidewater Railroad ran a branch to this spot to service the mines surrounding old Tecopa.

One of the prominent mines in the area was the Gunsight Mine, located about 3 miles north of the small graveyard. The Gunsight Mine was part of the Tecopa property renowned for its lead. Exploration work at the Gunsight Mine found the lead-rich ledge had pinched out. This brought great concerns to investors. However, in late August 1908, a sigh of relief was heard in the lead-mining industry when the rich ledge was found to resume at a depth of 600 feet.

At that stage, 50 men were employed and 50 tons of ore a day were being hauled to the Tecopa Siding for shipment to the smelter at Salt Lake City. Early in 1909, plans were under way to construct a large concentrating plant. That same year, work began on a private railroad between Tecopa Station and the mine heads at Gunsight and Noonday. An impressive tramway was built up to the second level of the Gunsight Mine. Trains came close to the mine, where they were loaded under the large ore bin that, in turn, was loaded by ore carts traveling along narrow tracks to an elevated position above the bin.

Closer to the graveyard, the Noonday Mine lay over a faulted offset of the same ore body as the Gunsight Mine. Closer still, the War Eagle Mine, which developed after World War II, also worked the same ledge.

Description

Sperry Wash Route is a well-known OHV route that leads away from the open OHV area of Dumont Dunes. It follows part of the route of the Tonopah & Tidewater Railroad grade, as well as passing through the site of Sperry.

The trail leaves California 127 and travels the graded road to Dumont Dunes OHV Area. The OHV area is open for use by ATVs, motorbikes, sand rails, and 4WD vehicles. The tall dunes have many varying faces for vehicle play. There is a large open area that is suitable for RVs and tent camping, although it can be extremely windy.

The start of the wash route is well marked by an overhead sign. The formed trail leads down to the Amargosa River and

Old Tonopah & Tidewater Railroad embankment alongside the trail

follows alongside the river in the main channel for the first few miles. There are many fords through the main river; these are normally shallow and easy to negotiate. The raised grade of the Tonopah & Tidewater Railroad is visible in places on the east side of the wash.

At the town site of Sperry, the trail leaves the Amargosa River and travels up the smaller, rockier Sperry Wash between the Sperry and Dumont Hills. The narrow canyon twists its way up the range before running over the Sperry Hills and down to the graded Western Talc Road at the Western Talc Mine.

The trail is marked along its length by cairns with a large paw print on the face. Navigation is relatively easy.

The trail ends by passing the remains of various talc mines. The Old Tecopa Cemetery is located 0.1 miles west of the eastern end of the trail along Furnace Creek Road. A few graves, marked by piles of stone and small crosses, sit on a rise overlooking the wash. The coordinates of the cemetery are N35°48.13' W116°05.99'.

Current Road Information

Bureau of Land Management
Needles Field Office
101 West Spikes Road
Needles, CA 92363
(760) 326-7000

Map References

BLM Owlshead Mts.
USGS 1:24,000 Saddle Peak Hills, Dumont Dunes, Tecopa, Tecopa Pass
1:100,000 Owlshead Mts.
Maptech CD-ROM: Barstow/San Bernardino County
Southern & Central California Atlas & Gazetteer, pp. 55, 56
California Road & Recreation Atlas, pp. 96, 97

Route Directions

Mileage		Direction
▼ 0.0		Trail commences on California 127, 23 miles south of Shoshone. Zero trip meter and turn northeast on graded dirt road at the sign for Dumont Dunes. Dunes are visible directly ahead after the turn.
3.7 ▲		Trail ends at T-intersection with California 127. Turn right for Shoshone; turn left for Baker.
		GPS: N35°41.53' W116°18.11'
▼ 3.7	BL	Bear left onto smaller trail and pass under entrance marking the Sperry Wash Route. Graded road continues 0.5 miles to the right into the Dumont Dunes OHV Area. Zero trip meter.
0.0 ▲		Continue to the west.
		GPS: N35°41.92' W116°15.16'
▼ 0.0		Continue to the east.
3.2 ▲	SO	Join graded dirt road from Dumont Dunes. Road on left goes 0.5 miles into the Dumont Dunes OHV Area. Zero trip meter.
▼ 0.3	SO	Follow alongside Amargosa River in main line of wash.
2.9 ▲	SO	Leave Amargosa River Wash.
▼ 0.7	BR	Bear right and ford through Amargosa River.
2.5 ▲	BL	Ford through Amargosa River.
		GPS: N35°42.21' W116°14.47'
▼ 0.9	SO	Track on right.
2.3 ▲	SO	Track on left.
▼ 1.3	SO	Track on left.
1.9 ▲	SO	Track on right.
		GPS: N35°42.54' W116°14.10'
▼ 1.4	SO	Track on right; then ford through Amargosa River.
1.8 ▲	SO	Ford through Amargosa River; then track on left.
		GPS: N35°42.65' W116°14.06'
▼ 1.6	BL	Ford through Amargosa River; then bear left.
1.6 ▲	BR	Bear right; then ford through Amargosa River.
▼ 2.1	SO	Track on right.
1.1 ▲	BR	Track on left.
▼ 2.2	SO	Track on right.
1.0 ▲	SO	Track on left.
▼ 2.3	SO	Track on right.
0.9 ▲	BR	Track on left.
▼ 2.4	SO	Ford river twice.
0.8 ▲	SO	Ford river twice.
▼ 2.6	SO	Track on right.
0.6 ▲	SO	Track on left.
▼ 2.7	SO	Track on right up wash.
0.5 ▲	SO	Track on left up wash.
▼ 3.0	SO	Track on right.
0.2 ▲	SO	Track on left.
▼ 3.1	SO	Ford through Amargosa River.
0.1 ▲	SO	Ford through Amargosa River.
		GPS: N35°43.80' W116°13.21'
▼ 3.2	SO	Entering Kingston Range Wilderness corridor at sign. Zero trip meter.
0.0 ▲		Continue to the south.
		GPS: N35°43.87' W116°13.22'
▼ 0.0		Continue to the north.
1.1 ▲	SO	Leaving wilderness corridor at sign. Zero trip meter.
▼ 0.1	BL	Ford through river; then bear left alongside old Tonopah & Tidewater Railroad embankment. Track on right.
1.0 ▲	BR	Track on left; then bear right and ford through river, leaving railroad embankment.
▼ 0.7	SO	Entering Amargosa Canyon ACEC—wildlife habitat.
0.4 ▲	SO	Leaving Amargosa Canyon ACEC—wildlife habitat.
		GPS: N35°44.46' W116°13.24'
▼ 1.1	BR	Bear right up Sperry Canyon. This is Sperry

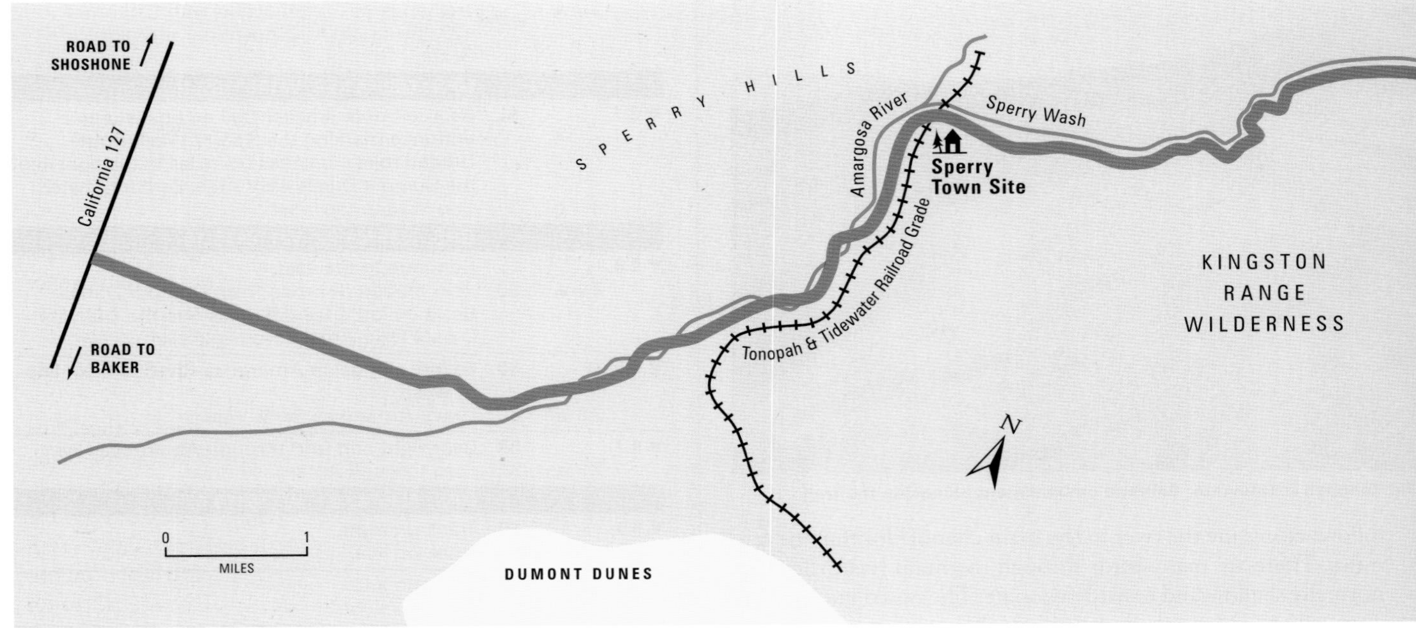

town site. Follow sign to Tecopa and Furnace Creek Road. Zero trip meter.

0.0 ▲ Continue to the south.

GPS: N35°44.77′ W116°13.22′

▼ 0.0 Continue to the northeast.

4.2 ▲ BL Leave Sperry Canyon and bear left down Amargosa River Wash. This is Sperry town site. Zero trip meter.

▼ 3.6 BR Bear right out of canyon and wash.

0.6 ▲ BL Bear left into wash and enter canyon.

GPS: N35°46.21′ W116°10.77′

▼ 4.0 SO Cross through wash.

0.2 ▲ SO Cross through wash.

▼ 4.2 SO Leaving wilderness corridor at sign. Zero trip meter.

0.0 ▲ Continue to the southwest.

GPS: N35°46.48′ W116°10.24′

▼ 0.0 Continue to the northeast.

2.0 ▲ SO Entering Kingston Range Wilderness corridor at sign. Zero trip meter.

▼ 0.4 SO Enter line of wash.

1.6 ▲ SO Exit line of wash.

▼ 1.9 BR Track on left; bear right at cairn. Exit line of wash.

0.1 ▲ BL Enter line of wash. Track on right; bear left at cairn.

GPS: N35°46.54′ W116°08.28′

▼ 2.0 TL T-intersection. Intersection is unmarked. Zero trip meter. Track on right is Desert #27: Alexander Hills Trail.

0.0 ▲ Continue to the west.

GPS: N35°46.54′ W116°08.20′

▼ 0.0 Continue to the northwest.

0.8 ▲ TR Turn right onto well-used trail. Track ahead is Desert #27: Alexander Hills Trail. Intersection is unmarked. Zero trip meter.

▼ 0.1 SO Cross through wash.

0.7 ▲ SO Cross through wash.

▼ 0.6 SO Track on right.

0.2 ▲ BR Track on left.

▼ 0.7 SO Track on right into talc mine.

0.1 ▲ SO Track on left into talc mine.

▼ 0.8 SO Pass under Sperry Wash Route sign and bear left onto Western Talc Road. Road on right goes into Western Talc Mine. Zero trip meter.

0.0 ▲ Continue to the southeast.

GPS: N35°47.10′ W116°08.33′

▼ 0.0 Continue to the northwest.

3.6 ▲ BR Road on left goes into Western Talc Mine. Bear right and pass under Sperry Wash Route sign. Zero trip meter.

▼ 0.2 SO Track on right and track on left.

3.4 ▲ SO Track on right and track on left.

▼ 0.3 SO Track on left and track on right into mine workings.

3.3 ▲ SO Track on right and track on left into mine workings.

▼ 0.4 SO Track on left and track on right; then track on right goes to overlook over open cut mine.

3.2 ▲ SO Track on left goes to overlook over open cut mine; then track on right and track on left.

▼ 0.5 BR Two tracks on left.

3.1 ▲ BL Two tracks on right.

▼ 0.6 BR Track on left.

3.0 ▲ BL Track on right.

▼ 0.7 SO Track on right.

2.9 ▲ SO Track on left.

▼ 0.8 BL Paved road on right is blocked. Bear left and join paved road.

2.8 ▲ BR Paved road continues on left but is blocked. Bear right onto graded dirt road.

GPS: N35°47.43′ W116°08.27′

▼ 1.1 SO Track on right.

2.5 ▲ SO Track on left.

▼ 1.4 SO Track on right.

2.2 ▲ SO Track on left.

▼ 2.8 SO Track on left.

0.8 ▲ SO Track on right.

▼ 3.4 SO Track on right; then second track on right before mill; then track on left.

0.2 ▲ SO Track on right; then track on left after mill; then second track on left.

▼ 3.5 SO Remains of mill on right. Track on right is

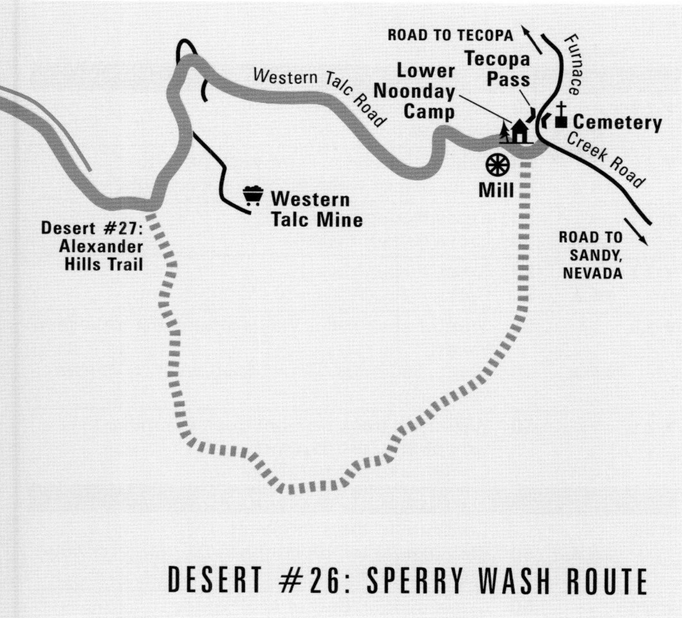

		Desert #27: Alexander Hills Trail.
0.1 ▲	SO	Remains of mill on left. Track on left is Desert #27: Alexander Hills Trail.
		GPS: N35°47.98' W116°05.95'
▼ 3.6		Trail ends at T-intersection with paved Furnace Creek Road. Turn left for Tecopa; turn right for Sandy.
0.0 ▲		From Furnace Creek Road, 9 miles southeast of Tecopa, zero trip meter and turn south on graded dirt road marked Western Talc Road and cross through wash on concrete ford. Past the wash on the right is the first trail marker for Sperry Wash Route—a small cairn bears the imprint of a large paw print.
		GPS: N35°48.07' W116°05.84'

DESERT #27

Alexander Hills Trail

Starting Point:	**Desert #26: Sperry Wash Route, 0.1 miles southwest of Furnace Creek Road**
Finishing Point:	**Desert #26: Sperry Wash Route, 3.6 miles southwest of Furnace Creek Road**
Total Mileage:	**6.4 miles**
Unpaved Mileage:	**6.4 miles**
Driving Time:	**1 hour**
Elevation Range:	**2,100–3,000 feet**
Usually Open:	**Year-round**
Best Time to Travel:	**September to June**
Difficulty Rating:	**4**
Scenic Rating:	**8**
Remoteness Rating:	**+0**

Special Attractions

- Remains of many talc mines.
- Narrow shelf road provides panoramic views of Valjean Valley and the Ibex Hills.
- Can be combined with Desert #26: Sperry Wash Route to make a longer, 4-rated trail.

Description

This short, moderate trail can be combined with Desert #26: Sperry Wash Route to provide an alternate exit to Furnace Creek Road that maintains a 4 difficulty rating. The trail leaves alongside the mill site at the northern end of Western Talc Road. It climbs a ridge, and not until you are on top do you see the trail stretching into the distance.

The formed trail follows a wash line for some distance. The most spectacular section of trail is along a very narrow shelf road, which winds around the southern end of the Alexander Hills. Panoramic views of Valjean Valley spread out to the southwest. This section of road is a very narrow single-track with extremely limited passing places. If you encounter an oncoming vehicle along this stretch, be prepared to back up for quite some distance.

A spur off the main trail leads 0.5 miles to a viewpoint over Valjean Valley and the Ibex Hills. It terminates in a loop that travels past a large adit. Other adits and mining remains can be found in the vicinity.

The main trail continues down the wash, passing the Acme Mine. Trails within the mine area lead to several viewpoints. The trail rejoins Desert #26: Sperry Wash Route, 3.6 miles from the northern end. Vehicles can exit via Western Talc Road back to Furnace Creek Road, or they can travel Sperry Wash Route to the Dumont Dunes.

Current Road Information

Bureau of Land Management
Needles Field Office
101 West Spikes Road
Needles, CA 92363
(760) 326-7000

Map References

BLM Owlshead Mts.
USGS 1:24,000 Tecopa Pass, Tecopa
1:100,000 Owlshead Mts.
Maptech CD-ROM: Barstow/San Bernardino County
Southern & Central California Atlas & Gazetteer, pp. 55, 56
California Road & Recreation Atlas, p. 97

Route Directions

▼ 0.0	From Desert #26: Sperry Wash Route, 0.1 miles from its northern end at Furnace Creek Road, zero trip meter and turn south on unmarked formed trail that climbs ridge toward an old water tank, keeping mill remains on the right.
3.9 ▲	Mill remains on left; then trail finishes back on Desert #26: Sperry Wash Route, immediately south of Furnace Creek Road. Turn left to travel Sperry Wash Route to Dumont Dunes; turn right for Furnace Creek Road.
	GPS: N35°47.98' W116°05.95'

Adit lined with branches and timbers

▼ 0.1		BL	Track on right returns to Sperry Wash Route. Bear left on formed trail leading away from mill.
	3.8 ▲	BR	Track on left leads down to Sperry Wash Route.
			GPS: N35°47.91′ W116°05.95′
▼ 0.6		SO	Pass through wire gate.
	3.3 ▲	SO	Pass through wire gate.
			GPS: N35°47.52′ W116°05.67′
▼ 1.2		BR	Track on left.
	2.7 ▲	SO	Track on right.
			GPS: N35°47.05′ W116°05.39′
▼ 2.9		SO	Enter line of wash.
	1.0 ▲	BL	Bear left away from line of wash.
▼ 3.0		BR	Exit line of wash. Faint track on left.
	0.9 ▲	BL	Enter line of wash. Faint track on right.
▼ 3.1		SO	Cross through wash.
	0.8 ▲	SO	Cross through wash.
▼ 3.3		SO	Cross through wash.
	0.6 ▲	SO	Cross through wash.
▼ 3.5		SO	Start of shelf road. Views southwest to Valjean Valley.
	0.4 ▲	SO	Shelf road ends. Views southwest to Valjean Valley.
▼ 3.9		SO	Well-used track on right goes 0.5 miles to viewpoint. Zero trip meter.
	0.0 ▲		Continue to the northeast.
			GPS: N35°45.49′ W116°06.53′
▼ 0.0			Continue to the southwest.
	2.5 ▲	SO	Well-used track on left goes 0.5 miles to viewpoint. Zero trip meter.
▼ 0.3		SO	Cross saddle. End of shelf road.
	2.2 ▲	SO	Cross saddle. Start of shelf road.
▼ 0.5		SO	Enter down line of wash.
	2.0 ▲	SO	Exit line of wash.
▼ 1.1		SO	Small track on right.
	1.4 ▲	BR	Small track on left.

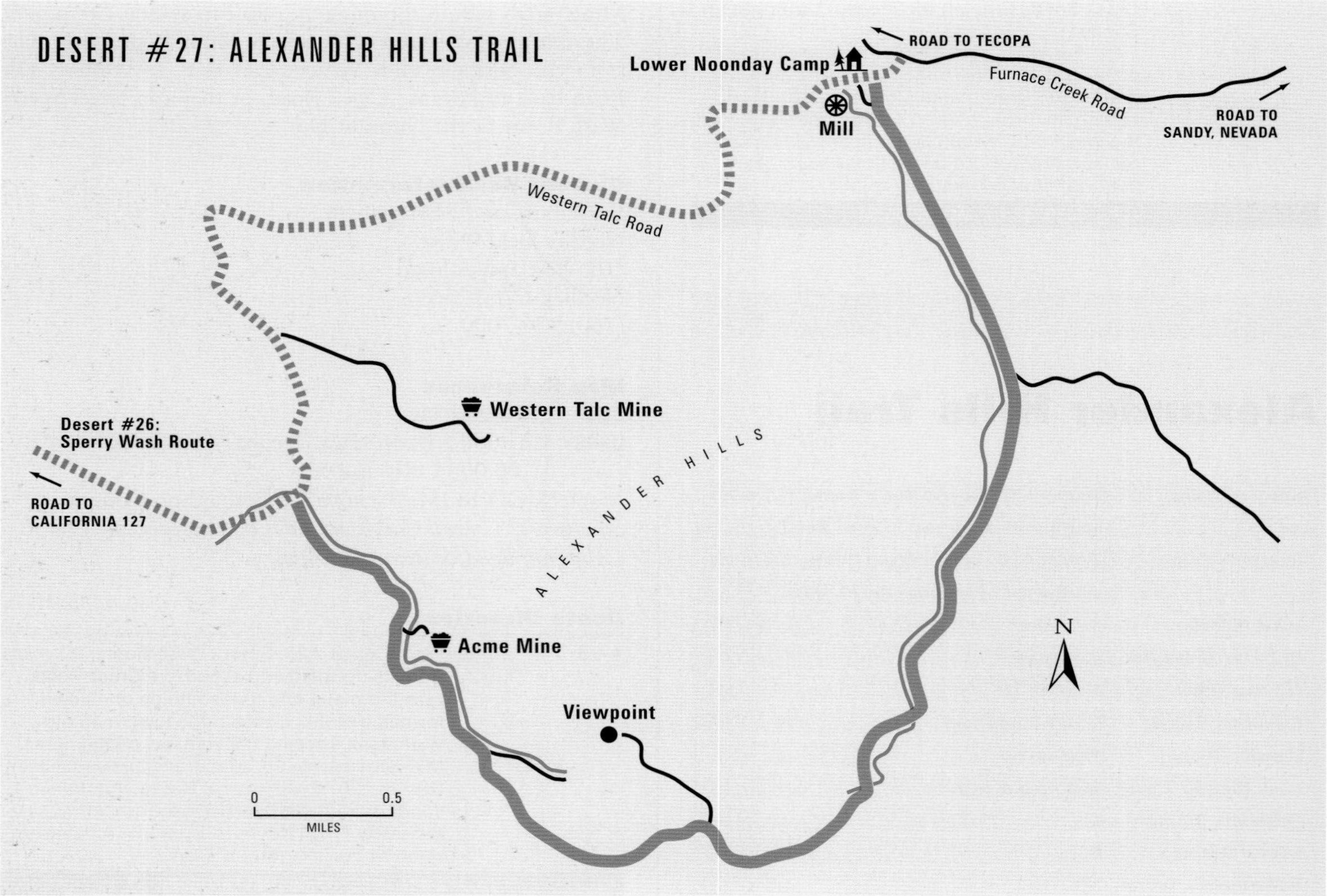

DESERT #27: ALEXANDER HILLS TRAIL

ROAD TO TECOPA
Lower Noonday Camp
Furnace Creek Road
Mill
ROAD TO SANDY, NEVADA
Western Talc Road
Western Talc Mine
Desert #26: Sperry Wash Route
ROAD TO CALIFORNIA 127
ALEXANDER HILLS
Acme Mine
Viewpoint
N
0 0.5 MILES

			GPS: N35°45.72′ W116°07.43′
▼ 1.8		SO	Two tracks on right. Both lead up to the Acme Mine and loop through the mine.
	0.7 ▲	BR	Two tracks on left. Both lead up to the Acme Mine and loop through the mine.
			GPS: N35°46.17′ W116°07.77′
▼ 2.4		SO	Exit line of wash.
	0.1 ▲	SO	Enter line of wash.
▼ 2.5			Trail ends at intersection with Desert #26: Sperry Wash Route. Turn left to continue along Sperry Wash; turn right to exit back to Western Talc Road.
	0.0 ▲		Trail starts on Desert #26: Sperry Wash Route, 3.6 miles from the northern end at Furnace Creek Road. Zero trip meter and turn southeast on unmarked formed trail. Sperry Wash Route turns to the west at this point.
			GPS: N35°46.54′ W116°08.19′

DESERT #28

Harry Wade Exit Route

Starting Point:	**California 127 at Ashford Junction**
Finishing Point:	**California 127, 27 miles south of Shoshone**
Total Mileage:	**30.5 miles**
Unpaved Mileage:	**30.5 miles**
Driving Time:	**1.5 hours**
Elevation Range:	**0–500 feet**
Usually Open:	**Year-round**
Best Time to Travel:	**September to June**
Difficulty Rating:	**2**
Scenic Rating:	**8**
Remoteness Rating:	**+0**

Special Attractions

- Easy graded trail through the southern end of Death Valley.
- Trail follows the approximate route used by Harry Wade and party to escape Death Valley in 1849.

History

The Harry Wade Exit Route is thought to have been the southerly exit from Death Valley used by the Wade family in 1849. Most of the family was born in England and had come to America in search of opportunity out West. They were the only members of the lost wagon train of 1849 to escape with their wagons intact. Other members of the group, including the Jayhawkers and the Bennett-Arcane party, either abandoned or burned their wagons. Their wagon train had attempted to follow a shortcut to the California goldfields. All of the members experienced starvation and extreme hardships trying to cope with the impossible terrain and extreme weather. Their oxen could barely pull the wagons because they were malnourished and dehydrated as well. It became a situation in which every man had to fend for himself. The wagon train split up near Furnace Creek, where it was confronted with the insurmountable Panamint Range dead ahead. The Wade party bore south, initially following an old Indian trail. They remained with their wagons, unlike some who had burned theirs to cook and smoke ox meat. Fortunately, the family managed to negotiate its way through Death Valley, and on to civilization.

The Confidence Mine is in the Black Mountains approximately 7 miles northeast of the Confidence Mill site. Mary Scott discovered what she thought was a silver vein in the early 1890s and moved on. Just a few years later, George Montgomery bought the claim for $36,000, once he realized that the vein contained gold. The mine was worked extensively, but the Confidence Mining Co. faced exorbitant haulage costs to ship ore out of Death Valley and to have supplies shipped in. As a result, Montgomery sought financial partners. The Confidence Mill was constructed late in 1895 in the valley below this trail. More than 20 men were employed by the company at the time. A well was dug nearby, which unfortunately produced very salty water that required additional treatment to render it useful. Despite such investments, the mill only ran for a few months because it was unable to sufficiently reduce the ore. Funds had run out and employees walked off the job because of non-payment, leaving the mine and mill idle.

By 1897, Montgomery managed to sell out for more than $80,000 to a partner named Cannon. Cannon tried unsuccessfully to sell the mine to outsiders. Two separate investors failed to make the mine profitable, one in 1911 and the other in 1913. By the mid-1920s, the mill was dismantled and the mine was quiet. A rumored reopening in the 1940s was the last mention of the old mine.

Harry Wade Exit Route passes through the southern end of Death Valley

Looking across the wide Amargosa River Wash

Description

Harry Wade Exit Route leaves the southern end of Death Valley, traveling through the sandy valley floor to intersect with California 127. The trail leaves from Ashford Junction, turning off the paved road to run south along the wide valley. The valley is framed by the Owlshead Mountains to the west and the Black Mountains to the east.

The road is suitable for high-clearance vehicles for its entire length. Soft sandy sections, particularly around the Amargosa River Wash, make it unsuitable for passenger vehicles. The road is often very washboardy. It is likely to be impassable after rain, when deep powder-fine sand traps turn to a sticky morass.

The trail intersects with the Desert #31: Owlshead Mountains Trail and Desert #29: Ibex Dunes Trail before it finishes on California 127.

Current Road Information

Death Valley National Park
PO Box 579
Death Valley, CA 92328-0579
(760) 786-2331

Map References

BLM Owlshead Mts.
USGS 1:24,000 Shore Line Butte, Epaulet Peak, Confidence Hills East, East of Owl Lake, Old Ibex Pass, Saddle Peak Hills
1:100,000 Owlshead Mts.
Maptech CD-ROM: Barstow/San Bernardino County
Southern & Central California Atlas & Gazetteer, pp. 54, 55
California Road & Recreation Atlas, p. 96

Route Directions

▼ 0.0		From California 178 at Ashford Junction, 25 miles west of the intersection with California 127, zero trip meter and turn southeast on graded dirt road, following sign to Baker.
18.3 ▲		Trail ends on paved California 178. Turn right for Shoshone; turn left for Furnace Creek.
		GPS: N35°53.99' W116°39.35'
▼ 6.5	SO	Confidence Mill site on right—nothing remains. The site is unmarked.
11.8 ▲	SO	Confidence Mill site on left—nothing remains. The site is unmarked.
		GPS: N35°50.59' W116°33.65'
▼ 11.8	SO	Start to cross wide Amargosa River Wash.
6.6 ▲	SO	Exit Amargosa River Wash.
		GPS: N35°46.11' W116°31.62'
▼ 12.5	SO	Exit Amargosa River Wash.
5.8 ▲	SO	Start to cross wide Amargosa River Wash.
▼ 14.1	SO	Cross through wash.
4.2 ▲	SO	Cross through wash.
▼ 15.9	SO	Cross through wash.
2.4 ▲	SO	Cross through wash.

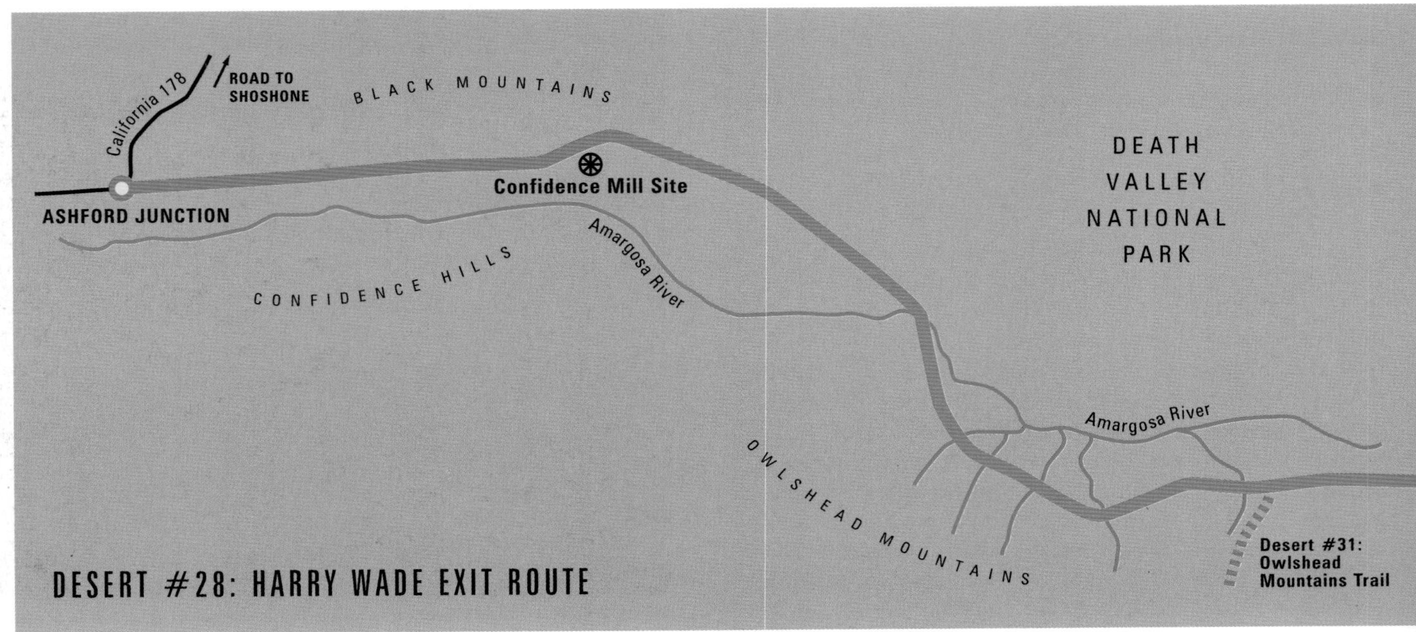

Mileage	Direction	Description
▼ 16.0	SO	Cross through wash.
2.3 ▲	SO	Cross through wash.
▼ 17.5	SO	Cross through wash.
0.8 ▲	SO	Cross through wash.
▼ 18.3	SO	Graded road on right is Desert #31: Owlshead Mountains Trail. Zero trip meter.
0.0 ▲		Continue to the northwest.
		GPS: N35°41.57' W116°29.42'
▼ 0.0		Continue to the southeast.
6.4 ▲	BR	Graded road on left is Desert #31: Owlshead Mountains Trail. Zero trip meter and follow sign to Furnace Creek.
▼ 4.9	SO	Track on right.
1.5 ▲	SO	Track on left.
		GPS: N35°39.09' W116°24.93'
▼ 5.1	SO	Leaving Death Valley National Park.
1.3 ▲	SO	Entering Death Valley National Park.
▼ 5.8	SO	Track on right.
0.6 ▲	SO	Track on left.
		GPS: N35°38.82' W116°24.18'
▼ 6.4	SO	Track on left is Desert #29: Ibex Dunes Trail, sign-posted to Saratoga Spring. Zero trip meter.
0.0 ▲		Continue to the west.
		GPS: N35°38.80' W116°23.47'
▼ 0.0		Continue to the east.
5.8 ▲	SO	Track on right is Desert #29: Ibex Dunes Trail, sign-posted to Saratoga Spring. Zero trip meter.
▼ 4.0	SO	Track on right.
1.8 ▲	SO	Track on left.
		GPS: N35°38.56' W116°19.19'
▼ 5.8		Trail ends at T-intersection with California 127, 27 miles south of Shoshone. Turn right for Shoshone; turn left for Baker.
0.0 ▲		Trail commences on California 127, 27 miles south of Shoshone. Zero trip meter and turn west on graded dirt road. There is a historical marker at the start of the trail for Harry Wade Exit Route, but otherwise the trail is unmarked. Start of the road is called Saratoga Spring Road on some maps.
		GPS: N35°37.99' W116°17.40'

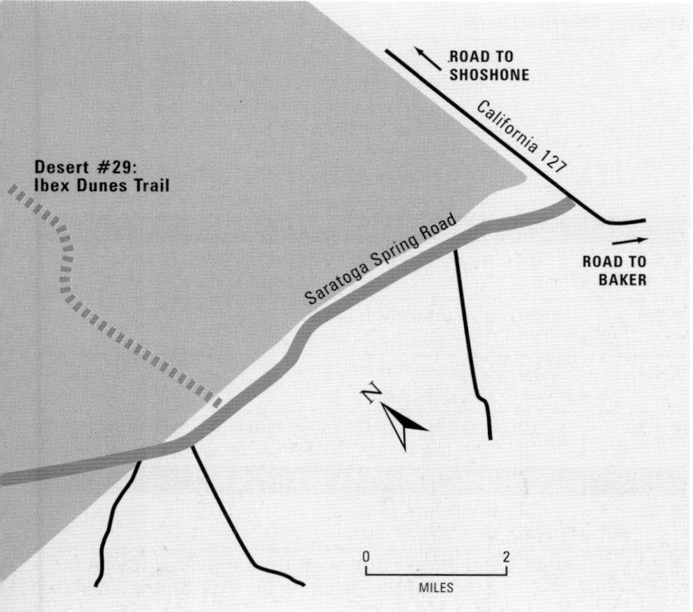

DESERT #29

Ibex Dunes Trail

Starting Point:	**California 127, 16 miles south of Shoshone**
Finishing Point:	**Desert #28: Harry Wade Exit Route, 5.8 miles west of California 127**
Total Mileage:	**11.1 miles**
Unpaved Mileage:	**11.1 miles**
Driving Time:	**1 hour**
Elevation Range:	**200–1,600 feet**
Usually Open:	**Year-round**
Best Time to Travel:	**October to May**
Difficulty Rating:	**3**
Scenic Rating:	**9**
Remoteness Rating:	**+0**

Special Attractions

- Ibex Sand Dunes.
- Saratoga Spring.
- Bird-watching and photography opportunities.

History

Saratoga Spring is one of the largest freshwater springs in the northern Mojave Desert. The Southern Paiute are thought to have had regular camps at Saratoga Spring, then known as Muta, before Euro-American arrivals. In a region of low rainfall and extreme weather conditions, these waters were essential for Indians, prospectors, and teamsters in the southern end of Death Valley. The spring was named by G. K. Gilbert during a mapping survey in 1871.

When the price of borax fell in the mid-1880s, William Tell Coleman of the Amargosa Borax Works had to find ways to reduce the cost of freighting borax to the railroad at Mojave. When his contract with hauler Charles Bennett was up, Cole-

Saratoga Spring

man developed his own freighting business with the assistance of his foreman, John Perry. They constructed massive wagons capable of carrying 10 tons of borax each. The wagons were then towed by 20-mule teams. This was the beginning of what was to become the Pacific Coast Borax Company's trademark, "20 Mule Team Borax."

Although the company claimed that it never lost a single animal on these death-defying, record-breaking trips, it did lose one teamster at Saratoga Spring in 1886. In a San Bernardino court hearing, Sterling Wassam, the swamper who operated the brakes on the wagon, claimed that he was attacked by teamster Al Bryson while lunching at the spring. He said he hit Bryson in self-defense with the nearest item at hand—a shovel. The teamster did not live to argue the point and Bryson was acquitted.

In 1905, prospector W. A. Kelly found rock salt near Saratoga Spring and formed a company with partner Jonas Osborne. The pair was unable to finance the freight costs out of Death Valley and the mining venture did not pay off. In 1912, Kelly sold out to millionaire William Kerckhoff. With the proper financing available, things looked promising; a railroad was planned and sample shafts were dug. Kerckhoff acquired nearby gypsum mines also but none paid well enough to warrant further investment.

In 1909, the Pacific Nitrate Company began to explore for minerals. The company enlarged the small Saratoga Spring to serve as a water source for its processing plant. The nitrate deposits were never worked because they were too poor in quality, but the enlarged pools remained. In the 1930s, the Saratoga Water Company bottled the water as a health cure. A resort was built around the pools, where people could "take the waters."

Description

The Ibex Dunes sit at the southern tip of Death Valley, in the small valley between the Saddle Peak Hills and the Ibex Hills. This trail runs along the western side of the dunes, far enough away that deep sand is not too much of a problem and near enough that photographers and others who appreciate the shape and form of the dunes can see them clearly.

Initially the trail leaves California 127 and runs down a sandy wash, descending steadily to Ibex Valley. Out of the wash, the trail forks, with the trail to Ibex ghost town and spring leaving to the northwest. Ibex Dunes Trail follows around the edge of the valley, passing the warning sign for deep sand. The sandy patches are deep enough that 4WD is preferred, especially in the reverse direction, when you tackle them heading uphill. However, they are short and interspersed with firmer ground.

The trail joins the graded road that leads to Saratoga Spring. The very beautiful reed-fringed pools support vast bird and animal populations, as well as the Saratoga Springs pupfish found nowhere else in the world. Late afternoon is a good time to visit the spring, when the low afternoon light brings out the colors of the surrounding rocks. No camping is permitted at the spring, and because of the unique wildlife populations, access is limited. An excellent view can be obtained by climbing the small ridge from the parking area.

Ibex Dunes

Current Road Information

Death Valley National Park
PO Box 579
Death Valley, CA 92328-0579
(760) 786-2331

Map References

BLM Owlshead Mts.
USGS 1:24,000 Ibex Pass, Old Ibex Pass, Ibex Spring
1:100,000 Owlshead Mts.
Maptech CD-ROM: Barstow/San Bernardino County
Southern & Central California Atlas & Gazeteer, p. 55
California Road & Recreation Atlas, p. 96
Trails Illustrated, Death Valley National Park (221)

Route Directions

Mileage		Direction
▼ 0.0		From California 127, 16 miles south of Shoshone, zero trip meter and turn southwest on unmarked graded dirt road. The road initially leads toward a communications tower.
2.7 ▲		Trail ends on California 127. Turn left for Shoshone; turn right for Baker and I-15.
		GPS: N35°46.33' W116°19.49'
▼ 0.3	BR	Track on left to communications tower.
2.4 ▲	BL	Track on right to communications tower.
▼ 0.6	SO	Cross through wash.
2.1 ▲	SO	Cross through wash.
▼ 1.1	SO	Track on left.
1.6 ▲	BL	Track on right.
▼ 1.2	SO	Entering Death Valley National Park at sign.
1.5 ▲	SO	Leaving Death Valley National Park at sign.
		GPS: N35°45.84' W116°20.52'
▼ 1.6	SO	Enter line of wash.
1.1 ▲	SO	Exit line of wash.
▼ 2.7	BL	Road forks. Track on right at warning sign for deep sand is Desert #30: Ibex Spring Trail. Zero trip meter.

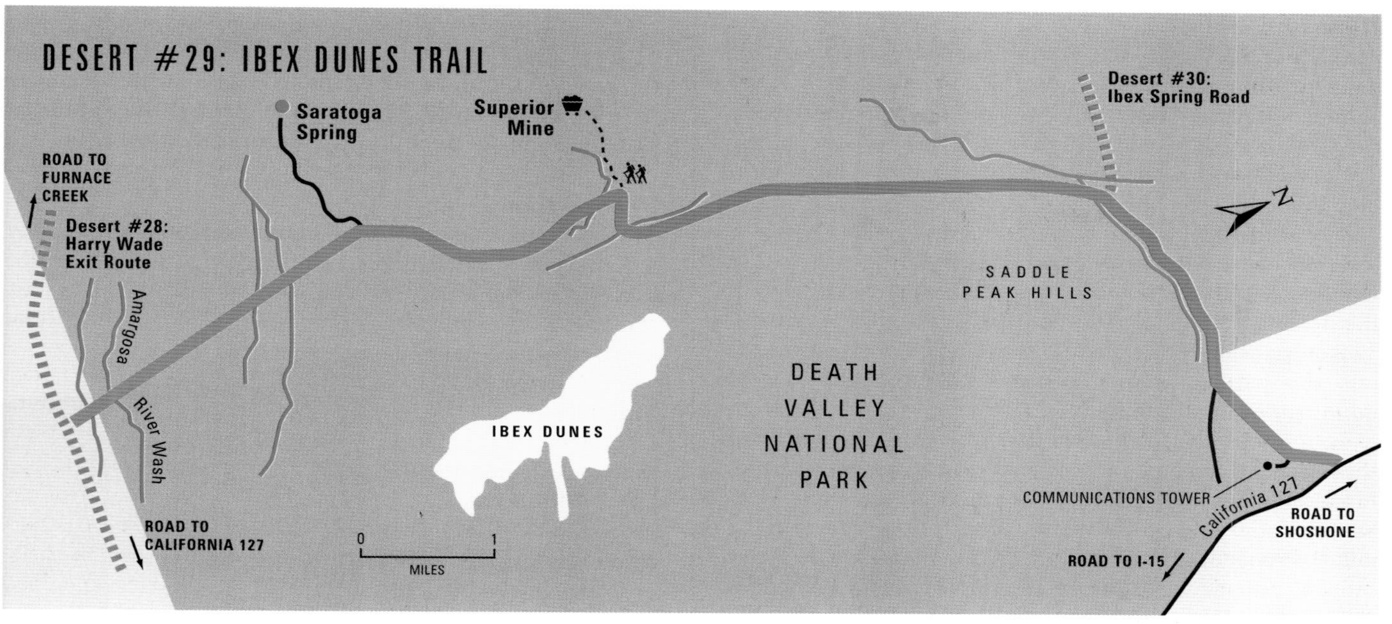

	0.0 ▲		Continue to the northeast.
			GPS: N35°45.62' W116°22.17'
▼ 0.0			Continue to the southwest.
	5.8 ▲	SO	Track on left is Desert #30: Ibex Spring Trail. Zero trip meter.
▼ 3.1		SO	Enter wash.
	2.7 ▲	SO	Exit wash.
			GPS: N35°42.96' W116°23.25'
▼ 3.3		SO	Exit wash.
	2.5 ▲	SO	Enter wash.
▼ 3.8		BL	Old vehicle trail (now a hiking trail) on right leads to Superior Mine.
	2.0 ▲	BR	Old vehicle trail (now a hiking trail) on left leads to Superior Mine.
			GPS: N35°42.71' W116°23.63'
▼ 3.9		SO	Cross through wash.
	1.9 ▲	SO	Cross through wash.
▼ 5.8		BL	Join larger graded road on bend. Zero trip meter. Road on right goes 1.2 miles to Saratoga Spring.
	0.0 ▲		Continue to the north
			GPS: N35°41.09' W116°24.11'
▼ 0.0			Continue to the south.
	2.6 ▲	BR	Bear right onto smaller, formed track. Intersection is unmarked, but is on a left-hand curve. There is a deep sand warning sign at the start of the track. Graded road continues on left for 1.2 miles to Saratoga Spring. Zero trip meter.
▼ 0.7		SO	Cross through wash.
	1.9 ▲	SO	Cross through wash.
▼ 1.7		SO	Cross through wash.
	0.9 ▲	SO	Cross through wash.
▼ 2.1		SO	Cross through wash.
	0.5 ▲	SO	Cross through wash.
▼ 2.2		SO	Cross through Amargosa River Wash.
	0.4 ▲	SO	Cross through Amargosa River Wash.
			GPS: N35°39.11' W116°23.56'
▼ 2.3		SO	Leaving Death Valley National Park at sign.
	0.3 ▲	SO	Entering Death Valley National Park at sign.
			GPS: N35°39.03' W116°23.54'
▼ 2.4		SO	Cross through wash.
	0.2 ▲	SO	Cross through wash.
▼ 2.6			Trail ends at T-intersection with Desert #28: Harry Wade Exit Route. Turn left for Tecopa; turn right to continue along Harry Wade Exit Route toward Furnace Creek.
	0.0 ▲		Trail commences on Desert #28: Harry Wade Exit Route, 5.8 miles west of California 127. Zero trip meter and turn north on graded dirt road at sign for Saratoga Spring.
			GPS: N35°38.81' W116°23.47'

DESERT #30

Ibex Spring Road

Starting Point:	**Desert #29: Ibex Dunes Trail, 2.7 miles west of California 127**
Finishing Point:	**Ibex Mine**
Total Mileage:	**7.8 miles (one-way)**
Unpaved Mileage:	**7.8 miles**
Driving Time:	**1 hour (one-way)**
Elevation Range:	**200–500 feet**
Usually Open:	**Year-round**
Best Time to Travel:	**October to May**
Difficulty Rating:	**3**
Scenic Rating:	**9**
Remoteness Rating:	**+1**

Special Attractions

- Ibex ghost town.
- Several well-preserved talc mines.
- Sand dunes in Buckwheat Wash Valley.

History

Ibex Spring and nearby Saratoga Spring are small yet valuable oases in this desert region. They are both noted for their abundance of arrowheads. Some low stone structures against the hills near Ibex Spring were thought to have housed miners before the Lost Buthane Mining Company established a mining town.

The Ibex Mine was first opened in 1882. The silver- and lead-bearing ore looked promising and a dry-roasting mill was constructed the following year. As was often the case in this region, the remote location worked against the mine. The overwhelming heat, lack of water, and hefty freight costs into this part of Death Valley proved too much for the mine's survival.

In 1906, new prospectors were reworking the Ibex and Rusty Pick Mines, both in Buckwheat Wash. But again, the returns could not make up for the expenses of operating mines in this remote location. A low level of activity continued at the mines throughout the years. One family moved to the other climatic extreme in Alaska in an effort to make a financial comeback. Several more unsuccessful attempts at working the mines were undertaken in the following decades, with prospecting continuing in the area into the 1970s.

A different kind of mining occurred in the twentieth century. The Ibex Spring talc claims were established by Charles Moorehouse in the 1930s. Moorehouse successfully operated his mines into the 1940s, when he then leased them to the Sierra Talc Company. Massive quantities of talc were removed from the Moorehouse region up until the 1960s. The Monarch Talc Mines took off in the late 1930s and the nearby Pleasanton Talc Mines did the same in the early 1940s. These mines, all leased by the Sierra Talc Company, were on the eastern side of the Ibex Hills. The late 1960s brought a close to activity in the region. Many mining structures have succumbed to time and weather over the decades since.

Ibex ghost town

Description

This short spur trail leads away from Desert #29: Ibex Dunes Trail and passes several historic points of interest along its length. The formed trail is well used and is easy to follow as far as Ibex ghost town. Erosion is a constant problem along the way; several deep gully washouts have to be negotiated or bypassed.

Sand-covered hills along Buckwheat Wash

At Ibex, easily spotted from a distance by the large palm trees at the spring, the trail branches in four directions. Continuing straight ahead leads into the center of the camp, where the Mojave River Valley Museum of Barstow (which has adopted the site) has placed a marker and visitors book. Many of the old houses and structures around Ibex are still standing. These date from the days of the talc mining operations in the 1930s. Past Ibex, the trail continues for 0.9 miles to the Moorehouse Talc Mine, where you can see extensive remains of the wooden loading chutes and tramway. Photographers will find some excellent viewpoints from this location. Bearing right at the 4-way intersection and remaining in the wash takes you to Ibex Spring itself, which is surrounded by palm trees.

The main trail turns to the southeast at the 4-way intersection, and travels along the wash for a short distance. Route finding is tricky along this section. The trail is lightly used and can be hard to follow, especially in the washes. It comes out of the first wash and turns west along the original road. Although this road seems to lead back to the main trail, a major washout has rendered it impassable.

The route winds west through the Ibex Hills, following a wash into the wide Buckwheat Wash Valley. On the far side of the valley (the southern end of the Black Mountains), sand has collected against the eastern face. These spectacular sand dunes are especially attractive in the low light of afternoon. The trail turns north up the wash and heads toward the most challenging section to navigate. Set your GPS to guide you to the exit point so that you don't miss it.

The trail leaves the wash and finishes at the Ibex Mine. An old corrugated iron cabin sits out of the wash here. You can spend some time exploring the rusting hulks of mine machinery scattered around the hill.

Exit the trail the way you came in. You have the choice of returning to California 127 or exiting via the equally pretty Desert #29: Ibex Dunes Trail. Past Ibex Spring, the trail is only marked on the *Southern & Central California Atlas & Gazetteer.*

Current Road Information

Death Valley National Park
PO Box 579
Death Valley, CA 92328-0579
(760) 786-2331

Map References

BLM Owlshead Mts.
USGS 1:24,000 Ibex Pass, Ibex Spring
1:100,000 Owlshead Mts.
Maptech CD-ROM: Barstow/San Bernardino County
Southern & Central California Atlas & Gazetteer, p. 55
California Road & Recreation Atlas, p. 96
Trails Illustrated, Death Valley National Park (221)

Route Directions

▼ 0.0		From Desert #29: Ibex Dunes Trail, 2.7 miles west of California 127, zero trip meter and turn west on unmarked formed trail. There is a sign for deep sand ahead on the Ibex Dunes Trail, but otherwise the intersection is unmarked.
		GPS: N35°45.62' W116°22.17'
▼ 0.1	SO	Cross through wash.
▼ 0.4	SO	Cross through deep washout.
▼ 1.1	SO	Cross through deep washout.
▼ 2.2	SO	Track on right goes 0.5 miles to remains of the Monarch Talc Mine.
▼ 2.3	TL	Turn first left down small wash. Track straight ahead goes 0.9 miles to the Moorehouse Mine and the historical marker at Ibex ghost town. Track on right continues in the wash for 0.3 miles to Ibex Spring. Zero trip meter.
		GPS: N35°46.14' W116°24.51'
▼ 0.0		Continue to the southeast.
▼ 0.1	SO	Old cans and remains of vehicle on right.
▼ 0.2	TR	4-way intersection.
		GPS: N35°45.92' W116°24.49'
▼ 0.6	SO	Small washout in trail.
▼ 1.1	SO	Small track on right.
▼ 1.3	SO	Enter wash.
▼ 2.2	SO	Exit wash and start to cross alluvial fan toward Buckwheat Wash.
▼ 2.8	BR	Old track on left was once the mule team trail (now a hiking trail) to Saratoga Spring. Trail bears right up wash.
		GPS: N35°46.26' W116°27.01'
▼ 3.8	SO	Trail dips down to enter wash.
		GPS: N35°47.16' W116°27.19'
▼ 4.9	SO	Mine on left.
		GPS: N35°48.18' W116°27.11'
▼ 5.1	BL	Bear left at fork in wash.
		GPS: N35°48.30' W116°27.04'
▼ 5.3	TL	Turn left onto formed trail out of wash.
		GPS: N35°48.47' W116°27.04'
▼ 5.4	BL	Fork in trail. Bear left toward the mine at the edge of mine diggings.
▼ 5.5		Trail ends at the Ibex Mine cabin.
		GPS: N35°48.52' W116°27.17'

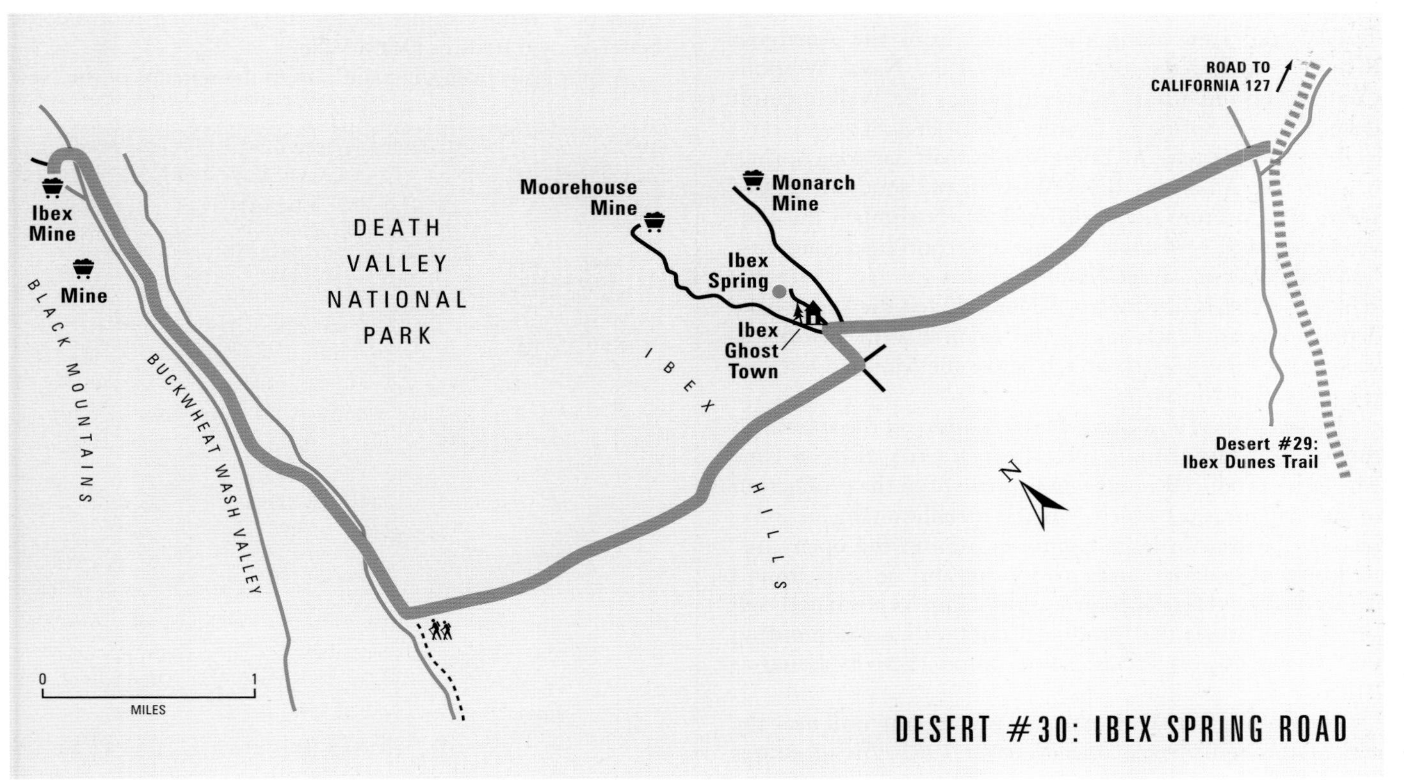

DESERT #31

Owlshead Mountains Trail

Starting Point:	**Desert #28: Harry Wade Exit Route, 12.2 miles north of California 127**
Finishing Point:	**Communications tower within the Owlshead Mountains**
Total Mileage:	**28.7 miles, plus 4.8-mile spur to Black Magic Mine**
Unpaved Mileage:	**28.7 miles, plus 4.8-mile spur**
Driving Time:	**2 hours (one-way)**
Elevation Range:	**50–1,200 feet**
Usually Open:	**Year-round**
Best Time to Travel:	**September to June**
Difficulty Rating:	**2**
Scenic Rating:	**8**
Remoteness Rating:	**+1**

Special Attractions

- Very remote desert experience, partially within Death Valley National Park.
- Panoramic views from the end of the trail.
- Backcountry camping.

History

This trail traces part of the old borax road from Mojave to Tecopa that was used by Charles Bennett's 20-mule teams. Today's trail runs along the section from the Amargosa Riverbed to the edge of the China Lake Naval Weapons Center. The mule trail followed part of the Walker cutoff from Saratoga Spring to Granite Wells. Freight teams traveled from the Amargosa Borax Works, past Saratoga Spring, to cross the Amargosa River Wash in the southern end of Death Valley. From there, the trail slowly climbed the alluvial fan toward Owl Hole Springs and continued southwest into today's China Lake Naval Weapons Center, where this vehicle trail bears northwest. Wagons skirted the Leach Lake depression, past Leach Spring and Granite Wells, before traversing the long straight stretch across the Mojave Desert to the railroad at Mojave.

The New Deal and Black Magic Mines, on the spur from this trail, extracted manganese from a series of open cuts. The latter produced a high-grade ore used in the production of steel. Pyrolusite, which is black metallic manganese oxide, can be seen in large quantities around the open cuts. Red-brown hematite (iron oxide) can also be seen around the mine. Owl Hole Springs was the camp location and mill site for the mines that produced military hardware during the 1910s, '40s, and '50s. Some mining activity lasted as late as 1991.

The Epsom Salt Works, located on a hiking trail near the end of this trail, began operations in 1921. An ingenious monorail was constructed to transport the ore to Trona. The 20-mile route traveled west over Wingate Pass, across Panamint Valley, over the Slate Range, and across the southern end of Searles Lake into Trona. A single rail was laid on top of timbers that were suspended 4 feet above the ground by A-frames set 10 feet apart. Dodge engines powered the locomotive, which was a double-flanged, two-wheel, in-line model built for this project. It was guided and balanced by rollers running along a timber guide that was attached to the A-frames approximately 1 foot above the ground. This form of transportation required very little grading and appropriate inclines were chosen when setting up the A-frames. By 1925, the mine was deemed too expensive for the grade of ore extracted when compared to new mines being discovered. Sinking problems on Searles Lake associated with a replacement heavy-duty train combined to bring the Epsom Salt Works to a close. Some remnants of the unusual monorail supposedly lie within the boundaries of China Lake Naval Weapons Center.

Description

Owlshead Mountains Trail is a long spur that leads from Desert #28: Harry Wade Exit Route into the Owlshead Mountains. The trail crosses a mixture of BLM land and the southernmost part of Death Valley National Park. It also skirts the north end of Fort Irwin Military Reservation. The road is roughly graded for its entire length. It is maintained to service the communications tower at the end of the trail. However, because generators have been replaced with solar panels, the tower needs fewer service visits and the trail consequently receives less maintenance, so it can be rough and eroded in places. The trail is also lightly traveled. There are some very quiet backcountry campsites for those wanting to avoid the better-known trails in Death Valley.

A spur leads from the main trail to the remains of the New

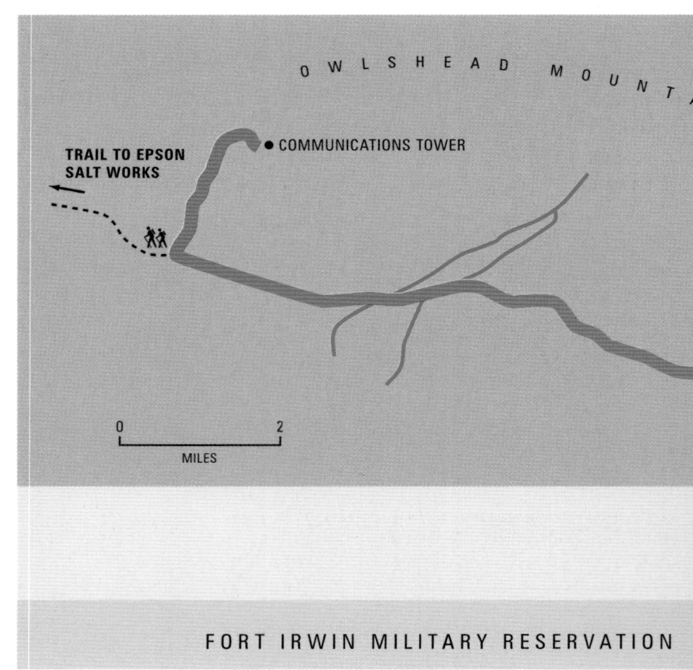

Overlooking the alluvial wash of Lost Lake from the end of the trail

Deal and Black Magic Mines, which are set above the main trail in the Owlshead Mountains. This rough spur is 3-rated for difficulty, but offers a wonderful panoramic view of the area.

At the western extreme of the trail, a remote hiking trail leads to the site of the old Epsom Salt Works. The faint trail runs close to the China Lake Naval Weapons Center and care must be taken not to enter the naval area for safety and security reasons. The main trail terminates a short distance past the hiking trailhead at a communications tower. At the trail's end, there are panoramic views over the dry pan of Lost Lake as well as the Owlshead Mountains, Death Valley, Black Mountains, and Quail Mountains.

Current Road Information

Death Valley National Park
PO Box 579
Death Valley, CA 92328-0579
(760) 786-2331

Map References

BLM Owlshead Mts.
USGS 1:24,000 Old Ibex Pass, East of Owl Lake, Owl Lake, Quail Spring, Hidden Spring
1:100,000 Owlshead Mts.
Maptech CD-ROM: Barstow/San Bernardino County
Southern & Central California Atlas & Gazetteer, pp. 54, 55
California Road & Recreation Atlas, p. 96

Route Directions

▼ 0.0		From Desert #28: Harry Wade Exit Route, 12.2 miles north of California 127, zero trip meter and turn west on graded dirt road. Harry Wade Exit Route continues to the northwest at this point and is sign-posted to Furnace Creek. Owlshead Mountains Trail is unmarked.
		GPS: N35°41.57' W116°29.42'
▼ 0.7	SO	Cross through wash.
▼ 5.8	SO	Leaving Death Valley National Park and entering BLM land. Boundary is not clearly marked.
		GPS: N35°38.96' W116°34.92'
▼ 9.4	SO	Track on right to diggings.
		GPS: N35°38.28' W116°38.67'
▼ 9.5	BL	Track on right is the spur to Black Magic Mine. Zero trip meter. Owl Hole Springs on right at intersection.
		GPS: N35°38.33' W116°38.81'

Spur to Black Magic Mine

▼ 0.0		From Owl Hole Springs, zero trip meter and turn northwest.

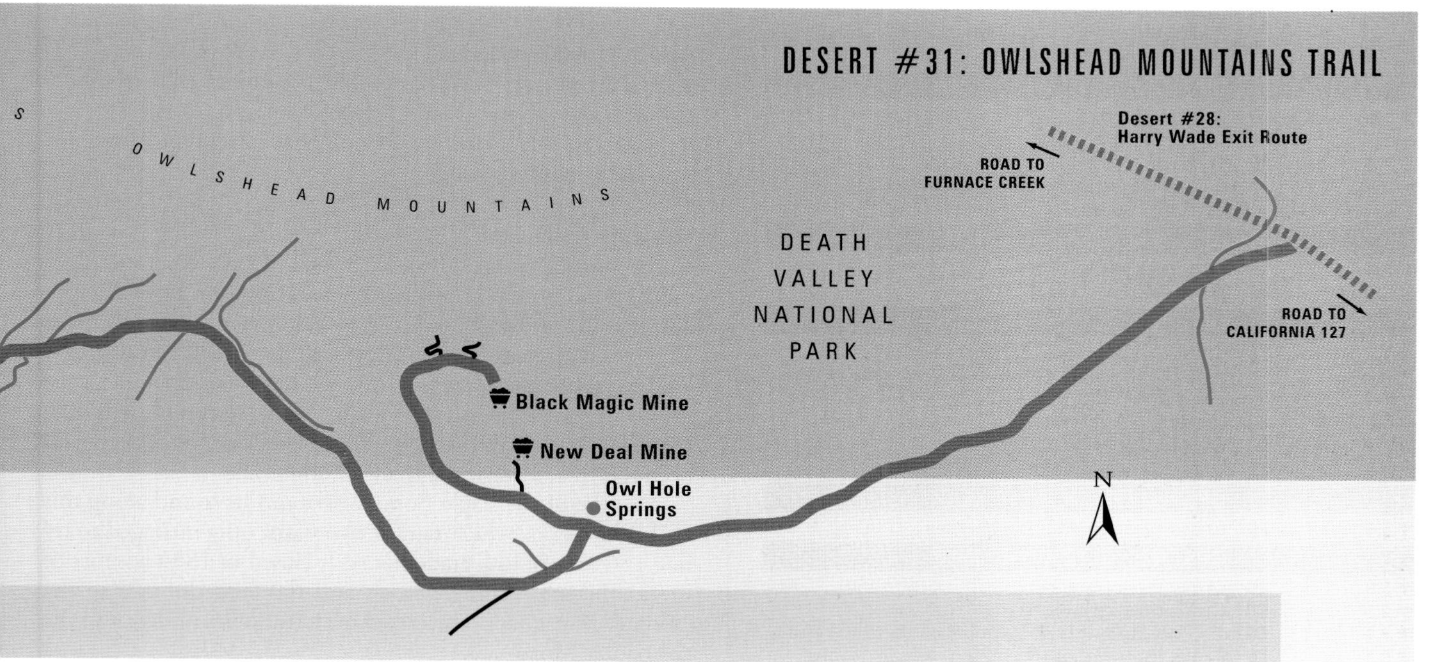

The rough spur trail offers panoramic views over the Owlshead Mountains

▼ 0.9	SO	Track on right to New Deal diggings.
▼ 1.6	SO	Entering Death Valley National Park at sign.
		GPS: N35°38.78' W116°40.43'
▼ 2.8	SO	Track on left.
▼ 2.9	SO	Track on left.
▼ 3.2	SO	Tailings on right.
▼ 3.8	SO	Loading hopper on left; then track on left at saddle goes 0.2 miles to diggings and view over the dry Owl Lake. Zero trip meter.
		GPS: N35°40.18' W116°40.79'
▼ 0.0		Continue to the northeast.
▼ 0.2	SO	Track on left.
▼ 1.0	UT	Spur ends at workings of the Black Magic Mine.
		GPS: N35°39.81' W116°40.08'

Continuation of Main Trail

▼ 0.0		Continue to the southwest.
▼ 0.3	SO	Track on left.
▼ 0.5	SO	Cross through wash.
▼ 1.2	BR	Graded road on left enters Fort Irwin Military Reservation—no unauthorized entry. Bear right onto smaller, graded dirt road.
		GPS: N35°37.64' W116°39.66'
▼ 1.5	SO	Track on right.
▼ 1.6	SO	Track on right.
▼ 1.8	SO	Track on right.
▼ 3.9	SO	Entering Death Valley National Park at sign. Zero trip meter.
		GPS: N35°38.81' W116°41.91'
▼ 0.0		Continue to the north.
▼ 0.6	BL	Track on right.
		GPS: N35°39.21' W116°42.19'
▼ 1.1	SO	Enter line of wash.
▼ 2.7	SO	Exit line of wash. Dry bed of Owl Lake is visible on the right in the valley.
▼ 3.0	SO	Cross through wash.
▼ 4.1	SO	Cross through wide wash.
▼ 4.8	SO	Cross through wash.
		GPS: N35°40.23' W116°46.12'
▼ 5.5	SO	Cross through wash.
		GPS: N35°40.12' W116°46.86'
▼ 5.9	SO	Cross through wash.
▼ 6.5	SO	Cross through wash.
▼ 8.0	SO	The dry bed of Lost Lake is visible to the right.
▼ 9.4	SO	Cross through wash.
		GPS: N35°41.12' W116°50.85'
▼ 10.3	SO	Cross through wash.
▼ 11.1	SO	Cross through wash.
▼ 13.0	BR	Closed vehicle track on left is now hiking trail to Epsom Salt Works. Zero trip meter.
		GPS: N35°41.45' W116°54.40'
▼ 0.0		Continue to the north.
▼ 1.6	SO	Cross through wash.
▼ 2.3		Trail ends at communications tower on a peak in the Owlshead Mountains.
		GPS: N35°42.59' W116°53.24'

DESERT #32

Death Valley West Side Road

Starting Point:	**California 178, 40 miles south of Furnace Creek Visitor Center, 28 miles west of Shoshone**
Finishing Point:	**California 178, 6 miles south of Furnace Creek Visitor Center**
Total Mileage:	**34.2 miles**
Unpaved Mileage:	**34.2 miles**
Driving Time:	**2 hours**
Elevation Range:	**-80–0 feet**
Usually Open:	**Year-round**
Best Time to Travel:	**October to May**
Difficulty Rating:	**1**
Scenic Rating:	**8**
Remoteness Rating:	**+0**

Special Attractions

- Trail crosses the dried-up, prehistoric bed of Lake Manly.
- Historic sites, graves, and points of interest.
- Access to three 4WD spur trails that travel up canyons into the Panamint Range.

History

This trail runs around the ancient bed of Lake Manly, a Pleistocene lake formed indirectly by glaciation during the last ice age. Twenty thousand years ago, Lake Manly was 90 miles long, an average of 8 miles wide, and up to 600 feet deep. As glaciers in the Sierra Nevada melted, the water drained to the south, eventually reaching Death Valley. Although it is currently subject to seasonal flooding, Lake Manly has been predominantly dry for more than 10,000 years.

The site of the Eagle Borax works can be found along this trail. The works, which ran for two years, only managed to refine 150 tons of low-grade borax. It closed in 1884 because of the inefficient refining process and the long distance to the railroad. Borax had to be carted over 160 miles of desert to the railroad at Mojave.

Graves of Shorty Harris and Jim Dayton

A historical marker along the trail commemorates the site of Bennett's Long Camp. On its way west to the California goldfields, the Bennett-Arcane group of Death Valley forty-niners became stranded for a month. The group was saved when two of its members, William Lewis Manly and John Rogers, crossed the mountains on foot and made their way to Mission San Fernando. The rugged individuals returned with supplies, and the party eventually made its way to safety.

The graves of two good friends can also be found alongside the trail. Jim Dayton died in 1899 and was buried in this remote Death Valley spot. His friend Shorty Harris died in 1934. It was Shorty's wish to be buried beside his friend in the valley that they both loved.

Description

The main paved highway, California 178, travels along the east side of Death Valley near the foot of the Amargosa Range. On the west side of the valley, the graded dirt West Side Road travels an alternate route, closer to the Panamint Range, that crosses the prehistoric bed of Lake Manly. Along the 40-mile route to Furnace Creek, the road passes many historic points of interest as well as accessing three 4WD trails that penetrate west into the Panamint Range.

The road is graded dirt for its entire length and is suitable for passenger vehicles in dry weather. However, the surface can be extremely washboardy and slow going. There is a 25 mph speed limit. In wet weather, the crossing of the Amargosa River can be impassable, and the road may be closed by the National Park Service.

The trail passes the site of the Eagle Borax works, the graves of Jim Dayton and Shorty Harris, and several springs that were important water sources for early travelers through this harsh landscape.

The far end of the trail crosses Salt Creek in the middle of Death Valley where the road is slightly elevated above the salt plains. The uneven texture and ridges of the salt-encrusted ground are known as frost heaves, which are the result of evaporation and cold weather on the salt plains.

Current Road Information

Death Valley National Park
PO Box 579
Death Valley, CA 92328-0579
(760) 786-2331

Map References

BLM Owlshead Mt., Death Valley Junction
USGS 1:24,000 Mormon Point, Badwater, Hanaupah Canyon, Devils Speedway, Devils Golf Course, Shore Line Butte, Anvil Spring Canyon East
1:100,000 Owlshead Mt., Death Valley Junction
Maptech CD-ROM: Barstow/San Bernardino County; Kings Canyon/Death Valley
Southern & Central California Atlas & Gazetteer, pp. 54, 42
California Road & Recreation Atlas, p. 88
Trails Illustrated, Death Valley National Park (221)
Other: Free NPS Death Valley map

Route Directions

▼ 0.0			From California 178, 40 miles south of Furnace Creek Visitor Center and 28 miles west of Shoshone, zero trip meter and turn southwest on wide graded dirt road, sign-posted West Side Road, and pass through gates. The intersection is 1.7 miles north of Ashford Mill on California 178.
	2.8 ▲		Trail ends on California 178. Turn left to return to Furnace Creek; turn right for Shoshone.
			GPS: N35°56.27′ W116°42.23′
▼ 0.7		SO	Cross through Amargosa River Wash. Crossing is impassable after rain.
	2.1 ▲	SO	Cross through Amargosa River Wash. Crossing is impassable after rain.
▼ 2.8		SO	Graded road on left is Desert #33: Mengel Pass Trail, sign-posted to Butte Valley. Zero trip meter and follow the sign to Furnace Creek.
	0.0 ▲		Continue to the southeast.
			GPS: N35°57.25′ W116°44.75′
▼ 0.0			Continue to the northwest through gate.
	6.9 ▲	SO	Gate; then graded road on right is Desert #33: Mengel Pass Trail, sign-posted to Butte Valley. Zero trip meter and follow the sign to Shoshone.
▼ 6.9		SO	Tank on right opposite track on left is Salt Well. Zero trip meter.

Salt-encrusted shapes along the Devils Golf Course

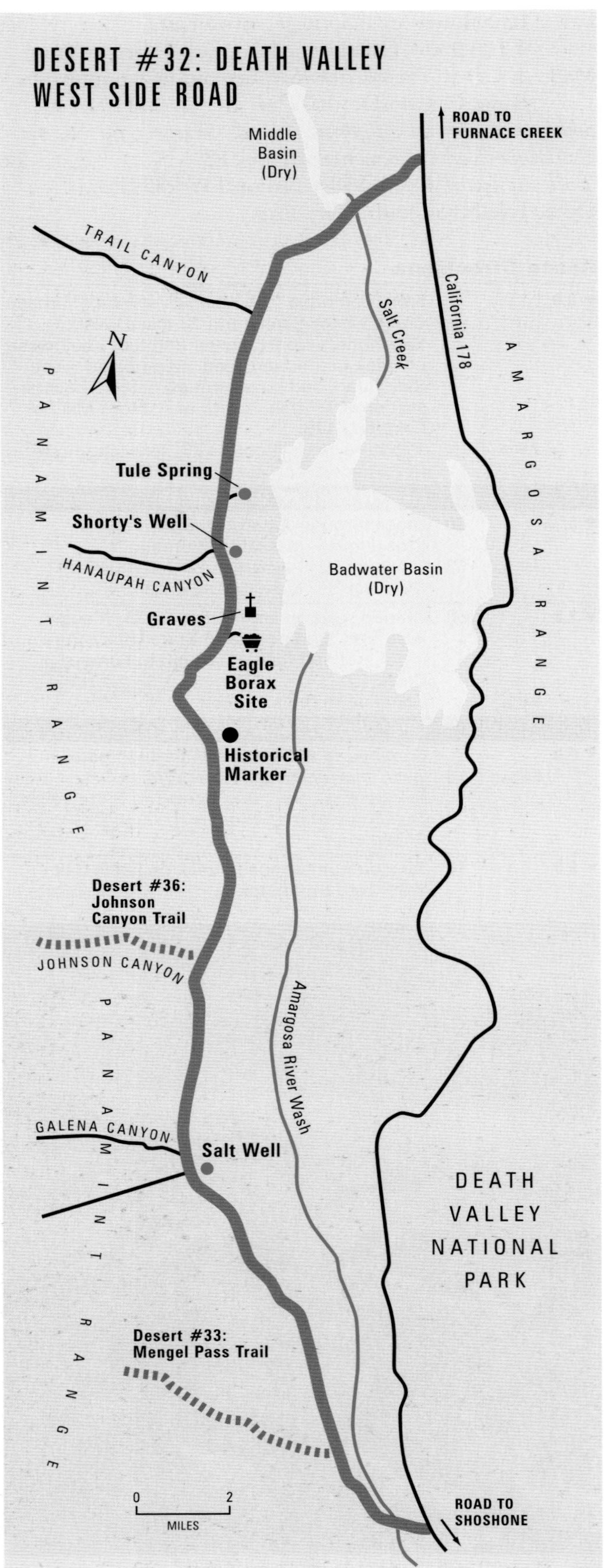

▼	▲		
	0.0 ▲		Continue to the southeast.
			GPS: N36°01.80' W116°49.70'
▼ 0.0			Continue to the northwest.
	4.7 ▲	SO	Tank on left opposite track on right is Salt Well. Zero trip meter.
▼ 0.1		SO	Track on left travels toward Galena Canyon.
	4.6 ▲	SO	Track on right travels toward Galena Canyon.
			GPS: N36°01.92' W116°49.81
▼ 4.7		SO	Desert #36: Johnson Canyon Trail on left. Zero trip meter.
	0.0 ▲		Continue to the south.
			GPS: N36°05.89' W116°50.67'
▼ 0.0			Continue to the north.
	7.7 ▲	SO	Desert #36: Johnson Canyon Trail on right. Zero trip meter.
▼ 4.6		SO	Historical marker on right for Bennett's Long Camp.
	3.1 ▲	SO	Historical marker on left for Bennett's Long Camp.
			GPS: N36°09.81' W116°51.74'
▼ 7.7		SO	Track on right goes 0.1 miles into Eagle Borax works site. Zero trip meter.
	0.0 ▲		Continue to the south.
			GPS: N36°12.01' W116°52.18'
▼ 0.0			Continue to the north.
	1.9 ▲	SO	Track on left goes 0.1 miles into Eagle Borax works site. Zero trip meter.
▼ 0.5		SO	Jim Dayton and Shorty (Frank) Harris graves on right, set back from the road.
	1.4 ▲	SO	Jim Dayton and Shorty (Frank) Harris graves on left, set back from the road.
			GPS: N36°12.45' W116°52.20'
▼ 1.9		SO	4-way intersection. Track on left is Hanaupah Canyon Trail, track on right goes 0.1 miles to Shortys Well. Zero trip meter.
	0.0 ▲		Continue to the southeast.
			GPS: N36°13.55' W116°52.83'
▼ 0.0			Continue to the northwest.
	1.1 ▲	SO	4-way intersection. Track on right is Hanaupah Canyon Trail, track on left goes 0.1 miles to Shortys Well. Zero trip meter.
▼ 1.1		SO	Track on right goes 0.2 miles to Tule Spring. Zero trip meter.
	0.0 ▲		Continue to the south.
			GPS: N36°14.56' W116°53.03'
▼ 0.0			Continue to the north.
	4.0 ▲	SO	Track on left goes 0.2 miles to Tule Spring. Zero trip meter.
▼ 4.0		SO	Track on left travels up Trail Canyon. Zero trip meter.
	0.0 ▲		Continue to the south.
			GPS: N36°18.18' W116°53.38'
▼ 0.0			Continue to the north.
	5.1 ▲	SO	Track on right travels up Trail Canyon. Zero trip meter.
▼ 3.3		SO	Cross over Salt Creek.
	1.8 ▲	SO	Cross over Salt Creek.
▼ 5.1			Trail ends at T-intersection with California 178. Turn left for Furnace Creek; turn right for Shoshone.
	0.0 ▲		Trail commences on California 178, 6 miles south of Furnace Creek Visitor Center. Zero trip meter and turn south on graded dirt road, following sign for West Side Road.
			GPS: N36°21.95' W116°50.64'

Mengel Pass Trail

Starting Point:	**Panamint Valley Road (California 178), at the turn to Ballarat, 21.5 miles north of Trona**
Finishing Point:	**Desert #32: Death Valley West Side Road, 2.8 miles from the southern end**
Total Mileage:	**50.1 miles, plus 0.6-mile spur to Barker Ranch House**
Unpaved Mileage:	**50.1 miles, plus 0.6-mile spur**
Driving Time:	**5.5 hours**
Elevation Range:	**0–4,400 feet**
Usually Open:	**Year-round**
Best Time to Travel:	**October to May**
Difficulty Rating:	**4**
Scenic Rating:	**10**
Remoteness Rating:	**+1**

Special Attractions

- Site of the police capture of Charles Manson.
- Many old mining remains and historic cabins.
- Beautiful scenery and panoramic vistas within Death Valley National Park.
- Warm Springs natural mineral springs.

History

Ballarat, at the western end of this trail, is named after an Australian gold town of the same name. Between 1897 and 1917, the small settlement served the many mining camps scattered throughout the Panamint Range. Between them, these mines produced nearly a million dollars worth of gold. Ballarat housed many of the miners who worked in the Radcliff Mine in Pleasant Canyon. The miners traveled to work up the canyon each day. Little remains of Ballarat now. However, you can still see a few adobe remains, the jail, and the graveyard. A small general store continues to operate.

In more recent years, the Barker Ranch in Goler Wash made headlines when one of America's most notorious killers, Charles Manson, and his followers were captured in 1969, following an apparent tip-off by a BLM officer. The officer became suspicious during a routine visit when he saw what seemed like too many vehicles at the remote ranch. Suspecting a possible vehicle theft ring, he notified police, who in turn made a multiagency raid on the ranch. The so-called Manson Family was taken into custody and initially charged with arson and grand theft auto. However, it was quickly established that they were homicide suspects as well. Manson himself was not found right away. He was hiding in a bathroom cupboard and was found in due course. The cupboard has since been removed from the house.

Mengel Pass is named after prospector Carl Mengel, who had a number of small claims in the area. Born in San Bernardino in 1868, Carl constructed a 3-stamp mill near Redlands Canyon in 1898. Some of the red and green timbers Carl used in the construction of the mill are said to have been salvaged timbers carted all the way from Los Angeles. However, controversy does exist regarding their actual origin. The words "Baker Iron Works – Los Angeles" were stamped into some of the stamp casings.

In 1912, Carl bought the Oro Fino Mine in Goler Wash and discovered an even more promising mine farther down the wash. Sadly most of his claims played out too quickly and Carl managed only a meager living during his life in the Panamints. The stone cabin at Greater View Spring was his home; its builder is uncertain. A rock shelter nearby is thought to have been used by Native Americans. Carl is buried on top of Mengel Pass (4,328 feet) just outside the boundary of the old Death Valley National Monument. He died in 1944.

Striped Butte, on the east side of the pass in Butte Valley, was originally named Curious Butte by Hugh McCormack, who passed through the region in the 1860s. The sedimentary outcropping is unusual in this area; most of the surrounding rock is granitic.

Prospectors are thought to have made claims in the Anvil Springs region as early as the 1850s. Mormon prospectors were among the first to find riches within Butte Valley. However, the mines changed hands many times because the potential for great wealth was always thwarted by the inaccessibility of the valley. The name Anvil dates from 1866, when a party of prospectors from San Bernardino worked this region under the leadership of Joseph Clews. Disillusioned after just three months, they threw a large anvil into the spring near their camp and left.

Asa Merton Russell, also known as "Panamint Russ," is said to have discovered and then lost the location of a very high-

This old arrastra was part of the Gold Hill Mill in Warm Spring Canyon

grade claim while prospecting in Butte Valley in 1925. He is credited with building what is known as the Geologist's Cabin in 1930. He also lined Anvil Spring with rocks and built a cistern with a wooden trap door. Big Blue #1 Mine is just one of the mines worked by Panamint Russ. By 1962, Stella and Clinton Anderson were manually working the mines within the Greater View Springs claim, having been granted them by Panamint Russ. They chose to live on the remote property without electricity, phone service, or plumbing. Clinton died in 1973, but Stella remained until the late 1970s, when she moved to Trona.

Warm Spring Canyon leads out of the eastern end of Butte Valley. Warm Spring, known to the Panamint Shoshone as *pabuna,* was a winter camp for the native people. During the 1880s, "Panamint Tom" ran a ranch and orchard in Warm Spring Canyon until a flash flood wiped out his crops and 150 fruit trees in July 1887. Because water was available from the springs, a mill was set up in 1932 to recover gold from the ore mined at Gold Hill, somewhat farther up the canyon on the north side. The remains of the mill can still be seen between the camp and the current trail. The hot-shot diesel engine, Blake jaw crusher, cylindrical ball-mill, cone crusher, ore bin, and stone arrastra are relatively intact and offer an exceptional example of a gold-processing site.

Forty-niners William Lewis Manly and John Rogers traveled up Warm Spring Canyon during their epic journey out of Death Valley. They returned a month later with supplies and led the Bennett and Arcane families, who were stranded at Bennett Spring, to safety. They took a shorter route just north of Warm Spring. Their harsh trek proceeded up Galena Canyon, joining Warm Spring Canyon just before it enters Butte Valley. From there they headed slightly north to refresh at Arrastre Spring. Continuing southwest through Butte Valley, they passed Striped Butte on the north side and exited the valley to the west via Redlands Canyon. Exhausted, they made their next camp deep in the canyon at Redlands Spring. From there, the families exited into Panamint Valley and traveled over the Slate Range to the west.

Mine adit at Warm Springs

Arrastre Spring seems to have been popular with Paleo-Indians who frequented this region; their early history can be seen near the spring in the form of petroglyphs. Native Americans also labored at the nearby Gold Hill mines during the 1800s transporting ore to an arrastra at the spring for reduction.

The name Manly appears throughout this region in honor of William Manly's heroic efforts to save members of his party. Geologist's Cabin sits at the eastern foot of Manly Peak. The vehicle trail up Redlands Canyon stops at the edge of Manly Peak Wilderness Area, and Manly Fall was a spectacular dry-fall located at Redlands Canyon's exit into Panamint Valley. This fall was later excavated by the Briggs gold mine.

Almost a century after the Bennett and Arcane families passed through Warm Spring Canyon, Louise Grantham and Ernest Huhn found a wealth of talc near Warm Spring. The demand for talc was running high for use in such products as paint, wall tiles, and insulators. Initial operations were sporadic, but by the late 1930s, large underground talc mines were developed. The ore-bearing rock was transported by truck to Dunn Siding, located west of Barstow on Desert #13: Mojave Road. World War II increased the demand for talc, particularly for use in paint. Massive quantities of paint were needed for naval vessels, and this region became one of the biggest suppliers in the western states. A talc-mining camp operated here at various levels of activity from the late 1930s to 1988.

The talc miners had quite a community based around the warm spring; it was regarded as one of the finest camps in Death Valley. Reports from the 1950s list a dormitory, two small houses, a mess hall, Mrs. Grantham's house, generator buildings, and a large swimming pool fed by the warm spring. Some of its structures remain today. In 1974, open pit mines were developed. They can still be seen today in Warm Spring Canyon. The talc-mining claims changed hands many times over the decades. Health and safety requirements improved some and closed others. The last claim holder, a man named Pfizer, donated the site to a conservation fund for eventual transfer to the National Park Service.

Description

Mengel Pass Trail is one of the few trails to traverse the Panamint Range, a rugged and barren range on the western edge of Death Valley National Park. The trail leaves from Ballarat, which has an operating general store. The store's hours of service are limited and there is no fuel.

The trail swings south from Ballarat, following Wingate Road, and hugs the western face of the Panamint Range, which rises abruptly from the sage-covered valley floor. Initially, the road is extremely smooth and well graded because it serves as the access road for trucks going to the active Briggs Open Cut Mine. The road drops in standard past the mine, and although graded, it receives considerably less maintenance and can be dusty, very washboardy, and slow going. There are views along the face of the Panamint Range, as well as to the west over the Panamint Valley to the Slate Range.

The trail turns east and enters the range along the narrow and steep-sided Goler Wash. It immediately drops in standard to become a narrow, loose surfaced trail that travels up the wash. This spectacular section of the trail climbs steadily into the Panamint Range, passing between high rock walls studded with cotton top cactus. Wild burros and bighorn sheep can sometimes be spotted in the canyon. A well-preserved cabin, which is the headquarters of the Newman Mine, sits in the wash a few yards from the trail.

This well-constructed swimming pool stands next to old cabins at Warm Springs

Immediately past the entrance to Death Valley National Park, there is a major fork in the trail. The right-hand fork is a worthwhile detour that travels a short distance to the well-preserved Barker Ranch house. This cabin, now operated by the National Park Service, is available for public use. It is sparsely furnished, but very picturesque in its canyon setting. The park service has posted warnings for users to beware of hantavirus, a rare but deadly disease spread by contact with rodent droppings. Warnings about this disease are currently posted at all the cabins along this trail. For more information on hantavirus, see page 13.

A short distance past the Barker Ranch house is the Meyer Ranch, which is posted as private property.

The main trail becomes rocky as it approaches Mengel Pass; the surface is uneven and some large embedded rocks require careful wheel placement. Large vehicles will need to take extra care because of the tight clearance between some rocks. This 4-rated section extends over both sides of Mengel Pass, the highest point of the trail.

From Mengel Pass, the trail drops into the wide-open Butte Valley, passing the small stone cabin known as Geologist's Cabin for one of its original occupants. Like the Barker Ranch house, this cabin is available for use on a first-come, first-served basis. It is situated above Anvil Spring. Past the spring, the trail passes beside the distinctive Striped Butte, which rises 900 feet above the valley floor.

The trail continues along the open valley before dropping farther down Warm Spring Canyon. There are extensive mining remains at the site of Warm Spring. A well-preserved cabin as well as a tiled, concrete-lined swimming pool that used to tap the warm mineral waters can still be seen. The swimming pool was full as recently as 1999. The natural warm spring is a short distance up the hillside behind the cabin. There are two small natural pools where the water comes out of the rock. Each pool can fit one or two people for a shallow soak. The water temperature is tepid to warm. The park service has created two small picnic/camping areas next to the cabins, which are also available for use. Watch out for cheeky coyotes and kit foxes that will steal your food and trash given the chance.

Past Warm Spring, the trail continues in the line of the wash and heads out to descend into Death Valley. The trail ends on Desert #32: Death Valley West Side Road.

Current Road Information

Death Valley National Park
PO Box 579
Death Valley, CA 92328-0579
(760) 786-2331

Bureau of Land Management
Ridgecrest Field Office
300 South Richmond Road
Ridgecrest, CA 93555
(760) 384-5400

Map References

BLM Darwin Hills, Ridgecrest, Owlshead Mts.
USGS 1:24,000 Maturango Peak SE, Ballarat, Manly Fall, Copper Queen Canyon, Sourdough Spring, Manly Peak, Anvil Spring Canyon West, Anvil Spring Canyon
1:100,000 Darwin Hills, Ridgecrest, Owlshead Mts.
Maptech CD-ROM: Kings Canyon/Death Valley; Barstow/San Bernardino County
Southern & Central California Atlas & Gazetteer, pp. 41, 53, 54
California Road & Recreation Atlas, pp. 88, 95
Trails Illustrated, Death Valley National Park (221)
Other: Free NPS Death Valley map

Route Directions

▼ 0.0		From Panamint Valley Road (California 178, also shown as Trona Wildrose Road on some maps), 21.5 miles north of Trona, zero trip meter and turn northeast on Ballarat Road, following the sign to Ballarat. There is a historical marker at the intersection.
3.5 ▲		Trail ends on Panamint Valley Road (California 178). Turn left for Trona; turn right for Panamint Springs.
		GPS: N36°02.02' W117°16.84'
▼ 0.7	SO	Track on left.
2.8 ▲	SO	Track on right.
▼ 3.3	SO	Graded road on right cuts across to Wingate Road. Road enters ghost town of Ballarat.
0.2 ▲	SO	Graded road on left returns to Wingate Road. Leaving Ballarat.
▼ 3.4	SO	Track on left is Indian Road.
0.1 ▲	SO	Track on right is Indian Road.
▼ 3.5	TR	4-way intersection at Ballarat General Store. Turn right onto Wingate Road and zero trip meter. Road on left is Indian Ranch Road to Surprise Canyon. Road ahead is Desert #35: Pleasant Canyon Loop Trail.
0.0 ▲		Continue to the southwest on Ballarat Road.
		GPS: N36°02.86' W117°13.40'

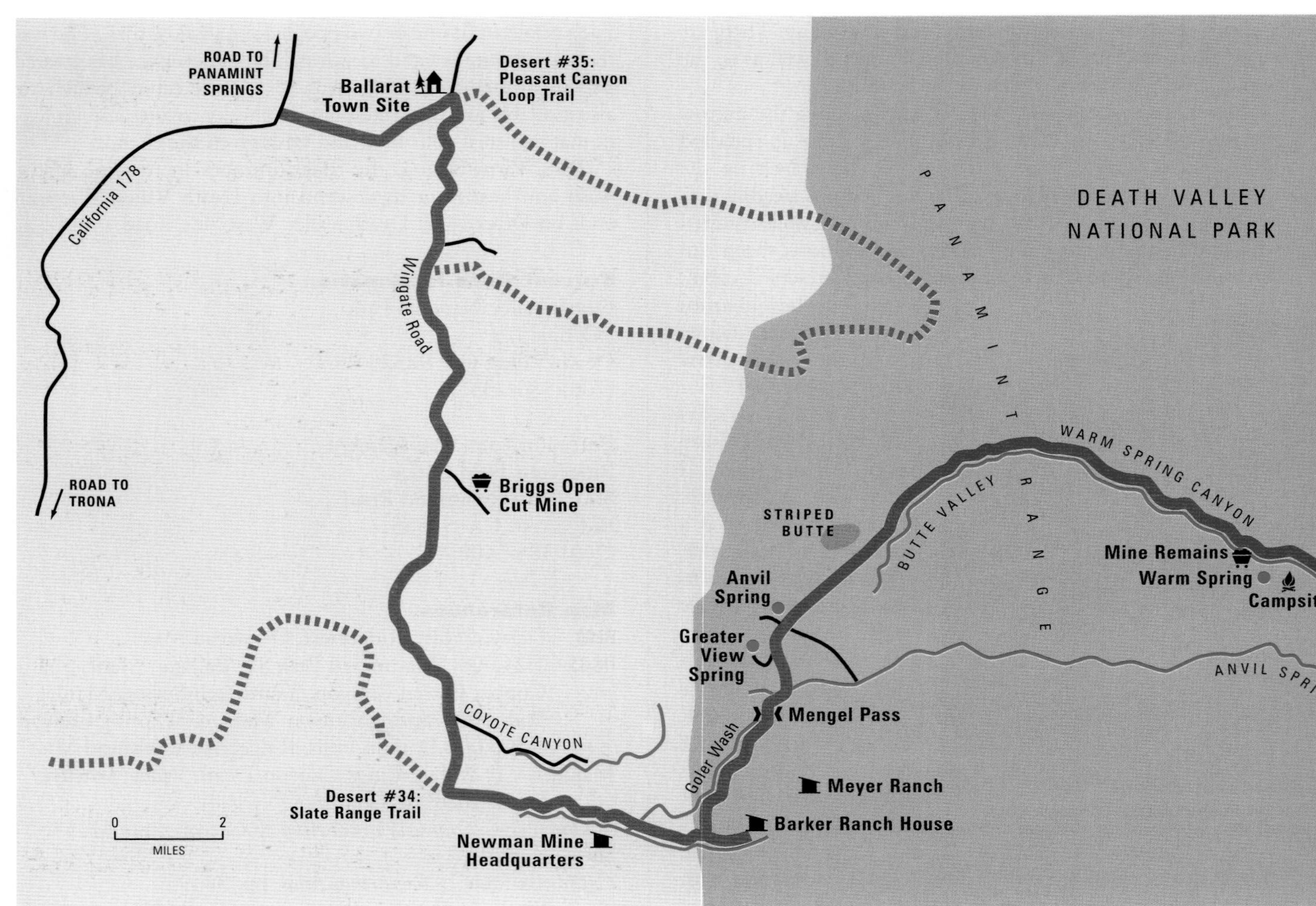

▼ 0.0			Continue to the southeast on Wingate Road.
	3.7 ▲	TL	4-way intersection at Ballarat General Store. Turn left onto Ballarat Road and zero trip meter. Road straight ahead is Indian Ranch Road to Surprise Canyon. Road on right is Desert #35: Pleasant Canyon Loop Trail.
▼ 0.1		SO	Road on right cuts across to Ballarat Road.
	3.6 ▲	BR	Road on left cuts across to Ballarat Road.
▼ 1.3		BR	Road on left.
	2.4 ▲	BL	Road on right.
▼ 3.1		SO	Track on left.
	0.6 ▲	SO	Track on right.
			GPS: N36°00.51' W117°13.17'
▼ 3.7		SO	Unmarked track on left is Desert #35: Pleasant Canyon Loop Trail. Zero trip meter.
	0.0 ▲		Continue to the north.
			GPS: N36°00.01' W117°13.17'
▼ 0.0			Continue to the south.
	3.7 ▲	SO	Unmarked track on right is Desert #35: Pleasant Canyon Loop Trail. Zero trip meter.
▼ 1.7		SO	Track on left.
	2.0 ▲	SO	Track on right.
▼ 2.1		SO	Track on left.
	1.6 ▲	SO	Track on right.
▼ 2.4		SO	Track on left.
	1.3 ▲	SO	Track on right.
▼ 3.7		BR	Road on left goes into Briggs Open Pit Mine. Mine is active, so do not enter. Zero trip meter.
	0.0 ▲		Continue to the north.
			GPS: N35°57.11' W117°12.13'
▼ 0.0			Continue to the south.
	7.0 ▲	SO	Road on right goes into Briggs Open Pit Mine. Mine is active, so do not enter. Zero trip meter.
▼ 5.0		SO	Faint track on left.
	2.0 ▲	SO	Faint track on right.
▼ 5.4		SO	Track on left travels up Coyote Canyon.
	1.6 ▲	SO	Track on right travels up Coyote Canyon.
			GPS: N35°52.93' W117°10.98'
▼ 6.1		SO	Track on left.
	0.9 ▲	SO	Track on right.
▼ 6.2		SO	Small track on left.
	0.8 ▲	SO	Small track on right.
▼ 7.0		TL	Turn left, following marker for P52, suitable for 4WDs, ATVs, and motorbikes. Track straight ahead marked P70 is Desert #34: Slate Range Trail. Zero trip meter.
	0.0 ▲		Continue to the northwest.
			GPS: N35°51.55' W117°10.74'
▼ 0.0			Continue to the east and travel up the alluvial fan.
	3.6 ▲	TR	Turn right at T-intersection, following marker for P52. Track on left marked P70 is Desert #34: Slate Range Trail. Zero trip meter.
▼ 1.3		SO	Track on left to mine.
	2.3 ▲	SO	Track on right to mine.

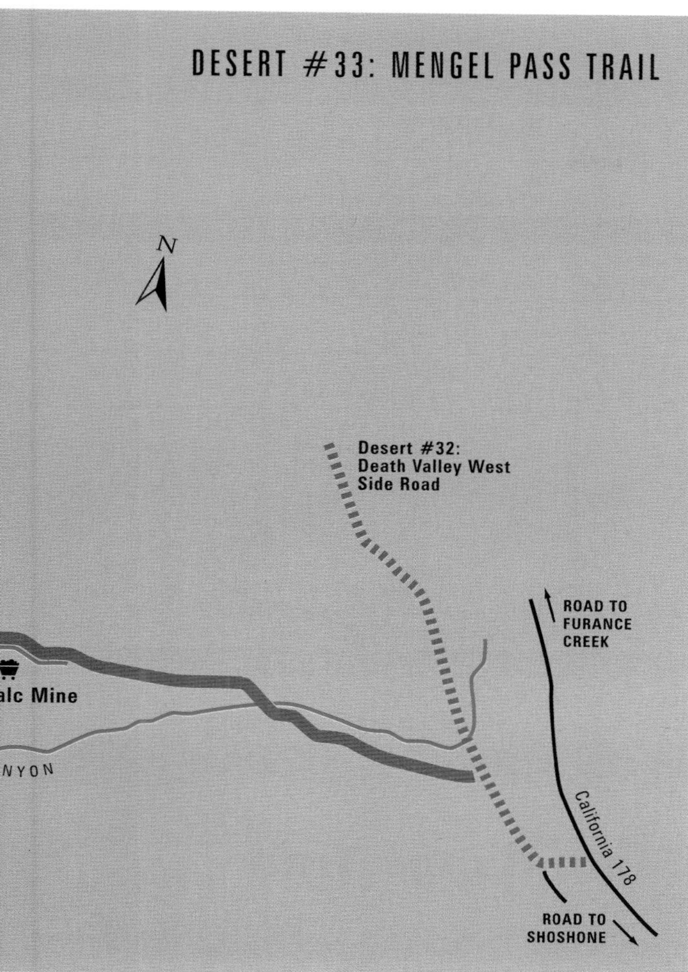

GPS: N35°51.61′ W117°09.39′

▼ 1.4 BL Bear left and enter Goler Wash.
2.2 ▲ BR Bear right and exit Goler Wash.

GPS: N35°51.55′ W117°09.24′

▼ 2.9 SO Loading hopper on right. Aerial tramway crosses to the workings high on the cliffs to the left.
0.7 ▲ SO Loading hopper on left. Aerial tramway crosses to the workings high on the cliffs to the right.

GPS: N35°51.78′ W117°08.25′

▼ 3.3 SO Aerial tramway anchors on left.
0.3 ▲ SO Aerial tramway anchors on right.

GPS: N35°51.60′ W117°07.91′

▼ 3.6 BL Trail forks in wash. Track on right goes to old cabin of Newman Mine Headquarters. Zero trip meter.
0.0 ▲ Continue to the south.

GPS: N35°51.71′ W117°07.62′

▼ 0.0 Continue to the north.
2.0 ▲ SO Track on sharp left goes to old cabin of Newman Mine Headquarters. Zero trip meter.

▼ 0.1 SO Old cabin on right of trail is Newman Mine Headquarters.
1.9 ▲ SO Old cabin on left of trail is Newman Mine Headquarters.

GPS: N35°51.73′ W117°07.55′

▼ 0.7 SO Track on right into mining activities.
1.3 ▲ SO Track on left into mining activities.

GPS: N35°51.64′ W117°07.01′

▼ 1.2 SO Track on right; then stone ruin on right.
0.8 ▲ SO Stone ruin on left; then track on left.

GPS: N35°51.58′ W118°06.57′

▼ 1.8 BL Track on right in wash, which peters out after short distance.
0.2 ▲ BR Track on left in wash, which peters out after short distance.

GPS: N35°51.52′ W117°05.90′

▼ 1.9 SO Entering Death Valley National Park.
0.1 ▲ SO Leaving Death Valley National Park.

GPS: N35°51.60′ W117°05.81′

▼ 2.0 SO Track on right is spur to Barker Ranch House. Zero trip meter.
0.0 ▲ Continue to the southwest.

GPS: N35°51.64′ W117°05.75′

Spur to Barker Ranch House

▼ 0.0 0.1 miles north of the boundary of Death Valley National Park, zero trip meter and turn southeast on unmarked, well-used trail.
▼ 0.3 SO Track on left goes to mine dump and mine workings.
▼ 0.6 UT Track on left to Barker Ranch House. Meyer Ranch is 0.2 miles farther and is posted as private property.

GPS: N35°51.54′ W117°05.25′

Continuation of Main Trail

▼ 0.0 Continue to the northeast.
3.2 ▲ SO Track on left is spur to Barker Ranch House. Zero trip meter.

GPS: N35°51.64′ W117°05.75′

▼ 0.2 SO Track on right.
3.0 ▲ SO Track on left.

▼ 0.5 BL Bear left out of Goler Wash.
2.7 ▲ SO Enter Goler Wash.

▼ 0.7 BR Trail forks and rejoins almost immediately.
2.5 ▲ BL Trail forks and rejoins almost immediately.

▼ 1.1 SO Enter line of wash, rising gradually toward Mengel Pass.
2.1 ▲ SO Exit line of wash.

▼ 2.3 SO Trail forks and rejoins almost immediately.
0.9 ▲ SO Trail forks and rejoins almost immediately.

▼ 2.7 SO Cross through rocky wash.
0.5 ▲ SO Cross through rocky wash.

GPS: N35°53.65′ W117°04.97′

▼ 3.2 SO Mengel Pass. Cairn on left is Carl Mengel's grave. Track on right. Zero trip meter.
0.0 ▲ Continue to the south.

GPS: N35°54.00′ W117°04.88′

▼ 0.0 Continue to the north.
1.7 ▲ SO Mengel Pass. Cairn on right is Carl Mengel's grave. Track on left. Zero trip meter.

▼ 1.3 SO Track on left goes toward cabin at Greater View Spring.
0.4 ▲ SO Second entrance to cabin.

GPS: N35°54.86′ W117°04.90′

▼ 1.4 SO Second entrance to cabin.
0.3 ▲ BL Track on right goes toward cabin at Greater View Spring.

▼ 1.6 SO Track on left.
0.1 ▲ BL Track on right.

Mileage		Direction	Description
▼ 1.7		BR	Track on left goes to small stone cabin at Anvil Spring. Zero trip meter.
	0.0 ▲		Continue to the south.
			GPS: N35°55.26' W117°04.99'
▼ 0.0			Continue to the northeast.
	6.9 ▲	SO	Track on right goes to small stone cabin at Anvil Spring. Zero trip meter.
▼ 0.2		SO	4-way intersection. Track on left goes to Anvil Spring and cabin, track on right goes to Anvil Spring Canyon Hiking Trail.
	6.7 ▲	SO	4-way intersection. Track on right goes to Anvil Spring and cabin, track on left goes to Anvil Spring Canyon Hiking Trail.
			GPS: N35°55.42' W117°04.90'
▼ 2.0		SO	Track on left. Striped Butte is directly on the left.
	4.9 ▲	SO	Track on right. Striped Butte is directly on the right.
			GPS: N35°56.69' W117°03.71'
▼ 6.8		SO	Enter line of wash.
	0.1 ▲	SO	Exit line of wash.
			GPS: N35°59.11' W117°00.05'
▼ 6.9		SO	Well-used track on left marked with small stone cairn. Zero trip meter.
	0.0 ▲		Continue to the west.
			GPS: N35°59.13' W116°59.97'
▼ 0.0			Continue to the east.
	4.4 ▲	SO	Well-used track on right marked with small stone cairn. Zero trip meter.
▼ 2.0		SO	Mine on left.
	2.4 ▲	SO	Mine on right.
			GPS: N35°58.57' W116°58.08'
▼ 2.6		SO	Small track on right and small track on left.
	1.8 ▲	SO	Small track on left and small track on right.
▼ 4.3		SO	Old mining remains and cabin at Warm Spring on right.
	0.1 ▲	SO	Old mining remains and cabin at Warm Spring on left.
			GPS: N35°58.13' W116°55.83'
▼ 4.4		SO	Track on right to large mine adit. Adit is visible immediately to the right. Zero trip meter.
	0.0 ▲		Continue to the northwest.
			GPS: N35°58.14' W116°55.71'
▼ 0.0			Continue to the northeast.
	1.8 ▲	SO	Track on left to large mine adit. Adit is visible immediately to the left. Zero trip meter.
▼ 0.1		SO	Track on right leads into Warm Spring area.
	1.7 ▲	BR	Track on left leads into Warm Spring area.
▼ 0.4		SO	Faint track on right.
	1.4 ▲	SO	Faint track on left.
▼ 1.2		SO	Open cut talc mine on right.
	0.6 ▲	SO	Open cut talc mine on left.
			GPS: N35°57.92' W116°54.46'
▼ 1.3		SO	Track on right.
	0.5 ▲	BR	Track on left.
▼ 1.7		SO	Track on right into loading hopper.
	0.1 ▲	SO	Track on left into loading hopper.
▼ 1.8		SO	Track on right leads into talc mine. Zero trip meter.
	0.0 ▲		Continue to the west.
			GPS: N35°57.73' W116°53.83'
▼ 0.0			Continue to the east.
	8.6 ▲	SO	Track on left leads into talc mine. Zero trip meter.
▼ 1.6		SO	Exit line of wash.
	7.0 ▲	SO	Enter line of wash.
▼ 1.7		SO	Graded road on right.
	6.9 ▲	BR	Graded road on left.
			GPS: N35°57.61' W116°52.01'
▼ 4.4		SO	Start to cross wide wash.
	4.2 ▲	SO	Exit wash crossing.
▼ 4.7		SO	Exit wash crossing.
	3.9 ▲	SO	Start to cross wide wash.
			GPS: N35°57.71' W116°48.89'
▼ 4.8		SO	Cross through wash.
	3.8 ▲	SO	Cross through wash.
▼ 4.9		SO	Track on right.
	3.7 ▲	SO	Track on left.
▼ 5.4		SO	Cross through wash.
	3.2 ▲	SO	Cross through wash.
▼ 8.6			Trail ends at T-intersection with Desert #32: Death Valley West Side Road. Turn left to continue along the trail; turn right to exit to California 178.
	0.0 ▲		Trail commences on Desert #32: Death Valley West Side Road, 2.8 miles from the south end. Zero trip meter and turn west on graded dirt road, sign-posted to Butte Valley. Turn is immediately in front of gates. A sign after the intersection says High Clearance 4x4 Recommended.
			GPS: N35°57.25' W116°44.75'

DESERT #34

Slate Range Trail

Starting Point:	**California 178, 7.5 miles north of the railroad crossing in Trona**
Finishing Point:	**Desert #33: Mengel Pass Trail, 14.4 miles south of Ballarat**
Total Mileage:	**13.9 miles**
Unpaved Mileage:	**13.9 miles**
Driving Time:	**2 hours**
Elevation Range:	**1,100–3,100 feet**
Usually Open:	**Year-round**
Best Time to Travel:	**September to June**
Difficulty Rating:	**3**
Scenic Rating:	**8**
Remoteness Rating:	**+1**

Special Attractions

- Trail travels part of the historic Forty-niner's Escape Trail from Death Valley.
- Ridge top trail with fantastic views over the Panamint and Searles Valleys.
- Silent Sepulchre.

History

The eastern end of Slate Range Trail commences at Valley Wells, which was a depot for the Rinaldi and Clark freight teams. The freight company delivered passengers and supplies to the Panamint mines on trails that were often worse than this particular one.

The forty-niner families, the Bennetts and Arcanes, who managed to escape death in Death Valley, crossed the Slate Range from the Panamint Valley on part of their long and painful journey to the West Coast. They passed through Fish Canyon on the east side of the range. Their quest for better times in the West saw them abandon their wagons in Death Valley and continue on foot with the assistance of William Lewis Manly and John Rogers. An earlier section of their escape route, where they descended into Panamint Valley near today's open cut Briggs Mine, is discussed in Desert #33: Mengel Pass Trail. Some weeks earlier, Manly and Rogers had made it on foot to Mission San Fernando to purchase supplies for the families left behind in Death Valley. They returned to the stranded party with the supplies and retraced their steps, escorting the Bennetts and Arcanes to safety. The journey of approximately 250 miles was difficult for all concerned. Swollen joints, blistered feet, sick children, and extremely limited fresh water were all compounded by the extreme desert heat.

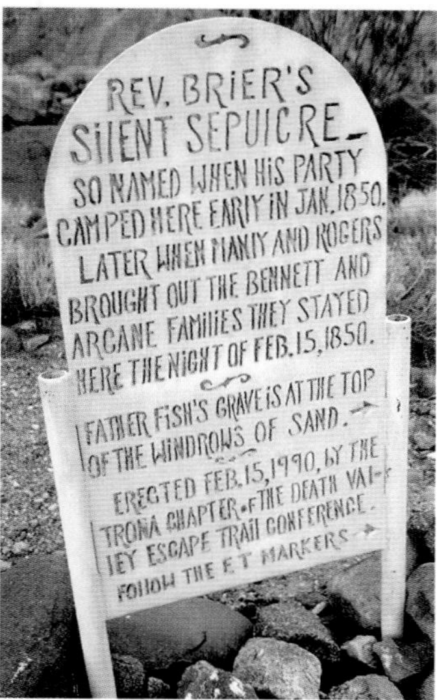

Silent Sepulchre sign

From Panamint Valley, they crossed the southern end of the valley to camp in Fish Canyon in the Slate Range. Just a month earlier, another forty-niner named Father Fish died here in an attempt to escape Death Valley. Fish had been a friend of Manly's, so respects were paid before they departed up the canyon.

Reverend Brier, who was Fish's travel companion, referred to the tight canyon as "a silent sepulchre of dismal appearance." He noticed Indians observing them from above on the canyon rims and he was concerned about the possibility of an ambush. Sickness and death were constant companions of forty-niners heading west through the harsh environment. The Bennetts and Arcanes were surprised to find Fish's body intact under some light sage bushes when they camped here on February 15, 1850. Fish Canyon is named after him and his grave is a short distance north of the Silent Sepulchre.

From here the party scaled its way up to what became known as Manly Pass. They then descended to the west down the middle fork of Isham Canyon, just north of the path of this trail. Isham was another forty-niner who had taken the supposed shortcut and died en route. Both oxen and humans had great difficulty in crossing the sharp rocks of the Slate Range. Cattle were given leather boots to protect against the rocks, but the makeshift gear quickly wore through, and progress was slow. Once over the Slate Range, Manly and Rogers led the party across Searles Lake toward Indian Joe Spring, passing close to where Isham was buried.

Description

Slate Range Trail provides a scenic and historic alternate entry into the Panamint Valley from Trona that avoids a long loop of paved highway. It is the shortest, although not necessarily the quickest, access point to Desert #33: Mengel Pass Trail and Desert #35: Pleasant Canyon Loop Trail.

The trail leaves California 178, 7.5 miles north of Trona, along a graded dirt road that also serves as the access road for a gravel pit. The trail diverges from this road and turns onto a smaller, formed trail that climbs up stony Goff Canyon into the Slate Range. The trail is small, but well used and easy to follow. There are a few turns that might be slightly confusing. Sections of the canyon are rugged and rocky, with a mixture of embedded rock and loose material that provides poor traction at times.

The trail makes its way up to a saddle and starts the long descent into the Panamint Valley. This ridge top section is the most spectacular part of the trail. Views extend 2,000 feet down into the Panamint Valley with the Panamint Range on the far side. The trail surface is loose and scrabbly in places.

As you descend into Fish Canyon, a keen eye will spot the marker placed there by the Death Valley Escape Trail Conference, which details part of the route taken by the forty-niners out of Death Valley. A side trail leads 1.1 miles up Fish Canyon to the rocky grotto of the Silent Sepulchre. The grave of Father Fish is a short distance farther up the hillside. This short trail is very narrow and rough, involves slow rock crawling for most of the way, and is rated a 5 for difficulty.

The main trail slowly descends Fish Canyon to spill out into the Panamint Valley. The road here is initially rough, but it becomes smooth as it travels around the edge of the Panamint Valley near the foot of the Slate Range. The trail finishes at the intersection of Desert #33: Mengel Pass Trail at the base of Goler Wash, 14.4 miles south of Ballarat.

Looking northeast into Panamint Valley

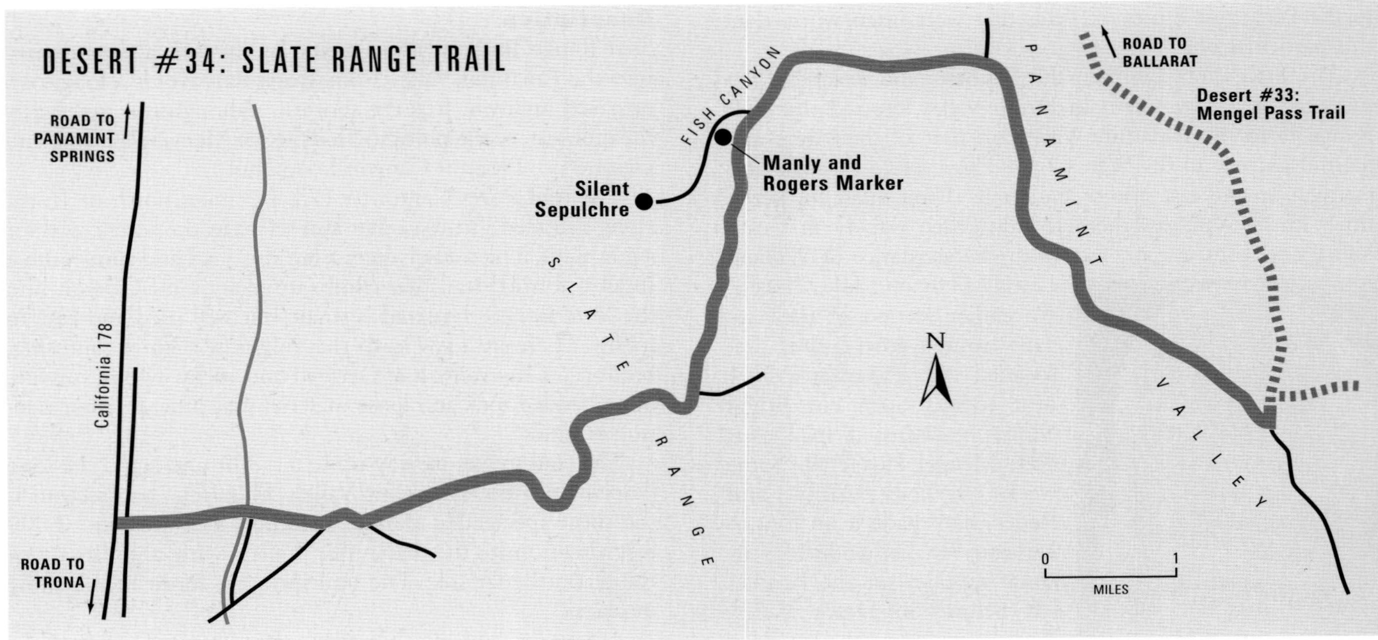

The trail is absent from or poorly marked on topographical maps of the region. The trail is sporadically marked with BLM route markers. A GPS unit is extremely useful for route finding along this trail.

Current Road Information

Bureau of Land Management
Ridgecrest Field Office
300 South Richmond Road
Ridgecrest, CA 93555
(760) 384-5400

Map References

BLM Ridgecrest
USGS 1:24,000 Trona East, Slate Range Crossing, Manly Fall, Copper Queen Canyon
1:100,000 Ridgecrest
Maptech CD-ROM: Barstow/San Bernardino County
Southern & Central California Atlas & Gazetteer, p. 53
California Road & Recreation Atlas, p. 95

Route Directions

▼ 0.0			From California 178, 7.5 miles north of the railroad crossing in Trona, zero trip meter and turn east on graded dirt road. The road is marked as #82 by a BLM marker. It is also the entrance for Valley Sand and Gravel.
	1.9 ▲		Trail ends on California 178. Turn left for Trona; turn right for Panamint Springs.
			GPS: N35°50.70′ W117°20.13′
▼ 0.1		SO	Graded road on right and left along power lines.
	1.8 ▲	SO	Graded road on right and left along power lines.
▼ 0.9		SO	Track on left.
	1.0 ▲	SO	Track on right.
▼ 1.0		SO	Track on left; then cross through wash. Track on right down wash.
	0.9 ▲	SO	Cross through wash. Track on left down wash; then track on right.
▼ 1.1		SO	Track on left and track on right.
	0.8 ▲	SO	Track on left and track on right.
▼ 1.6		BL	Graded road on right. Follow brown BLM route marker.
	0.3 ▲	BR	Graded road on left. Follow brown BLM route marker.
			GPS: N35°50.73′ W117°18.37′
▼ 1.7		SO	Cross through wash. Track on left in wash.
	0.2 ▲	SO	Cross through wash. Track on right in wash.
			GPS: N35°50.75′ W117°18.31′
▼ 1.9		BL	Bear left onto smaller, formed trail marked P 168, suitable for 4WDs, ATVs, and motorbikes, and zero trip meter. Graded road straight ahead enters a quarry.
	0.0 ▲		Continue to the west.
			GPS: N35°50.74′ W117°18.10′
▼ 0.0			Continue to the northeast.
	3.4 ▲	BR	Bear right, joining larger, graded road. A quarry entrance is on the left. Zero trip meter.
▼ 0.5		SO	Cross through wash.
	2.9 ▲	SO	Cross through wash.
▼ 0.9		SO	Enter line of wash.
	2.5 ▲	SO	Exit line of wash.
▼ 1.4		SO	Track on right exits wash.
	2.0 ▲	SO	Track on left exits wash.
			GPS: N35°50.95′ W117°16.67′
▼ 1.6		BL	Bear left into a side wash. Track continues in main wash.
	1.8 ▲	BR	Bear right into main wash. Track on left up wash.
			GPS: N35°50.83′ W117°16.49′
▼ 2.3		BL	Bear left out of wash up ridge.
	1.1 ▲	BR	Drop down from ridge and enter wash.
▼ 2.4		SO	Well-used track on left.
	1.0 ▲	SO	Well-used track on right.
▼ 2.6		SO	Enter wash.
	0.8 ▲	SO	Exit wash.
▼ 3.1		SO	Exit wash.
	0.3 ▲	SO	Enter wash.

▼ 3.3		SO	Track on right; cross through wash.
	0.1 ▲	BR	Cross through wash; track on left.
			GPS: N35°51.63′ W117°15.41′
▼ 3.4		SO	Saddle in the Slate Range. The Panamint Valley and Panamint Range are visible to the north. Well-used track on right. Zero trip meter.
	0.0 ▲		Continue to the south.
			GPS: N35°51.67′ W117°15.39′
▼ 0.0			Continue to the north.
	2.4 ▲	SO	Saddle in the Slate Range. Trail now leaves the Panamint Valley and starts to descend toward Searles Valley. Well-used track on left. Zero trip meter.
▼ 0.2		SO	Well-used track on left; then cross through wash.
	2.2 ▲	SO	Cross through wash; then well-used track on right.
▼ 0.4		SO	Cross through wash.
	2.0 ▲	SO	Cross through wash.
▼ 2.3		SO	Marker on left commemorates Manly and Rogers. Trail now enters Fish Canyon wash.
	0.1 ▲	BL	Bear left and exit Fish Canyon up ridge. Marker on right commemorates Manly and Rogers.
			GPS: N35°53.44′ W117°15.04′
▼ 2.4		SO	Track on left up wash goes 1.1 miles to the Silent Sepulchre. Zero trip meter.
	0.0 ▲		Continue to the southwest.
			GPS: N35°53.54′ W117°14.95′
▼ 0.0			Continue to the northeast.
	2.1 ▲	BL	Track on right up wash goes 1.1 miles to the Silent Sepulchre. Zero trip meter.
▼ 0.5		SO	Exit Fish Canyon wash and Fish Canyon.
	1.6 ▲	SO	Enter Fish Canyon wash and Fish Canyon.
			GPS: N35°53.85′ W117°14.65′
▼ 0.9		SO	Cross through wash.
	1.2 ▲	SO	Cross through wash.
▼ 1.6		SO	Cross through wash.
	0.5 ▲	SO	Cross through wash.
▼ 2.1		TR	Well-used, formed track on left and right is P 170. Small trail straight ahead. Zero trip meter and turn right onto P 170.
	0.0 ▲		Continue to the southwest.
			GPS: N35°53.89′ 117°13.04′
▼ 0.0			Continue to the southeast.
	4.1 ▲	TL	Well-used, formed track on left is P 168. P 170 continues straight ahead and small track on right. Zero trip meter and turn left onto P 168.
▼ 1.3		BL	Track on right.
	2.8 ▲	BR	Track on left.
			GPS: N35°52.82′ W117°12.76′
▼ 3.9		SO	Cross through wash.
	0.2 ▲	SO	Cross through wash.
▼ 4.0		TL	T-intersection. Turn left following sign for P 70.
	0.1 ▲	TR	Turn right following sign for P 70. Track straight ahead.
			GPS: N35°51.51′ W117°10.74′
▼ 4.1			Trail finishes at intersection with Desert #33: Mengel Pass Trail (P 52). Turn right to continue over Mengel Pass; turn left to exit to Ballarat and California 178.
	0.0 ▲		Trail commences on Desert #33: Mengel Pass Trail, 14.4 miles south of Ballarat, in the Panamint Valley. Zero trip meter and proceed south on P 70 at the trail marker. Mengel Pass Trail (P 52) swings due east at this point into Goler Wash.
			GPS: N35°51.55′ W117°10.74′

DESERT #35

Pleasant Canyon Loop Trail

Starting Point:	**Desert #33: Mengel Pass Trail, 3.7 miles south of Ballarat**
Finishing Point:	**Desert #33: Mengel Pass Trail in Ballarat**
Total Mileage:	**23.5 miles**
Unpaved Mileage:	**23.5 miles**
Driving Time:	**6.5 hours**
Elevation Range:	**300–7,400 feet**
Usually Open:	**Year-round**
Best Time to Travel:	**Spring and fall**
Difficulty Rating:	**7**
Scenic Rating:	**10**
Remoteness Rating:	**+2**

Special Attractions

- Long loop trail suitable for experienced drivers in high-clearance 4WD vehicles.
- Many mining remains, including the Briggs Mine Cabin.
- Unparalleled views into Death Valley from the ridge top.

History

Mining prospectors entered Pleasant Canyon in the early 1890s, and by 1896, Henry C. Ratcliff's Never Give Up claim was one of the early payers. With time, it became known as the Ratcliff Mine. Some early maps and publications spell the mine's name as Radcliff and others as Radcliffe.

Late in 1896, Bob and George Montgomery's World Beater Mine was successfully operating and the labor force in the canyon grew to 200 men. The only problem was the lack of suitable places to house workers. In 1897, the makeshift camp moved to the floor of Panamint Valley at the mouth of

Inside the old mill at Clair Camp

Old boiler at Clair Camp

Pleasant Canyon, where miners established a town that would fulfill their needs.

The new town needed a name and the townsfolk gathered to hear suggestions. A young Australian named George Riggins suggested that they look for a name associated with other rich gold discoveries throughout the world. He suggested Ballarat, after the rich Ballarat goldfields in Victoria, Australia. Many people already knew the name; the Australian Ballarat had attracted many gold-seeking Californians, and the name was adopted for the new Death Valley settlement. It was hoped that the well-known name would bring investors to the Panamint Valley.

Ballarat's population grew to almost 500. It supported two stores, several saloons, a Wells Fargo station, and the Calloway Hotel. By 1899, Ballarat had a small school and a jail. By 1900, seven mills were busy stamping away in the area. A mass exodus occurred in 1901 when large strikes at Tonopah, Nevada, drew miners away.

However, the World Beater Mine got its second wind, and combined with other smaller claims, it kept the town relatively active until 1905. By 1906, Skidoo was attracting most of the workforce away from Ballarat. The Montgomery brothers found further mining success at Skidoo. Because of Ballarat's location in the Panamint Valley, the town continued to operate as a supply center for the region's mining settlements. By 1917, the post office shut down and the last saloon closed its doors. A few people stayed on in the town. Seldom Seen Slim, referred to as the last resident of early Ballarat, was buried in 1968.

Mining continued to some degree in the following decades. A reworking of the Ratcliff Mine tailings brought profitable rewards to the Clair family. The family name remains in Pleasant Canyon at Clair Camp. The impressive 10-stamp mill that was attached to the World Beater Mine was burned down in the late 1980s, supposedly by thrill seekers.

In March 1908, a car competing in the world's longest race, from New York to Paris, passed through Ballarat. The car, a Thomas Flyer, won the race by traveling the 13,341-mile route in a total of 169 days. Today, Ballarat has a small general store with few residents or none at all.

Ingenuity has always played a major role in establishing mines and conquering the odds to survive in Death Valley. One of the more cheerful tales of such determination is about a cook in Pleasant Canyon. The enormous Panamint Range did not deter a Chinese migrant from getting food to his hungry miners. He reportedly placed dinners on an aerial tramway for delivery to men in the mine. The food was then passed along the mountain crest and down to workers in the narrows of South Park Canyon.

Thorndike Mine, sometimes referred to as Honolulu Mine, was discovered by John Thorndike in 1907, on the south side of South Park Canyon. Ore from the mine was lowered to the canyon floor via an aerial tramway; mules then hauled the ore out of the canyon along a long and dangerous route. It was not until 1924 that Thorndike managed to construct a narrow shelf road down South Park Canyon. The hand-built stone embankments of this twisting road are still visible today. The mine was last worked in the early 1940s. Thorndike's name is still attached to the old cabin alongside Briggs Mine Cabin. Both are now part of the Adopt-A-Cabin program.

Briggs Mine Cabin in South Park Canyon takes its name from Harry Briggs. In the early 1930s, Briggs took over the operation of a mill and cyanide plant below Manly Fall. This remarkable ancient dry fall was named after William Lewis Manly, who along with John Rogers led the stranded and starving Bennett and Arcane families to safety through the Death Valley region. Their escape route descended through Redlands Canyon and passed just south of these falls. This same dry fall, located near the mouth of Redlands Canyon, was destroyed by the expanding open cut mine and mill just a few miles south of the southern approach to this trail.

In 1850, Manly and Rogers climbed to the highest point on this trail (over 7,000 feet above Death Valley floor) in their attempts to exit Death Valley. It seems they did not actually cross the range here; their climb was an effort to get their bearings for the best possible route over the Panamint Range. The semblance of an old burro trail leads down to Arrastre Spring in Butte Valley, where the rest of the Bennett and Arcane group made camp while awaiting directions from the duo. This ascent was just the start of their arduous 250-mile trek to the safety of California's coastal mountains.

Modern Native Americans are believed to have frequented the upper reaches of Pleasant Canyon in order to escape the unpleasant summer heat of Panamint Valley. The remainder of a stone corral is visible near a water source about a mile and a half below Rita's Cabin. Apparently, this was where they penned their livestock while off gathering food. Farther down Pleasant Canyon is the World Beater Mine, which installed a well near the stone corral. The pipe that supplied the mine with water can still be seen in places.

Description

This long loop road is slow and rough at times. However, for a high-clearance 4WD with an experienced driver, this is one of the more rewarding trails within Death Valley National Park. This challenging drive takes you from 300 to 7,400 feet in elevation and back offers plenty of history as it climbs through the picturesque Panamint Range.

The trail leaves Desert #33: Mengel Pass Trail, 3.7 miles south of Ballarat. The start of the trail is well used, but has no markers of any kind. Those with a GPS unit will have no problem; the trail starts exactly along the 36-degree latitude line. Almost immediately, it starts a slow climb toward South Park Canyon. The shelf road is narrow and loose-surfaced, climbing steadily and steeply. Four-wheel drive is needed to maintain traction on the loose surface.

The trail dips down slightly as it enters South Park Canyon, before resuming the steady climb. South Park Canyon is very narrow in places, with towering rock walls on either side of the stony wash. The trail surface here is rough, alternating between uneven stony surface with some large embedded rocks and softer powdery sand that makes it easy to spin an opposing wheel. Sections within the canyon have some very large, embedded rocks that must be negotiated. Take special care with wheel placement. These sections make the trail unsuitable for vehicles with sidesteps, low-hanging skirts, or low-slung bull bars. Vehicles with roof racks will need to take care on some sections with overhanging canyon walls. Large tires and a suspension lift are an advantage; longer vehicles may find sections potentially damaging.

The narrow shelf road to the Suitcase Mine is steep and loose. There are five extremely tight switchbacks on a steep shelf road that require nerves of steel. Drivers of long wheelbase vehicles may prefer to reverse up a couple of them rather than turn, but this also has its dangers. It is best to make sure that there are no oncoming vehicles at each section between passing points. The spectacular endpoint above the mine has a wide turning area. The mine has collapsed shafts and the remains of a cable tramway.

A short distance past the turn to the Suitcase Mine, you will reach three cabins on the edge of the canyon. The cabins are maintained by the Briggs and Thorndike Volunteers under

Stunning views over Striped Butte Valley and Mengel Pass

the Adopt-A-Cabin program. The first, Stone Cabin, is built of rock and corrugated iron and is sandwiched between a large boulder and the canyon wall. The old workshop next door is badly burned. The second and larger of the two is Briggs Mine Cabin. These cabins are a credit to the volunteers who maintain and enjoy them. Both are habitable. They have running hot water, a refrigerator, and a cooker, all powered by gas. All need to be activated carefully with the appropriate fuel. Although they are comfortable, the cabins are not suited for travelers expecting a luxury setting. There are shaded outdoor eating areas with barbecues, large bunk beds, and even an intercom between the two cabins. On our visit, the cabins were spotlessly clean with no sign of the rodent activity that can make using many of these idyllic backcountry cabins a dangerous business. It seems each visitor contributes to further enhance the historic and practical qualities of the cabins.

Log bridge along the narrow shelf road

All are welcome to use the cabins on a first-come, first-served basis. However, you must be aware of the dangers of hantavirus (see page 13). Leave the cabins tidy, preferably in better order than you found them. Let us hope that these cabins remain in similar condition so those who venture this way can enjoy this historic and scenic region for years to come.

Immediately past the cabins is one of the narrowest sections of shelf road along the trail. It snakes precariously around an edge of the canyon wall, and because of the tight twists, it is not recommended for extra long or wide vehicles. The weight limit on the shelf bridge is 3 tons. It is recommended that you walk ahead for the short distance involved before committing your vehicle. Most SUVs will be fine if driven with care. The log bridge crossing part of the fallen shelf road is similarly narrow. This section of shelf road was blown out sometime in the late 1980s. The perpetrator and motive is unknown, but they succeeded in closing the trail until the log bridge was constructed by the same volunteers who maintain the cabin.

Other sections of this very narrow shelf road are rocky and rough, with an extremely low margin for error. Past the shelf road, the trail continues to climb steadily, entering Death Valley National Park past Coulter Spring. The waters from the spring flow down the track at this point. In winter this can ice up and make it difficult or impossible to gain enough traction to climb the somewhat steep grade.

The trail exits South Park Canyon into South Park and becomes easygoing and smooth as it runs through sagebrush. There is a major fork in the trail in South Park. Those wanting to explore farther can drive a slightly longer loop that travels for a longer time along the ridge tops before rejoining this trail.

Additional miners' cabins and mining remains are passed before the trail drops from a saddle and enters Middle Park. Again, the road is smooth and easygoing, a pleasant change from the rock crawling in the canyon. It climbs out of Middle Park to the ridge top, where it undulates steeply through pinyons and junipers to Rogers Pass, which is marked by a historical marker. There are unparalleled views over Striped Butte Valley, Mengel Pass, and Death Valley from this section of the trail.

From Rogers Pass, the trail descends toward Pleasant Canyon, passing Rita's Cabin. The cabin is not in as good order as the Briggs Mine Cabin, but there are picnic tables under some small trees, and it makes a pleasant place for a picnic or overnight camp.

The trail within Pleasant Canyon is generally smoother and easier than in South Park Canyon. However, in the lower sections there are a couple of very tricky sections that maintain the overall 7 difficulty rating of the trail. In addition, flowing springs turn the lower section of the canyon into a creek bed. When temperatures are low enough in winter and early spring, this section turns to a slick sheet of ice and can become totally impassable. The abundance of water from the spring means that long sections of lower Pleasant Canyon are moderately brushy. The trail finishes at Ballarat. There is no fuel available in Ballarat.

In winter, the ridge top sections of the trail can have snow on them. Although this trail is often passable all year, high summer temperatures make it unpleasant and hard on vehicles at lower elevations. The optimum travel times are spring and fall, although snow melt in early spring may make sections of trail around the springs extremely boggy.

Current Road Information

Death Valley National Park
PO Box 579
Death Valley, CA 92328-0579
(760) 786-2331

Bureau of Land Management
Ridgecrest Field Office
300 South Richmond Road
Ridgecrest, CA 93555
(760) 384-5400

Map References

BLM Ridgecrest, Darwin Hills
USGS 1:24,000 Manly Fall, Panamint, Ballarat
1:100,000 Ridgecrest, Darwin Hills
Maptech CD-ROM: Barstow/San Bernardino County; Kings Canyon/Death Valley
Southern & Central California Atlas & Gazetteer, pp. 41, 53
California Road & Recreation Atlas, p. 88
Trails Illustrated, Death Valley National Park (221)
Other: Free NPS Death Valley map (does not show road on map)

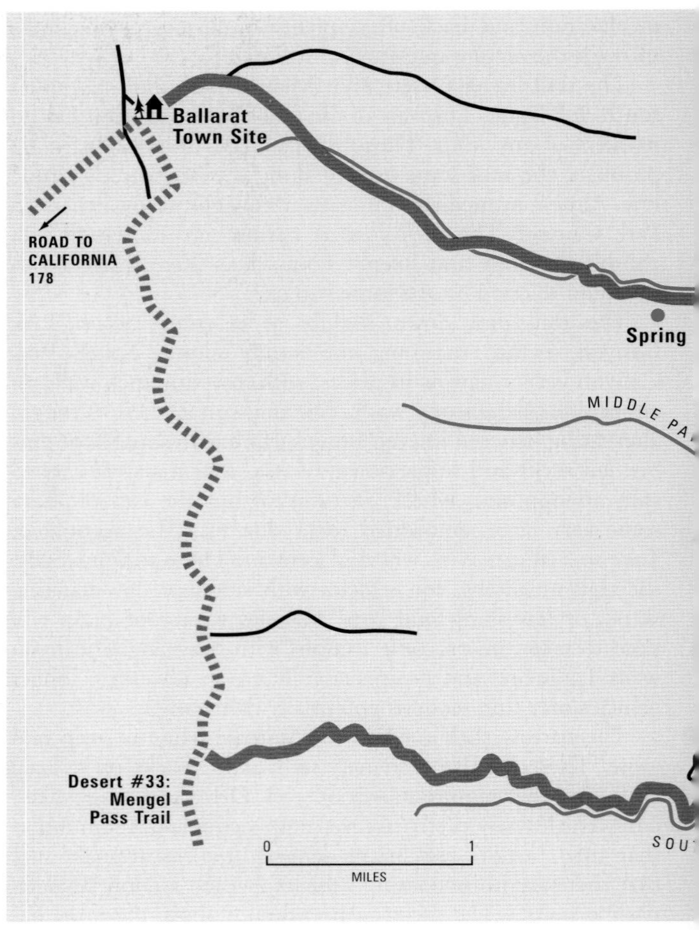

Route Directions

▼ 0.0		From Desert #33: Mengel Pass Trail, 3.7 miles south of Ballarat and 0.4 miles north of mile marker 8, zero trip meter and turn east on unmarked, formed trail. There is no sign at the intersection.
4.0 ▲		Trail finishes on Desert #33: Mengel Pass Trail in the Panamint Valley. Turn right for Ballarat; turn left to continue along Mengel Pass Trail.
		GPS: N36°00.01' W117°13.17'
▼ 0.2	SO	Start of shelf road.
3.8 ▲	SO	End of shelf road.
▼ 1.9	SO	Track on right is a shortcut up the ridge. This is very steep and loose and not recommended for travel uphill because the last section is extremely difficult. Proceed straight ahead to remain on main trail.
2.1 ▲	SO	Track on left is end of steep shortcut.
		GPS: N35°59.85' W117°11.73'
▼ 2.3	SO	Shortcut up ridge rejoins on right.
1.7 ▲	BR	Track on right is a very steep shortcut down the ridge. It is not recommended because of low traction.
▼ 2.6	SO	Trail enters South Park Canyon.
1.4 ▲	SO	Trails exits South Park Canyon.
▼ 2.7	SO	Enter South Park Canyon wash. End of shelf road.
1.3 ▲	SO	Exit South Park Canyon wash. Start of shelf road.
		GPS: N35°59.70' W117°11.24'

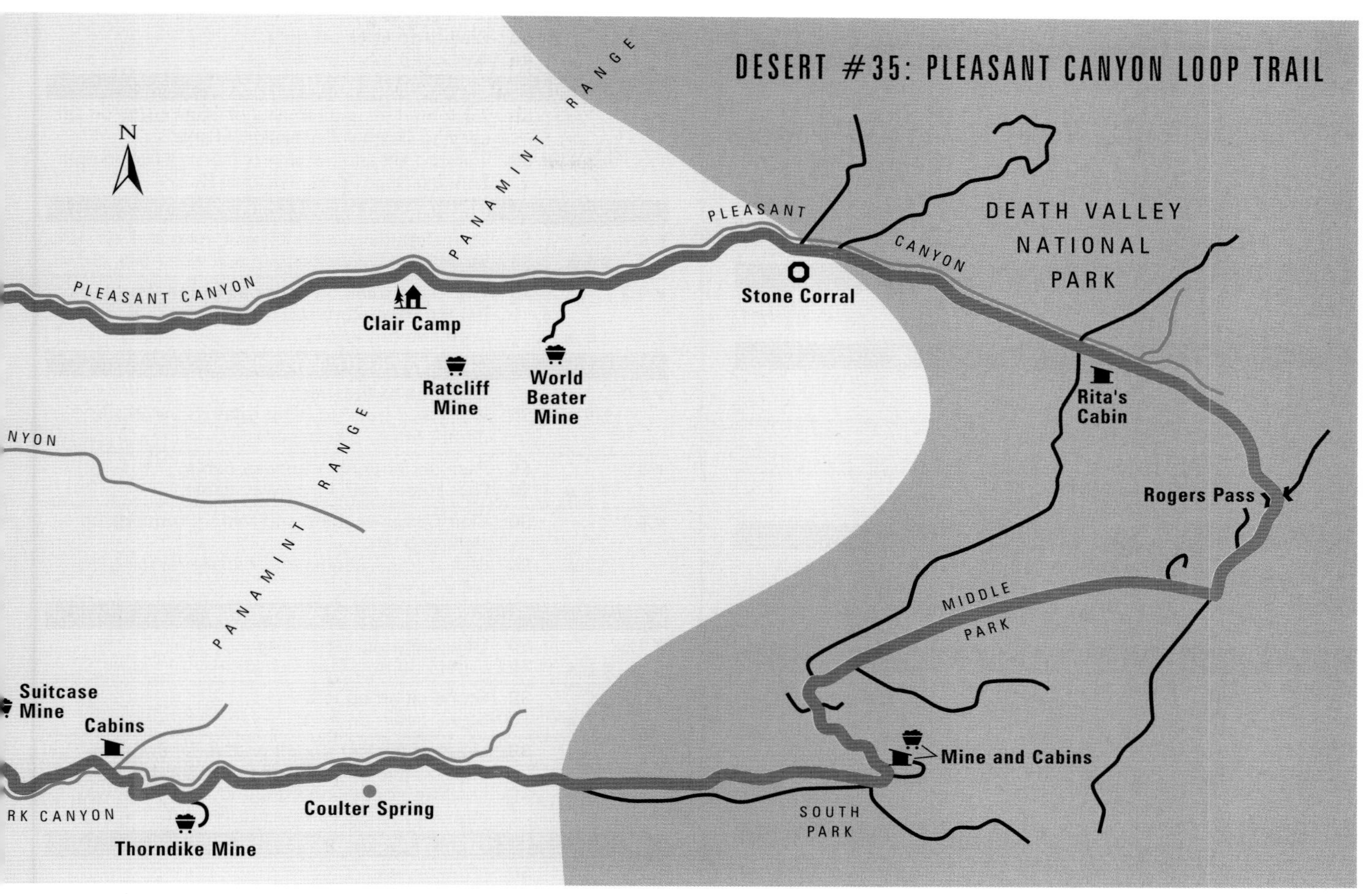

▼ 3.5 SO Track on left is old, washed out mining road that rejoins almost immediately.
0.5 ▲ SO Track on right is old, washed out mining road that rejoins almost immediately.

GPS: N35°59.70' W117°10.66'

▼ 4.0 SO Well-used track on left goes 1 mile to the Suitcase Mine. Zero trip meter.
0.0 ▲ Continue to the west down South Park Canyon.

GPS: N35°59.75' W117°10.42'

▼ 0.0 Continue to the east up South Park Canyon.
3.5 ▲ BL Well-used track on right goes 1 mile to the Suitcase Mine. Zero trip meter.

▼ 0.7 BR Two cabins on left. The first is Stone Cabin; the second is Briggs Mine Cabin. Track on left to cabins.
2.8 ▲ SO Two cabins on right. The first is Briggs Mine Cabin; the second is Stone Cabin. Track on right to cabins.

GPS: N35°59.72' W117°09.83'

▼ 0.9 BR Bear right out of wash. Start of narrow shelf road with no turnaround for 0.5 miles. Wide or long vehicles may wish to walk this section first.
2.6 ▲ BL End of shelf road. Bear left down wash.

GPS: N35°59.63' W117°09.56'

▼ 1.2 SO Narrow log bridge.
2.3 ▲ SO Narrow log bridge.

GPS: N35°59.59' W117°09.50'

▼ 1.3 SO End of shelf road. Enter wash.
2.2 ▲ SO Exit wash. Start of narrow shelf road with no turnaround for 0.5 miles. Wide or long vehicles may wish to walk this section first.

▼ 1.4 SO Track on right goes to the Thorndike Mine.
2.1 ▲ SO Track on left goes to the Thorndike Mine.

GPS: N35°59.58' W117°09.28'

▼ 2.4 SO Coulter Spring on right.
1.1 ▲ SO Coulter Spring on left.

GPS: N35°59.67' W117°08.40'

▼ 3.1 SO Exit line of wash.
0.4 ▲ SO Enter line of wash.

▼ 3.5 BL Trail forks. Well-used track on right. Zero trip meter. Entering South Park.
0.0 ▲ Continue to the west and start to descend into South Park Canyon.

GPS: N35°59.55' W117°07.27'

▼ 0.0 Continue to the northeast.
1.6 ▲ SO Well-used track on left. Continue out of South Park. Zero trip meter.

▼ 1.5 SO Track on right.
0.1 ▲ BR Track on left.

GPS: N35°59.51' W117°05.58'

▼ 1.6 SO Well-used track on right can be used to travel a longer loop within South Park. Continue toward mine and zero trip meter.
0.0 ▲ Continue to the west across South Park.

GPS: N35°59.49' W117°05.48'

▼ 0.0 Continue to the northeast past track on right.
3.0 ▲ BR Track on left; then well-used track on left is the end of the longer loop. Zero trip meter.

▼ 0.1 SO Pass two derelict cabins; then mine on right.

2.9 ▲ SO Mine on left; then pass two derelict cabins.

GPS: N35°59.55' W117°05.42'

▼ 0.2 SO Track on right into mine.
2.8 ▲ BR Track on left into mine.

▼ 0.6 SO 4-way intersection on saddle. Track on right to old mining truck and track on left. Descend to Middle Park.
2.4 ▲ SO 4-way intersection on saddle. Track on left to old mining truck and track on right. Descend to South Park.

GPS: N35°59.84' W117°05.81'

▼ 0.8 BR Two well-used tracks on left.
2.2 ▲ BL Two well-used tracks on right.

GPS: N35°59.97' W117°05.82'

▼ 1.0 SO Track on right.
2.0 ▲ SO Track on left.

▼ 2.0 SO Track on left.
1.0 ▲ SO Track on right.

▼ 2.9 SO Track on left.
0.1 ▲ SO Track on right.

GPS: N36°00.33' W117°03.64'

▼ 3.0 TL T-intersection at ridge top. Track on right is end of longer loop. Turn left and continue to climb ridge. Zero trip meter.
0.0 ▲ Continue to the west.

GPS: N36°00.32' W117°03.60'

▼ 0.0 Continue to the north.
0.6 ▲ TR Turn right onto well-used track and descend to Middle Park. Track ahead can be taken to travel a longer loop to South Park. Zero trip meter.

▼ 0.1 SO Track on left.
0.5 ▲ BL Track on right.

GPS: N36°00.44' W117°03.56'

▼ 0.5 SO Two tracks on left.
0.1 ▲ SO Two tracks on right.

▼ 0.6 TL Rogers Pass. There is a marker at the pass. Steep track straight ahead. Old indistinct pack trail on right goes to Arrastre Spring. Zero trip meter at marker.
0.0 ▲ Continue to the southwest.

GPS: N36°00.75' W117°03.22'

▼ 0.0 Continue to the northwest.
4.2 ▲ TR Rogers Pass. There is a marker at the pass. Continue to climb steeply. Steep track on left. Old indistinct pack trail straight ahead goes to Arrastre Spring. Zero trip meter at marker.

▼ 1.3 SO Track on left and Rita's Cabin on left. Entering Pleasant Canyon.
2.9 ▲ SO Track on right and Rita's Cabin on right. Exiting Pleasant Canyon.

GPS: N36°01.48' W117°04.19'

▼ 1.4 SO Well-used track on left is shorter, steeper route back into Middle Park that bypasses Rogers Pass.
2.8 ▲ BL Well-used track on right is shorter, steeper route into Middle Park that bypasses Rogers Pass.

▼ 1.5 SO Track on right.
2.7 ▲ SO Track on left.

▼ 1.6 BR Track on left.
2.6 ▲ SO Track on right.

▼ 2.0 BL Track on right.
2.2 ▲ SO Track on left.

GPS: N36°01.83' W117°04.85'

▼ 2.2 SO Track on left rejoins. Trail enters line of wash.
2.0 ▲ BL Track on right. Exit line of wash.

GPS: N36°01.85' W117°05.02'

▼ 2.8 SO Well-used track on right.
1.4 ▲ BR Well-used track on left.

GPS: N36°02.00' W117°05.66'

▼ 2.9 SO Track on right and remains of stone corral on left. Leaving Death Valley National Park.
1.3 ▲ SO Track on left and remains of stone corral on right. Entering Death Valley National Park.

GPS: N36°02.02' W117°05.77'

▼ 4.1 SO Stone foundations on left and water tank on right.
0.1 ▲ SO Stone foundations on right and water tank on left.

▼ 4.2 SO Well-used track on left goes to the World Beater Mine. Zero trip meter
0.0 ▲ Continue to the east.

GPS: N36°01.91' W117°06.99'

▼ 0.0 Continue to the west.
6.6 ▲ SO Well-used track on right goes to the World Beater Mine. Zero trip meter.

▼ 0.6 SO Pass under aerial tramway cable.
6.0 ▲ SO Pass under aerial tramway cable.

▼ 0.9 SO Clair Camp—cabins and mining remains on right and left.
5.7 ▲ SO Clair Camp—cabins and mining remains on left and right.

GPS: N36°01.98' W117°07.89'

▼ 1.0 SO Gate. Leaving Clair Camp.
5.6 ▲ SO Gate. Entering Clair Camp.

▼ 1.3 SO Stone cabin on left.
5.3 ▲ SO Stone cabin on right.

▼ 2.3 SO Loading hopper on left and aerial tramway high on the canyon wall to the right.
4.3 ▲ SO Loading hopper on right and aerial tramway high on the canyon wall to the left.

GPS: N36°01.76' W117°09.39'

▼ 2.6 SO Mine on left.
4.0 ▲ SO Mine on right.

▼ 2.9 SO Pass under aerial tramway cable.
3.7 ▲ SO Pass under aerial tramway cable.

▼ 3.0 SO Spring.
3.6 ▲ SO Spring.

GPS: N36°01.90' W117°10.50'

▼ 3.5 SO Adit on left.
3.1 ▲ SO Adit on right.

▼ 4.1 SO Exit line of wash.
2.5 ▲ SO Enter line of wash.

▼ 4.7 SO Cross through wash; then track on left; then cross through wash.
1.9 ▲ SO Cross through wash; then track on right; then cross through wash.

▼ 4.8 SO Cross through wash.
1.8 ▲ SO Cross through wash.

▼ 5.3 SO Cross through wash.
1.3 ▲ SO Cross through wash.

▼ 5.6 SO Cross through wash. Exit Pleasant Canyon.
1.0 ▲ SO Cross through wash. Enter Pleasant Canyon.

▼ 6.1 SO Track on right.
0.5 ▲ BR Track on left.

▼ 6.6 Trail ends in Ballarat. Continue straight ahead to exit to California 178; turn left to travel Desert #33: Mengel Pass Trail.
0.0 ▲ Trail commences in Ballarat in the Panamint Valley, along Desert #33: Mengel Pass Trail, 4 miles east of Trona Wildrose Road. Zero trip meter at the general store and proceed north-east on formed trail.

GPS: N36°02.87' W117°13.38'

DESERT #36

Johnson Canyon Trail

Starting Point:	**Desert #32: Death Valley West Side Road, 14.4 miles from the south end**
Finishing Point:	**Johnson Canyon**
Total Mileage:	**10 miles (one-way)**
Unpaved Mileage:	**10 miles**
Driving Time:	**1.5 hours (one-way)**
Elevation Range:	**-200–3,800 feet**
Usually Open:	**Year-round**
Best Time to Travel:	**October to May**
Difficulty Rating:	**3**
Scenic Rating:	**8**
Remoteness Rating:	**+1**

Special Attractions

- Rugged trail that penetrates the Panamint Range up Johnson Canyon.
- Hungry Bills Ranch site.

History

The Timbisha Shoshone have been associated with this area for many generations. Their ancestors roamed the land, using it in seasonal patterns. One seasonal dwelling area was in the canyon now referred to as Johnson Canyon. The Timbisha Shoshone valued the cooler temperatures of the canyon and the availability of springwater during the sweltering summer months.

The arrival of the forty-niners meant change for the native people's way of life. Word was spreading about the mineral wealth that could be found within this harsh landscape. Control of the intermittent water holes became an early source of conflict as whites arrived in search of mineral deposits. Native plants used for food by Indians were seen as fuel and construction materials by the new arrivals and hostilities quickly escalated into bloodshed. The Treaty of Ruby Valley, ratified by Congress in 1866, sought a peaceful solution to the situation. It granted new arrivals right of passage across Western Shoshone lands. However, miners were not easily placated and they continued to squeeze out the native Timbisha Shoshone.

Traveling across an alluvial fan to Death Valley can be deceptively slow

With the influx of miners to the Panamints and, in particular, the boom at Panamint City in 1873, the demand for fresh fruit and vegetables far outweighed the available supply. Two Swiss men saw the opportunity for a fresh produce supply business and they began their market gardening operation in the upper reaches of Johnson Canyon, about 10 miles across the range from Panamint City. Having an obvious monopoly on the supply of fresh goods to the mining town, the entrepreneurs found they could charge phenomenal prices and still sell all they produced. Cabbage was reportedly fetching a price of approximately $1.20 a head, well above the average market price of 1875.

A spring at the end of the vehicle trail marks the start of the hiking trail

But when the boom times of Panamint City declined, so did the demand for fresh produce. The property was vacated and almost forgotten until a Shoshone named Hungry Bill stepped in to reclaim his family's land rights in the region. The aging ruins and orchard of Hungry Bills Ranch can be seen along the hiking trail from the end of the vehicle trail.

Description

This spur trail leaves Desert #32: Death Valley West Side Road to travel a slow and bumpy path up the rocky, barren bajada on the east side of the Panamint Range. The formed trail travels steadily for 6 miles up the alluvial fan, or bajada, following alongside Johnson Canyon Wash. The hardy creosote bush is the main plant that manages to survive in the open, windswept area.

After 6 miles, the trail descends to join Johnson Canyon Wash and the surface becomes slightly harder, rougher, and lumpier with some larger embedded rocks to negotiate. The canyon is fairly open. Its walls support sparse creosote bush and sagebrush.

Nearly 10 miles from the start, the vehicle trail finishes at a spring surrounded by large cottonwood trees and the site of an old corral. It is possible to hike past the spring to visit the remains of Hungry Bills Ranch. The well-prepared hiker can continue over Panamint Pass to the site of Panamint ghost town.

There is no camping for the first 2 miles of the trail from Desert #32: Death Valley West Side Road, and there are extremely limited choices after that.

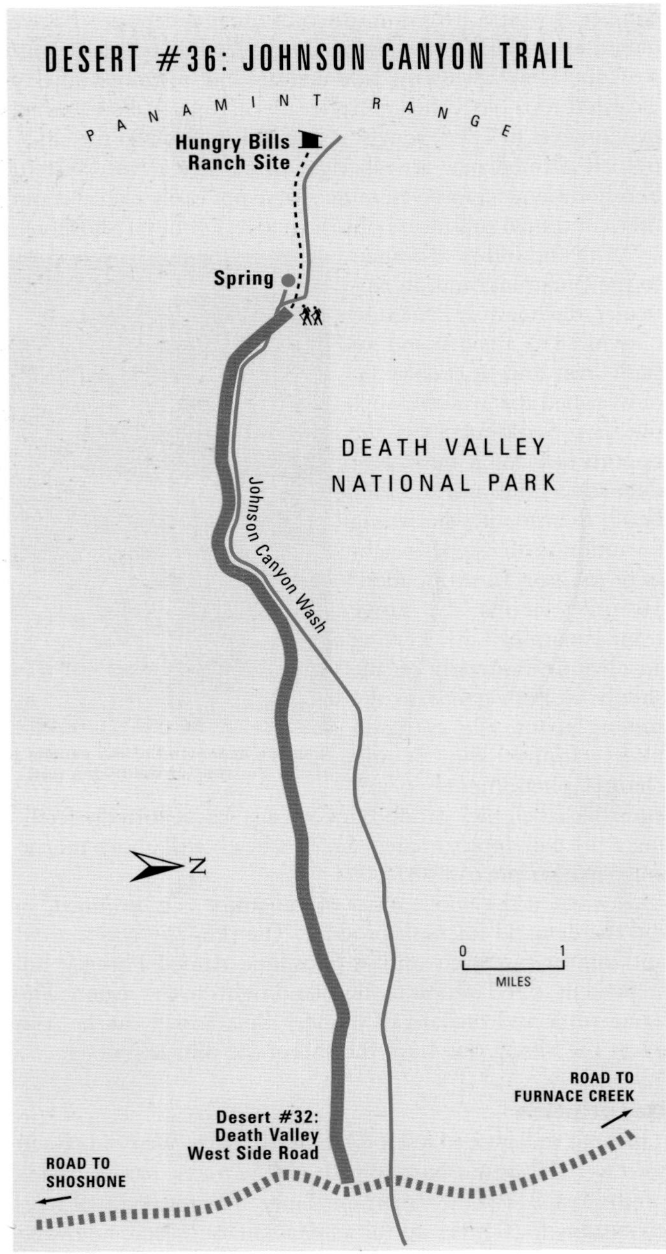

Current Road Information

Death Valley National Park
PO Box 579
Death Valley, CA 92328-0579
(760) 786-2331

Map References

BLM Death Valley Junction, Darwin Hills
USGS 1:24,000 Mormon Point, Galena Canyon, Panamint
1:1,000,000 Death Valley Junction, Darwin Hills
Maptech CD-ROM: Kings Canyon/Death Valley
Southern & Central California Atlas & Gazetteer, p. 42
California Road & Recreation Atlas, p. 88
Trails Illustrated, Death Valley National Park (221)
Other: Free NPS Death Valley map

Route Directions

▼ 0.0		From Desert #32: Death Valley West Side Road, 14.4 miles from the southern end of the trail, zero trip meter and turn west on formed dirt trail sign-posted to Johnson Canyon.
		GPS: N36°05.89' W116°50.67'
▼ 6.0	SO	Trail descends toward Johnson Canyon Wash.
		GPS: N36°05.17' W116°57.12'
▼ 6.2	SO	Enter Johnson Canyon Wash.
▼ 9.9	SO	Cross through creek formed by flowing spring.
▼ 10.0		Trail ends at spring. Vehicle trail does not continue past this point. From here, hike up the canyon past the spring to reach Hungry Bills Ranch site.
		GPS: N36°05.33' W117°00.33'

DESERT #37

Deadman Pass Trail

Starting Point:	**California 127, 7.1 miles south of Death Valley Junction**
Finishing Point:	**Gold Valley**
Total Mileage:	**27.5 miles**
Unpaved Mileage:	**27.5 miles**
Driving Time:	**1 hour for Deadman Pass section; 2.5 hours (one-way) for Gold Valley, including all 3 spurs**
Elevation Range:	**2,100–4,500 feet**
Usually Open:	**Year-round**
Best Time to Travel:	**September to June**
Difficulty Rating:	**3**
Scenic Rating:	**8**
Remoteness Rating:	**+0**

Special Attractions

- Alternate entry/exit to Nevada from Death Valley.
- Beautiful and varied Gold Valley.
- Chance to see bighorn sheep around Willow Spring.

History

In February 1908, the nearby town of Greenwater was almost deserted because the population headed for Gold Valley in search of a lucky strike. Prospectors Harry Ramsey and O. P. Grover found promising ore and formed the Willow Creek Gold Mining Company, located in Gold Valley about 20 miles southwest of Greenwater. The initial ore from their seven claims was reported in the *Inyo Independent* as returning an average of $148 to the ton. Ore from the nearby LeCry property was only returning an average of $37 to the ton. This was enough to cause a mild rush to Gold Valley. The Goldfield Review section of the *Inyo Independent* announced that Andy Kane had seven men working his claims. One had produced a sample of ore that assayed at 2,000 ounces silver; another produced copper ore at 40 to 60 percent. An assay office with a furnace was set up by Brockinghams of Boston. Bill Brong's auto line provided transportation to the new camp from the Tonopah & Tidewater Railroad's Death Valley Junction, located north of Deadman Pass.

The Willow Creek Gold Mining Company's ore could be handled by the stamp and plate process. Willow Creek's location near the claim, the farthest point on this trail, was noted as having enough water to run a 20-stamp mill without any further development. Transportation of the ore—always a concern to Death Valley prospectors—seemed under control as the Tonopah & Tidewater Railroad was expected to complete a branch to nearby Greenwater. All the elements seemed in order for another booming mining region similar to the one at Rhyolite, Nevada. Unfortunately, like Greenwater, not much development came to Gold Valley, and prospectors moved on in their never-ending search for the big one.

Description

This trail is really two separate trails divided by Greenwater Valley Road. The Deadman Pass section can be driven alone as a way of accessing the southern end of Death Valley National Park. The Gold Valley section can be treated as a detour off the long north-south Greenwater Valley Road.

Deadman Pass Trail leaves California 127 south of Death Valley Junction. Initially, the trail travels in a very loose, gravelly wash. This section can be slow and difficult, especially in hot weather. Leaving the wash, the trail climbs the gentle gradient to Deadman Pass, a wide pass in the Greenwater Range. There is a USGS bench mark at the pass but no sign. On the western side of the pass, the trail runs in a plumb line to join Greenwater Valley Road. The trail joins this road for 0.5 miles before turning west onto the Gold Valley section of the route.

USGS bench mark at Deadman Pass

Initially the trail is graded, but it quickly reverts to a well-used formed trail. Much of the trail's early section crosses an area of desert pavement. There are many faint tracks leading off on the right and left; remain on the main trail. As you approach Gold Valley, the trail becomes uneven and rougher, twisting up to a saddle with a view of the valley ahead and the Panamint Range beyond.

The trail follows a loop within Gold Valley, passing around the bowl of the valley through deep red rocks and pretty hills. There are three side trails that branch off from the loop. The first goes 0.6 miles south to some mine tailings. Two thirds of the way along this trail, it passes through a narrow crevice in the rocks, which will stop wider vehicles. The second side trail leads 2.3 miles west down Willow Creek to a spring. The lush vegetation and reliable water supply make this creek a favorite spot for bighorn sheep and other animal and bird life. The third side trail meanders north through the hills toward Sheep Canyon and various mine tailings. The third side trail is the least used of the three.

Looking back toward Nevada from Deadman Pass

When the loop is completed, you must exit back to Greenwater Valley Road. From here, you can travel south to Shoshone and the hot springs at Tecopa, north to Furnace Creek, or retrace your steps over Deadman Pass to Death Valley Junction.

Current Road Information

Death Valley National Park
PO Box 579
Death Valley, CA 92328-0579
(760) 786-2331

Map References

BLM Death Valley Junction
USGS 1:24,000 West of Eagle Mt., Deadman Pass, Funeral Peak, Gold Valley
1:100,000 Death Valley Junction
Maptech CD-ROM: Kings Canyon/Death Valley
Southern & Central California Atlas & Gazetteer, pp. 42, 43
California Road & Recreation Atlas, pp. 89, 88
Trails Illustrated, Death Valley National Park (221)
Other: Free NPS Death Valley map (trail is not marked)

Route Directions

▼ 0.0		From California 127, 7.3 miles south of Death Valley Junction, zero trip meter and turn south on unmarked, small formed trail. Trail is opposite the north end of Eagle Mountain and 0.1 miles west of the 2,000 feet elevation sign.
3.5 ▲		Trail ends at intersection with California 127. Turn left for Death Valley Junction; turn right for Shoshone.
		GPS: N36°12.60' W116°23.68'
▼ 0.1	BR	Bear right into line of wash. Very loose, deep gravel for next 1.2 miles.
3.4 ▲	BL	Bear left out of line of wash.
▼ 1.3	SO	Track on right.

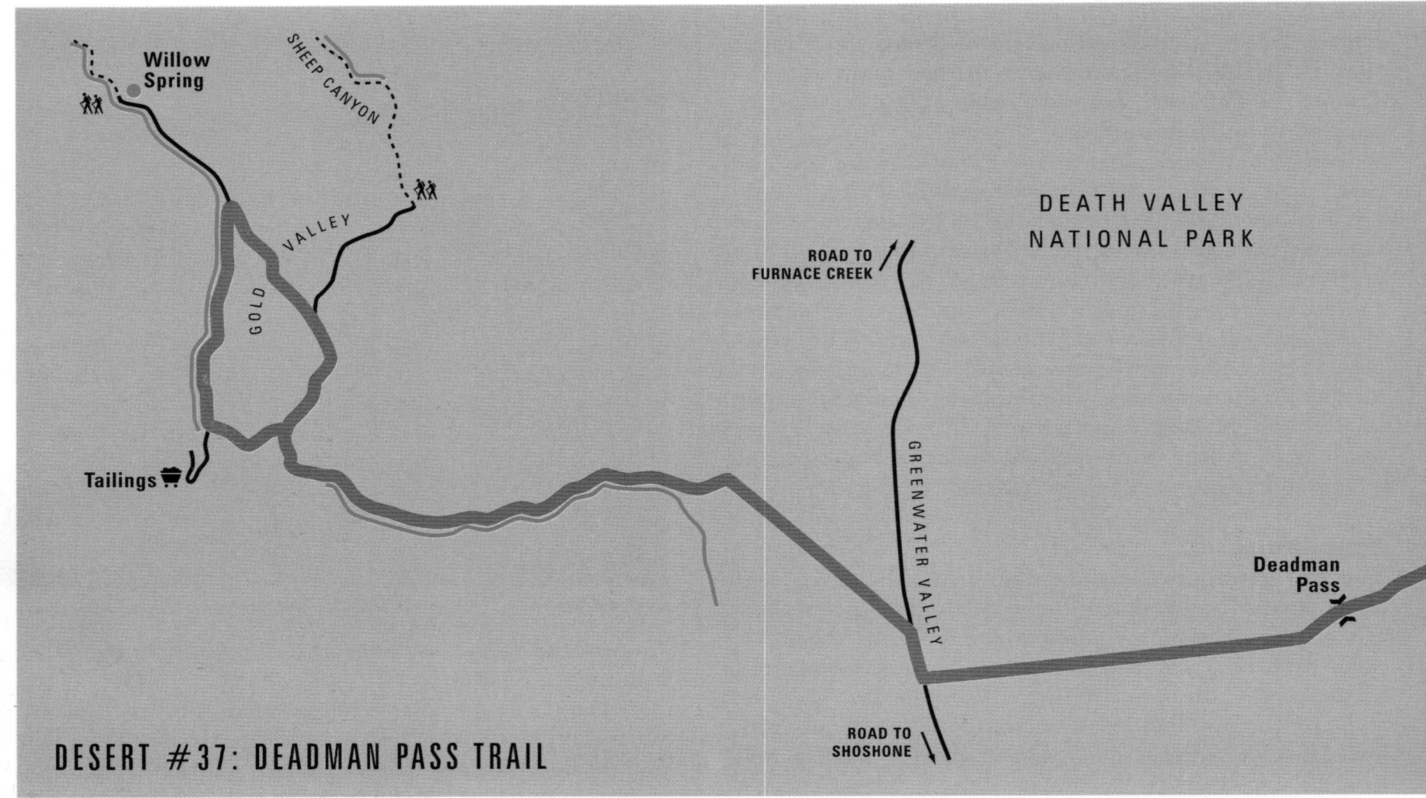

2.2 ▲ BR Track on left is alternate exit to California 127 that avoids a section of loose, deep gravel. Remain in wash. Very loose, deep gravel for next 1.2 miles.

GPS: N36°11.85′ W116°24.26′

▼ 1.4 SO Track on left.
2.1 ▲ SO Track on right.

▼ 1.5 BL Track on right out of wash. Exit wash.
2.0 ▲ SO Enter wash. Track on left out of wash.

GPS: N36°11.69′ W116°24.38′

▼ 1.6 SO Cross through wash.
1.9 ▲ SO Cross through wash.

▼ 1.7 SO Cross through wash.
1.8 ▲ SO Cross through wash.

▼ 3.5 SO Entering Death Valley National Park at sign. Zero trip meter.
0.0 ▲ Continue to the north.

GPS: N36°10.01′ W116°24.65′

▼ 0.0 Continue to the south.
5.1 ▲ SO Leaving Death Valley National Park at sign. Zero trip meter.

▼ 5.1 SO Deadman Pass. Zero trip meter at the top. There is a USGS bench mark on the left at the pass but no other marker. Trail now gradually descends.
0.0 ▲ Continue to the north.

GPS: N36°05.88′ W116°26.68′

▼ 0.0 Continue to the south.
4.3 ▲ SO Deadman Pass. Zero trip meter at the top. There is a USGS bench mark on the right at the pass but no other marker. Trail now gradually descends.

▼ 1.9 SO Track on right.
2.4 ▲ SO Track on left.

▼ 4.3 TR T-intersection with roughly graded Greenwater Valley Road. Zero trip meter.
0.0 ▲ Continue to the northeast.

GPS: N36°03.06′ W116°29.97′

▼ 0.0 Continue to the northwest.
0.5 ▲ TL Turn left onto well-used, unmarked trail and zero trip meter.

▼ 0.5 TL Turn left onto unmarked, roughly graded smaller trail. There is a metal post opposite the intersection but no sign. Zero trip meter. Trail is a spur from this point.
0.0 ▲ Continue to the southeast.

GPS: N36°03.35′ W116°30.39′

▼ 0.0 Continue to the west.
▼ 0.2 SO Cross through wash.
▼ 3.2 SO Enter line of wash.

GPS: N36°03.02′ W116°33.75′

▼ 7.0 SO Trail exits line of wash.

GPS: N36°01.23′ W116°36.93′

▼ 7.2 SO Pull-in on right.
▼ 7.7 BL Trail forks at the start of loop. Zero trip meter.

GPS: N36°01.29′ W116°37.31′

▼ 0.0 Continue to the west.
▼ 1.0 TR Track on left goes 0.6 miles to some tailings piles and the wilderness boundary. Zero trip meter.

GPS: N36°00.95′ W116°38.09′

▼ 0.0 Continue to the northwest.
▼ 0.8 SO Enter line of wash.
▼ 2.4 TR Turn sharp right to continue around loop and zero trip meter. Track on left goes 1.7 miles to Willow Spring. A hiking trail continues down Willow Creek from that point.

GPS: N36°02.74′ W116°39.47′

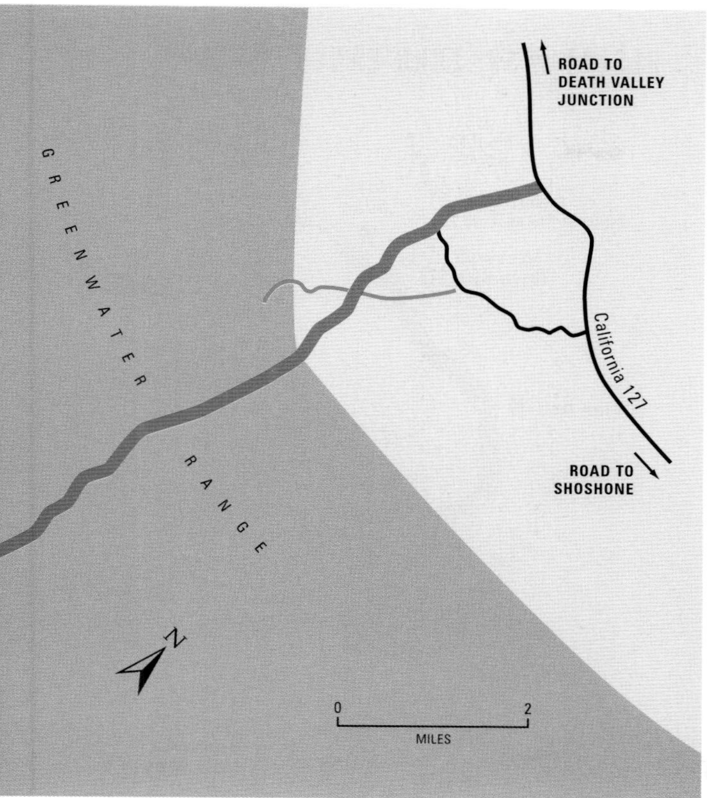

▼ 0.0		Continue to the east.
▼ 1.5	SO	Track on left goes 2.3 miles toward old dugouts, mines, and hiking trail in Sheep Canyon. Zero trip meter.
		GPS: N36°02.36' W116°37.93'
▼ 0.0		Continue to the east.
▼ 1.5		End of loop. Continue straight ahead to exit the way you came to Greenwater Valley Road.
		GPS: N36°01.29' W116°37.31'

DESERT #38

Echo Canyon Trail

Starting Point:	**California 190, 2 miles east of intersection with Death Valley Road at Furnace Creek**
Finishing Point:	**Inyo Mine**
Total Mileage:	**9.1 miles (one-way)**
Unpaved Mileage:	**9.1 miles**
Driving Time:	**1 hour (one-way)**
Elevation Range:	**400–3,700 feet**
Usually Open:	**Year-round**
Best Time to Travel:	**October to May**
Difficulty Rating:	**3**
Scenic Rating:	**9**
Remoteness Rating:	**+0**

Special Attractions

- Historic Travertine Hot Springs at the start of the trail.
- The natural rock window, Eye of the Needle.
- The remains of the Inyo Mine camp.

History

Members of an 1849 wagon train camped at Travertine Springs along their nightmare "shortcut" route to the goldfields of the West. The Brier family and the Mississippi Boys had been forced to abandon their wagons in western Nevada when their weakened oxen could no longer pull the weight of their possessions. Crossing the Funeral Mountains had been an arduous trip for all concerned, with no water to be found along the way. They reached the welcome waters of Travertine Springs on Christmas Day and feasted on the only food available—another ox. With malnourished children in tow, the Bennett and Ar-

Inyo Mine

cane families struggled over the mountains two days later. They also camped and rested by the warm Travertine Springs.

Prior to this, local Indians had little interaction with new settlers. They used Death Valley as a winter retreat and regularly camped at the mouth of Furnace Creek (close to where the inn is located today). Seeing the emigrants' oxen as food, the Indians attacked a beast with arrows. The forty-niners took this to be an assault against them personally, and they moved on into Death Valley as quickly as they could gather the strength. Unfortunately, their problems in Death Valley had only begun! Nearly five weeks later, they would barely escape with their lives.

The earliest mining claims in the Echo Canyon region were made by Chet Leavitt and Maroni Hicks in 1905. Within months, the two prospectors were receiving offers to buy out their claims. Charles Schwab was among the first investors. He did not actually take up his earliest options, yet his name remains on the map to this day. Many such investors came and paid initial monies, but they did not follow up on their options. Within a year, two dozen claims were located along Echo Canyon.

Production at the Inyo Mine began in 1906 with a good deal of success. The Inyo Mining Company went public in 1907, but because of the economic panic of that year, it turned out to be a bad time to put the company stock up for sale. Mining investors were nowhere to be found and the Inyo Mining Company was forced to wind down its operations. Little happened at the mine for the next 30 years. The mines were sold and resold. The last serious attempt to work the mine ended in 1941.

At the mouth of Furnace Creek, Greenland Ranch was part of the growing borax empire of William Tell Coleman. Coleman's ranch was the largest and most profitable in Death Valley. It later became known as Furnace Creek Ranch. The impressive date grove at the ranch was planted in the 1920s by the Pacific Coast Borax Company. It began providing quality dates in the early 1930s. Date palms are not native to North America; these were imported from Algeria around the turn of the twentieth century. The ranch offered accommodations for visitors to Death Valley and housed the headquarters of Death Valley National Park. In 1927, the Pacific Coast Borax Company opened the Furnace Creek Inn, with attractions such as a golf course, tennis courts, swimming pool, and auto tours of Death Valley. By 1933, the Pacific Coast Borax Company expanded Furnace Creek Ranch into a resort, offering less expensive accommodation options.

Description

Echo Canyon Trail is a lightly traveled canyon trail within Death Valley National Park. Along the way, it passes some beautiful scenery as well as the remains of what was once a large mining camp.

At the start of the trail, a thicket of palms immediately to the west marks the Travertine Hot Springs. The waters are tapped and there is no pool for bathing. However, the small oasis is interesting and worth the short hike to view the cluster of palms. The spring is situated 0.3 miles northwest of the start of the trail on the north side of California 190.

In the wash of Echo Canyon

The well-formed trail leaves California 190 and travels up the bajada to the mouth of Echo Canyon. No camping is permitted for the first 2 miles and no camping is permitted at the Inyo Mine. This is not a good trail for camping because the majority of it travels in a wash or canyon. Campers are better off selecting a site in one of the developed campgrounds at Furnace Creek.

Within Echo Canyon, the trail winds along in the wash. There are a couple of rocky sections, but the main reason for the difficulty rating is the very

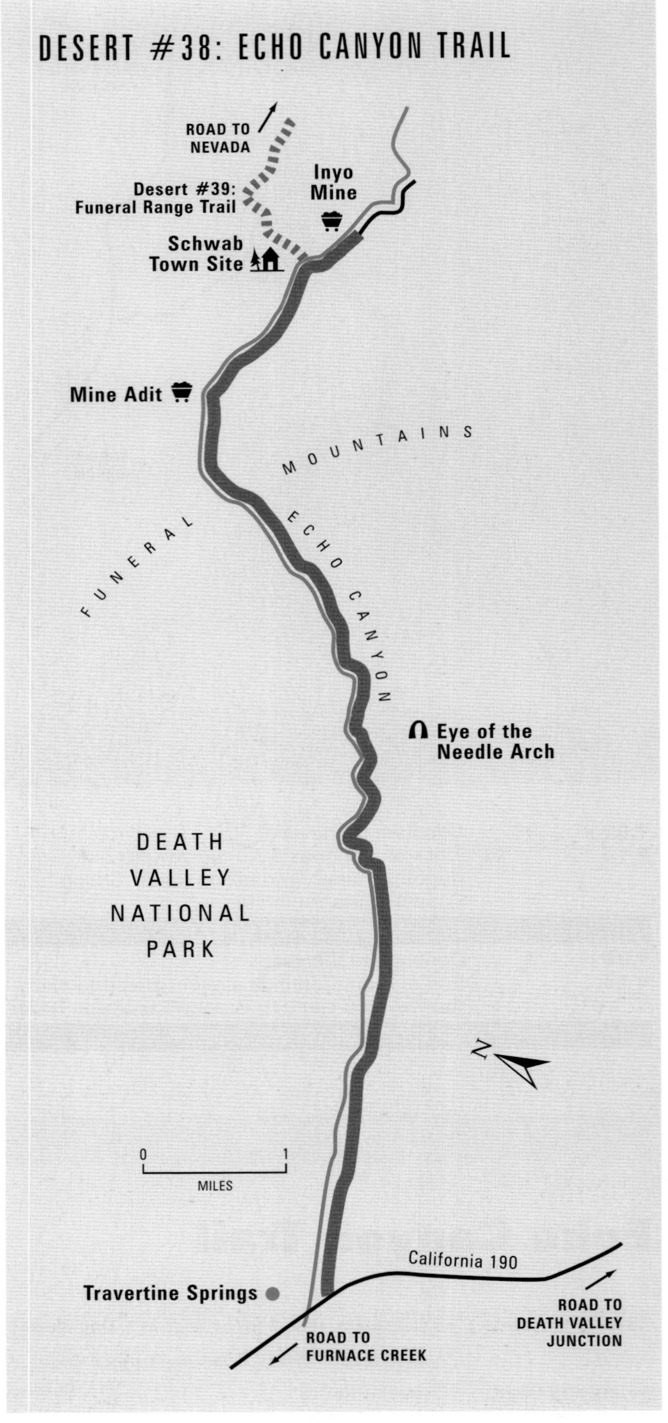

deep, loose gravel in the wash. In warmer months, this can quickly cause a vehicle to overheat.

The Eye of the Needle is located 5.1 miles from the start of the trail. The small rock window, or natural arch, is easy to spot, and it is possible to scramble up to it. Shortly after the window, the canyon opens out to a wider valley. Desert #39: Funeral Range Trail leaves to the northeast. This difficult trail is an alternate exit from Echo Canyon to the Amargosa Valley. The Inyo Mine is a short distance past the intersection with the Funeral Range Trail. There are many old cabins and mining remains scattered over the hillside at the site. The trail ends at the wilderness boundary a short distance past the mine.

Current Road Information

Death Valley National Park
PO Box 579
Death Valley, CA 92328-0579
(760) 786-2331

Map References

BLM Death Valley Junction
USGS 1:24,000 Furnace Creek, Echo Canyon
1:100,000 Death Valley Junction
Maptech CD-ROM: Kings Canyon/Death Valley
Southern & Central California Atlas & Gazetteer, p. 42
California Road & Recreation Atlas, p. 88
Trails Illustrated, Death Valley National Park (221)
Other: Free NPS Death Valley map

Route Directions

Mileage		Directions
▼ 0.0		From California 190, 2 miles southeast of the intersection with Death Valley Road at Furnace Creek, zero trip meter and turn northeast on formed trail. There is a small sign for Echo Canyon at the start. No camping for the first 2 miles. Trail travels up the alluvial fan.
8.6 ▲		Trail ends on California 190. Turn right for Furnace Creek; turn left for Death Valley Junction.
		GPS: N36°26.25' W116°49.40'
▼ 2.8	SO	Entering Echo Canyon wash.
5.8 ▲	SO	Exiting Echo Canyon wash. Trail now travels over alluvial fan.
▼ 3.3	SO	Entering Echo Canyon.
5.3 ▲	SO	Exiting Echo Canyon.
		GPS: N36°27.56' W116°46.26'
▼ 4.5	SO	Eye of the Needle on right at top of cliff.
4.1 ▲	SO	Eye of the Needle on left at top of cliff.
		GPS: N36°27.98' W116°45.52'
▼ 5.1	SO	Small rock window directly ahead above tight gap.
3.5 ▲	SO	Small rock window directly behind above tight gap.
		GPS: N36°28.19' W116°45.12'
▼ 5.2	SO	Turnout on left. Leave narrow section of Echo Canyon.
3.4 ▲	SO	Turnout on right. Enter narrow section of Echo Canyon.
		GPS: N36°28.28' W116°45.10'
▼ 7.7	SO	Mine adit on left.
0.9 ▲	SO	Mine adit on right.
		GPS: N36°29.84' W116°43.86'
▼ 8.6	SO	Track on left at small sign to Amargosa is the start of Desert #39: Funeral Range Trail. Zero trip meter.
0.0 ▲		Continue to the west.
		GPS: N36°29.78' W116°42.59'
▼ 0.0		Continue to the east on dead end trail.
▼ 0.5	SO	Remains of the Inyo Mine. Trail continues for 0.8 miles past this point to wilderness boundary. Retrace your steps to exit to California 190. Take Desert #39: Funeral Range Trail to continue into Nevada.
		GPS: N36°29.61' W116°42.18'

DESERT #39

Funeral Range Trail

Starting Point:	**Desert #38: Echo Canyon Trail, 8.6 miles northeast of California 190**
Finishing Point:	**Nevada 373, 5 miles south of Amargosa Valley**
Total Mileage:	**25.4 miles**
Unpaved Mileage:	**14.0 miles**
Driving Time:	**2 hours**
Elevation Range:	**2,300–4,900 feet**
Usually Open:	**Year-round**
Best Time to Travel:	**September to June**
Difficulty Rating:	**6**
Scenic Rating:	**9**
Remoteness Rating:	**+2**

Special Attractions

- Difficult trail through a variety of spectacular scenery.
- An alternate entry into Death Valley National Park from Nevada when coupled with Desert #38: Echo Canyon Trail.
- Site of historic Lees Camp.

History

It was through the harsh landscape of the Funeral Mountains that the Jayhawkers wagon party attempted to reach the goldfields of California by way of a supposed shortcut. Although four members of the party died in this region, the mountain range's name is thought to come from something else. It is attributed more to the natural black, cape-like lacing of basalt rock that sits above the light-colored rocks at the base, somewhat like mourning attire.

The town site of Schwab is near the junction of this trail and Desert #38: Echo Canyon Trail in the northern, or upper, branch of Echo Canyon. Named after Pennsylvania steel magnate Charles Schwab, the settlement served as a center for local miners during its brief existence. Founded in 1906, the town was deserted within a year. The remains in the area are remnants from the Inyo Mine, which operated on and off from 1906 to 1941.

Rough, rocky section of the trail

Farther to the north along this trail is the town site of Echo. The Lee Golden Gate Mining Company located the town near the summit of the Funeral Range, expecting the mines in the region to invest in town property. It is doubtful if any allotments were actually sold because most of the surrounding mines were unsuccessful.

The site of Lees Camp is close to the Nevada border. A small mining camp existed here between 1906 and 1912. The settlement was founded to compete with another town named Lee just over the Nevada border. A good source of water enabled the California Lee to flourish while its rival floundered. Foundation walls and mine shafts mark the site.

Description

This difficult trail travels through the spectacular Funeral Mountains, part of the larger Amargosa Range that runs along the California-Nevada border. The trail commences on Desert #38: Echo Canyon Trail, 8.6 miles from the start. The turn is easy to spot, and there is a small sign for Amargosa at the intersection. Although this trail is rated a 6 overall, the majority of it is rated a 4. The 6 rating comes from three separate places where the trail climbs or descends some rocky waterfalls within the tight canyon. There is no alternate route around these places, which means that the trail is best driven by an excellent stock high-clearance 4WD with good tires. Additional clearance from larger tires and/or a suspension lift is an advantage. These sections will put vehicles with low hanging front or rear bars or side steps at a definite disadvantage; such vehicles risk body damage. The difficulty of these rock falls is not the steepness, rather it is the loose piles of boulders and unforgiving embedded rock and rock faces that makes any error of judgment potentially very costly. Take them slowly and plan your line of approach beforehand. Use a spotter to help with wheel placement and to ensure that you are not in danger of damaging the undercarriage of your vehicle.

The trail is well formed as it twists along the washes and ridge tops of the Funeral Mountains. There are some spectacular sections of canyon narrows; one in particular is the final canyon before the trail spills out into the Amargosa Valley. In addition, the ridge top sections provide long ranging views, particularly over the Amargosa Valley.

One of the many beautiful, tight canyons along this trail

At the mouth of the canyon is the site of Lees Camp, once a booming mining camp. Little remains now except for some stone foundations and rusting piles of tin cans. Past the town site, the trail simultaneously exits California and Death Valley National Park and enters Nevada. There are no signs. From here it is an easy trail down the bajada to join paved Amargosa Farm Road, which takes you out to join Nevada 373.

Current Road Information

Death Valley National Park
PO Box 579
Death Valley, CA 92328-0579
(760) 786-2331

Map References

BLM Death Valley Junction, Beatty
USGS 1:24,000 Echo Canyon, Lees Camp, Leeland, South of Amargosa Valley
1:100,000 Death Valley Junction, Beatty
Maptech CD-ROM: Kings Canyon/Death Valley
Southern & Central California Atlas & Gazetteer, pp. 42, 30
Nevada Atlas & Gazetteer, p. 64
California Road & Recreation Atlas, pp. 88, 89
Trails Illustrated, Death Valley National Park (221)
Other: Free NPS Death Valley map (trail is not marked)

Route Directions

▼ 0.0		From Desert #38: Echo Canyon Trail, 8.6 miles northeast of California 190, zero trip meter and turn northeast on small formed trail following the sign to Amargosa.
3.6 ▲		Trail ends at intersection with Desert #38: Echo Canyon Trail. Turn left to visit the Inyo Mine; turn right to exit to California 190 via Echo Canyon.
		GPS: N36°29.78' W116°42.59'
▼ 0.3	SO	Track on right.
3.3 ▲	SO	Track on left rejoins.
▼ 0.4	SO	Enter wash.
3.2 ▲	SO	Exit wash.
▼ 0.5	SO	Track on right rejoins.
3.1 ▲	SO	Track on left.
▼ 1.0	SO	Enter canyon.
2.6 ▲	SO	Exit canyon.
▼ 2.5	SO	Track on right.
1.1 ▲	SO	Track on left.
		GPS: N36°30.42' W116°41.22'
▼ 2.8	SO	Track on right out of wash to stone foundations.
0.8 ▲	SO	Track on left out of wash to stone foundations.
		GPS: N36°30.65' W116°41.10'
▼ 2.9	SO	Narrow section of rough trail climbs small rock fall in a tight section of the canyon.
0.7 ▲	SO	Narrow section of rough trail descends small rock fall in a tight section of the canyon.
		GPS: N36°30.64' W116°40.99'
▼ 3.4	BL	Faint track on left; then track on right; then well-used track on left. Track continues up narrow wash ahead. Bear left out of wash on well-used track.
0.2 ▲	BR	Drop down and enter wash. Bear right in

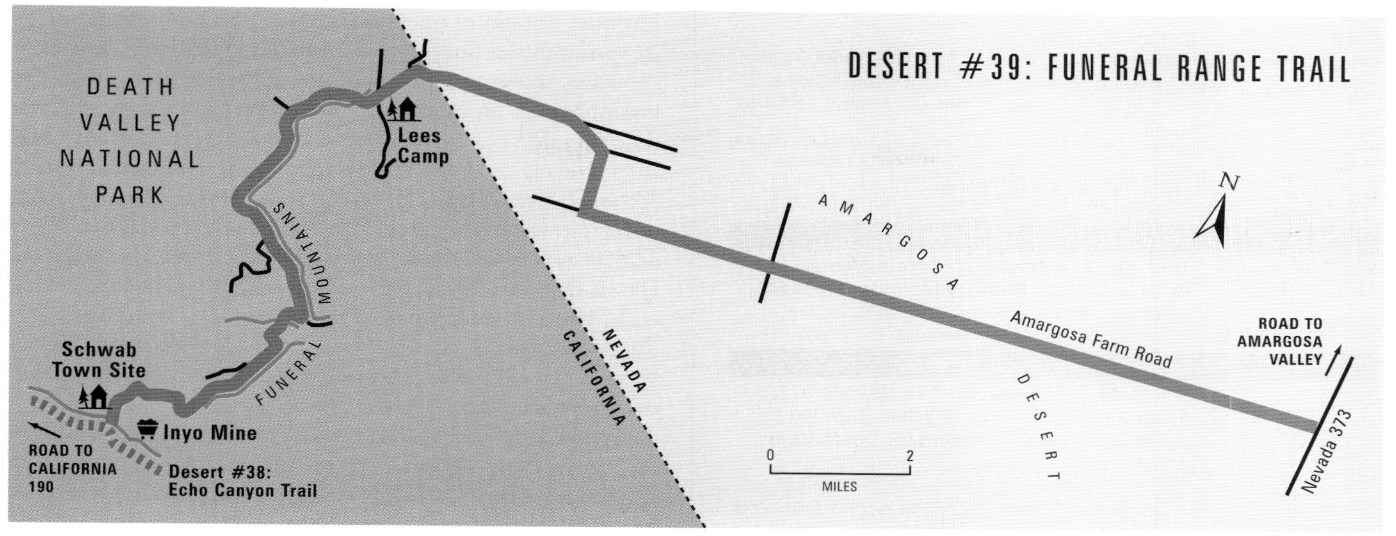

wash. Track on left up wash; then second track on left; then faint track on right.

GPS: N36°30.85′ W116°40.68′

▼ 3.6 SO 4-way intersection on saddle. Well-used track on left and right on top of saddle. Zero trip meter.
0.0 ▲ Continue to the southwest.

GPS: N36°30.99′ W116°40.66′

▼ 0.0 Continue to the northeast.
10.3 ▲ SO 4-way intersection on saddle. Well-used track on right and left on top of saddle. Zero trip meter.

▼ 0.1 SO Track on left. Enter line of wash.
10.2 ▲ BL Track on right. Bear left out of line of wash.

▼ 0.6 SO Exit line of wash and crest ridge; then enter another wash line.
9.7 ▲ SO Exit line of wash and crest ridge; then enter line of wash.

GPS: N36°31.39′ W116°40.59′

▼ 0.8 TR Well-used track on left leaves wash. Remain in smaller wash.
9.5 ▲ TL Well-used track on right leaves wash. Join larger wash.

GPS: N36°31.42′ W116°40.62′

▼ 1.0 SO Exit line of wash.
9.3 ▲ SO Enter line of wash.

▼ 1.3 SO Cross through wash.
9.0 ▲ SO Cross through wash.

▼ 1.5 SO Saddle. Views ahead of the Amargosa Desert and Nevada.
8.8 ▲ SO Saddle. Views behind of the Amargosa Desert and Nevada.

GPS: N36°31.80′ W116°40.29′

▼ 1.7 TL Turn left down line of wash. Track on right up wash is closed.
8.6 ▲ TR Turn right out of wash. Track up wash ahead is closed.

GPS: N36°31.84′ W116°40.12′

▼ 3.0 SO Rocky waterfall. Choice of staying to the left and riding a pile of loose rubble or staying to the right and riding a large, water-smoothed boulder.
7.3 ▲ SO Rocky waterfall. Choice of staying to the right and riding a pile of loose rubble or staying to the left and riding a large water-smoothed boulder.

GPS: N36°32.54′ W116°40.84′

▼ 3.2 SO Well-used track on left.
7.1 ▲ BL Well-used track on right.

GPS: N36°32.71′ W116°41.03′

▼ 3.9 BR Bear right down canyon past track on left.
6.4 ▲ BL Bear left up canyon past track on right. Track on right looks smoother and better used at this stage. Track on left appears lumpy and less used but it is the correct trail.

GPS: N36°32.96′ W116°41.55′

▼ 5.2 SO Exit canyon narrows.
5.1 ▲ SO Enter canyon narrows.

▼ 5.4 TR Turn right, heading down wash. Track on left goes up another wash.
4.9 ▲ TL Turn left on well-used track. Track straight ahead goes up another wash.

GPS: N36°34.04′ W116°41.35′

▼ 5.6 BR Well-used track on left out of wash. Remain in wash.
4.7 ▲ SO Well-used track on right out of wash. Remain in wash.

GPS: N36°34.25′ W116°41.28′

▼ 6.7 SO Exit wash.
3.6 ▲ SO Enter wash.

GPS: N36°34.68′ W116°40.29′

▼ 6.9 SO Track on right at Lees Camp.
3.4 ▲ SO Track on left at Lees Camp.

▼ 7.0 SO Track on left and track on right.
3.3 ▲ SO Track on left and track on right.

▼ 7.6 BR Well-used track on left.
2.7 ▲ BL Well-used track on right.

GPS: N36°35.28′ W116°39.65′

▼ 8.0 SO Exiting Death Valley National Park and California into Nevada. State line is unmarked.
2.3 ▲ SO Exiting Nevada into California and Death Valley National Park. State line is unmarked.

GPS: N36°35.24′ W116°39.26′

▼ 8.2 SO Track on left.
2.1 ▲ SO Track on right.

▼ 9.8 BR Track on left. Remain on main graded road.
0.5 ▲ SO Track on right. Remain on main graded road.

▼ 10.3 TL Turn left onto larger graded road and zero trip meter.
0.0 ▲ Continue to the northwest.

GPS: N36°35.01′ W116°36.71′

▼ 0.0		Continue to the east.
11.5 ▲	TR	Turn right onto smaller, roughly graded road. Turn is unmarked, but is opposite an orchard. Turn is hard to spot in this direction. Zero trip meter.
▼ 0.1	TR	Turn right onto paved Saddleback Drive at sign. Remain on paved road.
11.4 ▲	TL	Turn left onto graded dirt Frontier Drive at sign.
		GPS: N36°35.00' W116°36.56'
▼ 1.1	TL	Turn left at T-intersection onto paved Amargosa Farm Road. Remain on this road, ignoring turns to the left and right.
10.4 ▲	TR	Turn right onto paved Saddleback Drive.
		GPS: N36°34.14' W116°36.56'
▼ 11.5		Trail ends at intersection with Nevada 373, 5 miles south of Amargosa Valley. Turn left for Amargosa Valley; turn right for Death Valley Junction.
0.0 ▲		Trail commences on Nevada 373, 5 miles south of Amargosa Valley. Zero trip meter and turn northeast on paved road, marked Farm Road. Remain on this paved road, ignoring turns to the left and right for the next 10.4 miles.
		GPS: N36°34.13' W116°24.78'

DESERT #40

Titus Canyon Trail

Starting Point:	**Nevada 374, 6 miles southwest of Beatty, NV**
Finishing Point:	**North Highway, 15 miles north of the intersection with California 190**
Total Mileage:	**25.4 miles**
Unpaved Mileage:	**25.4 miles**
Driving Time:	**2.5 hours**
Elevation Range:	**200–5,300 feet**
Usually Open:	**October to May**
Best Time to Travel:	**Dry weather**
Difficulty Rating:	**2**
Scenic Rating:	**10**
Remoteness Rating:	**+0**

Special Attractions

- Leadfield ghost town.
- Petroglyphs at Klare Spring.
- Popular, easy trail within Death Valley National Park.

History

In the summer of 1905, Titus Canyon was the scene of an incident that claimed two lives and gave the canyon its name. Edgar Morris Titus, Earle Weller, and their mining companion John Mullan had set out from Rhyolite, Nevada, to prospect in the Panamint Range. Sadly, they never made their destination. Although they were well provisioned and had a burro team in tow, they got lost in unfamiliar territory and missed an expected spring in the Grapevine Mountains. They made camp instead at a tiny seep. Titus continued down the canyon with several burros in an attempt to find a better water supply. He didn't return. His brother-in-law, Weller, went out after him the following morning, taking more burros. He didn't return. Although Titus and Weller found each other, they were too weak to travel farther. Both men died because of lack of water. Mullan was found about two weeks later, still at the seep and almost delirious. Yet he managed to survive the horrific ordeal.

In 1905, an attorney in Rhyolite named Clay Tollman produced worthwhile ores from the Titus Canyon region, but it wasn't until 1926 that Leadfield was established. Buildings left over from this mining boom can still be found along the trail. Although Leadfield sprang up very quickly, it was based on false advertising—there were no fortunes to be made from mining in Titus Canyon. Three hundred people came to Leadfield. A post office opened in 1926 but only lasted six months. Leadfield was listed on the National Register of Historic Places in June 1975.

Titanothere Canyon, close to the Nevada state line, contains many fossils, some dating back nearly 35 million years. In 1933, the fossilized skull of an enormous creature resembling a rhino, a *Titanothere,* was discovered. A replica of the skull is on display at the Furnace Creek Visitor Center. Titanothere Canyon is a popular day hike within the region.

Description

Titus Canyon is one of the most popular dirt roads within Death Valley National Park, and justly so. The meandering dirt road travels down a narrow canyon, passing the ghost town of Leadfield and the Klare Spring petroglyphs.

The trail can only be traveled from east to west, commencing southwest of Beatty in Nevada. The first few miles can be washboardy as the trail travels across the creosote- and sagebrush-covered flats toward the Amargosa Range. Entering Death Valley National Park, the trail first crosses the Von Schmidt Line, the original boundary between California and

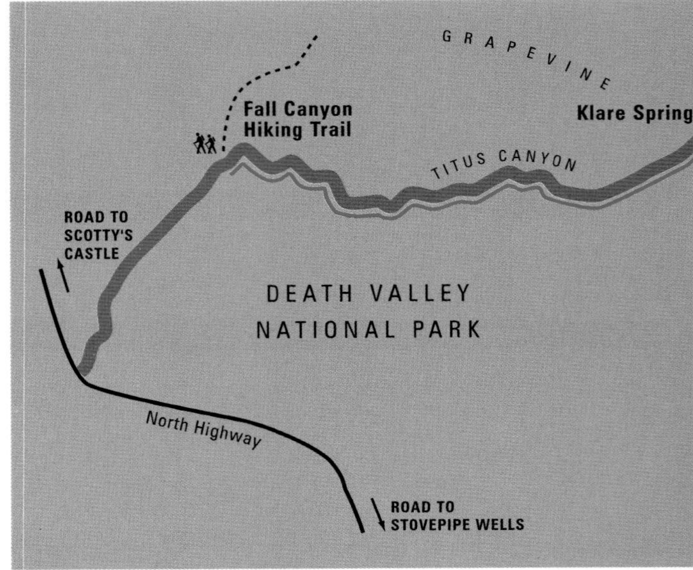

Nevada, and then the present-day state line into California. Neither is marked.

The trail winds into the Grapevine Mountains toward the aptly named Red Pass. The undulating trail, red-colored hills, and spectacular geology make this a trail best driven on a sunny day. On cloudy days, the colors of the rocks are muted.

The trail passes the ghost town of Leadfield, where there are several old cabins and remains, before entering the tight, narrow Titus Canyon. This canyon is one of the most spectacular within the Death Valley area, with high, tight canyon walls that have been smoothed by thousands of years of floodwaters. The trail surface is smooth and gravelly and is easygoing for the most part.

The lower end of the Titus Canyon is tight with rock smoothed by flood waters

Palm trees at the oasis of Klare Spring provide a splash of green within the red and gray canyon. Human visitors have been coming to the spring for many years, as is evidenced by the petroglyphs on a large gray boulder alongside the spring. The water source is important to the bighorn sheep that frequent the canyon. They can often be seen high on the rocky cliffs around the spring.

Past the spring, the trail continues in the wash, before opening out abruptly into Death Valley. The final 2 miles of the trail are suitable for two-way traffic.

Titus Canyon floods easily, so it may be closed for a few days after rain or snow. It is closed to vehicular traffic during the hot summer months. Check with the park service for the latest road conditions.

Current Road Information

Death Valley National Park
PO Box 579
Death Valley, CA 92328-0579
(760) 786-2331

Bureau of Land Management
Bishop Field Office
785 North Main Street, Suite E
Bishop, CA 93514
(760) 872-4881

Map References

BLM Beatty, Saline Valley
USGS 1:24,000 Gold Center, Daylight Pass, Thimble Peak, Fall Canyon
1:100,000 Beatty, Saline Valley
Maptech CD-ROM: Kings Canyon/Death Valley; Las Vegas/Henderson/Laughlin
Nevada Atlas & Gazatteer, p. 64
Southern & Central California Atlas & Gazetteer, pp. 29, 30
California Road & Recreation Atlas, p. 81
Trails Illustrated, Death Valley National Park (221)
Other: Free NPS Death Valley map

Route Directions

▼ 0.0		From Nevada 374, 6 miles southwest of Beatty, NV, zero trip meter and turn west on the graded dirt road, sign-posted to Titus Canyon.
		GPS: N36°51.56′ W116°50.70′
▼ 0.9	SO	Track on left and track on right.
		GPS: N36°51.45′ W116°51.67′
▼ 1.8	SO	Cattle guard and closure gate. Entering Death Valley National Park. Zero trip meter.
		GPS: N36°51.31′ W116°52.68′
▼ 0.0		Continue to the southwest.
▼ 4.1	SO	Enter line of wash. Look back to see Bare Mountain.

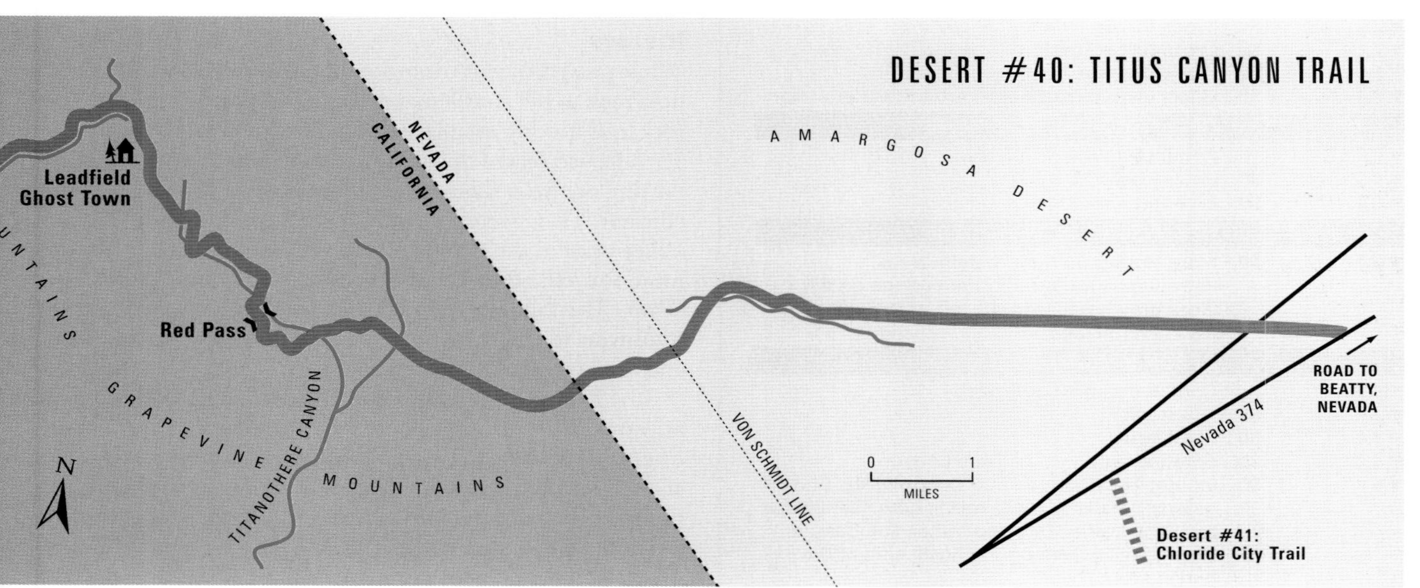

Looking west from Red Pass over the site of Leadfield

▼ 5.3	SO	Exit line of the wash and cross the old Von Schmidt state line of 1873.
		GPS: N36°50.20' W116°57.58'
▼ 5.5	SO	Re-enter line of wash.
▼ 5.9	SO	Entering California—no sign.
		GPS: N36°49.69' W116°58.47'
▼ 7.2	SO	Exit line of wash.
▼ 7.3	SO	Saddle. Trail starts to descend.
▼ 8.4	SO	Cross through wash.
▼ 8.6	SO	Cross through wash.
▼ 8.8	SO	Cross through wash.
		GPS: N36°49.68' W117°01.27'
▼ 8.9	SO	Cross over wash.
		GPS: N36°49.62' W117°01.33'
▼ 10.1	SO	Red Pass. Trail now descends toward Titus Canyon. Zero trip meter in the cutting of the pass.
		GPS: N36°49.72' W117°01.89'
▼ 0.0		Continue to the west.
▼ 0.7	SO	Cross through wash.
▼ 1.2	SO	Cross through wash.
▼ 1.7	SO	Mine adit on far side of canyon.
		GPS: N36°50.20' W117°02.80'
▼ 2.2	SO	Pull-in on left and mine on left.
▼ 2.6	SO	Cross through wash.
▼ 2.7	SO	Cross through wash.
▼ 2.9	SO	Cross through wash.
▼ 3.0	SO	Ghost town of Leadfield. Zero trip meter at sign.
		GPS: N36°50.90' W117°03.50'
▼ 0.0		Continue to the northwest.
▼ 0.3	SO	Enter wash.
▼ 0.7	SO	Entering Titus Canyon.
		GPS: N36°51.19' W117°03.96'
▼ 2.4	SO	Klare Spring on right at palm trees. Petroglyphs are around the springs on the large gray boulder to the left of the sign. Zero trip meter at sign.
		GPS: N36°50.47' W117°05.38'
▼ 0.0		Continue to the southwest.
▼ 1.2	SO	Exit wash.
▼ 1.4	SO	Enter wash.
▼ 4.0	SO	Entering tight part of Titus Canyon.
▼ 5.6	SO	Exiting Titus Canyon into Death Valley. Closure gate and parking area. Trail is now suitable for two-way traffic. Zero trip meter. Fall Canyon Hiking Trail leaves on the north side of the parking lot.
		GPS: N36°49.25' W117°10.41'
▼ 0.0		Continue to the southwest.
▼ 2.5		Closure gate; then trail ends at T-intersection with North Highway. Turn right for Scotty's Castle; turn left for Stovepipe Wells.
		GPS: N36°47.27' W117°11.44'

DESERT #41

Chloride City Trail

Starting Point:	**Daylight Pass Road, 10 miles northeast of intersection with California 190**
Finishing Point:	**Nevada 374 at the boundary of Death Valley National Park, 9.5 miles southwest of Beatty, NV**
Total Mileage:	**15.4 miles, plus 2.4-mile spur to Chloride Cliff**
Unpaved Mileage:	**15.4 miles, plus 2.4-mile spur**
Driving Time:	**1.5 hours**
Elevation Range:	**3,300–5,200 feet**
Usually Open:	**Year-round**
Best Time to Travel:	**October to May**
Difficulty Rating:	**3**
Scenic Rating:	**10**
Remoteness Rating:	**+1**

Special Attractions

- Unparalleled view from Chloride Cliff overlooking Death Valley and the Amargosa and Panamint Ranges.
- Historic site of Chloride City.
- Quiet trail through Death Valley National Park and the Amargosa Desert.

History

While prospecting in the region in 1871, A. J. Franklin picked up a rock to kill a rattlesnake. He found silver ore beneath the rock and quickly established a mine at the site. However, by 1873 he had ceased operations, realizing that the cost of transporting ore from this remote location made the operation inefficient. There were no roads to the eastern section of Death Valley prior to the development of the Chloride Cliff Mine. A route was established from Barstow to the mine via Wingate Wash. This allowed Death Valley to be accessed from the southwest for the first time. In time, the road was improved and used by borax mule trains.

In 1905, one year after Franklin's death and with the mine now owned by his son George, the success of the nearby Bullfrog strike spilled over to Chloride City. Water for the mines and its workers, a scarcity in these parts, was carted and later pumped from Keane Spring, just a few miles to the north in the Funeral Mountains.

Activity halted once again when the 1906 earthquake rat-

The windy trail is rough in places

tled San Francisco. Investors disappeared and life around Chloride City was quiet. The mines and cabins lay abandoned for the next few years. George sold the mine to a Pittsburgh syndicate. A resurgence in 1909 saw another wave of mining activity, which came and went, finally halting by 1940.

There are few structural remains in Chloride City today because most buildings were flimsy, temporary structures. A stamp mill and a half dozen wooden structures were built in the region; the rest of the miners were housed in tents.

Keane Wonder Mine, situated southwest of the spectacular Chloride Cliff, was an important mine in this region. Founded by an Irishman named Jack Keane and his partner Domingo Etcharren in 1904, the mine sold for more than $50,000, quite a sum of money at the time. It went on to produce almost $1 million. The new owners constructed a monumental 4,700-foot-long aerial tramway between the mine and mill.

Description

The undulating trail to Chloride City sees little vehicle traffic. Located on the eastern edge of Death Valley National Park, the well-formed trail travels between California and Nevada, passing through the northern end of the Funeral Mountains (part of the Amargosa Range).

The trail is rough in places, enough so that high-clearance 4WD is advised. There are few side trails, but one worthwhile spur travels a short distance down a narrow canyon to a deep pour-off in the wash. A hiking trail follows an old pack trail farther down the canyon. It heads past Monarch Spring on its way to Death Valley.

Climbing into the Grapevine Mountains

The ghost town of Chloride City and its associated mining area is a short distance from the main trail. The spur leads past the remains of the town and finishes on top of Chloride Cliff, arguably the best overlook in Death Valley. The final 0.1 miles of the spur is 4-rated. If you don't wish to tackle the final steep pinch, leave your vehicle at the bottom and hike the remaining distance. The view from the elevated point is stupendous. Death Valley and the Amargosa Range are spread out below you, and the Panamint Range borders the valley on the west side. This viewpoint alone makes this trail worthwhile.

There is a network of short trails to explore around Chloride City; many will take you past mines and old cabins.

Back on the main trail, the standard improves slightly, becoming smoother and easier going as it travels into Nevada. The trail comes to an end on Nevada 374 at the boundary of Death Valley National Park.

Current Road Information

Death Valley National Park
PO Box 579
Death Valley, CA 92328-0579
(760) 786-2331

Map References

BLM Beatty
USGS 1:24,000 Daylight Pass, Chloride City, East of Chloride City, Gold Center
1:100,000 Beatty
Maptech CD-ROM: Kings Canyon/Death Valley
Nevada Atlas & Gazatteer, p. 64
Southern & Central California Atlas & Gazetteer, p. 30
California Road & Recreation Atlas, pp. 81, 88
Trails Illustrated, Death Valley National Park (221)
Other: Free NPS Death Valley map

Route Directions

▼ 0.0		From Daylight Pass Road in California, 10 miles northeast of intersection with California 190, zero trip meter and turn northeast on unmarked, formed dirt trail. There is no signpost at the intersection but the road is marked as recommended for high-clearance 4x4. Trail is traveling in the wash.
2.1 ▲		Trail ends on Daylight Pass Road in California, which becomes Nevada 374. Turn left for Stovepipe Wells; turn right for Beatty, NV.
		GPS: N36°45.03' W116°56.15'
▼ 1.0	SO	Exit wash.
1.1 ▲	SO	Enter wash.
▼ 1.5	SO	Enter line of wash.
0.6 ▲	SO	Exit line of wash.
▼ 2.1	TL	Track on right travels 0.6 miles down a tight canyon to a large pour-off before turning into a hiking trail to Monarch Spring and Death Valley. Zero trip meter.
0.0 ▲		Continue to the north up wash.
		GPS: N36°44.20' W116°54.71'

View over Death Valley from Chloride Cliff

▼ 0.0 Continue to the east up wash.
2.9 ▲ TR Track on left travels 0.6 miles down a tight canyon to a large pour-off before turning into a hiking trail to Monarch Spring and Death Valley. Zero trip meter.

▼ 0.3 SO Tank on left. Exit line of wash.
2.6 ▲ SO Enter line of wash. Tank on right.

GPS: N36°44.29' W116°54.37'

▼ 1.0 SO Cross through wash.
1.9 ▲ SO Cross through wash.

▼ 1.3 SO Cross through wash.
1.6 ▲ SO Cross through wash.

▼ 1.6 SO Cross through wash.
1.3 ▲ SO Cross through wash.

▼ 2.2 BL Bear left up wash.
0.7 ▲ BR Bear right out of wash.

GPS: N36°43.08' W116°53.74'

▼ 2.4 SO Track on right.
0.5 ▲ SO Track on left.

GPS: N36°43.04' W116°53.59'

▼ 2.8 SO Exit line of wash.
0.1 ▲ SO Enter line of wash.

▼ 2.9 BL Track on right at Mine Hazard sign is spur to Chloride City and Chloride Cliff. Zero trip meter.
0.0 ▲ Continue to the west.

GPS: N36°43.06' W116°53.06'

Spur to Chloride Cliff

▼ 0.0 Proceed southwest on formed trail at Mine Hazard sign.
▼ 1.0 TL T-intersection. Site of Chloride City. Zero trip meter.

GPS: N36°42.42' W116°53.07'

▼ 0.0 Continue to the east.
▼ 0.3 SO Track on right, track on left, and second track on right.
▼ 0.4 SO Track on right to cabin and mine.
▼ 0.5 SO Second entrance to cabin and mine on right.
▼ 0.8 TL Track ahead, two tracks on right, and track on left. Turn first left.

GPS: N36°41.97' W116°52.68'

▼ 1.1 SO Track on right.
▼ 1.2 SO Track straight ahead and track on left; then bear left at second track on left.

GPS: N36°41.82' W116°52.68'

▼ 1.3 SO Adit and tailings on right.
▼ 1.4 UT Spur ends at Chloride Cliff-unparalleled viewpoint over the Amargosa Range, Death Valley, and the Panamint Range.

GPS: N36°41.69' W116°52.75'

Continuation of Main Trail

▼ 0.0 Continue to the east.
3.9 ▲ BR Track on left at Mine Hazard sign is spur to Chloride City and Chloride Cliff. Zero trip meter.

GPS: N36°43.06' W116°53.06'

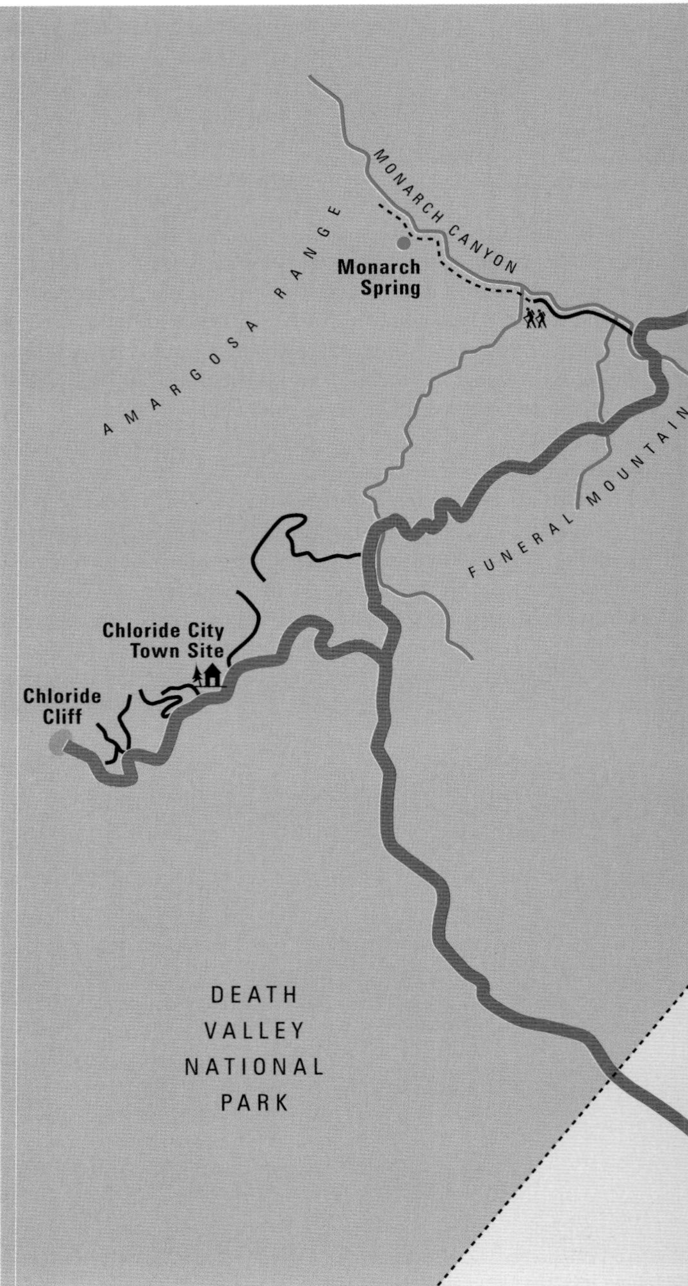

▼ 2.4	SO	Entering Nevada and leaving Death Valley National Park (no signs).
1.5 ▲	SO	Entering California and Death Valley National Park. Only sign is a "High Clearance 4x4 Recommended" sign.
		GPS: N36°43.82' W116°50.94'
▼ 2.9	SO	Track on right.
1.0 ▲	SO	Track on left.
▼ 3.9	BL	Trail forks. Well-used track on right. Zero trip meter.
0.0 ▲		Continue to the south.
		GPS: N36°44.82' W116°49.83'
▼ 0.0		Continue to the northwest. There are many small wash crossings for the next 6.5 miles.
6.5 ▲	BR	Well-used track on left. Zero trip meter.
▼ 1.1	SO	Cross through wash. Track on left up wash.
5.4 ▲	SO	Cross through wash. Track on right up wash.
▼ 1.5	SO	Faint track on left.
5.0 ▲	SO	Faint track on right.
▼ 6.5		Trail ends on Nevada 374 at the boundary of Death Valley National Park at the "Welcome to Nevada" sign. Trail is unmarked. Turn right for Beatty, NV; turn left for Death Valley.
0.0 ▲		Trail commences on Nevada 374, 9.5 miles southwest of Beatty, NV, on the boundary of Death Valley National Park at the "Welcome to Nevada" sign. Turn is unmarked. Zero trip meter and turn southeast on formed dirt trail across the bajada. There are many small wash crossings for the first 6.5 miles.
		GPS: N36°49.94' W116°52.76'

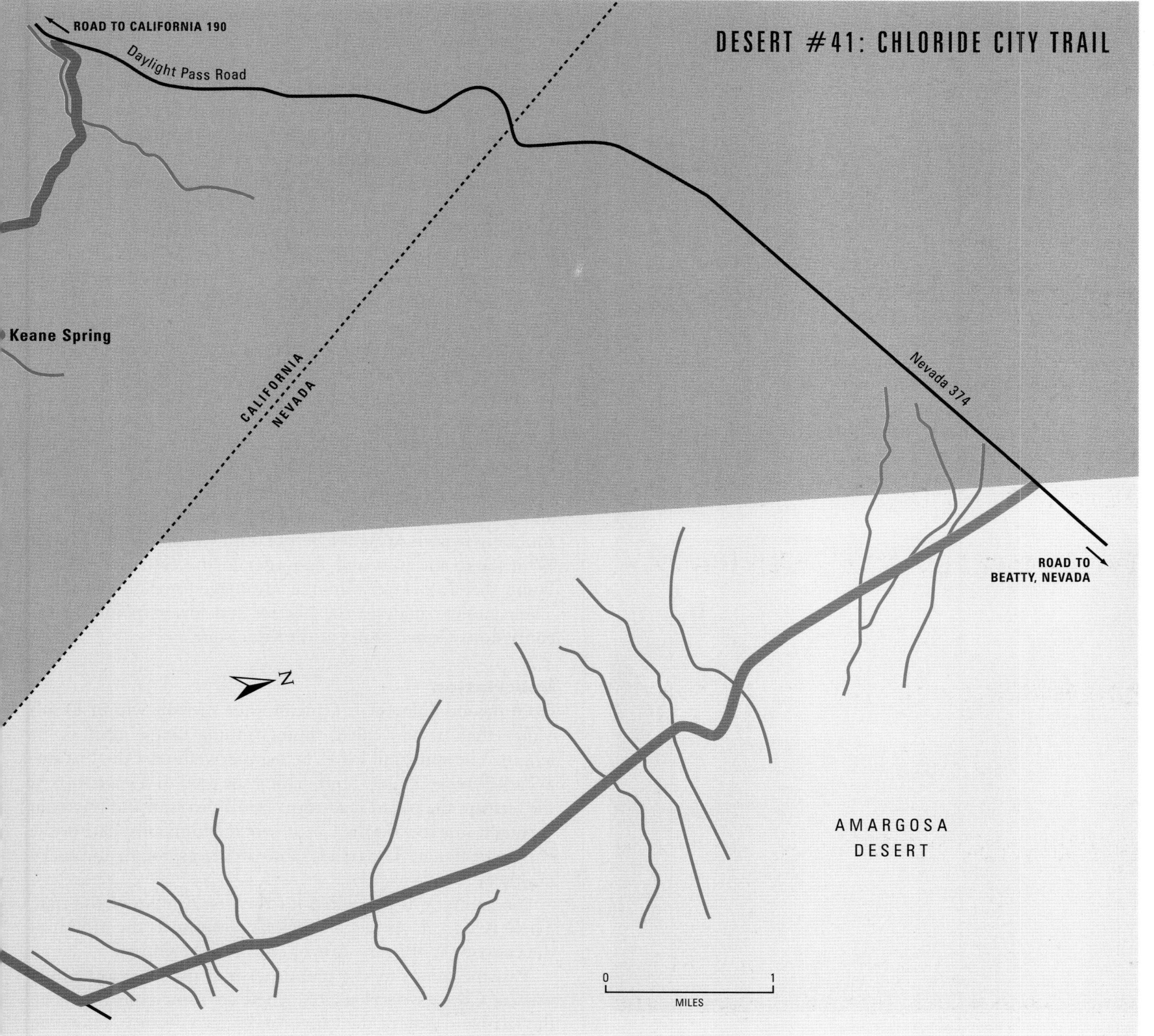

Cottonwood Canyon Trail

Starting Point:	**California 190 at Stovepipe Wells**
Finishing Point:	**Wilderness boundary in Cottonwood Canyon**
Total Mileage:	**17.4 miles (one-way)**
Unpaved Mileage:	**16.6 miles**
Driving Time:	**2 hours (one-way)**
Elevation Range:	**0–2,500 feet**
Usually Open:	**Year-round**
Best Time to Travel:	**October to May**
Difficulty Rating:	**3**
Scenic Rating:	**8**
Remoteness Rating:	**+0**

Special Attractions

- Remote desert canyon within Death Valley National Park.
- Petroglyphs in Marble Canyon.

History

Native American occupancy of Cottonwood Canyon is evidenced by the rock art inscribed at the lower entrance to this peaceful canyon. The upper canyon provided cool relief from the sweltering summer heat of the desert floor. The cottonwood trees that grow here, after which the canyon is named, are sometimes felled by flash flood waters.

The name at the starting point of this trail, Stovepipe Wells, comes from the original well that was located in the sand dune area of Death Valley. This water source was greatly valued by early inhabitants and travelers alike. Because shifting sands made finding the water difficult at times, a length of stovepipe was placed upright to mark the well. With time, the well became known as "stovepipe well." As the nearby mining town of Skidoo developed in late 1906, the need for a stage line increased. Stovepipe Wells became a stage stop before the stagecoach tackled the long climb to Skidoo. A tent saloon, lodging house, and store all operated during this period.

Cottonwood Canyon opens out to this beautiful vista

In 1925, Herman Eichbaum and his wife realized that Death Valley might have a lot to offer as a backcountry vacation destination. They set about constructing a toll road from the base of Darwin Wash, across the wide depression of Panamint Valley, over Towne Pass in the Panamint Range, and down to the proposed location of their Death Valley resort. By 1926, they opened their resort, named Bungalow City, near Stovepipe Wells. Later the name Stovepipe Wells was transposed to their resort. Initially, it consisted of 20 tent platforms, a restaurant, tennis courts, and even a swimming pool. The first airstrip was built so visitors could reach the desert resort without enduring the long rough roads into the region.

The Eichbaums soon found themselves competing with the revamped Furnace Creek Ranch. Both properties discovered their visitors were fascinated by the extremes of Death Valley. The Furnace Creek owners commissioned an access road to an excellent viewpoint. The outcome was Dantes View, set in the Black Mountains to the south of the Furnace Creek resort of the 1920s.

The Eichbaums counteracted in the winter of 1929 by constructing a road past Harrisburg to the crest of the Panamint Range, calling the spot Grand View. This viewpoint later became known as Aguereberry Point after a nearby prospector. Pierre "Pete" Aguereberry, from the Basque region, had been a shepherd until he was struck by gold fever at Rhyolite and Goldfield. From 1905 until his death in 1945, Pete and his friend Shorty Harris worked several claims in the surrounding region. At Aguereberry Point, visitors can see Mount Whitney to the west and Badwater to the east. Aguereberry Point, therefore, held a unique advantage for the Eichbaums. Their guests could see the highest and lowest points in the contiguous United States at the same time.

Description

Cottonwood Canyon is a picturesque canyon within Death Valley that has a vehicle route running along most of its length. The spur trail leaves Stovepipe Wells past the National Park Service campground, taking the road to the airstrip. At the airstrip, the paved road turns into a dirt trail and travels in a straight line toward the Cottonwood Mountains, part of the Panamint Range. The trail is sandy in places, rough and rocky in others.

No camping is permitted for the first 8 miles of the trail. There is a good, although exposed, campsite at the mouth of the canyon. Within the canyon, options are limited.

Past the campsite, the trail drops into the loose and sandy wash of Cottonwood Canyon. There are some petroglyphs on the left-hand wall of the canyon near the entrance. However,

Looking out from the natural cavern carved in the sediment of Cottonwood Canyon

the majority of rock art to be found along this trail is within Marble Canyon, an offshoot of the main trail.

Past an initial narrow section, the trail opens out to travel up the valley for a couple of miles before re-entering canyon narrows. A surprisingly large wind- and water-eroded cave is encountered on the eastern side of the canyon; camping is not advised in such a large wash setting. The trail finishes at the wilderness boundary where an indistinct hiking trail ultimately connects north to Marble Canyon, south to Lemoigne Canyon, and west to the old Goldbelt mining camp.

Current Road Information

Death Valley National Park
PO Box 579
Death Valley, CA 92328-0579
(760) 786-2331

Map References

BLM Saline Valley
USGS 1:24,000 Stovepipe Wells, East of Sand Flat, Cottonwood Canyon
1:100,000 Saline Valley
Maptech CD-ROM: Kings Canyon/Death Valley
Southern & Central California Atlas & Gazetteer, p. 29
California Road & Recreation Atlas, p. 88
Trails Illustrated, Death Valley National Park (221)
Other: Free NPS Death Valley map

Route Directions

▼ 0.0		At Stovepipe Wells on California 190, immediately west of the general store, zero trip meter and turn northwest into the entrance to the campground. Immediately bear left, leaving the campground on your right, and follow the paved road toward the airstrip.
		GPS: N36°36.38' W117°08.77'
▼ 0.8	BR	Bear right onto graded dirt trail. Airstrip is on the left. No vehicle entry into the airstrip.
		GPS: N36°36.42' W117°09.26'
▼ 8.4	BL	Campsite on right. Zero trip meter at sign.
		GPS: N36°38.56' W117°16.17'
▼ 0.0		Drop down and enter Cottonwood Canyon Wash, bearing northwest up wash.
▼ 0.4	SO	Petroglyphs on rock wall on left. Enter Cottonwood Canyon.
		GPS: N36°38.68' W117°16.63'
▼ 1.0	SO	Enter canyon narrows.
▼ 2.1	BL	Marble Canyon on right. Bear left at old signpost, remaining in Cottonwood Canyon, and zero trip meter.
		GPS: N36°37.92' W117°17.64'
▼ 0.0		Continue to the southwest.
▼ 6.9		Trail ends at wilderness boundary.
		GPS: N36°33.40' W117°20.10'

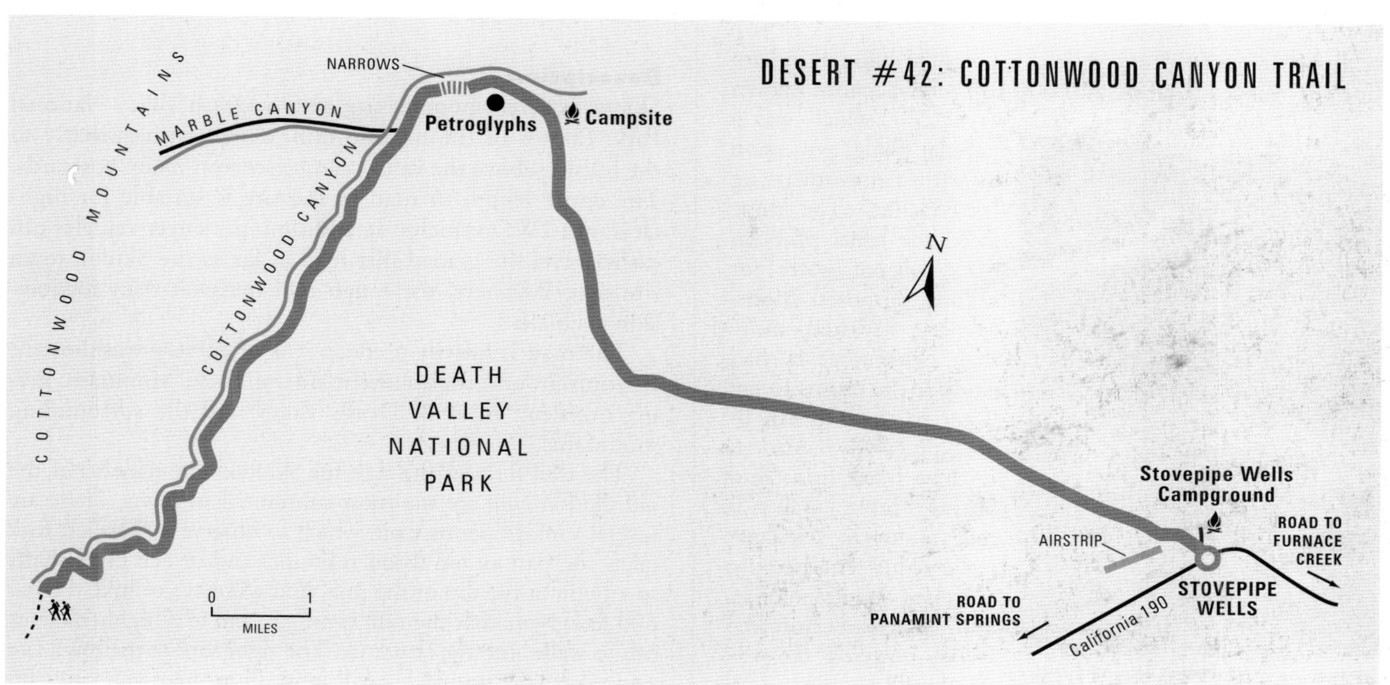

DESERT #43

Skidoo Road

Starting Point:	**Wildrose Road, 9 miles southeast of California 190**
Finishing Point:	**Skidoo**
Total Mileage:	**8.7 miles, plus 0.9-mile spur**
Unpaved Mileage:	**8.7 miles, plus 0.9-mile spur**
Driving Time:	**1 hour**
Elevation Range:	**4,900–5,900 feet**
Usually Open:	**Year-round**
Best Time to Travel:	**October to May**
Difficulty Rating:	**2**
Scenic Rating:	**9**
Remoteness Rating:	**+0**

Special Attractions

- Historic site of Skidoo and Skidoo Mill.
- Landscape and historic photography.

History

In 1905, prospectors Pete Aguereberry and Shorty Harris made a gold discovery at a location near Skidoo, which Shorty named Harrisburg. Very soon, other prospectors were drawn into the region. Two such hopefuls, John "One-eye" Thompson and John Ramsey, were prepared to join the strike at Harrisburg when they chanced upon some promising colored ledges to the north. The duo filed claims in 1906 that covered a broad region near their find, and they tried to keep things quiet. Word leaked out, though, and eventually reached the town of Rhyolite, Nevada.

Bob Montgomery recognized a potential winner and reportedly paid a total of $60,000 for what became known as Skidoo, which was a popular slang expression of the time meaning "skeedaddle." The mine faced the usual problem of a lack of water for milling purposes. Montgomery invested more than twice what he had paid for the claims to get water to the site. An 8-inch pipe was hauled in to draw water from Bird Spring, more than 20 miles away on Telescope Peak. This engineering feat was completed in 1907, and water from the spring powered the 15-stamp mill.

The easygoing road passes around Tucki Mountain

By this time, Skidoo had attracted more than 400 inhabitants. Several stores opened and restaurants, saloons, and associated businesses soon followed. Permanent commercial buildings were erected and a telephone line and stagecoach connected the new town to Rhyolite, the focal mining center of the region.

Skidoo was noted for, and often avoided because of, its peaceful nature. The town was considered to be boring. Interestingly enough, it was also the site of the only known hanging in the Death Valley region. In April 1908, a drunken Joe L. "Hootch" Simpson gunned down a local man named Jim Arnold. The townspeople wasted no time in retaliating, and Hootch Simpson was strung up on a telephone pole.

Skidoo's old stamp mill sits at the head of a tight canyon

Skidoo endured highs and lows and remained active for more than 10 years. At its peak, almost 700 people lived here. But like all such mining towns, once the mine ceased operation the town's lifeline ended and the townsfolk moved away. Skidoo was just about the last real gold town in Death Valley. Many found it hard to just walk away from their town. Because it was too far to haul them away to erect elsewhere, many of the buildings remained. One prospector known as Old Tom Adams remained until 1922.

Skidoo was listed on the National Register of Historic Places in April 1974.

Description

Skidoo is a very popular site within Death Valley National Park. Photos of the historic mill, clinging precariously to the hillside above the valley, can be seen on many postcards. The entire length of road to the site is suitable for high-clearance 2WD vehicles. In addition, passenger vehicles can easily travel the graded dirt road as far as the Skidoo town site sign. Past here, the rough trail makes it risky for low-slung vehicles.

The road is heavily used, so it is often very washboardy. It winds around the southern side of Tucki Mountain, giving excellent views of Death Valley and the surrounding mountains.

The trail forks at the sign for Skidoo. The remains of the old Skidoo Mill are the most substantial in town. There are several vantage points from which to observe it. The left fork takes you past an old wooden hopper and several mine shafts to a point at the top of the mill. You will have to hike the last 600 feet. Note that the mill is unsafe, and it is highly dangerous to walk onto the structure. The right fork at the town site sign takes you around a small loop. From here you can gain excellent views of the mill from across the canyon, or you can hike to the base of it. The loop continues around the hilltop, giving excellent views of the Panamint Range, before returning to its starting point. The loop is 2-rated in the direction mapped. If driven in reverse it is 3-rated and requires 4WD to ascend the hill.

The entire area is for day use only. Camping is prohibited, and trailers or vehicles longer than 25 feet are not permitted along the road. Skidoo Road is suitable for mountain bikes as well as vehicles.

Current Road Information

Death Valley National Park
PO Box 579
Death Valley, CA 92328-0579
(760) 786-2331

Map References

BLM Darwin Hills
USGS 1:24,000 Emigrant Canyon, Tucki Wash
1:100,000 Darwin Hills
Maptech CD-ROM: Kings Canyon/Death Valley
Southern & Central California Atlas & Gazetteer, p. 41
California Road & Recreation Atlas, p. 88
Trails Illustrated, Death Valley National Park (221)
Other: Free NPS Death Valley map

Route Directions

▼ 0.0	From Wildrose Road, 9 miles southeast of California 190, zero trip meter and turn east on graded dirt road at the sign for Skidoo. The trail initially crosses Harrisburg Flats.
	GPS: N36°23.15' W117°09.00'

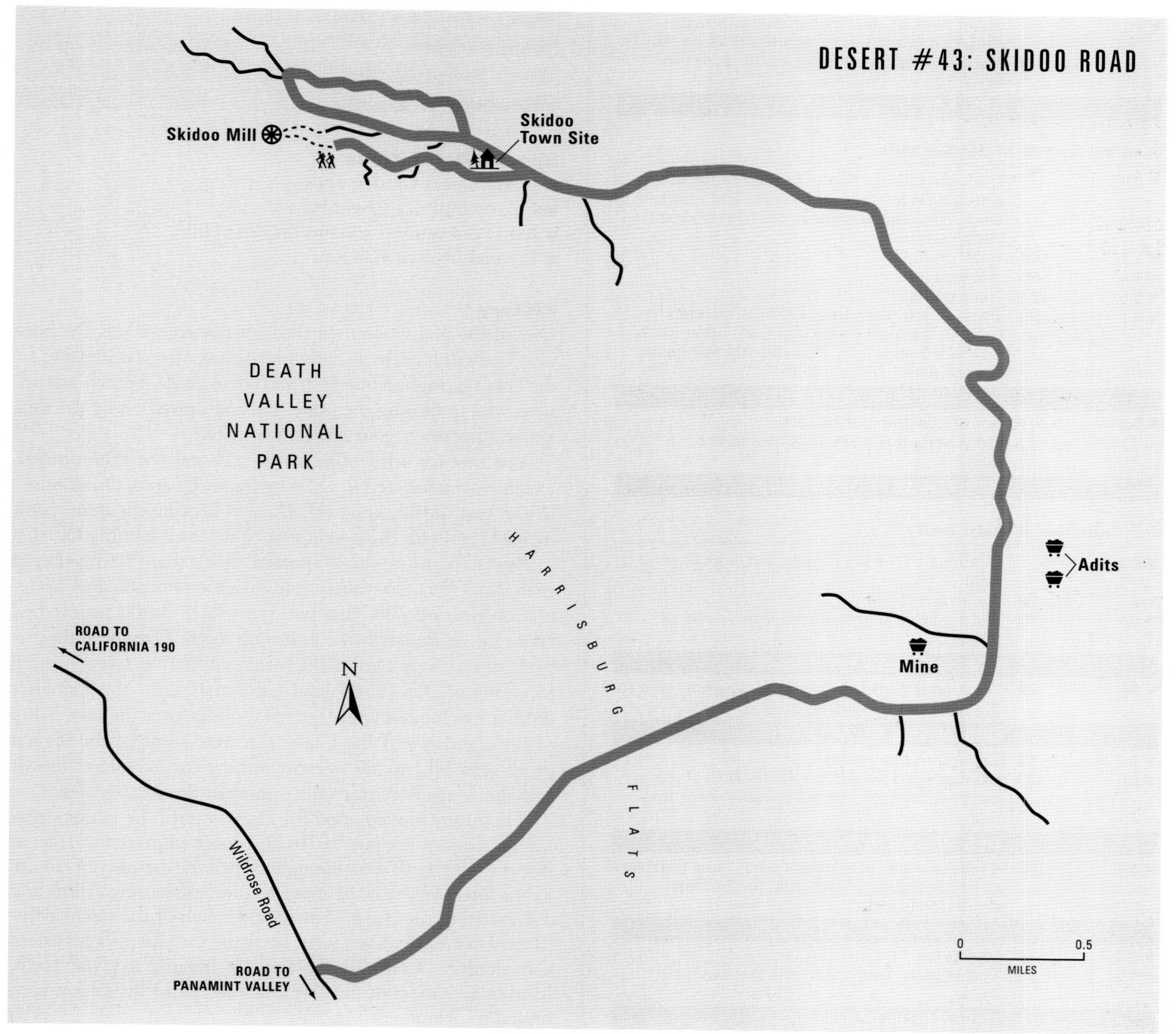

▼ 2.7	SO	Track on left passes mine shaft on its way to a cabin; then track on right to mine. Zero trip meter at track on right.
		GPS: N36°24.18' W117°06.53'
▼ 0.0		Continue to the east.
▼ 0.2	SO	Track on right.
		GPS: N36°24.18' W117°06.30'
▼ 0.5	SO	Track on left to mines and old cabin.
		GPS: N36°24.39' W117°06.15'
▼ 0.9	SO	Timber-lined adits in hillside on left.
		GPS: N36°24.73' W117°06.11'
▼ 1.4	SO	Faint track on right.
▼ 1.9	SO	Pull-in on right for a view over Death Valley.
▼ 3.2	SO	Track on right.
▼ 3.7	SO	Two tracks on left.
▼ 3.8	SO	Track on left.
		GPS: N36°26.00' W117°07.97'
▼ 4.1	SO	Small track on left; then continue straight ahead on graded road. Graded road on left is spur to the top of Skidoo Mill. Zero trip meter.
		GPS: N36°26.07' W117°08.22'

Spur to the Top of Skidoo Mill

▼ 0.0		From the intersection of graded roads at the sign for Skidoo, zero trip meter and proceed west. This spur is suitable for high-clearance 2WD vehicles.
▼ 0.1	SO	Track on right.
▼ 0.4	SO	Track on left.
▼ 0.5	SO	Track on left.
▼ 0.7	BL	Track on left; then bear left past wooden hopper. Track on right. There are other tracks on the left and right. Pass directly alongside the hopper.
		GPS: N36°26.13' W117°08.88'
▼ 0.9	UT	Spur ends at a locked gate. From here, it is a 600-foot hike to the mill.
		GPS: N36°26.16' W117°09.10'

Continuation of Main Trail

▼ 0.0		Continue to the northwest. Small track on right.
▼ 0.2	SO	Track on left.
▼ 0.3	SO	Track on left; then track on right is end of loop.
		GPS: N36°26.18' W117°08.48'
▼ 0.5	BR	Track on left goes to a gate and a short hike to the base of the mill.
		GPS: N36°26.19' W117°08.76'
▼ 0.7	SO	Cross through wash.
▼ 0.9	SO	Skidoo Mill is visible on the far side of the canyon. Track on left to viewpoint over the mill.
		GPS: N36°26.29' W117°09.15'
▼ 1.0	TR	4-way intersection. Track on left goes 0.8 miles to more diggings. Turn right to continue around the loop.
		GPS: N36°26.39' W117°09.25'
▼ 1.4	SO	Viewpoint.
▼ 1.9		End of loop. Turn left to exit the way you came.
		GPS: N36°26.18' W117°08.48'

DESERT #44

Darwin Falls Trail

Starting Point:	**Main Street in Darwin**
Finishing Point:	**California 190, 1 mile west of Panamint Springs**
Total Mileage:	**12.1 miles, plus 1.2-mile spur to China Garden Spring**
Unpaved Mileage:	**12 miles, plus 1.2-mile spur**
Driving Time:	**1.5 hours**
Elevation Range:	**2,100–5,000 feet**
Usually Open:	**Year-round**
Best Time to Travel:	**October to June**
Difficulty Rating:	**3**
Scenic Rating:	**9**
Remoteness Rating:	**+0**

Special Attractions

- Pretty China Garden Spring.
- Hiking trail to Darwin Falls.
- Many old mining remains on Zinc Hill.
- Rugged Darwin Canyon.

History

One of the first white men through this region was Dr. Erasmus Darwin French, an early prospector who was hunting for the Lost Gunsight Mine with an Indian guide. French was unsuccessful in finding the mine. He had moved on by the time Darwin became a gold fever town in 1874.

The first recorded mine in the area was the Promontoria, which was established in 1874 by Rafael Cuervo. Other mines in the area quickly took off. Darwin became the main commercial center for the developing New Cosco Mining District.

By 1875 the town supported more than 70 businesses with 2 smelters, 20 mines, many wooden houses, and a population nearing 700. Just two years later, 3,000 people had taken up residency in the booming town. Darwin and nearby Lookout were two of the most productive desert mining locations of the 1870s. The Christmas Gift, the Defiance (which was named after legal wranglings over the ownership of the claims), and the Lucky Jim were some of the biggest producers. Like many western mining towns, saloon brawls and shootings were not uncommon in these early years.

The future looked good for Darwin until the nation's economic woes of the late 1870s and more impressive strikes at Bodie to the north were enough to spell the demise of Darwin. Labor forces were on the move to more promising claims and a devastating fire in 1879 destroyed much of the town's commercial center. As has always been the case for this persistent community, Darwin never actually became a ghost town. Mining activity continued at a low level and the saloon continued to operate.

Old commercial building in Darwin

Changing market needs brought a resurgence to Darwin around 1906, with copper now a valued mineral. Earlier tailings that contained copper-bearing ore were greatly valued. By the late 1910s, silver was the sought-after commodity. The Darwin region was a notable producer, putting the town back on the map. In fact, most metallic minerals were being found in the region during the 1920s. Silver, lead, copper, gold, and tungsten were all in production. By the 1930s, more than $3 million worth of ore had been extracted from the region. Mining and milling activities continued in varying degrees until the 1950s. Though many mining structures have been torn down over the decades, several latter-day structures have survived. These remains provide a slight insight into a town driven mainly by mining prospectors.

Darwin Falls Trail follows a section of the old toll road, officially known as Eichbaum Toll Road, which was developed in 1925 by the Eichbaums as the first vehicle route into Panamint Valley and Death Valley from the west. The influx of visitors to their resort near Stovepipe Wells brought a lot of auto traffic through Darwin, which was developing quite a name for its fine Panamint Shoshone basketry.

In 1937, Darwin was bypassed by the construction of California 190 to the north. The passing tourist trade was gone. Darwin seemed like a dead end street to Death Valley visitors; it was no longer the Gateway to Death Valley. Advertisements put out by the Death Valley Hotel Company in 1938 renamed Lone Pine as the new "Gateway." Darwin was left off their mileage charts. These changes may have played a part in the economic demise of the town, yet they may also have been the town's savior. Darwin persists with its own ever-evolving character and characters.

Darwin Falls is fed by an underground spring that surfaces at the canyon floor. Over the centuries, the spring and the falls have been enjoyed by natives and travelers alike. During Darwin's early mining days in the 1870s, this spring was an asset to one settler who established vegetable gardens downstream from the falls. He had an excellent market for his produce with the booming population of nearby Darwin.

Description

The small town of Darwin still has a number of year-round residents, but it is a lot smaller now than it was at the height of its mining boom. As you enter the town from California 190, the old Ophir Mine and its extensive buildings are on the left, perched on the flank of Ophir Mountain. This mine is privately owned and posted, but a good view can be obtained from the main road. It has been renamed the Darwin Mine by the owners.

There are many old buildings in Darwin that are worth a look—the old dance hall, the post office, and many buildings constructed of corrugated iron, a common construction material in mining camps throughout the West.

The trail starts at the intersection in the center of Darwin and heads east toward the Darwin Hills. There are many tracks on the left and right, many of which lead to the remains of what were once active mines. The road is roughly graded as it snakes through the Darwin Hills to drop into the loose and gravelly Darwin Canyon wash. Darwin Canyon is not deep, but its striated layers of rock and twisting path make it an interesting drive.

A worthwhile spur trail leads 1.2 miles to China Garden Spring. This little oasis is sheltered under large cottonwoods. The clear waters of the spring contain large numbers of introduced goldfish. The spring makes an excellent spot for a picnic. The remains of a mine and cabin are nearby. The spur trail ends at the wilderness boundary. A 20-minute hike along the canyon floor takes you to Darwin Falls and a second lush spring. Darwin Falls is easiest approached from the northern end of the canyon, farther along the main trail.

The main trail leaves the canyon to wind around the western side of Zinc Hill where more mining remains dot the hillside. The trail around Zinc Hill is the roughest part, with some loose, rocky sections.

The main hiking access to Darwin Falls is passed at a small parking area. The 1-mile hike (each way) includes a year-round stream crossing and some rock scrambling. The small metal pipeline that you see coming out of the canyon at this point is the public water supply for the Panamint Springs Resort in Death Valley. Darwin Falls is a wetland

Goldfish in the clear waters of China Garden Spring

Mine on western face of Zinc Hill overlooks Darwin Canyon

habitat, and there are many birds, amphibians, reptiles, and mammals that use the springs for water. The 30-foot-high falls are fed by an underground spring, which bubbles to the surface through the volcanic rock of Darwin Canyon.

Past the hiking access, the trail is an easygoing graded road as it heads out to join California 190, 1 mile west of Panamint Springs.

Current Road Information

Death Valley National Park
PO Box 579
Death Valley, CA 92328-0579
(760) 786-2331

Bureau of Land Management
Bishop Field Office
785 North Main Street, Suite E
Bishop, CA 93514
(760) 872-4881

Map References

BLM Darwin Hills
USGS 1:24,000 Darwin, Panamint Springs
1:100,000 Darwin Hills
Maptech CD-ROM: Kings Canyon/Death Valley
Southern & Central California Atlas & Gazetteer, p. 40
California Road & Recreation Atlas, p. 87
Trails Illustrated, Death Valley National Park (221)
Other: Free NPS Death Valley map, Tom Harrison Maps—Death Valley National Park Recreation map

Route Directions

Mileage		Dir.	Directions
▼ 0.0			At the 4-way intersection in the center of Darwin, zero trip meter and turn northeast on paved road. The Darwin Dance Hall, old Out Post store, and gas station are at the intersection. Pass many side streets on the way out of town.
	6.1 ▲		Trail ends at Main Street intersection in Darwin. Turn right onto Main Street to exit to California 190.
			GPS: N36°16.10' W117°35.47'
▼ 0.1		SO	Road turns to graded dirt.
	6.0 ▲	SO	Road is now paved.
▼ 0.4		BL	Track on right goes to mines. Remain on main dirt road.
	5.7 ▲	SO	Track on left goes to mines.
▼ 0.6		SO	Track on right.
	5.5 ▲	SO	Track on left.

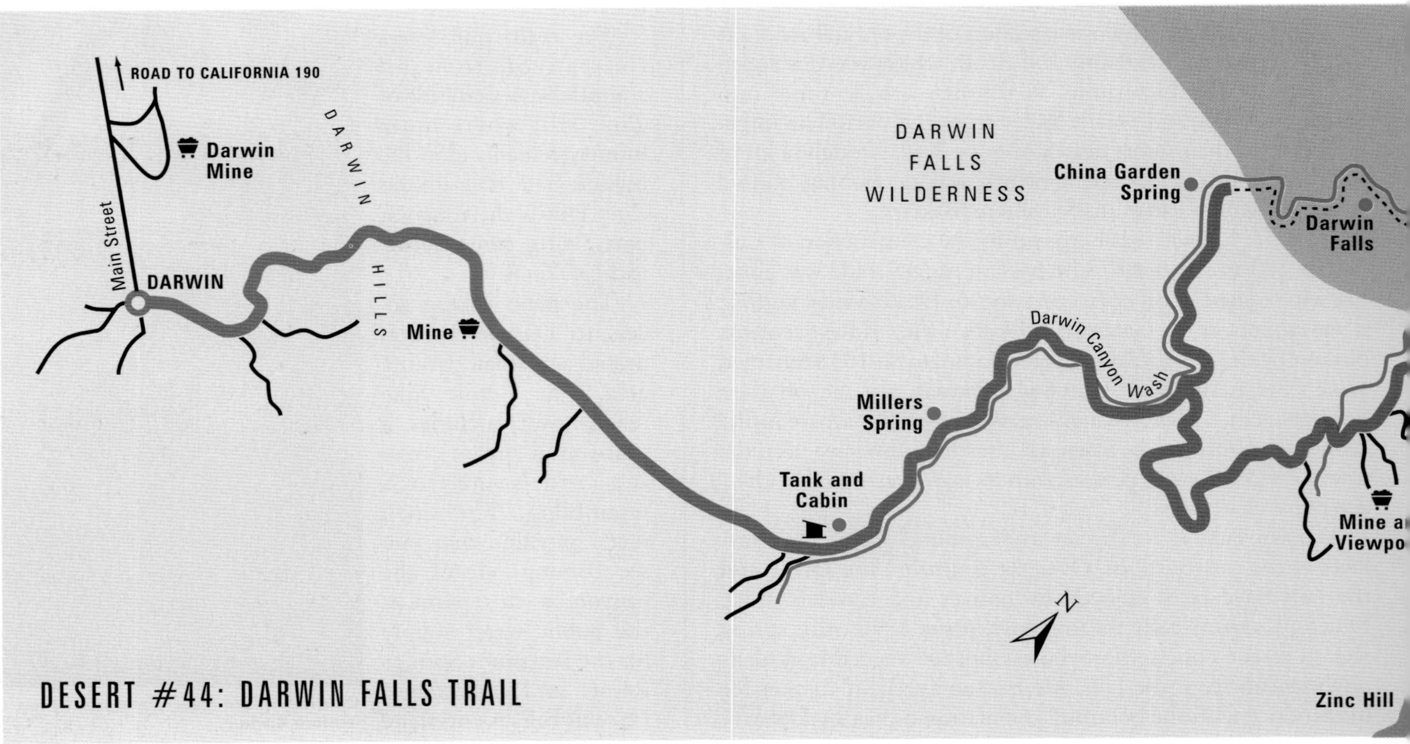

ROAD TO CALIFORNIA 190
Darwin Mine
DARWIN HILLS
Main Street
DARWIN
Mine
DARWIN FALLS WILDERNESS
China Garden Spring
Darwin Falls
Darwin Canyon Wash
Millers Spring
Tank and Cabin
Mine a
Viewpo
N
Zinc Hill

DESERT #44: DARWIN FALLS TRAIL

▼ 0.8	SO	Track on right.
5.3 ▲	SO	Track on left.
▼ 1.0	SO	Track on left.
5.1 ▲	SO	Track on right.
▼ 1.8	SO	Track on left.
4.3 ▲	SO	Track on right.
▼ 2.1	SO	Mine on right.
4.0 ▲	SO	Mine on left.
		GPS: N36°16.86' W117°34.21'
▼ 2.2	SO	Track on right.
3.9 ▲	SO	Track on left.
▼ 2.3	SO	Faint track on right.
3.8 ▲	SO	Faint track on left.
▼ 2.7	SO	Track on right.
3.4 ▲	SO	Track on left.
▼ 3.3	SO	Faint track on right.
2.8 ▲	SO	Faint track on left.
▼ 3.6	SO	Track on right to mine.
2.5 ▲	SO	Track on left to mine.
		GPS: N36°16.82' W117°32.50'
▼ 3.8	BL	Enter wash down narrow Darwin Canyon. Vehicles travel up wash to the right.
2.3 ▲	BR	Exit Darwin Canyon; then bear right and exit wash. Vehicles continue up wash.
		GPS: N36°16.88' W117°32.31'
▼ 3.9	SO	Tank and old cabin on left.
2.2 ▲	SO	Tank and old cabin on right.
▼ 4.1	SO	Two tracks on left to mine.
2.0 ▲	SO	Two tracks on right to mine.
		GPS: N36°17.07' W117°32.14'
▼ 4.6	SO	Millers Spring on left.
1.5 ▲	SO	Millers Spring on right.
		GPS: N36°17.54' W117°32.17'
▼ 6.1	TR	Well-used track on right leads out of Darwin Canyon wash up a smaller side canyon. Turn right up this track and zero trip meter. Trail continuing down the wash is spur to China Garden Spring.
0.0 ▲		Continue to the southeast up the wash.
		GPS: N36°18.19' W117°31.43'

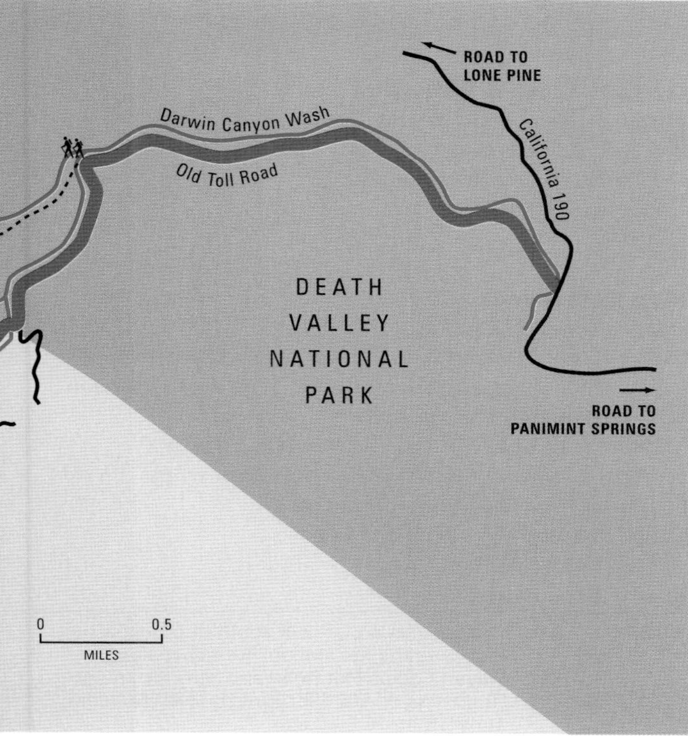

Spur to China Garden Spring

▼ 0.0		Continue down wash to the northwest.
▼ 1.0	SO	China Garden Spring on left under large cottonwoods. Stone and brick foundations of old pump house; then track on left to cabin and mine.
		GPS: N36°18.84' W117°31.85'
▼ 1.2	UT	Spur ends at boundary of the Darwin Falls Wilderness.
		GPS: N36°18.91' W117°31.79'

Continuation of Main Trail

▼ 0.0		Continue to the east and climb out of Darwin Canyon.
2.1 ▲	TL	T-intersection with wash in Darwin Canyon. Zero trip meter. Track down wash to the right is spur to China Garden Spring.
		GPS: N36°18.19' W117°31.43'
▼ 0.9	SO	Two tracks on right.
1.2 ▲	SO	Two tracks on left.
▼ 1.9	SO	Cross through wash.
0.2 ▲	SO	Cross through wash.
▼ 2.1	SO	Two tracks on right. Take first track on right to travel 0.3 miles to a mine on the hillside with an excellent view of the Darwin Hills. Zero trip meter.
0.0 ▲		Continue to the southwest.
		GPS: N36°18.48' W117°30.66'
▼ 0.0		Continue to the north.
1.6 ▲	SO	Two tracks on left. Take second track on left to travel 0.3 miles to a mine on the hillside with an excellent view of the Darwin Hills. Zero trip meter.
▼ 0.1	SO	Track on right at loading hoppers and stone ruins on right.
1.5 ▲	SO	Track on left at loading hoppers and stone ruins on left.
		GPS: N36°18.58' W117°30.66'
▼ 0.8	SO	Cross through wash. Track on right up wash. Trail now follows line of wash.
0.8 ▲	SO	Exit wash. Track on left up wash.
		GPS: N36°19.02' W117°30.57'
▼ 0.9	SO	Track on left.
0.7 ▲	SO	Track on right.
▼ 1.6	SO	Parking area on left for hiking trail to Darwin Falls. Zero trip meter.
0.0 ▲		Continue to the southeast up line of wash.
		GPS: N36°19.68' W117°30.81'
▼ 0.0		Continue to the north, re-entering Darwin Canyon and following line of wash.
2.3 ▲	BL	Parking area on right for hiking trail to Darwin Falls. Zero trip meter.
▼ 2.3		Trail ends at T-intersection with California 190. Turn right for Panamint Springs and Death Valley; turn left for Lone Pine.
0.0 ▲		Trail commences on California 190, 1 mile west of Panamint Springs. Zero trip meter and turn west on graded dirt road at sign for Darwin Falls.
		GPS: N36°20.40' W117°28.76'

DESERT #45

Cactus Flat Road

Starting Point:	**US 395, 2 miles south of Olancha, opposite the Olancha Fire Station**
Finishing Point:	**US 395, at Coso Junction**
Total Mileage:	**23.5 miles**
Unpaved Mileage:	**22.2 miles**
Driving Time:	**2 hours**
Elevation Range:	**3,300–5,400 feet**
Usually Open:	**Year-round**
Best Time to Travel:	**Dry weather, fall to spring**
Difficulty Rating:	**3**
Scenic Rating:	**8**
Remoteness Rating:	**+1**

Special Attractions

- Joshua trees at the northern limit of their range.
- Many mining remains.
- Lightly traveled network of trails in the Inyo Mountains.

History

Haiwee Reservoir is named after the Panamint word for dove. Coso, a name that applies to both Coso Junction and the Coso Range, comes from the Panamint word for a burned region. The Coso Range contains a number of petroglyphs. Current land divisions place the range within the China Lake Naval Weapons Center.

The navy has used China Lake Naval Weapons Center since 1943 for the deployment, testing, and development of air to target missiles and weaponry. At approximately 1 million acres, China Lake is the largest region available to the navy for such activities.

The Coso Petroglyphs have been conserved by the navy, which allows controlled entry to the sites at certain times of the year. Details of entry and tours can be obtained from the interagency office in Lone Pine. The sites were listed on the National Register of Historic Places in 1964 as Little Petroglyphs Canyon.

Description

The trail travels through a band of BLM land in the Inyo Mountains. It is bounded on the east by the China Lake Naval Weapons Center, and on the west by US 395. The area contains many Joshua trees, the signature plant of the Mojave Desert. Although this area is the northernmost extremity of their distribution, Joshua trees grow in abundance on Cactus Flat and in other valleys throughout the region.

The trail leaves Olancha along a graded dirt road that drops in standard to become a well-used, formed trail after the entrance to a pumice mine. The trail becomes smaller and lesser used as it winds along Cactus Flat, offering wide ranging views of the Inyo Mountains.

A few mining remains can be seen along the trail. There is a small stone cabin tucked under a large granite overhang at the McCloud Mine, and a well-preserved wooden headframe near the Five Tunnels Mine. Both mines have tailings heaps, shafts, and adits.

From the McCloud Mine on, the trail earns its 3-rating for difficulty, becoming rougher and more eroded. Navigation also becomes more difficult, especially around the Five Tunnels Mine, where small tracks intersect frequently. The trail crosses a claypan, which quickly becomes impassable when wet. Please remain on the main trail through the claypan to avoid leaving scars of additional tire tracks.

Old stone cabin at the McCloud Mine built under a granite overhang

The trail leaves McCloud Flat through a gap in the range, running close to the China Lake Naval Weapons Center. The area is fenced, and there is no public admittance to the center. Please be sure to remain on public land. The trail follows a good, graded dirt road before joining paved Gill Station Road to exit to Coso Junction.

Generally, animal life in the area is not readily apparent, although coyotes, jackrabbits, and a wide variety of reptiles live in the region. Raptors are occasionally seen circling overhead. Overall, the area is incredibly quiet and still, and it is a wonderful place for solitude and relaxation.

Current Road Information

Bureau of Land Management
Bishop Field Office
785 North Main Street, Suite E
Bishop, CA 93514
(760) 872-4881

Map References

BLM Darwin Hills
USGS 1:24,000 Vermilion Canyon, Haiwee Reservoirs, Upper Centennial Flat, Cactus Peak, Coso Junction
1:100,000 Darwin Hills
Maptech CD-ROM: Kings Canyon/Death Valley
Southern & Central California Atlas & Gazetteer, pp. 39, 40
California Road & Recreation Atlas, p. 87
Other: Panamint Desert Access Guide

Route Directions

▼ 0.0	Trail begins on US 395 south of Olancha, opposite the fire station. Turn east along paved Cactus Flat Road and zero trip meter.
4.1 ▲	Trail ends on US 395. Turn right for Olancha; turn left for Ridgecrest.

		GPS: N36°15.31′ W117°59.52′
▼ 0.4	SO	Graded road on left into private property.
3.7 ▲	SO	Graded road on right into private property.
▼ 1.3	SO	Road turns to graded dirt.
2.8 ▲	SO	Road is now paved.
▼ 1.6	SO	Cattle guard.
2.5 ▲	SO	Cattle guard.
▼ 2.1	SO	Track on right.
2.0 ▲	SO	Track on left.
▼ 2.4	SO	Cross through wash. Track on left up wash.
1.7 ▲	SO	Cross through wash. Track on right up wash.
▼ 2.5	SO	Haiwee Reservoir on right.
1.6 ▲	SO	Haiwee Reservoir on left.
▼ 2.6	SO	Road is paved as it ascends the hill; then track on right.
1.5 ▲	SO	Track on left; then road is paved as it descends the hill.
▼ 2.9	SO	Track on right.
1.2 ▲	SO	Track on left.
▼ 3.6	SO	Two tracks on left.
0.5 ▲	SO	Two tracks on right.
▼ 4.1	SO	Graded road on left into pumice mine. Continue along smaller graded road and zero trip meter. Small track on right. Road is marked with BLM marker for 4WDs, ATVs, and motorbikes.
0.0 ▲		Continue to the northwest.
		GPS: N36°13.21′ W117°56.07′
▼ 0.0		Continue to the southeast.
4.4 ▲	SO	Graded road on right into pumice mine. Join larger, graded dirt road and zero trip meter. Small track on left.
▼ 0.2	SO	Cross through wash.
4.2 ▲	SO	Cross through wash.
▼ 0.7	SO	Cross through wash.
3.7 ▲	SO	Cross through wash.

Cactus Flat Road passes alongside Haiwee Reservoir

▼ 1.0	BL	Track on right down wash.
3.4 ▲	BR	Track on left down wash.
		GPS: N36°12.54′ W117°55.37′
▼ 1.5	SO	Cross through wash.
2.9 ▲	SO	Cross through wash.
▼ 2.1	SO	Track on right.
2.3 ▲	SO	Track on left.
▼ 2.3	SO	Track on left.
2.1 ▲	SO	Track on right.
▼ 2.4	SO	Track on left. Trail is entering Cactus Flat.
2.0 ▲	SO	Track on right. Trail is leaving Cactus Flat.
		GPS: N36°12.28′ W117°53.88′

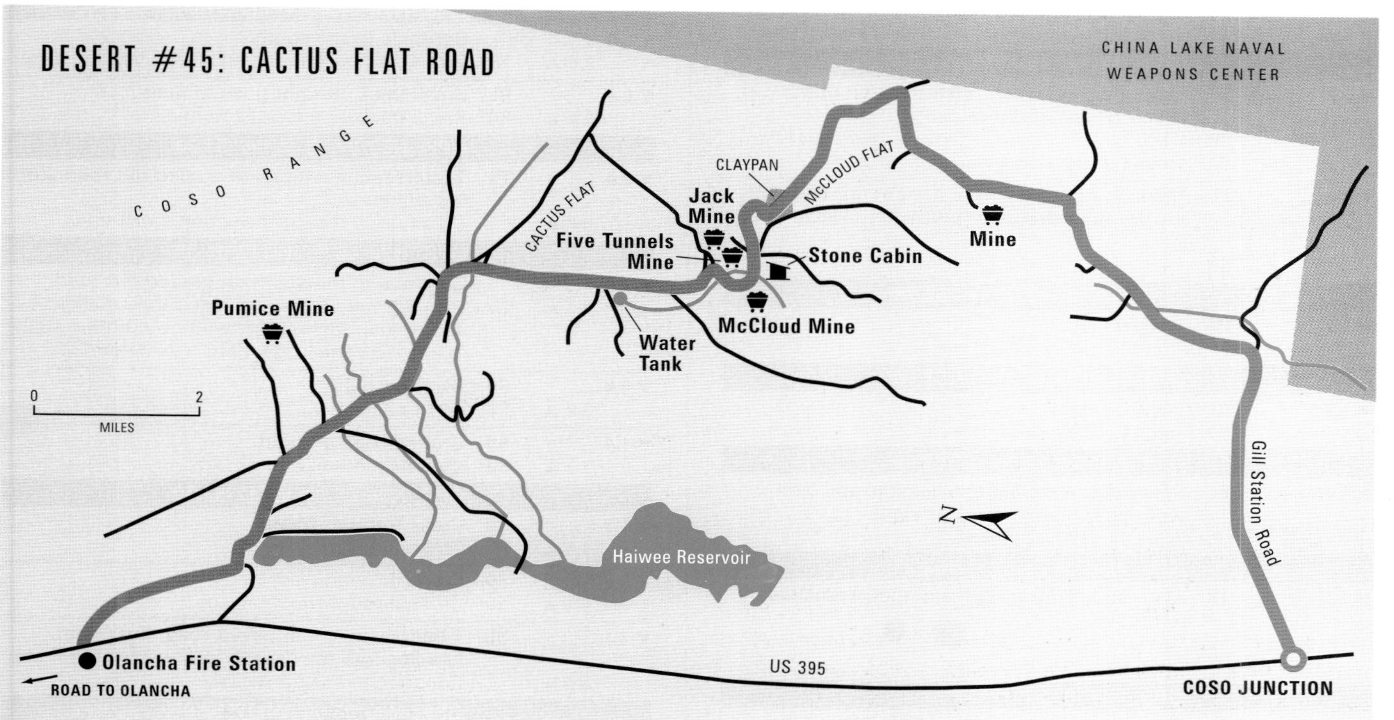

▼ 2.5	SO	Track on left.
1.9 ▲	SO	Track on right.
▼ 2.8	SO	Track on left; then cross through wash; then second track on left.
1.6 ▲	SO	Track on right; then cross through wash; then second track on right.
▼ 4.3	SO	Track on right.
0.1 ▲	SO	Track on left.
▼ 4.4	SO	Track on right at water tank. BLM trail marker at intersection. Road is marked for 4WDs, ATVs, and motorbikes. Zero trip meter.
0.0 ▲		Continue to the north.
		GPS: N36°10.60' W117°53.49'
▼ 0.0		Continue to the south.
1.3 ▲	SO	Track on left at water tank. BLM trail marker at intersection. Road is marked for 4WDs, ATVs, and motorbikes. Zero trip meter.
▼ 0.7	SO	Track on right.
0.6 ▲	SO	Track on left.
		GPS: N36°09.95' W117°53.40'
▼ 1.3	BR	Bear right onto smaller trail. Track ahead goes 0.1 miles to remains of the Jack Mine—a stone chimney and mine are visible farther up the hillside. Zero trip meter.
0.0 ▲		Continue to the west.
		GPS: N36°09.55' W117°53.08'
▼ 0.0		Continue to the southeast.
4.9 ▲	BL	Bear left onto larger formed trail. Track on right goes 0.1 miles to remains of the Jack Mine—a stone chimney and mine are visible on hillside to the right. Zero trip meter.
▼ 0.1	SO	Second entrance to Jack Mine on left.
4.8 ▲	SO	Track on right to Jack Mine, which is visible on hillside to the right.
▼ 0.2	SO	Cross through wash.
4.7 ▲	SO	Cross through wash.
▼ 0.6	SO	Cross through wash. Remains of the McCloud Mine on right. Small stone cabin on right.
4.3 ▲	SO	Remains of the McCloud Mine on the left. Small stone cabin on left. Cross through wash.
		GPS: N36°09.12' W117°53.07'
▼ 0.7	SO	Cross through wash; then track on right, which rejoins at top of rise.
4.2 ▲	SO	Track on left, which rejoins immediately; then cross through wash.
▼ 0.9	BL	Track on right and track straight on; bear left toward the headframe visible on hillside to the left.
4.0 ▲	SO	Two tracks on left.
		GPS: N36°09.07' W117°52.78'
▼ 1.1	BR	Track on left.
3.8 ▲	BL	Track on right.
		GPS: N36°09.15' W117°52.60'
▼ 1.2	BL	Track on right.
3.7 ▲	SO	Track on left.
		GPS: N36°09.17' W117°52.48'
▼ 1.4	BL	Bear left toward mine, tailings heaps, and wooden remains. Track on right.
3.5 ▲	SO	Track on left.
		GPS: N36°09.21' W117°52.31'
▼ 1.5	TR	Mine on left. Turn right and then immediately left.
3.4 ▲	TL	Turn right toward the mine and immediately left, just below the mine.
		GPS: N36°09.22' W117°52.22'
▼ 1.6	SO	Track on left; then bear right following around edge of claypan. Do not cut across the claypan.
3.3 ▲	BL	Swing left away from the claypan toward the mine visible on the hill; then bear left, leaving a second track on right.
▼ 1.7	TL	Rejoin track that bypassed the mine. Turn left (southeast), skirting edge of the claypan.
3.2 ▲	TR	Turn right (northeast) around edge of claypan.
		GPS: N36°09.08' W117°52.22'
▼ 1.8	BL	Bear left and cross claypan. Trail you are heading for is visible on the far side. Track on right and track straight ahead.
3.1 ▲	BR	Leave claypan and bear right alongside it. Track on left and track straight ahead.
		GPS: N36°09.02' W117°52.17'
▼ 2.1	SO	Exit claypan. Track on right and track on left.
2.8 ▲	SO	Start to cross claypan. Track on right and track on left.
		GPS: N36°08.90' W117°51.95'
▼ 3.0	SO	Trail passes through gate.
1.9 ▲	SO	Trail passes through gate.
		GPS: N36°08.60' W117°51.07'
▼ 3.3	BR	Bear right, remaining on most-used trail. Track on left goes to the boundary of the China Lake Naval Weapons Center.
1.6 ▲	BL	Bear left, remaining on most-used trail. Track on right goes to the boundary of the China Lake Naval Weapons Center.
		GPS: N36°08.55' W117°50.69'
▼ 4.1	TR	Turn right onto well-used track that can be seen leading out of the valley. Track straight ahead leads to the boundary of the China Lake Naval Weapons Center.
0.8 ▲	TL	T-intersection with well-used track. Track on right leads to the boundary of the China Lake Naval Weapons Center.
		GPS: N36°07.90' W117°50.30'
▼ 4.9	TL	Pass through wire fence line; then T-intersection. Turn left down valley. Zero trip meter.
0.0 ▲		Continue to the northeast.
		GPS: N36°07.60' W117°51.04'
▼ 0.0		Continue to the south.
2.0 ▲	TR	Turn right through wire fence line. Zero trip meter.
▼ 0.6	BL	Small track on right goes to mine.
1.4 ▲	BR	Small track on left goes to mine.
		GPS: N36°07.10' W117°51.30'
▼ 2.0	TR	T-intersection with main graded dirt road. Zero trip meter.
0.0 ▲		Continue to the northwest on small trail.
		GPS: N36°05.95' W117°51.38'
▼ 0.0		Continue to the south on graded dirt road.
3.1 ▲	TL	Turn left onto small well-used trail, marked by a BLM jeep trail marker with no number. Trail heads over the ridge. Zero trip meter.
▼ 0.9	SO	Track on right.
2.2 ▲	SO	Track on left.
▼ 1.4	SO	Graded road on right.
1.7 ▲	SO	Graded road on left.
		GPS: N36°05.09' W117°52.39'
▼ 1.7	SO	Cross through wash.
1.4 ▲	SO	Cross through wash.
▼ 3.0	SO	Cross through wash.
0.1 ▲	SO	Cross through wash.
▼ 3.1	BR	T-intersection with paved road. Bear right, heading into the Owens Valley. Zero trip meter.
0.0 ▲		Continue to the northeast.
		GPS: N36°03.68' W117°52.98'

▼ 0.0			Continue to the west.
	3.7 ▲	BL	Bear left onto large graded dirt road at unmarked intersection. Zero trip meter.
▼ 3.7			Trail ends at intersection with US 395 at Coso Junction.
	0.0 ▲		Trail commences on US 395 at Coso Junction. Zero trip meter and turn east on paved road. There is a rest area at the intersection.
			GPS: N36°02.76′ W117°56.76′

DESERT #46

Saline Valley Road

Starting Point:	**California 190, 9.5 miles east of the intersection with California 136.**
Finishing Point:	**California 168, 2.5 miles east of Big Pine and the intersection with US 395**
Total Mileage:	**91.4 miles**
Unpaved Mileage:	**78.8 miles**
Driving Time:	**5.5 hours**
Elevation Range:	**1,000–7,600 feet**
Usually Open:	**Year-round, higher elevations may be closed during winter**
Best Time to Travel:	**October to May, for the lower elevations**
Difficulty Rating:	**2**
Scenic Rating:	**10**
Remoteness Rating:	**+2**

Special Attractions

- Old salt works and tramway.
- Saline Valley Dunes.
- Many old mining camps and remains in Saline Valley and Marble Canyon.
- Remote desert experience.

History

Saline Valley, along with the Death Valley area in general, has a long history of mining activity. Saline Valley is best known for salt and borax mining operations. Borax was discovered in Saline Valley in 1874. The Conn and Trudo Borax Works operated in the valley from the late 1880s to the early 1900s. Saline Valley, along with Calico in San Bernardino County, was the principal producer of borax between 1888 and 1893. The valley's salt reserves were first worked around the same time, but they didn't become a large concern until 1903. The need to freight salt to the ferry and railroad on the western side of the Inyo Mountains for shipment across what was then Owens Lake led to the development of the salt tramway. The tramway, which was constructed between 1911 and 1913, runs from the floor of Saline Valley, up and over the Inyo Mountains, to Swansea in the Owens Valley. More about the tramway can be read in the history attached to Desert #48: Swansea-Cerro Gordo Road. The Saline Valley Salt Tram claims to be "the most scenic, historic, best preserved, oldest, and largest of its kind remaining today." It is listed on the National Register of Historic Places.

Salt-encrusted pilings at evaporation ponds at Salt Marsh

Gold mining activity in Marble Canyon, to the north of Saline Valley, began as limited placer mining in 1882. Lack of transportation into the region meant that the canyon remained quiet until the 1930s, when there was a slight revival of gold mining. The gold in Marble Canyon is unusual in that large nuggets can be found on top of the bedrock beneath a deep gravel layer. The region was active until 1960, when it once again became quiet.

In October 1944, a B-24 bomber with a crew of seven was on a routine training mission when engine trouble developed. The plane crashed on the dry lake in Saline Valley. With their radios damaged in the crash, the crew, which had one man seriously injured, wrote the word "plasma" in 6-foot-long letters on the dry salt bed. A rescue team was dispatched to the site. After hours of arduous travel and numerous flat tires, the team reached the crash site. The injured man had a severed leg, and although the rescue team tried their best, he died on the way to Big Pine.

Description

Saline Valley Road is a long, mainly dirt road that takes the traveler from California 190 to California 168, finishing near Big Pine. The historic road is suitable for high-clearance 2WDs in dry weather, but it is not a journey to be taken lightly by anyone. The dusty road can be extremely corrugated and there are no facilities or fuel anywhere along the way. In summer, temperatures reach extreme levels at the lower elevations,

Saline Valley Dunes

Large jumbled boulders at the south end of Saline Valley

and in winter, there is often snow at the higher elevations that may require the use of chains in order to pass through safely.

The trail commences along the original Saline Valley Road, which is now less used than the new route that begins farther east on California 190. The old and new routes merge 8.3 miles from the start of the trail. The first part of the route travels through the Talc City Hills, close to the site of several old mines, before ending at the broad Santa Rosa Flat. The Santa Rosa Hills separate the flat from Lee Flat, a broad valley with abundant Joshua trees.

From the intersection with Desert #49: Hidden Valley Road, the trail winds down the twisting Grapevine Canyon. The trail crosses the creek several times. These crossings are likely to be dry in summer but may be icy in winter. The route spills out of Grapevine Canyon and heads down into the wide, sage-covered Saline Valley. A well-used track to the right is the rougher, more difficult Desert #50: Lippincott Mine Road, which connects with Desert #51: Racetrack Road. Saline Valley Road is well defined but dusty and washboardy, as it runs down the length of Saline Valley with the Nelson Range on the left. There are several small tracks that lead to the base of the range and the remains of various mining camps. One noteworthy feature is the remains of the old salt works at Salt Marsh. A spur leads a short distance to the edge of the marsh, where you can view the evaporation ponds and remains of the tramway.

The Saline Valley Dunes, a low range of sand dunes that are lightly vegetated with creosote bush, are a great place for photographs. No vehicles are allowed on the dunes, which are in a wilderness area. However, the road runs close enough that it is a very short, easy hike to the dunes.

The start of the more difficult Steels Pass Trail is the next major intersection. Travelers who do not wish to drive this route may still wish to detour for the first few miles of this trail to check out Palm Spring Hot Springs. Nudity is the norm at these popular springs, so if this offends you, you are better off staying on the main road.

The trail continues down the broad Saline Valley, passing side tracks that lead to old mining camps. The trail climbs out of the valley into the higher elevations up to 7,000 feet. There are several higher elevation campsites tucked into the pinyons and junipers. No campfires are allowed at any time of year within Death Valley National Park.

The trail joins paved Eureka Canyon Road and passes the northern end of Harkless Flat Trail and Papoose Flat Trail, before finishing at the intersection with California 168, a short distance east of Big Pine. The trail is normally open year-round, but some sections may be impassable at times. Even light rainfall can make the trails in this region impassable, and they may be temporarily closed by the National Park Service.

Current Road Information

Death Valley National Park
PO Box 579
Death Valley, CA 92328-0579
(760) 786-2331

Maps References

BLM Saline Valley, Last Chance Range, Bishop, Darwin Hills
USFS Inyo National Forest
USGS 1:24,000 Talc City Hills, Santa Rosa Flat, Lee Wash, Jackass Canyon, Nelson Range, West of Ubehebe Peak, Craig Canyon, Lower Warm Springs, Pat Keyes Canyon, Waucoba Canyon, Waucoba Spring, Waucoba Mt., Cowhorn Valley, Uhlmeyer Spring, Big Pine
1:100,000 Saline Valley, Last Chance Range, Bishop, Darwin Hills

Southern & Central California Atlas & Gazetteer, pp. 40, 28, 27
Northern California Atlas & Gazetteer, p. 124
California Road & Recreation Atlas, pp. 87, 80, 79
Trails Illustrated, Death Valley National Park (221)
Other: Free NPS Death Valley map, Tom Harrison Maps—Death Valley National Park Recreation Map

Route Directions

Mileage		Directions
▼ 0.0		Trail commences on California 190, 9.5 miles east of the intersection with California 136. Zero trip meter and turn north on small paved road. Intersection is unmarked.
1.9 ▲		Small paved road on left is Talc City Road; then trail ends at intersection with California 190. Turn right for Lone Pine; turn left for Death Valley.
		GPS: N36°19.84' W117°42.84'
▼ 0.1	SO	Track on left.
1.8 ▲	SO	Track on right.
▼ 0.7	SO	Track on left joins S9.
1.2 ▲	SO	Track on right joins S9.
▼ 1.2	SO	Track on left and track on right; then second track on left to Viking and White Swan Mines; then second track on right.
0.7 ▲	SO	Track on left; then track on right to Viking and White Swan Mines; then second track on left and second track on right.
		GPS: N36°20.65' W117°42.22'
▼ 1.4	SO	Cross through wash.
0.5 ▲	SO	Cross through wash.
▼ 1.8	SO	Track on right is S5, suitable for 4WDs, ATVs,

and motorbikes, and goes toward the Sierra Mine.
0.1 ▲ SO Track on left is S5, suitable for 4WDs, ATVs, and motorbikes, and goes toward the Sierra Mine.

▼ 1.9 SO Track on left is S9, suitable for 4WDs, ATVs, and motorbikes, and goes to the Viking Mine, which is visible on the hillside to the left. Zero trip meter.
0.0 ▲ Continue to the south.

GPS: N36°21.20′ W117°41.74′

▼ 0.0 Continue to the north.
4.6 ▲ SO Track on right is S9, suitable for 4WDs, ATVs, and motorbikes, and goes to the Viking Mine, which is visible on the hillside to the right. Zero trip meter.

▼ 0.5 SO Track on left to mine.
4.1 ▲ SO Track on right to mine.

GPS: N36°21.56′ W117°41.50′

▼ 1.6 SO Track on left.
3.0 ▲ SO Track on right.

▼ 1.7 SO Cross through wash.
2.9 ▲ SO Cross through wash.

▼ 2.1 SO Track on right.
2.5 ▲ SO Track on left.

▼ 3.1 SO Many small wash crossings for the next 1.5 miles.
1.5 ▲ SO End of wash crossings.

▼ 3.7 BR Graded road on left is Santa Rosa Road.
0.9 ▲ SO Graded road on right is Santa Rosa Road.

GPS: N36°23.95′ W117°40.25′

▼ 4.6 BR Track on left is S5 for 4WDs, ATVs, and motorbikes. Zero trip meter.
0.0 ▲ Continue to the south. Trail is leaving Santa Rosa Flat. Many small wash crossings for the next 1.5 miles.

GPS: N36°24.72′ W117°39.91′

▼ 0.0 Continue to the northeast. End of wash crossings.
1.8 ▲ BL Track on right is S5 for 4WDs, ATVs, and motorbikes. Zero trip meter.

▼ 0.4 SO Cross through large wash.
1.4 ▲ SO Cross through large wash.

GPS: N36°24.86′ W117°39.49′

▼ 1.1 SO Faint track on right.
0.7 ▲ SO Faint track on left.

▼ 1.5 SO Cross through two channels of Santa Rosa Wash.
0.3 ▲ SO Cross through two channels of Santa Rosa Wash.

▼ 1.8 SO Join larger road that was once paved and zero trip meter. Alternate Saline Valley Road on right returns to California 190 in 4.7 miles. Intersection is unmarked.
0.0 ▲ Continue to the southwest toward Santa Rosa Flat.

GPS: N36°25.71′ W117°38.39′

▼ 0.0 Continue to the northeast through the Santa Rosa Hills.
3.3 ▲ BR Bear right onto smaller graded road, which is the original Saline Valley Road. Larger road ahead that was once paved is Alternate Saline Valley Road, which joins California 190 in 4.7 miles. Intersection is unmarked. Zero trip meter.

▼ 0.5 SO Track on left past cabin.
2.8 ▲ SO Track on right past cabin.

▼ 1.1 SO Track on right to Lee Mines.
2.2 ▲ SO Track on left to Lee Mines.

GPS: N36°26.10′ W117°37.33′

▼ 1.3 SO Track on left to mine.
2.0 ▲ SO Track on right to mine.

▼ 2.5 SO Entering Death Valley National Park at sign.
0.8 ▲ SO Leaving Death Valley National Park at sign.

GPS: N36°27.20′ W117°37.38′

▼ 3.3 BR Desert #47: Cerro Gordo Road on left. Intersection is large, but unmarked. Small track on right. Zero trip meter.
0.0 ▲ Continue to the southeast.

GPS: N36°27.91′ W117°37.55′

▼ 0.0 Continue to the north.
7.1 ▲ SO Desert #47: Cerro Gordo Road on right. Intersection is large, but unmarked. Small track on left. Zero trip meter.

▼ 1.5 SO Track on left. Track on right to site of Wilson Ranch.
5.6 ▲ SO Track on left to site of Wilson Ranch. Track on right.

GPS: N36°29.13′ W117°36.97′

▼ 3.1 SO Cross through wash.
4.0 ▲ SO Cross through wash.

▼ 4.9 SO Diggings on left.
2.2 ▲ SO Diggings on right.

GPS: N36°30.53′ W117°34.44′

▼ 5.4 SO Track on left past corral.
1.7 ▲ SO Track on right past corral.

GPS: N36°30.82′ W117°34.04′

▼ 6.8 SO Turnout on right gives views of the Panamint Dunes.
0.3 ▲ SO Turnout on left gives views of the Panamint Dunes.

▼ 7.1 SO Well-used track on right is Desert #49: Hidden Valley Road. Zero trip meter. Intersection is unmarked.
0.0 ▲ Continue to the south.

GPS: N36°31.62′ W117°32.75′

▼ 0.0 Continue to the northwest.
10.0 ▲ SO Well-used track on left is Desert #49: Hidden Valley Road. Zero trip meter. Intersection is unmarked.

▼ 2.6 SO Cross through Grapevine Canyon creek many times in the next 1.6 miles.
7.4 ▲ SO Final crossing of Grapevine Canyon creek.

GPS: N36°32.91′ W117°34.37′

▼ 4.2 SO Final crossing of Grapevine Canyon creek.
5.8 ▲ SO Cross through Grapevine Canyon creek many times in the next 1.6 miles.

▼ 4.8 SO Track on right.
5.2 ▲ SO Track on left.

▼ 7.8 SO Cross through wash.
2.2 ▲ SO Cross through wash.

▼ 10.0 SO Graded track on right is Desert #50: Lippincott Mine Road. Intersection is unmarked apart from a large cairn. Zero trip meter.
0.0 ▲ Continue to the southeast.

GPS: N36°37.20′ W117°38.88′

▼ 0.0 Continue to the northwest.
10.6 ▲ SO Graded track on left is Desert #50: Lippincott Mine Road. Intersection is unmarked apart from a large cairn. Zero trip meter.

▼ 2.9 SO Track on right.
7.7 ▲ SO Track on left.

GPS: N36°39.38′ W117°40.58′

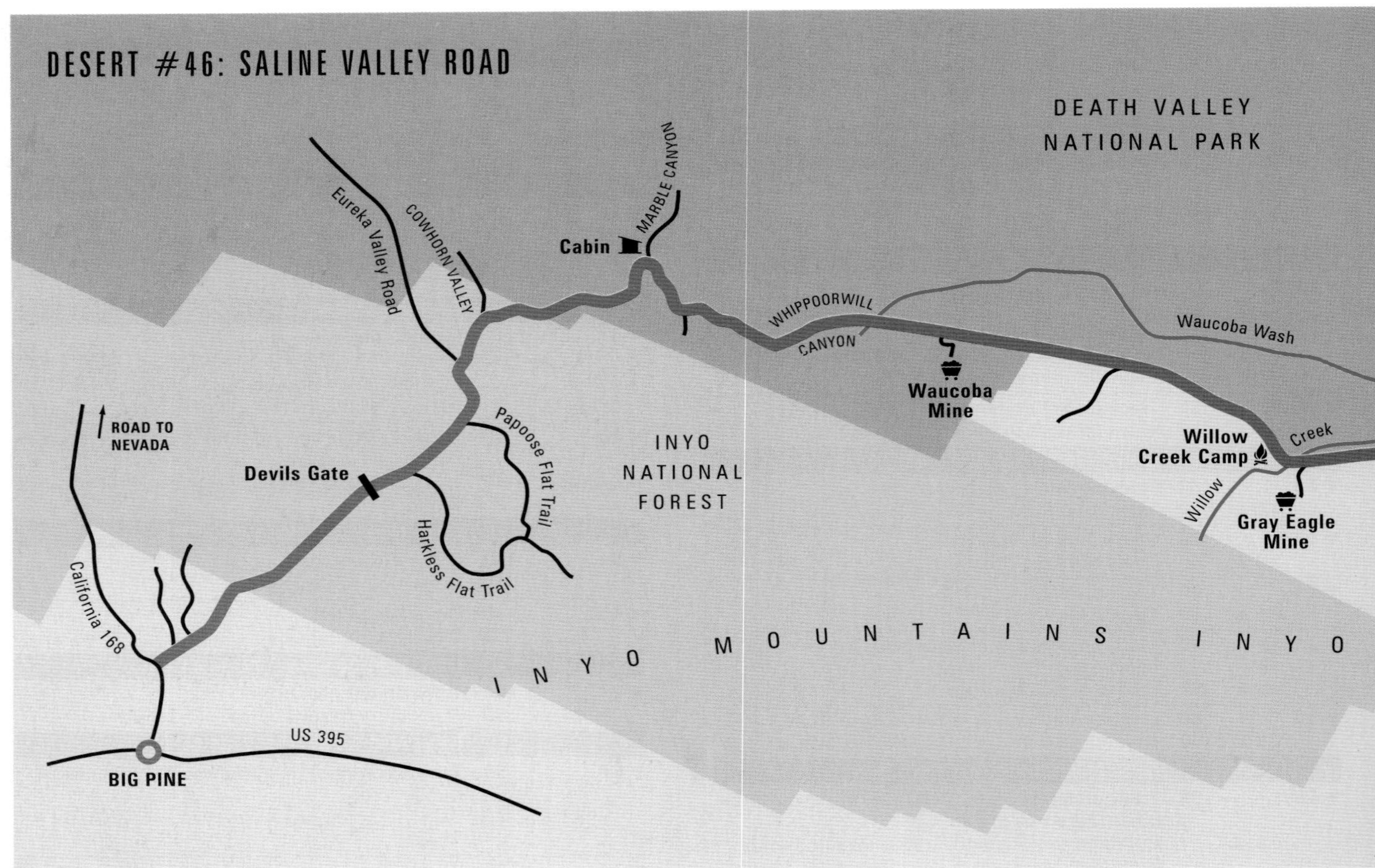

Mileage		Description
▼ 10.3	SO	Track on left.
0.3 ▲	SO	Track on right.
▼ 10.6	SO	Track on left follows route of abandoned aerial tramway and heads toward Big Silver Mine. Track on right goes to the edge of Salt Lake with its old salt evaporator and some remains of the salt tramway. Zero trip meter.
0.0 ▲		Continue to the east.
		GPS: N36°41.07' W117°48.90'
▼ 0.0		Continue to the west.
8.1 ▲	SO	Track on right follows the route of the abandoned aerial tramway and heads toward Big Silver Mine. Track on left goes to the edge of Salt Lake with its old salt evaporators and some remains of the salt tramway. Zero trip meter.
▼ 0.1	SO	Track on left.
8.0 ▲	SO	Track on right.
▼ 1.4	SO	Track on right across cattle guard.
6.7 ▲	SO	Track on left across cattle guard.
		GPS: N36°41.91' W117°49.86'
▼ 1.8	SO	Track on left toward Vega Mine and the start of the old steep pack route to Burgess Mine in the Inyo Mountains. Track on right.
6.3 ▲	SO	Track on right toward Vega Mine and the start of the old steep pack route to Burgess Mine in the Inyo Mountains. Track on left.
		GPS: N36°42.25' W117°49.67'
▼ 2.2	SO	Track on right.
5.9 ▲	SO	Track on left.
▼ 2.4	SO	Track on left goes to old works area.
5.7 ▲	SO	Track on right goes to old works area.
		GPS: N36°42.74' W117°49.90'
▼ 2.5	SO	Track on right.
5.6 ▲	SO	Track on left.
▼ 4.2	SO	Track on left to Snowflake Mine.
3.9 ▲	SO	Track on right to Snowflake Mine.
		GPS: N36°43.85' W117°50.51'
▼ 4.3	SO	Track on left to Snowflake Mine and track on right.
3.8 ▲	SO	Track on right to Snowflake Mine and track on left.
		GPS: N36°43.89' W117°50.52'
▼ 4.7	SO	Track on right.
3.4 ▲	SO	Track on left.
▼ 4.9	SO	Track on left to Snowflake Mine.
3.2 ▲	SO	Track on right to Snowflake Mine.
		GPS: N36°44.37' W117°50.96'
▼ 5.0	SO	Track on left and track on right.
3.1 ▲	SO	Track on right and track on left.
▼ 5.6	BR	Graded road on left.
2.5 ▲	SO	Graded road on right rejoins.
		GPS: N36°44.81' W117°51.41'
▼ 6.3	SO	Saline Valley Dunes are on the right.
1.8 ▲	SO	Saline Valley Dunes are on the left.
▼ 6.6.	SO	Graded road on left rejoins.
1.5 ▲	BL	Graded road on right.
▼ 7.1	SO	Track on left.
1.0 ▲	SO	Track on right.
▼ 8.1	SO	Well-used track on right is Steel Pass Trail.

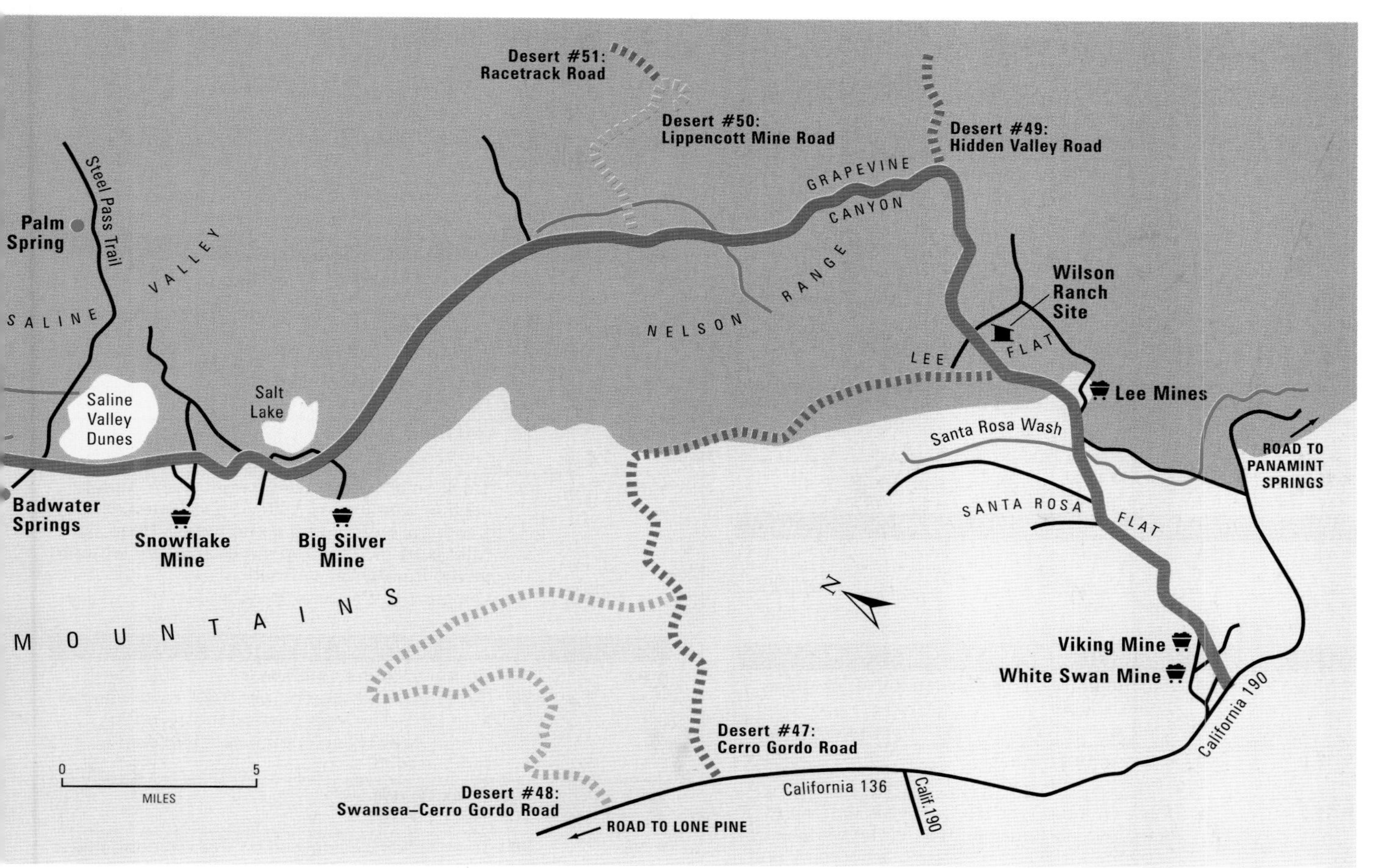

▼	▲		
	0.0 ▲		Zero trip meter. Intersection is unmarked. Continue to the southeast.
			GPS: N36°46.68' W117°52.74'
▼ 0.0			Continue to the northwest.
	4.5 ▲	SO	Well-used track on left is Steel Pass Trail. Zero trip meter. Intersection is unmarked.
▼ 0.4		SO	Track on left to Badwater Springs.
	4.1 ▲	SO	Track on right to Badwater Springs.
▼ 0.8		SO	Track on left.
	3.7 ▲	SO	Track on right.
▼ 1.7		SO	Cross through wash.
	2.8 ▲	SO	Cross through wash.
▼ 3.3		SO	Track on left.
	1.2 ▲	SO	Second entrance to track on right.
			GPS: N36°49.30' W117°54.35'
▼ 3.4		SO	Second entrance to track on left.
	1.1 ▲	SO	Track on right.
▼ 4.1		SO	Track on left to Gray Eagle Mine.
	0.4 ▲	SO	Second track on right to Gray Eagle Mine.
			GPS: N36°49.89' W117°54.79'
▼ 4.2		SO	Second track on left to Gray Eagle Mine.
	0.3 ▲	SO	Track on right to Gray Eagle Mine.
▼ 4.4		SO	Track on left; then cross through Willow Creek wash.
	0.1 ▲	SO	Cross through Willow Creek wash; then track on right.
▼ 4.5		BR	Graded road on left goes into Willow Creek Camp. Zero trip meter.
	0.0 ▲		Continue to the southeast.
			GPS: N36°50.16' W117°54.97'

▼	▲		
▼ 0.0			Continue to the north, following sign for Big Pine, and cross through wash.
	19.3 ▲	BL	Cross through wash; then graded road on right goes into Willow Creek Camp. Zero trip meter.
▼ 0.1		SO	Track on left.
	19.2 ▲	SO	Track on right.
▼ 0.6		SO	Cross through many washes for the next 3.4 miles.
	18.7 ▲	SO	Cross through wash. End of wash crossings.
▼ 4.0		SO	Cross through wash. End of wash crossings.
	15.3 ▲	SO	Cross through many washes for the next 3.4 miles.
▼ 5.4		SO	Well-used track on left.
	13.9 ▲	SO	Well-used track on right.
			GPS: N36°54.69' W117°54.50'
▼ 7.8		SO	Cross through wash.
	11.5 ▲	SO	Cross through wash.
▼ 8.6		SO	Track on left.
	10.7 ▲	SO	Track on right.
▼ 8.7		SO	Cross through wash.
	10.6 ▲	SO	Cross through wash.
▼ 9.8		SO	Track on left goes to Waucoba Mine.
	9.5 ▲	SO	Track on right goes to Waucoba Mine.
			GPS: N36°58.54' W117°55.88'
▼ 10.7		SO	Cross through wash.
	8.6 ▲	SO	Cross through wash.
▼ 11.5		SO	Cross through Waucoba Wash.
	7.8 ▲	SO	Cross through Waucoba Wash.

Mileage		Direction
▼ 12.0	SO	Cross through wash.
7.3 ▲	SO	Cross through wash.
		GPS: N37°00.41′ W117°56.54′
▼ 12.3	SO	Cross through wash.
7.0 ▲	SO	Cross through wash.
▼ 12.6	SO	Enter line of wash. Trail follows in or alongside wash, crossing it often for the next 2 miles.
6.7 ▲	SO	Exit line of wash.
▼ 14.6	SO	Exit line of wash and Whippoorwill Canyon.
4.7 ▲	SO	Enter line of wash and Whippoorwill Canyon. Trail follows in or alongside wash, crossing it often for the next 2 miles.
▼ 15.0	SO	Track on left. Entering Whippoorwill Flat.
4.3 ▲	SO	Track on right. Exiting Whippoorwill Flat.
		GPS: N37°02.06′ W117°58.41′
▼ 15.3	SO	Track on left.
4.0 ▲	SO	Track on right.
▼ 16.2	SO	Track on left.
3.1 ▲	SO	Track on right.
		GPS: N37°03.06′ W117°58.47′
▼ 17.3	SO	Track on left.
2.0 ▲	SO	Track on right.
▼ 17.6	SO	Track on left.
1.7 ▲	SO	Second entrance to track on right.
		GPS: N37°04.27′ W117°58.65′
▼ 17.8	SO	Second entrance to track on left. Trail enters Opal Canyon.
1.5 ▲	SO	Track on right. Trail enters Whippoorwill Flat.
▼ 18.0	SO	Cross through wash.
1.3 ▲	SO	Cross through wash.
▼ 19.3	BL	Track on right goes down Marble Canyon to many mining remains. Bear left up Marble Canyon, remaining on main graded road, and zero trip meter. Marble Canyon intersects with Opal Canyon at this point.
0.0 ▲		Continue to the south.
		GPS: N37°05.47′ W117°57.82′
▼ 0.0		Continue to the west.
7.6 ▲	BR	Track straight ahead continues down Marble Canyon. Bear right up Opal Canyon, remaining on main graded road, and zero trip meter. Marble Canyon intersects with Opal Canyon at this point.
▼ 0.1	SO	Old miner's cabin on right. There are many mining remains scattered along the floor of Marble Canyon.
7.5 ▲	SO	Old miner's cabin on left. There are many mining remains scattered along the floor of Marble Canyon.
▼ 0.7	SO	Track on right to mine.
6.9 ▲	SO	Track on left to mine.
		GPS: N37°05.35′ W117°58.53′
▼ 1.0	SO	Entering Inyo National Forest.
6.6 ▲	SO	Entering Death Valley National Park.
		GPS: N37°05.29′ W117°58.88′
▼ 1.2	SO	Track on left.
6.4 ▲	SO	Track on right.
▼ 1.3	SO	Track on left; then cross through wash; then second track on left.
6.3 ▲	SO	Track on right; then cross through wash; then second track on right.
▼ 1.5	SO	Track on right.
6.1 ▲	SO	Track on left.
▼ 4.4	SO	Track on left to game tank.
3.2 ▲	SO	Track on right to game tank.
▼ 4.5	SO	Track on left.
3.1 ▲	SO	Track on right.
▼ 4.8	SO	Track on left.
2.8 ▲	SO	Track on right.
▼ 4.9	SO	Track on right.
2.7 ▲	SO	Track on left.
▼ 5.9	SO	Track on right enters Cowhorn Valley.
1.7 ▲	SO	Track on left enters Cowhorn Valley.
		GPS: N37°08.15′ W118°01.52′
▼ 6.0	BR	Trail forks. Take either trail.
1.6 ▲	SO	Trail rejoins.
▼ 6.3	SO	Trail rejoins.
1.3 ▲	SO	Trail forks. Take either trail.
▼ 6.5	SO	Old road cutting on left.
1.1 ▲	SO	Old road rejoins.
▼ 6.6	SO	Old road rejoins.
1.0 ▲	SO	Old road cutting on right.
▼ 7.6	TL	Track on left and track on right; then T-intersection with Eureka Valley Road (listed as Death Valley Road on some maps). Road on right is 9S18. Zero trip meter and turn left onto paved Eureka Valley Road.
0.0 ▲		Continue to the east. Track on left and track on right.
		GPS: N37°08.24′ W118°03.15′
▼ 0.0		Continue to the southwest.
1.8 ▲	TR	Turn right onto graded dirt road, following the sign for Saline Valley Road, and zero trip meter. Paved road continues ahead and is marked 9S18.
▼ 1.2	SO	Track on left.
0.6 ▲	SO	Track on right.
▼ 1.8	SO	Track on left is Papoose Flat Trail. Zero trip meter.
0.0 ▲		Continue to the northeast.
		GPS: N37°07.38′ W118°04.60′
▼ 0.0		Continue to the west.
2.0 ▲	SO	Track on right is Papoose Flat Trail. Zero trip meter.
▼ 0.6	SO	Track on right.
1.4 ▲	SO	Track on left.
▼ 2.0	SO	Track on left is Harkless Flat Trail (9S13). Zero trip meter.
0.0 ▲		Continue to the southeast.
		GPS: N37°08.04′ W118°06.64′
▼ 0.0		Continue to the northwest.
5.5 ▲	SO	Track on right is Harkless Flat Trail (9S13). Zero trip meter.
▼ 0.2	SO	Track on right.
5.3 ▲	SO	Track on left.
▼ 1.1	SO	Pass through Devils Gate; then cross through wash.
4.4 ▲	SO	Cross through wash; then pass through Devils Gate.
		GPS: N37°08.66′ W118°07.47′
▼ 2.7	SO	Track on left.
2.8 ▲	SO	Track on right.
▼ 4.9	SO	Track on left.
0.6 ▲	SO	Track on right.
▼ 5.3	SO	Track on right.
0.2 ▲	SO	Track on left.
▼ 5.5	SO	Exiting Inyo National Forest at sign. Zero trip meter.
0.0 ▲		Continue to the east.
		GPS: N37°10.20′ W118°11.81′

▼ 0.0			Continue to the west.
	3.3 ▲	SO	Entering Inyo National Forest at sign. Zero trip meter.
▼ 0.8		SO	Cross through wash.
	2.5 ▲	SO	Cross through wash.
▼ 1.1		SO	Track on right.
	2.2 ▲	SO	Track on left.
▼ 1.9		SO	Track on right.
	1.4 ▲	SO	Track on left.
▼ 2.5		SO	Track on right.
	0.8 ▲	SO	Track on left.
▼ 3.3		SO	Trail ends at intersection with California 168. Turn left for Big Pine; turn right for Nevada.
	0.0 ▲		Trail commences on California 168, 2.5 miles east of US 395 and Big Pine. Zero trip meter and turn southeast on paved Saline Valley Road. It is sign-posted as Death Valley Road to Scotty's Castle.
			GPS: N37°11.10' W118°15.13'

DESERT #47

Cerro Gordo Road

Starting Point:	**California 136 at Keeler, 12 miles east of Lone Pine**
Finishing Point:	**Desert #46: Saline Valley Road, 11.6 miles north of California 190**
Total Mileage:	**23.7 miles**
Unpaved Mileage:	**23.7 miles**
Driving Time:	**2.5 hours**
Elevation Range:	**3,600–8,100 feet**
Usually Open:	**Year-round (may be blocked by snow in winter)**
Best Time to Travel:	**Spring and fall**
Difficulty Rating:	**2**
Scenic Rating:	**9**
Remoteness Rating:	**+1**

Special Attractions

- Lee Flat Joshua tree forest.
- Cerro Gordo ghost town.
- Alternate entry point to Desert #46: Saline Valley Road and Death Valley National Park.
- Views of the Sierra Nevada, Saline Valley, and Panamint Range.

History

Perched high in the Inyo Mountains, Cerro Gordo (Spanish for "fat hill") was the greatest producer of silver and lead in California's history. Rival cities competed to trade with the mining district. Los Angeles won out and Cerro Gordo became crucial in the development of the young city. Mexican prospectors discovered the first silver deposits in 1865, but the area was largely ignored until 1867 when Spanish-speaking miners began bringing silver ore samples to Virginia City, Nevada. Scores of fortune seekers hurried to the region and the town of Cerro Gordo soon sprang up to accommodate them.

American Hotel in Cerro Gordo

The two biggest investors in Cerro Gordo were San Francisco mining engineer M. W. Belshaw and his partner, store-owner Victor Beaudry. Belshaw constructed the Old Yellow Grade Road, an expensive toll road whose high rates helped bankrupt poor miners. This allowed the investors to form a monopoly on mining operations.

The ore was transported out of Cerro Gordo using mule teams. After several years, ferries began to carry silver over Owens Lake (which was not yet dry). At its peak in the mid-1870s, Cerro Gordo boasted a population of more than 2,000 and had many stores. Soon, though, the silver and iron mines played out, and the residents and store owners moved to other locations. The town reawakened several times, for zinc and limestone mining, but in 1959 the remaining equipment was sold and Cerro Gordo assumed its present, ghost town state. It is now private property, and its current owner rents out restored buildings to help fund preservation of the site. (For more information on Cerro Gordo, see "Towns, Ghost Towns, and Interesting Places.")

Description

Cerro Gordo Road follows close to the route of the old toll road into Death Valley. It travels up a steep canyon in the Inyo Mountains to Cerro Gordo ghost town and down the east side to Desert #46: Saline Valley Road in Lee Flat. The road leaves from Keeler, a small settlement on California 136.

The Old Yellow Grade Road made its way up the best possible route through the canyon

The route is well

graded, but surprisingly steep as it travels into the Inyo Mountains. Vehicles traveling the route in the reverse direction will need to watch their brakes. There are some mining remains visible along the length of the route. The upper sections of the trail approaching Cerro Gordo travel a narrow shelf road. The ghost town of Cerro Gordo is privately owned. Please remain on the through-routes while on private property. Tours of the ghost town are offered; call ahead for details at (760) 876-5030.

Cerro Gordo sits on a saddle under the shadow of the hill from which it takes its name. From the saddle the road descends the east side of the range. The grade here is less steep than the west side, although the trail is slightly rougher. The vegetation is different on each side; the west has bare, sparsely vegetated hills scattered with a few Joshua trees, the east has pinyon and juniper at the higher elevations.

The trail comes to a T-intersection with the east-west running San Lucas Canyon. The trail is rougher and prone to washouts, but it is usually suitable for high-clearance vehicles. San Lucas Canyon spills out onto Lee Flat, where there are some of the densest stands of Joshua trees to be found in Death Valley. The trail then comes to an end at Desert #46: Saline Valley Road.

With care, passenger vehicles can access the trail as far as Cerro Gordo. High-clearance is required east of the town site.

Current Road Information

Death Valley National Park
PO Box 579
Death Valley, CA 92328-0579
(760) 786-2331

Map References

BLM Saline Valley, Darwin Hills
USGS 1:24,000 Keeler, Cerro Gordo Peak, Nelson Range, Santa Rosa Flat
1:100,000 Saline Valley, Darwin Hills
Maptech CD-ROM: Kings Canyon/Death Valley

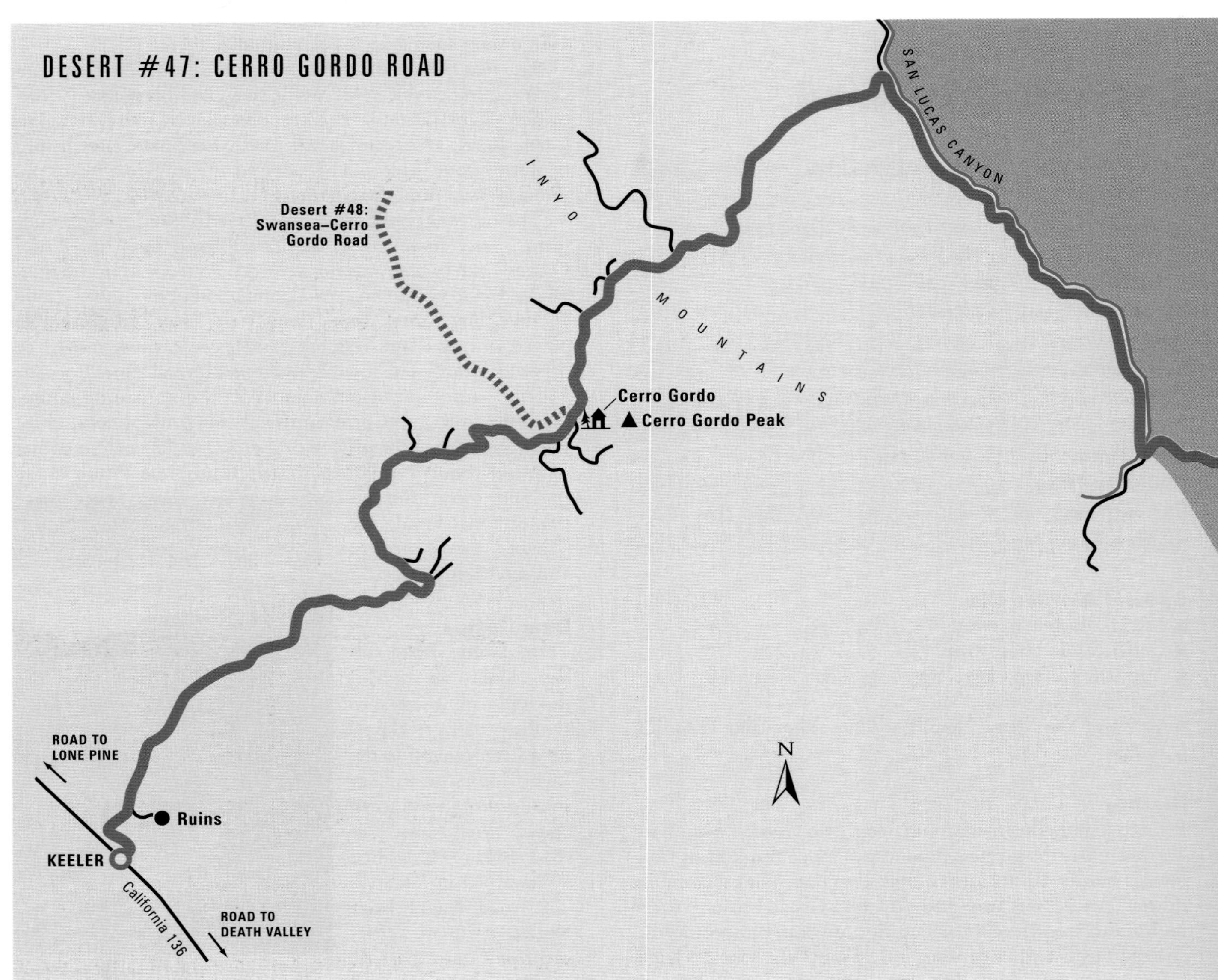

Southern & Central California Atlas & Gazetteer, pp. 40, 28
California Road & Recreation Atlas, p. 87
Trails Illustrated, Death Valley National Park (221)
Other: Free NPS Death Valley map, Tom Harrison Maps—
Death Valley National Park Recreation Map

Route Directions

▼ 0.0			From California 136 on the east side of Keeler, 12 miles east of Lone Pine, zero trip meter and turn northeast on graded dirt Cerro Gordo Road. There is a historical marker for Cerro Gordo at the intersection.
	4.2 ▲		Trail ends on California 136. Turn left for Death Valley; turn right for Lone Pine. There is a historical marker for Cerro Gordo at the intersection.
			GPS: N36°29.19' W117°51.94'
▼ 0.4		SO	Track on left along power lines.
	3.8 ▲	SO	Track on right along power lines.
▼ 0.6		SO	Track on right to stone ruins.
	3.6 ▲	SO	Track on left to stone ruins.
			GPS: N36°29.60' W117°51.87'
▼ 3.4		SO	Track on right.
	0.8 ▲	SO	Track on left.
			GPS: N36°30.97' W117°49.76'
▼ 4.2		BL	Two tracks on right—first passes salt tramway tower. Zero trip meter.
	0.0 ▲		Continue to the south, remaining on main graded road.
			GPS: N36°31.11' W117°49.04'
▼ 0.0			Continue to the northwest, remaining on main graded road. Cross through wash.
	3.4 ▲	BR	Cross through wash; then two tracks on left—second passes salt tramway tower. Zero trip meter.
▼ 0.3		SO	Track on right.
	3.1 ▲	SO	Track on left.
▼ 1.5		SO	Track on left.
	1.9 ▲	SO	Track on right.
▼ 1.7		SO	Track on left.
	1.7 ▲	SO	Track on right.
			GPS: N36°32.09' W117°48.85'
▼ 2.0		SO	Loading hopper on left.
	1.4 ▲	SO	Loading hopper on right.
▼ 3.1		SO	Cross through wash.
	0.3 ▲	SO	Cross through wash.
▼ 3.2		SO	Track on right on edge of Cerro Gordo.
	0.2 ▲	SO	Track on left on edge of Cerro Gordo.
▼ 3.3		SO	Track on right is entrance to Cerro Gordo.
	0.1 ▲	SO	Track on left is entrance to Cerro Gordo.
			GPS: N36°32.27' W117°47.64'
▼ 3.4		SO	Track on left is Desert #48: Swansea-Cerro Gordo Road. Track on right is private road into Cerro Gordo. Zero trip meter. Cerro Gordo Peak is on the right.
	0.0 ▲		Continue to the south.
			GPS: N36°32.36' W117°47.62'
▼ 0.0			Continue to the north over the saddle and drop toward Saline Valley.
	4.9 ▲	SO	Track on right is Desert #48: Swansea-Cerro Gordo Road. Track on left is private road into Cerro Gordo. Zero trip meter. Cerro Gordo Peak is on the left.
▼ 0.6		SO	Track enters line of wash.
	4.3 ▲	SO	Track exits line of wash.
▼ 1.0		SO	Track on right is private.
	3.9 ▲	SO	Track on left is private.
▼ 1.2		SO	Leaving private property of Cerro Gordo Mining District at sign.
	3.7 ▲	SO	Entering private property of Cerro Gordo Mining District at sign.
			GPS: N36°33.08' W117°47.49'
▼ 1.3		SO	Track on left.
	3.6 ▲	SO	Track on right.
▼ 1.6		SO	Two tracks on left.
	3.3 ▲	SO	Two tracks on right.
▼ 2.2		SO	Track on left.
	2.7 ▲	SO	Track on right.
			GPS: N36°33.52' W117°46.66'
▼ 2.3		SO	Track on right.
	2.6 ▲	SO	Track on left.
▼ 4.9		TR	T-intersection with bottom of San Lucas Canyon. Turn right and continue up wash in San Lucas Canyon. Zero trip meter.
	0.0 ▲		Continue to the southwest.
			GPS: N36°34.85' W117°44.67'

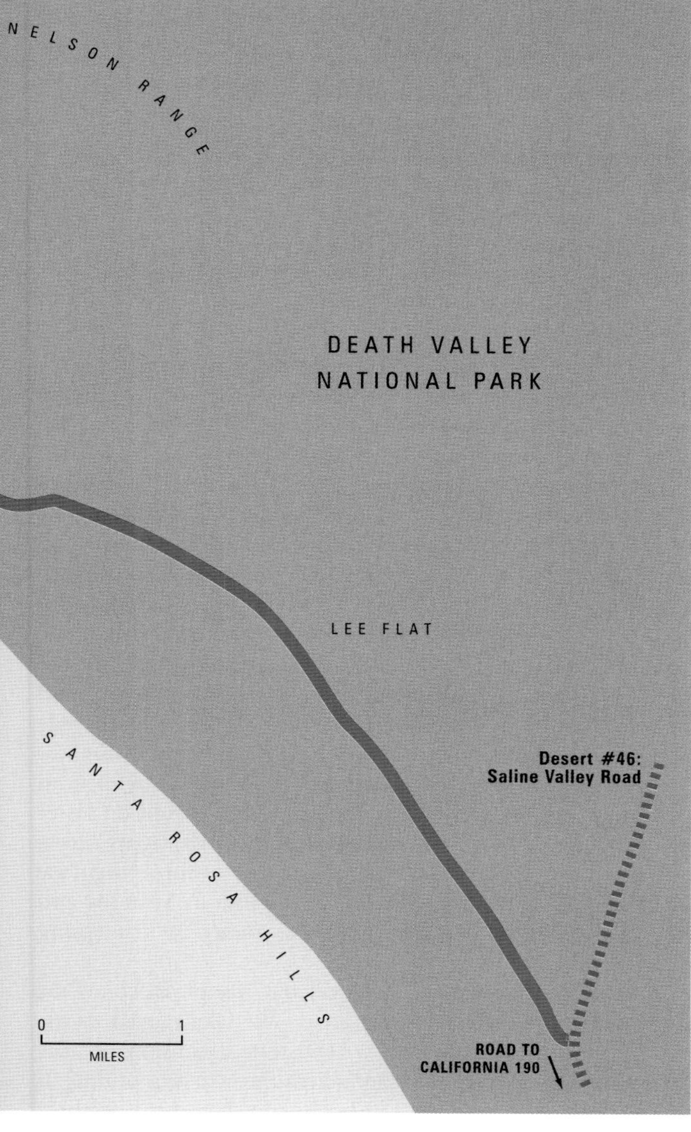

Mileage		Directions
▼ 0.0		Continue to the southeast.
4.4 ▲	TL	Turn left into line of wash, following BLM road marker for Cerro Gordo. Road continues ahead in San Lucas Canyon. Zero trip meter.
▼ 4.1	SO	Trail exits line of the wash.
0.3 ▲	SO	Trail enters line of the wash.
		GPS: N36°32.06′ W117°42.55′
▼ 4.4	TL	T-intersection. Track on right is S5 for 4WDs, ATVs, and motorbikes. Remain on main graded road. Zero trip meter. Trail is now entering Death Valley National Park (no sign).
0.0 ▲		Continue to the northwest.
		GPS: N36°31.85′ W117°42.55′
▼ 0.0		Continue to the northeast.
6.8 ▲	TR	Track straight ahead is S5 for 4WDs, ATVs, and motorbikes. Turn right, remaining on graded road. Zero trip meter. Trail leaves Death Valley National Park (no sign).
▼ 2.2	SO	Cross through wash.
4.6 ▲	SO	Cross through wash.
▼ 2.3	SO	Cross through wash.
4.5 ▲	SO	Cross through wash.
▼ 2.4	SO	Cross through wash.
4.4 ▲	SO	Cross through wash.
▼ 3.0	SO	Well-used track on left.
3.8 ▲	SO	Well-used track on right.
		GPS: N36°30.78′ W117°39.62′
▼ 3.1	SO	Track on left.
3.7 ▲	SO	Track on right.
▼ 5.1	SO	Track on left.
1.7 ▲	SO	Track on right.
		GPS: N36°29.23′ W117°38.48′
▼ 6.6	SO	Track on left.
0.2 ▲	SO	Track on right.
▼ 6.8		Trail ends at intersection with Desert #46: Saline Valley Road in Lee Flat. Turn right for California 136; turn left to travel Saline Valley Road.
0.0 ▲		Trail commences on Desert #46: Saline Valley Road, 11.6 miles north of California 190 in Lee Flat. Zero trip meter at unmarked, well-used intersection with graded dirt road and proceed northwest at the Y-intersection. Saline Valley Road continues to the north at this point.
		GPS: N36°27.91′ W117°37.55′

Sierra Talc Company plant at Keeler

DESERT #48

Swansea-Cerro Gordo Road

Starting Point	**California 136 at the site of Swansea, 9.1 miles east of Lone Pine**
Finishing Point:	**Desert #47: Cerro Gordo Road at Cerro Gordo**
Total Mileage:	**23 miles, plus 1.5-mile spur to Burgess Mine**
Unpaved Mileage:	**23 miles, plus 1.5-mile spur**
Driving Time:	**4.5 hours**
Elevation Range:	**3,700–9,500 feet**
Usually Open:	**Year-round**
Best Time to Travel:	**October to May**
Difficulty Rating:	**5**
Scenic Rating:	**10**
Remoteness Rating:	**+1**

Special Attractions

- Remote, rugged trail that follows a corridor through the Inyo Mountains Wilderness.
- Excellent example of an aerial tramway.
- The privately owned ghost town of Cerro Gordo.

History

The Owens Lake Silver and Lead Company constructed a smelter at Swansea in 1869 to process ores from the many mining claims around Cerro Gordo. A section of the furnace is all that remains today. This was one of three smelters handling ores from the booming mining district. By the late 1860s, Mortimer Belshaw of San Francisco had gained control of a high percentage of the claims, and he was making every effort to develop full control. Victor Beaudry, a merchant from Lone Pine, moved in and set up a store. Beaudry also had a smelter in operation on the mountain. Belshaw and Beaudry joined forces and attempted to squeeze out the smelter operation at Swansea. They constructed a toll road down from the mountain that they called the Yellow Grade Road and charged enormous fees to the miners who used it.

James Brady, who ran the smelter at Swansea, was eager to cut ore transportation costs. He realized it would be faster and cheaper to ferry the enormous number of ingots across Owens Lake rather than hauling them around the lake through soft sand. He constructed a wharf at Swansea and acquired a steamboat, named *Bessie Brady* by his young daughter.

In 1872, a violent earthquake killed 27 people in Lone Pine and altered the bed of Owens Lake. The lake moved to the west, thereby necessitating a 150-foot extension to the planned wharf. The first voyage across the lake to a landing at Cartago was made in May 1872. The trip shaved two to three

High above Saline Valley, aerial tramway timbers are preserved by the dry climate

days off the traditional freight time. Belshaw and Beaudry built their own wharf at Keeler, where the Yellow Grade Road exited the Inyo Mountains, and bought the *Bessie Brady* as part of their expanding Cerro Gordo Freighting Company.

The aerial tramway encountered along this trail was part of the ambitious salt works located at Saline Lake. The salt was reportedly so pure that it was sold at market in an unrefined state. Like all other mining activities in Death Valley, freighting costs and the time involved were prohibitive. In order to cut several days off the transportation route, construction of the monumental aerial tramway was started in 1911, with the first shipment made in 1913. The tramway was almost 14 miles long, making it one of the longest in the world at the time. It traversed extremely rugged terrain. Twenty tons of salt an hour were hauled up nearly 7,000 feet to then drop down more than 5,000 feet to Swansea on the edge of Owens Lake for shipment to market. Three hundred buckets were constantly on the go.

The family who lived and maintained the tower at the top of the crest had a lonely existence. They greeted any visitors who came their way. The family could only occupy the cabin during the summer; winters were much too harsh.

Mining operations lasted into the early 1930s, when salt supplies were depleted. Investors moved on and the salt works closed down. A restoration program, coordinated by the Bishop office of the Bureau of Land Management, is attempting to save the remainder of the controller's cabin and the aerial tramway tower.

Description

The dramatic road that runs over the ridge tops of the Inyo Mountains is one of the most beautiful in the region. The trail also passes the well-preserved remains of the salt tramway.

The trail leaves Swansea, beside the tumbledown stone building that was once a stagecoach stop, and follows a single-lane, stony formed trail toward the Inyo Mountains. The trail is easy to follow for the most part; it is well used with few turns. It climbs up the alluvial fan to enter a canyon. As it climbs, there are good views back over Owens Lake to the Sierra Nevada.

The trail within the wash is lumpy, loose, and gravelly as it climbs gradually to enter a vehicle corridor through the Inyo Mountains Wilderness. As you climb into the mountains, the salt tramway becomes visible. Look for it standing out starkly on the crests of the hills. The wooden tramway towers are well preserved in this dry climate.

The trail undulates steeply as it enters the range, at times with grades up to 25 degrees. At some spots, it is difficult to get traction on the shale surface. The views improve as you climb, with the Sierra Nevada coming fully into view. The driver will want to keep his eyes on the road, particularly around some of the narrow and rough sections of shelf road. The shelf road is narrow, with very limited passing places at times.

A spur leads 1.5 miles to the site of the Burgess Mine, where there is an excellent view over Saline Valley and the Nelson and Panamint Ranges. There is a small cabin left at the mine, plus tailings heaps, diggings, and some stone foundations.

The main trail now runs around the head of Craig Canyon, with a dizzying, sheer drop-off into the canyon, and down toward Saline Valley. It passes under a section of the salt tramway, which sits next to the control station tender's cabin. The cabin and tramway are listed on the National Register of Historic Places. This is one of the most accessible points along the trail to reach the tramway, where it plunges down off the range, heading north toward Saline Valley.

The trail finishes by wrapping down off the range to join Desert #47: Cerro Gordo Road at the ghost town of Cerro Gordo. The town site is privately owned, but tours can be arranged by calling ahead at (760) 876-5030. The final section of the trail crosses private property around Cerro Gordo. Please remain on the main trail.

Overlooking Owens Valley and the Sierra Nevada

Current Road Information

Death Valley National Park
PO Box 579
Death Valley, CA 92328-0579
(760) 786-2331

Bureau of Land Management
Bishop Field Office
785 North Main Street, Suite E
Bishop, CA 93514
(760) 872-4881

Map References

BLM Saline Valley
USGS 1:24,000 Dolomite, New York Butte, Cerro Gordo Peak
1:100,000 Saline Valley
Maptech CD-ROM: Kings Canyon/Death Valley
Southern & Central California Atlas & Gazetteer, pp. 27, 28
California Road & Recreation Atlas, p. 87
Trails Illustrated, Death Valley National Park (221)
Other: Free NPS Death Valley map, Tom Harrison Maps—Death Valley National Park Recreation Map

Route Directions

▼ 0.0		From California 136 at the site of Swansea, 9.1 miles east of US 395 and Lone Pine, zero trip meter and turn east on formed dirt trail. The turn is not well marked. It leaves immediately north of a private house and there is a small wooden "Welcome to Swansea" sign at the turn. The historical marker is opposite, set back from the road. There is a sign once you are on the road for the Swansea-Cerro Gordo Road.
12.3 ▲		Trail ends on California 136 at the site of Swansea. Turn right for US 395 and Lone Pine; turn left for Death Valley.
		GPS: N36°31.46' W117°54.26'
▼ 0.3	SO	Track on left.
12.0 ▲	SO	Track on right.
▼ 1.2	SO	Cross through wash.
11.1 ▲	SO	Cross through wash.
		GPS: N36°32.43' W117°53.97'
▼ 1.4	SO	Cross through wash. Trail follows along line of wash.
10.9 ▲	SO	Cross through wash. Trail leaves line of wash.
▼ 1.6	SO	Track on left.
10.7 ▲	SO	Track on right.

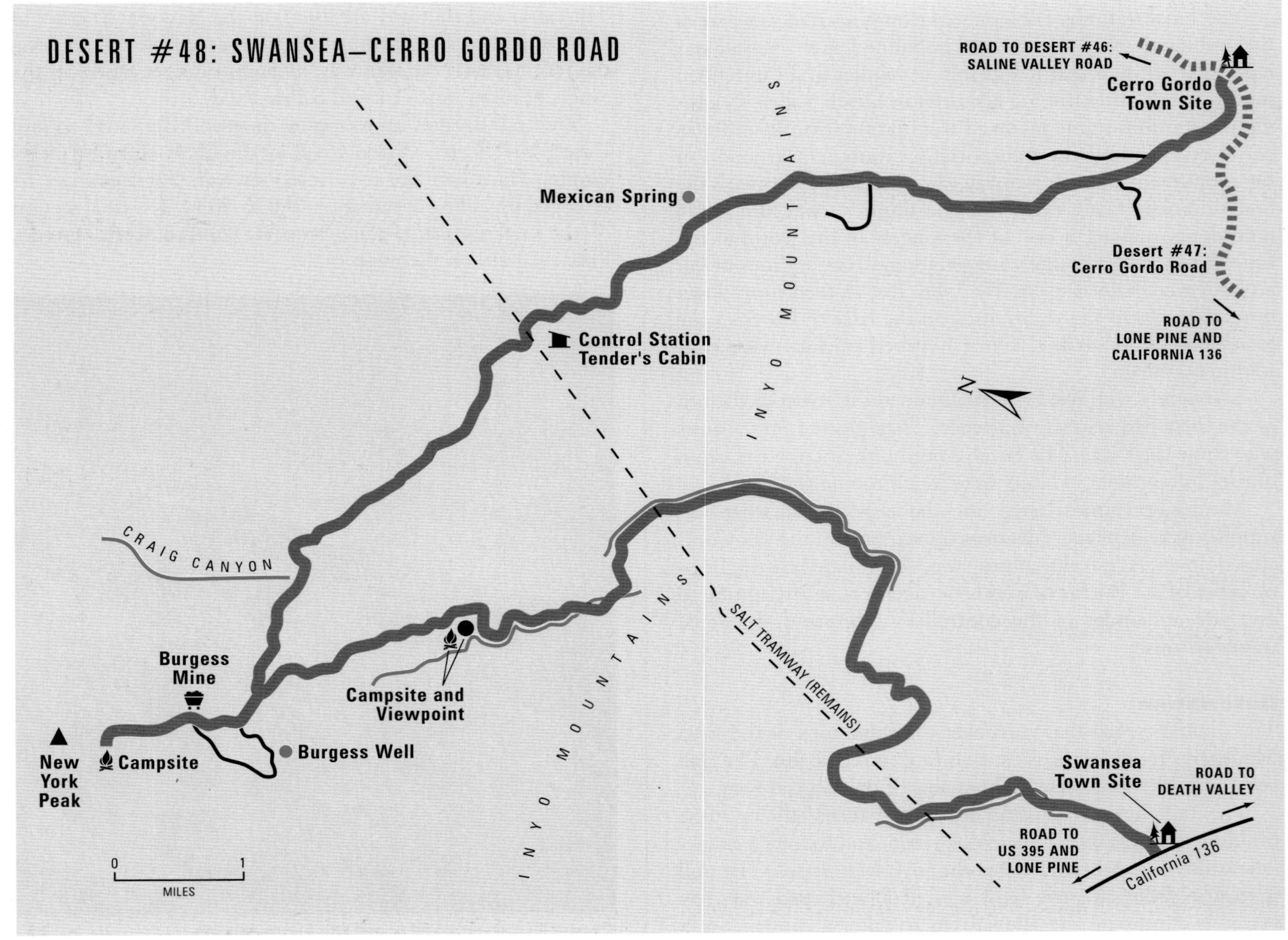

▼ 2.0	SO	Remains of salt tramway on left and right on hill.
10.3 ▲	SO	Remains of salt tramway on right and left on hill.
		GPS: N36°33.04' W117°54.04'
▼ 2.7	SO	Enter wash in tight canyon.
9.6 ▲	SO	Exit wash.
▼ 3.1	SO	Exit wash up steep pinch; then cross through wash.
9.2 ▲	SO	Cross through wash; then descend steep pinch to enter wash.
		GPS: N36°33.72' W117°54.03'
▼ 3.2	SO	Hiking trail on saddle on right goes to tramway support.
9.1 ▲	SO	Hiking trail on saddle on left goes to tramway support.
▼ 3.5	SO	Cross through wash and start to climb.
8.8 ▲	SO	End of descent. Cross through wash.
▼ 4.2	SO	End of climb.
8.1 ▲	SO	Start to descend.
▼ 4.6	SO	Enter wash.
7.7 ▲	SO	Exit wash.
▼ 4.9	SO	Exit wash.
7.4 ▲	SO	Enter wash.
▼ 5.4	SO	Enter wash.
6.9 ▲	SO	Exit wash.
		GPS: N36°33.68' W117°52.66'
▼ 7.9	SO	Salt tramway remains up hillside on right and fallen remains on left.
4.4 ▲	SO	Salt tramway remains up hillside on left and fallen remains on right.
		GPS: N36°35.31' W117°52.04'
▼ 8.9	BL	Exit wash.
3.4 ▲	BR	Enter wash.
		GPS: N36°35.46' W117°53.22'
▼ 9.0	SO	Cross through wash. Enter line of wash, crossing it often.
3.3 ▲	SO	Cross through wash. Exit line of wash.
▼ 10.0	SO	Exit line of wash.
2.3 ▲	SO	Enter line of wash, crossing it often.
		GPS: N36°36.21' W117°53.68'
▼ 10.1	SO	Campsite and viewpoint on left.
2.2 ▲	SO	Campsite and viewpoint on right.
▼ 10.8	SO	Track on left.
1.5 ▲	SO	Track on right.
		GPS: N36°36.63' W117°53.82'
▼ 12.3	TR	Well-used track on left in open flat area is spur to Burgess Mine. Zero trip meter. Intersection is unmarked.
0.0 ▲		Continue to the southeast.
		GPS: N36°37.53' W117°54.69'

Spur to the Burgess Mine

▼ 0.0		Zero trip meter and proceed west on formed trail.
▼ 0.2	BR	Track on left is a 1.3-mile loop past Burgess Well.
		GPS: N36°37.62' W117°54.92'
▼ 0.7	BL	Burgess Mine on right—many tailings heaps, old miner's cabin, and stone foundations remain. There is an exceptional view from this point east over Saline Valley and the Nelson and Panamint Ranges.
		GPS: N36°37.96' W117°54.98'
▼ 1.4	SO	Track on left.
▼ 1.5		Spur ends at turning circle and campsite at the base of New York Peak.
		GPS: N36°38.49' W117°55.34'

Continuation of Main Trail

▼ 0.0		Continue to the east.
4.0 ▲	TL	Well-used track straight ahead in open flat area is spur to Burgess Mine. Zero trip meter. Intersection is unmarked.
		GPS: N36°37.53' W117°54.69
▼ 0.8	SO	Sheer drop-off on left into Craig Canyon and down to Saline Valley.
3.2 ▲	SO	Sheer drop-off on right into Craig Canyon and down to Saline Valley.
▼ 3.8	SO	Salt tramway remains on left, immediately on the hill and farther down.
0.2 ▲	SO	Salt tramway remains on right, immediately on the hill and farther down.
		GPS: N36°36.54' W117°51.30'
▼ 4.0	SO	Pass under aerial tramway. Zero trip meter.
0.0 ▲		Continue to the northwest.
		GPS: N36°36.46' W117°51.18'
▼ 0.0		Continue to the southeast. Control station tender's cabin on right.
6.7 ▲	SO	Control station tender's cabin on left; then pass under aerial tramway. Zero trip meter.
▼ 1.9	BR	Two tracks on left lead into wilderness and are closed to vehicles.
4.8 ▲	BL	Two tracks on right lead into wilderness and are closed to vehicles.
		GPS: N36°35.43' W117°49.76'
▼ 2.5	SO	Mine below trail on left.
4.2 ▲	SO	Mine below trail on right.
		GPS: N36°34.98' W117°49.36'
▼ 3.1	SO	Track on right. Start of steep, loose descent.
3.6 ▲	SO	Track on left. End of climb.
		GPS: N36°34.54' W117°49.21'
▼ 4.2	SO	Enter wash.
2.5 ▲	SO	Exit wash.
		GPS: N36°33.69' W117°49.19'
▼ 4.6	SO	End of descent. Trail starts to climb again.
2.1 ▲	SO	End of descent. Trail starts to climb again.
▼ 5.6	SO	End of climb. Well-used track on right; then track on left. Start of shelf road.
1.1 ▲	SO	End of shelf road. Track on right; then well-used track on left. Trail starts to descend.
		GPS: N36°32.73' W117°48.48'
▼ 6.6	SO	Gate. Entering private property of Cerro Gordo.
0.1 ▲	SO	Gate. Leaving private property.
▼ 6.7		Join larger graded road and bear right, leaving both graded roads on left. Trail finishes on Desert #47: Cerro Gordo Road, immediately north of Cerro Gordo ghost town. Turn left to exit to Desert #46: Saline Valley Road; turn right to exit back to California 136 and Lone Pine.
0.0 ▲		Trail starts 0.1 miles north of Cerro Gordo ghost town on Desert #47: Cerro Gordo Road. Zero trip meter and proceed northwest on graded road and immediately swing left onto unmarked, formed trail that wraps around the hill, leaving two graded roads on the right. You know you are on the correct trail when you pass the Swansea-Cerro Gordo Road warning sign, 0.1 miles from the start of the formed trail.
		GPS: N36°32.36' W117°47.62'

DESERT #49

Hidden Valley Road

Starting Point:	**Desert #51: Racetrack Road, 21.3 miles from intersection with Big Pine Road**
Finishing Point:	**Desert #46: Saline Valley Road, 15.5 miles north of California 190**
Total Mileage:	**28.5 miles, including both spurs**
Unpaved Mileage:	**28.5 miles**
Driving Time:	**3 hours**
Elevation Range:	**4,100–7,300 feet**
Usually Open:	**Year-round**
Best Time to Travel:	**October to April**
Difficulty Rating:	**2**
Scenic Rating:	**9**
Remoteness Rating:	**+1**

Special Attractions

- Extensive remains of the Lost Burro Mine.
- The Ubehebe Talc Mine and other mining camps.
- Hiking access into Death Valley Wilderness.
- Can be combined with Desert #51: Racetrack Road and Desert #46: Saline Valley Road to form a loop trail from Scotty's Castle or Panamint Springs.

History

The site of the Lost Burro Mine was discovered in 1907 by Bert Shively. The prospector was chasing his straying burro when he picked up a rock that contained gold. There was a water-powered 5-stamp mill at the site, running on water piped in from Burro Spring, 8 miles away. The mine had many different owners; its most profitable years were between 1912 and 1917.

Description

Hidden Valley Road leaves Desert #51: Racetrack Road at Teakettle Junction. The name of the intersection has resulted in a number of teakettles being hung from the signpost, many of them inscribed with the thoughts of passing travelers. The National Park Service removes some of them periodically, but they are typically replaced as quickly as they are removed. This unique piece of folk art makes the start of Hidden Valley Road difficult to miss.

A short distance from the start, the trail enters Lost Burro Gap, a narrow canyon of tilted, striated rock. The trail follows a gravelly wash through this short but picturesque gap.

A very worthwhile detour from the main trail is the short side trail to Lost Burro Mine. The site includes extensive mining remains set in a tight, small canyon. A miner's cabin, outhouse, and various wooden structures remain. Opposite the turn to Lost Burro Mine, a second trail leads to White Top Mountain.

Lost Burro Mine is well preserved in the dry atmosphere of the Panamint Range

Continuing along Hidden Valley Road, the trail dips down to enter the long, wide Hidden Valley. A saddle divides the valley from Ulida Flat. Several spur trails on both sides lead to the remains of old mining camps on the flat. One worthwhile trail is the spur to Ubehebe Talc Mine, where various remains can still be seen and photographed.

Past the flats and mining areas, the road climbs above 7,000 feet. The wide shelf road is easygoing as it twists through pinyons and junipers to wind along the top of Hunter Mountain. In winter, this section can be icy and may be blocked by snow. Chains should be carried in winter months.

The trail finishes by descending from Hunter Mountain to join Desert #46: Saline Valley Road at South Pass. The Panamint Dunes and Panamint Dry Lake can be seen to the south from this intersection.

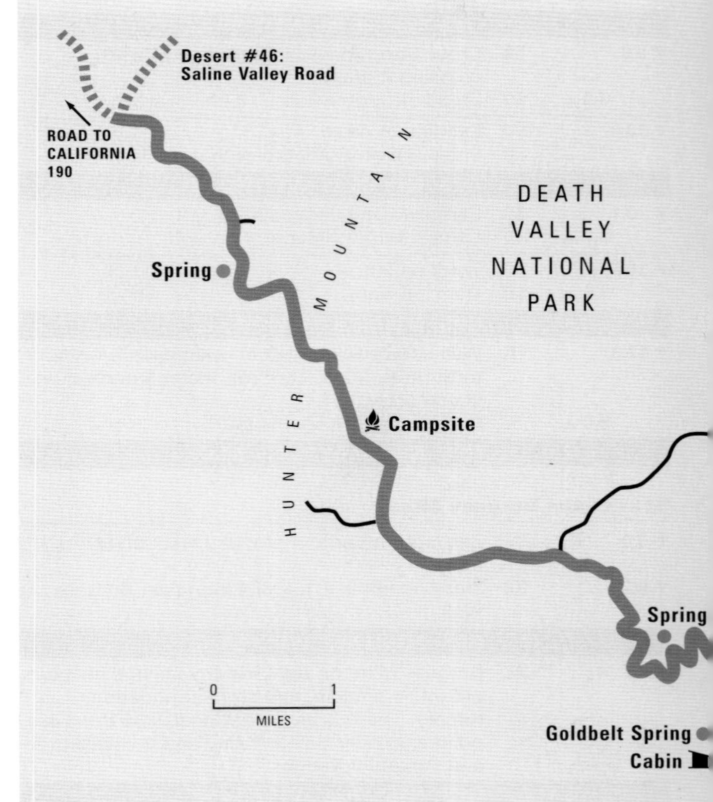

Current Road Information

Death Valley National Park
PO Box 579
Death Valley, CA 92328-0579
(760) 786-2331

Map References

BLM Saline Valley
USGS 1:24,000 Teakettle Junction, Ubehebe Peak, Sand Flat, Harris Hill, Jackass Canyon
1:100,000 Saline Valley
Maptech CD-ROM: Kings Canyon/Death Valley
Southern & Central California Atlas & Gazetteer, p. 28
California Road & Recreation Atlas, p. 87
Trails Illustrated, Death Valley National Park (221)
Other: Free NPS Death Valley map

Route Directions

Mileage		Direction
▼ 0.0		From Desert #51: Racetrack Road at Teakettle Junction, 21.3 miles south of the intersection with Big Pine Road near Grapevine, zero trip meter and turn southeast on graded dirt trail, following sign to Hunter Mountain.
3.1 ▲		Trail ends at Teakettle Junction on Desert #51: Racetrack Road. Turn left to visit The Racetrack; turn right to exit via Racetrack Road to Scotty's Castle.
		GPS: N36°45.61' W117°32.48'
▼ 0.1	SO	Cross through wash.
3.0 ▲	SO	Cross through wash.

Striated rock within Lost Burro Gap

Mileage		Direction
▼ 1.2	SO	Entering Lost Burro Gap. Trail is traveling in wash.
1.9 ▲	SO	Exiting Lost Burro Gap and wash.
		GPS: N36°44.91' W117°31.49'
▼ 1.8	SO	Exiting Lost Burro Gap.
1.3 ▲	SO	Entering Lost Burro Gap.
▼ 2.4	SO	Exit line of wash.
0.7 ▲	SO	Enter line of wash.
▼ 3.1	SO	4-way intersection. Track on right goes 1.2 miles to Lost Burro Mine. Track on left travels

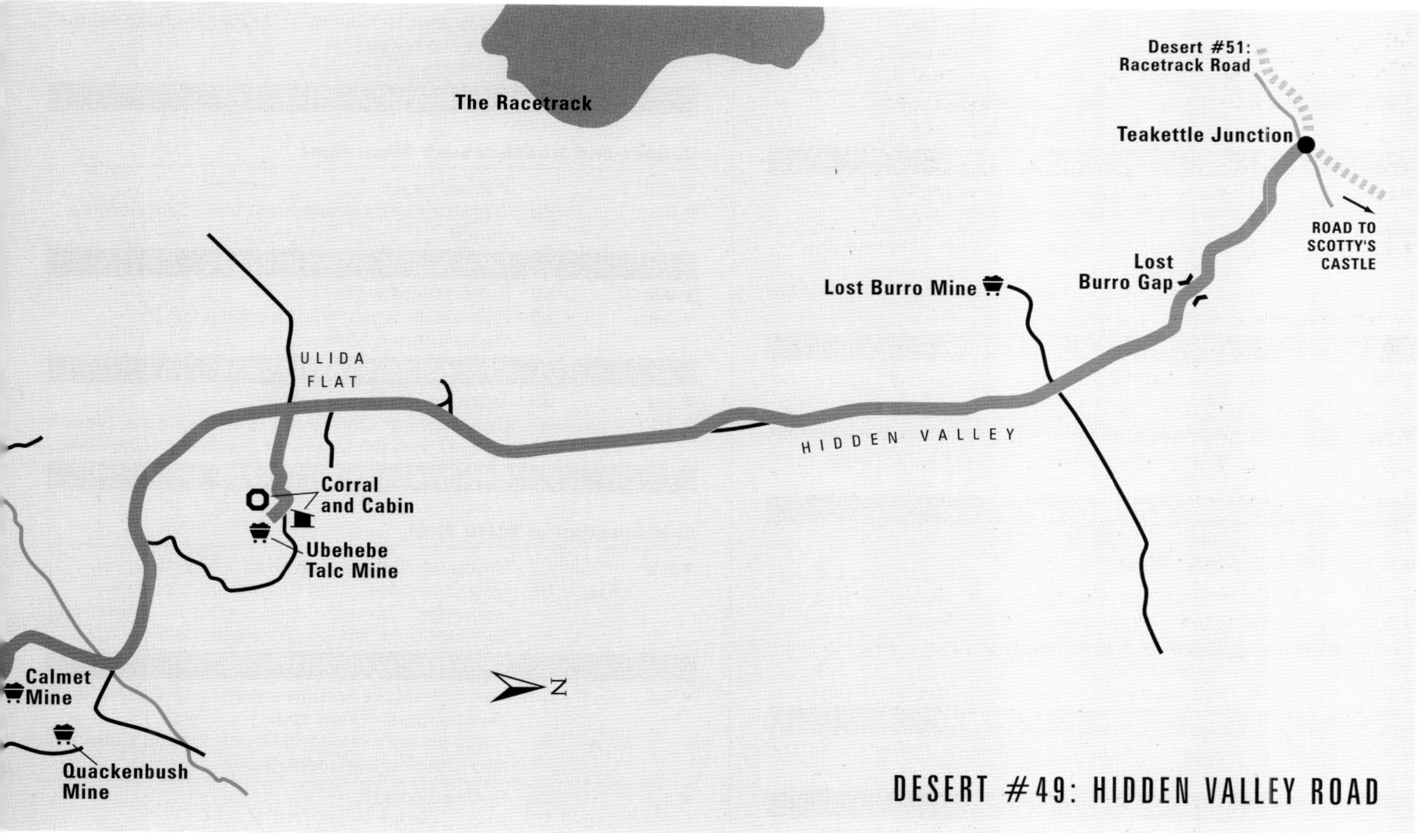

The Racetrack
Desert #51: Racetrack Road
Teakettle Junction
ROAD TO SCOTTY'S CASTLE
Lost Burro Mine
Lost Burro Gap
ULIDA FLAT
HIDDEN VALLEY
Corral and Cabin
Ubehebe Talc Mine
Calmet Mine
Quackenbush Mine
N

DESERT #49: HIDDEN VALLEY ROAD

Lost Burro Mine cabin remains intact. High winds can be one of the most destructive forces in this region

toward White Top Mountain. Zero trip meter.
0.0 ▲ Continue to the northwest, exiting Hidden Valley.

GPS: N36°43.78' W117°30.26'

▼ 0.0 Continue to the southeast, entering Hidden Valley.
6.4 ▲ SO 4-way intersection. Track on left goes 1.2 miles to Lost Burro Mine. Track on right travels toward White Top Mountain. Zero trip meter.

▼ 1.4 SO Track on left.
5.0 ▲ SO Track on right.

▼ 2.3 BR Track on left is old road (not used). Deep, fine dirt traps for next 0.7 miles.
4.1 ▲ SO Track on right is old road rejoining.

▼ 3.0 SO Track on left is old road rejoining.
3.4 ▲ BL Track on right is old road (not used). Deep, fine dirt traps for next 0.7 miles.

▼ 5.0 SO Track on right is a short dead end.
1.4 ▲ SO Second entrance to track on left.

GPS: N36°39.38' W117°29.95'

▼ 5.2 SO Second entrance to track on right.
1.2 ▲ SO Track on left is a short dead end.

▼ 5.3 SO Saddle. Leaving Hidden Valley and entering Ulida Flat.
1.1 ▲ SO Saddle. Leaving Ulida Flat and entering Hidden Valley.

GPS: N36°39.21' W117°30.08'

▼ 6.1 SO Track on left.
0.3 ▲ SO Track on right.

▼ 6.4 SO Well-used track on left is spur to Ubehebe Talc Mine. Also track on right. Zero trip meter.
0.0 ▲ Continue to the north.

GPS: N36°38.20' W117°30.07'

Spur to Ubehebe Talc Mine

▼ 0.0 Proceed east on well-used, unmarked trail.
▼ 0.1 SO Track on right returns to main trail. Sign for Ubehebe Talc Mine.
▼ 0.4 SO Enter line of wash.
▼ 0.6 SO Exit line of wash and climb up side of hill.

GPS: N36°38.15' W117°29.41'

▼ 0.9 SO Saddle. Remains of mine are visible ahead and on the right.

GPS: N36°38.21' W117°29.21'

▼ 1.0 BR Cabin on left and old corral on right; then track on left down line of wash.
▼ 1.2 UT Trail ends at Ubehebe Talc Mine.

GPS: N36°38.04' W117°29.08'

Continuation of Main Trail

▼ 0.0 Continue to the south.
3.1 ▲ SO Well-used track on right is spur to Ubehebe Talc Mine. Also track on left. Zero trip meter.

GPS: N36°38.20' W117°30.07'

▼ 0.2 SO Track on left is second entrance to Ubehebe Talc Mine spur.
2.9 ▲ SO Track on right is alternate entrance to Ubehebe Talc Mine spur.

▼ 1.6 SO Saddle. Exiting Ulida Flat.
1.5 ▲ SO Saddle. Entering Ulida Flat.

GPS: N36°37.10' W117°29.24'

▼ 1.9 SO Small track on left goes to mining camp.
1.2 ▲ SO Small track on right goes to mining camp.

GPS: N36°37.15' W117°28.85'

▼ 2.3 SO Cross through wash.
0.8 ▲ SO Cross through wash.

▼ 2.6 SO Enter line of wash.
0.5 ▲ SO Exit line of wash.

▼ 2.8 SO Exit line of wash.
0.3 ▲ SO Enter line of wash.

▼ 3.1 BR Trail forks. Track on left goes to mine. Bear right and zero trip meter.
0.0 ▲ Continue to the north.

GPS: N36°36.97' W117°27.73'

▼ 0.0 Continue to the south and cross through wash.
0.9 ▲ SO Cross through wash. Track on right goes to mine. Zero trip meter.

▼ 0.9 BR Trail forks. Intersection is unmarked. Track on left is spur to Calmet and Quackenbush Mines. Zero trip meter.
0.0 ▲ Continue to the west.

GPS: N36°36.20' W117°27.84'

Calmet and Quackenbush Mine Spur

▼ 0.0 Proceed east.
▼ 0.3 SO Track on right rejoins main trail. Calmet Mine on left.

GPS: N36°36.11' W117°27.57'

▼ 0.5 SO Enter line of wash.
▼ 0.8 SO Exit line of wash; then track on left to Quackenbush Mine.

GPS: N36°36.04' W117°26.99'

▼ 1.0 BR Track on left to old cabin.
▼ 1.1 UT Spur ends at old mining remains near Goldbelt Spring, once the locality of Goldbelt mining camp.

GPS: N36°35.89' W117°26.83'

Continuation of Main Trail

▼ 0.0 Continue to the south. Trail starts to climb.
3.6 ▲ BL End of descent. Trail forks. Intersection is unmarked. Track on right is spur to Calmet and Quackenbush Mines. Zero trip meter.

GPS: N36°36.20' W117°27.84'

▼ 0.4 SO Track on left is second entrance to Calmet and Quackenbush Mine spur.
3.2 ▲ BL Track on right is alternate entrance to Calmet and Quackenbush Mine spur.

▼ 1.2 SO Spring on right.
2.4 ▲ SO Spring on left.

▼	▲		
			GPS: N36°35.55' W117°27.82'
▼ 3.1		SO	End of climb. Trail is now running over Hunter Mountain.
	0.5 ▲	SO	Start of descent off Hunter Mountain.
▼ 3.5		SO	Cattle guard.
	0.1 ▲	SO	Cattle guard.
			GPS: N36°34.78' W117°28.65'
▼ 3.6		SO	Well-used track on right. Zero trip meter.
	0.0 ▲		Continue to the north.
			GPS: N36°34.72' W117°28.70'
▼ 0.0			Continue to the south.
	6.8 ▲	SO	Well-used track on left. Zero trip meter.
▼ 1.6		SO	Track on left over cattle guard.
	5.2 ▲	SO	Track on right over cattle guard.
			GPS: N36°33.45' W117°29.02'
▼ 2.6		SO	Track on right and campsite on right.
	4.2 ▲	SO	Track on left and campsite on left.
▼ 4.0		SO	Trail starts to descend toward Mill Canyon.
	2.8 ▲	SO	End of climb. Trail is now running over Hunter Mountain.
▼ 4.9		SO	Spring on left.
	1.9 ▲	SO	Spring on right.
			GPS: N36°32.44' W117°31.40'
▼ 5.2		SO	Track on right.
	1.6 ▲	SO	Track on left.
			GPS: N36°32.39' W117°31.75'
▼ 5.7		SO	Track on right.
	1.1 ▲	SO	Track on left.
▼ 6.8			Trail ends at intersection with Desert #46: Saline Valley Road on South Pass, 15.5 miles north of California 190. Turn left for California 190; turn right to travel along Saline Valley Road.
	0.0 ▲		Trail commences on Desert #46: Saline Valley Road on South Pass, 15.5 miles north of California 190. Zero trip meter and turn north on unmarked, well-used graded dirt road that starts to climb Hunter Mountain. There are views south of Panamint Dry Lake and the Panamint Dunes.
			GPS: N36°31.62' W117°32.75'

DESERT #50

Lippincott Mine Road

Starting Point:	**Desert #46: Saline Valley Road, 10 miles north of intersection with Desert #49: Hidden Valley Road**
Finishing Point:	**Lippincott Mine**
Total Mileage:	**8 miles**
Unpaved Mileage:	**8 miles**
Driving Time:	**1.5 hours**
Elevation Range:	**2,000–3,900 feet**
Usually Open:	**Year-round**
Best Time to Travel:	**October to May**
Difficulty Rating:	**4**
Scenic Rating:	**9**
Remoteness Rating:	**+1**

Special Attractions

- Rugged, moderately challenging 4WD trail within Death Valley National Park.
- Remains of the Lippincott Mine.
- Trail provides a link between Desert #51: Racetrack Road and Desert #46: Saline Valley Road for high-clearance 4WD vehicles.

Description

Lippincott Mine Road is not sign-posted at either end, and it does not appear on the free map handed out by the rangers when you enter the park. However, the road does exist and it is well traveled by those in the know. The trail connects dusty Desert #46: Saline Valley Road with Desert #51: Racetrack Road, both roughly graded dirt roads suitable for high-clearance vehicles. Lippincott Mine Road, however, requires a 4WD vehicle because of the loose and lumpy nature of the trail and the narrowness of the shelf road. In addition, the trail receives little maintenance and is quite eroded. Even a scant inch of rain can cause the loose trail to wash out to the point of impassability.

Old mining equipment at the upper level of the Lippincott Mine overlooking The Racetrack

The intersection at the start of the trail is marked by a cairn and a sign warning about the rough road ahead. The trail begins by heading east from Saline Valley Road and gradually climbing the bajada to the canyon. It winds into an unnamed, tight canyon and starts to climb, gaining nearly 2,000 feet in the next 5 miles.

The trail within the canyon is slow going. Large embedded boulders require careful wheel placement and some washouts reduce the trail to a single vehicle width. However, with a careful driver, the trail is traversable by most high-clearance 4WDs. Drivers should be aware that conditions can be worse than those described here because the trail receives little maintenance.

The trail snakes its way up, giving excellent views back toward the Saline Valley and the mountains beyond. From the top of the trail, the Lippincott Mine is visible on the far side of the canyon. The trail briefly joins the final run of the grader from Desert #51: Racetrack Road, passing the end of this trail before dropping in standard again to a rough, loose 4WD trail. Two separate spurs lead to different parts of the Lippincott Mine; both have various remains.

The trail is usually open all year, though it may be closed after heavy rain. It is uncomfortably hot for both you and your vehicle in summer and it may be icy in winter.

Lippincott Mine Road descends to Saline Valley

Current Road Information

Death Valley National Park
PO Box 579
Death Valley, CA 92328-0579
(760) 786-2331

Map References

BLM Saline Valley
USGS 1:24,000 Nelson Range, West of Ubehebe Peak, Ubehebe Peak
1:100,000 Saline Valley
Maptech CD-ROM: Kings Canyon/Death Valley
Southern & Central California Atlas & Gazetteer, p. 28
California Road & Recreation Atlas, p. 87
Trails Illustrated, Death Valley National Park (221)
Other: Free NPS Death Valley map (does not show road on map)

Route Directions

▼ 0.0			Trail commences on Desert #46: Saline Valley Road, 10 miles north of the end of Desert #49: Hidden Valley Road. Zero trip meter and turn northeast on graded dirt track. Intersection is unmarked apart from a large cairn.
	6.7 ▲		Trail ends on Desert #46: Saline Valley Road. Turn left to exit to California 190 and Lone Pine; turn right to exit to California 168 and the Owens Valley.
			GPS: N36°37.20' W117°38.88'
▼ 0.1		SO	Warning sign for Lippincott Road.
	6.6 ▲	SO	Warning sign for Lippincott Road.
▼ 0.3		SO	Cross through wash.
	6.4 ▲	SO	Cross through wash.
▼ 0.7		SO	Cross through wash.
	6.0 ▲	SO	Cross through wash.
▼ 0.8		SO	Cross through wash.
	5.9 ▲	SO	Cross through wash.
▼ 1.0		SO	Cross through wide wash.
	5.7 ▲	SO	Cross through wide wash.
▼ 1.2		SO	Cross through wash.
	5.5 ▲	SO	Cross through wash.
▼ 1.3		SO	Cross through wash.
	5.4 ▲	SO	Cross through wash.
▼ 1.4		SO	Cross through wash.
	5.3 ▲	SO	Cross through wash.
▼ 1.9		SO	Cross through wide wash.
	4.8 ▲	SO	Cross through wide wash.

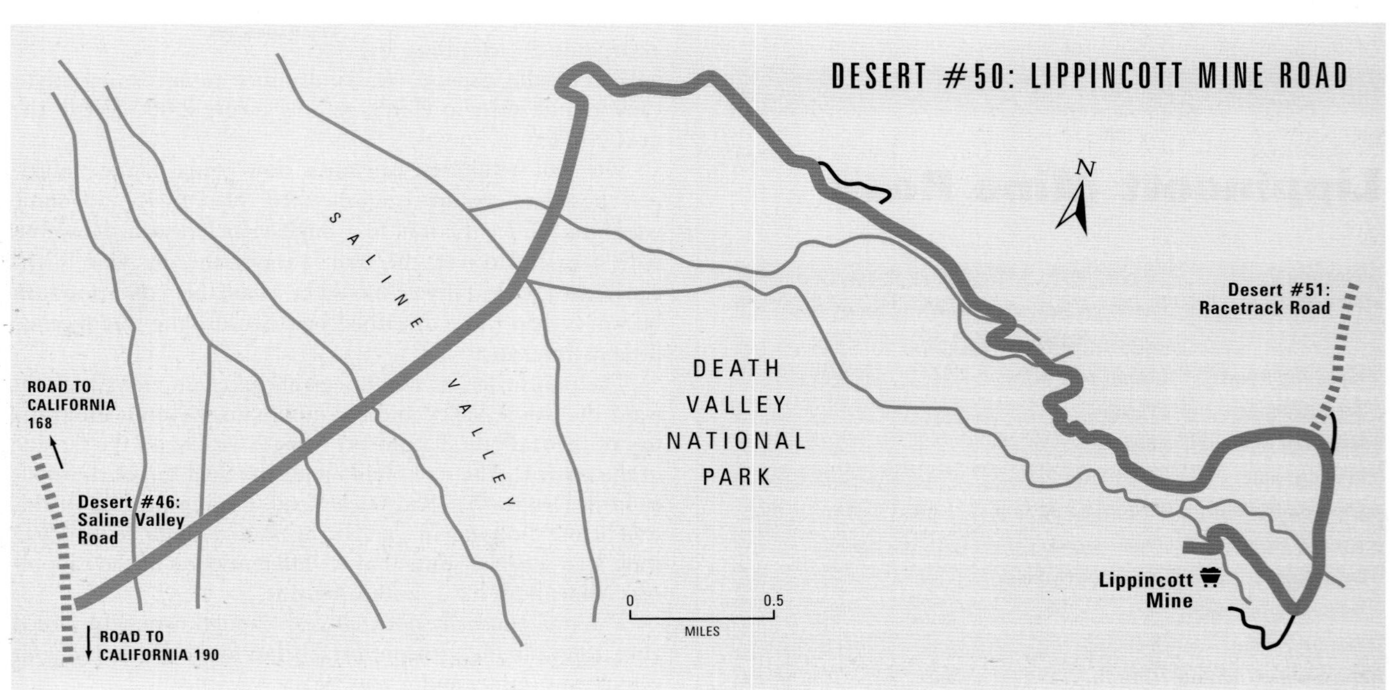

▼ 2.1	SO	Cross through wide wash.
4.6 ▲	SO	Cross through wide wash.
▼ 2.3	SO	Cross through wide wash. Leave bajada and start to climb away from Saline Valley.
4.4 ▲	SO	End of descent. Start to cross bajada. Cross through wide wash.
		GPS: N36°38.81' W117°37.41'
▼ 2.5	SO	Start of shelf road.
4.2 ▲	SO	End of shelf road.
▼ 3.7	SO	Faint track on left.
3.0 ▲	SO	Faint track on right.
▼ 3.9	SO	Track on left to mine.
2.8 ▲	SO	Track on right to mine.
		GPS: N36°38.89' W117°36.34'
▼ 4.1	SO	Adit on left.
2.6 ▲	SO	Adit on right.
▼ 4.2	SO	Old Death Valley National Park boundary at metal sign.
2.5 ▲	SO	Old Death Valley National Park boundary at metal sign.
		GPS: N36°38.82' W117°36.13'
▼ 4.4	SO	Cross through wash.
2.3 ▲	SO	Cross through wash.
▼ 4.6	SO	Cross through wash.
2.1 ▲	SO	Cross through wash.
▼ 4.8	SO	Cross through wash.
1.9 ▲	SO	Cross through wash.
▼ 5.2	SO	Cross through wash.
1.5 ▲	SO	Cross through wash.
▼ 5.9	SO	End of climb from Saline Valley. The Lippincott Mine is visible on the south side of the canyon wall.
0.8 ▲	SO	Start of descent to Saline Valley.
▼ 6.5	SO	Road standard improves to graded dirt at a small turning circle.
0.2 ▲	SO	Warning sign for Lippincott Road. Road standard is now a rough, formed trail that starts to descend toward Saline Valley.
		GPS: N36°38.44' W117°34.70'
▼ 6.7	BR	Trail forks. Graded road on left is Desert #51: Racetrack Road. Zero trip meter. Intersection is unsigned.
0.0 ▲		Continue to the south.
		GPS: N36°38.47' W117°34.51'
▼ 0.0		Continue to the east. Trail is now a spur.
▼ 0.1	SO	Second entrance to Desert #51: Racetrack Road.
▼ 0.2	SO	Start of Lippincott Mine Area. Camping permitted for next 0.2 miles.
		GPS: N36°38.36' W117°34.43'
▼ 0.3	BR	Track on left. There are a few exposed campsites in this area.
▼ 0.4	SO	Track on right joins. Trail drops to cross through wash.
▼ 0.5	SO	Cross through wide wash.
▼ 0.7	BR	Old yellow water tank on left; then track on left goes 0.5 miles to an upper level of the Lippincott Mine.
		GPS: N36°37.93' W117°34.43'
▼ 1.2	SO	Cross through wash.
▼ 1.3		Trail ends at the Lippincott Mine. Adit and various remains, including the loading hopper and part of the old tramway, are scattered around.
		GPS: N36°38.08' W117°34.84'

DESERT #51

Racetrack Road

Starting Point:	**Big Pine Road, 2.7 miles west of Grapevine on North Highway**
Finishing Point:	**Desert #50: Lippincott Mine Road, 1.3 miles west of Lippincott Mine**
Total Mileage:	**30.5 miles**
Unpaved Mileage:	**27.8 miles**
Driving Time:	**2.25 hours**
Elevation Range:	**2,000–5,000**
Usually Open:	**Year-round**
Best Time to Travel:	**October to May**
Difficulty Rating:	**2**
Scenic Rating:	**9**
Remoteness Rating:	**+1**

Special Attractions

- Ubehebe Crater.
- Racetrack Playa and the mysterious moving rocks.

History

Ubehebe Crater was formed several thousand years ago by a volcanic explosion. Magma rose to the surface, contacting groundwater. The build-up of steam pressure caused an explosion of such force that it created the crater you see today. The crater is 500 feet deep and half a mile wide. Rock debris from the explosion covers an area of several square miles. Several smaller craters, formed at a later time, can be found to the south of the main crater. *Ubehebe* (pronounced "yew-beh-HEE-bee") is an Indian word meaning "big basket in the rock."

South of the crater, the Ubehebe Mine was first established

The huge pit of Ubehebe Crater was formed several thousand years ago by a volcanic explosion

in 1875, but was not developed until 1906. The mine produced copper, lead, and zinc. However, its remote location meant that it would not be profitable until the value of copper increased. This finally happened when copper wiring became essential for domestic electricity.

In 1906, Jack Salsberry purchased the mine. A tent city known as Salina City sprang up to service the mine. Situated in Racetrack Valley, Salina City had two saloons, a store, and a stage station. However it did not have a post office. Most of the workers lived in tents on the valley floor.

Jack Salsberry also surveyed a railroad grade that would connect the Ubehebe Mine to the Las Vegas & Tonopah Railroad tracks at Bonnie Claire, Nevada. The grade was supposed to run up Grapevine Canyon. Although construction of the line was started, the mine did not warrant the outlay and the railroad was abandoned. Racetrack Road follows the surveyed grade from Ubehebe Crater to the mine. The mine was last worked in 1951.

The famous moving rocks at The Racetrack are not the only example of this phenomenon to be found near Death Valley, but they are the best known. Other playas in the area also show evidence of the mysterious movement. The real reason the rocks move is unknown. It was originally thought that magnetic forces somehow caused the rocks to move. The current theory is that a combination of rain or ice on the playa makes its surface slick enough that the rocks are moved by gusts of high wind. Although it is a little hard to believe—some of the rocks weigh up to 500 pounds and the force needed to move them under any conditions would be considerable—nobody has come up with a more plausible explanation.

Description

Racetrack Road is a long, graded dirt road that runs from Ubehebe Crater down a long valley to The Racetrack—a dry lakebed, famous for its legendary moving rocks.

Initially, the road follows a small, one-way loop past the large deep pit of Ubehebe Crater. The graded dirt road starts here and heads south, down the long valley between the Panamint Range to the east and the Last Chance Range to the west. The valley is carpeted with sagebrush and creosote bush, interspersed with clumps of cotton top cactus growing on the alluvial fan. The road can be very washboardy depending on how recently it was graded. But apart from the bumpy ride, it is an easy drive for high-clearance 2WD vehicles; on occasion passenger vehicles can make the trip.

The Grandstand on the Racetrack playa

Teakettle Junction

The intersection with Desert #49: Hidden Valley Road comes at Teakettle Junction. The signpost is always adorned with a number of teakettles, some brand new, some old and battered. The kettles are hung in disarray on the signpost and passing travelers often leave their names and thoughts inscribed on them. When there are too many, park rangers remove some of the kettles, but they always leave a good selection.

The Racetrack playa comes into view 5.6 miles after Teakettle Junction. The smooth surface of the dry lake is broken by The Grandstand, an outcropping of rock that protrudes through the lakebed. The moving rocks can be found at the southern end of the playa. It is approximately a half-mile walk over the flat surface to reach the rocks. You can see rocks that have traveled (often a great distance) across the bed. The imprint of their tracks can clearly be seen. Why the rocks move is a mystery but it is these moving rocks that give The Racetrack its name.

Racetrack Road ends a couple of miles farther, at the intersection with Desert #50: Lippincott Mine Road. This rough trail is a shorter exit to Desert #46: Saline Valley Road, but it is suitable for high-clearance 4WD vehicles only.

Current Road Information

Death Valley National Park
PO Box 579
Death Valley, CA 92328-0579
(760) 786-2331

Map References

BLM Last Chance Range, Saline Valley
USGS 1:24,000 Ubehebe Crater, Tin Mt., Dry Mt., White Top Mt., Teakettle Junction, Ubehebe Peak
1:100,000 Last Chance Range, Saline Valley
Maptech CD-ROM: Kings Canyon/Death Valley
Southern & Central California Atlas & Gazetteer, p. 28
California Road & Recreation Atlas, pp. 80, 87
Trails Illustrated, Death Valley National Park (221)
Other: Free NPS Death Valley map

Route Directions

Mileage		Directions
▼ 0.0		From Big Pine Road, 2.7 miles west of Grapevine on North Highway, zero trip meter and proceed northwest on paved road following the sign to Ubehebe Crater. Big Pine Road continues as a graded dirt road to the north.
2.4 ▲		Trail ends on Big Pine Road. Continue to the east on Big Pine Road to exit to Grapevine and Scotty's Castle.
		GPS: N37°01.07' W117°24.63'
▼ 0.3	SO	Cross through Death Valley Wash.
2.1 ▲	SO	Cross through Death Valley Wash.
▼ 2.4	BR	Road on left is exit from Ubehebe Crater. Start of one-way road section. Zero trip meter and continue reading Forward Directions
0.0 ▲	SO	Road on left is entry to Ubehebe Crater. End of one-way road.
		GPS: N37°00.86' W117°27.18'

Forward Directions

Mileage		Directions
▼ 0.0		Continue to the northwest.
▼ 0.3	TR	Turn right onto graded dirt Racetrack Road at sign. Zero trip meter. Ubehebe Crater is straight ahead. To visit the crater, follow around the loop and return to this point.
		GPS: N37°00.78' W117°27.41'

Reverse Directions

Mileage		Directions
0.0 ▲		Continue to the southeast.
0.3 ▲	SO	Ubehebe Crater on right.
		GPS: N37°00.67' W117°27.24'
0.6 ▲		End of one-way section. Zero trip meter. Turn left to continue along Racetrack Road; turn right to continue the trail in the reverse direction to Big Pine Road.
		GPS: N37°00.86' W117°27.18'

Continuation of Main Trail

Mileage		Directions
▼ 0.0		Continue to the west on graded dirt road. End of one-way road. No camping allowed for next 2 miles.
18.6 ▲		Turn right onto paved road into Ubehebe Crater. No entry to road on left, part of the one-way system around the crater. Zero trip meter and continue reading Reverse Directions.
		GPS: N37°00.78' W117°27.41'
▼ 2.9	SO	Track on left.
15.7 ▲	SO	Track on right.
		GPS: N36°58.40' W117°28.16'
▼ 3.2	SO	Cross through wash.
15.4 ▲	SO	Cross through wash.
▼ 12.8	SO	Largest peak on left is Tin Mountain.
5.8 ▲	SO	Largest peak on right is Tin Mountain.
		GPS: N36°50.27' W117°30.15'
▼ 16.4	SO	Cross through wash.
2.2 ▲	SO	Cross through wash.
▼ 18.5	SO	Cross through wash.
0.1 ▲	SO	Cross through wash.
▼ 18.6	SO	Teakettle Junction. Zero trip meter and continue on Racetrack Road, following sign to The Racetrack. Track on left is Desert #49: Hidden Valley Road.
0.0 ▲		Continue to the northeast.
		GPS: N36°45.61' W117°32.48'

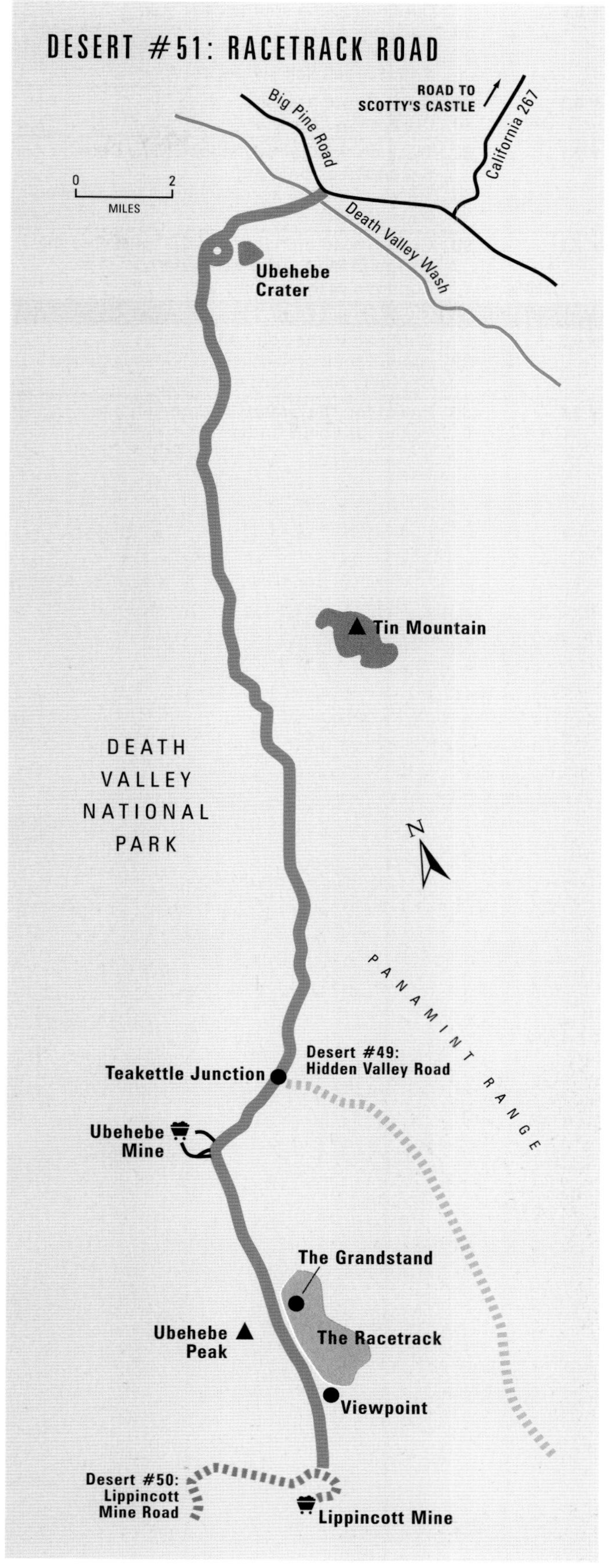

▼ 0.0			Continue to the southwest.
	2.2 ▲	SO	Teakettle Junction. Zero trip meter and continue on Racetrack Road. Track on right is Desert #49: Hidden Valley Road.
▼ 0.3		SO	Cross through wash.
	1.9 ▲	SO	Cross through wash.
▼ 2.1		BL	Track on right joins Ubehebe Mine track. Second track on right.
	0.1 ▲	SO	Track on left and second entrance to Ubehebe Mine on left.
▼ 2.2		SO	Graded road on right goes 0.7 miles into the Ubehebe Mine. Zero trip meter.
	0.0 ▲		Continue to the north.
			GPS: N36°44.66′ W117°34.45′
▼ 0.0			Continue to the southeast.
	5.3 ▲	BR	Graded road on left goes 0.7 miles into the Ubehebe Mine. Zero trip meter.
▼ 3.4		SO	Pull-in for The Grandstand on left.
	1.9 ▲	SO	Pull-in for The Grandstand on right.
			GPS: N36°41.66′ W117°34.24′
▼ 5.3		SO	Turnout on left is viewing point for the moving rocks. Zero trip meter.
	0.0 ▲		Continue to the north.
			GPS: N36°39.95′ W117°34.04′
▼ 0.0			Continue to the south.
	1.7 ▲	SO	Turnout on right is viewing point for the moving rocks. Zero trip meter.
▼ 1.7			Trail ends at T-intersection with Desert #50: Lippincott Mine Road. Turn left to visit the Lippincott Mine; turn right to exit to Desert #46: Saline Valley Road. NOTE that Lippincott Mine Road is 4-rated and suitable for high-clearance 4WD vehicles only.
	0.0 ▲		Trail commences along Desert #50: Lippincott Mine Road, 1.3 miles west of the Lippincott Mine. Zero trip meter and turn north on graded dirt road. Intersection is unmarked.
			GPS: N36°38.47′ W117°34.51′

Selected Further Reading

Massey, Peter, and Jeanne Wilson. *4WD Adventures: Colorado.* Castle Rock, Colo.: Swagman Publishing, Inc., 1999.

—. *4WD Adventures: Utah.* Castle Rock, Colo.: Swagman Publishing, Inc., 2000.

—. *Backcountry Adventures: Arizona.* Castle Rock, Colo.: Swagman Publishing, Inc., 2001.

Bauer, Helen. *California Mission Days.* New York: Doubleday & Company, Inc., 1951.

Beck, Warren A., and Ynez D. Haase. *Historical Atlas of California.* Norman, Okla.: University of Oklahoma Press, 1974.

Belden, L. Burr, and Mary DeDecker. *Death Valley to Yosemite: Frontier Mining Camps and Ghost Towns.* Bishop, Calif.: Spotted Dog Press, Inc., 1998.

Boessenecker, John. *Gold Dust and Gunsmoke.* New York: John Wiley & Sons, Inc., 1999.

Braasch, Barbara. *California's Gold Rush Country.* Medina, Wash.: Johnston Associates International, 1996.

Bright, William. *1500 California Place Names.* Berkeley and Los Angeles: University of California Press, 1998.

Broman, Mickey, and Russ Leadabrand. *California Ghost Town Trails.* Baldwin Park, Calif.: Gem Guides Book Co., 1985.

Brown, Vinson. *The Californian Wildlife Region.* Happy Camp, Calif.: Naturegraph Publishers, Inc., 1999.

Bukowski, Charles. *Hollywood.* Santa Rosa, Calif.: Black Sparrow Press, 1999.

Casebier, Dennis G. *Mojave Road Guide.* Essex, Calif.: Tales of the Mojave Road Publishing Company, 1999.

Clarke, Herbert. *An Introduction To Southern California Birds.* Missoula, Mont.: Mountain Press Publishing Company, 1997.

Conrotto, Eugene L. *Lost Gold and Silver Mines of the Southwest.* Mineola, N.Y.: Dover Publications, Inc., 1991.

Crampton, C. Gregory, and Stephen K. Madsen. *In Search of the Spanish Trail: Santa Fe to Los Angeles, 1829-1848.* Salt Lake City: Gibbs-Smith Publishing, 1994.

DeDecker, Mary. *Mines of the Eastern Sierra.* Glendale, Calif.: La Siesta Press, 1993.

Dunn, Jerry Camarillo, Jr. *National Geographic's Driving Guides to America: California and Nevada and Hawaii.* Washington, D.C.: The Book Division National Geographic Society, 1996.

Durham, David L. *Durham's Place-Names of California's Central Coast.* Clovis, Calif.: Word Dancer Press, 2000.

—. *Durham's Place-Names of San Diego County.* Clovis, Calif.: Word Dancer Press, 2000.

—. *Durham's Place-Names of Greater Los Angeles.* Clovis, Calif.: Word Dancer Press, 2000.

—. *Durham's Place-Names of California's Eastern Sierra.* Clovis, Calif.: Word Dancer Press, 2001.

—. *Durham's Place-Names of Central California.* Clovis, Calif.: Word Dancer Press, 2001.

—. *Durham's Place-Names of California's Desert Counties.* Clovis, Calif.: Word Dancer Press, 2001.

Fink, Augusta. *Monterey County: The Dramatic Story of Its Past.* Santa Cruz, Calif.: Western Tanager Press, 1972.

Florin, Lambert. *Ghost Towns of The West.* New York: Promontory Press, 1993.

Gersch-Young, Marjorie. *Hot Springs and Hot Pools of the Southwest.* Santa Cruz, Calif.: Aqua Thermal Access, 2001.

Gudde, Erwin G. *1000 California Place Names.* Berkeley and Los Angeles: University of California Press, 1959.

—. *California Place Names.* Berkeley and Los Angeles: University of California Press, 1998.

Hart, James D. *A Companion to California.* New York: Oxford University Press, 1978.

Heizer, Robert F. *The Destruction of California Indians.* Lincoln, Nebr.: University of Nebraska Press, 1993.

Historical Guide to North American Railroads, The. Waukesha, Wisc.: Kalmbach Publishing, 2000.

Hirschfelder, Arlene. *Native Americans.* New York: Dorling Kindersley Publishing, Inc., 2000.

Holmes, Robert. *California's Best-Loved Driving Tours.* New York: Macmillan Travel, 1999.

Hoxie, Frederick E., ed. *Encyclopedia of North American Indians.* Boston: Houghton Mifflin Company, 1996.

Huegel, Tony. *California Desert Byways.* Idaho Falls, Idaho: The Post Company, 1995.

Indians of California, The. Alexandria, Va.: Time-Life Books, 1994.

Jameson, E. W., Jr., and Hans J. Peeters. *California Mammals.* Berkeley and Los Angeles: University of California Press, 1988.

Jameson, W. C. *Buried Treasures of California.* Little Rock, Ark.: August House Publishers, Inc., 1995.

Johnson, William Weber. *The Old West: The Forty-niners.* New York: Time-Life Books, 1974.

Kavanagh, James, ed. *The Nature of California.* Helena, Mont.: Waterford Press Ltd., 1997.

Keyworth, C. L. *California Indians.* New York: Checkmark Books, 1991.

Kirk, Ruth. *Exploring Death Valley.* Stanford, Calif.: Stanford University Press, 1981.

Kroeber, A. L. *Handbook of the Indians of California.* New York: Dover Publications, Inc., 1976.

Kyle, Douglas E. *Historic Spots in California.* Stanford, Calif.: Stanford University Press, 1990.

Lamar, Howard R., ed. *The New Encyclopedia of the American West.* New Haven, Conn.: Yale University Press, 1998.

Lawlor, Florine. *Mohave Desert OHV Trails.* Glendale, Calif.: La Siesta Press, 1989.

Lewis, Donovan. *Pioneers of California.* San Francisco: Scottwall Associates, 1993.

Lindsay, Lowell, and Diana Lindsay. *The Anza-Borrego Desert Region.* Berkeley: Wilderness Press, 1998.

Lewellyn, Harry. *Backroad Trips and Tips.* Costa Mesa, Calif.: Glovebox Publications, 1993.

Martin, Don W., and Betty Woo Martin. *California-Nevada Roads Less Traveled.* Henderson, Nev.: Pine Cone Press, Inc., 1999.

Milner, Clyde A., II, Carol A. O'Conner, and Martha A. Sandweiss, eds. *The Oxford History of the American West.* Oxford: Oxford University Press, 1996.

Mitchell, James R. *Gem Trails of Southern California.* Baldwin Park, Calif.: Gem Guides Book Co., 1998.

Mitchell, John D. *Lost Mines and Buried Treasures Along the Old Frontier.* Glorieta, N. Mex.: 1995.

Mitchell, Roger. *Death Valley Jeep Trails.* Glendale, Calif.: La Siesta Press, 1969.

Mouchet, Paulette. *Horseback Riding Trails of Southern California, Volume I.* Acton, Calif.: Crown Valley Press, 1995.

Munz, Philip A. *California Spring Wildflowers.* Berkeley and Los Angeles: University of California Press, 1961.

Nadeau, Remi. *Ghost Towns and Mining Camps of California.* Santa Barbara, Calif.: Crest Publishing, 1999.

Nash, Jay Robert. *Encyclopedia of Western Lawmen and Outlaws.* New York: Da Capo Press, 1994.

National Audubon Society Field Guide to California. New York: Alfred A. Knopf, Inc., 1998.

National Audubon Society Field Guide to North American Birds: Western Region. New York: Alfred A. Knopf, Inc., 1998.

National Audubon Society Field Guide to North American Trees: Western Region. New York: Alfred A. Knopf, Inc., 1996.

National Audubon Society Field Guide to North American Mammals. New York: Alfred A. Knopf, Inc., 1996.

National Audubon Society Field Guide to North American Wildflowers: Western Region. New York: Alfred A. Knopf, Inc., 1998.

North American Wildlife. New York: Readers Digest Association, Inc., 1982.

O'Neal, Bill. *Encyclopedia of Western Gunfighters.* Norman, Okla.: University of Oklahoma Press, 1979.

Pepper, Choral. *Desert Lore of Southern California.* San Diego: Sunbelt Publications, 1999.

Pierce, L. Kingston. *America's Historic Trails with Tom Bodett.* San Francisco: KQED Books, 1997.

Poshek, Lucy, and Roger Naylor, comps. *California Trivia.* Nashville, Tenn.: Rutledge Hill Press, 1998.

Powers, Stephen. *Tribes of California.* Berkeley and Los Angeles: University of California Press, 1976.

Rae, Cheri, and John Mckinney. *Mojave National Preserve: A Visitor's Guide.* Santa Barbara, Calif.: Olympus Press, 1999.

Richards, Elizabeth W. *Guideposts to History: Origins of Place and Street Names in San Bernardino County.* Santa Fe: Santa Fe Federal Savings and Loan Association, 1966.

Robertson, Donald B. *Encyclopedia of Western Railroad History, Volume IV: California.* Caldwell, Idaho: The Caxton Printers, Ltd., 1998.

Rolle, Andrew. *California: A History.* Wheeling, Ill.: Harlan Davidson, Inc., 1998.

Sagstetter, Beth, and Bill Sagstetter. *The Mining Camps Speak.* Denver: Benchmark Publishing, 1998.

Schmoe, Floyd. *The Big Sur: Land of Rare Treasures.* San Francisco: Chronicle Books, 1975.

Schuler, Stanley, ed. *Cacti and Succulents.* New York: Simon and Schuster, Inc., 1985.

Secrest, William B. *California Desperadoes.* Clovis, Calif.: Word Dancer Press, 2000.

—. *Lawmen and Desperadoes.* Spokane, Wash.: The Arthur H. Clark Company, 1994.

Sharp, Robert P., and Allen F. Glazner. *Geology Underfoot in Southern California.* Missoula, Mont.: Mountain Press Publishing Company, 1993.

Starry, Roberta Martin, and Suzanne Knudson. *Exploring the Ghost Town Desert: A Guide to the Rand Mining Area.* Woodland Hills, Calif.: Engler Publishing, 2000.

Stein, Lou. *San Diego County Place-Names.* Leucadia, Calif.: Tofua Press, 1988.

Stob, Ron. *Exploring San Luis Obispo County and Nearby Coastal Areas.* San Luis Obispo, Calif.: Central Coast Press, 2000.

Sullivan, Noelle. *It Happened in Southern California.* Helena, Mont.: Falcon Publishing, Inc., 1996.

Taylor, Colin F. *The Native Americans: The Indigenous People of North America.* London: Salamander Books Ltd., 2000.

Tefertiller, Casey. *Wyatt Earp: The Life Behind the Legend.* New York: John Wiley & Sons, Inc., 1997.

Teie, William C. *4Wheeler's Guide: Trails of the San Bernardino Mountains.* Rescue, Calif.: Deer Valley Press, 1999.

Thrap, Dan L. *Encyclopedia of Frontier Biography.* 3 vols. Lincoln, Nebr.: University of Nebraska Press, 1988.

Varney, Philip. *Southern California's Best Ghost Towns.* Norman, Okla.: University of Oklahoma Press, 1990.

Waldman, Carl. *Encyclopedia of Native American Tribes.* New York: Facts on File, 1988.

Wright, Ralph B., ed. *California's Missions.* Los Angeles: The Stirling Press, 1967.

Wurman, Richard Saul. *Access Los Angeles.* Dunmore, Pa.: Harper Collins Publishers, 1999.

http://palmdale.lib.ca.us/history

http://palmsprings.com

http://pubs.usgs.gov/gip/earthq3

http://southmontereycounty.org/html/comm/soledad/solehis.html

http://rnrs.com/20MuleTeam/history.htm

http://www.29palms.com/History29.htm

http://www.395.com

http://www.Brawleyca.net

http://www.ca.blm.gov

http://www.calexico.ca.gov

http://www.calhist.org

http://www.califcity.com

http://www.californiamissions.com

http://www.cdc.gov/ncidod/diseases/hanta/hps

http://www.chocodog.com

http://www.cityofsoledad.com/history.html

http://www.ci.san-bernardino.ca.us/site/htm/history.htm

http://www.ci.san-luis-obispo.ca.us

http://www.ci.riverside.ca.us/city/blythe

http://www.ci.visalia.ca.us

http://www.desertusa.com

http://www.fieler.com

http://www.geocities.com/ghosttownexplorers

http://www.getty.edu

http://www.gist.com/tv/article.jsp

http://www.gorp.com

http://www.hhjm.com/66/history.htm

http://www.historyinslocounty.com

http://www.joshua.tree.national-park.com/info.htm

http://www.lone-pine.com

http://www.monrovia.acityline.com

http://www.nps.gov

http://www.oriflamme.net/ABDSP/intro.html

http://www.outwestnewspaper.com/Scotty.html

http://www.parkfield.com

http://www.pcta.org

http://www.pozosaloon.com

http://www.ramonamall.com

http://www.SanJuanCapistrano.org

http://www.socialhistory.org/Biographies

http://www.sbnature.org/chumash/pcart.htm

http://www.sdrm.org/history

http://www.tws-west.org

http://www.wemweb.com/traveler/towns

25 Favorite Trails

	Trail Name	Difficulty rating (Hardest = 10)	Scenic Rating (Best = 10)	Length (miles)
1	Desert #13: Mojave Road	4	10	128.6
2	Desert #48: Swansea–Cerro Gordo Road	5	10	23
3	Desert #35: Pleasant Canyon Loop Trail	7	10	23.5
4	South Coast #44: Red Canyon Trail	4	9	13.8
5	South Coast #20: North Coyote Canyon Trail	7	9	15.9
6	South Coast #37: Los Pinos Trail	5	9	18.6
7	Central Mountains #17: Jawbone Canyon Road	2	9	30.3
8	Central Mountains #33: Big Caliente Spring Trail	1	9	28.9
9	South Coast #30: Fish Creek–Sandstone Canyon Trail	3	10	14.3
10	Desert #33: Mengel Pass Trail	4	10	50.1
11	Central Mountains #32: Nordhoff Ridge Trail	4	9	28.8
12	Central Mountains #25: Sheep Spring Trail	3	9	12
13	Desert #26: Sperry Wash Route	4	9	18.6
14	Desert #5: Whipple Mountains Trail	3	8	23.4
15	Desert #40: Titus Canyon Trail	2	10	25.4
16	Desert #22: Grass Valley Trail	3	9	50.6
17	South Coast #42: Brooklyn Mine Road	6	9	12.3
18	Desert #41: Chloride City Trail	3	10	15.4
19	Desert #39: Funeral Range Trail	6	9	25.4
20	Central Mountains #23: Last Chance Canyon Trail	5	10	10.6
21	South Coast #34: Painted Gorge–Carrizo Mountain Trail	5	9	8.9
22	Central Mountains #16: Piute Mountain Road	2	9	30.5
23	Desert #10: Sunflower Spring Road	4	10	45
24	Desert #18: Cima Dome Trail	2	8	19.4
25	Central Mountains #43: Sand Highway	3	9	5.3

25 Longest Trails

	Trail Name	Length (Miles)	Difficulty Rating (Hardest = 10)	Scenic Rating (Best = 10)
1	Desert #13: Mojave Road	128.6	4	10
2	Desert #46: Saline Valley Road	91.4	2	10
3	South Coast #45: Bradshaw Trail	79.4	2	8
4	Desert #15: New York Mountains Trail	62.1	2	9
5	Desert #22: Grass Valley Trail	50.6	3	9
6	Desert #33: Mengel Pass Trail	50.1	4	10
7	Desert #14: East Lanfair Valley Trail	49.1	4	9
8	Desert #6: Cadiz Road	47.1	1	8
9	Desert #10: Sunflower Spring Road	45	4	10
10	South Coast #49: Indian Pass Road	43.4	3	10
11	Desert #17: Nipton Desert Road	41.4	2	8
12	Desert #21: Black Canyon Road	35.4	3	10
13	Central Mountains #12: Rancheria Road	35.3	1	9
14	South Coast #17: Rodman Mountains Trail	34.8	3	8
15	Desert #32: Death Valley West Side Road	34.2	1	8
16	Desert #1: Palen Pass Trail	33.8	3	8
17	Desert #28: Harry Wade Exit Route	30.5	2	8
18	Central Mountains #16: Piute Mountain Road	30.5	2	9
19	Desert #51: Racetrack Road	30.5	2	9
20	South Coast #5: Santa Clara Divide Road	30.5	1	9
21	Central Mountains #17: Jawbone Canyon Road	30.3	2	9
22	Desert #25: Kingston Wash Trail	30	3	8
23	South Coast #15: Ord Mountains Trail	29.7	3	8
24	Central Mountains #37: Sierra Madre Road	29.7	2	8
25	South Coast #1: Liebre Mountain Trail	29.3	2	9

25 Shortest Trails

	Trail Name	Length (Miles)	Difficulty Rating (Hardest=10)	Scenic Rating (Best=10)
1	Desert #9: Amboy Crater Road	1.7	4	9
2	South Coast #29: Calcite Mine Trail	1.9	7	9
3	Central Mountains #15: Bull Run Basin Trail	2.3	3	8
4	Central Mountains #42: Paradise Road	3.4	3	8
5	Central Mountains #7: Buck Road	3.6	5	9
6	Central Mountiains #36: Buckhorn Ridge Trail	3.6	3	9
7	Desert #2: Blythe Intaglios Trail	4	3	10
8	South Coast #27: Fonts Point Trail	4.1	2	9
9	Central Mountains #39: Big Rocks Trail	4.4	2	8
10	South Coast #24: Mine Wash Trail	4.5	2	8
11	Central Mountains #22: Nightmare Gulch Overlook Trail	5	4	8
12	South Coast #22: Santa Ysabel Creek Trail	5	2	8
13	Central Mountains #43: Sand Highway	5.3	3	9
14	Central Mountains #4: Whitaker Research Forest Trail	5.4	1	9
15	Central Mountains #40: Twin Rocks Trail	5.6	7	9
16	Desert #4: Gold Rice Mine Trail	6.2	6	8
17	Central Mountains #21: Opal Canyon Road	6.3	5	9
18	Desert #27: Alexander Hills Trail	6.4	4	8
19	Central Mountains #50: Cone Peak Trail	6.4	1	8
20	Central Mountains #14: Portuguese Pass Trail	6.9	1	8
21	South Coast #8: Pinyon Ridge Trail	7	2	9
22	Desert #8: Black Metal Mine Road	7.1	3	8
23	Central Mountains #41: Branch Creek Trail	7.3	5	8
24	Central Mountains #48: Willow Creek Road	7.4	1	9
25	Central Mountains #2: Delilah Fire Lookout Trail	7.5	2	8

25 Hardest Trails

	Trail Name	Difficulty rating (Hardest = 10)	Scenic Rating (Best = 10)	Length (miles)
1	South Coast #20: North Coyote Canyon Trail	7	9	15.9
2	Desert #35: Pleasant Canyon Loop Trail	7	10	23.5
3	South Coast #29: Calcite Mine Trail	7	9	1.9
4	Central Mountains #40: Twin Rocks Trail	7	9	5.6
5	South Coast #48: Black Mountain Road	6/7	9	15.5
6	South Coast #25: South Coyote Canyon Trail	6	10	13.2
7	Desert #39: Funeral Range Trail	6	9	25.4
8	South Coast #42: Brooklyn Mine Road	6	9	12.3
9	Desert #4: Gold Rice Mine Trail	6	8	6.2
10	Desert #48: Swansea–Cerro Gordo Road	5	10	23
11	South Coast #34: Painted Gorge–Carrizo Mountain Trail	5	9	8.9
12	Central Mountains 23: Last Chance Canyon Trail	5	10	10.6
13	South Coast #31: Arroyo Seco del Diablo Trail	5	9	8.2
14	Central Mountains #7: Buck Road	5	9	3.6
15	South Coast #37: Los Pinos Trail	5	9	18.6
16	Central Mountains #41: Branch Creek Trail	5	8	7.3
17	Central Mountains #27: Government Peak Trail	5	10	7.9
18	Central Mountains #21: Opal Canyon Road	5	9	6.3
19	South Coast #26: Truckhaven Trail	5	8	11.3
20	Desert #50: Lippincott Mine Road	4	9	8
21	Desert #27: Alexander Hills Trail	4	8	6.4
22	Desert #33: Mengel Pass Trail	4	10	50.1
23	Central Mountains #29: San Emigdio Mountain Trail	4	8	14.9
24	Desert #26: Sperry Wash Route	4	9	18.6
25	South Coast #44: Red Canyon Trail	4	9	13.8

25 Easiest Trails

	Trail Name	Difficulty rating (Hardest = 10)	Scenic Rating (Best = 10)	Length (miles)
1	Central Mountains #33: Big Caliente Spring Trail	1	9	28.9
2	South Coast #13: Big Pine Flat Trail	1	9	26.6
3	Desert #6: Cadiz Road	1	8	47.1
4	Central Mountains #11: Capinero Saddle Trail	1	7	8.2
5	Central Mountains #20: Chimney Peak Byway	1	8	14
6	South Coast #47: Cibola Wildlife Refuge Trail	1	9	21
7	Central Mountains #51: Coast Road	1	9	10.1
8	Central Mountains #50: Cone Peak Trail	1	8	6.4
9	Desert #32: Death Valley West Side Road	1	8	34.2
10	South Coast #50: Ferguson Lake Road	1	9	13.4
11	Central Mountains #46: Hi Mountain Road	1	8	12.1
12	South Coast #35: McCain Valley Road	1	8	14
13	Central Mountains #1: Movie Flat Trail	1	9	11.7
14	Central Mountains #47: Parkfield Grade Trail	1	8	18.4
15	Central Mountains #45: Pine Mountain Road	1	9	8.8
16	Central Mountains #14: Portuguese Pass Trail	1	8	6.9
17	Central Mountains #44: Pozo Road	1	8	18.2
18	Central Mountains #12: Rancheria Road	1	9	35.3
19	South Coast #5: Santa Clara Divide Road	1	9	30.5
20	Central Mountains #4: Whitaker Research Forest Trail	1	9	5.4
21	Central Mountains #48: Willow Creek Road	1	9	7.4
22	Central Mountains #9: Windy Gap Trail	1	8	13.5
23	Central Mountains #52: Tassajara Road	2	8	13.6
24	Central Mountains #34: Camino Cielo Road	2	9	25.2
25	Desert #28: Harry Wade Exit Route	2	8	30.5

25 Scenic Trails

	Trail Name	Scenic rating (Best = 10)	Difficulty Rating (Hardest = 10)	Length (miles)
1	Desert #13: Mojave Road	10	4	128.6
2	Desert #33: Mengel Pass Trail	10	4	50.1
3	South Coast #25: South Coyote Canyon Trail	10	6	13.2
4	Desert #48: Swansea–Cerro Gordo Road	10	5	23
5	Desert #21: Black Canyon Road	10	3	35.4
6	South Coast #30: Fish Creek–Sandstone Canyon Trail	10	3	14.3
7	South Coast #49: Indian Pass Road	10	3	43.4
8	South Coast #7: Rincon-Shortcut OHV Route	10	2	25.2
9	Desert #2: Blythe Intaglios Trail	10	3	4
10	Desert #40: Titus Canyon Trail	10	2	25.4
11	Desert #10: Sunflower Spring Road	10	4	45
12	Central Mountains #27: Government Peak Trail	10	5	7.9
13	Central Mountains #23: Last Chance Canyon Trail	10	5	10.6
14	Desert #35: Pleasant Canyon Loop Trail	10	7	23.5
15	Desert #41: Chloride City Trail	10	3	15.4
16	Desert #46: Saline Valley Road	10	2	91.4
17	South Coast #47: Cibola Wildlife Refuge Trail	9	1	21
18	South Coast #37: Los Pinos Trail	9	5	18.6
19	Central Mountains #4: Whitaker Research Forest Trail	9	1	5.4
20	Central Mountains #12: Rancheria Road	9	1	35.3
21	Central Mountains #16: Piute Mountain Road	9	2	30.5
22	South Coast #31: Arroyo Seco del Diablo Trail	9	5	8.2
23	South Coast #20: North Coyote Canyon Trail	9	7	15.9
24	Central Mountains #13: Rhymes Road	9	2	22.1
25	South Coast #38: Otay Mountain Truck Trail	9	2	16.2

Photograph Credits

Unless otherwise indicated in the following list of acknowledgments (which is organized by section and page number), all color photographs were taken by Peter Massey and are copyrighted by Swagman Publishing Inc., or by Peter Massey.

Abbreviations: California Historical Society, San Francisco (CHS); California Academy of Sciences Special Collections, San Francisco (CalPhotos); San Francisco Botanical Gardens, Strybing Arboretum Society (Strybing); San Diego Museum of Man (SDMOM); University of Southern California (USC); Arizona State Library (ASL); Brother Alfred Brousseau Project (Brousseau); Denver Botanical Garden (DBG); Denver Public Library Western History Collection (DPL); Corel Stock Photo Library (Corel); PhotoDisc (PD); Tucson Botanical Gardens (TBG).

24 CHS; **25** (upper left) USC; (lower left) CHS; **26** CHS; **28** CHS; **29** CHS; **31** CHS; **33** USC; **34** CHS; **35** USC; **37** USC; **38** CHS; **39** CHS; **40** CHS; **42** CHS; **43** (left) CHS; (right) USC; **44** CHS; **45** CHS; **46** CHS; **47** CHS; **49** Bushducks; **50** CHS; **51** CHS; **52** CHS; **53** CHS; **54** CHS; **56** USC; **57** (upper) Bushducks; (lower) CHS; **58** CHS; **59** USC; **65** (upper) USC; (lower) CHS; **66** (left) USC; (right) CHS; **67** DPL; **68** DPL; **69** (upper) USC; (lower) CHS; **70** (left) CHS; (right) ASL; **71** CHS; **73** (left) Utah State Historical Society; **74** (left) CHS; (right) DPL; **75** (left) CHS; (right) USC; **76** CHS; **78** ASL; **80** CHS; **81** CHS; **82** CHS; **83** CHS; **84** CHS; **85** CHS; **86** CHS; **88** SDMOM; **89** SDMOM; **91** SDMOM; **92** SDMOM; **93** SDMOM; **94** SDMOM; **95** (left) SDMOM; (right) Bushducks; **98** CHS; **100** ASL; **101** CHS; **104** Bushducks; **105** CHS; **106** CHS; **109** Corel; **110** Corel; **111** (upper left) PD; (lower left & right) Corel; **112** (left) Corel; (upper right) Earle Robinson; (lower right) Paul Berquist; **113** (left) Corel; (upper right) CalPhotos courtesy of Alden M. Johnson; (lower right) Corel; **114** (left) Corel; (upper right) Corel; (lower right) Paul Berquist; **115** (upper left) Corel; (lower left) Bushducks; (upper right) Paul Berquist; (lower right) Corel; **116** (left) Corel; (upper right) Corel; (middle right) Doug Von Gausig; (lower right) PD; **117** (left & upper right) Corel; (lower right) PD; **118** (upper left) Bushducks; (lower left) PD; (right) Corel; **119** (upper & middle left) Corel; (lower left) Corel; (upper & lower right) Corel; (middle right) Doug Von Gausig; **120** (left) Corel; (upper & lower right) Corel; (middle right) Bushducks; **121** (upper & middle left) Corel; (lower left) Bushducks; (upper right) Lauren Livo & Steve Wilcox; (lower right) Earle Robinson; **122** (upper left) Earle Robinson; (upper middle left) Corel; (middle & lower left) Corel; (right) Corel; **123** Corel; **124** (upper left) Earle Robinson; (lower left) Doug Von Gausig; (upper right) Lauren Livo & Steve Wilcox; (lower right) Don Baccus; **125** (left) Corel; (upper right) Bushducks; (lower right) Corel; **126** (upper left) CalPhotos courtesy Vannoy Davis; (middle left) Don Baccus; (lower left & upper right) Earle Robinson; (middle right) Corel; (lower right) PD; **127** (upper left) PD; (middle left) Corel; (lower left) CalPhotos #1 courtesy of Charles Webber and #3 courtesy of Dr. Lloyd Glen Engles; (right) Earle Robinson; **128** (left) Corel; (upper right) Don Baccus; (middle & lower right) Earle Robinson; **129** Corel; **130** (upper left) Corel; (middle left) PD; (lower left) Corel; (upper right) Don Baccus; (lower right) Earle Robinson; **131** (upper left) Earle Robinson; (middle left) Corel; (lower left) Don Baccus; (upper right) Earle Robinson; (lower right) Corel; **132** (upper left) Alison Sheehey; (upper middle left) Brousseau; (lower middle left) Bushducks; (lower left) Doug Von Gausig; (upper right) Bushducks; (middle & lowerright) DBG; **133** (upper left) DGBG; (middle left) Bushducks; (lower left) TBG; (upper right) Doug Von Gausig; (middle right) TBG; (lower right) PD; **134** (upper & upper middle left) Doug Von Gausig; (middle left) DBG; (lower middle left) Stybring; (lower left) DGBG; (upper & upper middle right) DBG; (upper middle right) PD; (lower right) DBG; **135** (upper & upper middle left) Strybing; (lower middle & lower left) TBG; (upper & upper middle right) DBG; (lower middle right) TBG; (lower right) Strybing; **136** (upper & upper middle left) Strybing; (middle left) Bushducks; (lower middle left) TBG; (lower left) Bushducks; (upper right) Bushducks; (upper middle right) Doug Von Gausig; (lower middle & lower right) Bushducks; **137** (upper & upper middle left) Bushducks; (middle & lower middle left) Bushducks; (lower left & upper right) CalPhotos courtesy of Charles Webber; (upper middle right) TBG; **138** (upper left) Brousseau; (upper, upper middle & middle right) Bushducks; (lower middle right) Brousseau; (lower right) CalPhotos courtesy of Charles Webber; **139** (left) Bushducks; (upper right) Bushducks; (upper middle right) Brousseau; (middle right) CalPhotos courtesy of Charles Webber; (lower middle & lower right) Bushducks; **140** (upper & upper middle left) Bushducks; (middle & lower middle right) Bushducks; (lower right) Strybing; **141** (upper left) CalPhotos courtesy of Charles Webber; (upper middle left) Brousseau; (middle left) Strybing; (upper middle left) CalPhotos courtesy of Charles Webber; (lower left & upper right) Brousseau; (upper middle right) Strybing; (lower middle left) DBG; (lower right) Bushducks; **142** (upper left) Corel; (upper middle left) TBG; (both lower left) Bushducks; (upper right) Corel; (lower right) Bushducks; **143** (upper left) Corel; (middle left) Bushducks; (lower left) CalPhotos courtesy of Charles Webber; (upper right & lower middle right) Corel; (upper middle right) Bushducks; (lower right) Corel; **148-559** Bushducks (except pages 265-266, 270 (upper), 274, 277-287 courtesy of Tim Duggan)

Front cover photography: Bushducks

Rear cover photography: (Beavertail cactus flowers) Corel; (Kit foxes) Corel; (Desert #47) Bushducks; (Central Mountains #23) Bushducks; ("Death Valley Scotty") CHS

Index

T

U

V

W

Y

Z

ABOUT THE SERIES OF swagman guides

71 TRAILS
232 PAGES
209 PHOTOGRAPHS
PRICE $29.95
ISBN: 0-9665675-5-2

The Adventures series of backcountry guidebooks are the ultimate for both adventurous four-wheelers and scenic sightseers. Each volume in the Adventures series covers an entire state or a distinct region. In addition to meticulously detailed route directions and trail maps, these full-color guides include extensive information on the history of towns, ghost towns, and regions passed along the way, as well as a history of the American Indian tribes who lived in the area prior to Euro-American settlement. The guides also provide wildlife information and photographs to help readers identify the great variety of native birds, plants, and animals they are likely to see. All you need is your SUV and your Adventures book to confidently explore all the best sites in each state's backcountry.

4WD Adventures: Colorado gets you safely to the banks of the beautiful Crystal River or over America's highest pass road, Mosquito Pass. This book guides you to the numerous lost ghost towns that speckle Colorado's mountains. In addition to the enormously detailed trail information, there are hundreds of photos of historic mining operations, old railroad routes, wildflowers, and native animals. Trail history is brought to life through the accounts of sheriffs and gunslingers like Bat Masterson and Doc Holliday; millionaires like Horace Tabor and Thomas Walsh; and American Indian warriors like Chiefs Ouray and Antero.

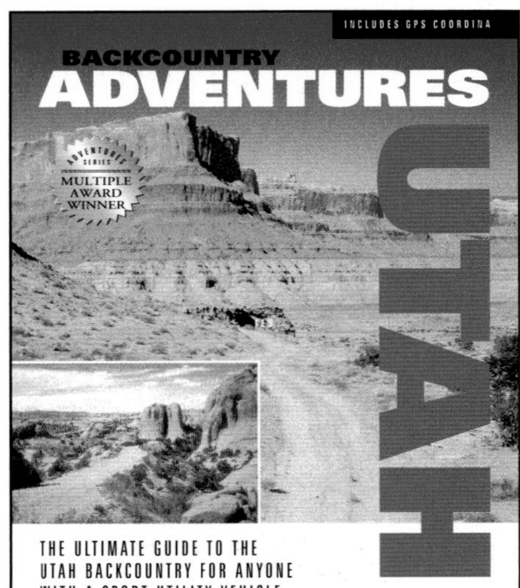

175 TRAILS
544 PAGES
525 PHOTOGRAPHS
PRICE $34.95
ISBN: 1-930193-12-2

Backcountry Adventures: Utah navigates you along 3,721 miles through the spectacular Canyonlands region of Utah, to the top of the Uinta Range, across vast salt flats, and along trails unchanged since the late 19th century when riders of the Pony Express sped from station to station and daring young outlaws wreaked havoc on newly established stage lines, railroads, and frontier towns. In addition to enormously detailed trail information, there are hundreds of photos of frontier towns, historic mining operations, old rail-

153 TRAILS
640 PAGES
647 PHOTOGRAPHS
PRICE $34.95
ISBN: 1-930193-04-1

157 TRAILS
576 PAGES
524 PHOTOGRAPHS
PRICE $34.95
ISBN: 0-9665675-0-1

road routes, wildflowers, and native animals. Trail history is brought to life through the accounts of outlaws like Butch Cassidy and his Wild Bunch; explorers and mountain men like Jim Bridger; and early Mormon settlers led by Brigham Young.

Backcountry Adventures: Arizona guides you along the back roads of the state's most remote and scenic regions, from the lowlands of the Yuma Desert to the high plains of the Kaibab Plateau. In addition to the enormously detailed trail information, there are hundreds of photos of frontier towns, historic mining operations, old railroad routes, wildflowers, and native animals. Trail history is brought to life through the accounts of Indian warriors like Cochise and Geronimo; trailblazers like Edward F. Beale; and the famous lawman Wyatt Earp, a survivor of the Shoot-out at the O.K. Corral in Tombstone.

Backcountry Adventures: Southern California takes you from the beautiful mountain regions of Big Sur, through the arid Mojave Desert, and straight into the heart of the aptly named Death Valley. In addition to the enormously detailed trail information, there are hundreds of photos of frontier towns, historic mining operations, old railroad routes, wildflowers, and native animals. Trail history is brought to life through the accounts of Spanish missionaries who first settled the coastal regions of Southern California; eager prospectors looking to cash in during California's gold rush; and legends of lost mines still hidden in the state's expansive backcountry.

Additional titles in the series will cover other states with four-wheel driving opportunities. Northern California is scheduled for release during 2002. Information on all upcoming books, including special pre-publication discount offers, can be found on the Internet at www.4WDbooks.com.

backcountry adventures series

WINNER OF FOUR PRESTIGIOUS BOOK AWARDS

"The 540-page tome is an incredible resource for getting to, and returning from, almost anywhere in Utah. Concise maps, backed with GPS, make getting lost something you'd have to do on purpose...To borrow a line from a well-known company: Don't leave home without it."

— Truck Trend

"Based on our initial experience, we expect our review copy of *Backcountry Adventures: Arizona* to be well used in the coming months... To say we'd strongly recommend this book is an understatement."

— Auto Week

"*4WD Adventures*...serves as a regional travel guide, complete with glossaries and color photos of wildflowers, animals, famous towns, and natural wonders."

— Four Wheeler Magazine

"Tired of being cooped up in your house because of the weather? This book, designed for owners of SUVs will get you out of the suburbs, off the highways, out of the cities, and into the backcountry..."

— Salt Lake Magazine

"The authors have compiled information that every SUV owner will find handy...Whether you want to know more about four-wheel driving techniques or if you are a snowmobiler or SUV owner looking for places to explore, *4WD Adventures* is the ultimate book...[They] bring the history of these trails to life through their accounts of the pioneers who built them to open up the territory to mining, ranching, and commerce in the 1800s."

— The Denver Post

"[The book]...is a massive undertaking, a textbook-size guide that seems well worth its price. Using this book, SUV owners should be able to explore areas they never knew existed, plus identify plants, animals, ghost towns and Indian history they'll see along the way."

— The Arizona Republic

"Similar to any good history book, once you get started, it's hard to put it down. Not only will it help flesh out your adventures off road, it will also broaden your appreciation of this beautiful country...The wealth of information is second to none, and the presentation makes it a pleasure to read."

— 4 Wheel Drive & Sport Utility Magazine

"This comprehensive book provides over 500 pages of photographs, maps, and detailed information about the trails and sights that make for fun 'wheeling in the Beehive State."

— Peterson's 4Wheel & Off-Road Magazine

"This book is a 10. It contains, in one volume, every kind of information I would want on a 4WD excursion."

— Awards Judge